Man, Economy, and State

A Treatise on Economic Principles

Some Other Books by Murray N. Rothbard

America's Great Depression

An Austrian Perspective on the History of Economic Thought
- Volume I: Economic Thought Before Adam Smith
- Volume II: Classical Economics

The Case Against the Fed

The Case for a 100 Percent Gold Dollar

Conceived in Liberty
- Volume I: A New Land, A New People, The American Colonies
- Volume II: "Salutary Neglect": The American Colonies in the First Half of the Eighteenth Century
- Volume III: Advance to Revolution, 1760–1774
- Volume IV: The Revolutionary War, 1775–1784

Education: Free and Compulsory

Egalitarianism as a Revolt Against Nature and Other Essays

The Ethics of Liberty

The Logic of Action One:
Method, Money, and the Austrian School

The Logic of Action Two:
Applications and Criticism from the Austrian School

Ludwig von Mises: Scholar, Creator, Hero

Making Economic Sense

Power and Market

What Has Government Done to Our Money?

Man, Economy, and State

A Treatise on Economic Principles

MURRAY N. ROTHBARD

Library of Congress Catalog Card Number: 76-167504
ISBN: 0-945466-32-3

Published by The Ludwig von Mises Institute, 518 West Magnolia Avenue, Auburn, Alabama, 36832-4528; www.mises.org.

TO

LUDWIG VON MISES

The Ludwig von Mises Institute gratefully acknowledges the generosity of its Members, who made the publication of this book possible. In particular, it wishes to thank the following Patrons:

Mark M. Adamo
O. P. Alford, III
Anonymous (2)
Cliff Beittel
G. Stanley Berge
Walter E. Bixby
Burton S. Blumert
John Hamilton Bolstad
J. R. Bost
Franklin M. Buchta
Samuel O. Campbell
Ed and Betty Capen
Christopher P. Condon
Doug Cook
Cook Brothers Manufacturing
Kerry E. Cutter
Charles G. Dannelly
Mr. and Mrs. William C. Daywitt
Tad Dekko
Robert T. Dofflemyer
Leo E. Eickhoff, Jr.
Mrs. Card G. Elliott, Jr.
Dr. James W. Esler, Jr.
Willard Fischer
Jim Feutz
Thomas E. Gee
Henry Getz
Morton Buildings, Inc.
The Greene View Foundation
Gary Gunter
David A. Haddad
Albert L. Hillman, Jr.
Brian Jedrick
Franklin Lee Johnson
Michael L. Keiser
Paul Kennedy
John F. Kieser
H. E. King
The M. H. King Foundation
Dr. Richard J. Kossmann
Hugh E. Ledbetter
Joe R. Lee
Arthur L. Loeb
Dr. Walter Marcyan
Henry J. Molloy
Molloy and Associates
M. K. Morse
Edward D. Muir
Charles A. and Elaine L. Nelson
Jeff and Vicky Neumeyer
Bruce M. Norman
Mr. and Mrs. George D. O'Neill
Arthur Peterson
Ellis L. Phillips, Jr.
Dr. Francis M. Powers
James M. Rodney
Sheldon Rose
Daniel Rosenthal
Rosenthal and Associates
Charles A. Ross, Jr.
E. D. Shaw, Jr.
Shaw Oxygen Company
Thomas W. Singleton
Richard J. Stephenson
Stephenson Family Foundation
Dr. Jonas C. Strouth
top dog
William Valliant
Lawrence Van Someren, Sr.
Fred Vreeland
Vreeland Tire Supply Company
Thomas G. Winter
Robert S. Young
Young Electric Company
Thomas V. Zignego
The Zignego Company

Preface
Revised Edition

One of the unhappy casualties of World War I, it seems, was the old-fashioned treatise on economic "principles." Before World War I, the standard method, both of presenting and advancing economic thought, was to write a disquisition setting forth one's vision of the corpus of economic science. A work of this kind had many virtues wholly missing from the modern world. On the one hand, the intelligent layman, with little or no previous acquaintance with economics, could read it. On the other hand, the author did not limit himself, textbook-fashion, to choppy and oversimplified compilations of currently fashionable doctrine. For better or worse, he carved out of economic theory an architectonic—an edifice. Sometimes the edifice was an original and noble one, sometimes it was faulty; but at least there *was* an edifice, for beginners to see, for colleagues to adopt or criticize. Hyperrefinements of detail were generally omitted as impediments to viewing economic science as a whole, and they were consigned to the journals. The university student, too, learned his economics from the treatise on its "principles"; it was not assumed that special works were needed with chapter lengths fitting course requirements and devoid of original doctrine. These works, then, were read by students, intelligent laymen, and leading economists, all of whom profited from them.

Their spirit is best illustrated by a prefatory passage from one of the last of the species:

> I have tried in this book to state the principles of economics in such form that they shall be comprehensible to an educated and intelligent person who has not before made any systematic study of the subject. Though designed in this sense for beginners, the book does not gloss

over difficulties or avoid severe reasoning. No one can understand economic phenomena or prepare himself to deal with economic problems who is unwilling to follow trains of reasoning which call for sustained attention. I have done my best to be clear, and to state with care the grounds on which my conclusions rest, as well as the conclusions themselves, but have made no vain pretense of simplifying all things." [1]

Since the brilliant burst that gave us the works of Wicksteed (1910), Taussig (1911), and Fetter (1915), this type of treatise has disappeared from economic thought, and economics has become appallingly fragmented, dissociated to such a degree that there hardly *is* an *economics* any more; instead, we find myriad bits and pieces of uncoordinated analysis. Economics has, first, been fragmented into "applied" fields—"urban land economics," "agricultural economics," "labor economics," "public finance economics," etc., each division largely heedless of the others. More grievous still has been the disintegration of what has been confined to the category of "economic theory." Utility theory, monopoly theory, international trade theory, etc., down to linear programming and games theory—each moves in its sharply isolated compartment, with its own hyperrefined literature. Recently, growing awareness of this fragmentation has led to vague "interdisciplinary" admixtures with all the other "social sciences." Confusion has been worse confounded, with resulting invasive forays of numerous other disciplines into economics, rather than the diffusion of economics elsewhere. At any rate, it is somewhat foolhardy to attempt to integrate economics with everything else before economics has *itself* been made whole. Only then will the proper place of economics among the other disciplines become manifest.

I think it fair to say that, with only a single exception (Ludwig von Mises' *Human Action*) *not one* general treatise on economic principles has appeared since World War I. Perhaps the closest approach was Frank H. Knight's *Risk, Uncertainty, and Profit,* and *that* was published far back in 1921. Since then there has been no book of remotely as broad a scope.

[1] Frank W. Taussig, *Principles of Economics* (New York: Macmillan, 1911), p. vii.

The only place where we can find economics treated with any degree of breadth is in the elementary textbooks. These textbooks, however, are sorry substitutes for a genuine Principles. Since they must, by their nature, present only currently received doctrine, their work is uninteresting to the established economist. Furthermore, since they may only boil down the existing literature, they must of necessity present to the student a hodgepodge of fragmented chapters, each with little or no relation to the other.

Many economists see no loss in all this; in fact, they herald these developments as signs of the enormous progress the science has made on all fronts. Knowledge has grown so vast that no man can encompass it all. Yet economists should at least be responsible for knowing *economics*—the essentials of the body of their discipline. Certainly, then, these essentials could have been presented by this time. The plain fact is that economics is fragmented precisely *because* it is no longer regarded as an edifice; since it is considered a congeries of isolated splinters, it is treated as such.

Perhaps the key to this change is that formerly economics was regarded as a logical structure. Fundamentally, whatever the differences of degree, or even of proclaimed methodology, economics was considered a deductive science using verbal logic. Grounded on a few axioms, the edifice of economic thought was deduced step by step. Even when the analysis was primitive or the announced methodology far more inductive, this was the essence of economics during the nineteenth century. Hence, the treatise on economic "principles"—for if economics proceeds by deductive logic grounded on a few simple and evident axioms, then the corpus of economics can be presented as an interrelated whole to the intelligent layman with no loss of ultimate rigor. The layman is taken step by step from simple and evident truths to more complex and less evident ones.

The "Austrian" economists best perceived this method and used it most fully and cogently. They were the classic employers, in short, of the "praxeologic" method. In the present day, however, the prevailing epistemology has thrown over praxeology for methods at once too empirical and too "theoretical." Empiricism has disintegrated economics to such an extent that no one thinks to look for a complete edifice; and, paradoxically, it has falsified economics by making economists eager to introduce admittedly false and short-cut assumptions in order to make their theories more readily "testable." Alfred Marshall's distrust of "long chains of deduction," as well as the whole Cambridge impetus toward such short cuts, has contributed a great deal to this breakdown. On the other hand, verbal logic in economic theory has been replaced by mathematics, seemingly more precise and basking in the reflected glory of the physical sciences. The dominant econometric wing of mathematical economists also looks for empirical verifications and thereby compounds the errors of both methods. Even on the level of pure theoretical integration, mathematics is completely inappropriate for any sciences of human action. Mathematics has, in fact, contributed to the compartmentalization of economics—to specialized monographs featuring a hyperrefined maze of matrices, equations, and geometric diagrams. But the really important thing is *not* that nonmathematicians cannot understand them; the crucial point is that mathematics cannot contribute to economic knowledge. In fact, the recent conquest of mathematical economics by econometrics is a sign of recognition that pure mathematical theory in economics is sterile.

This book, then, is an attempt to fill part of the enormous gap of forty years' time. Since the last treatise on economic "principles," economics has proceeded a long way in many areas, and its methodology has been immeasurably improved and strengthened by those continuing to work in the praxeological tradition. Furthermore, there are still great gaps in the praxeological corpus, since so few economists have worked at shaping it. Hence, the attempt in this book to develop the edifice of economic science in the manner of the old-fashioned works on its "principles"—slowly and logically to build on the basic axioms an integrated and coherent edifice of economic truth. Hyperrefinements have been shunned as much as possible. In short, Professor Taussig's quoted statement of intention has been mine also, with the addition that I have felt it necessary to include, at pertinent points, refutation of some of the main opposing doctrines. This was especially needed because economic fallacy prevails far more widely than in Taussig's time.

I have indicated briefly that there has been *one* general treatise since World War I. Professor Paul Samuelson has written rhapsodically of the joy of being under thirty at the time of publication of Keynes' *General Theory*. I can say the same for the publication of Ludwig von Mises' *Human Action* in 1949. For here at last was economics *whole* once more, once again an edifice. Not only that—here was a structure of economics with many of the components newly contributed by Professor Mises himself. There is no space here to present or expound Mises' great contributions to economic science. That will have to be done elsewhere. Suffice it to say that from now on, little constructive work can be done in economics unless it starts from *Human Action.*

Human Action is a general treatise, but not an old-style Principles. Instead, it assumes considerable previous economic knowledge and includes within its spacious confines numerous philosophic and historical insights. In one sense, the present work attempts to isolate the economic, fill in the interstices, and spell out the detailed implications, as I see them, of the Misesian structure. It must not be thought, however, that Professor Mises is in any way responsible for these pages. Indeed, he may well differ strongly with many sections of this volume. Yet it is my hope that this work may succeed in adding a few bricks to the noble structure of economic science that has reached its most modern and developed form in the pages of *Human Action.*

The present work deduces the entire corpus of economics from a few simple and apodictically true axioms: the Fundamental Axiom of *action*—that men employ means to achieve ends, and two subsidiary postulates: that there is a *variety* of human and natural resources, and that leisure is a consumers' good. Chapter 1 begins with the action axiom and deduces its immediate implications; and these conclusions are applied to "Crusoe economics"—that much maligned but highly useful analysis that sets individual man starkly against Nature and analyzes his resulting actions. Chapter 2 introduces other men and, consequently, social relations. Various types of interpersonal relations are analyzed, and the economics of *direct exchange* (barter) is set forth. Exchange cannot be adequately analyzed until property rights are fully defined—so chapter 2 analyzes property in a free society. Chapter 2, in fact, marks the beginning of the body of the book—an analysis of the economics of voluntary exchange. Chapter 2 discusses the free market of barter, and the subsequent chapters treat the economics of *indirect*—or monetary—exchange. Thus, analytically, the book deals fully with the economics of the free market, from its property relations to the economics of money.

Chapter 3 introduces money and traces the patterns of indirect exchange on the market. Chapter 4 treats the economics of consumption and the pricing of consumers' goods. Chapters 5–9 analyze production on the free market. One of the features of this consumption and production theory is the resurrection of Professor Frank A. Fetter's brilliant and completely neglected theory of *rent*—i.e., the concept of rent as the hire price of a unit service. *Capitalization* then becomes the process of determining the present values of the expected future rents of a good. The Fetter-Mises pure time-preference theory of interest is synthesized with the Fetter rent theory, with the Austrian theory of the structure of production, and with separation of *original* from *produced* factors of production. One "radical" feature of our analysis of production is a complete break with the currently fashionable "short-run" theory of the firm, substituting for this a general theory of marginal value productivity and capitalization. It is a "general equilibrium" analysis in the dynamic Austrian, and not in the static, currently popular Walrasian sense.

Chapter 10 expounds a completely new theory of monopoly—that monopoly can be meaningfully defined only as a grant of privilege by the State, and that a monopoly price can be attained only from such a grant. In short, there can be no monopoly or monopoly price on the free market. The theory of monopolistic competition is also discussed. And chapter 11 sets forth the theory of money on the free market, along with an extensive discussion of the Keynesian theories.

Having completed the theory of the purely free market, I then turn, in the final chapter, to applying praxeological analysis to a systematic discussion of various forms and degrees of coercive intervention and their consequences. The effects of coercive intervention can be studied only after fully analyzing the construct of a purely free market. Chapter 12 presents a typology of intervention, discusses its direct and indirect consequences and the effects on utility, and sets forth a necessarily brief analysis of the various major types of intervention, including price control, monopoly grants, taxation, inflation, and government enterprise and expenditures. The chapter and the book conclude with a brief summary assessment of the free market, as contrasted to interventionist and other coercive systems.

For this revised edition, I have decided to keep the original text and footnotes intact, and to confine any changes to this revised preface. Professor Mises died in 1973, and the following year, as luck would have it, the Austrian school of economics that Mises had kept alive in an almost underground existence burst forward into a spectacular revival. It is no accident that this revival coincided with the virtual collapse of the previously dominant Keynesian paradigm. Keynesians had promised to steer the economy easily away from the recurring pitfalls of inflationary boom, and recession and unemployment; instead, they would insure permanent and stable prosperity, bringing us full employment without inflation. And yet, after three decades of Keynesian planning, we faced a new phenomenon that cannot even exist, much less be explained, in the Keynesian paradigm: inflation *combined with* recession and high unemployment. This unwelcome specter first appeared in the inflationary recession of 1973–74, and has been repeated since, the last time being the recession of 1990—?

The Austrian revival of 1974 was also spurred by F. A. Hayek's receiving the Nobel prize for economics that year, the first free-market and non-mathematical economist to be accorded that honor. The economics profession's obsession with the Nobel reawakened interest in Hayek and in the Austrian school. But this award to Hayek itself can be no coincidence, since it reflects disillusion by economists in Keynesian macro-models.

Since 1974, the number of Austrians, books and articles by Austrians, and interest in the school, has greatly multiplied. It is a reflection of the difference in the quality of academia in the two countries that, even though there are proportionately fewer Austrian school economists in Britain than in the United States, Austrian economics is accorded a great deal more respect in Britain. In British textbooks and surveys of thought, Austrian economics, while not often winning agreement, is treated objectively and fairly as a respectable wing of economic thought. In the United States, on the contrary, while there are a large number of sympathizers as well as adherents in the profession, Austrians are still marginalized, unheeded, and unread by the bulk of economists.

Intellectual curiosity has a habit of breaking through, however, especially among college and graduate students. As a result, the Austrian school has flourished over the last two decades, despite severe institutional obstacles.

In fact, the number of Austrians has grown so large, and the discussion so broad, that differences of opinion and branches of thought have arisen, in some cases developing into genuine clashes of thought. Yet they have all been conflated and jammed together by non-Austrians and even by some within the school, giving rise to a great deal of intellectual confusion, lack of clarity, and outright error. The good side of these developing disputes is that each side has clarified and sharpened its underlying premises and world-view. It has indeed become evident in recent years that there are three very different and clashing paradigms within Austrian economics: the original Misesian or praxeological paradigm, to which the present author adheres; the Hayekian paradigm, stressing "knowledge" and "discovery" rather than the praxeological "action" and "choice," whose leading exponent now is Professor Israel Kirzner; and the nihilistic view of the late Ludwig Lachmann, an institutionalist anti-theory approach taken from the English "subjectivist"-Keynesian G. L. S. Shackle. Fortunately, there is now a scholarly journal, *The Review of Austrian Economics*, where the reader can keep apprised of ongoing developments in Austrian economics, as well as other publications, conferences, and instructional courses of the Ludwig von

Mises Institute. The Mises Institute, founded on the centenary of his birth, keeps alive the spirit of Mises as well as the paradigm that he has bequeathed to scholarship and to the world. For the latest on the three Austrian paradigms, the reader is referred to the Mises Institute Working Paper by the present author, *The Present State of Austrian Economics* (November, 1992).

My overriding intellectual debt, of course, is to Ludwig von Mises. But apart from that, I can never fully express my personal debt. His wisdom, kindness, enthusiasm, good humor, and unflagging encouragement of even the slightest signs of productivity among his students were a lifelong inspiration to those who knew him. He was one of the great teachers of economics, as well as one of the great economists, and I am grateful to have had the opportunity of studying for many years at his Seminar in Advanced Economic Theory at New York University.

I can also never fully express my gratitude to Llewellyn H. Rockwell, Jr., who, at a low point in Misesian economics, with no endowment, no large pledges of support, and armed only with an idea, founded and dedicated his life to the Ludwig von Mises Institute. Lew has done a remarkable job of building and expanding the Institute, and of devoting himself to the Misesian paradigm. In addition, Lew has been a close and valued friend and intellectual colleague for many years. It is obvious that, without his efforts, this new edition would never have seen the light of day.

Finally, I must at least try to convey how grateful I am to another long-time colleague, Burton S. Blumert, of the Mises Institute and head of the Center for Libertarian Studies, Burlingame, California. Self-effacing and indispensable, Burt is always there—with wit, wisdom, kindness, and friendship.

It is impossible to list all the friends and acquaintances who, over the many years, have taught and inspired me in the area of Austrian economics, or in the wider arena of political economy, and in the nature of coercion of freedom. I am grateful to them all. None of them, of course, is responsible for any errors herein.

Murray N. Rothbard
Las Vegas, Nevada
May, 1993

Table of Contents

1

Fundamentals of Human Action[1]

1. *The Concept of Action*

The distinctive and crucial feature in the study of man is the concept of *action. Human action is defined simply as purposeful behavior.* It is therefore sharply distinguishable from those observed movements which, from the point of view of man, are not purposeful. These include all the observed movements of inorganic matter and those types of human behavior that are purely reflex, that are simply involuntary responses to certain stimuli. *Human action,* on the other hand, can be *meaningfully interpreted* by other men, for it is governed by a certain *purpose* that the actor has in view.[2] The purpose of a man's act is his *end;* the desire to achieve this end is the man's *motive* for instituting the action.

All human beings *act* by virtue of their existence and their nature as human beings.[3] We could not conceive of human beings who do not act purposefully, who have no ends in view that they desire and attempt to attain. Things that did not *act,* that did not behave purposefully, would no longer be classified as human.

It is this fundamental truth—this axiom of human action—that forms the key to our study. The entire realm of praxeology and its best developed subdivision, economics, is based on an analysis of the necessary logical implications of this concept.[4] The fact that men act by virtue of their being human is indisputable and incontrovertible. To assume the contrary would be an absurdity. The contrary—the absence of motivated behavior—would apply only to plants and inorganic matter.[5]

2. *First Implications of the Concept*

The first truth to be discovered about human action is that *it can be undertaken only by individual "actors."* Only individuals have ends, and can act to attain them. There are no such things as ends of or actions by "groups," "collectives," or "States," which do not take place as actions by various specific individuals. "Societies" or "groups" have no independent existence aside from the actions of their individual members. Thus, to say that "governments" act is merely a metaphor; actually, certain individuals are in a certain relationship with other individuals and act in a way that they and the other individuals recognize as "governmental." [6] The metaphor must not be taken to mean that the collective institution itself has any reality apart from the acts of various individuals. Similarly, an individual may contract to act as an agent in representing another individual or on behalf of his family. Still, only individuals can desire and act. The existence of an institution such as government becomes meaningful only through influencing the actions of those individuals who are and those who are not considered as members.[7]

In order to institute action, it is not sufficient that the individual man have unachieved ends that he would like to fulfill. *He must also expect that certain modes of behavior will enable him to attain his ends.* A man may have a desire for sunshine, but if he realizes that he can do nothing to achieve it, he does not act on this desire. He must have certain *ideas* about how to achieve his ends. Action thus consists of the behavior of individuals directed towards ends in ways that they believe will accomplish their purpose. Action requires an image of a desired end and "technological ideas" or plans on how to arrive at this end.

Men find themselves in a certain *environment,* or *situation.* It is this situation that the individual decides to change in some way in order to achieve his ends. But man can work only with the numerous elements that he finds in his environment, by rearranging them in order to bring about the satisfaction of his ends. With reference to any given act, the environment external to the individual may be divided into two parts: those elements which he believes he cannot control and must leave unchanged, and those which he can alter (or rather, thinks he can alter) to arrive at his ends. The former may be termed the *general conditions* of the action; the latter the *means* used. Thus, the individual actor is faced with an environment that he would like to change in order to attain his ends. To act, he must have technological ideas about how to use some of the elements of the environment as *means,* as pathways, to arrive at his ends. Every act must therefore involve the employment of means by individual actors to attempt to arrive at certain desired ends. In the external environment, the general conditions cannot be the objects of any human action; only the means can be employed in action.[8]

All human life must take place *in time*. Human reason cannot even conceive of an existence or of action that does not take place through time. At a time when a human being decides to act in order to attain an end, his goal, or end, can be finally and completely attained only at some point *in the future*. If the desired ends could all be attained instantaneously in the present, then man's ends would all be attained, and there would be no reason for him to act; and we have seen that action is necessary to the nature of man. Therefore, an actor chooses means from his environment, in accordance with his ideas, to arrive at an expected end, completely attainable only at some point in the future. For any given action, we can distinguish among three periods of time involved: the period before the action, the time absorbed by the action, and the period after the action has been completed. All action aims at rendering conditions at some time in the future more satisfactory for the actor than they would have been without the intervention of the action.

A man's *time* is always scarce. He is not immortal; his time on earth is limited. Each day of his life has only twenty-four hours in which he can attain his ends. Furthermore, all actions must take place through time. Therefore time is a *means* that man must use to arrive at his ends. It is a means that is omnipresent in all human action.

Action takes place by *choosing* which ends shall be satisfied by the employment of means. Time is *scarce* for man only because whichever ends he chooses to satisfy, there are others that must remain unsatisfied. When we must use a means so that some ends remain unsatisfied, the necessity for a *choice among ends* arises. For example, Jones is engaged in watching a baseball game on television. He is faced with the choice of spending the next hour in: (*a*) continuing to watch the baseball game, (*b*) playing bridge, or (*c*) going for a drive. He would like to do all three of these things, but his means (time) is insufficient. As a result, he must *choose;* one end can be satisfied, but the others must go unfulfilled. Suppose that he decides on course A. This is a clear indication that he has *ranked* the satisfaction of end A higher than the satisfaction of ends B or C.

From this example of action, many implications can be deduced. In the first place, *all means are scarce,* i.e., limited with respect to the ends that they could possibly serve. If the means are in unlimited abundance, then they need not serve as the object of attention of any human action. For example, air in most situations is in unlimited abundance. It is therefore not a means and is not employed as a means to the fulfillment of ends. It need not be allocated, as time is, to the satisfaction of the more important ends, since it is sufficiently abundant for all human requirements. Air, then, though indispensable, is not a means, but a *general condition* of human action and human welfare.

Secondly, these scarce means must be allocated by the actor to serve certain ends and leave other ends unsatisfied. This act of *choice* may be called *economizing* the means to serve the most desired ends. Time, for example, must be economized by the actor to serve the most desired ends. The actor may be interpreted as ranking his alternative ends in accordance with their *value* to him. This scaling of ends may be described as assigning ranks of *value* to the ends by the actor, or as a process of *valuation*. Thus, suppose that Jones ranked his alternative ends for the use of an hour of time as follows:

(First) 1. Continuing to watch the baseball game
(Second) 2. Going for a drive
(Third) 3. Playing bridge

This was his *scale of values* or *scale of preferences.* The supply of means (time) available was sufficient for the attainment of only one of these ends, and the fact that he chose the baseball game shows that he ranked that highest (or first). Suppose now that he is allocating two hours of his time and can spend an hour on each pursuit. If he spends one hour on the game and then a second hour on the drive, this indicates that his ranking of preferences is as above. The lowest-ranking end—playing bridge—goes unfulfilled. Thus, the larger the supply of means available, the more ends can be satisfied and the lower the rank of the ends that must remain unsatisfied.

Another lesson to be derived is that *action* does not necessarily mean that the individual is "active," as opposed to "passive," in the colloquial sense. Action does not necessarily mean that an individual must stop doing what he has been doing and do something else. He also acts, as in the above case, who chooses to continue in his previous course, even though the opportunity to change was open to him. Continuing to watch the game is just as much *action* as going for a drive.

Furthermore, action does not at all mean that the individual must take a great deal of time in deliberating on a decision to act. The individual may take a decision to act hastily, or after great deliberation, according to his desired choice. He may decide on an action coolly or heatedly; none of these courses affects the fact that action is being taken.[9]

Another fundamental implication derived from the existence of human action is the *uncertainty of the future.* This must be true because the contrary would completely negate the possibility of action. If man knew future events completely, he would never act, since no act of his could change the situation. Thus, the fact of action signifies that the future is uncertain to the actors. This uncertainty about future events stems from two basic sources: the unpredictability of human acts of choice and insufficient knowledge about natural phenomena. Man does not know enough about natural phenomena to predict all their future developments, and he cannot know the content of future human choices. All human choices are continually changing as a result of changing valuations and changing ideas about the most appropriate means of arriving at ends. This does not mean, of course, that people do not try their best to estimate future developments. Indeed, any actor, when employing means, estimates that he will thus arrive at his desired goal. But he never has certain knowledge of the future. All his actions are of necessity *speculations* based on his *judgment* of the course of future events. The omnipresence of uncertainty introduces the ever-present possibility of *error* in human action. The actor may find, after he has completed his action, that the means have been *inappropriate* to the attainment of his end.

To sum up what we have learned thus far about human action: The distinguishing characteristic of human beings is that all humans *act*. Action is purposeful behavior directed toward the attainment of ends in some future period which will involve the fulfillment of wants otherwise remaining unsatisfied. Action involves the expectation of a less imperfectly satisfied state as a result of the action. The individual actor chooses to employ elements in his environment as means to the expected achievement of his ends, *economizing* them by directing them toward his most valued ends (leaving his least valued ones unsatisfied), and in the ways that his reason tells him are most appropriate to attain these ends. His method—his chosen means—may or may not turn out to be inappropriate.

3. *Further Implications: The Means*

The *means* to satisfy man's wants are called *goods*. These goods are all the objects of economizing action.[10] Such goods may all be classified in either of two categories: (*a*) they are immediately and *directly serviceable* in the satisfaction of the actor's wants, or (*b*) they may be transformable into directly serviceable goods only at some point in the future—i.e., are *indirectly serviceable* means. The former are called *consumption goods* or *consumers' goods* or *goods of the first order.* The latter are called *producers' goods* or *factors of production* or *goods of higher order.*

Let us trace the relations among these goods by considering a typical human end: *the eating of a ham sandwich.* Having a desire for a ham sandwich, a man decides that this is a want that should be satisfied and proceeds to act upon his judgment of the methods by which a ham sandwich can be assembled. *The consumers' good* is the ham sandwich at the point of being eaten. It is obvious that there is a scarcity of this consumers' good as there is for all direct means; otherwise it would always be available, like air, and would not be the object of action. But if the consumers' good is scarce and not obviously available, how can it be made available? The answer is that man must rearrange various elements of his environment in order to *produce* the ham sandwich at the desired place—the consumers' good. In other words, man must use various *indirect* means as co-operating factors of production to arrive at the direct means. This necessary process involved in all action is called *production;* it is the use by man of available elements of his environment as indirect means—as co-operating factors—to arrive eventually at a consumers' good which he can use directly to arrive at his end.

Let us consider the pattern of some of the numerous co-operating factors that are involved in a modern developed economy to produce one ham sandwich as a consumers' good for the use of one consumer. Typically, in order to produce a ham sandwich for Jones in his armchair, it is necessary for his wife to expend energy in unwrapping the bread, slicing the ham, placing the ham between bread slices, and carrying it to Jones. All this work may be called the *labor* of the housewife. The co-operating factors that are directly necessary to arrive at the consumers' good are, then: the housewife's labor, bread in the kitchen, ham in the kitchen, and a knife to slice the ham. Also needed is the land on which to have room to live and carry on these activities. Furthermore, this process must, of course, take *time,* which is another indispensable co-operating factor. The above factors may be called *first-order producers' goods,* since, in this case, these co-operate in the production of the consumers' good. Many of the first-order producers' goods, however, are also unavailable in nature and must be *produced* themselves, with the help of other producers' goods. Thus, bread in the kitchen must be produced with the co-operation of the following factors: *bread-in-retail-shop* and *housewife's labor* in carrying it (plus the ever-present land-as-standing-room, and time). In this procedure, these factors are second-order producers' goods, since they co-operate in producing first-order goods. Higher-order factors are those co-operating in the production of factors of lower order.

Thus, any process (or *structure*) of production may be analyzed as occurring in different *stages*. In the *earlier* or "higher" stages, producers' goods must be produced that will later co-operate in producing other producers' goods that will finally co-operate in producing the desired consumers' good. Hence, in a developed economy, the structure of production of a given consumers' good might be a very complex one and involve numerous stages.

Important general conclusions can, however, be drawn that apply to all processes of production. In the first place, each stage of production takes *time*. Secondly, the factors of production may all be divided into two classes: *those that are themselves produced,* and *those that are found already available in nature—in man's environment.* The latter may be used as indirect means without having been previously produced; the former must first be produced with the aid of factors in order to aid in the *later* (or "lower") stages of production. The former are the *produced factors of production;* the latter are the *original factors of production.* The original factors may, in turn, be divided into two classes: *the expenditure of human energy,* and *the use of nonhuman elements provided by nature.* The first is called *Labor;* the latter is Nature or *Land.*[11] Thus, the classes of factors of production are Labor, Land, and the produced factors which are termed *Capital Goods.*

Labor and Land, in one form or another, enter into each stage of production. Labor helps to transform seeds into wheat, wheat into flour, pigs into ham, flour into bread, etc. Not only is Labor present at every stage of production, but so also is Nature. Land must be available to provide room at every stage of the process, and time, as has been stated above, is required for each stage. Furthermore, if we wish to trace each stage of production far enough back to original sources, we must arrive at a point where only labor and nature existed and there were no capital goods. This must be true by logical implication, since all capital goods must have been produced at earlier stages with the aid of labor. If we could trace each production process far enough back in time, we must be able to arrive at the point—the earliest stage—where man combined his forces with nature unaided by produced factors of production. Fortunately, it is not necessary for human actors to perform this task, since action uses materials available in the present to arrive at desired goals in the *future,* and there is no need to be concerned with development in the *past.*

There is another unique type of factor of production that is indispensable in every stage of every production process. This is the "technological idea" of how to proceed from one stage to another and finally to arrive at the desired consumers' good. This is but an application of the analysis above, namely, that for any action, there must be some *plan* or idea of the actor about how to use things as means, as definite pathways, to desired ends. Without such plans or ideas, there would be no action. These plans may be called *recipes;* they are ideas of recipes that the actor uses to arrive at his goal. A *recipe* must be present at each stage of each production process from which the actor proceeds to a later stage. The actor must have a recipe for transforming iron into steel, wheat into flour, bread and ham into sandwiches, etc.

The distinguishing feature of a recipe is that, *once learned,* it generally does not have to be learned again. It can be noted and remembered. Remembered, it no longer has to be produced; it remains with the actor as an *unlimited* factor of production that never wears out or needs to be economized by human action. It becomes a general condition of human welfare in the same way as air.[12]

It should be clear that the end of the production process—the consumers' good—is valued because it is a direct means of satisfying man's ends. The consumers' good is *consumed,* and this act of *consumption* constitutes the satisfying of human wants. This consumers' good may be a material object like bread or an immaterial one like friendship. Its important quality is not whether it is material or not, but whether it is valued by man as a means of satisfying his wants. This function of a consumers' good is called its *service* in ministering to human wants. Thus, the material bread is valued not for itself, but for its service in satisfying wants; just as an immaterial thing, such as music or medical care, is obviously valued for such service. All these services are "consumed" to satisfy wants. "Economic" is by no means equivalent to "material."

It is also clear that the factors of production—the various higher-order producers' goods—*are valued solely because of their anticipated usefulness in helping to produce future consumers' goods or to produce lower-order producers' goods that will help to bring about consumers' goods.* The valuation of factors of production is derived from actors' evaluation of their products (lower stages), all of which eventually derive their valuation from the end result—the consumers' good.[13]

Furthermore, the omnipresent fact of the scarcity of consumers' goods must be reflected back in the sphere of the factors of production. The scarcity of consumers' goods must imply a scarcity of their factors. If the factors were unlimited, then the consumers' goods would also be unlimited, which cannot be the case. This does not exclude the possiblity that *some* factors, such as recipes, may be unlimited and therefore general conditions of welfare rather than scarce indirect means. But other factors at each stage of production must be in scarce supply, and this must account for the scarcity of the end product. Man's endless search for ways to satisfy his wants—i.e., to *increase his production of consumers' goods*—takes two forms: increasing his available supply of factors of production and improving his recipes.

Although it has seemed evident that there are several co-operating factors at each stage of production, it is important to realize that for each consumers' good *there must always be more than one scarce factor of production.* This is implied in the very existence of human action. It is impossible to conceive of a situation where only one factor of production produces a consumers' good or even advances a consumers' good from its previous stage of production. Thus, if the sandwich in the armchair did not require the co-operating factors at the previous stage (labor of preparation, carrying, bread, ham, time, etc.), then it would always be in the status of a consumers' good—sandwich-in-the-armchair. To simplify the example, let us suppose the sandwich already prepared and in the kitchen. Then, to produce a consumers' good from this stage forward requires the following factors: 1) the sandwich; 2) carrying it to the armchair; 3) time; 4) the land available. If we assume that it required only one factor—the sandwich—then we would have to assume that the sandwich was magically and instantaneously moved from kitchen to armchair without effort. But in this case, the consumers' good would not have to be produced at all, and we would be in the impossible assumption of Paradise. Similarly, at each stage of the productive process, the good must have been produced by at least *more than one* (higher-order) scarce co-operating factor; otherwise this stage of production could not exist at all.

4. *Further Implications: Time*

Time is omnipresent in human action as a means that must be economized. Every action is related to time as follows:

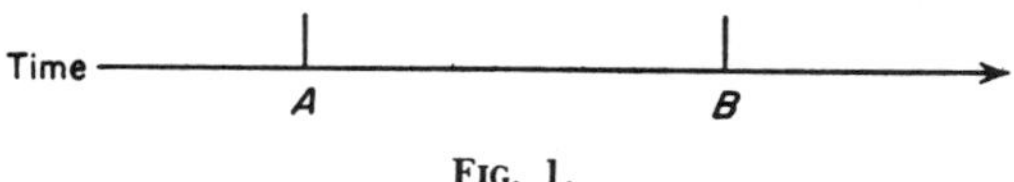

FIG. 1.

. . . *A* is the period before the beginning of the action; *A* is the point in time at which the action begins; *AB* is the period during which the action occurs; *B* is the point at which the action ends; *B* . . . is the period after the end of the action.

AB is defined as the *period of production*—the period from the beginning of the action to the time when the consumers' good is available. This period may be divided into various stages, each itself taking a period of time. The time expended during the period of production consists of the time during which *labor energy* is expended (*or working time*) and *maturing time,* i.e., time required without the necessity of concurrent expenditure of labor. An obvious example is the case of agriculture. There might be six months between the time the soil is tilled and the time the harvest is reaped. The total time during which labor must be expended may be three weeks, while the remaining time of over five months consists of the time during which the crop must mature and ripen by the processes of nature. Another example of a lengthy maturing time is the aging of wine to improve its quality.

Clearly, each consumers' good has its own period of production. The differences between the time involved in the periods of production of the various goods may be, and are, innumerable.

One important point that must be emphasized when considering action and the period of production is that acting man does *not* trace back past production processes to their original sources. In the previous section, we traced back consumers' goods and producers' goods to their original sources, demonstrating that all capital goods were *originally* produced solely by labor and nature. Acting man, however, is not interested in past processes, but only in using *presently available means* to achieve anticipated future ends. At any point in time, when he begins the action (say *A*), he has available to him: labor, nature-given elements, and *previously produced capital goods.* He begins the action at *A* expecting to reach his end at *B*. For *him,* the period of production is *AB,* since he is not concerned with the amount of time spent in past production of his capital goods or in the methods by which they were produced.[14] Thus, the farmer about to use his soil to grow crops for the coming season does not worry about whether or to what extent his soil is an original, nature-given factor or is the result of the improvements of previous land-clearers and farmers. He is not concerned about the previous time spent by these past improvers. He is concerned only with the capital (and other) goods in the present and the future. This is the necessary result of the fact that action occurs in the present and is aimed at the future. Thus, acting man considers and values the factors of production available in the present in accordance with their anticipated services in the future production of consumers' goods, and never in accordance with what has happened to the factors in the past.

A fundamental and constant truth about human action is that *man prefers his end to be achieved in the shortest possible time.* Given the specific satisfaction, the sooner it arrives, the better. This results from the fact that time is always scarce, and a means to be economized. The sooner any end is attained, the better. Thus, with any *given end* to be attained, the shorter the period of action, i.e., production, the more preferable for the actor. *This is the universal fact of time preference.* At any point of time, and for any action, the actor most prefers to have his end attained in the immediate present. Next best for him is the immediate future, and the further in the future the attainment of the end appears to be, the less preferable it is. *The less waiting time,* the more preferable it is for him.[15]

Time enters into human action not only in relation to the waiting time in production, but also in *the length of time in which the consumers' good will satisfy the wants of the consumer.* Some consumers' goods will satisfy his wants, i.e., attain his ends, for a short period of time, others for a longer period. They can be consumed for shorter or longer periods. This may be included in the diagram of any action as shown in Fig. 2. This length of time, *BC,*

FIG. 2. PERIOD OF PRODUCTION AND CONSUMPTION

is the *duration of serviceableness* of the consumers' good. It is the length of the time the *end* served by the consumers' good continues to be attained. This duration of serviceableness differs for each consumers' good. It may be four hours for the ham sandwich, after which period of time the actor desires other food or another sandwich. The builder of a house may expect to use it to serve his wants for ten years. Obviously, the expected durative power of the consumers' good to serve his end will enter into the actor's plans.[16]

Clearly, all other things being equal, the actor will prefer a consumers' good of greater durability to one of lesser, since the former will render more total service. On the other hand, if the actor values the total service rendered by two consumers' goods equally, he will, because of time preference, choose the less durable good since he will acquire its total services sooner than the other. He will have to wait less for the total services of the less durable good.

The concepts of period of production and duration of serviceableness are present in all human action. There is also a third time-period that enters into action. Each person has a general time-horizon, stretching from the present into the future, for which he plans various types of action. Whereas period of production and duration of serviceableness refer to specific consumers' goods and differ with each consumers' good, the *period of provision* (the time-horizon) is the length of future time for which each actor plans to satisfy his wants. The period of provision, therefore, includes planned action for a considerable variety of consumers' goods, each with its own period of production and duraction. This period of provision differs from actor to actor in accordance with his choice. Some people live from day to day, taking no heed of later periods of time; others plan not only for the duration of their own lives, but for their children as well.

5. *Further Implications*

A. ENDS AND VALUES

All action involves the employment of scarce means to attain the most valued ends. Man has the choice of using the scarce means for various alternative ends, and the ends that he chooses are the ones he values most highly. The less urgent wants are those that remain unsatisfied. Actors can be interpreted as *ranking* their ends along a scale of values, or scale of preferences. These scales differ for each person, both in their content and in their orders of preference. Furthermore, they differ for the same individual at different times. Thus, at some other point in time, the actor mentioned in section 2 above might choose to go for a drive, or to go for a drive and then to play bridge, rather than to continue watching the game. In that case, the ranking on his preference scale shifts to this order:

(First) 1. Going for a drive
(Second) 2. Playing bridge
(Third) 3. Continuing to watch the baseball game

Moreover, a new end might have been introduced in the meantime, so that the actor might enjoy going to a concert, and this may change his value scale to the following:

(First) 1. Going for a drive
(Second) 2. Going to a concert
(Third) 3. Playing bridge
(Fourth) 4. Continuing to watch the baseball game

The choice of which ends to include in the actor's value scale and the assignment of rank to the various ends constitute the process of *value judgment.* Each time the actor ranks and chooses between various ends, he is making a judgment of their value to him.

It is highly useful to assign a *name* to this value scale held by all human actors. We are not at all concerned with the specific *content* of men's ends, but only with the fact that various ends are ranked in the order of their importance. These scales of preference may be called *happiness* or *welfare* or *utility* or *satisfaction* or *contentment.* Which name we choose for value scales is not important. At any rate, it permits us to say, whenever an actor has attained a certain end, that he has *increased* his state of satisfaction, or his contentment, happiness, etc. Conversely, when someone considers himself worse off, and fewer of his ends are being attained, his satisfaction, happiness, welfare, etc., have *decreased.*

It is important to realize that there is never any possibility of *measuring* increases or decreases in happiness or satisfaction. Not only is it impossible to measure or compare changes in the satisfaction of different people; it is not possible to measure changes in the happiness of any given person. In order for any measurement to be possible, there must be an eternally fixed and objectively given unit with which other units may be compared. There is no such objective unit in the field of human valuation. The individual must determine subjectively for himself whether he is better or worse off as a result of any change. His preference can only be expressed in terms of simple choice, or *rank*. Thus, he can say, "I am better off" or "I am happier" because he went to a concert instead of playing bridge (or "I will be better off" for going to the concert), but it would be completely meaningless for him to try to assign units to his preference and say: "I am two and a half times happier because of this choice than I would have been playing bridge." Two and a half times *what?* There is no possible unit of happiness that can be used for purposes of comparison, and hence of addition or multiplication. Thus, values cannot be measured; values or utilities cannot be added, subtracted, or multiplied. They can only be ranked as better or worse. A man may know that he is or will be happier or less happy, but not by "how much," not by a measurable quantity.[17]

All action is an attempt to exchange a less satisfactory state of affairs for a more satisfactory one. The actor finds himself (or expects to find himself) in a nonperfect state, and, by attempting to attain his most urgently desired ends, expects to be in a better state. He cannot measure the gain in satisfaction, but he does know which of his wants are more urgent than others, and he does know when his condition has improved. Therefore, *all action involves exchange*—an exchange of one state of affairs, *X*, for *Y*, which the actor anticipates will be a more satisfactory one (and therefore higher on his value scale). If his expectation turns out to be correct, the value of *Y* on his preference scale will be higher than the value of *X*, and he has made a *net gain* in his state of satisfaction or utility. If he has been in error, and the value of the state that he has given up—*X*—is higher than the value of *Y*, he has suffered a *net loss*. This psychic gain (or *profit*) and loss cannot be measured in terms of units, but the actor always knows whether he has experienced psychic profit or psychic loss as a result of an action-exchange.[18]

Human actors value *means* strictly in accordance with their valuation of the ends that they believe the means can serve. Obviously, consumers' goods are graded in value in accordance with the ends that men expect them to satisfy. Thus, the value placed on the enjoyment contributed by a ham sandwich or a house will determine the value a man will place on the ham sandwich or the house themselves. Similarily, producers' goods are valued in accordance with their expected contribution in producing consumers' goods. Higher-order producers' goods are valued in accordance with their anticipated service in forming lower-order producers' goods. Hence, those consumers' goods serving to attain more highly valued ends will be valued more highly than those serving less highly valued ends, and those producers' goods serving to produce more highly valued consumers' goods will themselves be valued more highly than other producers' goods. Thus, the *process of imputing values to goods* takes place in the opposite direction to that of the process of production. Value proceeds from the ends to the consumers' good to the various first-order producers' goods, to the second-order producers' goods, etc.[19] The original source of value is the ranking of ends by human actors, who then impute value to consumers' goods, and so on to the orders of producers' goods, in accordance with their expected ability to contribute toward serving the various ends.[20]

B. THE LAW OF MARGINAL UTILITY

It is evident that things are valued as means in accordance with their ability to attain ends valued as more or less urgent. *Each physical unit of a means* (direct or indirect) that enters into human action is valued separately. Thus, the actor is interested in evaluating only those units of means that enter, or that he considers will enter, into his concrete action. Actors choose between, and evaluate, not "coal" or "butter" in general, but specific units of coal or butter. In choosing between acquiring cows or horses, the actor does not choose between the class of cows and the class of horses, but between specific units of them—e.g., two cows vs. three horses. Each unit that enters into concrete action is graded and evaluated separately. Only when several units together enter into human action are all of them evaluated together.

The processes that enter into valuation of specific units of different goods may be illustrated in this example: [21] An individual possessing two cows and three horses might have to choose between giving up one cow or one horse. He may decide in this case to keep the horse, indicating that in this state of his stock, a horse is more valuable to him than a cow. On the other hand, he might be presented with the choice of keeping either his entire stock of cows or his stock of horses. Thus, his stable and cowshed might catch fire, and he is presented with the choice of saving the inhabitants of one or of the other building. In this case, two cows might be more valuable to him than three horses, so that he will prefer to save the cows. When deciding between units of his stock, the actor may therefore prefer good *X* to good *Y*, while he may choose good *Y* if he must act upon his *whole stock of each good.*

This process of valuation according to the specific units involved provides the solution for the famous "value paradox" which puzzled writers for centuries. The question was: How can men value bread less than platinum, when "bread" is obviously more useful than "platinum"? The answer is that acting man does not evaluate the goods open to him by abstract classes, but in terms of the specific units available. He does not wonder whether "bread-in-general" is more or less valuable to him than "platinum-in-general," but whether, given the present available stock of bread and platinum, a "loaf of bread" is more or less valuable to him than "an ounce of platinum." That, in most cases, men prefer the latter is no longer surprising.[22]

As has been explained above, value, or utility, cannot be measured, and therefore cannot be added, subtracted, or multiplied. This holds for specific units of the same good in the same way as it holds for all other comparisons of value. Thus, if butter is an object serving human ends, we know that two pounds of butter will be valued more highly than one pound. This will be true until a point is reached when the butter is available in unlimited quantities to satisfy human wants and will then be transferred from the status of a means to that of a general condition of human welfare. However, we *cannot* say that two pounds of butter are "twice as useful or valuable" as one pound.

What has been involved in this key concept of "specific units of a good"? In these examples, the units of the good have been *inter-*

changeable from the point of view of the actor. Thus, any concrete pound of butter was evaluated in this case perfectly equally with any other pound of butter. Cow A and cow B were valued equally by the individual, and it made no difference to him which cow he was faced with the choice of saving. Similarly, horse A was valued equally with horse B and with horse C, and the actor was not concerned which particular horse he had to choose. When a commodity is in such a way available in *specific homogeneous units equally capable of rendering the same service to the actor,* this available stock is called a *supply.* A *supply of a good* is available in specific units each perfectly substitutable for every other. The individual above had an available supply of two cows and three horses, and a supply of pounds of butter.

What if one pound of butter was considered by the actor as of better quality than another pound of butter? In that case, the two "butters" are really *different goods* from the point of view of the actor and will be evaluated differently. The two pounds of butter are now two different goods and are no longer two units of a supply of one good. Similarly, the actor must have valued each horse or each cow identically. If he preferred one horse to each of the others, or one cow to the other, then they are no longer units of the supply of the same good. No longer are his horses interchangeable for one another. If he grades horse A above the others and regards horses B and C indifferently, then he has supplies of two different goods (omitting the cows): say, "Grade A horses—1 unit"; and "Grade B horses—2 units." If a specific unit is differently evaluated from all other units, then the supply of that good is only one unit.

Here again, it is very important to recognize that what is significant for human action is *not* the physical property of a good, but the evaluation of the good by the actor. Thus, physically there may be no discernible difference between one pound of butter and another, or one cow and another. But if the actor chooses to evaluate them differently, they are no longer part of the supply of the same good.

The interchangeability of units in the supply of a good does not mean that the concrete units are actually valued equally. They may and will be valued differently whenever their *position in the supply* is different. Thus, suppose that the isolated individual successively finds one horse, then a second, then a third. Each horse may be identical and interchangeable with the others. The first horse will fulfill the most urgent wants that a horse can serve; this follows from the universal fact that action uses scarce means to satisfy the most urgent of the not yet satisfied wants. When the second horse is found, he will be put to work satisfying the most urgent of the wants remaining. These wants, however, must be ranked lower than the wants that the previous horse has satisfied. Similarly, the third horse acquired might be capable of performing the same service as the others, but he will be put to work fulfilling the highest of the remaining wants—which, however, will yet be lower in value than the others.

The important consideration is the *relation between the unit to be acquired or given up and the quantity of supply* (*stock*) *already available to the actor.* Thus, if no units of a good (whatever the good may be) are available, the first unit will satisfy the most urgent wants that such a good is capable of satisfying. If to this supply of one unit is added a second unit, the latter will fulfill the most urgent wants remaining, but these will be less urgent than the ones the first fulfilled. Therefore, the value of the second unit to the actor will be less than the value of the first unit. Similarly, the value of the third unit of the supply (added to a stock of two units) will be less than the value of the second unit. It may not matter to the individual *which* horse is chosen first and which second, or *which* pounds of butter he consumes, but those units which he does use first will be the ones that he values more highly. *Thus, for all human actions, as the quantity of the supply* (*stock*) *of a good increases, the utility* (*or value*) *of each additional unit decreases.*

Let us now consider a supply from the point of view of a possible *decrease,* rather than an increase. Assume that a man has a supply of six (interchangeable) horses. They are engaged in fulfilling his wants. Suppose that he is now faced with the necessity of giving up one horse. It now follows that this smaller stock of means is not capable of rendering as much service to him as the larger supply. This stems from the very existence of the good as a means.[23] Therefore, *the utility of X units of a good is always greater than the utility of X – 1 units.* Because of the impossibility of measurement, it is impossible to determine *by how much greater* one value is than the other. Now, the question arises: Which utility, which end, does the actor give up because he is deprived of one unit? Obviously, he gives up the *least urgent of the wants which the larger stock would have satisfied.* Thus, if the individual was using one horse for pleasure riding, and he considers this the least important of his wants that were fulfilled by the six horses, the loss of a horse will cause him to give up pleasure riding.

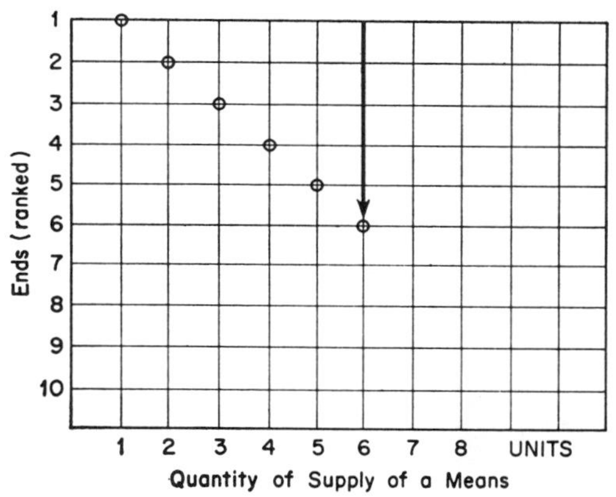

FIG. 3. VALUE-SCALE DIAGRAM

The principles involved in the utility of a supply may be illustrated in the accompanying value-scale diagram (Fig. 3). We are considering any given means, which is divisible into homogeneous units of a supply, each interchangeable and capable of giving service equal to that of the other units. The supply must be scarce in relation to the ends that it is capable of fulfilling; otherwise it would not be a good, but a condition of human welfare. We assume for simplicity that there are 10 ends which the means could fulfill, and that each unit of means is capable of serving one of the ends. If the supply of the good is 6 units, then the first 6 ends, ranked in order of importance by the valuing individual, are the ones that are being satisfied. Ends ranked 7–10 remain unsatisfied. If we assume that the stock arrived in successive units, then the first unit went to satisfy end 1, the second unit was used to serve end 2, etc. The sixth unit was used to serve end 6. The dots indicate how the units were used for the different ends, and the arrow indicates the direction the process took, i.e., that the most important ends were served first; the next, second, etc. The diagram illustrates the aforementioned laws that the utility (value) of more units is greater than the utility of fewer units and that the utility of each successive unit is less as the quantity of the supply increases.

Now, suppose the actor is faced with the necessity of giving up one unit of his stock. His total will be five instead of six units. Obviously, he gives up satisfying the end ranked sixth, and continues to satisfy the more important ends 1–5. As a result of the interchangeability of units, it does not matter to him *which* of the six units he must lose; the point is that he will give up serving this sixth end. Since action considers only the present and the future and not the past, it does not matter to him *which* units he acquired first in the past. He deals only with his presently available stock. In other words, suppose that the sixth horse that he had previously acquired (named "Seabiscuit") he had placed in the service of pleasure riding. Suppose that he now must lose another horse ("Man o' War") which had arrived earlier, and which was engaged in the more important duty (to him) of leading a wagon. He will still give up end 6 by simply transferring Seabiscuit from this function to the wagon-leading end. This consequence follows from the defined interchangeability of units and from disregard of past events which are of no consequence for the present and the future.

Thus, the actor gives up the lowest-ranking want that the original stock (in this case, six units) was capable of satisfying. This one unit that he must consider giving up is called *the marginal unit*. It is the unit "at the margin." This least important end fulfilled by the stock is known as the *satisfaction provided by the marginal unit,* or the *utility of the marginal unit*—in short: the marginal satisfaction, or *marginal utility*. If the marginal unit is one unit, then the *marginal utility of the supply* is the end that must be given up as the result of a loss of the unit. In the diagram above, the marginal utility is ranked sixth among the ends. If the supply consisted of four units, and the actor were faced with the necessity of giving up one unit, then the value of the marginal unit, or the *marginal utility,* would have a rank of 4. If the stock consisted of one unit, and this had to be given up, the value of the marginal unit would be 1—the value of the highest-ranked end.

We are now in a position to complete an important law indicated above, but with different phraseology: *The greater the supply of a good, the lower the marginal utility; the smaller the supply, the higher the marginal utility.* This fundamental law of economics has been derived from the fundamental axiom of human action; it is the *law of marginal utility,* sometimes known as the *law of diminishing marginal utility.* Here again, it must be emphasized that "utility" is not a cardinal quantity subject to the processes of measurement, such as addition, multiplication, etc. It is a *ranked number* expressible only in terms of higher or lower order in the preferences of men.

This law of marginal utility holds for all goods, regardless of the size of the unit considered. The size of the unit will be the one that enters into concrete human action, but whatever it is, the same principle applies. Thus, if in certain situations, the actor must consider only *pairs of horses* as the units to add or subtract from his stock, instead of the individual horses, he will construct a new and shorter scale of ends with fewer units of supply to consider. He will then go through a similar process of assigning means to serve ends and will give up the least valued end should he lose a unit of supply. The ends will simply be ranked in terms of the alternative uses of pairs of horses, instead of single horses.

What if a good cannot be divided into homogeneous units for purposes of action? There are cases where the good must be treated as a whole in human action. Does the law of marginal utility apply in such a case? The law does apply, since we then treat the supply as consisting of *one unit.* In this case, the marginal unit is equal in size to the total supply possessed or desired by the actor. The value of the marginal unit is equal to the *first rank of the ends which the total good could serve.* Thus, if an individual must dispose of his whole stock of six horses, or acquire a stock of six horses together, the six horses are treated as one unit. The marginal utility of his supply would then be equal to the first-ranking end that the unit of *six horses* could supply.

If, as above, we consider the case of *additions* instead of decreases to stock, we recall that the law derived for this situation was that as the quantity of supply increases, the utility of each additional unit decreases. Yet this additional unit is precisely the *marginal unit.* Thus, if instead of decreasing the supply from six to five horses, we *increase* it from five to six, the value of the additional horse is equal to the value of the sixth-ranking end—say, pleasure riding. This is the same marginal unit, with the same utility, as in the case of decreasing the stock from six to five. Thus, the law derived previously was simply another form of the law of marginal utility. The greater the supply of a good, the lower the marginal utility; the smaller the supply, the higher the marginal utility. This is true whether or not the marginal unit is the unit of decrease of stock or the unit of addition to stock, when these are considered by the actor. If a man's supply of a good equals X units, and he is considering the addition of one unit, this is the marginal unit. If his supply is $X + 1$ units, and he is considering the loss of one unit, this too is his marginal unit, and its value is identical with the former (provided that his ends and their ranking are the same in both cases).

We have dealt with the laws of utility as they apply to each good treated in human action. Now we must indicate the relationship among various goods. It is obvious that more than one good exists in human action. This has already been definitely proven, since it was demonstrated that more than one factor of production, hence more than one good, must exist. Fig. 4 below demonstrates the relationship between the various goods in human action. Here the value scales of two goods are considered—X and Y. For each good, the law of marginal utility holds, and the relation between supply and value is revealed in the diagram for each good. For simplicity, let us assume that X is horses and Y cows, and that the value scales representing those held by the individual are as follows (horizontal lines are drawn through each end to demonstrate the relationship in the ranking of the ends of the two goods): End *Y*-1 is ranked highest (say, cow 1); then ends *X*-1, *X*-2, and *X*-3 (horses 1, 2, and 3); *Y*-2; *Y*-3; *X*-4; *Y*-4; *X*-5; *Y*-5; *X*-6; *X*-7; *Y*-6; *Y*-7.

Now, the man's value scales will reveal his choices involving alternatives of action in regard to these two goods. Suppose that his

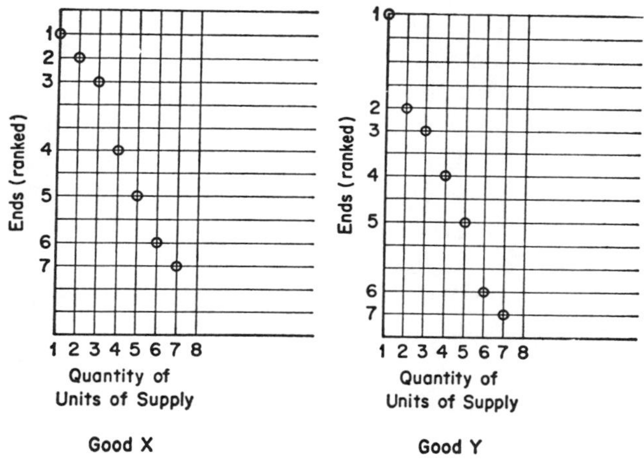

FIG. 4. VALUE SCALES

stock is: 3*Y* (cows) and 4*X* (horses). He is faced with the alternative of giving up: *either one cow or one horse.* He will choose the alternative which will deprive him of the least valued end possible. Since the marginal utility of each good is equal to the value of the least important end of which he would be deprived, *he compares the marginal utility of X with the marginal utility of Y.* In this case, the marginal unit of *X* has a rank of *X*-4, and the marginal unit of *Y* has a rank of *Y*-3. But the end *Y*-3 is ranked higher on his value scale than *X*-4. Hence the marginal utility of *Y* is in this case higher than (or greater than) the marginal utility of *X*. Since he will give up the lowest possible utility, he will give up one unit of *X*. *Thus, presented with a choice of units of goods to give up, he will give up the good with units of lowest marginal utility on his value scale.* Suppose another example: that his stock is three horses and two cows. He has the alternative of giving up 1*X* or 1*Y*. In this case, the marginal utility of *Y* is ranked at *Y*-2, and that of *X* is ranked at *X*-3. But *X*-3 occupies a higher position on his value scale than *Y*-2, and therefore the marginal utility of *Y* is at this point lower than the marginal utility of *X*. He gives up a unit of *Y*.

The converse occurs if the man must choose between the alternative of *increasing* his stock by either one unit of *X* or a unit of *Y*. Thus, suppose that his stock is 4 units of *X* and 4 units of *Y*. He must choose between adding one horse or one cow. He then compares the marginal utility of increase, i.e., the value of the most important of the not yet satisfied wants. The marginal utility of *X* is then ranked at *X*-5; of *Y* at *Y*-5. But *X*-5 ranks higher than *Y*-5 on his value scale, and he will therefore choose the former. *Thus, faced with the choice of adding units of goods, he will choose the unit of highest marginal utility on his value scale.*

Another example: Previously, we saw that the man in a position of (4*X*, 3*Y*) would, if faced with the choice of giving up one unit of either *X* or *Y*, give up the unit of *X*, with a lower marginal utility. In other words, he would prefer a position of (3*X*, 3*Y*) to (4*X*, 2*Y*). Now suppose he is in a position of (3*X*, 3*Y*) and faced with the choice of adding 1 unit of *X* or 1 unit of *Y*. Since the marginal utility of the increased *X* is greater than that of *Y*, he will choose to add the unit of *X* and to arrive at a position of (4*X*, 3*Y*) rather than (3*X*, 4*Y*). The reader can work out the hypothetical choices for all the possible combinations of the actor's stock.

It is evident that in the act of choosing between giving up or adding units of either *X* or *Y*, the actor must have, in effect, placed both goods on a *single, unitary value scale*. Unless he could place *X* and *Y* on *one* value scale for comparison, he could not have determined that the marginal utility of the fourth unit of *X* was higher than that of the fourth unit of *Y*. The very fact of action in choosing between more than one good implies that the units of these goods must have been ranked for comparison on one value scale of the actor. The actor may not and cannot *measure* differences in utility, but he must be engaged in ranking all the goods considered on one value scale. Thus, we should actually consider the ends served by the two means as ranked on one value scale as follows:

Ends (*Ranked*)

1—*Y*-1
2—*X*-1
3—*X*-2
4—*X*-3
5—*Y*-2
6—*Y*-3
7—*X*-4
8—*Y*-4
9—*X*-5
10—*Y*-5
11—*X*-6
12—*X*-7
13—*Y*-6
14—*Y*-7

These principles permit of being extended from two to any number of goods. Regardless of the number of goods, any man will always have a certain combination of units of them in his stock. He may be faced with the choice of giving up one unit of any good that he might choose. By ranking the various goods and the ends served by the relevant units, the actor will give up the unit of that good of which the marginal utility to him is the lowest. Similarly, with any given combination of goods in his stock, and faced with the choice of adding one unit of any of the goods available, the actor will choose that good whose marginal utility of increase will be highest. In other words, all the goods are ranked on one value scale in accordance with the ends they serve.

If the actor has no units of some goods in his possession, this does not affect the principle. Thus, if he has no units of *X* or *Y* in his possession, and he must choose between adding a unit of *X* or one unit of *Y*, he will choose the marginal unit of greatest utility, in this case, *Y*. The principle is easily extended to the case of *n* goods.

It must be reiterated here that value scales do not exist in a void apart from the concrete choices of action. Thus, if the actor has a stock of (3*X*, 4*Y*, 2*Z*, etc.), his choices for adding and subtracting from stock take place in this region, and there is no need for him to formulate hypothetical value scales to determine what his choices would have been if his stock were (6*X*, 8*Y*, 5*Z*, etc.). No one can predict with certainty the course of his choices except that they will follow the law of marginal utility, which was deduced from the axiom of action.

The solution of the value paradox mentioned above is now fully clear. If a man prefers one ounce of platinum to five loaves of bread, he is choosing between units of the two goods based on the supply available. On the basis of the available supply of platinum and of bread, the marginal utility of a unit of platinum is greater than the marginal utility of a unit of bread.[24]

6. *Factors of Production: The Law of Returns*

We have concluded that the value of each unit of any good is equal to its marginal utility at any point in time, and that this value is determined by the relation between the actor's scale of wants and the stock of goods available. We know that there are two types of goods: consumers' goods, which directly serve human wants, and producers' goods, which aid in the process of production eventually to produce consumers' goods. It is clear that the utility of a consumers' good is the end directly served. The utility of a producers' good is its contribution in producing consumers' goods. With value imputed backward from ends to consumers' goods through the various orders of producers' goods, the utility of any producers' good is its contribution to its product—the lower-stage producers' good or the consumers' good.

As has been discussed above, the very fact of the necessity of producing consumers' goods implies a scarcity of factors of production. If factors of production at each stage were not scarce, then there would be unlimited quantities available of factors of the next lower stage. Similarly, it was concluded that at each stage of production, the product must be produced by *more than one* scarce higher-order factor of production. If only one factor were necessary for the process, then the process itself would not be necessary, and consumers' goods would be available in unlimited abundance. Thus, at each stage of production, the produced goods must have been produced with the aid of more than one factor. These factors *co-operate* in the production process and are termed *complementary factors.*

Factors of production are available as units of a homogeneous supply, just as are consumers' goods. On what principles will an actor evaluate a unit of a factor of production? He will evaluate a unit of supply on the basis of the least importantly valued product which he would have to forgo were he deprived of the unit factor. In other words, he will evaluate each unit of a factor as equal to the satisfactions provided by its marginal unit—in this case, *the utility of its marginal product.* The marginal product is the product forgone by a loss of the marginal unit, and its value is determined either by *its* marginal product in the next stage of production, or, if it is a consumers' good, by the utility of the end it satisfies. Thus, the value assigned to a unit of a factor of production is equal to the *value of its marginal product,* or its *marginal productivity.*

Since man wishes to satisfy as many of his ends as possible, and in the shortest possible time (see above), it follows that he will strive for the *maximum product from given units of factors at each stage of production.* As long as the goods are composed of homogeneous units, their quantity can be measured in terms of these units, and the actor can know when they are in greater or lesser supply. Thus, whereas value and utility cannot be measured or subject to addition, subtraction, etc., quantities of homogeneous units of a supply can be measured. A man knows how many horses or cows he has, and he knows that four horses are twice the quantity of two horses.

Assume that a product *P* (which can be a producers' good or a consumers' good) is produced by three complementary factors, *X, Y,* and *Z.* These are all higher-order producers' goods. Since supplies of goods are quantitatively definable, and since in nature quantitative causes lead to quantitatively observable effects, we are always in a position to say that: *a* quantities of *X,* combined with *b* quantities of *Y,* and *c* quantities of *Z,* lead to *p* quantities of the product *P.*

Now let us assume that we hold the quantitative amounts *b* and *c* unchanged. The amounts *a* and therefore *p* are free to vary. The value of *a* yielding the maximum *p/a,* i.e., the maximum average return of product to the factor, is called the *optimum* amount of *X*. The *law of returns states that with the quantity of complementary factors held constant, there always exists some optimum amount of the varying factor.* As the amount of the varying factor decreases or increases from the optimum, *p/a,* the *average unit product* declines. The quantitative extent of that decline depends on the concrete conditions of each case. As the supply of the varying factor increases, just below this optimum the average return of product to the varying factor is increasing; after the optimum, it is decreasing. These may be called states of *increasing returns* and *decreasing returns* to the factor, with the maximum return at the optimum point.

The law that such an optimum must exist can be proved by contemplating the implications of the contrary. If there were no optimum, the average product would increase indefinitely as the quantity of the factor *X* increased. (It could not increase indefinitely as the quantity *decreases,* since the product will be zero when the quantity of the factor is zero.) But if *p/a* can always be increased merely by increasing *a,* this means that any desired quantity of *P* could be secured by merely increasing the supply of *X*. This would mean that the proportionate supply of factors *Y* and *Z* can be ever so small; any decrease in their supply can always be compensated to increase production by increasing the supply of *X*. This would signify that factor *X* is perfectly substitutable for factors *Y* and *Z* and that the scarcity of the latter factors would not be a matter of concern to the actor so long as factor *X* was available in abundance. But a lack of concern for their scarcity means that *Y* and *Z* would *no longer be scarce factors.* Only one scarce factor, *X*, would remain. But we have seen that there must be more than one factor at each stage of production. Accordingly, the very existence of various factors of production implies that the average return of product to each factor must have some maximum, or optimum, value.

In some cases, the optimum amount of a factor may be the

only amount that can effectively co-operate in the production process. Thus, by a known chemical formula, it may require precisely two parts of hydrogen and one part of oxygen to produce one unit of water. If the supply of oxygen is fixed at one unit, then anv supply of hydrogen under two parts will produce no product at all, and all parts beyond two of hydrogen will be quite useless. Not only will the combination of two hydrogen and one oxygen be the optimum combination, but it will be the only amount of hydrogen that will be at all useful in the production process.

The relationship between *average product* and *marginal product* to a varying factor may be seen in the following hypothetical example:

TABLE 1

FACTOR Y b UNITS	FACTOR X a UNITS	TOTAL PRODUCT p UNITS	AVERAGE UNIT PRODUCT p/a	MARGINAL PRODUCT $\Delta p/\Delta a$
3	0	0	0	...
3	1	4	4	4
3	2	10	5	6
3	3	18	6	8
3	4	30	7.5	12
3	5	40	8	10
3	6	45	7.5	5
3	7	49	7	4

Here is a hypothetical picture of the returns to a varying factor, with other factors fixed. The average unit product increases until it reaches a peak of 8 at 5 units of *X*. This is the optimum point for the varying factor. The *marginal product is the increase in total product provided by the marginal unit.* At any given supply of units of factor *X*, a loss of one unit will entail a loss of total product equal to the marginal product. Thus, if the supply of *X* is increased from 3 units to 4 units, total product is increased from 18 to 30 units, and this increase is the marginal product of *X* with a supply of 4 units. Similarly, if the supply is cut from 4 units to 3 units, the total product must be cut from 30 to 18 units, and thus the marginal product is 12.

It is evident that the amount of *X* that will yield the optimum of average product is not necessarily the amount that maximizes the marginal product of the factor. Often the marginal product reaches its peak before the average product. The relationship that always holds mathematically between the average and the marginal product of a factor is that *as the average product increases (increasing returns), the marginal product is greater than the average product. Conversely, as the average product declines (diminishing returns), the marginal product is less than the average product.*[25]

It follows that when the average product is at a maximum, it equals the marginal product.

It is clear that, with one varying factor, it is easy for the actor to set the proportion of factors to yield the optimum return for the factor. But how can the actor set an optimum combination of factors if all of them can be varied in their supply? If one combination of quantities of *X, Y,* and *Z* yields an optimum return for *X,* and another combination yields an optimum return for *Y,* etc., how is the actor to determine which combination to choose? Since he cannot quantitatively compare units of *X* with units of *Y* or *Z,* how can he determine the optimum proportion of factors? This is a fundamental problem for human action, and its methods of solution will be treated in subsequent chapters.

7. *Factors of Production: Convertibility and Valuation*

Factors of production are valued in accordance with their anticipated contribution in the eventual production of consumers' goods. Factors, however, differ in the *degree of their specificity,* i.e., the variety of consumers' goods in the production of which they can be of service. Certain goods are *completely specific*—are useful in producing only one consumers' good. Thus, when, in past ages, extracts from the mandrake weed were considered useful in healing ills, the mandrake weed was a completely specific factor of production—it was useful purely for this purpose. When the ideas of people changed, and the mandrake was considered worthless, the weed lost its value completely. Other producers' goods may be relatively nonspecific and capable of being used in a wide variety of employments. They could never be perfectly nonspecific—equally useful in all production of consumers' goods —for in that case they would be general conditions of welfare available in unlimited abundance for all purposes. There would be no need to economize them. Scarce factors, however, including the relatively nonspecific ones, must be employed in their most urgent uses. Just as a supply of consumers' goods will go first toward satisfying the most urgent wants, then to the next most urgent wants, etc., so a supply of factors will be allocated by actors first to the most urgent uses in producing consumers' goods, then to the next most urgent uses, etc. The loss of a unit of a supply of a factor will entail the loss of the least urgent of the presently satisfied uses.

The less specific a factor is, the more *convertible* it is from one use to another. The mandrake weed lost its value because it could not be converted to other uses. Factors such as iron or wood, however, are convertible into a wide variety of uses. If one type of consumers' good falls into disuse, iron output can be shifted from that to another line of production. On the other hand, once the iron ore has been transformed into a machine, it becomes less easily convertible and often completely specific to the product. When factors lose a large part of their value as a result of a decline in the value of the consumers' good, they will, if possible, be converted to another use of greater value. If, despite the decline in the value of the product, there is no better use to which the factor can be converted, it will stay in that line of product or cease being used altogether if the consumers' good no longer has value.

For example, suppose that cigars suddenly lose their value as consumers' goods; they are no longer desired. Those cigar machines which are not usable in any other capacity will become valueless. Tobacco leaves, however, will lose some of their value, but may be convertible to uses such as cigarette production with little loss of value. (A loss of all desire for tobacco, however, will result in a far wider loss in the value of the factors, although part of the land may be salvaged by shifting from tobacco to the production of cotton.)

Suppose, on the other hand, that some time after cigars lose their value this commodity returns to public favor and regains its former value. The cigar machines, which had been rendered valueless, now recoup their great loss in value. On the other hand, the tobacco leaves, land, etc., which had shifted from cigars to other uses will reshift into the production of cigars. These factors will gain in value, but their gain, as was their previous loss, will be less than the gain of the completely specific factor. These are examples of a general law that *a change in the value of the product causes a greater change in the value of the specific factors than in that of the relatively nonspecific factors.*

To further illustrate the relation between convertibility and valuation, let us assume that complementary factors 10*X*, 5*Y*, and 8*Z* produce a supply of 20*P*. First, suppose that each of these factors is completely specific and that none of the supply of the factors can be replaced by other units. Then, if the supply of one of the factors is lost (say 10*X*), the entire product is lost, and the other factors become valueless. In that case, the supply of that factor which must be given up or lost equals in value the value of the entire product—20*P*, while the other factors have a zero value. An example of production with purely specific factors is a pair of shoes; the prospect of a loss of one shoe is valued at the value of the entire pair, while the other shoe becomes valueless in case of a loss. Thus, *jointly*, factors 10*X*, 5*Y*, and 8*Z* produce a product that is valued, say, as rank 11 on the actor's value scale. Lose the supply of one of the factors, and the other complementary factors become completely valueless.

Now, let us assume, secondly, that each of the factors is nonspecific: that 10*X* can be used in another line of production that will yield a product, say, ranked 21st on the value scale; that 5*Y* in another use will yield a product ranked 15th on the actor's value scale; and that 8*Z* can be used to yield a product ranked 30th. In that case, the loss of 10*X* would mean that instead of satisfying a want of rank 11, the units of *Y* and *Z* would be shifted to their next most valuable use, and wants ranked 15th and 30th would be satisfied instead. We know that the actor preferred the satisfaction of a want ranked 11th to the satisfaction of wants ranked 15th and 30th; otherwise the factors would not have been engaged in producing *P* in the first place. But now the loss of value is far from total, since the other factors can still yield a return in other uses.

Convertible factors will be allocated among different lines of production according to the same principles as consumers' goods are allocated among the ends they can serve. Each unit of supply will be allocated to satisfy the most urgent of the not yet satisfied wants, i.e., where the value of its marginal product is the highest. A loss of a unit of the factor will deprive the actor of only the least important of the presently satisfied uses, i.e., that use in which the value of the marginal product is the lowest. This choice is analogous to that involved in previous examples comparing the marginal utility of one good with the marginal utility of another. This lowest-ranked marginal product may be considered the value of the marginal product of any unit of the factor, with all uses taken into account. Thus, in the above case, suppose that *X* is a convertible factor in a myriad of different uses. If one unit of *X* has a marginal product of say, 3*P*, a marginal product in another use of 2*Q*, 5*R*, etc., the actor ranks the values of these marginal products of *X* on his value scale. Suppose that he ranks them in this order: 4*S*, 3*P*, 2*Q*, 5*R*. In that case, suppose he is faced with the loss of 1 unit of *X*. He will give up the use of a unit of *X* in production of *R*, where the marginal product is ranked lowest. Even if the loss takes place in the production of *P*, he will not give up 3*P*, but shift a unit of *X* from the less valuable use *R* and give up 5*R*. Thus, just as the actor gave up the use of a horse in pleasure riding and not in wagon-pulling by shifting from the former to the latter use, so the actor who (for example) loses a cord of wood intended for building a house will give up a cord intended for a service less valuable to him—say, building a sled. Thus, the value of the marginal product of a unit of a factor will be equal to its value in its marginal use, i.e., that use served by the stock of the factor whose marginal product is ranked lowest on his value scale.

We can now see further why, in cases where products are made with specific *and* convertible factors, the general law holds that the value of convertible factors changes less than that of specific factors in response to a change in the value of *P* or in the conditions of its production. The value of a unit of a convertible factor is set, not by the conditions of its employment in *one* type of product, but by the value of its marginal product when *all* its uses are taken into consideration. Since a specific factor is usable in only one line of production, its unit value is set as equal to the value of the marginal product in that line of production alone. Hence, in the process of valuation, the specific factors are far more responsive to conditions in *any given process of production* than are the nonspecific factors.[26]

As with the problem of optimum proportions, the process of value imputation from consumers' good to factors raises a great many problems which will be discussed in later chapters. Since one product cannot be measured against other products, and units of different factors cannot be compared with one another, how can value be imputed when, as in a modern economy, the structure of production is very complex, with myriads of products and with convertible and inconvertible factors? It will be seen that value imputation is easy for isolated Crusoe-type actors, but that special conditions are needed to enable the value-imputing process, as well as the factor-allocating process, to take place in a complex economy. In particular, the various units of products and factors (*not* the values, of course) must be made commensurable and comparable.

8. *Factors of Production: Labor vs. Leisure*

Setting aside the problem of allocating production along the most desired lines and of measuring one product as against another, it is evident that every man desires *to maximize his production of consumers' goods per unit of time.* He tries to satisfy as many of his important ends as possible, and at the earliest possible time. But in order to increase the production of his consumers' goods, he must relieve the scarcity of the scarce factors of production; he must increase the available supply of these scarce factors. The *nature-given* factors are limited by his environment and therefore cannot be increased. This leaves him with the choice of increasing his supply of *capital goods* or of increasing his *expenditure of labor.*

It might be asserted that another way of increasing his production is to improve his technical knowledge of how to produce the desired goods—to improve his recipes. A recipe, however, can only set *outer limits* on his increases in production; the actual increases can be accomplished solely by an increase in the supply of productive factors. Thus, suppose that Robinson Crusoe lands, without equipment, on a desert island. He may be a competent engineer and have full knowledge of the necessary processes involved in constructing a mansion for himself. But without the necessary supply of factors available, this knowledge could not suffice to construct the mansion.

One method, then, by which man may increase his production per unit of time is by increasing his expenditure of labor. In the first place, however, the possibilities for this expansion are strictly limited—by the number of people in existence at any time and by the number of hours in the day. Secondly, it is limited by the ability of each laborer, and this ability tends to vary. And, finally, there is a third limitation on the supply of labor: whether or not the work is directly satisfying in itself, labor always involves the forgoing of *leisure,* a desirable good.[27]

We can conceive of a world in which leisure is not desired and labor is merely a useful scarce factor to be economized. In such a world, the total supply of available labor would be equal to the total quantity of labor that men would be capable of expending. Everyone would be eager to work to the maximum of capacity, since increased work would lead to increased production of desired consumers' goods. All time not required for maintaining and preserving the capacity to work would be spent in labor.[28] Such a situation could conceivably exist, and an economic analysis could be worked out on that basis. We know from empirical observation, however, that such a situation is very rare for human action. For almost all actors, *leisure is a consumers' good,* to be weighed in the balance against the prospect of acquiring other consumers' goods, including possible satisfaction from the effort itself. The more a man labors, the less leisure he can enjoy. Increased labor therefore reduces the available supply of leisure and the utility that it affords. Consequently, "people work only when they value the return of labor higher than the decrease in satisfaction brought about by the curtailment of leisure." [29] It is possible that included in this "return" of satisfaction yielded by labor may be satisfaction in the labor itself, in the voluntary expenditure of energy on a productive task. When such satisfactions from labor do not exist, then simply the expected value of the product yielded by the effort will be weighed against the *disutility* involved in giving up leisure—the utility of the leisure forgone. Where labor does provide intrinsic satisfactions, the utility of the product yielded will include the utility provided by the effort itself. As the quantity of effort increases, however, the utility of the satisfactions provided by labor itself declines, and the utility of the successive units of the final product declines as well. Both the marginal utility of the final product and the marginal utility of labor-satisfaction decline with an increase in their quantity, because both goods follow the universal law of marginal utility.

In considering an expenditure of his labor, man not only takes into account which are the most valuable ends it can serve (as he does with all other factors), these ends possibly including the satisfaction derived from productive labor itself, but he *also* weighs the prospect of abstaining from the expenditure of labor *in order* to obtain the consumers' good, leisure. Leisure, like any other good, is subject to the law of marginal utility. The first unit of leisure satisfies a most urgently felt desire; the next unit serves a less highly valued end; the third unit a still less highly valued end, etc. The marginal utility of leisure decreases as the supply increases, and this utility is equal to the value of the end that would have to be forgone with the loss of the unit of leisure. But in that case, the marginal disutility of work (in terms of leisure forgone) *increases* with every increase in the amount of labor performed.

In some cases, labor itself may be positively disagreeable, not only because of the leisure forgone, but also because of specific conditions attached to the particular labor that the actor finds disagreeable. In these cases, the marginal disutility of labor includes both the disutility due to these conditions and the disutility due to leisure forgone. The painful aspects of labor, like the forgoing of leisure, are endured for the sake of the yield of the final product. The addition of the element of disagreeableness in certain types of labor may reinforce and certainly does not counteract the increasing marginal disutility imposed by the cumulation of leisure forgone as the time spent in labor increases.

Thus, for each person and type of labor performed, the balancing of the marginal utility of the product of prospective units of effort as against the marginal disutility of effort will include the satisfaction or dissatisfaction with the work itself, in addition to the evaluation of the final product and of the leisure forgone. The labor itself may provide positive satisfaction, positive pain or dissatisfaction, or it may be neutral. In cases where the labor itself provides positive satisfactions, however, *these are intertwined with and cannot be separated from the prospect of obtaining the final product.* Deprived of the final product, man will consider his labor senseless and useless, and the labor itself will no longer bring positive satisfactions. Those activities which are engaged in *purely* for their own sake are not labor but pure *play,* consumers' goods in themselves. Play, as a consumers' good, is subject to the law of marginal utility as are all goods, and the time spent in play will be balanced against the utility to be derived from other obtainable goods.[30]

In the expenditure of any hour of labor, therefore, man weighs the disutility of the labor involved (including the leisure forgone plus any dissatisfaction stemming from the work itself) against the utility of the contribution he will make in that hour to the production of desired goods (including future goods and any pleasure in the work itself), i.e., with the *value of his marginal product.*

In each hour he will expend his effort toward producing *that* good whose marginal product is highest on his value scale. If he must give up an hour of labor, he will give up a unit of that good whose marginal utility is lowest on his value scale. At each point he will balance the utility of the product on his value scale against the disutility of further work. We know that a man's marginal utility of goods provided by effort will decline as his expenditure of effort increases. On the other hand, with each new expenditure of effort, the marginal disutility of the effort continues to increase. Therefore, a man will expend his labor as long as the marginal utility of the return *exceeds* the marginal disutility of the labor effort. A man will stop work when the marginal disutility of labor is greater than the marginal utility of the increased goods provided by the effort.[31]

Then, as his consumption of leisure increases, the marginal utility of leisure will decline, while the marginal utility of the goods forgone increases, until finally the utility of the marginal products forgone becomes greater than the marginal utility of leisure, and the actor will resume labor again.

This analysis of the laws of labor effort has been deduced from the implications of the action axiom and the assumption of leisure as a consumers' good.

9. *The Formation of Capital*

With the nature-given elements limited by his environment, and his labor restricted both by its available supply and its disutility, there is only one way by which man can increase his production of consumers' goods per unit of time—by increasing the quantity of capital goods. Beginning with unaided labor and nature, he must, to increase his productivity, mix his labor energy with the elements of nature to form capital goods. These goods are not immediately serviceable in satisfying his wants, but must be transformed by further labor into lower-order capital goods, and finally into the desired consumers' goods.

In order to illuminate clearly the nature of capital formation and the position of capital in production, let us start with the hypothetical example of Robinson Crusoe stranded on a desert island. Robinson, on landing, we assume, finds himself without the aid of capital goods of any kind. All that is available is his own labor and the elements given him by nature. It is obvious that without capital he will be able to satisfy only a few wants, of which he will choose the most urgent. Let us say that the only goods available without the aid of capital are berries and leisure. Say that he finds that he can pick twenty edible berries an hour, and, on this basis, works ten hours in berry-picking and enjoys fourteen hours a day of leisure. It is evident that, without the aid of capital, the only goods open to him for consumption are goods with the *shortest period of production.* Leisure is the one good that is produced almost instantaneously, while berries have a very short production period. Twenty berries have a production period of one hour. Goods with longer periods of production are not available to him unless he acquires capital goods.

There are two ways in which longer processes of production through the use of capital may increase productivity: (1) they may provide a greater production of the *same* good per unit of time; or (2) they may allow the actor to consume goods that are *not available at all* with shorter processes of production.

As an example of the first type of increase in productivity: Robinson may decide that if he had the use of a long stick, he could shake many berries off the trees instead of picking them by hand. In that way he might be able to step up his production to fifty berries an hour. How might he go about acquiring the stick? Obviously, he must expend labor in getting the materials, transporting them, shaping them into a stick, etc. Let us say that ten hours would be necessary for this task. This means that to obtain the stick, Crusoe must *forgo* ten hours' production of consumers' goods. He must either sacrifice ten hours of leisure or ten hours of berries at twenty per hour (two hundred berries), or some combination of the two. He must sacrifice, for ten hours, the enjoyment of consumers' goods, and expend his labor on producing a *capital good*—the stick—which will be of no *immediate* use to him. He will be able to begin using the capital good as an indirect aid to future production only after the ten hours are up. In the meantime, he must forgo the satisfaction of his wants. He must *restrict his consumption* for ten hours and *transfer his labor* for that period from producing immediately satisfying consumers' goods into the production of capital goods, which will prove their usefulness only *in the future.* The restriction of consumption is called *saving,* and the transfer of labor and land to the formation of capital goods is called *investment.*

We see now what is involved in the process of capital formation. The actor must decide whether or not to restrict his consumption and invest in the production of capital goods, by weighing the following factors: Does the utility yielded by the increased productivity of the longer process of production outweigh the sacrifice that I must make of *present* goods to acquire consumers' goods in the *future?* We have already seen above the universal fact of *time preference*—that a man will always prefer obtaining a given satisfaction earlier than later. Here, the actor must balance his desire to acquire *more satisfactions per unit of time* as against the fact that, to do so, he must give up satisfactions in the *present* to increase his production in the *future.* His time preference for present over future accounts for his *disutility of waiting,* which must be balanced against the utility that will be eventually provided by the capital good and the longer process of production. How he chooses depends on his scale of values. It is possible, for example, that if he thought the stick would provide him with only thirty berries an hour and would take twenty hours to make, he would not make the saving-investment decision. On the other hand, if the stick took five hours to make and could provide him with one hundred berries an hour, he might make the decision readily.

If he decides to invest ten hours in adding to his capital goods, there are many ways in which he might restrict his consumption. As mentioned above, he can restrict any combination of berries or leisure. Setting aside leisure for purposes of simplification, he may decide to take a whole day off at once and produce no berries at all, completing the stick in one day. Or, he may decide to pick berries for eight hours instead of ten, and devote the other two hours a day to making the stick, in which case the completion of the stick will take five days. Which method he will choose depends on the nature of his value scale. In any case, he must restrict his consumption by ten hours' worth of labor—two hundred berries. The *rate* of his restriction will depend on how urgently he wants the increased production, as compared with the urgency with which he desires to maintain his present supply of berries.

Analytically, there is little difference between working on consumers' goods, accumulating a stock of them, and *then* working full time on the capital good, and working on the capital good and consumer goods simultaneously. Other things being equal, however, it is possible that one of the methods will prove more productive; thus, it may be that the actor can complete the task in less time if he works on it continuously. In that case, he will tend to choose the former method. On the other hand, the berries might tend to spoil if accumulated, and this would lead him to choose the latter route. A balance of the various factors on his value scale will result in his decision.

Let us assume that Robinson has made his decision, and, after five days, begins to use the stick. On the sixth day and thereafter, then, five hundred berries a day will begin to pour forth, and he will harvest the fruits of his investment in capital goods.

Crusoe can use his increased productivity to *increase his hours of leisure* as well as to increase his output of berries. Thus, he might decide to cut his daily labor from ten hours to eight. His output of berries will then be increased, because of the stick, from two hundred to four hundred berries per day, while Crusoe is able to increase his hours of leisure from fourteen to sixteen per day. Obviously, Crusoe can choose to take his increased productivity in various combinations of increased output of the good itself and of increased leisure.[32]

Even more important than its use in increasing output per unit of time is the function of capital in enabling man to acquire goods which he could not *at all* obtain otherwise. A very short period of production enables Crusoe to produce leisure and at least some berries, but without the aid of capital he cannot attain *any* of his other wants at all. To acquire meat he must have a bow and arrows, to acquire fish he must have a pole or net, to acquire shelter he must have logs of wood, or canvas, and an axe to cut the wood. To satisfy any such wants, he must restrict his consumption and invest his labor in the production of capital goods. In other words, he must embark on lengthier processes of production than had been involved in culling berries; he must take time out to produce the capital goods themselves before he can use them to enjoy consumers' goods. In each case, the decisions that he makes in embarking on capital formation will be a result of weighing on his value scale the utility of the expected increased productivity as against the disutility of his time preference for present as compared to future satisfactions.

It is obvious that the factor which holds every man back from investing more and more of his land and labor in capital goods is his time preference for present goods. If man, other things being equal, did not prefer satisfaction in the present to satisfaction in the future, he would never consume; he would invest all his time and labor in increasing the production of future goods. But "never consuming" is an absurdity, since consuming is the end of all production. Therefore, at any given point in time, all men will have invested in all the *shorter* periods of production to satisfy the most urgently felt wants that their knowledge of recipes allows; *any further formation of capital will go into longer processes of production.* Other things being equal (i.e., the relative urgency of wants to be satisfied, and the actor's knowledge of recipes), any further investment will be in a longer process of production than is now under way.

Here it is important to realize that "a period of production" does not involve only the amount of time spent on making the actual capital good, but refers to the amount of waiting-time from the start of producing the capital good until the *consumers' good* is produced. In the case of the stick and the berries, the two times are identical, but this was so only because the stick was a first-order capital good, i.e., it was but one stage removed from the output of consumers' goods. Let us take, for example, a more complex case—the building by Crusoe of an axe in order to chop wood to produce a house for himself. Crusoe must decide whether or not the house he will gain will be worth the consumers' goods forgone in the meantime. Let us say it will take Crusoe fifty hours to produce the axe, and then a further two hundred hours, with the help of the axe, to chop and transport wood in order to build a house. The longer process of production which Crusoe must decide upon is now a three-stage one, totaling two hundred fifty hours. First, labor and nature produce the axe, a second-order capital good; second, labor, plus the axe, plus nature-given elements, produces logs-of-wood, a first-order capital good; finally, labor and the logs of wood combine to yield the desired consumers' good—a house. The length of the process of production is the entire length of time from the point at which an actor must begin his labor to the point at which the consumers' good is yielded.

Again, it must be observed that, in considering the length of a process of production, the actor is not interested in past history as such. The length of a process of production for an actor is the *waiting-time from the point at which his action begins.* Thus, if Crusoe were lucky enough to find an axe in good condition left by some previous inhabitant, he would reckon his period of production at two hundred hours instead of two hundred fifty. The axe would be given to him by his environment.

This example illustrates a fundamental truth about capital goods. Capital is a way station along the road to the enjoyment of consumers' goods. He who possesses capital is that much *further advanced in time* on the road to the desired consumers' good. Crusoe without the axe is two hundred fifty hours away from his desired house; Crusoe with the axe is only two hundred hours away. If the logs of wood had been piled up ready-made on his arrival, he would be that much closer to his objective; and if the house were there to begin with, he would achieve his desire immediately. He would be further advanced toward his goal without the necessity of further restriction of consumption. Thus, the role of capital is to advance men in time toward their objective in producing consumers' goods. This is true for both the case where *new* consumers' goods are being produced and the case where *more old goods* are being produced. Thus, in the previous case, without the stick, Crusoe was twenty-five hours away from an output of five hundred berries; with the stick, he is only ten hours away. In those cases where capital enables the acquisition of new goods—of goods which could not be obtained otherwise—it is an *absolutely indispensable,* as well as a convenient, way station toward the desired consumers' good.

It is evident that, for any formation of capital, there must be *saving*—a restriction of the enjoyment of consumers' goods in the present—and the investment of the equivalent resources in the production of capital goods. This enjoyment of consumers' goods—the satisfaction of wants—is called *consumption.* The saving might come about as a result of an increase in the available supply of consumers' goods, which the actor decides to save in part rather than consume fully. At any rate, consumption must always be less than the amount that could be secured. Thus, if the harvest on the desert island improves, and Crusoe finds that he can pick two hundred forty berries in ten hours without the aid of a stick, he may now save forty berries a day for five days, enabling him to invest his labor in a stick, without cutting back his berry consumption from the original two hundred berries. Saving involves the restriction of consumption compared to the amount that *could* be consumed; it does not always involve an actual reduction in the amount consumed over the previous level of consumption.

All capital goods are perishable. Those few products that are not perishable but permanent become, to all intents and purposes, part of the *land.* Otherwise, all capital goods are perishable, used up during the processes of production. We can therefore say that capital goods, during production, are *transformed* into their products. With some capital goods, this is physically quite evident. Thus, it is obvious, for example, that when a hundred pounds of bread-at-wholesale are combined with other factors to produce a hundred pounds of bread at retail, the former factor is immediately and completely transformed into the latter factor. The using up of capital goods is here dramatically clear. The whole of the capital good is used up in each production-event. The other capital goods, however, are also used up, but not as suddenly. A truck transporting bread may have a life of fifteen years, amounting to, say, three thousand of such conversions of bread from the wholesale to the retail stage. In this case we may say that 1/3,000 of the truck is used up each time the production process occurs. Similarly, a mill converting wheat into flour may have a useful life of twenty years, in which case we could say that 1/20 of the mill was used up in each year's production of flour. Each particular capital good has a different useful life and therefore a different rate of being used up, or, as it is called, of *depreciation.* Capital goods vary in the duration of their serviceableness.

Let us now return to Crusoe and the stick. Let us assume that the stick will have a useful life of ten days, and is so estimated by Crusoe, after which it wears out, and Crusoe's output reverts to its previous level of twenty berries per hour. He is back where he started from.

Crusoe is therefore faced with a choice, after his stick comes into use. His "standard of living" (now, say, at five hundred berries a day plus fourteen hours of leisure) has improved, and he will not like the prospect of a reduction to two hundred when the stick gives out. If he wishes to maintain his standard of living intact, therefore, he must, during the ten days, work on building another stick, which can be used to replace the old one when it wears out. This act of building another stick involves a *further act of saving.* In order to invest in a replacement for the stick, he must again save—restrict his consumption as compared to the production that might be available. Thus, he will again have to save ten hours' worth of labor in berries (or leisure) and devote them to investing in a good that is only indirectly serviceable for future production. Suppose that he does this by shifting one hour a day from his berry production to the labor of producing another stick. By doing so, he restricts his berry consumption, for ten days, to four hundred fifty a day. He has restricted consumption from his maximum, although he is still much better off than in his original, unaided state.

Thus, the *capital structure* is renewed at the end of the ten days, by saving and investing in a replacement. After that, Crusoe is *again* faced with the choice of taking his maximum production of five hundred berries per day and finding himself back to a two-hundred-per-day level at the end of ten more days, or of making a *third* act of saving in order to provide for replacement of the second stick when it wears out.[33]

If Crusoe decides *not* to replace the first or the second stick, and accepts a later drop in output to avoid undergoing present saving, he is *consuming capital.* In other words, he is electing to consume instead of to save and maintain his capital structure and future rate of output. Consuming his capital enables Crusoe to increase his consumption *now* from four hundred fifty to five hundred berries per day, but at some point in the future (here in ten days), he will be forced to cut his consumption back to two hundred berries. It is clear that what has led Crusoe to consume capital is his *time preference,* which in this case has led him to prefer more present consumption to greater losses in future consumption.

Thus, any actor, at any point in time, has the choice of: (*a*) adding to his capital structure, (*b*) maintaining his capital intact, or (*c*) consuming his capital. Choices (*a*) and (*b*) involve acts of saving. The course adopted will depend on the actor's weighing his disutility of waiting, as determined by his time preference, against the utility to be provided in the future by the increase in his intake of consumers' goods.

At this point in the discussion of the wearing out and replacement of capital goods we may observe that a capital good rarely retains its full "powers" to aid in production and then suddenly loses all its serviceability. In the words of Professor Benham, "capital goods do not usually remain in perfect technical condition and then suddenly collapse, like the wonderful 'one-hoss shay.' "[34] Crusoe's berry output, instead of remaining five hundred for ten days and then falling back to two hundred on the eleventh day, is likely to decline at some rate before the stick becomes completely useless.

Another method of maintaining capital may now prove available. Thus, Crusoe may find that, by spending a little time repairing the stick, breaking off weaker parts, etc., he may be able to prolong its life and maintain his output of berries longer. In short, he may be able to add to his capital structure via *repairs*.

Here again he will balance the added increase in future output of consumers' goods against the *present* loss in consumers' goods which he must endure by expending his labor on repairs. Making repairs therefore requires an independent act of saving and a choice to save. It is entirely possible, for example, that Crusoe will decide to replace the stick, and spend his labor on that purpose, but will not consider it worthwhile to repair it. Which course he decides to take depends on his valuation of the various alternative outputs and his rate of time preference.

An actor's decision on what objects to invest in will depend on the expected utility of the forthcoming consumers' good, its durability, and the length of his waiting-time. Thus, he may first invest in a stick and then decide it would not be worthwhile to invest in a second stick; instead, it would be better to begin building the axe in order to obtain a house. Or he may first make a bow and arrows with which to hunt game, and after that begin working on a house. Since the marginal utility of the stock of a good declines as the stock increases, the more he has of the stock of *one* consumers' good, the more likely he will be to expend his new savings on a different consumers' good, since the second good will now have a higher marginal utility of product to his invested labor and waiting, and the marginal utility of the first will be lower.

If two consumers' goods have the same expected marginal utility in daily serviceability and have the same period of waiting time, but one is more durable than the other, then the actor will choose to invest in production of the former. On the other hand, if the total serviceableness of two expected consumers' goods is the same, and their length of period of production is the same, the *less* durable good will be invested in, since its total satisfactions arrive earlier than the other. Also, in choosing between investing in one or the other of two consumers' goods, the actor will, other things being equal, choose that good with the shorter period of production, as has been discussed above.

Any actor will continue to save and invest his resources in various expected future consumers' goods as long as the utility, considered in the present, of the marginal product of each unit saved and invested is greater than the utility of present consumers' goods which he could obtain by not performing that saving. The latter utility—of present consumers' goods forgone—is the "disutility of waiting." Once the latter becomes greater than the utility of obtaining more goods in the future through saving, the actor will cease to save.

Allowing for the relative urgency of wants, man, as has been demonstrated above, tends to invest first in those consumers' goods with the shortest processes of production. Therefore, any given saving will be invested either in maintaining the present capital structure or in adding to it capital in *more and more remote* stages of production, i.e., in longer processes of production. Thus, any new saving (beyond maintaining the structure) will tend to lengthen production processes and invest in *higher and higher orders* of capital goods.

In a modern economy, the capital structure contains goods of almost infinite remoteness from the eventual consumers' goods. We saw above some of the stages involved in the production of a comparatively very simple good like a ham sandwich. The laborer in an iron mine is far removed indeed from the ham sandwich in Jones' armchair.

It is evident that the problems of measurement that arose in previous sections would be likely to pose a grave difficulty in saving and investing. How do actors know when their capital structure is being added to or consumed, when the types of capital goods and consumers' goods are numerous? Obviously, Crusoe knows when he has more or fewer berries, but how can a modern complex economy, with innumerable capital goods and consumers' goods, make such decisions? The answer to this problem, which also rests on the commensurability of different goods, will be discussed in later chapters.

In observing the increased output made possible by the use of capital goods, one may very easily come to attribute some sort of independent productive power to capital and to say that three types of productive forces enter into the production of consumers' goods: labor, nature, and capital. It would be easy to draw this conclusion, but completely fallacious. Capital goods have no independent productive power of their own; in the last analysis they are completely reducible to labor and land, which produced them, and time. Capital goods are "stored-up" labor, land, and time; they are intermediate way stations on the road to the eventual attainment of the consumers' goods into which they are transformed. At every step of the way they must be worked on by labor, in conjunction with nature, in order to continue the process of production. Capital is not an independent productive factor like the other two. An excellent illustration of this truth has been provided by Böhm-Bawerk:

> The following analogy will make it perfectly clear. A man throws a stone at another man and kills him. Has the stone killed the man? If the question is put without laying any special emphasis it may be answered without hesitation in the affirmative. But how if the murderer, on his trial, were to defend himself by saying that it was not he but the stone that had killed the man? Taking the words in this sense, should we still say that the stone had killed the man, and acquit the murderer? Now it is with an emphasis like this that economists inquire as to the independent productivity of capital . . . We are not asking about dependent intermediate causes, but about ultimate independent elements. The question is not whether capital plays a part in the bringing about of a productive result—such as the stone does in the killing of the man—but whether, granted the productive result, some part of it is due to capital so entirely and peculiarly that it simply cannot be put to the credit of the two other recognized elementary factors, nature and labour.

Böhm-Bawerk replies in the negative, pointing out that capital goods are purely way stations in the process of production, worked on at every possible stage by the forces of labor and land:

> If, today, by allying my labor with natural powers, I make bricks out of clay, and tomorrow, by allying my labor with natural gifts, I obtain lime, and the day after that make mortar and so construct a wall, can it be said of any part of the wall that I and the natural powers have *not* made it? Again, before a lengthy piece of work, such as the

> building of a house, is quite finished, it naturally must be at one time a fourth finished, then a half finished, then three-quarters finished. What now would be said if one were to describe these inevitable stages of the work as independent requisites of house-building, and maintain that, for the building of a house, we require, besides building materials and labor, a quarter-finished house, a half-finished house, a three-quarters finished house? In form perhaps it is less striking, but in effect it is not a whit more correct, to elevate those intermediate steps in the progress of the work, which outwardly take the shape of capital, into an independent agent of production by the side of nature and labor.[35]

And this holds true regardless of how many stages are involved or how remote the capital good is from the ultimate consumers' good.

Since investment in capital goods involves looking toward the future, one of the risks that an actor must always cope with is the *uncertainty* of future conditions. Producing consumers' goods directly involves a very short period of production, so that the uncertainty incurred is not nearly as great as the uncertainty of longer processes of production, an uncertainty that becomes more and more important as the period of production lengthens.[36]

Suppose that Crusoe, while deciding on his investment in the stick, believes that there is a good possibility of his finding a grove where berries are in abundance, giving him an output of fifty or more berries per hour without the aid of a stick, and also where the berries would be so close as to render the stick useless. In that case, the more likely he thinks are the chances of finding the grove, the less likely he is to make the decision to invest in the stick, which would then be of no help to him. The greater the doubt about the usefulness the stick will have after it is ready, the less likelihood of investing in it, and the more likelihood of either investing in another good or of consuming instead of saving. We can consider that there is a sort of "uncertainty discount" on the expected future utility of the investment that may be so large as to induce the actor not to make the investment. The uncertainty factor in this case works with the time-preference factor to the disadvantage of the investment, against which the actor balances the expected utility of future output.

On the other hand, uncertainty may work as an added spur to making the investment. Thus, suppose that Crusoe believes that a blight may strike the berries very shortly and that if this happens, his unaided berry-output would dangerously decline. If the blight struck, Crusoe would be in great need of the stick even to maintain his output at the present low level. Thus, the possibility that the stick may be of even greater use to him than he anticipates will add to the expected utility of his investment, and the greater the chance of this possibility in Crusoe's view, the more likely he will be to invest in the stick. Thus, the uncertainty factor may work in either direction, depending on the specific situation involved.

We may explain the entire act of deciding whether or not to perform an act of capital formation as the balancing of relative utilities, "discounted" by the actor's rate of time preference and also by the uncertainty factor. Thus, first let us assume, for purposes of simplification, that Crusoe, in making the stick, forgoes 10 hours' worth of present goods, i.e., 200 berries, and has acquired 1,500 berries three days later as a result of the investment decision. If the 1,500 berries had been immediately available, there would be no doubt that he would have given up 200 berries to acquire 1,500. Thus, 1,500 berries in the present might have a rank of 4 on his value scale, while 200 berries have a rank of 11:

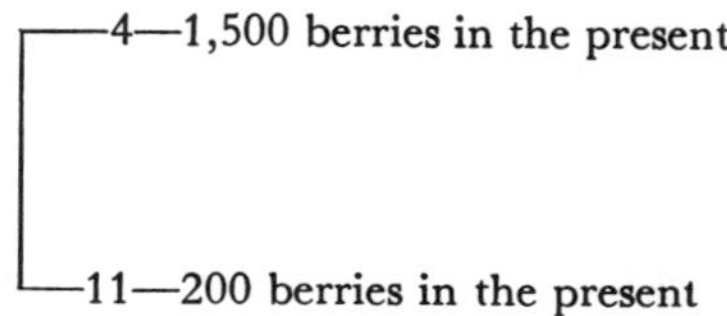

Now, how will Crusoe decide between 200 berries in the present and 1,500 three days from now? Since all choices have to be made on one value scale, Crusoe must grade the utility of 1,500 berries three days from now as against the utility of 200 berries now. If the former is greater (higher on his value scale) he will make the decision to save and invest in the stick. If the latter is greater, and his 200 berries forgone have a greater value than the expectation of 1,500 berries three days from now, then his time preference has conquered the increased utility of stock, and he will not make the saving-investment decision. Thus, the actor's value scale may be:

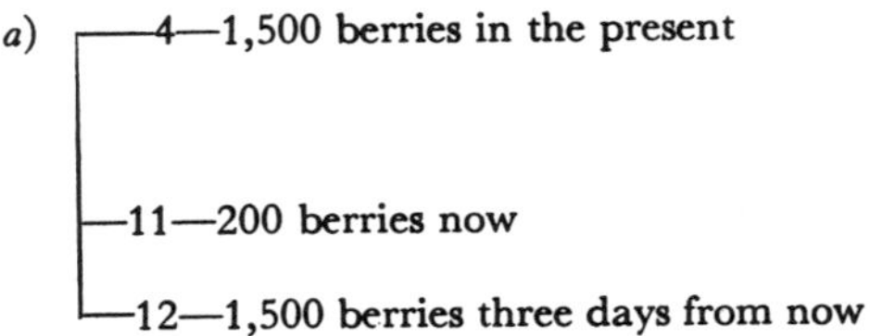

or it may be:

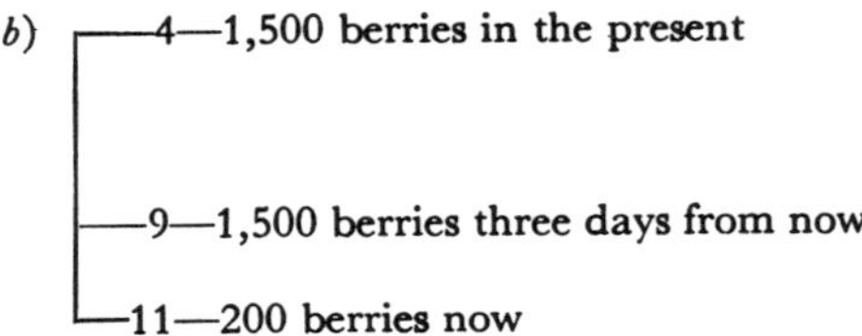

In case (*b*) he will make the decision to invest; in case (*a*) he will not. We can say that the value of 1,500 berries three days from now is the *present value of the future good*. The expected future good is discounted by the actor according to his *rate of time preference*. The present value of his expected future good is compared to the present value of the present good on the actor's value scale, and the decision to save and invest is made accordingly. It is clear that the higher the rate of discount, the lower the present value of the future good will be, and the greater the likelihood of abstaining from the investment. On the other hand, the lower the rate of discount, the higher the present value of future goods will be on the actor's value scale, and the greater the likelihood of its being greater than the value of present goods forgone, and hence of his making the investment.

Thus, the investment decision will be determined by which is greater: the present value of the future good or the present value of present goods forgone. The present value of the future good, in turn, is determined by the value that the future good would have if immediately present (say, the "expected future value of the future good"); and by the rate of time preference. The greater the former, the greater will be the present value of the future good; the greater the latter (the rate of discount of future compared to present goods), the lower will be the present value.

At any point in time, an actor has a range of investment decisions open to him of varying potential utilities for the products that will be provided.[37] He also has a certain rate of time preference by which he will discount these expected future utilities to their present value. How much he will save and invest in any period will be determined by comparing these present values with the value of the consumers' goods forgone in making the investment decision. As he makes one investment decision after another, he will choose to allocate his resources first to investments of highest present value, then to those of next highest, etc. As he continues investing (at any given time), the present value of the future utilities will decline. On the other hand, since he is giving up a larger and larger supply of consumers' goods in the present, the utility of the consumers' goods that he forgoes (leisure and others) will increase—on the basis of the law of marginal utility. He will cease saving and investing at the point at which the value of goods forgone exceeds the present value of the future utilities to be derived. This will determine an actor's *rate* of saving and investing at any time.

It is evident that the problem again arises: How can actors decide and compare time-preference rates for innumerable possible goods and in a complex, modern economy? And here too, the answer for a complex economy lies in establishing commensurability among all the various commodities, present and future, as will be discussed in later chapters.

Now, the uncertainty factors enter into the actor's decision in one way or the other. The delicate procedure of weighing all the various factors in the situation is a complex process that takes place in the mind of every actor according to his understanding of the situation. It is a decision depending purely on the individual judgment, the subjective estimates, of each actor. The "best" decision cannot be exactly, or quantitatively, decided upon in advance by objective methods. This process of *forecasting* the future conditions that will occur during the course of his action is one that must be engaged in by every actor. This necessity of guessing the course of the relevant conditions and their possible change during the forthcoming action is called the *act of entrepreneurship*. Thus, to some extent at least, every man is an entrepreneur. Every actor makes his estimate of the uncertainty situation with regard to his forthcoming action.

The concepts of *success* or *failure* in entrepreneurship are thus deducible from the existence of action. The relatively successful entrepreneur is the one who has guessed correctly the changes in conditions to take place during the action, and has invested accordingly. He is the Crusoe who has decided not to build the stick because his judgment tells him that he will soon find a new grove of berries, which he then finds. On the other hand, the relatively unsuccessful entrepreneur is the one who has been badly mistaken in his forecast of the relevant changes in conditions taking place during the course of his action. He is the Crusoe who has failed to provide himself with a stick against the blight. The successful actor, the successful entrepreneur, makes correct estimates; the unsuccessful entrepreneur is the one who makes erroneous estimates.

Suppose now that an investment has already been made, and capital goods have already been built with a goal in view, when changing conditions reveal that an error has been made. The actor is then faced with the problem of determining what to do with the capital good. The answer depends on the *convertibility* of the capital good. If the good becomes worthless in the use for which it is intended, the actor, though having made an error in investing in it in the first place, now has it on his hands and has to make the best of it. If there is another use to which the actor can conveniently transfer the capital good, he will do so. Thus, if Crusoe finds that a new grove has rendered his stick useless for berry-picking, he may use it as a walking stick. He would not have invested in it originally if he had known it would be useless for berry-picking, but now that he has it, he turns it to its most urgent available use. On the other hand, he may feel that it is hardly worthwhile to spend time replacing the stick, now that it is usable only for walking purposes. Or, after working fifty hours and building an axe, he may find a house left by some previous inhabitant. The axe, however, may be convertible to use in something just a bit lower in value—say, building a bow and arrows for hunting or building a boat for fishing. The axe may be so valuable in these uses that Crusoe will still work to replace and maintain it in operation.

It is clear that the accumulated stock of capital goods (or, for that matter, durable consumers' goods) imposes a conservative force on present-day action. The actor in the present is influenced by his (or someone else's) actions in the past, even if the latter were to some extent in error. Thus, Crusoe might find an axe already available, built by a previous inhabitant. It might not be the sort of axe that Crusoe would consider the best available. However, he may decide, if it is a serviceable axe, to use it as a capital good and to wait until it wears out before replacing it with one of his choosing. On the other hand, he may feel that it is so blunt as to be of little use, and begin immediately to work on an axe of his own.

The conservatism of the past exercises a similar influence on the question of *location,* another aspect of the same problem. Thus, Crusoe may already have built his house, cleared a field, etc., in one portion of the island. Then, one day, in walking around the island, he might find a section at the other end with far greater advantages in fishing, fruits, etc. If he had not invested in any capital goods or durable consumers' goods, he would immediately shift his location to this more abundant area. However, he has already invested in certain capital goods: some, such as the axe, are easily convertible to the new location; others, such as the cleared field and house, cannot be converted in their location. Therefore, he has to decide on his value scale between the advantages and disadvantages of moving: the more abundant fish and fruits vs. the necessity of working to build a new house, new clearing, etc. He might decide, for example, to stay in the house and clearing until they have worn down to a certain point, without working on a replacement, and then shift to the new location.

If an actor decides to abandon nonconvertible capital, such as the stick or the cleared field, in favor of producing other capital and consumers' goods, he is *not,* as some may think, wasting his resources by allowing the emergence of "unused capacity" of his resources. When Crusoe abandons his clearing or stick or house (which may be considered in this connection as equivalent to capital), he is abandoning nonconvertible capital for the sake of using his labor in combination with natural elements or capital goods which he believes will yield him a greater utility. Similarly, if he refuses to go deep into a jungle for berries, he is not "wasting" his nonconvertible supply of land-and-berries, for he judges doing so of far less utility than other uses that he could make of his labor and time. The existence of a capital good not in use reveals an error made by this or by some previous actor *in the past,* but indicates that the actor expects to acquire a greater utility from other uses of his labor than he could obtain by continuing the capital good in its originally intended use or by converting it to some other use.[38]

This discussion provides the clue to an analysis of how actors will employ the original nature-given factors of production. In many cases, actors have their choice among the varying elements provided by nature. Thus, suppose that Crusoe, in his explorations of the island, finds that among the possible locations where he can settle, some are abundant in their output of berries (setting aside their production of other consumers' goods), some less so, and some useless and barren. Clearly, other considerations being equal, he will settle on the most fertile—the "best" land—and employ this factor as far as is determined by the utility of its product, the possibility of investing in useful capital goods on the land, the value he places on leisure, etc. The poorer areas of land will remain unused. As stated above, this development is to be expected; there is no reason to be surprised at such evidence of "unused resources." On the other hand, if the better areas are used up, then Crusoe will go on to utilize some of the next best areas, until the utility of the supply produced fails to exceed the utility of his leisure forgone. ("Next best" includes all the relevant factors, such as productivity, convenient access to the best land, etc.)

Areas of potential use, but which the actor chooses *not* to bring into use because it would not "pay" in terms of utilities forgone, are called submarginal areas. They are not objects of action at the moment, but the actor has them in mind for possible future use.

On the other hand, Crusoe's island may be so small or so barren that all his available useful land or water areas must be pressed into use. Thus, Crusoe might have to explore the whole island for his daily output of two hundred berries. In that case, if his resources are such that he must always employ all the possibly useful nature-given factors, it is obvious that the actor is pretty close to the bare survival level.

In those cases where nature-given factors are worked on, "improved," and maintained by human labor, these are, in effect, thereby changed into capital goods. Thus, land that has been cleared, tilled, ploughed, etc., by human labor has become a capital good. This land is a produced good, and not an originally given good. Decisions concerning whether and how much to improve the soil, or whether to maintain it or extract the maximum present consumers' goods at the expense of future losses ("erosion"), are on exactly the same footing as all capital-formation decisions. They depend on a comparison of the expected utility of future production as against the utility of present consumers' goods forgone.

It is clear that capital formation and the concomitant lengthening of the period of production prolong the *period of provision* of the actor. Capital formation lengthens the period in the future for which he is providing for the satisfaction of wants. *Action* involves the anticipation of wants that will be felt in the future, an estimate of their relative urgency, and the setting about to satisfy them. The more capital men invest, the longer their period of provision will tend to be. Goods being directly and presently consumed are *present goods.* A *future good* is the present expectation of enjoying a consumers' good at some point in the future. A future good may be a claim on future consumers' goods, or it may be a capital good, which will be transformed into a consumers' good in the future. Since a capital good is a way station (and nature-given factors are original stations) on the route to consumers' goods, capital goods and nature-given factors are both future goods.

Similarly, the period of provision can be prolonged by lengthening the duration of serviceableness of the consumers' goods being produced. A house has a longer durability than a crop of berries, for example, and Crusoe's investment in a house considerably lengthens his period of provision. A durable consumers' good is consumed only partially from day to day, so that each day's consumption is that of a present good, while the stock of the remainder is a future good. Thus, if a house is built and will last 3,000 days, one day's use will consume 1/3,000 of it, while the remainder will be consumed in the future. 1/3,000 of the house is a present good, while the remaining part is a future good.[39]

It may be added that another method of lengthening the period of production is the simple accumulation of stocks of consumers' goods to be consumed in the future instead of the present. For example, Crusoe might save a stock of one hundred berries to be consumed a few days or a week later. This is often called *plain saving,* as distinguished from *capitalist saving,* in which saving enters into the process of capital formation.[40] We shall see, however, that there is no essential difference between the two types of saving and that plain saving is also capitalist saving in that it too results in capital formation. We must keep in mind the vital fact that the concept of a "good" refers to a thing the units of which the actor believes afford equal serviceability. It does not refer to the physical or chemical characteristics of the good. We remember our critique of the popular fallacious objection to the universal fact of time preference—that, in any given winter, ice the next summer is preferred to ice now.[41] This was not a case of preferring the consumption of the *same* good in the future to its consumption in the present. If Crusoe has a stock of ice in the winter and decides to "save" some until next summer, this means that "ice-in-the-summer" is a *different* good, with a different intensity of satisfaction, from "ice-in-the-winter," despite their physical similarities. The case of berries or of any other good is similar. If Crusoe decides to postpone consuming a portion of his stock of berries, this must mean that this portion will have a greater intensity of satisfaction if consumed later than now—enough greater, in fact, to overcome his time preference for the present. The reasons for such difference may be numerous, involving anticipated tastes and conditions of supply on that future date. At any rate, "berries-eaten-a-week-from-now" become a more highly valued good than "berries-eaten-now," and the number of berries that will be shifted from today's to next week's consumption will be determined by the behavior of the diminishing marginal utility of next week's berries (as the supply increases), the increasing marginal utility of today's berries (as the supply decreases), and the rate of time preference. Suppose that as a resultant of these factors, Crusoe decides to shift one hundred berries for this purpose. In that case, these hundred berries are removed from the category of consumers' goods and shifted to that of capital goods. These are the sort of capital goods, however, which, like wine, needs only *maturing time* to be transferred into consumers' goods, without the expenditure of labor (except the possible extra labor of storing and unstoring the berries).

It is clear, therefore, that the accumulation of a stock of consumers' goods is also saving that goes into capital formation.[42] The saved goods immediately become capital goods, which later mature into more highly valued consumers' goods. There is no essential difference between the two types of saving.

10. *Action as an Exchange*

We have stated that all action involves an exchange—a giving up of a state of affairs for what the actor expects will be a more satisfactory state.[43] We may now elaborate on the implications of this truth, in the light of the numerous examples that have been given in this chapter. Every aspect of action has involved a *choice* among alternatives—a giving up of some goods for the sake of acquiring others. Wherever the choice occurred—whether among uses of durable consumers' goods, or of capital goods; saving vs. consumption; labor vs. leisure; etc.—such choices among alternatives, such renouncing of one thing in favor of another, were always present. In each case, the actor adopted the course that he believed would afford him the highest utility on his value scale; and in each case, the actor gave up what he believed would turn out to be a lesser utility.

Before analyzing the range of alternative choices further, it is necessary to emphasize that *man must always act.* Since he is always in a position to improve his lot, even "doing nothing" is a form of acting. "Doing nothing"—or spending all of his time in leisure—is a choice that will affect his supply of consumers' goods. Therefore, man must always be engaged in choosing and in action.

Since man is always acting, he must always be engaged in trying to attain the *greatest height on his value scale,* whatever the type of choice under consideration. There must *always* be room for improvement in his value scale; otherwise all of man's wants would be perfectly satisfied, and action would disappear. Since this cannot be the case, it means that there is always open to each actor the prospect of improving his lot, of attaining a value higher than he is giving up, i.e., of *making a psychic profit.* What he is giving up may be called his *costs,* i.e., the utilities that he is forgoing in order to attain a better position. Thus, an actor's costs are his forgone opportunities to enjoy consumers' goods. Similarly, the (greater) utility that he expects to acquire because of the action may be considered his *psychic income,* or *psychic revenue,* which in turn will be equal to the utility of the goods he will consume as a result of the action. Hence, at the inauguration of any action, the actor will believe that this course of action will, among the alternatives, *maximize his psychic income or psychic revenue,* i.e., attain the greatest height on his value scale.

APPENDIX A: PRAXEOLOGY AND ECONOMICS

This chapter has been an exposition of part of *praxeological analysis*—the analysis which forms the body of economic theory. This analysis takes as its fundamental premise the existence of human action. Once it is demonstrated that human action is a necessary attribute of the existence of human beings, the rest of praxeology (and its subdivision, economic theory) consists of the elaboration of the logical implications of the concept of action. Economic analysis is of the form:

1) Assert *A*—action axiom.
2) If *A*, then *B*; if *B*, then *C*; if *C*, then *D*, etc.—by rules of logic.
3) Therefore, we assert (the truth of) *B*, *C*, *D*, etc.

It is important to realize that economics does not propound any laws about the *content* of man's ends. The examples that we have given, such as ham sandwich, berries, etc., are simply illustrative instances, and are not meant to assert anything about the content of a man's goals at any given time. The concept of action involves the use of scarce means for satisfying the most urgent wants at some point in the future, and the truths of economic theory involve the formal relations between ends and means, and not their specific contents. A man's ends may be "egoistic" or "altruistic," "refined" or "vulgar." They may emphasize the enjoyment of "material goods" and comforts, or they may stress the ascetic life. Economics is not concerned with their content, and its laws apply regardless of the nature of these ends.

Praxeology, therefore, differs from *psychology* or from the *philosophy of ethics*. Since all these disciplines deal with the subjective decisions of individual human minds, many observers have believed that they are fundamentally identical. This is not the case at all. Psychology and ethics deal with the content of human ends; they ask, *why* does the man choose such and such ends, or *what* ends *should* men value? Praxeology and economics deal with *any* given ends and with the formal implications of the fact that men have ends and employ means to attain them. Praxeology and economics are therefore disciplines separate and distinct from the others.

Thus, all explanations of the law of marginal utility on psychological or physiological grounds are erroneous. For example, many writers have based the law of marginal utility on an alleged "law of the satiation of wants," according to which a man can eat so many scoops of ice cream at one time, etc., and then becomes satiated. Whether or not this is true in psychology is completely irrelevant to economics. These writers erroneously concluded that, at the beginning of the supply, a second unit may be more enjoyable than the first, and therefore that marginal utility may increase at first before declining. This is completely fallacious. The law of marginal utility depends on no physiological or psychological assumptions, but is based on the praxeological truth that the first unit of a good will be used to satisfy the most urgent want, the second unit the next most urgent want, etc. It must be remembered that these "units" must be of equal potential serviceability.

For example, it is erroneous to argue as follows: Eggs are the good in question. It is possible that a man needs four eggs to bake a cake. In that case, the second egg may be used for a less urgent use than the first egg, and the third egg for a less urgent use than the second. However, since the fourth egg allows a cake to be produced that would not otherwise be available, the marginal utility of the fourth egg is greater than that of the third egg.

This argument neglects the fact that a "good" is not the physical material, but any material whatever of which the units will constitute an equally serviceable supply. Since the fourth egg is not equally serviceable and interchangeable with the first egg, the two eggs are *not* units of the same supply, and therefore the law of marginal utility does not apply to this case at all. To treat eggs in this case as homogeneous units of one good, it would be necessary to consider *each set of four eggs* as a unit.

To sum up the relationship and the distinctions between praxeology and each of the other disciplines, we may describe them as follows:

Why man chooses various ends: *psychology.*
What men's ends should be: *philosophy of ethics.*
also: *philosophy of aesthetics.*
How to use means to arrive at ends: *technology.*
What man's ends are and have been, and how man has used means in order to attain them: *history.*
The formal implications of the fact that men use means to attain various chosen ends: *praxeology.*

What is the relationship between praxeology and economic analysis? Economics is a subdivision of praxeology—so far the only fully elaborated subdivision. With praxeology as the general, formal theory of human action, economics includes the analysis of the action of an isolated individual (Crusoe economics) and, especially elaborate, the analysis of interpersonal exchange (catallactics). The rest of praxeology is an unexplored area. Attempts have been made to formulate a logical theory of war and violent action, and violence in the form of government has been treated by political philosophy and by praxeology in tracing the effects of violent intervention in the free market. A theory of games has been elaborated, and interesting beginnings have been made in a logical analysis of voting.

The suggestion has been made that, since praxeology and economics are logical chains of reasoning based on a few universally known premises, to be really scientific it should be elaborated according to the symbolic notations of mathematical logic.[44] This represents a curious misconception of the role of mathematical logic, or "logistics." In the first place, it is the great quality of verbal propositions that *each one* is meaningful. On the other hand, algebraic and logical symbols, as used in logistics, are not in themselves meaningful. Praxeology asserts the action axiom as true, and from this (together with a few empirical axioms—such as the existence of a variety of resources and individuals) are deduced, by the rules of logical inference, all the propositions of economics, each one of which is verbal and meaningful. If the logistic array of symbols were used, each proposition would not be meaningful. Logistics, therefore, is far more suited to the physical sciences, where, in contrast to the science of human action, the conclusions rather than the axioms are known. In the physical sciences, the premises are only hypothetical, and logical deductions are made from them. In these cases, there is no purpose in having meaningful propositions at each step of the way, and therefore symbolic and mathematical language is more useful.

Simply to develop economics verbally, then to translate into logistic symbols, and finally to retranslate the propositons back into English, makes no sense and violates the fundamental scientific principle of Occam's razor; which calls for the greatest possible simplicity in science and the avoidance of unnecessary multiplication of entities or processes.

Contrary to what might be believed, the use of verbal logic is not inferior to logistics. On the contrary, the latter is merely an auxiliary device based on the former. For formal logic deals with the necessary and fundamental laws of thought, which must be verbally expressed, and logistics is only a symbolic system that uses this formal verbal logic as its foundation. Therefore, praxeology and economics need not be apologetic in the slightest for the use of verbal logic—the fundamental basis of symbolic logic, and meaningful at each step of the route.[45]

APPENDIX B: ON MEANS AND ENDS

It is often charged that any theory grounded on a logical separation of *means* and *ends* is unrealistic because the two are often amalgamated or fused into one. Yet if man acts purposively, he therefore drives toward *ends,* and whatever route he takes, he must, *ipso facto,* employ *means* to achieve them. The distinction between means and ends is a necessary logical distinction rooted in all human—indeed, all purposive—action. It is difficult to see the sense in any denial of this primordial truth. The only sense to the charge concerns those cases where certain *objects,* or rather certain *routes of action,* become ends in themselves as well as means to other ends. This, of course, can often happen. There is no difficulty, however, in incorporating them into an analysis, as has been done above. Thus, a man may work at a certain job not only for the pay, but also because he enjoys the work or the location. Moreover; any desire for money is a desire for a means to other ends. The critics of praxeology confuse the necessary and eternal separation of ends and means as *categories* with their frequent coincidence in a particular concrete resource or course of action.

2

Direct Exchange

1. *Types of Interpersonal Action: Violence*

The analysis in chapter 1 was based on the logical implications of the assumption of action, and its results hold true for all human action. The *application* of these principles was confined, however, to "Crusoe economics," where the actions of isolated individuals are considered by themselves. In these situations there are no interactions between persons. Thus, the analysis could easily and directly be applied to *n* number of isolated Crusoes on *n* islands or other isolated areas. The next task is to apply and extend the analysis to consider interactions between individual human beings.

Let us suppose that Crusoe eventually finds that another individual, say Jackson, has also been living an isolated existence at the other end of the island. What types of interaction may now take place between them? One type of action is *violence*. Thus, Crusoe may entertain a vigorous hatred toward Jackson and decide to murder or otherwise injure him. In that case, Crusoe would gain his end—murder of Jackson—by committing violence. Or Crusoe may decide that he would like to expropriate Jackson's house and collection of furs and murder Jackson as a means to that end. In either case, the result is that Crusoe gains in satisfaction at the expense of Jackson, who, to say the least, suffers great psychic loss. Fundamentally similar is action based on a *threat of violence,* or *intimidation.* Thus, Crusoe may hold up Jackson at the point of a knife and rob him of his accumulated furs and provisions. Both examples are cases of *violent action* and involve gain for one at the expense of another.

The following factors, singly or in combination, might work to induce Crusoe (or Jackson) to *refrain* from any violent action against the other:

1) He may feel that the use of violence against any other human being is *immoral,* i.e., that refraining from violence against another person is an end in itself, whose rank in his value scale is higher that that of any advantages in the form of capital or consumers' goods that he might gain from such action.

2) He may decide that instituting violent action might well establish an unwelcome precedent, causing the other person to take up arms against him, so that he may end by being the victim instead of the victor. If he begins a type of action where one must gain at the expense of another, then he must face the fact that *he* might turn out to be the loser as a result of the action.

3) Even if he feels that his violent action will eventually result in victory over the other, he may conclude that the "costs of the war" would exceed his net gain from the victory. Thus, the disutility of time and labor-energy spent in *fighting the war* (war may be defined as violent action used by two or more opponents), in accumulating *weapons* for the war (capital goods for war uses), etc., might, in prospect, outweigh the spoils of conquest.

4) Even if Crusoe feels reasonably certain of victory and believes that the costs of fighting will be far less than the utility of his spoils of victory, this short-run gain may well be outweighed in his decision by long-run losses. Thus, his conquest of Jackson's furs and house may add to his satisfaction for a while after the "period of production" (= preparing for the war + the length of time of the war itself), but, after a time, his house will decay and his furs become worthless. He may then conclude that, by his murder of Jackson, he has lost permanently many services which Jackson's continued existence might have furnished. This might be companionship or other types of consumers' or capital goods. *How* Jackson might have served Crusoe without resort to violence will be indicated below, but, at any rate, Crusoe may

be detained from using violence by estimating the disutility of the long-run consequences more highly than the utility of the expected short-run gains. On the other hand, his time preference may be so high as to cause his short-run gains to override the long-run losses in his decision.

It is possible that Crusoe may institute violent action without taking into consideration the costs of the war or the long-run consequences, in which case his actions will turn out to be erroneous, i.e., the means he used were not the appropriate ones to maximize his psychic revenue.

Instead of murdering his opponent, Crusoe might find it more useful to *enslave* him, and, under continual threat of violence, to force Jackson to agree to expend his labor for the satisfaction of Crusoe's wants rather than his own.[1] Under *slavery,* the master treats the slave as he does his livestock, horses, and other animals, using them as factors of production to gratify his wants, and feeding, housing them, etc., just enough to enable them to continue in the master's service. It is true that the slave agrees to this arrangement, but this agreement is the result of a choice between working for the master and injury through violence. Labor under these conditions is qualitatively different from labor not under the threat of violence, and may be called *compulsory labor* as compared to *free labor* or *voluntary labor.* If Jackson agrees to continue working as a slave under Crusoe's dictates, it does *not* mean that Jackson is an enthusiastic advocate of his own slavery. It simply means that Jackson does not believe that *revolt* against his master will better his condition, because of the *costs* of the revolt in terms of possible violence inflicted on him, the labor of preparing and fighting, etc.

The argument that the slave might be an enthusiastic supporter of the system because of the food, etc., provided by his master ignores the fact that, in that case, violence and the threat of violence by the master would not be necessary. Jackson would simply voluntarily place himself in Crusoe's service, and this arrangement would not be slavery, but another type considered in the next section.[2,3] It is clear that the slave is always worse off than he would be without the threat of violence by the master, and therefore, that the master always gains at the expense of the slave.

The interpersonal relation under slavery is known as *hegemonic.*[4] The relationship is one of command and obedience, the commands being enforced by threats of violence. The master uses the slaves as instruments, as factors of production, for gratifying his wants. Thus, slavery, or hegemony, is defined as a system in which one must labor under the orders of another under the threat of violence. Under hegemony, the man who does the obeying—the "slave," "serf," "ward," or "subject"—makes only one choice among two alternatives: (1) to subject himself to the master or "dictator"; or (2) to revolt against the regime of violence by use of his own violence or by refusing to obey orders. If he chooses the first course, he submits himself to the hegemonic ruler, and all the other decisions and actions are made by that ruler. The subject chooses *once* in choosing to obey the ruler; the other choices are made by the ruler. The subject acts as a passive factor of production for use by the master. After that one act of (continual) choice made by the slave, he engages in coerced or compulsory labor, and the dictator alone is free to choose and act.

Violent action may result in the following developments: (*a*) inconclusive fighting, with neither opponent the victor, in which case the war may continue intermittently for a long period of time, or violent action may cease, and *peace* be established (the absence of war); (*b*) the victor may kill the victim, in which case there is no further interpersonal action between the two; (*c*) the victor may simply rob the victim and leave, to return to isolation, or perhaps with intermittent violent forays; or (*d*) the victor may establish a continuing hegemonic tyranny over the victim by threats of violence.

In course (*a*), the violent action has proved abortive and erroneous; in (*b*), there is no further interpersonal interaction; in (*c*), there is an alternation between robbery and isolation; and in (*d*), a continuing hegemonic bond is established.

Of these results, only in (*d*) has a continuing pattern of interpersonal relationship been constituted. These relations are compulsory, involving the following coerced "exchanges": the slaves are treated as factors of production in exchange for food and other provisions; the masters acquire factors of production in exchange for supplying the provisions. Any continuing pattern of interpersonal exchanges is called a *society,* and it is clear that a society has been established only in case (*d*).[5] In the case of Crusoe's enslavement of Jackson, the society established is a totally hegemonic one.

The term "society," then, denotes a pattern of interpersonal exchanges among human beings. It is obviously absurd to treat "society" as "real," with some independent force of its own. There is no reality to society apart from the individuals who compose it and whose actions determine the type of social pattern that will be established.

We have seen in chapter 1 that all action is an exchange, and we may now divide exchanges into two categories. One is *autistic exchange.* Autistic exchange consists of any exchange that does not involve some form of interpersonal exchange of services. Thus, all of isolated Crusoe's exchanges were autistic. On the other hand, the case of slavery did involve *interpersonal exchange,* in which each gives up some goods in order to acquire other goods from the other. In this form of compulsory exchange, however, only the ruler benefits from the exchange, since he is the only one who makes it of his own free choice. Since he must impose the threat of violence in order to induce the subject to make the exchange, it is clear that the latter loses by the exchange. The master uses the subject as a factor of production for his own profit at the latter's expense, and this hegemonic relationship may be called *exploitation.* Under hegemonic exchange, the ruler exploits the subject for the ruler's benefit.[6]

2. *Types of Interpersonal Action: Voluntary Exchange and the Contractual Society*[7]

From this point on, we shall develop an analysis of the workings of a society based purely on voluntary action, entirely *unhampered* by violence or threats of violence. We shall examine interpersonal actions that are purely voluntary, and have no trace of hegemonic relations. Then, after working out the laws of the *unhampered market,* we shall trace the nature and results of hegemonic relations—of actions based on violence or the threat of violence. We shall note the various effects of violent interference with voluntary actions and shall consider the consequences of approaches to a regime of total hegemony, of pure slavery or subjection. At present, we shall confine our discussion to an analysis of actions unhampered by the existence of violence of man against man.

The major form of voluntary interaction is voluntary interpersonal exchange. A gives up a good to B in exchange for a good that B gives up to A. The essence of the exchange is that *both people make it because they expect that it will benefit them; otherwise they would not have agreed to the exchange.* A necessary condition for an exchange to take place is that the *two goods have reverse valuations on the respective value scales of the two parties to the exchange.* Thus, suppose A and B are the two exchangers, and A gives B good *X* in exchange for good *Y*. In order for this exchange to take place, the following must have been their value scales before making the exchange:

A	*B*
1—(Good *Y*)	1—(Good *X*)
2—Good *X*	2—Good *Y*

(Parentheses around the good indicate that the party does not have it in his stock; absence of parentheses indicates that he has.) A possesses good *X,* and B possesses good *Y,* and each evaluates the good of the other more highly than his own. After the exchange is made, both A and B have shifted to a higher position on their respective value scales.

Thus, the conditions for an exchange to take place are that the goods are valued in reverse order by the two parties and that each of the parties *knows* of the existence of the other and the goods that he possesses. Without knowledge of the other person's assets, no exchange of these assets could take place.

It is clear that the things that must be exchanged are *goods,* which will be useful to the receiving party. The goods may be present or future goods (or claims to future goods, which may be considered as equivalent to future goods), they may be capital goods or consumers' goods, labor or nature-given factors. At any rate, the objects of an exchange must be *scarce means* to human ends, since, if they were available in abundance for all, they would be general conditions of human welfare and not objects of human action. If something were a general condition of human welfare, there would be no need to give something up to acquire it, and it would not become the object of exchange.

If the goods in question are unique goods with a supply of one unit, then the problem of when exchanges will or will not be made is a simple one. If A has a vase and B a typewriter, if each knows of the other's asset, and if A values the typewriter more highly, and B values the vase more highly, there will be an exchange. If, on the other hand, *either* A or B values whatever he has more highly than what the other has, then an exchange will not take place. Similarly, an exchange will not take place if either party has no knowledge that the other party has a vase or a typewriter.

On the other hand, if the goods are available in *supplies* of homogeneous units, the problem becomes more complex. Here, in determining how far exchanges of the two goods will go, the law of marginal utility becomes the decisive factor.[8] If Jones and Smith have certain quantities of units of goods *X* and *Y* in their possession, then in order for Jones to trade *one unit* of *X* for *one unit* of *Y*, the following conditions have to be met: To Jones, the marginal utility of the added unit of *Y* must be greater than the marginal utility of the unit of *X* given up; and to Smith, the marginal utility of the added unit of *X* must be greater than the marginal utility of the unit of *Y* given up. Thus:

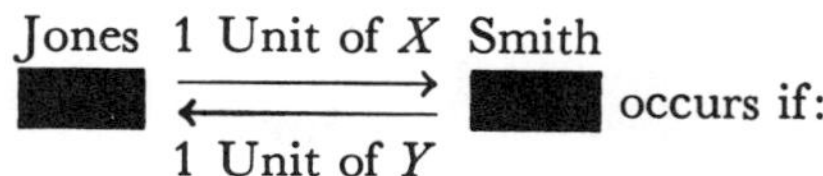

to Jones, M.U. of Addition of *Y* > M.U. of *X*.

to Smith, M.U. of Addition of *X* > M.U. of *Y*.

(The marginal utilities of the goods to Jones and to Smith are, of course, not comparable, since they cannot be measured, and the two value scales cannot be reduced to one measure or scale.)

However, as Jones continues to exchange with Smith units of *X* for units of *Y*, the marginal utility of *X* to Jones increases, because of the law of marginal utility. Furthermore, the marginal utility of the added unit of *Y* continues to decrease as Jones' stock of *Y* increases, because of the operation of this law. Eventually, therefore, Jones will reach a point where, in any further exchange of *X* for *Y*, the marginal utility of *X* will be greater than the marginal utility of the added unit of *Y*, so that he will make no further exchange. Furthermore, Smith is in a similar position. As he continues to exchange *Y* for *X*, for him the marginal utility of *Y* increases, and the marginal utility of the added unit of *X* decreases, with the operation of the law of marginal utility. He too will eventually reach a point where a further exchange will lower rather than raise his position on his value scale, so that he will decline to make any further exchange. Since it takes two to make a bargain, Jones and Smith will exchange units of *X* for units of *Y* *until one of them* reaches a point beyond which further exchange will lead to loss rather than profit.

Thus, suppose that Jones begins with a position where his *assets* (*stock of goods*) consist of a supply of 5 horses and 0 cows, while Smith begins with assets of 5 cows and 0 horses. How much, if any, exchanges of one cow for one horse will be effected is reflected in the value scales of the two people. Thus, suppose that Jones' value diagram is as shown in Fig. 5. The dots represent the value of the marginal utility of each additional cow, as Jones makes exchanges of one horse for one cow. The crosses represent the increasing marginal utility of each horse given up as Jones makes exchanges. Jones will stop trading after the third exchange, when his assets consist of 2 horses and 3 cows, since a further such exchange will make him worse off.

On the other hand, suppose that Smith's value diagram appears as in Fig. 6. The dots represent the marginal utility to Smith of each additional horse, while the crosses represent the marginal utility of each cow given up. Smith will stop trading after two exchanges, and therefore Jones will have to stop after two exchanges also. They will end with Jones having a stock of 3 horses and 2 cows, and Smith with a stock of 3 cows and 2 horses.

It is almost impossible to overestimate the importance of exchange in a developed economic system. Interpersonal exchanges have an enormous influence on productive activities. Their existence means that goods and units of goods have not only *direct use-value* for the producer, but also *exchange-value*. In other

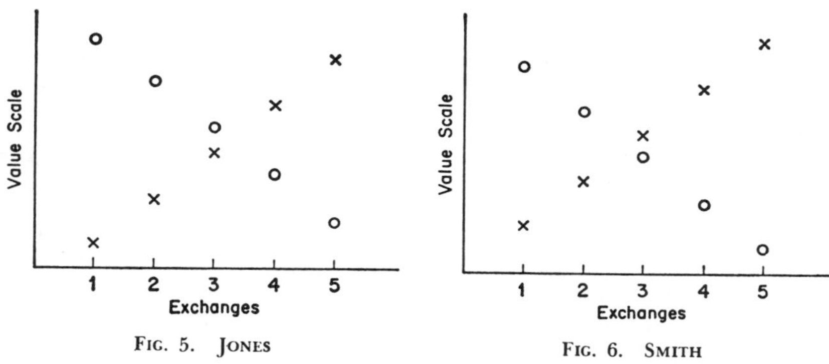

FIG. 5. JONES

FIG. 6. SMITH

words, goods may now be exchanged for other goods of greater usefulness to the actor. A man will exchange a unit of a good so long as the goods that it can command in exchange have greater value to him than the value it had in direct use, i.e., so long as its exchange-value is greater than its direct use-value. In the example above, the first two horses that Jones exchanged and the first two cows surrendered by Smith had a greater exchange value than direct use-value to their owners. On the other hand, from then on, their respective assets had greater use-value to their owners than exchange-value.[9]

The existence and possibilities of exchange open up for producers the avenue of producing for a "market" rather than for themselves. Instead of attempting to maximize his product in isolation by producing goods solely for his own use, each person can now produce goods in anticipation of their exchange-value, and exchange these goods for others that are more valuable to him. It is evident that since this opens a new avenue for the utility of goods, it becomes possible for each person to increase his productivity. Through praxeology, therefore, we know that only gains can come to every participant in exchange and that each must benefit by the transaction; otherwise he would not engage in it. Empirically we know that the exchange economy has made possible an enormous increase in productivity and satisfactions for all the participants.

Thus, any person can produce goods either for his own direct use or for purposes of exchange with others for goods that he desires. In the former case, *he* is the *consumer* of his own product; in the latter case, he produces in the service of *other consumers,* i.e., he "produces for a market." In either case, it is clear that, on the unhampered "market," it is the consumers who dictate the course of production.

At any time, a good or a unit of a good may have for its possessor either direct use-value or exchange-value or a mixture of both, and whichever is the greater is the determinant of his action. Examples of goods with only direct use-value to their owner are those in an isolated economy or such goods as eyeglasses ground to an individual prescription. On the other hand, producers of such eyeglasses or of surgical instruments find no direct use-value in these products, but only exchange-value. Many goods, as in the foregoing example of exchange, have both direct and exchange-value for their owners. For the latter goods, changing conditions may cause direct use-value to replace exchange-value in the actor's hierarchy of values, or vice versa. Thus, if a person with a stock of wine happens to lose his taste for wine, the previous greater use-value that wine had for him will change, and the wine's exchange-value will take precedence over its use-value, which has now become almost nil. Similarly, a grown person may exchange the toys that he had used as a child, now that their use-value has greatly declined.

On the other hand, the exchange-value of goods may decline, causing their possessors to use them directly rather than exchange them. Thus, a milliner might make a hat for purposes of exchange, but some minor defect might cause its expected exchange-value to dwindle, so that the milliner decides to wear the hat herself.

One of the most important factors causing a change in the relationship between direct use-value and exchange-value is an increase in the number of units of a supply available. From the law of marginal utility we know that an increase in the supply of a good available decreases the marginal utility of the supply for direct use. Therefore, the more units of supply are available, the more likely will the exchange-value of the marginal unit be greater than its value in direct use, and the more likely will its owner be to exchange it. The more horses that Jones had in his stock, and the more cows Smith had, the more eager would they be to exchange them. Conversely, a decrease in supply will increase the likelihood that direct use-value will predominate.

The network of voluntary interpersonal exchanges forms a society; it also forms a pattern of interrelations known as *the market.* A society formed solely by the market has an *unhampered market,* or a *free market,* a market not burdened by the interference of violent action. A society based on voluntary exchanges is called a *contractual society.* In contrast to the hegemonic society based on the rule of violence, the contractual type of society is based on freely entered contractual relations between individuals. Agreements by individuals to make exchanges are called *contracts,* and a society based on voluntary contractual agreements is a contractual society. It is the society of the unhampered market.

In a contractual society, each individual benefits by the exchange-contract that he makes. Each individual is an actor free to make his own decisions at every step of the way. Thus, the relations among people in an unhampered market are "symmetrical"; there is equality in the sense that each person has equal power to make his own exchange-decisions. This is in contrast to a hegemonic relationship, where power is asymmetrical—where the dictator makes all the decisions for his subjects except the one decision to obey, as it were, at bayonet point.

Thus, the distinguishing features of the contractual society, of the unhampered market, are self-responsibility, freedom from violence, full power to make one's own decisions (except the decision to institute violence against another), and benefits for all participating individuals. The distinguishing features of a hegemonic society are the rule of violence, the surrender of the power to make one's own decisions to a dictator, and exploitation of subjects for the benefit of the masters. It will be seen below that existing societies may be totally hegemonic, totally contractual, or various mixtures of different degrees of the two, and the nature and consequences of these various "mixed economies" and totally hegemonic societies will be analyzed.

Before we examine the exchange process further, it must be considered that, in order for a person to exchange anything, he must first possess it, or *own* it. He gives up the *ownership* of good *X* in order to obtain the *ownership* of good *Y*. Ownership by one or more owners implies exclusive control and use of the goods owned, and the goods owned are known as *property*. Freedom from violence implies that no one may seize the property of another by means of violence or the threat of violence and that each person's property is safe, or "secure," from such aggression.

What goods become property? Obviously, only *scarce means* are property. General conditions of welfare, since they are abundant to all, are not the objects of any action, and therefore cannot be owned or become property. On the free market, it is nonsense to say that someone "owns" the air. Only if a good is scarce is it necessary for anyone to obtain it, or ownership of it, for his use. The only way that a man could assume ownership of the air is to use violence to enforce this claim. Such action could not occur on the unhampered market.

On the free, unhampered market, a man can acquire property in scarce goods as follows: (1) In the first place, *each man has ownership over his own self,* over his will and actions, and the manner in which he will exert his own labor. (2) He acquires scarce nature-given factors either by appropriating hitherto unused factors for his own use or by receiving them as a gift from someone else, who in the last analysis must have appropriated them as hitherto unused factors.[10] (3) He acquires capital goods or consumers' goods either by mixing his own labor with nature-given factors to produce them or by receiving them as a gift from someone else. As in the previous case, gifts must eventually resolve themselves into some actor's production of the goods by the use of his own labor. Clearly, it will be nature-given factors, capital goods, and *durable* consumers' goods that are likely to be handed down through gifts, since nondurable consumers' goods will probably be quickly consumed. (4) He may *exchange* any type of factor (labor service, nature-given factor, capital good, consumers' good) for any type of factor. It is clear that gifts and exchanges as a source of property must eventually be resolved into: *self-ownership, appropriation of unused nature-given factors,* and *production of capital and consumers' goods,* as the ultimate sources of acquiring property in a free economic system. In order for the giving or exchanging of goods to take place, they must first be obtained by individual actors in one of these ways. The logical sequence of events is therefore: A man owns himself; he appropriates unused nature-given factors for his ownership; he uses these factors to produce capital goods and consumers' goods which become his own; he uses up the consumers' goods and/or gives them and the capital goods away to others; he exchanges some of these goods for other goods that had come to be owned in the same way by others.[11,12] These are the methods of acquiring goods that obtain on the free market, and they include all but the method of violent or other *invasive* expropriation of the property of others.[13]

In contrast to general conditions of welfare, which on the free market cannot be subject to appropriation as property, scarce goods in use in production must always be under *someone's* control, and therefore must always be *property*. On the free market, the goods will be owned by those who either produced them, first put them to use, or received them in gifts. Similarly, under a system of violence and hegemonic bonds, someone or some people must superintend and direct the operations of these goods. Whoever performs these functions in effect owns these goods as property, regardless of the legal definition of ownership. This applies to persons and their services as well as to material goods. On the free market, each person is a complete owner of himself, whereas under a system of full hegemonic bonds, he is subject to the ownership of others, with the exception of the one decision not to revolt against the authority of the owner. Thus, violent or hegemonic regimes do not and cannot *abolish* property, which derives from the fundamentals of human action, but can only transfer it from one person or set of people (the producers or natural self-owners) to another set.

We may now briefly sum up the various types of human action in the following table:

HUMAN ACTION

I. Isolation (Autistic Exchange)
II. Interpersonal Action
  A. Invasive Action
    1. War
    2. Murder, Assault
    3. Robbery
    4. Slavery
  B. Noninvasive Action
    1. Gifts
    2. Voluntary Exchange

This and subsequent chapters are devoted to an analysis of a noninvasive society, particularly that constituted by voluntary interpersonal exchange.

3. *Exchange and the Division of Labor*

In describing the conditions that must obtain for interpersonal exchange to take place (such as reverse valuations), we implicitly assumed that it must be *two different goods* that are being exchanged. If Crusoe at his end of the island produced only berries, and Jackson at his end produced only the same kind of berries, then no basis for exchange between them would occur. If Jackson produced two hundred berries and Crusoe one hundred fifty, it would be nonsensical to assume that any exchange of berries would be made between them.[14] The only voluntary interpersonal action in relation to berries that could occur would be a gift from one to another.

If exchangers must exchange two different goods, this implies that each party must have a different proportion of assets of goods in relation to his wants. He must have relatively *specialized* in the acquisition of different goods from those the other party produced. This specialization by each individual may have occurred for any one of three different reasons or any combination of the three: (*a*) differences in suitability and yield of the nature-given factors; (*b*) differences in given capital and durable consumers' goods, and (*c*) differences in skill and in the desirability of different types of labor.[15] These factors, in addition to the potential exchange-value and use-value of the goods, will determine the line of production that the actor will pursue. If the production is directed toward exchange, then the exchange-value will play a major role in his decision. Thus, Crusoe may have found abundant crops on his side of the island. These resources, added to his greater skill in farming and the lower disutility of this occupation for him because of a liking for agriculture, might cause him to take up farming, while Jackson's greater skill in hunting and more abundant game supply induce him to specialize in hunting and trapping. Exchange, a productive process for both participants, implies specialization of production, or *division of labor.*

The extent to which division of labor is carried on in a society depends on the *extent of the market for the products.* The latter determines the exchange-value that the producer will be able to obtain for his goods. Thus, if Jackson knows that he will be able to exchange part of his catch of game for the grains and fruits of Crusoe, he may well expend all his labor on hunting. Then he will be able to devote all his labor-time to hunting, while Crusoe devotes his to farming, and their "surplus" stocks will be exchanged up to the limits analyzed in the previous section. On the other hand, if, for example, Crusoe has little use for meat, Jackson will not be able to exchange much meat, and he will be forced to be far more directly self-sufficient, producing his own grains and fruits as well as meat.

It is clear that, praxeologically, the very fact of exchange and the division of labor implies that it must be more productive for all concerned than isolated, autistic labor. Economic analysis alone, however, does not convey to us knowledge of the enormous increase in productivity that the division of labor brings to society. This is based on a further empirical insight, viz., the enormous *variety* in human beings and in the world around them. It is a fact that, superimposed on the basic unity of species and objects in nature, there is a great diversity. Particularly is there variety in the aforementioned factors that would give rise to specialization: in the locations and types of natural resources and in the ability, skills, and tastes of human beings. In the words of Professor von Mises:

> One may as well consider these two facts as one and the same fact, namely, the manifoldness of nature which makes the universe a complex of infinite varieties. If the earth's surface were such that the physical conditions of production were the same at every point and if one man were . . . equal to all other men . . . division of labor would not offer any advantages for acting man.[16]

It is clear that conditions for exchange, and therefore increased productivity for the participants, will occur *where each party has a superiority in productivity in regard to one of the goods exchanged*—a superiority that may be due either to better nature-given factors or to the ability of the producer. If individuals abandon attempts to satisfy their wants in isolation, and if each devotes his working time to that specialty in which he excels, it is clear that total productivity for each of the products is increased. If Crusoe can produce more berries per unit of time, and Jackson can kill more game, it is clear that productivity in both lines is increased if Crusoe devotes himself wholly to the production of berries and Jackson to hunting game, after which they can exchange some of the berries for some of the game. In addition to this, full-time specialization in a line of production is likely to improve each person's productivity in that line and intensify the relative superiority of each.

More puzzling is the case in which one individual is superior to another in all lines of production. Suppose, for example, that Crusoe is superior to Jackson both in the production of berries and in the production of game. Are there any possibilities for exchange in this situation? Superficially, it might be answered that there are none, and that both will continue in isolation. Actually, it pays for Crusoe to specialize in that line of production in which he has the greatest *relative* superiority in production, and to exchange this product for the product in which Jackson specializes. It is clear that the inferior producer benefits by receiving some of the products of the superior one. The latter benefits also, however, by being free to devote himself to that product in which his productive superiority is the greatest. Thus, if Crusoe has a great superiority in berry production and a small one in game production, it will still benefit him to devote his full working time to berry production and then exchange some berries for Jackson's game products. In an example mentioned by Professor Boulding:

> A doctor who is an excellent gardener may very well prefer to employ a hired man who as a gardener is inferior to himself, because thereby he can devote more time to his medical practice.[17]

This important principle—that exchange may beneficially take place even when one party is superior in both lines of production—is known as the *law of association,* the *law of comparative costs,* or the *law of comparative advantage.*

With all-pervasive variation offering possibilities for specialization, and favorable conditions of exchange occurring even when one party is superior in both pursuits, great opportunities abound for widespread division of labor and extension of the market. As more and more people are linked together in the exchange network, the more "extended" is the market for each of the products, and the more will exchange-value predominate, as compared to direct use-value, in the decisions of the producer. Thus, suppose that there are five people on the desert island, and each specializes in that line of product in which he has a comparative or absolute advantage. Suppose that each one concentrates on the following products:

A. . . . . berries
B. . . . . game
C. . . . . fish
D. . . . . eggs
E. . . . . milk.

With more people participating in the market process, the opportunities for exchange for each actor are now greatly increased. This is true even though each particular act of exchange takes place between just two people and involves two goods. Thus, as shown in Fig. 7, the following network of exchange may take place: Exchange-value now takes a far more dominant place in the decisions of the producers. Crusoe (if A is Crusoe) now knows that if he specializes in berries, he does not now have to rely solely

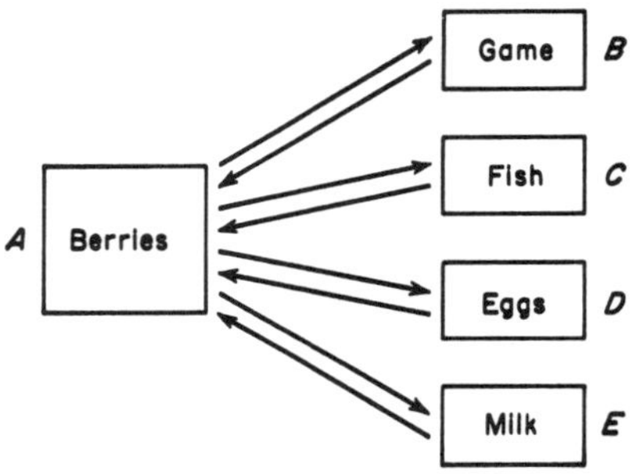

This diagram depicts the pattern of *A's exchanges*. He engages in exchange with each one of the other actors. For each of the other actors, the pattern would be similar.

FIG. 7. PATTERN OF A'S EXCHANGES

on Jackson to accept them, but can exchange them for the products of several other people. A sudden loss of taste for berries by Jackson will not impoverish Crusoe and deprive him of all other necessities as it would have before. Furthermore, berries will now bring to Crusoe a wider variety of products, each in far greater abundance than before, some being available now that would not have been earlier. The greater productivity and the wider market and emphasis on exchange-value obtain for all participants in the market.

It is evident, as will be explained further in later sections on indirect exchange, that the contractual society of the market is a genuinely *co-operative society*. Each person specializes in the task for which he is best fitted, and each serves his fellow men in order to serve himself in exchange. Each person, by producing for exchange, co-operates with his fellow men voluntarily and without coercion. In contrast to the hegemonic form of society, in which one person or one group of persons exploits the others, a contractual society leaves each person free to benefit himself in the market and as a consequence to benefit others as well. An interesting aspect of this praxeological truth is that this benefit to others occurs regardless of the *motives* of those involved in exchange. Thus, Jackson may specialize in hunting and exchange the game for other products even though he may be indifferent to, or even cordially detest, his fellow participants. Yet regardless of his motives, the other participants are benefited by his actions as an indirect but necessary consequence of his own benefit. It is this almost marvelous process, whereby a man in pursuing his own benefit also benefits others, that caused Adam Smith to exclaim that it almost seemed that an "invisible hand" was directing the proceedings.[18]

Thus, in explaining the origins of society, there is no need to conjure up any mystic communion or "sense of belonging" among individuals. Individuals recognize, through the use of reason, the advantages of exchange resulting from the higher productivity of the division of labor, and they proceed to follow this advantageous course. In fact, it is far more likely that feelings of friendship and communion are the *effects* of a regime of (contractual) social co-operation rather than the cause. Suppose, for example, that the division of labor were not productive, or that men had failed to recognize its productivity. In that case, there would be little or no opportunity for exchange, and each man would try to obtain his goods in autistic independence. The result would undoubtedly be a fierce struggle to gain possession of the scarce goods, since, in such a world, each man's gain of useful goods would be some other man's loss. It would be almost inevitable for such an autistic world to be strongly marked by violence and perpetual war. Since each man could gain from his fellows only at their expense, violence would be prevalent, and it seems highly likely that feelings of mutual hostility would be dominant. As in the case of animals quarreling over bones, such a warring world could cause only hatred and hostility between man and man. Life would be a bitter "struggle for survival." On the other hand, in a world of voluntary social co-operation through mutually beneficial exchanges, where one man's gain is another man's *gain,* it is obvious that great scope is provided for the development of social sympathy and human friendships. It is the peaceful, co-operative society that creates favorable conditions for feelings of friendship among men.

The mutual benefits yielded by exchange provide a major incentive (as in the case of Crusoe above) to would-be *aggressors* (initiators of violent action against others) to restrain their aggression and co-operate peacefully with their fellows. Individuals then decide that the advantages of engaging in specialization and exchange outweigh the advantages that war might bring.

Another feature of the market society formed by the division of labor is its permanence. The wants of men are renewed for each period of time, and so they must try to obtain for themselves anew a supply of goods for each period. Crusoe wants to have a steady rate of supply of game, and Jackson would like to have a continuing supply of berries, etc. Therefore, the social relations formed by the division of labor tend to be permanent as individuals specialize in different tasks and continue to produce in those fields.

There is one, less important, type of exchange that does *not* involve the division of labor. This is an exchange of the *same types of labor* for certain tasks. Thus, suppose that Crusoe, Jackson, and Smith are trying to clear their fields of logs. If each one engaged solely in the work of clearing his own field, it would take a long period of time. However, if each put in some time in a joint effort to roll the other fellow's logs, the productivity of the log-rolling operations would be greatly increased. Each man could finish the task in a shorter period of time. This is particularly true for operations such as rolling heavy logs, which each man alone could not possibly accomplish at all and which they could perform only by agreed-upon joint action. In these cases, each man gives up his own labor in someone else's field in exchange for receiving the labor of the others in his field, the latter being worth more to him. Such an exchange involves a *combination* of the same type of labor, rather than a division of labor into different types, to perform tasks beyond the ready capacity of an isolated individual. This type of co-operative "log-rolling," however, would entail merely temporary alliances based on specific tasks, and, would not, as do specialization and division of labor, establish permanent exchange-ties and social relations.[19]

The great scope of the division of labor is not restricted to situations in which each individual makes all of one particular product, as was the case above. Division of labor may entail the specializing by individuals in the different *stages of production* necessary to produce a particular consumers' good. Thus, with a wider market permitting, different individuals specialize in the different stages, for example, involved in the production of the ham sandwich discussed in the previous chapter. General productivity is greatly increased as some people and some areas specialize in producing iron ore, some in producing different types of machines, some in baking bread, some in packaging meat, some in retailing, etc. The essence of developed market economies consists in the framework of co-operative exchange emerging with such specialization.[20]

4. *Terms of Exchange*

Before analyzing the problem of the terms of exchange, it is well to recall the reason for exchange—the fact that each individual values more highly the good he gets than the good he gives up. This fact is enough to elminate the fallacious notion that, if Crusoe and Jackson exchange five thousand berries for one cow, there is some sort of "equality of value" between the cow and the five thousand berries. Value exists in the valuing minds of individuals, and these individuals make the exchange precisely because for each of them there is an *inequality* of values between the cow and the berries. For Crusoe the cow is valued more than the five thousand berries; for Jackson it is valued less. Otherwise, the exchange could not be made. Therefore, for each exchange there is a *double inequality of values,* rather than an equality, and hence there are no "equal values" to be "measured" in any way.[21]

We have already seen what conditions are needed for exchange to occur and the extent to which exchange will take place on given terms. The question then arises: Are there any principles that decide the *terms* on which exchanges are made? Why does Crusoe exchange with Jackson at a rate of five thousand berries for one cow; or two thousand berries for one cow?

Let us take the hypothetical exchange of 5,000 berries for 1 cow. These are the terms, or the *rate of exchange* (5,000 berries for 1 cow). If we express one commodity in terms of the other, we obtain the *price* of the commodity. Thus, *the price of one good in terms of another is the amount of the other good divided by the amount of the first good in exchange.* If 2 cows exchange for 1,000 berries, then the *price* of cows in terms of berries ("the berry-price of cows") is 500 berries per cow. Conversely, the *price* of berries in terms of cows ("the cow-price of berries") is 1/500 cow per berry. The *price* is the rate of exchange between two commodities expressed in terms of one of the commodities.

Other useful concepts in the analysis of exchange are those of "selling" and "buying." Thus, in the above exchange, we may say that Crusoe *sold* a thousand berries and *bought* two cows in exchange. On the other hand, Jackson *sold* two cows and *bought* a thousand berries. The *sale* is the good given up in exchange, while the *purchase* is the good received.

Let us again focus attention on the object of exchange. We remember from chapter 1 that the object of all action is to *maximize psychic revenue,* and to do this the actor tries to see to it that the psychic revenue from the action exceeds the psychic cost, so that he obtains a psychic profit. This is no less true of interpersonal exchange. The object in such an exchange for each party is to maximize revenue, to exchange so long as the expected psychic revenue exceeds the psychic cost. The psychic revenue from any exchange is the value of the goods received in the exchange. This is equal to the marginal utility to the purchaser of adding the goods to his stock. More complicated is the problem of the psychic costs of an exchange. *Psychic costs* include all that the actor gives up by making the exchange. This is equal to the *next best use* that he could have made of the resources that he has used.

Suppose, for example, that Jackson possesses five cows and is considering whether or not to sell one cow in exchange. He decides on his value scale that the following is the rank in value of the possible uses of the cow:

1. 5,000 berries offered by Crusoe
2. 100 bbls. of fish offered by Smith
3. 4,000 berries offered by Jones
4. Marginal utility of the cow in direct use.

In this case, the top three alternatives involve the exchange-value of the cow, and the fourth its value in direct use. Jackson will make the best use of his resource by making the exchange with Crusoe. The 5,000 berries of Crusoe will be his psychic revenue from the exchange, while the loss of the 100 barrels of fish constitutes his psychic cost. We saw above that, in order for exchange to take place, the marginal utility of the goods received must be greater than the marginal utility of the goods given up. We now see that for any *specific* exchange to occur, the marginal utility of the goods received must also be greater than the marginal utility forgone—that which could have been received in another type of exchange.

It is evident that Jackson will always prefer an offer of more units of one type of good to an offer of fewer units of the same good. In other words, the seller will always prefer *the highest possible selling price for his good.* Jackson will prefer the price of 5,000 berries per cow offered by Crusoe to the price of 4,000 berries per cow offered by Jones. It might be objected that this may not always be true and may be offset by other factors. Thus, the prospect of 4,000 berries from Jones may be evaluated higher than the prospect of 5,000 berries from Crusoe, if: (*a*) the psychic disutility of labor and time, etc., for delivery over a longer distance to the latter renders the prospect of sale to Crusoe less attractive despite the higher price in berries; or (*b*) special feelings of friendship for Crusoe or hatred for Jones serve to change the utilities on Jackson's value scale. On further analysis, however, these turn out *not* to be vitiating factors at all. The rule that the actor will prefer the highest selling price for his good in terms of the other good always holds. It must be reiterated that a *good* is not defined by its physical characteristics, but by the equal serviceability of its units to the actor. Now, clearly, a berry from a longer distance, since it must call forth the disutility of labor to move it, is *not* the same good as the berry from a shorter distance, even though it is physically the same berry. The very fact that the first is further away means that it is not as serviceable as the other berry, and hence not the same good. For one "price" to be comparable with another, the good must be the same. Thus, if Jackson prefers to sell his cow for 4,000 berries from Jones as compared to 5,000 berries from Crusoe, it does *not* mean that he chooses a *lower* price for his product in terms of the same good (berries), but that he chooses a price in terms of one good (berries from Jones) over a price in terms of an entirely different good (berries from Crusoe). Similarly, if, because of feelings of friendship or hostility, receiving berries from Crusoe takes on a different quality from that of receiving berries from Jones, the two packets of berries are no longer of equal serviceability to Jackson, and therefore they become for him *two different goods.* If these feelings cause him to sell to Jones for 4,000 berries rather than to Crusoe for 5,000 berries, this does not mean that he chooses a lower price for the same good; he chooses between two different goods—berries from Crusoe and berries from Jones. Thus, at all times, an actor will sell his product at the highest possible price in terms of the good received.

Clearly, the converse is true for the buyer. *The buyer will always purchase his good at the lowest possible price.* This truth can be traced in the example just discussed, since, at the point that Jackson was a seller of the cow, he was also a *buyer of the berries.* Where the good in question—berries—was comparable, he bought at the lowest possible price—say 1/5,000 cow per berry in preference to 1/4,000 cow per berry. In cases where Jackson chooses the latter price, the two berries are no longer the same, but different, goods. If, to buy berries, the purchaser has to range further afield or buy from someone he dislikes, then this good becomes a different one in kind from the good closer by or sold by a friend.

5. *Determination of Price: Equilibrium Price*[22]

One of the most important problems in economic analysis is the question: What principles determine the formation of prices on the free market? What can be said by logical derivation from the fundamental assumption of human action in order to explain the determination of all prices in interpersonal exchanges, past, present, and future?

It is most convenient to begin with a case of *isolated exchange,* a case where only two isolated parties are involved in the exchange of two goods. For example, Johnson and Smith are considering a possible exchange of a horse of the former for some barrels of fish possessed by the latter. The question is: What can economic analysis say about the determinants of the exchange rate established between the two goods in the exchange?

An individual will decide whether or not to make an exchange on the basis of the relative positions of the two goods on his value scale. Thus, suppose the value scale of Smith, the possessor of the fish, is as follows:

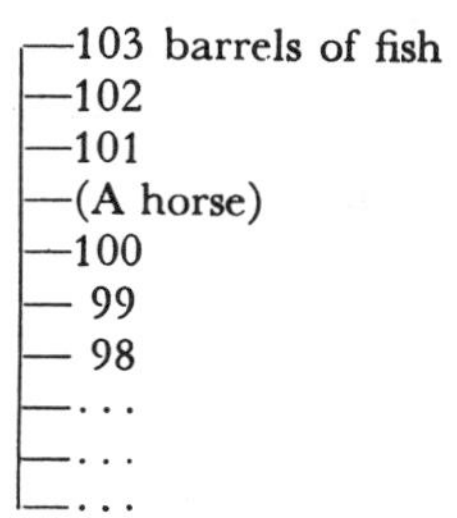

Fig. 8. Smith's Value Scale

(Any desired numbers of rank could be assigned to the various quantities, but these are not necessary here.)

It is clear that Smith would be willing to acquire a horse from Johnson if he could give up *100 barrels of fish or less.* 100 barrels or less are less valuable to Smith than the horse. On the other hand, 101 or more barrels of fish are more valuable to him than the horse. Thus, if the *price* of the horse in terms of the fish offered by Smith is *100 barrels or less,* then Smith will make the exchange. If the price is 101 barrels or more, then the exchange will not be made.

Suppose Johnson's value scale looks like this:

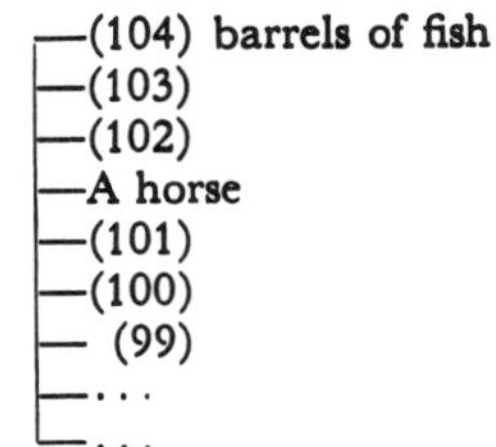

FIG. 9. JOHNSON'S VALUE SCALE

Then, Johnson will not give up his horse for less than 102 barrels of fish. If the price offered for his horse is less than 102 barrels of fish, he will not make the exchange. Here, it is clear that *no exchange will be made;* for at Johnson's minimum selling price of 102 barrels of fish, it is more beneficial for Smith to keep the fish than to acquire the horse.

In order for an exchange to be made, then, the *minimum selling price of the seller must be lower than the maximum buying price of the buyer* for that good. In this case, it must be lower than the price of 100 barrels of fish per horse. Suppose that this condition is met, and Johnson's value scale is as follows:

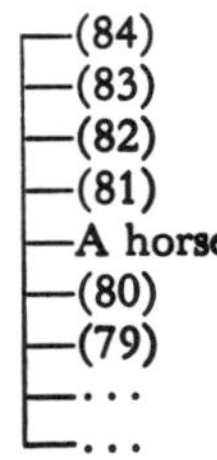

FIG. 10. JOHNSON'S VALUE SCALE

Johnson will sell the horse for any amount of fish at or above 81 barrels. This, then, is his minimum selling price for the horse. With this as Johnson's value scale, and Smith's as pictured above, what price will they agree upon for the horse (and, conversely, for the fish)? All analysis can say about this problem is that, since the exchange must be for the mutual benefit of both parties, *the price of the good in isolated exchange will be established somewhere between the maximum buying price and the minimum selling price,* i.e., the price of the horse will be somewhere between 100 and 81 barrels of fish. (Similarly, the price of the fish will be set somewhere between $\frac{1}{81}$ and $\frac{1}{100}$ of a horse per barrel.) We cannot say at which point the price will be set. That depends on the data of each particular case, on the specific conditions prevailing. In particular, it will depend upon the *bargaining skill* of the two individuals. Clearly, Johnson will try to set the price of the horse as high as possible, while Smith will try to set the price as low as possible. This is based on the principle that the seller of the product tries to obtain the highest price, while the buyer tries to secure the lowest price. We cannot predict the point that the two will agree on, except that it will be somewhere in this range set by the two points.[28]

Now, let us gradually remove our assumption of isolated exchange. Let us first assume that Smith has a competitor, Brown, a rival in offering fish for the desired horse of Johnson's. We assume that the fish offered by Brown is of identical serviceability to Johnson as the fish offered by Smith. Suppose that Smith's value scale is the same as before, but that Brown's value scale is such that the horse is worth more than 90 barrels of fish to him, but less than 91 barrels. The value scales of the three individuals will then appear as follows:

Smith		*Brown*	*Johnson*	
103		93	(84)	
102		92	(83)	
101		91	(82)	
(A horse)		(A horse)	(81)	←Minimum
100	←Maximum→	90	A horse	selling
99	buying	98	(80)	price
98	prices	88	(79)	

FIG. 11. VALUE SCALES OF THREE INDIVIDUALS

Brown and Smith are competing for the purchase of Johnson's horse. Clearly, only one of them can make the exchange for the horse, and since their goods are identical to Johnson, the latter's decision to exchange will be decided by the price offered for the horse. Obviously, Johnson will make the exchange with that potential buyer who will offer the highest price. Their value scales are such that Smith and Brown can continue to overbid each other as long as the price range is between 81 and 90 barrels of fish per horse. Thus, if Smith offers Johnson an exchange at 82 barrels per horse, Brown can compete by raising the bid to 84 barrels of fish per horse, etc. This can continue, however, only until Brown's maximum buying price has been exceeded. If Smith offers 91 barrels for the horse, it no longer pays for Brown to make the exchange, and he drops out of the competition. Thus. the price in the exchange will be high enough to exclude the "less capable" or "less urgent" buyer—the one whose value scale does not permit him to offer as high a price as the other, "more capable," buyer. We do not know exactly what the price will be, but we do know that it will be set by bargaining *somewhere at or below the maximum buying price of the most capable buyer and above the maximum buying price of the next most capable buyer.* It will be somewhere between 100 barrels and 91 barrels, and the exchange will be made with Smith. We see that the addition of another competing buyer for the product considerably narrows the zone of bargaining in determining the price that will be set.

This analysis can easily be extended to a case of one seller and *n* number of buyers (each offering the same commodity in exchange). Thus, suppose that there are five potential buyers for the horse, all offering fish, whose value scales are as follows:

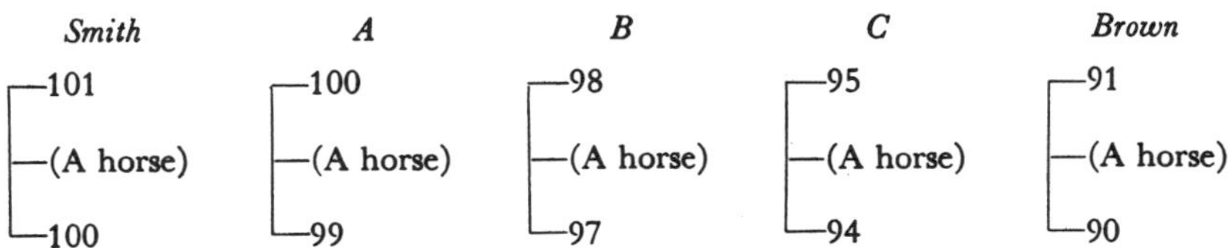

FIG. 12. VALUE SCALES OF FIVE POTENTIAL PURCHASERS

With only one horse to be disposed of to one buyer, the buyers overbid each other until each must drop out of the competition.

Finally, Smith can outbid A, his next most capable competitor, only with a price of 100. We see that in this case, the price in the exchange is uniquely determined—once the various value scales are given—at 100, since at a lower price A is still in the bidding, and, at a higher price, no buyer will be willing to conclude the exchange. At any rate, even if the value scales are not such as to determine the price uniquely, the addition of more competitors greatly narrows the bargaining zone. The general rule still holds: The price will be between the maximum buying price of the most capable and that of the next most capable competitor, including the former and excluding the latter.[24]

It is also evident that the narrowing of the bargaining zone has taken place in an upward direction, and to the advantage of the seller of the product.

The case of one-sided competition of *many sellers with just one buyer* is the direct converse of the above and may be considered by merely reversing the example and considering the price of the fish instead of the price of the horse. As more sellers of the fish competed to conclude the exchange with the one buyer, the zone of determination of the price of fish narrowed, although this time in a downward direction and to the further advantage of the buyer. As more sellers were added, each tried to *underbid* his rival—to offer a lower price for the product than his competitors. The sellers continued to underbid each other until all but the one seller were excluded from the market. In a case of many sellers and one buyer, the price will be set at a *point between the minimum selling price of the second most capable and that of the most capable competitor*—strictly, at a point below the former and down to or including the latter. In the final example above, the point was pushed down to be uniquely determined at the latter point—$1/100$ horse per barrel.

We have so far considered the cases of one buyer and more than one seller, and of one seller and more than one buyer. We now come to the only case with great importance in a modern, complex economy based on an intricate network of exchanges: *two-sided competition of buyers and sellers*. Let us therefore consider a market with any number of competing buyers and sellers.

Any product could be considered, but our hypothetical example will continue to be the sale of horses in exchange for fish (with the horses as well as the fish considered by all parties as homogeneous units of the same good). The following is a list of the maximum buying prices of the various buyers, based on the valuations on their respective value scales:

Buyers of Horses	*Maximum Buying Prices*
*X*1	100 barrels of fish
*X*2	98
*X*3	95
*X*4	91
*X*5	89
*X*6	88
*X*7	86
*X*8	85
*X*9	83

The following is a list of the minimum selling prices of the various sellers on the market:

Sellers of Horses	*Minimum Selling Prices*
*Z*1	81 barrels of fish
*Z*2	83
*Z*3	85
*Z*4	88
*Z*5	89
*Z*6	90
*Z*7	92
*Z*8	96

The "most capable buyer" of fish we recognize as Smith, with a buying price of 100 barrels. Johnson is the "most capable seller"—the seller with the lowest minimum selling price—at 81 barrels. The problem is to find the principle by which the price, or prices, of the exchanges of horses will be determined.

Now, let us first take the case of *X*1—Smith. It is clear that it is to the advantage of Smith to make the exchange at a price of 100 barrels for the horse. Yet it is to Smith's greater advantage to buy the good at the lowest possible price. He is not engaged in overbidding his competitors merely for the sake of overbidding. He will try to obtain the good for the lowest price that he can. Therefore, Smith will prefer to begin bidding for a horse at the lowest prices offered by his competitors, and only raise the offered price if it becomes necessary to do so in order to avoid being shut out of the market. Similarly, Johnson would make an advantageous sale at a price of 81 barrels. However, he is interested in selling his product at the highest possible price. He will underbid his competitor only if it becomes necessary to do so in order to avoid being shut out of the market without making a sale.

It is evident that buyers will tend to start negotiations by offering as low prices as possible, while sellers will tend to start by asking for as high a price as they think they can obtain. Clearly, this preliminary "testing of the market" will tend to be more prolonged in a "new" market, where conditions are unfamiliar, while it will tend to be less prolonged in an "old" market, where the participants are relatively familiar with the results of the price-formation process in the past and can estimate more closely what the results will be.

Let us suppose that buyers begin by offering the low price of 82 barrels for a horse. Here is a price at which each of the buyers would be glad to make a purchase, but only one seller, *Z*1, would be willing to sell at 82. It is possible that *Z*1, through ignorance, might conclude the exchange with some one of the buyers at 82, without realizing that he could have obtained a higher price. It is also possible that the other buyers will, through ignorance, permit the buyer to get away with this windfall without overbidding him for this cheap horse. But such a result is not very likely. It seems most likely that *Z*1 will not sell at such a low price, and that the buyers would immediately overbid any attempt by one of their number to conclude an exchange at that price. Even if, by some chance, one exchange was concluded at 82, it is obvious that such a price could not last. Since no other seller would make an exchange at that price, the price of further exchanges would have to rise further, as a result of upbidding by buyers.

Let us assume at this point that no exchange will be made at this price because of the further upbidding of the buyers and the knowledge of this by the sellers. As the offering price rises, the least capable buyers, as in the previous case, begin to be excluded from the market. A price of 84 will bring two sellers into the market, but will exclude X9 from the buyer's side. As the offering price rises, the disproportion between the *amount offered for sale* and the *amount demanded for purchase* at the given price diminishes, but as long as the latter is greater than the former, mutual overbidding of buyers will continue to raise the price. The amount offered for sale at each price is called the *supply;* the amount demanded for purchase at each price is called the *demand.* Evidently, at the first price of 82, the supply of horses on the market is 1; the demand for horses on the market is 9. Only one seller would be willing to sell at this price, while all nine buyers would be willing to make their purchase. On the basis of the above tabulations of maximum buying prices and minimum selling prices, we are able to present a list of the quantities of the good that will be demanded and supplied at each hypothetical price.

TABLE 2

PRICE	SUPPLIED	DEMANDED	PRICE	SUPPLIED	DEMANDED
80........	0 horses	9 horses	91........	6 horses	4 horses
81........	1	9	92........	7	3
82........	1	9	93........	7	3
83........	2	9	94........	7	3
84........	2	8	95........	7	3
85........	3	8	96........	8	2
86........	3	7	97........	8	2
87........	3	6	98........	8	2
88........	4	6	99.	8	1
89........	5	5	100	8	1
90........	6	4	101	8	0

This table reflects the progressive entry into the market of the sellers as the price increases and the dropping out of the buyers as the price increases. As was seen above, as long as the demand exceeds the supply at any price, buyers will continue to overbid and the price will continue to rise.

The converse occurs if the price begins near its highest point. Thus, if sellers first demand a price of 101 barrels for the horse, there will be eight eager sellers and no buyers. At a price of 99, the sellers may find one eager buyer, but chances are that a sale will not be made. The buyer will realize that there is no point in paying such a high price, and the other sellers will eagerly underbid the one who tries to make the sale at the price of 99. Thus, when the price is so high that the *supply exceeds the demand* at that price, underbidding of suppliers will drive the price downwards. As the tentative price falls, more sellers are excluded from the market, and more buyers enter it.

If the overbidding of buyers will drive the price up whenever the quantity demanded is greater than the quantity supplied, and the underbidding of sellers drives the price down whenever supply is greater than demand, it is evident that the price of the good will find a resting point where the quantity demanded is equal to the quantity supplied, i.e., where supply equals demand. At this price and at this price only, *the market is cleared,* i.e., there is no incentive for buyers to bid prices up further or for sellers to bid prices down. In our example, this final, or *equilibrium price,* is 89, and at this price, five horses will be sold to five buyers. This equilibrium price is the price at which the good will tend to be set and sales to be made.[25]

Specifically, the sales will be made to the five most capable buyers at that price: *X*1, *X*2, *X*3, *X*4 and *X*5. The other less capable (or less urgent) buyers are excluded from the market, because their value scales do not permit them to buy horses at that price. Similarly, sellers *Z*1–*Z*5 are the ones that make the sale at 89; the other sellers are excluded from the market, because their value scales do not permit them to be in the market at that price.

In this horse-and-fish market, *Z*5 is the least capable of the sellers who have been able to stay in the market. *Z*5, whose minimum selling price is 89, is just able to make his sale at 89. He is the *marginal seller*—the seller at the margin, the one who would be excluded with a slight fall in price. On the other hand, *X*5 is the least capable of the buyers who have been able to stay in the market. He is the *marginal buyer*—the one who would be excluded by a slight rise in price. Since it would be foolish for the other buyers to pay more than they must to obtain their supply, they will also pay the same price as the marginal buyer, i.e., 89. Similarly, the other sellers will not sell for less than they could obtain; they will sell at the price permitting the marginal seller to stay in the market.

Evidently, the more capable or "more urgent" buyers (and sellers)—the *supramarginal* (which includes the marginal)—obtain a psychic surplus in this exchange, for they are better off than they would have been if the price had been higher (or lower). However, since goods can be ranked only on each individual's value scale, and no *measurement* of psychic gain can be made either for one individual or between different individuals, little of value can be said about this psychic gain except that it exists. (We cannot even make the statement, for example, that the psychic gain in exchange obtained by *X*1 is greater than that of *X*5.) The excluded buyers and sellers are termed *submarginal.*

The specific feature of the "clearing of the market" performed by the equilibrium price is that, at this price alone, all those buyers and sellers who are willing to make exchanges can do so. At this price five sellers with horses find five buyers for the horses; all who wish to buy and sell at this price can do so. At any other price, there are either frustrated buyers or frustrated sellers. Thus, at a price of 84, eight people would like to buy at this price, but only two horses are available. At this price, there is a great amount of "unsatisfied demand" or *excess demand.* Conversely, at a price of, say, 95, there are seven sellers eager to supply horses, but only three people willing to demand horses. Thus, at this price, there is "unsatisfied supply," or *excess supply.* Other terms for excess demand and excess supply are "shortage" and "surplus" of the good. Aside from the universal fact of the scarcity of all goods, a price that is below the equilibrium price creates an additional shortage of supply for demanders, while a price above equilibrium creates a surplus of goods for sale as compared to demands for purchase. We see that the market process always tends to eliminate such shortages and surpluses and establishes a price where demanders can find a supply, and suppliers a demand.

It is important to realize that this process of overbidding of buyers and underbidding of sellers always takes place in the market, even if the surface aspects of the specific case make it appear that only the sellers (or buyers) are setting the price. Thus, a good might be sold in retail shops, with prices simply "quoted" by the individual seller. But the same process of bidding goes on in such a market as in any other. If the sellers set their prices below the equilibrium price, buyers will rush to make their purchases, and the sellers will find that shortages develop, accompanied by queues of buyers eager to purchase goods that are unavailable. Realizing that they could obtain higher prices for their goods, the sellers raise their quoted prices accordingly. On the other hand, if they set their prices above the equilibrium price, surpluses of unsold stocks will appear, and they will have to lower their prices in order to "move" their accumulation of unwanted stocks and to clear the market.

The case where buyers quote prices and therefore appear to set them is similar. If the buyers quote prices below the equilibrium price, they will find that they cannot satisfy all their demands at that price. As a result, they will have to raise their quoted prices. On the other hand, if the buyers set the prices too high, they will find a stampede of sellers with unsalable stocks and will take advantage of the opportunity to lower the price and clear the market. Thus, regardless of the *form* of the market, the result of the market process is always to tend toward the establishment of the equilibrium price via the mutual bidding of buyers and sellers.

It is evident that, if we eliminate the assumption that no preliminary sales were made before the equilibrium price was established, this does not change the results of the analysis. Even if, through ignorance and error, a sale was made at a price of 81 or 99, these prices will still be ephemeral and temporary, and the final price for the good will tend to be the equilibrium price.

Once the market price is established, *it is clear that one price must rule over the entire market.* This has already been implied by the fact that all buyers and sellers will tend to exchange at the same price as their marginal competitors. There will always be a tendency on the market to establish one and only one price at any time for a good. Thus, suppose that the market price has been established at 89, and that one crafty seller tries to induce a buyer to buy at 92. It is evident that no buyer will buy at 92 when he knows that he can buy on the regular market at 89. Similarly, no seller will be willing to sell at a price below the market if he knows that he can readily make his sale at 89. If for example, an ignorant seller sells a horse at 87, the buyer is likely to enter the market as a seller to sell the horse at 89. Such drives for *arbitrage gains* (buying and selling to take advantage of discrepancies in the price of a good) act quickly to establish one price for one good over the entire market. Such market prices will tend to change only when changing supply and demand conditions alter the equilibrium price and establish a condition of excess supply or excess demand where before the market had been cleared.

A clearer picture of equilibrium prices as determined by supply and demand conditions will be derived from the graphical representation in Fig. 13.

It is evident that, as the price increases, new suppliers with higher minimum selling prices are brought into the market, while demanders with low maximum buying prices will begin to drop out. Therefore, as the price decreases, the quantity demanded must always either remain the same or increase, never decrease. Similarly, as the price decreases, the amount offered in supply must always decrease or remain the same, never increase. Therefore, the demand curve must always be vertical or rightward-sloping as the price decreases, while the supply curve must always be vertical or leftward-sloping as the price decreases. The curves will intersect at the equilibrium price, where supply and demand are equal.

Clearly, once the zone of intersection of the supply and demand curves has been determined, it is the buyers and sellers at the margin—in the area of the equilibrium point—that determine what the equilibrium price and the quantity exchanged will be.

The tabulation of supply offered at any given price is known as the *supply schedule,* while its graphical presentation, with the points connected here for the sake of clarity, is known as the

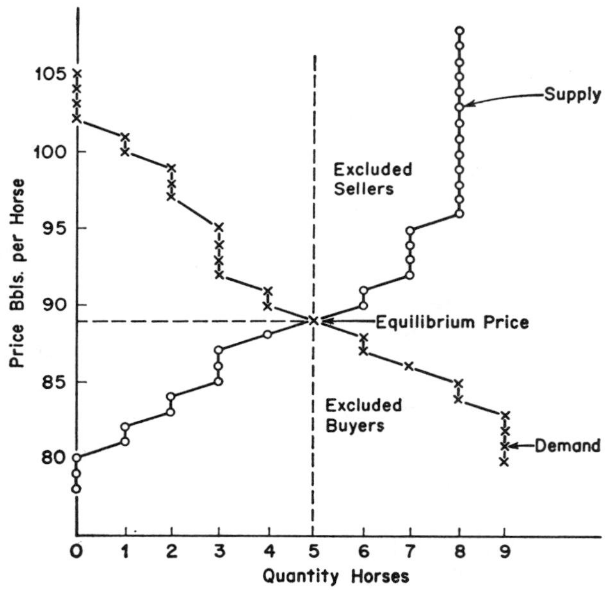

FIG. 13. DETERMINATION OF EQUILIBRIUM PRICE

supply curve. Similarly, the tabulation of demand is the *demand schedule,* and its graphical representation the *demand curve,* for each product and market. Given the point of intersection, the demand and supply curves above and below that point could take many conceivable shapes without affecting the equilibrium price. The direct determinants of the price are therefore the marginal buyers and sellers, while the valuations of the supramarginal people are important in determining *which* buyers and sellers will be at the margin. The valuations of the *excluded buyers and sellers* far beyond the margin have no direct influence on the price and will become important only if a change in the market demand and supply schedules brings them near the intersection point.

Thus, given the intersection point, the pattern of supply and demand curves (represented by the solid and dotted lines) could be at least any one of the variants shown in Fig. 14.

Up to this point we have assumed, for the sake of simplicity and clarity, that each demander, as well as each supplier, was limited to one unit of the good the price of which we have been concentrating on—the horse. Now we can remove this restriction and complete our analysis of the real world of exchange by permitting suppliers and demanders to exchange any number of horses that they may desire. It will be seen immediately that the removal of our implicit restriction makes no substantial change in the analysis. Thus, let us revert to the case of Johnson, whose minimum selling price for a horse was 81 barrels of fish. Let us now assume that Johnson has a stock of several horses. He is willing to sell one horse—the first—for a minimum price of 81 barrels, since on his value scale, he places the horse between 81 and 80 barrels of fish. What will be Johnson's minimum selling price to part with his second horse? We have seen earlier in this chapter that, according to the law of marginal utility, as a man's stock of goods declines, the value placed on each unit remaining increases; conversely, as a man's stock of goods increases, the marginal utility of each unit declines. Therefore, the marginal utility of the second horse (or, strictly, of each horse after the first horse is gone), will be greater than the marginal utility of the first horse. This will be true even though each horse is capable of the same service as every other. Similarly, the value of parting with a third horse will be still greater. On the other hand, while the marginal utility placed on each horse given

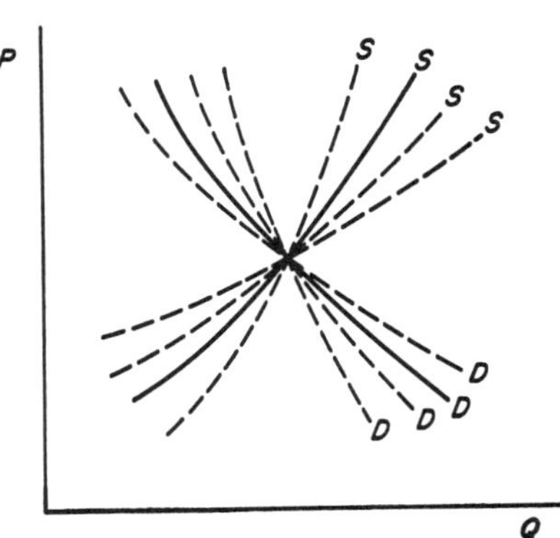

Fig. 14. Possible Patterns of Supply and Demand Curves

up increases, the marginal utility of the additional fish acquired in exchange will decline. The result of these two factors is inevitably to raise the minimum selling price for each successive horse sold. Thus, suppose the minimum selling price for the first horse is 81 barrels of fish. When it comes to the second exchange, the value forgone of the second horse will be greater, and the value of the same barrels in exchange will decline. As a result, the minimum selling price below which Johnson will not sell the horse will increase, say, to 88. Thus, as the seller's stock dwindles, his minimum selling price increases. Johnson's value scale may appear as follows:

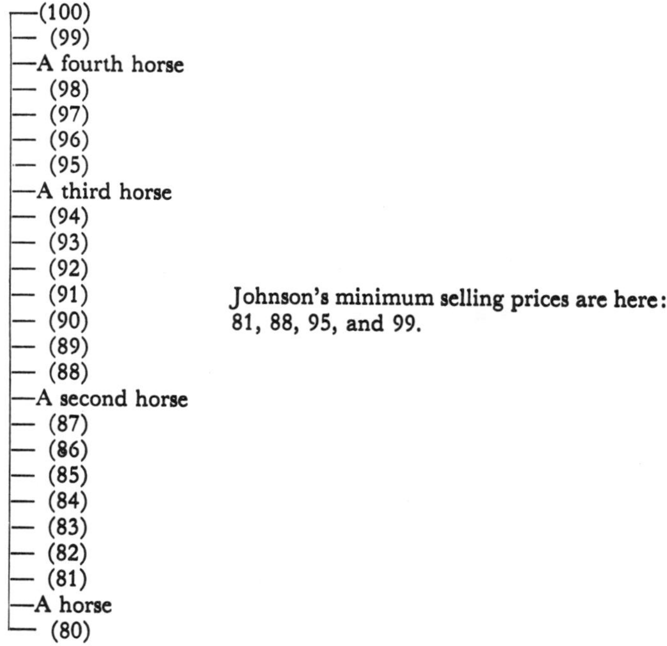

FIG. 15. JOHNSON'S VALUE SCALE

On the basis of this value scale, Johnson's own individual supply schedule can be constructed. He will supply 0 horses up to a price of 80, 1 horse at a price between 81 and 87, 2 horses with the price between 88 and 94, 3 horses at a price of 95 to 98, and 4 horses at a price of 99 and above. The same can be done for each seller in the market. (Where the seller has only one horse to sell, the supply schedule is constructed as before.) It is clear that a market-supply schedule can be constructed simply by adding the supplies that will be offered by the various individual sellers in the market at any given price.

The essentials of the foregoing analysis of market supply remain unchanged. Thus, the effect of constructing the market-supply schedule in this case *is the same as if there were four sellers, each supplying one horse, and each with minimum selling prices of 81, 88, 95, and 99*. The fact that it is one man that is supplying the new units rather than different men does not change the results of the analysis. What it does is to reinforce the rule that the supply curve must always be vertical or rightward-sloping as the price increases, i.e., *that the supply must always remain unchanged or increase with an increase in price.* For, in addition to the fact that new suppliers will be brought into the market with an increase in price, the same supplier will offer more units of the good. Thus, the operation of the law of marginal utility serves to reinforce the rule that the supply cannot decrease at higher prices, but must increase or remain the same.

The exact converse occurs in the case of demand. Suppose that we allow buyers to purchase any desired number of horses. We remember that Smith's maximum buying price for the first horse was 100 barrels of fish. If he considers buying a second horse, the marginal utility of the additional horse will be less than the utility of the first one, and the marginal utility of the same amount of fish that he would have to give up will increase. If the marginal utility of the purchases declines as more are made, and the marginal utility of the good given up increases, these factors result in lower maximum buying prices for each successive horse bought. Thus, Smith's value scale might appear as in Fig. 16.

Such individual demand schedules can be made for each buyer on the market, and they can be added to form a resultant demand curve for all buyers on the market.

It is evident that, here again, there is no change in the essence of the market-demand curve. Smith's individual demand curve, with maximum buying prices as above, is analytically equivalent to four buyers with maximum buying prices of 83, 89, 94, and 100, respectively. The effect of allowing more than one unit to be demanded by each buyer brings in the law of marginal utility to reinforce the aforementioned rule that the demand curve is

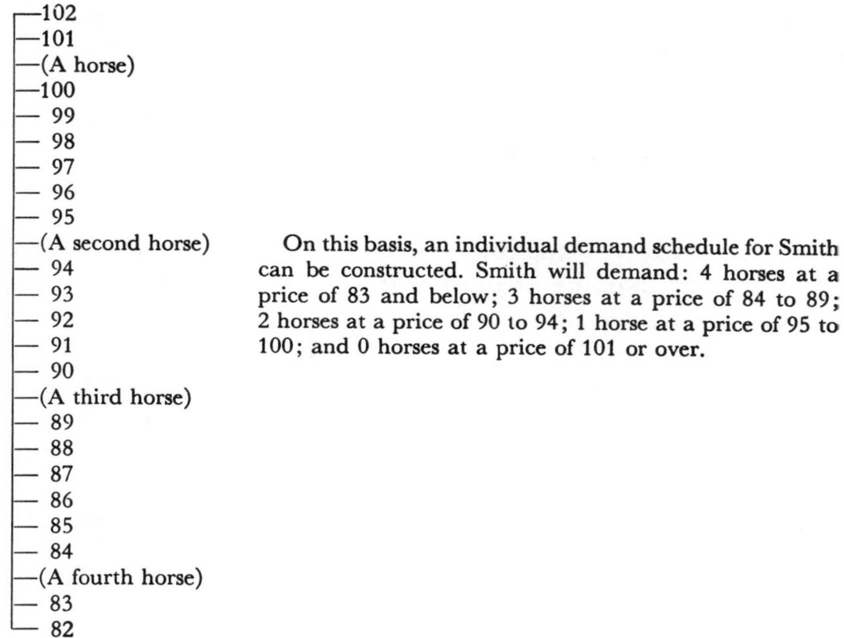

FIG. 16. SMITH'S VALUE SCALE

rightward-sloping as the price decreases, i.e., that *the demand must either increase or remain unchanged as the price decreases.* For, added to the fact that lower prices bring in previously excluded buyers, each individual will tend to demand more as the price declines, since the maximum buying prices will be lower with the purchase of more units, in accordance with the law of marginal utility.

Let us now sum up the factors determining prices in interpersonal exchange. One price will tend to be established for each good on the market, and that price will tend to be the equilibrium price, determined by the intersection of the market supply and demand schedules. Those making the exchanges at this price will be the supramarginal and marginal buyers and sellers, while the less capable, or submarginal, will be excluded from the sale, because their value scales do not permit them to make an exchange. Their maximum buying prices are too low, or their minimum selling prices too high. The market supply and demand schedules are themselves determined by the minimum selling prices and maximum buying prices of all the individuals in the market. The latter, in turn, are determined by the placing of the units to be bought and sold on the individuals' value scales, these rankings being influenced by the law of marginal utility.

In addition to the law of marginal utility, there is another factor influencing the rankings on each individual's value scale. It is obvious that the amount that Johnson will supply at any price is limited by the *stock* of goods that he has available. Thus, Johnson may be willing to supply a fourth horse at a price of 99, but if this exhausts his available stock of horses, no higher price will be able to call forth a larger supply from Johnson. At least this is true as long as Johnson has no further stock available to sell. Thus, at any given time, the total stock of the good available puts a maximum limit on the amount of the good that can be supplied in the market. Conversely, the total stock of the purchasing good will put a maximum limit on the total of the sale good that any one individual, or the market, can demand.

At the same time that the market supply and demand schedules are setting the equilibrium price, they are *also* clearly setting the equilibrium *quantity* of both goods that will be exchanged. In our previous example, the equilibrium quantities exchanged are 5 horses, and 5 × 89, or 445 fish, for the aggregate of the market.

6. *Elasticity of Demand* [26]

The demand schedule tells us how many units of the purchase good will be bought at each hypothetical price. From this schedule we may easily find the *total number of units of the sale good that will be expended at each price.* Thus, from Table 2, we find that at a price of 95, three horses will be demanded. If three horses are demanded at a price of 95 barrels of fish, then the total number of units of the sale good that will be offered in exchange will be 3 × 95, or 285 barrels of fish. This, then, is the *total outlay* of the sale good that will be offered on the market at that price.

The total outlay of the sale good at each hypothetical price is shown in Table 3.

TABLE 3

	BUYERS	
PRICE	DEMANDED	TOTAL OUTLAY SALE GOOD
80	9 horses	720 barrels of fish
81	9	729
82	9	738
83	9	747
84	8	672
85	8	680
86	7	602
87	6	522
88	6	528
89	5	445
90	4	360
91	4	364
92	3	276
93	3	279
94	3	282
95	3	285
96	2	192
97	2	194
98	2	196
99	1	99
100	1	100
101	0	0

Fig. 17 is a graphic presentation of the total outlay curve. It is evident that this is a logical derivation from the demand curve and that therefore it too is a curve of outlay by buyers at each hypothetical price.

A striking feature of the total outlay curve is that, in contrast to the other curves (such as the demand curve), it can slope in either direction as the price increases or decreases. The possibility of a slope in either direction stems from the operation of the two factors determining the position of the curve. Outlay = Price × Quantity Demanded (of purchase good). But we know that as the price decreases, the demand must either increase or remain the same. Therefore, a decrease in price tends to be counteracted by an increase in quantity, and, as a result, the total outlay of the sale good may either increase or decrease as the price changes.

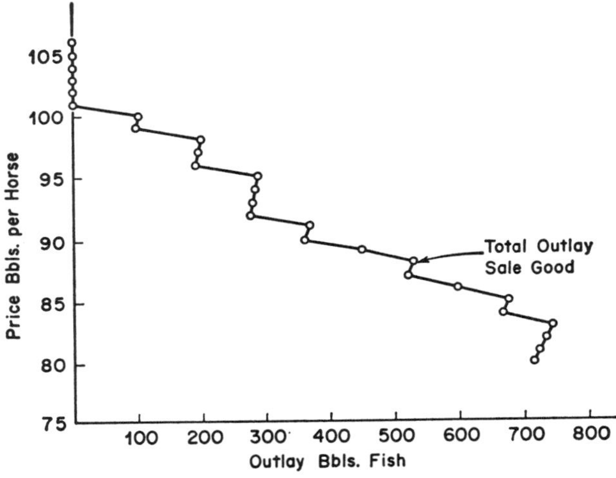

FIG. 17. TOTAL OUTLAY CURVE

For any two prices, we may compare the total outlay of the sale good that will be expended by buyers. If the lower price yields a greater total outlay than the higher price, the total outlay curve is defined as being *elastic* over that range. If the lower price yields a lower total outlay than the higher price, then the curve is *inelastic* over that range. Alternatively, we may say that the former case is that of an *elasticity greater than unity,* the latter of an *elasticity less than unity,* and the case where the total outlay is the same for the two prices is one of *unit elasticity,* or elasticity equal to 1. Since numerical precision in the concept of elasticity is not important, we may simply use the terms "inelastic," "elastic," and (for the last case) "neutral."

Some examples will clarify these concepts. Thus, suppose that we examine the total outlay schedule at prices of 96 and 95. At 96, the total outlay is 192 barrels; at 95, it is 285 barrels. The outlay is greater at the lower price, and hence the outlay schedule is *elastic* in this range. On the other hand, let us take the prices 95 and 94. At 94, the outlay is 282. Consequently, the schedule here is *inelastic.* It is evident that there is a simple geometrical device for deciding whether or not the demand curve is elastic or inelastic between two hypothetical prices: if the outlay curve is further to the right at the lower price, the demand curve is elastic; if further to the left, the latter is inelastic.

There is no reason why the concept of elasticity must be confined to two prices next to each other. Any two prices on the schedule may be compared. It is evident that an examination of the entire outlay curve demonstrates that the foregoing demand curve is basically elastic. It is elastic over most of its range, with the exception of a few small gaps. If we compare any two rather widely spaced prices, it is evident that the outlay is less at the higher price. If the price is high enough, the demand for any good will dwindle to zero, and therefore the outlay will dwindle to zero.

Of particular interest is the elasticity of the demand curve at the equilibrium price. Going up a step to the price of 90, the curve is clearly elastic—total outlay is less at the higher price. Going down a step to 88, the curve is also elastic. This particular demand curve is elastic in the neighborhood of the equilibrium price. Other demand curves, of course, could possibly be inelastic at their equilibrium price.

Contrary to what might be thought at first, the concept of "elasticity of supply" is not a meaningful one, as is "elasticity of demand." If we multiply the quantity supplied at each price by the price, we shall obtain the number of barrels of fish (the sale good) which the sellers will demand in exchange. It will easily be seen, however, that this quantity *always increases* as the price increases, and *vice versa.* At 82 it is 82, at 84 it is 168, at 88 it is 352, etc. The reason is that its other determinant, quantity supplied, changes in the *same* direction as the price, not in the inverse direction as does quantity demanded. As a result, supply is always "elastic," and the concept is an uninteresting one.[27]

7. *Speculation and Supply and Demand Schedules*

We have seen that market price is, in the final analysis, determined by the intersection of the supply and demand schedules. It is now in order to consider further the determinants of these particular schedules. Can we establish any other conclusions concerning the causes of the shape and position of the supply and demand schedules themselves?

We remember that, at any given price, the amount of a good that an individual will buy or sell is determined by the position of the sale good and the purchase good on his value scale. He will demand a good if the marginal utility of adding a unit of the purchase good is greater than the marginal utility of the sale good that he must give up. On the other hand, another individual will be a seller if his valuations of the units are in a reverse order. We have seen that, on this basis, and reinforced by the law of marginal utility, the market demand curve will never decrease when the price is lowered, and the supply curve will never increase when the price decreases.

Let us further analyze the value scales of the buyers and sellers. We have seen above that the two sources of value that a good may have are direct use-value and exchange-value, and that the higher value is the determinant for the actor. An individual, therefore, can demand a horse in exchange for one of two reasons: its direct use-value to him or the value that he believes it will be able to command in exchange. If the former, then he will be a consumer of the horse's services; if the latter, then he purchases in order to make a more advantageous exchange later. Thus, suppose in the foregoing example, that the existing market price has not reached equilibrium—that it is now at 85 barrels per horse. Many demanders may realize that this price is below the equilibrium and that therefore they can attain an arbitrage profit by buying at 85 and reselling at the final, higher price.

We are now in a position to refine the analysis in the foregoing section, which did not probe the question whether or not sales took place before the equilibrium price was reached. We now assume explicitly that the demand schedule shown in Table 2 referred to demand for direct use by consumers. Smoothing out the steps in the demand curve represented in Fig. 13, we may, for purposes of simplicity and exposition, portray it as in Fig. 18. This, we may say, is the demand curve for direct use. For this demand curve, then, the approach to equilibrium takes place through *actual* purchases at the various prices, and then the shortages or the surpluses reveal the overbidding or underbidding, until the equilibrium price is finally reached. To the extent that buyers foresee the final equilibrium price, however, they will not buy at a higher price (even though they would have done so if *that* were the final price), but will wait for the price to fall. Similarly, if the price is below the equilibrium price, to the extent that the buyers foresee the final price, they will tend to buy some of the good (e.g., horses) in order to resell at a profit at the final price. Thus, if exchange-value enters the picture, and a good number of buyers act on their anticipations, the demand curve might change as shown in Fig. 19. The old demand curve, based only on demand for use, is *DD,* and the new demand curve, including anticipatory forecasting of the equilibrium price, is *D′D′*. It is clear that such anticipations render the demand curve

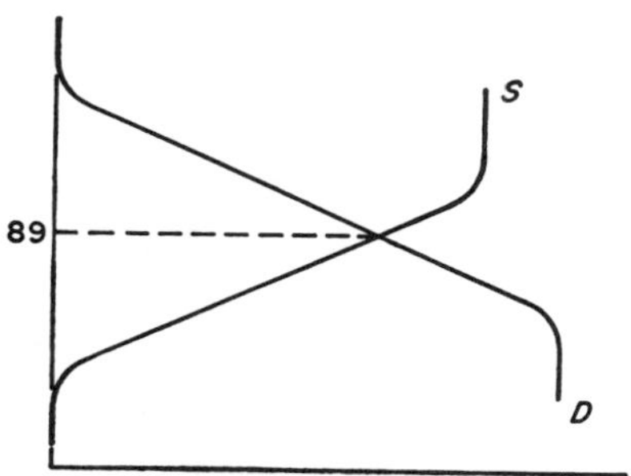

FIG. 18. SIMPLIFIED DEMAND CURVE

far more *elastic,* since more will be bought at the lower price and less at the higher.

Thus, the introduction of exchange-value can restrict demand above the anticipated equilibrium price and increase it below that price, although the final demand—to consume—at the equilibrium price will remain the same.

Now, let us consider the situation of the seller of the commodity. The supply curve in Fig. 13 treats the amount supplied

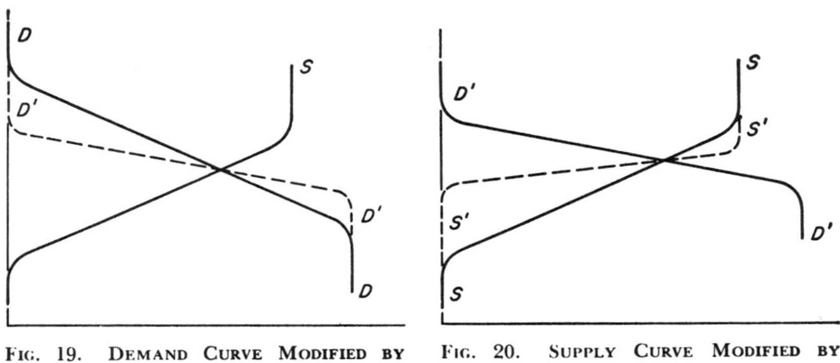

FIG. 19. DEMAND CURVE MODIFIED BY SPECULATION

FIG. 20. SUPPLY CURVE MODIFIED BY SPECULATION

at any price without considering possible equilibrium price. Thus, we may say that, with such a supply curve, sales will be made en route to the equilibrium price, and shortages or surpluses will finally reveal the path to the final price. On the other hand, suppose that many sellers anticipate the final equilibrium price. Clearly, they will refuse to make sales at a lower price, even though they would have done so if *that* were the final price. On the other hand, they will sell more above the equilibrium price, since they will be able to make an arbitrage profit by selling their horses above the equilibrium price and buying them back at the equilibrium price. Thus, the supply curve, with such anticipations, may change as shown in Fig. 20. The supply curve changes, as a result of anticipating the equilibrium price, from *SS* to *S'S'*.

Let us suppose the highly unlikely event that *all* demanders and suppliers are able to forecast *exactly* the final, equilibrium price. What would be the pattern of supply and demand curves on the market in such an extreme case? It would be as follows: At a price above equilibrium (say 89) no one would demand the good, and suppliers would supply their entire stock. At a price below equilibrium, no one would supply the good, and everyone would demand as much as he could purchase, as shown in Fig. 21. Such unanimously correct forecasts are not likely to take place in human action, but this case points up the fact that, the

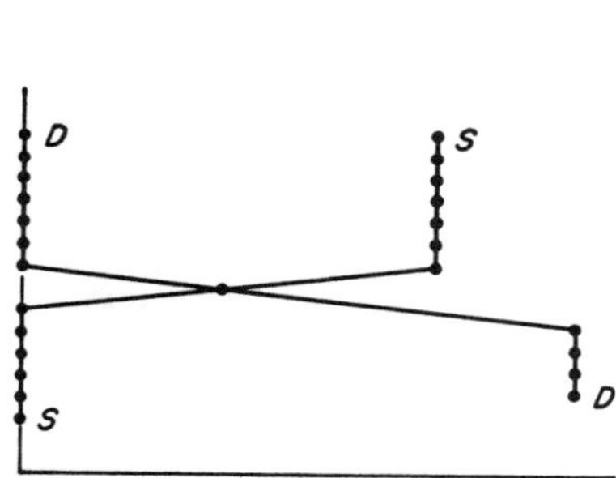

FIG. 21. UNANIMOUSLY CORRECT FORECASTS OF FINAL PRICE

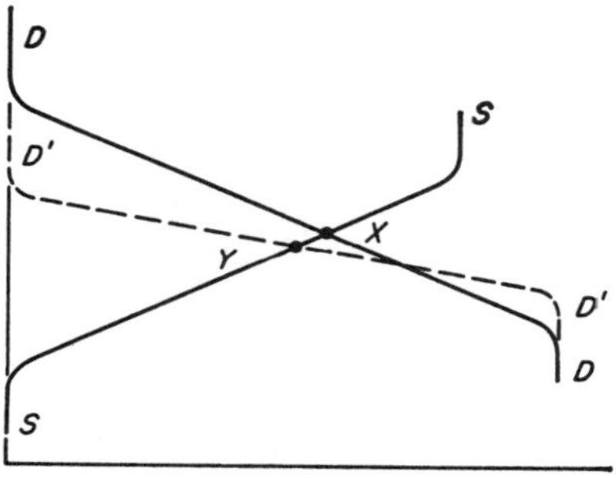

FIG. 22. DEMAND CURVE MODIFIED BY ERRONEOUS ANTICIPATION

more this anticipatory, or *speculative,* element enters into supply and demand, the more quickly will the market price tend toward equilibrium. Obviously, the more the actors anticipate the final price, the further apart will be supply and demand at any price differing from equilibrium, the more drastic the shortages and surpluses will be, and the more quickly will the final price be established.

Up to now we have assumed that this *speculative* supply and demand, this anticipating of the equilibrium price, has been correct, and we have seen that these correct anticipations have hastened the establishment of equilibrium. Suppose, however, that most of these expectations are erroneous. Suppose, for example, that the demanders tend to assume that the equilibrium price will be lower than it actually is. Does this change the equilibrium price or obstruct the passage to that price? Suppose that the demand and supply schedules are as shown in Fig. 22. Suppose that the basic demand curve is *DD,* but that the demanders anticipate lower equilibrium prices, thus changing and lowering the demand curve to *D′D′*. With the supply curve given at *SS,* this means that the intersection of the supply and demand schedules will be at *Y* instead of *X,* say at 85 instead of 89. It is clear, however, that this will be only a provisional resting point for the price. As soon as the price settles at 85, the demanders see that shortages develop at this price, that they would like to buy more than is available, and the overbidding of the demanders raises the price again to the genuine equilibrium price.

The same process of revelation of error occurs in the case of errors of anticipation by suppliers, and thus the forces of the market tend inexorably toward the establishment of the genuine equilibrium price, undistorted by speculative errors, which tend to reveal themselves and be eliminated. As soon as suppliers or demanders find that the price that their speculative errors have set is not really an equilibrium and that shortages and/or surpluses develop, their actions tend once again to establish the equilibrium position.

The actions of both buyers and sellers on the market may be related to the concepts of psychic revenue, profit, and cost. We remember that the aim of every actor is the highest position of psychic revenue and thus the making of a psychic profit compared to his next best alternative—his cost. Whether or not an individual *buys* depends on whether it is his best alternative with his given resources—in this case, his fish. His expected revenue in any action will be balanced against his expected cost—his next best alternative. In this case, the revenue will be either (*a*) the satisfaction of ends from the direct use of the horse or (*b*) expected resale of the horse at a higher price—whichever has the highest utility to him. His cost will be either (*a*) the marginal utility of the fish given up in direct use or (*b*) (possibly) the exchange-value of the fish for some other good or (*c*) the expected future purchase of the horse at a lower price—whichever has the highest utility. He will buy the horse if the expected revenue is greater; he will fail to buy if the expected cost is greater. The expected revenue is the marginal utility of the added horse for the buyer; the expected cost is the marginal utility of the fish given up. For either revenue or cost, the higher value in direct use or in exchange will be chosen as the marginal utility of the good.

Now let us consider the seller. The seller, as well as the buyer, attempts to maximize his psychic revenue by trying to attain a revenue higher than his psychic cost—the utility of the next best alternative he will have to forgo in taking his action. The seller will weigh the marginal utility of the added sale-good (in this case, fish) against the marginal utility of the purchase-good given up (the horse), in deciding whether or not to make the sale at any particular price.

The psychic revenue for the seller will be the higher of the utilities stemming from one of the following sources: (*a*) the value in direct use of the sale-good (the fish) or (*b*) the speculative value of re-exchanging the fish for the horse at a lower price in the future. The cost of the seller's action will be the highest utility forgone among the following alternatives: (*a*) the value in direct use of the horse given up or (*b*) the speculative value of selling at a higher price in the future or (*c*) the exchange-value of acquiring some other good for the horse. He will sell the horse if the expected revenue is greater; he will fail to sell if the expected cost is greater. We thus see that the situations of the sellers and the buyers are comparable. Both act or fail to act in accordance with their estimate of the alternative that will yield them the highest utility. It is the position of the utilities on the two sets of value scales—of the individual buyers and sellers—that determines the market price and the amount that will be exchanged at that price. In other words, it is, for every good, *utility* and utility alone that determines the price and the quantity exchanged. Utility and utility alone determines the nature of the supply and demand schedules.

It is therefore clearly fallacious to believe, as has been the popular assumption, that utility and "costs" are equally and independently potent in determining price. "Cost" is simply the utility of the next best alternative that must be forgone in any action, and it is therefore part and parcel of utility on the individual's value scale. This cost is, of course, always a *present* consideration of a *future* event, even if this "future" is a very near one. Thus, the forgone utility in making the purchase might be the direct consumption of fish that the actor might have engaged in within a few hours. Or it might be the possibility of exchanging for a cow, whose utility would be enjoyed over a long period of time. It goes without saying, as has been indicated in the previous chapter, that the present consideration of revenue and of cost in any action is based on the present value of expected future revenues and costs. The point is that both the utilities derived and the utilities forgone in any action refer to some point in the future, even if a very near one, and that *past costs* play no role in human action, and hence in determining price. The importance of this fundamental truth will be made clear in later chapters.

8. *Stock and the Total Demand to Hold*

There is another way of treating supply and demand schedules, which, for some problems of analysis, is more useful than the schedules presented above. At any point on the market, suppliers are engaged in offering some of their stock of the good and withholding their offer of the remainder. Thus, at a price of 86, suppliers supply three horses on the market and withhold the other five in their stock. This withholding is caused by one of the factors mentioned above as possible costs of the exchange: either the direct use of the good (say the horse) has greater utility than the receipt of the fish in direct use; or else the horse could be exchanged for some other good; or, finally, the seller expects the final price to be higher, so that he can profitably delay the sale. The amount that sellers will withhold on the market is termed their *reservation demand.* This is not, like the demand studied above, a demand for a good *in exchange;* this is a demand to *hold stock.* Thus, the concept of a "demand to hold a stock of goods" will always include both demand-factors; it will include the demand for the good in exchange by nonpossessors, *plus* the demand to hold the stock by the possessors. The demand for the good in exchange is also a demand to hold, since, regardless of what the buyer intends to do with the good in the future, he must h 'd the good from the time when it comes into his ownership and possession by means of exchange. We therefore arrive at the concept of a "total demand to hold" for a good, differing from the previous concept of exchange-demand, although including the latter in addition to the reservation demand by the sellers.

If we know the total stock of the good in existence (here, 8 horses), we may, by inspecting the supply and demand schedules, arrive at a "total demand to hold"—or *total demand schedule* for the market. For example, at a price of 82, 9 horses are demanded by the buyers, in exchange, and 8 – 1 = 7 horses are withheld by the sellers, i.e., demanded to be held by the sellers. Therefore, the total demand to hold horses on the market is 9 + 7 = 16 horses. On the other hand, at the price of 97, no horses are withheld by sellers, whose reservation demand is therefore 0, while the demand by buyers is 2. Total demand to hold at this price is 0 + 2 = 2 horses.

Table 4 shows the total demand to hold derived from the sup-

TABLE 4

PRICE	TOTAL DEMAND TO HOLD	TOTAL STOCK	PRICE	TOTAL DEMAND TO HOLD	TOTAL STOCK
80	17 horses	8 horses	91	6 horses	8 horses
81	16	8	92	4	8
82	16	8	93	4	8
83	15	8	94	4	8
84	14	8	95	4	8
85	13	8	96	2	8
86	12	8	97	2	8
87	11	8	98	2	8
88	10	8	99	1	8
89	8	8	100	1	8
90	6	8	101	0	8

ply and demand schedule in Table 2, along with the total stock, which is, for the moment, considered as fixed. Figure 23 represents the total demand to hold and the stock.

It is clear that the rightward-sloping nature of the total demand curve is even more accentuated than that of the demand curve. For the demand schedule increases or remains the same as the price falls, while the reservation demand schedule of the

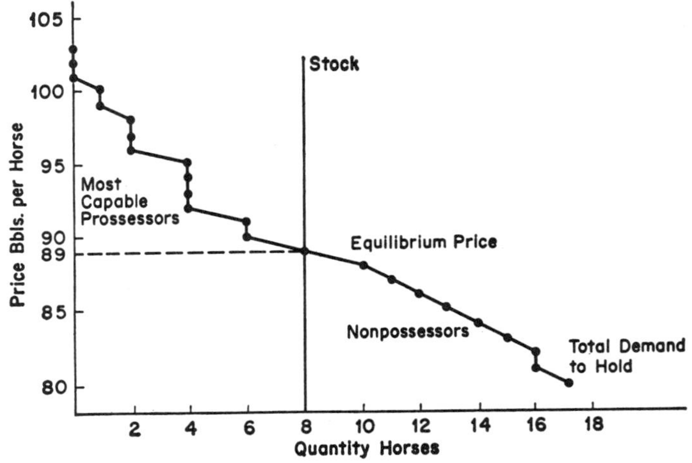

FIG. 23. STOCK AND TOTAL DEMAND TO HOLD

sellers also tends to increase as the price falls. The total demand schedule is the result of adding the two schedules. Clearly, the reservation demand of the sellers increases as the price falls for the same reason as does the demand curve for buyers. With a lower price, the value of the purchase-good in direct use or in other and future exchanges relatively increases, and therefore the seller tends to withhold more of the good from exchange. In other words, the reservation demand curve is the obverse of the supply curve.

Another point of interest is that, at the equilibrium price of 89, the total demand to hold is 8, equal to the total stock in existence. Thus, the equilibrium price not only equates the supply and demand on the market; *it also equates the stock of a good to be held with the desire of people to hold it, buyers and sellers included.* The total stock is included in the foregoing diagram at a fixed figure of 8.

It is clear that the market always tends to set the price of a good so as to equate the stock with the total demand to hold the stock. Suppose that the price of a good is higher than this equilibrium price. Say that the price is 92, at which the stock is 8 and the total demand to hold is 4. This means that four horses exist which their possessors do not want to possess. It is clear that *someone* must possess this stock, since all goods must be property; otherwise they would not be objects of human action. Since all the stock must at all times be possessed by someone, the fact that the stock is greater than total demand means that there is an imbalance in the economy, that some of the possessors are unhappy with their possession of the stock. They tend to lower the price in order to sell the stock, and the price falls until finally the stock is equated with the demand to hold. Conversely, suppose that the price is below equilibrium, say at 85, where 13 horses are demanded compared to a stock of 8. The bids of the eager nonpossessors for the scarce stock push up the price until it reaches equilibrium.

In cases where individuals correctly anticipate the equilibrium price, the speculative element will tend to render the total demand curve even more "elastic" and flatter. At a higher-than-equilibrium price few will want to keep the stock—the buyers will demand very little, and the sellers will be eager to dispose of the good. On the other hand, at a lower price, the demand to hold will be far greater than the stock; buyers will demand heavily, and sellers will be reluctant to sell their stock. The discrepancies between total demand and stock will be far greater, and the underbidding and overbidding will more quickly bring about the equilibrium price.

We saw above that, at the equilibrium price, the most capable (or "most urgent") buyers made the exchanges with the most capable sellers. Here we see that the result of the exchange process is that the stock finally goes into the hands of the *most capable possessors.* We remember that in the sale of the eight horses, the most capable buyers, X1–X5, purchased from the most capable sellers of the good, Z1–Z5. At the conclusion of the exchange, then, the possessors are X1–X5, and the excluded sellers Z6–Z8. It is these individuals who finish by possessing the eight horses, and these are the most capable possessors. At a price of 89 barrels of fish per horse, these were the ones who preferred the horse on their value scales to 89 barrels of fish, and they acted on the basis of this preference. For five of the individuals, this meant exchanging their fish for a horse; for three it meant refusing to part with their horses for the fish. The other nine individuals on the market were the less capable possessors, and they concluded by possessing the fish instead of the horse (even if they started by possessing horses). These were the ones who ranked 89 barrels of fish above one horse on their value scale. Five of these were original possessors of horses who exchanged them for fish; four simply retained the fish without purchasing a horse.

The total demand-stock analysis is a useful twin companion to the supply-demand analysis. Each has advantages for use in different spheres. One relative defect of the total demand-stock analysis is that it does not reveal the differences between the buyers and the sellers. In considering total demand, it abstracts from actual exchanges, and therefore does not, in contrast to the supply-demand curves, determine the quantity of exchanges. It reveals only the equilibrium price, without demonstrating the equilibrium quantity exchanged. However, it focuses more sharply on the fundamental truth that price is determined solely by *utility*. The supply curve is reducible to a *reservation demand curve* and to a *quantity of physical stock*. The demand-stock analysis therefore shows that the supply curve is not based on some sort of "cost" that is independent of utility on individual value scales. We see that the fundamental determinants of price are the value scales of all individuals (buyers and sellers) in the market and that the physical stock simply assumes its place on these scales.[28]

It is clear, in these cases of direct exchange of useful goods, that even if the utility of goods for buyers or sellers is at present determined by its subjective exchange-value for the individual, the sole *ultimate* source of utility of each good is its direct use-value. If the major utility of a horse to its possessor is the fish or the cow that he can procure in exchange, and the major value of the latter to their possessors is the horse obtainable in exchange, etc., the ultimate determinant of the utility of each good is its direct use-value to its individual consumer.

9. *Continuing Markets and Changes in Price*

How, then, may we sum up the analysis of our hypothetical horse-and-fish market? We began with a stock of eight horses in existence (and a certain stock of fish as well), and a situation where the relative positions of horses and fish on different people's value scales were such as to establish conditions for the exchange of the two goods. Of the original possessors, the "most capable sellers" sold their stock of horses, while among the original non-possessors, the "most capable buyers" purchased units of the stock with their fish. The final price of their sale was the equilibrium price determined ultimately by their various value scales, which also determined the quantity of exchanges that took place at that price. The net result was a shift of the stock of each good into the hands of its most capable possessors in accordance with the relative rank of the good on their value scales. The exchanges having been completed, the relatively most capable possesors own the stock, *and the market for this good has come to a close.*

With arrival at equilibrium, the exchanges have shifted the goods to the most capable possessors, and there is no further motive for exchange. The market has ended, and there is no longer an active "ruling market price" for either good because there is no longer any motive for exchange. Yet in our experience the markets for almost all goods are being continually renewed.

The market can be renewed again only if there is a change in the relative position of the two goods under consideration on the value scales of at least two individuals, one of them a possessor of one good and the other a possessor of the second good. Exchanges will then take place in a quantity and at a final price determined by the intersection of the *new* combination of supply and demand schedules. This may set a different quantity of exchanges at the old equilibrium price or at a new price, depending on their specific content. Or it may happen that the new combination of schedules—in the new period of time—will be identical with the old and therefore set the same quantity of exchanges and the same price as on the old market.

The market is always tending quickly toward its equilibrium position, and the wider the market is, and the better the communication among its participants, the more quickly will this position be established for any set of schedules. Furthermore, a growth of specialized speculation will tend to improve the forecasts of the equilibrium point and hasten the arrival at equilibrium. However, in those cases where the market does not arrive at equilibrium before the supply or demand schedules themselves change, the market does not reach the equilibrium point. It becomes *continuous,* moving toward a new equilibrium position before the old one has been reached.[29]

The types of change introduced by a shift in the supply and/or the demand schedule may be depicted by the diagrams in Fig. 24.

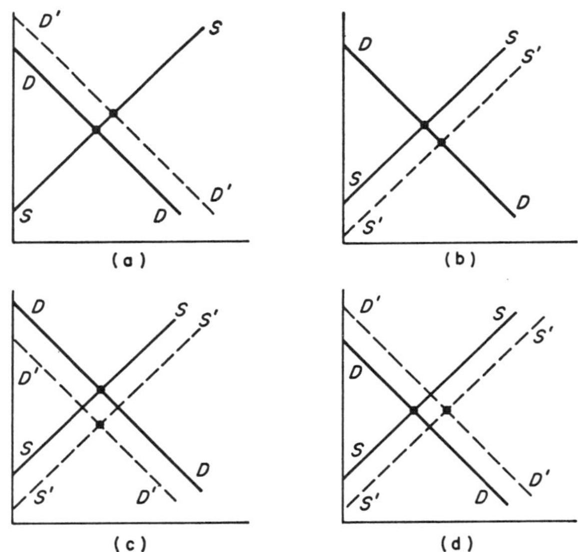

FIG. 24. CHANGES IN SUPPLY AND DEMAND SCHEDULES

These four diagrams depict eight types of situations that may develop from changes in the supply and demand schedules. It must be noted that these diagrams may apply *either* to a market that has already reached equilibrium and is then *renewed* at some later date *or* to one continuous market that experiences a change in supply and/or demand conditions before reaching the old equilibrium point. Solid lines depict the old schedules, while broken lines depict the new ones.

In all these diagrams straight lines are assumed purely for convenience, since the lines may be of any shape, provided the aforementioned restrictions on the slope of the schedules are met (rightward-sloping demand schedules, etc.).

In diagram *A*, the *demand schedule* of the individuals on the market *increases.* At each hypothetical price, people will wish to add more than before to their stock of the good—and it does not matter whether these individuals already possess some units of the good or not. The supply schedule remains the same. *As a result, the new equilibrium price is higher than the old, and the quantity of exchanges made at the new equilibrium position is greater than at the old position.*

In diagram *B*, the *supply schedule increases,* while the demand schedule remains the same. At each hypothetical price, people will wish to dispose of more of their stock. The result is that the new equilibrium price is *lower* than the old, and the equilibrium *quantity exchanged is greater.*

Diagrams *A* and *B* also depict what will occur when the demand curve decreases and the supply curve decreases, the other schedule remaining the same. All we need do is think of the broken lines as the old schedules, and the solid lines as the new ones. On diagram *A* we see that a *decrease in the demand schedule* leads to a fall in price and a fall in the quantity exchanged. On diagram *B*, we see that a *decrease in the supply schedule* leads to a rise in price and a fall in the quantity exchanged.

For diagrams *C* and *D*, the restriction that one schedule must remain the same while the other one changes is removed. In diagram *C*, the demand curve decreases and the supply curve increases. This will definitely lead to a *fall in equilibrium price,* although what will happen to the quantity exchanged depends on the relative proportion of change in the two schedules, and therefore this result cannot be predicted from the fact of an increase in the supply schedule and a decrease in the demand schedule. On the other hand, a decrease in the supply schedule plus an increase in the demand schedule will definitely lead to a *rise in the equilibrium price.*

Diagram *D* discloses that an *increase* in both demand and supply schedules will definitely lead to an *increase in the quantity exchanged,* although whether or not the price falls depends on the relative proportion of change. Also, a decrease in both supply and demand schedules will lead to a *decline in the quantity exchanged.* In diagram *C* what happens to the quantity, and in diagram *D* what happens to the price, depends on the specific shape and change of the curves in question.

The conclusions from these diagrams may be summarized in Table 5.

TABLE 5

If DEMAND SCHEDULE	and SUPPLY SCHEDULE	Then EQUILIBRIUM PRICE	and QUANTITY EXCHANGED
Increases	The Same	Increases	Increases
Decreases	The Same	Decreases	Decreases
The Same	Increases	Decreases	Increases
The Same	Decreases	Increases	Decreases
Decreases	Increases	Decreases	
Increases	Decreases	Increases	
Increases	Increases		Increases
Decreases	Decreases		Decreases

If these are the effects of changes in the demand and supply schedules from one period of time to another, the next problem is to explain the causes of these changes themselves. A change in the demand schedule is due purely to a change in the relative utility-rankings of the two goods (the purchase-good and the sale-good) on the value scales of the individual buyers on the market. An increase in the demand schedule, for example, signifies a general rise in the purchase-good on the value scales of the buyers. This may be due to either (*a*) a rise in the direct use-value of the good; (*b*) poorer opportunities to exchange the sale-good for some other good—as a result, say, of a higher price of cows in terms of fish; or (*c*) a decline in speculative waiting for the price of the good to fall further. The last case has been discussed in detail and has been shown to be self-correcting, impelling the market more quickly towards the true equilibrium. We can therefore omit this case now and conclude that an increase in the demand schedule is due either to an increase in the direct use-value of the good or to a higher price of other potential purchase-goods in terms of the sale-good that buyers offer in exchange. A decrease in demand schedules is due precisely to the converse cases—a fall in the value in direct use or greater opportunities to buy other purchase-goods for this sales-good. The latter would mean a greater exchange-value—of fish, for example—in other fields of exchange. Changes in opportunities for other types of exchange may be a result of higher or lower prices for the other purchase-goods, or they may be the result of the fact that new types of goods are being offered for fish on the market. The sudden appearance of cows being offered for fish where none had been offered before is a widening of exchange opportunities for fish and will result in a general decline of the demand curve for *horses* in terms of fish.

A change in the market supply curve is, of course, also the result of a change in the relative rankings of utility on the sellers' value scales. This curve, however, may be broken down into the amount of physical stock and the reservation-demand schedule of the sellers. If we assume that the *amount of physical stock is constant* in the two periods under comparison, then a shift in supply curves is purely the result of a change in reservation-demand curves. A decrease in the supply curve caused by an increase in reservation demand for the stock may be due to either (*a*) an increase in the direct use-value of the good for the sellers; (*b*) greater opportunities for making exchanges for other purchase-goods; or (*c*) a greater speculative anticipation of a higher price in the future. We may here omit the last case for the same reason we omitted it from our discussion of the demand curve. Conversely, a fall in the reservation-demand schedule may be due to either (*a*) a decrease in the direct use-value of the good to the sellers or (*b*) a dwindling of exchange opportunities for other purchase-goods.

Thus, with the total stock constant, changes in both supply and demand curves are due solely to changes in the demand to hold the good by either sellers or buyers, which in turn are due to shifts in the relative utility of the two goods. Thus, in both diagrams *A* and *B* above, the *increase* in the demand schedule and a *decrease* in the supply schedule from *S'S'* to *SS* are a result of increased total demand to hold. In one case the increased total demand to hold is on the part of the buyers, in the other case of the sellers. The relevant diagram is shown in Fig. 25. In both cases of an increase in the total demand-to-hold schedule, say from *TD* to *T'D'*, the *equilibrium price increases.* On the contrary, when the demand schedule declines, and/or when the supply schedule increases, these signify a general decrease in the total demand-to-hold schedule and consequently a *fall in equilibrium price.*

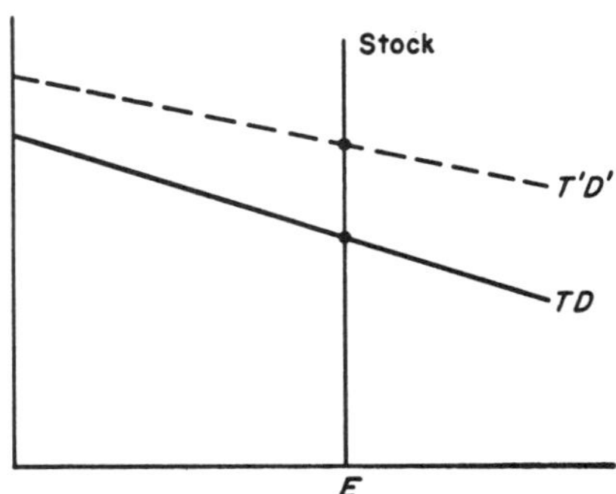

FIG. 25. INCREASE IN THE TOTAL DEMAND TO HOLD

A total demand-stock diagram can convey no information about the quantity exchanged, but only about the equilibrium price. Thus, in diagram *C*, the broken lines both represent a fall in demand to hold, and we could consequently be sure that the total demand to hold declined, and that therefore price declined. (The opposite would be the case for a shift from the broken to the solid lines.) In diagram *D*, however, since an increase in the supply schedule represented a fall in demand to hold, and an increase in demand was a rise in the demand to hold, we could not always be sure of the net effect on the total demand to hold and hence on the equilibrium price.

From the beginning of the supply-demand analysis up to this point we have been assuming the existence of a constant physical stock. Thus, we have been assuming the existence of eight horses and have been considering the principles on which this stock will go into the hands of different possessors. The analysis above applies to *all goods*—to all cases where an existing stock is being exchanged for the stock of another good. For some goods this point is as far as analysis can be pursued. This applies to those goods of which the stock is fixed and cannot be increased through production. They are either once produced by man or given by nature, but the stock cannot be increased by human action. Such a good, for example, is a Rembrandt painting after the death of Rembrandt. Such a painting would rank high enough on individual value scales to command a high price in exchange for other goods. The stock can never be increased, however, and its exchange and pricing is solely in terms of the previously analyzed exchange of existing stock, determined by the relative rankings of these and other goods on numerous value scales. Or assume that a certain quantity of diamonds have been produced, and no more diamonds are available anywhere. Again, the problem would be solely one of exchanging the existing stock. In these cases there is no further problem of *production*—of deciding how much of a stock should be produced in a certain period of time. For most goods, however, the problem of deciding how much to produce is a crucial one. Much of the remainder of this volume, in fact, is devoted to an analysis of the problem of production.

We shall now proceed to cases in which the existing stock of a good *changes* from one period to another. A stock may increase from one period to the next because an amount of the good has been *newly produced* in the meantime. This amount of new production constitutes an *addition to the stock*. Thus, three days after the beginning of the horse-market referred to above, two new horses might be produced and added to the existing stock. If the demand schedule of buyers and the reservation demand schedule of sellers remain the same, what will occur can be represented as in Fig. 26.

The increased stock will lower the price of the good. At the old equilibrium price, individuals find that their stock is in excess of the total demand to hold, and the consequence is an underbidding to sell that lowers the price to the new equilibrium.

In terms of supply and demand curves, an increase in stock, with demand and reservation-demand schedules remaining the same, is equivalent to a *uniform increase in the supply schedule*

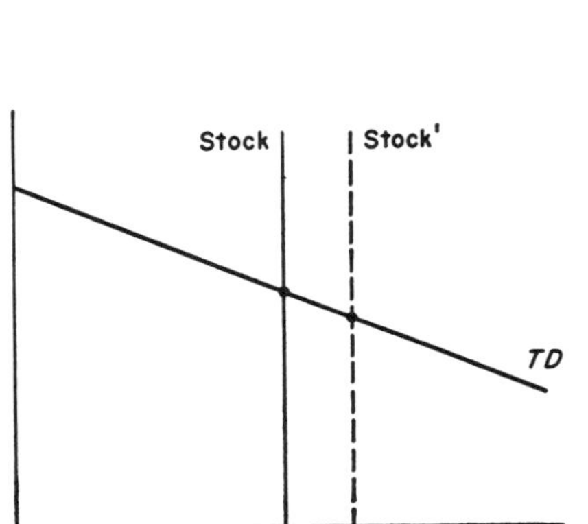

FIG. 26. EFFECT OF AN INCREASE IN STOCK

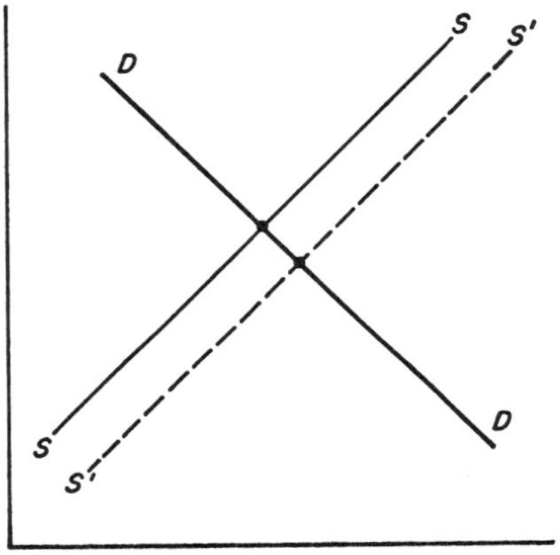

FIG. 27. EFFECT OF AN INCREASE IN THE SUPPLY SCHEDULE

by the amount of the increased stock—in this case by two horses. The amount supplied would be the former total plus the added two. Possessors with an excess of stock at the old equilibrium price must underbid each other in order to sell the increased stock. If we refer back to Table 2, we find that an increase in the supply schedule by 2 lowers the equilibrium price to 88, where the demand is 6 and the new supply is 6.

Diagrammatically, the situation may be depicted as in Fig. 27. The increased stock is reflected in a uniform increase in the supply curve, and a consequent fall in price and an increase in the quantity exchanged.

Of course, there is no reason to assume that, in reality, an increased stock will necessarily be accompanied by an unchanged reservation-demand curve. But in order to study the various causal factors that interact to form the actual historical result, it is necessary to isolate each one and consider what would be its effect if the others remained unchanged. Thus, if an increased stock were at the same time absorbed by an equivalent increase in the reservation-demand schedule, the supply curve would not increase at all, and the price and quantity exchanged would remain unchanged. (On the total demand-stock schedule, this situation would be reflected in an increase in stock, accompanied by an offsetting rise in the total-demand curve, leaving the price at the original level.)

A *decrease* in stock from one period to another may result from the *using up* of the stock. Thus, if we consider only consumers' goods, a part of the stock may be consumed. Since goods are generally used up in the process of consumption, if there is not sufficient production during the time considered, the total stock in existence may decline. Thus, one new horse may be produced, but two may die, from one point of time to the next, and the result may be a market with one less horse in existence. A *decline* in stock, with demand remaining the same, has the exactly reverse effect, as we may see on the diagrams by moving from the broken to the solid lines. At the old equilibrium price, there is an excess demand to hold compared to the stock available, and the result is an upbidding of prices to the new equilibrium. The supply schedule uniformly decreases by the decrease in stock, and the result is a higher price and a smaller quantity of goods exchanged.

We may summarize the relation between stock, production, and time, by stating that the stock at one period (assuming that a period of time is defined as one during which the stock remains unchanged) is related to the stock at a previous period as follows:

If S_t equals stock at a certain period (t)
S_{t-n} equals stock at an earlier period ($t - n$) which is n units of time before period (t)
P_n equals production of the good over the period n
U_n equals amount of the good used up over the period n

Then: $$S_t = S_{t-n} + P_n - U_n$$

Thus, in the case just mentioned, if the original stock is 8 horses, and one new horse is produced while two die, the new stock of the good is 8 + 1 − 2 = 7 horses.

It is important to be on one's guard here against a common confusion over such a term as "an increase in demand." Whenever this phrase is used by itself in this work, it always signifies an *increase in the demand schedule,* i.e., an increase in the amounts that will be demanded at each hypothetical price. This "shift of the demand schedule to the right" always tends to cause an increase in price. It must never be confused with the "increase in quantity demanded" that takes place, for example, in response to an increased supply. An increased supply schedule, by lowering price, induces the market to demand the larger quantity offered. This, however, is *not* an increase in the demand schedule, but an *extension along the same demand schedule.* It is a larger quantity demanded in response to a more attractive price offer. This simple movement along the same schedule must not be confused with an increase in the demand schedule at *each* possible price. The diagrams in Fig. 28 highlight the difference:

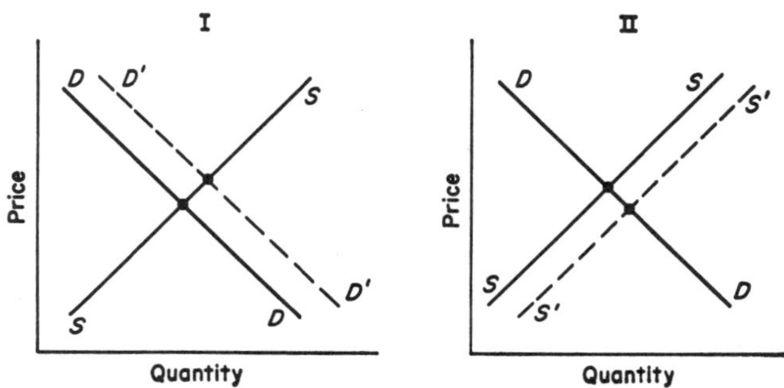

FIG. 28. INCREASE IN THE DEMAND SCHEDULE AND IN THE QUANTITY DEMANDED

Diagram I depicts an increase in the demand schedule, while diagram II depicts an extension of quantity demanded along the same schedule as a result of an increase in the supply offered. In both cases, the value scales of the various individuals determine the final result, but great confusion can ensue if the concepts are not clearly distinguished when such terms as "increase" or "decrease" in demand are being used.

10. *Specialization and Production of Stock*

We have analyzed the exchanges that take place in existing stock and the effect of *changes* in the stock of a good. The question still remains: On what principles is the size of the stock itself determined? Aside from the consumers' or producers' goods given directly by nature, *all goods must be produced by man.* (And even seemingly nature-given products must be searched for and then used by man, and hence are ultimately products of human effort.) The size of the stock of any good depends on the rate at which the good has been and is being *produced.* And since human wants for most goods are continuous, the goods that are worn out through use must constantly be replaced by new production. An analysis of the rate of production and its determinants is thus of central importance in an analysis of human action.

A complete answer to this problem cannot be given at this point, but certain general conclusions on production can be made. In the first place, while any one individual can at different times be both a buyer and a seller of existing stock, in the *production* of that stock there must be *specialization.* This omnipresence of specialization has been treated above, and the further an exchange economy develops, the further advanced will be the specialization process. The basis for specialization has been shown to be the varying abilities of men and the varying location of natural resources. The result is that a good comes first into existence by production, and then is sold by its producer in exchange for some other good, which has been produced in the same way. The initial sales of any new stock will all be made by original producers of the good. Purchases will be made by buyers who will use the good either for their direct use or for holding the good in speculative anticipation of later reselling it at a higher price. At any given time, therefore, new stock will be sold by its original producers. The old stock will be sold by: (*a*) original producers who through past reservation demand had accumulated old stock; (*b*) previous buyers who had bought in speculative anticipation of reselling at a higher price; and (*c*) previous buyers on whose value scales the relative utility of the good for their direct use has fallen.

At any time, then, the *market supply schedule* is formed by the addition of the supply schedules of the following groups of sellers:[30]

a) The supply offered by *producers* of the good.
   1. The initial supply of new stock.
   2. The supply of old stock previously reserved by the producers.

b) The supply of old stock offered by previous buyers.
   1. Sales by speculative buyers who had anticipated reselling at a higher price.
   2. Sales by buyers who had purchased for direct use, but on whose value scales the relative utility of the good has fallen.

The market demand schedule at any time consists of the sum of the demand schedules of:

c) Buyers for direct use.
d) Speculative buyers for resale at a higher price.

Since the good consists of equally serviceable units, the buyers are necessarily indifferent as to whether it is old or new stock that they are purchasing. If they are not, then the "stock" refers to two different goods, and not the same good.

The supply curve of the class (*b*) type of sellers has already been fully analyzed above, e.g., the relationship between stock and reservation demand for speculative resellers and for those whose utility position has changed. What more can be said, however, of the supply schedule of the class (*a*) sellers—the original producers of the good?

In the first place, the stock of newly produced goods in the hands of the producers is also *fixed* for any given point in time. Say that for the month of December the producers of copper decide to produce 5,000 tons of copper. At the end of that month their stock of newly produced copper is 5,000 tons. They might regret their decision and believe that if they could have made it again, they would have produced, say, 1,000 tons. But they have their stock, and they must use it as best they can. The distinguishing feature of the original producers is that, as a result of specialization, the direct use-value of their product to them is likely to be almost nonexistent. The further specialization proceeds, the less possible use-value can the product have for its producer. Picture, for example, how much copper a copper manufacturer could consume in his personal use, or the direct use-value of the huge number of produced automobiles to the Ford family. Therefore, in the supply schedule of the producers, the direct-use element in their reservation demand disappers. The only reason for a producer to reserve, to hold on to, any of his stock is speculative—in anticipation of a higher price for the good in the future. (In direct exchange, there is also the possibility of exchange for a third good—say cows instead of fish, in our example.)

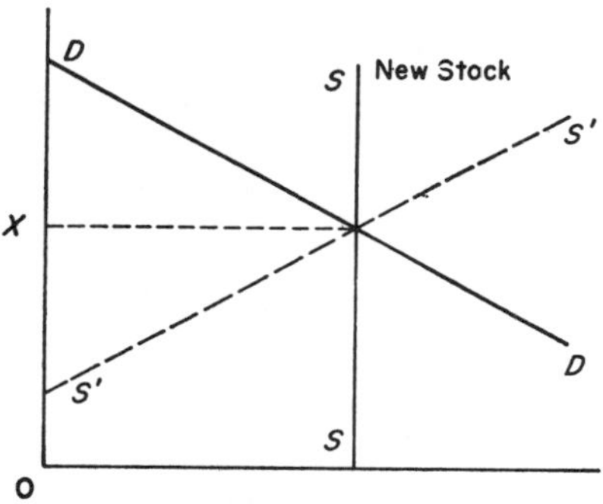

FIG. 29. EFFECT OF NEW STOCK OF CLASS (A) PRODUCERS

If, for the moment, we make the restrictive assumptions that there are no class (*b*) sellers on the market and that the producers have no present or accumulated past reservation demand, then the market supply-demand schedules can be represented as *SS, DD* in Fig. 29. Thus, with no reservation demand, the supply curve will be a vertical straight line (*SS*) at the level of the new stock. It seems more likely, however, that a price below equilibrium will tend to call forth a reservation demand to hold by the producers in anticipation of a higher price (called "building up inventory"), and that a price above equilibrium will result in the unloading of old stock that had been accumulated as a result of past reservation demand (called "drawing down inventory").

In that case, the supply curve assumes a more familiar shape (the broken line above—*S′S′*).

The removal of direct use-value from the calculation of the sellers signifies that all the stock must eventually be sold, so that *ultimately* none of the stock can be reserved from sale by the producers. The producers will make their sales at that point at which they expect the market price to be the greatest that they can attain—i.e., at the time when the market demand for the given stock is expected to be the greatest.[31] The length of time that producers can reserve supply is, of course, dependent on the durability of the good; a highly perishable good like strawberries, for example, could not be reserved for long, and its market supply curve is likely to be a vertical line.

Suppose that an equilibrium price for a good has been reached on the market. In this case, the speculative element of reservation demand drops out. However, in contrast to the market in re-exchange of *existing stock,* the market for *new production* does not end. Since wants are always being renewed in each successive period of time, new stock will also be produced in each period, and if the amount of stock is the same and the demand schedule given, the same amount will continue to be sold at the same equilibrium price. Thus, suppose that the copper producers produce 5,000 tons in a month; these are sold (no reservation demand) at the equilibrium price of *OX* on the foregoing diagram. The equilibrium quantity is *OS*. The following month, if 5,000 tons are produced, the equilibrium price will be the same. If more is produced, then, as we saw above, the equilibrium price is lower; if less, the equilibrium price will be higher.

If the speculative elements are also excluded from the demand schedule, it is clear that this schedule will be determined solely by the utility of the good in direct use (as compared with the utility of the sale-good). The only two elements in the value of a good are its direct use-value and its exchange-value, and the demand schedule consists of demand for direct use plus the speculative demand in anticipation of reselling at a higher price. If we exclude the latter element (e.g., at the equilibrium price), the only ultimate source of demand is the direct use-value of the good to the purchaser. If we abstract from the speculative elements in a market, therefore, the *sole* determinant of the market price of the stock of a good is its relative direct use-value to its purchasers.

It is clear, as has been shown in previous sections, that production must take place over a period of time. To obtain a certain amount of new stock at some future date, the producer must first put into effect a series of acts, using labor, nature, and capital goods, and the process must take time from the initial and intermediary acts until the final stock is produced. Therefore, the essence of specialized production is *anticipation of the future state of the market by the producers.* In deciding whether or not to produce a certain quantity of stock by a future date, the producer must use his judgment in estimating the market price at which he will be able to sell his stock. This market price is likely to be at some equilibrium, but an equilibrium is not likely to last for more than a short time. This is especially true when (as a result of ever-changing value scales) the demand curve for the good continually shifts. Each producer tries to use his resources—his labor and useful goods—in such a way as to obtain, in the production of stock, the maximum psychic revenue and hence a psychic profit. He is ever liable to error, and errors in anticipating the market will bring him a psychic loss. The essence of production for the market, therefore, is entrepreneurship. The key consideration is that the demand schedules, and consequently the future prices, are not and can never be definitely and automatically known to the producers. They must estimate the future state of demand as best they can.

Entrepreneurship is also the dominant characteristic of buyers and sellers who act speculatively, who specialize in anticipating higher or lower prices in the future. Their entire action consists in attempts to anticipate future market prices, and their success depends on how accurate or erroneous their forecasts are. Since, as was seen above, correct speculation quickens the movement toward equilibrium, and erroneous speculation tends to correct itself, the activity of these speculators tends to hasten the arrival of an equilibrium position.

The direct users of a good must *also anticipate their desires for a good* when they purchase it. At the time of purchase, their actual use of a good will be at some date in the future, even if in the very near future. The position of the good on their value scales is an estimate of its expected future value in these periods, discounted by time preferences. It is very possible for the buyer to make an erroneous forecast of the value of the good to him in the future, and the more durable the good, the greater the likelihood of error. Thus, it is more likely that the buyer of a house will be in error in forecasting his own future valuation than the buyer of strawberries. Hence, entrepreneurship is also a feature of the buyer's activity—even in direct use. However, in the case of specialized producers, entrepreneurship takes the form of estimating *other people's* future wants, and this is obviously a far more difficult and challenging task than forecasting one's *own* valuations.

Human action occurs in stages, and at each stage an actor must make the best possible use of his resources in the light of expected future developments. The past is forever bygone. The role of errors in different stages of human action may be considered in the comparatively simple case of the man who buys a good for direct use. Say that his estimate of his future uses is such that he purchases a good—e.g., 10 quarts of milk—in exchange for 100 barrels of fish, which also happens to be his maximum buying price for 10 quarts of milk. Suppose that after the purchase is completed he finds, for some reason, that his valuations have changed and that the milk is now far lower on his value scale. He is now confronted with the question of the best use to make of the 10 quarts of milk. The fact that he has made an error in using his resources of 100 barrels of fish does not remove the problem of making the best use of the 10 quarts of milk. If the price is still 100 barrels of fish, his best course at present would be to resell the milk and reobtain the 100 barrels of fish. If the price is now above 100, he has made a speculative gain, and he can resell the milk for more fish. And if the price of milk has fallen, but the fish is still higher on his value scale than the 10 quarts of milk, it would maximize his psychic revenue to sell the milk for less than 100 barrels of fish.

It is important to recognize that it is absurd to criticize such an action by saying that he suffered a clear loss of *X* barrels of fish from the two exchanges. To be sure, if he had correctly forecast later developments, the man would not have made the original exchange. His *original* exchange can therefore be termed erroneous in retrospect. But once the first exchange has been made, he must make the best possible present and future use of the milk, regardless of past errors, and therefore his second exchange was his best possible choice under the circumstances.

If, on the other hand, the price of milk has fallen below his new maximum buying price, then his best alternative is to use the milk in its most valuable direct use.

Similarly, a producer might decide to produce a certain amount of stock, and, after the stock has been made, the state of the market turns out to be such as to make him regret his decision. However, he must do the best he can with the stock, once it has been produced, and obtain the maximum psychic revenue from it. In other words, if we consider his action from the beginning—when he *invested* his resources in production—his act in retrospect was a psychic loss because it did not yield the best available alternative from these resources. But once the stock is produced, *this* is his available resource, and its sale at the best possible price now nets him a psychic gain.

At this point, we may summarize the expected (psychic) revenue and the expected (psychic) cost, factors that enter into the decision of buyers and sellers in any direct exchange of two goods.

Buyer Revenue	*Seller Revenue*
Either	Either
* A. Direct use of purchase-good	* A. Direct use of sale-good
or B. Anticipated later sale at higher price	or B. Anticipated later purchase at lower price
(whichever is the greater on his value scale)	(whichever is the greater on on his value scale)

Buyer Cost	*Seller Cost*
Either	Either
A. Direct use of sale-good	A. Direct use of purchase-good
or B. Anticipated later purchase at lower price	or * B. Exchange for a third good
or * C. Exchange for a third good	or C. Later sale at a higher price
(whichever is the greatest on his value scale)	(whichever is the greatest on his value scale)

If we eliminate the temporary speculative element, we are left with factors: revenue *A*, cost *A*, cost *C* for buyers; and revenue *A*, cost *A*, cost *B* for sellers. Similarly, if we consider the sellers as the specialized original producers—and this will be more true the greater the proportion of the rate of production to accumulated stock—cost *A* drops out for the sellers. If we also remember that, since the exchange involves two goods, the set of buyers for one good *is* the set of sellers for the other good, cost *A* is eliminated as a factor for buyers as well. Only the factors asterisked above ultimately remain. The revenue for both the buyers and the sellers is the expected direct use of the goods acquired; the costs are the exchange for a third good that is forgone because of this exchange.

The revenue and costs that are involved in making *the original decision regarding the production of stock* are, as we have indicated, of a different order, and these will be explored in subsequent chapters.

11. *Types of Exchangeable Goods*

For the sake of clarity, the examples of exchangeable goods in this chapter have mainly been taken from tangible *commodities,* such as horses, fish, eggs, etc. Such commodities are not the only type of goods subject to exchange, however. A may exchange his *personal services* for the commodity of B. Thus, for example, A may give his *labor* services to farmer B in exchange for farm produce. Furthermore, A may give personal services that function directly as *consumers' goods* in exchange for another good. An individual may thus exchange his medical advice or his musical performance for food or clothing. These services are as legitimately consumers' goods as those goods that are embodied in tangible, physical commodities. Similarly, individual labor services are as much producers' goods as are tangible capital goods. As a matter of fact, tangible goods are valued not so much for their physical content as for their *services* to the user, whether he is a consumer or a producer. The actor values the bread for its services in providing nourishment, the house for its services in providing shelter, the machine for its service in producing a lower-order good. In the last analysis, tangible commodities are also valued for their services, and are thus on the same plane as intangible personal "services."

Economics, therefore, is *not* a science that deals particularly with "material goods" or "material welfare." It deals in general with the action of men to satisfy their desires, and, specifically, with the process of exchange of goods as a means for each individual to "produce" satisfactions for his desires. These goods may be tangible commodities or they may be intangible personal services. The principles of supply and demand, of price determination, are exactly the same for any good, whether it is in one category or the other. The foregoing analysis is applicable to all goods.

Thus, the following types of possible exchanges have been covered by our analysis:

a) A commodity for a commodity; such as horses for fish.
b) A commodity for a personal service; such as medical advice for butter, or farm labor for food.
c) A personal service for a personal service; such as mutual log-rolling by two settlers, or medical advice for gardening labor, or teaching for a musical performance.[32]

In cases where there are several competing homogeneous units, supply and demand schedules can be added; in cases where one or both parties are isolated or are the only ones exchanging, the zone of price determination will be established as indicated above. Thus, if one arithmetic teacher is bargaining with one violinist for an exchange of services, their respective utility rankings will set the zone of price determination. If several arithmetic teachers and several violinists who provide homogeneous services form a market for their two goods, the market price will be formed with the addition and intersection of supply and demand schedules. If the services of the different individuals are not considered as of equal quality by the demanders, they will be evaluated separately, and each service will be priced separately.[33] The supply curve will then be a supply of units of a commodity possessed by only *one* individual. This individual supply curve is, of course, sloped upward in a rightward direction. Where only one individual is the supplier of a good on the market, his supply curve is identical with the market supply curve.

One evident reason for the confusion of exchange with a mere trade of material objects is the fact that much intangible property *cannot,* by its very nature, be exchanged. A violinist may *own* his musicianly ability and exchange units of it, in the form of service, for the services of a physician. But other personal attributes, which cannot be exchanged, may be desired as goods. Thus, Brown might have a desired end: to gain the genuine approval of Smith. This is a particular consumers' good which he cannot purchase with any other good, for what he wants is the genuine approval rather than a show of approval that might be purchased. In this case, the consumers' good is a property of Smith's that cannot be exchanged; it might be acquired in some way, but not by exchange. In relation to exchange, this intangible good is an *inalienable* property of Smith's, i.e., it cannot be given up. Another example is that a man cannot permanently transfer his will, even though he may transfer much of his services and his property. As mentioned above, a man may not agree to permanent bondage by contracting to work for another man for the rest of his life. He might change his mind at a later date, and then he cannot, in a free market, be compelled to continue working thereafter. Because a man's self-ownership over his will is inalienable, he cannot, on the unhampered market, be compelled to continue an arrangement whereby he submits his will to the orders of another, even though he might have agreed to this arrangement previously.[34, 35] On the other hand, when property that *can* be alienated is transferred, it, of course, becomes the property—under the sole and exclusive jurisdiction—of the person who has received it in exchange, and no later regret by the original owner can establish any claim to the property.

Thus, exchange may occur with alienable goods; they may be consumers' goods, of varying degrees of durability; or they may be producers' goods. They may be tangible commodities or intangible personal services. There are other types of exchangeable items, which are based on these alienable goods. For example, suppose that Jones deposits a good—say 1,000 bushels of wheat—in a warehouse for safekeeping. He retains ownership of the good, but transfers its physical possession to the warehouse owner, Green, for safekeeping. Green gives Jones a *warehouse receipt* for the wheat, certifying that the wheat is there for safekeeping and giving the owner of the receipt a *claim* to receive the wheat whenever he presents the receipt to the warehouse. In exchange for this service as a guardian of the wheat, Jones pays him a certain agreed amount of some other good, say emeralds. Thus, the claim originates from an exchange of a commodity for a service—emeralds for storage—and the price of this exchange is determined according to the principles of the foregoing analysis. Now, however, the warehouse receipt has come into existence as a claim to the wheat. On an unhampered market, the claim would be regarded as absolutely secure and certain to be honored, and therefore Jones would be able to exchange the claim as a *substitute* for actual physical exchange of the wheat. He might find another party, Robinson, who wishes to purchase the wheat in exchange for horses. They agree on a price, and then Robinson accepts the *claim* on the warehouse as a perfectly good substitute for actual transfer of the wheat. He knows that when he wants to use the wheat, he will be able to *redeem* the claim at the warehouse; the claim therefore functions here as a *goods-substitute.* In this case, the claim is to a *present good,* since the good can be redeemed at any time that the owner desires.

Here, the nature and function of the claim is simple. The claim is a secure evidence of ownership of the good. Even simpler is a case where ownership of property, say a farm, is transferred from A to B by transferring written *title,* or evidence of ownership, which may be considered a claim. The situation becomes more complicated, however, when ownership is divided into pieces, and these pieces are transferred from person to person. Thus, suppose that Harrison is the owner of an iron mine. He decides to divide up the ownership, and sell the various divided pieces, or *shares,* of the good to other individuals. Assume that he creates a hundred tickets, with the total constituting the full ownership of the mine, and then sells all but ten tickets to numerous other individuals. The owner of two shares then becomes a $\frac{2}{100}$ owner of the mine. Since there is very little practical scope for such activity in a regime of *direct* exchange, analysis of this situation will be reserved for later chapters. It is clear, however, that the $\frac{2}{100}$ owner is entitled to his proportionate share of direction and control of, and revenue from, the jointly owned property. In other words, the *share* is evidence of part-ownership, or a claim to part-ownership, of a good. This property right in a proportionate share of the use of a good can also be sold or bought in exchange.

A third type of claim arises from a *credit exchange* (or *credit transaction*). Up to this point we have been discussing exchanges of one *present good* for another, i.e., the good can be used *at present*—or at any desired time—by each receiver in the exchange. In a credit transaction, a present good is exchanged for a *future good,* or rather, a *claim on a future good.* Suppose, for example, that Jackson desires to acquire 100 pounds of cotton at once. He makes the following exchange with Peters: Peters to give Jackson 100 pounds of cotton now (a present good); and, in return, Jackson gives Peters a *claim* on 110 pounds of cotton one year from now. This is a claim on a future good—110 pounds of cotton one year from now. The price of the present good in terms of the future good is 1.1 pounds of future cotton (one year from now) per pound of present cotton. Prices in such exchanges are determined by value scales and the meeting of supply and demand schedules, just as in the case of exchanges of present goods. Further analysis of the pricing of credit transactions must be left for later chapters; here it may be pointed out that, as explained in the previous chapter, every man will evaluate a homogeneous good more highly the earlier in time is his prospect of attaining it. A present good (a good consisting of units capable of rendering equivalent satisfaction) will always be valued more highly than the same good in the future, in accordance with the individual's rate of time preference. It is evident that the various rates of time preference—ultimately determined by relative positions on individual value scales—will act to set the price of credit exchanges. Moreover, the receiver of the present good—*the debtor*—will always have to repay *a greater amount* of the good in the future to the *creditor*—the man who receives the claim, since the same number of units is worth more as a present than as a future good. The creditor is rendering the debtor the service of using a good in the *present,* while the debtor pays for this service by repaying a greater amount of the good in the future.

At the date when the claim finally falls due, the creditor redeems the claim and acquires the good itself, thus ending the existence of the claim. In the meanwhile, however, the claim is in existence, and it can be bought and sold in exchange for other goods. Thus, Peters, the creditor, might decide to sell the claim—or promissory note—to Williams in exchange for a wagon. The price of this exchange will again be determined by supply and demand schedules. Demand for the note will be based on its security as a claim to the cotton. Thus, Williams' demand for the note (or Peter's demand to hold) in terms of wagons will be based (*a*) on the direct utility and exchange-value of the wagon, and (*b*) the marginal utility of the added units of cotton, *discounted* by him on two possible grounds: (1) the length of time the claim has left until the date of "maturity," and (2) the estimate of the security of the note. Thus, the less time there remains to elapse for a claim to any given good, the higher will it tend to be valued in the market. Also, if the eventual payment is considered less than absolutely secure, because of possible failure to redeem, the claim will be valued less highly in accordance with people's estimates of the likelihood of its failure. After a note has been transferred, it becomes the property of the new owner, who becomes the creditor and will be entitled to redeem the claim when due.

When a claim is thus transferred in exchange for some other good (or *claim*), this in itself is *not* a credit transaction. A credit exchange sets up an *unfinished payment* on the part of the debtor; in this case, Peters pays Williams the claim in return for the other good, and the transaction is finished. Jackson, on the other hand, remains the debtor as a result of the original transaction, which remains unfinished until he makes his agreed-upon payment to the creditor on the date of maturity.[36]

The several types of claims, therefore, are: on present goods, by such means as warehouse receipts or shares of joint ownership in a good; and on future goods, arising from credit transactions. These are evidences of ownership, or, as in the latter case, objects that *will become* evidence of ownership at a later date.

Thus, in addition to the three types of exchanges mentioned above, there are three other types whose terms and principles are included in the preceding analysis of this chapter:

d) A commodity for a claim; examples of this are: (1) the deposit of a commodity for a warehouse receipt—the claim to a present good; (2) a credit transaction, with a commodity exchanged for a claim to a future commodity; (3) the purchase of shares of stock in a commodity by exchanging another type of commodity for them; (4) the purchase of promissory notes on a debtor by exchanging a commodity. All four of these cases have been described above.

e) A claim for a service; an example is personal service being exchanged for a promissory note or warehouse receipt or stock.

f) A claim for a claim; examples would be: exchange of a promissory note for another one; of stock shares for a note; of one type of stock share for another; of a warehouse receipt for any of the other types of claims.

With all goods analyzable into categories of tangible commodities, services, or claims to goods (goods-substitutes), all six possible types of exchanges are covered by the utility and supply-demand analysis of this chapter. In each case, different concrete considerations enter into the formation of the value scales—such as time preference in the case of credit exchanges; and this permits more to be said about the various specific types of exchanges. The level of analysis presented in this chapter, however, encompasses all possible exchanges of goods. In later chapters, when *indirect exchange* has been introduced, the present analysis will apply also, but further analysis will be made of production and exchange problems involved in credit exchanges (time preference); in exchanges for capital goods and consumer goods; and in exchanges for labor services (wages).

12. *Property: The Appropriation of Raw Land*

As we have stated above, the origin of all property is ultimately traceable to the appropriation of an unused nature-given factor by a man and his "mixing" his labor with this natural factor to produce a capital good or a consumers' good. For when we trace back through gifts and through exchanges, we must reach a man and an unowned natural resource. In a free society, any piece of nature that has never been used is *unowned* and is subject to a man's ownership through his first use or mixing of his labor with this resource.

How will an individual's title to the nature-given factor be determined? If Columbus lands on a new continent, is it legitimate for him to proclaim all the new continent his own, or even that sector "as far as his eye can see"? Clearly, this would not be the case in the free society that we are postulating. Columbus or Crusoe would have to *use* the land, to "cultivate" it in some way, before he could be asserted to own it. This "cultivation" does not have to involve tilling the soil, although that is one possible form of cultivation. If the natural resource is land, he may clear it for a house or a pasture, or care for some plots of timber, etc. If there is more land than can be used by a limited labor supply, then the unused land must simply remain unowned until a first user arrives on the scene. Any attempt to claim a new resource that someone does not use would have to be considered invasive of the property right of whoever the first user will turn out to be.

There is no requirement, however, that land *continue* to be used in order for it to continue to be a man's property. Suppose that Jones uses some new land, then finds it is unprofitable, and lets it fall into disuse. Or suppose that he clears new land and therefore obtains title to it, but then finds that it is no longer useful in production and allows it to remain idle. In a free society, would he lose title? No, for once his labor is mixed with the natural resource, it remains his owned land. His labor has been irretrievably mixed with the land, and the land is therefore his or his assigns' in perpetuity. We shall see in later chapters that the question whether or not labor has been mixed with land is irrelevant to its market price or capital value; in catallactics, the past is of no interest. In establishing the ownership of property, however, the question is important, for once the mixture takes place, the man and his heirs have appropriated the nature-given factor, and for anyone else to seize it would be an invasive act.

As Wolowski and Levasseur state:

> Nature has been appropriated by him (man) for his use; she has become his *own;* she is his *property*. This property is legitimate; it constitutes a right as sacred for man as is the free exercise of his faculties. It is his because it has come entirely from himself, and is in no way anything but an emanation from his being. Before him, there was scarcely anything but matter; since him, and by him, there is interchangeable wealth. The producer has left a fragment of his own person in the thing which has thus become valuable, and may hence be regarded as a prolongation of the faculties of man acting upon external nature. As a free being he belongs to himself; now, the cause, that is to say, the productive force, is himself; the effect, that is to say, the wealth produced, is still himself. Who shall dare contest his title of ownership so clearly marked by the seal of his personality?[37]

Some critics, especially the Henry Georgists, assert that, while a man or his assigns may be entitled to the produce of his own labor or anything exchanged for it, he is not entitled to an original, nature-given factor, a "gift of nature." For one man to appropriate this gift is alleged to be an invasion of a common heritage that all men deserve to use equally. This is a self-contradictory position, however. A man cannot produce anything without the co-operation of original nature-given factors, if only as standing room. In order to produce and possess any capital good or consumers' good, therefore, he must appropriate and use an original nature-given factor. He cannot form products purely out of his labor alone; he *must* mix his labor with original nature-given factors. Therefore, if property in land or other nature-given factors is to be denied man, he cannot obtain property in the fruits of his labor.

Furthermore, in the question of land, it is difficult to see what better title there is than the first bringing of this land from a simple unvaluable thing into the sphere of production. For that is what the first user does. He takes a factor that was previously unowned and unused, and therefore worthless to anyone, and converts it into a tool for production of capital and consumers' goods. While such questions as communism of property will be discussed in later parts of this book, it is difficult indeed to see why the mere fact of being born should automatically confer upon one some aliquot part of the world's land. For the first user has mixed his labor with the land, while neither the newborn child nor his ancestors have done anything with the land at all.

The problem will be clearer if we consider the case of *animals*. Animals are "economic land," because they are equivalent to physical land in being original, nature-given factors of production. Yet will anyone deny title to a cow to the man that finds and domesticates her, putting her to use? For this is precisely what occurs in the case of land. Previously valueless "wild" land, like wild animals, is taken and transformed by a man into goods useful for man. The "mixing" of labor gives equivalent title in one case as in the other.

We must remember, also, what "production" entails. When man "produces," he does not create matter. He uses given materials and transforms and rearranges them into goods that he desires. In short, he moves matter further toward consumption. His finding of land or animals and putting them to use is also such a transformation.

Even if the value accruing to a piece of land at present is substantial, therefore, it is only "economic land" because of the innumerable past efforts of men at work on the land. When we are considering legitimacy of title, the fact that land always embodies past labor becomes extremely important.[38]

If animals are also "land" in the sense of given original nature factors, so are water and air. We have seen that "air" is inappropriable, a condition of human welfare rather than a scarce good that can be owned. However, this is true only of air for breathing under usual conditions. For example, if some people want their air to be changed, or "conditioned," then they will have to pay for this service, and the "conditioned air" becomes a scarce good that *is* owned by its producers.

Furthermore, if we understand by "air" the medium for the transmission of such things as radio waves and television images, there is only a limited quantity of wave lengths available for radio and for television purposes. This scarce factor *is* appropriable and ownable by man. In a free society, ownership of these channels would accrue to individuals just like that of land or animals: the first users obtain the property. The first user, Jones, of the wave length of 1,000 kilocycles, would be the absolute owner of this length for his wave area, and it will be his right to continue using it, to abandon it, to sell it, etc. Anyone else who set up a transmitter on the owner's wave length would be as guilty of invasion of another's property right as a trespasser on someone else's land or a thief of someone else's livestock.[39,40]

The same is true of *water*. Water, at least in rivers and oceans, has been considered by most people as also inappropriable and unownable, although it is conceded to be ownable in the cases of (small) lakes and wells. Now it is true that the high seas, in relation to shipping lanes, are probably inappropriable, because of their abundance in relation to shipping routes.[41] This is *not* true, however, of *fishing* rights in oceans. Fish are definitely not available in unlimited quantities relatively to human wants. Therefore, they are appropriable—their stock and source just as the captured fish themselves. Indeed, nations are always quarreling about "fishing rights." In a free society, fishing rights to the appropriate areas of oceans would be owned by the first users of those areas and then usable or salable to other individuals. Ownership of areas of water that contain fish is directly analogous to private ownership of areas of land or forests that contain animals to be hunted. Some people raise the difficulty that water flows, and has no fixed position, as land does. This is a completely invalid objection, however. Land "moves" too, as when soil is uprooted in dust storms. Most important, water can definitely be marked off in terms of latitudes and longitudes. These boundaries, then, would circumscribe the area owned by individuals, in the full knowledge that fish and water can move from one person's property to another. The value of the property would be gauged according to this knowledge.[42]

Another argument is that appropriation of ownership by a first user would result in an uneconomic allocation of the nature-given factors. Thus, suppose that one man can fence, cultivate, or otherwise use, only five acres of a certain land, while the most economic allocation would be units of fifteen acres. However, the rule of *first ownership by the first user,* followed in a free society, would not mean that ownership must end with this allocation. On the contrary. In this case, either the owners would pool their assets in one corporate form, or the most efficient individual owners would buy out the others, and the final size of each unit of land in production would be fifteen acres.

It must be added that the theory of land ownership in a free society set forth here, i.e., first ownership by the first user, has nothing in common with another superficially similar theory of land ownership—that advanced by J. K. Ingalls and his disciples in the late nineteenth century. Ingalls advocated *continuing* ownership only for actual occupiers and personal users of the land. This is in contrast to *original* ownership by the first user.

The Ingalls system would, in the first place, bring about a highly uneconomic allocation of land factors. Land sites where small "homestead" holdings are uneconomic would be forced into use in spite of this, and land would be prevented from entering other lines of use greatly demanded by consumers. Some land would be artificially and coercively withdrawn from use, since land that could not be used by owners *in person* would have to lie idle. Furthermore, this theory is self-contradictory, since it would not really permit ownership at all. One of the prime conditions of ownership is the right to buy, sell, and dispose of property as the owner or owners see fit. Since small holders would not have the right to sell to nonoccupying large holders, the small holders would not really be owners of the land at all. The result is that on the ownership question, the Ingalls thesis reverts, in the final analysis, to the Georgist view that Society (in the alleged person of the State) should own the land.[43]

13. *Enforcement against Invasion of Property*

This work is largely the analysis of a market society unhampered by the use of violence or theft against any man's person or property. The question of the *means* by which this condition is best established is not at present under consideration. For the present purpose, it makes no difference whether this condition is established by every man's deciding to *refrain from invasive action* against others or whether some agency is established to enforce the abandonment of such action by every individual. (*Invasive action* may be defined as any action—violence, theft, or fraud—taking away another's personal freedom or property without his consent.) Whether the enforcement is undertaken by each person or by some sort of agency, we assume here that such a condition—the existence of an unhampered market—is maintained in some way.

One of the problems in maintaining the conditions of a free market is the role of the enforcing agency—whether individual or organizational—in exchange contracts. What type of contracts are to be enforced to maintain the conditions of an unhampered market? We have already seen that contracts assigning away the will of an individual cannot be enforced in such a market, because the will of each person is by its nature inalienable. On the other hand, if the individual made such a contract and received another's property in exchange, he must forfeit part or all of the property when he decides to terminate the agreement. We shall see that fraud may be considered as theft, because one individual receives the other's property but does not fulfill his part of the exchange bargain, thereby taking the other's property without his consent. This case provides the clue to the role of contract and its enforcement in the free society. Contract must be considered as an agreed-upon exchange between two persons of two goods, present or future. Persons would be free to make any and all property contracts that they wished; and, for a free society to exist, all contracts, where the good is naturally alienable, must be enforced. Failure to fulfill contracts must be considered as theft of the other's property. Thus, when a debtor purchases a good in exchange for a promise of future payment, the good cannot be considered his property until the agreed contract has been fulfilled and payment made. Until then, it remains the creditor's property, and nonpayment would be equivalent to theft of the creditor's property.

An important consideration here is that contract *not* be enforced because a promise has been made that is not kept. It is not the business of the enforcing agency or agencies in the free market to enforce promises merely because they are promises; its business is to enforce against theft of property, and contracts are enforced because of the implicit theft involved.

Evidence of a *promise to pay property* is an enforceable claim, because the possessor of this claim is, in effect, the owner of the property involved, and failure to redeem the claim is equivalent to theft of the property. On the other hand, take the case of a promise to contribute personal services without an advance exchange of property. Thus, suppose that a movie actor agrees to act in three pictures for a certain studio for a year. Before receiving any goods in exchange (salary), he breaks the contract and decides not to perform the work. Since his personal will is inalienable, he cannot, on the free market, be forced to perform the work there. Further, since he has received none of the movie company property in exchange, he has committed no theft, and thus the contract cannot be enforced on the free market. Any suit for "damages" could not be entertained on an unhampered market. The fact that the movie company may have made considerable plans and investments on the expectation that the actor would keep the agreement may be unfortunate for the company, but it could not expect the actor to pay for its lack of foresight and poor entrepreneurship. It pays the penalty for placing too much confidence in the man. The movie actor has not received and kept any of the company's property and therefore cannot be held accountable in the form of payment of goods as "damages."[44] Any such enforced payment would be an invasion of his property rights on the free market rather than an attack upon invasion. It may be considered more moral to keep promises than to break them, but the condition of a free market is that each individual's rights of person and property be maintained, and not that some *further* standard of morals be coercively imposed on all. Any coercive enforcement of such a moral code, going beyond the abolition of invasive acts, would in itself constitute an invasion of individual rights of person and property and be an interference in the free market.[45]

It certainly would be consonant with the free market, however, for the movie company to ask the actor to pay a certain sum in consideration of his breaking the contract, and, if he refuses, to refuse to hire him again, and to notify other prospective contracting parties (such as movie companies) of the person's action. It seems likely that his prospect of making exchanges in the future will suffer because of his action. Thus, the "blacklist" is permissible on the free market. Another legitimate action on the free market is the *boycott,* by which A urges B not to make an exchange with C, for whatever reason. Since A's and B's actions are purely voluntary and noninvasive, there is no reason for a boycott not to be permitted on the unhampered market. On the contrary, any coercive action against a boycott is an invasion against the rights of free persons.

If default on contracted debts is to be considered as equivalent to theft, then on the unhampered market its treatment by the enforcing agency will be similar to that of theft. It is clear—for example, in the case of burglary—that the recovery of the stolen property to its owner would be the fundamental consideration for the enforcing agency. Punishment of the wrongdoer would be a consideration subsidiary to the former. Thus, suppose A has stolen 100 ounces of gold from B. By the time A has been apprehended by the enforcing agency, he has dissipated the 100 ounces and has no assets by which the 100 ounces can be obtained. The main goal of the enforcement agency should be to force A to return the 100 ounces. Thus, instead of simply idle imprisonment, the agency could force the thief to labor and to attach his earnings to make up the amount of the theft, plus a compensation for the delay in time. Whether this forced labor is done in or out of prison is immaterial here. The main point is that the invader of another's rights on the free market gives up his rights to the same extent. The first consideration in the punishment of the aggressor against property in the free market is the forced return of the equivalent property.[46] On the other hand, suppose that B voluntarily decides to forgive A and grant the latter a gift of the property; he refuses to "press charges" against the thief. In that case, the enforcement agency would take no action against the robber, since he is now in the position of the receiver of a gift of property.

This analysis provides the clue to the treatment of defaulting debtors on the free market. If a creditor decides to forget about the debt and not press charges, he in effect grants a gift of his property to the debtor, and there is no further room for enforcement of contract. What if the creditor insists on keeping his property? It is clear that if the debtor can pay the required amount but refuses to do so, he is guilty of pure fraud, and the enforcing agency would treat his act as such. Its prime move would be to make sure that the debtor's assets are transferred to their rightful owner, the creditor. But suppose that the debtor has not got the property and would be willing to pay if he had it? Does this entitle him to special privilege or coerced elimination of the debt, as in the case of bankruptcy laws? Clearly not. The prime consideration in the treatment of the debtor would be his continuing and primary responsibility to redeem the property of the creditor. The only way by which this treatment could be eliminated would be for the debtor and the creditor to agree, as part of the original contract, that if the debtor makes certain investments and fails to have the property at the date due, the creditor will forgive the debt; in short, he grants the debtor the rights of a partial co-owner of the property.

There could be no room, in a free society such as we have outlined, for "negotiable instruments." Where the government designates a good as "negotiable," if A steals it from B and then sells it to C without the latter's knowledge of the theft, B cannot take the good back from C. Despite the fact that A was a thief and had no proper title to the good, C is decreed to be the legitimate owner, and B has no way of regaining his property. The law of negotiability is evidently a clear infringement of property right. Where property rights are fully defended, theft cannot be compounded in this manner. The buyer would have to purchase at his own risk and make sure that the good is not stolen; if he nonetheless does buy stolen goods, he must try to obtain restitution from the thief, and not at the expense of the rightful owner.

What of a cartel agreement? Would that be enforceable in a free society? If there has been no exchange of property, and A, B, C . . . firms agree among themselves to set quotas on their production of a good, this agreement would surely not be illegal, but neither would it be enforceable. It could be only a simple promise and not an enforceable case of implicit theft.[47]

One difficulty often raised against a free society of individual property rights is that it ignores the problem of "external diseconomies" or "external costs." But cases of "external diseconomy" all turn out to be instances of failure of *government*—the enforcing agency—adequately to enforce individual property rights. The "blame," therefore, rests not on the institution of private property, but on the failure of the government to enforce this property right against various subtle forms of invasion—the failure, e.g., to maintain a free society.

One instance of this failure is the case of smoke, as well as air pollution generally. In so far as the outpouring of smoke by factories pollutes the air and damages the persons and property of others, it is an invasive act. It is equivalent to an act of vandalism and in a truly free society would have been punished after court action brought by the victims. Air pollution, then, is not an example of a defect in a system of absolute property rights, but of failure on the part of the government to preserve property rights. Note that the remedy, in a free society, is not the creation of an administrative State bureau to prescribe regulations for smoke control. The remedy is *judicial* action to punish and proscribe pollution damage to the person and property of others.[48]

In a free society, as we have stated, every man is a self-owner. No man is allowed to own the body or mind of another, that being the essence of slavery. This condition completely overthrows the basis for a law of defamation, i.e., libel (written defamation) or slander (oral defamation). For the basis of outlawing defamation is that every man has a "property in his own reputation" and that therefore any malicious or untruthful attack on him or his character (or even more, a truthful attack!) injures his reputation and therefore should be punished. However, a man has no such objective property as "reputation." His reputation is simply what others think of him, i.e., it is purely a function of the *subjective* thoughts of others. But a man cannot own the minds or thoughts of others. Therefore, I cannot invade a man's property right by criticizing him publicly. Further, since I do not own others' minds either, I cannot force anyone else to think less of the man because of my criticism.[49]

The foregoing observations should firmly remind us that what the enforcing agency combats in a free society is invasion of the *physical* person and property, *not* injury to the *values* of property. For physical property is what the person owns; he does not have any ownership in monetary values, which are a function of what *others* will pay for his property. Thus, someone's vandalism against, or robbery of, a factory is an invasion of physical property and is outlawed. On the other hand, someone's shift from the purchase of this factory's product to the purchase of a competing factory's product may lower the monetary value of the former's property, but this is certainly not a punishable act. It is precisely the condition of a free society that a property owner have no unearned *claim* on the property of anyone else; therefore, he has no vested right in the value of his property, only in its physical existence. As for the value, this must take its chance on the free market. This is the answer, for example, to those who believe that "undesirable" businesses or people must be legally prevented from moving into a certain neighborhood because this may or will "lower the existing property value."

One method of acquiring property that we have so far not discussed, is *fraud*. Fraud involves cases where one party to an agreed-upon exchange deliberately refuses to fulfill his part of the contract. He thus acquires the property of the other person, but he sacrifices either none of the agreed-upon goods or less than he had agreed. We have seen that a debtor's deliberate failure to pay his creditor is equivalent to an outright theft of the creditor's property.

Another example of fraudulent action is the following exchange: Smith agrees to give up fifteen ounces of gold to Jones in exchange for a package of certain specified chinaware. When he receives the package, after having given up the gold, Smith finds that he has received an empty crate instead of the goods that the two had agreed to exchange. Jones has falsely represented the goods that he would exchange, and here again this is equivalent to outright theft of Smith's property. Since the exchange has been made falsely, the actual form of which might not have been contracted had the other party not been deceived, this is not an example of voluntary exchange, but of one-sided theft. We therefore exclude both explicit violence and the implicit violence of fraud from our definition of the market—the pattern of voluntary interpersonal exchanges. At this point we are dealing only with an analysis of the market unhampered by fraud or violence.

We have not here been discussing what type of enforcing agency will be set up or the means it will use, but what type of actions the agency will combat and what type will be permissible. In a free market, all invasive acts by one person against another's property, either against his person or his material goods, will be combatted by the enforcing agency or agencies. We are here assuming that there are no invasive acts in the society, either because no individuals commit them or because they are successfully combatted and prevented by some sort of enforcing agency. The problem then becomes one of defining invasive, as distinguished from noninvasive, acts, and this is what has been done here in various typical examples. Each man would be entitled to ownership over his own person and over any property that he has acquired by production, by appropriation of unowned factors, by receiving gifts, or by voluntary exchange.

Never has the basis of the free, noninvasive, or "voluntaryist" society been described more clearly in a brief space than by the British political philosopher Auberon Herbert:

> 1) The great natural fact of each person being born in possession of a separate mind and separate body implies the ownership of such mind and body by each person, and rights of direction over such mind and body; it will be found on examination that no other deduction is reasonable.
>
> 2) Such self-ownership implies the restraint of violent or fraudulent aggressions made upon it.
>
> 3) Individuals, therefore, have the right to protect themselves by force against such aggressions made forcibly or fraudulently, and they may delegate such acts of self-defence to a special body called a government . . .
>
> Condensed into a few words, our Voluntaryist formula would run: "The sovereignty of the individual must remain intact, except where the individual coerced has aggressed upon the sovereignty of another unaggressive individual."

Elaborating on the first point, Herbert continued:

> If there is one thing on which we can safely build, it is the great natural fact that each human being forms with his or her body and mind a separate entity—from which we must conclude that the entities belong to themselves and not to each other. As I have said, no other deduction is possible. If the entities do not belong to themselves, then we are reduced to the most absurd conclusion. A or B cannot own himself; but he can own, or part own, C or D.[50]

3

The Pattern of Indirect Exchange

1. *The Limitations of Direct Exchange*

We have seen in the previous chapter how exchange benefits each participant and how the division of labor on a market increases productivity. The only exchange so far discussed, however, has been *direct exchange,* or *barter*—the exchange of one useful good for another, each for purposes of direct use by the party to the exchange. Although a treatment of direct exchange is important for economic analysis, the scope for direct exchange in society is extremely limited. In a very primitive society, for example, Crusoe could employ Jackson to labor on his farm in exchange for a part of the farm produce. There could, however, be no advanced system of production in a direct-exchange society and no accumulation of capital in higher stages of production—indeed no production at all beyond the most primitive level. Thus, suppose that A is a house-builder; he builds a house on contract and employs masons, carpenters, etc. In a regime of direct exchange, how would it be possible to pay these men? He could not give pieces of the house to each of the laborers. He would have to try to sell the house for precisely that combination of useful goods that each of the laborers and each of the sellers of raw material would accept. It is obvious that production could not be carried on and that the difficulties would be insuperable.

This problem of the lack of "coincidence of wants" holds even for the simple, direct exchange of consumers' goods, in addition to the insoluble problem of production. Thus, suppose that A, with a supply of eggs for sale, wants a pair of shoes in exchange. B has shoes but does not want eggs; there is no way for the two to get together. For anyone to sell the simplest commodity, he must find not only one who wants to purchase it, but one who has a commodity for sale that he must want to acquire. The market for anyone's commodities is therefore extremely limited, the extent of the market for any product is very small, and the scope for division of labor negligible. Furthermore, someone with a less divisible commodity, such as a plow, is in worse straits. Suppose that D, with a plow, would like to exchange it for eggs, butter, shoes, and various other commodities. Obviously, he cannot divide his plow into several pieces and then exchange the various pieces for eggs, butter, etc. The value of each piece to the others would be practically nil. Under a system of direct exchange, a plow would have almost no *marketability* in exchange, and few if any would be produced.

In addition to all these difficulties, which render a regime of direct exchange practically impossible, such a society could not solve the various problems of estimation, which (as was seen in chapter 1) even Crusoe had to face.[1] Since there would be no common denominator of units, there could be no way of estimating which line of production various factors should enter. Is it better to produce automobiles or tractors or houses or steel? Is it more productive to employ fewer men and more land on a certain product or less land and more men? Is the capital structure being maintained or consumed? None of these questions could be answered, since, in the stages beyond immediate consumption, there would be no way of comparing the usefulness or the productivity of the different factors or products.

The conclusion is evident that no sort of civilized society can be built on the basis of direct exchange, and that direct exchange, as well as Crusoe-like isolation, could yield only an economy of the most primitive type.[2]

2. *The Emergence of Indirect Exchange*

The tremendous difficulties of direct exchange can be overcome only by *indirect exchange,* where an individual buys a commodity in exchange, not as a consumers' good for the direct satisfaction of his wants or for the production of a consumers' good, but simply *to exchange again* for another commodity that he does desire for consumption or for production. Offhand, this might seem a clumsy and roundabout operation. Actually, it is indispensable for any economy above the barely primitive level.

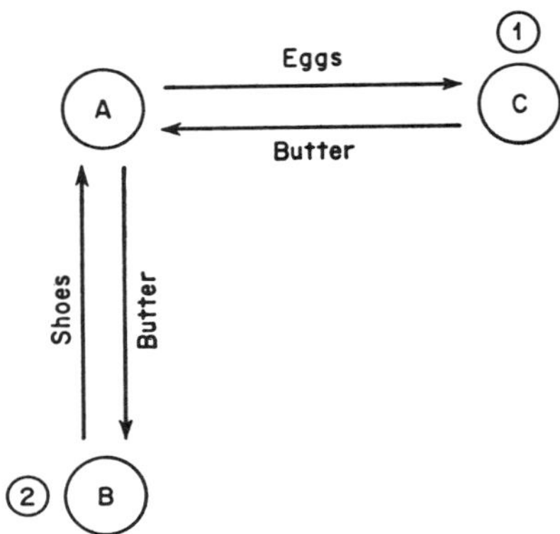

Fig. 30. Pattern of Indirect Exchange

Let us return, for example, to the case of A, with a supply of eggs, who wants a pair of shoes in exchange. B, the shoemaker, has shoes for sale but does not desire any more eggs than he has in stock. A cannot acquire shoes by means of direct exchange. If A wants to purchase a pair of shoes, he must find out what commodity B does want in exchange, and procure it. If A finds that B wants to acquire butter, A may exchange his eggs for the butter of C, and *then* exchange this butter for B's shoes. In this case, butter has been used as a *medium* of indirect exchange. The butter was worth more to A than the eggs (say the exchange was ten dozen eggs for ten pounds of butter, then for one pair of shoes), *not* because he wanted to consume the butter or to use the butter to produce some other good in a later stage of production, but because the butter greatly facilitated his obtaining the shoes in exchange. Thus, for A, the butter was more *marketable* than his eggs and was worth purchasing *because* of its superior marketability. The pattern of the exchange was as shown in Fig. 30.

Or consider the enormous benefit that D, the owner of a plow, acquires by using a medium of exchange. D, who would like to acquire many commodities but finds that his plow has a very limited marketability, can sell it in exchange for quantities of a more marketable commodity, e.g., butter. Butter, for one thing, is more marketable because, unlike the plow, its nature is such that it does not lose its complete value when divided into smaller pieces. D now uses the butter as a medium of indirect exchange to obtain the various commodities that he desires to consume.

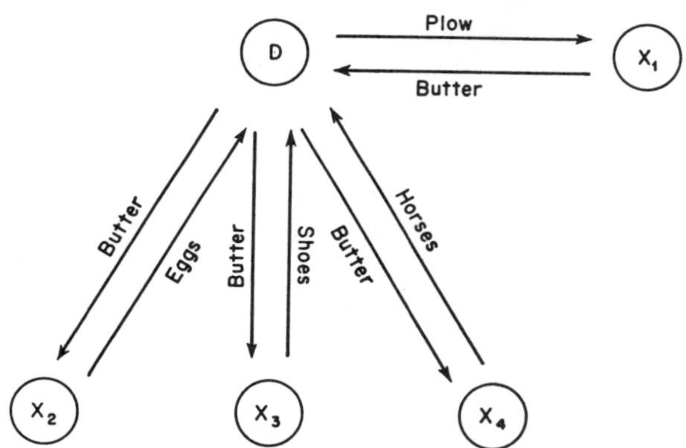

FIG. 31. EFFECT OF EXCHANGING A LESS MARKETABLE FOR A MORE MARKETABLE COMMODITY

Just as it is fundamental to human experience that there is great variety in resources, goods desired, and human skills, so is there great variety in the marketability of various commodities. Tending to increase the marketability of a commodity are its demand for use by more people, its divisibility into small units without loss of value, its durability, and its transportability over large distances. It is evident that people can vastly increase the extent of the market for their own products and goods by exchanging them for more marketable commodities and using the latter as media to exchange for goods that they desire. Thus, the pattern of D's, the plow-producer's, exchanges will be as shown in Fig. 31.

D first exchanges his plow for X_1's butter, and then uses the butter to exchange for the various goods that he desires to use, with X_2 for eggs, X_3 for shoes, X_4 for horses, etc.

As the more marketable commodities in any society begin to be picked by individuals as media of exchange, their choices will quickly focus on the few *most marketable* commodities available. If D saw, for example, that eggs were a more marketable commodity than butter, he would exchange his plow for eggs instead and use them as his medium in other exchanges. It is evident that, as the individuals center on a few selected commodities as the media of exchange, the demand for these commodities on the market greatly increases. For commodities, in so far as they are used as media, have an additional component in the demand for them—not only the demand for their direct use, but also a demand for their use as a medium of indirect exchange. This demand for their use as a medium is superimposed on the demand for their direct use, and this increase in the composite demand for the selected media *greatly increases their marketability*. Thus, if butter begins as one of the most marketable commodities and is therefore more and more chosen as a medium, this increase in the market demand for butter greatly increases the very marketability that makes it useful as a medium in the first place. The process is cumulative, with the most marketable commodities becoming enormously more marketable and with this increase spurring their use as media of exchange. The process continues, with an ever-widening gap between the marketability of the medium and the other commodities, until finally one or two commodities are far more marketable than any others and are in general use as media of exchange.[3]

Economic analysis is not concerned about *which* commodities are chosen as media of exchange. That is subject matter for economic *history*. The economic analysis of indirect exchange holds true regardless of the type of commodity used as a medium in any particular community. Historically, many different commodities have been in common use as media. The people in each community tended to choose the most marketable commodity available: tobacco in colonial Virginia, sugar in the West Indies, salt in Abyssinia, cattle in ancient Greece, nails in Scotland, copper in ancient Egypt, and many others, including beads, tea, cowrie shells, and fishhooks.[4] Through the centuries, gold and silver (specie) have gradually evolved as the commodities most widely used as media of exchange. Among the factors in their high marketability have been their great demand as ornaments, their scarcity in relation to other commodities, their ready divisibility, and their great durability. In the last few hundred years their marketable qualities have led to their general adoption as media throughout the world.

A commodity that comes into *general use* as a medium of exchange is defined as being a *money*. It is evident that, whereas the concept of a "medium of exchange" is a precise one, and indirect exchange can be distinctly separated from direct exchange, the concept of "money" is a less precise one. The point at which a medium of exchange comes into "common" or "general" use is not strictly definable, and whether or not a medium is a money can be decided only by historical inquiry and the judgment of the historian. However, for purposes of simplification, and since we have seen that there is a great impetus on the market for a medium of exchange to become money, we shall henceforth refer to all media of exchange as *moneys*.

3. *Some Implications of the Emergence of Money*

The establishment of a money on the market enormously increases the scope for specialization and division of labor, immensely widens the market for every product, and makes possible a society on a civilized productive level. Not only are the problems of coincidence of wants and indivisibility of goods eliminated, but individuals can now construct an ever-expanding edifice of remote stages of production to arrive at desired goods. Intricate and remote stages of production are now possible, and specialization can extend to every part of a production process as well as to the type of good produced. Thus, an automobile producer can sell an automobile in exchange for the money, e.g., butter or gold, and then exchange the gold partly for labor, partly for steel, partly for chrome, partly for rubber tires, etc. The steel producers can exchange the gold partly for labor, partly for iron, partly for machines, etc. Then the various laborers, landowners, etc., who receive the gold in the production process can use it as a medium to purchase eggs, automobiles, or clothing, as they desire.

The whole pattern of a modern society is thus built on the use of money, and the enormous importance of the use of money will become clearer as the analysis continues.[5] It is evident that it is a mistake on the part of many writers who wish to set forth the doctrines of modern economics to analyze direct exchange only and then to insert money somewhere at the end of the analysis, considering the task finished. On the contrary, the analysis of direct exchange is useful only as an introductory aid to the analysis of a society of indirect exchange; direct exchange would leave very little scope for the market or for production.

With the great variety in human skills and natural resources resulting in enormous advantages from the division of labor, the existence of money permits the splitting of production into minute branches, each man selling his product for money and using money to buy the products that he desires. In the field of consumers' goods, a doctor can sell his services, or a teacher his, for money, and then use the money to purchase goods that he demands. In production, a man can produce a capital good, sell it for money, and use the gold received to purchase the labor, land, and capital goods of a higher order needed for its production. He may use the surplus of money income over money outlay on factors to purchase consumers' goods for his own needs. Thus, at any stage in the production of any product, a man employs land and labor factors, exchanging money for their services as well as for the needed capital goods, and then sells the product for money to help in the next lower stage of production. This process continues until the final consumers' goods are sold to consumers. These consumers, on the other hand, obtain their money by *purchasing* it through the sale of their own goods—either durable consumers' goods or services in production. The latter may include the sale of labor services, the sale of services of their land, the sale of their capital goods, or inheritance from those who had previously contributed such services.[6]

Thus, nearly all exchanges are made against money, and money impresses its stamp upon the entire economic system. Producers of consumers' goods as well as owners of durable consumers' goods, owners of capital goods, and sellers of labor services, all sell their goods against money and purchase with money the factors that they need. They use their net money income to purchase consumers' goods produced by others in the society. Thus, all individuals, in their capacity as producers and owners, supply goods (commodities and services) and demand money in exchange. And, in their capacity as producers purchasing factors, as well as in their capacity as consumers, they supply money and demand an almost infinite variety of goods in exchange. The economy is therefore a "money economy," and almost all goods are compared with and exchanged against the money commodity. This fact is of crucial importance to the analysis of any society beyond the most primitive level. We may sum up the complex pattern of exchanges in a money economy in the following way:

Men in their capacity as:

Producers

Sell:	*Buy:*
Consumers' Goods,	*Producers' Goods*
Producers' Goods	Labor
Labor	Land
Land	Capital Goods
Capital Goods	
For Money	*With Money*

Consumers

	Buy:
	Consumers' Goods
	With Money

---

4. *The Monetary Unit*

We have seen that every good is "in supply" if it can be divided into units, each of which is homogeneous with every other. Goods can be bought and sold only in terms of such units, and those goods which are indivisible and unique may be described as being in a supply of one unit only. Tangible commodities are generally traded in terms of *units of weight,* such as tons, pounds, ounces, grains, grams, etc. The money commodity is no exception to this rule. The most universally traded commodity in the community, it is bought and sold always in terms of units of its weight. It is characteristic of units of weight, as of other metrical scales, that each unit is convertible into every other. Thus, one pound equals 16 ounces; and one ounce equals 437.5 grains or 28.35 grams. Therefore, if Jones sells his tractor for 15 pounds of gold, he may also be described as having sold the tractor for 240 ounces of gold, or for 6,804 grams of gold, etc.

It is clear that the size of the unit of the money commodity chosen for any transaction is irrelevant for economic analysis and is purely a matter of convenience for the various parties. All the units will be units of weight, and they will be convertible into pounds, ounces, etc., by multiplying or dividing by some constant number, and therefore will all be convertible into one another in the same manner. Thus, one pound of gold will equal 16 ounces and will, of course, exchange for 16 ounces, should such an exchange be desired on the market. The economic irrelevance of the names or sizes of the units may be seen from the following example. Suppose that the residents of Texas use, in their exchanges, a unit known as the Houston, equalling 20 grains of gold, while the residents of Massachusetts use the Adams, equalling 10 grains. The citizens of the respective areas may make their exchanges and calculations in these terms, e.g., Jones sells his car for "2,000 Houstons of gold," or, more simply, "2,000 Houstons," or Jones might consider the money price of eggs as being "½ Houston per dozen." On the other hand, Smith might buy a house for "10,000 Adamses." It is obvious that the use of the different names will complicate matters but is economically *insignificant.* The "Houston" is still a unit of weight of gold, and is a shorthand name for "20 grains of gold." It is clear that, on the market, 1 Houston will exchange for 2 Adamses.[7]

To avoid unnecessary complications and to clarify the analysis, therefore, the names of the monetary units in this work will be in terms of universally acceptable units of weight (such as ounces, grams, etc.) rather than in terms of accidental names of only local significance (such as dollars or francs).

Obviously, the more valuable the units of a commodity are, the smaller the size of the units used in daily transactions; thus, platinum will be traded in terms of ounces, while iron is traded in terms of tons. Relatively valuable money commodities like gold and silver will tend to be traded in terms of smaller units of weight. Here again, this fact has no particular economic significance.

The *form* in which a unit weight of any commodity is traded depends on its usefulness for any specific, desired purpose. Thus, iron may be sold in the form of bars or chunks, cheese in rectangular or triangular shape, etc. Whereas other commodities will be traded in those forms suitable for production or consumption, money will be traded in forms suitable for exchange or storing until an exchange is made. Historically, the shapes of money have been innumerable.[8] In recent centuries large bars of gold or silver have been used for storage or for exchange in larger transactions, while smaller, circular pieces, known as *coins,* are used for smaller transactions.

5. *Money Income and Money Expenditures*

In a money economy, each individual sells goods and services that he owns for money and uses the money to buy desired goods. Each person may make a record of such monetary exchanges for any period of time. Such a record may be called his *balance of payments* for that period.

One record may be the transactions of goods sold for money in a certain period to other individuals. Suppose, for example, that Mr. Brown draws up the record of goods sold for money for the month of September, 1961. Suppose that he has sold his services as a carpenter to a Mr. Jones in building the latter's house and has sold his services also as a handyman to Messrs. Jones and Smith during the same period. Also, he has disposed of an old radio to Mr. Johnson. His account of money received, i.e., money *purchased* for goods and services *sold,* is as follows:

September, 1961—James Brown

Money Purchased	*For Goods and Services Sold*
20 ounces of gold	Labor as Carpenter to Jones
5 ounces of gold	Labor as Handyman to Jones & Smith
1 ounce of gold	Old Radio to Johnson
26 ounces of gold	

From the account, we know that by his sales of goods and services during this period, Brown has purchased 26 ounces of gold. This total of money purchased is his total of *money income* for that period.

It is clear that the more money income a man receives during any period, the more money he will be able to spend on desired goods. *Other things being equal* (an important qualification that will be examined in later sections), *he will strive to earn as much money income in any prospective period as he can.*

Mr. Brown acquired his income by selling his labor services and a durable consumers' good. There are other ways of acquiring money income on an unhampered market. The owner of land may sell it for agricultural, locational, or industrial, as well as other, purposes. The owner of capital goods may sell them to those interested in using them as factors of production. Tangible land and capital goods may be sold for money outright, or the owner may retain ownership of the good while selling ownership of its *services* over a certain period of time. Since any good is bought only for the services that it can bestow, there is no reason why a certain period of service of a good may not be purchased. This can be done, of course, only where it is technically possible. Thus, the owner of a plot of land or of a sewing machine or of a house may "rent it out" for a certain period of time in exchange for money. While such *hire* may leave legal ownership of the good in the hands of the "landlord," the actual owner of the good's service *for that period* is the renter, or "tenant." At the end of the hire period, the good is returned to the original owner, who may use or sell the remainder of the services.

In addition to the sale of goods and services, a man may receive money as a gift. A man does not *purchase* the money he receives in gifts. His money income for any period equals his money purchased, plus the money he receives in gifts. (One common form of receipt of gift is an inheritance, the result of a bequest at death.)

Thus, Mr. Green's account of money income for June to December, 1961, may be as follows:

Money Income		*From Sale of Goods and Services*
	28 ounces of gold	Rent of Land to Mr. Jones
PURCHASED	300 ounces of gold	Sale of (other) Land to Mr. Forrest
	15 ounces of gold	Sale of a Threshing Machine to Mr. Woods
		From Gifts
GIVEN	400 ounces of gold	Inheritance from Uncle
	753 ounces of gold	

As was seen in the previous chapter, in order first to acquire the good or service that a man can sell for money, he must first either produce it himself or buy it from someone who has produced it (or who, in turn, has bought it from the original producer). If he has been given money, the original owner must have acquired it through producing a good, etc. Thus, in the last analysis, the first seller of a capital good or a durable consumers' good is the original producer, and later purchasers must have produced some service of their own in order to obtain the money to acquire it. The seller of labor service, of course, produces the service directly at the time. The seller of pure land must originally have appropriated unused land which he had found and transformed. On the unhampered market of a money economy, producers of commodities and services sell their goods for the money commodity, then use the money acquired to buy other desired goods.

Money is acquired in this way by all except the producers of the original gold on the market—those who mined and marketed it. However, the production of the money commodity, as with all other valuable commodities, itself requires the use of land, labor, and capital goods, and these must be paid for by the use of money. The gold miner, then, receives no money by gift, but must actively find and produce gold to acquire his money.

With the use of money acquired in these various ways, individuals purchase desired goods. They do so in two capacities: as consumers and as producers. As consumers, they purchase consumers' goods that they desire; in the case of durable goods, they may purchase the entire good, or they may hire the services of goods for some specified period of time. As producers, they use money to purchase the services of factors of production needed to produce consumers' goods or lower-order capital goods. Some factors they may purchase outright, to use *all* their anticipated future services; some they may hire for their services for a specified period of time. Thus, they may purchase capital goods that function as "raw material"; they may purchase some capital goods called "machines" and hire others; they may hire or purchase the land that they need to work on. In general, just as consumers cannot very well hire short-lived, nondurable goods, so producers cannot very well hire capital goods, dubbed "raw material" or "inventory," that are used up quickly in the process of production. On a free market, they cannot purchase labor services outright, as was explained in the preceding chapter. Since man's personal will is inalienable, he cannot, in a voluntary society, be compelled to work for another against his present will, and therefore no contracts can be made for purchase of his future will. Labor services, therefore, can only be bought for "hire," on a "pay-as-you-go" basis.

Any individual may draw up an account of his purchases of other goods with money for any period of time. The total amount of money given up in such exchanges is his *money expenditures* or *money outlays* for that period. Here it must be noted that his expenditure account, as well as his income account, can be itemized for each transaction or may be grouped into various classes.

Thus, in Brown's account above, he might have tabulated his income as 25 ounces from labor in general, and 1 ounce from his radio. How broad or narrow the classes are depends purely on the convenience of the person drawing up the account. The total, of course, is always unaffected by the type of classification chosen.

Just as money income equaled *money purchased* for goods and services sold *plus* money received as gifts, so money expenditure equals *money sold* for goods and services bought *plus* money given away as gifts. Thus, Mr. Brown's money expenditure account for September, 1961, might be the following:

September 1961—James Brown
Money Expended

Money Sold	*For Goods and Services Bought*
12 ounces of gold	Food
6 ounces of gold	Clothing
3 ounces of gold	Rent of House
2 ounces of gold	Entertainment
Money Given	
1 ounce of gold	Charity
24 ounces of gold	

In this account, Brown is spending money purely as a *consumer,* and his total money expenditures for the period are 24 ounces. If he had desired it, he could have subdivided the account further into such items as apples, 1/5 ounce; hat, 1 ounce, etc.

Here it may be noted that an individual's total money income for any period may be termed his *exports,* and the goods sold may be termed the "goods exported"; on the other hand, his total money expenditure may be termed his *imports,* and the goods and services bought are the "goods imported." These terms apply to goods purchased by producers or consumers.

Now, let us observe and compare Mr. Brown's income and expenditure accounts for September, 1961. Brown's total money income was 26 ounces of gold, his money expenditures 24 ounces. This must mean that 2 ounces of the 26 earned in this period *remained unspent.* These 2 ounces remain in the possession of Mr. Brown, and are therefore added to whatever previous stock of gold Brown might have possessed. If Brown's stock of money on September 1, 1961, was 6 ounces of gold, his stock of money on October 1, 1961, is 8 ounces of gold. The stock of money owned by any person at any point in time is called his *cash holding* or *cash balance* at that time. The 2 ounces of income remaining unspent on goods and services constituted a *net* addition to Brown's cash balance over the month of September. For any period, therefore, a person's money income is equal to his money outlay plus his addition to cash balance.

If we subdivide this income-expenditure account into smaller periods of time, the picture of what is happening to the cash balance within the larger period is likely to be far different from a simple addition of 2 ounces. Thus, suppose that all of Brown's money income came in two chunks on the first and the fifteenth of September, while his expenditures occurred every day in varying amounts. As a result, his cash balance rose drastically on September 1, say to 6 plus 13 or a total of 19 ounces. Then, the cash balance was gradually drawn down each day until it equaled 6 again on the 15th; then it rose sharply again to 19, finally being reduced to 8 at the month's end.

The pattern of Brown's supplies and demands on the market is clear. Brown *supplied* various goods and services on the market and *demanded* money in exchange. With this money income, he *demanded* various goods and services on the market and supplied money in exchange. The money *must go into the cash balance* before it can be spent on goods and services.[9]

Suppose, on the other hand, that Brown's expenditures for September had been 29 ounces instead of 24 ounces. This was accomplished by drawing down Brown's previous cash balance by 3 ounces and leaving him with 3 ounces in his cash holding. In this case, his money expenditures for the period equaled his money income *plus* the decrease in his cash balance. In sum, the following formula always holds true for any individual over any period of time:

Money Income = Money Expenditures + Net Additions to Cash Balance − Net Subtractions from Cash Balance

Alternatively, the term Exports can be substituted for Income, and Imports for Expenditures, in the above equation.

Let us assume for purposes of simplification that the total stock of the money commodity in the community has remained unchanged over the period. (This is not an unrealistic assumption, since newly mined gold is small compared to the existing stock.) Now it is obvious that, like all valuable property, all money must, at any point in time, be owned by *someone*. At any point in time, the sum of the cash holdings of all individuals is equal to the total *stock* of money in the community. Thus, if we consider Brown among a *group* of five persons living in a village, and their respective cash balances on September 1 were: 6, 8, 3, 12, and 5 ounces, then the total stock of money held in the village on that date was 34 ounces. If the data were available, the same sort of summation could be performed for the world as a whole, and the total stock of money discovered. *Now it is obvious that Brown's addition of 2 ounces to his cash balance for September must have been counterbalanced by a subtraction of 2 ounces from the cash balances of one or more other individuals.* Since the stock of money has not changed, Brown's addition to his cash balance must have been acquired by drawing down the cash balances of other individuals. Similarly, if Brown had drawn down his cash balance by 3 ounces, this must have been counterbalanced by the addition of 3 ounces to the cash balance of one or more individuals.

It is important to recognize that the additions to, or subtractions from, a cash balance are all voluntary acts on the part of the individuals concerned. In each period, some individuals decide to add to their cash balances, and others decide to reduce them, and each makes that decision which he believes will benefit him most.[10] For centuries, however, fallacious popular usage has asserted that one whose income is greater than expenditures (exports greater than imports) has a "favorable balance of trade," while one whose expenditures have been greater than income for a period (imports greater than exports) has suffered an "unfavorable balance of trade." Such a view implies that the active, important part of the balance of payments is the "trade" part, the exports and imports, and that the changes in the individual's cash balance are simply passive "balancing factors," serving to keep the total payments always in balance. In other words, it assumes that the individual spends as much as he wants to on goods and services and that the addition or subtraction from his cash balance appears as an afterthought. On the contrary, changes in cash balance are actively decided upon by each individual in the course of his market actions. Thus, Brown decided to increase his cash balance by 2 ounces and sold his labor services to obtain the money, forgoing purchases of consumers' goods to the extent of 2 ounces. Conversely, in the later example, when he spent 3 ounces more than he earned in the month, he decided that his cash balance had been excessive and that he would rather spend some of it on consumers' goods and services. *There is therefore never a need for anyone to worry about anyone else's balance of payments.* A person's "unfavorable" balance of trade will continue so long as the individual wishes to reduce his cash balance (and others are willing to purchase his money for goods). His maximum limit is, of course, the point when his cash balance is reduced to zero. Most likely, however, he will stop reducing his cash balance long before this point.[11]

6. *Producers' Expenditures*

The previous section concentrated on the case of Mr. Brown, whose entire money expenditures were on *consumers'* goods. His money income, aside from the sale of old, previously produced goods, came from the sale of current productive labor services. His expenditures were purely on consumption; his income was derived almost solely from his production of labor services. Every man must be a consumer, and therefore this analysis of consumer spending applies to all persons. Most people earn their income from the sale of their labor services. However, if we except previously produced goods, because someone must have originally produced them, all other money incomes must derive from new production of capital goods or consumers' goods. (This is apart from the sellers of land or its services, whose ownership must have originally derived from the finding and reshaping of unappropriated land.)

Producers of capital goods and consumers' goods are in a different position from sellers of labor service only. Mr. Brown, for example, a seller solely of labor service, need not spend any money on purchasing capital goods. Purely from his expenditure on desired consumers' goods, he derives the energy to be able to produce and sell labor services on the market. But the producers of capital goods and consumers' goods—the nub of any civilized society, since labor services alone could produce very little—are not and cannot be in such a fortunate position. For a man to produce a consumers' good, he must obtain labor services and the services of land and capital goods, in order to use the technological "know-how" available in the production of the good. Pushing the problem back, we find that, in order to produce a capital good, the would-be producer must obtain the necessary land, labor, and capital goods. Each such individual producer (or group of individuals in partnership) obtains the required factors and then directs the combination of factors into producing a capital good. This process is repeated among numerous individuals, until the lowest stage of production is reached and a consumers' good is produced. The producer of the capital good must obtain the needed factors (land, labor, and capital) by purchasing them for money, and, when the (lower-order) capital good is completed, he sells it for money. This capital good is, in turn, used for the production of a still lower-order capital good, and the latter is sold for money. This process continues until the final producer of the consumers' good sells it for money to the ultimate consumer.

A simplified schematic representation of this process is shown in Fig. 32.

The solid arrows depict the movement of *goods* in exchange, as factors are bought by the producers at each stage, worked into a lower-order capital good, and then sold to lower-order producers. The broken arrows in the reverse direction depict the movement of *money* in the same exchanges. The producer of a capital good

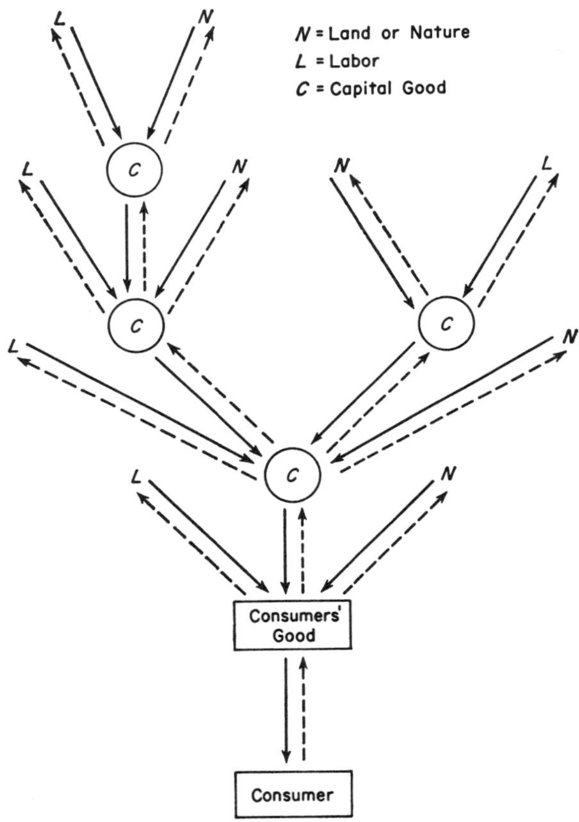

Fig. 32. Stages in the Process of Production for the Ultimate Consumer

employed money that he owned to purchase factors of production. He then used these owned factors, along with hired labor services, to produce a lower-order capital good that he owned until he could sell it for money to another producer. The producer of a consumers' good went through the same process, except that his final sale for money was to the ultimate consumer.

Now let us call those producers who use their money to *invest* in the purchase of factors (either outright or for hire) *capitalists.* The capitalists then produce and own the various stages of capital goods, exchanging them for money until their products reach the consumers. Those who participate in the productive process are therefore the capitalists and the sellers of land and labor services. The capitalists are the only ones who *spend money on producers' goods,* and they, therefore, may here be termed "the producers."

It is evident that a dominant characteristic of the production process is that each individual must produce *in anticipation* of the sale of his product. Any investment in production is made in anticipation of later sale to lower-order producers and, finally, to consumers.

Clearly, the consumer must have money in his cash balance in order to spend it on consumers' goods, and, likewise, the producer must have the original money to invest in factors. Where does the consumer get the money? As has been shown above, he may obtain it from gifts or from the sale of previously produced goods, but in the last analysis he must have obtained it from the sale of some productive service. The reader can inspect the final destinations of the broken arrows; these are the sellers of labor services and of the services of land. These laborers and landowners use the money thus obtained to buy the final products of the production system. The capitalist-producers also receive income at each stage of the production process. Evidently, the principles regulating these incomes require careful investigation, which will be undertaken below. Here it might be noted that the net incomes accruing to the owners of capital goods are not simply the result of the contribution to production by the capital goods, since these capital goods are in turn the products of other factors.

Where, then, do the *producers* acquire their money for investment? Clearly, from the same sources only. From the income acquired in production, individuals can, in addition to buying consumers' goods, purchase factors of production and engage in the productive process as producers of a good that is not simply their own labor service. In order to obtain the money for investment, then, an individual must *save money* by restricting his possible consumption expenditures. This saved money first goes into his cash balance and then is *invested* in the purchase of factors in the anticipation of a later sale of the produced good. It is obvious that investment can come only from funds that are saved by individuals from their possible consumption spending. The producers restrict their consumption expenditures, save their money, and "go into business" by investing their funds in factors that will yield them products in the future.[12]

Thus, while every man must spend part of his money income in consumption, some decide to become producers of capital or consumers' goods and to save money to invest in the required factors. Every person's income may be spent on consumption, on investment in the production of goods, or on an addition to his cash balance. For any period, an individual's *Money Income = his Consumption Expenditures + Investment Expenditures + Additions to Cash Balance – Subtractions from Cash Balance.* (Investment expenditures may be defined as the sum of the money expenditures made in investment in factors of production.)

Let us take the hypothetical case of Mr. Fred Jones and his "balance of payments" for November, 1961. Suppose his income from various sources during this month is 50 ounces. He decides to spend, during the month, 18 ounces on consumers' goods; to add 2 ounces to his cash balance; and to invest the other 30 ounces in a "business" for the production of some good. It must be emphasized that this business can involve the production of any good at all; it could be a steel factory, a farm, or a retail shoe store. It could be for the purchase of wheat in one season of the year in anticipation of sale in another season. All of this is productive enterprise, since, in each instance, a good is produced, i.e., goods are moved a step forward in their progress to the ultimate consumer. Since the investment is always in anticipation of later sale, the investors are also engaged in *entrepreneurship,* in enterprise.

Let us assume that Jones expends the saved funds on investment in a paper factory. His income-expenditure account for November may appear as follows:

November, 1961—Fred Jones

Income		*Expenditures*	
From sale of land	20 oz.	Food	7 oz.
From sale of a building	30 oz.	Clothing	4 oz.
		Shelter	4 oz.
		Entertainment	3 oz.
	50 oz.	Consumption Expenditures	18 oz.
		On Paper Machinery	12 oz.
		On Wood Pulp	10 oz.
		On Labor Services	8 oz.
		Investment Expenditures	30 oz.
		Addition to Cash Balance	2 oz.
		Total	50 oz.

Of course, these figures are purely illustrative of a possible situation; there are innumerable other illustrations; e.g., there could have been a subtraction from cash balance to enable greater investment.

Investment expenditures are always made in anticipation of future sale. Factors are purchased, they are transformed into the product, and the product is then sold by the enterpriser for money. The "businessman" makes his outlays with the expectation of being able to sell the product at a certain price on a certain future date. Suppose that Jones makes the investment of 30 ounces with the expectation of being able to transform his factors into the product (in this case, paper) and sell the product for 40 ounces at some date in November, 1962. If his expectation proves correct, he will succeed in selling the paper for 40 ounces at that date, and his income account, for any period that includes that date in November, 1962, will include "40 ounces from sale of paper."

It is obvious that, other things being equal, an investor will attempt to acquire the greatest possible net income from his investment, just as, with the same qualification, everyone attempts to acquire the greatest income from other types of sales. If Jones is confronted with investment opportunities for his 30 ounces in different possible lines or processes of production, and he expects that one will net him 40 ounces in a year, another 37 ounces, and another 34, etc., Jones will choose that investment promising the greatest return. A crucial difference, then, between man as an entrepreneur and man as a consumer is that in the latter case there is no drive to have exports greater than imports. A man's imports are his purchase of consumers' goods and are therefore the ends of his activity. The goods he imports are a source of satisfaction to him. On the other hand, the businessman is "importing" only producers' goods, which by definition are useless to him directly. He can gain from them only by selling them or their product, and therefore his imports are merely the necessary means to his later "exports." Therefore, he tries to attain the greatest net income, or, in other words, to attain the largest surplus of exports over imports. The larger his business income, the more the owner of the business will be able to spend (i.e., to import) on consumers' goods that he desires.

It is clear, however, that the man, *considered as a whole,* has no particular desire to export more than he imports or to have a "favorable balance of trade." He tries to export more than he imports *of producers' goods* in his business; then he uses this surplus to spend on *imports of consumers' goods* for his personal wants. On total balance, he may, like Mr. Brown above, choose to add to his cash balance or subtract from his cash balance, as he sees fit and considers most desirable.[13] Let us take as an example Mr. Jones, after he has been established in his business. Over a certain period, he may decide to subtract 5 ounces from his cash balance. Even though he tries his best to achieve the largest net income from business and thus add to his cash balance as much as possible from *this source,* in total he may well decide to reduce his cash balance. Thus:

Fred Jones

Income		*Expenditures*	
From business . . .	150 oz.	In business, on factors of production (producers' goods) . .	100 oz.
		For consumers' goods	55 oz.
			155 oz.
		Subtraction from cash balance .	5 oz.

7. *Maximizing Income and Allocating Resources*

We have seen that, in the money economy, *other things being equal,* men will attempt to attain the highest possible money income: if they are investors, they will try to obtain the largest net return; if they sell their labor service, they will sell it for the largest return. The higher their money income, the more money they will have available for expenditure on consumers' goods. Before we proceed to a deeper analysis of the money economy, it is important to examine the "other things being equal," or the *ceteris paribus,* qualification.

In chapter 1, we examined the truth that in every action, men try to obtain the greatest advantage, i.e., to attain the end located on the highest possible point on their value scale. This was also called attempting to "maximize psychic revenue" or "psychic income." This is a praxeological truth, a general law holding for all human action, with no qualification whatsoever. Now the establishment of indirect exchange, or a money economy, enables every person to obtain a vast number of consumers' goods that he could not obtain, or could barely obtain, in isolation or by way of barter. As we have demonstrated in this chapter, these consumers' goods are acquired by producing and selling a good for the money commodity and then using money to purchase them. Despite this development, however, by no means all goods can be bought and sold on the market. Some goods are attainable in this way; some cannot be. As was explained in chapter 2, some goods cannot be alienated from a person and therefore cannot be exchanged. They cannot come within the money nexus; they cannot be bought or sold for money. This fact does not mean that individuals disparage or revere them on that account. To some people, many of the unexchangeable consumers' goods are very precious and hold a high place on their value scale. To others, these goods mean little, as compared to those consumers' goods that can be bought in exchange. The ranking on his value scale depends entirely on the voluntary choice of each individual. It is nonsense to place the blame on "money" for the tendencies of some people to value exchangeable goods highly as compared to some nonexchangeable goods. There is no force in the existence of the money economy that compels men to make such choices; money simply enables men to expand enormously their acquisition of exchangeable goods. But the existence of the market leaves it to each individual to decide how he will value money and the goods that money will buy, as against other goods that are unexchangeable.

As a matter of fact, the existence of the money economy has the reverse effect. Since, as we know from the law of utility, the marginal utility of a unit of any good diminishes as its supply increases, and the establishment of money leads to an enormous increase in the supply of exchangeable goods, it is evident that this great supply enables men to enjoy unexchangeable goods to a far greater extent than would otherwise be the case. *The very fact that exchangeable consumers' goods are more abundant enables each individual to enjoy more of the nonexchangeable ones.*

There are many possible examples of grading exchangeable and nonexchangeable goods on one's value scale. Suppose that a man owns a piece of land containing an historic monument, which he prizes on aesthetic grounds. Suppose also that he has an offer for sale of the property for a certain sum of money, knowing that the purchaser intends to destroy the monument and use it for other purposes. To decide whether or not to sell the property, he must weigh the value to him of keeping the monument intact as against the value to him of the consumers' goods that he could eventually buy with the money. Which will take precedence depends on the constitution of the individual's value scale at that particular time. But it is evident that a greater abundance of consumers' goods already at his disposal will tend to raise the value of the (unexchangeable) aesthetic good to him as compared with the given sum of money. Contrary, therefore, to the common accusation that the establishment of a money economy tends to lead men to slight the importance of nonexchangeable goods, the effect is precisely the reverse. A destitute person is far less likely to prefer the nonexchangeable to the exchangeable than one whose "standard of living" in terms of the latter is high.[14]

Examples such as these are of great importance for human action, but of little importance for the rest of this volume, which is mainly concerned with analysis of the market under a system of indirect exchange. In this study of money exchanges—the subdivision of praxeology known as *catallactics*—there is not much more that could be said about this problem. Other examples of such choices, however, are more important for catallactics. Consider the case of a man who has three offers for the purchase of his labor services, one of a money income of 30 ounces per month, another of 24 ounces, and a third of 21 ounces. Now—and here we return to the original problem of this section—the man will clearly choose to accept the offer of 30 ounces, *provided* that the psychic, or more precisely, the nonexchangeable, factors are "equal" between the various alternatives. If the man is indifferent to any variations in conditions of work among the three offers, then no factors enter into his choice except money income and leisure, and, if he works at all, he will choose the income of 30 ounces. On the other hand, he may well have great differences in taste for the work itself and the varying conditions; thus, the job earning 30 ounces may be for a firm, or in a type of labor, which he dislikes. Or the job offering 24 ounces may have positive qualities that the man likes a great deal. We have seen in chapter 1 that labor is evaluated on the basis, not only of the monetary return, but also in terms of the individual's liking for or dislike of the work itself. The valuations that a man attaches to the work itself are nonexchangeable positive or negative goods, because they are, for the actor, inseparable attachments to the work itself. They may be weighed against monetary considerations, but they cannot be exchanged away or ignored. Thus, in the above case, along with the prospective money income, the man must weigh the nonexchangeable "consumers' goods" attached to the different jobs in his value scale. What he is weighing, in essence, is two "bundles" of utility: (*a*) the utility of 30 ounces per month plus work in what he considers an immoral trade or in unpleasant surroundings, vs. (*b*) the utility of 24 ounces per month plus work in a job which he likes. The choice will be made in accordance with the value scale of each individual; one man may choose the 30-ounce job, and another may choose the 24-ounce job. The important fact for catallactics is that a man always chooses a bundle of *money income plus other psychic factors* and that he will maximize his money income only if psychic factors are neutral with respect to his choices. If they are not, then these factors must always be kept in view by the economist.

Another similar example is the case of a prospective investor. Suppose that an investor faces the choice of investing his saved money in various alternative production projects. He can, say, invest 100 ounces, with the prospect of earning a net return of 10% in a year, in one project; 8% in a second; and 6% in a third. Other nonexchangeable psychic factors being equal, he will tend to invest in that line where he expects the greatest net money return—in this case, the 10% line. Suppose, however, that he has a great dislike for the product that would offer a 10% return, while he has a great fondness for the process and the product promising the 8% return. Here again, each prospect of investment carries with it a nondetachable positive or negative psychic factor. The pleasure in producing one product as against the distaste for producing another are *nonexchangeable consumers' goods,* positive and negative, which the actor has to weigh in deciding where to make his investment. He will weigh not simply 10% vs. 8%, but "10% plus a disliked production process and product" vs. "8% plus a delightful production process." Which alternative he chooses depends on his individual value scale. Thus, in the case of enterprise as well as in the case of labor, we must say that the entrepreneur will tend to choose the course that maximizes his prospective money income, *provided* that other nonexchangeable factors are neutral with respect to the various alternatives. In all cases whatsoever, of course, each man will move to maximize the *psychic* income on his value scale, on which scale all exchangeable and unexchangeable goods are entered.[15]

In deciding on the course that will maximize his psychic income, man therefore considers all the relevant factors, exchangeable and nonexchangeable. In considering whether to work and at what job, he must also consider the almost universally desired consumers' good, leisure. Suppose that, on the basis of the money return and the nonexchangeable values attached, the laborer in the example given above chooses to work at the 24-ounce job. As he continues to work at the job, the marginal utility of the money wage per unit of time that he earns (whether it be 24 ounces per month or ¼ ounce per hour, etc.), will decline. The marginal utility of money income will tend to decline as more money is acquired, since money is a good. In so far as money is desired for a nonmonetary use (such as ornaments) or for use as an addition to one's cash balance (see below for a discussion of the components in the demand for money), addition to its stock will lead to a decline in its marginal utility just as in the case of any other good. In so far as money is desired for the purchase of consumers' goods, an "ounce-worth" of consumers' goods will also decline in utility as new ounces are acquired. The first ounce of money spent on consumers' goods will fulfill the highest-ranking wants on the person's value scale, the next ounce spent the wants ranking second highest, etc. (Of course, this will not be true for a good costing more than one ounce, but this difficulty can be met by increasing the size of the monetary units so that each is homogeneous in what it can buy.) Consequently, the marginal utility of money income tends to decline as the income is increased.

On the other hand, as the input of labor increases, the stock of possible units of leisure declines, and the marginal utility of leisure forgone increases. As was seen in chapter 1, labor will tend to be supplied until the point at which the marginal utility reaped from labor no longer outweighs the marginal utility of leisure on the individual's value scale. In the money economy, labor will cease when the marginal utility of the additional money income per unit of time no longer exceeds the marginal utility of the leisure forgone by working for the additional time.[16]

Thus, man allocates his time between leisure and productive labor, between labor for money and labor on unexchangeable items, etc., in accordance with the principle of maximizing his psychic income. In deciding between labor and leisure, he weighs the marginal advantages of work with the marginal advantages of leisure.

Similarly, man as a prospective investor must weigh, not only the advantages and disadvantages, monetary and otherwise, from each prospective investment, but also whether or not to invest at all. *Every man must allocate his money resources in three and only three ways: in consumption spending, in investment expenditure, and in addition to his cash balance.* Assume that to the investor cited above, the 10% project is highest in utility in his value scale, all factors considered. But then he must decide: Shall he invest at all, or shall he buy consumers' goods now, or add to his cash balance? The marginal advantage of making the investment will be the prospective money return, weighted by the nonexchangeable utilities or disutilities involved. The advantage of a money return will be that he will have more money, in the future, that he could spend on consumers' goods. If he has 100 ounces of money now and invests it, in a year he might have 110 ounces which he could spend on consumers' goods. On the other hand, what chiefly militates against investment, as was explained in chapter 1, is the fact of time preference, the fact that he is giving up possible consumption *in the present*. If we assume that an ounce of money will buy the same quantity of goods as an ounce a year from now (an assumption that will be removed in later chapters), then one ounce of money now will always be worth *more* than one ounce a year from now, simply because enjoyment *of a given good* is always preferred as early as possible. Therefore, in deciding whether or not to invest, he must balance the *additional* return against his desire to consume in the present rather than the future. He must decide: if I value 100 ounces now more than 100 ounces a year from now, do I value 100 ounces now more or less than *110* ounces a year from now? He will decide in accordance with his value scale. Similarly, he must weigh each against the marginal utility of adding to his cash balance (in what this consists will be examined below).

Thus, every unit of the money commodity in a man's stock (his money resources owned) is always being allocated to the three categories of use in accordance with his value scale. The more money that he allocates to consumption, the lower will be the marginal utility of the goods consumed. Each further unit spent will be devoted to less urgently desired goods. And each further unit so spent will decrease his available stock of investment goods and his available cash balance, and therefore will, in accordance with the law of utility, raise the marginal utility forgone in each of these uses. The same will be true for each of the other uses; the more money he spends on each use, the less will be the marginal utility from that use, and the higher will be the marginal utility of other uses forgone. Every man will allocate his money resources on the same principles that the hypothetical actor allocated his stock of horses in chapter 1 above; each unit will be used for the most useful end not yet achieved. It is in accordance with these principles—the maximizing of his psychic income—that each man will allocate his money stock. In accordance with his value scale, each man will judge the respective marginal utilities to be obtained by each monetary unit in each use, and his allocation of money expenditures as revealed in his balance of payments will be determined by such judgments.

Just as, within the general category of investment expenditure, there are different projects with different expected returns, so there are an innumerable variety of consumers' goods within the general category of consumption. On what principles does a man allocate his expenditures among the numerous types of consumers' goods available? On precisely corresponding principles. His first unit of money spent on consumers' goods will be spent on that good satisfying the most highly valued end, the next unit on the next most highly valued end, etc. Each parcel of a consumers' good bought decreases the marginal utility of this good to the man and increases the marginal utility of all other goods forgone. Again, a man will allocate his money resources within the consumption category by apportioning each unit of money to that good with the highest marginal utility on his value scale. A judgment of relative marginal utilities determines the allocation of his money expenditures. It is evident that we may eliminate the words "within the consumption category" in the sentence before the preceding, to arrive at the rule which governs all a man's money allocation within and between categories.

Our analysis may now be generalized still further. Each man, at every point in time, has in his ownership a certain stock of useful goods, a certain stock of *resources,* or *assets.* These resources may include not only *money,* but also *consumers' goods, nonpersonal producers' goods* (land and capital goods), *personal energy,* and *time.* He will allocate *each one* of these resources according to the same principles by which he has allocated money—so that each unit goes into the use with the highest prospective marginal utility on his value scale.

Here we must note that the sale of personal labor service is not always made to an investing "employer" who purchases the labor service for money and then tries to sell the resulting product. In many cases, the man who invests also works directly in the production of the product. In some cases, the investor spends saved funds on factors of production and hires the labor of someone to direct the actual production operation. In other cases, the investor also spends his labor-time in the details of the production process. It is clear that this is just as much "labor" as the labor of an employee who does not own and sell the product.

What principles will decide whether a prospective investor uses his labor in his own investment in production (i.e., will be "self-employed") or will invest only his money and sell his labor elsewhere as an employee? Clearly, the principle again will be the best psychic advantage from the action. Thus, suppose that Jones finds what he considers to be the best and most remunerative investment project, which he estimates will yield him a net money income of 150 ounces for the forthcoming year, provided that he does not labor on the project itself, but hires others for its direction and management. He also estimates that, if he were to perform the direction himself instead of hiring a manager to do it, he would be able to net a further income from the project of 50 ounces a year. With his own labor involved, then, the net income from the project will be 200 ounces for the year. This figure will be the higher, the more skilled his direction would be than the man he replaces, and the lower, the less comparatively skilled he is. In this case, the 200-ounce net income would include a 150-ounce investment income and 50 ounces for the labor income of direction. Whether or not he takes this course depends (setting leisure aside) on whether he can sell his labor service for a greater income elsewhere. This "greater income" will, of course, be in terms of psychic income, but, if nonexchangeable factors are assumed in this case to be neutral, then the "greater income" will be the greater money income. If, *ceteris paribus,* Jones can earn 60 ounces as an employee for some other investing producer, then he will take this job and hire someone else to use labor on his investment. His total money income will then be: 150 ounces from the project plus 60 ounces from the sale of his labor services to a producer, totaling 210 ounces. Of course, if nonexchangeable psychic factors countervail, such as a great preference for being self-employed in the use of his labor, then he may accept the 200-ounce income.

It is clear from this discussion that the common concept of the productive laborer, limited to the man who works in the fields or on an assembly line, is completely fallacious. Laborers are all those who expend their labor in the productive process. This labor is expended for a money income (which may be weighted by other psychic factors). If the labor service is sold to an investing employer who owns the final good produced by the co-operating factors, it might be rendered in any required task from that of a ditchdigger to that of a company president. On the other hand, labor income may be the result of the "self-employment" of the investing enterpriser. This type of laborer is also the owner of the final product, and his net monetary return from the sale of the product will include his labor income as well as his return from the money invested. The larger and more complex the enterprise and the production process, the greater will tend to be the development of specialized skill in management, and therefore the less will be the tendency for self-employment by the enterpriser. The smaller the enterprise, and the more direct the production methods, the more likely is self-employment to be the rule.

We have so far specifically treated the principles of allocating labor and money. The other exchangeable resources that a man may possess (and it is the *exchangeable* resources that catallactics is interested in) are consumers' goods and nonpersonal producers' goods (land and capital goods).

The consumers' goods in a man's stock are the *durable* ones. The nondurable goods and services will have disappeared in the process of consuming them. Now, as we have seen in chapter 2, any good may have either *direct use-value* to its owner or *exchange-value* or a mixture of both. At any time, each owner of a consumers' good must judge on his value scale whether its exchange-value or its highest direct use-value is the greater. In the money economy, the problem of exchange-value is simplified, since it will be exchange for *money* that will be especially important. The utility on his value scale of the highest direct use-value will be compared to the utility of the sum of money the good could procure in exchange. Suppose, for example, that Mr. Williams owns a house; he determines that he could sell the house for 200 ounces of gold. Now he judges the ranking of the direct use as against the exchange-value on his value scale. Thus, he might have three alternative direct uses for the house (*a*) living in it; (*b*) living in it part of the time and letting his brother live in it part of the time; (*c*) living in it part of the time, with no participation by his brother, and he may weigh each of these against the exchange-value as follows:

Williams' Value Scale

Ranking

1. Direct Use (*a*).
2. Exchanging good for 200 ounces of money.
3. Direct Use (*b*).
4. Direct Use (*c*).

In this case, Williams will decide to live in the house and not sell it. His decision will be determined solely by his value scale; someone else might rank the exchange above the direct use and therefore sell the house for money.

It is obvious that it is true, without qualification, for any *given good,* that the seller will try to obtain as high a money price for it as possible. The proof of this is analogous to the demonstration given in chapter 2 that the seller of a given good always tries to obtain the highest price, except that here the markets are simplified by being exchanges solely for *money,* and therefore it is the *money price* that is important. *The money income that a man will get from the sale of a good will always equal the money price of the sale times the quantity of units of the good.* Thus, if he sells one house at a money price of 200 ounces per house, his total money income from the good will be 200 ounces. His desire to sell at the highest price does not, of course, mean that he will *always* sell at that price. The highest money price for a good may still be lower than the psychic value of direct use to him, as was the case with Williams. It is possible, however, that if the money price for selling the house rose to 250 ounces, the exchange-value of the house would have ranked higher than Direct Use (*a*), and he would have sold the house.

It is clear that, if the owner of the consumers' good is also the original producer, the direct use-value to him will be almost nil. The specialized producer who produces and owns houses or television sets or washing machines finds that the direct use-value to him of this stock is practically nonexistent. For him, the exchange-value is the only important factor, and his interest lies *solely* in maximizing his money income from the stock and therefore in attaining the highest money prices in the sale of each good. The nonexchangeable factors that might loom large to the prospective investor or laborer in a certain line of production will be negligible to the producer who already has a stock of goods, since he had already taken the nonexchangeable factors into account when he made his original investment or his original choice of occupation. Thus, to the producer of a consumers' good, the way to maximize his psychic income from this revenue is to obtain the highest possible money price from its sale.

When will an owner sell the good, and when will he rent out its services? Clearly, he will take the course that he believes will yield him the highest money income, or, more precisely, the highest present value of money income.

What of the owner of a stock *of nonpersonal producers' goods?* How will he allocate these goods to attain the highest psychic income? In the first place, it is clear that, by definition, producers' goods can have no direct use-value to him as consumers' goods. But they may well have direct use-value *as producers' goods,* i.e., as factors of production in the making of a product further along in the process of being transformed into consumers' goods. For any given stock of a producers' good, or for any unit of that stock, there might be an exchange-value, a value in use for transformation into another product that would then have exchange-value, or both. It is also true for the owner of producers' goods that nonexchangeable factors will generally play a negligible role. The fact that he has already invested and perhaps worked in producing or purchasing these goods signifies that he has already accounted for the possible positive or negative psychic values in the work itself. Furthermore, in the economy of indirect exchange, it is only exchange of goods produced for money that is important, as there will be very little scope for barter. The owner of producers' goods is therefore interested in judging whether the goods will yield a higher money income from exchanging them directly for money or from transforming them via production into a product of "lower-order," and then selling the product for money.

As an example of the choices facing the owner of producers' goods, let us take Robertson. Robertson has invested in, and therefore owns, the following factors:

10 units of Producers' Good *X*
5 units of Producers' Good *Y*
6 units of Producers' Good *Z*

He knows, because of his technological knowledge, that he can transform these units of co-operating factors *X, Y,* and *Z,* into

10 units of a final product *P*. (The various "units," of course, are purely physical units of the various goods and are therefore completely incommensurable with one another.) He estimates that he will be able to sell these units of *P* for 15 ounces each, a total money income of *150 ounces.*

On the other hand, he sees that he could sell (or resell) the factors directly for money, without himself transforming them into *P*, as follows:

10 units of *X* @ 6 oz. of gold per unit (the money price of *X*) a money income from stock of *X* of	*60 ounces*
5 units of *Y* @ 9 oz. per unit, a money income of	*45 ounces*
6 units of *Z* @ 4 oz. per unit, a money income of	*24 ounces*

His total money income from the sale of the stock of each producers' good separately and directly is *129 ounces.* However, Robertson must also consider the money expenditures that he would have to make in buying labor services to help in this transformation. In a free economy, he cannot own a stock of laborers. If his expenditure on labor service is less than *21 ounces,* then it will pay him to transform the factors and sell the product *P* for 150 ounces; if the required expenditures on labor-service are more than 21 ounces, then it will pay him to sell the producers' goods directly for money.

In each one of these prospective sales, of course, it is to the owner's interest to be able to sell at the highest possible price, thus yielding the highest money income from each good.

Suppose, now, that Robertson had decided to go ahead with the production and that he now has in his stock 10 units of *P*. There is no prospect of his immediately going into the business that would make use of *P* as a factor in making another product. Therefore, there is only one alternative left to this owner—to sell the product for money, for the highest price that he can acquire. However, in those cases where *P* is durable, he still has the option of holding off the sale if he believes that its money price in the future will be higher, and provided that the higher price will cover the disadvantage to him of waiting (his time preference) and the expenses of storing P until the sale is made.

The owner of a producers' good, whether a product to him or a factor, may rent it out if he does not sell the entire good. In order for this to be feasible, of course, the good would have to be relatively durable. Here again, as in the case of a consumers' good, the owner will decide on outright sale of the good or hiring out of its services over a period of time in accordance with his judgment of which alternative will yield him the highest money income (precisely, the highest present value).

We have thus analyzed the actions of an owner of a stock of consumers' goods or of producers' goods in attempting to attain his most highly valued ends, i.e., to maximize his psychic income. Nonexchangeable factors for him will generally be negligible in importance, since they had already been discounted when the investment in them was made. If we set aside the value of the durable consumers' good in direct use for some owners, the aim of the owners will be to maximize their money income from the stock of the good. Since money income from sale of a good is the money price of the good multiplied by the quantity sold, this means that the sellers will try to attain the highest money price for their stock.

At this point we may, at least briefly, begin to answer the question which we did not have the information to answer in chapter 2: Granted the behavior of the owner of a given stock, what determines the *size* of that stock of goods? Now obviously, except in the case of personal energy, these goods must have been *previously produced by someone* (or previously found and transformed in the case of pure nature-given factors). This previous production was undertaken either by the present owner or by someone in the past, from whom he had acquired, by exchange or gift, this stock of goods. The past investment must have been made for the reason that we saw above: the expectation of a future money return from the investment, compensating for the sacrifice of waiting to consume in the future instead of the present. This previous investor expected that he would be able to sell the good for a money income greater than the money expenditures that he had to make on the factors of its production. As an example, let us take Robertson with a stock of ten units of *P*. How did he acquire this stock? By investing money in buying factors of its production, and then producing it, in the hope of making a certain net money income, i.e., in the expectation that the money income from the sale of *P* would be greater by a certain amount than the money expenditures invested in the various factors. Now how did the previously produced stock of the factors *X, Y,* and *Z* come into existence? By the same process. Various investors engaged in the production of these factors in the expectation of a net money income from the investment (total money income from the investment greater than total money expenditures). This investment decision accounts for the existence of all the stock of all producers' goods and durable consumers' goods for any community at any given point in time. In addition, the stock of pure nature-given factors was acquired through the owner's or some previous person's finding and using previously unused factors in a production process. The stock of the money commodity was, like that of the consumers' and producers' goods, the result of an investment decision by an investing producer, who expected his money income to be higher than his money expenditure. On the other hand, the stock of *personal energy* owned by any person is inherent in his nature as a human being.

We have thus analyzed each type of exchangeable resource that a person may have, what governs his use of them in order to maximize his psychic income, and to what extent such maximization involves attempted maximization of money income from the resource. In analyzing the determinants of the money income from any sale, we have seen that they are the quantity and the money price, and we have just seen how the quantities involved in the "given stock" of any good can be accounted for. What yet remains unaccounted for is the money prices. All we know about them so far is that the *seller* of any good—consumers' or producers' good or labor service—wishes to sell it for as *high a money price as possible.* Nonexchangeable goods on the owner's value scale may modify this rule, but generally these modifications will be important only for sellers of labor services.

We have so far been considering man as the allocator, or seller, of a given good. What of man as a *buyer* of a good? (And here we recall the discussion in the early parts of this chapter.) As a buyer, he uses money for investment expenditures and for consumption expenditures. In our discussion of an individual's consumption expenditures, we saw that he decided on them upon considering a "unit's worth" of goods. But what determines what his unit's worth shall be? What is an ounce of money's worth of eggs, or hats, or butter, etc.? This can be determined only by the *money price* that the buyer would have to pay for the good. If a man can buy eggs at $\frac{1}{10}$ of an ounce per dozen, then one ounce's worth of eggs is 10 dozen. Now it is obvious that man, in his capacity as a buyer of consumers' goods with money, will seek to buy each particular good at the *lowest money price possible*. For a man who owns money and seeks to buy consumers' goods, it is clear that the lower the money prices of the goods he seeks to buy, the *greater is his psychic income;* for the more goods he can buy, the more uses he can make with the same amount of his money. The buyer will therefore seek the lowest money prices for the goods he buys.

Thus, *ceteris paribus,* the psychic income of man as a seller for money is maximized by selling the good at the highest money price obtainable; the psychic income of man as a buyer with money is maximized by buying the good for the lowest money price obtainable.

Let us now sum up the results of the analysis of this chapter. We have seen how the common medium of exchange emerges in the market out of direct exchange; we have noted the pattern of exchanges with and for money in an economy of indirect exchange; we have described how each individual has a pattern of money income and money expenditures. Then, we investigated what is involved in the maximization of psychic income in a money economy, how this principle governs the actions of people in their various functions—as owners of different types of resources and as laborers or investors. We have seen to what extent such pursuit after the most highly valued ends involves the maximization of money income in the various cases, and to what extent it does not. We have just concluded that such maximization of psychic income always leads the seller of a good to seek the highest money price for it, and the buyer of a good to seek the lowest money price, with such exceptions as the laborer who spurns a higher money price for his labor because of the nonexchangeable conditions attached to the work, or the investor who spurns a greater prospective income for a line of production that he prefers for its own sake. These exceptions aside, pursuit of the rule: "Buy on the cheapest market and sell on the dearest" leads to satisfaction of the most highly valued ends for each individual, both as a consumer and as a producer.

Although we know that man tries to maximize his psychic income, and therefore his money income, *ceteris paribus,* we still do not know on what basis the money income that he does acquire is determined. We know that the nonexchangeable values are simply determined by the value scales of each individual. But though we know that, *ceteris paribus,* a man will sell a service or a good for a greater rather than a lesser money price and income, we do not yet know what makes the money prices what they are. What determines the money prices of consumers' goods, of labor services, of capital goods, of nature-given factors? What determines the money price of the entire durable good and the money price of the "hired-out" services? And, with the enormous importance of investment as the determinant of the given stock of every good, what determines the spread between gross money income from goods and the money expenditures on the factors needed to produce them? It is only the anticipation of this spread between money income from the sale of the product, and money expenditure on factors, that brings about investment and production. And what, if any, are the relations that tend to be established among the various prices?

To put it differently, all human action uses scarce resources to attempt to arrive at the most highly valued of not-yet-attained ends, i.e., to maximize psychic income. We have seen how this is done by individuals in isolation and by individuals in direct exchange—although these can exist only to a drastically limited extent. We have seen how it is done, on an immensely greater scale, in the money economy; and we have seen that the specific components of psychic maximization in the money economy are, ultimately, nonexchangeable values, quantities of goods in stock, and the money prices that these goods can exchange for on the market. We have explained the operations of the nonexchangeable values, and we have very briefly indicated how the quantity of the given stock of each good is determined. We have now to investigate the classic problem in the analysis of indirect exchange: *the determination of money prices.* The analysis of money prices, moreover, will enable investigation into the reasons for, and the determinants of, the "spread" between expected gross money income from sales and the expenditure on factors, which induces people to invest in the production of stock.

4

Prices and Consumption

1. *Money Prices*

We have seen the enormous importance of the money prices of goods in an economy of indirect exchange. The money income of the producer or laborer and the psychic income of the consumer depend on the configuration of these prices. How are they determined? In this investigation, we may draw extensively from almost all of the discussion in chapter 2 above. There we saw how the prices of one good in terms of others are determined under conditions of direct exchange. The reason for devoting so much consideration to a state of affairs that can have only a very limited existence was that a similar analysis can be applied to conditions of indirect exchange.

In a society of barter, the *markets* that established prices (assuming that the system could operate) were innumerable markets of one good for every other good. With the establishment of a money economy, the *number* of markets needed is immeasurably reduced. A large variety of goods exchange against the money commodity, and the money commodity exchanges for a large variety of goods. Every single market, then (with the exception of isolated instances of barter) includes the money commodity as one of the two elements.

Aside from loans and claims (which will be considered below), the following types of exchange are made against money:

Old Consumer Goods	against Money
New Consumer Goods and Services	against Money
Capital Goods	against Money
Labor Services	against Money
Land Factors	against Money

For durable goods, each unit may be sold *in toto,* or it may be hired out for its services over a certain period of time.

Now we remember from chapter 2 that the price of one good in terms of another is the amount of the other good divided by the amount of the first good in the exchange. If, in a certain exchange, 150 barrels of fish exchanged for 3 horses, then the price of horses in terms of fish, the "fish-price of horses," was 50 barrels of fish per horse in that exchange. Now suppose that, in a money economy, 3 horses exchange for 15 ounces of gold (money). The *money price* of horses in this exchange is *5 ounces per horse.* The money price of a good in an exchange, therefore, is the quantity of units of gold, divided by the quantity of units of the good, yielding a numerical ratio.

To illustrate how money prices may be computed for any exchange, suppose that the following exchanges are made:

15 ounces of gold for 3 horses
5 ounces of gold for 100 barrels of fish
$\frac{1}{8}$ ounces of gold for 2 dozen eggs
24 ounces of gold for 3 hours of *X*'s labor

The money prices of these various exchanges were:

$$\frac{15 \text{ oz.}}{3 \text{ horses}} = \frac{5 \text{ oz.}}{1 \text{ horse}}$$

$$\frac{5 \text{ oz.}}{100 \text{ bbls. of fish}} = \frac{1 \text{ oz.}}{20 \text{ bbls. of fish}} = \frac{\frac{1}{20} \text{ oz.}}{1 \text{ bbl. of fish}}$$

$$\frac{\frac{1}{8} \text{ oz.}}{2 \text{ doz. eggs}} = \frac{\frac{1}{16} \text{ oz.}}{1 \text{ doz. eggs}}$$

$$\frac{24 \text{ oz.}}{8 \text{ hrs. of } X\text{'s labor}} = \frac{3 \text{ oz.}}{1 \text{ hr. of } X\text{'s labor}}$$

The last ratios on each line are the money prices of the units of each good for each exchange.

It is evident that, with money being used for all exchanges, money prices serve as a *common denominator* of all exchange ratios. Thus, with the above money prices, anyone can calculate that if 1 horse exchanges for 5 ounces, and 1 barrel of fish exchanges for 1/20 ounces, then 1 horse can, indirectly, exchange for 100 barrels of fish, or for 80 dozen eggs, or 5/3 of an hour of *X*'s labor, etc. Instead of a myriad of isolated markets for each good and every other good, each good exchanges for money, and the exchange ratios between every good and every other good can easily be estimated by observing their money prices. Here it must be emphasized that these exchange ratios are only hypothetical, and can be computed at all only because of the exchanges against money. It is only through the use of money that we can hypothetically estimate these "barter ratios," and it is only by intermediate exchanges against money that one good can finally be exchanged for the other at the hypothetical ratio.[1] Many writers have erred in believing that money can somehow be abstracted from the formation of money prices and that analysis can accurately describe affairs "as if" exchanges really took place by way of barter. With money and money prices pervading all exchanges, there can be no abstraction from money in analyzing the formation of prices in an economy of indirect exchange.

Just as in the case of direct exchange, there will always be a tendency on the market for *one money price to be established for each good.* We have seen that the basic rule is that each seller tries to sell his good for the highest attainable money price, and each buyer tries to buy the good for the lowest attainable money price. The actions of the buyers and sellers will always and rapidly tend to establish one price on the market at any given time. If the "ruling" market price for 100 barrels of fish, for example, is 5 ounces—i.e., if sellers and buyers believe that they can sell and buy the fish they desire for 5 ounces per 100 barrels—then no buyer will pay 6 ounces, and no seller will accept 4 ounces for the fish. Such action will obtain for all goods on the market, establishing the rule that, for the entire market society, every homogeneous good will tend to be bought and sold at one particular money price at any given time.

What, then, are the forces that determine at what point this uniform money price for each good tends to be set? We shall soon see that, as demonstrated in chapter 2, the determinants are the individual value scales, expressed through demand and supply schedules.

We must remember that, in the course of determining the "fish-price of horses" in the direct exchange of fish as against horses, at the same time there was also determined the "horse-price of fish." In the exchanges of a money economy, what is the "goods-price of money" and how is it determined?

Let us consider the foregoing list of typical exchanges against money. These exchanges established the money prices of four different goods on the market. Now let us reverse the process and divide the quantities of goods by the quantity of money in the exchange. This gives us:

$$\frac{\text{1/5 horse}}{\text{1 oz.}}; \quad \frac{\text{20 bbls. of fish}}{\text{1 oz.}}; \quad \frac{\text{16 doz. eggs}}{\text{1 oz.}}; \quad \frac{\text{1/8 hr. of } X\text{'s labor}}{\text{1 oz.}}$$

This sort of list, or "array," goes on and on for each of the myriad exchanges of goods against money. *The inverse of the money price of any good gives us the "goods-price" of money in terms of that particular good.* Money, in a sense, is the only good that remains, as far as its prices are concerned, in the same state that every good was in a regime of barter. In barter, every good had only its ruling market price in terms of *every other good:* fish-price of eggs, horse-price of movies, etc. In a money economy, every good except money now has *one* market price in terms of money. Money, on the other hand, still has an almost infinite *array* of "goods-prices" that establish the "goods-price of money." The entire array, considered together, yields us the general "goods-price of money." For if we consider the whole array of goods-prices, we know what one ounce of money will buy in terms of any desired combination of goods, i.e., we know what that "ounce's worth" of money (which figures so largely in consumers' decisions) will be.

Alternatively, we may say that the money price of any good discloses what its "purchasing power" on the market will be. Suppose that a man possesses 200 barrels of fish. He estimates that the ruling market price for fish is 6 ounces per 100 barrels, and that therefore he can sell the 200 barrels for 12 ounces. The "purchasing power" of 100 barrels on the market is 6 ounces of money. Similarly, the purchasing power of a horse may be 5 ounces, etc. *The purchasing power of a stock of any good is equal to the amount of money it can "buy" on the market* and is therefore directly determined by the money price that it can obtain. As a matter of fact, *the purchasing power of a unit of any quantity of a good is equal to its money price.* If the market money price of a dozen eggs (the unit) is ⅛ of an ounce of gold, then the purchasing power of the dozen eggs is also ⅛ of an ounce. Similarly, the purchasing power of a horse, above, was 5 ounces; of an hour of X's labor 3 ounces; etc.

For every good except money, then, the purchasing power of its unit is identical with the money price that it can obtain on the market. *What is the purchasing power of the monetary unit?* Obviously, the purchasing power of, e.g., an ounce of gold can be considered only in relation to *all* the goods that the ounce could purchase or help to purchase. *The purchasing power of the monetary unit consists of an array of all the particular goods-prices in the society in terms of the unit.*[2] It consists of a huge array of the type above: ⅕ horse per ounce; 20 barrels of fish per ounce; 16 dozen eggs per ounce; etc.

It is evident that the money commodity and the determinants of its purchasing power introduce a complication in the demand and supply schedules of chapter 2 that must be worked out; there cannot be a mere duplication of the demand and supply schedules of barter conditions, since the demand and supply situation for money is a unique one. Before investigating the "price" of money and its determinants, we must first take a long detour and investigate the determination of the money prices of all the other goods in the economy.

2. *Determination of Money Prices*

Let us first take a typical good and analyze the determinants of its money price on the market. (Here the reader is referred back to the more detailed analysis of price in chapter 2.) Let us take a homogeneous good, Grade A butter, in exchange against money.

The money price is determined by actions decided according to individual value scales. For example, a typical buyer's value scale may be ranked as follows:

—7 grains of gold
—(1st pound of butter)
—6 grains of gold
—5 grains of gold
—(2nd pound of butter)
—4 grains of gold
—3 grains of gold
—(3rd pound of butter)
—2 grains of gold

The quantities in parentheses are those which the person does not possess but is considering adding to his ownership; the others are those which he has in his possession. In this case, the buyer's *maximum buying money price* for his first pound of butter is 6 grains of gold. At any market price of 6 grains or under, he will exchange these grains for the butter; at a market price of 7 grains or over, he will not make the purchase. His maximum buying price for a second pound of butter will be considerably lower. This result is always true, and stems from the law of utility; as he adds pounds of butter to his ownership, the marginal utility of each pound declines. On the other hand, as he dispenses with grains of gold, the marginal utility to him of each remaining grain increases. Both these forces impel the maximum buying price of an additional unit to decline with an increase in the quantity purchased.[3] From this value scale, we can compile this buyer's *demand schedule,* the amount of each good that he will consume at each hypothetical money price on the market. We may also draw his demand curve, if we wish to see the schedule in graphic form. The individual demand schedule of the buyer considered above is as shown in Table 6.

TABLE 6

MARKET PRICE	QUANTITY DEMANDED (PURCHASED)
Grains of gold per pound of butter	Pounds of butter
8	0
7	0
6	1
5	1
4	2
3	2
2	3
1	3

We note that, because of the law of utility, an individual demand curve must be either "vertical" as the hypothetical price declines, or else rightward-sloping (i.e., the quantity demanded, as the money price falls, must be either the same or greater), not leftward-sloping (not a lower quantity demanded).

If this is the necessary configuration of every buyer's demand schedule, it is clear that the existence of more than one buyer will tend greatly to *reinforce* this behavior. There are two and only two possible classifications of different people's value scales: either they are all identical, or else they differ. In the extremely unlikely case that everyone's relevant value scales are identical with everyone else's (extremely unlikely because of the immense variety of valuations by human beings), then, for example, buyers B, C, D, etc. will have the same value scale and therefore the same individual demand schedules as buyer A who has just been described. In that case, the shape of the aggregate market-demand curve (the sum of the demand curves of the individual buyers) will be identical with the curve of buyer A, although the aggregate quantities will, of course, be much greater. To be sure, the value scales of the buyers will almost always differ, which means that their maximum buying prices for any given pound of butter will differ. The result is that, as the market price is lowered, more and more buyers of different units are brought into the market. This effect greatly reinforces the rightward-sloping feature of the market-demand curve.

As an example of the formation of a market-demand schedule from individual value scales, let us take the buyer described above as buyer A and assume two other buyers on the market, B and C, with the following value scales:

Buyer B	*Buyer C*
—6 grains	—5 grains
—(1st lb. of butter)	—4 grains
—5 grains	—(1st lb. of butter)
—(2nd lb. of butter)	—3 grains
—4 grains	—(2nd lb. of butter)
—3 grains	—(3rd lb. of butter)
—2 grains	—2 grains
—(3rd lb. of butter)	—(4th lb. of butter)
—(4th lb. of butter)	—(5th lb. of butter)
—1 grain	—1 grain

From these value scales, we can construct their individual demand schedules (Table 7).

TABLE 7

Buyer B		Buyer C	
PRICE Grains/lb.	QUANTITY DEMANDED lbs. butter	PRICE Grains/lb.	QUANTITY DEMANDED lbs. butter
7	0	5	0
6	0	4	0
5	1	3	1
4	2	2	3
3	2	1	5
2	2		
1	4		

We notice that, in each of the varied patterns of individual demand schedules, none can ever be leftward-sloping as the hypothetical price declines.

Now we may summate the individual demand schedules, A, B, and C, into the *market-demand schedule*. The market-demand schedule yields the total quantity of the good that will be bought by all the buyers on the market at any given money price for the good. The market-demand schedule for buyers A, B, and C is as shown in Table 8.

TABLE 8

AGGREGATE MARKET-DEMAND SCHEDULE

PRICE	QUANTITY DEMANDED
8	0
7	0
6	1
5	2
4	4
3	5
2	8
1	12

Fig. 33 is a graphical representation of these schedules and their addition to form the market-demand schedule.

The principles of the formation of the market-supply schedule are similar, although the causal forces behind the value scales will differ.[4] Each supplier ranks each unit to be sold and the amount of money to be obtained in exchange on his value scale. Thus, one seller's value scale might be as follows:

Seller X

—(7 grains)
—(6 grains)
—6th lb. of butter
—(5 grains)
—5th lb. of butter
—4th lb. of butter
—(4 grains)
—3rd lb. of butter
—(3 grains)
—2nd lb. of butter
—1st lb. of butter
—(2 grains)
—(1 grain)

If the market price were 2 grains of gold, this seller would sell no butter, since even the first pound in his stock ranks above the acquisition of 2 grains on his value scale. At a price of 3 grains, he would sell 2 pounds, each of which ranks below 3 grains on his value scale. At a price of 4 grains, he would sell three

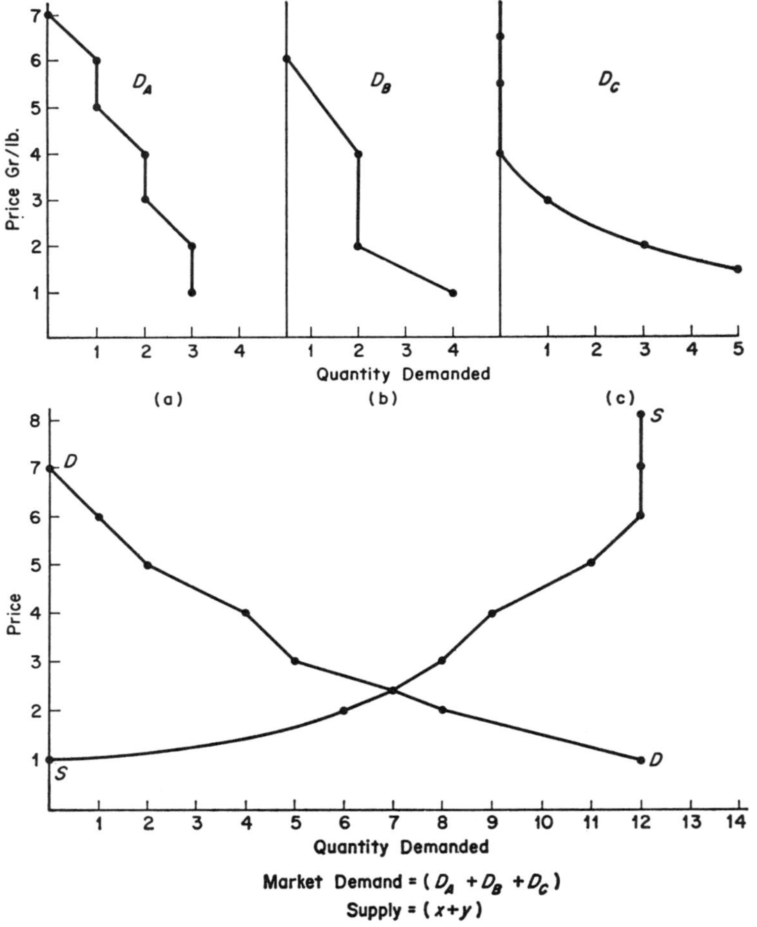

FIG. 33. EFFECT OF ADDING MARKET-DEMAND AND MARKET-SUPPLY SCHEDULES

pounds, etc. It is evident that, as the hypothetical price is lowered, the individual supply curve must be either vertical or leftward-sloping, i.e., a lower price must lead either to a lesser or to the same supply, never to more. This is, of course, equivalent to the statement that as the hypothetical price *increases,* the supply curve is either vertical or rightward-sloping. Again, the reason is the law of utility; as the seller disposes of his stock, its marginal utility to him tends to rise, while the marginal utility of the money acquired tends to fall. Of course, if the marginal utility of the stock to the supplier is nil, and if the marginal utility of money to him falls only slowly as he acquires it, the law may not change his quantity supplied during the range of action on the market, so that the supply curve may be vertical throughout almost all of its range. Thus, a supplier *Y* might have the following value scale:

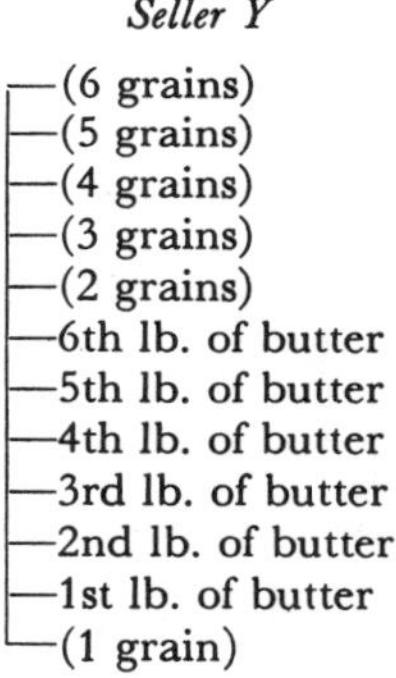

Seller Y

—(6 grains)
—(5 grains)
—(4 grains)
—(3 grains)
—(2 grains)
—6th lb. of butter
—5th lb. of butter
—4th lb. of butter
—3rd lb. of butter
—2nd lb. of butter
—1st lb. of butter
—(1 grain)

This seller will be willing to sell, above the minimum price of 1 grain, every unit in his stock. His supply curve will be shaped as in Fig. 34.

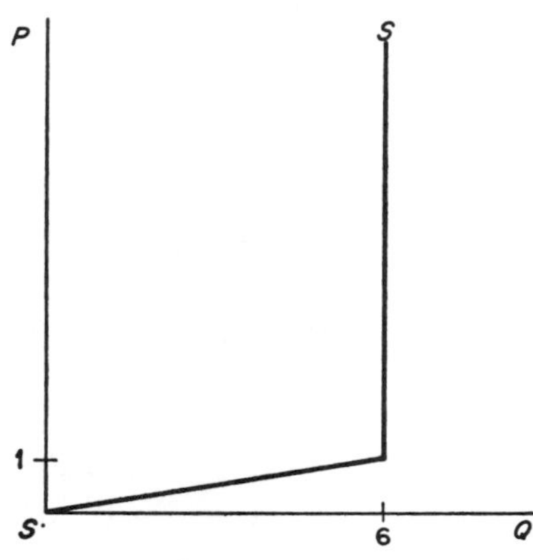

FIG. 34. SELLER Y'S SUPPLY CURVE

In seller *X's* case, his minimum selling price was 3 grains for the first and second pounds of butter, 4 grains for the third pound, 5 grains for the fourth and fifth pounds, and 6 grains for the sixth pound. Seller *Y*'s minimum selling price for the first pound and for every subsequent pound was 1 grain. In no case, however, can the supply curve be rightward-sloping as the price declines; i.e., in no case can a lower price lead to more units supplied.

Let us assume, for purposes of exposition, that the suppliers of butter on the market consist of just these two, *X* and *Y*, with the foregoing value scales. Then their individual and aggregate market-supply schedules will be as shown in Table 9.

TABLE 9

	QUANTITY SUPPLIED		
Price	*X*	*Y*	Market
8	6	6	12
7	6	6	12
6	6	6	12
5	5	6	11
4	3	6	9
3	2	6	8
2	0	6	6
1	0	0	0

This market-supply curve is diagramed above in Fig. 33.

We notice that the *intersection* of the market-supply and market-demand curves, i.e., the price at which the quantity supplied and the quantity demanded are equal, here is located at a point *in between* two prices. This is necessarily due to the lack of *divisibility* of the units; if a unit grain, for example, is indivisible, there is no way of introducing an intermediate price, and the *market-equilibrium price* will be at *either* 2 or 3 grains. This will be the best approximation that can be made to a price at which the market will be *precisely* cleared, i.e., one at which the would-be suppliers and the demanders at that price are satisfied. Let us, however, assume that the monetary unit can be further divided, and therefore that the equilibrium price is, say, 2½ grains. Not only will this simplify the exposition of price formation; it is also a realistic assumption, since one of the important characteristics of the money commodity is precisely its *divisibility* into minute units, which can be exchanged on the market. It is this divisibility of the monetary unit that permits us to draw continuous lines between the points on the supply and demand schedules.

The money price on the market will tend to be set at the equilibrium price—in this case, at 2½ grains. At a higher price, the quantity offered in supply will be greater than the quantity demanded; as a result, part of the supply could not be sold, and the sellers will underbid the price in order to sell their stock. Since only one price can persist on the market, and the buyers always seek their best advantage, the result will be a general lowering of the price toward the equilibrium point. On the other hand, if the price is below 2½ grains, there are would-be buyers at this price whose demands remain unsatisfied. These demanders bid up the price, and with sellers looking for the highest attainable price, the market price is raised toward the equilibrium point. Thus, the fact that men seek their greatest utility sets forces into motion that establish the money price at a certain equilibrium point, at which further exchanges tend to be made. The money price will remain at the equilibrium point for further exchanges of the good, *until* demand or supply schedules change. Changes in demand or supply conditions establish a new equilibrium price, toward which the market price again tends to move.

What the equilibrium price will be depends upon the configuration of the supply and demand schedules, and the causes of these schedules will be subjected to further examination below.

The stock of any good is the total quantity of that good in existence. Some will be supplied in exchange, and the remainder will be *reserved.* At any hypothetical price, it will be recalled, adding the demand to buy and the *reserved* demand of the supplier gives the *total demand to hold* on the part of both groups.[5] The total demand to hold includes the demand in exchange by present nonowners and the reservation demand to hold by the present owners. Since the supply curve is either vertical or increasing with a rise in price, the sellers' reservation demand will fall with a rise in price or will be nonexistent. In either case, the total demand to hold rises as the price falls.

Where there is a rise in reservation demand, the increase in the total demand to hold is greater—the curve far more elastic—than the regular demand curve, because of the addition of the reservation-demand component.[6] Thus, the higher the market price of a stock, the less the willingness on the market to hold and own it and the greater the eagerness to sell it. Conversely, the lower the price of a good on the market, the greater the willingness to own it and the less the willingness to sell it.

It is characteristic of the total demand curve that it *always* intersects the physical stock available at the same equilibrium price as the one at which the demand and supply schedules intersect. The Total Demand and Stock lines will therefore yield the same market equilibrium price as the other, although the quantity exchanged is not revealed by these curves. They do disclose, however, that, since all units of an existing stock must be possessed by someone, the market price of any good tends to be such that the aggregate demand to keep the stock will equal the stock itself. Then the stock will be in the hands of the most eager, or most capable, possessors. These are the ones who are willing to demand the most for the stock. That owner who would just sell his stock if the price rose slightly is the *marginal possessor:* that nonowner who would buy if the price fell slightly is the *marginal nonpossessor.*[7]

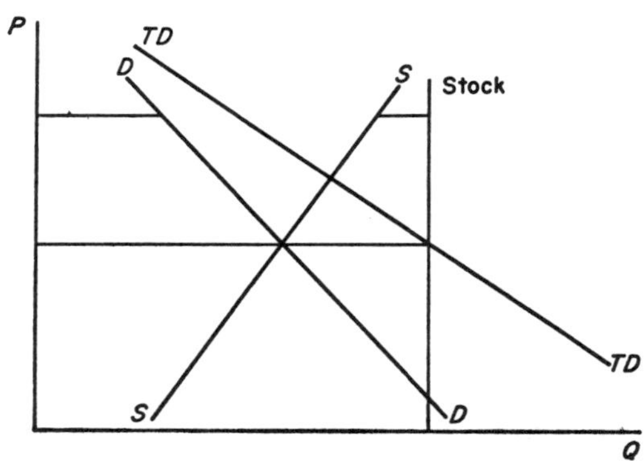

FIG. 35. SUPPLY, DEMAND, TOTAL DEMAND, AND STOCK CURVES

Fig. 35 is a diagram of the supply, demand, total demand, and stock curves of a good.

The total demand curve is composed of demand plus reserved supply; both slope rightward as prices fall. The equilibrium price is the same both for the intersection of the *S* and *D* curves, and for *TD* and Stock.

If there is no reservation demand, then the supply curve will be vertical, and equal to the stock. In that case, the diagram becomes as in Fig. 36.

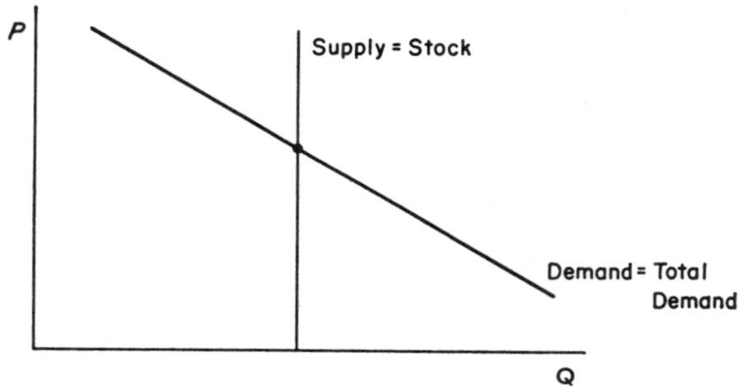

FIG. 36. EFFECT OF THE ABSENCE OF RESERVATION DEMAND

3. *Determination of Supply and Demand Schedules*

Every money price of a good on the market, therefore, is determined by the supply and demand schedules of the individual buyers and sellers, and their action tends to establish a uniform equilibrium price on the market at the point of intersection, which changes only when the schedules do.[8] Now the question arises: What are the determinants of the demand and supply schedules themselves? Can any conclusions be formed about the value scales and the resulting schedules?

In the first place, the analysis of speculation in chapter 2 can be applied directly to the case of the money price. There is no need to repeat that analysis here.[9] Suffice it to say, in summary, that, in so far as the equilibrium price is anticipated correctly by speculators, the demand and supply schedules will reflect the fact: above the equilibrium price, demanders will buy less than they otherwise would because of their anticipation of a later drop in the money price; below that price, they will buy more because of an anticipation of a rise in the money price. Similarly, sellers will sell more at a price that they anticipate will soon be lowered; they will sell less at a price that they anticipate will soon be raised. The general effect of speculation is to make both the supply and demand curves more elastic, viz., to shift them from *DD* to *D′D′* and from *SS* to *S′S′* in Fig. 37. The more people engage in such (correct) speculation, the more elastic will be the

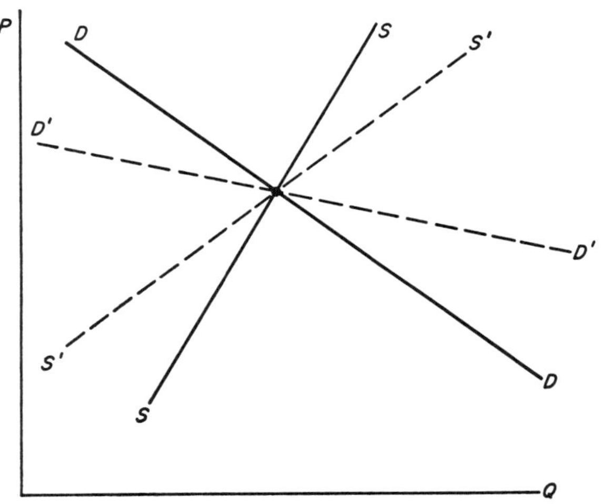

FIG. 37. EFFECT OF SPECULATION ON SUPPLY AND DEMAND CURVES

curves, and, by implication, the more rapidly will the equilibrium price be reached.

We also saw that preponderant errors in speculation tend inexorably to be self-correcting. If the speculative demand and supply schedules (*D′D′*–*S′S′*) preponderantly do not estimate the correct equilibrium price and consequently intersect at another price, then it soon becomes evident that that price does not really clear the market. Unless the equilibrium point set by the speculative schedules is identical with the point set by the schedules minus the speculative elements, the market again tends to bring the price (and quantity sold) to the true equilibrium point. For if the speculative schedules set the price of eggs at 2 grains, and the schedules without speculation would set it at 3 grains, there is an excess of quantity demanded over quantity supplied at 2 grains, and the bidding of buyers finally brings the price to 3 grains.[10]

Setting speculation aside, then, let us return to the buyer's demand schedules. Suppose that he ranks the unit of a good above a certain number of ounces of gold on his value scale. What can be the possible *sources* of his *demand for the good?* In other words, what can be the sources of the utility of the good to him? There are three and only three sources of utility that any purchase good can have for any person.[11] One of these is (*a*) the *anticipated later sale* of the same good for a higher money price. This is the speculative demand, basically ephemeral—a useful path to uncovering the more fundamental demand factors. This demand has just been analyzed. The second source of demand is (*b*) direct use as a consumers' good; the third source of demand is (*c*) direct use as a producers' good. Source (*b*) can apply only to consumers' goods; (*c*) to producers' goods. The former are directly consumed; the latter are used in the production process and, along with other co-operating factors, are transformed into lower-order capital goods, which are then sold for money. Thus, the third source applies solely to the investing producers in their purchases of producers' goods; the second source stems from consumers. If we set aside the temporary speculative source, (*b*) is the source of the individual demand schedules for all consumers' goods, (*c*) the source of demands for all producers' goods.

What of the *seller* of the consumers' good or producers' good —why is he demanding money in exchange? The seller demands money because of the marginal utility of money to him, and for this reason he ranks the money acquired above possession of the goods that he sells. The components and determinants of the utility of money will be analyzed in a later section.

Thus, the buyer of a good demands it because of its direct use-value either in consumption or in production; the seller demands money because of its marginal utility in exchange. This, however, does not exhaust the description of the components of the market supply and demand curves, for we have still not explained the rankings of the good on the seller's value scale and the rankings of money on the buyer's. When a seller keeps his stock instead of selling it, what is the source of his *reservation demand* for the good? We have seen that the quantity of a good reserved at any point is the quantity of stock that the seller refuses to sell at the given price. The sources of a reservation demand by the seller are two: (*a*) anticipation of later sale at a higher price; this is the speculative factor analyzed above; and (*b*) direct use of the good by the seller. This second factor is not often applicable to producers' goods, since the seller produced the producers' good for sale and is usually not immediately prepared to use it directly in further production. In some cases, however, this alternative of direct use for further production does exist. For example, a producer of crude oil may sell it or, if the money price falls below a certain minimum, may use it in his own plant to produce gasoline. In the case of consumers' goods, which we are treating here, direct use may also be feasible, particularly in the case of a sale of an old consumers' good previously used directly by the seller—such as an old house, painting, etc. However, with the great development of specialization in the money economy, these cases become infrequent.

If we set aside (*a*) as being a temporary factor and realize that (*b*) is frequently not present in the case of either consumers' or producers' goods, it becomes evident that many market-supply curves will tend to assume an almost vertical shape. In such a case, *after* the investment in production has been made and the stock of goods is on hand, the producer is often willing to sell it at any money price that he can obtain, regardless of how low the market price may be. This, of course, is by no means the same as saying that *investment in further production* will be made if the seller *anticipates* a very low money price from the sale of the product. In the latter case, the problem is to determine how much to invest *at present* in the production of a good to be produced and sold at a point *in the future*. In the case of the market-supply curve, which helps set the day-to-day equilibrium price, we are dealing with already given stock and with the reservation demand for this stock. In the case of production, on the other hand, we are dealing with investment decisions concerning how much stock to produce for some later period. What we have been discussing has been the market-supply curve. Here the seller's problem is *what to do with given stock,* with already produced goods. The problem of production will be treated in chapter 5 and subsequent chapters.

Another condition that might obtain on the market is a previous buyer's re-entering the market and reselling a good. For him to be able to do so, it is obvious that the good must be *durable.* (A violin-playing service, for example, is so nondurable that it is not resalable by the purchasing listeners.) The total stock of the good in existence will then equal the producers' new supply *plus* the producers' reserved demand *plus* the supply offered by old possessors *plus* the reserved demand of the old possessors (i.e., the amount the old buyers retain). The market-supply curve of the old possessors will increase or be vertical as the price rises; and the reserved-demand curve of the old possessors will increase or be constant as the price falls. In other words, their schedules behave similarly to their counterpart schedules among the producers. The aggregate market-supply curve will be formed simply by adding the producers' and old possessors' supply curves. The total-demand-to-hold schedule will equal the demand by buyers plus the reservation demand (if any) of the producers and of the old possessors.

If the good is Chippendale chairs, which cannot be further produced, then the market-supply curves are *identical* with the supply curves of the old possessors. There is no new production, and there are no additions to stock.

It is clear that the greater the proportion of old stock to new production, other things being equal, the greater will tend to be the importance of the supply of old possessors compared to that of new producers. The tendency will be for old stock to be more important the greater the durability of the good.

There is one type of consumers' good the supply curve of which will have to be treated in a later section on labor and earnings. This is *personal service,* such as the services of a doctor, a lawyer, a concert violinist, a servant, etc. These services, as we have indicated above, are, of course, nondurable. In fact, they are consumed by the seller immediately upon their production. Not being material objects like "commodities," they are the direct emanation of the effort of the supplier himself, who produces them instantaneously upon his decision. The supply curve depends on the decision whether or not to produce—supply—personal effort, not on the sale of already produced stock. There is no "stock" in this sphere, since the goods disappear into consumption immediately on being produced. It is evident that the concept of "stock" is applicable only to tangible objects. The price of personal services, however, is determined by the intersection of supply and demand forces, as in the case of tangible goods.

For all goods, the establishment of the equilibrium price tends to establish a *state of rest,* a cessation of exchanges. After the price is established, sales will take place until the stock is in the hands of the most capable possessors, in accordance with the value scales. Where new production is continuing, the market will tend to be *continuing,* however, because of the inflow of new stock from producers coming into the market. This inflow alters the state of rest and sets the stage for new exchanges, with producers eager to sell their stock, and consumers to buy. When total stock is fixed and there is no new production, on the other hand, the state of rest is likely to become important. Any changes in price or new exchanges will occur as a result of changes of valuations, i.e., a change in the relative position of money and the good on the value scales of at least two individuals on the market, which will lead them to make further exchanges of the good against money. Of course, where valuations are changing, as they almost always are in a changing world, markets for old stock will again be continuing.[12]

An example of that rare type of good for which the market may be intermittent instead of continuous is Chippendale chairs, where the stock is very limited and the money price relatively high. The stock is always distributed into the hands of the most eager possessors, and the trading may be infrequent. Whenever one of the collectors comes to value his Chippendale below a certain sum of money, and another collector values that sum in his possession below the acquisition of the furniture, an exchange is likely to occur. Most goods, however, even nonreproducible ones, have a lively, continuing market, because of continual changes in valuations and a large number of participants in the market.

In sum, buyers decide to buy consumers' goods at various ranges of price (setting aside previously analyzed speculative factors) because of their *demand for the good for direct use.* They decide to *abstain from buying* because of their *reservation demand for money,* which they prefer to retain rather than spend on that particular good. Sellers supply the goods, in all cases, because of their *demand for money,* and those cases where they reserve a stock for themselves are due (aside from speculation on price increases) to their demand for the good for direct use. Thus, the general factors that determine the supply and demand schedules of any and all consumers' goods, by *all persons on the market,* are the balancing on their value scales of their demand for the good for direct use and their demand for money, either for reservation or for exchange. Although we shall further discuss investment-production decisions below, it is evident that decisions to invest are due to the demand for an expected money return *in the future.* A decision *not* to invest, as we have seen above, is due to a competing demand to use a stock of money *in the present.*

4. *The Gains of Exchange*

As in the case considered in chapter 2, the sellers who are included in the sale at the equilibrium price are those whose value scales make them the most capable, the most eager, sellers. Similarly, it will be the most capable, or most eager, buyers who will purchase the good at the equilibrium price. With a price of 2½ grains of gold per pound of butter, the sellers will be those for whom 2½ grains of gold is worth more than one pound of butter; the buyers will be those for whom the reverse valuation holds. Those who are excluded from sale or purchase by their own value scales are the "less capable," or "less eager," buyers and sellers, who may be referred to as "submarginal." The "marginal" buyer and the "marginal" seller are the ones whose schedules just barely permit them to stay in the market. The marginal seller is the one whose minimum selling price is just 2½; a slightly lower selling price would drive him out of the market. The marginal buyer is the one whose maximum buying price is just 2½; a slightly higher selling price would drive him out of the market. Under the law of price uniformity, all the exchanges are made at the equilibrium price (once it is established), i.e., between the valuations of the marginal buyer and those of the marginal seller, with the demand and supply schedules and their intersection determining the point of the margin. It is clear from the nature of human action that all buyers will benefit (or decide they will benefit) from the exchange. Those who abstain from buying the good have decided that they would lose from the exchange. These propositions hold true for all goods.

Much importance has been attached by some writers to the "psychic surplus" gained through exchange by the most capable buyers and sellers, and attempts have been made to measure or compare these "surpluses." The buyer who would have bought the same amount for 4 grains is obviously attaining a subjective benefit because he can buy it for 2½ grains. The same holds for the seller who might have been willing to sell the same amount for 2 grains. However, the psychic surplus of the "supramarginal" cannot be contrasted to, or measured against, that of the marginal buyer or seller. For it must be remembered that the marginal buyer or seller also receives a psychic surplus: he gains from the exchange, or else he would not make it. Value scales of each individual are *purely ordinal,* and there is no way whatever of measuring the distance between the rankings; indeed, any concept of such distance is a fallacious one. Consequently, there is no way of making interpersonal comparisons and measurements, and no basis for saying that one person subjectively benefits more than another.[13]

We may illustrate the impossibility of measuring utility or benefit in the following way. Suppose that the equilibrium market price for eggs has been established at 3 grains per dozen. The following are the value scales of some selected buyers and would-be buyers:

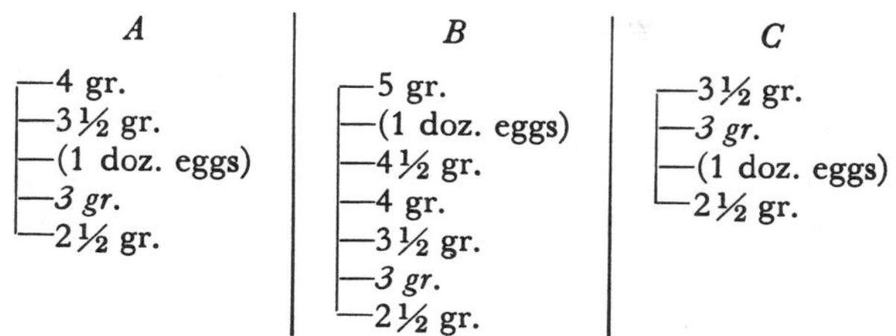

The money prices are divided into units of ½ grain; for purposes of simplification, each buyer is assumed to be considering the purchase of *one unit*—one dozen eggs. C is obviously a submarginal buyer; he is just excluded from the purchase because 3 grains is higher on his value scale than the dozen eggs. A and B, however, will make the purchase. Now A is a marginal buyer; he is just able to make the purchase. At a price of 3½ grains, he would be excluded from the market, because of the rankings on his value scale. B, on the other hand, is a supramarginal buyer: he would buy the dozen eggs even if the price were raised to 4½ grains. But can we say that B benefits from his purchase *more than A? No, we cannot.* Each value scale, as has been explained above, is purely ordinal, a matter of rank. Even though B prefers the eggs to 4½ grains, and A prefers 3½ grains to the eggs, we still have no standard for comparing the two surpluses. All we can say is that *above* the price of 3 grains, B has a psychic surplus from exchange, while A becomes submarginal, with no surplus. But, even if we assume for a moment that the concept of "distance" between ranks makes sense, for all we know, A's surplus over 3 grains may give him a far greater subjective utility than B's surplus over 3 grains, even though the latter is also a surplus over 4½ grains. There can be no interpersonal comparison of utilities, and the relative rankings of money and goods on different value scales cannot be used for such comparisons.

Those writers who have vainly attempted to measure psychic gains from exchange have concentrated on "consumer surpluses." Most recent attempts try to base their measurements on the price a man would have paid for the good if confronted with the possibility of being deprived of it. These methods are completely fallacious. The fact that A would have bought a suit at 80 gold grains as well as at the 50 grains' market price, while B would not have bought the suit if the price had been as high as 52 grains, does not, as we have seen, permit any measurement of the psychic surpluses, nor does it permit us to say that A's gain was in any way "greater" than B's. The fact that even if we could identify the marginal and supramarginal purchasers, we could never assert that one's gain is greater than another's is a conclusive reason for the rejection of all attempts to measure consumers' or other psychic surpluses.

There are several other fundamental methodological errors in such a procedure. In the first place, individual value scales are here separated from concrete action. But economics deals with the universal aspects of real action, not with the actors' inner psychological workings. We deduce the existence of a specific value scale on the basis of the *real act;* we have no knowledge of that part of a value scale that is not revealed in real action. The question how much one would pay if threatened with deprivation of the whole stock of a good is strictly an academic question with no relation to human action. Like all other such constructions, it has no place in economics. Furthermore, this particular concept is a reversion to the classical economic fallacy of dealing with the whole supply of a good as if it were relevant to individual action. It must be understood that only *marginal* units are relevant to action and that there is no determinate relation at all between the marginal utility of a unit and the utility of the supply as a whole.

It is true that the total utility of a supply increases with the size of the supply. This is deducible from the very nature of a good. Ten units of a good will be ranked higher on an individual's value scale than four units will. But this ranking is completely unrelated to the utility ranking of *each unit* when the supply is 4, 9, 10 or any other amount. This is true regardless of the size of the unit. We can affirm only the trivial ordinal relationship, i.e., that five units will have a higher utility than one unit, and that the first unit will have a higher utility than the second unit, the third unit, etc. But there is no determinate way of lining up the single utility with the "package" utility.[14] Total utility, indeed, makes sense as a real and relevant rather than as a hypothetical concept only when actual decisions must be made concerning the whole supply. In that case, it is still *marginal* utility, although with the size of the margin or unit now being the whole supply.

The absurdity of the attempt to measure consumers' surplus would become clearer if we considered, as we logically may, *all* the consumers' goods at once and attempted to measure in any way the undoubted "consumers' surplus" arising from the fact that production for exchange exists at all. This has never been attempted.[15]

5. *The Marginal Utility of Money*

A. THE CONSUMER

We have not yet explained one very important problem: the ranking of money on the various individual value scales. We know that the ranking of units of goods on these scales is determined by the relative ranking of the marginal utilities of the units. In the case of barter, it was clear that the relative rankings were the result of people's evaluations of the marginal importance of the direct uses of the various goods. In the case of a monetary economy, however, the direct use-value of the money commodity is overshadowed by its exchange-value.

In chapter 1, section 5, on the law of marginal utility, we saw that the marginal utility of a unit of a good is determined in the following way: (1) if the unit is in the possession of the actor, the marginal utility of the unit is equal to the ranked value he places on the least important end, or use, which he would have to *give up* on losing the unit; or (2) if the unit is not yet in his possession, the marginal utility *of adding* the unit is equal to the value of the most important end that the unit could serve. On this basis, a man allocates his stock of various units of a good to his most important uses first, and his less important uses in succession, while he gives up his *least* important uses first. Now we saw in chapter 3 how every man allocates his stock of money among the various uses. The money commodity has numerous different uses, and the number of uses multiplies the more highly developed and advanced are the money economy, division of labor, and the capital structure. Decisions concerning numerous consumer goods, numerous investment projects, consumption at present versus expected increased returns in the future, and addition to cash balance, must all be made. We say that each individual allocates each unit of the money commodity to its most important use first, then to the next most important use, etc., thus determining the allocation of money in each possible use and line of spending. The least important use is given up first, as with any other commodity.

We are not interested here in exploring all aspects of the analysis of the marginal utility of money, particularly the cash-balance decision, which must be left for later treatment. We are interested here in the marginal utility of money as relevant to consumption decisions. Every man is a consumer, and therefore the analysis applies to everyone taking part in the nexus of monetary exchange.

Each succeeding unit that the consumer allocates among different lines of spending, he wishes to allocate to the most highly valued use that it can serve. His *psychic revenue* is the marginal utility—the value of the most important use that will be served. His *psychic cost* is the next most important use which must be forgone—the use which must be sacrificed in order to attain the most important end. The highest ranked utility *forgone,* therefore, is defined as the *cost* of any action.

The utility a person derives or expects to derive from an act of exchange is the marginal utility of adding the good purchased, i.e., the most important use for the units to be acquired. The utility that he forgoes is the highest utility that he could have derived from the units of the good that he gives up in the exchange. When he is a consumer purchasing a good, his marginal utility of addition is the most highly valued use to which he could put the units of the good; this is the psychic revenue that he expects from the exchange. On the other hand, what he forgoes is the use of the units of money that he "sells" or gives up. His *cost,* then, is the value of the most important use to which he could have put the money.[16] Every man strives in action to achieve a psychic revenue greater than his psychic cost, and thereby a psychic profit; this is true of the consumer's purchases as well. Error is revealed when his choice proves to be mistaken, and he realizes that he would have done better to have pursued the other, forgone course of action.

Now, as the consumer adds to his purchases of a good, the marginal utility which the added good has for him must *diminish,* in accordance with the law of marginal utility. On the other hand, as he gives up units of a good in sale, the marginal utility that this good has for him becomes greater, in accordance with the same law. Eventually, he must cease purchasing the good, because the marginal utility of the good forgone becomes greater than the marginal utility of the good purchased. This is clearly true of direct goods, but what of money?

It is obvious that money is not only a useful good, but one of the most useful in a money economy. It is used as a medium in practically every exchange. We have seen that one of a man's most important activities is the allocation of his money stock to various desired uses. It is obvious, therefore, *that money obeys the law of marginal utility, just as any other commodity does.* Money is a commodity divisible into homogeneous units. Indeed, one of the reasons the commodity is picked as money is its ready divisibility into relatively small homogeneous units. The first unit of money will be allocated to its most important and valued use to an individual; the second unit will be allocated to its second most valued use, etc. Any unit of money that must be given up will be surrendered at the sacrifice of the least highly valued use previously being served or which would have been served. Therefore, it is true of money as of any other commodity, that *as its stock increases, its marginal utility declines; and that as its stock declines, its marginal utility to the person increases.*[17] Its marginal utility of addition is equal to the rank of the most highly valued end the monetary unit can attain; and its marginal utility is equal in value to the most highly valued end *that would have to be sacrificed* if the unit were surrendered.

What are the various ends that money can serve? They are: (*a*) the nonmonetary uses of the money commodity (such as the use of gold for ornament); (*b*) expenditure on the many different kinds of consumers' goods; (*c*) investment in various alternative combinations of factors of production; and (*d*) additions to the cash balance. Each of these broad categories of uses encompasses a large number of types and quantities of goods, and each particular alternative is ranked on the individual's value scale. It is clear what the uses of consumption goods are: they provide immediate satisfaction for the individual's desires and are thus immediately ranked on his value scale. It is also clear that when money is used for nonmonetary purposes, it becomes a direct consumers' good itself instead of a medium of exchange. Investment, which will be further discussed below, aims at a greater level of future consumption through investing in capital goods at present.

What is the usefulness of keeping or adding to a cash balance? This question will be explored in later chapters, but here we may state that the desire to keep a cash balance stems from fundamental *uncertainty* as to the right time for making purchases, whether of capital or of consumers' goods. Also important are a basic *uncertainty* about the individual's own future value scale and the desire to keep cash on hand to satisfy any changes that might occur. Uncertainty, indeed, is a fundamental feature of all human action, and uncertainty about changing prices and changing value scales are aspects of this basic uncertainty. If an individual, for example, anticipates a rise in the purchasing power of the monetary unit in the near future, he will tend to postpone his purchases toward that day and add now to his cash balance. On the other hand, if he anticipates a fall in purchasing power, he will tend to buy more at present and draw down his cash balance. An example of general uncertainty is an individual's typical desire to keep a certain amount of cash on hand "in case of a rainy day" or an emergency that will require an unanticipated expenditure of funds in some direction. His "feeling safer" in such a case demonstrates that money's only value is not simply when it makes exchanges; because of its very marketability, its mere *possession* in the hands of an individual performs a service for that person.

That money in one's cash balance is performing a service demonstrates the fallacy in the distinction that some writers make between "circulating" money and money in "idle hoards." In the first place, all money is *always* in someone's cash balance. It is never "moving" in some mysterious "circulation." It is in A's cash balance, and then when A buys eggs from B, it is shifted to B's cash balance. Secondly, regardless of the length of time any given unit of money is in one person's cash balance, it is performing a service to him, and is therefore never in an "idle hoard."

What is the marginal utility and the cost involved in any act of consumption exchange? When a consumer spends five grains of gold on a dozen eggs, this means that he anticipates that the most valuable use for the five grains of gold is to acquire the dozen eggs. This is his marginal utility of addition of the five grains. This utility is his anticipated psychic revenue from the exchange. What, then, is the "opportunity cost" or, simply, the "cost," of the exchange, i.e., the next best alternative forgone? This is the most valuable use that he could have made with the five grains of gold. This could be any one of the following alternatives, whichever is the highest on his value scale: (*a*) expenditure on some other consumers' good; (*b*) use of the money commodity for purposes of direct consumption; (*c*) expenditure on some line of investment in factors of production to increase future monetary income and consumption; (*d*) addition to his cash balance. It should be noted that since this cost refers to a decision on a marginal unit, of whatever size, this is also the "marginal cost" of the decision. This cost is subjective and is ranked on the individual's value scale.

The nature of the cost, or utility forgone, of a decision to spend money on a particular consumers' good, is clear in the case where the cost is the value that could have been derived from another act of consumption. When the cost is forgone investment, then what is forgone is expected future increases in consumption, expressed in terms of the individual's rate of time preference, which will be further explored below. At any rate, when an individual buys a particular good, such as eggs, the more he continues to buy, the lower will be the marginal utility of addition that each successive unit has for him. This, of course, is in accordance with the law of marginal utility. On the other hand, the more money he spends on eggs, the greater will be the marginal utility forgone in whatever is the next best good—e.g., butter. Thus, the more he spends on eggs, the less will be his marginal utility derived from eggs, and the greater will be his marginal cost of buying eggs, i.e., the value that he must forgo. Eventually, the latter becomes greater than the former. When this happens and the marginal cost of purchasing eggs becomes greater than the marginal utility of addition of the commodity, he switches his purchases to butter, and the same process continues. With any stock of money, a man's consumption expenditures come first, and expenditures on each good follow the same law. In some cases, the marginal cost of consumption on a consumers' good becomes investment in some line, and the man may invest some money in factors of production. This investment continues until the marginal cost of such investment, in terms of forgone consumption or cash balance, is greater than the present value of the expected return. Sometimes, the most highly valued use is an addition to one's cash balance, and this continues until the marginal utility derived from this use is less than the marginal cost in some other line. In this way, a man's monetary stock is allocated among all the most highly valued uses.

And in this way, individual demand schedules are constructed for every consumers' good, and market-demand schedules are determined as the summation of the individual demand schedules on the market. Given the stocks of all the consumers' goods (this *given* will be analyzed in succeeding chapters), their market prices are thereby determined.

It might be thought, and many writers have assumed, that money has here performed the function of measuring and rendering comparable the utilities of the different individuals. It has, however, done nothing of the sort. The marginal utility of money differs from person to person, just as does the marginal utility of any other good. The fact that an ounce of money can buy various goods on the market and that such opportunities may be open to all does not give us any information about the ways in which various people will rank these different combinations of goods. *There is no measuring or comparability in the field of values or ranks.* Money permits only *prices* to be comparable, by establishing money prices for every good.

It might seem that the process of ranking and comparing on value scales by each individual has established and determined the prices of consumers' goods without any need for further analysis. The problem, however, is not nearly so simple. Neglect or evasion of the difficulties involved has plagued economics for many years. Under a system of barter, there would be no analytic difficulty. All the possible consumers' goods would be ranked and compared by each individual, the demand schedules of each in terms of the other would be established, etc. Relative utilities would establish individual demand schedules, and these would be summed up to yield market-demand schedules. But, in the monetary economy, a grave analytic difficulty arises.

To determine the price of a good, we analyze the market-demand schedule for the good; this in turn depends on the individual demand schedules; these in their turn are determined by the individuals' value rankings of units of the good and units of money as given by the various alternative uses of money; *yet the latter alternatives depend in turn on given prices of the other goods.* A hypothetical demand for eggs must assume as given some money price for butter, clothes, etc. *But how, then, can value scales and utilities be used to explain the formation of money prices, when these value scales and utilities themselves depend upon the existence of money prices?*

B. The Money Regression

It is obvious that this vitally important problem of *circularity* (*X* depends on *Y*, while *Y* depends on *X*) exists not only in regard to decisions by consumers but also in regard to any exchange decision in the money economy. Thus, let us consider the *seller* of the stock of a consumers' good. At a given offered money price, he must decide whether to sell the units of his stock or whether to hold on to them. His eagerness to sell in exchange for acquiring money is due to the use that the money would have for him. The money would be employed in its most important uses for him, and this will determine his evaluation of the money—or its marginal utility of addition. But the *marginal utility of addition of money to the seller of the stock* is based *on its already being money* and its ready command of other goods that the seller will buy—consumers' goods and factors of production alike. The seller's marginal utility therefore also depends on the previous existence of money prices for the various goods in the economy.

Similarly, for the laborer, landowner, investor, or owner of a capital good: in selling his services or goods, money has a marginal utility of addition, which is a necessary prior condition to his decision to sell the goods and therefore a determinant in his supply curve of the good for money. And yet this marginal utility always depends on there being a previous array of money prices in existence. The seller of any good or service for money, therefore, ranks the marginal utility of the money that he will obtain against the marginal utility of holding on to the good or service. Whoever spends money to buy any good or service ranks the marginal utility which keeping the money has for him against the marginal utility of acquiring the good. These value scales of the various buyers and sellers determine the individual supply-demand schedules and hence all money prices; yet, in order to rank money and goods on his value scale, money must *already* have a marginal utility for each person, and this marginal utility *must* be based on the fact of pre-existing money prices of the various goods.[18]

The solution of this crucial problem of circularity has been provided by Professor Ludwig von Mises, in his notable theory of the money regression.[19] The theory of money regression may be explained by examining the period of time that is being considered in each part of our analysis. Let us define a "day" as the period of time just sufficient to determine the market prices of every good in the society. On day *X*, then, the money price of each good is determined by the interactions of the supply and demand schedules of money and the good by the buyers and sellers on that day. Each buyer and seller ranks money and the given good in accordance with the relative marginal utility of the two to him. Therefore, a money price at the *end* of day *X* is determined by the marginal utilities of money and the good as they existed at the *beginning* of day *X*. But the marginal utility of money is based, as we have seen above, on a *previously* existing array of money prices. Money is demanded and considered useful because of its *already existing* money prices. Therefore, the price of a good on day *X* is determined by the marginal utility of the good on day *X* and the marginal utility of money on day *X*, which last in turn depends on the prices of goods on day $X - 1$.

The economic analysis of money prices is therefore *not* circular. If prices today depend on the marginal utility of money today, the latter is dependent on money prices *yesterday*. Thus, in every money price in any day, there is contained a *time component*, so that this price is partially determined by the money prices of yesterday. This does *not* mean specifically that the price of eggs today is partially determined by the price of eggs yesterday, the price of butter today by that of yesterday, etc. On the contrary, the time component essential to each specific price today is the *general array* of yesterday's money prices for all goods, and, of course, the subsequent evaluation of the monetary unit by the individuals in the society. If we consider the *general array* of today's prices, however, an essential time component in their determination is the general array of yesterday's prices.

This time component is purely on the money side of the determining factors. *In a society of barter, there is no time component* in the prices of any given day. When horses are being exchanged against fish, the individuals in the market decide on the relative marginal utilities solely on the basis of the direct uses of the commodities. These direct uses are immediate and do not require any previously existing prices on the market. Therefore, the marginal utilities of direct goods, such as horses and fish, have no previous time components. And, therefore, there is no problem of circularity in a system of barter. In such a society, if all previous markets and knowledge of previous prices were somehow wiped out, there would, of course, be an initial period of confusion while each individual consulted his value scales and tried to estimate those of others, but there would be no great difficulty in speedily re-establishing the exchange markets. The case is different in a monetary economy. Since the marginal utility of the money commodity depends on previously existing money prices, a wiping out of existing markets and knowledge of money prices would render impossible the direct re-establishment of a money economy. The economy would be wrecked and thrown back into a highly primitive state of barter, after which a money economy could only slowly be re-established as it had been before.

Now the question may be raised: Granted that there is no circularity in the determination of money prices, does not the fact that the causes partially *regress* backward in time simply push the unexplained components back further without end? If today's prices are partly determined by yesterday's prices, and yesterday's by those of the day before yesterday, etc., is not the regression simply pushed back infinitely, and part of the determination of prices thus left unexplained?

The answer is that the regression is not infinite, and the clue to its stopping point is the distinction just made between conditions in a money economy and conditions in a state of barter. We remember that the utility of money consists of *two* major elements: the utility of the money as a medium of exchange, and the utility of the money commodity in its direct, commodity use (such as the use of gold for ornaments). In the modern economy, after the money commodity has fully developed as a medium of exchange, its use as a medium tends greatly to overshadow its direct use in consumption. The demand for gold as money far exceeds its demand as jewelry. However, the latter use and demand continue to exist and to exert some influence on the total demand for the money commodity.

In any day in the money economy, the marginal utility of gold and therefore the demand for it enter into the determination of every money price. The marginal utility of gold and the demand for it today depend on the array of money prices existing yesterday, which in turn depended on the marginal utility of gold and the demand for it yesterday, etc. Now, as we regress backwards in time, we must eventually arrive at the original point when people first began to use gold as a medium of exchange. Let us consider the *first* day on which people passed from the system of pure barter and began to use gold as a medium of exchange. On that day, the money price, or rather, the gold price, of every other good depended partially on the marginal utility of gold. This marginal utility had a *time component,* namely, the previous array of gold prices, which had been determined in barter. In other words, when gold first began to be used as a medium of exchange, its marginal utility for use in that capacity depended on the existing previous array of gold prices established through *barter.* But if we regress one day further *to the last day of barter,* the gold prices of various goods on that day, like all other prices, had *no* time components. They were determined, as were all other barter prices, solely by the marginal utility of gold and of the other goods on that day, and the marginal utility of gold, since it was used *only* for direct consumption, had *no* temporal component.

The determination of money prices (gold prices) is therefore completely explained, with no circularity and no infinite regression. The demand for gold enters into every gold price, and today's demand for gold, in so far as it is for use as a *medium of exchange,* has a time component, being based on yesterday's array of gold prices. This time component regresses until the last day of barter, the day before gold began to be used as a medium of exchange. On that day, gold had no utility in that use; the demand for gold was solely for direct use, and consequently, the determination of the gold prices, for that day and for all previous days, had no temporal component whatever.[20, 21]

The causal-temporal pattern of the regression may be portrayed as in the diagram in Fig. 38. Consecutive days are numbered 1, 2, 3, etc., and, for each period, arrows depict the underlying causal factors determining the gold prices of goods on the market. For each period of time, the gold prices of goods are fundamentally determined by the relative marginal utilities of gold and other goods on individual value scales, and the marginal utilities of gold are based on the gold prices during the preceding period. This temporal component, depicted by an arrow, continues back-

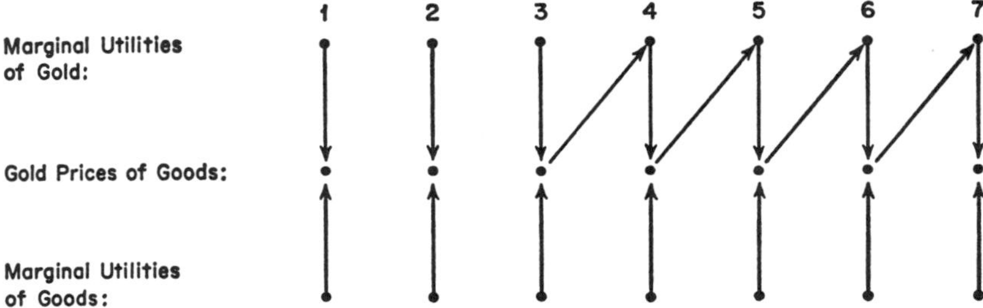

FIG. 38. CAUSAL-TEMPORAL PATTERN OF THE MONEY REGRESSION

ward until the period of barter, when gold is used only for direct consumption or production purposes and not as a medium of exchange. At that point there is no temporal dependence on preceding gold prices, and the temporal arrow disappears. In this diagram, a system of barter prevails on days 1, 2, and 3, and gold is used as a medium of exchange on day 4 and thereafter.

One of the important achievements of the regression theory is its establishment of the fact that money *must* arise in the manner described in chapter 3, i.e., it must develop out of a commodity already in demand for direct use, the commodity then being used as a more and more general medium of exchange. Demand for a good as a medium of exchange *must* be predicated on a previously existing array of prices in terms of other goods. A medium of exchange can therefore *originate only* according to our previous description and the forgoing diagram; it can arise only out of a commodity previously *used directly in a barter situation,* and therefore having had an array of prices in terms of other goods. *Money must develop out of a commodity with a previously existing purchasing power, such as gold and silver had.* It cannot be created out of thin air by any sudden "social compact" or edict of government.

On the other hand, it does *not* follow from this analysis that if an extant money were to lose its direct uses, it could no longer be used as money. Thus, if gold, after being established as money, were suddenly to lose its value in ornaments or industrial uses, it would not necessarily lose its character as a money. Once a medium of exchange has been established as a money, money prices continue to be set. If on day X gold loses its direct uses, there will still be previously existing money prices that had been established on day $X - 1$, and these prices form the basis for the marginal utility of gold on day X. Similarly, the money prices thereby determined on day X form the basis for the marginal utility of money on day $X + 1$. From X on, gold could be demanded for its exchange value alone, and not at all for its direct use. Therefore, while it is absolutely necessary that a money *originate* as a commodity with direct uses, it is not absolutely necessary that the direct uses continue after the money has been established.

The money prices of consumers' goods have now been completely explained in terms of individual value scales, and these value scales have been explained up to the point of the content of the subjective use-valuations of each good. Economics is not concerned with the specific content of these ends, but with the explanation of various phenomena of action based on *any* given ends, and therefore its task in this sphere is fully accomplished by tracing these phenomena back to subjective valuations of useful goods.[22]

C. UTILITY AND COSTS

We may sum up the utility and cost considerations in decisions of buyers and sellers of consumers' goods—or, rather, of potential buyers and sellers (cf. chapter 2, pp. 139 f.)—as follows:

Seller:

Revenue: Marginal Utility of Addition of the Units of Money = value rank in most valuable prospective use

Cost:

Either
1) Marginal Utility of good in direct use —highest-ranked use that would have to be sacrificed

Or

2) Marginal Utility of holding for anticipated future sale at higher price —whichever is the higher on his value scale

In cases where neither cost item is present, the sale is costless.

Buyer:

Revenue: Marginal Utility of Addition of the Units of the Good = highest-ranked direct use of units

Cost: Marginal Utility of Units of Money—value rank in highest-ranked use that will have to be sacrificed in making the exchange

The aim of the actor is always to achieve a psychic profit from an action by having his marginal revenue exceed his marginal cost. Only after the decision has been made, the action taken, and the consequences assessed, can the actor know if his decision was correct, i.e., if his psychic revenue really did exceed his cost. It is possible that his cost may prove to have been greater than his revenue and that therefore he lost on the exchange.

It is convenient to distinguish the two vantage points by which an actor judges his action as *ex ante* and *ex post*. *Ex ante* is his position when he must decide on a course of action; it is the relevant and dominant consideration for human action. It is the actor considering his alternative courses and the consequences of each. *Ex post* is his recorded observation of the results of his past action. It is the judging of his past actions and their results. *Ex ante,* then, he will always take the most advantageous course of action, and will always have a psychic profit, with revenue exceeding cost. *Ex post,* he may have profited or lost from a course of action. Revenue may or may not have exceeded cost, depending on how good an entrepreneur he has been in making his original action. It is clear that his *ex post* judgments are mainly useful to him in the weighing of his *ex ante* considerations for future action.

Suppose that an ultimate consumer buys a product and then finds that he was mistaken in this purchase and that the good has little or no value to him. Thus, a man might buy a cake and find that he does not like it at all. *Ex ante* the (expected) utility of the cake was greater than the marginal utility of the money forgone in purchasing it; *ex post* he finds that he was in error and that if he had it to do over again, he would not have bought the cake. The purchase was the consumer's responsibility, and he must bear the loss as well as the gain from his voluntary transaction. Of course, no one can relive the past, but he can use this knowledge, for example, to avoid purchasing such a cake again. It should be obvious that the cake, once purchased, may have little or no value even though the man originally paid several grains of gold for it. The *cost* of the cake was the forgone marginal utility of the three grains of gold paid for it. But this cost incurred *in the past* cannot confer any value on the cake *now*. This would seem obvious, and yet economics has always suffered from neglect of this truth, particularly during the nineteenth century, in the form of various "cost" theories of value. These cost theories asserted that the value of goods is conferred by the costs or sacrifices incurred in their acquisition in the past. On the contrary, it is clear that value can be conferred on a good only by individuals' desires to use it directly in the *present* or in the present expectation of selling to such individuals in the *future*.[23]

We may modify the buyer summary above by considering the case in which the buyer is not an ultimate consumer, but rather a speculative buyer anticipating a future price rise. In that case, a higher revenue for him will be the marginal utility of holding for anticipated future sale at a higher price, which he considers net of the cost of storage.

D. PLANNING AND THE RANGE OF CHOICE

It should be evident that the the establishment of money tremendously broadens the range of choice open to everybody. The range of alternative uses that can be satisfied by units of money is far wider than the number of uses to which individual goods can be put. Horses or houses can be allocated to several uses, raw materials to many areas of production, but money can be allocated in expenditure on *every* single type of exchangeable good in the society, whether a tangible commodity or an intangible service, a consumers' or a capital or a natural good or claims to these goods. Money serves greatly to expand the range of choice; and it itself becomes a key *means* to be allocated to the most highly valued of alternative ends.[24]

It might be worth while to consider at this point what each person does in action. He is always engaged in allocating means to the most highly valued of his alternative ends, as ranked on his value scale. His actions in general, and his actions *in exchange* in particular, are always the result of certain expectations on his part, expectations of the most satisfactory course that he could follow. He always follows the route that he *expects* will yield him the most highly ranked available end at a certain future time (which might in some cases be so near as to be almost immediate) and therefore a psychic profit from the action. If he proves to have acted erroneously, so that another course of action would have yielded him a greater psychic revenue, then he has incurred a loss. *Ex ante* he appraises his situation, present and prospective future, chooses among his valuations, tries to achieve the highest ones according to his "know-how," and then chooses courses of action on the basis of these *plans*. Plans are his decisions concerning future action, based on his ranking of ends and on his assumed knowledge of how to attain the ends. Every individual, therefore, is constantly engaged in *planning*. This planning may range from an impressive investment in a new steel plant to a small boy's decision to spend two cents on candy, but it is planning nevertheless.[25] It is erroneous, therefore, to assert that a free market society is "unplanned"; on the contrary, each individual plans for himself.

But does not "chaos" result from the fact that individual plans do not seem to be co-ordinated? On the contrary, the exchange system, in the first place, co-ordinates individual plans by benefiting *both* parties to every exchange. In the second place, the bulk of the present volume is devoted to an explanation and analysis of the principles and order that determine the various exchange phenomena in a monetary economy: prices, output, expenditures, etc. Far from being chaotic, the structure of the monetary economy presents an intricate, systematic picture and is deducible from the basic existence of human action and indirect exchange.[26]

6. *Interrelations among the Prices of Consumers' Goods*

Thus, at any given point in time, the consumer is confronted with the previously existing money prices of the various consumers' goods on the market. On the basis of his utility scale, he determines his rankings of various units of the several goods and of money, and these rankings determine how much money he will spend on each of the various goods. Specifically, *he will spend money on each particular good until the marginal utility of adding a unit of the good ceases to be greater than the marginal utility that its money price on the market has for him.* This is the law of consumer action in a market economy. As he spends money on a good, the marginal utility of the new units declines, while the marginal utility of the money forgone rises, until he ceases spending on that good. In those cases where the marginal utility of even one unit of a good is lower than the marginal utility of its money price, the individual will not buy any of that good.

In this way are determined the individual demand schedules for each good and, consequently, the aggregate market-demand schedules for all buyers. The position of the market-demand schedule determines what the market price will be in the immediate future. Thus, if we consider action as divided into periods consisting of "days," then the individual buyers set their rankings and demand schedules on the basis of the prices existing at the end of day 1, and these demand schedules determine what the prices will be by the end of day 2.

The reader is now referred back to the discussion in chapter 2 above, sections 9 and 10. The analysis, there applied to barter conditions, applies to money prices as well. At the end of each day, the demand schedules (or rather, the total demand schedules) and the stock in existence on that day set the market equilibrium price for that day. In the money economy, these factors determine the money prices of the various goods during that day. The analysis of changes in the prices of a good, set forth in chapter 2, is directly applicable here. In the money economy, the most important markets are naturally continuous, as goods continue to be produced in each day. Changes in supply and demand schedules or changes in total demand schedules and quantity of stock have exactly the same directional effect as in barter. An increase in the market's total demand schedule over the previous day tends to increase the money price for the day; an increase in stock available tends to lower the price, etc. As in barter, the stock of each good, at the end of each day, has been transferred into the hands of the most eager possessors.

Up to this point we have concentrated on the determination of the money price of each consumers' good, without devoting much attention to the relations among these prices. The interrelationships should be clear, however. The available goods are ranked, along with the possibility of holding the money commodity in one's cash balance, on each individual's value scale. Then, in accordance with the rankings and the law of utility, the individual allocates his units of money to the most highly valued uses: the various consumers' goods, investment in various factors, and addition to his cash balance. Let us here set aside the question of the distribution chosen between consumption and investment, and the question of addition to the cash balance, until later chapters, and consider the interrelations among the prices of consumers' goods alone.

The law of the interrelation of consumers' goods is: *The more substitutes are available for any given good, the more elastic will tend to be the demand schedules (individual and market) for that good.* By the definition of "good," two goods cannot be "perfect substitutes" for each other, since if consumers regarded two goods as completely identical, they would, by definition, be one good. *All* consumers' goods are, on the other hand, *partial* substitutes for one another. When a man ranks in his value scale the myriad of goods available and balances the diminishing utilities of each, he is treating them all as partial substitutes for one another. A change in ranking for one good by necessity changes the rankings of all the other goods, since all the rankings are ordinal and relative. A higher price for one good (owing, say, to a decrease in stock produced) will tend to shift the demand of consumers from that to other consumers' goods, and therefore their demand schedules will tend to increase. Conversely, an increased supply and a consequent lowering of price for a good will tend to shift consumer demand from other goods to this one and lower the demand schedules for the other goods (for some, of course, more than for others).

It is a mistake to suppose that only technologically similar goods are substitutes for one another. The more money consumers spend on pork, the less they have to spend on beef, or the more money they spend on travel, the less they have to spend on TV sets. Suppose that a reduction in its supply raises the price of pork on the market; it is clear that the quantity demanded, and the price, of beef will be affected by this change. *If the demand schedule for pork is more than unitarily elastic in this range,* then the higher price will cause less money to be spent on pork, and more money will tend to be shifted to such a substitute as beef. The demand schedules for beef will increase, and the price of beef will tend to rise. On the other hand, if the demand schedule for pork is *inelastic,* more consumers' money will be spent on pork, and the result will be a fall in the demand schedule for beef and consequently in its price. Such interrelations of substitute goods, however, hold true in some degree for all goods, since all goods are substitutes for one another; for every good is engaged in competing for the consumers' stock of money. Of course, some goods are "closer" substitutes than others, and the interrelations among them will be stronger than among the others. The closeness of the substitution depends, however, on the particular circumstances of the consumer and his preferences rather than on technological similarity.

Thus, consumers' goods, in so far as they are substitutes for one another, are related as follows: When the stock of *A* rises and the price of *A* therefore *falls,* (1) *if* the demand schedule for *A* is elastic, there will be a tendency for a decline in the demand schedules for *B, C, D,* etc., and consequent declines in their prices; (2) if the demand schedule for *A* is inelastic, there will be a rise in the demand schedules for *B, C, D,* etc., and a consequent *rise* in their prices; (3) if the demand schedule has exactly neutral (or unitary) elasticity, so that there is no change in the amount of money expended on *A,* there will be no effect on the demands for and the prices of the other goods.

As the money economy develops and civilization flowers, there is a great expansion in the types of goods available and therefore in the number of goods that can be substituted for one another. Consequently, there is a tendency for the demands for the various consumers' goods to become more elastic, although they will continue to vary from highly elastic to highly inelastic. In so far as the multiplication of substitutes tends to render demand curves for individual goods elastic, the first type of interaction will tend to predominate. Furthermore, when *new* types of goods are established on the market, these will clearly draw monetary demand away from other, substitute products, and hence bring about the first type of reaction.

The substitutive interrelations of consumers' goods were cogently set forth in this passage by Philip Wicksteed:

> It is sufficiently obvious that when a woman goes into the market uncertain whether she will or will not buy new potatoes, or chickens, the price at which she finds that she can get them may determine her either way . . . For the price is the first and most obvious indication of the nature of the alternatives that she is foregoing, if she makes a contemplated purchase. But it is almost equally obvious that not only the price of these particular things, but the price of a number of other things also will affect the problem. If good, sound, old potatoes are to be had at a low price, the marketer will be less likely to pay a high price for new ones, because there is a good alternative to be had on good terms . . . If the housewife is thinking of doing honour to a small party of neighbours by providing a couple of chickens for their entertainment at supper, it is possible that she could treat them with adequate respect, though not with distinction, by substituting a few pounds of cod. And in that case not only the price of chickens but the price of cod will tend to affect her choice. . . .
>
> But on what does the significance . . . [of the price difference between chicken and cod] depend? Probably upon the price of things

that have no obvious connection with either chicken or cod. A father and mother may have ambitions with respect to the education or accomplishments of their children, and may be willing considerably to curtail their expenditure on other things in order to gratify them. Such parents may be willing to incur . . . entertaining their guests less sumptuously than custom demands, and at the same time getting French or violin lessons for their children. In such cases the question whether to buy new or old potatoes, or whether to entertain friends with chicken or cod, or neither, may be affected by the terms on which French or music lessons of a satisfactory quality can be secured.[27]

While all consumers' goods compete with one another for consumer purchases, some goods are also *complementary* to one another. These are goods whose uses are closely linked together by consumers, so that movements in demand for them are likely to be closely tied together. An example of complementary consumers' goods is *golf clubs* and *golf balls,* two goods the demands for which tend to rise and fall together. In this case, for example, an increase in the supply of golf balls will tend to cause a *fall* in their prices, which will tend to raise the demand schedule for golf *clubs* as well as to increase the quantity of golf balls demanded. This will tend to *increase* the price of golf clubs. In so far, then, as two goods are *complementary* to each other, when the stock of *A* rises, and the price of *A* therefore *falls,* the demand schedule for *B* increases and its price will tend to *rise.* Since a fall in the price of a good will always increase the quantity of the good demanded (by the law of demand), this will always stimulate the demand schedule for a complementary good and thus tend to raise its price.[28] For this effect the elasticity of demand for the original good has no relevance.

Summing up these interrelations among consumers' goods:

Substitutable goods:

If stock of *A* rises, and price of *A* *falls,* and
Demand curve for A is:

Inelastic:	Demand for, Price of, *B, C, D,* . . . *rise*
Elastic:	Demand for, Price of, *B, C, D,* . . . *fall*
Neutral:	No effect on *B, C, D* . . .

Complementary goods:

If stock of *A* rises, price of *A falls,* and: Demand for, and Price of, *B, C, D, . . . rise.*

(Unless Demand Curve for *A* is vertical, then there is no effect.)

All goods are substitutable for one another, while fewer are complementary. When they are also complementary, then the complementary effect will be mixed with the substitutive effect, and the nature of each particular case will determine which effect will be the stronger.

This discussion of the interrelation of consumers' goods has treated the effect only of changes from the *stock,* or supply, side. The effects are different when the change occurs in *the demand schedule* instead of in the quantity of stock. Suppose that the market-demand schedule for good *A increases*—shifts to the right. This means that, for every hypothetical price, the quantity of *A* bought, and therefore the amount of money spent on *A, increases.* But, given the supply (stock) of money in the society, this means that there will be decreases in the demand schedules for one or more other goods.[29] More money spent on good *A,* given the stock of money, signifies that less money is spent on goods *B, C, D . . .* The demand curves for the latter goods "shift to the left," and the prices of these goods *fall.* Therefore, the effect of the substitutability of all goods for one another is that an increased demand for *A,* resulting in a *rise* in the price of *A,* will lead to decreased demand schedules and *falling* prices for goods *B, C, D . . .* We can see this relation more fully when we realize that the demand schedules are determined by individual value scales and that a rise in the marginal utility of a unit of *A* necessarily means a relative fall in the utility of the other consumers' goods.

In so far as two goods are complementary, another effect tends to occur. If there is an increase in the demand schedule for golf clubs, it is likely to be accompanied by an increase in the demand schedule for golf balls, since both are determined by increased relative desires to play golf. When changes come from the demand side, the prices of complementary goods tend to rise and fall together. In this case, we should not say that the rise in demand for *A led* to a rise in demand for its complement *B,* since both increases were due to an increased demand for the consumption "package" in which the two goods are intimately related.

We may now sum up both sets of interrelations of consumers' goods, for changes in stock and in demand (suppliers' reservation demand can be omitted here, since this speculative element tends toward correct estimates of the basic determinant, consumer demand).

Table 10 indicates the reactions of other goods, *B, C, D,* to changes in the determinants for good *A,* in so far as these goods are substitutable for it or complementary to it. A + sign signifies that the prices of the other goods react in the *same* direction as the price of good *A;* a – sign signifies that the prices of the other goods react in the *opposite* direction:

TABLE 10

CHANGE IN PRICES OF *B, C, D,* . . .

If *A* and the Good are:	If Change in Stock of *A*	If Change in Demand for *A*
Substitutable for each other	+ if Demand for *A* is *elastic* – if Demand for *A* is *inelastic* None 0 if Demand for *A* is *unitary*	–
Complementary to each other	–	+

In some cases, an *old* stock of a good may be evaluated differently from the *new* and therefore may become a separate good. Thus, while well-stored old nails might be considered the same good as newly produced nails, an old Ford will not be considered the same as a new one. There will, however, definitely be a close relation between the two goods. If the supply schedule for the new Fords decreases and the price rises, consumers will tend to shift to the purchase of old Fords, tending to raise the price of the latter. Thus, old and new commodities, technologically similar, tend to be very close substitutes for each other, and their demands and prices tend to be closely related.

Much has been written in the economic literature of consumption theory on the "assumption" that each consumers' good is desired quite independently of other goods. Actually, as we have seen, the desires for various goods are of necessity interdependent, since all are ranged on the consumers' value scales. Utilities of each of the goods are relative to one another. These ranked values for goods and money permit the formation of individual, and then aggregate, demand schedules in money for each particular good.

7. *The Prices of Durable Goods and Their Services*

Why does a man purchase a consumers' good? As we saw back in chapter 1, a consumers' good is desired and sought because the actor believes that it will serve to satisfy his urgently valued desires, that it will enable him to attain his valued ends. In other words, the good is valuable because of the expected *services* that it will provide. Tangible commodities, then, such as food, clothing, houses, etc., and intangible personal services, such as medical attention and concert performances, are similar in the life of the consumer. Both are evaluated by the consumer in terms of their services in providing him with satisfactions.

Every type of consumers' good will yield a certain amount of *services per unit of time*. These may be called *unit services*. When they are exchangeable, these services may be sold individually. On the other hand, when a good is a physical commodity and is durable, it may be sold to the consumer in one piece, thereby embodying an expected future accrual of many unit services.

What are the interrelations among the markets for, and prices of, the unit services and the durable good as a whole?

Other things being equal, it is obvious that a *more* durable good is more valuable than a *less* durable good, since it embodies more future unit services. Thus, suppose that there are two television sets, each identical in service to the viewer, but that *A* has an expected life of five years, and *B* of ten. Though the service is identical, *B* has twice as many services as *A* to offer the consumer. On the market, then, the price of *B* will tend to be twice the price of *A*.[30]

For nondurable goods, the problem of the separate sale of the service of the good and of the good itself does not arise. Since they embody services over a relatively short span of time, they are almost always sold as a whole. Butter, eggs, Wheaties, etc., are sold as a whole, embodying all their services. Few would think of "renting" eggs. Personal services, on the other hand, are never sold as a whole, since, on the free market, slave contracts are not enforceable. Thus, no one can purchase a doctor or a lawyer or a pianist for life, to perform services at will with no further payment. Personal services, then, are always sold in their individual units.

The problem whether services should be sold separately or with the good as a whole arises in the case of durable commodities, such as houses, pianos, tuxedos, television sets, etc. We have seen that goods are sold, not as a total class, e.g., "bread" or "eggs," but in separate homogeneous units of their supply, such as "loaves of bread," or "dozens of eggs." In the present discussion, a good can be sold either as a complete physical unit—a house, a television set, etc.—or in service units over a period of time. This sale of service units of a durable good is called *renting* or *renting out* or *hiring out* the good. The price of the service unit is called the *rent*.

Since the good itself is only a bundle of expected service units, it is proper to base our analysis on the *service unit*. It is clear that the demand for, and the price of, a service unit of a consumers' good will be determined on exactly the same principles as those set forth in the preceding analysis of this chapter.

A durable consumers' good embodies service units as they will accrue over a period of time. Thus, suppose that a house is expected to have a life of 20 years. Assume that a year's rental of the house has a market price, as determined by the market supply and demand schedules, of 10 ounces of gold. Now, what will be the market price of the house itself should it be sold? Since the annual rental price is 10 ounces (and if this rental is expected to continue), the buyer of the house will obtain what amounts to 20 $\times$ 10, or 200 ounces, of prospective rental income. The price of the house as a whole will tend inexorably to equal the present value of the 200 ounces. Let us assume for convenience at this point that there is no phenomenon of time preference and that the present value of 200 ounces is therefore equal to 200 ounces. In that case, the price of the house as a whole will tend to equal 200 ounces.

Suppose that the market price of the house as a whole is 180 ounces. In that case, there will be a rush to buy the house, since there is an expected monetary profit to be gained by purchasing for 180 ounces and then renting out for a total income of 200 ounces. This action is similar to speculative purchasers' buying a good and expecting to resell at a higher price. On the other hand, there will be a great reluctance by the present owners of such houses (or of *the* house, if there is no other house adjudged by the market as the same good), to sell at that price, since it is far more profitable to rent it out than to sell it. Thus, under these conditions, there will be a considerable excess of demand over supply of this type of house for sale, at a price of 180 ounces. The upbidding of the excess demand tends to raise the price toward 200. On the other hand, suppose that the market price is above 200. In that case, there will be a paucity of demand to purchase, since it would be cheaper to pay rental for it instead of paying the sum to purchase it. On the contrary, possessors will be eager to sell the house rather than rent it out, since the price for sale is better. The excess supply over demand at a price over 200 will drive the price down to the equilibrium point.

Thus, while every type of market price is determined as in the foregoing sections of this chapter, the market also determines price *relations.* We see that there is a definite relationship between the price of the unit services of a durable consumers' good and the price of the good as a whole. If that relationship is disturbed or does not apply at any particular time, the actions of individuals on the market will tend to establish it, because prospects of monetary gain arise until it is established, and action to obtain such gain inevitably tends to eliminate the opportunity. This is a case of "arbitrage" in the same sense as the establishment of *one price* for a good on the market. If two prices for one good exist, people will tend to rush to purchase in the cheaper market and sell more of the good in the more expensive market, until the play of supply and demand on each market establishes an "equilibrium" price and eliminates the arbitrage opportunity. In the case of the durable good and its services, there is an *equilibrium-price relation,* which the market tends to establish. *The market price of the good as a whole is equal to the present value of the sum of its expected (future) rental incomes or rental prices.*

The expected future rental incomes are, of course, not necessarily a simple extrapolation of present rental prices. Indeed, since prices are always changing, it will almost always be the case that rental prices will change in the future. When a person buys a durable good, he is buying its services for a length of time extending into the future; hence, he is more concerned with *future* than with *present* rates; he merely takes the latter as a possible guide to the future.[31] Now, suppose that the individuals on the market generally estimate that rents for this house over the next decade or so will be much lower than at present. The price of the house will then not be 20×10 ounces, but some correspondingly smaller amount.

At this point we shall define the "price of the good as whole" as its *capital value* on the market, even though there is risk of confusion with the concept of "capital good." The *capital value* of any good (be it consumers' or capital good or nature-given factor) is the money price which, as a durable good, it presently sells for on the market. The concept applies to durable goods, embodying future services.[32] The capital value of a consumers' good will tend to equal the present value of the sum of expected unit rentals.

The capital value at any time is based on expectations of future rental prices. What happens when these expectations are erroneous? Suppose, for example, that the market expects the rental prices of this house to increase in the next few years and therefore sets the capital value higher than 200 ounces. Suppose, further, that the rental prices actually decline instead. This means that the original capital value on the market had overestimated the rental income from the house. Those who had sold the house at, say, 250, have gained, while those who bought the house in order to rent it out have lost, on the transaction. Thus, those who have forecast better than their fellows gain, while the poorer forecasters lose, as a result of their speculative transactions.

It is obvious that such monetary profits come *not* simply from correct forecasting, *but from forecasting more correctly than other individuals.* If all the individuals had forecast correctly, then the original capital value would have been below 200, say, 150, to account for the eventually lower rental prices. In that case no such monetary profit would have appeared.[33] It should be clear that the gains or losses are the consequences of the freely undertaken action of the gainers and losers themselves. The man who has bought a good to rent out at what proves to be an excessive capital value has only himself to blame for being overoptimistic about the monetary return on his investment. The man who sells at a capital value higher than the eventual rental income is rewarded for his sagacity through decisions voluntarily taken by all parties. And since successful forecasters are, in effect, rewarded, and poor ones penalized, and in proportion to good and poor judgment respectively, the market tends to establish and maintain as high a quality of forecasting as is humanly possible to achieve.

The equilibrium relation between the capital value on the market and the sum of *expected* future rents is a day-to-day equilibrium that tends always to be set by the market. It is similar to the day-to-day *market equilibrium* price for a good set by supply and demand. On the other hand, the equilibrium relation between present capital value and *actual* future rents is only a long-range tendency fostered by the market's encouragement of successful forecasters. This relation is a *final* equilibrium, similar to the *final equilibrium* prices that set the goal toward which the day-to-day prices tend.

Study of capital value and rental prices requires additional supply-demand analysis. The determination of the unit rental price presents no problem. Price determination of the capital value, however, needs to be modified to account for this dependence on, and relationship to, the rental price. The *demand* for the durable good will now be, not only for direct use, but *also,* on the part of others, *demand for investment in future renting out.* If a man feels that the market price of the capital value of a good is lower than the income he can obtain from future rentals, he will purchase the good and enter the renting-out market as a supplier. Similarly, the *reserved demand* for the good as a whole will be not only for direct use or for speculative price increases, but *also* for future renting out of the good. If the possessor of a durable good believes that the selling price (capital value) is lower than what he can get in rents, he will reserve the supply and rent out the good. The capital value of the good will be such as to clear the total stock, and the total of all these demands for the good will be in equilibrium. The reserved demand of the buyers will, as before, be due to their reserved demand for money, while the sellers of both the good as a whole and of its unit services will be demanding money in exchange.

In other words, for any consumers' good, the possessors have the choice of either consuming it directly or selling it for money. In the case of durable consumers' goods, the possessors can do any one of the following with the good: use it directly, sell it whole, or *hire it out*—selling its unit services over a period of time. We have already seen that if using it directly is highest on his value scale, then the man uses the good and reserves his stock from the market. If selling it whole is highest on his value scale, he enters the "capital" market for the good as a supplier. If renting it out is highest on his value scale, then he enters the "renting" market for the good as a supplier. Which of these latter alternatives will be higher on his value scale depends on his estimate of which course will yield him the higher money income. The shape of the supply curves in both the capital and rental markets will be either rightward- and upward-sloping or vertical, since the greater the expected income, the less will be the amount reserved for direct use. It is clear that the supply schedules on the two markets are interconnected. They will tend to come into equilibrium when the equilibrium-price relation is established between them.

Similarly, the nonpossessors of a good at any given time will choose between (*a*) not buying it and reserving their money, (*b*) buying it outright, and (*c*) renting it. They will choose the course highest on their value scales, which depends partially on their demand for money and on their estimate of which type of purchase will be cheaper. If they decide to buy, they will buy on what they estimate is the cheaper market; then they can either use the good directly or resell it on the more expensive market. Thus, if the capital value of the house is 200 and a buyer estimates that total rental prices will be 220, he buys outright at 200, after which he may either use it directly or enter the rental market as a supplier in order to earn the expected 220 ounces. The latter choice again depends on his value scale. This is another example of the arbitrage action already explained, and the effect is to link the demand curves for the two types of markets for durable goods.

Here it must be pointed out that in some cases the renting contract itself takes on the characteristics of a capital contract and the estimating of future return. Such is the case of a *long-term* renting contract. Suppose that A is planning to rent a house to B for thirty years, at a set annual price. Then, instead of continual changes in the rental price, the latter is *fixed* by the original contract. Here again, the demand and supply schedules are set according to the various individual estimates of the changing course of other varying rents for the same type of good. Thus, if there are two identical houses, and it is expected that the sum of the varying rents on house *A* for the next thirty years will be

300 ounces, then the long-term renting price for house *B* will tend to be set at 10 ounces per year. Here again, there is a similar connection between markets. *The price of presently established long-term rents will tend to be equal to the present value of the sum of the expected fluctuating rents for identical goods.* If the general expectation is that the sum of rents will be 360 ounces, then there will be a heavy demand for long-term rent purchases at 300 ounces and a diminished supply for rent at that price, until the long-term rental price is driven to 12 ounces per year, when the sum will be the same. And here again, the ever-present uncertainty of the future causes the more able forecasters to gain and the less able ones to lose.[34]

In actuality, time preference exists, and the present value of the future rentals is always less by a certain discount than the sum of these rentals. If this were not so, the capital value of very durable goods, goods which wear out only imperceptibly, would be almost infinite. An estate expected to last and be in demand for hundreds of years would have an almost infinitely high selling price. The reason this does not happen is that *time preference* discounts future goods in accordance with the length of time being considered. How the rate of time preference is arrived at will be treated in later chapters. However, the following is an illustration of the effect of time preference on the capital-value of a good. Assume a durable good, expected to last for 10 years, with an expected rental value of 10 ounces each year. If the rate of time preference is 10% per annum, then the future rents and their *present* value are as follows:

Years:	1	2	3	4	5	6	7	8	9	10
Expected Rents:	10	10	10	10	10	10	10	10	10	10
Present Value: (assuming first year payment at one year from present date)	9	8.1	7.3	6.7	6.0	5.4	4.9	4.4	4.0	3.6

Sum of these present values = 59.4 ounces = Capital value, as compared to a sum of 100 ounces of future rent.

As the date of time recedes into the future, the compounded discount becomes greater, finally reducing the present value to a negligible amount.

It is important to recognize that the time-preference factor does *not*, as does relatively correct forecasting of an uncertain situation, confer monetary profits or losses. If the time-preference rate is 10%, purchasing the aforementioned good for 59.4 ounces, holding it, and renting it out for 10 years to acquire 100 ounces does *not* constitute a monetary profit. Present money was at this premium over future money, and what this man earned was simply the amount of future income that the market had evaluated as equal to 59.4 ounces of present money.

In general, we may sum up the action of entrepreneurs in the field of durable consumers' goods by saying that they will tend to *invest* in the outright purchase of (already existing) durable consumers' goods when they believe that the present capital value of the good on the market is less than the sum of future rentals (discounted by time preference) that they will receive. They will sell such goods outright when they believe that the present capital value is higher than the discounted sum of future rentals. Better forecasters will earn profits, and poorer ones will suffer losses. In so far as the forecasting is correct, these "arbitrage" opportunities will tend to disappear.

Although we have analyzed the arbitrage profits and losses of entrepreneurship in the case of selling outright as against renting, we have yet to unravel fully the laws that govern entrepreneurial incomes—the incomes that the producers strive to obtain in the process of production. This problem will be analyzed in later chapters.[35]

8. *Welfare Comparisons and the Ultimate Satisfactions of the Consumer*

In our preoccupation with analysis of the action of man in the monetary economy, it must not be thought that the general truths presented in chapter 1 remain no longer valid. On the contrary, in chapter 1 they were applied to isolated Crusoe-type situations because we logically begin with such situations in order to be able to analyze the more complex interrelations of the monetary economy. However, the truths formulated in the first chapter are applicable still, not only through logical inferences applied to the monetary nexus, but also directly to all situations in the monetary economy in which money is not involved.

There is another sense in which the analysis of the first chapter is directly applicable in a money economy. We may be primarily concerned in the analysis of exchange with the consumer's allocation of money to the most highly valued of its uses—based on the individual's value scales. We must not forget, however, the *ultimate* goal of the consumers' expenditures of money. This goal is the actual use of the purchased goods in attaining his most highly valued ends. Thus, for the purposes of analysis of the *market,* once Jones has purchased three pounds of butter, we have lost interest in the butter (assuming there is no chance of Jones' re-entering the market to sell the butter). We call the retail sale of the butter the sale of the *consumers' good,* since this is its *last sale for money* along the path of the butter's production. Now the good is in the hands of the ultimate consumer. The consumer has weighed the purchase on his value scale and has decided upon it.

Strictly, we must never lose sight of the fact that this purchase by the consumer is *not* the last stopping point of the butter, when we consider human action in its entirety. The butter must be carried to the man's home. Then, Jones allocates the units of butter to their most highly valued uses: buttered toast, butter in a cake, butter on a bun, etc. To use the butter in a cake or sandwich, for example, Mrs. Jones bakes the cake and prepares the sandwich and then brings it to the table where Jones eats it. We can see that the analysis of chapter 1 holds true, in that useful goods—horses, butter, or anything else—in the hands of the consumer are allocated, in accordance with their utility, to the most highly valued uses. Also, we can see that actually the *butter when last sold for money* was not a consumers' good, but a *cap-*

ital good—albeit one of lower order than at any other previous stage of its production. Capital goods are produced goods that must be combined still further with other factors in order to provide the consumers' good—the good that finally yields the ultimate satisfaction to the consumer. From the full praxeological point of view, the butter becomes a consumers' good only when it is actually being eaten or otherwise "consumed" by the ultimate consumer.

From the standpoint of praxeology proper—the complete formal analysis of human action in all its aspects—it is inadmissible to call the good at its last retail sale to the consumer a "consumers' good." From the point of view of that subdivision of praxeology that covers traditional economics—that of *catallactics,* the science of monetary exchanges—however, it becomes convenient to call the good at the last retail stage a "consumers' good." This is the last stage of the good in the monetary nexus—the last point, in most cases, at which it is open to producers to invest money in factors. To call the good at this final monetary stage a "consumers' good" is permissible, provided we are always aware of the foregoing qualifications. We must always remember that without the final stages and the final allocation by consumers, there would be no *raison d'être* for the whole monetary exchange process. Economics cannot afford to dismiss the ultimate consumption stage simply because it has passed beyond the monetary nexus; it is the final goal and end of the monetary transactions by individuals in society.

Attention to this point will clear up many confusions. Thus, there is the question of consumers' income. In chapter 3, we analyzed consumers' money income and the universal goal of maximizing psychic income, and we indicated to some extent the relation between the two. Everyone attempts to maximize the latter, which includes on its value scale a vast range of all consumers' goods, both exchangeable and nonexchangeable. Exchangeable goods are generally in the monetary nexus, and therefore can be purchased for money, whereas nonexchangeable goods are not. We have indicated some of the consequences of the fact that it is *psychic* and not *monetary* income that is being maximized, and how this introduces qualifications into the expenditure of effort or labor and in the investment in producers' goods. It is also true that psychic income, being purely subjective, cannot be measured. Further, from the standpoint of praxeology, we cannot even ordinally compare the psychic income or utility of one person with that of another. We cannot say that A's income or "utility" is greater than B's.

We can, at least theoretically, measure monetary incomes by adding the amount of money income each person obtains, but this is by no means a measure of psychic income. Furthermore, it does not, as we perhaps might think, give any exact indication of the amount of services that each individual obtains purely from *exchangeable* consumers' goods. An income of 50 ounces of gold in one year may not, and most likely will not, mean the same to him in terms of services from exchangeable goods as an income of 50 ounces in some other year. The purchasing power of money in terms of all other commodities is continually changing, and there is no way to measure such changes.

Of course, as historians rather than economists, we can make imprecise judgments comparing the "real" income rather than the monetary income between periods. Thus, if Jones received 1,000 ounces of income in one year and 1,200 in the next, and prices generally rose during the year, Jones' "real income" in terms of goods purchasable by the money has risen considerably less than the nominal monetary increase or has perhaps fallen. However, as we shall see further below, there is no precise method of measuring or even identifying the purchasing power of money and its changes.

Even if we confine ourselves to the same period, monetary incomes are not an infallible guide. There are, for example, many consumers' goods that are obtainable *both* through monetary exchange and outside the money nexus. Thus, Jones may be spending 18 ounces a month on food, rent, and household maintenance, while Smith spends only 9 ounces a month. This does not necessarily mean that Jones obtains twice as much of these services as Smith. Jones may live in a hotel, which provides him with these services in exchange for money. Smith, on the other hand, may be married and may obtain household and cooking services outside the monetary nexus. Smith's psychic income from these services may be equal to, or greater than, Jones', despite the lower monetary expenditures.

Neither can we measure psychic incomes if we confine ourselves to goods in the monetary nexus. A and B might live in the same sort of house, but how can the economist-observer deduce from this that the two are deriving the same amount of enjoyment from the house? Obviously, the degree of enjoyment will most likely differ, but the mere fact of the income or property will provide no clue to the direction or extent of the difference.

It follows that the law of the diminishing marginal utility of money applies only to the valuations of *each individual* person. There can be no comparison of such utility between persons. Thus, we cannot, as some writers have done, assert that an extra dollar is enjoyed less by a Rockefeller than by a poor man. If Rockefeller were suddenly to become poor, each dollar would be worth more to him than it is now; similarly, if the poor man were to become rich, his value scales remaining the same, each dollar would be worth less than it is now. But this is a far cry from attempting to compare different individuals' enjoyments or subjective valuations. It is certainly possible that a Rockefeller enjoys the services of each dollar more than a poor, but highly ascetic, individual does.

9. *Some Fallacies Relating to Utility*

A doctrine commonly held by writers on utility is that the consumer acts so as to bring the marginal utility that any good has for him into *equality* with the price of that good. To understand this thesis, let us examine the preference scale of Mr. Jones in contemplating the purchase of one or more suits (and we shall assume that each suit is of the same quality—the same "good"). Suppose his value scale is as follows:

—3.4 grains of gold
—3.3 " " "
—(1st suit)
—3.2 " " "
—3.1 " " "
—(2nd suit)
—3.0 " " "
—2.9 " " "
—2.8 " " "
—(3rd suit)
—2.7 " " "

And suppose also that the market price is 2.9 grains per suit. Jones will buy not one or three, but two, suits. *He will buy up to the last unit at which the diminishing marginal utility that the suit has for him exceeds the increasing marginal utility of money.*[36] This is obvious. Now, if a writer couches the exposition in terms of highly divisible goods, such as butter, and in terms of small units of money, such as pennies, it is easy to leap unthinkingly to the conclusion that the consumer for each good will act in such a way as to equalize, at the market price, the marginal utility of the sum of money and the marginal utility of the good. It should be clear, however, that there is never any such "equalization." In the case of the suit, the rank of the second suit is still considerably above the rank of the 2.9 grains. So there is no equalization. Even in the case of the most divisible of goods, there will still be a *difference in rank,* not an equalization, between the two utilities. A man may buy 11 ounces of butter at 10 cents an ounce, until there is nothing ranking between the 11th ounce and the 10 cents on his utility scale; yet there is still no *equality,* but a difference in rank, with the last ounce bought ranking higher than the last sum of money spent. Of course, the consumer tries to spend his money so as to bring the two as close as possible, but they can never be equal.

Furthermore, the marginal utility of each particular good, after the purchases are made, differs in rank from that of every other. Thus, let us take one grain of gold as the monetary unit under consideration. Let us say that the given market-prices of various goods are as follows:

eggs—1 dozen per grain;
butter—1 pound per grain;
bread—1 loaf per grain;
candy—1 bar per grain.

Now each individual will purchase each commodity until the last point at which the marginal utility of the unit exceeds the marginal utility of a grain of gold. For one man this might mean the purchase of 5 pounds of butter, 3 loaves of bread, 2 bars of candy, etc. This would mean that either a sixth pound of butter or a third loaf of bread would have a lower marginal utility than a grain of gold forgone. However, the marginal utility of each good will still differ in rank from that of every other and will not be equal to that of any other.

Another, even more curious doctrine holds that in equilibrium the ratio of the marginal utilities of the various goods equals the ratio of their prices. Without entering in detail into the manner by which these writers arrive at this conclusion, we can see its absurdity clearly, since utilities are not quantities and therefore cannot be divided.

These fallacies stem from a related one: the idea that an individual will act so as to *equalize* the marginal utility that any good will have in each of its uses. Applied to money, this would imply that the marginal utility of a unit of money is equal for each field of expenditure for each person. This is incorrect, as we have just seen that the marginal utilities of the various goods are not equalized. Successive units of a good are allocated to the most desired end, then to the next most desired satisfaction, etc. If there are several uses for the good, each one involving many possible units, the marginal utility of a unit in each use continues to decline as the supply increases. As goods are purchased, the marginal utility of each good purchased diminishes, and a man may allocate his money first to one use, then to another, and then to the first use again. However, in no case is there any equalization of marginal utilities.

The dogma of the equalization of marginal utilities may best be illustrated in the following passage from perhaps the originator of this line of argument:

Let s be the whole stock of some commodity, and let it be capable of two distinct uses. Then we may represent the two quantities appropriated to these uses by x_1 and y_1, it being a condition that x_1 plus y_1 equal s. The person may be conceived as successively expending small quantities of the commodity; now it is the inevitable tendency of human nature to choose that course which appears to offer the greatest advantage at the moment. Hence, when the person remains satisfied with the distribution he has made, it follows that no alteration would yield him more pleasure; which amounts to saying that an increment of commodity would yield exactly as much utility in one use as in another. Let Δu_1, Δu_2, be the increments of utility, which might arise respectively from consuming an increment of commodity in the two different ways. When the distribution is completed, we ought to have $\Delta u_1 = \Delta u_2$ . . . The same reasoning . . . will evidently apply to any two uses, and hence to all uses simultaneously, so that we obtain a series of equations less numerous by a unit than the number of ways of using the commodity. The general result is that the commodity, if consumed by a perfectly wise being, must be consumed with a maximum production of utility.[37]

The chief errors here consist in conceiving utility as a certain quantity, a definite function of an increment in the commodity, and in treating the problem in terms of infinitely small steps. Both procedures are fallacious. Utilities are not quantities, but ranks, and the successive amounts of a commodity that are used are always discrete units, not infinitely small ones. If the units are discrete, then the rank of each unit differs from that of every other, and there can be no equalization.

Many errors in discussions of utility stem from an assumption that it is some sort of quantity, measurable at least in principle. When we refer to a consumer's "maximization" of utility, for example, we are *not* referring to a definite stock or quantity of something to be maximized. We refer to the *highest-ranking position* on the individual's value scale. Similarly, it is the assumption of the infinitely small, added to the belief in utility as a quantity, that leads to the error of treating marginal utility as the mathematical derivative of the integral "total utility" of several units of a good. Actually, there is no such relation, and there is no such thing as "total utility," only the marginal utility of a *larger-*

sized unit. The size of the unit depends on its relevance to the particular action.[38]

This illustrates one of the grave dangers of the mathematical method in economics, since this method carries with it the bias of the assumption of continuity, or the infinitely small step. Most writers on economics consider this assumption a harmless, but potentially very useful, fiction, and point to its great success in the field of physics. They overlook the enormous differences between the world of physics and the world of human action. The problem is not simply one of acquiring the microscopic measuring tools that physics has developed. The crucial difference is that physics deals with inanimate objects that *move* but do not *act*. The movements of these objects can be investigated as being governed by precise, quantitatively determinate laws, well expressed in terms of mathematical functions. Since these laws precisely describe definite paths of movement, there is no harm at all in introducing simplified assumptions of continuity and infinitely small steps.

Human beings, however, do not move in such fashion, but act purposefully, applying means to the attainment of ends. Investigating causes of human action, then, is radically different from investigating the laws of motion of physical objects. In particular, human beings act on the basis of things that are *relevant* to their action. The human being cannot see the infinitely small step; it therefore has no meaning to him and no relevance to his action. Thus, if one ounce of a good is the smallest unit that human beings will bother distinguishing, then the ounce is the basic unit, and we cannot simply assume infinite continuity in terms of small fractions of an ounce.

The key problem in utility theory, neglected by the mathematical writers, has been *the size of the unit*. Under the assumption of mathematical continuity, this is not a problem at all; it could hardly be when the mathematically conceived unit is infinitely small and therefore literally *sizeless*. In a praxeological analysis of human action, however, this becomes a basic question. The relevant size of the unit varies according to the particular situation, and in each of these situations this relevant unit becomes the *marginal* unit. There is none but a simple ordinal relation among the utilities of the variously sized units.

The tendency to treat problems of human action in terms of equality of utility and of infinitely small steps is also apparent in recent writings on "indifference maps." Almost the entire edifice of contemporary mathematical economics in consumption theory has been built on the "indifference" assumption. Its basis is the treatment of large-sized classes of combinations of two goods, between which the individual is indifferent in his valuations. Furthermore, the differences between them are infinitely small, so that smooth lines and tangents can be drawn. The crucial fallacy is *that "indifference" cannot be a basis for action.* If a man were really indifferent between two alternatives, he could not make any choice between them, and therefore the choice could not be revealed in action. We are interested in analyzing human action. Any action demonstrates choice based on preference: preference for one alternative over others. There is therefore no role for the concept of indifference in economics or in any other praxeological science. If it is a matter of indifference for a man whether he uses 5.1 or 5.2 ounces of butter, for example, because the unit is too small for him to take into consideration, then there will be no occasion for him to act on this alternative. He will use butter in ounce units, instead of tenths of an ounce. For the same reason, there are no infinitely small steps in human action. Steps are only those that are significant to human beings; hence, they will always be finite and discrete.

The error in reasoning on the basis of "indifference" is the failure to appreciate the fact that a problem important in the field of *psychology* may have no significance in the realm of praxeology, to which economics belongs. Psychology deals with the problem of *how* or why the individual forms value scales, and for this question it is relevant to consider whether the individual is decisive or inclined to be "indifferent" between various alternatives. Praxeology, however, is a logical science based on the existence of action *per se;* it is interested in explaining and interpreting real action in its universal sense rather than in its concrete content. Its discussion of value scales is therefore a deduction from the nature of human action and not a speculative essay on the internal workings of the mind. It is consequently irrelevant for praxeology whether a man, in having to decide between alternatives *A* and *B*, makes a choice firmly and decisively, or whether he decides by tossing a coin. This is a problem for psychology; praxeology is concerned only with the fact that he chooses, for example, *A* rather than *B*, and that therefore *A* ranked higher in his preference scale than *B*. Utility theory is not concerned with psychology or the internal operations of the mind, but is part of a separate science based on the logical consequences of the simple existence of action.

Neither is praxeology based on behaviorist psychology. In fact, in so far as praxeology touches on psychology, its principles are the reverse of those of behaviorism. As we have seen, far from simply observing action in the same way as we observe and record the movements of stones, praxeology is based on a fundamental distinction between human action and the motion of inorganic matter, namely, that human action is *motivated* toward the achievement of certain ends. Means and resources are used for the achievement of these ends. Far from leaving mind out of the picture, praxeology rests fundamentally on the basic axiom of action, action caused and put into effect by human minds. However, praxeology is not concerned with the content of these ends, the manner of arriving at them, or their order; it is concerned with analysis of the logical implications of the existence of these ends.

Some writers, in their artificial separation of value scales from real action, have actually gone to the length of attempting to discover people's indifference maps by means of questionnaires. These attempts, besides being open to the stricture that indifference is not praxeologically valid, fail to realize that value scales may and do change continually and that therefore such questionnaires have no relevance to the business of economics. Economics is interested not in value scales professed in response to questionnaires, but in the values implied by real action. As Ludwig von Mises states, with regard to all attempts to separate value scales from action:

> . . . the scale of value is nothing but a constructed tool of thought. The scale of value manifests itself only in real acting; it can be discerned only from the observation of real acting. It is therefore impermissible to contrast it with real acting and to use it as a yardstick for the appraisal of real actions.[39]

Since indifference is not relevant to human action, it follows that two alternatives for choice cannot be ranked equally on an individual's value scale. If they are really ranked equally, then they cannot be alternatives for choice, and are therefore not relevant to action. Hence, not only are alternatives ranked ordinally on every man's value scale, but they are ranked *without ties;* i.e., every alternative has a different rank.

The famous illustration used by the indifference theorists to demonstrate the relevance of indifference to human action is the case of Buridan's ass. This is the fable of the ass who stands, hungry, equidistant from two equally attractive bales of hay, or, thirsty, equidistant from two water holes. Since the two bales or water holes are equally attractive in every way, the ass can choose neither one and must therefore starve. This example is supposed to prove the great relevance of indifference to action and to be an indication of the way that indifference is *revealed* in action. Compounding confusion, Schumpeter refers to this ass as "perfectly rational." [40]

In the first place, it is of course difficult to conceive of an ass or a person that could be *less* rational. He is confronted not with *two* choices, but with *three,* the third being to starve where he is. Even on the indifferentists' own grounds, this third choice will be ranked lower than the other two on the actor's value scale. He will *not* choose starvation.

If both left and right water holes are equally attractive, and he can find no reason for preferring one or the other, the ass or the man will allow pure chance, such as a flip of a coin, to decide on either one. But on one he must and will decide. Again, we are interested in preference *as revealed through choice* and not in the *psychology* of preferences. If the flipped coin indicated the left water hole, then the left water hole was finally placed higher on the actor's value scale, as was revealed when he went toward it. Far from being a proof of the importance of indifference, the case of Buridan's ass is an excellent demonstration of the fact that indifference can play no part whatever in an analysis of human action.

Another way of attempting a justification of the indifference analysis is to suppose that a man, Jones, chooses each of two alternatives *A* and *B* about fifty per cent of the time, upon repeated opportunities. This shifting is alleged to be a demonstration that Jones is really indifferent as between the two alternatives. Yet what is the reasonable inference? Clearly, that in some cases, *A* was *preferred* to *B* on Jones' value scale, and that in the others, the positions were shifted so that *B* was *preferred* to *A*. *In no case* was there indifference between the two alternatives. The shift of choice indicates a shift in the preference scale, and not indifference on a constant value scale. Of course, if we were dealing with psychology, we could enter into a discussion of intensities of preferences and opine that the man, with respect to his underlying personality, was relatively indifferent rather than intensely biassed, as between the two alternatives. But in praxeology we are not interested in the concrete content of his value scales nor in his underlying personality. We are interested in value scales as revealed through choice.

APPENDIX A: THE DIMINISHING MARGINAL UTILITY OF MONEY

Some writers, while admitting the validity of the law of diminishing marginal utility for all other goods, deny its application to money. Thus, for example, a man may allocate each ounce of money to his most preferred uses. However, suppose that it takes 60 ounces of gold to buy an automobile. Then the acquisition of the 60th ounce, which will enable him to buy an automobile, will have considerably more value than the acquisition of the 58th or of the 59th ounce, which will not enable him to do so.

This argument involves a misconception identical with that of the argument about the "increasing marginal utility of eggs" discussed in chapter 1, above.[41] There we saw that it is erroneous to argue that because a fourth egg might enable a man to bake a cake, which he could not do with the first three, the marginal utility of the eggs has increased. We saw that a "good" and, consequently, the "unit" of a good are defined in terms of whatever quantity of which the units give an *equally serviceable supply*. This last phrase is the key concept. The fourth egg was not equally serviceable as, and therefore not interchangeable with, the first egg, and therefore a *single egg* could not be taken as the *unit*. The units of a good must be homogeneous in their serviceability, and it is only to such units that the law of utility applies.

The situation is similar in the case of money. The serviceability of the money commodity lies in its use in exchange rather than in its direct use. Here, therefore, a "unit" of money, in its relevance to individual value scales, must be such as to be homogeneous with every other unit in exchange-value. If another ounce permits a purchase of an automobile, and the issue is relevant to the case in question, then the "unit" of the money commodity must be taken not as one ounce, but as sixty ounces.

All that needs to be done, then, to account for and explain "discontinuities" because of possible large purchases is to *vary the size of the monetary unit* to which the law of utility and the preferences and choices apply.[42] This is what each man actually does in practice. Thus, suppose that a man is considering what to do with 60 ounces of gold. Let us assume, for the sake of simplicity, that he has a choice of parceling out the 60 ounces into 5-ounce units. This, we will say, is alternative *A*. In that case, he decides that he will parcel out each 5 ounces in accordance with the highest rankings on his utility scale. The first 5 ounces will be allocated to, or spent on, the most highly valued use *that can be served by 5 ounces;* the next 5 ounces to the next most highly valued use, and so on. Finally, his twelfth 5 ounces he will allocate to his twelfth most highly valued use. Now, however, he is also confronted with alternative *B*. This alternative is to spend the entire 60 ounces on whatever single use will be most valuable on his value scale. This will be the single highest-ranked use for a *unit* of 60 ounces of money. Now, to decide which alternative course he will take, the man compares the utility of the highest-ranked single use of a lump sum of 60 ounces (say, the purchase of a car) with the utility of the "package"—the expenditure of 5 ounces on *a*, 5 ounces on *b*, etc. Since the man knows his own preference scale—otherwise he could never choose any action—it is no more difficult to assume that he can rank the utility of the whole package with the utility of purchasing a car than to assume that he can rank the uses of each 5 ounces. In other words, he posits a unit of 60 ounces and determines which alternative ranks higher on his value scale: purchase of the car or a certain package distribution by 5-ounce (or other-sized) units. At any rate, the 60 ounces are distributed to what each man believes will be its highest-ranking use, and the same can be said for each of his monetary exchange decisions.

Here we must stress the fact that there is no numerical relation—aside from pure ordinal rank—between the marginal utilities of the various 5-ounce units and the utilities of the 60-ounce units, and this is true even of the package combination of distribution that we have considered. All that we can say is that the utility of 60 ounces will clearly be higher than any *one* of the utilities of 5 ounces. But there is no way of determining the numerical difference. Whether or not the rank of the utility of this *package* is higher or lower than the utility of the car purchase, moreover, can be determined only by the individual himself.

We have reiterated several times that utility is only ranked, and never measurable. There is no numerical relationship whatever between the utility of large-sized and smaller-sized units of a good. Also, there is no numerical relationship between the utilities of one unit and several units of the same size. Therefore, there is no possible way of adding or combining marginal utilities to form some sort of "total utility"; the latter can only be a *marginal* utility of a large-sized unit, and there is no numerical relationship between that and the utilities of small units.

As Ludwig von Mises states:

> Value can rightly be spoken of only with regard to specific acts of appraisal. . . . Total value can be spoken of only with reference to a particular instance of an individual . . . having to choose between the total available quantities of certain economic goods. Like every other act of valuation, this is complete in itself . . . When a stock is valued as a whole, its marginal utility, that is to say, the utility of the last available unit of it, coincides with its total utility, since the total supply is one indivisible quantity.[48]

There are, then, two laws of utility, both following from the apodictic conditions of human action: first, that *given the size of a unit of a good, the (marginal) utility of each unit decreases as the supply of units increases;* second, that *the (marginal) utility of a larger-sized unit is greater than the (marginal) utility of a smaller-sized unit.* The first is the law of diminishing marginal utility. The second has been called the law of increasing total utility. The relationship between the two laws and between the items considered in both is purely one of rank, i.e., ordinal. Thus, 4 eggs (or pounds of butter, or ounces of gold) are worth more on a value scale than 3 eggs, which in turn are worth more than 2 eggs, 2 eggs more than 1 egg, etc. This illustrates the second law. One egg will be worth more than a second egg, which will be worth more than a third egg, etc. This illustrates the first law. But there is no arithmetical relationship between the items apart from these rankings.[44]

The fact that the units of a good must be homogeneous in serviceability means, in the case of money, that the given array of money prices remains constant. The serviceability of a unit of money consists in its direct use-value and especially in its exchange-value, which rests on its power to purchase a myriad of different goods. We have seen in our study of the money regression and the marginal utility of money that the evaluation and the marginal utility of the money commodity rests on an already given structure of money prices for the various goods. It is clear that, in any given application of the foregoing law, the money prices cannot change in the meantime. If they do, and for example, the fifth unit of money is valued more highly than the fourth unit because of an intervening change in money prices, then the "units" are no longer equally serviceable and therefore cannot be considered as homogeneous.

As we have seen above, this power of the monetary unit to purchase quantities of various goods is called the *purchasing power of the monetary unit.* This purchasing power of money consists of the *array* of all the given money prices on the market at any particular time, considered in terms of the prices of goods per unit of money. As we saw in the regression theorem above, today's purchasing power of the monetary unit is determined by today's marginal utilities of money and of goods, expressed in demand schedules, while today's marginal utility of money is directly dependent on yesterday's purchasing power of money.[45]

APPENDIX B: ON VALUE

Economics has made such extensive use of the term "value" that it would be inexpedient to abandon it now. However, there is undoubtedly confusion because the term is used in a variety of different ways. It is more important to keep distinct the subjective use of th· term in the sense of *valuation* and preference, as against the "objective" use in the sense of *purchasing power* or price on the market. Up to this chapter, "value" in this book has meant the subjective individual "valuing" process of ranking goods on individual "value scales."

In this chapter, the term "value of capital" signifies the purchasing power of a durable good in terms of money on the market. If a house can be sold on the market for 250 ounces of gold, then its "capital value" is 250 ounces. The difference between this and the subjective type of value is apparent. When a good is being subjectively valued, it is ranked by someone in relation to other goods on his value scale. When a good is being "evaluated" in the sense of finding out its capital value, the evaluator *estimates* how much the good could be sold for in terms of money. This sort of activity is known as *appraisement* and is to be distinguished from subjective evaluation. If Jones says: "I shall be able to sell this house next week for 250 ounces," he is "appraising" its purchasing power, or "objective exchange-value," at 250 ounces of gold. He is not thereby ranking the house and gold on his own value scale, but is estimating the money price of the house at some point in the future. We shall see below that appraisement is fundamental to the entire economic system in an economy of indirect exchange. Not only do the renting and selling of consumers' goods rest on appraisement and on hope of monetary profits, but so does the activity of all the investing producers, the keystone of the entire productive system. We shall see that the term "capital value" applies, not only to durable consumers' goods, but to all nonhuman factors of production as well—i.e., land and capital goods, singly and in various aggregates. The use and purchase of these factors rest on appraisement by entrepreneurs of their eventual yield in terms of monetary income on the market, and it will be seen that their capital value on the market will also tend to be equal to the discounted sum of their future yields of money income.[46]

5

Production: The Structure

1. *Some Fundamental Principles of Action*

The analysis of production activities—the actions that eventually result in the attainment of consumers' goods—is a highly intricate one for a complex, monetary market economy. It is best, therefore, to summarize now some of the most applicable of the fundamental principles formulated in chapter 1. In that chapter we applied those principles to a Crusoe economy only. Actually, however, they are applicable to any type of economy and are the indispensable keys to the analysis of the complex modern economy. Some of these fundamental principles are:

1) Each individual acts so that the expected psychic revenue, or achievement of utility, from his action will exceed its psychic cost. The latter is the forgone utility of the next best alternative that he could adopt with the available means. Both the psychic revenue and the psychic cost are purely subjective to the individual. Since all action deals with units of supply of a good, we may refer to these subjective estimates as marginal utility and marginal cost, the *marginal* signifying action in steps.

2) Each person acts in the *present* instant, on the basis of present value scales, to obtain *anticipated* end results *in the future.* Each person acts, therefore, to arrive at a certain satisfactory state in the future. Each has a temporal horizon of future dates toward which his actions are directed. He uses present given *means,* according to his technological ideas, to attain his ends in the future.

3) Every person prefers and will attempt to achieve the satis-

faction of a given end in the present to the satisfaction of that end in the future. This is the law of time preference.

4) All goods are distributed by each individual in accordance with their utility to him. A stock of the units of a good is allocated first to its most highly valued uses, then to its next most highly valued use, etc. The definition of a *good* is that it consists of an interchangeable supply of one or more units. Therefore, every unit will always be valued equally with every other. If a unit of a stock is given up or disposed of, the *least highly valued use* for one unit will be the one given up. Therefore, the value of each unit of the supply of a good is equal to the utility of the least highly valued of its present uses. This marginal utility diminishes as the stock of each good increases. The marginal utility of *addition* of a unit to the stock equals the utility of a unit in its next most highly valued use, i.e., *the most highly valued of the not yet satisfied ends.* This provides us with the law of marginal utility and the law of allocation of goods.

5) In the technical combination of factors of production to yield a product, as one factor varies and the others remain constant, there is an optimum point—a point of maximum average product produced by the factor. This is the law of returns. It is based on the very fact of the existence of human action.

6) And we know from chapter 2 that the price of any good on the market will tend to be *uniform* throughout the market. The price is determined by supply and demand schedules, which are themselves determined by the value scales of the individuals in the market.

2. *The Evenly Rotating Economy*

Analysis of the activities of production in a monetary market economy is a highly complex matter. An explanation of these activities, in particular the determination of prices and therefore the return to factors, the allocation of factors, and the formation of capital, can be developed only if we use the mental construction of the *evenly rotating economy.*

This construction is developed as follows: We realize that the real world of action is one of continual change. Individual value scales, technological ideas, and the quantities of means available are always changing. These changes continually impel the economy in various directions. Value scales change, and consumer demand shifts from one good to another. Technological ideas change, and factors are used in a different way. Both types of change have differing effects on prices. Time preferences change, with certain effects on interest and capital formation. The crucial point is this: before the effects of any one change are completely worked out, other changes intervene. What we must consider, however, by the use of reasoning, is what would happen if no changes intervened. In other words, what would occur if value scales, technological ideas, and the given resources remained constant? What would then happen to prices and production and their relations? Given values, technology, and resources, whatever their concrete form, remain constant. In that case, the economy tends toward a state of affairs in which it is *evenly rotating,* i.e., in which the same activities tend to be repeated in the same pattern over and over again. Rates of production of each good remain constant, all prices remain constant, total population remains constant, etc. Thus, if values, technology, and resources remain constant, we have two successive states of affairs: (*a*) the period of transition to an unchanging, evenly rotating economy, and (*b*) the unchanging round of the evenly rotating economy itself. This latter stage is the state of *final equilibrium.* It is to be distinguished from the market equilibrium prices that are set each day by the interaction of supply and demand. *The final equilibrium state is one which the economy is always tending to approach.* If our *data*—values, technology, and resources—remained constant, the economy would move toward the final equilibrium position and remain there. In actual life, however, the data are always changing, and therefore, before arriving at a final equilibrium point, the economy must shift direction, towards some other final equilibrium position.

Hence, the final equilibrium position is always changing, and consequently no one such position is ever reached in practice. But even though it is never reached in practice, it has a very real importance. In the first place, it is like the mechanical rabbit being chased by the dog. It is never reached in practice and it is always changing, but it explains the direction in which the dog is moving. Secondly, the complexity of the market system is such that we cannot analyze factor prices and incomes in a world of continual change unless we first analyze their determination in an evenly rotating world where there is no change and where given conditions are allowed to work themselves out to the full.

Certainly at this stage of inquiry we are not interested in ethical evaluations of our knowledge. We are attaching no ethical merit to the equilibrium position. It is a concept for scientific explanation of human activity.

The reader might ask why such an "unrealistic" concept as final equilibrium is permissible, when we have already presented and will present grave strictures against the use of various unrealistic and antirealistic premises in economics. For example, as we shall see, the theory of "pure competition," so prevalent among writers today, is based on impossible premises. The theory is then worked out along these lines and not only applied uncritically to the real world, but actually used as an ethical base from which to criticize the real "deviations" from this theory. The concepts of "indifference classes" and of infinitely small steps are other examples of false premises that are used as the basis of highly elaborate theoretical structures. The concept of the evenly rotating economy, however, when used with care, is not open to these criticisms. For this is an ever-present force, since it is the goal toward which the actual system is always moving, the *final position of rest,* at which, on the basis of the given, actually existing value scales, all individuals would have attained the highest positions on their value scales, given the technology and resources. This concept, then, is of legitimate and realistic importance.

We must always remember, however, that while a final equilibrium is the goal toward which the economy is moving at any particular time, changes in the data alter this position and therefore shift the direction of movement. Therefore, *there is nothing in a dynamic world that is ethically better about a final equilib-*

rium position. As a matter of fact, since wants are unsatisfied (otherwise there would be no action), such a position of no change would be most unfortunate, since it would imply that no further want-satisfaction would be possible. Furthermore, we must remember that a final equilibrium situation tends to be, though it can never actually be, the *result* of market activity, and not the *condition* of such activity. Far too many writers, for example, discerning that in the evenly rotating economy entrepreneurial profits and losses would all be zero, have somehow concluded that this must be the *condition* for any legitimate activity on the market. There could hardly be a greater misconception of the market or a greater abuse of the equilibrium concept.

Another danger in the use of this concept is that its purely static, essentially timeless, conditions are all too well suited for the use of mathematics. Mathematics rests on *equations,* which portray mutual relationships between two or more "functions." Of themselves, of course, such mathematical procedures are unimportant, since they do not establish causal relationships. They are of the greatest importance in physics, for example, because that science deals with certain observed regularities of motion by particles of matter that we must regard as unmotivated. These particles move according to certain precisely observable, exact, quantitative laws. Mathematics is indispensable in formulating the laws among these variables and in formulating theoretical explanations for the observed phenomena. In human action, the situation is entirely different, if not diametrically opposite. Whereas in physics, causal relations can only be assumed hypothetically and later approximately verified by referring to precise observable regularities, in praxeology we *know* the causal force at work. This causal force is human action, *motivated,* purposeful behavior, directed at certain ends. The universal aspects of this behavior can be logically analyzed. We are not dealing with "functional," quantitative relations among variables, but with human reason and will causing certain action, which is not "determinable" or reducible to outside forces. Furthermore, since the data of human action are always changing, there are no precise, quantitative relationships in human history. In physics, the quantitative relationships, or laws, are constant; they are considered to be valid for any point in human history, past, present, or future. In the field of human action, there are no such quantitative constants. There are no constant relationships valid for different periods in human history. The only "natural laws" (if we may use such an old-fashioned but perfectly legitimate label for such constant regularities) in human action are *qualitative* rather than *quantitative*. They are, for example, precisely the laws educed in praxeology and economics—the fact of action, the use of means to achieve ends, time preference, diminishing marginal utility, etc.[1]

Mathematical equations, then, are appropriate and useful where there are constant quantitative relations among unmotivated variables. They are singularly inappropriate in praxeology and economics. In the latter fields, verbal, logical analysis of action and its processes through time is the appropriate method. It is not surprising that the main efforts of the "mathematical economists" have been directed toward describing the final equilibrium state by means of equations. For in this state, since activities merely repeat themselves, there seems to be more scope for describing conditions by means of functional equations. These equations, at best, however, can do no more than describe this equilibrium state.

Aside from doing no more than verbal logic can do, and therefore violating the scientific principle of *Occam's razor*—that science should be as simple and clear as possible—such a use of mathematics contains grave errors and defects within itself. In the first place, it cannot describe the *path* by which the economy approaches the final equilibrium position. This task can be performed only by verbal, logical analysis of the causal action of human beings. It is evident that this task is the important one, since it is this analysis that is significant for human action. Action moves along a path and is not describable in an unchanging, evenly rotating world. The world is an uncertain one, and we shall see shortly that we cannot even pursue to its logical conclusion the analysis of a static, evenly rotating economy. The assumption of an evenly rotating economy is only an auxiliary tool in aiding us in the analysis of real action. Since mathematics is least badly accommodated to a static state, mathematical writers have tended to be preoccupied with this state, thus providing a particularly misleading picture of the world of action. Finally, the mathematical equations of the evenly rotating economy describe only a static situation, outside of time.[2] They differ drastically from the mathematical equations of physics, which describe a *process through time;* it is precisely through this description of constant, quantitative relations in the *motion* of elements that mathematics renders its great service in natural science. How different is economics, where mathematics, at best, can only inadequately describe a timeless end result![3]

The use of the mathematical concept of "function" is particularly inappropriate in a science of human action. On the one hand, action itself is *not* a function of anything, since "function" implies definite, unique, mechanical regularity and determination. On the other hand, the mathematics of simultaneous equations, dealing in physics with unmotivated motion, stresses mutual determination. In human action, however, the known causal force of action unilinearly determines the results. This gross misconception by mathematically inclined writers on the study of human action was exemplified during a running attack on Eugen Böhm-Bawerk, one of the greatest of all economists, by Professor George Stigler:

> . . . yet the postulate of continuity of utility and demand functions (which is unrealistic only to a minor degree, and essential to analytic treatment) is never granted. A more important weakness is Böhm-Bawerk's failure to understand some of the most essential elements of modern economic theory, the concepts of mutual determination and equilibrium (developed by the use of the theory of simultaneous equations). Mutual determination is spurned for the older concept of cause and effect.[4]

The "weakness" displayed here is not that of Böhm-Bawerk, but of those, like Professor Stigler, who attempt vainly and fallaciously to construct economics on the model of mathematical physics, specifically, of classical mechanics.[5]

To return to the concept of the evenly rotating economy, the error of the mathematical economists is to treat it as a real and even ideal state of affairs, whereas it is simply a mental concept enabling us to analyze the market and human activities on the market. It is indispensable because it is the goal, though ever-shifting, of action and exchange; on the other hand, the data can never remain unchanged long enough for it to be brought into being. We cannot conceive in all consistency of a state of affairs without change or uncertainty, and therefore without action. The evenly rotating state, for example, would be incompatible with the existence of money, the very medium at the center of the entire exchange structure. For the money commodity is demanded and held only because it is more marketable than other commodities, i.e., because the holder is more sure of being able to exchange it. In a world where prices and demands remain perpetually the same, such demand for money would be unnecessary. Money is demanded and held only because it gives greater assurance of finding a market and because of the uncertainties of the person's demands in the near future. If everyone, for example, knew his spending precisely over his entire future—and this would be known under the evenly rotating system—there would be no point in his keeping a cash balance of money. It would be invested so that money would be returned in precisely the needed amounts on the day of expenditure. But if no one wishes to hold money, there will be no money and no system of money prices. The entire monetary market would break down. Thus, the evenly rotating economy is unrealistic, for it cannot actually be established and we cannot even conceive consistently of its establishment. But the idea of the evenly rotating economy is indispensable in analyzing the real economy; through hypothesizing a world where all change has worked itself out, we can analyze the directions of actual change.

3. *The Structure of Production: A World of Specific Factors*

Crucial to understanding the process of production is the question of the *specificity* of factors, a problem we touched on in chapter 1. A *specific* factor is one suitable to the production of only one product. A *purely nonspecific* factor would be one equally suited to the production of *all* possible products. It is clear that not all factors could be purely nonspecific, for in that case all factors would be purely interchangeable, i.e., there would be need for only one factor. But we have seen that human action implies more than one existing factor. Even the existence of *one* purely nonspecific factor is inconceivable if we properly consider "suitability in production" in *value* terms rather than in *technological* terms.[6] In fact, if we analyze the concept, we find that there is no sense in saying that a factor is "equally suitable" in purely technological terms, since there is no way of comparing the physical quantities of one product with those of another. If *X* can help to produce three units of *A* or two units of *B*, there is no way by which we can compare these units. Only the *valuation* of consumers establishes a hierarchy of valued goods, their interaction setting the prices of the consumers' goods. (Relatively) nonspecific factors, then, are allocated to those products that the consumers have valued most highly. It is difficult to conceive of any good that would be purely nonspecific and equally valuable in all processes of production. Our major distinction, then, is between the *specific* factor, which can be used in only one line of production, and the *nonspecific* factor (of varying degrees of convertibility), which can be used in more than one production process.

Now let us for a time consider a world where every good is produced *only* by several *specific* factors. In this world, a world that is conceivable, though highly unlikely, every person, every piece of land, every capital good, would necessarily be irrevocably committed to the production of one particular product. There would be no alternative uses of any good from one line of production to another. In the entire world of production, then, there would be little or no "economic problem," i.e., no problem of allocating scarce means to alternative ends. Certainly, the *consumers* would still have to allocate their scarce monetary resources to the most preferred consumers' goods. In the nonmarket sphere, everyone—again as a consumer—would have to allocate his time and energies to the enjoyment of various consumers' goods.

There would still, in the sphere of production of exchangeable goods, be *one* allocation that every man would make: how much time to devote to labor and how much to leisure. But there would be no problem of *which* field to labor in, no problem of what to do with any piece of land, no problem of how to allocate capital goods. The employment of the factors would all depend on the consumers' demand for the final product.

The structure of production in such a world of purely specific

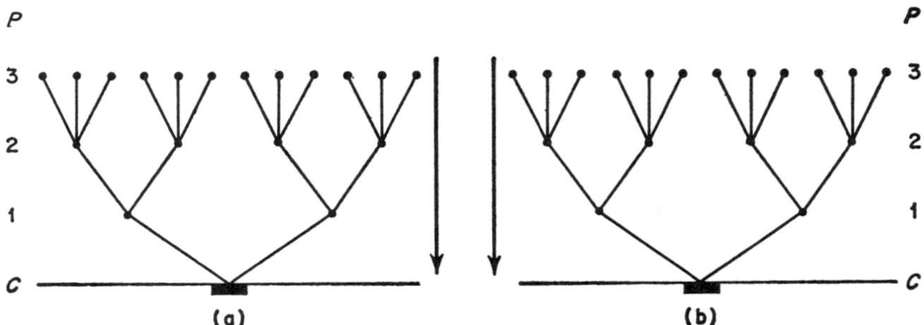

FIG. 39. STRUCTURE OF PRODUCTION IN A WORLD OF PURELY SPECIFIC FACTORS

factors would be somewhat as in Fig. 39. In this diagram, we see two typical consumers' goods, *A* and *B*. Each, depicted as a solid rectangle at the bottom of the diagram, is produced by co-operating factors of the next higher rank, designated *P* 1, or the first order of producers' goods. The *capital goods* of the first rank are, in turn, produced with the help of co-operating factors, these being of the second-rank, and so on upward. The process logically continues upward until capital goods are produced completely by land and labor factors, although this stage is not depicted on the diagram. Lines connect the dots to designate the causal pattern of the factors. In the diagram, all factors are purely *specific,* since no good is used at different stages of the process or for different goods. The center arrows indicate the causal direction of *effort* downward, from the highest ranked producers' goods through the intermediate ranks, finally concluding in consumers' goods. At each stage, labor uses nature-given factors to produce capital goods, and the capital goods are again combined with labor and nature-given factors, transformed into lower and lower orders of capital goods, until consumers' goods are reached.

Now that we have traced the direction of productive effort, we must trace the direction of monetary income. This is a reverse one, from the consumers back to the producers. The consumers purchase the stock of a consumers' good at a price determined on the market, yielding the producers a certain income. Two of the crucial problems of production theory are the method by which the monetary income is allocated and the corollary problem of the pricing of the factors of production. First, let us consider only the "lowest" stage of production, the stage that brings about the *final* product. In that stage, numerous factors, all now assumed to be specific, co-operate in producing the consumers' good. There are three types of such factors: labor, original nature and produced capital goods.[7] Let us assume that on a certain day, consumers purchase a certain quantity of a good *X* for, say, 100 ounces of gold. Given the quantity of the good sold, the *price* of the total quantity is equal to the (gross) income obtained from the sale of the good. How will these 100 ounces be allocated to the producing factors?

In the first place, we must make an assumption about the *ownership* of the consumers' good just before it is sold. It is obvious that this owner or these owners will be the *immediate* recipients of the 100 ounces of gold income. Let us say that, in the final stage, there have been seven factors participating in the production: two types of labor, two types of land, and three types of capital goods. There are two alternatives in regard to the final ownership of the product (*before* it is sold to the consumer): (*a*) all the owners of these factors *jointly* own the final product; or (*b*) the owner of each of the factors sells the services of his factor to someone else, and the latter (who may himself contribute a factor) sells the good at a later date to the consumer. Although the latter is the nearly universal condition, it will be convenient to begin by analyzing the first alternative.

Those who own the final product, whatever the alternative adopted, are "capitalists," since they are the owners of capital goods. It is better, however, to confine the term "capitalists" to those who have saved money capital with which to buy factors. This, by definition, does not occur under the first alternative, where owners of factors are joint owners of the products. The term "product-owner" suffices for designating the owner of the capital assets, whatever the alternative adopted. Product-owners are also "entrepreneurs," since they assume the major entrepreneurial burden of adjusting to uncertain future conditions. To call them "entrepreneurs" alone, however, is to run the danger of forgetting that they are also capitalists or product-owners and that they would continue to perform that function in an evenly rotating economy.

4. *Joint Ownership of the Product by the Owners of the Factors*

Let us first consider the case of joint ownership by the owners of all the final co-operating factors.[8] It is clear that the 100 ounces of gold accrue to the owners jointly. Let us now be purely arbitrary and state that a total of 80 ounces accrues to the owners of capital goods and a total of 20 ounces to the owners of labor and nature-given factors. It is obvious that, whatever the allocation, it will be, on the unhampered market, in accordance with the voluntary contractual agreement of each and every factor-owner concerned. Now it is clear that there is an important difference between what happens to the monetary income of the *laborer* and the *landowner,* on the one hand, and of the owner of *capital goods,* on the other. For the capital goods must in turn be produced by labor, nature, and other capital goods. Therefore, while the contributor of personal "labor" energy (and this, of course, includes the energy of direction as well as what are called "laborers" in popular parlance) has earned a pure return, the owner of capital goods has previously spent some money for the production or the purchase of *his* owned factors.

Now it is clear that, since only factors of production may obtain income from the consumer, *the price of the consumers' good, i.e., the income from the consumers' good, equals the sum of the prices accruing to the producing factors, i.e., the income accruing to the factors.* In the case of joint ownership, this is a truism, since *only a factor* can receive income from the sale of a good. It is the same as saying that 100 ounces equals 100 ounces.

But what of the 80 ounces that we have arbitarily allocated to the owners of capital goods? To whom do they finally accrue? Since we are assuming in this example of joint ownership that all products are owned by their factor-owners, it also follows that capital goods, which are *also* products, are *themselves* jointly owned by the factors on the second rank of production. Let us say that each of the three first-order capital goods was produced by five co-operating factors: two types of labor, one type of land, two types of capital goods. All these factor-owners jointly own the 80 ounces. Let us say that each of the first-order capital goods had obtained the following:

Capital good *A*: 30 ounces
Capital good *B*: 30 ounces
Capital good *C*: 20 ounces

The income to each capital good will then be owned by five factor-owners on the second rank of production.

It is clear that, conceptually, *no one, in the last analysis, receives a return as the owner of a capital good.* Since every capital good analytically resolves itself into original nature-given and labor factors, it is evident that no money could accrue to the owner of a capital good. All 100 ounces must eventually be allocated to labor and owners of nature-given factors exclusively. Thus, the 30 ounces accruing to the owners of capital good *A* will be allocated to the five factor-owners, while the, say, four ounces accruing to one of the capital goods of third rank helping to produce good *A* will, in turn, be allocated to land, labor, and capital-goods factors of the fourth rank, etc. Eventually, all the money is allocated to labor and nature-given factors only. The diagram in Fig. 40 illustrates this process.

At the bottom of the diagram, we see that 100 ounces of gold are transferred from the consumers to the producers. Some of this money goes to owners of capital goods, some to landowners, some to owners of labor. (The proportion going to one group and the other is arbitrarily assumed in the example and is of no importance for this analysis.) The amount accruing to the capital-goods owners is included in the *shaded* portion of the diagram and the amount accruing *both* to labor and nature-owners is included in the clear portion of the diagram. In the lowest, the

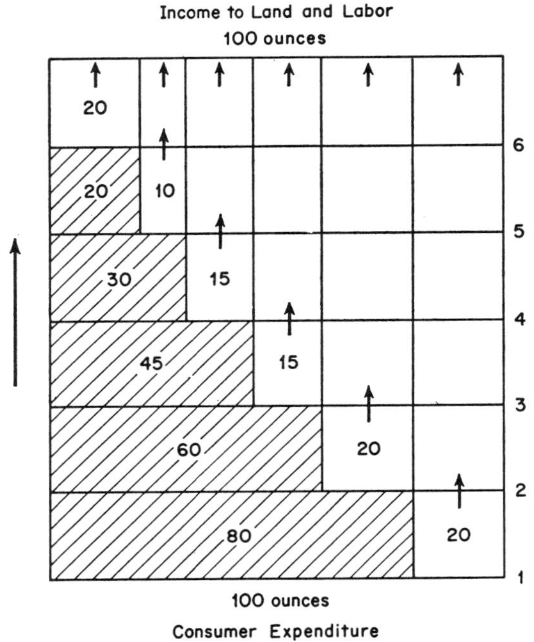

FIG. 40. INCOME ACCRUING TO THE FACTORS OF PRODUCTION

first, block, the 20 ounces received by owners of land and of labor factors is marked with an upward arrow, followed by a similar upward arrow at the top of the diagram, the top line designating the money ultimately received by the owners of the various factors. The width of the top line (100 ounces) must be equal to the width of the bottom line (100 ounces), since the money ultimately received by the owners of the factors must equal the money spent by the consumers.

Moving up to line 2, we follow the fortunes of the 80 ounces which had accrued to the owners of capital goods of the first order. We assume that 60 ounces accrue to the owners of second-order capital goods and 20 ounces to second-order labor and nature-given factors. Once again, the 20 ounces' clear area is marked with an upward arrow designating the ultimate receipt of money by the owners of the factors and is equally marked off on the top line of the diagram. The same process is repeated as we go further and further upward in the order of capital goods. At each point, of course, the amount obtained by owners of capital goods becomes smaller, because more and more has accrued to labor and nature owners. Finally, at the highest conceivable stage, all the remaining 20 ounces earned by the owners of capital goods accrue to land and labor factors only, since eventually we must come to the stage where no capital good has yet been produced and only labor and nature remain. The result is that the 100 ounces are all eventually allocated to the clear spaces, to the land and labor factors. The large upward arrow on the left signifies the general upward course of the monetary income.

To the truism that the income from sale of the consumers' good equals the consumers' expenditure on the good, we may add a corresponding truism for each stage of production, namely, that *the income from sale of a capital good equals the income accruing to the factors of its production.*

In the world that we have been examining, where all products, at whatever stage, are owned jointly by the owners of their factors, it is clear that *first* work is done on the highest stage. Owners of land and of labor *invest* their land and labor to produce the highest-order (in this case the fifth) capital good; then these owners turn the good over to the owners of labor and land at the next lower stage; these produce the fourth-order capital good, which in turn co-operates with labor and land factors on that stage to produce the lower-order good, etc. Finally, the lowest stage is reached, and the final factors co-operate to produce the consumers' good. The consumers' good is then sold to consumers.[9]

In the case of joint ownership, then, there does not arise any separate class of owners of capital goods. All the capital goods produced are jointly owned by the owners of the producing land and labor factors; the capital goods of the next lower order are owned by the owners of the land and labor factors at the next lower stage along with the previously co-operating owners, etc. In sum, the entire capital-goods structure engaged in any line of production is jointly owned by the owners of land and labor. And the income gained from the final sale of the product to the consumers accrues only to the owners of land and labor; there is no separate group of owners of capital goods to whom income accrues.[10]

It is obvious that the production process takes *time,* and the more complex the production process the more time must be taken. During this time, all the factors have had to work without earning any remuneration; they have had to work only in *expectation* of *future* income. Their income is received only at a much later date.

The income that would be earned by the factors, in a world of purely specific factors, depends entirely on consumer demand for the particular final product. If consumers spend 100 ounces on the good, then the factors will jointly earn 100 ounces. If they spend 500 ounces, the factors will earn that amount. If they spend nothing on the product, and the producers have made the enormous entrepreneurial error of working on a product that the consumers do not buy, the factors earn precisely zero. The joint monetary income earned by the owners of the factors fluctuates *pari passu* with consumer demand for the product.

At this point, a question naturally arises: What happens to owners of factors who earn a zero return? Must they "starve"? Fundamentally, we cannot answer this question for concrete individual persons, since economics demonstrates truths about "functional" earnings in production, and not about the entire earnings of a given person. A particular person, in other words, may experience a zero return on this good, while at the same time earning a substantial return on ownership of another piece of land. In cases where there is no such ownership in another area, the individual may pursue isolated production that does not yield a monetary return, or, if he has an accumulated monetary cash balance, he may purchase goods by reducing the balance. Furthermore, if he has such a balance, he may invest in land or capital goods or in a production organization owning them, in some other line of production. His labor, on our assumptions, may be a specific factor, but his *money* is usable in every line of production.

Suppose we assume the worst possible case—a man with no cash balance, with no assets of capital, and whose labor is a *specific* factor the product of which has little or no consumer demand.[11] Is he not truly an example of an individual led astray by the existence of the market and of the specialization prevalent on it? By subjecting himself to the consumer has he not placed his happiness and existence in jeopardy? Even granting that people chose a market, could not the choice turn out to be tragic for many people?

The answer is that there is no basis whatever for such strictures on the market process. For even in this impossible case, the individual is no worse off than he would have been in isolation or barter. He can always revert to isolation if he finds he cannot attain his ends via the market process. The very fact that we consider such a possibility ludicrous is evidence of the enormous advantages that the market confers upon everyone. Indeed, empirically, we can certainly state that without the modern, developed market, and thrown back into isolation, the overwhelming majority of individuals could not obtain enough exchangeable goods to exist at all. Yet this choice always remains open to anyone who, for any reason, voluntarily prefers isolation to the vast benefits obtainable from the market system. Certainly, therefore, complaints against the market system by disgruntled persons are misplaced and erroneous. Any person or group, on the unhampered market, is free to abandon the social market at any time and to withdraw into any other desired form of co-operative arrangement. People may withdraw into individual isolation or establish some sort of group isolation or start from the beginning to re-create their own market. In any case, on the free market, their choice is entirely their own, and they decide according to their preferences unhampered by the use or threat of violence.[12]

Our example of the "worst possible case" enables us to analyze one of the most popular objections to the free society: that "it leaves people free to starve." First, from the fact that this objection is so widespread, we can easily conclude that there will be enough charitable people in the society to present these unfortunates with gifts. There is, however, a more fundamental refutation. It is that the "freedom-to-starve" argument rests on a basic confusion of "freedom" with "abundance of exchangeable goods." The two must be kept conceptually distinct. Freedom is meaningfully definable only as absence of interpersonal restrictions. Robinson Crusoe on the desert island is absolutely free, since there is no other person to hinder him. But he is not necessarily living an abundant life; indeed, he is likely to be constantly on the verge of starvation. Whether or not man lives at the level of poverty or abundance depends upon the success that he and his ancestors have had in grappling with nature and in transforming naturally given resources into capital goods and consumers' goods. The two problems, therefore, are logically separate. Crusoe is absolutely free, yet starving, while it is certainly possible, though not likely, for a given person at a given instant to be a slave while being kept in riches by his master. Yet there is an important connection between the two, for we have seen that a free market tends to lead to abundance for all of its participants, and we shall see below that violent intervention in the market and a hegemonic society tend to lead to general poverty. That a person is "free to starve" is therefore *not* a condemnation of the free market, but a simple fact of nature: every child comes into the world without capital or resources of his own. On the contrary, as we shall see further below, it is the free market in a free society that furnishes the only instrument to reduce or eliminate poverty and provide abundance.

5. *Cost*

At this point, let us reintroduce the concept of "cost" into the analysis. We have seen above that the cost, or "marginal" cost, of any decision is the next highest utility that must be forgone because of the decision. When a means M must be distributed among ends E_1, E_2, and E_3, with E_1 ranked highest on the individual's value scale, the individual attempts to allocate the means so as to attain his most highly valued ends and to forgo those ranked lower, although he will attain as many of his ends as he can with the means available. If he allocates his means to E_1 and E_2, and must forgo E_3, E_3 is the marginal cost of his decision. If he errs in his decision, and arrives at E_3 instead of E_2, then *ex post*—in retrospect—he is seen to have suffered a loss compared to the course he could have taken.

What are the costs involved in the decisions made by the owners of the factors? In the first place, it must be stressed that these costs are subjective and cannot be precisely determined by outside observers or be gauged *ex post* by observing accountants.[13] Secondly, it is clear that, *since* such factors as land and the produced capital goods have only one use, namely, the production of this product (by virtue of being purely specific), they involve *no cost* to their owner in being used in production. By the very terms of our problem, the only alternative for their owner would be to let the land lie unused, earning no return. The use of labor, however, does have a cost, in accordance with the value of the leisure forgone by the laborers. This value is, of course, unmeasurable in money terms, and necessarily differs for each individual, since there can be no comparison between the value scales of two or more persons.

Once the final product has been produced, the analysis of the previous chapter follows, and it becomes clear that, in most cases, the sale of the good at the market price, whatever the price may be, is *costless,* except for rare cases of direct consumption by the producer or in cases of anticipation of a price increase in the near future. This sale is *costless* from the proper point of view—the point of view of acting man at the relevant instant of action. The fact that he would not have engaged in the labor at all if he had known in advance of the present price might indicate a deplorable instance of poor judgment, but it does not affect the present situation. At present, with all the labor already exerted and the product finished, the original—subjective—cost has already been incurred and vanished with the original making of the decision. At present, there is no alternative to the sale of the good at the market price, and therefore the sale is costless.[14]

It is evident, therefore, that once the product has been made, "cost" has *no influence* on the price of the product. Past costs, being ephemeral, are irrelevant to present determination of prices. The agitation that often takes place over sales "below cost" is now placed in its proper perspective. It is obvious that, in the relevant sense of "cost," no such sales can take place. The sale of an already produced good is likely to be costless, and if it is not, and price is below its costs, then the seller will hold on to the good rather than make the sale.

That costs do have an influence in production is not denied by anyone. However, the influence is not directly on the price, but on the amount that will be produced or, more specifically, on the degree to which factors will be used. We have seen in our example that land and capital goods will be used to the fullest extent practicable, since there is no return or benefit in allowing them to remain idle.[15] But man laboring bears the cost of leisure forgone. What he expects will be the monetary return from his labor is the deciding factor in his decision concerning how much or whether or not to employ his labor on the product. The monetary return is ranked on his subjective value scale along with the costs of forgoing leisure, and his decision is made on the quantity of labor he will put forth in production. The height of costs on individual value scales, then, is *one* of the determinants of the quantity, the *stock,* that will be produced. This stock, of course, *later* plays a role in the determination of market price, since stock is evaluated by consumers according to the law of diminishing marginal utility. This, however, is a far cry from stating that cost either determines, or is co-ordinate with utility in determining, price. We may briefly summarize the law of price (which can be stated at this point only in regard to specific factors and joint ownership, but which will be later seen as true for any arrangement of production): Individuals, on their value scales, evaluate a given stock of goods according to their utilities, setting the prices of consumers' goods; the stock is produced according to previous decisions by producers, who had weighed on their value scales the expected monetary revenue from consumers against the subjective costs (themselves simply *utilities forgone*) of engaging in the production. In the former case, the utility valuations are generally (though by no means always) the ones made by *consumers;* in the latter case, they are made by *producers.* But it is clear that the determinants of price are *only the subjective utilities of individuals* in valuing given conditions and alternatives. There are no "objective" or "real" costs that determine, or are co-ordinate in determining, price.[16]

If we investigate the costs of laborers in production more closely, we see that what is involved is not simply a question of leisure forgone. There is another, though in this case intertwined, element: *present goods* are being forgone in exchange for an expectation of return *in the future.* Thus, added to the leisure-labor element, the workers, in this case, must wait for some time before earning the return, while they must give up their leisure in the present or in various periods earlier than the return is obtained. Time, therefore, is a critical element in production, and its analysis must pervade any theory of production.

When the owners of the factors embark on a process of production the yield of which will be necessarily realized in the future, they are giving up leisure and other consumers' goods that they either could have enjoyed without working or could have earned earlier from shorter processes of production. In order to *invest* their labor and land in a process of production, then, they must restrict their *present* consumption to less than its possible maximum. This involves forgoing either immediate consumption or the consumption made possible from shorter processes of production. *Present* consumption is given up in anticipation of *future* consumption. Since we have seen that the universal law of time preference holds that any given satisfaction will be preferred earlier than later, an equivalent satisfaction will be preferred as early as possible. Present consumption of a good will be given up only in anticipation of a *greater future* consumption, the degree of the premium being dependent on time preferences. This restriction of present consumption is *saving.* (See the discussion in chapter 1, above.)

In a world where products are all jointly owned by owners of factors, the original owners of land and labor must do their own saving; there is no monetary expression to represent total saving, even in a monetary economy. The owners of land and labor forgo a certain amount of present or earlier consumption and save in various amounts in order to invest their time and labor to produce the final product. Their income is finally earned, say after one year, when the good is sold to the consumers and the 100 ounces is received by the joint owners. It is impossible, however, for us to say what this saving or investment was in monetary terms.

6. *Ownership of the Product by Capitalists: Amalgamated Stages*

Up to this point we have discussed the case in which the owners of land and labor, i.e., of the original factors, restrict their possible consumption and invest their factors in a production process, which, after a certain time, produces a consumers' good to be sold to consumers for money. Now let us consider a situation in which the owners of the factors do *not* own the final product. How could this come about? Let us first forget about the various stages of the production process and assume for the moment that all the stages can be lumped together as one. An individual or a group of individuals acting jointly can then, *at present,* offer to pay money to the owners of land and labor, thus buying the services of their factors. The factors then work and produce the product, which, under the terms of their agreement, belongs to the new class of product-owners. These product-owners have purchased the services of the land and labor factors as the latter have been contributing to production; they then sell the final product to the consumers.

What has been the contribution of these product-owners, or "capitalists," to the production process? It is this: the saving and restriction of consumption, instead of being done by the owners of land and labor, has been done by the *capitalists.* The capitalists originally saved, say, 95 ounces of gold which they could have then spent on consumers' goods. They refrained from doing so, however, and, instead, *advanced* the money to the original owners of the factors. They *paid* the latter for their services while they were working, thus advancing them money before the product was actually produced and sold to the consumers. The capitalists, therefore, made an essential contribution to production. They relieved the owners of the original factors from the necessity of sacrificing present goods and waiting for future goods. *Instead,* the capitalists have supplied present goods *from their own savings* (i.e., money with which to buy present goods) to the owners of the original factors. In return for this supply of present goods, the latter contribute their productive services to the capitalists, who become the owners of the product. More precisely, the capitalists become the owners of the capital structure, of the whole structure of capital goods as they are produced. Keeping to our assumption that one capitalist or group of capitalists owns all the stages of any good's production, the capitalists continue to advance present goods to owners of factors as the "year" goes on. As the period of time continues, highest-order capital goods are first produced, are then transformed into lower-order capital goods, etc., and ultimately into the final product. At any given time this whole structure is owned by the capitalists. When one capitalist owns the whole structure, these capital goods, it must be stressed, *do him no good whatever.* Thus, suppose that a capitalist has already advanced 80 ounces over a period of many months to owners of labor and land in a line of production. He has in his ownership, as a result, a mass of fifth-, fourth-, and third-order capital goods. None of these capital goods is of any use to him, however, until the goods can be further worked on and the final product obtained and sold to the consumer.

Popular literature attributes enormous "power" to the capitalist and considers his owning a mass of capital goods as of enormous significance, giving him a great advantage over other people in the economy. We see, however, that this is far from the case; indeed, the opposite may well be true. For the capitalist has already saved from possible consumption and hired the services of factors to produce his capital goods. The owners of these factors have the money already for which they otherwise would have had to save and wait (and bear uncertainty), while the capitalist has only a mass of capital goods, a mass that will prove worthless to him unless it can be further worked on and the product sold to the consumers.

When the capitalist purchases factor services, what is the precise exchange that takes place? The capitalist gives money (a present good) in exchange for receiving factor services (labor and land), which work to supply him with capital goods. They supply him, in other words, with *future goods.* The capital goods for which he pays are way stations on the route to the final product—the consumers' good. At the time when land and labor are hired to produce capital goods, therefore, these capital goods, and therefore the services of the land and labor, are *future* goods; they represent the embodiment of the expected yield of a good in the future—a good that can then be consumed. The capitalist who buys the services of land and labor in year 1 to work on a product that will eventually become a consumers' good ready for sale in year 2 is advancing money (a present good) in exchange for a future good—for the present anticipation of a yield of money in the future from the sale of the final product. A present good is being exchanged for an expected future good.

Under the conditions of our example, we are assuming that the capitalists own *no* original factors, in contrast to the first case, in which the products were jointly owned by the owners of these factors. In our case, the capitalists originally owned money, with which they purchased the services of land and labor in order to produce capital goods, which are finally transformed by land and labor into consumers' goods. In this example we have assumed that the capitalists do not at any time own any of the co-operating labor or land factors. In actual life, of course, there may be and are capitalists who both work in some managerial capacity in the production process and also own the land on which they operate. Analytically, however, it is necessary to isolate these various functions. We may call those capitalists who own only the capital goods and the final product before sale "pure capitalists."

Let us now add another temporary restriction to our analysis —namely, that all producers' goods and services are only *hired,* never bought outright. This is a convenient assumption that will be maintained long after the assumption of specific factors is dropped. We here assume that the pure capitalists never purchase as a whole a factor that in itself could yield several units of service. They can only *hire* the services of factors per unit of time. This situation is directly analogous to the conditions described in chapter 4, section 7 above, in which consumers bought or "rented" the unit services of goods rather than the goods as a whole. In a free economy, of course, this hiring or renting must always occur in the case of labor services. The laborer, being a free man, *cannot be bought;* i.e., he cannot be paid a cash value for his total future anticipated services, after which he is at the permanent command of his buyer. This would be a condition of slavery, and even "voluntary slavery," as we have seen, cannot be enforced on the free market because of the inalienability of personal will. A laborer cannot be bought, then, but his *services* can be bought over a period of time; i.e., he can be rented or hired.

7. *Present and Future Goods: The Pure Rate of Interest*

We are deferring until later the major part of the analysis of the pricing of productive services and factors. At this point we can see, however, that the purchasing of labor and land services are directly analogous. The classical discussion of productive income treats labor as earning wages whereas land earns rents, and the two are supposed to be subject to completely different laws. Actually, however, the earnings of labor and land services are analogous. Both are original and productive factors; and in the case in which land is hired rather than bought, both are rented per unit of time rather than sold outright. Generally, writers on economics have termed those capitalists "entrepreneurs" who buy labor and land factors in expectation of a future monetary return from the final product. They are entrepreneurs, however, only in the actual economy of uncertainty. *In an evenly rotating economy,* where all the market actions are repeated in an endless round and there is therefore no uncertainty, *entrepreneurship* disappears. There is no uncertain future to be anticipated and about which forecasts are made. To call these capitalists simply entrepreneurs, then, is tacitly to imply that in the evenly rotating economy there will be no capitalists, i.e., no group that saves money and hires the services of factors, thereby acquiring capital and consumers' goods to be sold to the consumers. Actually, however, there is no reason why pure capitalists should not continue in the ERE (the evenly rotating economy). Even if final returns and consumer demand are certain, *the capitalists are still providing present goods to the owners of labor and land* and thus relieving them of the burden of waiting until the future goods are produced and finally transformed into consumers' goods. Their function, therefore, remains in the ERE to provide present goods and to assume the burden of waiting for future returns over the period of the production process. Let us assume simply that the sum the capitalists paid out was 95 ounces and that the final sale was for 100 ounces. The 5 ounces accruing to the capitalists is payment for their function of supplying present goods and waiting for a future return. In short, the capitalists, in year 1, bought future goods for 95 ounces and then sold the transformed product in year 2 for 100 ounces when it had become a *present* good. In other words, in year 1 the market price of an anticipated (certain) income of 100 ounces was only 95 ounces. It is clear that this arises out of the universal fact of time preference and of the resulting premium of a given good at present over the present *prospect* of its *future* acquisition.

In the monetary economy, since money enters into all transactions, the discount of a future good against a present good can, in all cases, be expressed in terms of one good: money. This is so because the money commodity is a present good and because claims to future goods are almost always expressed in terms of future money income.

The factors of production in our discussion have all been assumed to be purely *specific* to a particular line of production. When the capitalists have saved money ("money capital"), however, they are at liberty to purchase factor services in any line of production. *Money, the general medium of exchange, is precisely nonspecific.* If, for example, the saver sees that he can invest 95 ounces in the aforementioned production process and earn 100 ounces in a year, whereas he can invest 95 ounces in some other process and earn 110 ounces in a year, he will invest his money in the process earning the greater return. Clearly, the line in which he will feel impelled to invest will be the line that earns him the greatest *rate* of return on his investment.

The concept of *rate* of return is necessary in order for him to compare different potential investments for different periods of time and involving different sums of money. For any amount of money that he saves, he would like to earn the greatest amount of net return, i.e., the greatest rate of net return. The absolute amount of return has to be reduced to units of time, and this is done by determining the rate per unit of time. Thus, a return of 20 ounces on an investment of 500 ounces after 2 years is 2% per annum, while a return of 15 ounces on the same investment after 1 year is a return of 3% per annum.

After data work themselves out and continue without change, the rate of net return on the investment of money capital will, in the ERE, be the *same* in every line of production. If capitalists can earn 3% per annum in one production process and 5% per annum in another, they will cease investing in the former and invest more in the latter until the rates of return are uniform. In the ERE, there is no entrepreneurial uncertainty, and the rate of net return is the pure exchange ratio between present and future goods. This rate of return is *the rate of interest*. This *pure rate of interest* will be uniform for all periods of time and for all lines of production and will remain constant in the ERE.[17]

Suppose that at some time the rates of interest earned are not uniform as between several lines of production. If capitalists are generally earning 5% interest, and a capitalist is obtaining 7% in a particular line, other capitalists will enter this line and bid away the factors of production from him by raising factor prices. Thus, if a capitalist is paying factors 93 ounces out of 100 income, a competing capitalist can offer 95 ounces and outbid the first for the use of the factors. The first, then, forced to meet the competition of other capitalists, will have to raise his bid eventually to 95 (disregarding for simplicity the variation in percentages based on the investment figure rather than on 100). The same equalization process will occur, of course, between capitalists and firms within the same line of production—the same "industry." There is always competitive pressure, then, driving toward a uniform rate of interest in the economy. This competition, it must be pointed out, does not take place simply between firms in the same industry or producing "similar" products. Since money is the general medium of exchange and can be invested in all products, this close competition extends throughout the length and breadth of the production structure.

A fuller discussion of the determination of the rate of interest will take place in chapter 6 below. But one thing should here be evident. The classical writers erred grievously in their discussion of the income-earning process in production. They believed that wages were the "reward" of labor, rents the "reward" of land, and interest the "reward" of capital goods, the three supposedly co-ordinate and independent factors of production. But such a discussion of interest was completely fallacious. As we have seen and shall see further below, capital goods are *not* independently productive. They are the imputable creatures of land and labor (and time). Therefore, capital goods generate no interest income. We have seen above, in keeping with this analysis, that *no* income accrues to the owners of capital goods *as such.*[18]

If the owners of land and labor factors receive all the income (e.g., 100 ounces) when they own the product jointly, why do their owners consent to sell their services for a total of 5 ounces less than their "full worth"? Is this not some form of "exploitation" by the capitalists? The answer again is that the capitalists do *not* earn income from their possession of capital goods or because capital goods generate any sort of monetary income. The capitalists earn income in their capacity as *purchasers of future goods in exchange for supplying present goods to owners of factors.* It is this *time element,* the result of the various individuals' time preferences, and *not* the alleged independent productivity of capital goods, from which the interest rate and interest income arise.

The capitalists earn their interest income, therefore, by supplying the services of present goods to owners of factors in advance of the fruits of their production, acquiring their products by this purchase, and selling the products *at the later date when they become present goods.* Thus, capitalists supply present goods in exchange for future goods (the capital goods), hold the future goods, and have work done on them until they become present goods. They have given up money in the present for a greater sum of money in the future, and the interest rate that they have earned is the agio, or discount on future goods as compared with present goods, i.e., the premium commanded by present goods over future goods. We shall see below that this exchange rate between present and future goods is not only uniform in the production process, but throughout the entire market system. It is the "social rate of time preference." It is the "price of time" on the market as the resultant of all the individual valuations of that good.

How the agio, or pure interest rate, is determined, in the particular time-exchange markets, will be discussed below. Here we shall simply conclude by observing that there is some agio which will be established uniformly throughout the economy and which will be the pure interest rate on the certain expectation of future goods as against present goods.

8. *Money Costs, Prices, and Alfred Marshall*

In the ERE, therefore, every good sold to consumers will sell at a certain "final equilibrium" price and at certain total sales. These receipts will accrue in part to capitalists in the form of interest income, and the remainder to owners of land and labor. The payments of income to the producers have also been popularly termed "costs." These are clearly *money* costs, or money expenses, and are obviously not the same thing as "costs" in the psychic sense of subjective opportunity forgone. Money costs may be *ex post* as well as *ex ante.* (In the ERE, of course, *ex ante* and *ex post* calculations are always the same.) However, the two concepts become linked when psychic costs are appraised as much as possible in monetary terms. Thus, payment to factors may be

95 ounces and recorded as a cost, while the capitalist who earns an interest of five ounces considers 100 as an opportunity cost, since he could have invested elsewhere and earned five (actually, a bit higher) per cent interest.

If, *for the moment,* we include as *money costs* factor payments and interest,[19] then in the ERE, money costs equal total money sales for every firm in every line of production. A firm earns entrepreneurial *profits* when its return is more than interest, suffers entrepreneurial *losses* when its return is less. In our production process, consumers will pay 100 ounces (money sales) and money costs are 100 ounces (factor plus interest income) and there will be similar equality for all other goods and processes. What this means, in essence, is that there are no entrepreneurial profits or losses in the ERE, because there is no change of data or uncertainty about possible change. If total money sales equal total money costs, then it evidently follows that total money sales *per unit sold* will equal total money costs per unit sold. This follows from elementary rules of arithmetic. But the money sales per unit are equal to the *money price* of the good, by definition; while we shall call the total money costs per unit the *average money cost* of the good. It likewise follows, therefore, that *price will equal average money cost for every good in the ERE.*

Strange as it may seem, a great many writers on economics have deduced from this a curious conclusion indeed. They have deduced that "in the long run" (i.e., in the ERE), the fact that costs equal sales or that "cost equals price" implies that *costs determine price.* The price of the good discussed above is 100 ounces per unit, allegedly *because* the cost (average money cost) is 100 ounces per unit. This is supposed to be the law of price determination "in the long run." It would seem to be crystal clear, however, that the truth is precisely the reverse. The price of the final product is determined by the valuations and demands of the consumers, and this price *determines what the cost will be.* If the consumers value the product mentioned above so that its price is 50 ounces instead of 100 ounces, as a result, say, of a change in their valuations, then it is precisely in the "long run," when the effects of uncertainty are removed, that "costs of production" (here, factor payment plus interest payment) will equal the final price. We have seen above how factor incomes are at the mercy of consumer demand and fluctuate according to that demand. Factor payments are the *result* of sales to consumers and *do not determine the latter in advance.* Costs of production, then, are at the mercy of final price, and not the other way around. It is ironic that it is precisely in the ERE that this causative phenomenon should be the clearest. For in the ERE we see quite evidently that consumers pay and determine the final price of the product; that it is through these payments and these payments alone that factors and interest are paid; that therefore the amount of the payments and the total "costs of production" are determined by price and not vice versa. Money costs are the opposite of a basic, determining factor; they are dependent on the price of the product and on consumer demands.

In the real world of uncertainty it is more difficult to see this, because factors are paid in *advance* of the sale of the product, since the capitalist-entrepreneurs speculatively advance money to the factors in the *expectation* of being able to recoup their money with a surplus for interest and profit after sale to the consumers.[20] Whether they do so or not depends on their foresight regarding the state of consumer demand and the future prices of consumers' goods. In the real world of immediate market prices, of course, the existence of entrepreneurial profit and loss will always prevent costs and receipts, cost and price, from being identical, and it is obvious to all that price is solely determined by valuations of stock—by "utilities"—and not at all by money cost. But although most economists recognize that in the real world (the so-called "short-run") costs cannot determine price, they are seduced by the habit of the individual entrepreneur of dealing in terms of "cost" as the determining factor, and they apply this procedure to the case of the ERE and therefore to the inherent long-run tendencies of the economy. Their grave error, as will be discussed further below, comes from viewing the economy from the standpoint of an individual entrepreneur rather than from that of an economist. To the individual entrepreneur, the "cost" of factors is largely determined by forces outside himself and his own sales; the economist, however, must see how money costs are determined and, taking account of all the interrelations in the economy, must recognize that they are determined by final prices reflecting consumer demands and valuations.

The source of the error will become clearer below when we consider a world of nonspecific as well as specific factors. However, the essentials of our analysis and its conclusion remain the same in that more complex and realistic case.

The classical economists were under the delusion that the price of the final product is determined by "costs of production," or rather they fluctuated between this doctrine and the "labor theory of value," which isolated the money costs of labor and picked that segment of the cost of production as the determinant of price. They slurred over the determination of the prices of such goods as old paintings that already existed and needed no further production. The correct relation between prices and costs, as outlined above, was developed, along with other outstanding contributions to economics, by the "Austrian" economists, including the Austrians Carl Menger, Eugen von Böhm-Bawerk, and Friedrich von Wieser, and the Englishman W. Stanley Jevons. It was with the writings of the Austrian school in the 1870's and 1880's that economics was truly established as a science.[21]

Unfortunately, in the science of economics *retrogression* in knowledge has taken place almost as often as progression. The enormous advance provided by the Austrian school, on this point as on others, was blocked and reversed by the influence of Alfred Marshall, who attempted to rehabilitate the classicists and integrate them with the Austrians, while disparaging the contributions of the latter. It was unfortunately the Marshallian and not the Austrian approach that exerted the most influence over later writers. This influence is partly responsible for the current myth among economists that the Austrian school is effectively dead and has no more to contribute and that everything of lasting worth that it had to offer was effectively stated and integrated in Alfred Marshall's *Principles*.

Marshall tried to rehabilitate the cost-of-production theory of the classicists by conceding that, in the "short run," in the immediate market place, consumers' demand rules price. But in the long run, among the important reproducible goods, cost of production is determining. According to Marshall, both utility and money costs determine price, like blades of a scissors, but one blade is more important in the short run, and another in the long run. He concludes that

> as a general rule, the shorter the period we are considering, the greater must be the share of our attention which is given to the influence of demand on value; and the longer the period, the more important will be the influence of cost of production on value. . . . The actual value at any time, the market value as it is often called, is often more influenced by passing events and by causes whose action is fitful and short-lived, than by those which work persistently. But in long periods these fitful and irregular causes in large measure efface one another's influence; so that in the long run persistent causes dominate value completely.[22]

The implication is quite clear: if one deals with "short-run" market values, one is being quite superficial and dwelling only on fitful and transient causes—so much for the Austrians. But if one wants to deal with the "really basic" matters, the really lasting and permanent causes of prices, he must concentrate on costs of production—*pace* the classicists. This impression of the Austrians—their alleged neglect of the "long period," and "one-sided neglect of costs"—has been stamped on economics ever since.

Marshall's analysis suffers from a grave methodological defect —indeed, from an almost hopeless methodological confusion as regards the "short run" and the "long run." He considers the "long run" as actually existing, as being the permanent, persistent, observable element beneath the fitful, basically unimportant flux of market value. He admits (p. 350) that "even the most persistent causes are, however, liable to change," but he clearly indicates that they are *far less* likely to change than the fitful market values; herein, indeed, lies their long-run nature. He regards the long-run data, then, as underlying the transient market values in a way similar to that in which the basic sea level underlies the changing waves and tides.[23] For Marshall, then, the long-run data are something that can be spotted and marked by an observer;

indeed, since they change far more slowly than the market values, they can be observed more accurately.

Marshall's conception of the long run is completely fallacious, and this eliminates the whole groundwork of his theoretical structure. The long run, by its very nature, *never does and never can exist.* This does not mean that "long-run," or ERE, analysis is not important. On the contrary, only through the concept of the ERE can we subject to catallactic analysis such critical problems as entrepreneurial profit, the structure of production, the interest rate, and the pricing of productive factors. The ERE is the goal (albeit shifting in the concrete sense) toward which the market moves. But the point at issue is that it *is not observable,* or real, as are actual market prices.

We have seen above the characteristics of the evenly rotating economy. The ERE is the condition that comes into being and continues to obtain when the present, existing market data (valuations, technology, resources) remain constant. It is a theoretical construct of the economist that enables him to point out in what directions the economy tends to be moving at any given time; it also enables the economist to isolate various elements in his analysis of the economy of the real world. To analyze the determining forces in a world of change, he must construct hypothetically a world of nonchange. This is far different from, indeed it is the reverse of, saying that the long run exists or that it is somehow *more permanently* or more persistently existent than the actual market data. The actual market prices, on the contrary, are the only ones that *ever* exist, and they are the resultants of actual market data (consumer demands, resources, etc.) that themselves change continually. The "long run" is *not* more stable; its data necessarily change along with the data on the market. The fact that costs equal prices in the "long run" does not mean that costs will actually equal prices, but that the tendency exists, a tendency that is continually being *disrupted* in reality by the very fitful changes in market data that Marshall points out.[24]

In sum, rather than being in some sense more persistent and more real than the actual market, the "long run" of the ERE is not real at all, but a very useful theoretical construct that enables the economist to point out the direction in which the market is moving at any given time—specifically, toward the elimination of profits and losses if existing market data remain the same. Thus, the ERE concept is especially helpful in the analysis of profits and losses as compared to interest. But the market data are the only actual reality.

This is not to deny, and the Austrians never did deny, that subjective costs, in the sense of opportunity costs and utilities forgone, are important in the analysis of production. In particular, the disutilities of labor and of waiting—as expressed in the time-preference ratios—determine how much of people's energies and how much of their savings will go into the production process. This, in the broadest sense, will determine or help to determine the total supply of all goods that will be produced. But these costs are themselves subjective utilities, so that both "blades of the scissors" are governed by the subjective utility of individuals. This is a *monistic* and not a dualistic causal explanation. The costs, furthermore, have no direct influence on the relative amount of the stock of *each good* to be produced. Consumers will evaluate the various stocks of goods available. *How much* productive energy and savings will go into producing stock of one particular good and how much into producing another, in other words the relative stocks of each product, will depend in turn on entrepreneurial expectations of where the greatest monetary profit will be found. These expectations are based on the anticipated direction of consumer demand.

As a result of such anticipations, the *nonspecific* factors will move to the production of those goods where, *ceteris paribus,* their owners will earn the highest incomes. An exposition of this process will be presented below.

Marshall's treatment of subjective costs was also highly fallacious. Instead of the idea of opportunity costs, he had the notion that they were "real costs" that could be added in terms of measurable units. Money costs of production, then, became the "necessary supply prices" which entrepreneurs had to pay in order "to call forth an adequate supply of the efforts and waitings" to produce a supply of the product. These real costs were then supposed to be the fundamental, persisting element that backstops money costs of production, and allowed Marshall to talk of the more persisting, long-run, normal situation.[25]

Marshall's great error here, and it has permeated the works of his followers and of present-day writers, is to regard costs and production exclusively from the point of view of an isolated individual entrepreneur or an isolated individual industry, rather than viewing the whole economy in all of its interrelations.[26] Marshall is dealing, of necessity, with particular prices of different goods, and he is attempting to show that alleged "costs of production" determine these prices in the long run. But it is completely erroneous to tie up particular goods with labor vs. leisure and with consuming vs. waiting costs, for the latter are only *general* phenomena, applying and diffusing throughout the entire economic system. The price necessary to call forth a nonspecific factor is the highest price this factor can earn elsewhere—an opportunity cost. What it can attain elsewhere is basically determined by the state of consumer demand elsewhere. The forgone leisure-and-consumption costs, in general, only help to determine the size—the general stock—of labor and savings that will be applied to production. All this will be treated further below.

9. *Pricing and the Theory of Bargaining*

We have seen that, for all goods, total receipts to sellers will tend to equal total payments to factors, and this equality will be established in the evenly rotating economy. In the ERE, interest income will be earned at the same uniform rate by capitalists throughout the economy. The remainder of income from production and sale to consumers will be earned by the owners of the original factors: land and labor.

Our next task will be to analyze the determination of the prices of factor services and the determination of the interest rate, as they tend to be approached in the economy and would be reached in the ERE. Until now, discussion has centered on the capital-goods structure, treated *as if* it were in one composite stage of production. Clearly, there are numerous stages, but we have seen above that earnings in production ultimately resolve themselves, and certainly do so in the ERE, into the earnings of the original factors: land and labor. Later on, we shall expand the analysis to include the case of *many* stages in the production process, and we shall defend this type of temporal analysis of production against the very fashionable current view that production is "timeless" under modern conditions and that the original-factor analysis might have been useful for the primitive era but not for a modern economy. As a corollary to this, we shall develop further an analysis of the nature of capital and time in the production process.

What will be the process of pricing productive factors in a world of purely specific factors? We have been assuming that only *services* and not whole goods can be acquired. In the case of labor this is true because of the nature of the free society; in the case of land and capital goods, we are assuming that the capitalist product-owners hire or rent rather than own any of the productive factors outright. In our example above, the 95 ounces went to all the factor-owners jointly. By what *principles* can we determine how the joint income is allocated to the various *individual* factor services? If all the factors are purely specific, we can resort to what is usually called the *theory of bargaining*. We are in a very analogous situation to the *two-person* barter of chapter 2. For what we have is not relatively determinate prices, or proportions, but exchange ratios with wide zones between the "marginal pairs" of prices. The maximum price of one is widely separated from the minimum price of the other.

In the present case, we have, say, twelve labor and land factors, each of which is indispensable to the production of the good. None of the factors, furthermore, can be used anywhere else, in any other line of production. The question for these factor-owners to solve is the proportionate share of each in the total joint income. Each factor-owner's maximum goal is something slightly less than 100% of the income from the consumers. What the final decision will be cannot be indicated by praxeology. There is, for all practical purposes, no theory of bargaining; all that can be said is that since the owner of each factor wants to participate and earn some income, all will most likely arrive at some sort of voluntary contractual arrangement. This will be a formal type of partnership agreement if the factors jointly own the product; or it will be the *implicit* result if a pure capitalist purchases the services of the factors.

Economists have always been very unhappy about bargaining situations of this kind, since economic analysis is estopped from saying anything more of note. We must not pursue the temptation, however, to condemn such situations as in some way "exploitative" or bad, and thereby convert barrenness for economic analysis into tragedy for the economy. Whatever agreement is arrived at by the various individuals will be beneficial to every one of them; otherwise he would not have so agreed.[27]

It is generally assumed that, in the jockeying for proportionate shares, labor factors have less "bargaining power" than land factors. The only meaning that can be seen in the term "bargaining power" here is that some factor-owners might have minimum reservation prices for their factors, below which they would not be entered in production. In that case, these factors would *at least* have to receive the minimum, while factors with no minimum, with no reservation price, would work even at an income of only slightly more than zero. Now it should be evident that the owner of every labor factor has *some* minimum selling price, a price below which he will not work. In our case, where we are assuming (as we shall see, quite unrealistically) that *every* factor is specific, it is true that no laborer would be able to earn a return in any other type of work. But he could always enjoy leisure, and this sets a minimum supply price for labor service. On the other hand, the use of land sacrifices no leisure. Except in rare cases where the owner enjoys a valuable esthetic pleasure from contemplating a stretch of his own land not in use, there is no revenue that the land can bring him except a monetary return in production. Therefore, land has no reservation price, and the landowner would have to accept a return of almost zero rather than allow his land to be idle. The bargaining power of the owner of labor, therefore, is almost always superior to that of the owner of land.

In the real world, labor, as will be seen below, is uniquely the *nonspecific* factor, so that the theory of bargaining could never apply to labor incomes.[28]

Thus, when two or more factors are specific to a given line of production, there is nothing that economic analysis can say further about the allocation of the joint income from their product; it is a matter of voluntary bargaining between them. Bargaining and indeterminate pricing also take place even between two or more nonspecific factors in the rare case where the proportions in which these factors *must* be used are *identical* in each employment. In such cases, also, there is no determinate pricing for any of the factors separately, and the result must be settled by mutual bargaining.

Suppose, for example, that a certain machine, containing two necessary parts, can be used in several fields of production. The two parts, however, must always be combined in use in a certain fixed proportion. Suppose that two (or more) individuals owned these two parts, i.e., two different individuals produced the different parts by their labor and land. The combined machine will be sold to, or used in, that line of production where it will yield the highest monetary income. But the price that will be established for that machine will necessarily be a *cumulative* price so far as the two factors—the two parts—are concerned. The price of each part and the allocation of the income to the two owners must be decided by a process of bargaining. Economics cannot here determine separate prices. This is true because the proportions between the two are always the same, even though the combined product can be used in several different ways.[29]

Not only is bargaining theory rarely applicable in the real world, but zones of indeterminacy between valuations, and therefore zones of indeterminacy in pricing, tend to dwindle radically in importance as the economy evolves from barter to an advanced monetary economy. The greater the number and variety of goods available, and the greater the number of people with differing valuations, the more negligible will zones of indeterminacy become.[30]

At this point, we may introduce another rare, explicitly empirical, element into our discussion: that on this earth, labor has been a far scarcer factor than land. As in the case of Crusoe, so in the case of a modern economy, men have been able to choose which land to use in various occupations, and which to leave idle, and have found themselves with idle "no-rent" land, i.e., land yielding no income. Of course, as an economy advances, and population and utilization of resources grow, there is a tendency for this superfluity of land to diminish (barring discoveries of new, fertile lands).

6

Production: The Rate of Interest and Its Determination

1. *Many Stages: the Pure Rate of Interest* [1]

Up to this point we have been treating the structure of production as amalgamated into one stage. One or several firms have all been *vertically integrating* all the stages of production of a product (with all factors specific), until finally the product is sold to the consumer. This is certainly an unrealistic assumption. We shall now consider the production situation in the real world, where (*a*) factors are nonspecific as well as specific, and (*b*) production is divided into numerous stages, as the factors continue to work and advance from the higher to the lower stages of the production process.[2] Instead of assuming that one firm—one set of capitalists—purchases factors and retains ownership of the product up through the sale to consumers, let us suppose that there are different firms and different sets of capitalists at definite intervals, and at each interval the product, in the stage it has reached up to that point, is sold for money to another capitalist or group of capitalists. It is not necessary to make any restrictive assumptions about how many separate stages occur or what the time intervals between individual stages might be. For purposes of convenience, let us return to our example and the diagram in Fig. 40. We shall assume that exchanges of product and service take place at each line marked on the diagram. We shall further assume, for convenience only, that each stage takes the same length of time.

Now, instead of collecting interest income for services in one lump sum at the final stage, the capitalist or capitalists acquire interest income *at each stage*.[3] If each stage takes one year, then

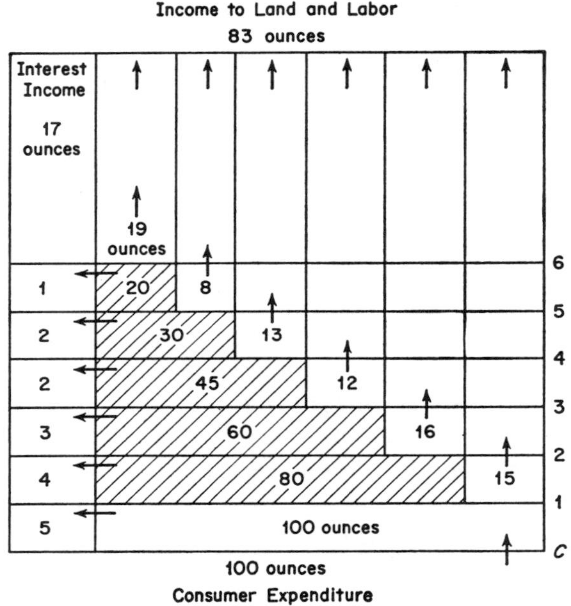

FIG. 41. INCOME ACCRUING TO FACTORS AT VARIOUS STAGES OF PRODUCTION

the entire production process for the good takes six years. When the stages are all lumped together, or vertically integrated, then one capitalist (or set of capitalists) advances the owners of original factors their money six years ahead of time and then waits for this period to acquire his revenue. (Strictly, since the work and pay of labor and land would be continual as the product advanced to its final form, the earliest hired labor and land would be paid, say, in year 1, and the latest toward the end of year 6.) With separate stages, however, each capitalist advances the money for only one year.

Let us see the picture on a diagram (Fig. 41). We must modify the previous diagram somewhat. A lower bar of 100 ounces is added, and the *interest* income that accrues to the capitalist at this lowest stage is indicated by an arrow going off to the left side. The upward arrow then represents the amount going to owners of original factors, land and labor, at this stage, and the shaded area the amount going to owners of capital-goods factors of a higher rank, i.e., intermediate products. The previous diagram did not depict interest income, but simply presented all income as going to the owners of original factors; the time element had not yet been introduced into our discussion.

The structure of production and payment depicted in this basic diagram is as follows: Consumers spend 100 ounces on the good in question. Of the 100 ounces, 5 ounces go as interest income to the sellers of the consumers' good, and 95 are paid out to the owners of factors. In our example, 15 ounces go for the use of land and labor (original) factors, and 80 go into the purchase of factor services of capital goods of a higher order. At the second stage, capitalists receive 80 ounces in revenue from the sale of their product.

Of the 80 ounces, 16 go into the purchase of land and labor factors, and 4 accrue as interest income to the second-level capitalists. The remaining 60 are used for the purchase of higher-order capital goods. The same process is repeated until, on the highest stage, the highest-order capitalists receive 20 ounces of revenue, retain 1 for themselves, and pay out 19 to land and labor factors. The sum total of income to land and labor factors is 83 ounces; total interest income is 17 ounces.

In the foregoing section on interest we showed that money is always nonspecific, and the result is that in the ERE the interest return on monetary investment (the pure rate of interest) is the same everywhere in the economy, regardless of the type of product or the specific conditions of its production. Here we see an amplification of this principle. *Not only must the interest rate be uniform for each good; it must be uniform for every stage of every good.* In our diagram, the interest rate return received by product-owners, i.e., by capitalists, is equal at each stage. At the lowest stage, producers have invested 95 ounces in factors (both capital goods and original factors) and receive 100 ounces from consumers—a net income of 5 ounces. This represents a return on the investment of 5/95, or approximately 5.2%. In the ERE, which we are considering, there are no profits or losses due to uncertainty, so that this return represents the rate of pure interest.[4] The capitalist at the next higher stage invests 60 plus 16 or 76 ounces in factors and receives a net return of 4 ounces, again approximately 5.2%. And so on for each stage of investment, where, except for the vagaries of the arithmetic in our example, the interest rate is uniform for each stage. At the highest stage, the capitalist has invested 19 ounces in land and labor, and receives a net return of 1, again about 5.2%.

The interest rate must be equal for each stage of the production process. For suppose that the interest rate were higher in the higher stages than in the lower stages. Then capitalists would abandon producing in the lower stage, and shift to the higher stage, where the interest return is greater. What is the effect of such a shift? We can answer by stressing the *implications* of differences in the interest rate. A higher interest rate in stage *A* than in stage *B* means that the *price* spread between the sum of factors entering into stage *A* and the selling price of its product, *is greater,* in percentage terms, than the price spread in stage *B*. Thus, if we compare stage 4 and stage 1 in the diagram in Fig. 41, we find a price spread of 43 to 45 in the former case, and 95 to 100 in the latter, for a net interest return of approximately 5.2% in each. Let us suppose, however, that the sum of the factor prices for stage 4 is 35 instead of 43, while the sum of factor prices in stage 1 is 98. (The sum of factor prices here *excludes* interest income, of course.) Capitalists investing in stage 4 would earn a net return of 8, or 23%, while investors in stage 1 earned about 2%. Capitalists would begin to stop investing in stage 1 and shift to stage 4. As a consequence of this shifting, the aggregate demand in stage 1 for its factors diminishes, and the prices of the factors used in stage 1 therefore decline. In the meanwhile, greater investment in stage 4 raises factor prices there, so that the cumulative price rises from 35. Products of stage 4 increase, and the increased supply lowers the selling price, which falls from 43. These arbitrage actions continue until the percentage spread in each of the two stages is equal.

It is important to realize that the *interest rate is equal to the rate of price spread in the various stages.* Too many writers consider the rate of interest as only the price of loans on the loan market. In reality, as we shall see further below, the rate of interest pervades all time markets, and the productive loan market is a strictly subsidiary time market of only derivative importance.[5]

Not only will the rate of interest be equal in each stage of any given product, but the *same* rate of interest will prevail in *all* stages of *all* products in the ERE. In the real world of uncertainty, the *tendency* of entrepreneurial actions is always in the direction of establishing a uniform rate of interest throughout all time markets in the economy. The reason for the uniformity is clear. If stage 3 of good *X* earns 8% and stage 1 of good *Y* earns 2%, capitalists will tend to cease investing in the latter and shift to greater investments in the former. The price spreads change accordingly, in response to the changing demands and supplies, and the interest rates become uniform.

We may now remove our restrictive assumption about the equality of duration of the various stages. Any stage of any product may be as long or as short as the techniques of production, and the organizational structure of industry require. Thus, a technique of production might require a year's harvest for any particular stage. On the other hand, a firm might "vertically integrate" two stages and advance the money to owners of factors for the period covering *both* stages before selling the product for money. The net return on the investment in any stage will adjust itself in accordance with the length of the stage. Thus, suppose that the uniform interest rate in the economy is 5%. This is 5% for a certain unit period of time, say a year. A production process or investment covering a period of two years will, in equilibrium, then earn 10%, the equivalent of 5% *per year.* The same will obtain for a stage of production of any length of time. Thus, *irregularity or integration of stages does not hamper the equilibrating process in the slightest.*

It is already clear that the old classical trinity of "land, labor, and capital" earning "wages, rents, and interest" must be drastically modified. It is *not* true that capital is an independent productive factor or that it earns interest for its owner, in the same way that land and labor earn income for their owners. As we have seen above and will discuss further below, capital is not an independently productive factor. Capital goods are vital and of crucial importance in production, but their production is, in the long run, imputable to land, labor, and time factors. Futhermore, land and labor are not homogeneous factors within themselves, but simply categories of *types* of uniquely varying factors. Each land and each labor factor, then, has its own physical features, its own power to serve in production; each, therefore, receives its own income from production, as will be detailed below. Capital goods too have infinite variety; but, in the ERE, they earn no incomes. What does earn an income is the conversion of future goods into present goods; because of the universal fact of time preference, future satisfactions are always at a discount compared to present satisfactions. The *owning* and holding of capital goods from date 1, when factor services are purchased, until the product is sold at date 2 is what capitalist investors accomplish. This is equivalent to the purchase of future goods (the factor services producing capital goods) with money, followed by the sale at a later date of the present goods for money. The latter occurs when consumers' goods are being sold, for consumers' goods *are* present goods. When intermediate, lower-order capital goods are sold for money, then it is not present goods, but *less distantly future* goods, that are sold. In other words, capital goods have been advanced from an earlier, *more distantly future* stage toward the consumption stage, to a later or *less distantly future* stage. The time for this transformation will be covered by a rate of time preference. Thus, if the market time preference rate, i.e., interest rate, is 5% per year, then a present good worth 100 ounces on the market will be worth about 95 ounces for a claim on it one year from now. The *present value* for a claim on 100 ounces one year from now will be 95 ounces. On this basis, the estimated worth of the good could be worked out for various points in time; thus, the claim for ½ year in the future will be worth roughly 97.5 ounces. The result will be a uniformity of rates over a period of time.

Thus, capitalists advance present goods to owners of factors in return for future goods; then, later, they sell the goods which have matured to become present or less distantly future goods in exchange for present goods (money). They have advanced present goods to owners of factors and, in return, wait while these factors, which are future goods, are transformed into goods that are *more nearly present* than before. The capitalists' function is thus a *time* function, and their income is precisely an income representing the agio of present as compared to future goods. This interest income, then, is *not* derived from the concrete, heterogeneous capital *goods,* but from the generalized investment of time.[6] It comes from a willingness to sacrifice present goods for the purchase of future goods (the factor services). As a result of the purchases, the owners of factors obtain their money in the present for a product that matures only in the future.

Thus, capitalists restrict their present consumption and use these *savings* of money to supply money (present goods) to factor owners who are producing only future goods. This is the service—an advance of time—that the capitalists supply to the owners of factors, and for which the latter voluntarily pay in the form of the interest rate.

2. *The Determination of the Pure Rate of Interest: The Time Market*[7]

It is clear that the rate of interest plays a crucial role in the system of production in the complex, monetary economy. How is the rate of interest determined? The *pure* rate of interest, with which we are now concerned, we have seen will tend to be equal throughout all stages of all production processes in the economy and thus will be uniform in the ERE.

The level of the pure rate of interest is determined by the market for the exchange of present goods against future goods, a market which we shall see permeates many parts of the economic system. The establishment of money as a general medium of exchange has greatly simplified the present-future market as compared to the laborious conditions under barter, where there were separate present-future markets for every commodity. In the monetary economy, the present-future market, or what we may call the "time market," is expressed completely in terms of money. *Money* is clearly the present good *par excellence.* For, aside from the consumption value of the monetary metal itself, the money commodity is the one completely marketable good in the entire society. It is the open sesame to exchange for consumption goods at any time that its owner desires. It is therefore a present good. Since consumers' goods, once sold, do not ordinarily re-enter the exchange nexus, money is the dominant present good in the market. Furthermore, since money is the medium for *all* exchanges, it is also the medium for exchanges on the time market.

What are the future goods that exchange for money? *Future goods are goods that are now expected to become present goods at some future date.* They therefore have a present value. Because of the universal fact of time preference, a particular good is worth more at present than is the present *prospect* of its becoming available as a present good at some time in the future. In other words, a good at present is worth more now than its present value as a future good. Because money is the general medium of exchange, for the time market as well as for other markets, money is the present good, and the future goods *are present expectations of the future acquisition of money.* It follows from the law of time preference that *present money is worth more than present expectations of the same amount of future money.* In other words, future money (as we may call present expectations of money in the future) will always exchange at a discount compared to present money.

This discount on future goods as compared with present goods (or, conversely, the premium commanded by present goods over future goods) is the rate of interest. Thus, if, on the time market, 100 ounces of gold exchange for the prospect of obtaining 105 ounces of gold one year from now, then the rate of interest is approximately 5% per annum. This is the time-discount rate of future to present money.

What do we mean specifically by "prospects for obtaining money in the future"? These prospects must be carefully analyzed in order to explain all the causal factors in the determination of the rate of interest. In the first place, in the real world, these prospects, like any prospects over a period of time, are always more or less *uncertain.* In the real world this ever-present uncertainty necessarily causes interest and profit-and-loss elements to be intertwined and creates complexities that will be analyzed further below. In order to separate the time market from the entrepreneurial elements, we must consider the certain world of the evenly rotating economy, where anticipations are all fulfilled and the pure rate of interest is equal throughout the economy. The *pure* rate of interest will then be the going rate of time discount, the ratio of the price of present goods to that of future goods.

What, then, are the specific types of future goods that enter the time market? There are two such types. One is a *written claim to a certain amount of money at a future date.* The exchange on the time market in this case is as follows: A gives money to B in exchange for a claim to future money. The term generally used to refer to A, the purchaser of the future money, is "lender," or "creditor," while B, the seller of the future money, is termed the "borrower" or "debtor." The reason is that this *credit transaction,* as contrasted to a *cash* transaction, remains *unfinished* in the present. When a man buys a suit for cash, he transfers money in exchange for the suit. The transaction is finished. In a credit transaction he receives simply a written I. O. U., or note, entitling him to claim a certain amount of money at a future date. The transaction remains to be completed in the future, when B, the borrower, "repays the loan" by transferring the agreed money to the creditor.

Although the loan market is a very conspicuous type of time transaction, it is by no means the only or even the dominant one. There is a much more subtle, but more important, type of transaction which permeates the entire production system, but which is not often recognized as a time transaction. This is the purchase of producers' goods and services, which are transformed over a period of time, finally to emerge as consumers' goods. When capitalists purchase the services of factors of production (or, as we shall later see, the factors themselves), they are purchasing a certain amount and value of net produce, discounted to the *present* value of that produce. For the land, labor, and capital services purchased are *future goods,* to be transformed into *final form as present goods.*

Suppose, for example, that a capitalist-entrepreneur hires labor services, and suppose that it can be determined that this amount of labor service will result in a net revenue of 20 gold ounces to the product-owner. We shall see below that the service will tend to be paid the net value of its product; but it will earn its product *discounted* by the time interval until sale. For if the labor service will reap 20 ounces five years from now, it is obvious that the owner of the labor cannot expect to receive from the capitalist the full 20 ounces *now,* in advance He will receive his net earnings discounted by the going agio, the rate of interest. And the interest income will be earned by the capitalist who has assumed the task of advancing present money. The capitalist then waits for five years until the product matures before recouping his money.

The pure capitalist, therefore, in performing a capital-advancing function in the productive system, plays a sort of intermediary role. He sells money (a present good) to factor-owners in exchange for the services of their factors (prospective future goods). He holds these goods and continues to hire work on them until they have been transformed into consumers' goods (present goods), which are then sold to the public for money (a present good). The premium that he earns from the sale of present goods, compared to what he paid for future goods, is the *rate of interest* earned on the exchange.

The time market is therefore not restricted to the loan market. It permeates the entire production structure of the complex economy. All productive factors are future goods: they provide for their owner the expectation of being advanced toward the final goal of consumption, a goal which provides the *raison d'être* for the whole productive enterprise. It is a time market where the future goods sold do not constitute a credit transaction, as in the case of the loan market. The transaction is complete in itself and needs no further payment by either party. In this case, the buyer of the future goods—the capitalist—earns his income through transforming these goods into present goods, rather than through the presentation of an I. O. U. claim on the original seller of a future good.

The time market, the market where present goods exchange for future goods, is, then, an aggregate with several component parts. In one part of the market, capitalists exchange their money savings (present goods) for the services of numerous factors (future goods). This is one part, and the most important part, of the time market. Another is the consumers' loan market, where savers lend their money in a credit transaction, in exchange for an I. O. U. of future money. The savers are the suppliers of present money, the borrowers the suppliers of future money, in the form of I. O. U.'s. Here we are dealing only with those who borrow to spend on consumption goods, and *not* with producers who borrow savings in order to invest in production. For the borrowers of savings for production loans are not independent forces on the time market, but are rather completely dependent on the interest agio between present and future goods as determined in the production system, equaling the ratio between the prices of consumers' and producers' goods, and between the various stages of producers' goods. This dependence will be seen below.

3. *Time Preference and Individual Value Scales*

Before considering the component parts of the time market further, let us go to the very root of the matter: the value scale of the individual. As we have seen in the problem of pricing and demand, the individual's value scale provides the key to the determination of all events on the market. This is no less true in regard to the interest rate. Here the key is the schedule of time-preference valuations of the individual.

Let us consider a hypothetical individual, abstracting from any particular role that he may play in the economic system. This individual has, of necessity, a diminishing marginal utility of money, so that each additional unit of money acquired ranks lower on his value scale. This is necessarily true. Conversely, and this also follows from the diminishing marginal utility of money, each successive unit of money given up will rank higher on his value scale. The same law of utility applies to future money, i.e., to prospects of future money. To both present money and future money there applies the general rule that *more* of a good will have greater utility than *less* of it. We may illustrate these general laws by means of the following hypothetical value scale of an individual:

John Smith

....(19 oz. future) (10 yrs. from now)
....................4th unit of 10 oz.
....(18 oz. future)
....(17 oz. future)
....(16 oz. future)
....................3rd unit of 10 oz.
....(15 oz. future)
....(14 oz. future)
....(13 oz. future)
....................2nd unit of 10 oz.
....(12 oz. future)
....................1st unit of 10 oz.
....(11 oz. future)
....................(1st added unit of 10 oz.)
....(10 oz. future)
....................(2nd added unit of 10 oz.)

We see in this value scale an example of the fact that all possible alternatives for choice are ranged in one scale, and the truths of the law of utility are exemplified. The "1st unit of 10 oz." refers to the rank accorded to the first unit of 10 ounces (the unit arbitrarily chosen here) to be given up. The "2nd unit of 10 ounces" of money to be given up is accorded higher rank, etc. The "1st added unit of 10 oz." refers to the rank accorded to the next unit of 10 ounces which the man is considering acquiring, with parentheses to indicate that he does not now have the good in his possession. Above we have a schedule of John Smith's value scale with respect to time, i.e., his scale of time preferences. Suppose that the market rate of interest, then, is 3%; i.e., he can obtain 13 ounces of future money (considered here as 10 years from now), by selling 10 ounces of present money. To see what he will do, we are privileged to be able to consult his time-preference scale. We find that 13 ounces of future money is preferred to his first unit of 10 ounces and also to the second unit of 10 ounces, but that the 3rd unit of 10 ounces stands higher in his valuation. Therefore, with a market rate of 3% per year, the individual will save 20 ounces of gold and sell them for future money on the time market. He is a supplier of present goods on the time market to the extent of 20 ounces.[8]

If the market rate of interest is 2%, so that 12 future ounces would be the price of 10 present ounces, then John Smith would be a *supplier of 10 ounces of present money*. He is never a *supplier of future money* because, in his particular case, there are no quantities of future money above 10 ounces that are ranked below "1st added unit of 10 oz."

Suppose, for example, that James Robinson has the following time-value scale:

James Robinson

....(19 oz. future) (10 yrs. from now)
....................2nd unit of 10 oz.
....(18 oz. future)
....(17 oz. future)
....................1st unit of 10 oz.
....(16 oz. future)
....(15 oz. future)
....(14 oz. future)
....................(1st added unit of 10 oz.)
....(13 oz. future)
....(12 oz. future)
....................(2nd added unit of 10 oz.)
....(11 oz. future)
....................(3rd added unit of 10 oz.)
....(10 oz. future)

If the market rate of interest is 3%, then Robinson's valuations are such that no savings will be supplied to the time market. On the contrary, 13 ounces future *is lower than* "1st added unit of 10 oz.," which means that Robinson would be willing to exchange 13 ounces of future money for 10 ounces of present money. Thereby he becomes, in contrast to Smith, a supplier of future money. If the rate of interest were 1%, then he would supply 22 ounces of future money in exchange for 20 ounces of present money, thus increasing his demand for present money at the lower price.

It will be noticed that there is no listing for less than 10 ounces of future goods, to be compared with 10 ounces of present goods. The reason is that every man's time preference is positive, i.e., 1 ounce of present money will always be preferred to 1 ounce or less of future money. Therefore, there will never be any question of a zero or negative pure interest rate. Many economists have made the great mistake of believing that the interest rate determines the time-preference schedule and rate of savings, rather than *vice versa.* This is completely invalid. The interest rates discussed here are simply hypothetical schedules, and they *indicate* and reveal the time-preference schedules of each individual. In the aggregate, as we shall see presently, the interaction of the time preferences and hence the supply-demand schedules of individuals on the time market determine the pure rate of interest on the market. They do so in the same way that individual valuations determine aggregate supply and demand schedules for goods, which in turn determine market prices. And once again, it is utilities and utilities alone, here in the form of time preferences, that determine the market result; the explanation does not lie in some sort of "mutually determining process" of preferences and market consequences.

Continuing with our analysis, let us tabulate the schedules of John Smith and James Robinson, from their time-value scales above, in relation to their position on the time market. John Smith's schedule is given in Table 11. James Robinson's schedule is given in Table 12.

The Robinson time schedule is of particular interest. Referring to his time-value scale, we find that at an interest rate of 9%, 19 ounces of future money is above the 2nd unit of 10 ounces of

TABLE 11

INTEREST RATE %	SUPPLY OF PRESENT MONEY = DEMAND FOR FUTURE MONEY = SAVINGS OZ. OF GOLD	SUPPLY OF FUTURE MONEY = DEMAND FOR PRESENT MONEY OZ. OF GOLD
9..........	40	0
8..........	30	0
7..........	30	0
6..........	30	0
5..........	20	0
4..........	20	0
3..........	20	0
2..........	10	0
1..........	0	0

TABLE 12

INTEREST RATE %	SUPPLY OF PRESENT MONEY = DEMAND FOR FUTURE MONEY = SAVINGS OZ. OF GOLD	SUPPLY OF FUTURE MONEY = DEMAND FOR PRESENT MONEY OZ. OF GOLD
9..........	20	0
8..........	10	0
7..........	10	0
6..........	0	0
5..........	0	0
4..........	0	0
3..........	0	10
2..........	0	10
1..........	0	20

present money and therefore also above the first unit. At this interest rate, his supply of present money on the time market, i.e., his savings, equals 20 ounces. Because his valuation of the first unit (of 10 ounces—an arbitrary size of unit that we have picked for this discussion) is between 16 and 17 ounces of future money, when the market interest rate is 6%, his return of 16 ounces is less valuable to him than his first unit. Therefore, he will not be a saver and supplier of present money at this rate. On the other hand, he will not be a supplier of future goods (i.e., a demander of present goods on the time market) either. In order to be a supplier of future goods, his valuation of the future money that he would have to give up at the ruling rate of interest has to be lower than the present money that he would get. In other words, what he gives up in prospective future money will have to be worth less to him than the utility of the "1st additional unit of 10 oz." on his scale. While the market rate is in the 4% to 6% range, this will not be true, for the 14 to 16 ounces of future money that he would have to supply would be worth more to him than the additional 10 ounces of present money that he would gain from the exchange. In Robinson's case, the critical point takes place when the hypothetical interest rate drops to 3%, for 13 future ounces are worth less than an additional 10 ounces of present money, and he will supply the future ounces on the market. If the interest rate were 1%, he would supply 20 ounces of future goods.[9]

It should be evident that an individual, at any one time, will either be a net saver (i.e., a net demander of future goods), a net supplier of future goods, or not be on the time market at all. The three categories are mutually exclusive.

The diagram in Fig. 42 sketches the schedules of Smith and Robinson in graphic form. Interest rate is on the vertical axis, and money on the horizontal. The supplies of present goods are also demands for future goods, and the demand for present goods is also the supply of future goods.

We cannot compare utilities or values between persons, but we certainly may say that Robinson's time-preference schedule is *higher* than Smith's. In other words, it cannot make sense to compare the rankings or utilities that the two men accord to any particular unit of a good, but we can (if we know them) compare their *schedules* based purely on their demonstrated time preferences. Robinson's time-preference schedule is *higher* than

Smith's, i.e., at each hypothetical rate of interest Robinson's values are such that he will part with less of his present goods in exchange for future goods.[10]

Let us explore the typical individual time-preference schedule, or time-supply-and-demand schedule, more closely. In the first place, there is no necessity for the unit chosen to be 10 ounces.

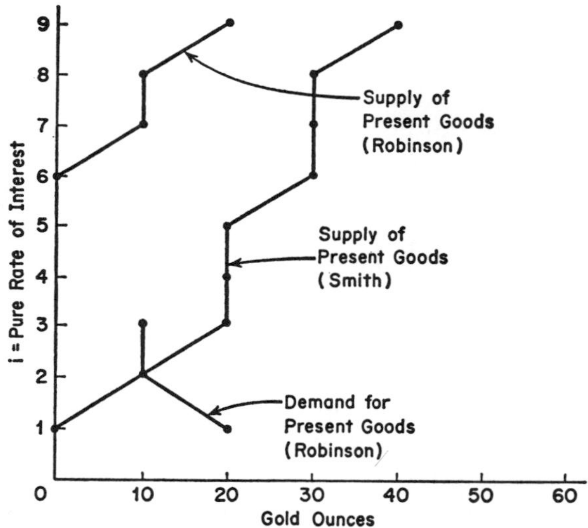

FIG. 42. COMPARISON OF TIME-PREFERENCE SCHEDULES

Since money is perhaps the most *divisible* of goods, it is possible to break down the units into far smaller sizes. Furthermore, because of the arbitrage of the market, the rate of interest return on investments of present in future goods will be equal for all the various sizes of units. We may therefore visualize a comparatively smooth curve, even for each individual.

One inevitable characteristic of an individual's time-preference schedule is that eventually, after a certain amount of present money has been supplied on the market, no conceivable interest rate could persuade him to purchase more future goods. The reason is that as present money dwindles and future money increases in a man's possession, the marginal utility of the former increases on the man's value scale, and the marginal utility of the latter decreases. In particular, every man must consume in the present, and this drastically limits his savings regardless of the interest rate. As a result, after a certain point, a man's time preference for the present becomes infinite, and the line representing his supply of present goods becomes vertical upward. At the other end of the scale, the fact of time preference will imply that at some minimum rate of interest the man will not save at all. At what point the supply curve hits the vertical axis depends on the valuations of the individual; but it must do so, as a result of the operation of the law of time preference. A man could not prefer 10 ounces or even less of future money to 10 ounces of present money.[11]

What happens after the individual supply curve hits the vertical axis depends entirely on the time preferences of the individual. In some cases, as in that of John Smith above, the person's marginal utility of money falls too fast, as compared with that of future money, for him to participate as a net demander of present goods at low rates of interest. In other words, Smith's time-preference ratio is too low in this area for him to become a demander of present goods and a supplier of future goods. On the other hand, Robinson's higher schedule of time preferences is such that, at low rates of interest, he becomes a supplier of future goods for present goods. (See Fig. 42.)

We may of course, diagram a typical individual's supply and demand curve conventionally, as we have done in Fig. 42. On the other hand, we may also modify this diagram, so as to make one continuous curve of the individual's activity on the time market. We may call this curve the "individual's time-market curve." At higher interest rates, down to where it hits the vertical axis, this curve is simply the individual's supply curve of present goods. But below this, we are *reversing* his demand curve and continuing it on to the left on the horizontal axis. (See Fig. 43.)

Every individual on the market has a similar type of time-market schedule, reflecting his particular value scale. The schedule of each will be such that at higher rates of interest there will be a greater tendency toward net saving, and at lower rates of interest, less saving, until the individual becomes a net demander.

At each *hypothetical* rate of interest there is a possible net saving, net demanding, or abstaining from the market, for each individual. For some changes in the rate of interest, there will be no change (vertical curve), but there will never be a situation where the supply will be greater, or demand less, with lower rates of interest.

The time-market schedules of all individuals are aggregated on

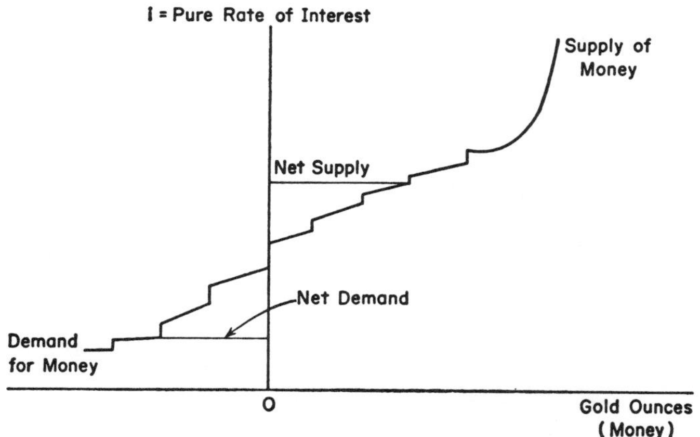

FIG. 43. INDIVIDUAL TIME-MARKET CURVE

the market to form market-supply and market-demand schedules for present goods in terms of future goods. The supply schedule will increase with an increase in the rate of interest, and the demand schedule will fall with the higher rates of interest.

A typical aggregate market diagram may be seen in Fig. 44. Aggregating the supply and demand schedules on the time market for all individuals in the market, we obtain curves such as *SS* and *DD*. *DD* is the demand curve for present goods in terms of the supply of future goods; it slopes rightward as the rate of interest falls. *SS* is the supply curve of present goods in terms of the demand for future goods; it slopes rightward as the rate of interest increases. The intersection of the two curves determines the *equilibrium rate of interest*—the rate of interest as it would tend to be in the evenly rotating economy. This pure rate of interest, then, is determined *solely by the time preferences of the individuals in the society, and by no other factor.*

The intersection of the two curves determines an equilibrium rate of interest, *BA, and* an equilibrium amount saved, *OB. OB* is the total amount of money that will be saved and invested in future money. At a higher interest rate than *BA,* present goods supplied would exceed future goods supplied in exchange, and

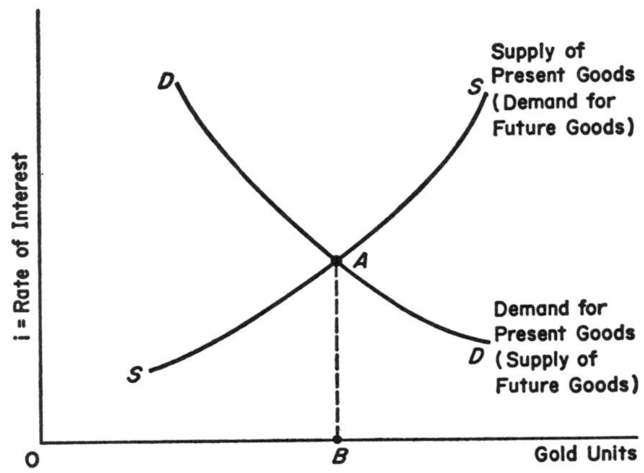

FIG. 44. AGGREGATE TIME-MARKET CURVES

the excess savings would compete with one another until the price of present goods in terms of future goods would decline toward equilibrium. If the rate of interest were below *BA,* the demand for present goods by suppliers of future goods would exceed the supply of savings, and the competition of this demand would push interest rates up toward equilibrium.

Perhaps more fallacies have been committed in discussions concerning the interest rate than in the treatment of any other aspect of economics. It took a long while for the crucial importance of time preference in the determination of the pure rate of interest to be realized in economics; it took even longer for economists to realize that time preference is the *only* determining factor. Reluctance to accept a monistic causal interpretation has plagued economics to this day.[12]

4. *The Time Market and the Production Structure*

The time market, like other markets, consists of component individuals whose schedules are aggregated to form the market supply and demand schedules. The intricacy of the time market (and of the money market as well) consists in the fact that it is also divided and subdivided into various distinguishable submarkets. These are aggregable into a total market, but the subsidiary components are interesting and highly significant in their own right and deserve further analysis. They themselves, of course, are composed of individual supply and demand schedules.

As we have indicated above, we may divide the present-future market into two main subdivisions: *the production structure* and the *consumer loan market.* Let us turn first to the production structure. This may be done most clearly by considering once again a typical production-structure diagram. This diagram is the one in Fig. 41, with one critical difference. Previously the diagram represented a typical production structure for any particular consumers' good. *Now the same diagram represents the aggregate production structure for all goods.* Money moves from consumers' goods back through the various stages of production, while goods flow from the higher through the lower stages of production, finally to be sold as consumers' goods. The pattern of production is not changed by the fact that both specific and nonspecific factors exist. Since the production structure is aggregated, the degree of specificity for a *particular product* is irrelevant in a discussion of the time market.

There is no problem in the fact that different production processes for different goods take unequal lengths of time. This is not a difficulty because the flow from one stage to another can be aggregated for any number of processes.

There are, however, two more serious problems that seem to be involved in aggregating the production structure for the entire economy. One is the fact that in various processes there will not necessarily be an exchange of capital goods for money at each stage. One firm may "vertically integrate" within itself one or more stages and thereby advance present goods for a greater period of time. We shall see below, however, that this presents no difficulty at all, just as it presented no difficulty in the case of particular processes.

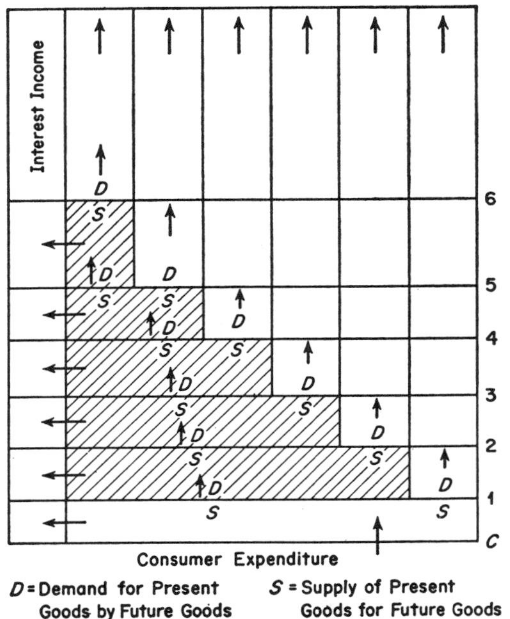

FIG. 45. AGGREGATE PRODUCTION STRUCTURE FOR ALL GOODS

A second difficulty is the purchase and use of *durable* capital goods. We have been assuming, and are continuing to assume, that no capital goods or land are *bought*—that they are only *hired*, i.e., "rented" from their owners. The purchase of durable goods presents complications, but again, as we shall see, this will lead to no essential change whatever in our analysis.

The production-structure diagram in Fig. 45 omits the numbers that indicated the size of payments between the various sectors and substitutes instead *D*'s and *S*'s to indicate the points where present-future transactions ("time transactions") take place and what groups are engaging in these various transactions. *D*'s indicate demanders of present goods, and *S*'s are suppliers of present goods, for future goods.

Let us begin at the bottom—the expenditure of consumers on consumers' goods. The movement of money is indicated by arrows, and money moves from consumers to the sellers of consumers' goods. This is *not* a time transaction, because it is an exchange of *present goods* (money) *for present goods* (consumers' goods).[13]

These producers of consumers' goods are necessarily capitalists who have invested in the services of factors to produce these goods and who then sell their products. Their investment in factors consisted of purchases of the services of land factors and labor factors (the original factors) and first-order capital goods (the produced factors). In both these two large categories of transactions (exchanges that are made a stage earlier than the final sale of consumers' goods), present goods are exchanging for future goods. In both cases, the capitalists are supplying *present money* in exchange for factor services whose yield will materialize in the future, and which therefore are *future goods.*

So the capitalists who are producing consumers' goods, whom we might call "first-stage capitalists," engage in time transactions in making their investments. The components of this particular subdivision of the time market, then, are:

Supply of Present Goods: Capitalists_1
Supply of Future Goods: Landowners, Laborers, Capitalists_2 (Demand for Present Goods)

Capitalists_1 are the first-stage capitalists who produce consumers' goods. They purchase capital goods from the producer-owners—the second-stage capitalists, or Capitalists_2. The appropriate *S*'s and *D*'s indicate these transactions, and the arrows pointing upward indicate the direction of money payment.

At the next stage, the Capitalists_2 have to purchase services of factors of production. They supply present goods and purchase future goods, goods which are even more distantly in the future than the product that they will produce.[14] These future goods are supplied by landowners, laborers, and Capitalists$_3$. To sum up, at the second stage:

Supply of Present Goods: Capitalists$_2$
Supply of Future Goods: Landowners, Laborers, Capitalists$_3$

These transactions are marked with the appropriate *S*'s and *D*'s, and the arrows pointing upward indicate the direction of money payment in these transactions.

This pattern is continued until the very last stage. At this final stage, which is here the sixth, the sixth-stage capitalists supply future goods to the fifth-stage capitalists, but also supply present goods to laborers and landowners in exchange for the extremely distant future services of the latter. The transactions for the two highest stages are, then, as follows (with the last stage designated as *N* instead of 6):

5th Stage:

Supply of Present Goods: Capitalists$_5$
Supply of Future Goods: Landowners, Laborers, Capitalists$_N$

*N*th Stage:

Supply of Present Goods: Capitalists$_N$
Supply of Future Goods: Landowners, Laborers.

We may now sum up our time market for any production structure of *N* stages:

Suppliers of Present Goods	*Suppliers of Future Goods (Demanders of Present Goods)*
Capitalists$_1$	All Landowners
Capitalists$_2$	All Laborers
Capitalists$_3$	Capitalists$_2$
....	Capitalists$_3$
....	....
....	....
Capitalists$_N$	Capitalists$_N$

To illustrate clearly the workings of the production structure, let us hark back to the numerical example given in Fig. 41 and summarize the quantities of present goods supplied and received by the various components of the time market. We may use the same figures here to apply to the *aggregate* production structure, although the reader may wish to consider the units as multiples of gold ounces in this case. The fact that different durations of production processes and different degrees of vertical integration make no difficulties for aggregation permits us to use the diagram almost interchangeably for a single production process and for the economy as a whole. Furthermore, the fact that the ERE interest rate will be the same for all stages and all goods in the economy especially permits us to aggregate the comparable stages of all goods. For if the rate is 5%, then we may say that for a certain stage of one good, payments by capitalists to owners of factors are 50 ounces, and receipts from sales of products are 52.5 ounces, while we can also assume that the aggregate payments for the whole economy in the same period are 5,000 ounces, and receipts 5,250 ounces. The same interest rate connotes the same rate of return on investments, whether considered separately or for all goods lumped together.

The following, then, are the supplies and demands for present goods from Fig. 41, the diagram now being treated as an aggregate for the whole economy:

(*Savers*) *Suppliers of Present Goods*			*Demanders of Present Goods* *Suppliers of Future Goods*	
Capitalists$_1$ . .	95 oz. →	15 oz.	Land and Labor Owners; Capitalists$_2$	80 oz.
Capitalists$_2$ . .	76 oz. →	16 oz.	Land and Labor Owners; Capitalists$_3$	60 oz.
Capitalists$_3$ . .	57 oz. →	12 oz.	Land and Labor Owners; Capitalists$_4$	45 oz.
Capitalists$_4$ . .	43 oz. →	13 oz.	Land and Labor Owners; Capitalists$_5$	30 oz.
Capitalists$_5$ . .	28 oz. →	8 oz.	Land and Labor Owners; Capitalists$_N$	20 oz.
Capitalists$_N$ . .	19 oz. →	19 oz.	Land and Labor Owners	
	318 oz.	83 oz.		235 oz.

The horizontal arrows at each stage of this table depict the movement of money as supplied from the savers to the recipient demanders at that stage.

From this tabulation it is easy to derive the *net* money income of the various participants: their *gross* money income minus their money payments, if we include the entire period of time for all of their transactions on the time market. The case of the owners of land and labor is simple: they receive their money in exchange for the future goods to be yielded by their factors; this money is their gross *and* their net money income from the productive system. The total of net money income to the owners of land and labor is 83 ounces. This is the sum of the money incomes to the various owners of land and labor at each stage of production.

The case of the capitalists is far more complicated. They pay out present goods in exchange for future goods and then sell the maturing less distantly future products for money to lower-stage capitalists. Their *net* money income is derived by subtracting their money outgo from their gross income over the period of the production stage. In our example, the various net incomes of the capitalists are as follows:

Net Incomes of Capitalists Producing Capital Goods

Capitalists_2	80 − 76 = 4 oz.
Capitalists_3	60 − 57 = 3 oz.
Capitalists_4	45 − 43 = 2 oz.
Capitalists_5	30 − 28 = 2 oz.
Capitalists_N	20 − 19 = 1 oz.
	12 oz.

The total net income of the capitalists producing capital goods (orders 2 through *N*) is *12 ounces.* What, then, of Capitalists_1, who apparently have not only no net income, but a deficit of 95 ounces? They are recouped, as we see from the diagram (in Fig. 41), *not* from the savings of capitalists, but from the expenditure of consumers, which totals 100 ounces, yielding a net income to Capitalists_1 of 5 ounces.

It should be emphasized at this point that the general pattern of the structure of production and of the time market will be the same in the real world of uncertainty as in the ERE. The difference will be in the amounts that go to each sector and in the relations among the various prices. We shall see later what the discrepancies will be; for example, the rate of return by the capitalists in each sector will not be uniform in the real market.

But the *pattern* of payments, the composition of suppliers and demanders, will be the same.

In analyzing the income-expenditure balance sheets of the production structure, writers on economic problems have seen that we may consolidate the various incomes and consider only the net incomes. The temptation has been simply to write off the various intercapitalist transactions as "duplications." If that is done here, then the total net income in the market is: capitalists, 17 ounces (12 ounces for capital-good capitalists and 5 ounces for consumers'-good capitalists); land and labor factors, 83 ounces. The grand total net income is then 100 ounces. This is exactly equal to the total of consumer spending for the period.

Total net income is 100 ounces, and consumption is 100 ounces. There is, therefore, no new *net* saving. We shall deal with savings and their change in detail below. Here the point is that, in the endless round of the ERE, zero *net* savings, as thus defined, would mean that there is just enough *gross* saving to keep the structure of productive capital intact, to keep the production processes rolling, and to keep a constant amount of consumers' goods produced per given period.

It is certainly legitimate and often useful to consider net incomes and net savings, but it is not always illuminating, and its use has been extremely misleading in present-day economics.[15] Use of the net "national" income figures (it is better to deal with "social income" extending throughout the market community using the money rather than to limit the scope to national boundaries) leads one to believe that the really important element maintaining the production structure is consumers' spending. In our ERE example, the various factors and capitalists receive their net income and plow it back into consumption, thus maintaining the productive structure and future standards of living, i.e., the output of consumers' goods. The inference from such concepts is clear: capitalists' savings are necessary to increase and deepen the capital structure, but even without any savings, consumption expenditure is alone sufficient to maintain the productive capital structure intact.

This conclusion seems deceptively clear-cut: after all, is not consumer spending the bulwark and end product of activity? This thesis, however, is tragically erroneous. There is no simple automatism in capitalists' spending, especially when we leave the certain world of the ERE, and it is in this real world that the conceptual error plays havoc. For with production divided into stages, it is not true that consumption spending is sufficient to provide for the maintenance of the capital structure. When we consider the maintenance of the capital structure, we must consider *all the decisions* to supply present goods on the present-future market. These decisions are *aggregated;* they do not cancel one another out. Total savings in the economy, then, are not zero, but the aggregation of all the present goods supplied to owners of future goods during the production process. This is the sum of the supplies of Capitalists_1 through Capitalists_N, which totals *318 ounces.* This is the total *gross* savings—the supply of present goods for future goods in production—and also equals total *gross* investment. Investment is the amount of money spent on future-good factors and necessarily equals savings. Total expenditures on production are: 100 (Consumption) plus 318 (Investment = Savings), equals *418 ounces.* Total gross income from production equals the gross income of Capitalists_1 (100 ounces) plus the gross income of other capitalists (235 ounces) plus the gross income of owners of land and labor (83 ounces), which also equals *418 ounces.*

The system depicted in our diagram of the production structure, then, is of an economy in which *418 gold ounces* are earned in gross income, and *100 ounces* are spent on consumption, while *318 ounces* are saved and invested in a certain order in the production structure. In this evenly rotating economy, 418 ounces are earned and then spent, with no net "hoarding" or "dishoarding," i.e., no net additions or subtractions from the cash balance over the period as a whole.[16]

Thus, instead of no savings being needed to maintain capital and the production structure intact, we see that a very heavy proportion of savings and investment—in our example three times the amount spent on consumption—is necessary simply to keep the production structure intact. The contrast is clear when we consider *who* obtains income and who is empowered to decide whether to consume or to invest. The net-income theorists implicitly assume that the only important decisions in regard to consuming vs. saving-investing are made by the factor-owners out of their net income. Since the net income of capitalists is admittedly relatively small, this approach attributes little importance to their role in maintaining capital. We see, however, that what maintains capital is *gross* expenditures and *gross* investment and not net investment. The capitalists at each stage of production, therefore, have a vital role in maintaining capital through their savings and investment, through heavy savings from gross income.

Concretely, let us take the case of the Capitalists$_1$. According to the net-income theorists, their role is relatively small, since their net income is only 5 ounces. But actually their gross income is 100 ounces, and *it is their decision how much of this to save and how much to consume that is decisive.* In the ERE, of course, we simply state that they save and invest 95 ounces. But when we leave the province of the ERE, we must realize that there is nothing automatic about this investment. There is no natural law that they must reinvest this amount. Suppose, for example, that the Capitalists$_1$ decide to break up the smooth flow of the ERE by spending all of the 100 ounces for their own consumption rather than investing the 95 ounces. It is evident that the entire market-born production structure would be destroyed. No income at all would accrue to the owners of all the higher-order capital goods, and all the higher-order capital processes, all the production processes longer than the very shortest, would have to be abandoned. We have seen above, and shall see in more detail below, that civilization advances by virtue of additional capital, which lengthens production processes. Greater quantities of goods are made possible only through the employment of more capital in longer processes. Should capitalists shift from saving-investment to consumption, all these processes would be necessarily abandoned, and the economy would revert to barbarism, with the employment of only the shortest and most primitive production processes. The standard of living, the quantity and variety of goods produced, would fall catastrophically to the primitive level.[17]

What could be the reason for such a precipitate withdrawal of savings and investment in favor of consumption? The only reason—on the free market—would be a sudden and massive increase in the time-preference schedules of the capitalists, so that present satisfactions become worth very much more in terms of future satisfactions. Their higher time preferences mean that the existing rate of interest is not enough to induce them to save and invest in their previous proportions. They therefore consume a greater proportion of their gross income and invest less.

Each individual, on the basis of his time-preference schedule, decides between the amount of his money income to be devoted to saving and the amount to be devoted to consumption. *The aggregate time-market schedules (determined by time preferences) determine the aggregate social proportions between (gross) savings and consumption.* It is clear that the higher the time-preference schedules are, the greater will be the proportion of consumption to savings, while lower time-preference schedules will lower this proportion. At the same time, as we have seen, higher time-preference schedules in the economy lead to higher rates of interest, and lower schedules lead to lower rates of interest.

From this it becomes clear that *the time preferences of the individuals on the market determine simultaneously and by themselves both the market equilibrium interest rate and the proportions between consumption and savings (individual and aggregate).*[18] Both the latter are the obverse side of the same coin. In our example, the increase in time-preference schedules has caused a decline in savings, absolute and proportionate, and a rise in the interest rate.

The fallacies of the net product figures have led economists to include some "grossness" in their product and income figures. At present the favorite concept is that of the "gross national product" and its counterpart, gross national expenditures. These concepts were adopted because of the obvious errors encountered with the net income concepts.[19] Current "gross" figures, however, are the height of illogicality, because they are not gross at all, but only partly gross. They include only gross purchases by capitalists of *durable* capital goods and the consumption of their self-owned durable capital, approximated by depreciation allowances set by the owners. We shall consider the problems of durable capital more fully below, but suffice it to say that there is no great difference between durable and less durable capital. Both are consumed in the course of the production process, and both must be paid for out of the gross income and gross savings of lower-order capitalists. In evaluating the payment pattern of the production structure, then, it is inadmissible to leave the consumption of nondurable capital goods out of the investment picture. It is completely illogical to single out durable goods, which are themselves only discounted embodiments of their nondurable services and are therefore no different from nondurable goods.

The idea that the capital structure is maintained intact without savings, as it were automatically, is fostered by the use of the "net" approach. If even zero savings will suffice to maintain capital, then it seems as if the aggregate value of capital is a permanent entity that cannot be reduced. This notion of the permanence of capital has permeated economic theory, particularly through the writings of J. B. Clark and Frank H. Knight, and through the influence of the latter has molded current "neoclassical" economic theory in America. To maintain this doctrine it is necessary to deny the stage analysis of production and, indeed, to deny the very influence of *time* in production.[20] The all-pervading influence of time is stressed in the period-of-production concept and in the determination of the interest rate and of the investment-consumption ratio by individual time-preference schedules. The Knight doctrine denies any role to time in production, asserting that production "now" (in a modern, complex economy) is timeless and that time preference has *no* influence on the interest rate. This doctrine has been aptly called a "mythology of capital." Among other errors, it leads to the belief that there is no economic problem connected with the replacement and maintenance of capital.[21, 22]

A common fallacy, fostered directly by the net-income approach, holds that the important category of expenditures in the production system is consumers' spending. Many writers have gone so far as to relate business prosperity directly to consumers' spending, and depressions of business to declines in consumers' spending. "Business cycle" considerations will be deferred to later chapters, but it is clear that there is little or no relationship between prosperity and consumers' spending; indeed almost the reverse is true. For business prosperity, the important consideration is the price spreads between the various stages—i.e., the rate of interest return earned. It is this rate of interest that induces capitalists to save and invest present goods in productive factors. The rate of interest, as we have been demonstrating, is set by the configurations of the time preferences of individuals in the society. It is not the total quantity of money spent on consumption that is relevant to capitalists' returns, but the *margins,* the spreads, between the product prices and the sum of factor prices at the various stages—spreads which tend to be proportionately equal throughout the economy.

There is, in fact, *never any need to worry about the maintenance of consumer spending*. There must always be consumption; as we have seen, after a certain amount of monetary saving, there is always an irreducible minimum of his monetary assets that every man will spend on current consumption. The fact of human action insures such an irreducible minimum. And as long as there is a monetary economy and money is in use, it will be spent on the purchase of consumers' goods. The proportion spent on capital in its various stages and *in toto* gives a clue to the *important* consideration—the real output of consumers' goods in the economy. The total amount of money spent, however, gives no clue at all. Money and its value will be systematically studied in a later chapter. It is obvious, however, that the number of units spent could vary enormously, depending on the quantity of the money commodity in circulation. 100 or 1,000 or 10,000 or 100,000 ounces of gold might be spent on consumption, without signifying anything except that the quantity of money units available was less or greater. The total amount of money spent on consumption gives no clue to the quantity of goods the economy may purchase.

The important consideration, therefore, is time preferences and the resultant proportion between expenditure on consumers' and producers' goods (investment). The lower the proportion of the former, the heavier will be the investment in capital structure, and, after a while, the more abundant the supply of consumers' goods and the more productive the economy. The obverse of the coin is the determining effect of time preferences on the price spreads that set the rate of interest, and the income of the capitalist savers-investors in the economy. We have already seen the effect of a lowering of investment on the first rank, and below we shall analyze fully the effect on production and interest of a lowering of time preferences and the effects of various changes in the quantity of money on time preferences and the production structure.

Before continuing with an analysis of time preference and the production structure, however, let us complete our examination of the components of the time market.[23]

The pure demanders of present goods on the time market are the various groups of laborers and landowners—the sellers of the services of original productive factors. Their price on the market, as will be seen below, will be set equal to the *marginal value product* of their units, *discounted* by the prevailing rate of interest. The greater the rate of interest, the less will the price of their service be, or rather, the greater will be the *discount* from their marginal value product considered as the matured present good. Thus, if the marginal value product of a certain labor or land factor is 10 ounces per unit period, and the rate of interest is 10%, its earning price will be approximately 9 ounces per year if the final product is one year away. A higher rate of interest would lead to a lower price, and a lower rate to a higher price, although the maximum price is one slightly below the full MVP (marginal value product), since the interest rate can never disappear.

It seems likely that the demand schedule for present goods by the original productive factors will be highly inelastic in response to changes in the interest rate. With the large base amount, the discounting by various rates of interest will very likely make little difference to the factor-owner.[24] Large changes in the interest rate, which would make an enormous difference to capitalists and determine huge differences in interest income and the profitableness of various lengthy productive processes, would have a negligible effect on the earnings of the owners of the original productive factors.

On the time market, we are considering all factors in the aggregate; the interest rate of the time market permeates all particular aspects of the present-future market, including all purchases of land and labor services. Therefore, when we are considering the supply of a certain factor on the market, we are considering it *in general,* and not its supply schedule for a specific use. A group of homogeneous pieces of land may have three alternative uses: say, for growing wheat, raising sheep, or serving as the site of a steel factory. Its supply schedule for each of the three uses will be elastic (relatively flat curve) and will be determined by the amount it can obtain in the next best use—i.e., the use in which its discounted MVP is next highest. In the present analysis, we are not considering the factor's supply curve for a *particular* industry or use; we are considering its supply curve for all users *in the aggregate,* i.e., its supply curve on the time market in exchange for present goods. We are therefore considering the behavior of all owners of a homogeneous factor of land (or of one owner if the land factor is unique, as it often is). Land is very likely to have *no* reservation price, i.e., it will have little subjective use-value to the owner. A few landlords may place a valuation on the possibility of contemplating the virgin beauty of the unused land; in practice, however, the importance of such reservation-demand for land is likely to be negligible. It will, of course, be greater where the owner can use the land to grow food for himself.

Labor services are also likely to be inelastic with respect to the interest discount, but probably less so than land, since labor has a reservation demand, a subjective use-value, even in the aggregate labor market. This special reservation demand stems from the value of leisure as a consumers' good. Higher prices for labor services will induce more units of labor to enter the market, while lower prices will increase the relative advantages of leisure. Here again, however, the difference that will be made by relatively large changes in the interest rate will not be at all great, so that the aggregate supply-of-labor curve (or rather curves, one for each homogeneous labor factor) will tend to be inelastic with regard to the interest rate.

The two categories of independent demanders of present goods for future goods, then, are the *landowners* and the *laborers*. The suppliers of present goods on the time market are clearly the *capitalists,* who save from their possible consumption and invest their savings in future goods. But the question may be raised: Do not the capitalists also *demand* present goods as well as supply them?

It is true that capitalists, after investing in a stage of production, demand present goods in exchange for their product. This particular demand is inelastic in relation to interest changes since these capital goods also can have no subjective use-value for their producers. This demand, however, is strictly derivative and dependent. In the first place, the product for which the owner demands present goods is, of course, a future good, but it is also one stage *less distantly future* than the goods that the owner purchased in order to produce it. In other words, Capitalists_3 will sell their future goods to Capitalists_2, but they had bought future goods from Capitalists_4, as well as from landowners and laborers. Every capitalist at every stage, then, *demands* goods that are *more* distantly future than the product that he supplies, and he supplies present goods for the duration of the production stage until this product is formed. He is therefore a *net supplier of present goods,* and a *net demander of future goods.* Hence, his activities are guided by his role as a supplier. The higher the rate of interest that he will be able to earn, i.e., the higher the price spread, the more he will tend to invest in production. If he were not essentially a supplier of present goods, this would not be true.

The relation between his role as a supplier and as a demander of present goods may be illustrated by the diagram in Fig. 46.

This diagram is another way of conveniently representing the structure of production. On the horizontal axis are represented the various stages of production, the dots furthest to the left being the highest stages, and those further to the right being the lower stages. From left to right, then, the stages of production are

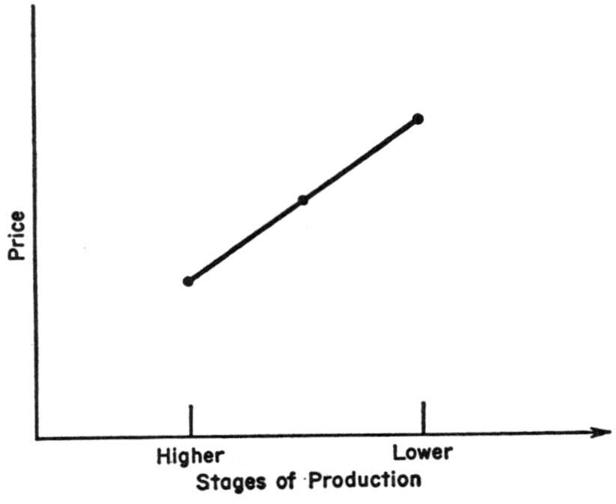

FIG. 46. RELATION OF CUMULATIVE FACTOR PRICES TO STAGES OF PRODUCTION

lower and eventually reach the consumers'-good stage. The vertical axis represents prices, and it could interchangeably be either the production structure of one particular good or of all the goods in general. The prices that are represented at each stage are the *cumulative* prices of the factors at each stage, *excluding* the interest return of the capitalists. At each stage rightward, then, the level of the dots is higher, the difference representing the interest return to the capitalists at that stage. In this diagram, the interest return to capitalists at two adjacent stages is indicated, and the constant slope indicates that this return is equal.

Let us now reproduce the above diagram in Fig. 47.[25] The original production structure diagram is marked at points *A, B,* and *C*. Capitalists *X* purchase factors at *A* price and sell their product at point *B;* while capitalists *Y* buy at *B* and sell their product at *C*. Let us first consider the highest stage here portrayed—that of capitalists *X*. They purchase the factors at point *A*. Here they *supply* present goods to owners of factors. Capitalists *X*, of course, would prefer that the prices of the factors be lower; thus, they would prefer paying *A′* rather than *A*. Their interest spread cannot be determined until their selling prices are determined. Their activities as suppliers of present goods in exchange for

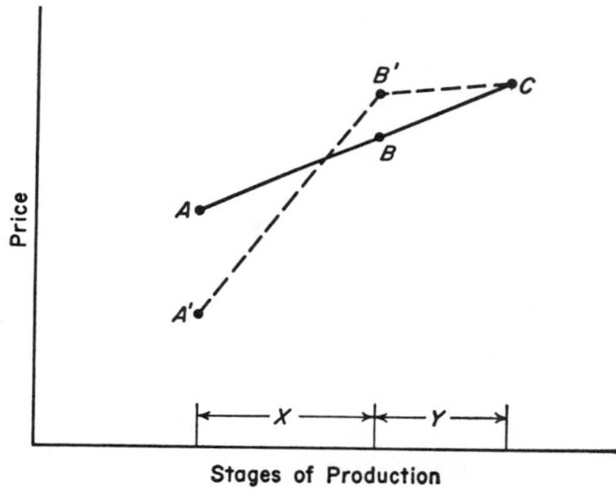

FIG. 47. EFFECT OF THE TENDENCY TOWARD A UNIFORM RATE OF INTEREST

interest return, therefore, are not really completed with their purchase of factors. Obviously, they could not be. The capitalists must transform the factors into products and sell their products for money before they obtain their interest return from their supply of present goods. The suppliers of future goods (landowners and laborers) *complete* their transactions immediately, as soon as they obtain present money. But the capitalists' transactions are incomplete until they obtain present money once again. Their demand for present goods is therefore strictly dependent on their previous supply.

Capitalists *X*, as we have stated, sell their products at *B* to the next lower rank of capitalists. Naturally, they would prefer a higher selling price for their product, and the point *B′* would be preferred to *B*. If we looked only at this sale, we might be tempted to state that, as demanders of present goods, capitalists *X* prefer a higher price, and therefore a lower discount for their product, i.e., a lower interest rate. This, however, would be a superficial point of view, for we must look at both of their exchanges, which are necessarily considered together if we consider their *complete* transaction. They prefer a lower buying point and a higher selling point, i.e., a more steeply sloped line, or a *higher rate of discount.* In other words, the capitalists prefer a higher rate of interest and therefore always act as *suppliers* of present goods. Of course, the result of this particular change (to a price spread of *A′B′*) is that the next lower rung of capitalists, capitalists *Y,* suffer a narrowing of their price spread, along the line *B′C.* It is, of course, perfectly agreeable to capitalists *X* if capitalists *Y* suffer a lowering of their interest return, so long as the return of the former improves. Each capitalist is interested in improving his own interest return and not necessarily the rate of interest in general. However, as we have seen, *there cannot for long be any differences in interest return between one stage and another or between one production process and another.* If the *A′B′C* situation were established, capitalists would pour out of the *Y* stage and into the *X* stage, the increased demand would bid up the price above *A′,* the sales at *B′* would be increased and the demand lowered, and the supply at *C* lowered, until finally the interest returns were equalized. There is always a tendency for such equalization, and this equalization is actually completed in the ERE.

5. *Time Preference, Capitalists, and Individual Money Stock*

When we state that the time-preference schedules of all individuals in the society determine the interest rate and the proportion of savings to consumption, we mean *all* individuals, and not some sort of separate class called "capitalists." There is a temptation, since the production structure is analyzed in terms of different classes—landowners, laborers, and capitalists—to conclude that there are three definite stratified groups of *people* in society corresponding to these classifications. Actually, in economic analysis of the market we are concerned with *functions* rather than *whole persons per se.* In reality, there is no special class of capitalists set off from laborers and landowners. This is not simply due to the trite fact that even capitalists must also be consumers. It is also due to the more important fact that *all* consumers *can be capitalists* if they wish. They will be capitalists if their time-preference schedules so dictate. Time-market diagrams such as shown above apply to every man, and not simply to some select group known as capitalists. The interchange of the various aggregate supply and demand diagrams throughout the entire time market sets the equilibrium rate of interest on the market. At this rate of interest, some individuals will be suppliers of present goods, some will be demanders, the curves representing the supply and demand schedules of others will be coinciding with their line of origin and they will not be in the time market at all. Those whose time-preference schedules at this rate permit them to be suppliers will be the *savers*—i.e., they will be the capitalists.

The role of the capitalists will be clarified if we ask the question: Where did they get the money that they save and invest? First, they may have obtained it in what we might call "current" production; i.e., they could have received the money in their current capacities as laborers, landowners, and capitalists. After they receive the money, they must then decide how to allocate it among various lines of goods, and between consumption and investment. Secondly, the source of funds could have been money earned in *past* rounds of production and previously "hoarded," now being "dishoarded." We are, however, leaving out hoarding and dishoarding at this stage in the analysis. The only other source, the third source, is *new* money, and this too will be discussed below.

For the moment, therefore, we shall consider that the money from which savings derive could only have come from recent earnings from production. Some earnings were obtained as capitalists, and some as owners of original factors.

The reader might here have detected an apparent paradox: How can a laborer or a landowner be a demander of present goods, and then turn around and be a supplier of present goods for investment? This seems to be particularly puzzling since we have stated above that one cannot be a demander and a supplier of present goods at the same time, that one's time-preference schedule may put one in one camp or the other, but not in both. The solution to this puzzle is that the two acts are *not performed at the same time,* even though both are performed to the same extent in their turn in the endless round of the evenly rotating economy.

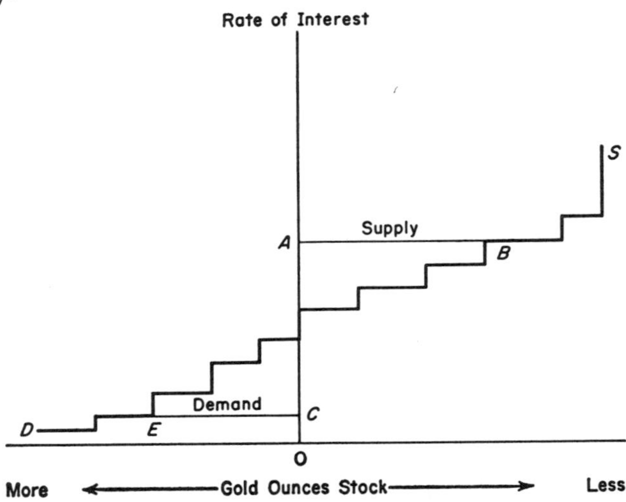

FIG. 48. RELATION OF INDIVIDUAL TIME-PREFERENCE SCHEDULE TO MONEY STOCK

Let us reproduce the typical individual time-preference schedule (see Fig. 48). At a market interest rate of *OA,* the individual would supply savings of *AB;* at a market interest rate of *OC,* he would demand money of amount *CE.* Here, however, we are analyzing more carefully the horizontal axis. The point *O* is the point of origin. It is the point at which the person deliberates on his course of action, i.e., the position he is in when he is consulting, so to speak, his time-preference scales. Specifically, this is his position with respect to the *size of his money stock* at the time of origin. At point *O,* he has a certain money stock, and he is considering how much of his stock he is willing to give up in exchange for future goods or how much new stock he would like to acquire while giving up future goods. Suppose that he is a saver.

As the curve moves to the right, he is giving up more and more of his present money stock in exchange for future goods; therefore, his minimum interest return becomes greater. The further the curve goes to the right, then, the lower will his final money stock be. On the other hand, consider the same individual when he is a demander of present goods. As the curve proceeds to the left, he increases his stock of present goods and gives up future goods. Considering both sides of the point of origin, then, we see that the further right the curve goes, the less stock he has; the further left, the greater his stock.

Given his time-preference schedule, therefore, he is bound to be in a greater supply position the more money he has, and in more of a demand position the less money he has. Before the laborer or landowner sells his services, he has a certain money stock—a cash balance that he apparently does not reduce below a certain minimum. After he sells his services, he acquires his money income from production, thereby adding to his money stock. He then allocates this income between consumption and savings-investment, and we are assuming no hoarding or dishoarding. At this point, then, when he is allocating, he is in a far different position and at a different point in time. For now he has had a considerable addition to his money stock.

Let us consider (Fig. 49) the individual's time-market graph with two different points of origin, i.e., two different sizes of money stock, one before he earns his income (I), and one immediately after (II).

Here we see how a laborer or a landowner can be a demander at one time, in one position of his money stock, and a supplier at another time. With very little money stock, as represented in the first diagram, he is a demander. Then, he acquires money in the productive arena, greatly increases his money stock, and therefore the point of origin of his decision to allocate his money income shifts to the left, so that he might well become a supplier out of his income. Of course, in many cases, he is still a demander or is not on the time market at all. To coin a phrase to distinguish these two positions, we may call his original condition a "pre-income position" (before he has sold his services for money), and the latter a "post-income position"—his situation when he is allocating his money income. Both points of origin are relevant to his real actions.

We have seen above that a landowner's pre-income demand

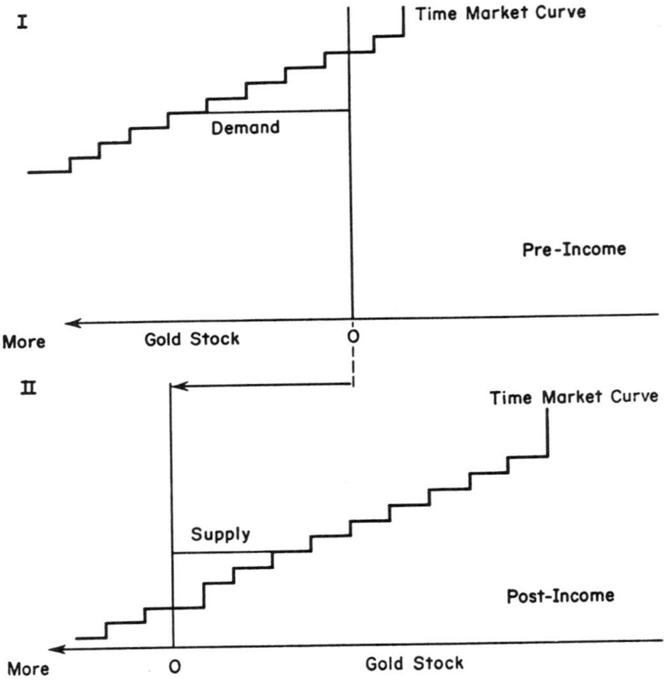

FIG. 49. EFFECT OF CHANGE IN INDIVIDUAL'S MONEY STOCK ON HIS ALLOCATION OF MONEY TO SAVINGS AND CONSUMPTION

for money is likely to be practically inelastic, or vertical, while a laborer's will probably be more elastic. Some individuals in a post-income position will be suppliers at the market rate of interest; some will be demanders; some will be neutral. The four diagrams in Fig. 50 depict various pre-income and post-income time-preference situations, establishing individual time-market curves, with the same market rate of interest applied to each one.

The line *AB,* across the page, is our assumed market rate of interest, equilibrated as a result of the individual time-preference scales. At this rate of interest, the landowner and the laborer (I and II) are shown with demands for present money (pre-income), and diagrams III and IV depict a demander at this rate and a neutral at this rate, one who is moved neither to supply nor to demand money in the time market. Both the latter are in post-income situations.

We conclude that any man can be a capitalist if only he wants to be. He can derive his funds solely from the fruits of previous

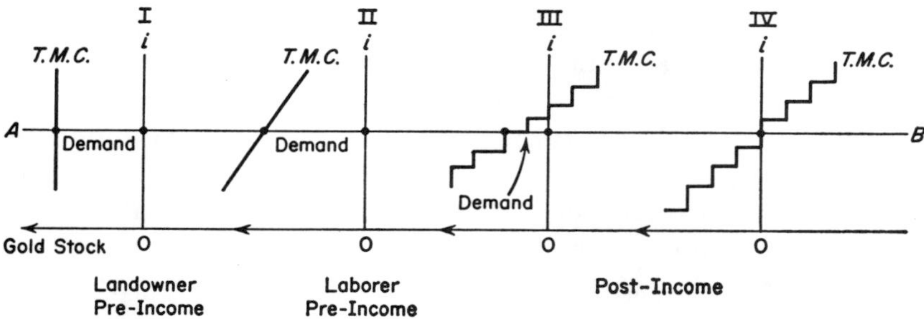

FIG. 50. DIFFERENT INDIVIDUALS' TIME-MARKET CURVES AT A GIVEN RATE OF INTEREST

capitalist investment or from past "hoarded" cash balances or solely from his income as a laborer or a landowner. He can, of course, derive his funds from several of these sources. *The only thing that stops a man from being a capitalist is his own high time-preference scale,* in other words, his stronger desire to consume goods in the present. Marxists and others who postulate a rigid stratification—a virtual *caste* structure in society—are in grave error. The same person can be at once a laborer, a landowner, and a capitalist, in the same period of time.[26]

It might be argued that only the "rich" can afford to be capitalists, i.e., those who have a greater amount of money stock. This argument has superficial plausibility, since from our diagrams above we saw that, for *any given individual* and a given time-preference schedule, a greater money stock will lead to a greater supply of savings, and a lesser money stock to a lesser supply of savings. *Ceteris paribus,* the same applies to changes in money income, which constitute additions to stock. We *cannot,* however, assume that a man with (post-income) assets of 10,000 ounces of gold will necessarily save more than a man with 100 ounces of gold. We *cannot compare time preferences interpersonally,* any more than we can formulate interpersonal laws for any other type of utilities. What we can assert as an economic law for one person we cannot assert in comparing two or more persons. Each person has his own time-preference schedule, apart from the specific size of his monetary stock. Each person's time-preference schedule, as with any other element in his value scale, is entirely of his own making. All of us have heard of the proverbially thrifty French peasant, compared with the rich playboy who is always running into debt. The common-sense observation that it is generally the rich who save more may be an interesting historical judgment, but it furnishes us with no scientific economic law whatever, and the purpose of economic science is to furnish us with such laws. As long as a person has any money at all, and he must have some money if he participates in the market society to any extent, he can be a capitalist.

6. *The Post-Income Demanders*

Up to this point we have analyzed the time-market demand for present goods by landowners and laborers, as well as the derived demand by capitalists. This aggregate demand we may call the *producers' demand* for present goods on the time market. This is the demand by those who are selling their services or the services of their owned property in the advancing of production. This demand is all *pre-income demand* as we have defined it; i.e., it takes place prior to the acquisition of money income from the productive system. It is all in the form of selling factor services (future goods) in exchange for present money. But there is another component of net demand for present goods on the time market. This is the *post-income* component; it is a demand that takes place even after productive income is acquired. Clearly, this demand cannot be a productive demand, since owners of future goods used in production exercise that demand *prior* to their sale. It is, on the contrary, a *consumers' demand.*

This subdivision of the time market operates as follows: Jones sells 100 ounces of future money (say, one year from now) to Smith in exchange for 95 ounces of present money. This future money is not in the form of an expectation created by a factor of production; instead, it is an I. O. U. by Jones promising to pay 100 ounces of money at a point one year in the future. He exchanges this *claim* on future money for present money—95 ounces. The discount on future money as compared with present money is precisely equivalent to that in the other parts of the time market that we have studied heretofore, except that the present case is more obvious. The rate of interest finally set on the market is determined by the aggregate net supply and net demand schedules throughout the entire time market, and these, as we have seen, are determined by the time preferences of all the individuals on the market. Thus, in the case of Fig. 50 above, in diagram III we have a case of a net (post-income) demander at the market rate of interest. The form that his demand takes is the sale of an I. O. U. of future money—usually termed the "borrowing" of present money. On the other hand, the person whose time-market curve is shown in diagram IV has such a time-preference configuration that he is neither a net supplier nor a net demander at the going rate of interest—he is not on the time market at all—in his post-income position.

The net borrowers, then, are people who have relatively higher time-preference rates than others at the going rate of interest, in fact so high that they will borrow certain amounts at this rate. It must be emphasized here that we are dealing *only* with consumption borrowing—borrowing to add to the present use of Jones' money stock for consumption. Jones' sale of future money differs from the sales of the landowners and laborers in another respect; their transactions are completed, while Jones has not yet completed his. His I. O. U. establishes a claim to future money on the part of the buyer (or "lender") Smith, and Smith, to complete his transaction and earn his interest payment, must present his note at the later date and claim the money due.

In sum, the *time market's components are as follows:*

I. *Supply of Present Goods for Future Goods:*
   Savings (of all)

II. *Demand for Present Goods by Suppliers of Future Goods:*
   a. *Producers' Demand*
      Landowners   Laborers
   b. *Consumers' Demand*
      Borrowing Consumers

These demands are aggregated without regard to whether they are post- or pre-income; they both occur within a relatively brief time period, and they recur continually in the ERE.

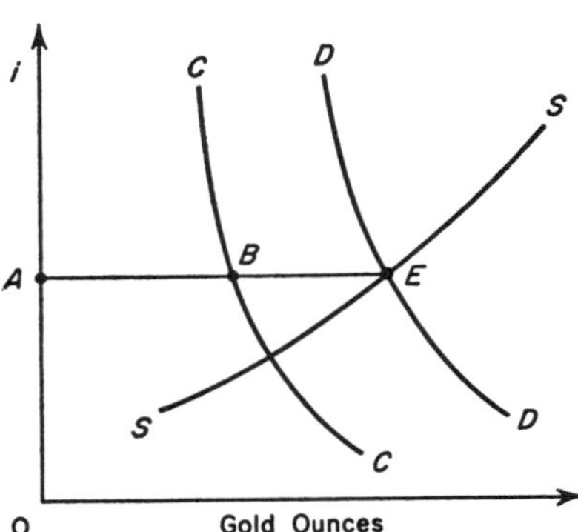

FIG. 51. DETERMINATION OF THE EQUILIBRIUM RATE OF INTEREST ON THE TIME MARKET

Although the consumption and the productive demands are aggregated to set the market rate of interest, a point of great importance for the productive system is revealed if we separate these demands analytically. The diagram in Fig. 51 depicts the establishment of the rate of interest on the time market.

The vertical axis is the rate of interest; the horizontal axis is gold ounces. The *SS* curve is the supply-of-savings schedule, determined by individual time preferences. The *CC* curve is the schedule of consumers' loan demands for present goods, consisting of the aggregate net demand (post-income) at the various hypothetical rates of interest. The *DD* curve is the total demand for present goods by suppliers of future goods, and it consists of the *CC* curve *plus* a curve that is not shown—the demand for present goods by the owners of original productive factors, i.e., land and labor. Both the *CC* and the *DD* curves are determined by individual time preferences. The equilibrium rate of interest will be set by the market at the point of intersection of the *SS* and *DD* curves—point *E*.

The point of intersection at *E* determines two important resultants: the rate of interest, which is established at *OA*, and the total supply of savings *AE*. A vital matter for the productive system, however, is the position of the *CC* curve: the larger *CC* is at any given rate of interest, the larger the amount of total savings that will be competed for and drawn away from production into consumers' loans. In our diagram, the total savings going into investment in production is *BE*.

The relative strength of productive and consumption demand for present goods in the society depends on the configurations of the time-preference schedules of the various individuals on the market. We have seen that the productive demand for present goods tends to be inelastic with respect to interest rates; on the other hand, the consumers' loan curve will probably display greater elasticity. It follows that, on the demand side, changes in time preferences will display themselves mostly in the consumption demand schedule. On the supply side, of course, a rise in time preferences will lead to a shift of the *SS* curve to the left, with less being saved and invested at each rate of interest. The effects of time-preference changes on the rate of interest and the structure of production will be discussed further below.

It is clear that the gross savings that maintain the production structure are the "productive" savings, i.e., those that go into productive investment, and that these exclude the "consumption" savings that go into consumer lending. From the point of view of the production system, we may regard borrowing by a consumer as dissaving, for this is the amount by which a *person's consumption expenditures exceed his income,* as contrasted to savings, the amount by which a person's income exceeds his consumption. In that case, the savings loaned are canceled out, so to speak, by the dissavings of the consumption borrowers.

The consumers' and producers' subdivisions of the time market are a good illustration of how the rate of interest is equalized over the market. The connection between the returns on investment and money loans to consumers is not an obvious one. But it is clear from our discussion that both are parts of one time market. It should also be clear that there can be no long-run deviation of the rate of interest on the consumption loan market from the rate of interest return on productive investment. Both are aspects of one time market. If the rate of interest on consumers' loans, for example, were higher than the rate of interest return from investment, savings would shift from buying future goods in the form of factors to the more remunerative purchase of I. O. U.'s. This shift would cause the price of future factors to fall, i.e., the interest rate in investment to rise; and the rate of interest on consumers' loans to fall, as a result of the competition of more savings in the consumer loan arena. The everyday arbitrage of the market, then, will tend to equalize the rate of interest in both parts of the market. Thus, the rate of interest will tend to be equalized for all areas of the economy, as it were in three dimensions—"horizontally" in every process of production, "vertically" at every stage of production, and "in depth," in the consumer loan market as well as in the production structure.

7. *The Myth of the Importance of the Producers' Loan Market*

We have completed our analysis of the determination of the pure rate of interest as it would be in the evenly rotating economy—a rate that the market tends to approach in the real world. We have shown how it is determined by time preferences on the time market and have seen the various components of that time market. This statement will undoubtedly be extremely puzzling to many readers. Where is the producers' loan market? This market is always the one that is stressed by writers, often to the exclusion of anything else. In fact, "rate of interest" generally refers to money loans, including loans to consumers and producers, but particularly stressing the latter, which is usually quantitatively greater and more significant for production. The rate of interest of money loans to the would-be producer is supposed to be the significant rate of interest. In fact, the fashionable neoclassical doctrine holds that the producers' loan market *determines* the rate of interest and that this determination takes place as in Fig. 52, where *SS* is the supply of savings *entering the loan market,* and *DD* is the *demand for these loans* by producers or entrepreneurs. Their intersection allegedly determines the rate of interest.

It will be noticed that this sort of approach completely overlooks the *gross savings of the producers* and, even more, the *demand for present goods by owners of the original factors.* Instead of being fundamentally suppliers of present goods, capitalists are portrayed as demanders of present goods. What determines the *SS* and *DD* schedules, according to this neoclassical doctrine? The *SS* curve is admittedly determined by time preferences; the *DD* curve, on the other hand, is supposed to be determined by the "marginal efficiency of capital," i.e., by the expected rate of return on the investment.

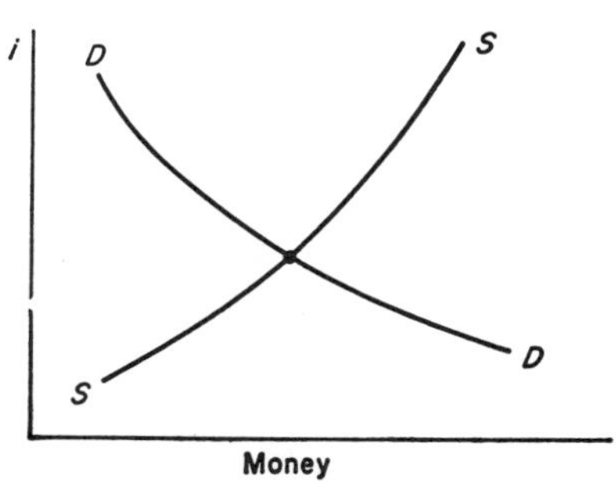

FIG. 52. NEOCLASSICAL CONCEPTION OF THE DETERMINATION OF THE RATE OF INTEREST

This approach misses the point very badly because it looks at the economy with the superficial eye of an average businessman. The businessman borrows on a producers' loan market from individual savers, and he judges how much to borrow on the basis of his expected rate of "profit," or rate of return. The writers assume that he has available a shelf of investment projects some of which would pay him, say 8%, some 7%, some 3%, etc., and that at each hypothetical interest rate he will borrow in order to invest in those projects where his return will be as high or higher. In other words, if the interest rate is 8%, he will borrow to invest in those projects that will yield him over 8%; if the rate is 4%, he will invest in many more projects—those that will yield him over 4%, etc. In that way, the demand curve for savings, for each individual, and still more for the aggregate on the market, will slope rightward as demand curves usually do, as the rate of interest falls. The intersection sets the market rate of interest.

Superficially, this approach might seem plausible. It usually happens that a businessman foresees such varying rates of return on different investments, that he borrows on the market from different individual savers, *and* that he is popularly considered the "capitalist" or entrepreneur, while the lenders are simply savers. This lends plausibility to terming the *DD* curve in Fig. 52, the demand by capitalists or entrepreneurs for money (present goods). And it seems to avoid mysterious complexities and to focus neatly and simply on the rate of interest for producers' loans—the loans from savers to businessmen—in which they and most writers on economics are interested. It is this rate of interest that is generally discussed at great length by economists.

Although popular, this approach is wrong through and through, as will be revealed in the course of this analysis. In the first place, let us consider the construction of this *DD* curve a little more closely. What is the basis for the alleged shelf of available projects, each with different rates of return? *Why does a particular investment yield any net monetary return at all?* The usual answer is that each dose of new investment has a "marginal value productivity," such as 10%, 9%, 4%, etc., that naturally the most productive investments will be made first and that therefore, as savings increase, further investments will be less and less value-productive. This provides the basis for the alleged "businessman's demand curve," which slopes to the right as savings increase and the interest rate falls. The cardinal error here is an old one in economics—the attribution of *value*-productivity to monetary investment. There is no question that investment increases the *physical* productivity of the productive process, as well as the productivity per man hour. Indeed, that is precisely why investment and the consequent lengthening of the periods of production take place at all. But what has this to do with value-productivity or with the monetary return on investment, especially in the long run of the ERE?

Suppose, for example, that a certain quantity of physical factors (and we shall set aside the question of how this quantity can be measured) produces 10 units of a certain product per period at a selling price of 2 gold ounces per unit. Now let us postulate that investment is made in higher-order capital goods to such an extent that productivity multiplies fivefold and that the same original factors can now produce 50 units per period. The selling price of the larger supply of product will be less; let us assume that it will be cut in half to 1 ounce per unit. The gross revenue per period is increased from 20 to 50 ounces. Does this mean that value-productivity has increased two and a half times, just as physical productivity increased fivefold? Certainly not! For, as we have seen, producers benefit, not from the gross revenue received, but from the *price spread* between their selling price and their aggregate factor prices. The increase in physical productivity will certainly increase revenue in the short run, but this refers to the profit-and-loss situations of the real world of uncertainty. The *long-run* tendency will be nothing of the sort. The long-run tendency, eventuating in the ERE, is toward an equalization of price spreads. How can there be any permanent benefit when the cumulative factor prices paid by this producer increase from, say, 18 ounces to 47 ounces? This is precisely what will happen on the market, as competitors vie to invest in these profitable situations. The price spread, i.e., the *interest rate,* will again be 5%.

Thus the productivity of production processes has no basic relation to the rate of return on business investment. This rate of return depends on the price spreads between stages, and these price spreads will tend to be equal. The size of the price spread, i.e., the size of the interest rate, is determined, as we have seen at length, by the time-preference schedules of all the individuals in the economy.

In sum, the neoclassical doctrine maintains that the interest rate, by which is largely meant the producers' loan market, is codetermined by time preference (which determines the supply of individual savings) and by marginal (value) productivity of investment (which determines the demand for savings by business men), which in turn is determined by the rates of return that can be achieved in investments. But we have seen that *these very rates of return are, in fact, the rate of interest* and that their size is determined by time preferences. The neoclassicists are partly right in only one respect—that the rate of interest in the producers' loan market is dependent on the rates of return on investment. They hardly realize the extent of this dependence, however. It is clear that these *rates of return,* which will be equalized into one uniform rate, *constitute the significant rate of interest in the production structure.*[27,28]

Discarding the neoclassical analysis, we may ask: What, then, is the role of the productive loan market and of the rate of interest set therein? This role is one of complete and utter dependence on the rate of interest as determined above, and manifesting itself, as we have seen, in the rate of investment return, on the one hand, and in the consumers' loan market, on the other. These latter two markets are the independent and important subdivisions of the general time market, with the former being the important market for the production system.

In this picture, the producers' loan market has a purely subsidiary and dependent role. In fact, from the point of view of fundamental analysis, there need not be any producers' loan market at all. To examine this conclusion, let us consider a state of business affairs without a producers' loan market. What is needed to bring this about? Individuals save, consuming less than their income. They then *directly invest* these savings in the production structure, the incentive for investment being the rate of interest return—the price spread—on the investment. This rate is determined, along with the rate on the consumers' loan market, by the various components of the time market that we have portrayed above. There is, in that case, no producers' loan market. There are no loans from a saving group to another group of investors. And it is clear that the rate of interest in the production structure still exists; it is determined by factors that have nothing to do with the usual discussion by economists of the producers' loan market.

8. *The Joint-Stock Company*

It is clear that, far from being the centrally important element, the producers' loan market is of minor importance, and it is easy to postulate a going productive system with no such market at all. But, some may reply, this may be all very well for a primitive economy where every firm is owned by just one capitalist-investor, who invests his own savings. What happens in our modern complex economy, where savings and investment are *separated,* are processes engaged in by different groups of people—the former by scattered individuals, the latter by relatively few directors of firms? Let us, therefore, now consider a second possible situation. Up to this point we have not treated in detail the question whether each factor or business was owned by one person or jointly by many persons. Now let us consider an economy in which factors are *jointly owned* by many people, as largely happens in the modern world, and we shall see what difference this makes in our analyses.

Before studying the effect of such jointly owned companies on the producers' loan market, we must digress to analyze the nature of these companies themselves. In a *jointly* owned firm, instead of each individual capitalist's making his own investments and making all his own investment and production decisions, various individuals pool their money capital in one organization, or *business firm,* and jointly make decisions on the investment of their joint savings. The firm then purchases the land, labor, and capital-goods factors, and later sells the product to consumers or to lower-order capitalists. Thus, the firm is the joint owner of the factor services and particularly of the *product* as it is produced and becomes ready for sale. The firm is the product-owner until the product is sold for money. The individuals who contributed their saved capital to the firm are the joint owners, successively, of: (*a*) the initial money capital—the pooled savings, (*b*) the services of the factors, (*c*) the product of the factors, and (*d*) the money obtained from the sale of the product. In the evenly rotating economy, their ownership of assets follows this same step-by-step pattern, period after period, without change. In a jointly owned firm, in actual practice, the variety of productive assets owned by the firm is large. Any one firm is usually engaged in various production processes, each one involving a different period of time, and is likely to be engaged in different stages of each process at any one particular time. A firm is likely to be producing so that its output is continuous and so that it makes sales of new units of the product every day.

It is obvious, then, that if the firm keeps continually in business, its operations at any one time will be a mixture of investment and sale of product. Its assets at any one time will be a mixture of cash about to be invested, factors just bought, hardly begun products, and money just received from the sale of products. The result is that, to the superficial, it looks as if the firm is an automatically continuing thing and as if the production is somehow timeless and instantaneous, ensuing immediately after the factor input.

Actually, of course, this idea is completely unfounded. There is no automatic continuity of investment and production. Production is continued because the owners are continually making decisions to proceed; if they did not think it profitable to do so, they could and do at any point alter, curtail, or totally cease operations and investments. And production takes *time* from initial investment to final product.

In the light of our discussion, we may classify the types of assets owned by any firm (whether jointly or individually owned) as follows:

A. *Money*

B. *Productive Assets*

Melange of factors, such as land and capital goods, embodying future services (this will be analyzed below); various stages of product; the completed product

On this entire package of assets, a monetary evaluation is placed by the market. How this is done will be examined in detail later.

At this point, let us revert to the simple case of a one-shot investment, an investment in factors on one date, and the sale of the resulting product a year later. This is the assumption involved in our original analysis of the production structure; and it will be seen below that the same analysis can be applied to the more complex case of a melange of assets at different stages of production and even to cases where one firm engages in several different production processes and produces different goods. Let us consider a group of individuals pooling their saved money capital to the extent of 100 ounces, purchasing factors with the 100 gold ounces, obtaining a product, and selling the product for 105 ounces a year later. The rate of interest in this society is 5% per annum, and the rate of interest return on this investment conforms with this condition. The question now arises: *On what principle do the individual owners mutually apportion their shares of the assets?* It will almost always be the case that every individual is vitally interested in knowing his share of the joint assets, and consequently firms are established in such a way that the principle of apportionment is known to all the owners.

At first one might be inclined to say that this is simply a case of bargaining, as in the case of the product jointly owned by all the owners of the factors. But the former situation does not apply here. For in the case discussed above, there was no principle whereby any man's share of ownership could be distinguished from that of anyone else. A whole group of people worked, contributed their land, etc., to the production process, and there was no way except simple bargaining by which the income from the sale of the product could be apportioned among them. Here, each individual is contributing a certain amount of money capital to begin with. Therefore, the proportions are naturally established from the outset. Let us say that the 100 ounces of capital are contributed by five men as follows:

A.	40 oz.
B.	20 oz.
C.	20 oz.
D.	15 oz.
E.	5 oz.

In other words, A contributes 40% of the capital, B 20%, C 20%, D 15%, E 5%. Each individual owner of the firm then owns the same percentage of all the assets that he contributed in the beginning. This holds true at each step of the way, and finally for the money obtained from the sale of the product. The 105 ounces earned from the sale will be either reinvested in or "dis-invested" from the process. At any rate, the ownership of these 105 ounces will be distributed in the same percentages as the capital invested.

This natural structure of a firm is essentially the structure of a *joint-stock company*. In the joint-stock company, each investor-owner receives a *share*—a certification of ownership in proportion to the amount he has invested in the total capital of the company. Thus, if A, B, . . . E above form a company, they may issue 100 shares, each share representing a value, or an asset, of 1 ounce. A will receive 40 shares; B, 20 shares; C, 20 shares, etc. After the sale of the product, each share will be worth five percent more than its original, or *par,* value.

Suppose that after the sale, or indeed at any time before the sale, another person, F, wishes to invest in this company. Suppose that he wishes to invest 30 ounces of gold. In that case, the investment of money savings in the company increases from 100 (if before the sale) or 105 (if after the sale) by 30 ounces. Thirty new shares will be issued and turned over to F, and the capital value of the firm increases by 30 ounces. In the vast majority of cases where reinvestment of monetary revenue is going on continuously, at any point in time the capital value of a firm's assets will be the appraised value of all the productive assets, including cash, land, capital goods, and finished products. The capital value of the firm is increased at any given time by new investment and is maintained by the reinvestments of the owners after the finished product is sold.

The shares of capital are generally known as *stock;* the total *par* value of capital stock is the amount originally paid in on the formation of the company. From that point on, the total capital value of assets changes as income is earned, or, in the world of uncertainty, as losses are suffered, and as capital is reinvested or withdrawn from the company. The total value of capital stock changes accordingly, and the value of each share will differ from the original value accordingly.

How will the group of owners decide on the affairs of the company? Those decisions that must be made jointly will be made by some sort of voting arrangement. The natural voting arrangement, which one would expect to be used, is to have one vote per share of voting stock, with a majority of the votes deciding. This is precisely the arrangement used in the joint-stock company and its modern form, the *corporation.*

Of course, some joint-stock company arrangements differ from this, according to the desires of the owners. *Partnerships* can be worked out between two or more people on various principles. Usually, however, if one partner receives more than his proportionate share of invested capital, it is because he is contributing more of his labor or his land to the enterprise and gets paid accordingly. As we shall see, the rate paid to the labor of the "working partner" will be approximately equal to what he could earn in labor elsewhere, and the same is true for payment to the land or any other originally owned factor contributed by a partner. Since partnerships are almost always limited to a few, the relationships are more or less informal and need not have the formal patterns of the joint-stock company. However, partnerships will tend to work quite similarly. They provide more room for idiosyncratic arrangements. Thus, one partner may receive more than his share of capital because he is loved and revered by the others; this is really in the nature of a gift to him from the rest of the partners. Joint-stock companies hew more closely to a formal principle.

The great advantage of the joint-stock company is that it provides a more ready channel for new investments of saved capital. We have seen how easy it is for new capital to be attracted through the issuance of new shares. It is also easier for any owner to withdraw his capital from the firm. This greater ease of withdrawal vastly increases the temptation to invest in the company. Later on we shall explore the pricing of stock shares in the real world of uncertainty. In this real world, there is room for great differences of opinion concerning the appraised value of a firm's assets, and therefore concerning the monetary appraised value of each share of the firm's stock. In the evenly rotating economy, however, all appraisals of monetary value will agree—the principles of such appraisal will be examined below—and therefore the appraised value of the shares of stock will be agreed upon by all and will remain constant.

While the share market of joint-stock companies provides a ready channel for accumulating savings, *the share market is strictly dependent on the price spreads.* The savings or dissavings of capitalists are determined by time preferences, and the latter establish the price spread in the economy. The value of capital invested in the enterprise, i.e., its productive assets, will be the sum of future earnings from the capital discounted by the rate of interest. If the price spreads are five per cent, the rate of interest return yielded on the share market (the ratio of earnings per share to the market price of the share) will tend to equal the rate of interest as determined elsewhere on the time market—in this case, five per cent.

We still have a situation in which capitalists supply their own saved capital, which is used to purchase factors in expectation of a net monetary return. The only complications that develop from joint-stock companies or corporations are that many capitalists contribute and own the firm's assets jointly and that the price of a certain quantum of ownership will be regulated by the market so that the rate of interest yield will be the same for each individual share of stock as it is for the enterprise as a whole. If the whole firm buys factors for a total price of 100 and sells the product a year later for 105, for a five per cent return, then, say, 1/5 of the shares of ownership of this firm will sell for an aggregate price of twenty, and earn an annual net return of one ounce. Thus, the rates of interest for the partial shares of capital will all tend to be equal to the rate of interest earned on the entire capital.[29]

Majority rule in the joint-stock companies, with respect to total shares owned, does not mean that the minority rights of owners are overridden. In the first place, the entire pooling of resources and the basis on which it is worked out are voluntary for all parties concerned. Secondly, all the stockholders, or owners, have one single interest in common—an increase in their monetary return and assets, although they may, of course, differ concerning the means to achieve this goal. Thirdly, the members of the minority may sell their stock and withdraw from the company if they so desire.

Actually, the partners may arrange their voting rights and ownership rights in any way they please, and there have been many variations of such arrangements. One such form of group ownership, in which each owner has one vote regardless of the number of shares he owns, has absurdly but effectively arrogated to itself the name of "co-operative." It is obvious that partnerships, joint-stock companies and corporations are *all* eminently *co-operative* institutions.[30]

Many people believe that economic analysis, while applicable to individually owned firms, does not hold true for the modern economy of joint-stock companies. Nothing could be further from the truth. The introduction of corporations has not fundamentally changed our analysis of the interest rate or the savings-investment process. What of the separation of "management" from ownership in a corporation? It is certainly true that, in a joint-stock firm, the owners hire managerial labor to supervise their workers, whereas individual owners generally perform their own managerial labor. A manager is just as much a hired laborer as any other worker. The president of a company, just like the ditchdigger, is hired by the owners; and, like the ditchdigger, he expends labor in the production process. The price of managerial labor is determined in the same way as that of other labor, as will be seen below. On the market, the income to an independent owner will *also* include the going wage for that type of managerial labor, which joint-stock owners, of course, will not receive. Thus, we see that, far from rendering economic analysis obsolete, the modern world of the corporation aids analysis by separating and simplifying functions in production—specifically, the managerial function.

In addition to the capital-supplying function, the corporate capitalists also assume the *entrepreneurial* function: the crucial directing element in guiding the processes of production toward meeting the desires of the consumers. In the real world of uncertainty, it takes sound judgment to decide how the market is operating, so that present investment will lead to future profits, and not future losses. We shall deal further with the nature of profit and loss, but suffice it to say here that the active entrepreneurial element in the real world is due to the presence of uncertainty. We have been discussing the determination of the pure rate of interest, the rate of interest as it always tends to be and as it will be in the certain world of the ERE. In the ERE, where all techniques, market demands and supplies, etc., for the future are known, the investment function becomes purely passive and waiting. There might still be a supervisory or managerial labor function, but this can be analyzed under prices of labor factors. But there will no longer be an entrepreneurial function because future events are known.

Some have maintained, finally, that joint-stock companies make for a separation of savings and investment. Stockholders save, and the managers do the investing. This is completely fallacious. The managers are *hired agents* of the stockholders and subject to the latters' dictation. Any individual stockholder not satisfied with the decisions of the majority of owners can dispose of his ownership share. As a result, it is effectively the *stockholders* who save and the *stockholders* who invest the funds.[31]

Some people maintain that since most stockholders are not "interested" in the affairs of their company, they do not effectively control the firm, but permit control to pass into the hands of the hired managers. Yet surely a stockholder's interest is a matter of his own preference and is under his own control. Preferring his lack of interest, he permits the managers to continue their present course; the fundamental control, however, is still his, and he has absolute control over his agents.[32] A typical view asserts: "The maximizing of dividend income for stockholders as a group is not an objective that is necessarily unique or paramount. Instead, management officials will seek to improve the long-run earnings and competitive position of the firm and their own prestige as managers."[33] But to "improve the long-run earnings" is identical with maximizing stockholders' income, and what else can develop the "prestige" of managers? Other theorists lapse into the sheer mysticism of considering the "corporation"—a conceptual name which we give to an institution owned by real individuals—as "really" existing and acting by itself.[34]

9. *Joint-Stock Companies and the Producers' Loan Market*

We are now ready to embark on an analysis of the effect of joint-stock companies on the producers' loan market.

Let us take the aforementioned firm with a total capital stock and capital value of 130 ounces and owned by six stockholders. The firm earns a net income of 5% per year for its owners, and this is the interest rate earned by all the firms in the economy.

We have already seen how the firm expanded its capital by 30 ounces through the sale of new capital stock to F. Let us see what happens when a productive loan is made. Suppose that the firm borrows 20 ounces from the producers' loan market for a five-year period. What has happened? The firm has exchanged a future good—a promise to pay money in the future—for present money. The present money has been supplied by a saver, G. It is clear that G has done the saving and is the capitalist in this transaction, while the joint stockholders A–F are here supplying future goods; and further, it is the stockholders who invest the new capital in the production system. On the surface, this seems to be a positive case of the separation of savings and investment.

However, let us look at the transaction further. G has supplied new capital, worth 20 ounces, to the firm, for a five-year period. The owners A–F take this new capital and invest it in future goods, i.e., factors of production. In other words, to the extent of 20 ounces, A–F are intermediary investors of the savings of the creditors. What will the rate of interest on this loan be? It is obvious that this rate of interest in the ERE, will be equal to 5%, i.e., it will be purely dependent on the rate of interest return that prevails in the price spreads of the production structure. The reason for this should be clear. We have already seen how the interest rate is determined in the production structure; we have assumed it to be 5% everywhere. Now, suppose that the firm offers to pay G 3% on the loan. Clearly, G will not lend the firm 20 ounces for a 3% return when he could get 5% as a stockholder either in the same firm or in any other firm. On the other hand, the firm is in no position to pay G any more than 5%, since its net return on the investment will be only 5%. If the maximum that the firm can pay in interest is 5%, and the minimum that the creditor can accept is 5%, it is obvious that the transaction will take place at 5%.

It is clear that, in essence, G, the creditor on the prospective loan market, is no different from F, the man who has invested in stock. Both have saved money instead of spending it on consumption, and both wish to sell their saved capital in exchange for future goods and to earn interest. The time-preference schedules of both F and G, as well as of everyone else, are aggregated on the time market to arrive at the rate of interest; both F and G are net savers at the market rate. The interest rate, then, is determined by the various time-preference schedules, and the final rate is set by the saving schedules, on the one hand, and by the demand-for-present-goods schedules, on the other. The demand schedules consist (and consist only) of the productive demand by laborers and landowners and the consumption demand by borrowing consumers. F and G are both net savers, interested in investing their capital for the highest return. There is no essential difference between F's method of investing his capital and G's method of investing his; *the difference between investing in stock and lending money to firms is mainly a technical one.* The separation between saving and investment that occurs in the latter case is completely unimportant. The interest return on investment, as set by total savings and total demands by owners of factors, *completely determines the rate of interest on the producers' loan market* as well as the rate of earning on stock. The producers' loan market is totally unimportant from the point of view of fundamental analysis; it is even useless to try to construct demand and supply schedules for this market, since its price is determined elsewhere.[35] Whether saved capital is channeled into investments *via* stocks or *via* loans is unimportant. The only difference is in the legal technicalities. Indeed, even the legal difference between the creditor and the owner is a negligible one. G's loan has increased the capital value of the assets in the firm from 130 to 150. The invested 150 pays 5%, or 7.5 ounces per year. Let us examine the situation and see who the actual owners of this capital are (see Fig. 53).

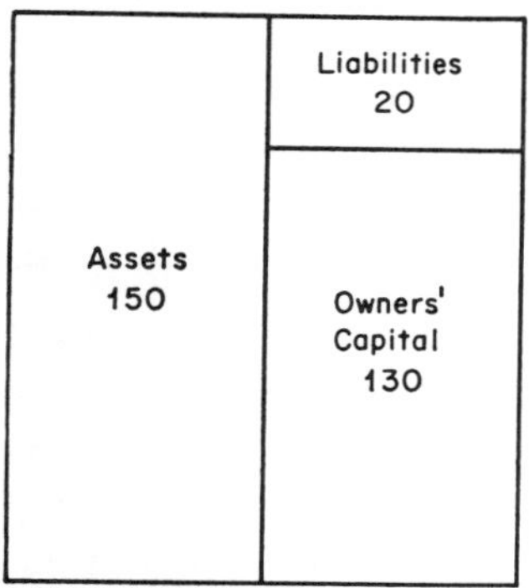

Fig. 53. Distribution of Ownership of Joint-Stock Company's Assets

In this diagram, the left-hand rectangle represents assets at any one point in time. We see in the right-hand rectangle that 130 ounces of these assets is represented by owners' capital, and 20 by liabilities—i.e., by I. O. U.'s due to creditors. But what does this "representation" mean? It means that if, for example, the firm were to liquidate and go out of business, 20 ounces of its assets would be used to pay off the creditors, and 130 would go to the legal owners. It means, further, that of the 7.5 ounces paid out as net earnings per year, 6.5 ounces go to the legal owners and 1 ounce to the creditors, each being 5% of their saving. In fact, each group gets 5% on its *investment,* for are not the creditors just as much investors as the stockholders? In fact, are not the creditors the *owners* of 20 ounces' worth of the firm's assets, and do they not own the prorata earnings of those 20 ounces? What functions of ownership do the creditors *not* have as compared to the stockholders? Even from the legal point of view, the creditors *get first claim* on the assets of a corporation, and they get paid before the stockholders. They are therefore definitely owners of these assets. It might be stated that since they are not shareholders, they do not vote on the decisions of the corporation, but there are many situations in which joint-stock companies issue *nonvoting* shares, the holders of which do not vote on company affairs, even though they receive their prorata value of the earnings.

We must conclude that economically and even in basic law, there is no difference between shareholders and productive creditors; both are equally suppliers of capital, both receive interest return as determined on the general time market, both own their proportionate share of the company's assets. The differences between the two are only technical and semantic. It is true that our discussion has so far applied only to the evenly rotating economy, but we shall see that the real world of uncertainty and entrepreneurship, while complicating matters, does not change the essentials of our analysis.[36]

In recent writings there has been a growing acknowledgment of the essential identity between shareholders and creditors, in contrast to the old tradition that postulated a sharp cleavage between them. But it is curious that the new literature interprets the identity in precisely the wrong way: instead of treating the creditors like shareholder-owners, it treats the shareholders like creditors. In other words, the correct approach is to consider creditors as actually part owners of the firm; but the new literature treats stockholders as merely creditors of the firm, in keeping with the new tradition of picturing the hired managers as its real controllers and owners. Managers are depicted as somehow owning the firm and paying out interest to creditors, as well as dividends to stockholders, just as any factor payment is made—as a grudging cost of production. In reality, the managers are only the hired agents of the stockholders, and it is the latter who decide how much of their earnings to reinvest in the firm and how much to "take out of the firm" in the form of "dividends."

The commonly made distinction between "dividends" and "retained earnings" is not a useful one for the purposes of economic analysis. Retained earnings are not necessarily reinvested; they may be held out of investment in a cash balance and later paid out as dividends. Dividends, on the other hand, are not necessarily spent on consumption; they may be invested in some other firm. Therefore, this distinction is a misleading one. Earnings are either reinvested or they are not; and all corporate earnings constitute earnings of the individual owners.

Savings may be channeled through intermediaries before entering the actual producers' loan (or the consumers' loan) market. *Finding* a productive investment is one of the tasks of entrepreneurs, and it is often far more convenient for all concerned when the individual, instead of making up his mind himself on the proper channels of investment, lends or invests his money in other institutions specially set up to be experts in investment. These institutions may serve as channels, gathering in the small savings of isolated individuals, whose investments by themselves are too small to be worth the cost of finding a market for them. The institutions then invest the funds knowledgeably in larger lump sums. A typical example is the *investment trust,* which sells its own stock to individuals and then uses this capital to buy stock of other companies. In the ERE, the interest that will be earned from individuals' savings via intermediaries will equal the interest earned from direct investments minus the cost of the intermediary's service, this price to be determined on the market just like other prices. Thus, if the interest rate throughout the market is 5%, and the cost of intermediary service is 1%, then, in the ERE, those who channel their savings via the convenient intermediary method will receive a 4% interest return on the investment of their savings.

We have thus seen the unimportance of the producers' loan market as an independent determining factor in the establishment of the market rate of interest or in the productive system.

In many cases it is convenient to designate by different terms the rate of interest on contractual loan markets and the rate of interest in the form of earnings on investments as a result of price spreads. The former we may call the *contractual rate of interest* (where the interest is fixed at the time of making the contract), and the latter the *natural rate of interest* (i.e., the interest comes "naturally" via investments in production processes, rather than being officially included in an exchange contract). The two interest rates will, of course, coincide in the ERE.

Throughout our analysis we have been making one underlying

assumption that might be modified: that individuals will always try to obtain the highest interest return. It is on this basis that we have traced the arbitrage actions and eventual uniformities of the ERE. We have assumed that each investor will try to earn as much as he can from his investment. This might not always be true, and critics of economics have never tired of reproaching economists for neglecting other than monetary ends. Economics does not neglect such ends, however. In fact, praxeological analysis explicitly includes them. As we have repeatedly pointed out, each individual attempts to maximize his *psychic* income, and this will translate itself into maximizing his *monetary* income only if other psychic ends are neutral. The ease with which economics can accommodate nonmonetary ends may readily be seen. Suppose that the interest rate in the society is 5%. Suppose, however, that there is a line of production that is distasteful to a large number of people, including investors. In a society, for example, where the making of arms is held in disfavor, simple arbitrage would not work to equate returns in the armament industry with those in other industries. We are not here referring to the displeasure of consumers of arms, which would, of course, reflect itself in a lowered demand for the product. We are referring to the particular displeasure of producers, specifically investors. Because of this psychic dislike, investors will require a higher return in the armament industry than in other industries. It is possible, for example, that they might require an interest return of 10% in the armament industry, even though the general rate of interest is 5%. What factors, then, will have to pay for this increased discount? We are not overly anticipating the results of our subsequent analysis if we state that the owners of *nonspecific* factors, i.e., those factors which can be employed elsewhere (or, strictly, the *services* of which can be thus employed) will certainly not accept a lower monetary return in the armament industry than in the other industries. In the ERE, their prices as determined in this industry will, then, be the same as in the other industries. In fact, they might be even higher, if the owners share the investors' specific antipathy toward engaging in the armament industry. The burden of the lower prices at each stage of production, then, falls on the *purely specific* factors in the industry, those which *must* be devoted to this industry if they are to be in the production system at all. In the long run of the ERE, these will not be capital goods, since capital goods always need to be reproduced, and the equivalent resources can gradually or rapidly leave the industry, depending in each case on the durability of the capital good and the length of the process of its production. The specific factor may be labor, but this is not empirically likely, since labor is almost always a nonspecific factor that may shift to several occupations. It is therefore likely to be specific *land* factors that bear the brunt of the lower return.

The opposite will occur in the case of an industry that most investors specifically are very eager to engage in for one reason or another. In that case, they will accept a lower interest return in this production process than in others. The force of competition on the market will, once again, keep nonspecific factors at the same price from industry to industry, although the price might be lower if the factor-owners were also particularly eager to work in this industry. The higher prices at the various stages are therefore reaped by the owners of specific factors, generally land factors.

The rate of interest, then, always tends toward equality throughout its various submarkets and in its various forms. In the ERE, the rates will be uniformly equal throughout. This conclusion must be modified, however, to state that the rates of interest will differ in accordance with a "psychic" component, either positive or negative, depending on whether there is an acute dislike or liking among investors for a particular production process.[37] We may say that, in the case of a particular liking, the investors are "consuming" the enjoyment of investing in the particular process and paying the price of a lower return; in the case of a particular dislike, they are charging more for a particular disutility. It must be emphasized, however, that these differences in return do not occur if merely *one person* particularly likes or dislikes a certain field, but only if there is a significant aggregate of strong preferences in one direction or another. This type of consumption, positive or negative, is intertwined in the production process and occurs directly with production, and thus differs from ordinary consumption, which occurs at the end of the production process.

10. *Forces Affecting Time Preferences*

Praxeology can never furnish an ultimate explanation for a man's time preferences. These are psychologically determined by each person and must therefore be taken, in the final analysis, as data by economists. However, praxeological analysis can supply some truths about time preferences, using *ceteris paribus* assumptions. Thus, as we have seen above, each person has a time-preference schedule relating to his money stock. A lower money stock will cause a higher time-preference rate for any unit of money remaining in his possession, until finally his time-preference rate will rise to infinity when the money stock—or rather, the money for consumption—is low enough. Here, one element, a man's money stock, is varied and his value scale is otherwise assumed to remain constant. Hence, we can in this way gauge the effects of a change in one determinant, the money stock.

Actually, it is not his *money* stock that is relevant to his time preferences, but the *real* value of his money stock. In the ERE, of course, where the purchasing power of the money unit remains unchanged, the two are identical. *Ceteris paribus,* an increase in his real income—real additions to his money stock—will lower the time-preference rate on his schedule. Of course, historically, there is no reason why his time-preference *schedule* should remain unchanged. It is important to know, however, that, given an unchanged schedule, his relevant time-preference rate will fall.

There are other elements that enter into the determination of the time-preference schedules. Suppose, for example, that people were certain that the world would end on a definite date in the near future. What would happen to time preferences and to the rate of interest? Men would then stop providing for future needs and stop investing in all processes of production longer than the shortest. Future goods would become almost valueless compared to present goods, time preferences for present goods would zoom, and the pure interest rate would rise almost to infinity. On the other hand, if people all became immortal and healthy as a result of the discovery of some new drug, time preferences would tend to be very much lower, there would be a great increase in investment, and the pure rate of interest would fall sharply.

11. *The Time Structure of Interest Rates*

It is clear that the natural interest rates are highly flexible; they tend toward uniformity and are easily changed as entrepreneurial expectations change. In the real world the prices of the various factors and intermediate products, as well as of the final products, are subject to continual fluctuation, as are the prices of stock and the interest return on them. It is also clear that the interest rate on short-term loans is easily changed with changed conditions. As the natural interest rate changes, the new loans for short periods can easily conform to the change.

A difficulty seems to arise, however, in the case of *long-term* producers' loans. Here is an apparently clear-cut rigid element in the system, and one which can conform to the natural rate of interest in investments only after a great lag. After all, a twenty-year loan is contracted at an original interest rate that remains fixed for the duration; is this not a fixed element that cannot conform to changing conditions and valuations? This superficial view is incorrect. Long-term I. O. U.'s can also be bought and sold in a market. Most of these long-term debts are called *bonds,* and they are traded in a flourishing and flexible bond market. The fixed rate of interest at the beginning is unimportant. Thus, a 100-ounce long-term loan is contracted at 5% fixed interest, or 5 ounces per year. If the general interest rate rises, people will tend to sell their bonds, which have been yielding them only 5%, and invest their money elsewhere—either in whole firms, stocks of firms, or short-term loans. This increased willingness to sell bonds—an increased supply schedule—depresses the *price* of the bond until the interest *yield* to the buyer is the same as the general interest rate elsewhere. Thus, if the general interest rate goes up from 5% to 10%, the price of the bond will fall from 100 to 50, so that the fixed annual return of 5 will provide an interest yield of 10%. The important element in bond investment is not the original interest rate (the fixed return on the so-called "par value" of the bond), but the interest *yield* on the market price of the bond. A general lowering of the interest rate will, on the other hand, raise the bond prices above par and push yield below 5%. As the day of redemption of the bond draws near, the market price of the bond will, of course, rapidly approach the par value, until it finally sells at par, since the amount redeemed will be the original par value, or principal, of the loan.

It is clear that, in the ERE, the interest rates for all periods of time will be equal. The *tendency* toward such equality at any one time, however, has been disputed in the case of *expected future changes* in the interest rate. Although surprisingly little attention has been devoted to this subject, the prevailing theory is that, on the loan market, there will not be a tendency toward equalization if a change in interest rates is expected in the near future.[38] Suppose that the interest rate is now 5%, and it is expected to remain there. Then the interest rate on loans of all maturities will be the same, 5%. Suppose, however, that the interest rate is expected to increase steadily in the near future, say to increase each year by 1% until it will be 9% four years from now. In that case, since the short-run rate (say the rate of interest on loans lasting one year or less) is expected to increase over the next four-year period, then the present long-run rate for that period—e.g., the present rate for five-year loans—will be an average of the expected future short-run rates during this period. Thus, the present rate on five-year loans will be 5% plus 6% plus 7% plus 8% plus 9% divided by 5, equaling 7%. The long-run rate will be the average of short-run rates over the relevant period. Consequently, the long-run rates will be proportionately higher than short-run rates when the latter are expected to increase, and lower when the later are expected to be lower. (See Fig. 54.)

This, however, is a completely question-begging theory. Suppose that a rise in interest rates is expected; why should this be simply confined to a rise in the *short-term rates?* Why should not the expectation be equally applicable to long-term rates so that they rise as well?[39] The theory rests on the quite untenable assumption that it sets out to prove, namely, that there is no tendency for short-term and long-term rates to be equal. The assumption that a change in the interest rate will take place only over the short term is completely unproved and goes against our demonstration that the short-run and long-run rates tend to move to-

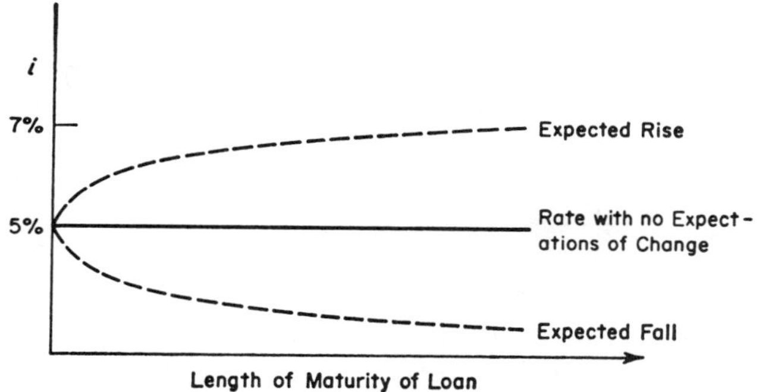

Fig. 54. Long-Run Interest Rates Conceived as Averages of Short-Run Interest Rates

gether. Further, the theory rests on the implicit assumption that individuals will be content to remain lenders in "shorts" at 5% while their fellow investors reap 7% on the long market, simply because they expect that eventually, if they stay in the short market, they will earn an average of 7%. *What is there to prevent a present lender in shorts from selling his currently earning 5% loan, purchasing a 7% long, waiting for the presumed rise in shorts above 7% after two years, and then re-entering the short market, earning 8% or 9%?* If he does this, he will not simply earn 7% as the foregoing diagram postulates (either directly in longs or in an average of 5%–9% in shorts); he will earn 7% plus 7% plus 7% plus 8% plus 9%, or an annual average of 7.6%. By striving to do so, he will set up an *irresistible* arbitrage movement from shorts to longs, with the rate of interest in the former thereby rising from the sales of loans on the market, and the rate of interest in longs falling, *until the rate of interest is uniform throughout the time structure.*

The same thing occurs in the case of an expectation of a future fall. Longs cannot remain in equilibrium below shorts for any length of time, since there will be a present movement from longs to shorts on the market, until the rates of interest for all time structures are equal and the arbitrage movement ceases.

The interest rate, then, always tends to be uniform throughout its time structure. What happens if the interest rate is expected to *change* in the near future? In that case, there will be a similar process as in the case of speculation in commodities. Speculators will bid up the interest rate in the expectation of an imminent rise or bid down the rate in expectation of a fall. Clearly, the earlier a rise or fall is expected to take place, the greater proportionately will be the effect on the speculators, and the greater impact it will have on current movement in the rate. In the case of a commodity, stocks would be withheld in expectation of a rise in demand and price, and then released, thereby effecting a more rapid transition to the price eventually established by underlying supply-and-demand forces. Similarly, in this case money will tend to be withheld from investments and held in cash balances until the rate reaches its expected higher level, or dislodged from cash balances and added to investment if the rate of interest is expected to be lower. This action will speed up the transition to the rate determined by the new alignment of basic time preferences. Just as speculative errors in regard to commodity prices cause losses and impel further change to the "real" underlying price, so speculative errors will be self-correcting here too and lead the rate of interest to the height determined by underlying time preferences.

The time-structure diagram of interest, then, will rather tend to be as depicted in Fig. 55.

The absurdity of separating the long-run and the short-run interest rates becomes evident when we realize that the basic interest rate is the natural rate of interest on investments, not interest on the producers' loan market. We have already seen the essential identity of the rate of earnings on the loan market with that on the stock market. If we consider the stock market, it becomes obvious that there is no distinction in rates between short-run and long-run investments. Different firms engage in stages of production of varying lengths; yet the stock market equates the rate of interest on all investments, obliterating the differences in time structure so thoroughly that it becomes difficult for many writers to grasp the very concept of period of production. But

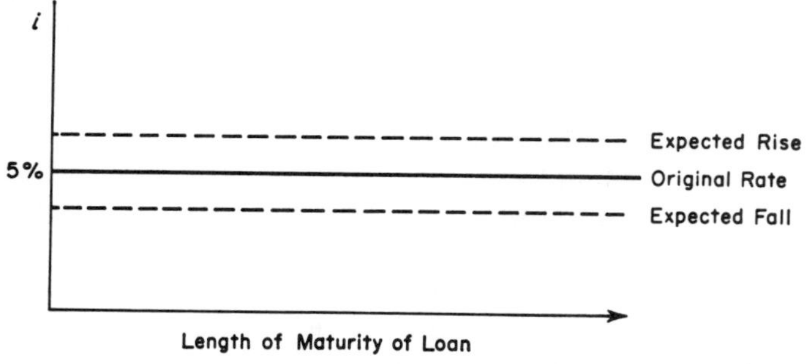

FIG. 55. TIME STRUCTURE OF INTEREST RATES

since the operations of the stock market and the loan market are essentially the same, it is obvious that there is no difference in causal explanation between short-run and long-run interest rates. Those writers who postulate an essential difference between the nature of long-run and short-run rates have been misled by a common penchant for considering the time market as confined exclusively to the loan market, when in fact the loan market is only a dependent one.[40]

In actual practice, it may well happen that either the short-run loan market or the long-run market may change first, with the other market following. Which market characteristically changes first is the outcome of the concrete conditions.[41]

APPENDIX: SCHUMPETER AND THE ZERO RATE OF INTEREST

The late Professor Joseph Schumpeter pioneered a theory of interest which holds that the rate of interest will be zero in the evenly rotating economy. It should be clear from the above discussion why the rate of interest (the *pure* rate of interest in the ERE) could never be zero. It is determined by individual time preferences, which are all positive. To maintain his position, Schumpeter was forced to assert, as does Frank Knight, that capital maintains itself permanently in the ERE. If there is no problem of maintenance, then there appears to be no necessity for the payment of interest in order to maintain the capital structure. This view, treated above, is apparently derived from the static state of J. B. Clark and seems to follow purely *by definition,* since the value of capital is maintained by definition in the ERE. But this, of course, is no answer whatever; the important question is: *How* is this constancy maintained? And the only answer can be that it is maintained by the decisions of capitalists induced by a rate of interest return. If the rate of interest paid were zero, complete capital consumption would ensue.[42]

The conclusive Mises-Robbins critique of Schumpeter's theory of the zero rate of interest, which we have tried to present above, has been attacked by two of Schumpeter's disciples.[43] First, they deny that constancy of capital is assumed by definition in Schumpeter's ERE; instead it is "deduced from the conditions of the system." What are these conditions? There is, first, the absence of uncertainty concerning the future. This, indeed, would seem to be the condition for any ERE. But Clemence and Doody add: "Neither is there time preference unless we introduce it as a special assumption, in which case it may be either positive or negative as we prefer, and there is nothing further to discuss." With such a view of time preference, there is indeed nothing to discuss. The whole basis for pure interest, requiring interest payments, is time preference, and if we casually assume that time preference is either nonexistent or has no discernible influence, then it follows very easily that the pure rate of interest is zero. The authors' "proof" simply consists of ignoring the powerful, universal fact of time preference.[44]

7

Production: General Pricing of the Factors

1. *Imputation of the Discounted Marginal Value Product*

Up to this point we have been investigating the rate of interest as it would be determined in the evenly rotating economy, i.e., as it always *tends* to be determined in the real world. Now we shall investigate the pricing of the various factors of production in the same terms, i.e., as they tend to be in the real world, and as they would be in the evenly rotating economy.

Whenever we have touched on the pricing of productive factors we have signified the prices of their *unit services,* i.e., their *rents.* In order to set aside consideration of the pricing of the factors as "wholes," as embodiments of a series of future unit services, we have been assuming that no businessmen purchase factors (whether land, labor, or capital goods) outright, but only unit services of these factors. This assumption will be continued for the time being. Later on, we shall drop this restrictive assumption and consider the pricing of "whole factors."

In chapter 5 we saw that when all factors are specific there is no principle of pricing that we can offer. Practically, the only thing that economic analysis can say about the pricing of the productive factors in such a case is that voluntary bargaining among the factor-owners will settle the issue. As long as the factors are all purely specific, economic analysis can say little more about the determinants of their pricing. What conditions must apply, then, to enable us to be more definite about the pricing of factors?

The currently fashionable account of this subject hinges on the *fixity* or *variability* in the proportions of the combined factors used per unit of product. If the factors can be combined only in certain fixed proportions to produce a given quantity of product, it is alleged, then there can be no determinate price; if the proportions of the factors can be varied to produce a given result, then the pricing of each factor can be isolated and determined. Let us examine this contention. Suppose that a product worth 20 gold ounces is produced by three factors, each one purely specific to this production. Suppose that the proportions are variable, so that a product worth 20 gold ounces can be produced either by 4 units of factor *A*, 5 units of factor *B*, and 3 units of factor *C*, or by 6 units of *A*, 4 units of *B*, and 2 units of *C*. How will this help the economist to say anything more about the pricing of these factors than that it will be determined by bargaining? The prices will still be determined by bargaining, and it is obvious that the variability in the proportions of the factors does not aid us in any determination of the specific value or share of each particular product. Since each factor is purely specific, there is no way we can analytically ascertain how a price for a factor is obtained.

The fallacious emphasis on variability of proportion as the basis for factor pricing in the current literature is a result of the prevailing method of analysis. A typical single firm is considered, with its selling prices and *prices of factors given*. Then, the proportions of the factors are assumed to be variable. It can be shown, accordingly, that if the price of factor *A* increases compared to *B*, the firm will use less of *A* and more of *B* in producing its product. From this, demand curves for each factor are deduced, and the pricing of each factor established.

The fallacies of this approach are numerous. The chief error is that of basing a causal explanation of factor pricing on the *assumption of given factor prices*. On the contrary, we cannot explain factor prices while assuming them as given from the very beginning of the analysis.[1] It is then assumed that the price of a factor changes. But *how* can such a change take place? In the market there are no uncaused changes.

It is true that this is the way that the market looks to a typical firm. But concentration on a single firm and the reaction of its owner is not the appropriate route to the theory of production; on the contrary, it is likely to be misleading, as in this case. In the current literature, this preoccupation with the single firm rather than with the interrelatedness of firms in the economy has led to the erection of a vastly complicated and largely valueless edifice of production theory.

The entire discussion of variable and fixed proportions is really technological rather than economic, and this fact should have alerted those writers who rely on variability as the key to their explanation of pricing.[2] The one technological conclusion that we know purely from *praxeology* is the law of returns, derived at the beginning of chapter 1. According to the law of returns, there is an optimum of proportions of factors, given other factors, in the production of any given product. This optimum may be the *only* proportion at which the good can be produced, or it may be one of many proportions. The former is the case of fixed proportions, the latter of variable proportions. Both cases are subsumed under the more general law of returns, and we shall see that our analysis of factor pricing is based only on this praxeological law and not on more restrictive technological assumptions.

The key question, in fact, is not variability, but *specificity* of factors.[3] For determinate factor pricing to take place, there must be *nonspecific* factors, factors that are useful in several production processes. It is the prices of these nonspecific factors that are determinate. If, in any particular case, only one factor is specific, then its price is also determined: it is the residual difference between the sum of the prices of the nonspecific factors and the price of the common product. When there is more than one specific factor in each process, however, only the *cumulative* residual price is determined, and the price of each specific factor singly can be determined solely by bargaining.

To arrive at the principles of pricing, let us first leap to the conclusion and then trace the process of arriving at this conclusion. Every capitalist will attempt to employ a factor (or rather, the service of a factor) at the price that will be at least *less than its discounted marginal value product.* The *marginal value product* is the monetary revenue that may be attributed, or "imputed," to one service unit of the factor. It is the "marginal" value product, because the supply of the factor is in discrete units. This MVP (marginal value product) is *discounted* by the social rate of time preference, i.e., by the going rate of interest. Suppose, for example, that a unit of a factor (say a day's worth of a certain acre of land or a day's worth of the effort of a certain laborer) will, imputably, produce for the firm a product one year from now that will be sold for 20 gold ounces. The MVP of this factor is 20 ounces. But this is a future good. The *present value of the future good,* and it is this present value that is *now* being purchased, will be equal to the MVP discounted by the going rate of interest. If the rate of interest is 5%, then the discounted MVP will be equal to 19 ounces. To the employer—the capitalist—then, the maximum amount that the factor unit is now worth is 19 ounces. The capitalist will be willing to buy this factor at any price up to 19 ounces.

Now suppose that the capitalist owner or owners of one firm pay for this factor 15 ounces per unit. As we shall see in greater detail later on, this means that the capitalist earns a *pure profit* of 4 ounces per unit, since he reaps 19 ounces from the final sale. (He obtains 20 ounces on final sale, but 1 ounce is the result of his time preference and waiting and is not pure profit; 19 ounces is the *present value* of his final sale.) But, seeing this happen, other entrepreneurs will leap into the breach to reap these profits. These capitalists will have to bid the factor away from the first capitalist and thus pay more than 15 ounces, say 17 ounces. This process continues until the factor earns its full DMVP (discounted marginal value product), and no pure profits remain. The result is that in the ERE every isolable factor will earn its DMVP, and this will be its price. As a result, each factor will earn its DMVP, and the capitalist will earn the going rate of interest for purchasing future goods with his savings. In the ERE, as we have seen, all capitalists will earn the same going rate of interest, and no pure profit will then be reaped. The sale price of a good will be necessarily equal to the sum of the DMVP's of its factors plus the rate of interest return on the investment.

It is clear that if the marginal value of a specific unit of factor service can be isolated and determined, then the forces of competition on the market will result in making *its price equal to its DMVP in the ERE.* Any price higher than the discounted marginal value product of a factor service will not long be paid by a capitalist; any price lower will be raised by the competitive actions of entrepreneurs bidding away these factors through offers of higher prices. These actions will lead, in the former case to the disappearance of losses, in the latter, to the disappearance of pure profit, at which time the ERE is reached.

When a factor is isolable, i.e., if its service can be separated out in appraised value from other factors, then its price will always tend to be set equal to its DMVP. The factor is clearly not isolable, if, as mentioned in note 3 above, it must always be combined with some other particular factor in fixed proportions. If this happens, then a price can be given only to the cumulative product of the factors, and the individual price can be determined only through bargaining. Also, as we have stated, if the factors are all purely specific to the product, then, regardless of any variability in the proportions of their combination, the factors will not be isolable.

It is, then, the nonspecific factors that are directly isolable; a specific factor is isolable if it is the only specific factor in the combination, in which case its price is the difference between the price of the product and the sum of the prices of the nonspecific factors. But by what process does the market isolate and determine the share (the MVP of a certain unit of a factor) of income yielded from production?

Let us refer back to the basic law of utility. What will be the marginal value of a unit of any good? It will be equal to the individual's valuation of the end that must remain unattained should this unit be removed. If a man possesses 20 units of a good, and the uses served by the good are ranked 1 to 20 on his value scale (1 being the ordinal highest), then his loss of a unit—

regardless of which end the unit is supplying *at present*—will mean a loss of the use ranked twentieth in his scale. Therefore, the marginal utility of a unit of the good is ranked at 20 on the person's value scale. Any further unit to be acquired will satisfy the next highest of the ends *not yet being served,* i.e., at 21—a rank which will necessarily be *lower* than the ends already being served. The greater the supply of a good, then, the lower the value of its marginal utility.

A similar analysis is applicable to a producers' good as well. A unit of a producers' good will be valued in terms of the revenue that will be lost should one unit of the good be lost. This can be determined by an entrepreneur's knowledge of his "production function," i.e., the various ways in which factors can technologically be combined to yield certain products, and his estimate of the demand curve of the buyers of his product, i.e., the prices that they would be willing to pay for his product. Suppose, now, that a firm is combining factors in the following way:

$$4X + 10Y + 2Z \rightarrow 100 \text{ gold oz.}$$

4 units of X plus 10 units of Y plus 2 units of Z produce a product that can be sold for 100 gold ounces. Now suppose that the entrepreneur estimates that the following would happen if one unit of X were eliminated;

$$3X + 10Y + 2Z \rightarrow 80 \text{ gold oz.}$$

The loss of one unit of X, other factors remaining constant, has resulted in the loss of *20 gold ounces of gross revenue.* This, then, is the marginal value product of the unit at this position and with this use.[4]

This process is reversible as well. Thus, suppose the firm is at present producing in the latter proportions and reaping 80 gold ounces. If it adds a fourth unit of X to its combination, keeping other quantities constant, it earns 20 more gold ounces. So that here as well, the MVP of this unit is *20 gold ounces.*

This example has implicitly assumed a case of variable proportions. What if the proportions are necessarily fixed? In that case, the loss of a unit of X would require that proportionate quantities of Y, Z, etc., be disposed of. The combination of factors built on $3X$ would then be as follows:

$$3X + 7.5Y + 1.5Z \rightarrow 75 \text{ gold oz. (assuming no price change in the final product)}$$

With fixed proportions, then, the marginal value product of the varying factor would be greater, in this case 25 gold ounces.[5]

Let us for the moment ignore the variations in MVP *within* each production process and consider only variations in MVP among different processes. This is basic since, after all, it is necessary to have a factor usable in more than one production process before its MVP can be isolated. Inevitably, then, the MVP will differ from process to process, since the various production combinations of factors and prices of products will differ. For every factor, then, there is available a sheaf of possible investments in different production processes, each differing in MVP. The MVP's (or, strictly, the discounted MVP's), can be arrayed in descending order. For example, for factor X:

25 oz.
24 oz.
22 oz.
21 oz.
20 oz.
19 oz.
18 oz.
etc.

Suppose, that we begin in the economy with a zero supply of the factor, and then add one unit. Where will this one unit be employed? It is obvious that it will be employed in the use with the highest DMVP. The reason is that capitalists in the various production processes will compete with one another for the use of the factor. But the use in which the DMVP is 25 can bid away the unit of the factor from the other competitors, and it can do this finally only by paying 25 gold ounces for the unit. When the second unit of supply arrives in society, it goes to the second highest use, and it receives a price of 24 ounces, and a similar process occurs as new units of supply are added. *As new supply is added, the marginal value product of a unit declines.* Conversely, *if the supply of a factor decreases* (i.e., the total supply in the economy), *the marginal value product of a unit increases.* The same laws apply, of course, to the DMVP, since this is just the MVP discounted by a common factor, the market's pure rate of interest. As supply increases, then, more and more of the sheaf of available employments for the factor are used, and lower and lower MVP's are tapped.

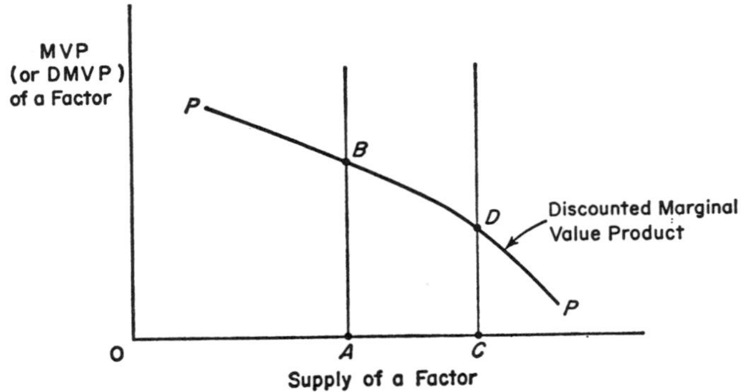

FIG. 56. INFLUENCE OF SUPPLY OF A FACTOR ON ITS MARGINAL VALUE PRODUCT

Diagrammatically, we may present this situation as in Fig. 56. The line *PP* is the curve of the marginal value product (or discounted MVP) of a factor. It is *always declining* as it moves to the right, because new units of supply always enter those uses that are most productive of revenue. On the horizontal axis is the quantity of supply of the factor. When the supply is *OA*, then the MVP is *AB*. When the supply is larger at *OC*, then the MVP is lower at *CD*.

Let us say that there are 30 units of factor *X* available in the economy, and that the MVP corresponding to such a supply is 10 ounces. The price of the thirtieth unit, then, will tend to be 10 ounces and will be 10 ounces in the ERE. This follows from the tendency of the price of a factor to be equal to its MVP. But now we must recall that there takes place the inexorable tendency in the market for the *price of all units of any good to be uniform throughout its market.* This must apply to a productive factor just as to any other good. Indeed, this result follows from the very basic law of utility that we have been considering. For, since factor units by definition are interchangeable, the value of one unit will be equal to the value of every other unit at any one time. The value of every unit of a good will be equal to the value of the lowest-ranking use now served by a unit. In the present case, every unit of the factor will be priced at 10 gold ounces.

Suppose, for example, that the owner of the factor unit serving the top-ranking use in our array should demand that he receive 24 ounces, instead of 10 ounces, as his price. In that case, the capitalist in that line of production can refuse to hire this factor and instead bid away the unit employed in the lowest-ranking use, say by paying for the latter 10.5 ounces. The only alternative left to the owner of the factor who had demanded 24 ounces is to replace the other factor in the lowest-ranking spot, at 10 ounces. Effectively, all factors will shift until the prices that they can attain will be uniform throughout the market for their services.

The price of *X*, then, is determined at 10 ounces. It is determined by the MVP (or rather DMVP) of the supply, which decreases as the supply increases, and *vice versa.* Let us assume that *Y* is also a nonspecific factor and that *Z* is a factor *specific* to the particular process considered above. Let us further assume that, by a similar process, the DMVP, and therefore the price, of *Y* is determined at 2 ounces.

At this point, we must reintroduce the concept of production *within* each line. We have been discussing MVP's of factors shifted from one use to another. In our example, a unit of *X* may have an MVP (or DMVP) of 20 ounces in a particular use; yet its price, as determined by the MVP of the lowest-ranking use for which it is employed, is 10 ounces. This means that, in this use, the capitalist is hiring a factor for 10 ounces which earns for him 20 ounces. Spurred on by this profit, he will hire more units of the factor until the MVP in this use will equal the MVP in the lowest-ranking use, i.e., the factor price, 10 ounces. The same process will occur in regard to each of the other uses. The tendency will always be, then (and this will always obtain in the ERE), *for the DMVP of any factor to be equal in each line of production.* We will see shortly why increased purchase of a factor even within each line will lower the MVP in that line.

Suppose, then, that the price of X and Y are 10 and 2 ounces respectively and that all the capitalists have so arranged their production as to equate the DMVP of each factor in each line with this price. Suppose, further, that the equilibrium point in this particular use is the combination:

$$3X + 10Y + 2Z \rightarrow 80 \text{ oz.}$$

Substituting the given prices of X and Y:

$$30 + 20 + 2Z \rightarrow 80 \text{ oz.}$$

$$2Z \rightarrow 30 \text{ oz.}$$

$$Z \rightarrow 15 \text{ oz.}$$

Therefore, $Z = 15$ oz.

The price of the specific factor Z, residual to the other factors, is thereby determined at 15 ounces.

It is obvious that the impact of a change in consumer demand on a specific factor will be far greater, in either direction, than it will be on the price of employment of a nonspecific factor.

It is now clear why the temptation in factor-price analysis is for the *firm* to consider that factor prices are given externally to itself and that it simply varies its production in accordance with these prices. However, from an analytic standpoint, it should be evident that the array of MVP's as a whole is the determining factor, and the lowest-ranking process in terms of MVP will, through the medium of factor prices, transmit its message, so to speak, to the various firms, each of which will use the factor to such an extent that its DMVP will be brought into alignment with its price. But the ultimate determining factor is the DMVP schedule, not the factor price. To make the distinction, we may term the full array of all MVP's for a factor, the *general DMVP schedule* of a factor, while the special array of DMVP's *within* any particular production process or stage, we may term the *particular DMVP schedule* of the factor. It is the *general* DMVP schedule that determines the price of the supply of the factor, and then the *particular* DMVP schedules within each production process are brought into alignment so that the DMVP's of the factor equal its price. Fig. 56 above was a *general* schedule. The particular MVP's are subarrays within the widest array of all the possible alternatives—the general MVP schedule.

In short, the prices of productive factors are determined as follows: Where a factor is isolable, its price will tend toward its discounted marginal value product and will equal its DMVP in the ERE. A factor will be isolable where it is nonspecific, i.e., is useful in more than one productive process, or where it is the *only* specific factor in a process. The nonspecific factor's price will be set equal to its DMVP as determined by its general DMVP schedule: the full possible array of DMVP's, given various units of supply of the factor in the economy. Since the most value-productive uses will be chosen first, and the least abandoned first, the curve of general MVP declines as the supply increases. The various particular MVP's in the various processes will be arranged so as to equal the factor price set by the general DMVP schedule. The specific factor's imputed DMVP is the residual difference between the price of the product and the sum of the prices of the nonspecific factors.

The marginal utility of a unit of a good is determined by a man's diminishing marginal utility schedule evaluating a certain supply or stock of that good. Similarly, the market's establishment of the price of a consumers' good is determined by the aggregate consumer demand schedules—diminishing—and their intersection with the given supply or stock of a good. We are now engaged in pursuing the problem still further and in finding the answer to two general questions: What determines the prices of factors of production on the market, and what determines the quantity of goods that will be produced? We have seen in this section that the price of a factor is determined by its diminishing general (discounted) marginal value productivity curve intersecting with the given supply (stock) of the factor in the economy.

2. *Determination of the Discounted Marginal Value Product*

A. DISCOUNTING

If the DMVP schedules determine the prices of nonspecific factor services, what determines the shape and position of the DMVP schedules? In the first place, by definition it is clear that the DMVP schedule is the MVP schedule for that factor *discounted.* There is no mystery about the *discounting;* as we have stated, the MVP of the factor is discounted in accordance with the going pure rate of interest on the market. The relation of the MVP schedule and the DMVP schedule may be diagrammed as in Fig. 57.

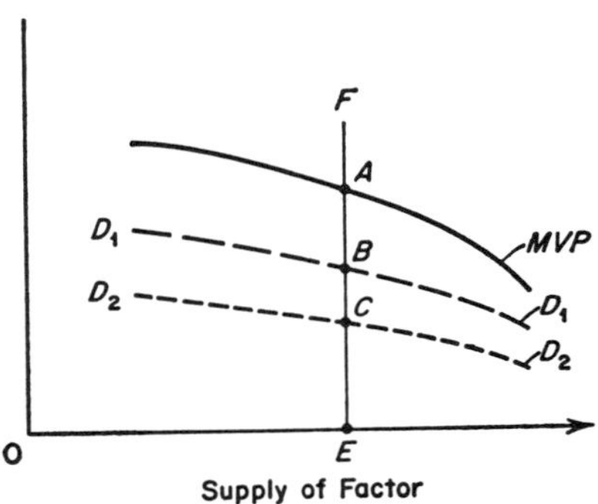

FIG. 57. EFFECT OF CHANGES IN THE RATE OF INTEREST ON THE DISCOUNTED MARGINAL VALUE PRODUCT AS SUPPLY OF THE FACTOR VARIES

The supply of the factor is the *EF* line at the given quantity *OE*. The solid line is the MVP schedule at various supplies. The MVP of the supply *OE* is *EA*. Now the broken line D_1D_1 is the discounted marginal value product schedule at a certain rate of interest. Since it is discounted, it is uniformly lower than the MVP curve. In absolute terms, it is relatively lower at the left of the diagram, because an equal percentage drop implies a greater absolute drop where the amount is greater. The DMVP for supply *OE* equals *EB*. *EB* will be the price of the factor in the evenly rotating economy. Now suppose that the rate of interest in the economy rises, as a result, of course, of rises in time-preference schedules. This means that the rate of discount for every hypothetical MVP will be greater, and the absolute levels lower. The new DMVP schedule is depicted as the dotted line

D_2D_2. The new price for the same supply of the factor is *EC*, a lower price than before.

One of the determinants of the DMVP schedule, then, is the rate of discount, and we have seen above that the rate of discount is determined by individual time preferences. The higher the rate of discount, the lower will tend to be the DMVP and, therefore, the lower the price of the factor; the lower the interest rate, the higher the DMVP and the price of the factor.

B. THE MARGINAL PHYSICAL PRODUCT

What, then, determines the position and shape of the MVP schedule? What is the marginal value product? It is the amount of revenue intake attributable to a unit of a factor. And this revenue depends on two elements: (1) the physical product produced and (2) the price of that product. If one hour of factor *X* is estimated by the market to produce a value of 20 gold ounces, this might be because one hour produces 20 units of the physical product, which are sold at a price of one gold ounce per unit. Or the same MVP might result from the production of 10 units of the product, sold at 2 gold ounces per unit, etc. In short, *the marginal value product of a factor service unit is equal to its marginal physical product times the price of that product.*[6]

Let us, then, investigate the determinants of the marginal physical product (MPP). In the first place, there can be no general schedule for the MPP as there is for the MVP, for the simple reason that *physical* units of various goods are not comparable. How can a dozen eggs, a pound of butter, and a house be compared in *physical* terms? Yet the same factor might be useful in the production of any of these goods. There can be an MPP schedule, therefore, only in *particular* terms, i.e., in terms of each particular production process in which the factor can be engaged. For each production process there will be for the factor a marginal physical production schedule of a certain shape. The MPP for a supply *in that process* is the amount of the physical product imputable to one unit of that factor, i.e., the amount of the product that will be lost if one unit of the factor is removed. If the supply of the factor in the process is increased by one unit, other factors remaining the same, then the MPP of the supply becomes the additional physical product that can be gained from the addition of the unit. The supply of the factor that is relevant for the MPP schedules is not the total supply in the society, but the supply *in each process,* since the MPP schedules are established for each process separately.

1) *The Law of Returns*

In order to investigate the MPP schedule further, let us recall the law of returns, set forth in chapter 1. According to the law of returns, an eternal truth of human action, if the quantity of one factor varies, and the quantities of other factors remain constant, there is a point at which the physical product per factor is at a maximum. Physical product per factor may be termed the *average physical product* (APP). The law further states that with either a lesser or a greater supply of the factor the APP must be lower. We may diagram a typical APP curve as in Fig. 58.

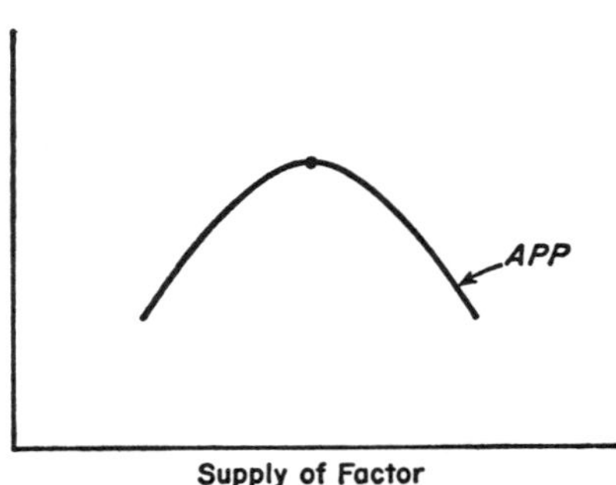

FIG. 58. AVERAGE PHYSICAL PRODUCT IN RELATION TO THE SUPPLY OF A FACTOR

2) *Marginal Physical Product and Average Physical Product*

What is the relationship between the APP and MPP? *The MPP is the amount of physical product that will be produced with the addition of one unit of a factor, other factors being given. The APP is the ratio of the total product to the total quantity of the variable factor, other factors being given.* To illustrate the meanings of APP and MPP, let us consider a hypothetical case in which all units of other factors are constant, and the number of units of one factor is variable. In Table 13 the first column lists the number of units of the variable factor, and the second column the total physical product produced when these varying units are combined with fixed units of the other factors. The third column is the APP = total product divided by the number of units of the factor, i.e., the average physical productivity of a unit of the factor. The fourth column is the MPP = the difference in total product yielded by adding one more unit of the variable factor, i.e., the total product of the current row minus the total product of the preceding row:

TABLE 13

UNITS OF VARIABLE FACTOR	TOTAL PRODUCT	AVERAGE PHYSICAL PRODUCT	MARGINAL PHYSICAL PRODUCT
0.	0	0	0
1.	3	3	3
2.	8	4	5
3.	15	5	7
4.	22	5.2	7
5.	27.5	5.5	5.5
6.	30	5	2.5
7.	28	4	−2

In the first place, it is quite clear that *no factor will ever be employed in the region where the MPP is negative.* In our example, this occurs where 7 units of the factor are being employed. 6 units of the factor, combined with given other factors, produced 30 units of the product. An addition of another unit results in a loss of two units of the product. The MPP of the factor when 7 units are employed is −2. Obviously, no factor will ever be employed in this region, and this holds true whether the factor-owner is also owner of the product, or a capitalist hires the factor to work on the product. It would be senseless and contrary to the principles of human action to expend either effort or money on added factors only to have the quantity of the total product decline.

In the tabulation, we follow the law of returns, in that the APP, beginning, of course, at zero with zero units of the factor, rises to a peak and then falls. We also observe the following from our chart: (1) *when the APP is rising* (with the exception of the very first step where TP, APP and MPP are all equal) *MPP is higher than APP:* (2) *when the APP is falling, MPP is lower than APP;* (3) *at the point of maximum APP, MPP is equal to APP.* We shall now prove, algebraically, that these three laws *always* hold.[7]

Let F be any number of units of a variable factor, other factors being given, and P be the units of the total product yielded by the combination. Then P/F is the Average Physical Product. When we add ΔF more units of the factor, total product increases by ΔP. Marginal Physical Product corresponding to the increase in the factor is $\Delta P/\Delta F$. The new Average Physical Product, corresponding to the greater supply of factors, is:

$$\frac{P + \Delta P}{F + \Delta F}$$

Now the new APP might be higher or lower than the previous one. Let us suppose that the new APP is higher and that therefore we are in a region where the *APP is increasing.* This means that:

$$\frac{P + \Delta P}{F + \Delta F} > \frac{P}{F}$$ > is the symbol for "is greater than."

or $$\frac{P + \Delta P}{F + \Delta F} - \frac{P}{F} > 0$$

Combining terms:

$$\frac{FP + F\Delta P - PF - P\Delta F}{F(F + \Delta F)} > 0$$

Then, surely:

$$FP + F\Delta P - PF - P\Delta F > 0$$

$$F\Delta P - P\Delta F > 0$$

$$F\Delta P > P\Delta F$$

$$\therefore \frac{\Delta P}{\Delta F} > \frac{P}{F}$$

Thus, the MPP is greater than the *old* APP. Since it is greater, this means that there exists a positive number k such that:

$$\frac{\Delta P}{\Delta F} = \frac{kP}{F}$$

Now there is an algebraic rule according to which, if:

$$\frac{a}{b} = \frac{c}{d},$$

then

$$\frac{a}{b} = \frac{c + a}{d + b}$$

Therefore,

$$\frac{\Delta P}{\Delta F} = \frac{kP + \Delta P}{F + \Delta F}$$

Since k is positive,

$$\frac{kP + \Delta P}{F + \Delta F} > \frac{P + \Delta P}{F + \Delta F}$$

Therefore,

$$\boxed{\frac{\Delta P}{\Delta F} > \frac{P + \Delta P}{F + \Delta F}}$$

In short, the MPP is *also* greater than the *new* APP.

In other words, *if APP is increasing, then the marginal physical product is greater than the average physical product* in this region. This proves the first law above. Now, if we go back in our proof and substitute "less than" signs for "greater than" signs and carry out similar steps, we arrive at the opposite conclusion: *where APP is decreasing, the marginal physical product is lower than the average physical product.* This proves the second of our three laws about the relation between the marginal and the average physical product. But if MPP is greater than APP when the latter is rising, and is lower than APP when the latter is falling, then it follows that when *APP is at its maximum, MPP must be neither lower nor higher than, but equal to, APP.* And this proves the third law. We see that these characteristics of our table apply to all possible cases of production.

The diagram in Fig. 59 depicts a typical set of MPP and APP

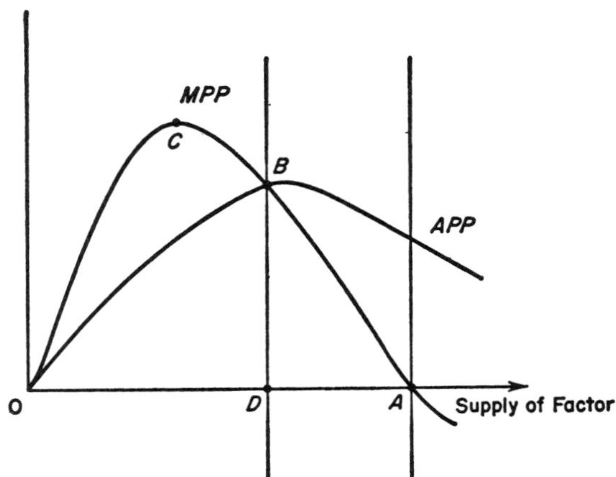

FIG. 59. RELATION BETWEEN MARGINAL PHYSICAL PRODUCT AND AVERAGE PHYSICAL PRODUCT

schedules. It shows the various relationships between APP and MPP. Both curves begin from zero and are identical very close to their origin. The APP curve rises until it reaches a peak at *B,* then declines. The MPP curve rises faster, so that it is higher than APP, reaches its peak earlier at *C,* then declines until it intersects with APP at *B.* From then on, the MPP curve declines faster than APP, until finally it crosses the horizontal axis and becomes negative at some point *A.* No firm will operate beyond the *OA* area.

Now let us explore further the area of *increasing APP,* between *O* and *D.* Let us take another hypothetical tabulation (Table 14), which will be simpler for our purpose.

TABLE 14

UNITS OF FACTOR	TOTAL PRODUCT	AVERAGE PHYSICAL PRODUCT
2.	10	5
3.	18	6
4.	25	6.2

This is a segment of the increasing section of the average physical product schedule, with the peak being reached at 4 units and 6.2 APP. The question is: What is the likelihood that this region will be settled upon by a firm as the right input-output combination? Let us take the top line of the chart. Two units of the variable factor, plus a bundle of what we may call *U* units of all the other factors, yield 10 units of the product. On the other hand, at the maximum APP for the factor, 4 units of it, plus *U* units of other factors, yield 25 units of the product. We have seen above that it is a fundamental truth in nature that the same quantitative causes produce the same quantitative effects. Therefore, if we halve the quantities of all of the factors in the third line, we shall get half the product. In other words, 2 units of the factor combined with *U*/2—with half of the various units of each of the other factors—will yield 12.5 units of the product.

Consider this situation. From the top line we see that 2 units of the variable factor, plus *U* units of given factors, yield 10 units of the product. But, extrapolating from the bottom line, we see that 2 units of the variable factor, plus *U*/2 units of given factors, yield 12.5 units of the product. It is obvious that, as in the case of going beyond *OA*, any firm that allocated factors so as to be in the *OD* region would be making a most unwise decision. Obviously, no one would want to spend *more* in effort or money on factors (the "other" factors) and obtain *less* total output or, for that matter, the same total output. It is evident that if the producer remains in the *OD* region, he is in an area of *negative marginal physical productivity of the other factors.* He would be in a situation where he would obtain a greater total product by throwing away some of the other factors. In the same way, after *OA,* he would be in a position to gain greater total output if he threw away some of the present variable factor. *A region of increasing APP for one factor,* then, signifies a region of *negative MPP for other factors,* and *vice versa.* A producer, then, will never wish to allocate his factor in the *OD* region or in the region beyond *A*.

Neither will the producer set the factor so that its MPP is at the points *B* or *A*. Indeed, the variable factor will be set so that it has zero marginal productivity (at *A*) *only if it is a free good.* There is however, no such thing as a free good; there is only a condition of human welfare not subject to action, and therefore not an element in productivity schedules. Conversely, the APP is at *B,* its maximum for the variable factor, only when the *other* factors are free goods and therefore have zero marginal productivity at this point. Only if all the other factors were free and could be left out of account could the producer simply concentrate on maximizing the productivity of one factor alone. However, there can be no production with only one factor, as we saw in chapter 1.

The conclusion, therefore, is inescapable. A factor will always be employed in a production process in such a way that *it is in a region of declining APP and declining but positive MPP* —between points *D* and *A* on the chart. In every production process, therefore, every factor will be employed in a region of diminishing MPP and diminishing APP *so that additional units of the factor employed in the process will lower the MPP, and decreased units will raise it.*

C. MARGINAL VALUE PRODUCT

As we have seen, the MVP for any factor is its MPP multiplied by the selling price of its product. We have just concluded that every factor will be employed in its region of diminishing marginal physical product in each process of production. What will be the shape of the marginal *value* product schedule? As the supply of a factor increases, and other factors remain the same, it follows that the total physical output of the product is greater. A greater stock, given the consumers' demand curve, will lead to a lowering of the market price. The price of the product will then fall as the MPP diminishes and rise as the latter increases. It follows that the MVP curve of the factor will always be falling, and falling at a *more rapid* rate than the MPP curve. *For each specific production process, any factor will be employed in the region of diminishing MVP.*[8] This correlates with the previous conclusion, based on the law of utility, that the factor in general, among various production processes, will be employed in such a way that its MVP is diminishing. Therefore, its *general MVP* (between various uses and within each use) is diminishing, and its various *particular MVP's* are diminishing (within each use). Its DMVP is, therefore, diminishing as well.

The price of a unit of any factor will, as we have seen, be established in the market as equal to its discounted marginal value product. This will be the DMVP as determined by the general schedule including all the various uses to which it can be put. Now the producers will employ the factor in such a way *that its DMVP will be equalized among all the uses.* If the DMVP in one use is greater than in another, then employers in the former line of production will be in a position to bid more for the factor and will use more of it until (according to the principle of diminishing MVP) the DMVP of the expanding use diminishes to the point at which it equals the increasing DMVP in the contracting use. The price of the factor will be set as equal to the general DMVP, which in the ERE will be uniform throughout all the particular uses.

Thus, by looking at a factor in all of its interrelations, *we have been able to explain the pricing of its unit service without previously assuming the existence of the price itself.* To focus the analysis on the situation as it looks from the vantage point of the firm is to succumb to such an error, for the individual firm obviously finds a certain factor price given on the market. The price of a factor unit will be established by the market as equal to its marginal value product, discounted by the rate of interest for the length of time until the product is produced, provided that this valuation of the share of the factor is isolable. It is isolable if the factor is nonspecific or is a single residual specific factor in a process. The MVP in question is determined by the general MVP schedule covering the various uses of the factor and the supply of the factor available in the economy. The general MVP schedule of a factor diminishes as the supply of the factor increases; it is made up of particular MVP schedules for the various uses of the factor, which in turn are compounded of diminishing Marginal Physical Product schedules and declining product prices. Therefore, if the supply of the factor increases, the MVP schedule in the economy remaining the same, the MVP and hence the price of the factor will drop; and as the supply of the factor dwindles, *ceteris paribus,* the price of the factor will rise.

To the individual firm, the price of a factor established on the market is the signal of its discounted marginal value product elsewhere. This is the opportunity cost of the firm's using the product, since it equals the value product that is forgone through failure to use the factor unit elsewhere. In the ERE, where all factor prices equal discounted marginal value products, it follows that factor prices and (opportunity) "costs" will be equal.

Critics of the marginal productivity analysis have contended that in the "modern complex world" all factors co-operate in producing a product, and therefore it is impossible to establish any sort of imputation of part of the product to various co-operating factors. Hence, they assert, "distribution" of product to factors is separable from production and takes place arbitrarily according to bargaining theory. To be sure, no one denies that many factors do co-operate in producing goods. But the fact that most factors (and all labor factors) are nonspecific, and that there is very rarely more than one purely specific factor in a production process, enables the market to isolate value productivity and to tend to pay each factor in accordance with this marginal product. On the free market, therefore, the price of each factor is not determined by "arbitrary" bargaining, but tends to be set strictly in accordance with its discounted marginal value product. The importance of this market process becomes *greater* as the economy becomes more specialized and complex and the adjustments more delicate. The more uses develop for a factor, and the more types of factors arise, the more important is this market "imputation" process as compared to simple bargaining. For it is this process that causes the effective allocation of factors and the flow of production in accordance with the most urgent demands of the consumers (including the nonmonetary desires of the producers themselves). In the free market process, therefore, there is no separation between production and "distribution." There is no heap somewhere on which "products" are arbitrarily thrown and from which someone does or can arbitrarily "distribute" them among various people. On the contrary, individuals produce goods and sell them to consumers for money, which they in turn spend on consumption or on investment in order to increase future consumption. There is no separate "distribution"; there is only production and its corollary, exchange.

It should always be understood, even where it is not explicitly stated in the text for reasons of exposition, that the MVP schedules used to set prices are *discounted* MVP schedules, discounting the final MVP by the length of time remaining until the final consumers' product is produced. It is the DMVP's that are equalized throughout the various uses of the factor. The importance of this fact is that it explains the market allocation of non-specific factors among various productive *stages* of the same or of different goods. Thus, if the DMVP of a factor is 6 gold ounces, and if the factor is employed on a process practically instantaneous with consumption, its MVP will be 6. Suppose that the pure rate of interest is 5%. If the factor is at work on a process that will mature in final consumption five years from now, a DMVP of 6 signifies an MVP of 7.5; if it is at work on a ten-year process, a DMVP of 6 signifies an MVP of 10; etc. The more remote the time of operation is from the time when the final product is completed, the greater must be the difference allowed for the annual interest income earned by the capitalists who advance present goods and thereby make possible the entire length of the production process. The *amount* of the discount from the MVP is greater here because the higher stage is more remote than the others from final consumption. Therefore, in order for investment to take place in the higher stages, their MVP has to be far higher than the MVP in the shorter processes.[9]

3. *The Source of Factor Incomes*

Our analysis permits us now to resolve that time-honored controversy in economics: Which is the source of wages—capital or consumption? Or, as we should rephrase it, which is the source of original-factor incomes (for labor and land factors)? It is clear that the ultimate goal of the investment of capital is future consumption. In that sense, consumption is the necessary requisite without which there would be no capital. Furthermore, for each particular good, consumption dictates, through market demands, the prices of the various products and the shifting of (nonspecific) factors from one process to another. However, consumption by itself provides nothing. Savings and investment are needed in order to permit any consumption at all, since very little consumption could be obtained with no production processes or capital structure at all—perhaps only the direct picking of berries.[10]

In so far as labor or land factors produce and sell consumers' goods *immediately,* no capital is required for their payment. They are paid directly by consumption. This was true for Crusoe's berry-picking. It is also true in a highly capitalistic economy for labor (and land) in the final stages of the production process. In these final stages, which include pure labor incomes earned in the sale of personal services (of doctors, artists, lawyers, etc.) to consumers, the factors earn MVP directly without being discounted in advance. All the other labor and land factors participating in the production process are paid by saved capital in advance of the produced and consumed product.

We must conclude that in the dispute between the classical theory that wages are paid out of capital and the theory of Henry George, J. B. Clark, and others that wages are paid out of the annual product consumed, the former theory is correct in the overwhelming majority of cases, and that this majority becomes more preponderant the greater the stock of capital in the society.[11]

4. *Land and Capital Goods*

The price of the unit service of every factor, then, is equal to its discounted marginal value product. This is true of *all* factors, whether they be "original" (land and labor) or "produced" (capital goods). However, as we have seen, there is no *net* income to the owners of capital goods, since their prices contain the prices of the various factors that co-operate in their production. Essentially, then, *net* income accrues only to owners of land and labor factors and to capitalists for their "time" services. It is still true, however, that the pricing principle—equality to discounted MVP—applies whatever the factor, whether capital good or any other.

Let us revert to the diagram in Fig. 41. This time, let us assume for simplicity that we are dealing with one unit of one consumers' good, which sells for 100 ounces, and that *one unit* of each particular factor enters into its production. Thus, on Rank 1, 80 refers to one unit of a capital good. Let us consider the first rank first. $Capitalists_1$ purchase one capital good for 80 ounces and (we assume) one labor factor for 8 ounces and one land factor for 7 ounces. The joint MVP for the three factors is 100. Yet their total price is 95 ounces. The remainder is the *discount* accruing to the capitalists because of the time element. The sum of the discounted MVP's, then, is 95 ounces, and this is precisely what the owners of three factors received in total. The discounted MVP of the labor factor's service was 8, the DMVP of the land's service was 7, the DMVP of the capital good's service was 80. Thus, each factor obtains its DMVP as its received price. But what happens in the case of the capital good? It has been sold for 80, but it has had to be produced, and this production cost money to pay the income of the various factors. The price of the capital good, then, is reduced to, say, another land factor, paid 8 ounces; another labor factor paid 8 ounces, and a capital-goods factor paid 60 ounces. The prices, and therefore the incomes, of all these factors are discounted again to account for the time, and this discount is earned by $Capitalists_2$. The sum of these factor incomes is 76, and once again each factor service earns its DMVP.

Each capital-goods factor must be produced and must continue to be produced in the ERE. Since this is so, we see that the capital-goods factor, though obtaining its DMVP, does not earn it *net*, for *its* owner, in turn, must pay money to the factors that produce it. Ultimately, only land, labor, and time factors earn net incomes.

This type of analysis has been severely criticized on the following grounds:

This "Austrian" method of tracing everything back to land and labor (and time!) may be an interesting historical exercise, and we may grant that, if we trace back production and investment far enough, we shall ultimately reach the world of primitive men, who began to produce capital with their bare hands. But of what relevance is this for the modern, complex world around us, a world in which a huge amount of capital already exists and can be worked with? In the modern world there is no production without the aid of capital, and therefore the whole Austrian capital analysis is valueless for the modern economy.

There is no question about the fact that we are not interested in historical analysis, but rather in an economic analysis of the complex economy. In particular, acting man has no interest in the historical origin of his resources; he is acting in the *present* on behalf of a goal to be achieved *in the future*.[12] Praxeological analysis recognizes this and deals with the individual acting at present to satisfy ends of varying degrees of futurity (from instantaneous to remote).

It is true, too, that the presentation by the master of capital and production theory, Böhm-Bawerk, sowed confusion by giving an historical interpretation to the structure of production. This is particularly true of his concept of the "average period of production," which attempted to establish an average length of production processes operating at present, but stretching back to the beginning of time. In one of the weakest parts of his theory, Böhm-Bawerk conceded that "The boy who cuts a stick with his knife is, strictly speaking, only continuing the work of the miner who, centuries ago, thrust the first spade into the ground to sink the shaft from which the ore was brought to make the blade."[13] He then tried to salvage the relevance of the production structure by averaging periods of production and maintaining that the effect in the present product of the early centuries' work is so small (being so remote) as to be negligible.

Mises has succeeded, however, in refining the Austrian production theory so as to eliminate reliance on an almost infinitely high production structure and on the mythical concept of an "average period of production."

As Mises states:

> Acting man does not look at his condition with the eyes of an historian. He is not concerned with how the present situation originated. His only concern is to make the best use of the means available today for the best possible removal of future uneasiness . . . He has at his disposal a definite quantity of material factors of production. He does not ask whether these factors are nature-given or the product of production processes accomplished in the past. It does not matter for him how great a quantity of nature-given, i.e., original material factors of production and labor, was expended in their production and how much time these processes of production have absorbed. He values the available means exclusively from the aspect of the services they can render him in his endeavors to make future conditions more satisfactory. The period of production and the duration of serviceableness are for him categories in planning future action, not concepts of academic retrospection. . . . They play a role in so far as the actor has to choose between periods of production of different length. . . .
>
> [Böhm-Bawerk] . . . was not fully aware of the fact that the period of production is a praxeological category and that the role it plays in action consists entirely in the choices acting man makes between periods of production of different length. The length of time expended in the past for the production of capital goods available today does not count at all.[14]

But if the past is not taken into account, how can we use the production-structure analysis? How can it apply to an ERE if the structure would have to go back almost endlessly in time? If we base our approach on the present, must we not follow the Knightians in scrapping the production-structure analysis?

A particular point of contention is the dividing line between land and capital goods. The Knightians, in scoffing at the idea of tracing periods of production back through the centuries, scrap the *land* concept altogether and include land as simply a part of capital goods. This change, of course, completely alters production theory. The Knightians point correctly, for example, to the fact that present-day land has many varieties and amounts of past labor "mixed" with it: canals have been dug, forests cleared, basic improvements have been made in the soil, etc. They assert that practically nothing is pure "land" anymore and therefore that the concept has become an empty one.

As Mises has shown, however, we can revise Böhm-Bawerk's theory and still retain the vital distinction between land and capital goods. We do not have to throw out, as do the Knightians, the land baby with the average-period-of-production bathwater. We can, instead, reformulate the concept of "land." Up to this point we have simply assumed land to be the original, nature-given factors. Now we must modify this, in keeping with our focus on the present and the future rather than the past. Whether or not a piece of land is "originally" pure land is in fact economically immaterial, so long as whatever alterations have been made are permanent—or rather, so long as these alterations do not have to be reproduced or replaced.[15] Land that has been irrigated by canals or altered through the chopping down of forests has become a present, permanent *given*. Because it is a present given, not worn out in the process of production, and not needing to be replaced, it becomes a *land* factor under our definition. In the ERE, this factor will continue to give forth its natural powers unstinted and without further investment; it is therefore *land* in our analysis. Once this occurs, and the permanent are separated from the nonpermanent alterations, we see that the structure of production no longer stretches back infinitely in time, but comes to a close within a relatively brief span of time.[16] The capital goods are those which are continually wearing out in the process of production and which labor and land factors must work to replace. When we consider physical wearing out and replacement, then, it becomes evident that it would not take many years for the whole capital-goods structure to collapse if no work were done on maintenance and replacement, and this is true even in the modern, highly capitalist economy. Of course, the higher the degree of "capitalist" development and the more stages in production, the longer will it take for all the capital goods to wear out.[17]

The "permanence" with which we are dealing refers, of course, to the *physical* permanence of the goods, and *not* to the permanence of their value. *The latter depends on the shifting desires of consumers and could never be called permanent.* Thus, there might be a land factor uniquely and permanently suitable as a vineyard. It is *land* and remains so, therefore, indefinitely. If, at some time, the consumers should completely lose their taste for wine, and the land becomes valueless and no longer used, it is *still* a permanent factor, and therefore is land, although now submarginal. It should be noted that the "permanence" is relevant to present considerations of human action. A piece of land might give forth a permanent marginal (physical) product, without necessity of maintenance, and suddenly a volcano might erupt or a hurricane strike in the area, and the permanence could be destroyed. Such conceivable natural events, however, are not *ex ante* relevant to human action, and therefore from the point of view of action this land is rightly considered as "permanent," until the natural changes occur.[18,19]

The concept of "land" as used throughout this book, then, is entirely different from the popular concept of land. Let us, in this section, distinguish between the two by calling the former *economic land* and the latter *geographic land.* The economic concept includes *all* nature-given sources of value: what is usually known as natural resources, land, water, and air in so far as they are not free goods. On the other hand, a large part of the value of what is generally considered "land"—i.e., that part that has to be maintained with the use of labor—is really a capital good.

That agricultural land is an example of the latter may surprise the reader who is likely to think of it as permanently productive. This is completely wrong; the marginal physical productivity of (geographic) land varies greatly in accordance with the amount of labor that is devoted to maintaining or improving the soil, as against such use or nonuse of the soil as leads to erosion and a lower MPP. The basic soil (and here we are referring to the soil that would remain *now* if maintenance were suspended, *not* to the soil as it was in the dim past before cultivation) is the *land element,* while the final product—which is popularly known as agricultural land—is usually a capital good containing this land element.

And Van Sickle and Rogge say about the soil:

> Land, as the top 12 to 18 inches from which grains, vegetables, grasses, and trees draw almost their entire nourishment, is highly destructible. Top soil can be washed or blown away (eroded), or its organic and mineral content can be dissolved and drawn down out of reach of plant life (leached) in a relatively few years, unless great care is exercised in its use. It can also be rebuilt by careful husbandry. Hence it can be said of all soils . . . that their maintenance requires saving.[20]

The indestructibility of land is much more clearly exemplified in what is commonly called "urban land." For land in urban areas (and this includes suburban land, land for factories, etc.) clearly evinces one of its most fundamentally indestructible features: *its physical space*—its part of the surface of the earth. For the surface area of the earth is, except in rare cases, eternally fixed, as is the geographic position of each piece of geographic land on the surface. This eternally fixed, permanent, *positional* aspect of geographic land is called the *site* aspect of the land, or as Mises aptly puts it, "the land as standing room." Since it is permanent and nonreproducible, it very clearly comes under the category of economic land. The permanence, once again, refers to its physical spatial aspect; its site *values,* of course, are always subject to change.[21] Midtown Manhattan is on the same site—the same geographical location—now as it was in the 1600's, although the monetary values accruing to it have changed.

Suppose that a piece of currently unused land can be used for various agricultural purposes or for urban purposes. In that case, a choice will be made according to its alternative values as nonreplaceable economic land: between its discounted MVP as a result of the fertility of its basic soil and its discounted MVP as an urban site. And if a decision must be made whether land *now* used in agriculture and being maintained for that purpose should remain in agriculture or be used as a site for building, the principles of choice are the same. The marginal value return to the agricultural or urban land is broken down by the owner of the land—the "landlord"—into the interest return on the capital maintenance and improvement and the discounted marginal value return to the basic economic land.

"Basic land" (or "ground land") in this treatise refers to the *soil without maintenance,* in the case of agriculture, or the *pure site without depreciating superstructure,* in the case of urban land. The basic land, therefore, whether it be soil or site, earns for its owner an ultimate unit price, or rent, equaling its DMVP. Working on this basic land, labor and investment create a finished capital good. This capital good, like all capital goods, also earns unit rents equal to its DMVP. However, this earning is broken down (and relevantly so in the *current* market, not as an historical exercise) into basic land rent and interest return on the capital invested (as well, of course, as returns to labor that works on the basic land, i.e., labor's wage or "rent-price," equaling its DMVP). This capital-good land we have variously termed "geographic land," "land in the popular sense," "final land," "finished land." When we speak simply of "land," on the other hand, we shall always be referring to the true economic land—the currently nature-given factor.

5. *Capitalization and Rent*

The subject of "rent" is one of the most confused in the entire economic literature. We must, therefore, reiterate the meaning of rent as set forth above. We are using "rent" *to mean the unit price of the services of any good.* It is important to banish any preconceptions that apply the concept of rent to land only. Perhaps the best guide is to keep in mind the well-known practice of "renting out." Rent, then, is the same as *hire:* it is the sale and purchase of the *unit services* of any good.[22] It therefore applies as well to prices of labor services (called "wages") as it does to land or to any other factor. The rent concept applies to all goods, whether durable or nondurable. In the case of a completely nondurable good, which vanishes fully when first used, its "unit" of service is simply identical in size with the "whole" good itself. In regard to a durable good, of course, the rent concept is more interesting, since the price of the unit service is distinguishable from the price of the "good as a whole." So far, in this work, we have been assuming that no durable producers' goods are ever bought outright, that only their *unit services* are exchanged on the market. Therefore, our entire discussion of pricing has dealt with rental pricing. It is obvious that *the rents are the fundamental prices.* The marginal utility analysis has taught us that men value goods in *units* and not as wholes; the *unit price* (or "rent") is, then, the fundamental price on the market.

In chapter 4 we analyzed rental pricing and the price of the "good as a whole" for durable consumers' goods. The principle is precisely the same for producers' goods. The rental value of the unit service is the basic one, the one ultimately determined on the market by individual utility scales. The price of the "whole good," also known as *the capital value of the good,* is equal to the sum of the expected future rents discounted by what we then vaguely called a time-preference factor and which we now know is the *rate of interest.* The capital value, or price of the good as a whole, then, is completely dependent on the rental prices of the good, its physical durability, and the rate of interest.[23] Obviously, the concept of "capital value" of a good has meaning only when that good is durable and does not vanish instantly upon use. If it did vanish, then there would only be pure rent, without separate valuations for the good as a whole. When we use the term "good as a whole," we are not referring to the aggregate supply of the whole good in the economy. We are referring, e.g., not to the total supply of housing of a certain type, but to *one* house, which can be rented out over a period of time. We are dealing with *units of "whole goods,"* and these units, being durable, are necessarily larger than their constituent unit services, which can be rented out over a period of time.

The principle of the determination of "capital values," i.e., prices of "whole goods," is known as *capitalization,* or the capitalizing of rents. This principle applies to *all* goods, not simply capital goods, and we must not be misled by similarity of terminology. Thus, capitalization applies to durable consumers' goods, such as houses, TV sets, etc. It also applies to all factors of production, including basic land. The rental price, or rent, of a factor of production is equal, as we have seen, to its discounted marginal value product. *The capital value of a "whole factor" will be equal to the sum of its future rents, or the sum of its DMVP's.*[24] This capital value will be the price for which the "whole good" will exchange on the market. It is at this capital value that a unit of a "whole good" such as a house, a piano, a machine, an acre of land, etc., will sell on the market. There is clearly no sense to capitalization if there is no market, or price, for the "whole good." The capital value is the appraised value set by the market on the basis of rents, durability, and the interest rate.

The process of capitalization can encompass many units of a "whole good," as well as one unit. Let us consider the example of chapter 4, section 7, and generalize from it to apply, not only to houses, but to all durable producers' goods. The good is a ten-year good; expected future rents are 10 gold ounces per year (determined by consumer utilities for consumers' goods, or by MVP's for producers' goods). The rate of interest is 10% per annum. The present capital value of this good is 59.4 gold ounces. But this "whole good" is itself a unit of a larger supply; one of many houses, machines, plants, etc. At any rate, since all units of a good have equal value, the capital value of two such houses, or two such machines, etc., added together equals precisely twice the amount of one, or 118.8 ounces. Since we are adding rents or DMVP's in money terms, we may keep adding them to determine capital values of larger aggregates of durable goods. As a matter of fact, in adding capital values, *we do not need to confine ourselves to the same good.* All we need do is to add the capital values in whatever bundle of durable goods we are interested in appraising. Thus, suppose a firm, Jones Construction Company, wishes to sell all its assets on the market. These assets, necessarily durable, consist of the following:

3 machines. Each machine has a capital value (based on the sum of the DMVP's) of 10 ounces. Therefore, total capital value is *30 ounces.*

1 building, with a capital value of *40 ounces.*
5 acres of land. Each acre has a capital value of 10 ounces. Total is *40 ounces.*
Total capital value of these assets: *110 ounces.*

But we must always remember, in adding capital values, that these are relevant only in so far as they are expressed in market price or potential market price. Many writers have fallen into the trap of assuming that they can, in a similar way, add up the entire capital value of the nation or world and arrive at a meaningful figure. Estimates of National Capital or World Capital, however, are completely meaningless. The world, or country, cannot sell all its capital on the market. Therefore, such statistical exercises are pointless. They are without possible reference to the very goal of capitalization: correct estimation of potential market price.

As we have indicated, capitalization applies to *all* factors of production, or rather, to all factors where there are markets for the whole goods that embody them. We may call these markets *capital markets.* They are the markets for exchange of ownership, total or partial, of durable producers' goods. Let us take the case of capital goods. The rent of a capital good is equal to its DMVP. The capitalized value of the capital good is the sum of the future DMVP's, or the discounted sum of the future MVP's. This is the *present* value of the good, and this is what the good will sell for on the capital market.

The process of capitalization, because it permeates all sectors of the economy, and because it is flexible enough to include different types of assets—such as the total capital assets of a firm—is a very important one in the economy. Prices of shares of the ownership of this capital will be set at their proportionate fraction of the total capital value of the assets. In this way, given the *MVP's, durability,* and the *rate of interest,* all the prices on the capital market are determined, and these will be the prices in the ERE. This is the way in which the prices of individual capital goods (machines, buildings, etc.) will be set on the market, and this is the way in which these values will be summed up to set the price of a bundle of capital assets, similar and dissimilar. Share prices on the stock market will be set according to the proportion that they bear to the capitalized value of the firm's total assets.

We have stated that *all* factors that can be bought and sold as "whole goods" on the market are capitalized. This includes capital goods, ground land, and durable consumers' goods. It is clear that capital goods and durable consumers' goods can be and are capitalized. But what of ground land? How can this be capitalized?

We have seen in detail above that the ultimate earnings of factors go to the owners of labor and of ground land and, as interest, to capitalists. If land can be capitalized, does this not mean that land and capital goods are "really the same thing" after all? The answer to the latter question is No.[25] It is still emphatically true that the earnings of basic land factors are ultimate and irreducible, as are labor earnings, while capital goods have to be constantly produced and reproduced, and therefore their earnings are always reducible to the earnings of ground land, labor, and time.

Basic land can be capitalized for one simple reason: it can be bought and sold "as a whole" on the market. (This cannot be done for labor, except under a system of slavery, which, of course, cannot occur on the purely free market.) Since this can be and is being done, the problem arises how the prices in these exchanges are determined. These prices are the capital values of ground land.

A major characteristic of land as compared to capital goods is that its series of future rents is generally *infinite,* since, whether as basic soil or site, it is physically indestructible. In the ERE, the series of future rents will, of course, always be the same. The very fact that any land is ever bought and sold, by the way, is a demonstration of the universality of time preference. If there were no time preference for the present, then an infinite series of future rents could never be capitalized. A piece of land would have to have an infinite present price and therefore could never be sold. The fact that lands *do* have prices is an indication that there is always a time preference and that future rents are discounted to reduce to a present value.

As in the case of any other good, the capital value of land is equal to the sum of its discounted future rents. For example, it can be demonstrated mathematically that if we have a constant rent expected to be earned in perpetuity, the capital value of the asset will equal the annual rent divided by the rate of interest.[26] Now it is obvious that on such land, the investor annually obtains the market rate of interest. If, in other words, annual rents will be 20, and the rate of interest is 5%, the asset will sell for 20/.05, or 1,000. The investor who purchases the asset for 1,000 ounces will earn 20 ounces a year from it, or 5%, the market rate of interest.

Ground land, then, is "capitalized" just as are capital goods, shares in capital-owning firms, and durable consumers' goods. All these owners will tend to receive the same rate of interest return, and all *will* receive the same rate of return in the ERE. In short, all owned assets will be capitalized. In the ERE, of course, the capital values of all assets will remain constant; they will also be equal to the discounted sum of the MVP's of their unit rents.

Above, we saw that a key distinction between land and capital goods is that the owners of the former sell future goods for present money, whereas the owners of the latter *advance* present money, buy future goods, and later sell their product when it is less distantly future. This is still true. But then we must ask the question: How does the landowner come to own this land? The answer is (excepting his or his ancestors' finding unused land and putting it to use) that he must have bought it from someone else. If he did so, then, in the ERE, he must have bought it *at its capitalized value*. If he buys the piece of land at a price of 1,000 ounces, and receives 20 ounces per annum in rent, then he earns *interest,* and *only* interest. He sells future goods (land service) in the production process, but *he too first bought the whole land with money*. Therefore, he too is a "capitalist-investor" earning interest.

"Pure rent," i.e., rent that is *not* simply a return on previous investment and is therefore not capitalized, *seems,* therefore, to be earned only by those who have *found* unused land themselves (or inherited it from the finders). But even *they* do not earn pure rent. Suppose that a man finds land, unowned and worth zero, and then fences it, etc., until it is now able to yield a perpetual rental of 20 ounces per annum. Could we not say that *he* earns pure rent, since he did not buy the land, capitalized, from someone else? But this would overlook one of the most important features of economic life: *implicit earnings.* Even if this man did not buy the land, the land is *now* worth a certain capital value, the one it *could obtain* on the market. This capital value is, say, 1,000. Therefore, the man could sell the land for 1,000 at any time. *His forgone opportunity cost of owning the land and renting out its services is sale of the land for 1,000 ounces.* It is true that he earns 20 ounces per year, but this is only at the sacrifice of not selling the whole land for 1,000 ounces. His land, therefore, is really as much capitalized as land that has been bought on the market.

We must therefore conclude that *no one* receives pure rent except laborers in the form of wages, that the *only* incomes in the productive ERE economy are *wages* (the term for the prices and incomes of labor factors) and *interest.* But there is still a crucial distinction between land and capital goods. For we see that a fundamental, irreducible element is the *capital value of land.* The capital value of capital goods still reduces to wages and the capital value of land. In a *changing* economy, there is another source of income: *increases in the capital value of ground land.* Typical was the man who found unused land and then sold its services. Originally, the capital value of the land was zero; it was worthless. Now the land has become valuable because it earns rents. As a result, the capital value has risen to 1,000 ounces. His income, or gain, consisted of the *rise* of 1,000 ounces in capital value. This, of course, cannot take place in the ERE. In the ERE, all capital values must remain constant; here, we see that a source of monetary gain is a *rise* in the capital value of land, a rise resulting from increases in expected rental yields of land.[27] If the economy becomes an ERE after this particular change from 0 to 1,000, then this income was a "one-shot" affair, rather than a continuing and recurring item. The capital value of the land rose from 0 to 1,000, and the owner can reap this income at any time. However, after this has been reaped once, it is never reaped again. If he sells the land for 1,000, the next buyer receives no gain from the increase in capital value; he receives only market interest. Only interest and wages accrue continuously. As long as the ERE continues, there will be no further gains or losses in capital value.[28]

6. *The Depletion of Natural Resources*

One category has been purposely omitted so far from the discussion of land factors. At first, we defined land as the *original, nature-given factor*. Then we said that land which had been improved by human hands but which is now permanently given must also be considered as *land*. Land, then, became the catallactically permanent, nonreproducible resource, while capital goods are those that are nonpermanent and therefore must be produced again in order to be replaced. But there is one type of resource that is nonreplaceable but also nonpermanent: the natural resource that is being depleted, such as a copper or a diamond mine. Here the factor is definitely original and nature-given; it cannot be produced by man. On the other hand, it is not permanent, but subject to *depletion* because any use of it leaves an absolutely smaller amount for use in the future. It is original, but nonpermanent. Shall it be classed as land or as a capital good?

The crucial test of our classificatory procedure is to ask: Must labor and land factors work in order to reproduce the good? In the case of permanent factors this is not necessary, since they do not wear out. But in this case, we must answer in the negative also, for these goods, though nonpermanent, *cannot* be reproduced by man despite their depletion. Therefore, the natural resource comes as a special division under the "land" category.[29]

Table 15, adapted from one by Professor Hayek, reveals our classification of various resources as either land or capital goods:[30]

TABLE 15

RESOURCES	PERMANENT	NONPERMANENT (CONSUMABLE)
Original (nonproducible)	Land	Land
Produced (producible)	Land	Capital Goods

Hayek criticizes the criterion of *reproducibility* for classifying a capital good. He declares: "The point that is relevant . . . is not that certain existing resources *can* be replaced by others which are in some technological sense similar to them, but that they *have* to be replaced by something, whether similar or not, if the income stream is not to decline." [31] But this is confusing *value* with *physical* considerations. We are attempting to classify *physical* goods here, not to discuss their possible values, which will fluctuate continually. The point is that the resources subject to depletion *cannot* be replaced, much as the owner would like to do so. They therefore earn a *net rent*. Hayek also raises the question whether a stream is "land" if a new stream can be created by collecting rain water. Here again, Hayek misconceives the issue as one of maintaining a "constant income stream" instead of classifying a physical concrete good. The stream is land because it does not *need* to be physically replaced. It is obvious that Hayek's criticism is valid against Kaldor's definition. Kaldor defined capital as a reproducible resource which it is *economically* profitable to produce. In that case, obsolete machines would no longer be capital goods. (Would they be "land"?) The definition should be: *physically* reproducible resources. Hayek's criticism that then the possibility of growing artificial fruit, etc., would make all land "capital" again misconceives the problem, which is one of the physical *need and possibility* of reproducing the agent. Since the basic *land—not* its fruit—needs no reproduction, it is excluded from the capital-good category.

The fact that the natural resources *cannot* be reproduced means that they earn a *net rent* and that their rent is not absorbed by land and labor factors that go into their production. Of course, from the net rents they earn the usual interest rate of the society for their owners, interest earnings being related to their capital value. Increases in capital values of natural resources go ultimately to the resource-owner himself and are not absorbed in gains by other land and labor factors.

There is no problem in capitalizing a resource that is subject to depletion, since, as we have seen, capitalization can take place for either a finite or an infinite series of future rental incomes.

There is, however, one striking problem that pervades any analysis of the resource subject to depletion and that distinguishes it from all other types of goods. This is the fact that there can be *no* use for such a resource in an evenly rotating economy. For the basis of the ERE is that all economic quantities continue indefinitely in an endless round. But this cannot happen in the case of a resource that is subject to depletion, for whenever it is used, the total stock of that good in the economy decreases. The situation at the next moment, then, cannot be the same as before. This is but one example of the insuperable difficulties encountered whenever the ERE is used, not as an auxiliary construction in analysis, but as some sort of ideal that the free economy must be forced to emulate.

There can be a reserve demand for a depletable resource, just as there is speculative reserve demand for any other stock of goods on the market. This speculation is not simple wickedness, however; it has a definite function, namely, that of allocating the scarce depletable resource to those uses *at those times* when consumer demand for them will be greatest. The speculator, waiting to use the resources until a future date, benefits consumers by shifting their use to a time when they will be more in demand than at present. As in the case of ground land, the permanent resource belongs to the first finder and first user, and often some of these initial capital gains are absorbed by interest on the capital originally invested in the business of resource-finding. The absorption can take place only in so far as the finding of new resources is a regular, continuing business. But this business, which by definition could not exist in the ERE, can never be completely regularized.

Minerals such as coal and oil are clearly prime examples of depletable resources. What about such natural resources as forests? A forest, although growing by natural processes, can be "produced" by man if measures are taken to maintain and grow more trees, etc. Therefore, forests would have to be classified as capital goods rather than depletable resources.

One of the frequent attacks on the behavior of the free market is based on the Georgist bugbear of natural resources held off the market for speculative purposes. We have dealt with this alleged problem above. Another, and diametrically opposite, attack is the common one that the free market wastes resources, especially depletable resources. Future generations are allegedly robbed by the greed of the present. Such reasoning would lead to the paradoxical conclusion that *none* of the resource be consumed at all. For whenever, at any time, a man consumes a depletable resource (here we use "consumes" in a broader sense to include "uses up" in production), he is leaving less of a stock for himself or his descendants to draw upon. It is a fact of life that *whenever* any amount of a depletable resource is used up, less is left for the future, and therefore *any* such consumption could just as well be called "robbery of the future," if one chooses to define robbery in such unusual terms.[32] Once we grant *any* amount of use to the depletable resource, we have to discard the robbery-of-the-future argument and accept the individual preferences of the market. There is then no more reason to assume that the market will use the resources too fast than to assume the opposite. The market will tend to use resources at precisely the rate that the consumers desire.[33]

Having developed, in Volume I, our basic analysis of the economics of the isolated individual, barter, and indirect exchange, we shall now proceed, in Volume II, to develop the analysis further by dealing with "dynamic" problems of a changing economy, particular types of factors, money and its value, and monopoly and competition, and discussing, in necessarily more summary fashion, the consequences of violent intervention in the free market.

APPENDIX A: MARGINAL PHYSICAL AND MARGINAL VALUE PRODUCT

For purposes of simplification, we have described *marginal value product* (MVP) as equal to *marginal physical product* (MPP) times *price.* Since we have seen that a factor must be used in the region of declining MPP, and since an increased supply of a factor leads to a fall in price, the conclusion of the analysis was that every factor works in an area where increased supply leads to a decline in MVP, and hence in DMVP. The assumption made in the first sentence, however, is not strictly correct.

Let us, then, find out what *is* the multiple of MPP that will yield an MVP. MVP is equal to an increase in revenue acquired from the addition of a unit, or lost from the loss of a unit, of a factor. MVP will then equal the difference in revenue from one position to another, i.e., the change in position resulting from an increase or decrease of a unit of a factor. Then, *MVP equals* R_2 *minus* R_1, where R is the gross revenue from the sale of a product, and a higher subscript signifies that *more* of a factor has been used in production. The *MPP* of this increase in a factor is $P_2 - P_1$, where P is the quantity of product produced, a higher subscript again meaning that more of a factor has been used.

So: $$\text{MVP} = R_2 - R_1 \quad \text{by definition.}$$

$$\text{MPP} = P_2 - P_1 \quad \text{by definition.}$$

Revenue is acquired by sale of the product; therefore, for any given point on the demand curve, total revenue equals the quantity produced and sold, multiplied by the price of the product.

Therefore, $R = P \cdot p$, where p is the price of the product.

So: $$R_2 = P_2 \cdot p_2$$

$$R_1 = P_1 \cdot p_1$$

Now, since the factors are economic goods, any increase in the use of a factor, other factors remaining constant, must *increase* the quantity produced. It would obviously be pointless for an entrepreneur to employ more factors which would not increase the product. Therefore, $P_2 > P_1$.

On the other hand, the price of the product falls as the supply increases, so that:

$$p_2 < p_1$$

Now, we are trying to find out what multiplied by MPP yields MVP. This unknown will be equal to:

$$\frac{\text{MVP}}{\text{MPP}} = \frac{R_2 - R_1}{P_2 - P_1}$$

This may be called the *marginal revenue,* which is the change in revenue divided by the change in output.

It is obvious that this figure, which we may call *MR,* will not equal either p_2 or p_1, or any average of the two. Simple multiplication of the denominator by either of the p's or both will reveal that this does not amount to the numerator. What *is* the relation between *MR* and price?

A price is the *average revenue,* i.e., it equals the total revenue divided by the quantity produced and sold. In short,

$$p = \frac{R}{P}$$

But above, in the discussion of marginal and average product, we saw the mathematical relationship between "average" and "marginal," and this holds for revenue as well as for productivity: namely, that in the range where the average is increasing, marginal is greater than average; in the range where average is decreasing, marginal is less than average. But we have established early in this book that the demand curve—i.e., the price, or average revenue curve—is always *falling* as the quantity increases. Therefore, the marginal revenue curve is falling also and is always below average revenue, or price. Let us, however, cement the proof by demonstrating that, for any two positions, p_2 is greater than *MR*. Since p_2 is smaller than p_1, as price falls when supply increases, the proposition that *MR* is less than both prices will be proved.

First, we know that $p_2 < p_1$
which means that

$$\frac{R_2}{P_2} < \frac{R_1}{P_1}$$

Now, we may take point 1 as the starting point and then consider the change to point 2, so that:

$$\frac{R + \Delta R}{P + \Delta P} < \frac{R}{P}$$

thus translating into the same symbols we used in the productivity proof above.

Now this means that

$$\frac{R}{P} - \frac{R + \Delta R}{P + \Delta P} > 0$$

Combining the two fractions, and then multiplying across, we get

$$R\Delta P - P\Delta R > 0$$

Or

$$R\Delta P > P\Delta R$$

So that

$$\frac{R}{P} > \frac{\Delta R}{\Delta P}$$

(We have here proved that MR is less than p_1, the higher of the two prices.)

Now this means that there is some unknown, constant positive *fraction* $1/k$ which, multiplied by the larger, will yield the smaller ratio (MR) in the last inequality. Thus

$$\frac{R}{kP} = \frac{\Delta R}{\Delta P}$$

Now, by algebra,

$$\frac{\Delta R}{\Delta P} = \frac{R + \Delta R}{kP + \Delta P}$$

And since k is a positive number,

$$\frac{R + \Delta R}{P + \Delta P} > \frac{R + \Delta R}{kP + \Delta P}$$

But this establishes that

$$\frac{R + \Delta R}{P + \Delta P} > \frac{\Delta R}{\Delta P}$$

i.e., *that MR is less than p_2*. Q.E.D.

Hence, when we consider that, strictly, *MR*, and not price, should be multiplied by MPP to arrive at MVP, we find that our conclusion—that production always takes place in the zone of a falling MVP curve—is *strengthened* rather than weakened. MVP falls even more rapidly in relation to MPP than we had been supposing. Furthermore, our analysis is not greatly modified, because no new basic determinants—beyond MPP and prices set by the consumer demand curve—have been introduced in our corrective analysis. In view of all this, we may continue to treat MVP as equaling MPP times price as a legitimate, simplified approximation to the actual result.[34]

APPENDIX B: PROFESSOR ROLPH AND THE DISCOUNTED MARGINAL PRODUCTIVITY THEORY

Of current schools of economic thought, the most fashionable have been the Econometric, the Keynesian, the Institutionalist, and the Neo-Classic. "Neo-Classic" refers to the pattern set by the major economists of the late nineteenth century. The dominant neoclassical strain at present is to be found in the system of Professor Frank Knight, of which the most characteristic feature is an attack on the whole concept of time preference. Denying time preference, and basing interest return solely on an alleged "productivity" of capital, the Knightians attack the doctrine of the *discounted* MVP and instead advocate a pure MVP theory. The clearest exposition of this approach is to be found in an article by a follower of Knight's, Professor Earl Rolph.[35]

Rolph defines "product" as any *immediate* results of "present valuable activities." These include work on goods that will be consumed only in the future. Thus, "workmen and equipment beginning the construction of a building may have only a few stakes in the ground to show for their work the first day, but this and not the completed structure is their immediate product. Thus, the doctrine that a factor receives the value of its marginal product refers to this immediate product. The simultaneity of production and product does not require any simplifying assumptions. It is a direct appeal to the obvious. Every activity has its immediate results."

Obviously, no one denies that people work on goods and move capital a little further along. But is the immediate result of this a *product* in any meaningful sense? It should be clear that the product is the end product—the good sold to the consumer. The whole purpose of the production system is to lead to final consumption. All the intermediate purchases are based on the expectation of final purchase by the consumer and would not take place otherwise. Every activity may have its immediate "results," but they are not results that would command any monetary income from anyone if the owners of the factors themselves were joint owners of all they produced until the final consumption stage. In that case, it would be obvious that they do not get paid immediately; hence, their product is not immediate. The only reason that they *are* paid immediately (and even here there is not strict immediacy) on the market is that capitalists *advance* present goods in exchange for those *future* goods for which they expect a premium, or interest return. Thus, the owners of the factors are paid the *discounted* value of their marginal product.

The Knight-Rolph approach, in addition, is a retreat to a real-cost theory of value. It assumes that present efforts will somehow always bring present results. But when? In "present valuable activities." But how do these activities *become* valuable? Only if their *future product* is sold, as expected, to consumers. Suppose, however, that people work for years on a certain good and are paid by capitalists, and then the final product is not bought by consumers. The capitalists absorb monetary losses. Where was the immediate payment according to marginal product? The payment was only an investment in future goods by capitalists.

Rolph then turns to another allegedly heinous error of the discount approach, namely, the "doctrine of *nonco-ordination of factors.*" This means that some factors, in their payment, receive the *discounted* value of their product and some do not. Rolph, however, is laboring under a misapprehension; there is no assumption of nonco-ordination in any sound discounting theory. As we have stated above, *all* factors —labor, land, and capital goods—receive their discounted marginal value product. The difference in regard to the owners of capital goods is that, in the ultimate analysis, they do not receive any *independent* payment, since capital goods are resolved into the factors that produced them, ultimately land and labor factors, and to interest for the time involved in the advance of payment by the capitalists.[36] Rolph believes that nonco-ordination is involved because owners of land and labor factors "receive a discounted share," and capital "receives an undiscounted share." But this is a faulty way of stating the conclusion. Owners of land and labor factors receive a discounted share, but owners of capital (money capital) receive *the discount.*

The remainder of Rolph's article is largely devoted to an attempt to prove that no time lag is involved in payments to owners of factors. Rolph assumes the existence of "production centers" within every firm, which, broken down into virtually instantaneous steps, produce and then implicitly receive payment instantaneously. This tortured and unreal construction misses the entire point. Even if there were atomized "production centers," the point is that some person or persons will have to make advances of present money along the route, in whatever order, until the final product is sold to the consumers. Let Rolph picture a production system, atomized or integrated as the case may be, with no one making the advances of present goods (money capital) that he denies exist. And as the laborers and landowners work on the intermediate products for years without pay, until the finished product is ready for the consumer, let Rolph exhort them not to worry, since they have been implicitly paid simultaneously as they worked. For this is the logical implication of the Knight-Rolph position.[87]

Notes

NOTES TO CHAPTER 1

1. For further reading on this topic, the best source is the epochal work of Ludwig von Mises, *Human Action* (New Haven: Yale University Press, 1949), pp. 1–143, and *passim.*
2. Cf. *ibid.,* p. 11; F. A. Hayek, "The Facts of the Social Sciences," *Individualism and Economic Order* (Chicago: University of Chicago Press, 1948), pp. 57–76; Hayek, *The Counter-Revolution of Science* (Glencoe, Ill.: The Free Press, 1952), pp. 25–35; and Edith T. Penrose, "Biological Analogies in the Theory of the Firm," *American Economic Review,* December, 1952, pp. 804–19 especially pp. 818–19.
3. Cf. Aristotle, *Ethica Nicomachea,* Bk. I, especially ch. vii.
4. This chapter consists solely of a development of the logical implications of the existence of human action. Future chapters—the further parts of the structure—are developed with the help of a very small number of subsidiary assumptions. Cf. Appendix below and Murray N. Rothbard, "Praxeology: Reply to Mr. Schuller," *American Economic Review,* December, 1951, pp. 943–46; and "In Defense of 'Extreme Apriorism,'" *Southern Economic Journal,* January, 1957, pp. 314–20.
5. There is no need to enter here into the difficult problem of animal behavior, from the lower organisms to the higher primates, which might be considered as on a borderline between purely reflexive and motivated behavior. At any rate, men can *understand* (as distinguished from merely observe) such behavior only in so far as they can impute to the animals motives that they can understand.
6. To say that only individuals act is not to deny that they are influenced in their desires and actions by the acts of other individuals, who might be fellow members of various societies or groups. We do not at all assume, as some critics of economics have charged, that individuals are "atoms" isolated from one another.
7. Cf. F. A. Hayek, *The Counter-Revolution of Science,* p. 34. Also cf. Mises, *Human Action,* p. 42.
8. Cf. Talcott Parsons, *The Structure of Social Action* (Glencoe, Ill.: The Free Press, 1949), pp. 44 ff.
9. Some writers have unfoundedly believed that praxeology and economics assume that all action is cool, calculating, and deliberate.
10. The common distinction between "economic goods" and "free goods" (such as air) is erroneous. As explained above, air is not a means, but a general condition of human welfare, and is not the object of action.
11. The term "land" is likely to be misleading in this connection because it is not used in the popular sense of the word. It includes such *natural* resources as water, oil, and minerals.

12. We shall not deal at this point with the complications involved in the original learning of any recipe by the actor, which is the object of human action.
13. Cf. Carl Menger, *Principles of Economics* (Glencoe, Ill.: The Free Press, 1950), pp. 51–67.
14. For each actor, then, the period of production is equivalent to his *waiting time*—the time that he must expect to wait for his end after the commencement of his action.
15. *Time preference* may be called the preference for *present satisfaction* over *future satisfaction* or *present good* over *future good,* provided it is remembered that it is the *same* satisfaction (or "good") that is being compared over the periods of time. Thus, a common type of objection to the assertion of universal time preference is that, in the winter time, a man will prefer the delivery of ice the next summer (future) to delivery of ice in the present. This, however, confuses the concept "good" with the material properties of a thing, whereas it actually refers to subjective satisfactions. Since ice-in-the-summer provides different (and greater) satisfactions than ice-in-the-winter, they are *not* the same, but *different* goods. In this case, it is different satisfactions that are being compared, despite the fact that the *physical* property of the thing may be the same.
16 It has become the custom to designate consumer goods with a longer duration of serviceableness as *durable goods,* and those of shorter duration as *nondurable goods.* Obviously, however, there are innumerable degrees of durability, and such a separation can only be unscientific and arbitrary.
17. Accordingly, the numbers by which ends are ranked on value scales are *ordinal,* not *cardinal,* numbers. Ordinal numbers are only ranked; they cannot be subject to the processes of measurement. Thus, in the above example, all we can say is that going to a concert is valued more than playing bridge, and either of these more than watching the game. We cannot say that going to a concert is valued "twice as much" as watching the game; the numbers 2 and 4 cannot be subject to processes of addition, multiplication, etc.
18. An example of suffering a loss as a result of an erroneous action would be going to the concert and finding that it was not at all enjoyable. The actor then realizes that he would have been much happier continuing to watch the game or playing bridge.
19. A large part of this book is occupied with the problem of how this process of value imputation can be accomplished in a modern, complex economy.
20. This is the solution of a problem that plagued writers in the economic field for many years: the source of the value of goods.
21. Cf. Ludwig von Mises, *The Theory of Money and Credit* (New Haven: Yale University Press, 1953), p. 46.
22. Also cf. T. N. Carver, *The Distribution of Wealth* (New York: Macmillan & Co., 1904), pp. 4–12. See below for a further discussion of the influences on man's valuation of specific units resulting from the size of the available stock.

23. This would not be true only if the "good" were not a means, but a general condition of human welfare, in which case one less unit of supply would make no difference for human action. But in that case it would not be a *good,* subject to the economizing of human action.
24. On the whole subject of marginal utility, *see* Eugen Von Böhm-Bawerk, *The Positive Theory of Capital* (New York: G. E. Stechert & Co., 1930), pp. 138–65, especially pp. 146–55.
25. For algebraic proof, *see* George J. Stigler, *The Theory of Price* (New York: Macmillan & Co., 1946), pp. 44–45.
26. For further reading on this subject, *see* Böhm-Bawerk, *op. cit.,* pp. 170–88; and F. A. Hayek, *The Counter-Revolution of Science,* pp. 32–33.
27. This is the first proposition in this chapter that has not been deduced from the axiom of action. It is a subsidiary assumption, based on empirical observation of actual human behavior. It is not deducible from human action because its contrary is conceivable, although not generally existing. On the other hand, the assumptions above of quantitative relations of cause and effect were logically implicit in the action axiom, since knowledge of definite cause-and-effect relations is necessary to any decision to act.
28. Cf. Mises, *Human Action,* p. 131.
29. *Ibid.,* p. 132.
30. Leisure is the amount of time not spent in labor, and play may be considered as one of the forms that leisure may take in yielding satisfaction. On labor and play, cf. Frank A. Fetter, *Economic Principles* (New York: The Century Co., 1915), pp. 171–77, 191, 197–206.
31. Cf. L. Albert Hahn, *Common Sense Economics* (New York: Abelard-Schuman Co., 1956), pp. 1 ff.
32. In this sense, the stick might be called a "labor-saving device," although the terminology is misleading. It is "labor-saving" only to the extent that the actor chooses to take the increased productivity in the form of leisure.
33. It is necessary to emphasize that independent acts of saving are necessary for replacement of goods, since many writers (e.g., J. B. Clark, Frank H. Knight) tend to assume that, once produced, capital, in some mystical way, reproduces itself without further need for acts of saving.
34. Cf. Frederic Benham, *Economics* (New York: Pitman Publishing Co., 1941), p. 162.
35. Böhm-Bawerk, *op. cit.,* pp. 95–96. *Also see* Mises, *Human Action,* pp. 480–90, and pp. 476–514.
36. This uncertainty is a subjective feeling ("hunch" or estimate) and cannot be measured in any way. The efforts of many popular writers to apply mathematical "probability theory" to the uncertainty of future historical events are completely vain. Cf. Mises, *Human Action,* pp. 105–18.
37. That such a range of investment decisions enabling him to achieve greater future output must always be open to him is a fundamental truth derived from the assumption of human action. If they were not open to him, it would mean that man could not (or rather, believed that he could not) act to improve his lot, and therefore there would be no possi-

bility of action. Since we cannot even conceive of human existence without action, it follows that "investment opportunities" are always available.

38. On the "unused capacity" bogey, *see* Benham, *op. cit.*, pp. 147–49.
39. Cf. Böhm-Bawerk, *op. cit.*, pp. 238–44.
40. Plain saving is not to be confused with an earlier example, when Crusoe saved stocks of consumers' goods to be consumed while devoting his labor to the production of capital.
41. See note 15 above.
42. The period of production will be equal to the time difference between the act of saving and the act of future consumption, as in all other cases of investment.
43. See page 16 above.
44. Cf. G. J. Schuller, "Rejoinder," *American Economic Review*, March, 1951, p. 188. For a reply, *see* Murray N. Rothbard, "Toward a Reconstruction of Utility and Welfare Economics" in M. Sennholz, ed., *On Freedom and Free Enterprise*, Essays in Honor of Ludwig von Mises (Princeton, N. J.: D. Van Nostrand Co., 1956), p. 227. *Also see* Boris Ischboldin, "A Critique of Econometrics," *Review of Social Economy*, September, 1960, pp. 110–27; and Vladimir Niksa, "The Role of Quantitative Thinking in Modern Economic Theory," *Review of Social Economy*, September, 1959, pp. 151–73.
45. Cf. René Poirier, "Sur Logique" in André Lalande, *Vocabulaire technique et critique de la philosophie* (Paris: Presses Universitaires de France, 1951), pp. 574–75.

NOTES TO CHAPTER 2

1. For a discussion of the transformation from murder to slavery, cf. Franz Oppenheimer, *The State* (New York: Vanguard Press, 1914, reprinted 1928), pp. 55–70 and *passim*.
2. It is true that man, being what he is, cannot absolutely guarantee lifelong service to another under a voluntary arrangement. Thus, Jackson, at present, might agree to labor under Crusoe's direction for life, in return for food, clothing, etc., but he cannot guarantee that he will not change his mind at some point in the future and decide to leave. In this sense, a man's own person and will is "inalienable," i.e., cannot be given up to someone else for any future period.
3. Such an arrangement is *not* a *guarantee* of "security" of provisions, since no one can guarantee a steady supply of such goods. It simply means that A *believes* that B is better able to furnish a supply of these goods than he is himself.
4. Cf. Mises, *Human Action*, pp. 196–99, and, for a comparison of slaves and animals, *ibid.*, pp. 624–30.
5. There is, of course, no judgment at this point concerning whether the establishment of a society or such a society is a good, bad, or indifferent development.

6. This system has sometimes been called "compulsory co-operation," but we prefer to restrict the term "co-operation" to the result of voluntary choices.
7. For an analysis of exchange, *see* Menger, *op. cit.*, pp. 175–90. For a vivid discussion of exchange, *see* Frédéric Bastiat, *Harmonies of Political Economy* (Santa Ana, Calif.: The Register Publishing Co., 1944), I, 96–130.
8. Strictly, the law of marginal utility is also applicable to the case where the supply is only one unit, and we can say that, in the example above, exchange will take place if, for A, the marginal utility of good *Y* is greater than the marginal utility of good *X*, and vice versa for B.
9. On use-value and exchange-value, *see* Menger, *op. cit.*, pp. 226–35.
10. Analytically, receiving a factor from someone as a gift simply pushes the problem back another stage. At some point, the actor must have appropriated it from the realm of unused factors, as Crusoe appropriated the unused land on the island.
11. On self-ownership and the acquisition of property, cf. the classic discussion of John Locke, "An Essay Concerning the True Original Extent and End of Civil Government, Second Treatise" in Ernest Barker, ed., *Social Contract* (London: Oxford University Press, 1948), pp. 15–30.
12. The problem of self-ownership is complicated by the question of *children*. Children cannot be considered self-owners, because they are not yet in possession of the powers of reason necessary to direct their actions. The fact that children are under the hegemonic authority of their parents until they are old enough to become self-owning beings is therefore not contrary to our assumption of a purely free market. Since children are not capable of self-ownership, authority over them will rest in some individuals; on an unhampered market, it would rest in their *producers*, the parents. On the other hand, the property of the parents in this unique case is not exclusive; the parents may not injure the children at will. Children, not long after birth, begin to acquire the powers of reasoning human beings and embody the potential development of full self-owners. Therefore the child will, on the free market, be defended from violent actions in the same way as an adult. On children, see *ibid.*, pp. 30–38.
13. For more on invasive and noninvasive acts in a free market, see section 13 below.
14. It is possible that Crusoe and Jackson, for the mutual fun of it, might pass fifty berries back and forth between them. This, however, would not be genuine exchange, but joint participation in an enjoyable consumers' good—a game or play.
15. Basically, class (*b*) is resolvable into differences in classes (*a*) and (*c*), which account for their production.
16. Mises, *Human Action*, pp. 157 ff. On the pervasiveness of variation, also cf. F. A. Harper, *Liberty, A Path to Its Recovery* (Irvington-on-Hudson, N. Y.: Foundation for Economic Education, 1949), pp. 65–77, 139–41.
17. Kenneth E. Boulding, *Economic Analysis* (1st ed., New York: Harper & Bros., 1941), p. 30; also *ibid.*, pp. 22–32.

18. Those critics of Adam Smith and other economists who accuse the latter of "assuming" that God or Nature directs the market process by an "invisible hand" for the benefit of all participants completely miss the mark. The fact that the market provides for the welfare of each individual participating in it is a *conclusion* based on scientific analysis, not an assumption upon which the analysis is based. The "invisible hand" was simply a metaphor used in commenting on this process and its results. Cf. William D. Grampp, "Adam Smith and the Economic Man," *Journal of Political Economy,* August, 1948, pp. 315–36, especially pp. 319–20.
19. See Mises, *Human Action,* pp. 157–58.
20. Such specialization of stages requires the adoption of *indirect exchange,* discussed in the following chapters.
21. Cf. Mises, *ibid.,* pp. 204–06, and Menger, *op. cit.,* pp. 192–94, 305–06.
22. Cf. Böhm-Bawerk, pp. 195–222. Also cf. Fetter, *op. cit.,* pp. 42–72; and Menger, *op. cit.,* pp. 191–97.
23. Of course, given other value scales, the final prices might be determinate at our point, or within a narrow range. Thus, if Smith's maximum buying price is 87, and Johnson's minimum selling price is 87, the price will be uniquely determined at 87.
24. Auction sales are examples of markets for one unit of a good with one seller and many buyers. Cf. Boulding, *op. cit.,* pp. 41–43.
25. It is possible that the equilibrium point will not be uniquely determined at one definite price. Thus, the pattern of supply and demand schedules might be as follows:

P	*S*	*D*
89	5	6
90	6	5

The inequality is the narrowest possible, but there is no one point of equality. In that case, if the units are further divisible, then the price will be set to clear the market at a point in between, say 89.5 barrels of fish per horse. If both goods being exchanged are indivisible further, however, such as cows against horses, then the equilibrium price will be either 89 or 90, and this will be the closest approach to equilibrium rather than equilibrium itself.

26. Cf. Benham, *op. cit.,* pp. 60–63.
27. The attention of some writers to the elasticity of supply stems from an erroneous approach to the entire analysis of utility, supply, and demand. They assume that it is possible to treat human action in terms of "infinitely small" differences, and therefore to apply the mathematically elegant concepts of the calculus, etc., to economic problems. Such a treatment is fallacious and misleading, however, since human action must treat all matters only in terms of discrete steps. If, for example, the utility of *X* is so little smaller than the utility of *Y* that it can be regarded as identical or negligibly different, then human action will treat them as such, i.e., as the same good. Because it is conceptually impossible to measure utility, even the drawing of continuous utility curves is

pernicious. In the supply and demand schedules, it is not harmful to draw continuous curves for the sake of clarity, but the mathematical concepts of continuity and the calculus are not applicable. As a result, the seemingly precise concept of "elasticity at a point" (percentage increase in demand divided by a "negligibly small" percentage decrease in price) is completely out of order. It is this mistaken substitution of mathematical elegance for the realities of human action that lends a seeming importance to the concept of "elasticity of supply," comparable to the concept of elasticity of demand.

28. On the total demand-stock analysis, *see* Philip H. Wicksteed, *The Common Sense of Political Economy and Selected Papers* (London: Routledge and Kegan Paul, 1933), I, 213–38; II, 493–526 and 784–88. *Also see* Boulding, *op. cit.*, pp. 51–80.
29. This situation is not likely to arise in the case of the *market equilibria* described above. Generally, a market tends quickly to "clear itself" by establishing its equilibrium price, after which a certain number of exchanges take place, leading toward what has been termed the *plain state of rest*—the condition after the various exchanges have taken place. These equilibrium market prices, however (as will be seen in later chapters), in turn tend to move toward certain long-run equilibria, in accordance with the demand schedule and the effect on the size of stock produced. The supply curve involved in this *final state of rest* involves the ultimate decisions in producing a commodity and differs from the market supply curve. In the movements toward this "final state," conditions, such as the demand curve, always change in the interim, thus setting a new final state as the goal of market prices. The final state is never reached. *See* Mises, *Human Action*, pp. 245 ff.
30. The *addition* of supply schedules is a simple process to conceive: if at a price X, the class (a) sellers will supply T tons of a good and the class (b) sellers will supply T' tons, the total market supply for that price is $T + T'$ tons. The same process applies to each hypothetical price.
31. Strictly, of course, costs of storage will have to be considered in their calculations.
32. On the importance of services, *see* Arthur Latham Perry, *Political Economy* (21st ed., New York: Charles Scribner's Sons, 1892), pp. 124–39.
33. This is not to deny, of course, that the existence of *several* violinists of different quality will affect the consumer's evaluations of each one.
34. If he has taken the property of another by means of such an agreement, he will, on the free market, have to return the property. Thus, if A has agreed to work for life for B in exchange for 10,000 grams of gold, he will have to return the proportionate amount of property if he terminates the arrangement and ceases the work.
35. In other words, he cannot make enforceable contracts binding his future personal actions. (On contract enforcement in an unhampered market, see section 13 below.) This applies also to *marriage contracts.* Since human self-ownership cannot be alienated, a man or a woman, on a free market, could not be compelled to continue in marriage if he or she no

longer desired to do so. This is regardless of any previous agreement. Thus, a marriage contract, like an individual labor contract, is, on an unhampered market, terminable at the will of *either one* of the parties.

36. In a credit transaction, it is not necessary for the present and the future goods exchanged to be the same commodity. Thus, a man can sell wheat now in exchange for a certain amount of corn at a future date. The example in the text, however, highlights the importance of time preference and is also more likely to occur in practice.
37. Léon Wolowski and Émile Levasseur, "Property," *Lalor's Cyclopedia of Political Science, etc.* (Chicago: M. B. Cary & Co., 1884), III, 392.
38. See the vivid discussion by Edmond About, *Handbook of Social Economy* (London: Strahan & Co., 1872), pp. 19–30. Even urban sites embody much past labor. Cf. Herbert B. Dorau and Albert G. Hinman, *Urban Land Economics* (New York: Macmillan & Co., 1928), pp. 205–13.
39. If a channel has to be a certain number of wave lengths in width in order to permit clear transmission, then the property would accrue to the first user, in terms of such width.
40. Professor Coase has demonstrated that Federal ownership of airwaves was arrogated, in the 1920's, not so much to alleviate a preceding "chaos," as to forestall this very acquisition of private property rights in air waves, which the courts were in the process of establishing according to common law principles. Ronald H. Coase, "The Federal Communications Commission," *The Journal of Law and Economics,* October, 1959, pp. 5, 30–32.
41. It is rapidly becoming evident that air lanes for planes *are* becoming scarce and, in a free society, would be owned by first users—thus obviating a great many plane crashes.
42. *Flowing* water should be owned in proportion to its rate of use by the first user—i.e., by the "appropriation" rather than the "riparian" method of ownership. However, the appropriator would then have absolute control over his property, might transfer his share, etc., something which cannot be done in those areas, e.g., states in the West, where an approach to appropriation ownership now predominates. *See* Murray N. Rothbard, "Concerning Water," *The Freeman,* March, 1956, pp. 61–64. Also see the excellent article by Professor Jerome W. Milliman, "Water Law and Private Decision-Making: A Critique," *The Journal of Law and Economics,* October, 1959, pp. 41–63; Milliman, "Commonality, the Price System, and Use of Water Supplies," *Southern Economic Journal,* April, 1956, pp. 426–37.
43. On Ingalls and his doctrines, *see* James J. Martin, *Men Against the State* (DeKalb, Ill.; Adrian Allen Associates, 1953), pp. 142–52, 220 ff., 246 ff. Also cf. Benjamin R. Tucker, *Instead of a Book* (2nd ed., New York: B. R. Tucker, 1897), pp. 299–357, for the views of Ingalls' most able disciple. Despite the underlying similarity and their many economic errors, the Ingalls-Tucker group launched some interesting and effective critiques of the Georgist position. These take on value in the light of the excessive kindness often accorded to Georgist doctrines by economists.

44. This is true *even* if the actor had previously agreed in a contract that he would pay damages. For this is still merely a promise; he has not implicitly seized someone else's property. The object of an enforcing agency in a free society is not to uphold promise-keeping by force, but to redress any invasions of person and property.
45. Sir Frederick Pollock thus describes original English contract law: "Money debts, it is true, were recoverable from an early time. But this was not because the debtor had promised to repay the loan; it was because the money was deemed still to belong to the creditor, as if the identical coins were merely in the debtor's custody. The creditor sued to recover money . . . in exactly the same form which he would have used to demand possession of land . . . and down to Blackstone's time the creditor was said to have a property in the debt—property which the debtor had granted him. Giving credit, in this way of thinking, is not reliance on the right to call thereafter for an act . . . to be performed by the debtor, but merely suspension of the immediate right to possess one's own particular money, as the owner of a house lot suspends his right to occupy it . . . The foundation of the plaintiff's right was not bargain or promise, but the unjust detention by the defendant of the plaintiff's money or goods." Sir Frederick Pollock, "Contract," *Encyclopaedia Britannica* (14th ed.; London, 1929), VI, 339–40.
46. "In Rome one could recover stolen goods, or damages for their loss, by what we should call a civil process, without in the least affecting the relation between the thief and the public by reason of the theft. Restitution first and punishment afterwards was the rule." Wordsworth Donisthorpe, *Law in A Free State* (London: Macmillan & Co., 1895), p. 135.
47. This reason for the unenforceability of a cartel agreement in a free society has no relation to any common-law hostility to agreements allegedly "in restraint of trade." However, it is very similar to the English common-law doctrine finally worked out in the *Mogul Steamship Case* (1892). *See* William L. Letwin, "The English Common Law Concerning Monopolies," *University of Chicago Law Review*, Spring, 1954, pp. 382 ff.
48. *Noise* is also an invasive act against another, a transmission of sound waves assaulting the eardrums of others. On "external diseconomies," the only good discussion by an economist is the excellent one in Mises, *Human Action*, pp. 650–53. For an appreciation of the distinction between judicial and administrative action in a free society, as well as a fine grasp of property rights and governmental enforcement, see the classic discussion of adulteration in Donisthorpe, *op. cit.*, pp. 132–58.
49. Similarly, *blackmail* would not be illegal in the free society. For blackmail is the receipt of money in exchange for the service of not publicizing certain information about the other person. No violence or threat of violence to person or property is involved.
50. Auberon Herbert, in A. Herbert and J. H. Levy, *Taxation and Anarchism* (London: The Personal Rights Assn., 1912), pp. 24, 36–39; and in "A Cabinet Minister's Vade Mecum" in Michael Goodwin, ed., *Nineteenth-Century Opinion* (London: Penguin Books, 1951), pp. 206–07.

NOTES TO CHAPTER 3

1. See, for example chapter 1 above, page 50.
2. For a vivid and accurate contrast between man's condition in a market society and that in a primitive society, *see* About, *op. cit.,* pp. 5–17.
3. For further analysis of this process of the emergence of common media, *see* Mises, *The Theory of Money and Credit,* pp. 30–33, and *Human Action,* pp. 402–04. *Also see* Menger, *op. cit.,* pp. 257–63. For an historical description, *see* J. Laurence Laughlin, *Money, Credit, and Prices* (Chicago: University of Chicago Press, 1931), I, 3–15, 28–31.
4. Cf. Adam Smith, *The Wealth of Nations* (New York: Modern Library, 1937), pp. 22–24; Menger, *op. cit.,* pp. 263–71; Laughlin, *op. cit.,* pp. 15–23, 38–43.
5. On the significance of money for civilized society, cf. Wicksteed, *op. cit.,* I, 140 ff.
6. Later sections will deal further with the receipt of money income in the production process. Here it must be noted that since the owner and seller of capital goods must pay for the land, labor, and capital goods in *their* production, in the last analysis the owner of capital receives income only as a holder of goods over a period of *time.*
7. The names of the units can be, and have been, anything conceivable, dependent on custom, language, etc. Such names as dollars, francs, marks, shekels, are examples. The "dollar" originated as the generally applied name of ounce weights of silver coined by the Count of Schlick in Bohemia. The Count, who lived in Joachim's valley (or Joachims*thal*) began coining ounces of silver in 1518, and their uniformity and fineness earned a reputation throughout Europe. They became known as Joachimsthalers, finally abbreviated to *thalers.* The name "dollar" is derived from "thaler." Cf. Charles A. Conant, *The Principles of Money and Banking* (New York: Harper & Bros., 1905), I, 135–40; Menger, *op. cit.,* p. 283.
8. Gold, for example, has been traded as money in the raw form of nuggets, as gold dust in sacks, or as jewelry and other ornaments. One interesting example of a money shape was the iron money of central Africa. Iron was a valuable commodity, in use as hoes. The money form was made to be divisible into two parts, easily shaped into hoes. *See* Laughlin, *op. cit.,* p. 40.
9. This is also true if the income is gradual and the expenditure is in discrete sums, or for any other pattern of money income and expenditures.
10. This section is limited to a discussion of expenditures on consumers' goods. A later section will discuss producers' expenditures on producers' goods. It will be seen, however, that even unwelcome losses from cash balances suffered by producers are purely the result of voluntary action that, in a later period, proved erroneous.
11. The assertion has also been made that a person who spends most or all of his income on food and clothing *must* also have an "unfavorable bal-

ance of trade," since his money expenditures *must* be at a certain minimum amount. However, if the man has spent all his cash balance, he can no longer continue to have an "unfavorable balance," regardless of what goods he buys or what his standard of living is.

12. Producers could also borrow the saved funds of others, but the whole process of lending and borrowing is omitted in this section in order to clarify the analysis. Loans will be analyzed in a later chapter.
13. It was partly confusion between the *total* action of the individual and his action as a businessman that led writers to extrapolate from the behavior of the businessman and conclude that "nations" are "better off" if "they" export more than "they" import.
14. The terms "nonexchangeable" (or "unexchangeable") and "exchangeable" goods are far superior to the terms "ideal" and "material." The latter classification errs on two counts, aside from failing to convey the essential difference between the two types of goods. In the first place, as has been stated above, many exchangeable goods are intangible services rather than tangible, "material" things. Secondly, many of the nonexchangeable goods valued by some persons would hardly be considered "ideal" by others, so that a less colored term is necessary.
15. The belief of the classical economists, notably John Stuart Mill, as well as their critics, that economics must postulate a mythical "economic man," who is interested only in acquiring money income, is thus a completely erroneous one.
16. Of course, the concrete result differs with the individual and with the *unit of time* selected for consideration. In terms of income per hour, the point at which labor stops may come fairly quickly; in terms of income per year, it may never come. Regardless of his money income per hour, in other words, he is likely to stop work after a certain number of hours worked, whereas he is likely to take a year off from work only if his annual income is substantial.

NOTES TO CHAPTER 4

1. The exceptions are direct exchanges that might be made between two goods on the basis of their hypothetical exchange ratios on the market. These exchanges, however, are relatively isolated and unimportant and depend on the money prices of the two goods.
2. Many writers interpret the "purchasing power of the monetary unit" as being some sort of "price level," a measurable entity consisting of some sort of average of "all goods combined." The major classical economists did not take this fallacious position: "When they speak of the value of money or of the level of prices without explicit qualification, they mean the array of prices, of both commodities and services, in all its particularity and without conscious implication of any kind of statistical average." Jacob Viner, *Studies in the Theory of International Trade* (New York: Harper & Bros., 1937), p. 314. Also cf. Joseph A. Schumpeter, *History of Economic Analysis* (New York: Oxford University Press, 1954), p. 1094.

3. The tabulations in the text are simplified for convenience and are not strictly correct. For suppose that the man had already paid 6 gold grains for 1 ounce of butter. When he decides on a purchase of another pound of butter, his ranking for *all* the units of money rise, since he now has a lower stock of money than he had before. Our tabulations, therefore, do not fully portray the rise in the marginal utility of money as money is spent. However, the correction *reinforces,* rather than modifies, our conclusion that the maximum demand-price falls as quantity increases, for we see that it will fall still further than we have depicted.
4. On market-supply schedules, cf. Friedrich von Wieser, *Social Economics* (London: George Allen & Unwin, 1927), pp. 179–84.
5. The reader is referred to the section on "Stock and the Total Demand to Hold" in chapter 2, pp. 118–23 above.
6. If there is no reservation-demand schedule on the part of the sellers, then the total demand to hold is *identical* with the regular demand schedule.
7. The proof that the two sets of curves always yield the same equilibrium price is as follows: Let, at any price, the quantity demanded = D, the quantity supplied = S, the quantity of existing stock = K, the quantity of reserved demand = R, and the total demand to hold = T. The following are always true, by definition:

$$S = K - R$$

$$T = D + R$$

Now, at the equilibrium price, where S and D intersect, S is obviously equal to D. But if $S = D$, then $T = K - R + R$, or $T = K$.
8. Of course, this equilibrium price might be a *zone* rather than a single price in those cases where there is a zone between the valuations of the marginal buyer and those of the marginal seller. See the analysis of one buyer and one seller in chapter 2, above, pp. 91–93. In such rare cases, where there generally must be very few buyers and very few sellers, there is a zone within which the market is cleared at any point, and there is room for "bargaining skill" to maneuver. In the extensive markets of the money economy, however, even one buyer and one seller are likely to have one determinate price or a very narrow zone between their maximum buying- and minimum selling-prices.
9. See chapter 2 above, pp. 112–17.
10. This and the analysis of chapter 2 refute the charge made by some writers that speculation is "self-justifying," that it distorts the effects of the underlying supply and demand factors, by tending to establish pseudoequilibrium prices on the market. The truth is the reverse; speculative errors in estimating underlying factors are self-correcting, and anticipation tends to establish the true equilibrium market-price more rapidly.
11. Compare this analysis with the analysis of direct exchange, chapter 2 above, p. 139.
12. See chapter 2 above, pp. 123–24.

13. We might, in some situations, make such comparisons as historians, using imprecise judgment. We cannot, however, do so as praxeologists or economists.
14. For more on these matters, *see* Rothbard, "Toward a Reconstruction, etc." *op. cit.*, pp. 224–43. *Also see* Mises, *Theory of Money and Credit*, pp. 38–47.
15. It is interesting that those who attempt to measure consumers' surplus explicitly rule out consideration of *all* goods or of any good that looms "large" in the consumers' budget. Such a course is convenient, but illogical, and glosses over fundamental difficulties in the analysis. It is, however, typical of the Marshallian tradition in economics. For an explicit statement by a leading present-day Marshallian, *see* D. H. Robertson, *Utility and All That* (London: George Allen & Unwin, 1952), p. 16.
16. See chapter 2 above, p. 139.
17. For a further discussion of this point, see Appendix A below, on "The Diminishing Marginal Utility of Money."
18. It is true that "he who considers acquiring or giving away money is, of course, first of all interested in its future purchasing power and the future structure of prices. But he cannot form a judgment about the future purchasing power of money otherwise than by looking at its configuration in the immediate past." Mises, *Human Action*, p. 407.
19. *See* Mises, *Theory of Money and Credit*, pp. 97–123, and *Human Action*, pp. 405–08. *Also see* Schumpeter, *op. cit.*, p. 1090. This problem obstructed the development of economic science until Mises provided the solution. Failure to solve it led many economists to despair of ever constructing a satisfactory economic analysis of money prices. They were led to abandon fundamental analysis of money prices and to separate completely the prices of goods from their money components. In this fallacious course, they assumed that individual prices are determined wholly as in barter, without money components, while the supply of and the demand for money determined an imaginary figment called the "general price level." Economists began to specialize separately in the "theory of price," which completely abstracted from money in its real functions, and a "theory of money," which abstracted from individual prices and dealt solely with a mythical "price level." The former were solely preoccupied with a particular price and its determinants; the latter solely with the "economy as a whole" without relation to the individual components—called "microeconomics" and "macroeconomics" respectively. Actually, such fallacious premises led inevitably to erroneous conclusions. It is certainly legitimate and necessary for economics, in working out an analysis of reality, to isolate different segments for concentration as the analysis proceeds; but it is not legitimate to falsify reality in this separation, so that the final analysis does not present a correct picture of the individual parts and their interrelations.
20. As we regress in time and approach the original days of barter, the exchange use in the demand for gold becomes relatively weaker as compared to the direct use of gold, until finally, on the last day of barter, it dies out altogether, the time component dying out with it.

21. It should be noted that the crucial stopping point of the regression is *not* the cessation of the use of gold as "money," but the cessation of its use as a *medium of exchange*. It is clear that the concept of a "general" medium of exchange (money) is not important here. As long as gold is used as a medium of exchange, gold prices will continue to have temporal components. It is true, of course, that for a commodity used as a *limited* medium of exchange only a limited array of prices has to be taken into account in considering its utility.

22. Professor Patinkin criticizes Mises for allegedly basing the regression theorem on the view that the marginal utility of money refers to the marginal utility of the goods for which money is exchanged rather than the marginal utility of holding money, and charges Mises with inconsistently holding the latter view in parts of his *Theory of Money and Credit*. In fact, Mises' concept of the marginal utility of money *does* refer to the utility of *holding* money, and Mises' point about the regression theorem is a different one, namely, that the marginal utility-to-hold is in itself based on the prior fact that money can exchange for goods, i.e., on the prior money prices of goods. Hence, it becomes necessary to break out of this circularity—by means of the regression theorem. In short, the prices of goods have to exist *in order* to have a marginal utility of money to hold.

    In his own theory, Patinkin very feebly tries to justify circularity, by saying that in analyzing the market (market "experiment") he begins with utility, and in analyzing utility he begins with prices (individual "experiment"), but the fact remains that he is caught inextricably in a circular trap, which a methodology of cause-and-effect (in contrast to a mathematical type of mutual determination) would quickly reveal. Don Patinkin, *Money, Interest, and Prices* (Evanston, Ill.: Row, Peterson & Co., 1956), pp. 71–72, 414.

23. As Wicksteed states: "Efforts are regulated by anticipated values, but values are not controlled by antecedent efforts," and "The value of what you have got is not affected by the value of what you have relinquished or forgone in order to get it. But the measure of the advantages you are willing to forgo in order to get a thing is determined by the value that you expect it to have when you have got it." Wicksteed, *op. cit.*, I, 88–93.

24. We shall see below, in chapter 11, that money is unique in not conferring any general benefit through an increase in the supply once money has been established on the market.

25. "Planning" does not necessarily mean that the man has pondered long and hard over a decision and subsequent action. He might have made his decision almost instantaneously. Yet this is still planned action. Since all action is purposive rather than reflexive, there must always, before an action, have been a decision to act as well as valuations. Therefore, there is always planning.

26. Economics "must at any rate include and imply a study of the way in which members of . . . society will spontaneously administer their own

resources and the relations into which they will spontaneously enter with each other." Wicksteed, *op. cit.,* I, 15–16.

27. Wicksteed, *op. cit.,* I, 21–22.
28. The exception is those cases in which the demand curve for the good is directly vertical, and there will then be no effect on the complementary good.
29. We omit at this point analysis of the case in which the increase in demand results from decreases of cash balance and/or decreases in investment.
30. Strictly, this is not correct, and the important qualification will be added below. Since, as a result of time preference, present services are worth more than the same ones in the future, and those in the near future more than those in the far future, the price of *B* will be *less* than twice the price of *A*.
31. It needs to be kept in mind that, strictly, there is no such thing as a "present" price established by the market. When a man considers the price of a good, he is considering that price agreed upon in the last recorded transaction in the market. The "present" price is always in reality the historically recorded price of the most immediate past (say, a half-hour ago). What always interests the actor is what various prices will be at various times in the future.
32. On the different uses of the term "value," see Appendix B, "On Value," below.
33. The concept of monetary profit and loss and their relation to capitalization will be explored below.
34. Cf. Fetter, *op. cit.,* pp. 158–60.
35. For a discussion of the value of durable goods, see the brilliant treatment in Böhm-Bawerk, *Positive Theory, etc.,* pp. 339–57; Fetter, *op. cit.,* pp. 111–21; and Wicksteed, *op. cit.,* I, 101–11.
36. We are omitting possible shifts in rank resulting from the increasing utility of money, which would only complicate matters unduly.
37. W. Stanley Jevons, *The Theory of Political Economy* (3rd ed.; London: Macmillan & Co., 1888), pp. 59–60.
38. See Appendix A below, "The Diminishing Marginal Utility of Money," and Rothbard, "Toward a Reconstruction, etc.," *loc. cit.*
39. Mises, *Human Action,* p. 102. Dr. Bernardelli justly says: "If someone asks me *in abstracto* whether my love for my country is greater than my desire for freedom, I am somewhat at a loss how to answer, but actually having to make a choice between a trip in my country and the danger of losing my freedom, the order of intensities of my desire becomes only too determinate." Harro F. Bernardelli, "What has Philosophy to Contribute to the Social Sciences, and to Economics in Particular?" *Economica,* November, 1936, p. 451. Also see our discussion of "consumer surplus" in section 4 above.
40. Schumpeter, *op. cit.,* pp. 94 n. and 1064.
41. See chapter 1, p. 64.
42. Cf. the excellent discussion of the sizes of units in Wicksteed, *op. cit.,* I, 96–101, and 84.

43. Mises, *Theory of Money and Credit,* pp. 46–47. *Also see* Harro F. Bernardelli, "The End of the Marginal Utility Theory?" *Economica,* May, 1938, pp. 205–07; and Bernardelli, "A Reply to Mr. Samuelson's Note," *Economica,* February, 1939, pp. 88–89.
44. It must always be kept in mind that "total" and "marginal" do not have the same meaning, or mutual relation, as they do in the calculus. "Total" is here another form of "marginal." Failure to realize this has plagued economics since the days of Jevons and Walras.
45. For further analysis of the determination of the purchasing power of money and of the demand for and the supply of money, see chapter 11 below on "Money and Its Purchasing Power."
46. On appraisement and valuation, cf. Mises, *Human Action,* pp. 328–30.

NOTES TO CHAPTER 5

1. Another difference is one we have already discussed: that mathematics, particularly the calculus, rests in large part on assumptions of infinitely small steps. Such assumptions may be perfectly legitimate in a field where behavior of unmotivated matter is under study. But *human action* disregards infinitely small steps precisely because they *are* infinitely small and therefore have no relevance to human beings. Hence, the action under study in economics must always occur in finite, discrete steps. It is therefore incorrect to say that such an assumption may just as well be made in the study of human action as in the study of physical particles. In human action, we may describe such assumptions as being not simply unrealistic, but *antirealistic.*
2. The mathematical economists, or "econometricians," have been trying without success for years to analyze the path of equilibrium as well as the equilibrium conditions themselves. The econometrician F. Zeuthen recently admitted that such attempts cannot succeed. All that mathematics can describe is the final equilibrium point. See the remarks of F. Zeuthen at the 16th European meeting of the Econometric Society, in *Econometrica,* April, 1955, pp. 199–200.
3. For a brilliant critique of the use of mathematics in economics, *see* Mises, *Human Action,* pp. 251, 347–54, 697–99, 706–11. *Also see* Mises, "Comments about the Mathematical Treatment of Economic Problems," *Studium Generale,* VI, 2 (1953), (Springer Verlag: unpublished translation by Helena Ratzka); Niksa, *loc. cit.;* Ischboldin, *loc. cit.;* Paul Painlevé, "The Place of Mathematical Reasoning in Economics" in Louise Sommer, ed., *Essays in European Economic Thought* (Princeton: D. Van Nostrand, 1960), pp. 120–32; and Wieser, *op. cit.,* pp. 51 ff. For a discussion of the logical method of economics. see *Human Action* and the neglected work, J. E. Cairnes, *The Character and Logical Method of Political Economy* (2nd ed.; London: Macmillan & Co., 1888). *Also see* Marian Bowley, *Nassau Senior and Classical Economics* (New York: Augustus M. Kelley, 1949), pp. 55–65. If any mathematics has been used in this treatise, it has been only along the lines charted by Cairnes: "I have no desire to deny that it may be possible to employ geometrical

diagrams or mathematical formulae for the purpose of exhibiting economic doctrines *reached by other paths. . . .* What I venture to deny is the doctrine which Professor Jevons and others have advanced—that economic knowledge can be extended by such means; that Mathematics can be applied to the development of economic truth, as it has been applied to the development of mechanical and physical truth; and unless it can be shown either that mental feelings admit of being expressed in precise quantitative forms, or, on the other hand, that economic phenomena do not depend on mental feelings, I am unable to see how this conclusion can be avoided." Cairnes, *op. cit.*, pp. iv–v.

4. George J. Stigler, *Production and Distribution Theories* (New York: Macmillan & Co., 1946), p. 181. For Carl Menger's attack on the concept of mutual determination and his critique of mathematical economics in general, *see* T. W. Hutchison, *A Review of Economic Doctrines, 1870–1929* (Oxford: The Clarendon Press, 1953), pp. 147–48, and the interesting article by Emil Kauder, "Intellectual and Political Roots of the Older Austrian School," *Zeitschrift für Nationalökonomie,* XVII, 4 (1958), 412 ff.
5. Stigler appends a footnote to the above paragraph, which is meant as the *coup de grace* to Böhm-Bawerk: "Böhm-Bawerk was not trained in mathematics," Stigler, *op. cit.* Mathematics, it must be realized, is only the servant of logic and reason, and not their master. "Training" in mathematics is no more necessary to the realization of its uselessness for and inapplicability to the sciences of human action than, for example, "training" in agricultural techniques is essential to knowing that they are not applicable on board an ocean liner. Indeed, training in mathematics, without adequate attention to the epistemology of the sciences of human action, is likely to yield unfortunate results when applied to the latter, as this example demonstrates. Böhm-Bawerk's greatness as an economist needs no defense at this date. For a sensitive tribute to Böhm-Bawerk, *see* Joseph A. Schumpeter, "Eugen von Böhm-Bawerk, 1851–1914" in *Ten Great Economists* (New York: Oxford University Press. 1951), pp. 143–90. For a purely assertive and unsupported depreciation of Böhm-Bawerk's stature as an economist, *see* Howard S. Ellis' review of Schumpeter's book in the *Journal of Political Economy,* October, 1952, p. 434.
6. The literature in economics has been immeasurably confused by writers on production theory who deal with problems in terms of technology rather than valuation. For an excellent article on this problem, cf. Lionel Robbins, "Remarks upon Certain Aspects of the Theory of Costs," *Economic Journal,* March, 1934, pp. 1–18.
7. We must hasten to add that this does *not* signify adoption of the old classical fallacy that treated each of these groups of factors as homogeneous. Clearly, they are heterogeneous and for pricing purposes and in human action are treated as such. Only the same good, homogeneous for human valuation, is treated as a common "factor," and all factors are treated alike—for their contribution to revenue—by producers. The categories "land, labor, and capital goods" are essential, however, for a

deeper analysis of production problems, in particular the analysis of various income returns and of the relation of time to production.

8. It must be understood that "factors of production" include *every* service that advances the product toward the stage of consumption. Thus, such services as "marketing costs," advertising, etc., are just as legitimately productive services as any other factors. The fallacy in the spurious distinction between "production costs" and "selling costs" has been definitely demonstrated by Mises, *Human Action,* p. 319.
9. On the structure of production, *see* Wieser, *op. cit.,* pp. 47 ff.
10. In practice, one or more persons can be the owners of any of the factors. Thus, the original factors might also be jointly owned by several persons. This would not affect our analysis. The only change would be that the joint owners of a factor would have to allocate the factor's income according to voluntary contract. But the type of allocation would remain the same.
11. Actually, this case cannot occur, since labor, as we shall see below, is always a nonspecific factor.
12. It is therefore our contention that the term "consumers' sovereignty" is highly inapt and that "individual sovereignty" would be a more appropriate term for describing the free market system. For an analysis of the concept of "consumers' sovereignty," see chapter 10 below.
13. Cf. the excellent discussion of cost by G. F. Thirlby, "The Subjective Theory of Value and Accounting 'Cost,'" *Economica,* February, 1946, pp. 33 f.; and especially Thirlby, "Economists' Cost Rules and Equilibrium Theory," *Economica,* May, 1960, pp. 148–53.
14. As Thirlby says, "Cost is ephemeral. The cost involved in a particular decision loses its significance with the making of a decision because the decision displaces the alternative course of action." Thirlby, "Subjective Theory of Value," *op. cit.,* p. 34. And Jevons: *"Labor once spent has no influence on the future value of any article:* it is gone and lost for ever. In commerce bygones are forever bygones and we are always starting clear at each moment, judging the values of things with a view to future utility. Industry is essentially prospective, not retrospective." Jevons, *op. cit.,* p. 164.
15. There will undoubtedly be exceptions, such as cases where the owner obtains enjoyment from the land or capital good from its lying idle—such as the esthetic enjoyment of using it as an uncultivated forest. These alternatives are then also costs, when a decision is made on the use of the land.
16. It is unfortunate that these truths, substantially set forth by the "Austrian School of economics" (which included some Englishmen and Americans) close to three-quarters of a century ago, should have been almost entirely obscured by the fashinable eclectic doctrine that "real costs" and utility are somehow co-ordinate in price determination, with "costs" being "really" more important "in the long run." How often has Alfred Marshall's homely analogy of utility and cost being "two blades of a scissors" been invoked as a substitute for analysis! Emil Kauder has supplied an interesting interpretation of the reason for the failure of

British thought to adopt the nascent subjective value approach in previous centuries. He attributes the emphasis on labor and real cost, as contrasted to subjective utility and happiness, to the Calvinist background of the British classicists, typified by Smith and Locke. Of particular interest here is his citation of the strongly Evangelical background of Marshall. Implicit in his treatment is the view that the second major reason for the classicists' failure to follow subjectivist leads was their search for an invariable measurement of value. This search embodied the "scientistic" desire to imitate the methods of the natural sciences. Emil Kauder, "The Retarded Acceptance of the Marginal Utility Theory," *Quarterly Journal of Economics,* November, 1953, pp. 564–75.

17. The term "pure rate of interest" corresponds to Mises' term "originary rate of interest." See *Human Action, passim.*
18. Here the reader is referred to one of the great works in the history of economic thought, Eugen von Böhm-Bawerk's *Capital and Interest* (New York: Brentano's, 1922), where the correct theory of interest is outlined; in particular, the various false theories of interest are brilliantly dissected. This is not to say that the present author endorses all of Böhm-Bawerk's theory of interest as presented in his *Positive Theory of Capital.*
19. Strictly, this assumption is incorrect, and we make it in this section only for purposes of simplicity. For interest may be an opportunity cost for an individual investor, but it is *not* a *money* cost, nor is it an opportunity cost for the aggregate of capitalists. For the implications of this widely held error in economic literature, *see* André Gabor and I. F. Pearce, "The Place of Money Capital in the Theory of Production," *Quarterly Journal of Economics,* November, 1958, pp. 537–57; and Gabor and Pearce, "A New Approach to the Theory of the Firm," *Oxford Economic Papers,* October, 1952, pp. 252–65.
20. Cf. Menger, *op. cit.,* pp. 149 ff.
21. The very interesting researches by Emil Kauder indicate that the essentials of the Austrian marginal utility theory (the basis of the view that price determines cost and not *vice versa* or mutually) had already been formulated by French and Italian economists of the seventeenth and eighteenth centuries and that the English classical school shunted economics onto a very wrong road, a road from which economics was extricated only by the Austrians. *See* Emil Kauder, "Genesis of the Marginal Utility Theory," *Economic Journal,* September, 1953, pp. 638–50; and Kauder, "The Retarded Acceptance of the Marginal Utility Theory," *loc. cit.*
22. Alfred Marshall, *Principles of Economics* (8th ed.; London: Macmillan & Co., 1920), pp. 349 ff.
23. This analogy, though not used in this context, was often used by classical economists as applied to prices and "the price level," an application equally erroneous.
24. On this error in Marshall, *see* F. A. Hayek, *The Pure Theory of Capital* (Chicago: University of Chicago Press, 1941), pp. 21, 27–28. Marshall is

here committing the famous fallacy of "conceptual realism," in which theoretical constructs are mistaken for actually existing entities. For other examples, cf. Leland B. Yeager, "Some Questions on Growth Economics," *American Economic Review,* March, 1954, p. 62.

25. Marshall, *op. cit.,* pp. 338 ff.
26. We must hasten to point out that this is by no means the same criticism as the neo-Keynesian charge that economists must deal in broad aggregates, and not with individual cases. The latter approach is even worse, since it begins with "wholes" that have no basis in reality whatever. What we are advocating is a theory that deals with all the individuals as they interact in the economy. Furthermore, this is the "Austrian," and not the Walrasian approach, which has recently come into favor. The latter deals with interrelations of individuals ("the general equilibrium approach") but only in the ERE and with mathematical abstractions in the ERE.
27. Little of value has been said about bargaining since Böhm-Bawerk. *See* Böhm-Bawerk, *Positive Theory,* pp. 198–99. This can be seen in J. Pen's "A General Theory of Bargaining," *American Economic Review,* March, 1952, pp. 24 ff. Pen's own theory is of little worth because it rests explicitly on an assumption of the measurability of utility. *Ibid.,* p. 34 n.
28. Contrast the discussion in most textbooks, where bargaining occupies an important place in explanation of market pricing *only* in the discussion of labor incomes.
29. See Mises, *Human Action,* p. 336.
30. Any zone of indeterminacy in pricing must consist of the coincidence of an absolutely vertical supply curve with an absolutely vertical market demand curve for the good or service, so that the equilibrium price is in a zone rather than at a point. As Hutt states, "It depends entirely upon the fortuitous coincidence of . . . an unusual and highly improbable demand curve with an absolutely rigid supply curve." W. H. Hutt, *The Theory of Collective Bargaining* (Glencoe, Ill.: The Free Press, 1954), pp. 90, and 79–109.

NOTES TO CHAPTER 6

1. The discussion in this chapter deals with the *pure* rate of interest, as determined by time preference. On the role of the purchasing-power component in the market rate of interest, cf. chapter 11 on money, below.
2. On production theory and stages of production, see the important works of F. A. Hayek, particularly *Prices and Production* (2nd ed.; London: Routledge and Kegan Paul, 1935); and *Profits, Interest, and Investment* (London: Routledge and Kegan Paul, 1939).
3. Cf. Böhm-Bawerk, *Positive Theory,* pp. 304–05, 320.
4. In the ERE of our example, the *pure* rate of interest is *the* rate of interest, since, as we shall see, deviations from the pure rate are due solely to uncertainty.
5. In the reams of commentary on J. M. Keynes' *General Theory,* no one has noticed the very revealing passage in which Keynes criticizes Mises'

discussion of this point. Keynes asserted that Mises' "peculiar" new theory of interest "confused" the "marginal efficiency of capital" (the net rate of return on an investment) with the rate of interest. The point is that the "marginal efficiency of capital" *is indeed* the rate of interest! It is a price on the time market. It was precisely this "natural" rate, rather than the loan rate, that had been a central problem of interest theory for many years. The essentials of this doctrine were set forth by Böhm-Bawerk in *Capital and Interest* and should therefore not have been surprising to Keynes. *See* John Maynard Keynes, *The General Theory of Employment, Interest and Money* (New York: Harcourt, Brace & Co., 1936), pp. 192–93. It is precisely this preoccupation with the relatively unimportant problems of the loan market that constitutes one of the greatest defects of the Keynesian theory of interest.

6. As Böhm-Bawerk declared: "Interest . . . may be obtained from any capital, no matter what be the kind of goods of which the capital consists: from goods that are barren as well as from those that are naturally fruitful; from perishable as well as from durable goods; from goods that can be replaced and from goods that cannot be replaced; from money as well as from commodities." Böhm-Bawerk, *Capital and Interest,* p. 1.
7. Cf. Mises, *Human Action,* pp. 521–42.
8. This is a highly simplified portrayal of the value scale. For purposes of exposition, we have omitted the fact that the *second* unit of 13 added future ounces will be worth less than the first, the third unit of 13 less than the second, etc. Thus, in actuality, the demand schedule of future goods will be lower than portrayed here. However, the essentials of the analysis are unaffected, since we can assume a demand schedule of any size that we wish. The only significant conclusion is that the demand curve is shaped so that an individual demands more future goods as the market rate of interest rises, and this conclusion holds for the actual as well as for our simplified version.
9. The reader may drop the parentheses around the future moneys at the lower end of the value scale, for Robinson is considering supplying them as well as demanding them.
10. In the same way, though we cannot compare utilities, we can compare (if we know them) individual *demand* schedules for goods.
11. It is not valid to object that some might prefer to *use* the money in the future rather than in the present. That is not the issue here, which is one of *availability* for use. If a man wants to "save" money for some future use, he may "hoard" it rather than spend it on a future good, and thus have it always available. We have abstracted from hoarding, which will be dealt with in the chapter on money; it would have no place, anyway, in the evenly rotating world of certainty.
12. The importance of time preference was first seen by Böhm-Bawerk in his *Capital and Interest.* The *sole* importance of time preference has been grasped by extremely few economists, notably by Frank A. Fetter and Ludwig von Mises. See Fetter, *Economic Principles,* pp. 235–316; *id.,* "Interest Theories, Old and New," *American Economic Review,* March, 1914, pp. 68–92; and Mises, *Human Action,* pp. 476–534.

13. The fact that consumers may physically consume all or part of these goods at a later date does not affect this conclusion, because any further consumption takes place outside the money nexus, and it is the latter that we are analyzing.
14. No important complication arises from the greater degree of futurity of the higher-order factors. As we have indicated above, a *more* distantly future good will simply be discounted by the market by a greater amount, though at the same rate per annum. The interest *rate,* i.e., the discount rate of future goods per unit of time, remains the same regardless of the degree of futurity of the good. This fact serves to resolve one problem mentioned above—vertical integration by firms over one or more stages. If the equilibrium rate of interest is 5% per year, then a one-stage producer will earn 5% on his investment, while a producer who advances present goods over three stages—for three years—will earn 15%, i.e., 5% per annum.
15. Very recently, greater realism has been introduced into social accounting by considering intercapitalist "money flows."
16. Problems of hoarding and dishoarding from the cash balance will be treated in chapter 11 on money and are prescinded from the present analysis.
17. Cf. Knut Wicksell, *Lectures on Political Economy* (London: Routledge and Kegan Paul, 1934), I, 189–91.
18. For more on the relations between the interest rate, i.e., the price spreads or margins, and the proportions invested and consumed, see below.
19. On gross and net product, *see* Milton Gilbert and George Jaszi, "National Product and Income Statistics as an Aid in Economic Problems" in W. Fellner and B. F. Haley, eds., *Readings in the Theory of Income Distribution* (Philadelphia: Blakiston, 1946), pp. 44–57; and Simon Kuznets, *National Income, A Summary of Findings* (New York: National Bureau of Economic Research, 1946), pp. 111–21, and especially p. 120.
20. If permanence is attributed to the mythical entity, the aggregate value of capital, it becomes an independent factor of production, along with labor, and earns interest.
21. The fallacy of the "net" approach to capital is at least as old as Adam Smith and continues down to the present. *See* Hayek, *Prices and Production,* pp. 37–49. This book is an excellent contribution to the analysis of the production structure, gross savings and consumption, and its application to the business cycle, based on the production and business cycle theories of Böhm-Bawerk and Mises respectively. *Also see* Hayek, "The Mythology of Capital" in *Readings in the Theory of Income Distribution,* pp. 355–83; *id., Profits, Interest, and Investment, passim.*
22. For a critique of the analogous views of J. B. Clark, *see* Frank A. Fetter, "Recent Discussions of the Capital Concept," *Quarterly Journal of Economics,* November, 1900, pp. 1–14. Fetter succinctly criticizes Clark's failure to explain interest on consumption goods, his assumption of a permanent capital fund, and his assumption of "synchronization" in production.

23. Cf. Böhm-Bawerk, *Positive Theory,* pp. 299–322, 329–38.
24. The rate of interest, however, will make a great deal of difference in so far as he is an owner and seller of a durable good. Land is, of course, durable almost by definition—in fact, generally permanent. So far, we have been dealing only with the sale of factor *services,* i.e., the "hire" or "rent" of the factor, and abstracting from the sale or valuation of durable factors, which embody future services. Durable land, as we shall see, is "capitalized," i.e., the value of the factor as a whole is the discounted sum of its future MVP's, and there the interest rate will make a significant difference. The price of durable land, however, is irrelevant to the supply schedule of land *services* in demand for present money.
25. Strictly, of course, the slope would not be constant, since the return is in equal *percentages,* not in equal absolute amounts. Slopes are treated as constant here, however, for the sake of simplicity in presenting the analysis.
26. This Marxian error stemmed from a very similar error introduced into economics by Adam Smith. Cf. Ronald L. Meek, "Adam Smith and the Classical Concept of Profit," *Scottish Journal of Political Economy,* June, 1954, pp. 138–53.
27. For brilliant dissections of various forms of the "productivity" theory of interest (the neoclassical view that investment earns an interest return because capital goods are *value*-productive), see the following articles by Frank A. Fetter: "The Roundabout Process of the Interest Theory," *Quarterly Journal of Economics,* 1902, pp. 163–80, where Böhm-Bawerk's highly unfortunate lapse into a productivity theory of interest is refuted; "Interest Theories Old and New," *op. cit.,* pp. 68–92, which presents an extensive development of time-preference theory, coupled with a critique of Irving Fisher's concessions to the productivity doctrine; *also see* "Capitalization Versus Productivity, Rejoinder," *American Economic Review,* 1914, pp. 856–59, and "Davenport's Competitive Economics," *Journal of Political Economy,* 1914, pp. 555–62. Fetter's only mistake in interest theory was to deny Fisher's assertion that time preference (or, as Fisher called it, "impatience") is a universal and *necessary* fact of human action. For a demonstration of this important truth, *see* Mises, *Human Action,* pp. 480 ff.
28. On Keynes' failure to perceive this point, see page 454 of this chapter, note 5 above.
29. The shares of stock, or the units of property rights, "have the characteristic of fungibility; one unit is exactly the same as another. . . . We have a mathematical division of the one set of rights. This fungible quality makes possible organized commodity and security markets or exchanges. . . . With these fungible units of . . . property rights we have a possible acceleration of changes of ownership and in membership of the groups. . . . If a course of market dealings arises, the unit of property has a swift cash conversion value. Its owner may readily resume the cash power to command the uses of wealth." Hastings Lyon, *Corporations and their Financing* (Boston: D. C. Heath, 1936), p. 11.

Thus, *shares* of property as well as total property have become readily marketable.

30. The literature on the so-called "co-operative movement" is of remarkably poor quality. The best source is *Co-operatives in the Petroleum Industry,* ed. by K. E. Ettinger (New York: Petroleum Industry Research Foundation, 1947), especially Pt. I, Ludwig von Mises, "Observations on the Co-operative Movement."
31. *See* Mises, *Human Action,* pp. 301–05, 703–05.
32. The proxy fights of recent years simply give dramatic evidence of this control.
33. Edgar M. Hoover, "Some Institutional Factors in Business Decisions," *American Economic Review, Papers and Proceedings,* May, 1954, p. 203.
34. For example, *see* Gerhard Colm, "The Corporation and the Corporation Income Tax in the American Economy," *American Economic Review, Papers and Proceedings,* May, 1954, p. 488.
35. As Frank Fetter brilliantly stated: "Contract [interest] is based on and tends to conform to economic interest [i.e., the 'natural interest' price differential between stages]. . . . It is economic interest that we seek to explain logically through the economic nature of the goods. Contract interest is a secondary problem—a business and legal problem—as to who shall have the benefit of the income arising with the possession of the goods. It is closely connected with the question of ownership." Fetter, "Recent Discussions of the Capital Concept," *op. cit.,* pp. 24–25.
36. "The creditor is always a virtual partner of the debtor or a virtual owner of the pledged and mortgaged property." Mises, *Human Action,* p. 536. *Also see* Fetter, "Recent Discussions of the Capital Concept," *op. cit.,* p. 43.
37. Similar psychic components may occur in the consumers' loan market—for example, if there is general strong liking or dislike for a certain borrower.
38. Thus, cf. Friedrich A. Lutz, "The Structure of Interest Rates" in *Readings in the Theory of Income Distribution,* pp. 499–532.
39. Since the writing of this text, Professor Luckett has published a critique of Lutz similar in part. *See* Dudley G. Luckett, "Professor Lutz and the Structure of Interest Rates," *Quarterly Journal of Economics,* February, 1959, pp. 131–44. *Also see* J. M. Culbertson, "The Term Structure of Interest Rates," *ibid.,* November, 1957, pp. 485–517.
40. It is remarkable that in his empirical study of the time structure of interest rates, Charls Walker found an irresistible tendency of interest rates to equalize, but was forced to multiply his assumptions in order to try to demonstrate that this was a proof of the theory that interest rates do not necessarily equalize. Charls E. Walker, "Federal Reserve Policy and the Structure of Interest Rates on Government Securities," *Quarterly Journal of Economics,* February, 1954, pp. 19–42. Walker's article has considerable merit in demonstrating the impossibilities of governmental maintenance of a differential interest pattern in the face of the market's drive to equality. Cf. Luckett, *op. cit.,* p. 143 n.
41. *See* Mises, *Human Action,* p. 541.

42. *See* Mises, *Human Action,* pp. 527–29. *Also see* Lionel Robbins, "On a Certain Ambiguity in the Conception of Stationary Equilibrium," in Richard V. Clemence, ed., *Readings in Economic Analysis* (Cambridge: Addison-Wesley Press, 1950), I, 176 ff.
43. Richard V. Clemence and Francis S. Doody, *The Schumpeterian System* (Cambridge: Addison-Wesley Press, 1950), pp. 28–30.
44. As has been the case with all theorists who have attempted to deny time preference, Clemence and Doody hastily brush *consumers' loans* aside. As Frank A. Fetter pointed out years ago, only time preference can integrate interest on consumers' as well as on producers' loans into a single unified explanation. Consumers' loans are clearly unrelated to "productivity" explanations of interest and are obviously due to time preference. Cf. Clemence and Doody, *op. cit.,* p. 29 n.

NOTES TO CHAPTER 7

1. The mathematical bent toward replacing the concepts of cause and effect by mutual determination has contributed to the willingness to engage in circular reasoning. *See* Rothbard, "Toward a Reconstruction of Utility and Welfare Economics," *op. cit.,* p. 236; and Kauder, "Intellectual and Political Roots of the Older Austrian School," *loc. cit.*
2. Clearly, the longer the period of time, the more variable will factor proportions tend to be. Technologically, varying amounts of time are needed to rearrange the various factors.
3. This justifies the conclusion of Mises, *Human Action,* p. 336, as compared, for example, with the analysis in George J. Stigler's *Production and Distribution Theories.* Mises adds the important proviso that if the factors have the same fixed proportions in *all* the processes for which they are nonspecific, then here too only bargaining can determine their prices.
4. Strictly, we should be dealing with *discounted* MVP's here, but treating just MVP's at this stage merely simplifies matters.
5. We are here postulating that equal quantities of factors produce equal quantities of results. The famous question whether this condition actually holds (sometimes phrased in pretentious mathematical language as whether the "production function is linear and homogeneous") is easily resolved if we realize that the proposition: equal causes produce equal results, is the major technological axiom in nature. Any cases that appear to confute this rule only do so in appearance; in reality, supposed exceptions always involve some "indivisibility" where one factor, in effect, cannot change proportionately with other factors.
6. This is not strictly true, but the technical error in the statement does not affect the causal analysis in the text. In fact, this argument is strengthened, for MVP actually equals MPP × "marginal revenue," and marginal revenue is always less than, or equal to, price. See Appendix A below, "Marginal Physical and Marginal Value Product."
7. It might be asked why we now employ mathematics after our strictures against the mathematical method in economics. The reason is that, in

this particular problem, we are dealing with a purely *technological* question. We are not dealing with human decisions here, but with the necessary technological conditions of the world as given to human factors. In this external world, given quantities of cause yield given quantities of effect, and it is this sphere, very limited in the over-all praxeological picture, that, like the natural sciences in general, is peculiarly susceptible to mathematical methods. The relationship between average and marginal is an obviously *algebraic,* rather than an ends-means, relation. Cf. the algebraic proof in Stigler, *Theory of Price,* pp. 44 ff.

8. This law applies to all factors, specific and nonspecific.
9. See the excellent discussion in Böhm-Bawerk, *Positive Theory of Capital,* pp. 304–12. For a further discussion of DMVP as against MVP, see Appendix B below, "Professor Rolph and the Discounted Marginal Productivity Theory."
10. *See* Wicksell, *op. cit.,* I, 108.
11. See the excellent analysis in Wicksell, *op. cit.,* I, 189–91, 193–95.
12. This was realized by Carl Menger. *See* F. A. Hayek, "Carl Menger" in Henry W. Spiegel, ed., *The Development of Economic Thought* (New York: John Wiley, 1952), pp. 530 ff.
13. Böhm-Bawerk, *Positive Theory of Capital,* p. 88.
14. Mises, *Human Action,* pp. 477, 485 f. *Also see* Menger, *op. cit.,* pp. 166–67.
15. "Nonreplaceable" as a criterion for *land,* in contrast to *capital goods,* is *not* equivalent to "permanent." "Permanent" is a subdivision of "nonreplaceable." It is clear that permanent improvements do not have to be replaced. However, *depletable* natural resources, such as coal, ores, etc., are not permanent, but are also nonreplaceable. The key question is whether a resource has to be *produced,* in which case it earns only *gross* rents. If it does not or cannot, it earns *net* rents as well. Resources that are being depleted obviously *cannot* be replaced and are therefore *land,* not capital goods. See the section on depletable resources below.
16. We may use "permanent" and "nonpermanent" in this section, because resources that are being depleted obviously cannot be included in any evenly rotating equilibrium. For more on depletable resources, see below. With depletable resources left aside, "permanent" becomes identical with "nonreproducible."
17. Cf. Wicksell, *op. cit.,* I, 186, and *passim;* and Hayek, *Pure Theory of Capital,* pp. 54–58.
18. Neither is there any relation between the present issue of permanence or nonpermanence and the cosmological question of the permanence of matter and energy. *See* Mises, *Human Action,* p. 634.
19. Stigler charges that the various distinctions between land and capital goods based on permanence or origin, such as are discussed herein, are physical rather than economic. These strictures miss the point. No one denies that these homogeneous factors can change greatly in *value* over time. But whether or not a given factor is original or improved, or permanent or needing to be maintained, *is* a physical question, and one that is very relevant to economic analysis. Certainly, the Knightian argu-

ment that all land is capital goods, because no land is original, is also an argument in the *physical* realm. Stigler, *Production and Distribution Theories,* p. 274.

20. John V. Van Sickle and Benjamin A. Rogge, *Introduction to Economics* (New York: D. Van Nostrand, 1954), p. 141.
21. But while the position is permanent, even the land itself was necessarily altered by man to prepare it for urban use. See chapter 2 above.
22. This concept of rent is based on the original contribution of Frank A. Fetter. Cf. Fetter, *Economic Principles,* pp. 143–70. Fetter's conception has, unfortunately, had little influence on economic thought. It is not only in accord with common usage; it provides a unifying principle, enabling a coherent explanation of the price determination of unit services and of the whole goods that embody them. Without the rental-price concept, it is difficult to distinguish between the pricing of unit services and of whole goods.

    Fetter used the rental concept to apply only to the services of durable goods, but it is clear that it can be extended to cover cases of non-durable goods where the unit service *is* the whole good.
23. See chapter 4 above. On capitalization, *see* Fetter, *Economic Principles,* pp. 262–84, 308–13; Böhm-Bawerk, *Positive Theory,* pp. 339–57.
24. It is often more convenient to define *rent* as equal to the MVP, rather than the DMVP. In that case, the capital value of the whole factor is equal to the *discounted* sum of its future rents.
25. Fetter's main error in capital theory was his belief that capitalization meant the scrapping of any distinction between capital goods and land.
26. Cf. Boulding, *Economic Analysis,* pp. 711–12.
27. In the *long run,* increases in the capital value of *capital goods* are unimportant, since they resolve into increases in wages and increases in the capital value of ground land.
28. The problem of gains from changes in capital values will be treated further below.
29. Cf. Fred R. Fairchild, Edgar S. Furniss, and Norman S. Buck, *Elementary Economics* (New York: Macmillan & Co., 1926), II, 147.
30. Hayek, *Pure Theory of Capital,* p. 58 n.
31. *Ibid.,* p. 92.
32. Unusual terms because robbery has been distinctively defined as seizure of *someone else's* property without his consent, not the use of one's *own* property.
33. As Stigler says in discussing the charge of "wasted" resources on the market, "It is an interesting problem to define 'wasteful' sensibly without making the word synonymous with 'unprofitable.'" Stigler, *Theory of Price,* p. 332 n. For a discussion of natural resources and a critique of the doctrines of "conservation," *see* Anthony Scott, *Natural Resources: The Economics of Conservation* (Toronto: University of Toronto Press, 1955).
34. A curious notion has arisen that considering *MR,* instead of price, as the multiplier somehow vitiates the optimum satisfaction of consumer

desires on the market. There is no genuine warrant for such an assumption.

35. Earl Rolph, "The Discounted Marginal Productivity Doctrine" in *Readings in Theory of Income Distribution,* pp. 278–93.

36. Rolph ascribes this error to Knut Wicksell, but such a confusion is not attributable to Wicksell, who engages in a brilliant discussion of capital and the production structure and the role of time in production. Wicksell demonstrates correctly that labor and land are the only ultimate factors, and that therefore the marginal productivity of capital goods is reducible to the marginal productivity of labor and land factors, so that money capital earns the interest (or discount) differential.

    Wicksell's discussion of these and related issues is of basic importance. He recognized, for example, that capital goods are fully and basically co-ordinate with land and labor factors *only from the point of view of the individual firm,* but not when we consider the total market in all of its interrelations. Current economic theorizing is, to its detriment, even more preoccupied than writers of his day with the study of an isolated firm instead of the interrelated market. Wicksell, *Lectures,* I, 148–54, 185–95.

37. Rolph ends his article, consistently, with a dismissal of any time-preference influences on interest, which he explains in Knightian vein by the "cost" of producing new capital goods.

8

Production: Entrepreneurship and Change

1. *Entrepreneurial Profit and Loss*

Having developed in Volume I our basic analysis of the market economy, we now proceed to discuss more dynamic and specific applications, as well as the consequences of intervention in the market.

In the evenly rotating economy, there are only two ultimate categories of producers' prices and incomes: interest (uniform throughout the economy), and "wages"—the prices of the services of various labor factors. In a changing economy, however, wage rates and the interest rate are not the only elements that can change. Another category of both positive and negative income appears: *entrepreneurial profit and loss.* We shall concentrate on the *capitalist-entrepreneurs,* economically the more important type of entrepreneur. These are the men who invest in "capital" (land and/or capital goods) used in the productive process. Their function is as we have described: the advance of money to owners of factors and the consequent use of the goods until the *more nearly present* product is later sold. We have worked out the laws of the ERE in detail: factor prices will equal DMVP, every factor will be allocated to its most value-productive uses, capital values will equal the sums of the DMVP's, the interest rate will be uniform and governed solely by time preferences, etc.

The difference in the dynamic, real world is this. None of these future values or events is known; all must be *estimated,* guessed at, by the capitalists. They must advance present money in a speculation upon the unknown future in the expectation that the future product will be sold at a remunerative price. In the real world, then, quality of judgment and accuracy of forecast play an enormous role in the incomes acquired by capitalists. As a result of the arbitrage of the entrepreneurs, the *tendency* is always toward the ERE; in consequence of ever-changing reality, changes in value scales and resources, the ERE never arrives.

The capitalist-entrepreneur buys factors or factor services in the present; his product must be sold in the future. He is always on the alert, then, for discrepancies, for areas where he can earn more than the going rate of interest. Suppose the interest rate is 5%; Jones can buy a certain combination of factors for 100 ounces; he believes that he can use this agglomeration to sell a product after two years for 120 ounces. His *expected* future return is 10% per annum. If his expectations are fulfilled, then he will obtain a 10% annual return instead of 5%. The difference between the general interest rate and his actual return is his *money profit* (from now on to be called simply "profit," unless there is a specific distinction between money profit and psychic profit). In this case, his money profit is 10 ounces for two years, or an extra 5% per annum.

What gave rise to this realized profit, this *ex post* profit fulfilling the producer's *ex ante* expectations? The fact that the *factors of production in this process were underpriced and undercapitalized*—underpriced in so far as their unit services were bought, undercapitalized in so far as the factors were bought as wholes. In either case, the general expectations of the market erred by underestimating the future rents (MVP's) of the factors. This particular entrepreneur saw better than his fellows, however, and acted on this insight. He reaped the reward of his superior foresight in the form of a profit. His action, his recognition of the general undervaluation of productive factors, results in the eventual elimination of profits, or rather in the tendency toward their elimination. By extending production in this particular process, he increases the demand for these factors and raises their prices. This result will be accentuated by the entry of competitors into the same area, attracted by the 10% rate of return. Not only will the rise in demand *raise* the prices of the factors, but the increase in output will *lower* the price of the product. The result will be a tendency for a fall in the rate of return back to the pure interest rate.

What function has the entrepreneur performed? In his quest for profits he saw that certain factors were underpriced vis à vis their potential value products. By recognizing the discrepancy and doing something about it, he shifted factors of production (obviously nonspecific factors) from other productive processes to this one. He detected that the factors' prices did not adequately reflect their potential DMVP's; by bidding for, and hiring, these factors, he was able to allocate them from production of lower DMVP to production of higher DMVP. He has served the consumers better by anticipating where the factors are more valuable. For the greater value of the factors is due solely to their being more highly demanded by the consumers, i.e., being better able to satisfy the desires of the consumers. That is the meaning of a greater discounted marginal value product.

It is clear that there is no sense whatever in talking of a going *rate of profit.* There is no such rate beyond the ephemeral and momentary. For any realized profit tends to disappear because of the entrepreneurial actions it generates. The basic *rate,* then, is the *rate of interest,* which does not disappear. If we start with a dynamic economy, and if we postulate given value scales and given original factors and technical knowledge throughout, the result will be a wiping out of profits to reach an ERE with a pure interest rate. Continual changes in tastes and resources, however, constantly shift the final equilibrium goal and establish a new goal toward which entrepreneurial action is directed —and again the final tendency in the ERE will be the disappearance of profits. For the ERE means the disappearance of uncertainty, and profit is the outgrowth of uncertainty.

A grave error is made by a host of writers and economists in considering only profits in the economy. Almost no account is taken of *losses*. The economy should not be characterized as a "profit economy," but as a "profit and loss economy." [1]

A *loss* occurs when an entrepreneur has made a poor estimate of his future selling prices and revenues. He bought factors, say, for 1,000 ounces, developed them into a product, and then sold it for 900 ounces. He erred in not realizing that the factors were *overpriced* and *overcapitalized* on the market in relation to their discounted marginal value products, i.e., to the prices of his output.

Every entrepreneur, therefore, invests in a process because he expects to make a profit, i.e., *because he believes that the market has underpriced and undercapitalized the factors* in relation to their future rents. If his belief is justified, he makes a profit. If his belief is unjustified, and the market, for example, has really *overpriced* the factors, he will suffer losses.

The nature of loss has to be carefully defined. Suppose an entrepreneur, the market rate of interest being 5%, buys factors at 1,000 and sells their product for 1,020 one year later. Has he suffered a "loss" or made a "profit"? At first, it might seem that he has not taken a loss. After all, he gained back the principal plus an extra 20 ounces, for a 2% net return or gain. However, closer inspection reveals that he could have made a 5% net return anywhere on his capital, since this is the going interest return. He could have made it, say, investing in any other enterprise or in lending money to consumer-borrowers. In this venture he did not even earn the interest gain. The "cost" of his investment, therefore, was not simply his expenses on factors—1,000—but also his forgone opportunity of earning interest at 5%, i.e., an additional 50. He therefore suffered a loss of 30 ounces.

The absurdity of the concept of "rate of profit" is even more evident if we attempt to postulate a *rate of loss*. Obviously, no meaningful use can be made of "rate of loss"; entrepreneurs will be very quick to leave the losing investment and take their capital elsewhere. With entrepreneurs leaving the line of production, the prices of the factors there will drop and the price of the product will rise (with reduced supply), until the net return in that branch of production will be the same as in every branch, and this return will be the uniform interest rate of the ERE. It is clear, therefore, that the process of equalization of rate of return throughout the economy, one that results in a uniform rate of interest, *is the very same process that brings about the abolition of profits and losses in the ERE.* A real economy, in other words, where line A yields a net return of 10% to some entrepreneur, and line B yields 2%, while other lines yield 5%, is one in which the rate of interest is 5%, A makes a pure profit of 5%, and B suffers a pure loss of 3%. A correctly estimated that the market had underpriced his factors in relation to their true DMVP's; B had incorrectly guessed that the market had underpriced (or, at the very least, correctly priced) *his* factors, but found to his sorrow that they had been overpriced in relation to the uses that he made of the factors. In the ERE, where all future values are known and there is therefore no underpricing or overpricing, there are no entrepreneurial profits or losses; there is only a pure interest rate.

In the real world, profits and losses are almost always intertwined with interest returns. Our separation of them is conceptually valid and very important, but cannot be made easily and quantitatively in practice.

Let us sum up the essence of an evenly rotating economy. It is this: all factors of production are allocated to the areas where their discounted marginal value products are the greatest. These are determined by consumer demand schedules. In the modern world of specialization and division of labor, it is almost always the consumers alone who decide, and this in effect excludes the capitalists, who rarely consume more than a negligible amount of their own products. It is the consumers, then, given the "natural" facts of stocks of resources (particularly labor and land factors), who make the decisions for the economic system. The consumers, through their buying and abstention from buying, decide how much of what will be produced, at the same time determining the incomes of all the participating factors. And every man is a consumer.

One obvious exception to this "rule" occurs when either capitalists or laborers have strong preferences or dislikes for a particular line of production. The equilibrium rate of return in the ERE for a strongly disliked line will be considerably higher than the uniform rate, and the equilibrium rate of return for a strongly liked line will be lower. These preferences, however, have to be strong enough to affect the investment or productive actions of a considerable number of potential investors or laborers in order to register as a change in the rate of return.

Do profits have a social function? Many critics point to the ERE, where there are no profits (or losses) and then attack entrepreneurs earning profits in the real world as if they were doing something mischievous or at best unnecessary. Are not profits an index of something wrong, of some maladjustment in the economy? The answer is: Yes, profits are an index of maladjustment, but in a sense precisely opposed to that usually meant. As we have seen above, *profits are an index that maladjustments are being met and combatted by the profit-making entrepreneurs.* These maladjustments are the inevitable concomitants of the real world of change. A man earns profits only if he has, by superior foresight and judgment, uncovered a maladjustment—specifically an undervaluation of certain factors by the market. By stepping into this situation and gaining the profit, he calls everyone's attention to that maladjustment and sets forces into motion that eventually eliminate it. If we must condemn anyone, it should not be the *profit-making* entrepreneur, but the one that has suffered losses. For losses are a sign that he has added further to a maladjustment, through allocating factors where they were overvalued as compared to the consumers' desire for their product. On the other hand, the profit-maker is allocating factors where they had been undervalued as compared to the consumers' desires. The greater a man's profit has been, the more praiseworthy his role, for then the greater is the maladjustment that he alone has uncovered and is combatting. The greater a man's losses, the more blameworthy he is, for the greater has been his contribution to maladjustment.[2]

Of course, we should not be too hard on the bumbling loser. He receives his penalty in the form of losses. These losses drive him from his poor role in production. If he is a consistent loser wherever he enters the production process, he is driven out of the entrepreneurial role altogether. He returns to the job of wage earner. In fact, the market tends to reward its efficient entrepreneurs and penalize its inefficient ones proportionately. In this way, consistently provident entrepreneurs see their capital and resources growing, while consistently imprudent ones find their resources dwindling. The former play a larger and larger role in the production process; the latter are forced to abandon entrepreneurship altogether. There is no inevitably self-reinforcing tendency about this process, however. If a formerly good entrepreneur should suddenly made a bad mistake, he will suffer losses proportionately; if a formerly poor entrepreneur makes a good forecast, he will make proportionate gains. The market is no respecter of past laurels, however large. Moreover, the size of a man's investment is no guarantee whatever of a large profit or against grievous losses. Capital does not "beget" profit. Only wise entrepreneurial decisions do that. A man investing in an unsound venture can lose 10,000 ounces of gold as surely as a man engaging in a sound venture can profit on an investment of 50 ounces.[3]

Beyond the market process of penalization, we cannot condemn the unfortunate capitalist who suffers losses. He was a man who voluntarily assumed the risks of entrepreneurship and suffered from his poor judgment by incurring losses proportionate to his error. Outside critics have no right to condemn him further. As Mises says:

> Nobody has the right to take offense at the errors made by the entrepreneurs in the conduct of affairs and to stress the point that people would have been better supplied if the entrepreneurs had been more skillful and prescient. If the grumbler knew better, why did he not himself fill the gap and seize the opportunity to earn profits? It is easy indeed to display foresight after the event.[4]

2. *The Effect of Net Investment*

Having considered the ERE and its relation to specific entrepreneurial profit and loss, let us now turn to the problem: When will there be *aggregate* profits or losses in the economy? This is connected with the question: What is the effect of a change in the level of aggregate saving or investment in the economy?

Let us begin with an economy in the equilibrium depicted in chapters 5 and 6 above. Production occurs in processes up to six years in total length; total gross income is 418 gold ounces, gross savings-investment is 318 ounces, total consumption 100 ounces, net savings-investment is 0. Of the 100 ounces of income, 83 ounces of net income are earned by land and labor owners, 17 ounces by capital owners. The production structure remains constant because the natural rates of interest coincide, and the resulting price spreads conform to the aggregate of individual time-preference schedules in the economy. As Hayek states:

> Whether the structure of production remains the same depends entirely upon whether entrepreneurs find it profitable to reinvest the usual proportion of the return from the sale of the product in turning out intermediate goods of the same sort. Whether this is profitable, again, depends upon the prices obtained for the product of this particular stage of production on the one hand and on the prices paid for the original means of production and for the intermediate products taken from the preceding stage of production on the other. The continuance of the existing degree of capitalistic organization depends, accordingly, on the prices paid and obtained for the product of each stage of production, and these prices are, therefore, a very real and important factor in determining the direction of production.[5]

What happens if, in a certain period, there are now net savings as a result of a lowering of time-preference schedules? Suppose, for example, that consumption decreases from 100 to 80 and that the saved 20 ounces enter the time market. Gross savings have increased by 20 ounces. During the transition period, net saving has changed from 0 to 20; after the new level of saving has been reached, however, there will be a new equilibrium with gross savings equalling 338 and net savings equalling 0. To the superficial, it might seem that all is lost. Has not consumption decreased from 100 to 80 ounces? What, then, will happen to the whole complex of productive activities that rest on final consumption sales? Will this not lead to a disastrous depression for all firms? And how can a *reduced* consumption profitably support an *increased* volume of expenditures on producers' goods? The latter has aptly been termed by Hayek the "paradox of saving," i.e., that saving is the necessary and sufficient condition for increased production, and yet that such investment seems to contain within itself the seeds of financial disaster for the investors.[6]

If we observe the diagram in Fig. 40 above, it is clear that the volume of money incomes to $Capitalists_1$ will be drastically reduced. $Capitalists_1$ will receive a total of 80 instead of 100 ounces. The amount that they have to apportion to original factors and to $Capitalists_2$ is therefore also considerably decreased. Thus, from the side of final consumers' spending, an impetus toward declining money incomes and prices is sent along the production structure. In the meanwhile, however, *another force* has concurrently come into play. The 20 ounces have not been lost to the system. They are in the process of being invested in the economy, their owners ranging throughout the economy looking for maximum interest returns on their investment. The new savings have changed the ratio of gross investment to consumption from 318:100 to 338:80. A "narrower" consumption base must support a larger amount of producers' spending. How can this happen, especially since the lower-rank capitalists must also receive a lower aggregate income? The answer is: in only one way—by shifting investment further up the ladder to the higher-order production stages. Simple investigation will reveal that the only way that so much investment can be shifted from the lower to the higher stages, while preserving uniform (lowered) interest differentials (cumulative price spreads) at each stage, is *to increase the number of productive stages in the economy,* i.e., to lengthen the structure of production. The impact of net saving on the economy, i.e., of increased total savings, is to lengthen and narrow the structure of production, and this procedure is viable and self-supporting, since it preserves essential price spreads from stage to stage. The diagram in Fig. 60 illustrates the impact of net saving.

In this diagram we see the narrowing and the lengthening of the structure of production. The heavy line *AA* outlines the original structure. The bottom rectangle—consumption—is nar-

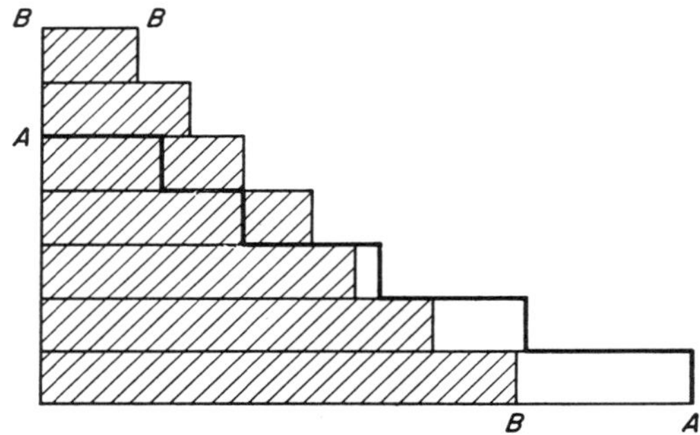

FIG. 60. THE IMPACT OF NET SAVING

rowed with the addition of new savings. As we go up in stepwise fashion—the steps in these diagrams accounting for the interest spreads [7]—the new production structure *BB* (its area covered by diagonal lines) becomes relatively less and less narrow compared to the original structure, until it becomes wider in the upper registers, and finally adds new and higher stages.

The reader will notice that the steps (differentials between stages) in the new production structure *BB* are considerably narrower than the ones in *AA*. This is not an accident. If the steps in *BB* were of the same width as in *AA*, there would be no lengthening of the structure, and total investment would diminish instead of increase. But what is the significance of the narrowing steps in the structure? On the assumptions on which we have drawn the diagram, it is equivalent to a lowering of the interest spreads, i.e., a lowering of the natural rate of interest. But we have seen above that the consequence of lower time-preference rates in the society is precisely a lowering of the rate of interest. Thus, lowered time preferences mean an increased proportion of savings-investment to consumption and lead to smaller price spreads and an equivalent lowering of the rate of interest.

The lowering of interest spreads may be portrayed by another diagram, as in Fig. 61.

In this diagram, cumulative prices are plotted against stages

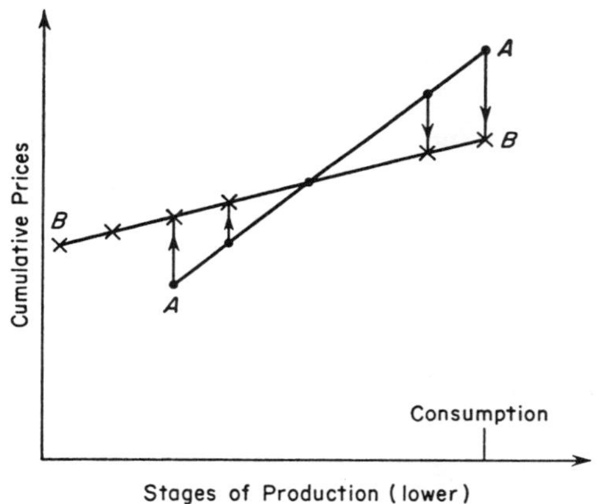

FIG. 61. LOWERING OF INTEREST SPREADS

of production, and the further right we go, the lower the stage of production, until consumption is reached. *AA* is the original curve with the topmost dot representing the highest cumulative price—the one for the final product consumed. The dots next to the left are the lower cumulative prices of the higher stages, and the differences between the dots represent the interest spread and therefore the rate of interest return from stage to stage. *BB* is the curve applicable to the new situation, after saving has increased. Consumption has declined; hence the rightmost dot in *B* is lower than the one in *A,* and the arrow depicts the change. The point next to the left on the *BB* curve is, of course, lower than the rightmost dot, but lower by a smaller amount than the corresponding dot in *AA,* because the lower interest rate signifies a smaller spread between the cumulative prices of the two stages.

The next dot to the left, having the same rate of interest return, will be on approximately the same slope. Therefore, since the *BB* curve is flatter then the *AA* curve—because of the lower interest spread—it crosses the *AA* curve and from that point leftward, i.e., in the higher productive stages, its prices are higher than *A*'s. Arrows depict this change as well.

In the previous diagram we saw the effect of additional saving, i.e., positive net savings, on the structure of production and on the rate of interest. Here we see that the change in the rate of interest lessens the spreads of cumulative prices, so that aggregate consumption is lower, the immediate next higher stages are less and less lower, until the lines cross, and the prices in the higher stages are higher than before. Let us consider the price changes in the various stages and the processes by which they occur. In the lower stages, prices fall because of the lower consumer demand and the resulting shift of investment capital from the stages nearest consumption. In the higher stages, on the other hand, demand for factors increases under the impact of the new savings and the shift in investment from the lower levels. The increased investment expenditure in the higher levels raises the prices of the factors in these stages. It is as if the impact of lower consumer demand tends to die out in the higher stages and is more and more counteracted by the increase and shift in investment funds.

The process of readjustment to lower price spreads caused by increased gross saving has been very lucidly described by Hayek. As he states:

> The final effect will be that, through the fall of prices in the later stages of production and the rise of prices in the earlier stages of production, price margins between the different stages of production will have decreased all round.[8]

The changes in cumulative prices in the various sectors will lead to changes in the prices of the particular goods that enter into the cumulation of factors. These factors are, of course, the capital goods, land, and labor factors, and are ultimately reducible to the latter two, since capital goods are produced (and reproduced) factors. It is clear that lower aggregate demand in the lower stages will cause the prices of the various factors there to decline. The *specific* factors will have to bear the brunt of the decline, since they have nowhere else to go. The nonspecific factors, on the other hand, *can* and do go elsewhere—to the earlier stages, where the monetary demand for factors has increased.

The pricing of capital goods is ultimately unimportant in this connection, because it is reducible to the prices of land, labor, and time, and because the slopes of the curves, the interest spread, indicate the mode of pricing of the capital goods. The ultimately important factors, then, are land, labor, and time. The time element has been extensively considered and accounts for the interest spread. It is the land and labor elements that constitute the fundamental resources being shifted or remaining in production. Some land is specific and some nonspecific; some can be used in several alternative types of productive processes; some can be used in only one type. Labor, on the other hand, is almost always nonspecific; very rare indeed is the person who could conceivably perform only one type of task.[9] Of course, there are different *degrees* of nonspecificity for any factor, and the less specific ones will be more readily shifted from one stage or product to another.

Those factors which are specific to only one particular stage and process will therefore fall in price in the later stages and rise in the earlier stages. What of the nonspecific factors, which include all labor factors? These will tend to shift from the later to the earlier stages. At first, there will be a difference in the price of each nonspecific factor; it will be lower in the lower stages and higher in the higher stages. In equilibrium, however, as we have seen time and again, there must be a uniform price for any factor throughout the economy. The lower demand in the lower stages, and the consequent lower price, coupled with the higher demand and higher price in the higher stages, causes the shift of the factor from later to earlier stages. The shift ceases when the price of the factor is again uniform throughout.

We have seen the impact of new saving, i.e., a shift from consumption to investment, on the prices of goods at various levels. What, however, is the *aggregate* impact of a change to a higher level of gross savings on the prices of factors? Here we reach a paradoxical situation. *Net income* is the total amount of money that ultimately goes to factors: land, labor, and time. In any equilibrium situation, net saving is zero by definition (since net saving means a change in the level of gross saving over the previous period of time), and net income equals consumption and consumption alone. If we look again at Fig. 41 above, we see that the total income for original factors and interest can come only from net, rather than gross, income. Let us consider the new ERE *after* the change has taken place to a higher level of saving (ignoring for a moment the relevant conditions *during* the period of change). Gross savings = gross investment has increased from 318 to 338. But consumption has declined from 100 to 80, and it is consumption that provides the net income in the equilibrium situation. Net income is, as it were, the "fund" out of which money prices and incomes are paid to original factors. And this fund has *declined.*

The recipients of the net income fund are the original factors (labor and land) and interest on time. We know that the interest rate declines, this is a corollary of the increased saving and investment in the productive system, caused by lowered time preference. However, the absolute amount of interest *income* is gross investment multiplied by the rate of interest. Gross investment has increased, so that it is impossible for economic analysis to determine whether interest *income* has fallen, increased, or remained the same. Any of these alternatives is a possibility.

What happens to total original-factor income is also indeterminate. Two forces are pulling different ways in a *progressing economy* (an economy with *increasing* gross investment). On the one hand, the total net income money fund is falling; on the other hand, if the interest decline is large enough, it is possible that the fall in interest income will outstrip the fall in total net income, so that total factor income actually increases. For this to occur is possible but empirically highly unlikely.

The one certain prospect is that total net income for factors *and* interest will fall. If the total original-factor income falls, then, since we have implicitly been assuming a given supply of original factors, the prices of these factors, as well as the interest rate, will "in general" also decline.

That the general trend of original-factor incomes and prices may well be downward is a startling conclusion, for it is difficult to conceive of a *progressing* economy as one in which factor prices, such as wage rates and ground rents, steadily *decline*. What interests us, however, is not the course of *money* incomes and prices of factors, but of *real* incomes and prices, i.e., the "goods-income" accruing to factors. If money wage rates or wage incomes fall, and the supply of consumers' goods increases such that the prices of these goods fall even more, the result is a rise in "real" wage rates and "real incomes" to factors. That this is precisely what does happen solves the paradox that a progressing economy experiences falling wages and rents. There may be a fall in money terms (although not in all conceivable cases); but there will always be a *rise in real terms.*

The rise in real rates and incomes is due to the increase in the marginal physical productivity of factors that always results from an increase in saving and investment.[10] The increased productivity of the longer production processes leads to a greater physical supply of capital goods, and, most important, of consumers' goods, with a consequent fall in the prices of consumers' goods. As a result, even if the money prices of labor and land fall, those of consumers' goods will *always* fall farther, so that real factor incomes will rise. That this is always true in a progressing economy can be seen from the following considerations.

At any time, the wage or rent of the service of an original factor of production will equal its DMVP, the discounted marginal value product. This DMVP is equal to the MVP (marginal value product) divided by a discount factor, say *d*, which is directly dependent on the rate of interest. The MVP, in turn, is approximately equal to the MPP (marginal physical product) of the factor times the selling price, i.e., the final price of the consumers' good product. Hence,

$$\text{Price of factor service} = \frac{\text{MPP} \times P}{d}$$

In this discussion, we are considering the prices of consumers' goods "in general" or in the aggregate. The "real" prices of the original factors equal the money prices divided by the prices of consumers' goods. Strictly, there is no precise praxeological way of measuring these aggregates, or "real" income, based on changes in the purchasing power of money, but we can make qualitative statements about these elements even though we cannot make precise quantitative measurements.

The *real* price of factor service, then, $= \frac{\text{MPP} \times P}{d \times P}$.

The *P*'s cancel, and the result:

$$\text{Real price of factor service} = \frac{\text{MPP}}{d} \text{ (roughly)}$$

Now the progressing economy consists of two leading features: an increase in the MPP of original factors resulting from more productive and longer production processes, and a fall in the discount or interest rate concomitant with falling time preference and increasing gross investment. Both elements—the increase in MPP and the fall in *d*—impel an increase in the real prices of factor services in a progressing economy.

The conclusion is that in a progressing economy, i.e., in an economy with increases in gross savings and investment, money wages and ground rents may well fall, but *real* wages and rents will rise.[11]

One question that immediately presents itself is: How can the prices of factors decline while the gross income remains the same and gross investment even increases? The answer is that the increase in investment goes into increasing the number of stages, pushing back the stages of production and employing longer production processes. It is this increasing "roundaboutness" that causes every increase in capital—even if unaccompanied by an advance in technological *knowledge*—to lead to higher physical productivity per original factor. The increase in gross investment, in particular, raises the prices of capital goods at the highest stages, encouraging new stages and inducing entrepreneurs to shift factors into this new and flowering field. The larger gross investment fund is absorbed, so to speak, by higher prices of high-order capital goods and by the consequent new stages of turnover of these goods.[12]

3. *Capital Values and Aggregate Profits in a Changing Economy*

Net saving, as we have seen, increases gross investment in the economy. This increase in gross investment at first accrues as profits to the firms doing the increased business. These profits will accrue particularly in the higher stages, toward which old capital is shifting and in which new capital is invested. An accrual of profits to a firm increases, by that amount, the capital value of its assets, just as the losses decrease the capital value. The first impact of the new investment, then, is to cause *aggregate profits* to appear in the economy, concentrated in the new production processes in the higher stages. As the transition to the new ERE begins to take place, however, these profits more and more become *imputed* to the factors for which these entrepreneurs must pay in production. Eventually, if no other interfering changes occur, the result will be a disappearance of profits in the economy, a settling into the new ERE, an increase in real wages and other real rents, and an increase in the real capital value of ground land. This latter result, of course, is in perfect conformity with the previous conclusion that a progressing economy will lead to an increase in the real rents of ground land and a fall in the rate of interest. These two factors in conjunction, both impel a rise in the real capital value of ground land.

Future rises in the real values of rents can be either anticipated or not anticipated. To the extent that they are *anticipated,* the rise in future rents is already accounted for, and discounted, in the capital value of the whole land. A rise in the far future may be anticipated, but will have no appreciable effect on the present price of land, simply because time preference places a very distant date beyond the effective "time horizon" of the present. To the extent that rises in the real rate are *not* foreseen, then, of course, entrepreneurial errors have been made, and the market has undercapitalized in the present price.[13] Throughout the whole history of landholding, therefore, income from *basic land* can be earned in only three ways (we are omitting *improving* the land): (1) through entrepreneurial profit in correcting the forecasting errors of others; (2) as interest return; or (3) by a rise in the capital value to the *first* finder and user of the land.

The first type of income is obvious and not unique. It is pervasive in any field of enterprise. The second type of income is the general income earned by ground land. Because of the market phenomenon of capitalization, income from ground land is largely interest return on investment, just as in any other business. The only unique component of income that ground land confers, therefore, is (3), accruing to the first user, whose land value began at zero and became positive. After that, the buyer of the land must pay its capitalized value. To earn rent on ground land, in other words, a man must either buy it or find it, and in the former case he earns only interest, and not pure rent. The capitalized value can increase from time to time and not be discounted in advance only if some new and unexpected development occurs (or if better knowledge of the future comes to light), in which case the previous owner has suffered an entrepreneurial loss in profit forgone for not having anticipated the new situation, and the current owner earns an entrepreneurial profit.

The only unique aspect to ground land, then, is that it is found and first put on the market at some particular time, so that the *first user* earns pure rent as a result of his initial discovery and use of the land. All later increases in the capital value of the land are accounted for in the value, either as entrepreneurial profits resulting from better forecasting or as interest return.

The first user earns his gain only at first and not at whatever later date he actually sells the land. After the capital value has increased, his refusal to sell the land involves an opportunity cost —the forgone utility of selling the land for its capital value. Therefore, his true gain was reaped earlier, when the capital value of his land increased, and not at the later date when he "took" his gain in the form of money.

If we set aside uncertainty and entrepreneurial profits for a moment, and assume the highly unlikely condition that all future changes can be anticipated correctly by the market,[14] then all future increases in the value of ground rents will be capitalized back into the land when it is first found and put into use. The first finder will reap the net gain immediately, and from then on all that will be earned by him and by successive heirs or purchasers is the usual interest return. When future rises are too remote to enter into the capitalized price, this is simply a phenomenon of time preference, not a sign of some mysterious breakdown in the market's process of adjustment. The fact that complete discounting never takes place is due to the presence of uncertainty, and the result is a continual accretion of entrepreneurial gains through rising capital values of land.

Thus, we see, this time from the landowner's point of view, that aggregate gains in capital value are synonymous with aggregate profits. Aggregate profits begin with the higher-order firms, then filter down until they increase real wages and the aggregate profits of landowners, particularly owners of land specific to the higher-order stages of production. (Land specific to the lower stages will, of course, bear the brunt of decreases in capital value, i.e., losses, in the progressing economy.)

As the only income to ground land that is not profit or interest, we are left with the original gains to the first finder of land. But, *here again,* there is capitalization and not a pure gain. Pioneering —finding new land, i.e., new natural resources—is a business like any other. Investing in it takes capital, labor, and entrepreneurial ability. The expected rents of finding and using are taken into account when the investments and expenses of exploration and shaping into use are made. Therefore, these gains are also capitalized backward in the original investment, and the tendency will be for them too to be the usual interest return on the investment. Deviations from this return will constitute entrepreneurial profits and losses. Therefore, we conclude that there is practically nothing unique about incomes from ground land and that all net income in the productive system goes to wages, to interest, and to profit.

A progressive economy is marked by aggregate net profits. When there is a shift from one savings-investment level to a higher one (therefore, a progressing economy), aggregate profits are earned in the economy, particularly in the higher stages of production. The increased gross investment first increases the aggregate capital value of firms that earn net profits. As production and investment increase in the higher stages, and the effects of the new saving continue, the profits disappear and become imputed to increases in real wage rates and in real ground rents. The latter effect, added to a fall in the rate of interest, leads to a rise in the real capital values of ground land.

What happens when there is a shift in the reverse direction—a changed proportion such that gross saving and investment *decline* and consumption *increases?* For the most part, we may simply trace the above analysis in reverse—that is, consider the shift from a 338:80 situation to a 318:100 situation. During the transition to a new equilibrium, there would be a *net dissaving* of 20 ounces, since gross saving decreases from 100 to 80. There would also be a *net disinvestment* of the same amount. The cause of such a shift would be an increase in the time-preference schedules of the individuals on the market. This would increase the rate of interest and widen the interest spread between cumulative prices in the production stages. It would broaden the consumption base, but leave less money available for saving and investment. We may simply reverse the diagrams above and consider the reverse shift, e.g., to a shorter and wider structure of production, to a steeper price curve with a smaller number of productive stages. The interest spread goes up, but the investment base declines. There would be higher prices for consumers' goods and therefore a greater demand for factors in this and other lower stages; on the other hand, there would be general abandonment of the higher stages in the face of the monetary attractions of the later stages, the decline in investment funds, and the shift of these funds from the higher to the lower stages. Specific factors will bear the brunt of lowered incomes and sheer abandonment in the higher stages, and they will gain in the lower stages.

There will be a rise in net income and consumption, in monetary terms, and therefore a rise in aggregate factor income. The interest rate increases, while the gross investment base declines.

In real terms the important result is a lowering in the physical productivity of labor (and of land) because of the abandonment of the most productive processes of production—the lengthiest ones. The lower output at every stage, the lower supply of capital goods, and the consequent lower output of consumers' goods leads to a lowering in the "standard of living." Money wage rates and money rents may rise (although this possibly might not occur because of the higher interest rate), but the prices of consumers' goods will rise further because of the reduced physical supply of goods.[15]

The case of decreasing gross capital investment is defined as a *retrogressing economy*.[16] The decreased investment is first revealed as aggregate losses in the economy, particularly losses to firms in the highest stages of production, the firms which are now losing customers. As time proceeds, these losses will tend to disappear, as firms leave the industry and abandon the now unprofitable production processes. The losses will thereby be imputed to factors in the form of lower real wage rates and lower real rents, which, combined with a higher interest rate, cause lower real capital values of ground land. Particularly hard hit will be the factors specific to these lines of production.

The reason why there are aggregate profits in the progressing economy and aggregate losses in the retrogressing economy, may be demonstrated in the following way. For profits to appear, there must be undercapitalization, or overdiscounting, of productive factors on the market. For losses to appear, there must be overcapitalization, or underdiscounting, of factors on the market. But if the economy is stationary, i.e., if from one period to another the total gross investment remains constant, the total value of capital remains constant. There might be an increase of investment in one line of production, but this is made possible only by a decrease elsewhere. Aggregate capital values remain constant, and therefore any profits (the result of mistaken undercapitalization) must be offset by equal losses (the result of mistaken overcapitalization). In the progressing economy, on the other hand, there are additional investment funds made available through new savings, and this provides a source for new revenue not yet capitalized anywhere in the system. These constitute the aggregate net profits during this period of change. In the retrogressing economy, investment funds are lowered, and this leaves net areas of overcapitalization of factors in the economy. Their owners suffer aggregate net losses during this period of change.[17]

Thus, another conclusion of our analysis is that aggregate profits will equal aggregate losses in a *stationary economy,* i.e., profits and losses will equal zero. This stationary economy is not the same construct as the evenly rotating economy that has played such a large role in our analysis. In the stationary economy, uncertainty does not disappear and no unending constant round pervades all elements in the system. There is, in fact, only *one* constancy: total capital invested. Clearly, the stationary economy (like all other economies) tends to evolve into the ERE, given constant data. After a time, market forces will tend to eliminate all *individual* profits and losses as well as aggregate profits and losses.

We might pause here to consider briefly the old problem: Are "capital gains"—increases in capital value—*income?* If we fully realize that profits and capital gains, and losses and capital losses, are identical, the solution becomes clear. No one would exclude business profits from money income. The same should be true of capital gains. In the ERE, of course, there are neither capital gains nor capital losses.

Let us now return to the case of the retrogressing economy and a decrease in capital investment. The greater the shift from saving to consumption, the more drastic will the effects tend to be, and the greater the lowering of productivity and living standards. The fact that such shifts can and do happen serves to refute easily the fashionable assumption that our capital structure is, by some magical provision or hidden hand, permanently and eternally self-reproducing once it is built. No positive acts of saving by capitalists are deemed necessary to maintain it.[18, 19] The ruins of Rome are mute illustrations of the error of this assumption.[20]

Refusal to maintain the value of capital, i.e., the process of net dissaving, is known as *consuming capital.* Granting the impossibility of measuring the value of capital in society with any precision, this is still a highly important concept. "Consuming capital" means, of course, not "eating machines," as some critics have scoffingly referred to it, but failing to maintain existing gross investment and the existing capital goods structure, using some of these funds instead for consumption expenditure.[21]

Professor Frank H. Knight has been the leader of the school of thought that assumes capital to be automatically permanent. Knight has contributed a great deal to economics in his analysis of profit theory and entrepreneurship, but his theories of capital and interest have misled a generation of American economists. Knight succinctly summed up his doctrine in an attack on the "Austrian" investment theory of Böhm-Bawerk and Hayek. Knight said that the latter involved two fallacies. One is that Böhm-Bawerk viewed production as the production of concrete goods, whereas "in reality, what is produced, and consumed, is services." There is no real problem here, however. It is not to be denied—in fact it has been stressed herein—that goods are valued *for their services*. Yet it is also undeniable that the concrete capital goods structure must be produced before its services can be obtained. The second alleged correction, and here we come directly to the problem of capital consumption, is that "the production of any service includes the maintenance of things used in the process, and this includes reproduction of any which are used up . . . really a detail of maintenance." [22] This is obviously incorrect. Services are yielded by things, at least in the cases relevant to our discussion, and they are produced through the using up of *things*, of capital goods. And this production does not necessarily "include" maintenance and reproduction. This alleged "detail" is a completely separate area of choice and involves the building up of more capital at a later date to replace the used-up capital.

The case of the retrogressing economy is our first example of what we may call a *crisis situation*. A crisis situation is one in which firms, in the aggregate, are suffering losses. The crisis aspect of the case is aggravated by a decline in production through the abandonment of the highest production stages. The troubles arose from "undersaving" and "underinvestment," i.e., a shift in people's values so that they do not *now* choose to save and invest enough to enable *continuation* of production processes begun in the past. We cannot simply be critical of this shift, however, since the people, given existing conditions, have decided voluntarily that their time preferences are higher, and that they wish to consume more proportionately at present, even at the cost of lowering future productivity.

Once an increase to a greater level of gross investment occurs, therefore, it is not maintained automatically. Producers have to maintain the gross investment, and this will be done only if their time preferences remain at the lower rates and they continue to be willing to save a greater proportion of gross monetary income. We have demonstrated, further, that this maintenance and further progress can take place without any increase in the money supply or other change in the money relation. Progress can occur, in fact, with falling prices of all products and factors.[23]

4. *Capital Accumulation and the Length of the Structure of Production*

We have been demonstrating that investment lengthens the structure of production. Now we may consider some criticisms of this approach.

Böhm-Bawerk is the great founder of production-structure analysis, but unfortunately he left room for misinterpretation by identifying capital accumulation with adopting "more roundabout" methods of production. Thus, consider his famous example of the Crusoe who must first construct (and then maintain) a net if he wishes to catch more than the number of fish he can catch without any capital. Böhm-Bawerk stated: "The roundabout ways of capital are fruitful but long; they procure us more or better consumption goods, but only at a later period of time." [24] Calling these methods "roundabout" is definitely paradoxical; for do we not know that men strive always to achieve their ends in the most direct and shortest manner possible? As Mises demonstrates, rather than speak of the higher productivity of roundabout methods of production, "it is more appropriate to speak of the higher physical productivity of production processes requiring more time" (longer processes).[25]

Now let us suppose that we are confronted with an array of possible production processes, based on their physical productivities. We may also rank the processes in accordance with their *length,* i.e., in terms of the waiting time between the input of the resources and the yielding of the final product. The longer the waiting period between first input and final output, the greater the disutility, *ceteris paribus,* since more time must elapse before the satisfaction is attained.

The first processes to be used will be those most productive (in value and physically) *and* the shortest. No one has maintained that *all* long processes are more productive than *all* short processes.[26] The point is, however, that all short *and* ultraproductive processes will be the first ones to be invested in and established. Given any present structure of production, a new investment will not be in a *shorter* process because the shorter, more productive process would have been chosen first.

As we have seen, there is only one way by which man can rise from the ultraprimitive level: through investment in capital. But this cannot be accomplished through short processes, since the short processes for producing the most valuable goods will be the ones first adopted. Any increase in capital goods can serve only to lengthen the structure, i.e., to enable the adoption of longer and longer productive processes. Men will invest in longer processes more productive than the ones previously adopted. They will be more productive in two ways: (1) by producing *more* of a previously produced good, and/or (2) by producing a new good that could not have been produced at all by the shorter processes. Within this framework these longer processes *are the most direct* that must be used to attain the goal—not more roundabout. Thus, if Crusoe can catch ten fish per day directly without capital and can catch a hundred fish per day with a net, building a net should not be considered as a "more roundabout method of catching fish," but as the "most direct method for catching a hundred fish a day." Furthermore, no amount of labor and land without capital could enable a man to produce an automobile; for this a certain amount of capital is required. The production of the requisite amount of capital is the shortest and most direct method of obtaining an automobile.

Any new investment will therefore be in a longer and more productive method of production. Yet, if there were no time preference, the most productive methods would be invested in *first,* regardless of time, and an increase in capital would not cause more productive methods to be used. The existence of time preference acts as a brake on the use of the more productive but longer processes. Any state of equilibrium will be based on the time-preference, or pure interest, rate, and this rate will determine the amount of savings and capital invested. It determines capital by imposing a limit on the length of the production processes and therefore on the maximum amount produced. A lowering of time preference, therefore, and a consequent lowering of the pure rate of interest signify that people are now more willing to wait for any given amount of future output, i.e., to invest more proportionately and in longer processes than heretofore. A rise in time preference and in the pure interest rate means that people are less willing to wait and will spend proportionately more on consumers' goods and less on the longer production processes, so that investments in the longest processes will have to be abandoned.[27]

One qualification to the law that increased investment lengthens production processes appears when investment turns to a type of good which is less useful than the goods previously acquired, yet which has a shorter process of production than some of the others. Here the investment in this process was checked, not by the length of the process, but by its inferior (value) productivity. Yet even here the structure of production was lengthened, since people have to wait longer for the new *and* the old goods than they previously did for the old good. New capital investment always lengthens the overall structure of production.

What of the case where a technological invention permits a more productive process with a lesser amount of capital investment? Is this not a case in which increased investment *shortens* the production structure? Up to this point we have been assuming technological knowledge as given. Yet it is not given in the dynamic world. Technological advance is one of the most dramatic features of the world of change. What then of these "capital-saving" inventions? One interesting example was cited by Horace White in a criticism of Böhm-Bawerk.[28] Oil was produced first by ships hunting in the Arctic for whales, the whale oil being processed from the whales, etc., an obviously lengthy production process. Later an invention permitted people to bore for oil in the ground, thereby immeasurably shortening the production period.

Aside from the fact that, empirically, most inventions do not shorten physical production processes, we must reply that the limits at any time on investment and productivity are a *scarcity of saved capital, not* the state of technological knowledge. In other words, there is always an unused shelf of technological projects available and idle. This is demonstrable by the fact that a new invention is not immediately and instantaneously adopted by all firms in the society. Therefore, any further investment will lengthen production processes, many of them more productive because of superior technique. A new invention does not automatically impel itself into production, but first joins the unused array. Further, in order for the new invention to be used, *more capital must be invested. The ships for whaling have already been built; the oil wells and machinery, etc., must be created anew.* Even the newly invented method will yield a greater product only through further investment in longer processes. In other words, the only way to obtain more oil now is to invest more capital in more machinery and lengthier production periods in the oil-drilling business. As Böhm-Bawerk pointed out, White's criticism would apply only if the invention were *progressively* capital-saving, so that the product would always increase with the shortening of the process. But in that case, boring for oil with one's bare hands, unaided by capital, would have to be more productive than drilling for oil with machinery.[29]

Böhm-Bawerk drew the analogy of an agricultural invention applied to two grades of land, one grade previously yielding a marginal product of 100 bushels of wheat, the lower grade yielding 80 bushels Now suppose use of the invention raises the marginal product of the lower-grade land to 110 bushels. Does this mean that the poorer land *now* yields more than the fertile land and that the effect of agricultural inventions is to make poorer lands more productive than fertile ones? Yet this is precisely analogous to White's position, which maintains that inventions may cause shorter production processes to be more productive! As Böhm-Bawerk pointed out, it is obvious that the source of the error is this: inventions increase the physical productivity of *both* grades of land. The better land becomes *still* better. Similarly, perhaps it is true that an invention will cause a shorter process to be more productive now than a longer process was previously. But this does not mean that it is superior to *all* longer processes; longer processes using the invention will still be more productive than the shorter ones. (Boring for oil *with* machinery is more productive than boring for oil without machinery.)

Technological inventions have received a far more important place than they deserve in economic theory. It has often been assumed that production is limited by the "state of the arts"—by technological knowledge—and therefore that any improvement in technology will immediately show itself in production. Technology does, of course, set a limit on production; no production process could be used at all without the technological knowledge of how to put it into operation. But while knowledge is a limit, *capital* is a narrower limit. It is logically obvious that while capital cannot engage in production beyond the limits of existing available knowledge, knowledge can and does exist without the capital necessary to put it to use. Technology and its improvement, therefore, play no *direct* role in the investment and production process; technology, while important, must always *work through* an investment of capital. As was stated above, even the most dramatic capital-saving invention, such as oil-drilling, can be put to use only by saving and investing capital.

The relative unimportance of technology in production as compared to the supply of saved capital becomes evident, as Mises points out, simply by looking at the "backward" or "underdeveloped" countries.[30] What is lacking in these countries is not knowledge of Western technological methods ("know-how"); that is learned easily enough. The service of imparting knowledge, in person or in book form, can be paid for readily. What is lacking is the supply of saved capital needed to put the advanced methods into effect. The African peasant will gain little from looking at pictures of American tractors; what he lacks is the saved capital needed to purchase them. That is the important limit on his investment and on his production.[31]

A businessman's new investment in a longer and more physically productive process will therefore be made from a sheaf of processes previously known but unusable because of the time-preference limitation. A lowering of time preferences and of the pure interest rate will signify an expansion of saved capital at the disposal of investors and therefore an expansion of the longer processes, the time limitation on investment having been weakened.

Some critics charge that not all net investment goes to lengthening the structure—that new investments might duplicate preexisting processes. This criticism misfires, however, because our theory does not assume that net saving must be invested in an actually longer process in some specific line of production. A longer production structure can just as well be achieved by a shift from consumption to investment that will lengthen the *aggregate* production structure by greater investment in already existing longer processes, accompanied by less investment in existing shorter processes. Thus, in the case of Crusoe mentioned above, suppose that Crusoe now invests in a *second* net, which will permit him to catch a total of a hundred fifty fish a day. The structure of production is now lengthened even though the second net may be no more productive than the first. For the total period of production, from the time he must build and rebuild his total capital until his product arrives, is now considerably longer. He must now cut down again on present consumption (including leisure) and work on his second net.[32]

5. *The Adoption of a New Technique*

At any given time, then, there will be a shelf of available and more productive techniques that remain unused by many firms continuing with older methods. What determines the extent to which these firms adopt new and more productive techniques?

The reason that firms do not scrap their old methods immediately and begin afresh is that they and their ancestors have invested in a certain structure of capital goods. As times and tastes, resources, and techniques change, much of this capital investment becomes an *ex post* entrepreneurial error. If, in other words, investors had been able to foresee the changed pattern of values and methods, they would have invested in a far different manner. Now, however, the investment has been made, and the resulting capital structure is a given residue from the past that supplies the resources they have to work with. Since costs in the *present* are only present and future opportunities forgone, and bygones are bygones, existing equipment must be used in the most profitable way. Thus, there undoubtedly would have been far less investment in railroads in late nineteenth-century America if investors had foreseen the rise of truck and plane competition.[33] Now that the existing railroad equipment remains, however, decisions concerning how much of it is to be used must be based on current and expected future costs, not on past expenses or losses.

An old machine will be scrapped for a new and better substitute if the superiority of the new machine or method is great enough to compensate for the additional expenditure necessary to purchase the machine. The same applies to the shifting of a plant from an old location to a superior new location (superior because of greater access to factors or consumers). At any rate, the adoption of new techniques or locations is limited by the usefulness of the already given (and specific) capital-goods structure. This means that those processes and methods will be adopted at any time which will best satisfy the desires of the consumers.

The fact that investment in a new technique or location is unprofitable means that the use of capital in the new process at the cost of scrapping the old equipment is a waste from the point of view of satisfying consumer wants. How fast equipment or location is scrapped as obsolescent, then, is not decided arbitrarily by businessmen; it is determined by the values and desires of consumers, who decide on the price and profitability of the various goods and on the values of the necessary nonspecific factors used to produce these goods.[34]

As is often true, critics of the free market have attacked it from two contradictory points of view: one, that it unduly slows down the rate of technological improvement from what it could and should be; and, two, that it unduly accelerates the rate of technological improvement, thereby unsettling the peaceful course of society. We have seen that a free market will, as far as the knowledge and foresight of entrepreneurs permit, produce so that factors are best allocated to satisfy the wishes of consumers. Improvement in productivity through new techniques and locations will be balanced against the opportunity costs forgone in value product from using the existing old plant.[35] And ability in entrepreneurial foresight will be assured as much as possible by the market's process of "selection" in "rewarding" good forecasters and "penalizing" poor ones proportionately.

THE ENTREPRENEUR AND INNOVATION

Under the stimulus of the late Professor Schumpeter, it has been thought that the essence of entrepreneurship is *innovation* —the disturbance of peaceful, unchanging business routine by bold innovators who institute new methods and develop new products. There is, of course, no denying the importance of the discovery and institution of more productive methods of obtaining a product or of the development of valuable new products. Analytically, however, there is danger of overrating the importance of this process. For innovation is only one of the activities performed by the entrepreneur. As we have seen above, most entrepreneurs are not innovators, but are in the process of investing capital within a large framework of available technological opportunities. Supply of product is limited by supply of capital goods rather than by available technological know-how.

Entrepreneurial activities are derived from the presence of *uncertainty*. The entrepreneur is an adjuster of the discrepancies of the market toward greater satisfaction of the desires of the consumers. When he innovates he is *also* an adjuster, since he is adjusting the discrepancies of the market as they present themselves in the potential of a new method or product. In other words, if the ruling rate of (natural) interest return is 5%, and a business man estimates that he could earn 10% by instituting a new process or product, then he has, as in other cases, discovered a discrepancy in the market and sets about correcting it. By launching and producing more of the new process, he is pursuing the entrepreneurial function of adjustment to consumer desires, i.e., what he estimates consumer desires will be. If he succeeds in his estimate and reaps a profit, then he and others will continue in this line of activity until the income discrepancy is eliminated and there is no "pure" profit or loss in this area.

6. *The Beneficiaries of Saving-Investment*

We have seen that an increase in saving and investment causes an increase in the real incomes of owners of labor and land factors. The latter is reflected in increases in the capital value of ground lands. The benefits to land factors, however, accrue only to particular lands. Other lands may lose in value, although there is an aggregate gain. This is so because usually lands are relatively specific factors. For the nonspecific factor *par excellence,* namely, labor, there is, on the contrary, a very general rise in real wages. These laborers are "external beneficiaries" of increased investment, i.e., they are beneficiaries of the actions of others without paying for these benefits. What benefits do the investors themselves acquire? In the long run, they are not great. In fact, their rate of interest return is reduced. This is not a loss, however, since it is the outcome of their changed time preferences. Their *real* interest return may well be increased, in fact, since the fall in the interest rate may be offset by the rise in the purchasing power of the monetary unit in an expanding economy.

The main benefits gained by the investors, therefore, are short-run entrepreneurial profits. These are earned by investors who see a profit to be gained by investing in a certain area. After a while, the profits tend to disappear as more investors enter this field, although changing data are always presenting new profit opportunities to enterprising investors. But the short-run benefits earned by the workers and landowners are more certain. The entrepreneur-capitalists take the risks of speculating on the uncertain market; their investment may result in profits, in breaking even with no profits at all, or in suffering outright losses. No one can guarantee profits to them.[36] Aggregate new investment will result in aggregate net profits, to be sure, but no one can predict with certainty in what areas the profits will appear. On the other hand, the workers and landowners in the fields of new investment gain *immediately,* as new investment bids up wages and rents in the longer processes. They gain even if the investment turns out to have been uneconomic and unprofitable. For in that case, the error in satisfying consumers is borne by the heavy losses of the capitalist-entrepreneurs. In the meanwhile, the workers and landowners have reaped a gain. This is hardly a clear gain, however, since consumers have, as a whole, suffered in real income through entrepreneurial error in producing the wrong kind of goods. Yet it is obvious that the brunt of the loss from making the error is suffered by the entrepreneurs.

7. *The Progressing Economy and the Pure Rate of Interest*

It is clear that a feature of the progressing economy must necessarily be a fall in the pure rate of interest. We have seen that in order for more capital to be invested, there must be a fall in the pure rate of interest, reflecting general declines in time preferences. If the pure rate remains the same, this is an indication that there will be no new investment or disinvestment, that time preferences are generally stable, and that the economy is *stationary.* A fall in the pure rate of interest is a corollary of a drop in time preferences and a rise in gross investment. A rise in the pure rate of interest is a corollary of a rise in time preferences and net disinvestment. Hence, for the economy to keep advancing, time preferences and the pure rate of interest must continue to fall. If the pure rate of interest remains the same, capital will only just be maintained at its same real level.

Since praxeology never establishes quantitative laws, there is no way by which we can determine any sort of *quantitative* relation between changes in the pure rate of interest and the amount that capital will change. All we can assert is the qualitative relation.

It should be noticed what we are *not* saying. We are *not* asserting that the pure rate of interest is determined by the quantity or value of capital goods available. We are not concluding, therefore, that an increase in the quantity or value of capital goods lowers the pure rate of interest because interest is the "price of capital" (or for any other reason). On the contrary, we are asserting *precisely the reverse:* namely, *that a lower pure rate of interest increases the quantity and value of capital goods available.* The causative principle is just the other way round from what is commonly believed. The pure rate of interest, then, can change at any time and is determined by time preferences. If it is lowered, the stock of invested capital will increase; if it is raised, the stock of invested capital will fall.

That a change in the pure rate of interest has an *inverse* effect on the stock of capital is discovered by deduction from accepted axioms and not inferred from uncertain and complex empirical data.[37] The law is not deduced, for example, by observing that the *market* rate of interest in backward nations is higher than in advanced nations. It is clear that this phenomenon is at least partly due to the higher entrepreneurial risk component in the backward countries and is not *necessarily* caused by differences in the *pure* rate of interest.

8. *The Entrepreneurial Component in the Market Interest Rate*

In the ERE, as we have seen, the interest rate throughout the economy will be uniform. In the real world there is an additional *entrepreneurial (or "risk") component,* which *adds* to the interest rate in particularly risky ventures, and in accordance with the degree of risk. (Since "risk" has an actuarially "certain" connotation, we may better call it "degree of uncertainty.") Thus, suppose that the basic social time preference rate, or *pure* rate of interest, in the economy is 5%. Capitalists will buy 100 ounces of future goods to sell less remotely future goods one year later at 105 ounces. Thus, a 5% return is a "pure" return, i.e., it is the return assuming that the 105 ounces will *definitely* be accruing. The pure rate, in other words, abstracts from any entrepreneurial uncertainty. It gauges the premium of present over future goods on the assumption that the future goods are known as *certain* to be forthcoming.

In the real world, of course, nothing is absolutely certain, and therefore the pure rate of interest (the result of time preference) can never appear alone. Now suppose that in one particular venture or industry it is fairly certain that 105 ounces will be earned from the sale of a product one year in the future. Then, with a social time preference rate of 5%, the capitalist-entrepreneurs will be willing to pay 100 ounces for factors and reap a 5% return. But suppose that there is another possible venture considered very risky by entrepreneurs. The product is expected to sell for 105 ounces, but there are definite possibilities that the price of the product might plummet. In that case, the entrepreneurs will not be willing to pay 100 ounces for factors. They would have to be compensated for the extra risks that they run; the price of the factors might finally be 90 ounces. Thus, the riskier a given venture appears *ex ante,* the higher will be the expected interest return that capitalists will require before they make the investment.

On the market, then, a whole structure of interest rates will be superimposed on the pure rate, varying positively in accordance with the expected risks of each venture. The counterpart of this structure will be a similar variety of interest rates on the loan market, which, as usual, is derivative from the goods market.[38] In the *long run,* of course, the tendency, given no changes of data, will be for people to realize that such and such a venture is pretty consistently yielding a higher than 5% return. The risk component for this venture will then fall, other entrepreneurs will enter this type of venture, and the interest rate will tend to fall back to 5% again. Thus, the varying risk structure of interest does not invalidate the tendency toward uniformity of the interest rate. On the contrary, any variety is something of an index of the various "risks" of uncertainty which still remain in the market and which would be eliminated if data were frozen and an ERE were reached. If data *did* remain constant, then the uniformity of the ERE would ensue. It is because data are always changing and thus setting up new uncertainties in place of the old that we do not have the uniformity of the ERE.

9. *Risk, Uncertainty and Insurance*

Entrepreneurship deals with the inevitable uncertainty of the future. Some forms of uncertainty, however, can be converted into *actuarial risk.* The distinction between "risk" and "uncertainty" has been developed by Professor Knight.[39] "Risk" occurs when an event is a member of a class of a large number of homogeneous events and there is fairly certain knowledge of the frequency of occurrence of this class of events. Thus, a firm may produce bolts and know from long experience that a certain almost fixed proportion of these bolts will be defective, say one per cent. It will not know whether any given bolt will be defective, but it will know the proportion of the total number defective. This knowledge can convert the percentage of defects into a definite cost of the firm's operations, especially where enough cases occur *within* a firm. In other situations, a given loss or hazard may be large and infrequent in relation to a firm's operations (such as the risk of fire), but over a large number of firms it could be considered as a "measurable" or actuarial risk. In such situations, the firms themselves could pool their risks, or a specialized firm, an "insurance company," could organize the pooling for them.

The principle of insurance is that firms or individuals are subject to risks which, in the aggregate, form a class of homogeneous cases. Thus, out of a class of a thousand firms, no one firm has any idea whether it will suffer a fire next year or not; but it is fairly well known that ten of them will. In that case, it may be advantageous for each of the firms to "take out insurance," to pool their risks of loss. Each firm will pay a certain premium, which will go into a pool to compensate those firms which suffer the fires.

As a result of competition, the firm organizing the insurance service will tend to obtain the usual interest income on its investment, no more and no less.

The contrast between risk and uncertainty has been brilliantly analyzed by Ludwig von Mises. Mises has shown that they can be subsumed under the more general categories of "class probability" and "case probability." [40] "Class probability" is the only scientific use of the term "probability," and is the only form of probability subject to numerical expression.[41] In the tangled literature on probability, no one has defined class probability as cogently as Ludwig von Mises:

> Class probability means: We know or assume to know, with regard to the problem concerned, everything about the behavior of a whole class of events or phenomena; but about the actual singular events or phenomena we know nothing but that they are elements of this class.[42]

Insurable risk is an example of class probability. The businessmen knew how many bolts would be defective out of a total number of bolts, but had no knowledge as to which particular bolt would be defective. In life insurance the mortality tables reveal the proportion of mortality of each age group in the population, but they tell nothing about the particular life expectancy of any given individual.

Insurance firms have their problems. As soon as something specific is known about individual cases, firms break down the cases into subaggregates in an effort to maintain homogeneity of classes, i.e., the similarity, as far as is known, of all individual members in the class with respect to the attribute in question. Thus, certain subgroups within one age group may have a higher mortality rate because of their occupation; these will be segregated, and different premiums applied to the two cases. If there were knowledge about differences between subgroups, and insurance firms charged the same premium rate to all, then this would mean that the healthy or "less risky" groups would be subsidizing the riskier. Unless they specifically desire to grant such subsidies, this result will never be maintained in the competitive free market. In the free market each homogeneous group will tend to pay premium rates in proportion to its actuarial risk, plus a sum for interest income and for necessary costs for the insurance firms.

Most uncertainties are uninsurable because they are unique, single cases, and not members of a class. They are unique cases facing each individual or business; they may bear resemblances to other cases, but are not homogeneous with them. Individuals or entrepreneurs know something about the outcome of the particular case, but not everything. As Mises defines it:

> Case probability means: We know, with regard to a particular event, some of the factors which determine its outcome; but there are other determining factors about which we know nothing.[43]

Estimates of future costs, demands, etc., on the part of entrepreneurs are all unique cases of uncertainty, where methods of specific understanding and individual judgment of the situation must apply, rather than objectively measurable or insurable "risk."

It is not accurate to apply terms like "gambling" or "betting" to situations either of risk or of uncertainty. These terms have unfavorable emotional implications, and for this reason: they refer to situations where *new* risks or uncertainties are *created* for the enjoyment of the uncertainties themselves. Gambling on the throw of the dice and betting on horse races are examples of the deliberate creation by the bettor or gambler of new uncertainties which otherwise would not have existed.[44] The entrepreneur, on the other hand, is not creating uncertainties for the fun of it. On the contrary, he tries to reduce them as much as possible. The uncertainties he confronts are already inherent in the market situation, indeed in the nature of human action; someone must deal with them, and he is the most skilled or willing candidate. In the same way, an *operator* of a gambling establishment or of a race track is not creating new risks; he is an entrepreneur trying to judge the situation on the market, and neither a gambler nor a bettor.

Profit and loss are the results of entrepreneurial *uncertainty*. Actuarial *risk* is converted into a cost of business operation and is not responsible for profits or losses except in so far as the actuarial estimates are erroneous.

9

Production: Particular Factor Prices and Productive Incomes

1. *Introduction*

Up to this point we have analyzed the determination of the rate of interest and of the prices of productive factors on the market. We have also discussed the role of entrepreneurship in the changing world and the consequences of changes in saving and investment. We now return to analysis of the particular ultimate factors—labor and land—and to a more detailed discussion of entrepreneurial incomes. Our analysis of general factor pricing in chapter 7 treated prices as they would be in the ERE, a state toward which they are always tending. Our discussion of entrepreneurship in chapter 8 showed that this tendency is a result of drives toward profits and away from losses by capitalist-entrepreneurs. Now let us return to the particular factors and analyze their pricing, their supplies and incomes, and the effects of a changing economy upon them.

2. *Land, Labor, and Rent*

A. RENT

We have been using the term *rent* in our analysis to signify the hire price of the services of goods. This price is paid for *unit services,* as distinguished from the prices of the *whole factors* yielding the service. Since all goods have unit services, *all* goods will earn rents, whether they be consumers' goods or any type of producers' goods. Future rents of durable goods tend to be capitalized and embodied in their capital value and therefore in the money presently needed to acquire them. As a result, the investors and producers of these goods tend to earn simply an interest return on their investment.

All goods earn *gross rent,* since all have unit services and prices for them. If a good is "rented out," it will earn gross rent in the hire charge. If it is bought, then its present price embodies discounted future rents, and in the future it will earn these rents by contributing to production. All goods, therefore, earn gross rents, and here there is no analytic distinction between one factor and another.

Net rents, however, are earned only by labor and land factors, and not by capital goods.[1] For the gross rents earned by a capital good will be imputed to gross rents paid to the owners of the factors that produced it. Hence, on net, only labor and land factors—the ultimate factors—earn rents, and, in the ERE, these, along with interest on time, will be the only incomes in the economy.

The Marshallian theory holds that durable capital goods earn "quasirents" temporarily, while permanent lands earn full rents. The fallacy of this theory is clear. Whatever their durability, capital goods receive gross rents just as lands do, whether in the changing real world or the ERE. In the ERE, they receive no *net* rents at all, since these are imputed to land and labor. In the real world, their capital value changes, but this does not mean that they earn net rents. Rather, these changes are *profits* or *losses* accruing to their owners as entrepreneurs. If, then, incomes in the real world are net rents (accruing to labor and land factors) and entrepreneurial profits, while the latter disappear in the ERE, there is no room in *either* world for the concept of "quasirent." Nowhere does this special type of income exist.

A *wage* is the term describing the payment for the unit services of a *labor* factor. *A wage, therefore, is a special case of rent;* it is labor's "hire." On a free market this rent cannot, of course, be capitalized, since the whole labor factor—the man—cannot be bought and sold for a price, his income to accrue to his owner. This is precisely what occurs, however, under a regime of slavery. The wage, in fact, is the only source of rent that *cannot* be capitalized on the free market, since every man is necessarily a self-owner with an inalienable will.

One distinction between wages and land rents, then, is that the latter are capitalized and transformed into interest return, while the former are not. Another distinction is purely *empirical* and not apodictically true for mankind. It has simply been an historical-empirical truth *that labor factors have always been relatively scarcer than land factors.* Land and labor factors can be ranged in order of their marginal value productivity. The result of a relative superfluity of land factors is that not all the land factors will be put to use, i.e., the poorest land factors will be left idle, so that labor will be free to work the most productive land (e.g., the most productive agricultural land, urban sites, fish hatcheries, "natural resources," etc.). Laborers will tend to use the most value-productive land first, the next most productive second, etc. At any given time, then, there will be some land —the most value-productive—under cultivation and use, and some not in use. The latter, in the ERE, will be free land, since its rental earnings are zero, and therefore its price will be zero.[2] The former land will be "supramarginal" and the latter land will be "submarginal." On the dividing line will be the poorest land now in use; this will be the "marginal" land, and it will be earning *close* to zero rent.

It is important to recognize the qualification that the marginal land will earn *not zero,* but only *close* to zero, rent.[3] The reason is that, in human action, there is no infinite continuity, and action cannot proceed in infinitely small steps. Mathematically-minded writers tend to think in such terms, so that the points before and after the point under consideration all tend to merge into one. Using marginal land, however, will pay only if it earns *some* rent, even though a small one. And, in cases where there are large discontinuities in the array of MVP's for different lands, the marginal land might be earning a substantial sum. It is obvious that there is no praxeological precision in terms like "close," "substantial," etc. All that we can say with certainty is that if we arrange the MVP's of lands in an array, the rents of the *sub*-marginal lands will be zero. We cannot say what the rent of the marginal land will be, except that it will be closer to zero than that of the supramarginal lands.[4]

Now we have seen above that the marginal value product of a factor decreases as its total supply increases, and increases as the supply declines. The three major categories of factors in the economy are land, labor, and capital goods. In the progressing economy, the supply of capital per person increases.[5] The supply of all ranks of capital goods increases, thereby decreasing the marginal value productivities of capital goods, so that the prices of capital goods fall. The *relative* MVP's of land and labor factors, in the aggregate, tend to rise, so that their income will rise in real terms, if not in monetary ones.

What if the supply of capital remained the same, while the supply of labor or land factors changed? Thus, suppose that, with the same capital structure, population increases, thus expanding the total supply of labor factors. The result will be a *general fall in the MVP of labor* and a *rise in the MVP of land factors.* This rise will cause formerly submarginal, no-rent lands to earn rent and to enter into cultivation by the new labor supply. This is the process particularly emphasized by Ricardo: population pressing on the land supply. The tendency for the MVP of labor to drop, however, may well be offset by a rise in the MPP schedules of labor, since a rise in population will permit a greater utilization of the advantages of specialization and the division of labor. The constant supply of capital would have to be reoriented to the changed conditions, but the constant amount of money capital will then be more physically productive. Hence, there will be an offsetting tendency for the MVP's of labor to rise. At any time, for any given conditions of capital and production processes, there will be an "optimum" population level that will maximize the total output of consumers' goods per head in the economy. A lower level will not take advantage of enough division of labor and opportunities for labor, so that the MPP of labor factors will be lower than at the optimum point; a higher level of population will decrease the MVP of labor and will therefore lower real wages per person.[6]

Recognition of the existence of a theoretical "optimum" population that maximizes real output per head, given existing land and capital, would go far to end the dreary Malthusian controversies in economic theory. For whether a given increase in population at any time will lead to an increase or decrease in real output per head is an *empirical* question, depending on the concrete data. It cannot be answered by economic theory.[7]

It might be wondered how the statement that increasing population might increase MPP and MVP's can be reconciled with the demonstration above that factors will always be put to work in areas of *diminishing* physical returns. The conditions here are completely different, however. In the previous problem we were assuming a given total supply of the various factors and considering the best method of their relative arrangement. Here we are dealing, not with particular production processes and given supplies of factors, but with the vague concept of "production" in general and with the effect of change in the total supply of a factor. Furthermore, we are dealing not with a true factor (homogeneous in its supply), but with a "class of factors," such as land-in-general or labor-in-general. Aside from the problem of vagueness, it is evident that the conditions of our present problem are completely different. For if the *total* supply of a factor changes and it has an effect on the productivity of the labor factor, this is equivalent to a *shift* in the MPP curves (or schedules) rather than a movement *along the curves* such as we considered above.[8]

Because we are accustomed to viewing labor implicitly as scarcer than land factors, we speak in terms of *zero-rent* land. If the situations were reversed, and lands were scarcer than labor factors, we would have to speak of zero-wage laborers, submarginal labor, etc. Theoretically, this is certainly possible, and it might be argued that in such static societies with institutionally limited markets as ancient Sparta and medieval or post-Medieval Europe, this condition actually obtained, so that the "surplus labor" earned a below-subsistence wage in production. Those who were "surplus" and did not own invested capital were curbed by infanticide or reduced to beggary.

That submarginal land earns no rent has given rise to an unfortunate tendency to regard the very concept of rent as a "differential" one—as referring particularly to *differences in quality* between factors. Sometimes the concept of "absolute" or pure rents is thrown overboard completely, and we hear only of rent in a "differential sense," as in such statements as the following:

If land A earns 100 gold ounces a month, and land B earns zero, land A is making a differential rent of 100.

If laborer A earns 50 gold ounces a month, and laborer B earns 30 gold ounces, A earns a "rent of ability" of 20 ounces.

On the contrary, rents are absolute and do not depend on the existence of a poorer factor of the same general category. The "differential" basis of rent is purely dependent on, and derived from, absolute rents. It is simply a question of arithmetical subtraction. Thus, land A may earn a rent of 100, and land B a rent of 0. Obviously, the difference between 100 and 0 is 100. In the case of the laborer, however, laborer A's "rent," i.e., wage, is 50 and B's is 30. If we want to compare the two earnings, we may say that A earns 20 more than B. There is little point, however, in adding to confusion by using "rent" in this sense.

The "differential rent" concept has also been used to contrast earnings by a factor in one use with those of the same factor in another use. Thus, if a factor, whether land or labor, earns 50 ounces per month in one use and *would* have earned 40 ounces in some other use, then its "rent" is 10 ounces. Here, "differential rent" is used to mean the difference between the actual DMVP and the opportunity forgone or the DMVP in the next best use. It is sometimes believed that the 10-ounce differential is in some way not "really" a part of costs to entrepreneurs, that it is surplus or even "unearned" rent acquired by the factor. It is generally admitted that it is not without cost to *individual firms,* which have bid the factor up to its MVP of 50. It is supposed, however, to be without cost from the "industry point of view." But there *is no* industry "point of view." Not "industries," but *firms,* buy and sell and seek profits.

In fact, the entire discussion concerning whether or not rent is "costless" or enters into cost is valueless. It belongs to the old classical controversies about whether rents are "price-determined" or "price-determining." The view that *any* costs can be price-determining is a product of the old cost-of-production theory of value and prices. We have seen that costs do not determine prices, but vice versa. Or more accurately, prices of consumers' goods, through market processes, determine the prices of productive factors (ultimately land and labor factors), and the brunt of price changes is borne by *specific* factors in the various fields.

B. THE NATURE OF LABOR

As we have mentioned earlier, "labor" is a category that includes a myriad variety of services. Generally, labor is the expenditure of pure human energy on a production process. Catallactically, labor is hired by entrepreneur-capitalists.[9] It is grossly unscientific to separate laborers into arbitrary categories and to refer to one group as "labor" and "workers," while the other group receives various other names. To give them other names implies a difference in *kind* between their contribution and the contribution of others, but this difference does not exist. Thus, the popular custom is to call some hired labor, "labor," while others are called "managers," "executives," etc. "Management" is a particularly popular category as contrasted with "labor," and we hear a great deal of the term "labor-management relations." But these categories are valueless. "Management" is hired by the owners or owner to direct production; managers are supposed to obey the orders of their superiors—something they consent to do as part of the terms of their employment. The lower-quality workers, further down the scale—the "laborers"—are treated by these writers as a different breed.[10] Their function is supposed to be not to obey orders and engage in a production process, but in some way to be different—to act as an independent entity, asserting its "rights," quarreling with "management," etc.

Yet there is no difference in kind between "workers" and "management." The vice-president of a company, if hired by its owners, has exactly the same amount of justification, or lack of justification, for joining a union as does a hired mechanic. Both are supposed to abide by the terms of their employment, i.e., to obey the relevant orders of their superiors. Both are free at any time to haggle over the terms of their employment, just as in any other voluntary exchange on the market. Both are *laborers,* who expend human energy in the production of goods. No special quality attaches to one set of laborers or another that makes it more or less justifiable for them to join a union.

The union question will be explored below, in chapter 10 on Monopoly and Competition. Here we might note that this false "labor-management" dichotomy crops up in an interesting way in the struggle over foremen's unions.[11] For some reason, even the most ardent union advocate thinks absurd the idea of unionizing the vice-presidents. Those more critical of unions think it monstrous if unions attempt to organize foremen, who are in the lower echelons of "management," and would of course be horrified at the very thought of unionizing vice-presidents. Yet if there is no real dichotomy and all employees are labor, then our views on unions must be altered accordingly. For if everyone admits that the unionizing of vice-presidents is absurd or evil, then perhaps the same adjective would have to apply to the unionization of *any* workers.

C. SUPPLY OF LAND

We have seen throughout that the processes of price determination for the unit services of land and labor are exactly the same. Both sets of factors tend to earn their DMVP; both receive advances of present money from capitalist-entrepreneurs; etc. The analysis of the pricing of unit services of original or "permanent" factors applies equally to each. There are three basic differences between the conditions of land and those of labor, however, that make separation of the two important. One we have already dealt with in detail: that (in the free economy) land can be capitalized in its price as a "whole factor" and therefore earns simply interest and entrepreneurial changes in asset value; while labor cannot be capitalized. A second difference we have been considering—the empirical fact that labor has been more scarce than land factors.

A corollary of this is that labor is pre-eminently the nonspecific factor, which is applicable to all processes of production, whereas land tends to be far more specific. A third difference derives from the fact that laborers are human beings and—also an empirical fact—that leisure is always a consumers' good. As a result, there will be reserve prices for labor against leisure, whereas land—in the broadest sense—will not have a reserve price. We shall deal with the effects of this distinction presently.

The fact that labor is scarcer and nonspecific means that there will always be *unused land.* Only the best and most productive land will be used, i.e., the land with the highest DMVP's. Similarly, in the real world of uncertainty, where errors are made, there will also be unused *capital goods,* i.e., in places where malinvestments had been made which turned out to be unprofitable.

We may now trace the supply and demand curves for land factors. We have shown above that, for any factor, the *particular* demand curve for any use, i.e., the particular MVP curve for a factor in that use, will slope downward in the region in which the factor is working. Also, we have seen that the *general* demand curve for the factor in the range of all its uses will slope downward. *What of the supply curves* for land factors? If we take the *general* supply curve (the factor considered in relation to all of its uses), then it is clear that there is no reservation demand curve for land; at least this will be true in the ERE. The *particular* supply curves for each use will depend on the alternate uses a piece of land may have. If it has any alternative uses, its supply curve for each use will slope upward as its price increases, since it can be shifted from one use to another as a use yields a higher rental return.

In its *particular* uses, the landowner will have a reservation demand, since he may obtain a higher return by shifting to another use. The greater the extent of alternate uses, the flatter each particular supply curve will tend to be.

In Fig. 62, the first diagram depicts the supply and demand curves for the general use of a land factor, including all uses. The supply curve will be the stock—a vertical straight line. The diagram to the right depicts typical demand and supply curves for a particular use; here, the supply curve slopes upward because it can shift to and from the alternative use or uses. The intersection of the supply and demand curves, in each instance, yields the rental price, equaling the discounted marginal value product for the total quantity of the factor available. The price for the general uses, *OC*, will be the same as the prices *OE*, etc., for any particular use, since the price of the factor must, in equilibrium,

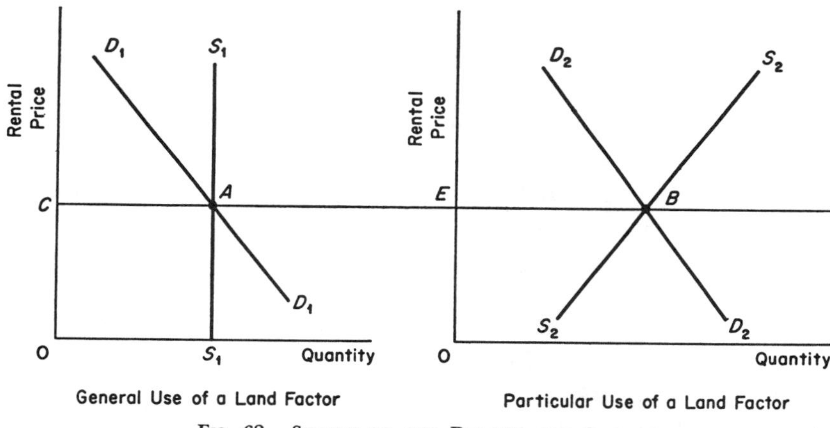

FIG. 62. SUPPLY OF AND DEMAND FOR LAND

be the same in all uses. The *general* diagram also yields the total quantity that will be sold for rent, OS_1, which will equal the total supply of the land factor available. The *sum* of the equilibrium quantities (such as *EB* on the diagram) supplied for particular uses would equal the total supplied for all uses, OS_1.

We have seen that the prices of consumers' goods are set by consumers' demand schedules, as determined by their value scales, i.e., by the way that the quantity supplied by producers (the first-rank capitalists) will be valued by consumers. When, in the changing economy, producers have speculative reservation demands, the price will, at any moment, be set by the total demand for the given stock, and this will always tend to approach the true consumers' demand price. A similar situation obtains in land. The prices of land factors will be determined by the general schedule of the factors' DMVP's and will be set according to the point of intersection of the total quantity, or stock, of the factor available, with its discounted marginal value productivity schedule. The DMVP, in turn, is, as we have seen at length, determined by the extent to which this factor serves the consumers. The MVP is determined directly by the degree that a factor unit serves the consumers, and the discount is determined by the extent that consumers choose saving-investment as against present consumption. Therefore, the *value scales of the consumers* determine, given the stocks of original factors, all the various results of the market economy that need to be explained: the prices of the original factors, the allocation of original factors, the incomes to original factors, the rate of time preferences and interest, the length of the production processes in use, and the amounts and types of the final products. In our changing real world, this beautiful and orderly structure of the free market economy tends to be attained through the drive of the entrepreneurs toward making profit and avoiding loss.[12]

At this point, let us consider a great bugaboo of the Henry Georgists—speculation in land that withholds productive land from use. According to the Georgists, a whole host of economic evils, including the depressions of the business cycle, stem from speculative withholding of ground land from use, causing an artificial scarcity and high rents for the sites in use. We have seen above that speculation in consumers' goods (and the same will also apply to capital goods) performs the highly useful function of speeding adjustment to the best satisfaction of consumer demand. Yet, curiously, speculation in *land* is far less likely to occur and is far less important than in the case of any other economic good. For consumers' or capital goods, being nonpermanent, can be used either now or at some later date. There is a choice between use in the present *or* use at various times in the future. If the owner of the good estimates that demand for the good will be higher in the future and therefore its price will be greater, he will, provided that the length of waiting time is not too costly in terms of time preference and storage, keep the goods on hand (in inventory) until that date. This serves the consumers by shifting the good from use at present to a more highly valued use in the future.

Land, however, is a permanent resource, as we have seen. It can be used all the time, *both* in the present *and* in the future. Therefore, any withholding of land from use by the owner is simply silly; it means merely that he is refusing monetary rents unnecessarily. The fact that a landowner may anticipate that his land value will increase (because of increases in future rents) in a few years furnishes no reason whatever for the owner to refuse to acquire rents in the meanwhile. Therefore, a site will remain unused simply because it would earn zero rent in production. In many cases, however, a land site, once committed to a certain line of production, could not easily or without substantial cost be shifted to another line. Where the landowner anticipates that a better line of use will soon become available or is in doubt on the best commitment for the land, he will withhold the land site from use if his saving in "change-over cost" will be greater than his opportunity cost of waiting and of forgoing presently obtainable rents. The speculative site-owner is, then, performing a great service to consumers and to the market in not committing the land to a poorer productive use. By waiting to place the land in a superior productive use, he is allocating the land to the uses most desired by the consumers.

What probably confuses the Georgists is the fact that many sites lie unused and yet command a capital price on the market. The capital price of the site might even *increase* while the site continues to remain idle. This does not mean, however, that some sort of villainy is afoot. It simply means that no rents on the site are expected for the first few years, although it will earn positive rents thereafter. The capital value of ground land, as we have seen, sums up the discounted total of all future rents, and these rental sums may exert a tangible influence from a considerable distance in the future, depending on the rate of interest. There is therefore no mystery in the fact of a capital value for an idle site, or in its rise. The site is not being villainously withheld from production.[13]

Let us now consider the effect of a change in the supply of a land factor. Suppose that there is an increase in the supply of land in general, the supply of labor and savings remaining constant. If the new land is submarginal in relation to land presently in use, it is obvious that the new land will not be used, but will, instead, join its fellow submarginal land sites in idleness. If, on the other hand, the new land is superior, and therefore would earn a positive rent, it comes into use. There has been, however, no increase in labor or capital, so that it will not be profitable for these factors to be employed on a greater total amount of land than before. The new productive land, competing with the older land, will therefore push the previously just-marginal land into the submarginal category. Labor will always employ capital on the best land, and so the new acquisition of supramarginal land will oust the previously marginal land from production. Since the new land is more value-productive than the old marginal land which it replaces, the change increases the total output of goods in the society.

D. SUPPLY OF LABOR

In the case of a labor factor, the particular demand curve for its use will slope downward, and the particular supply curve of a labor factor for a specific use will slope upward to the right. In fact, since labor is the relatively nonspecific factor, the par-

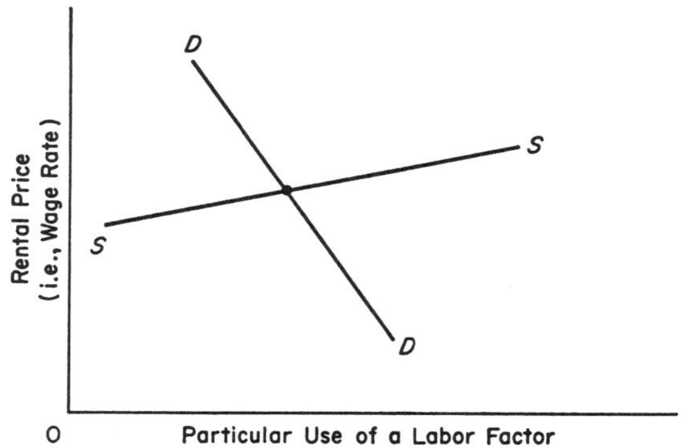

FIG. 63. SUPPLY OF AND DEMAND FOR LABOR FOR A PARTICULAR USE

ticular supply curve of a labor factor is likely to be flatter than the supply curve of the (usually more specific) land factor. Thus, the *particular* supply and demand curves for a labor factor may be as represented in Fig. 63.

The general demand curve for a labor factor will also slope downward in the relevant area. One of the complications in the analysis of labor is the alleged occurrence of a "backward supply curve of labor." This happens when workers react to higher wage rates by reducing their supply of labor hours, thus taking some of their higher incomes as increased leisure. This may very well occur, but it will not be relevant to the determination of the wages of a factor. In the first place, we saw that particular supply curves of a factor will be flat because of the competition of alternative uses. But even the *general* supply curve of a factor will be "forward-sloping," i.e., rightward-sloping. For labor, though hardly homogeneous, is a peculiarly nonspecific factor. Therefore, higher wage rates for one set of factors will tend to stimulate other laborers to train themselves or bestir themselves to enter this particular "market." Since skills differ, this does not mean that all wages will be equalized. It does mean, however, that *general* supply curves for a labor factor will also be forward-sloping. We might arrange an array of general supply and demand curves for various labor factors as in Fig. 64.

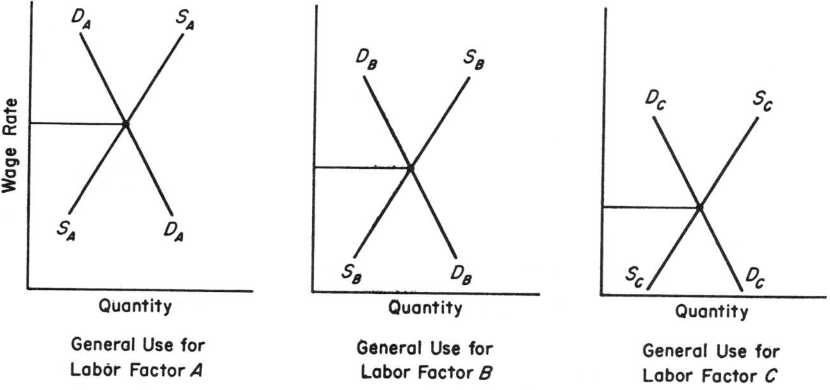

FIG 64. GENERAL SUPPLY AND DEMAND CURVES FOR VARIOUS LABOR FACTORS

The only case in which a backward supply curve may occur is for the total supply of *all* labor factors, and here the elements are so imprecise, since these factors are not homogeneous, that diagrams are of little avail in analysis. Yet this is an important question. As wage rates in general rise, in all their connexity between various specific labor markets, the supply of all labor (i.e., the quantity of labor-hours) can either increase or decrease, depending on the value scales of the individuals concerned. Rising wages may draw nonworking people into the labor force and induce people to work overtime or to obtain an extra part-time job. On the other hand, it may lead to increased leisure and a falling off in total hours worked. Rising wages may lead to population growth, swelling the total supply of labor "in general," or may lead to a cutback in population and the taking of some of the gains of increased wages in the form of increased leisure and an increased standard of living per person in the population.[14] Changes in the total supply or stock of labor-in-general will affect the particular markets by shifting all the specific schedules to the left if the stock decreases, or to the right if it increases.

A backward supply curve might conceivably take place for a land factor as well, when the owner has a high reserve demand for the land in order to enjoy its unused (in the catallactic sense) beauty. In that case, the land would have an increasing marginal disutility of visual enjoyment forgone, just as leisure is forgone in the process of expending labor. In the case of land, since there is not as great a connexity between land factors as there is between nonspecific labor factors, this circumstance will, in fact, impinge more directly on the market rental price. It may be revealed in a backward general supply curve for the *land factor*. Higher rental prices offered for his land will then induce the landowner to withhold more of it, taking the higher income partially in nonexchangeable consumption goods as well as in more money received. These cases may be rare in practice, but only because of the freely chosen values of the individuals themselves.

Thus, there is no reason for the would-be preserver of a monument or of a park to complain about the way the market treats his treasured objects. In the free society, these conservationists are at perfect liberty to purchase the sites and preserve them intact. They would, in effect, be deriving consumption services from such acts of preservation.

To return to labor, we have mentioned another component in wage rates. This is the *psychic* income, or psychic disutility, involved in any particular line of work. People, in other words, are often attracted to a certain line of work or to a specific job by other considerations than the monetary income. There may be positive psychic benefits and satisfactions derived from the particular type of work or from the particular firm employing the worker. Similarly, psychic disutilities may be attached to particular jobs.

These psychic elements will enter into the curves for particular uses. In order to isolate such elements, let us suppose for the moment that all laborers are equally value-productive, that labor is a homogeneous factor. In such a world, all wage rates in all occupations would be equal. All industries need not be equally value-productive for this result to occur. For as a result of the connexity of labor, i.e., its nonspecificity, laborers can enter wide ranges of occupations. If we assume, as we do for the moment, that all laborers are equally value-productive, then they will enter a high-wage industry to push the particular supply curve of labor in that industry downward, while quitting workers raise the supply curve of labor in the low-wage industry.

This conclusion follows from the general tendency toward the *uniformity of the price of any good on the market.* If all labor were homogeneous and therefore one factor, its price (wage rate) would be uniform throughout industry, just as the pure interest rate tends to be uniform.

Now let us relax one of the conditions of our hypothetical construct.[15] While retaining the assumption of equal productivity of all laborers, let us now introduce the possibility of psychic benefits or psychic disutilities accruing to workers at particular jobs. Some jobs are actively liked by most people, others actively disliked. These jobs may be common to certain industries or, more narrowly, to individual firms which may be considered particularly pleasant or unpleasant to work for. What will happen to money wage rates and to the supply of labor in the various occupations? It is obvious that, in the generally *disliked* occupation or firm, *higher* money wage rates will be necessary to attract and hold labor in that job. On the other hand, there will be so much labor competing in the generally liked jobs that they will pay *lower* wage rates. In other words, our amended conclusion is that not *money* wage rates, but *psychic* wage rates, will be equalized throughout—psychic wage rates being equal to money wage rates plus or minus a psychic benefit or psychic disutility component.

Many economists have assumed, implicitly or explicitly, an essential homogeneity among laborers. And they have made this assumption not, as we have done, as a purely temporary construct, but as an attempt to describe the real world. The question is an empirical one. It is a fundamental, empirically derived postulate of this book that there is a great variety among men in labor skills, in insight into future events, in ability, intelligence, etc. It seems empirically clear that this is the case.[16] The denials seem to be based on the simple faith that all men are "really" equal in all respects or could be made equal under proper conditions. Generally, the assumptions of uniformity and equality are made implicitly rather than explicitly, perhaps because the absurdities and obvious errors of the position would then become clear. For who would deny that not everyone could be an opera singer or a batting champion?

Some writers try to salvage the uniformity assumption by demonstrating that differences in wages occur solely because of the heavy *cost of training* for certain jobs. Thus, a doctor will earn more than a clerk because, in the nature of the task, a doctor will have to undergo the expenses of years of training (the expenses including actual money costs as well as opportunity costs forgone of earning money in such jobs as clerking). Therefore, in long-run equilibrium, money wage rates will not be uniform in the two fields, but income rates will be enough higher in medicine to just compensate for the loss, so that the *net* wage or income rates, considered over the person's lifetime, will be the same.

It is true that costs of training do enter in this way into market wage rates. But they do not account for all wage differentials by any means. Inherent differences in personal ability are also vital. Decades of training will not convert the average person into an opera star or a baseball champion.[17]

Many writers have based their analyses on the assumption of the homogeneity of all workers. Consequently, when they find that generally well-liked jobs, such as television-directing, pay more than such disliked jobs as ditch-digging, they tend to assume that there is injustice and chicanery afoot. A recognition of differences in labor productivity, however, eliminates this bugbear.[18] In such cases, a psychic component still exists that relatively lowers the wage of the better-liked job, but it is offset by the higher marginal value productivity and skill attached to the latter. Since TV-directing takes more skill than ditch-digging, or rather skill that fewer people have, the wage rates in the two occupations cannot be equalized.

E. PRODUCTIVITY AND MARGINAL PRODUCTIVITY

Great care must be taken in dealing with the productivity concept. In particular, there is danger in using a term such as "productivity of labor." Suppose, for example, we state that "the productivity of labor has advanced in the last century." The implication is that the cause of this increase came from within labor itself, i.e., because current labor is more energetic or personally skillful than previous labor. This, however, is not the case. An advancing capital structure increases the *marginal* productivity of labor, because the labor supply has increased less than the supply of capital goods. This increase in the marginal productivity of labor, however, is not due to some special improvement in the labor energy expended. It is due to the increased supply of capital goods. The causal agents of increased wage rates in an expanding economy, then, are *not* primarily the workers themselves, but the capitalist-entrepreneurs who have invested in capital goods. The workers are provided with more and better tools, and so their labor becomes relatively scarcer as compared to the other factors.[19]

That each man receives his marginal value product means

that each man is paid what he is worth in producing for consumers. But this does not mean that increases in his worth over the years are necessarily caused by his own improvement. On the contrary, as we have seen, the rise is primarily due to the increasing abundance of capital goods provided by the capitalists.

It is, then, clearly impossible to impute absolute "productivity" to any productive factor or class of factors. In the absolute sense, it is meaningless to try to impute productivity to any factor, since all the factors are necessary to the product. We can discuss productivity only in *marginal terms,* in terms of the productive contribution of a single unit of a factor, given the existence of other factors. This is precisely what entrepreneurs do on the market, adding and subtracting units of factors in an attempt to achieve the most profitable course of action.

Another illustration of the error in attempting to attribute increased "productivity" to the workers themselves occurs within the various segments of the labor market. As we have seen, there is a definite *connexity* between all the occupations on the labor market, since labor is the prime nonspecific factor. As a result, while wage rates are not equalized, psychic wage rates will all tend, in the long run, to move together and maintain a given skill-differential between each occupation. Therefore, when a certain branch of industry expands its capital and production, an increase in DMVP, and therefore in wage rates, is not confined to that particular branch. Because of the connexity of the supply of labor, labor tends to leave other industries and enter the new ones, until finally all the wage rates throughout the labor market have risen, while maintaining the same differentials as before.

Suppose, for example, that there is an expansion of capital in the steel industry.[20] The MVP of the steel worker increases, and his wage rates go up. The increase in wage rates, however, is governed by the fact that the rise will attract workers from more poorly paid industries. For example, suppose that steel workers are receiving 25 grains of gold per hour, while domestic servants receive 15 grains per hour. Now, under the impetus of expansion, the MVP and hence the wage rate of the steel workers go up to 30 grains. The differential has been increased, inducing domestic servants to enter the steel industry, lowering steel wages and especially raising servants' wages, until the differential is re-established. Thus, a rise in capital investment in steel will increase the wages of workers in domestic service. The latter increase is clearly not caused by some sort of increase in the "productivity" or in the quality of the output of the domestic servants. Rather, their *marginal* value productivity has increased as a result of the greater scarcity of labor in the service trades.

The differentials will not remain precisely constant in practice, of course, since changing investment and changing methods also alter the types of skills required in the economy.

The shift in labor supply will not usually be as abrupt as in our example. Generally, it will take place from one occupation or one grade to a closely similar grade or occupation. Thus, more ditchdiggers might become foremen, more foremen supervisors, etc., so that shifts will take place from grade to grade. It is as if the labor market consisted of linked segments, a change in one segment transmitting itself throughout the chain from each link to the next.

F. A NOTE ON OVERT AND TOTAL WAGE RATES

It is "total wage rates" that are determined on the market. They tend to be equalized on the market and to be set at the DMVP of the worker. *Total wage rates* are the money paid out by the employer for labor services. They do not necessarily correspond to the "take-home pay" of the worker. The latter may be called the "overt wage rates." Thus, suppose that there are two competing employers bidding for the same type of labor. One employer, Mr. A, pays out a certain amount of money, not in direct wages, but in pension funds or other "welfare" benefits. These benefits, it must be realized, will not be added as a gift from the employer to the workers. They will not be additions to the total wage rates. Overt wage rates paid out by Mr. A will instead be correspondingly *lower* than those paid out by his rival, Mr. B, who does not have to spend on the "welfare" benefits.

To the employer, in other words, it makes no difference in what form workers cost him money, whether in "take-home pay" or in welfare benefits. But he cannot pay more than the worker's DMVP; i.e., the worker's total wage income is set by this amount. The worker, in effect, chooses in what *form* he would like his pay and in what proportion of net wage rates to "welfare" benefits. Part of these benefits is money that the employer might spend to provide particularly pleasant or plush working conditions for all or some of his employees. This cost is part of the total and is deducted from the overt wage rates of the employee.

The institutional manner of paying wage rates is a matter of complete indifference to our analysis. Thus, while "piece rates" or "time rates" may be more convenient in any given industry, they do not differ in essentials; both are wage rates paid for a certain amount of work. With time rates, the employer has in mind a standard of performance which he expects from a worker, and he pays according to that rate.[21]

G. THE "PROBLEM" OF UNEMPLOYMENT

An economic bugbear of our times is "unemployment." Not only is this considered the pre-eminent problem of the "depression" in the "business cycle"; it is also generally considered the primary "problem" of the "capitalist system," i.e., of the developed free market economy. "Well, at least socialism solves the unemployment problem," is supposed to be the most persuasive argument for socialism.

Of particular interest to us is the sudden emergence of the "unemployment problem" in economic theory. The Keynesians, in the mid-1930's, inaugurated the fashion of declaiming: Neoclassical economics is all right for its special area, but it assumes "full employment." Since, "orthodox" economics "assumes full employment," it holds true only so long as "full employment" prevails. If it does not, we enter a Keynesian wonderland where all economic truths are vitiated or reversed.

"Full employment" is supposed to be the condition of no unemployment and therefore the goal at which everyone aims.

In the first place, it should be emphasized that economic theory does not "assume" full employment. Economics, in fact, "assumes" *nothing*. The whole discussion of alleged "assumptions" reflects the bias of the epistemology of physics, where "assumptions" are made without originally knowing their validity and are eventually tested to see whether or not their consequents are correct. The economist does not "assume"; he *knows.* He *concludes* on the basis of logical deduction from self-evident axioms, i.e., axioms that are either logically or empirically incontrovertible.

Now what does economics *conclude* on the matter of unemployment or "full employment"? In the first place, there is no "problem" involved in the unemployment of either land or capital goods factors. (The latter condition is often known as "idle" or "unused capacity.") We have seen above that a crucial distinction between land and labor is that labor is relatively scarce. As a result, there will always be land factors remaining unused, or "unemployed."[22] As a further result, *labor factors will always be fully employed on the free market to the extent that laborers are so willing.* There is no *problem* of "unemployed land," since land remains unused for a good reason. Indeed, if this were not so (and it is conceivable that some day it will not be), the situation would be most unpleasant. If there is ever a time when land is scarcer than labor, then land will be fully employed, and some labor factors will either get a zero wage or else a wage below minimum subsistence level. This is the old classical bugbear of population pressing the food supply down to below-subsistence levels, and certainly this is theoretically possible in the future.

This is the only case in which an "unemployment problem" might be said to apply in the free market. But even here, if we consider the problem carefully, we see that there is no unemployment problem *per se.* For if what a man wants is simply a "job," he could work for zero wages, or even pay his "employer" to work for him. In other words, he could earn a "negative wage." Now this could never happen, for the good reason that labor is a disutility, especially as compared to leisure or "play." Yet all the worry about "full employment" makes it appear that the "job," and not the income from the job, is the great desideratum. If that were really the case, then there *would* be negative wages, and there would be no unemployment problem either.

The fact that no one will work for zero or negative wages implies that in addition to whatever enjoyment he receives, the laborer requires a monetary income from his work. So what the worker wants is not just "employment" (which he could always get in the last resort by *paying* for it) but *employment at a wage.*

But once this is recognized, the whole modern and Keynesian emphasis on employment has to be revalued. For the great missing link in their discussion of unemployment is precisely *the wage rate.* To talk of unemployment or employment without reference to a wage rate is as meaningless as talking of "supply" or "demand" without reference to a price. And it is precisely analogous. The demand for a commodity makes sense only with reference to a certain price. In a market for goods, it is obvious that whatever stock is offered as supply, it will be "cleared," i.e., sold, at a price determined by the demand of the consumers. No good need remain unsold if the seller wants to sell it; all he need do is lower the price sufficiently, in extreme cases even below zero if there is no demand for the good and he wants to get it off his hands. The situation is precisely the same here. Here we are dealing with labor services. Whatever supply of labor service is brought to market can be sold, but only if wages are set at whatever rate will clear the market.

We conclude that there can never be, on the free market, an unemployment problem. If a man wishes to be employed, he will be, provided the wage rate is adjusted according to his DMVP. But since no one wants to be simply "employed" without getting what he considers sufficient payment, we conclude that employment *per se* is not even a desired goal of human action, let alone a "problem."

The problem, then, is not employment, but employment at an above-subsistence wage. There is no guarantee that this situation will always obtain on the free market. The case mentioned above —scarcity of land in relation to labor—can lead to a situation where a worker's DMVP is below a subsistence wage for him. There also may be so little capital invested per worker that any wage will be below-subsistence for many people. Even in a relatively prosperous society there may be individual workers so infirm or lacking in skill that their particular talents could not command an above-subsistence wage. In that case, they could survive only through the gifts of those who are making above-subsistence wages.

But what of the able-bodied worker who "can't find a job"? This situation cannot obtain. In those cases, of course, where a worker insists on a certain type of job or a certain minimum wage rate, he may well remain "unemployed." But he does so only of his own volition and on his own responsibility. Thus, suppose that perhaps half the labor force suddenly insisted that they would not work unless they received a job in New York City in the television industry. Obviously, "unemployment" would suddenly become enormous. This is only a large-scale example of something that is always going on. There may be a shift of industry away from one town or region and toward another. A worker may decide that he wants to remain in the old town and insists on looking for a job there. If he fails to get one, however, the fault lies with himself and not with the "capitalist system." The same is true of a clerk who insists on working only in the TV industry, or of a radio employee who refuses to leave for television and insists on working only in radio. We are not condemning these workers here. We are simply saying that by their decisions they are themselves choosing not to be employed.

The able-bodied in a developed economy can always find work, and work that will pay an over-subsistence wage. This is so because labor is scarcer than land, and enough capital has been invested to raise the marginal value product of laborers sufficiently to pay such a wage. But while this is true in the general labor market, it is not necessarily true for particular labor markets, for particular regions or occupations, as we have just seen.

If a worker can withdraw from the labor market by insisting on a certain type of work or location of work, he can also withdraw by insisting on a certain minimum wage payment. Suppose a man insisted that he would not work at any job unless he is paid 500 gold ounces per year. If his best available DMVP is only 100 gold ounces per year, he will remain unemployed. Whenever a man insists on a wage higher than his DMVP, he will remain unemployed, i.e., *unemployed at the wage that he insists upon.* But then this unemployment is not a "problem," but a voluntary choice on the part of the idle person.[23]

The "full employment" provided by the free market is employment to the extent that workers wish to be employed. If they refuse to be employed except at places, in occupations, or at wage rates they would like to receive, then they are likely to be choosing unemployment for substantial periods.[24]

It might be objected that workers often do not *know* what job opportunities await them. This, however, applies to the owner of *any* goods up for sale. The very function of *marketing* is the acquisition and dissemination of *information* about the goods or services available for sale. Except to those writers who posit a fantastic world where everyone has "perfect knowledge" of all relevant data, the marketing function is a vital aspect of the production structure. The marketing function can be performed in the labor market, as well as in any other, through agencies or other means for the discovery of who or where the potential buyers and sellers of a particular service may be. In the labor market this has been done through "want ads" in the newspapers, employment agencies used by both employer and employee, etc.

Of course "full employment," as an absolute ideal, is absurd in a world where leisure is a positive good. A man may choose idleness in order to obtain leisure; he benefits (or believes he benefits) more from this than from working at a job.[25] We can see this truth more clearly if we consider the hours of the work week. Will anyone maintain that an eighty-hour work week is necessarily better than a forty-hour week? Yet the former clearly represents a fuller employment of labor than the latter.

One alleged example of a possible case of involuntary unemployment on the free market has been suggested by Professor Hayek.[26] Hayek maintains that when there is a shift from investment to consumption, and therefore a shortening of the production structure on the market, there will be a necessary temporary unemployment of workmen thrown out of work in the higher stages, lasting until they can be reabsorbed in the shorter processes of the later stages. It is true that there is a loss in income, as well as a loss in capital, from a shift to shorter processes. It is also true that the shortening of the structure means that there is a transition period when, at final wage rates, there will be unemployment of the men displaced from the longer processes. However, during this transition period there is no reason why these workers cannot bid down wage rates until they are low enough to enable the employment of all the workers during the transition. This transition wage rate will be lower than the new equilibrium wage rate. But at no time is there a necessity for unemployment.

The ever-recurring doctrine of "technological unemployment" —man displaced by the machine—is hardly worthy of extended analysis. Its absurdity is evident when we look at the advanced economy and compare it with the primitive one. In the former there is an abundance of machines and processes completely unknown to the latter; yet in the former, standards of living are far higher *for far greater numbers of people.* How many workers have been "displaced" because of the invention of the shovel? The technological unemployment motif is encouraged by the use of the term "labor-saving devices" for capital goods, which to some minds conjure up visions of laborers being simply discarded. Labor needs to be "saved" because *it is the pre-eminently scarce good* and because man's wants for exchangeable goods are far from satisfied. Furthermore, these wants would not be satisfied at all if the capital-goods structure were not maintained. The more labor is "saved," the better, for then labor is using more and better capital goods to satisfy more of its wants in a shorter amount of time.

Of course, there will be "unemployment" if, as we have stated, workers insist on their own terms for work, and these terms cannot be met. This applies to technological changes as well as any other. The clerk who, for some reason, insists nowadays on working *only* for a blacksmith or in an old-fashioned general store may well have chosen a large dose of idleness. Any workers who insisted on working in the buggy industry or nothing found themselves, no doubt, unemployed after the development of the automobile.

A technological improvement in an industry will tend to *increase* employment in that industry if the demand for the product is elastic downward, so that the greater supply of goods induces greater consumer spending. On the other hand, an innovation in an industry with *inelastic* demand downward will cause consumers to spend less on the more abundant products, contracting employment in that industry. In short, the process of technological innovation shifts workers from the inelastic-demand to the elastic-demand industries. One of the major sources of new employment demand is in the industry making the new machines.[27]

3. *Entrepreneurship and Income*

A. COSTS TO THE FIRM

We have seen the basis on which the prices of the factors of production and the interest rate are determined. Looked at from the point of view of an individual entrepreneur, payments to factors are money *costs*. It is clear that we cannot simply rest on the old classical law that prices of products tend, in the long run, to be equal to their costs of production. Costs are not fixed by some Invisible Hand, but are determined precisely by the total force of entrepreneurial demand for factors of production. Basically, as Böhm-Bawerk and the Austrians pointed out, *costs conform to prices,* and not vice versa. Confusion may arise because, looked at from the point of view of the individual firm rather than of the economist, it *appears* as if costs (at least in the sense of the prices of factors) are somehow given, and beyond one's control.[28] If a firm can command a selling price that will more than cover its costs, it remains in business; if not, it will have to leave. The illusion of externally determined costs is prevalent because, as we shall presently see, most factors can be employed in a wide variety of firms, if not industries. If we take the broader view of the economist, however, the various "costs," i.e., prices of factors, determined by their various DMVP's in alternative uses, are ultimately determined solely by consumers' demand for all uses. It must not be forgotten, furthermore, that changes in demand and selling price will change the prices and incomes of *specialized factors* in the same direction. The "cost curves" so fashionable in current economics assume fixed factor prices, thereby ignoring their variability, even for the single firm.

It might be noted that, in this work, there is none of that plethora and tangle of "cost curves" which fill the horizon of almost every recent "neoclassical" work in economics.[29] This omission has been deliberate, since it is our contention that the cost curves are at best redundant (thus violating the simplicity principle of Occam's Razor), and at worst misleading and erroneous.

As an explanation of the pricing of factors and the allocation of output it is obvious that cost curves add nothing new to discussion in terms of marginal productivity. At best, the two are reversible. This can be clearly seen in such texts as E. T. Weiler's *The Economic System* and George J. Stigler's *Theory of Price.*[30] But, in addition, the shift brings with it many grave deficiencies and errors. This is revealed in the very passage in which Stigler explains the reasons for his switch from a perfunctory discussion of productivity to a lengthy treatment of cost curves:

> The law of variable proportions has now been explored sufficiently to permit a transition to the cost curves of the individual firm. The fundamentally new element in the discussion will, of course, be the introduction of prices of the productive services. The transition is made here only for the case of competition—that is, the prices of the productive services are constant because the firm does not buy enough of any service to affect its price.[31]

But by introducing *given* prices of productive services, the contemporary theorist really abandons any attempt to explain these prices. This is one of the cardinal errors of the currently fashionable theory of the firm. It is highly superficial. One of the aspects of this superficiality is the assumption that prices of productive services are given, without any attempt to explain them.

To furnish an explanation, marginal productivity analysis is necessary.

Marginal productivity analysis and the profit motive are sufficient to explain the prices of productive factors and their allocation to various firms and industries in the economy. Furthermore, there are in production theory two important and interesting concepts involving periods of time. One is what we may call the "immediate run"—the market prices of commodities and factors on the basis of given stocks and speculative demands and given consumer valuations. The immediate run is important, since it provides an explanation of the actual market prices of all goods at any time. The other important concept is that of the "final price," or the long-run equilibrium price, i.e., the price that would be established in the ERE. This is important because it reveals the direction in which the immediate-run market prices tend to move. It also permits the analytic isolation of interest, as compared to profit and loss, in entrepreneurial incomes. In the ERE all factors will receive their discounted marginal value product, and interest will be pure time preference; there will be no profit and loss.

The interesting phases, then, are the immediate run and the long run. Yet cost-curve analysis deals almost exclusively with a hybrid intermediate phase known as the "short run." In this short run, "costs" are sharply divided into two categories: fixed (which must be incurred regardless of the amount produced) and variable (which vary with output). This whole construction is a highly artificial one. There is no actual "fixity" of costs. Any alleged fixity depends purely on the length of time involved. In fact, suppose that production is zero. The "cost-curve theorists" would have us believe that even at zero output there are fixed costs that must be incurred: rent of land, payment of management, etc. However, it is clear that if data are frozen—as they should be in such an analysis—and the entrepreneurs *expect a situation of zero output to continue indefinitely,* these "fixed" costs would become "variable" and disappear very quickly. The rent contract for land would be terminated, and management fired, as the firm closed its doors.

There are no "fixed" costs; rather there are different degrees of variability for different productive factors. Some factors are best used in a certain quantity over a certain range of output, while others yield best results over other ranges of output. The result is not a dichotomy into "fixed" and "variable" costs, but a condition of many degrees of variability for the various factors.[32]

Even if none of these difficulties existed, it is hard to see why the "short run" should be picked out for detailed analysis, when it is merely one way station, or rather a series of way stations, between the *important* periods of time: the immediate run and the long run. Analytically, the cost-curve approach is at best of little interest.[33]

With these *caveats,* let us now turn to an analysis of the costs of the firm. Let us consider what will happen to costs at alternate hypothetical levels of output. There are two elements that determine the behavior of *average costs,* i.e., total costs per unit output.

a) There are "physical costs"—the amounts of factors that must be purchased in order to obtain a certain physical quantity of output. These are the obverse of "physical productivity"—the amounts of the physical product that can be produced with various amounts of factors. This is a technological problem. Here the question is *not* marginal productivity, where one factor is varied while others remain constant in quantity. Here we concentrate on the scale of output when *all* factors are permitted to vary. *Where all factors and the product are completely divisible, a proportionate increase in the quantities of all the factors must lead to an equally proportionate increase in physical output.*[34] This may be called the law of "constant returns to scale."

b) The second determinant of average costs is factor prices. "Pure competition" theorists assume that these prices remain unchanged with a changing scale of output, but this is impossible.[35] As any firm's scale of output increases, it necessarily bids factors of production away from other firms, raising their prices in the process. And this is particularly true for labor and land factors, which cannot be increased in supply via new production. The increase in factor prices as output increases, combined with constant physical costs, raises the average money cost per unit output. We may therefore conclude that *if factors and product were perfectly divisible, average cost would always be increasing.*

In the productive world, perfect divisibility does not always, or even usually, obtain. Units of factors and of output are *indivisible,* i.e., they are not purely divisible into very small units. First, the *product* may be indivisible. Thus, suppose that 3 units of factor A + 2 units of factor B may combine to produce one refrigerator. Now it may be true that $6A + 4B$ will produce two refrigerators, according to our law of returns to scale. But it is also true that $4A + 3B$ will *not* produce one-and-a-fraction refrigerators. There are bound to be *gaps* where an increased supply of factors will *not* lead to an increased product, because of the technological indivisibility of the unit product.

In the areas of the gaps, average costs increase rapidly, since new factors are being hired with no product forthcoming; then, when expenditures on factors are increased sufficiently to produce more of the product, there is a precipitate *decline* in average cost compared to the situation during the gap. As a result, no businessman will knowingly invest in the area of the gaps. To invest more without yielding a product is sheer waste, and so businessmen will invest only in the trough points outside the gap areas.[36]

Secondly, and more important, *the productive factors* may be indivisible. Because of this indivisibility, it is not possible simply to double or halve the quantities of input of every one of the productive services simultaneously. Each factor has its own technological unit size. As a result, almost all business decisions take place in zones in which many factors have to remain constant while others (the more divisible ones) may vary. And these relative divisibilities and indivisibilities are due, not to variations in periods of time, but to the technological size of the various units. In any productive operation there will be many varieties of indivisibility.

Professor Stigler presents the example of a railroad track, a factor capable of handling up to 200 trains a day.[37] The track is most efficiently utilized when train runs total precisely 200 a day. This is the technologically "ideal" output and may be the one for which the track was designed. Now what happens when output is below 200? Suppose output is only 100 per day. The *divisible* factors of production will then be cut in half by the owners of the railroad. Thus, if engineers are divisible, the railroad will hire half as many engineers or hire its engineers for half their usual number of hours. But (and this is the critical point here) the railroad cannot cut the track in half and operate on half a track. The technological unit of "track" being what it is, the number of tracks has to remain at 1. Conversely, when output increases to 200 again, other productive services may be doubled, but the quantity of track remains the same.[38]

What happens should output increase to 250 cars a day—a 25% increase over the planned quantity? Divisible services such as engineers may be increased by one-fourth; but the track must either remain at 1—and be overutilized—or be increased to 2. If it is increased, the tracks will again be underutilized at 250, because the "ideal" output from the point of view of utilizing the tracks is now 400.

When an important indivisible factor is becoming *less and less underutilized,* the tendency will be for "increasing returns," for *decreasing average costs* as output increases. When an important indivisible factor is becoming *more and more overutilized,* there is a tendency for *increasing average costs.*

In some spheres of production, indivisibilities may be such that full utilization of one indivisible factor requires full utilization of *all.*[39] In that case, all the indivisible factors move together and can be lumped together for our purposes; they become the equivalent of *one* indivisible factor, such as the railroad track. In such cases again, average costs will first decline with an increase in output, as the increased output remedies an underutilization of the lumped indivisible factors. After the technologically most efficient point is reached, however, costs will increase, given the indivisible factors. The tendency for costs to decline will, in addition, be offset by the rise in factor prices caused by the increase in output.

In the overwhelming majority of cases, however, each factor will *differ* from the others in size and degree of divisibility. As a consequence, any size or combination chosen might utilize one indivisible factor most efficiently, but at the expense of *not utilizing* some other indivisible factor at peak efficiency. Suppose we consider a hypothetical schedule of average money cost at each alternative output. When we start at a very low level of output, all the indivisible factors will be underutilized. Then, as we expand production, average costs will decrease *unless* offset by the price rise for those divisible factors needed to expand production. As soon as one of the indivisible factors is fully utilized and becomes overworked, average costs will rise sharply. Later, a tendency toward decreasing costs sets in again as another underutilized factor becomes more fully utilized. The result is an alternating series of decreases and increases in average costs as output increases. Eventually, a point will be reached at which more indivisible factors will be overutilized than underutilized, and from then on the general trend of average cost as output increases will be upward. Before that point, the trend will be downward.

Mingling with these influences from the technological side of costs are the continuing rises in factor prices, which also become more important as output increases.

In sum, as Mises states:

> Other things being equal, the more the production of a certain article increases, the more factors of production must be withdrawn from other employments in which they would have been used for the production of other articles. Hence—other things being equal—average production costs increase with the increase in the quantity produced. But this general law is by sections superseded by the phenomenon that not all factors of production are perfectly divisible and that, as far as they can be divided, they are not divisible in such a way that full utilization of one of them results in full utilization of the other imperfectly divisible factors.[40]

Some indivisible factors, such as the railroad track, can be available in only one particular size. Other indivisible factors, such as machinery, can be built in various sizes. Cannot a small factory, then, use small-scale machinery which will be just as efficient as large-scale machinery in a larger factory, and would this not eliminate indivisibilities and result in constant costs? No, for here too, one particular size will probably be most efficient. Below the most efficient size, operating the machine will be more costly. Thus, as Stigler says, "fitting together of the parts of a ten-horsepower motor does not require ten times the labor necessary to fit those of a one-horsepower motor. Similarly, a truck requires one driver, whether it has a half-ton or two-ton capacity."[41]

It is also true that an over-sized machine will be more costly than the optimum. But this will be no limitation on the size of the firm, for a large firm can simply use several (smaller) optimum-sized machines instead of one huge machine.

Labor is usually treated as a perfectly divisible factor, as one that varies directly with the size of the output. But this is not true. As we have seen, the truck driver is not divisible into fractions. Further, management tends to be an indivisible production factor. So also salesmen, advertising, cost of borrowing, research expenditures, and even insurance for actuarial risk. There are certain basic costs in borrowing which simply arise from investigating, paper work, etc. These will tend to be proportionately smaller the larger the size—another indivisibility, with returns increasing over a certain area. Also, the broader the coverage, the lower insurance premiums will be.[42]

Then there are the well-known gains from the increase in the division of labor with larger outputs. The benefits from the division of labor may be considered indivisible. They arise from the specialized machines that must first be used with a larger product, and similarly from the increased labor skills of specialists. Here too, however, there is a point beyond which no further specialization is possible or where specialization is subject to increasing costs. Management has usually been stressed as particularly subject to overutilization. Even more important is the factor of *ultimate-decision-making ability,* which cannot be enlarged to the extent that management can.

What any given firm's size and output will be is therefore subject to a host of conflicting determinants, some impelling a limitation, some an expansion, of size. At what point any firm will settle depends on the concrete data of the actual case and cannot be decided by economic analysis. Only the actual entrepreneur, through the give and take of the market, can decide where the maximum-profit size is and can set the firm at that point. This is the task of the businessman and not of the economist.[43]

Furthermore, the cost-curve diagrams, so simple and smooth in the textbooks, misinterpret real conditions. We have seen that there are a whole host of determinants which tend at any point toward increasing and toward decreasing costs. It is, of course, true that an entrepreneur will seek to produce at the point of maximum profit, i.e., of maximum net returns over costs. But the factors that influence his decision are too numerous and their interactions too complex to be captured in cost-curve diagrams.

It is clear to almost everyone that the optimum size of a firm in some industries is larger than in others. The economic optimum for a steel plant is larger than the optimum barbershop. In industries where large-scale firms have demonstrated the most efficiency, however, many people have worried a great deal about an alleged tendency for decreasing costs to continue permanently and therefore for "monopoly" to result from ever-larger firms. It should be obvious, however, that there is no infinite tendency for ever-larger size; this is clear from the very fact that *every firm, at any time, always has a finite size* and that, therefore, an economic limit must have been imposed upon it from *some* direction. Furthermore, we have seen that the general rule of operating in a zone of diminishing marginal productivity for each factor, as well as the tendency for product prices to decline and factor prices to increase as output increases, establishes limits on the size of each firm. And, as a neglected point, we shall see that ultimate limits are set on the relative size of the firm by the necessity for *markets* to exist in every factor, in order to make it possible for the firm to calculate its profits and losses.[44]

Money costs will equal opportunity costs to the businessman only when he *plans* an investment in factors. To the extent that his money costs are "sunk" in any production process, they are committed irrevocably, and any future plans must consider them as irretrievably spent.[45] The businessman's market-supply curve will depend on his *present opportunity cost, not* his past money cost. For the businessman sells his goods at any price that will more than cover any further costs that must be incurred in selling them. As capital goods move toward final output in any stage of the production structure, more and more investment has been sunk into the process. Therefore, the *marginal* cost of further production (roughly the opportunity cost) becomes ever lower as the product moves toward final output and sale. This is the simple meaning of the usual cost-curve morass. When, for example, some costs are not "fixed," but irrevocable from the point of view of *further* short-run production, they are not included in the businessman's estimated costs of such further production. As we have seen above, the sale of immediate stock completely ready for sale is virtually "costless," since there are no further costs for *its* production—in the immediate run.[46] In the ERE, of course, all costs and investments will be adjusted, and irrevocably incurred costs will present no problem. In the ERE average money costs for all firms will equal the price of the product minus pure interest return to the capitalist-entrepreneurs, and also, as we shall see, minus the return to the "discounted marginal productivity of the owner," a factor which does not enter into the firm's money costs.[47, 48]

B. BUSINESS INCOME

The net incomes in the economy accrue to labor in wages, to landowners in ground rents (both wages and ground rents being "rents," i.e., unit-prices of productive factors), to capitalists in interest—all of which continue in the ERE—and profits and losses to entrepreneurs, which do not. (Ground rents are capitalized in the capital value of land, which therefore earns the interest rate in the ERE.) But what of the owners? Are their incomes exhausted by the category of entrepreneurial profit and loss, which we have studied in chapter 8, or will they continue to earn income beyond interest in the ERE?

So far we have seen that owners of businesses perform an *entrepreneurial* function: the function of uncertainty-bearing in an ever-changing world. Owners are also capitalists, who advance present funds to labor and land factors and earn interest. They may also be their own managers; in that case, they earn an implicit *wage of management,* since they are performing work which could also be performed by employees.[49] We have seen that, catallactically, labor is the personal energy of nonowners in production, and that this factor receives wages. When the owner does laboring work himself, then he too earns an implicit wage. This wage, of course, continues also in the ERE.

But is there a function which owning businessmen perform, and would still perform in the ERE, beyond the advancing of capital or possible managerial work? The answer is that they do execute another function for which they *cannot* hire other factors. It goes beyond the simple capital-advancing function, and it still continues in the ERE. For want of a better term, it may be called the *decision-making function,* or the *ownership function.* Hired managers may successfully direct production or choose production processes. But the ultimate responsibility and control of production rests inevitably with the *owner,* with the businessman whose property the product is until it is sold. It is the owners who make the decision concerning how much capital to invest and in what particular processes. And particularly, it is the *owners* who must choose the managers. The ultimate decisions concerning the use of their property and the choice of the men to manage it must therefore be made by the owners and by no one else. It is a function necessary to production, and one that continues in the ERE, since even in the ERE there are skills needed to hire proper managers and invest in the most efficient processes; and even though these skills remain constant, the efficiency with which they are performed will differ from one firm to another, and differing returns will be received accordingly.[50]

The decision-making factor is necessarily *specific* to each firm. We cannot call what it earns a *wage* because it can never be hired, and thus it does not earn an implicit wage. We may therefore call the income of this factor, the "rent of decision-making ability." [51] It is clear that this rent will be equal to the factor's DMVP, the amount which it specifically contributes to the firm's revenue. Since this ability differs from one owner to the next, the rents will differ accordingly. This difference accounts for the phenomena of "high-cost" and "low-cost" firms in any industry and indicates that differences in efficiency among firms are not solely functions of ephemeral uncertainty, but would persist even in the ERE.

Granting that the "*supra*marginal" (i.e., the lower-cost) firms in an industry are earning *rents of decision-making ability* for their owners, what of the "marginal" firms in the industry, the "high-cost" firms just barely in business? Are *their* owners earning rents of decision-making ability? Many economists have believed that these marginal firms earn no such income, just as they have believed that the marginal land earns zero rent. We have seen, however, that the marginal land earns *some* rent, even if "close to" zero. Similarly, the marginal firm earns *some* rent of decision-making ability. We can never say quantitatively how much it will be, only that it will be less than the corresponding "decision rents" of the *supra*marginal firms.

The belief that marginal firms earn no decision rents whatever seems to stem from two errors: (1) the assumption of mathematical continuity, so that successive points blend together; and (2) the assumption that "rent" is basically differential and therefore that the most inferior working land or firm must earn zero to establish the differential. We have seen, however, that rents are "absolute"—the earnings and marginal value products of factors. There is no necessity, therefore, for the poorest factor to earn zero, as we can see when we realize that *wages* are a subdivision of rents and that there is clearly no one making a zero wage. And so neither does the marginal firm earn a decision rent of zero.

That the decision rent earned by the marginal firm *must* be positive and not zero becomes evident if we consider a firm whose decision rent is only zero. Its owner would then be performing certain functions—making and bearing responsibility for ultimate decisions about his property and choosing the top managers—and yet receiving no return. And this in the ERE, where it cannot be simply the unforeseen result of entrepreneurial mistakes! But there will be no reason for the owner to continue performing these functions without a return. He will not continue to earn what is *psychically* a negative return, for while he remained in business he would continue to expend energy in ownership while receiving nothing in return.

To sum up, the income accruing to a business owner, in a changing economy, will be a composite of four elements:

Remains in ERE	*a*) interest on capital invested (uniform in ERE) *b*) wages of management, when owner is self-employed (set according to DMVP) *c*) rents of ownership-decision (set according to DMVP)
Disappears in ERE	*d*) entrepreneurial profit or loss

We have, so far, been dealing almost exclusively with *capitalist*-entrepreneurs. Since the entrepreneur is the actor in relation to natural uncertainty, the capital investor, who hires and makes advances to other factors, plays a peculiarly important entrepreneurial role. Making decisions concerning how much and where to invest, he is the driving force of the modern economy. *Laborers* are also entrepreneurs in the sense of predicting demand in the markets for labor and choosing to enter certain markets accordingly. Someone who emigrates from one country to another in expectation of a higher wage is in this sense an entrepreneur and may obtain a monetary profit or loss from his move. One important distinction between capitalist-entrepreneurs and laborer-entrepreneurs is that only the former may suffer *negative incomes* in production. Even if a laborer emigrates to a nation where pay turns out to be lower than expected, he absorbs only a differential, or "opportunity," loss from what he might have earned elsewhere. But he still earns a positive wage in production. Even in the unlikely event of a labor surplus vis à vis land, the laborer earns zero and not *negative* wages. But the capitalist-entrepreneur, the man who hires the other factors, can and does incur actual monetary losses from his entrepreneurial effort.

C. PERSONAL CONSUMER SERVICE

A particularly important category of laborer-entrepreneurs is that of the sellers of personal services to consumers. These laborers are generally capitalists as well. The sellers of such services—doctors, lawyers, concert artists, servants, etc.—are self-employed businessmen, who, in addition to interest on whatever capital they have invested, earn an implicit "managerial" wage for their labor.[52,53] Thus, they earn a peculiar type of income: a business return consisting almost exclusively of labor income. We may call this type of work *direct labor,* since it is labor that serves *directly* as a consumers' good rather than hired as a factor of production. And since it is a consumers' good, this labor service is priced directly on the market.

The determination of the prices of these goods will be similar on the demand side to that of any consumers' good. Consumers evaluate marginal units of the service on their value scales and decide how much, if any, to purchase. There is a difference, however, on the supply side. The market-supply curves for most consumers' goods are vertical straight lines, since the sale of the product, *once produced,* is costless to the entrepreneur. He has no alternative use for it. The case of *personal service,* however, is different. In the first place, leisure is a definite alternative to work. In the second place, as a result of the connexity of the labor market, the worker can shift to a higher-paying occupation further up on the structure of production if his income in this occupation is unsatisfactory. As a result, for this type of consumers' good, the supply curve is likely to be a rather flat, forward-sloping one.

The seller of the service, or the *direct laborer,* earns, as do all factors, his DMVP to the consumer. He will allocate his labor to whatever branch, whether high or low in the structure of production, where his DMVP will be the highest, and where, as a consequence, his wage rate will be the greatest. The principles of allocation, then, between direct labor and indirect labor in production are the same as those among the various branches of indirect productive use.

D. MARKET CALCULATION AND IMPLICIT EARNINGS

We have seen that a musician or a doctor earns wages without being an employee; the wages of each are *implicit* in the income that he receives, even though they are received directly from the consumers.

In the real world, each *function* is not necessarily performed by a different person. The same person can be a landowner and a worker. Similarly, a particular firm, or rather its owner or owners, may own land and participate in the production of capital goods. The owner may *also* manage his own firm. In practice, the different sources of income can be separated only by referring to these incomes *as determined by prices on the market*. For example, suppose that a man owns a firm which invests its capital, owns its own ground land, and produces a capital good, and that he manages the plant himself. He receives a net income over a year's period of 1,000 gold ounces. How can he estimate the different *sources* of his income? Suppose that he had invested 5,000 gold ounces in the business. He looks around at the economy and finds that what he can pretty well call the ruling rate of interest, toward which the economy is tending, is 5%. He then concludes that 250 gold ounces of his net income was implicit interest. Next, he estimates approximately what he would have received in wages of management if he had gone to work for a competing firm rather than engaging in this business. Suppose he estimates that this would have been 500 gold ounces. He then looks to his ground land. What could he have received for the land if he had rented it out instead of using it himself in the business? Let us say that he could have received 400 ounces in rental income for the land.

Now, our owner received a net money income, as landowner-capitalist-laborer-entrepreneur, of 1,000 gold ounces for the year. He then estimates what his *costs* were, in money terms. These costs are not his explicit money expenses, which have already been deducted to find his net income, but his *implicit* expenses, i.e., his opportunities forgone by engaging in the business. Adding up these costs, he finds that they total:

250 gold ounces	interest
500 gold ounces	wages
400 gold ounces	rent
1150 gold ounces	total opportunity costs

Thus, the entrepreneur suffered a *loss* of 150 ounces over the period. If his opportunity costs had been less than 1,000, he would have gained an entrepreneurial profit.

It is true that such estimates are not precise. The estimates of what he would have received can never be wholly accurate. But this tool of *ex post calculation* is an indispensable one. It is the only way by which a man can guide his *ex ante* decisions, his future actions. By means of this calculation, he may realize that he is suffering a loss in this business. If the loss continues much longer, he will be impelled to shift his various resources to other lines of production. It is only by means of such estimates that an owner of more than one type of factor in the firm can determine his gains or losses in any situation and then allocate his resources to strive for the greatest gains.

A very important aspect of such estimates of implicit incomes has been overlooked: *there can be no implicit estimates without an explicit market!* When an entrepreneur receives income, in other words, he receives a complex of various functional incomes. To isolate them by calculation, *there must be in existence an external market to which the entrepreneur can refer.* This is an extremely important point, for, as we shall soon see in detail, this furnishes a most important limitation on the relative potential size of a single firm on the market.

For example, suppose we return for a moment to our old hypothetical example in which each firm is owned jointly by all its factor-owners. In that case, there is no separation at all between workers, landowners, capitalists, and entrepreneurs. There would be no way, then, of separating the wage incomes received from the interest or rent incomes or profits received. And now we finally arrive at the reason why the economy cannot consist completely of such firms (called "producers' co-operatives").[54] For, without an external market for wage rates, rents, and interest, there would be no rational way for entrepreneurs to allocate factors in accordance with the wishes of the consumers. No one would know where he could allocate his land or his labor to provide the maximum monetary gains. No entrepreneur would know how to arrange factors in their most value-productive combinations to earn the greatest profit. There could be no efficiency in production because the requisite knowledge would be lacking. The productive system would be in complete chaos, and everyone, whether in his capacity as consumer or as producer, would be injured thereby. It is clear that a world of producers' co-operatives would break down for any economy but the most primitive, because it could not calculate and therefore could not arrange productive factors to meet the desires of the consumers and hence earn the highest incomes for the producers.

E. VERTICAL INTEGRATION AND THE SIZE OF THE FIRM

In the free economy, there *is* an explicit time market, labor market, and land-rent market. It is clear that while chaos would ensue from a world of producers' co-operatives, other critical points even before that would, as it were, introduce *little bits of chaos* into the productive system. Thus, suppose that workers are separated from capitalists, but that *all* capitalists own their own ground land. Further, suppose, that for one reason or another, no capitalist will be able to rent out his land to some *other* firm. In that case, land and a particular capital and production process are indissolubly wedded to each other. There would be no rational way to allocate land in production, since it would have no explicit price anywhere. Since producers would suffer heavy losses, the *free market would never establish such a situation.* For the free market always tends to conduct affairs so that entrepreneurs make the greatest profit through serving the consumer best and most efficiently. Since absence of calculation creates grave inefficiencies in the system, it also causes heavy losses. Such a situation (absence of calculation) would therefore never be established on a free market, particularly after an advanced economy has already developed calculation and a market.

If this is true for such cases as a world of producers' co-operatives and the absence of a rent market, it also holds true, on a smaller scale, for "vertical integration" and the size of a firm. Vertical integration occurs when a firm produces not only at *one* stage of production, but over two or more stages. For example, a firm becomes so large that it buys labor, land, and capital goods of the fifth order, then works on these capital goods, producing other capital goods of the fourth order. In another plant, it then works on the fourth-order capital goods until they become third-order capital goods. It then sells the *third-order* product.

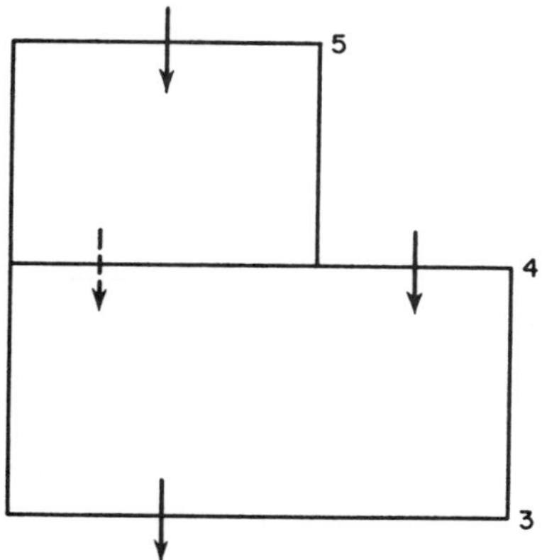

Fig. 65. Movement of Goods and Services in a Vertically Integrated Firm

Vertical integration, of course, lengthens the production period for *any firm,* i.e., it lengthens the time before *the firm* can recoup its investment in the production process. The interest return then covers the time for two or more stages rather than one.[55] There is a more important question involved, however. This is the role of implicit earnings and calculation in a vertically integrated firm. Let us take the case of the integrated firm mentioned above (see Fig. 65).

This diagram depicts a vertically integrated firm; the arrows represent the movement of goods and services (not of money). The firm buys labor and land factors at both the fifth and the fourth stages; it also makes the fourth-stage capital goods itself and uses them in another plant to make a lower-stage good. This movement *internal* to the firm is expressed by the dotted arrow.

Does such a firm employ calculation within itself, and if so, how? Yes. The firm assumes that it *sells itself* the fourth-rank capital good. It separates its net income as a producer of fourth-rank capital from its role as producer of third-rank capital. It calculates the net income for each separate division of its enterprise and allocates resources according to the profit or loss made in each division. *It is able to make such an internal calculation only because it can refer to an existing explicit market price for the fourth-stage capital good.* In other words, a firm can accurately estimate the profit or loss it makes in a stage of its enterprise only by finding out the *implicit* price of its internal product, and it can do this only if an *external* market price for that product is established elsewhere.

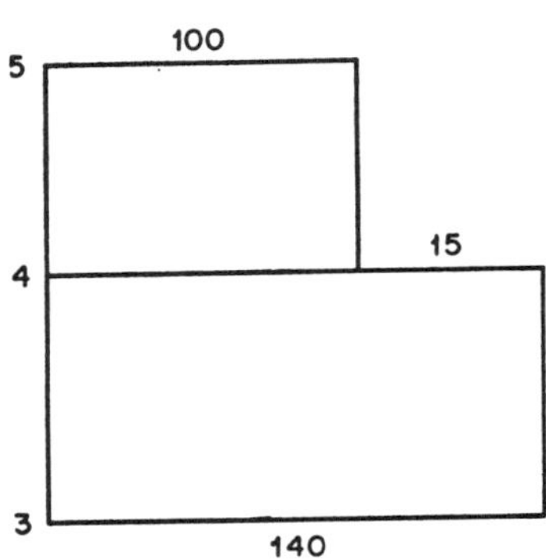

Fig. 66. Calculation within a Vertically Integrated Firm

To illustrate, suppose that a firm is vertically integrated over two stages, with each stage covering one year's time. The general rate of interest in the economy tends towards 5% (per annum). This particular firm, say, the Jones Manufacturing Company, buys and sells its factors as shown in Fig. 66.

This vertically integrated firm buys factors at the fifth rank for 100 ounces and original factors at the fourth rank for 15 ounces; it sells the final product at 140 ounces. It *seems* that it has made a handsome entrepreneurial profit on its operations, but can it find out which stage or stages is making this profitable showing? If there is an external market for the product of the stage that the firm has vertically integrated (stage 4), the Jones Company is able to calculate the profitability of specific *stages* of its operations. Suppose, for example, that the price of the fourth-order capital good on the external market is 103 ounces. The Jones Company then estimates its *implicit* price for this intermediate product at what it *would have brought on the market* if it had been sold there. This price will be about 103 ounces.[56] Assuming that the price is estimated at 103, then the total amount of money spent by Jones' lower-order plant on factors is 15 (explicit, on original factors) plus 103 (implicit, on capital goods) for a total of 118.

Now the Jones Company can calculate the profits or losses made at *each stage* of its operations. The "higher" stage bought factors for 100 ounces and "sold" them at 103 ounces. It made a 3% return on its investment. The lower stage bought its factors for 118 ounces and sold the product for 140 ounces, making a 29% return. It is obvious that, instead of enjoying a general profitability, the Jones Company suffered a 2% entrepreneurial loss on its earlier stage and gained a 24% profit on its later stage. Knowing this, it will shift resources from the higher to the lower stage in accordance with their respective profitabilities—and therefore in accordance with the desires of consumers. Perhaps it will abandon its higher stage altogether, buying the capital good from an external firm and concentrating its resources in the more profitable lower stage.

On the other hand, suppose that there is no external market, i.e., that the Jones Company is the only producer of the intermediate good. In that case, it would have no way of knowing which stage was being conducted profitably and which not. It would therefore have no way of knowing how to allocate factors to the various stages. There would be no way for it to estimate any implicit price or opportunity cost for the capital good at that particular stage. Any estimate would be completely arbitrary and have no meaningful relation to economic conditions.

In short, if there were no market for a product, and all of its exchanges were internal, there would be no way for a firm or for anyone else to determine a price for the good. A firm can estimate an implicit price when an external market exists; but when a market is absent, the good can have no price, whether implicit or explicit. Any figure could be only an arbitrary symbol. Not being able to calculate a price, the firm could not rationally allocate factors and resources from one stage to another.

Since the free market always tends to establish the most efficient and profitable type of production (whether for type of good, method of production, allocation of factors, or size of firm), we must conclude that complete vertical integration for a capital-good product can never be established on the free market (above the primitive level). *For every capital good, there must be a definite market in which firms buy and sell that good.* It is obvious that this economic law *sets a definite maximum to the relative size of any particular firm on the free market.*[57] Because of this law, firms cannot merge or cartelize for complete vertical integration of stages or products. Because of this law, there can never be One Big Cartel over the whole economy or mergers until One Big Firm owns all the productive assets in the economy. The force of this law multiplies as the area of the economy increases and as islands of noncalculable chaos swell to the proportions of masses and continents. As the area of incalculability increases, the degrees of irrationality, misallocation, loss, impoverishment, etc., become greater. Under *one* owner or *one* cartel for the whole productive system, there would be no possible areas of calculation at all, and therefore complete economic chaos would prevail.[58]

Economic calculation becomes ever more important as the market economy develops and progresses, as the stages and the complexities of type and variety of capital goods increase. Ever more important for the maintenance of an advanced economy, then, is the preservation of *markets* for all the capital and other producers' goods.

Our analysis serves to expand the famous discussion of the possibility of economic calculation under socialism, launched by Professor Ludwig von Mises over forty years ago.[59] Mises, who has had the last as well as the first word in this debate, has demonstrated irrefutably that a socialist economic system cannot calculate, since it lacks a market, and hence lacks prices for producers' and especially for capital goods.[60] Now we see that, paradoxically, the reason why a socialist economy cannot calculate is *not* specifically because it is socialist! Socialism is that system in which the State forcibly seizes control of all the means of production in the economy. The reason for the impossibility of calculation under socialism is that *one agent* owns or directs the use of all the resources in the economy. It should be clear that it does not make any difference whether that one agent is the State or one private individual or private cartel. Whichever occurs, there is no possibility of calculation anywhere in the production structure, since production processes would be only internal and without markets. There could be no calculation, and therefore complete economic irrationality and chaos would prevail, whether the single owner is the State or private persons.

The difference between the State and the private case is that our economic law debars people from ever establishing such a system in a free-market society. Far lesser evils prevent entrepreneurs from establishing even islands of incalculability, let alone infinitely compounding such errors by eliminating calculability altogether. But the State does not and cannot follow such guides of profit and loss; its officials are not held back by fear of losses from setting up all-embracing cartels for one or more vertically integrated products. The State is free to embark upon socialism without considering such matters. While there is therefore no possibility of a one-firm economy or even a one-firm vertically integrated product, there is much danger in an attempt at socialism by the State. A further discussion of the State and State intervention will be found in chapter 12 of this book.

A curious legend has become quite popular among the writers on the socialist side of the debate over economic calculation. This runs as follows: Mises, in his original article, asserted "theoretically" that there could be no economic calculation under socialism; Barone proved mathematically that this is false and that calculation is possible; Hayek and Robbins conceded the validity of this proof but then asserted that calculation would not be "practical." The inference is that the argument of Mises has been disposed of and that all socialism needs is a few practical devices (perhaps calculating machines) or economic advisers to permit calculation and the "counting of the equations."

This legend is almost completely wrong from start to finish. In the first place, the dichotomy between "theoretical" and "practical" is a false one. In economics, all arguments are theoretical. And, since economics discusses the real world, these theoretical arguments are by their nature "practical" ones as well.

The false dichotomy disposed of, the true nature of the Barone "proof" becomes apparent. It is not so much "theoretical" as irrelevant. The proof-by-listing-of-mathematical-equations is no proof at all. It applies, at best, only to the evenly rotating economy. Obviously, our whole discussion of the calculation problem applies to the real world and *to it only. There can be no calculation problem in the ERE because no calculation there is necessary.* Obviously, there is no need to calculate profits and losses when all future data are known from the beginning and where there *are no* profits and losses. In the ERE, the best allocation of resources proceeds automatically. For Barone to demonstrate that the calculation difficulty does not exist in the ERE is not a solution; it is simply a mathematical belaboring of the obvious.[61] The difficulty of calculation applies to the real world only.[62]

4. *The Economics of Location and Spatial Relations*

One very popular subdivision of economics has been "international trade." In a purely free market, such as we are analyzing in the bulk of this work, there can be no such thing as an "international trade" problem. For nations might then possibly continue as cultural expressions, but not as economically meaningful units. Since there would be neither trade nor other barriers between nations nor currency differences, "international trade" would become a mere appendage to a general study of interspatial trade. It would not matter whether the trade was within or outside a nation.[63]

The laws of the free market that we have been enunciating apply, therefore, to the whole extent of the market, i.e., to the "world" or the "civilized world." In the case of a completely isolated country, the laws would apply throughout that area. Thus, the pure interest rate will tend to be uniform throughout the world, prices for the same good will tend to be uniform throughout, and, therefore, so will wages for the same type of labor.

Wage rates will tend toward uniformity for the same labor in different geographical areas in precisely the same way as from industry to industry or firm to firm. Any temporary differential will induce laborers to move from the low- to the high-wage area and businesses to move from the latter to the former, until equilibrium is reached. Once again, just as in the more general case considered above, workers may have particular positive or negative attachments toward working in a certain *area,* just as we saw they may have toward working in a certain industry. There may be a general psychic benefit from living and working in a certain place, and a psychic disutility involved in working at some other location. Since it is *psychic,* not money, wage rates that are being equalized, money wage rates will be equalized throughout the world *plus* or *minus* negative or positive psychic attachment components.

That the prices of each good will be uniform throughout the world rests on a precise definition of the term "good." Suppose, for example, that wheat is grown in Kansas and that the bulk of the consumers of the wheat are in New York. The wheat in Kansas, even when ready for shipment, is *not* the same good as the wheat in New York. It may be the same physical-chemical bundle, but it is not the same *good* vis à vis its objective use-value to the consumers. In short, wheat in Kansas is a higher-stage capital good than wheat in New York (when the consumer is in New York rather than in Kansas.) Transporting the wheat to New York is a stage in the process of production. The price of wheat in Kansas will then tend to equal the price of wheat in New York *minus* the necessary costs of transport from Kansas to New York.

What determines how people and businesses will be distributed over the face of the earth? Obviously, the major factor is the marginal productivity of labor. This will differ from location to location in accordance with the distribution of natural resources and the distribution of capital equipment inherited from ancestors. Another factor influencing location will be positive or negative attachments to certain areas, as we have seen above. The actual dispersal over the face of the earth is caused chiefly by the distribution of productive land and natural resources over the earth's surface. This has been one of the chief forces limiting the concentration of industry, the size of each firm, and population in purely industrial areas.[64]

In considering the location of industry, entrepreneurs must account for costs of transportation from raw material sites to the centers of consumer population. Certain areas of the world will tend to have higher costs of transportation than other parts. Wheat is further away in New York than in Kansas, and the theater further away in Kansas. Some areas may enjoy lower transport costs for the bulk of consumers' goods, while others may have higher transport costs. Thus, Alaska will probably have higher transport costs for its consumers' goods than less remote areas such as San Francisco. Therefore, to obtain the same products, Alaskan consumers must be willing to pay higher prices in Alaska than in San Francisco, even though purchasing power and prices are uniform throughout the world. As a result, the "cost component" for anyone working in Alaska will be a certain positive amount. Because of the transport problem, the same money wage in Alaska will buy fewer goods than in San Francisco. This increased "cost of living" establishes a positive cost component in the wage, so that for similar labor a worker would require a higher money wage to work in Alaska than elsewhere.

If the costs attached to a geographical area are particularly high or low, a positive or a negative cost component will be attached to the wage rate in that area. Instead of saying that money wage rates for the same type of labor will be equalized throughout the world, we must say rather that there will be a tendency for equalization of money wage rates *plus* or *minus* the attachment component, and *plus* or *minus* the cost component, for every geographic area.[65]

The purchasing power of the monetary unit will also be equalized throughout the world. This case will be treated below in chapter 11 on Money.

The tendency of an advancing market economy, of course, is to lower transportation costs, i.e., to increase labor productivity in the transport field. Other things being equal, then, the cost components tend to become relatively less important as the economy progresses.

We have seen that a "good" must be considered as homogeneous in *use-value,* and not in physical substance.[66] Wheat in Kansas was a different good from wheat in New York. Some economists have taken the law that all goods tend to be uniform in price throughout the world economy to mean that all *physically* homogeneous things will be equal in price. But a difference in position with respect to consumers makes a physically identical thing a different good. Suppose, for example, that two firms are producing a certain product, say cement, and that one is located in Rochester and one in Detroit. Let us say that the bulk of the consumers of cement are in New York City.

Let us call the cement produced in Rochester, C_r, and the cement produced in Detroit, C_d. Now, in equilibrium, the price of C_r in New York City will equal the price of C_r in Rochester plus the freight cost from Rochester to New York. Also, in equilibrium, the price of C_d in New York City will equal the price of C_d in Detroit plus the freight cost from Detroit to New York. Which cement prices will be equal *to each other* in equilibrium? Many writers maintain that the price of C_r in Rochester will be equal to the price of C_d in Detroit, i.e., that the "mill prices," or the "f.o.b. prices," of cement will be equal in each of the two localities in equilibrium. But it is clear that these writers have adopted the confusion of treating "good" in the technological rather than in the use-value sense.[67]

We must, in short, take the point of view of the *consumer*—the man who uses the good—and he is in New York City. From his point of view, cement in Detroit is a far different good from cement in Rochester, since Rochester is closer to him and freight costs are greater from Detroit. From his point of view, the *homogeneous* goods are: C_r in New York City and C_d in New York City. Wherever it comes from, cement *at the place where he must use it* is the homogeneous good for the consumer.

Therefore, in equilibrium, it is C_r in New York City that will be equal to C_d in New York City—and these are the "delivered prices" of cement to the consumer.[68] Substituting this equality in the above equations, we see that it implies that the price of C_r in Rochester, plus freight cost from Rochester to New York, will equal the price of C_d in Detroit, plus freight cost from Detroit to New York. The freight costs at any time are readily calculable, and *ceteris paribus,* they will be greater for longer distances. In other words, in equilibrium on the free market, the price of C_r

in Rochester is equal to the price of C_d in Detroit *plus* the *differential* in freight costs for the longer as compared to the shorter distance to the consumer. Generalizing, *the "mill price" of cement at a shorter distance from the consumer will equal the "mill price" of cement at the longer distance plus the freight differential.* This is applicable not only to cement, but to every product in the economic system, and not only to products serving ultimate consumers, but also to those to be "consumed" by lower-order capitalists.

In proportion as firms are more distantly located from the consumer, they will then not be able to remain in business unless their average costs at the mill are sufficiently lower than those of their competitors to compensate for the increased freight costs. This is not, as might be thought, a "penalty" on the "technological superiority" of the distant firm, for the latter is *inferior* with respect to the important economic factor of location. It is precisely this mechanism that helps to determine the location of firms and assures that firms will be economically located in relation to the consumer. The influence of the location-difference factor in the price of a product will, of course, depend upon the proportion that freight costs bear to the other costs of producing the good. The higher the proportion, the greater the influence.

A firm with a location closer to the consumer market therefore has a spatial advantage conferred by its location. Given the same costs in other fields as its competitors, it earns a profit from its superior location. The gains of location will be imputed to the site value of the ground land of the plant. The owner of the site obtains its marginal value product. Therefore, gains to a firm resulting from improvement in locational advantage, as well as losses resulting from a locational disadvantage, will accrue as changes in ground rent and capital value to the owner of the specific site, whether the owner be the firm itself or someone else.

5. *A Note on the Fallacy of "Distribution"*

Ever since the days of early classical economics, many writers have discussed "distribution theory" as if it were completely separate and isolated from production theory.[69] Yet we have seen that "distribution" theory is simply production theory. The receivers of income earn wages, rent, interest, and increases in capital values; and these earnings are the prices of productive factors. The theory of the market determines the prices and incomes accruing to productive factors, thereby also determining the "functional distribution" of the factors. "Personal distribution"—how much money each *person* receives from the productive system—is determined, in turn, by the functions that he or his property performs in that system. There is no separation between production and distribution, and it is completely erroneous for writers to treat the productive system as if producers dump their product onto some stockpile, to be later "distributed" in some way to the people in the society. "Distribution" is only the other side of the coin of production on the market.

Many people criticize the free market as follows: Yes, we agree that production and prices will be allocated on the free market in a way best fitted to serve the needs of the consumers. But this law is necessarily based on a *given initial distribution of income* among the consumers; some consumers begin with only a little money, others with a great deal. The market system of production can be commended only if the original distribution of income meets with our approval.

This initial distribution of income (or rather of money assets) did not originate in thin air, however. It, too, was the necessary consequence of a market allocation of prices and production. It was the consequence of serving the needs of previous consumers. It was not an arbitrarily given distribution, but one that itself emerged from satisfying consumer needs. It too was inextricably bound up with production.

As we saw in chapter 2, a person's presently owned property could have been ultimately obtained in only one of the following ways: through personal production, voluntary exchange for a personal product, the finding and first using of unappropriated land, or theft from a producer. On a free market, only the first three can obtain, so that any "distribution" served by producers was in itself the result of free production and exchange.

Suppose, however, that at some preceding time the bulk of the wealthy consumers had acquired their property through theft and not through serving other consumers on the free market. Does this not instill a "built-in bias" into the market economy, since future producers must satisfy demands ensuing from unjust incomes?

The answer is that after the initial period, the effect of unjust incomes becomes less and less important. For in order to keep and increase their ill-gotten gains, the former robbers, now that a free economy is established, have to invest and recoup their funds so as to serve consumers correctly. If they are not fit for this task, and their exploits in predation have certainly not trained them for it, then entrepreneurial losses will diminish their assets and shift them to more able producers.

6. *A Summary of the Market*

The explanation of the free economic system constitutes a great architectural edifice. Starting from human action and its implications, proceeding to individual value scales and a money economy, we have demonstrated that the quantity of goods produced, the prices of consumers' goods, the prices of productive factors, the interest rate, profits and losses, all can be explained by the same deductive apparatus. Given a stock of land and labor factors, given existing capital goods inherited from the past, given individual time preferences (and, more broadly, technological knowledge), the capital goods structure and total production is determined. Individual preferences set prices for the various consumers' goods, and the alternative combinations of various factors in their production set the marginal value-productivity schedules of these factors. Ultimately, the marginal value product accruing to capital goods is resolved into returns to land, labor, and interest for time. The point at which a land or labor factor will settle on its DMVP schedule will be determined by the stock available. Since each factor will operate in an area of diminishing physical and certainly diminishing value returns, any increased stock of the factor, other things being equal, will enter at a lower DMVP point. The intersecting points on the DMVP schedules will yield the prices of the factors, also known as "rents" and "wage rates" (in the case of labor factors). The pure interest rate will be determined by the time-preference schedules of all individuals in the economy. Its chief expression will be not in the loan market, but in the discounts between prices in the various stages of production. Interest on the loan market will be a reflection of this "natural" interest rate. All the prices of each good, as well as the interest rate, will be uniform throughout the entire market. The capital value of every durable good will equal the discounted value of the sum of future rents to be obtained from the good, the discount being the rate of interest.

All this is a picture of the evenly rotating economy—the equilibrium situation toward which the real economy is always tending. If consumer valuations and the supply of resources remained constant, the relevant ERE would be reached. The forces driving toward the ERE are the profit-seeking entrepreneurs, who take the lead in meeting the uncertainties of the real world. By seeking out discrepancies between existing conditions and the equilibrium situation and remedying them, entrepreneurs make profits; those businessmen who unwittingly add to the maladjustments on the market are penalized with losses. Thus, to the extent that producers wish to make money, they drive toward ever more efficient servicing of the desires of the consumers—allocating resources to the most value-productive areas and away from the least value-productive. The (monetary) value productivity of a course of action depends on the extent to which it serves consumer needs.

But consumer valuations and supplies of resources are always changing, so that the ERE goal always changes as well and is never reached. We have analyzed the implications of changing elements in the economy. An increase in the labor supply may lower the DMVP of labor and hence wage rates, or raise them because of the further advantages of the division of labor and a more extended market. Which will occur depends on the optimum population level. Since labor is relatively more scarce than land, and relatively nonspecific, there will always be idle and zero-rent land, while there will never be involuntarily idle or zero-wage labor. An increase or decrease in the supply of "submarginal" land will have no effect on production; an increase in *supra*marginal land will increase production and render hitherto marginal land submarginal.

Lower time preferences will increase capital investment and thereby lengthen the structure of production. Such lengthening of the production structure, increasing the supply of capital goods, is the only way for man to advance from his bare hands and empty acres of land to more and more civilized standards of living. These capital goods are the necessary way stations on the road to higher total production. But they must be maintained and replaced as well as initially produced if people wish to keep their higher standard over any length of time.

To expand production, the important consideration is not so much technological improvement as greater capital investment. At no time has invested capital exhausted the best technological opportunities available. Many firms still use old, unimproved processes and techniques simply because they do not have the capital to invest in new ones. They would know how to improve their plant if capital were available. Thus, while the state of technology is ultimately a very important consideration, at no given time does it play a *direct* role, since the *narrower* limit on production is always the supply of capital.

In a progressing economy, given a constant supply of money, increased investment and a longer capital structure bring about lower money prices for factors and still lower prices for consumers' goods. "Real" factor prices (corrected for changes in the purchasing power of the monetary unit) increase. In net terms, this means that real land rents and real wage rates will increase in the progressing economy. Interest rates will fall as time-preference rates drop and the proportion of gross investment to consumption increases.

If rents are earned by a durable factor, they can be and are "capitalized" on the market, i.e., they have a capital value equivalent to the discounted sum of their expected future rents. Since land is a form of investment on the market just as are shares of a firm, its future rents will be capitalized so that land will tend to earn the same uniform interest rate as any other investment. In a progressing economy, the real capital value of land will increase, although the value will fall in money terms. To the extent that future changes in the value of land can be foreseen, they will be immediately incorporated into its present capital value. Therefore, future owners of land will benefit by future increases in its real capital value only to the extent that previous owners failed to anticipate the increase. To the extent that it was anticipated, the future owners will have paid it in their purchase price.

The course of change in a retrogressing economy will be the opposite. In a *stationary* economy, total production, the capital structure, real wages per capita, real capital values of land, and the rate of interest will remain the same, while the allocation of factors of production and the relative prices of various products will vary.[70]

10

Monopoly and Competition

1. *The Concept of Consumers' Sovereignty*

A. CONSUMERS' SOVEREIGNTY VS. INDIVIDUAL SOVEREIGNTY

We have seen that in the free market economy people will tend to produce those goods most demanded by the consumers.[1] Some economists have termed this system "consumers' sovereignty." Yet there is no compulsion about this. The choice is purely an independent one by the producer; his dependence on the consumer is purely voluntary, the result of his own choice for the "maximization" of utility, and it is a choice that he is free to revoke at any time. We have stressed many times that the pursuit of monetary return (the consequence of consumer demand) is engaged in by each individual *only to the extent that other things are equal.* These other things are the individual producer's psychic valuations, and they may counteract monetary influences. An example is a laborer or other factor-owner engaged in a certain line of work at less monetary return than elsewhere. He does this because of his enjoyment of the particular line of work and product and/or his distaste for other alternatives. Rather than "consumers' sovereignty," it would be more accurate to state that in the free market there is *sovereignty of the individual:* the individual is sovereign over his own person and actions and over his own property.[2] This may be termed *individual self-sovereignty.* To earn a monetary return, the individual producer must satisfy consumer demand, but the extent to which he obeys this expected monetary return, and the extent to which he pursues other, nonmonetary factors, is entirely a matter of his own free choice.

The term "consumers' sovereignty" is a typical example of the abuse, in economics, of a term ("sovereignty") appropriate only to the *political* realm and is thus an illustration of the dangers of the application of metaphors taken from other disciplines. "Sovereignty" is the quality of ultimate political power; it is the power resting on the use of violence. In a purely free society, each individual is sovereign over his own person and property, and it is therefore this self-sovereignty which obtains on the free market. No one is "sovereign" over anyone else's actions or exchanges. Since the consumers do not have the power to coerce producers into various occupations and work, the former are not "sovereign" over the latter.

B. PROFESSOR HUTT AND CONSUMERS' SOVEREIGNTY

The metaphorical shibboleth of "consumers' sovereignty" has misled even the best economists. Many writers have used it as an ideal with which to contrast the allegedly imperfect free market system. An example is Professor W. H. Hutt of the University of Capetown, who has made the most careful defense of the concept of consumers' sovereignty.[3] Since he is the originator of this concept and his use of the term is widespread in the literature, his article is worth particular attention. It will be used as the basis for a critique of the concept of consumers' sovereignty and its implications for the problems of competition and monopoly.

In the first part of his article, Hutt defends his concept of consumers' sovereignty against the criticism that he has neglected the desires of *producers*. He does this by asserting that if a producer desires a *means* as an *end* in itself, then he is "consuming." In this *formal* sense, as we have seen, consumers' sovereignty, by definition, always obtains. Formally, there is nothing wrong with such a definition, for we have stressed throughout this book that an individual evaluates ends (consumption) on his value scale and that his valuation of means (for production) is dependent upon the former. In this sense, then, consumption always rules production.

But this formal sense is not very useful for analyzing the situation on the *market*. And it is precisely the latter sense that Hutt and others employ. Thus, suppose producer A withholds his labor or land or capital service from the market. For whatever reason, he is exercising his sovereignty over his person and property. On the other hand, if he supplies them to the market, he is, to the extent that he aims at monetary return, submitting himself to the demands of the consumers. In the aforementioned general sense, "consumption" rules in any case. But the critical question is: *which* "consumer"? The market consumer of exchangeable goods who buys these goods with money, or the market producer of exchangeable goods who sells these goods for money? To answer this question, it is necessary to distinguish between the "producer of exchangeable goods" and the "consumer of exchangeable goods," since the market, by definition, can deal only in such goods. In short, we can designate people as "producers" and as "consumers," even though every man must act as a consumer, and every man must also act, in another context, as a producer (or as the receiver of a gift from a producer).

Making this distinction, we find that, contrary to Hutt, each individual has *self-sovereignty* over his person and property on the free market. The producer, and the producer alone, decides whether or not he will keep his property (including his own person) idle or sell it on the market for money, the results of his production then going to the consumers in exchange for their money. This decision—concerning how much to allocate to the market and how much to withhold—is the decision of the individual producer and of him alone.

Hutt implicitly recognizes this, however, since he soon shifts his argument and begins inconsistently to hold up "consumers' sovereignty" as an *ethical ideal against which the activities of the free market are to be judged*. Consumers' sovereignty becomes almost an Absolute Good, and any action by producers to thwart this ideal is considered as little less than moral treason. Wavering between consumers' sovereignty as a *necessary fact* and the contradictory concept of consumers' sovereignty as an *ideal* that can be violated, Hutt attempts to establish various criteria to determine when this sovereignty *is* being violated. For example, he asserts that when a producer withholds his person or property out of a desire to use it for enjoyment *as a consumers' good,* then this is a legitimate act, in keeping with rule by the consumer. On the other hand, when the producer acts to withhold his property in order to attain more monetary income than otherwise (presumably, although Hutt does not state this, by taking advantage of an inelastic demand curve for his product), then he is engaging in a vicious infringement on the consumers' will. He may do so by acting to restrict production of his own personal product, or, if he makes the same product as other producers, by acting in concert with them to restrict production in order to raise the price. This is the doctrine of monopoly price, and it is this monopoly price that is allegedly the instrument by which producers pervert their rightful function.

Hutt recognizes the enormous difficulty of distinguishing among the producer's motives in any concrete case. The individual who withholds his own labor may be doing so in order to obtain leisure; and even the owner of land or capital may be withholding it in order to derive, say, an esthetic enjoyment from the contemplation of his unused property. Suppose, indeed, that there is a *mixture* of motives in both cases. Hutt is definitely inclined to solve these difficulties by *not* giving the producer the benefit of the doubt, particularly in the case of property.

But the difficulty is far greater than Hutt imagines. Every individual producer is always engaged in an attempt to maximize his "psychic income," to arrive at the highest place on his value scale. To do so, he balances on this scale monetary income and various nonmonetary factors, in accordance with his particular valuations. Let us take the producer first as a *seller of labor.* In judging how much of his labor to sell and at what price, the producer will take into consideration the monetary income to be gained, the psychic return from the type of work and the "working conditions," and the leisure forgone, balancing them in accordance with the operation of his various marginal utilities. Certainly, if he can earn a higher income by working less, he will do so, since he also gains leisure thereby. And the question arises: Why is this immoral?

Moreover, (1) it is *impossible,* not simply impracticable, to separate the leisure from monetary considerations here, since both elements are involved, and only the person himself will know the intricate balancing of his own valuations. (2) More important, this act does *not* contravene the truth that the producer can earn money only by serving the consumers. Why has he been able to extract a "monopoly price" through restricting his production? Only because the demand for his services (either directly by consumers or indirectly from them through lower-order producers) is *inelastic,* so that a decreased production of the good and a higher price will lead to increased expenditure on his product and therefore increased income for him. Yet this inelastic demand schedule is purely the result of the *voluntary demands* of the consumers. If the consumers were really angry at this "monopolistic action," they could easily make their demand curves *elastic* by *boycotting* the producer and/or by increasing their demands at the "competitive" production level. The fact that they do not do so signifies their satisfaction with the existing state of affairs and demonstrates that they, as well as the producer, benefit from the resulting voluntary exchanges.

What about the producer in his capacity as a seller of property—the main target of the "anti-monopoly-price" school? The principle, first of all, is virtually the same. Individual producers may restrict the production and sale of their land or capital goods, either individually or in concert (by means of a "cartel") in order to increase their expected monetary incomes from the sale. Once again, there is nothing distinctively immoral about such action. The producers, other things being equal, are attempting to maximize the monetary income from their factors of production. This is no more immoral than any other attempt to maximize monetary income. Furthermore, they can do so only *by serving the consumers,* since, once again, the sale is voluntary on the part of both producers and consumers. Again, such a "monopoly price," to be established either by one individual or by individuals co-operating together in a cartel, is possible only if the demand curve (directly or indirectly of the consumers) is *inelastic,* and this inelasticity *is the resultant of the purely voluntary choices of consumers in their maximization of satisfaction.* For this "inelasticity" is simply a label for a situaion in which consumers spend more money on a good at a higher than at a lower price. If the consumers were really opposed to the cartel action, and if the resulting exchanges really hurt them, they would boycott the "monopolistic" firm or firms, they would lower their purchasing so that the demand curve became *elastic,* and the firm would be forced to increase its production and reduce its price again. If the "monopolistic price" action had been taken by a cartel of firms, and the cartel had no other advantages for rendering production more efficient, it would then have to disband, because of the now demonstrated elasticity of the demand schedule.

But, it may be asked, is it not true that the consumers would *prefer* a lower price and that therefore achievement of a "monopoly price" constitutes a "frustration of consumers' sovereignty"? The answer is: Of course, consumers would prefer lower prices; they always would. In fact, the lower the price, the more they would like it. Does this mean that the ideal price is zero, or close to zero, for all goods, because this would represent the greatest degree of producers' sacrifice to consumers' wishes?

In their role as consumers, men would always like lower prices for their purchases; in their capacity as producers, men always like higher prices for their wares. If Nature had originally provided a material Utopia, then all exchangeable goods would be free for the taking, and there would be no need for any labor to earn a money return. This Utopia would also be "preferred," but it too is a purely imaginary condition. Man must necessarily work within a given *real* environment of inherited land and durable capital.

In *this* world, there are two, and only two, ways to settle what the prices of goods will be. One is the way of the free market, where prices are set voluntarily by each of the participating individuals. In this situation, exchanges are made on terms benefiting all the exchangers. The other way is by violent intervention in the market, the way of hegemony as against contract. Such hegemonic establishment of prices means the outlawing of free exchanges and the institution of exploitation of man by man —for exploitation occurs whenever a coerced exchange is made. If the free market route—the route of mutual benefit—is adopted, then there can be no other criterion of justice than the free market price, and this includes alleged "competitive" and "monopoly" prices, as well as the actions of cartels. In the free market, consumers and producers adjust their actions in voluntary cooperation.

In the case of barter, this conclusion is evident; the various producer-consumers either determine their mutual exchange rates voluntarily in the free market, or else the ratios are set by violence. There seems to be no reason why it should be more or less "moral," on any grounds, for the horse-price of fish to be higher or lower than it is on the free market, or, in other words, why the fish-price of horses should be lower or higher. Yet it is no more evident why any money price should be lower or higher than it is on the market.[4]

2. *Cartels and Their Consequences*

A. CARTELS AND "MONOPOLY PRICE"

But is not monopolizing action a restriction of production, and is not this restriction a demonstrably antisocial act? Let us first take what would seem to be the worst possible case of such action: the actual destruction of part of a product by a cartel. This is done to take advantage of an inelastic demand curve and to raise the price to gain a greater monetary income for the whole group. We can visualize, for example, the case of a coffee cartel burning great quantities of coffee.

In the first place, such actions will surely occur very seldom. Actual destruction of its product is clearly a highly wasteful act, even for the cartel; it is obvious that the factors of production which the growers had expended in producing the coffee have been spent in vain. Clearly, the production of the total quantity of coffee itself has proved to be an error, and the burning of coffee is only the aftermath and reflection of the error. Yet, because of the uncertainty of the future, errors are often made. Man could labor and invest for years in the production of a good which, it may turn out, consumers hardly want at all. If, for example, consumers' tastes had changed so that coffee would not be demanded by anyone, regardless of price, it would again have to be destroyed, with or without a cartel.

Error is certainly unfortunate, but it cannot be considered immoral or antisocial; nobody aims deliberately at error.[5] If coffee were a durable good, it is obvious that the cartel would *not* destroy it, but would store it for gradual future sale to consumers, thus earning income on the "surplus" coffee. In an evenly rotating economy, where errors are barred by definition, there would be no destruction, since optimum stocks for the attainment of money income would be produced in advance. Less coffee would be produced from the beginning. *The waste lies in the excessive production of coffee* at the expense of other goods that could have been produced. *The waste does not lie in the actual burning of the coffee.* After the production of coffee is lowered, the other factors which would have gone into coffee production will not be wasted; the other land, labor, etc., will go into other and more profitable uses. It is true that excess specific factors will remain idle; but this is always the fate of specific factors when the realities of consumer demand do not sustain their use in production. For example, if there is a sudden dwindling of consumer demand for a good, so that it becomes unremunerative for labor to work with certain specialized machines, this "idle capacity" is *not* a social waste, but is rather socially useful. It is proved an error to have produced the machines; and now that the machines *are* produced, working on them turns out to be less profitable than working with other lands and machines to produce some other result. Therefore, the economical step is to leave them idle or perhaps to transform their material stuff into other uses. Of course, in an errorless economy, no excessive specific capital goods will be produced.

Suppose, for example, that before the coffee cartel went into operation, *X* amount of labor and *Y* amount of land co-operated to produce 100 million pounds of coffee a year. The coffee cartel determined, however, that the most remunerative production was 60 million pounds and therefore reduced annual output to this level. It would have been absurd, of course, to continue wasteful production of 100 million pounds and then to burn 40 millions. But what of the now surplus labor and land? These shift to the production, say, of 10 million pounds of rubber, 50,000 hours of service as jungle guides, etc. Who is to say that the second structure of production, the second allocation of factors, is less "just" than the first? In fact, we may say it is *more* just, since the new allocation of factors will be more profitable, and hence more *value-productive,* to consumers. In the value sense, then, over-all production has now *expanded,* not contracted. It is clear we cannot say that production, over-all, has been *restricted,* since output of goods other than coffee has increased, and the only comparison between the decline of one good and the increase in another must be made in these broad valuational terms. Indeed, the shifting of factors to rubber and jungle guidance no more *restricts* coffee production than a previous shift of factors to coffee *restricted* the production of the former goods.

The whole concept of "restricting production," then, is a fallacy when applied to the free market. In the real world of scarce resources in relation to possible ends, *all* production involves choice and the allocation of factors to serve the most highly valued ends. In short, the production of *any* product is necessarily always "restricted." Such "restriction" follows simply from the universal scarcity of factors and the diminishing marginal utility of any one product. But then it is absurd to speak of "restriction" at all.[6]

We cannot, then, say that the cartel has "restricted production." After the final allocation has eliminated the producer's error, the cartel's action will effect a maximization of producers' incomes in the service of the consumers, as do all other free-market allocations. This is the result that people on the market tend to attain, in consonance with their skill as forecasting entrepreneurs, and this is the only situation in which man as consumer harmonizes with man as producer.

It follows from our analysis that the producers' original production of 100 million pounds was an unfortunate error, later corrected by them. Instead of being a vicious restriction of production to the detriment of the consumers, the cutback in coffee production was, on the contrary, a correction of the previous error. Since only the free market can allocate resources to serve the consumer, in accordance with monetary profitability, it follows that in the previous situation, "too much" coffee and "too little" rubber, jungle guide service, etc., were being produced. The cartel's action, in reducing the production of coffee and causing an increase in the production of rubber, jungle guiding, etc., led to an *increase* in the power of the productive resources to satisfy consumer desires.

If there are anticartelists who disagree with this verdict and believe that the *previous* structure of production served the consumers better, they are always at perfect liberty to bid the land, labor, and capital factors away from the jungle-guide agencies and rubber producers, *and themselves* embark on the production of the allegedly "deficient" 40 million pounds of coffee. Since *they* are not doing so, they are hardly in a position to attack the *existing* coffee producers for not doing so. As Mises succinctly stated: "Certainly those engaged in the production of steel are not responsible for the fact that other people did not likewise enter this field of production. . . . If somebody is to blame for the fact that the number of people who joined the voluntary civil defense organization is not larger, then it is not those who have already joined but those who have not." [7] The position of the anticartelists implies that someone else is producing *too much* of some *other* product; yet they offer no standards except their own arbitrary decrees to determine *which* production is excessive.

Criticism of steel owners for not producing "enough" steel or of coffee growers for not producing "enough" coffee also implies the existence of a caste system, whereby a certain caste is permanently designated to produce steel, another caste to grow coffee, etc. Only in such a caste society would such criticism make sense. Yet the free market is the reverse of the caste system; indeed, choice between alternatives implies mobility between alternatives, and this mobility obviously holds for entrepreneurs or lenders with money to invest in production.

Furthermore, as we have stated above, an inelastic demand curve is purely the result of consumers' choice. Thus, suppose that 100 million pounds of coffee have been produced and lie in stock, and a group of growers jointly decide that a burning of 40 million pounds of coffee will, say, double the price from 1 gold grain per pound to 2 gold grains per pound, thus giving them a higher total income acting jointly. This would be impossible if the growers knew that they would be confronted with an effective consumer boycott at the higher price. Further, consumers have another way, *if they so desire,* to prevent destruction of the good. Various consumers, acting either individually or jointly, could offer to purchase the existing coffee *at higher than present prices.* They could do this either because of their desire for coffee or because of their philanthropic dismay at the destruction of a useful good, or from a combination of both motives. At any rate, if they did so, they would prevent the producers' cartel from decreasing the supply sold on the market. The boycott at a higher price and/or increased offers at the lower price would change the demand curve and render it elastic at the present stock level, thereby removing any incentive or need for the formation of a cartel.

To regard a cartel as immoral or as hampering some sort of consumers' sovereignty is therefore completely unwarranted. And this is true even in the seemingly "worst" case of a cartel that we may assume is founded *solely* for "restrictive" purposes, and where, as a result of previous error and the perishability of product, actual destruction will occur. If consumers really wish to prevent this action, they need only change their demand schedules for the product, either by an actual change in their taste for coffee or by a combination of boycott and philanthropy. The fact that such a development does not take place in any given circumstance signifies that the producers are still maximizing their monetary income in the service of the consumers—by a cartel action, as well as by any other action. Some readers might object that, in offering higher demands for existing stock, the consumers would be bribing the producers, and that this constitutes an unwarranted extortion on the part of the producers. But this charge is untenable. Producers are guided by the goal of maximizing monetary income; they are not extorting, but simply producing where their gains are at a maximum, through exchanges concluded voluntarily by producers and consumers alike. This is no more nor less a case of "extortion" than when a laborer shifts from a lower-paying to a higher-paying job or when an entrepreneur invests in what he thinks will be a more rather than a less profitable project.

It must be recognized that once an error has been committed, as it had been in the aforementioned situation, the rational course is not to bewail the past, nor to attempt to "recover" historical costs, but to make the best (*ceteris paribus,* the most money) of the present situation. We recognize this when previously produced machines or other capital goods face a loss of demand for their product. In the production process, as we have seen, labor energies work on natural and produced factors to arrive at the most urgently demanded consumers' goods. Since error is inevitable, this process is bound to lead to a considerable amount of "idle" capital goods at any given time. Similarly, much original land area will remain idle because existing labor has more profitable work to do on other lands. In short, the "idle" coffee is the result of an error in forecasting and should be no more shocking or reprehensible than "idle capacity" in any other type of capital good.

Our argument is just as applicable to a single firm producing a unique product with an inelastic demand as it is to a cartel of firms. A single firm, with inelastic demand for its product, could also destroy part of its stock after committing a forecasting error. Our critique of the "anti-monopoly-price" and consumers'-sovereignty doctrines applies equally well to such a case.

B. CARTELS, MERGERS, AND CORPORATIONS

A common argument holds that cartel action involves *collusion.* For one firm may achieve a "monopoly price" as a result of its natural abilities or consumer enthusiasm for its particular product, whereas a cartel of many firms allegedly involves "collusion" and "conspiracy." These expressions, however, are simply emotive terms designed to induce an unfavorable response. What is actually involved here is *co-operation* to increase the incomes of the producers. For what is the essence of a cartel action? Individual producers agree to pool their assets into a common lot, this single central organization to make the decisions on production and price policies for all the owners and then to allocate the monetary gain among them. *But is this process not the same as any sort of joint partnership or the formation of a single corporation?* What happens when a partnership or corporation is formed? Individuals agree to pool their assets into a central management, this central direction to set the policies for the owners and to allocate the monetary gains among them. In both cases, the pooling, lines of authority, and allocation of monetary gain take place according to rules agreed upon by all from the beginning. *There is therefore no essential difference between a cartel and an ordinary corporation or partnership.* It might be objected that the ordinary corporation or partnership covers only *one* firm, while the cartel includes an entire "industry" (i.e., all firms producing a certain product). But such a distinction does not necessarily hold. Various firms may refuse to enter a cartel, while, on the other hand, a single firm may well be a "monopolist" in the sale of its particular unique product, and therefore it may also encompass an entire "industry."

The correspondence between a co-operative partnership or corporation—not generally considered reprehensible—and a cartel is further enhanced when we consider the case of a *merger* of various firms. Mergers have been denounced as "monopolistic," but not nearly as vehemently as have cartels. Merging firms pool their capital assets, and the owners of the individual firms now become part owners of the single merged firm. They will agree on rules for the exchange ratios of the shares of the different companies. If the merging firms encompass the entire industry, then a merger is simply a permanent form of cartel. Yet clearly the only difference between a merger and the *original forming of a single corporation* is that the merger pools existing capital-goods assets, while the original birth of a corporation pools *money* assets. It is clear that, economically, there is little difference between the two. A merger is the action of individuals with a certain quantity of already produced capital goods, adjusting themselves to their present and expected future conditions by co-operative pooling of assets. The formation of a new company is an adjustment to expected future conditions (before any specific investment has been made in capital goods) by co-operative pooling of assets. The essential similarity lies in the voluntary pooling of assets in a more centralized organization for the purpose of increasing monetary income.

The theorists who attack cartels and monopolies do not recognize the identity of the two actions. As a result, a merger is considered less reprehensible than a cartel, and a single corporation far less menacing than a merger. Yet an industry-wide merger is, in effect, a permanent cartel, a permanent combination and fusion. On the other hand, a cartel that maintains by voluntary agreement the separate identity of each firm is by nature a highly transitory and ephemeral arrangement and, as we shall see below, generally tends to break up on the market. In fact, in many cases, a cartel can be considered as simply a tentative step in the direction of permanent merger. And a merger and the original formation of a corporation do not, as we have seen, essentially differ. The former is an adaptation of the size and number of firms in an industry to new conditions or is the correction of a previous error in forecasting. The latter is a *de novo* attempt to adapt to present and future market conditions.

C. ECONOMICS, TECHNOLOGY, AND THE SIZE OF THE FIRM

We do not know, and economics cannot tell us, the optimum size of a firm in any given industry. The optimum size depends on the concrete technological conditions of each situation, as well as on the state of consumer demand in relation to the given supply of various factors in this and in other industries. All these complex questions enter into the decisions of producers, and ultimately of consumers, concerning how large the firms in various lines of production will be. In line with consumer demand and with opportunity costs for the various factors, factor-owners and entrepreneurs will produce in those industries and firms in which they can maximize their monetary income or profit (other psychic factors being equal). Since forecasting is the function of entrepreneurs, successful entrepreneurs will minimize their errors and hence their losses as well. As a result, *any existing situation on the free market will tend to be the most desirable for the satisfaction of consumers' demands (including herein the nonmonetary wishes of the producers).*

Neither economists nor engineers can decide the most efficient size of a firm in any situation. Only the entrepreneurs themselves can determine what size of firm will operate most efficiently, and it is presumptuous and unwarranted for economists or for any other outside observers to attempt to dictate otherwise. In this and other matters, the wishes and demands of the consumers are "telegraphed" through the price system, and the resulting drive for maximum monetary income and profits will always tend to bring about the optimum allocation and pricing. There is no need for the external advice of economists.

It is clear that when several thousand individuals decide *not* to produce and own individual steel plants by themselves, but rather to pool their capital into an organized corporation—which will purchase factors, invest and direct production, and sell the product, later allocating the monetary gains among the owners—they are enormously increasing their efficiency. Compared to production in hundreds of tiny plants, the quantity of production per given factors will be greatly increased. The large firm will be able to purchase heavily capitalized machinery and to finance better organized marketing and distributing outlets. All this is quite clear when thousands of individuals pool their capital into the establishment of a steel firm. But why may it not be equally true when *several small steel firms merge into one large company?*

It might be replied that in the latter merger, particularly in the case of a cartel, joint action is taken, not to increase efficiency, but solely to increase income by restricting sales. Yet there is no way that an outside observer can distinguish between a "restrictive" and an efficiency-increasing operation. In the first place, we must not think of the plant or factory as being the only productive factors the efficiency of which can increase. Marketing, advertising, etc., are also *factors of production;* for "production" is not simply the physical transformation of a product, but also consists in transporting it and placing it into the hands of users. The latter implies the expenses of informing the user about the existence and nature of the product and of selling that product to him. Since a cartel always engages in joint marketing, who can deny that the cartel might render marketing more efficient? How, therefore, can this efficiency be separated from the "restrictive" aspect of the operation? [8]

Furthermore, technological factors in production can never be considered in a vacuum. Technological knowledge tells us of a whole host of alternatives that are open to us. But the crucial questions—in what to invest? how much? what production method to choose?—can be answered only by economic, i.e., by *financial* considerations. They can be answered only on a market actuated by a drive for money incomes and profits. Thus, how is a producer to decide, in digging a subway tunnel, what material to use in its construction? From a purely technological point of view, solid platinum may be the best choice, the most durable, etc. Does this mean that he should choose platinum? He can make a choice among factors, methods, goods to produce, etc., only by comparing the necessary monetary expenses (which are equal to the income the factors could earn elsewhere) with expected monetary income from the production. Only by maximizing monetary gain can factors be allocated in the service of consumers; otherwise, and on purely technological grounds, there would be nothing to prevent the building of platinum-lined subway tunnels the breadth of the continent. The only reason this cannot be done under present conditions is the heavy money "cost" caused by the waste of drawing away factors and resources from uses far more urgently demanded by the consumers. But the fact of this urgent alternative demand—and thus *the fact of the waste*—can be discovered only through being recorded by a price system actuated by a drive by producers for money incomes. Only empirical observation of the market reveals to us the full absurdity of such a transcontinental subway.

Moreover, there are no physical units with which we can compare the different types of physical factors and physical products. Thus, suppose a producer attempts to determine the most efficient use of two hours of his labor. In a romantic moment, he tries to determine this efficiency by purely abstracting from "sordid" considerations of monetary gain. Assume that he is confronted with three technologically known alternatives. These are tabulated as follows:

Factors		*Product*
A		
2 hours of labor 5 pounds of clay 1 oven-hour	:	1 pot
B		
2 hours of labor 1 block of wood 1 oven-hour	:	1 pipe
C		
2 hours of labor 1 block of wood 1 oven-hour	:	1 model boat

Which of these alternatives, *A, B,* or *C,* is the most efficient, the most technologically "useful," way of allocating his labor? It is clear that the "idealistic," self-sacrificing producer has no way of knowing! He has no rational way of deciding whether or not to produce the pot, the pipe, or the boat. Only the "selfish" money-seeking producer has a rational way of determining the allocation. In seeking maximum monetary gain, the producer compares the money costs (necessary expenses) of the various factors with the prices of the products. Considering *A* and *B*, for example, if the purchase of the clay and oven-hour would cost 1 gold ounce, and the pot could sell for 2 gold ounces, his labor would earn 1 gold ounce. On the other hand, if the wood and oven-hour would cost 1½ gold ounces, and the pipe could sell for 4 gold ounces, he would earn 2½ ounces for his two hours of labor and would choose to make this product. The prices of both the product and the factors are reflections of consumer demand and of producers' attempts to earn money in its service. The only way the producer could determine which product to make is to compare expected monetary gains. If the boat would sell for 5 gold ounces, he would produce the boat rather than the pipe, and thus satisfy a more urgent consumer demand, as well as his own desire for monetary income.

There can therefore be no separation of technological efficiency from financial considerations. The only way that we can determine whether one product is more demanded than another, or one process more efficient than another, is through concrete actions of the free market. We may think it self-evident, for example, that the optimum efficient size of a steel plant is larger than that of a barber shop. But we know this not as economists from a priori or praxeological reasoning, but purely by empirical observation of the free market. There is no way that economists or any other outside observers can set the technological optimum for any plant or firm. This can be done only on the market itself. But if this is true in general, it is also true in the specific cases of mergers and cartels. The impossibility of isolating a technological element becomes even clearer when we remember that the critical problem is not the size of the *plant*, but the size of the *firm*. The two are by no means synonymous. It is true that the firm will consider the optimum-sized plant for whatever scale its operations will be on, and, further, that a larger-sized plant will, *ceteris paribus*, require a larger-sized firm. But its range of decisions cover a much broader ground: how much to invest, what good or goods to produce, etc. A firm may encompass one or more plants or products and always encompasses marketing facilities, financial organization, etc., which are overlooked when only the plant is held in view.[9]

These considerations, incidentally, serve to refute the very popular distinction between "production for use" and "production for profit." In the first place, *all* production is for use; otherwise it would not take place. In the market economy, this almost always means goods for the use of *others*—the consumers. Profit can be earned only through servicing consumers with produced goods. On the other hand, there can be no rational production, above the most primitive level, based on technological or utilitarian considerations abstracted from monetary gain.[10]

It is important to realize what we have *not* said in this section. We have not said that cartels will always be more efficient than individual firms or that "big" firms will always be more efficient than small ones. Our conclusion is that economics can make few valid statements about the optimal size of a firm *except* that the free market will come as close as possible to rendering maximum service to consumers, whether we are considering the size of a firm or any other aspect of production. All the concrete problems in production—the size of the firm, the size of the industry, the location, price, size and nature of the output, etc.—are for entrepreneurs, not economists, to solve.

We should not leave the problem of the size of the firm without considering a common worry of economic writers: What if the average cost curve of a firm continues to fall indefinitely? Would not the firm then grow so big as to constitute a "monopoly"? There is much lamentation that competition "breaks down" in such a situation. Much of the emphasis on this problem comes, however, from preoccupation with the case of "pure competition," which, as we shall see below, is an impossible figment. Secondly, it is obvious that no firm ever has been or can be infinitely large, so that limiting obstacles—rising or less rapidly falling costs—must enter somewhere, and relevantly, for every firm.[11] Thirdly, if a firm, through greater efficiency, does obtain a "monopoly" in some sense in its industry, it clearly does so, in the case we are considering (falling average cost), by lowering prices and benefiting the consumers. And if (as all the theorists who attack "monopoly" agree) what is wrong with "monopoly" is precisely a *restriction* of production and a *rise* in price, there is obviously nothing wrong with a "monopoly" achieved by pursuing the directly opposite path.[12]

D. THE INSTABILITY OF THE CARTEL

Analysis demonstrates that a cartel is an inherently unstable form of operation. If the joint pooling of assets in a common cause proves in the long run to be profitable for each of the individual members of the cartel, then they will act formally to *merge* into one large firm. The cartel then disappears in the merger. On the other hand, if the joint action proves unprofitable for one or more members, the dissatisfied firm or firms will break away from the cartel, and, as we shall see, any such independent action almost always destroys the cartel. The cartel form, therefore, is bound to be highly evanescent and unstable.

If joint action is the most efficient and profitable course for each member, a merger will soon take place. The very fact that each member firm retains its potential independence in the cartel means that a breakup could take place at any time. The cartel will have to assign production totals and quotas to each of the member firms. This is likely to lead first to a good deal of bickering among the firms over the assignment of quotas, with each member attempting to gain a larger share of the assignment. Whatever basis quotas are assigned on will necessarily be arbitrary and will always be subject to challenge by one or more members.[13] In a merger, or in the formation of one corporation, the stockholders, by majority vote, form a decision-making organization. In the case of a cartel, however, disputes arise among *independent* owning entities.

Particularly likely to be restive under the imposed joint action will be the more efficient producers, who will be eager to expand their business rather than be fettered by shackles and quotas to provide shelter for their less efficient competitors. Clearly, the more efficient firms will be the ones to break up the cartel. This will be increasingly true as time goes on and conditions change from the time the cartel was first formed. The quotas, the jealously made agreements that formerly seemed plausible to all, now become intolerable restrictions for the more efficient firms, and the cartel soon breaks up; for once one firm breaks away, expands output and cuts prices, the others must follow.

If the cartel does not break up from within, it is even more likely to do so from without. To the extent that it has earned unusual monopoly profits, outside firms and outside producers will enter the same field of production. Outsiders, in short, rush in to take advantage of the higher profits. But once one strong competitor arises to challenge it, the cartel is doomed. For as the firms in the cartel are bound by production quotas, they must watch new competitors expand and take away sales from them at an accelerating rate. As a result, the cartel must break up under the pressure of the newcomers' competition.[14]

E. FREE COMPETITION AND CARTELS

There are other arguments that opponents of cartels use in decrying cartel action. One thesis asserts that there is something wicked about formerly competing firms now uniting, e.g., "restricting competition" or "restraining trade." Such restriction is supposed to injure the consumers' freedom of choice. As Hutt phrased it in his previously cited article: "Consumers are free . . . and consumers' sovereignty is realizable, only to the extent to which the power of substitution exists."

But surely this is a complete misconception of the meaning of freedom. Crusoe and Friday bargaining on a desert island have very little *range* or *power* of choice; their power of substitution is limited. Yet if neither man interferes with the other's person or property, each one is absolutely *free*. To argue otherwise is to adopt the fallacy of confusing freedom with abundance or range of choice. *No individual producer is or can be responsible for other people's power to substitute.* No coffee grower or steel producer, whether acting singly or jointly, is responsible to anyone because he chose not to produce more. If Professor X or consumer Y believes that there are not enough coffee producers in existence or that they are not producing enough, these critics are free to enter the coffee or steel business as they see fit, thus increasing both the number of competitors and the quantity of the good produced.

If consumer demand had really justified more competitors or more of the product or a greater variety of products, then entrepreneurs would have seized the opportunity to profit by satisfying this demand. The fact that this is not being done in any given case demonstrates that no such unsatisfied consumer demand exists. But if this is true, then it follows that *no man-made actions can improve the satisfaction of consumer demand more than is being done on the unhampered market.* The false confusion of freedom with abundance rests on a failure to distinguish between the *conditions given by nature* and *man-made actions to transform nature.* In a state of raw nature, there is no abundance; in fact, there are few, if any, goods at all. Crusoe is *absolutely free,* and yet on the point of starvation. Of course, it would be pleasanter for everyone if the nature-given conditions had been far more abundant, but these are vain fantasies. For vis à vis nature, this *is* the best of all *possible* worlds, because it is the *only* possible one. Man's condition on earth is that he must work with the given natural conditions and improve them by human action. *It is a reflection on nature, not on the free market, that everyone is "free to starve."*

Economics demonstrates that individuals, entering into mutual relations in a free market in a free society—and *only* in such relations—can provide abundance for themselves and for the entire society. ("Free," as always in this book, is used in the interpersonal sense of being unmolested by other persons.) To employ freedom as itself equivalent to abundance obstructs understanding of these truths.

The free market in the world of production may be termed "free competition" or "free entry," meaning that in a free society anyone is free to compete and produce in any field he chooses. "Free competition" is the application of liberty to the sphere of production: the freedom to buy, sell, and transform one's property without violent interference by an external power.

We have seen above that in a regime of free competition consumers' satisfaction will, at any time, tend to be at the maximum possible, given natural conditions. The best forecasters will tend to emerge as the dominant entrepreneurs, and if anyone sees an opportunity passed up, he is free to take advantage of his superior foresight. The regime that tends to maximize consumers' satisfaction, therefore, is not "pure competition" or "perfect competition" or "competition without cartel action,"[15] or anything other than one of simple *economic liberty.*

Some critics charge that there is no "real" free entry or free competition in a free market. For how can anyone compete or enter a field when an enormous amount of money is needed to invest in efficient plants and firms? It is easy to "enter" the pushcart peddling "industry" because so little capital is required, but it is almost impossible to establish a new automobile firm, with its heavy requirements of capital.

This argument is but another variant of the prevailing confusion between freedom and abundance. In this case, the abundance refers to the money capital which a man has been able to amass. Every man is perfectly free to become a baseball player; but this freedom does not imply that he will be as good a baseball player as the next man. A man's range or power of action, dependent on his ability and the exchange-value of his property, is something completely distinct from his freedom. As we have said, a free society will in the long run lead to general abundance and is the necessary condition for that abundance. But the two must be kept conceptually distinct, and not confused by phrases such as "real freedom" or "true freedom." Therefore, the fact that everyone is *free* to enter an industry does not mean that everyone is *able,* either in terms of personal qualities or monetary capital, to do so. In industries requiring more capital, fewer people will be able to take advantage of their freedom to set up a new firm than in those requiring less capital, just as fewer laborers will be able to take advantage of freedom of entry in a very highly skilled profession than in a menial position. There is no mystery about either situation.

In fact, the disability is much more relevant in the case of labor than in the case of business competition. What are modern devices such as corporations but means of pooling capital by many people of greater and lesser wealth? The "difficulty" of investing in a new automobile firm should be considered, not in terms of the hundreds of millions of dollars required for total investment, but in terms of the fifty or so dollars required to purchase one share of stock. But while capital can be pooled, beginning with the smallest units, labor ability cannot be pooled.

Sometimes the argument reaches absurd lengths. For example, it is often asserted that now, in this modern world, firms are so large that new people "cannot" compete or enter the industry because the capital cannot be raised. These critics do not seem to see that the aggregate capital and wealth of individuals have advanced along with the increase in wealth required to launch a new enterprise. In fact, these are two sides of the same coin. There is no reason to suppose that it was easier to raise the capital to launch a new retail shop many centuries ago than it is to raise capital for the automobile firm today. If there is enough capital to finance the large firms currently existing, there is enough to finance one more; in fact, capital could be withdrawn from existing large firms and shifted to new ones if there is a need for them. Of course, if the new enterprise would be unprofitable and therefore unserviceable to consumers, it is easy to see why there is reluctance in the free market to embark on the venture.

That there is inequality of ability or monetary income on the free market should surprise no one. As we have seen above, men are not "equal" in their tastes, interests, abilities, or locations. Resources are not distributed "equally" over the earth.[16] This inequality or diversity in abilities and distribution of resources insures inequality of income on the free market. And, since a man's monetary assets are derived from his and his ancestors' abilities in serving consumers on the market, it is not surprising that there is inequality of monetary *wealth* as well.

The term "free competition," then, will prove misleading unless it is interpreted to mean free action, i.e., freedom to compete or not to compete as the individual wills.

It should be clear from the foregoing discussion that there is nothing particularly reprehensible or destructive of consumer freedom in the establishment of a "monopoly price" or in a cartel action. A cartel action, if it is a voluntary one, cannot injure freedom of competition and, if it proves profitable, *benefits* rather than injures the consumers. It is perfectly consonant with a free society, with individual self-sovereignty, and with the earning of money through serving consumers.

As Benjamin R. Tucker brilliantly concluded in dealing with the problem of cartels and competition:

> The right to cooperate is as unquestionable as the right to compete; the right to compete involves the right to refrain from competition; cooperation is often a method of competition, and competition is always, in the larger view, a method of cooperation . . . each is a legitimate, orderly, non-invasive exercise of the individual will under the social law of equal liberty . . .
>
> Viewed in the light of these irrefutable propositions, the trust, then, like every other industrial combination endeavoring to do collectively nothing but what each member of the combination might fully endeavor to do individually, is, *per se*, an unimpeachable institution. To assail or control or deny this form of cooperation on the ground that it is itself a denial of competition is an absurdity. It is an absurdity because it proves too much. *The trust is a denial of competition in no other sense than that in which competition itself is a denial of competition.* (Italics ours.) The trust denies competition only by producing and selling more cheaply than those outside of the trust can produce and sell; but in that sense every successful individual competitor also denies competition . . . The fact is that there is one denial of competition which is the right of all, and that there is another denial of competition which is the right of none. All of us, whether out of a trust or in it, have a right to deny competition by competing, but none of us, whether in a trust or out of it, have a right to deny competition by arbitrary decree, by interference with voluntary effort, by forcible suppression of initiative.[17]

This is not to say, of course, that joint co-operation or combination is necessarily "better than" competition among firms. We simply conclude that the relative extent of areas *within* or *between* firms on the free market will be precisely that proportion most conducive to the well-being of consumers and producers alike. This is the same as our previous conclusion that the size of a firm will tend to be established at the level most serviceable to the consumers.[18]

F. THE PROBLEM OF ONE BIG CARTEL

The myth of the evil cartel has been greatly bolstered by the nightmare image of "one big cartel." "This is all very well," one may say, "but suppose that all the firms in the country amalgamated or cartelized into One Big Cartel. What of the horrors then?"

The answer can be obtained by referring to chapter 9, pp. 547 ff. above, where we saw that the free market placed definite limits on the size of the firm, i.e., the limits of *calculability* on the market. In order to calculate the profits and losses of each branch, a firm must be able to refer its internal operations to *external markets* for *each* of the various factors and intermediate products. When any of these external markets disappears, because all are absorbed *within* the province of a single firm, calculability disappears, and there is no way for the firm rationally to allocate factors to that specific area. The more these limits are encroached upon, the greater and greater will be the sphere of irrationality, and the more difficult it will be to avoid losses. One big cartel would not be able rationally to allocate producers' goods at all and hence could not avoid severe losses. Consequently, it could never really be established, and, if tried, would quickly break asunder.

In the production sphere, socialism is equivalent to One Big Cartel, compulsorily organized and controlled by the State.[19] Those who advocate socialist "central planning" as the more efficient method of production for consumer wants must answer the question: If this central planning is really more efficient, why has it not been established by profit-seeking individuals on the free market? The fact that One Big Cartel has never been formed voluntarily and that it needs the coercive might of the State to be formed demonstrates that it could not possibly be the most efficient method of satisfying consumer desires.[20]

Let us assume for a moment that One Big Cartel could be established on the free market and that the calculability problem does not arise. What would the economic consequences be? Would the cartel be able to "exploit" anyone? In the first place, *consumers* could not be "exploited." For consumers' demand curves would still be elastic or inelastic, as the case may be. Since, as we shall see further below, consumers' demand curves for a firm are always elastic above the free-market equilibrium price, it follows that the cartel will not be able to raise prices or earn more from consumers.

What about the factors? Could not *their* owners be exploited by the cartel? In the first place, the universal cartel, to be effective, would have to include owners of primary land; otherwise whatever gains they might have might be imputed to land. To put it in its strongest terms, then, could a universal cartel of all land *and* capital goods "exploit" laborers by systematically paying the latter less than their discounted marginal value products? Could not the members of the cartel agree to pay a very low sum to these workers? If that happened, however, there would be created great opportunities for entrepreneurs either to spring up outside the cartel or to break away from the cartel and profit by hiring workers for a higher wage. This competition would have the double effect of (*a*) breaking up the universal cartel and (*b*) tending again to yield to the laborers their marginal product. As long as competition is free, unhampered by governmental restrictions, no universal cartel could either exploit labor or remain universal for any length of time.[21]

3. *The Illusion of Monopoly Price*

So far we have established that there is nothing "wrong" with a monopoly price, either when instituted by one firm or by a cartel; that, in fact, whatever price the free market (unhampered by violence or the threat of violence) establishes will be the "best" price. We have also shown the impossibility of separating "monopolizing" from efficiency considerations in cartel actions or of separating technology from profitability in general; and we have seen the great instability of the cartel form.

In this section we investigate a further problem: Granted that there is nothing "wrong" with monopoly prices, how tenable is the very concept of "monopoly price" on the free market? Can it be distinguished at all from "competitive price," its supposed polar opposite? To answer this question, we must explore what the theory of monopoly price is all about.

A. DEFINITIONS OF MONOPOLY

Before investigating the theory of monopoly price, we must begin by defining *monopoly*. Despite the fact that monopoly problems occupy an enormous quantity of economic writings, little or no clarity of definition exists.[22] There is, in fact, enormous vagueness and confusion on the subject. Very few economists have formulated a coherent, meaningful definition of monopoly.

A common example of a confused definition is: "Monopoly exists when a firm has control over its price." This definition is a mixture of confusion and absurdity. In the first place, on the free market there is no such thing as "control" over the price in an exchange; in any exchange the price of the sale is *voluntarily* agreed upon by both parties. No "control" is exercised by either party; the only control is each person's control over *his own* actions—stemming from his self-sovereignty—and consequently his control will be over his own decision to enter or not to enter into an exchange at any hypothetical price. There is no direct control over price because price is a *mutual* phenomenon. On the other hand, each person has *absolute* control over his own action and therefore over the price which he will *attempt* to charge for any particular good. Any man can set any price that he wants for any quantity of a good that he sells; the question is whether he can find any buyers at that price. Similarly, of course, any buyer can set any price at which he will purchase a certain good; the question is whether he can find a seller at that price. It is this process, indeed, of mutual bids and offers that yields the daily prices on the market.

There is an all-too-common assumption, however, that if we compare, say, Henry Ford and a small wheat farmer, the two differ enormously in their respective powers of control. It is believed that the wheat farmer finds his price "given" to him by the market, while Ford can "administer" or "set his own" price. The wheat farmer is allegedly subject to the impersonal forces of the market, and ultimately to the consumer, while Ford is, to a greater or lesser extent, the master of his own fate, if not indeed the ruler of the consumers. Further, it is believed that Ford's "monopoly power" stems from his being "large" in relation to the automobile market, while the farmer is a "pure competitor" because he is "small" compared to the total supply of wheat. Usually, Ford is not considered an "absolute" monopolist, but someone with a vague "degree of monopoly power."

In the first place, it is completely false to say that the farmer and Ford differ in their control over price. Both have exactly the same degree of control and of noncontrol: i.e., both have absolute *control* over the quantity they produce and the price which they attempt to get; [23] and absolute *noncontrol* over the price-and-quantity transaction that finally takes place. The farmer is free to ask any price he wants, just as Ford is, and is free to look for a buyer at such a price. He is not in the least compelled to sell his produce to the organized "markets" if he can do better elsewhere. Every producer of every product is free, in a free-market society, to produce as much as he wants of whatever he possesses or can purchase and to try to sell it, at whatever price he can get, to anyone he can find.[24] Naturally, every seller, as we have repeatedly stated, will attempt to sell his produce for the highest possible price; similarly, every buyer will attempt to purchase goods at the lowest possible price. It is precisely the voluntary interaction of these buyers and sellers that establishes the entire supply and demand structure for consumers' and producers' goods. To accuse Ford or a waterworks or any other producer of "charging whatever the traffic will bear" and to take this as a sign of monopoly is pure nonsense, for this is precisely the action of everyone in the economy: the small wheat farmer, the laborer, the landowner, etc. "Charging whatever the traffic will bear" is simply a rather emotive synonym for charging as high a price as can be freely obtained.

Who officially "sets" the price in any exchange is a completely trivial and irrelevant technological question—a matter of institutional convenience rather than economic analysis. The fact that Macy's posts its prices each day does not mean that Macy's has some sort of mysterious "control" of its price over the consumer;[25] similarly, that large-scale industrial buyers of raw materials often post their bid prices does not mean that they exercise some sort of extra control over the price obtained by the growers. Rather than acting as a means of control, in fact, posting simply furnishes needed information to all would-be buyers and/or sellers. The process of price determination through the interaction of value scales occurs in precisely the same way regardless of the concrete details and institutional conditions of market arrangements.[26]

Each individual producer, then, is sovereign over his own actions; he is free to buy, produce, and sell whatever he likes and to whoever will purchase. The farmer is not compelled to sell to any particular market or to any particular company, any more than Ford is compelled to sell to John Brown if he does not wish to do so (say, because he can get a higher price elsewhere). But, as we have seen, in so far as a producer wishes to maximize his monetary return, he does submit himself to the control of consumers, and he sets his output accordingly. This is true of the farmer, of Ford, or of anyone else in the entire economy—landowner, laborer, service-producer, product-owner, etc. Ford, then, has no more "control" over the consumer than the farmer has.

One common objection is that Ford is able to acquire "monopoly power" or "monopolistic power" because his product has a recognized brand name or trade-mark, which the wheat farmer has not. This, however, is surely a case of putting the cart before the horse. The brand name and the wide knowledge of the brand come from consumers' desire for the product attached to that particular brand and are therefore a *result* of consumer demand rather than a pre-existing means for some sort of "monopolistic power" over the consumers. In fact, farmer Hiram Jones is perfectly free to stamp the brand name "Hiram Jones Wheat" on his product and attempt to sell it on the market. The fact that he has not done so signifies that it would not be a profitable step in the concrete market condition of his product. The chief point is that in some cases consumers and lower-order entrepreneurs consider each individual brand name as representing a *unique* product, while in other cases purchasers consider the output of one firm—one product-owner or set of product-owners operating jointly—as identical in use-value with products of other firms. Which situation will occur is entirely dependent on the buyers' valuations in each concrete case.

Later in this chapter we shall analyze in greater detail the tangled web of fallacies involved in the various theories of "monopolistic competition"; at this point we are attempting to arrive at a definition of monopoly *per se*. To proceed: There are three possible coherent definitions of monopoly. One is derived from its linguistic roots: *monos* (only) and *polein* (to sell) i.e., *the only seller of any given good* (definition 1). This is certainly a legitimate definition, but it is an extraordinarily broad one. It means that, whenever there is any differentiation at all among individual products, the individual producer and seller is a "monopolist." John Jones, lawyer, is a "monopolist" over the legal services of John Jones; Tom Williams, doctor, is a "monopolist" over his own unique medical services, etc. The owner of the Empire State Building is a "monopolist" over the rental services in his building. This definition, therefore, labels all consumer distinctions between individual products as establishing "monopolies."

It must be remembered that only *consumers* can decide whether two commodities offered on the market are one good or two different goods. This issue cannot be settled by a physical inspection of the product. The elemental physical nature of the good may be only *one* of its properties; in most cases, a brand name, the "good will" of a particular company, or a more pleasant atmosphere in the store will differentiate the product from its rivals in the view of many of its customers. The products then become *different goods* for the consumers. No one can ever be certain in advance—least of all the economist—whether a commodity sold by A will be treated on the market as homogeneous with the same basic physical good sold by B.[27, 28]

Hence, there is hardly any way that definition 1 of "monopoly" can be successfully used. For this definition depends on how we choose a "homogeneous good," and this can never be decided by an economist. What constitutes a "homogeneous commodity" (i.e., an industry)—neckties, bow ties, bow ties with polka dots, etc., or bow ties made by Jones? Only consumers will decide, and they, as different consumers, will be likely to decide differently in each concrete case. Use of definition 1, therefore, will probably reduce to the barren definition of monopoly as *each man's exclusive ownership of his own property*—and this, absurdly, would make every single person a monopolist! [29]

Definition 1, then, is coherent, but highly inexpedient. Its usefulness is very limited, and the term has acquired highly charged emotional connotations from past use of quite different definitions. For reasons detailed below, the term "monopoly" has sinister and evil connotations to most people. "Monopolist" is generally a word of abuse; to apply the term "monopolist" to at least the vast majority of the population and perhaps to every man would have a confusing and even ludicrous effect.

The second definition is related to the first, but differs very significantly. It, in fact, was the *original* definition of monopoly and the very definition responsible for its sinister connotations in the public mind. Let us turn to its classic expression by the great seventeenth-century jurist, Lord Coke:

> A monopoly is an institution or allowance by the king, by his grant, commission, or otherwise . . . to any person or persons, bodies politic or corporate, for the *sole* buying, selling, making, working, or using of anything, whereby any person or persons, bodies politic or corporate, are sought to be restrained of any freedom or liberty that they had before, or hindered in their lawful trade.[30]

In other words, by this definition, *monopoly* is a *grant of special privilege by the State, reserving a certain area of production to one particular individual or group*. Entry into the field is prohibited to others and this prohibition is enforced by the gendarmes of the State.

This definition of monopoly goes back to the common law and acquired great political importance in England during the sixteenth and seventeenth centuries, when an historic struggle took place between libertarians and the Crown over the issue of monopoly as opposed to freedom of production and enterprise. Under this definition of the term, it is not surprising that "monopoly" took on connotations of sinister interest and tyranny in the public mind. The enormous restrictions on production and trade, as well as the establishment by the State of a monopoly caste of favorites, were the objects of vehement attack for several centuries.[31]

That this definition was formerly important in economic analysis is clear in the following quotation from one of the first American economists, Francis Wayland:

> A monopoly is an exclusive right granted to a man, or to a monopoly of men, to employ their labor or capital in some particular manner.[32]

It is obvious that this type of monopoly can *never* arise on a free market, unhampered by State interference. In the free economy, then, according to this definition, there can be *no* "monopoly problem."[33] Many writers have objected that brand names and trade-marks, generally considered as part of the free-market, really constitute grants of special privilege by the State. No other firm can "compete" with Hershey chocolates by producing its own product and calling it Hershey chocolates.[34] Is this not a State-imposed restriction on freedom of entry? And how can there be "real" freedom of entry under such conditions?

This argument, however, completely misconceives the nature of liberty and of property. Every individual in the free society has a right to ownership of his *own self* and to the exclusive use of his own property. Included in his property is his *name,* the linguistic label which is uniquely his and is identified with him. A name is an essential part of a man's identity and therefore of his property. To say that he is a "monopolist" over his name is saying no more than that he is a "monopolist" over his own will or property, and such an extension of the word "monopolist" to every individual in the world would be an absurd usage of the term. The "governmental" function of defense of person and property, vital to the existence of a free society so long as any people are disposed to invade them, involves the defense of each person's particular name or trade-mark against the fraud of *forgery* or *imposture.* It means the outlawing of John Smith's pretending to be Joseph Williams, a prominent lawyer, and selling his own legal advice after stating to clients that he is selling that of Williams. This fraud is not only implicit theft of the consumer, but it is also abusing the property right of Joseph Williams to his unique name and individuality. And the use by some other chocolate firm of the Hershey label would be an equivalent perpetration of an invasive act of fraud and forgery.[35]

Before adopting this definition of monopoly as the proper one, we must consider a final alternative: the defining of a monopolist as *a person who has achieved a monopoly price* (definition 3). This definition has never been explicitly set forth, but it has been implicit in the most worthwhile of the neoclassical writings on this subject. It has the merit of focusing attention on the important economic question of monopoly price, its nature and consequences. In this connection, we shall now investigate the neoclassical theory of monopoly price and inquire whether it really has the substance it seems at first glance to possess.

B. THE NEOCLASSICAL THEORY OF MONOPOLY PRICE [36]

In previous sections we have referred to a monopoly price as one established either by a monopolist or by a cartel of producers. At this point we must investigate the theory more closely. A succinct definition of monopoly price has been supplied by Mises:

> If conditions are such that the monopolist can secure higher net proceeds by selling a smaller quantity of his product at a higher price than by selling a greater quantity of his supply at a lower price, there emerges a *monopoly price* higher than the potential market price would have been in the absence of monopoly.[37]

The monopoly price doctrine may be summed up as follows: A certain quantity of a good, when produced and sold, yields a *competitive price* on the market. A monopolist or a cartel of firms can, if *the demand curve is inelastic at the competitive-price point,* restrict sales and raise the price, to arrive at the point of maximum returns. If, on the other hand, the demand curve as it presents itself to the monopolist or cartel is *elastic* at the competitive-price point, the monopolist will not restrict sales to attain a higher price. As a result, as Mises points out, there is no need to be concerned with the "monopolist" (in the sense of definition 1 above); whether or not he is the sole producer of a commodity is unimportant and irrelevant for catallactic problems. It becomes important only if the configuration of his demand curve enables him to restrict sales and achieve a higher income at a monopoly price.[38] If he learns about the inelastic demand curve *after* he has erroneously produced too great a stock, he must destroy or withhold part of his stock; after that, he restricts production of the commodity to the most remunerative level.

The monopoly price analysis is portrayed in the diagram in Fig. 67. The basic assumption, usually only implicit, is that there is some identifiable stock, say *OA,* and some identifiable market

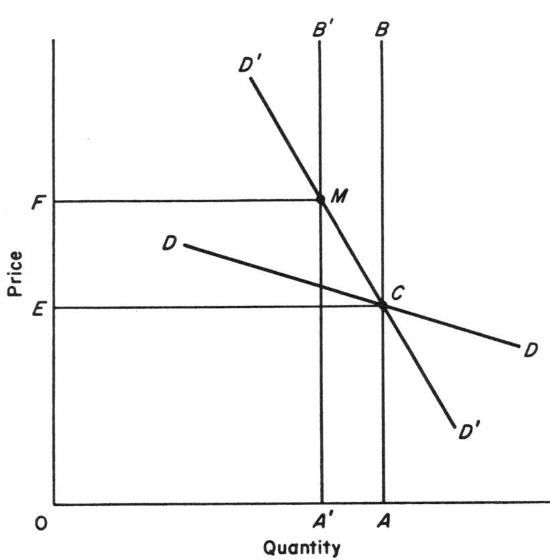

FIG. 67. FORMATION OF A MONOPOLY PRICE ACCORDING TO NEOCLASSICAL DOCTRINE

price, say, *AC,* which will result from *competitive* conditions. *AB* then represents the stock line under "competition." Then, according to the theory, if the demand curve is *elastic* above this price, there will be no occasion to restrict sales and obtain a higher, or "monopoly," price. Such a demand curve is *DD*. On the other hand, if the demand curve is inelastic above the competitive-price point, as in *D′D′,* it will pay the monopolist to restrict sales to, say, *OA′* (stock line represented by *A′B′*) and achieve a monopoly price, *A′M*. This would yield the maximum monetary income for the monopolist.[39]

The inelastic demand curve, giving rise to an opportunity to monopolize, may present itself either to a single monopolist of a given product or to "an industry as a whole" when organized into a cartel of the different producers. In the latter case, *the demand curve, as it presents itself to each firm, is elastic.* At the competitive price, if one firm raises its price, the customers preponderantly shift to purchasing from its competitors. On the other hand, if the firms are cartelized, in many cases the lesser range of substitution by consumers would render *the demand curve, as presented to the cartel, inelastic.* This condition serves as the impetus to the formation of the cartels studied above.

C. CONSEQUENCES OF MONOPOLY-PRICE THEORY

1) *The Competitive Environment*

Before engaging in a critical analysis of the monopoly-price theory itself, we might explore some of the consequences which do or do not follow from it. In this section we for the moment assume that the monopoly-price theory is valid.[40] In the first place, it is *not* true that the "monopolist" (used here in the sense of definition 3—*an obtainer of a monopoly price*) is removed from the influence of competition or has the power to dictate to consumers at will. The best of the monopoly-price theorists admit that the monopolist is as subject to the forces of competition as are other firms. The monopolist cannot set prices as high as he would like, being limited by the configurations of consumer demand. By definition, in fact, the demand curve as presented to the monopolist *becomes elastic above the monopoly-price point.* There has been an unfortunate tendency of writers to refer to an "elastic demand curve" or an "inelastic demand curve" without pointing out that every curve has different *ranges* along which there will be varying degrees of elasticity or inelasticity. By definition, the monopoly-price point is that which maximizes the firm's or the cartel's income; above that price any further "restriction" of production and sales will lower the monopolist's monetary income. This implies that the *demand curve will become elastic above that point,* just as it is also elastic above the *competitive-price* point when that is established on the market. Consumers make the curve elastic by their power of substituting purchases of other goods. Many other goods compete "directly" in their use-value to the consumer. If some firm or combination of firms should, for example, achieve a monopoly-price for cake soap, housewives can shift to detergents and thus limit the height of the monopoly price. But, in addition, *all goods,* without exception, compete for the consumer's dollar or gold ounce. If the price of yachts becomes too high, the consumer can substitute expenditure on mansions, or he can substitute books for television sets, etc.[41]

Furthermore, as the market advances, as capital is invested and the market becomes more and more specialized, the demand curve for each product tends to become more and more *elastic.* As the market develops, the range of consumers' goods available increases enormously. The more consumers' goods are available, the more goods can be purchased by consumers, and the more elastic, *ceteris paribus,* the demand curve for each good will tend to be. As a result, the opportunities for the establishment of monopoly prices will tend to diminish as the market and "capitalist" methods develop.

2) *Monopoly Profit vs. Monopoly Gain to a Factor*

Many monopoly-price theorists have declared that establishment of the monopoly price means that the monopolist is able to attain permanent "monopoly profits." This is then contrasted with "competitive" profits and losses, which, as we have seen, disappear in the evenly rotating economy. Under "competition," if one firm is seen to be making great profits in a particular productive process, other firms rush in to take advantage of the anticipated opportunities, and the profits disappear. But in the case of the monopolist, it is asserted, his unique position allows him to keep making these profits permanently.[42]

To use such terminology is to misconceive the nature of "profit" and "loss." Profits and losses are purely the results of entrepreneurial activity, and that activity is the consequence of the uncertainty of the future. Entrepreneurship is the action on the market that takes advantage of estimated discrepancies between selling prices and buying prices of factors. The better forecasters make profits, and the incorrect ones suffer losses. In the evenly rotating economy, where everyone has settled down to an unchanging round of activity, there can be no profit or loss because there is no uncertainty on the market. The same is true for the monopolist. In the evenly rotating economy, he obtains his "specific monopoly gain," *not* as an entrepreneur, but as the owner of the product which he sells. His monopoly gain is an added *income* to his monopolized product; whether for an individual or for a cartel, it is this product which earns more income through restriction of its supply.

The question arises: Why cannot other entrepreneurs seize the gainful opportunity and enter into the production of this good, thereby tending to eliminate the opportunity? In the case of the cartel, this is precisely the tendency that will always prevail and lead to the breakup of a monopoly-price position. Even if new firms entering the industry are "bought off" by being offered quotal positions in the old cartel, and both the new and the old firms have been able to agree on allocations of production and income, such actions will not suffice to preserve the cartel. For new firms will be tempted to acquire a share in the monopoly gains, and ever more will be created until the entire cartel operation is rendered unprofitable, there being too many firms to share the benefits. In such situations, the pressure will become greater and greater for the more efficient firms to cut loose from the cartel and to refuse further to provide a comfortable shelter for the host of inefficient firms.

In the case of a single monopolist, either his brand name and unique good will with the consumers prevents others from taking away his monopoly gains, or else he is a recipient of special monopoly privilege from the government, in which case other producers are prevented by force from producing the same good.

Our analysis of monopoly gain must be pursued further. We have said that the gain is derived from income from the sale of a certain product. But this product must be produced by *factors,* and we have seen that the return to any product is resolved into returns to the factors which produce it. Such "imputation," in the market, must also take place for monopoly gains. Let us say, for example, that the Staunton Washing Machine Company has been able to achieve a monopoly price for its product. It is clear that the monopoly gain cannot be attributed to the machines, the plant, etc., which produce the washers. If the Staunton Company bought these machines from other producers, then any monopoly gains would, in the long run, as the machines were replaced, accrue to the producers of the machines. In the evenly rotating economy, where entrepreneurial profits and losses disappear, and the price of a product equals the sum of the prices of its factors, all the monopoly gain would accrue to a *factor* and not a product. Furthermore, *no* income, except time income, could accrue to the owner of a capital good, because every capital good must, in turn, be produced by higher-order factors. Ultimately, all capital goods are resolvable into *labor, land,* and *time* factors. But if the Staunton Washing Machine Company cannot *itself* achieve a monopoly gain from a monopoly price, then obviously it does not benefit by restricting production in order to obtain this gain. Therefore, just as *no* income in the evenly rotating economy can accrue specifically to owners of capital goods, neither can specific monopoly gains.

The monopoly gains must, then, be imputed to either labor or land factors. In the case of a *brand* name, for example, a certain *kind* of labor factor is being monopolized. A name, as we have seen, is a unique identifying label for a person (or a group of persons acting co-operatively), and is therefore an attribute of the *person* and his energy. Considered *generally,* labor is the term designating the productive efforts of personal energy, whatever its concrete content. A brand name, therefore, *is an attribute of a labor factor,* specifically the owner or owners of the firm. Or, considered *catallactically,* the brand name represents the *decision-making rent* accruing to the owner and his name. If a monopoly price is achieved by the baseball prowess of Mickey Mantle, this is a specific monopoly gain attributable to a labor factor. In both of these cases, then, the monopoly price stems, not simply from the unique possession of the final product, but, more basically, *from the unique possession of one of the factors necessary to the final product.*

A monopoly gain might also be imputable to ownership of a unique natural resource or "land" factor. Thus, a monopoly price for diamonds may be attributable to a monopoly of diamond mines, from which diamonds must be ultimately produced.

Under the analysis of monopoly price, then, there cannot be, in the evenly rotating system, any such thing as "monopoly profits"; there are only specific monopoly income gains to owners of labor or land factors. No monopoly gain can accrue to an owner of a capital good. If a monopoly price has been imposed because of a grant of monopoly privilege by the State, then obviously the monopoly gain is attributable to this special privilege.[43]

3) *A World of Monopoly Prices?*

Is it possible, within the framework of monopoly-price theory, to assert that *all prices* on the free market may be *monopoly* prices?[44] *Can* all selling prices be monopoly prices?

There are two ways in which we may analyze this problem. One is by turning our attention to the monopolized industry. As we have seen, the industry with a monopoly price restricts production in that industry (either by a cartel or a single firm), thereby releasing nonspecific factors to enter other fields of production. But it is evidently impossible to conceive of a world of monopoly prices, because this would imply a piling up of unused nonspecific factors. Since wants do not remain unfulfilled, labor and other nonspecific factors will be used somewhere, and the industries that acquire *more* factors and produce more cannot be monopoly-price industries. *Their* prices will be *below* the competitive price level.

We may also consider consumer demand. We have seen that a necessary condition for the establishment of monopoly price is a consumers' demand schedule inelastic above the competitive-price point. Obviously, it is impossible for *every* industry to have such an inelastic demand schedule. For the definition of *inelastic* is that consumers will spend a greater total sum of money on the good when the price is higher. But consumers have a certain given total stock of money assets and money income, as well as a given amount, at any one time, which they may allocate to consumption spending. If they spend more on a certain good, they have less to spend on other goods. Therefore, they cannot spend more on *every* good, and not all prices can be monopoly prices.

There can never, then, be a world of monopoly prices, even assuming monopoly-price theory. Because of the fixity of consumers' monetary stock and the employment of displaced factors, monopoly prices could not be established in more than approximately half of the economy's industries.

4) *"Cutthroat" Competition*

A popular theme in the literature is the alleged evil of "cutthroat competition." Curiously, cutthroat, or "excessive," competition, is linked by critics to the achievement of a monopoly price. The usual charge is that a "big" firm, for example, deliberately sells below the most profitable price, even to the extent of suffering losses. The firm acts so peculiarly in order to force another firm producing the same product to cut its price also. The "stronger" firm, with the capital resources to endure the losses, then drives the "weaker" firm out of business and establishes a monopoly of the field.

But, first, what is wrong with such a monopoly (definition 1)? What is wrong with the fact that the firm more efficient in serving the consumer remains in business, while consumers refuse to patronize the inefficient firm? A firm's suffering losses signifies that it is not as successful as other firms in serving consumer desires. Factors then shift from the inefficient to the efficient firms. A firm's going out of business harms no owner of any factor it employs and injures only the entrepreneur who miscalculated in his advance-production decisions. A firm goes out of business precisely because it suffers entrepreneurial losses, i.e., its monetary revenues in sales to consumers are less than the money it paid out previously to owners of factors. But so much money had to be paid out for factors, i.e., costs were so high, because these factors could earn as much money elsewhere. If this entrepreneur cannot profitably employ the factors at their given prices, the reason is that factor-owners can sell their services to other firms. In so far as factors may be specific to the firm, and to the extent that their owners will accept a reduced price and income as the price of the firm's product is reduced, total money costs can be reduced and the firm can be maintained in operation. Therefore, failure by business firms is due solely to entrepreneurial error in forecasting and to entrepreneurial inability to secure the factors of production by outbidding those firms more successful in serving the consumer.[45] Thus, the elimination of inefficient firms cannot harm factor-owners or lead to their "unemployment," since their failure was due precisely to the more attractive competing bids made by other firms (or, in some cases, to the alternatives of leisure or production outside the market). Their failure also helps consumers by transferring resources from wasteful to efficient producers. It is largely the entrepreneurs who suffer from their own errors, errors incurred through their own voluntarily adopted risks.

It is curious that the critics of "cutthroat competition" are generally the same as those who complain about the market's subversion of "consumers' sovereignty." For selling a product at very low prices, even at short-term losses, is a bonanza to the consumers, and there is no reason why this gift to the consumers should be deplored. Furthermore, if the consumers were really indignant about this form of competition, they would scornfully refuse to accept this gift and instead continue to patronize the allegedly "victimized" competitor. When they do not do so and instead rush to acquire the bargains, they are indicating their perfect contentment with this state of affairs. From the point of view of consumers' sovereignty or individual sovereignty, there is nothing at all wrong with "cutthroat competition."

The only conceivable problem is the one usually cited: that after the single firm has driven everyone else out of business through sustained selling at very low prices, *then* the final monopolist will restrict sales and raise its price to a monopoly price. Even granting for a moment the tenability of the monopoly-price concept, this does not seem a very likely occurrence. In the first place, it is time enough to complain *after* the monopoly price is established, especially since we have seen that we cannot consider "monopoly" *per se* (definition 1) as an evil.[46] Secondly, a firm will not always be able to achieve a monopoly price. In all such cases, including (*a*) where not all the other firms in the industry can be driven out, or (*b*) where the demand curve is such that the monopolist cannot achieve a monopoly price, the "cutthroat competition" is then a pure boon with no harmful effects.

Incidentally, it is by no means true that the *large* firms will always be the strongest in a "price-cutting war." Often, depending on the concrete conditions, it is the smaller, more mobile firm, not burdened with heavy investments, that is able to "cut its costs" (particularly when its factors are more specific to it, such as the labor of its management) and outcompete the larger firm. In such cases, of course, there is no monopoly-price problem whatever. The fact that the lowly pushcart peddler for centuries has been set upon by governmental violence at the behest of his more lordly and heavily capitalized competitors bears witness to the practical possibilities of such a situation.[47]

Suppose, however, that after this lengthy and costly process, a firm has finally been able to achieve a monopoly price by the route of "cutthroat competition." What is there to prevent this monopoly gain from attracting other entrepreneurs who will try to undercut the existing firm and achieve some of the gain for themselves? What is to prevent new firms from coming in and driving the price down to competitive levels again? Is the firm to resume "cutthroat competition" and the same deliberate losing process once more? In that case, we are likely to find that consumers of the good will be receiving gifts far more often than facing a monopoly price.[48]

Professor Leeman has pointed out[49] that the smaller firm, driven out by "cutthroat competition," may simply close down, wait for the larger firm to reap its expected gain of a higher "monopoly price," and then reopen! More important, even if the small firm is driven into bankruptcy, its *physical plant* remains intact, and it may be bought by a new entrepreneur at bargain prices. As a result, the new firm will be able to produce at very low cost and damage the "victor" firm considerably. To avoid this threat, the big firm would have to delay raising its price for the very long time required for the small plant to wear out or become obsolete.

Leeman also demonstrates that the big firm could not keep new, small firms out by a mere *threat* of cutthroat competition. For (*a*) new firms will probably interpret the high price charged by the "monopolist" as a sign of inefficiency, providing a ripe opportunity for profits; and (*b*) the "monopolist" can demonstrate his power satisfactorily only by *actually* selling at low prices for long periods of time. Hence, only by keeping its costs down and its prices low, i.e., by *not* extracting a monopoly price, can the "victor" firm keep out potential rivals. But this means that the cutthroat competition, far from being a route to a monopoly price, was a pure gift to consumers and a pure loss to the "victor."[50]

But what of a standard problem brought forward by critics of "cutthroat competition"? Cannot the big firm check the entry of efficient small firms by simply buying up the new rival's plant and putting it out of production? Perhaps a short period of cutthroat price-cutting will convince the new small firm of the advantage of selling out and will permit the monopolist to avoid the long periods of losses just mentioned.

No one seems to realize, however, the high costs such buying will entail. Leeman points out that the really efficient small firm can demand such a high price for its assets as to make the whole procedure prohibitively expensive. And, further, any later attempt by the large firm to recoup its losses by charging the monopoly price will only invite new entry by other firms and redouble the expensive buying-out process again and again. Buying out competitors, then, will be even more costly than simple cutthroat competition, which we have seen to be unprofitable.[51, 52]

A final argument against the doctrines of "cutthroat competition" is that *it is impossible to determine whether it is taking place or not.* The fact that a monopoly might ensue afterward does not even establish the motive and is certainly no *criterion* of cutthroat procedures. One proposed criterion has been selling "below costs"—most cogently, below what is usually termed "variable costs," the expenses of using factors in production, assuming previously sunk investment in a fixed plant. But this is no criterion at all. As we have already declared, *there is no such thing as costs* (apart from speculation on a higher future price) *once the stock has been produced.* Costs take place along the path of decisions to produce—at each step along the way that investments (of money and effort) are made in factors. The allocations, the opportunities forgone, take place at each step as future production decisions must be taken and commitments made. Once the stock has been produced, however (and there is no expectation of a price rise), the sale is *costless,* since there are no advantages forgone by selling the product (costs in making the sale being here considered negligible for purposes of simplification). Therefore, the stock will tend to be sold at whatever price is obtainable. There is no such thing, then, as "selling below costs" on stock already produced. The cutting of price may just as well be due to inability to dispose of stock at any higher price as to "cutthroat" competition, and it is impossible for an observer to separate the two elements.

D. THE ILLUSION OF MONOPOLY PRICE ON THE UNHAMPERED MARKET

Up to this point we have explained the neoclassical theory of monopoly price and have pointed out various misconceptions about its consequences. We have also shown that there is nothing bad about monopoly price and that it constitutes no infringement on any legitimate interpretation of individuals' sovereignty or even of consumers' sovereignty. Yet there has been a great deficiency in the economic literature on this whole issue: a failure to realize *the illusion in the entire concept of monopoly price.*[53] If we turn to the definition of monopoly price on page 593 above, or the diagrammatic interpretation in Fig. 67, we find *that there is assumed to be* a "competitive price," to which a higher "monopoly price"—an outcome of restrictive action—is contrasted. Yet, if we analyze the matter closely, it becomes evident that the entire contrast is an illusion. In the market, *there is no discernible, identifiable competitive price,* and therefore there is no way of distinguishing, even conceptually, any given price as a "monopoly price." The alleged "competitive price" can be identified neither by the producer himself nor by the disinterested observer.

Let us take a firm which is considering the production of a certain good. The firm can be a "monopolist" in the sense of producing a unique good, or it can be an "oligopolist" among a few firms. Whatever its position, it is irrelevant, because we are interested only in whether or not it can achieve a monopoly price as compared to a competitive price. This, in turn, depends on the elasticity of the demand curve as it is presented to the firm *over a certain range.* Let us say that the firm finds itself with a certain demand curve (Fig. 68).

The producer must decide how much of the good to produce and sell in a future period, i.e., at the time when this demand curve will become relevant. He will set his output at whatever point is expected to maximize his monetary earnings (other psychic factors being equal), taking into consideration the necessary monetary expenses of production for each quantity, i.e., the amounts that can be produced for each amount of money invested. As an entrepreneur he will attempt to maximize profits, as a labor-owner to maximize his monetary income, as a landowner to maximize his monetary income from that factor.

On the basis of this logic of action, the producer sets his in-

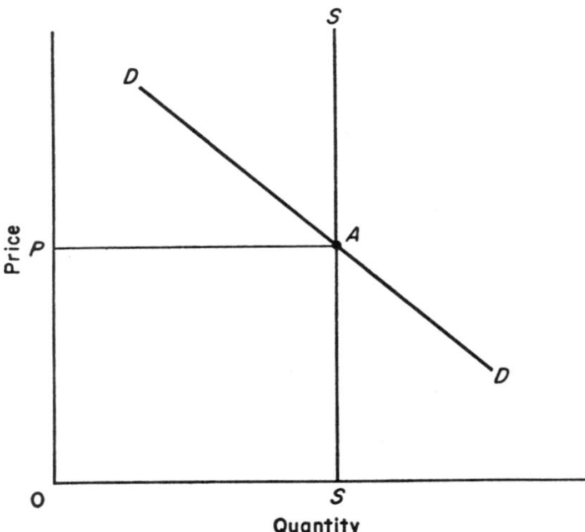

FIG. 68. PRICE FORMATION IN A FREE MARKET

vestment to produce a certain stock, or as a factor-owner to sell a certain amount of service, say *OS*. Assuming that he has correctly estimated his demand curve, the intersection of the two will establish the market-equilibrium price, *OP* or *SA*.

The critical question is this: Is the market price, *OP*, a "competitive price" or a "monopoly price"? The answer is that *there is no way of knowing*. Contrary to the assumptions of the theory, there is no "competitive price" which is clearly established somewhere, and which we may compare *OP* with. Neither does the elasticity of the demand curve establish any criterion. Even if all the difficulties of discovering and identifying the demand curve were waived (and this identifying can be done, of course, only by the producer himself—and only in a tentative fashion), we have seen that the price, if accurately estimated, will always be set by the seller so that the *range above the market price will be elastic*. How is anyone, including the producer himself, to know whether or not this market price is competitive or monopoly?

Suppose that, after having produced *OS*, the producer decides that he will make more money if he produces less of the good in the next period. Is the higher price to be gained from such a cutback necessarily a "monopoly price"? Why could it not just as well be a movement from a *subcompetitive* price to a competitive price? In the real world, a demand curve is not simply "given" to a producer, but must be estimated and discovered. If a producer has produced too much in one period and, in order to earn more income, produces less in the next period, *this is all that can be said about the action.* For there is no criterion that will determine whether or not he is moving from a price *below* the alleged "competitive price" or moving *above* this price. Thus, we cannot use "restriction of production" as the test of monopoly vs. competitive price. A movement from a subcompetitive to a competitive price also involves a "restriction" of production of this good, coupled, of course, with an expansion of production in other lines by the released factors. *There is no way whatever to distinguish such a "restriction" and corollary expansion from the alleged "monopoly-price" situation.*

If the "restriction" is accompanied by increased leisure for the owner of a labor factor rather than increased production of some other good on the market, it is still an expansion of the yield of a consumers' good—leisure. There is still no way of determining whether the "restriction" resulted in a "monopoly" or a "competitive" price or to what extent the motive of increased leisure was involved.

To define a *monopoly price* as a price attained by selling a smaller quantity of a product at a higher price is therefore meaningless, since the same definition applies to the "competitive price" as compared with a subcompetitive price. There is no way to define "monopoly price" because there is also no way of defining the "competitive price" to which the former must refer.

Many writers have attempted to establish some criterion for distinguishing a monopoly price from a competitive price. Some call the monopoly price that price achieving permanent, long-run "monopoly profits" for a firm. This is contrasted to the "competitive price," at which, in the evenly rotating economy, profits disappear. Yet, as we have already seen, there are never permanent monopoly profits, but only monopoly gains to owners of land or labor factors. Money costs to the entrepreneur, who must buy factors of production, will tend to equal money revenues in the evenly rotating economy, whether the price is competitive or monopoly. The monopoly gains, however, are secured as *income* to labor or land factors. *There is therefore never any identifiable element that could provide a criterion of the absence of monopoly gain.* With a monopoly gain, the factor's income is greater; without it, it is less. But where is the criterion for distinguishing this from a change in the income of a factor for "legitimate" demand and supply reasons? How distinguish a "monopoly gain" from a simple increase in factor income?

Another theory attempts to define a monopoly gain as income to a factor greater than that received by another, similar factor. Thus, if Mickey Mantle receives a greater monetary income than another outfielder, that difference represents the "monopoly gain" resulting from his natural monopoly of unique ability. The crucial difficulty with this approach is that it implicitly adopts the old classical fallacy of treating all the various labor factors, as well as all the various land factors, as somehow homogeneous. If all the labor factors are somehow *one* good, then the variations in income accruing to each must be explained by reference to some sort of "monopolistic" or other mysterious element. Yet a good with a homogeneous supply is only a *good* if all its units are interchangeable, as we saw at the beginning of this work. But the very fact that Mantle and the other outfielder are treated differently in the market signifies that they are selling *different,* not the same, goods. Just as in tangible commodities, so in personal labor services (whether sold to other producers or to consumers directly): each seller may be selling a unique good, and yet he is "competing" with more or less close substitutability against all the other sellers for the purchases of consumers (or lower-order producers). But since each good or service is unique, we cannot state that the difference between the prices of any two represents any sort of "monopoly price"; monopoly price vis à vis competitive price can refer only to alternative prices *of the same good.* Mickey Mantle may indeed be a person of unique ability and a "monopolist" (*as is everyone else*) over the disposition of his own talents, but whether or not he is achieving a "monopoly price" (and therefore a monopoly gain) from his service can never be determined.

This analysis is equally applicable to land. It is just as illegitimate to dub the difference between the income of the site of the Empire State Building and that of a rural general store a "monopoly gain" as to apply the same concept to the additional income of Mickey Mantle. The fact that both areas are land makes them no more homogeneous on the market than the fact that Mickey Mantle and Joe Doakes are both baseball players or, in a broader category, both laborers. The fact that each is remunerated at a different price and income signifies that they are considered different on the market. To treat differential gains for *different* goods as instances of "monopoly gain" is to render the term completely devoid of significance.

Neither is the attempt to establish the existence of idle resources as a criterion of monopolistic "withholding" of factors any more valid. Idle labor resources will always mean increased leisure, and therefore the leisure motive will always be intertwined with any alleged "monopolistic" motive. It therefore becomes impossible to separate them. The existence of idle land may always be due to the fact of the relative scarcity of labor as compared with available land. This relative scarcity makes it more serviceable to consumers, and hence more remunerative, to invest labor in certain areas of land, and not in others. The land areas least productive of potential earnings will be forced to lie idle, the amount depending on how much labor supply is available. We must stress that all "land" (i.e., every nature-given resource) is involved here, including urban sites and natural resources as well as agricultural areas. The allocation of labor to land is comparable to Crusoe's having to decide on which plot of ground to build his shelter or in which stream to fish. Because of the natural, as well as voluntary, limitations on his labor effort, that area of land on which he produces the highest utility will be cultivated, and the rest will be left idle. This element also cannot be separated from any alleged monopolistic element. For if someone objects that the "withheld" land is of the *same quality* as the land in use and therefore that monopolistic restriction is afoot, it may always be answered that the two pieces of land *necessarily* differ—in *location* if in no other attribute—and that the very fact that the two are treated differently on the market tends to confirm this difference. By what mystical criterion, then, does some outsider assert that the two lands are economically identical? In the case of capital goods it is also true that the limitations of available labor supply will often make idle those goods which are expected to yield a lesser return as compared with other capital that can be employed by labor. The difference here is that idle capital goods are always the result of previous *error* by producers, since no such idleness would be necessary if the present events—demands, prices, supplies—had all been forecast correctly by all the producers. But though error is always unfortunate, the keeping idle of unremunerative capital is the best course to follow; it is making the best of the *existing* situation, not of the situation that would have obtained if foresight had been perfect. In the evenly rotating economy, of course, there would never be idle capital goods; there would be only idle land and idle labor (to the extent that leisure is voluntarily preferred to money income). In no case is it possible to establish an identification of purely "monopolistic" withholding action.

A similar proposed criterion for distinguishing a monopoly price from a competitive price runs as follows: In the competitive case, the marginal factor produces no rent; in the monopoly-price case, however, use of the monopolized factor is restricted, so that its marginal use *does* yield a rent. We may answer, in the first place, that there is no reason to say that every factor will, in the competitive case, always be worked until it yields *no* rent. On the contrary, every factor is worked in a region of *diminishing* but positive marginal product, not zero product. Indeed, as we have shown above, if the value product of a unit of a factor is zero, it will not be used at all. Every unit of a factor is used because it yields a value product; otherwise, it would not be used in production. And if it yields a value product, it will earn its discounted value product in income.

It is clear, further, that this criterion could never be applied to a monopolized labor factor. What labor factor earns a *zero* wage in a competitive market? Yet many monopolized (definition 1) factors are labor factors—such as brand names, unique services, decision-making ability in business, etc. Land is more abundant than labor, and therefore some lands will be idle and receive zero rent. Even here, however, it is only the *sub*marginal lands that receive no rent; the *marginal* lands in use receive *some* rent, however small.

Furthermore, even if it were true that marginal lands received zero rent, this would be irrelevant for our discussion. It would apply only to "poorer" or "inferior," as compared with more productive, lands. But a criterion of monopoly or competitive price must apply, *not* to factors of *different* quality, but to homogeneous factors. The monopoly-price problem is one of a supply of units of *one* homogeneous factor, *not* of various different factors within the one broad category, land. In this case, as we have stated, every factor will earn some value product in a diminishing zone, and not zero.[54]

Since, in the "competitive" case, all factors in use will earn some rent, there is still no basis for distinguishing a "competitive" from a "monopoly" price.

Another very common attempt to distinguish between a competitive and a monopoly price rests on the alleged ideal of "marginal-cost pricing." Failure to set prices equal to marginal cost is considered an example of "monopoly" behavior. There are several fatal errors in this analysis. In the first place, as we shall see further below, there *can be* no such thing as "pure competition," that hypothetical state in which the demand curve for the output of a firm is infinitely elastic. Only in this never-never land does price equal marginal cost in equilibrium. Otherwise, marginal cost equals "marginal revenue" in the ERE, i.e., the revenue that a given increment of cost will yield to the firm. (Only if the demand curve were perfectly elastic would marginal revenue boil down to "average revenue," or price.) There is now no way of distinguishing "competitive" from "monopolistic" situations, since marginal cost will in *all* cases tend to equal marginal revenue.

Secondly, this equality is only a *tendency* that *results from* competition; it is not a *precondition* of competition. It is a property of the equilibrium of the ERE that the market economy always tends toward, but never can reach. To uphold it as a "welfare ideal" for the real world, an ideal with which to gauge existing conditions, as so many economists have done, is to misconceive completely the nature of the market and of economics itself.

Thirdly, there is no reason why firms should ever deliberately balk at being guided by marginal-cost considerations. Their aiming at maximum net revenue will see to that. But there is no one simple, determinate "marginal cost," because, as we have seen above, there is no one identifiable "short-run" period, such as is assumed by current theory. The firm faces a gamut of variable periods of time for the investment and use of factors, and its pricing and output decisions depend on the future period of time which it is considering. Is it buying a new machine, or is it selling old output piled up in inventory? The marginal cost considerations will differ in the two cases.

It is clear that it is impossible to distinguish competitive or monopolistic behavior on the part of a firm. It is no more possible to speak of monopoly price in the case of a cartel. In the first place, a cartel, when it sets the amount of its production in advance for the next period, is in *exactly the same* position as the single firm: it sets the amount of its production at that point which it believes will maximize its monetary earnings. There is still no way of distinguishing a monopoly from a competitive or a subcompetitive price.

Furthermore, we have seen that there is no essential difference between a cartel and a merger, or between a merger of producers with money assets and a merger of producers with previously existing capital assets to form a partnership or corporation. As a result of the tradition, still in evidence in the literature, of identifying a *firm* with a *single* individual entrepreneur or producer, we tend to overlook the fact that most existing firms are constituted through the voluntary merging of monetary assets. To pursue the similarity further, suppose that firm A wishes to expand its production. Is there an essential difference between its buying new land and building a new plant, and its purchasing an old plant owned by another firm? Yet the latter case, if the plant constitutes all the assets of firm B, will involve, in fact, a merger of the two firms. The degree of merger or the degree of independence in the various parts of the productive system will depend entirely upon the most remunerative method for the producers concerned. This will also be the method most serviceable to the consumers. And there is no way of distinguishing between a cartel, a merger, and one larger firm.

It might be objected at this point that there are many useful, indeed indispensable, theoretical concepts which cannot be practically isolated in their pure form in the real world. Thus, the interest rate, in practice, is not strictly separable from profits, and the various components of the interest rate are not separable in practice, but they can be separated in analysis. But these concepts *are each definable in terms independent of one another and of the complex reality being investigated.* Thus, the "pure" interest rate may never exist in practice, but the market interest rate is theoretically analyzable into its components: pure interest rate, price-expectation component, risk component. They are so analyzable because each of these components is *definable independently* of the complex market-interest rate and, *moreover, is independently deducible from the axioms of praxeology.* The existence and determination of the pure interest rate is strictly deducible from the principles of human action, time preference, etc. Each of these components, then, is arrived at *a priori* in relation to the concrete market interest rate itself and is deduced from previously established truths about human action. In all such cases, the components are definable through independently established theoretical criteria. In this case, however, there is, as we have seen, *no independent way by which we can define and distinguish a "monopoly price" from a "competitive price."* There is no prior rule available to guide us in framing the distinction. To say that the monopoly price is formed when the configuration of demand is inelastic above the competitive price tells us nothing because we have no way of independently defining the "competitive price."

To reiterate, the seemingly unidentifiable elements in other areas of economic theory are independently deducible from the axioms of human action. Time preference, uncertainty, changes in purchasing power, etc., can all be independently established by prior reasoning, and their interrelations analyzed through the method of mental constructions. The evenly rotating economy can be seen as the ever-moving goal of the market, through our analysis of the direction of action. But here, all that we know from prior analysis of human action is that individuals co-operate on the market to sell and purchase factors, transform them into products, and expect to sell the products to others—eventually to final consumers; and that the factors are sold, and entrepreneurs undertake the production, in order to obtain monetary income from the sale of their product. How much any given person will produce of any given good or service is determined by his expectations of greatest monetary income, other psychic considerations being equal. But nowhere in the analysis of such action is it possible to separate conceptually an alleged "restrictive" from a nonrestrictive act, and nowhere is it possible to define "competitive price" in any way that would differ from the *free-market price.* Similarly, there is no way of conceptually distinguishing "monopoly price" from *free-market price.* But if a concept has no possible grounding in reality, then it is an empty and illusory, and not a meaningful, concept. On the free market there is no way of distinguishing a "monopoly price" from a "competitive price" or a "subcompetitive price" or of establishing any changes as movements from one to the other. No criteria can be found for making such distinctions. The concept of monopoly price as distinguished from competitive price is therefore untenable. We can speak only of the *free-market price.*

Thus, we conclude not only that there is nothing "wrong" with "monopoly price," but also that the entire concept is meaningless. There is a great deal of "monopoly" in the sense of a single owner of a unique commodity or service (definition 1). But we have seen that this is an inappropriate term and, further, that it has no catallactic significance. A "monopoly" would be of importance only if it led to a monopoly price, and we have seen that there is no such thing as a monopoly price or a competitive price on the market. There is only the "free-market price."

E. SOME PROBLEMS IN THE THEORY OF THE ILLUSION OF MONOPOLY PRICE

1) *Location Monopoly*

It might be objected that in the case of a *location monopoly,* a monopoly price *can* be distinguished from a competitive price on a free market. Let us consider the case of cement. There are cement consumers, say, who live in Rochester. A cement firm in Rochester could competitively charge a mill price of X gold grams per ton. The nearest competitor is stationed in Albany, and freight costs from Albany to Rochester are 3 gold grams per ton. The Rochester firm is then able to increase its price to obtain $(X + 2)$ gold grams per ton from Rochester consumers. Does its locational advantage not confer upon it a monopoly, and is not this higher price a monopoly price?

First, as we have seen above, the good that we must consider is the good in the hands of the consumers. The Rochester firm is superior locationally for the Rochester market; the fact that the Albany firm cannot compete is not to be blamed on the Rochester firm. Location is also a factor of production. Furthermore, another firm could, if it wished, set itself up in Rochester to compete.

Let us, however, be generous to the location-monopoly theorists and grant that, in a sense (definition 1) this monopoly is enjoyed by *all* individual sellers of any good or service. This is due to the eternal law of human action, and indeed of all matter, *that only one thing can be in one place at one time.* The retail grocer on Fifth Street enjoys a monopoly of the sale of groceries *for that street;* the grocer on Fourth Street enjoys a monopoly of grocery service for *his street,* etc. In the case of stores which all cluster together in the same block, say radio stores, there are still a few feet of sidewalk over which each owner of a radio store exercises a location monopoly. Location is as specific to a firm or plant as ability is to a person.

Whether this element of location takes on any importance in the market depends on the configuration of consumer demand and on which policy is most profitable for each seller in the concrete case. In some cases a grocer, for example, can charge higher prices for his goods than another because of his monopoly of the block. In that case, his monopoly over the good "eggs available on Fifth Street" has taken on such a significance for the consumers in his block that he can charge them a higher price than the Fourth Street grocer and still retain their patronage. In other cases, he cannot do so because the bulk of his customers will desert him for the neighboring grocer if the latter's prices are lower.

Now, a good is homogeneous if consumers evaluate its units in the same way. If that condition holds, its units will be sold for a uniform price on the market (or rapidly tend to be sold at a uniform price). If, now, various grocers must adhere to a uniform price, then there *is* no location monopoly.

But what of the case where the Fifth Street grocer *can* charge a higher price than his competitor? Do we not have here a clear case of an identifiable monopoly price? Can we not say that the Fifth Street grocer who can charge more than his competitor for the same goods has found that the demand curve for his products is inelastic for a certain range above the "competitive price," the competitive price being taken as that equal to the price charged by his neighbor? Can we not say this even though we recognize that there is no "infringement on consumers' sovereignty" in this action, since it is due to the specific tastes of his consuming customers? The answer is an emphatic *No.* The reason is that the economist can never equate a good with some physical substance. A *good,* we remember, is a quantity of a thing divisible into a supply of homogeneous units. And this homogeneity, we repeat, must be in the minds of the consuming public, *not* in its physical composition. If a malted milk consumed at a luncheonette is the same good in the minds of consumers as the malted at a fashionable restaurant, then the price of the malted will be the same in both places. On the other hand, we have seen that the consumer buys not only the physical good, *but all attributes of a thing,* including its name, the wrappings, and the atmosphere in which it is consumed. If most of the consumers differentiate sufficiently between food consumed in the restaurant and food consumed at the luncheonette, so that a higher price can be charged in one case than in the other, then the food *is* a different good in each case. A malted consumed in the restaurant becomes, for a significant body of consumers, a *different good* from a malted consumed at the luncheonette. The same situation obtains for brand names, even in those situations where a minority of the consumers do regard several brands as "actually" the same good. As long as the bulk of the consumers regard them as different goods, then they *are* different goods, and their prices will differ. Similarly, goods may differ physically, but as long as they are regarded by consumers as the same, they *are* the same good.[55]

The same analysis applies to the case of location. Where the Fifth Street consumers regard groceries at Fifth Street as a significantly better good than groceries at Fourth Street, so that they are willing to pay more rather than walk the extra distance, *then the two will become different goods*. In the case of location, there will always be a tendency for the two to be different goods, but very often this will not be significant on the market. For a consumer may and almost always will prefer groceries available on this block to groceries available on the next block, but often this preference will *not be enough* to overcome any higher price for the former goods. If the bulk of the consumers shift to the latter good at a higher price, the *two, on the market, will be the same good*. And it is action on the market, real action, that we are interested in, not the nonsignificant pure valuations by themselves. In praxeology we are interested only in preferences that result in, and are therefore demonstrated by, *real choices,* not in the preferences themselves.

A good cannot be independently established as such apart from consumer preference on the market. Groceries on Fifth Street may be higher in price than groceries on Fourth Street to the Fifth Street consumers. If so, it will be because the former is a different good to the consumers. In the same way, Rochester cement may cost more than Albany cement *in Albany* to Rochester consumers, but the two are different goods by virtue of their difference in location. And there is no way of determining whether or not the price in Rochester or on Fifth Street is a "monopoly price" or a "competitive price" or of determining what the "competitive price" might be. It certainly could not be the price charged by the other firm elsewhere, since these prices are really for two different goods. There is no theoretical criterion by which we can distinguish simple locational income to sites from alleged "monopoly" income to sites.

There is another reason for abandoning any theory of locational monopoly price. If all sites are purely specific in locational value, there is no sense to the statement that they earn a "monopoly rent." For monopoly price, according to the theory, can be established only by selling less of a good and thus commanding a higher price. But *all* locational properties of a site differ in quality because they differ in location, and therefore there can be no restriction of sales to *part* of a site. Either a site is in production, or it is idle. But the idle sites necessarily differ in location from the sites in use and are therefore idle *because their value productivity is inferior*. They are idle because they are submarginal, not because they are "monopolistically" withheld parts of a certain homogeneous supply.

The locational-monopoly-price theorist, then, is refuted whichever way he turns. If he takes a limited view of locational monopoly (in the sense of definition 1) and confines it to such examples as Rochester vs. Albany, he can never establish a criterion for monopoly price, for another firm can enter Rochester, either actually or potentially, to bid away any locational profit that the first firm may earn. His prices cannot be compared with those of his competitors, because they are selling different goods. If the theorist takes an extensive view of locational monopoly—which would take into consideration the fact that every location necessarily differs from every other—and compares locations a few feet apart, then there is no sense at all in talking of "monopoly price," for (*a*) the price of a product at one location cannot be precisely compared with another, because they are different goods, and (*b*) each site is different in locational quality, and therefore no site can be conceptually split up into different homogeneous units —some to be sold and some to be withheld from the market. Each site is a unit in itself. But such a splitting is essential for the establishment of a monopoly-price theory.

2) *Natural Monopoly*

A favorite target of the critics of "monopoly" is the so-called "natural monopoly" or "public utility," where "competition is naturally not feasible." A typically cited case is the water supply of a city. It is supposed to be technologically feasible for only one water company to exist for serving a city. No other firms are therefore able to compete, and special interference is alleged to be necessary to curb monopoly pricing by this utility.

In the first place, such a "limited-space monopoly" is just one case in which only one firm in a field is profitable. How many firms will be profitable in any line of production is an institutional question and depends on such concrete data as the degree of consumer demand, the type of product sold, the physical productivity of the processes, the supply and pricing of factors, the forecasting of entrepreneurs, etc. Spatial limitations may be unimportant; as in the case of the grocers, the spatial limits may allow only the narrowest of "monopolies"—the monopoly over the portion of sidewalk owned by the seller. On the other hand, conditions may be such that only one firm may be feasible in the industry. But we have seen that this is irrelevant; "monopoly" is a meaningless appellation, unless monopoly price is achieved, and, once again, there is no way of determining whether the price charged for the good is a "monopoly price" or not. And this applies to *all* circumstances, including a nation-wide telephone firm, a local water company, or an outstanding baseball player. All these persons or firms will be "monopolies" within their "industry." And in all these cases, the dichotomy between "monopoly price" and "competitive price" is still an illusory one. Furthermore, there are no rational grounds by which we can preserve a separate sphere for "public utilities" and subject them to special harassment. A "public utility" industry does not differ conceptually from any other, and there is no nonarbitrary method by which we can designate certain industries to be "clothed in the public interest," while others are not.[56]

In no case, therefore, on the free market can a "monopoly price" be conceptually distinguished from a "competitive price." *All* prices on the free market are competitive.[57]

4. *Labor Unions*

A. RESTRICTIONIST PRICING OF LABOR

It might be asserted that labor unions, in exacting higher wage rates on the free market, are achieving identifiable monopoly prices. For here two *identifiable* contrasting situations exist: (*a*) where individuals sell their labor themselves; and (*b*) where they are members of labor unions which bargain on their labor for them. Furthermore, it is clear that while cartels, to be successful, must be economically more efficient in serving the consumer, no such justification can be found for unions. Since it is always the individual laborer who works, and since efficiency in organization comes from management hired for the task, forming unions *never* improves the productivity of an individual's work.

It is true that a union provides an identifiable situation. However, it is *not* true that a union wage rate could ever be called a monopoly price.[58] For the characteristic of the monopolist is precisely that he monopolizes a factor or commodity. To obtain a monopoly price, he sells only part of his supply and *withholds* selling the other part, because selling a lower quantity raises the price on an inelastic demand curve. It is the unique characteristic of labor in a free society, however, that it *cannot* be monopolized. Each individual is a self-owner and cannot be owned by another individual or group. Therefore, in the labor field, no one man or group can own the total supply and withhold part of it from the market. Each man owns himself.

Let us call the total supply of a monopolist's product P. When he withholds W units in order to obtain a monopoly for $P - W$, the increased revenue he obtains from $P - W$ must more than compensate him for the loss of revenue he suffers from not selling

W. A monopolist's action is always limited by loss of revenue from the withheld supply. But in the case of labor unions, this limitation does not apply. Since each man owns himself, the "withheld" suppliers are *different people* from the ones getting the increased income. If a union, in one way or another, achieves a higher price than its members could command by individual sales, its action is *not* checked by the loss of revenue suffered by the "withheld" laborers. If a union achieves a higher wage, some laborers are earning a higher price, while others are excluded from the market and lose the revenue they would have obtained. Such a higher price (wage) is called a *restrictionist price.*

A restrictionist price, by any sensible criterion, is "worse" than a "monopoly price." Since the restrictionist union does not have to worry about the laborers who are excluded and suffers no revenue loss from such exclusion, restrictionist action is not curbed by the elasticity of the demand curve for labor. For unions need only maximize the net income of the *working* members, or, indeed, of the union bureaucracy itself.[59]

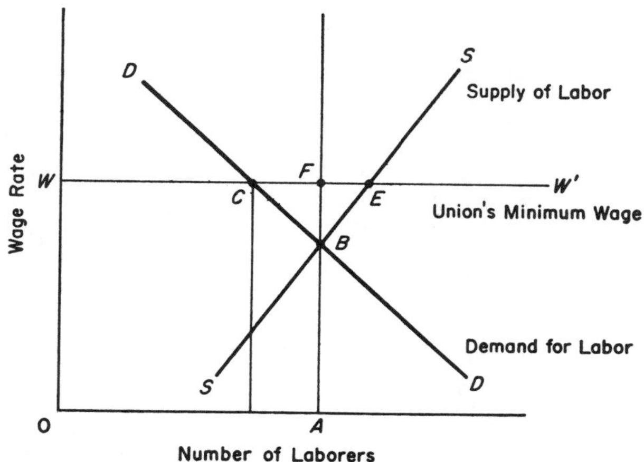

FIG. 69. FORMATION OF A RESTRICTIONIST WAGE RATE

How may a union achieve a restrictionist price? Fig. 69 will illustrate. The demand curve is the demand curve for a labor factor in an industry. *DD* is the demand curve for the labor in the industry; *SS*, the supply curve. Both curves relate the number of laborers on the horizontal axis and the wage rate on the vertical. At the market equilibrium, the supply of laborers offering their work in the industry will intersect the demand for the labor, at number of laborers *OA* and wage rate *AB*. Now, suppose that a union enters this labor market, and the union decides that its members will insist on a higher wage than *AB*, say *OW*. What unions do, in fact, is to insist upon a certain wage rate as a minimum below which they will not work in that industry.

The effect of the union decision is to shift the supply curve of labor available to the industry to a horizontal one at the wage rate *WW'*, rising after it joins the *SS* curve at *E*. The minimum reserve price of labor for this industry has risen, and has risen for all laborers, so that there are no longer laborers with lower reserve prices who would be willing to work for less. With a supply curve changing to *WE*, the new equilibrium point will be *C* instead of *B*. The number of workers hired will be *WC*, and the wage rate *OW*.

The union has thus achieved a restrictionist wage rate. It can be achieved regardless of the shape of the demand curve, granting only that it is falling. The demand curve falls because of the diminishing DMVP of a factor and the diminishing marginal utility of the product. But a sacrifice has been made—specifically, there are now fewer workers hired, by an amount *CF*. *What happens to them?* These discharged workers are the main losers in this procedure. Since the union represents the remaining workers, it does not have to concern itself, as the monopolist would, with the fate of these workers. At best, they must shift (being a nonspecific factor, they can do so) to some other—nonunionized—industry. The trouble is, however, that the workers are less suited to the new industry. Their having been in the now unionized industry implies that their DMVP in that industry was higher than in the industry to which they must shift; consequently, their wage rate is now lower. Moreover, their entry into the other industry depresses the wage rates of the workers already there.

Consequently, at best, a union can achieve a higher, restrictionist wage rate for its members only at the expense of lowering the wage rates of all other workers in the economy. Production efforts in the economy are also distorted. But, in addition, the wider the scope of union activity and restrictionism in the economy, the more difficult it will be for workers to shift their locations and occupations to find nonunionized havens in which to work. And more and more the tendency will be for the displaced workers to remain permanently or quasi-permanently unemployed, eager to work but unable to find nonrestricted opportunities for employment. The greater the scope of unionism, the more a permanent mass of unemployment will tend to develop.

Unions try as hard as they can to plug all the "loop-holes" of nonunionism, to close all the escape hatches where the dispossessed workmen can find jobs. This is termed "ending the unfair competition of nonunion, low-wage labor." A universal union control and restrictionism would mean permanent mass unemployment, growing ever greater in proportion to the degree that the union exacted its restrictions.

It is a common myth that only the old-style "craft" unions, which deliberately restrict their occupational group to highly skilled trades with relatively few numbers, can restrict the supply of labor. They often maintain stringent standards of membership and numerous devices to cut down the supply of labor entering the trade. This direct restriction of supply doubtless makes it easier to obtain higher wage rates for the remaining workers. But it is highly misleading to believe that the newer-style "industrial" unions do not restrict supply. The fact that they welcome as many members in an industry as possible cloaks their restrictionist policy. The crucial point is that the unions insist on a minimum wage rate higher than what would be achieved for the given labor factor without the union. By doing so, as we saw in Fig. 69, they necessarily cut the number of men whom the employer can hire. *Ergo,* the consequence of their policy is to restrict the supply of labor, while at the same time they can piously maintain that they are inclusive and democratic, in contrast to the snobbish "aristocrats" of craft unionism.

In fact, the consequences of industrial unionism are more devastating than those of craft unionism. For the craft unions, being small in scope, displace and lower the wages of only a few workers. The industrial unions, larger and more inclusive, depress wages and displace workers on a large scale and, what is even more important, can cause permanent mass unemployment.[60]

There is another reason why an openly restrictionist union will cause less unemployment than a more liberal one. For the union which restricts its membership serves open warning on workers hoping to enter the industry that they are barred from joining the union. As a result, they will swiftly look elsewhere, where jobs can be found. Suppose the union is democratic, however, and open to all. Then, its activities can be described by the above figure; it has achieved a higher wage rate *OW* for its working members. But such a wage rate, as can be seen on the *SS* curve, attracts more workers into the industry. In other words, while *OA* workers were hired by the industry at the previous (non-union) wage *AB*, now the union has won a wage *OW*. At this wage, only *WC* workers can be employed in the industry. But this wage also *attracts more* workers than before, namely *WE*. As a result, instead of only *CF* workers becoming unemployed from the union's restrictionist wage rate, more—*CE*—will be unemployed in the industry.

Thus, an open union does not have the one virtue of the closed union—rapid repulsion of the displaced workers from the unionized industry. Instead, it attracts even more workers *into* the industry, thus aggravating and swelling the amount of unemployment. With market signals distorted, it will take a much longer time for workers to realize that no jobs are available in the industry. The larger the scope of open unions in the economy, and the greater the differential between their restrictionist wage rates and the market wage rates, the more dangerous will the unemployment problem become.

The unemployment and the misemployment of labor, caused by restrictionist wage rates need not always be directly visible. Thus, an industry might be particularly profitable and prosperous, either as a result of a rise in consumer demand for the product or from a cost-lowering innovation in the productive process.

In the absence of unions, the industry would expand and hire more workers in response to the new market conditions. But if a union imposes a restrictionist wage rate, it may not cause the unemployment of any current workers in the industry; it may, instead, simply prevent the industry from expanding in response to the requirements of consumer demand and the conditions of the market. Here, in short, the union destroys *potential* jobs in the making and imposes a misallocation of production by preventing expansion. It is true that, without the union, the industry will bid up wage rates *in the process* of expansion; but if unions impose a higher wage rate at the beginning, the expansion will not occur.[61]

Some opponents of unionism go to the extreme of maintaining that unions can *never* be free-market phenomena and are always "monopolistic" or coercive institutions. Although this might be true in actual practice, it is not *necessarily* true. It is very possible that labor unions might arise on the free market and even gain restrictionist wage rates.

How can unions achieve restrictionist wage rates on the free market? The answer can be found by considering the displaced workers. They key problem is: Why do the workers *let themselves* be displaced by the union's *WW* minimum? Since they were willing to work for less before, why do they now meekly agree to being fired and looking for a poorer-paying job? Why do some remain content to continue in a quasi-permanent pocket of unemployment in an industry, waiting to be hired at the excessively high rate? The only answer, in the absence of coercion, is that they have adopted on a commandingly high place on their value scales the goal of *not undercutting union wage rates.* Unions, naturally, are most anxious to persuade workers, both union and nonunion, as well as the general public, to believe strongly in the sinfulness of undercutting union wage rates. This is shown most clearly in those situations where union members refuse to continue working for a firm at a wage rate below a certain minimum (or on other terms of employment). This situation is known as a *strike.* The most curious thing about a strike is that the unions have been able to spread the belief throughout society that the striking members are still "really" working for the company even when they are deliberately and proudly *refusing* to do so. The natural answer of the employer, of course, is to turn somewhere else and to hire laborers who *are* willing to work on the terms offered. Yet unions have been remarkably successful in spreading the idea through society that anyone who accepts such an offer—the "strikebreaker"—is the lowest form of human life.

To the extent, then, that nonunion workers feel ashamed or guilty about "strike-breaking" or other forms of undercutting union-proclaimed wage scales, the displaced or unemployed workers agree to their own fate. These workers, in effect, are being displaced to poorer and less satisfying jobs voluntarily and remain unemployed for long stretches of time *voluntarily*. It is voluntary because that is the consequence of their voluntary acceptance of the *mystique* of "not crossing the picket line" or of not being a strikebreaker.

The economist *qua* economist can have no quarrel with a man who voluntarily comes to the conclusion that it is more important to preserve union solidarity than to have a good job. But there is one thing an economist *can* do: he can point out to the worker the consequences of his voluntary decision. There are undoubtedly countless numbers of workers who do not realize that their refusal to cross a picket line, their "sticking to the union," may result in their losing their jobs and remaining unemployed. They do not realize this because to do so requires knowledge of a chain of praxeological reasoning (such as we have been following here). The consumer who purchases directly enjoyable services does not have to be enlightened by economists; he needs no lengthy chain of reasoning to know that his clothing or car or food is enjoyable or serviceable. He can see each perform its service before his eyes. Similarly, the capitalist-entrepreneur does not need the economist to tell him what acts will be profitable or unprofitable. He can see and test them by means of his profits or losses. But for a grasp of the consequences of acts of governmental intervention in the market or of union activity, knowledge of praxeology is requisite.[62]

Economics cannot itself decide on ethical judgments. But in order for anyone to make ethical judgments rationally, he must know the consequences of his various alternative courses of action. In questions of government intervention or union action, economics supplies the knowledge of these consequences. Knowledge of economics is therefore necessary, though not sufficient, for making a rational ethical judgment in these fields. As for unions, the consequences of their activity, when discovered (e.g., displacement or unemployment for oneself or others), will be considered unfortunate by most people. Therefore, it is certain that when knowledge of these consequences becomes widespread, far fewer people will be "prounion" or hostile to "nonunion" competitors.[63]

Such conclusions will be reinforced when people learn of another consequence of trade union activity: that a restrictionist wage raises costs of production for the firms in the industry. This means that the marginal firms in the industry—the ones whose entrepreneurs earn only a bare rent—will be driven out of business, for their costs have risen above their most profitable price on the market—the price that had *already* been attained. Their ejection from the market and the general rise of average costs in the industry signify a general fall in productivity and output, and hence a loss to the consumers.[64] Displacement and unemployment, of course, also impair the general standard of living of the consumers.

Unions have had other important economic consequences. Unions are not *producing* organizations; they do not work for capitalists to improve production.[65] Rather they attempt to persuade workers that they can better their lot at the expense of the employer. Consequently, they invariably attempt as much as possible to establish work rules that hinder management's directives. These work rules amount to preventing management from arranging workers and equipment as it sees fit. In other words, instead of agreeing to submit to the work orders of management in exchange for his pay, the worker now sets up not only minimum wages, but also work rules without which he refuses to work. The effect of these rules is to *lower the marginal produc-*

tivity of all union workers. The lowering of marginal value-product schedules has a twofold result: (1) it itself establishes a restrictionist wage scale with its various consequences, for the marginal value product has fallen while the union insists that the wage rate remain the same; (2) consumers lose by a general lowering of productivity and living standards. Restrictive work rules therefore also lower output. All this is perfectly consistent with a society of individual sovereignty, however, provided always that no force is employed by the union.

To advocate coercive abolition of these work rules would imply literal enslavement of the workers to the dictates of catallactic consumers. But, once again, it is certain that knowledge of these various consequences of union activity would greatly weaken the voluntary adherence of many workers and others to the *mystique* of unionism.[66]

Unions, therefore, are theoretically compatible with the existence of a purely free market. In actual fact, however, it is evident to any competent observer that unions acquire almost all their power through the wielding of force, specifically force against strikebreakers and against the property of employers. An implicit license to unions to commit violence against strikebreakers is practically universal. Police commonly either remain "neutral" when strikebreakers are molested or else blame the strikebreakers for "provoking" the attacks upon them. Certainly, few pretend that the institution of mass picketing by unions is simply a method of advertising the fact of a strike to anyone passing by. These matters, however, are empirical rather than theoretical questions. Theoretically, we may say that it is possible to have unions on a free market, although empirically we may question how great their scope would be.

Analytically, we can also say that when unions are permitted to resort to violence, the state or other enforcing agency has implicitly delegated this power to the unions. The unions, then, have become "private states."[67]

We have, in this section, investigated the consequences of unions' achieving restrictionist prices. This is not to imply, however, that unions *always* achieve such prices in collective bargaining. Indeed, because unions do not own workers and therefore do not sell their labor, the collective bargaining of unions is an artificial replacement for the smooth workings of "individual bargaining" on the labor market. Whereas wage rates on the non-union labor market will always tend toward equilibrium in a smooth and harmonious manner, its replacement by collective bargaining leaves the negotiators with little or no rudder, with little guidance on what the proper wage rates would be. Even with both sides trying to *find* the market rate, neither of the parties to the bargain could be sure that a given wage agreement is too high, too low, or approximately correct. Almost invariably, furthermore, the union is not *trying* to discover the market rate, but to impose various arbitrary "principles" of wage determination, such as "keeping up with the cost of living," a "living wage," the "going rate" for comparable labor in other firms or industries, an annual average "productivity" increase, "fair differentials," etc.[68]

B. SOME ARGUMENTS FOR UNIONS: A CRITIQUE

1) *Indeterminacy* [69]

A favorite reply of union advocates to the above analysis is this: "Oh, that is all very well, but you are overlooking the indeterminacy of wage rates. Wage rates are determined by marginal productivity in a *zone* rather than at a point; and within that zone unions have an opportunity to bargain collectively for increased wages without the admittedly unpleasant effects of unemployment or displacement of workers to poorer jobs." It is curious that many writers move smoothly through rigorous price analysis until they come to wage rates, when suddenly they lay heavy stress on indeterminacy, the huge zones within which the price makes no difference, etc.

In the first place, the scope of indeterminacy is very small in the modern world. We have seen above that, in a two-person barter situation, there is likely to be a large zone of indeterminacy between the buyer's maximum demand price and the seller's minimum supply price for a quantity of a good. Within this zone, we can only leave the determination of the price to bargaining. However, it is precisely the characteristic of an advanced monetary economy that these zones are ever and ever narrowed and lose their importance. The zone is only between the "marginal pairs" of buyers and sellers, *and this zone is constantly dwindling as the number of people and alternatives in the market increase.* Growing civilization, therefore, is always narrowing the importance of indeterminacies.

Secondly, there is no reason whatever why a zone of indeterminacy should be more important for the labor market than for the market for the price of any other good.

Thirdly, suppose that there *is* a zone of indeterminacy for a labor market, and let us assume that no union is present. This means that there is a certain zone, the length of which can be said to equal a zone of the discounted marginal value product of the factor. This, parenthetically, is far less likely than the existence of a zone for a consumers' good, since in the former case there is a specific amount, a DMVP, to be estimated. But the *maximum* of the supposed zone is the highest point at which the wage equals the DMVP. Now, competition among employers will tend to raise factor prices to precisely that height at which profits will be wiped out. In other words, wages will tend to be raised to the *maximum* of any zone of the DMVP.

Rather than wages being habitually at the bottom of a zone, presenting unions with a golden opportunity to raise wages to the top, the truth is quite the reverse. Assuming the highly unlikely case that any zone exists at all, wages will tend to be at the *top,* so that the only remaining indeterminacy is downward. Unions would have no room for increasing wages within that zone.

2) *Monopsony and Oligopsony*

It is often alleged that the buyers of labor—the employers—have some sort of monopoly and earn a monopoly gain, and that therefore there is room for unions to raise wage rates without injuring other laborers. However, such a "monopsony" for the purchase of labor would have to encompass all the entrepreneurs in the society. If it did not, then labor, a nonspecific factor, could move into other firms and other industries. And we have seen that one big cartel cannot exist on the market. Therefore, a "monopsony" cannot exist.

The "problem" of "oligopsony"—a "few" buyers of labor—is a pseudo problem. As long as there is no monopsony, competing employers will tend to drive up wage rates until they equal their DMVP's. The *number* of competitors is irrelevant; this depends on the concrete data of the market. Below, we shall see the fallacy of the idea of "monopolistic" or "imperfect" competition, of which this is an example. Briefly, the case of "oligopsony" rests on a distinction between the case of "pure" or "perfect" competition, in which there is an allegedly horizontal—infinitely elastic—supply curve of labor, and the supposedly less elastic supply curve of the "imperfect" oligopsony. Actually, since people do not move *en masse* and all at once, the supply curve is never infinitely elastic, and the distinction has no relevance. There is only free competition, and no other dichotomies, such as between pure competition and oligopsony, can be established. The shape of the supply curve, furthermore, makes no difference to the truth that labor or any other factor tends to get its DMVP on the market.

3) *Greater Efficiency and the "Ricardo Effect"*

One common prounion argument is that unions benefit the economy through forcing higher wages on the employers. At these higher wages the workers will become more efficient, and their marginal productivity will rise as a result. If this were true, however, no unions would be needed. Employers, ever eager for greater profits, would see this and pay higher wages now to reap the benefits of the allegedly higher productivity in the future. As a matter of fact, employers often train workers, paying higher wages than their *present* marginal product justifies, in order to reap the benefits of their increased productivity in later years.

A more sophisticated variant of this thesis was advanced by Ricardo and has been revived by Hayek. This doctrine holds that union-induced higher wage rates encourage employers to substitute machinery for labor. This added machinery increases the capital per worker and raises the marginal productivity of labor, thereby paying for the higher wage rates. The fallacy here is that only increased saving can make more capital available. Capital investment is limited by saving. Union wage increases do not increase the total supply of capital available. Therefore, there can be no general rise in labor productivity. Instead, the potential supply of capital is *shifted* (not increased) from other industries to those industries with higher wage rates. And it is shifted to industries where it would have been less profitable under nonunion conditions. The fact that an induced higher wage rate shifts capital to the industry does not indicate economic progress, but rather an attempt, never fully successful, to offset an economic retrogression—a higher cost in the manufacture of the product. Hence, the shift is "uneconomic."

A related thesis is that higher wage rates will spur employers to invent new technological methods to make labor more efficient. Here again, however, the supply of capital goods is limited by the savings available, and there is almost always a sheaf of technological opportunities awaiting more capital anyway. Furthermore, the spur of competition and the desire of the producer to keep and increase his custom is enough of an incentive to increase productivity in his firm, without the added burden of unionism.[70]

5. *The Theory of Monopolistic or Imperfect Competition*

A. MONOPOLISTIC COMPETITIVE PRICE

The theory of monopoly price has been generally superseded in the literature by the theories of "monopolistic" or "imperfect" competition.[71] As against the older theory, the latter have the advantage of setting up *identifiable* criteria for their categories—such as a perfectly elastic demand curve for pure competition. Unfortunately, these criteria turn out to be completely fallacious.

Essentially, the chief characteristic of the imperfect-competition theories is that they uphold as their "ideal" the state of "pure competition" rather than "competition" or "free competition." *Pure competition* is defined as that state in which the demand curve for each firm in the economy is *perfectly elastic,* i.e., the demand curve as presented to the firm is completely horizontal. In this supposedly pristine state of affairs, no one firm can, through its actions, possibly have any influence over the price of its product. Its price is then "set" for it by the market. Any amount it produces can and will be sold at this ruling price. In general, it is this state of affairs, or else this state without uncertainty ("perfect competition"), that has received most of the elaborate analysis in recent years. This is true both for those who believe that pure competition fairly well represents the real economy and for their opponents, who consider it only an ideal with which to contrast the actual "monopolistic" state of affairs. Both camps, however, join in upholding pure competition as the ideal system for the general welfare, in contrast to various vague "monopoloid" states that occur when there is departure from the purely competitive world.

The pure-competition theory, however, is an utterly fallacious one. It envisages an absurd state of affairs, never realizable in practice, and far from idyllic if it were. In the first place, there can be no such thing as a firm *without* influence on its price. The monopolistic-competition theorist contrasts this ideal firm with those firms that have some influence on the determination of price and are therefore in some degree "monopolistic." Yet it is obvious that the demand curve to a firm *cannot* be perfectly elastic throughout. At some points, it must dip downward, since the increase in supply will tend to lower market price. As a matter of fact, it is clear from our construction of the demand curve that there can be *no* stretch of the demand curve, however small, that is horizontal, although there can be small vertical stretches. In aggregating the market demand curve, we saw that for each hypothetical price, the consumers will decide to purchase a certain amount. If the producers attempt to sell a larger amount, they will have to conclude their sale at a lower price in order to attract an increased demand. Even a very small increase in supply will lead to a perhaps very small lowering of price. The individual firm, no matter how small, always has a perceptible influence on the total supply. In an industry of small wheat farms (the implicit model for "pure competition"), each small farm contributes a part of the total supply, and there can be no total without a contribution from each farm. Therefore, each farm has a perceptible, even if very small, influence. No perfectly elastic demand curve can, then, be postulated even in such a case. The error in believing in "perfect elasticity" stems from the use of such mathematical concepts as "second order of smalls," by which infinite negligibility of steps can be assumed. But economics analyzes real human action, and such real action must always be concerned with discrete, perceptible steps, and never with "infinitely small" steps.

Of course, the demand curve for each small wheat farm is likely to be very highly, *almost* perfectly, elastic. And yet the fact that it is *not* "perfect" destroys the entire concept of pure competition. For how does this situation differ from, say, the Hershey Chocolate Company if the demand curve for the latter firm is also elastic? Once it is conceded that all demand curves to firms must be falling, the monopolistic-competition theorist can make no further analytic distinctions.

We cannot compare or classify the curves on the basis of *degrees of elasticity,* since there is nothing in the Chamberlin-Robinson monopolistic-competition analysis, or in any part of praxeology for that matter, that permits us to do so, once the case of pure competition is rejected. For praxeology cannot establish *quantitative* laws, only *qualitative* ones. Indeed, the only recourse of monopolistic-competition theorists would be to fall back on the concepts of "inelastic" vs. "elastic" demand curves, and this would precisely plunge them right back into the old monopoly-price vs. competitive-price dichotomy. They would have to say, with the old monopoly-price theorists, that if the demand curve for the firm is more than unitarily elastic at the equilibrium point, the firm will remain at the "competitive" price; that if the curve is inelastic, it will rise to a monopoly-price position. But, as we have already seen in detail, the monopoly-competitive price dichotomy is untenable.

According to the monopolistic-competition theorists, the two influences sabotaging the possible existence of pure competition are "differentiation of product" and "oligopoly," or fewness of firms, where one firm influences the actions of others. As to the former, the producers are accused of creating an artificial differentiation among products in the mind of the public, thus carving out for themselves a portion of monopoly. And Chamberlin originally attempted to distinguish "groups" of producers selling "slightly" differentiated products from old-fashioned "industries" of firms making identical products. Neither of these attempts has any validity. If a producer is making a product different from that of another producer, then he is an unique "industry"; there is no rational basis for any grouping of varied producers, particularly in aggregating their demand curves. Furthermore, the consuming public decides on the differentiation of products on its value scales. There is nothing "artificial" about the differentiation, and indeed this differentiation serves to cater more closely to the multifarious wants of the consumers.[72] It is clear, of course, that Ford has a monopoly on the sale of Ford cars; but this is a full "monopoly" rather than a "monopolistic" tendency. Also, it is difficult to see what difference can come from the number of firms that are producing the same product, particularly once we discard the myth of pure competition and perfect elasticity. Much ado indeed has been made about strategies, "warfare," etc., between oligopolists, but there is little point to such discussions. Either the firms are independent and therefore competing, or they are acting jointly and therefore cartelizing. There is no third alternative.

Once the perfect-elasticity myth has been discarded, it becomes clear that all the tedious discussion about the number and size of firms and groups and differentiation, etc., becomes irrelevant. It becomes relevant only for economic history, and not for economic analysis.

It might be objected that there is a substantial problem of oligopoly: that, under oligopoly, each firm has to take into account the reactions of competing firms, whereas under pure competition or differentiated products without oligopoly, each firm can operate in the blissful awareness that no competitor will take account of its actions or change its actions accordingly. Hiram Jones, the small wheat farmer, can set his production policy without wondering what Ezra Smith will do when he discovers what Jones' policy is. Ford, on the other hand, must consider General Motors' reactions, and *vice versa*. Many writers, in fact, have gone so far as to maintain that economics can simply not be applied to these "oligopoly" situations, that these are indeterminate situations where "anything may happen." They define the buyers' demand curve that presents itself to the firm as *assuming no reaction* by competing firms. Then, since "few firms" exist and each firm takes account of the reactions of others, they proceed to the conclusion that in the real world all is chaos, incomprehensible to economic analysis.

These alleged difficulties are nonexistent, however. There is no reason why the demand curve to a firm cannot *include* expected reactions by other firms.[73] The demand curve to a firm is the set of a firm's expectations, at any time, of how many units of its product consumers will buy at an alternative series of prices. What interests the producer is the hypothetical set of consumer demands at each price. He is not interested in what consumer demand will be in various sets of nonexistent situations. His expectations will be based on his judgment of what would actually happen should he charge various alternative prices. If his rivals will react in a certain way to his charging a higher or a lower price, then it is each firm's business to *forecast and take account of this reaction* in so far as it will affect buyers' demand for its particular product. There would be little sense in ignoring such reactions if they were relevant to the demand for its product or in including them if they were not. A firm's estimated demand curve, therefore, *already includes* any expected reactions of rivals.

The relevant consideration is not the fewness of the firms or the state of hostility or friendship existing among firms. Those writers who discuss oligopoly in terms applicable to games of poker or to military warfare are entirely in error. The fundamental business of production is service to the consumers for monetary gain, and not some sort of "game" or "warfare" or any other sort of struggle *between* producers. In "oligopoly," where several firms are producing an identical product, there cannot persist any situation in which one firm charges a higher price than another, since there is always a tendency toward the formation of a uniform price for each uniform product. Whenever firm A attempts to sell its product higher or lower than the previously ruling market price, it is attempting to "discover the market," to find out what the equilibrium market price is, in accordance with the present state of consumer demand. If, at a certain price for the product, consumer demand is in excess of supply, the firms will tend to raise the price, and *vice versa* if the produced stock is not being sold. In this familiar pathway to equilibrium, all the stock that the firms wish to sell "clears the market" at the highest price that can be obtained. The jockeying and raising and lowering of prices that takes place in "oligopolistic" industries is not some mysterious form of warfare, but the visible process of attempting to find market equilibrium—that price at which the quantity supplied and the quantity demanded will be equal. The same process, indeed, takes place in any market, such as the "nonoligopolistic" wheat or strawberry markets. In the latter markets the process seems to the viewer more "impersonal," because the actions of any one individual or firm are not as important or as strikingly visible as in the more "oligopolistic" industries. But the process is essentially the same, and we must not be led to think differently by such often inapt metaphors as the "automatic mechanisms of the market" or the "soulless, impersonal forces on the market." All action on the market is necessarily *personal;* machines may move, but they do not purposefully *act*. And, in oligopoly situations, the rivalries, the feelings of one producer toward his competitors, may be historically dramatic, but they are unimportant for economic analysis.

To those who are still tempted to make the number of producers in any field the test of competitive merit, we might ask (setting aside the problem of proving homogeneity): How can the market create sufficient numbers? If Crusoe exchanges fish for Friday's lumber on their desert island, are they both benefiting, or are they "bilateral monopolists" exploiting each other and charging each other monopoly prices? But if the State is not justified in marching in to arrest Crusoe and/or Friday, how can it be justified in coercing a market where there are obviously many *more* competitors?

Economic analysis, in conclusion, fails to establish any criterion for separating any elements of the free-market price for a product. Such questions as the number of firms in an industry, the sizes of the firms, the type of product each firm makes, the personalities or motives of the entrepreneurs, the location of plants, etc., are entirely determined by the concrete conditions and data of the particular case. Economic analysis can have nothing to say about them.[74]

B. THE PARADOX OF EXCESS CAPACITY

Perhaps the most important conclusion of the theory of monopolistic or imperfect competition is that the real world of monopolistic competition (where the demand curve to each firm is necessarily falling) is inferior to the ideal world of pure competition (where no firm can affect its price). This conclusion was expressed simply and effectively by comparing two final equilibrium states: under conditions of pure and monopolistic competition (Fig. 70).

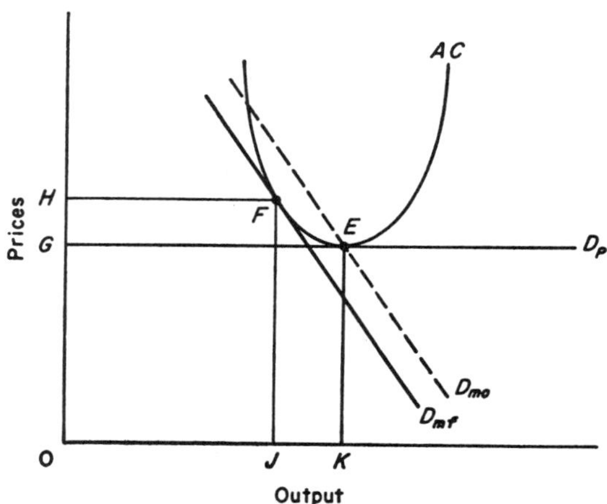

FIG. 70. FINAL EQUILIBRIUM STATES UNDER CONDITIONS OF PURE AND MONOPOLISTIC COMPETITION

AC is a firm's average total-cost curve—its alternative dollar costs per unit—with output on the horizontal axis and prices (including costs) on the vertical axis. The only assumption we need in drawing the average-cost curve is that, for any plant in any branch of production, there will be *some optimum* point of production, i.e., some level of output at which average unit cost is at a minimum. All levels of production lower or higher than the optimum have a higher average cost. In pure competition, where the demand curve for any firm is perfectly elastic, D_p, each firm will eventually adjust so that its *AC* curve will be tangent to D_p, in equilibrium; in this case, at point *E*. For if average revenue (price) is greater than average cost, then competition will draw in other firms, until the curves are tangent; if the cost curve is irretrievably higher than demand, the firm will go out of business. Tangency is at point *E,* price at *OG,* and output at *OK*. As in any definition of final equilibrium, total costs equal total revenues for each firm, and profits are zero.

Now contrast this picture with that of monopolistic competition. Since the demand curve (D_{mf}) is now sloping downward to the right, it must, given the same *AC* curve, be tangent at some point (*F*), where the price is higher (*JF*) and the production lower (*OJ*) than under pure competition. In short, monopolistic competition yields higher prices and less production—i.e., a lower standard of living—than pure competition. Furthermore, output will not take place at the point of minimum average cost—clearly a social "optimum," and each plant will produce at a lower than optimum level, i.e., it will have "excess capacity." This was the "welfare" case of the monopolistic-competition theorists.

By a process of revision in recent years, some of it by the originators of the doctrine themselves, this theory has been effectively riddled beyond repair. As we have seen, Chamberlin and others have shown that this analysis does not apply if we are to take consumer desire for diversity as a good to be satisfied.[75] Many other effective and sound attacks have been made from different directions. One basic argument is that the situations of pure and of monopolistic competition cannot be compared because the *AC* curves *would not,* in fact, be the same. Chamberlin has pursued his revisionism in this realm also, declaring that the comparisons are wholly illegitimate, that to apply the concept of pure competition to existing firms would mean, for example, assuming a very large number of similar firms producing the identical product. If this were done, say, with General Motors, it would mean that *either* GM must conceptually be divided up into numerous fragments, or else that it be multiplied. If divided, then unit costs would undoubtedly be higher, and then the "competitive firm" would suffer higher costs and have to subsist on higher prices. This would clearly injure consumers and the standard of living; thus, Chamberlin follows Schumpeter's criticism that the "monopolistic" firm may well have and probably will have lower costs than its "purely competitive" counterpart. If, on the other hand, we conceive of the multiplication of a very large number of General Motors corporations at existing size, we cannot possibly relate it to the present world, and the whole comparison becomes absurd.[76]

In addition, Schumpeter has stressed the superiority of the "monopolistic" firm for innovation and progress, and Clark has shown the inapplicability, in various ways, of this static theory to the dynamic real world. He has recently shown its fallacious asymmetry of argument with respect to price and quality. Hayek and Lachmann have also pointed out the distortion of dynamic reality, as we have indicated above.[77]

A second major line of attack has shown that the comparisons are much less important than they seem from conventional diagrams, because cost curves are empirically much flatter than they appear in the textbooks. Clark has emphasized that firms deal in *long-run* considerations, and that long-run cost and demand curves are both more elastic than short-run; hence the differences between E and F points will be negligible and may be nonexistent. Clark and others have stressed the vital importance of *potential* competition to any would-be reaper of monopoly price, from firms both within and without the industry, and also the competition of substitutes between industries. A further argument has been that the cost curves, empirically, are flat within the relevant range, even aside from the long- vs. short-run problems.[78]

All these arguments, added to our own analysis given above, have effectively demolished the theory of monopolistic competition, and yet more remains to be said. There is something very peculiar about the entire construction, even on its own terms, aside from the fallacious "cost-curve" approach, and practically no one has pointed out these other grave defects in the theory. In an economy that is almost altogether "monopolistically competitive," how can *every* firm produce too little and charge too much? What happens to the surplus factors? What are they doing? The failure to raise this question stems from the modern neglect of Austrian general analysis and from undue concentration on an isolated firm or industry.[79] The excess factors must go somewhere, and in that case must they not go to other monopolistically competive firms? In which case, the thesis breaks down as self-contradictory. But the proponents have prepared a way out. They take, first, the case of pure competition, with equilibrium at point *E*. Then, they assume a sudden shift to conditions of monopolistic competition, with the demand curve for the firm now sloping downward. The demand curve now shifts from D_p to D_{mo}. Then the firm restricts production and raises its price accordingly, reaps profits, attracts new firms entering the industry, the new competition reduces the output salable by each firm, and the demand curve shifts downward and to the left until it is tangent to the *AC* curve at point *F*. Hence, say the monopolistic-competition theorists, not only does monopolistic competition suffer from too little production in each firm and excessive costs and prices; it also suffers from *too many firms* in each industry. Here is what has happened to the excess factors: they are trapped in too many uneconomic firms.

This seems plausible, until we realize that the whole example has been constructed as a trick. If we isolate a firm or an industry, as does the example, we may just as well start from a position of monopolistic competition, at point *F,* and then suddenly shift to conditions of pure competition. This is certainly just as legitimate, or rather illegitimate, a base for comparison. What then? As we see in the next diagram, Fig. 71, the demand curve for each firm is now shifted from D_{mf} to D_{po}. It will now be profitable for each firm to expand its output, and it will then make profits. New firms will then be attracted into the industry, and the demand curve will fall vertically, until it again reaches tangency with the *AC* curve at point *E*. Are we now "proving" that there are *more* firms in an industry under *pure* than under monopolistic competition?[80] The fundamental error here is failure to see that, under the conditions established by the assumptions, *any* change opening up profits will bring new firms into an industry.

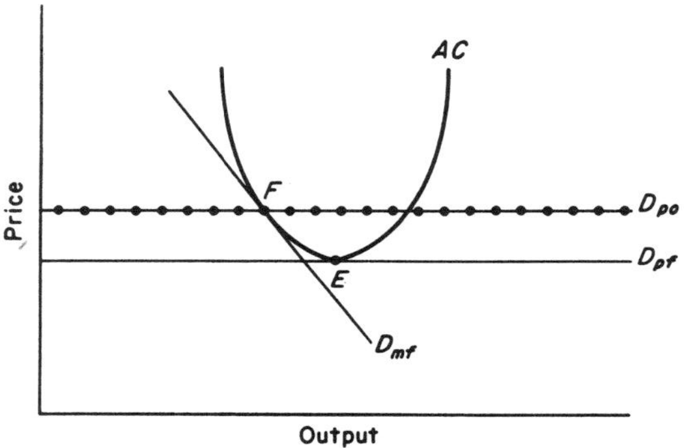

FIG. 71. CONSEQUENCE OF A SHIFT FROM MONOPOLISTIC TO PURE COMPETITION

Yet the theorists are supposed to be comparing two different static equilibria, of pure and of monopolistic competition, and not discussing paths from one to the other. Thus, the monopolistic-competition theorists have by no means solved their problem of surplus factors.

But, aside from this point, there are more difficulties in the theory, and Sir Roy Harrod, himself one of its originators, is the only one to have seized the essence of the remaining central difficulty. As Harrod says:

> If the entrepreneur foresees the trend of events, which will in due course limit his profitable output to x – y units, why not plan to have a plant that will produce x – y units most cheaply, rather than encumber himself with excess capacity? To plan a plant for producing x units, while knowing that it will only be possible to maintain an output of x – y units, is surely to suffer from schizophrenia.

And yet, asserts Harrod puzzledly, the "accepted doctrine" apparently deems it "impossible to be an entrepreneur and not suffer from schizophrenia!" [81] In short, the theory assumes that, in the long run, a firm having to produce at *F* will yet construct a plant with minimum costs at point *E*. Clearly, here is a patent contradiction with reality. What is wrong? Harrod's own answer is an excellent and novel discussion of the difference between long-run and short-run demand curves, with the "long run" always being a factor in entrepreneurial planning, but he does not precisely answer this question.

The paradox becomes "curiouser and curiouser" when we fully realize that it all hinges on a mathematical technicality. The reason why a firm can never produce at an optimum cost point is that (*a*) it must produce at a tangent of demand and average-cost curves in equilibrium, and (*b*) if the demand curve is falling, it follows that it can be tangent to a U-shaped cost curve only at some point higher than, and to the left of, the trough point. There are two considerations that we may now add. First, there is no reason why the cost "curve" should, in fact, be curved. In an older day, textbook demand curves used to be curves, and now they are often straight lines; there is even more reason for believing that cost curves are a series of angular lines. It is of course (*a*) more convenient for diagrams, and (*b*) essential to mathematical representation, for there to be continuous curves, but we must never let reality be falsified in order to fit the niceties of mathematics. In fact, production is a series of discrete alternatives, as all human action is discrete, and cannot be smoothly continuous, i.e., move in infinitely small steps from one production level to another. But once we recognize the discrete, angular nature of the cost curve, the "problem" of excess capacity immediately disappears (Fig. 72). Thus the falling demand curve to the "monopolistic" firm, D_m, can now be "tangent" to the *AC* curve at *E*, the minimum-cost point, and will be so in final equilibrium.

There is another way for this pseudo problem to disappear, and that is to call into question the entire assumption of tangency. The tangency of average cost and demand at equilibrium has appeared to follow from the property of equilibrium: that total costs and total revenues of the firm will be equal, since profits as well as losses will be zero. But a key question has been either overlooked or wrongly handled. Why should the firm produce *anything,* after all, if it earns nothing from doing so? But it will earn something, in equilibrium, and that will be *interest* return. Modern orthodoxy has fallen into this error, for one reason: because it does not realize that entrepreneurs are also capitalists and that

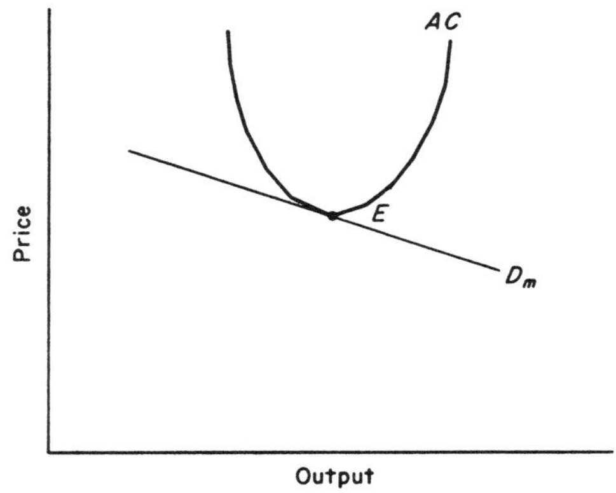

FIG. 72. DETERMINATION OF PRICE AT POINT OF MINIMUM COST

even if, in an evenly rotating economy, the strictly entrepreneurial function were no longer to be required, the capital-advancing function would still be emphatically necessary.

Modern theory also tends to view interest return as a *cost* to the firm. Naturally, if this is done, then the presence of interest does not change matters. But (and here we refer the reader to foregoing chapters) interest is *not* a cost to the firm; it is an earning *by* a firm. The contrary belief rests on a superficial concentration on loan interest and on an unwarranted separation between entrepreneurs and capitalists. Actually, loans are unimportant and are only another legal form of entrepreneurial-capitalist investment. In short, in the evenly rotating economy, the *firm* earns a "natural" interest return, dictated by social time preference. Hence, Fig. 72 must be altered to look like the diagram in Fig. 73 (setting aside the problem of curves vs. angles). The firm will produce *OK,* its optimum production level, at minimum average cost, *KE.* Its demand curve and cost curve will *not* be tangent to each other, but will allow room for equilibrium interest return, represented by the area *EFGH.* (Neither, as some may object, will the price be higher in this corrected version of monopolistic competition; for this *AC* curve is lower all around than the previous ones, which had included interest return in costs. If they did

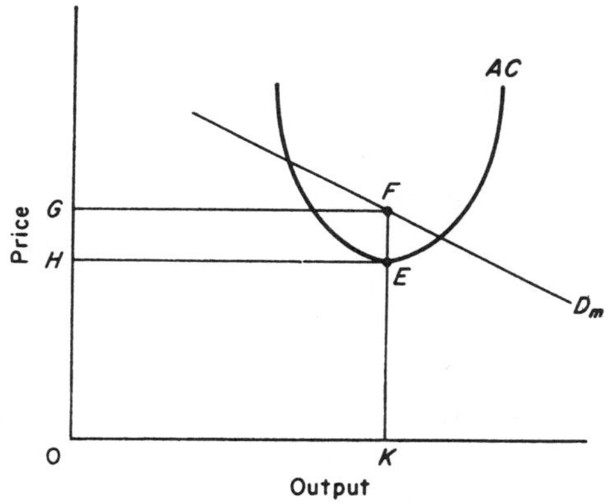

FIG. 73. EQUILIBRIUM INTEREST RETURN AS A COMPONENT OF PRICE

not include interest, and instead assumed that interest would be zero in the ERE, then they were wrong, as we have pointed out above.) [82] And so the paradox of the monopolistic-competition theory is finally and fully interred.[83]

C. CHAMBERLIN AND SELLING COST

One of Professor Chamberlin's most important contributions is alleged to have been his sharp distinction between "selling cost" and "production cost." [84] "Production costs" are supposed to be the legitimate expenses needed to increase supply in order to meet *given* consumer demand schedules. "Selling costs," on the other hand, are supposed to be directed toward influencing consumers and *increasing* their demand schedules for the firm's product.

This distinction is completely spurious.[85] Why does a businessman invest money and incur *any* costs whatever? To supply a hoped-for demand for his product. Every time he improves his product he is hoping that consumers will respond by increasing their demands. In fact, *all* costs expended on raw materials are incurred in an attempt to increase consumer demand beyond what it would have been in the absence of these costs. *Therefore, every production cost is also a "selling cost."*

Conversely, selling costs are not the sheer waste or even tyranny that monopolistic-competition theorists have usually assumed. The various expenses designated as "selling costs" perform definite services for the public. Basically, they furnish information to the public about the goods of the seller. We live in a world where there can be no "perfect knowledge" of products by anyone—especially consumers, who are faced with a myriad of available products. Selling costs are therefore important in providing information about the product as well as about the firm. In some cases, e.g., displays, the "selling cost" itself *directly* improves the quality of the product in the mind of the consumer. It must always be remembered that the consumer is not simply buying a *physical product;* he may also be buying "atmosphere," prestige, service, etc., all of which have tangible reality to him and are valued accordingly.[86]

The view that a selling cost is somehow an artifact of "monopolistic competition" stems only from the peculiar assumptions of "pure competition." In the "ideal" world of pure competition, we remember, each firm's demand is *given* to it as infinitely elastic, so that it can sell whatever it wants at the ruling price. Naturally, in such a situation, no selling costs are necessary, because a market for a product is automatically assured. In the real world, however, there is no perfect knowledge, and the demand curves are neither given nor infinitely elastic.[87] Therefore, firms have to try to increase demands for their products and to carve out market areas for themselves.

Chamberlin falls into another error in implying that selling costs, such as advertising, "create" consumer demands. This is the determinist fallacy. Every man as a self-owner freely decides his own scale of valuations. On the free market no one can force another to choose his product. And no other individual can ever "create" someone's values for him; he must adopt the value himself.[88]

6. *Multiform Prices and Monopoly*

Up to this point we have always concluded that the market tends, at any given time, to establish *one uniform market price* for any good, under competitive or monopoly conditions. One phenomenon that sometimes appears, however, is persistent *multiformity* of prices. (We must consider, of course, a good that is really homogeneous; otherwise, there would merely be price differences for different goods.) How, then, can multiformity come about, and does it in some sense violate the workings or the ethics of a free-market society?

We must first separate goods into two kinds: those that are *resalable* and those that are not. Under the latter category come all intangible services, which are either consumed directly or used up in the process of production; in any case, they themselves cannot be resold by the first buyer. Nonresalable services also include the *rental* use of a tangible good, for then the good itself is not being bought, but rather its unit services over a period of time. An example may be the "renting" of space in a freight car.

Let us first take resalable goods. When can there be persistent multiform pricing of such goods? One necessary condition is clearly *ignorance* on the part of some seller or buyer. The market price for a certain kind of steel, for example, may be one gold ounce per ton; but one seller, out of pure ignorance, may persist in selling it for half a gold ounce per ton. What will happen? In the first place, some enterprising person will buy the steel from this laggard and resell it at the market price, thus establishing effective uniformity. Secondly, other buyers will rush to outbid the first buyer for the bargain, thus informing the seller of his underpricing. Finally, the persistently ignorant seller will not long remain in business. (Of course, it may happen that the seller may have a strong desire to sell steel for lower than market price, for "philanthropic" reasons. But if he persists in doing so, then he is simply purchasing the consumers' good—to him—of philanthropy and paying the price for it in lower revenue. He is here acting as a consumer rather than as an entrepreneur, just as he would if he hired his ne'er-do-well nephew at the expense of a cut in profits. This, then, would not be a genuine case of multiform pricing, where the good must *always* be homogeneous.)

Nor is the buyer in a different condition. If a buyer were ignorant and continued to buy steel at two gold ounces a ton when the market price was one gold ounce, then some other seller would soon apprise the buyer of his error by offering to sell him the steel for much less. If there is only one seller, then the cheaper buyer can still resell at a profit to the buyer charged a higher price. And a persistently ignorant buyer will also go out of business.

There is only one case where a multiform price could possibly be established for a resalable good: where the good is being sold to consumers—the ultimate buyers. For while entrepreneurial buyers will be alert to price differentials, and a buyer of a good at a lower price can resell to another buyer charged a higher price, ultimate consumers do not usually consider reselling once they buy. A classic case is that of American tourists at a Middle Eastern bazaar.[89] The tourist has neither the time nor the inclination to make a thorough study of the consumer markets, and therefore each tourist is ignorant of the going price of any good. Hence, the seller can isolate each buyer, charging highest prices to the most eager buyers, less high prices to the next most eager, and much lower prices to the marginal buyers, of the same good. In that way the seller achieves a generally unfulfilled objective of all sellers: the tapping of more of the "consumers' surplus" of the buyers. Here the two conditions are fulfilled: the consumers are ignorant of the going price and are not in the market to resell.

Does multiform pricing, as has often been charged, distort the structure of production, and is it in some way immoral or exploitative? How is it immoral? The seller aims, as always, to maximize his earnings in voluntary exchange, and he certainly cannot be held responsible for the ignorance of the buyer. If buyers do not take the trouble to inform themselves of the state of the market, they must stand prepared to have some of their psychic surplus tapped by the bargaining of the seller. Neither is this action irrational on the part of the buyer. For we must deduce from the buyers' action that *he prefers to remain in ignorance rather than to make the effort or pay the money to inform himself of market conditions.* To acquire knowledge of any field takes time, effort, and often money, and it is perfectly reasonable for an individual on any given market to prefer to take his chances on the price and use his scarce resources in other directions. This choice is crystal clear in the case of a tourist on holiday, but it is also possible in any other given market. Both the impatient tourist, who prefers to pay a higher price and not spend time and money on learning about the market, and a companion who spends days on an intensive study of the bazaar market are exercising their preferences, and praxeology cannot call one or the other more rational. Furthermore, there is no way to measure the consumer surpluses lost or gained in the case of the two tourists. We must therefore conclude that multiform pricing, in the case of resalable goods, does not at all distort the allocation of productive factors, because, on the contrary, it is consistent with, and in the case of the tourist, the *only* pricing consistent with, the satisfaction of consumer preferences.

It must be emphasized here that no matter how much the seller at the bazaar taps of his customers' psychic surplus, he does not tap it *all;* otherwise the sale would not be made at all. Since the exchange is voluntary, both parties still benefit from making it.

What if the good is *not* resalable? In that case, there is far greater room for multiform pricing, since ignorance is not required. A vendor can sell an intangible service at a higher price to A than to B without fear that B can undercut him by reselling to A. Hence, most actual cases of multiform pricing take place in the realm of intangible goods.

Suppose now that seller X has managed to establish multiform prices for his customers. He might be a lawyer, for example, who charges higher fees for the same service to a wealthy than to a poor client. Since there is still competition among sellers, why does another lawyer Y not enter the field and undercut X's price to the wealthy clients? In fact, this is what will generally happen, and any attempt to establish "separate markets" among customers will lead to an invasion of the more profitable, higher-price field by other competitors, finally driving the price down, reducing revenues, and re-establishing uniform pricing. If a seller's service is unusual and it is universally recognized that he has no effective competitors, then he might be able to sustain a multiform structure.

There is one simple but very important condition that we have not mentioned which must be fulfilled to establish multiform pricing: the total proceeds from multiformity must be greater than from uniformity. Where one buyer can buy only one unit of a good, this is no problem. If there is and can be only one seller of a nonresalable good, *and* each buyer can buy no more than one unit, then multiform pricing will tend to be established (barring undercutting by competitors), since the total revenue to the seller will always be greater through tapping more of the consumer surpluses of each buyer.[90] But if a buyer can buy more than one unit, revenue becomes a problem. For then each buyer, confronted with a higher price, will restrict his purchases. This will leave an unsold stock, which the seller will then unload by *lowering* his prices below the hypothetical uniform price in order to tap the demands of hitherto submarginal buyers. Thus, suppose that the uniform price of a good is ten gold grains per unit, at which a hundred units are sold. The seller now decides to isolate each buyer as a separate market and tap more consumer surpluses. Aside from the barely marginal buyers, then, all the others will find their prices raised. They will restrict their purchases, say to an aggregate of eighty-five units, and the other fifteen units will be sold by lowering the price to new, hitherto submarginal buyers.

Multiformity can be established only when total proceeds are greater than uniformity provides. This is by no means always the case, for the supramarginal buyers may restrict their purchases by more than the submarginal buyers can compensate.[91]

Multiform pricing has been accorded a curious reception by economists and laymen. In some cases it is deemed vicious exploitation of the consumers; in others (e.g., medicine and education) it is considered praiseworthy and humanitarian. In reality, it is neither. It is certainly not the *rule* in pricing that the most eager *should* pay in proportion to their eagerness (in practice, usually gauged by their wealth), for then everyone would pay in proportion to his wealth for everything, and the entire monetary and economic system would break down; money would no longer function. (See chapter 12 below.) If this is clear in general, it is difficult to see a priori why specific goods should be singled out for this treatment. On the other hand, the consumers are not being "exploited" if there is multiformity. It is clear that the marginal and submarginal buyers are not exploited: the latter obviously gain. What of the *supra*marginal buyers who are receiving less consumer surplus? In some cases, they gain, because without the greater revenues provided by "price discrimination" the good would not be supplied at all. Consider, for example, a country doctor who would leave the area if he had to subsist on the lower revenues provided by uniformity. And even if the good were still supplied, *the fact* that the supramarginal buyers continue to patronize the seller at all shows that they are content with the seemingly discriminatory arrangement. Otherwise, they would quickly boycott the seller, either individually or in concert, and patronize competitors. They would simply refuse to pay more than the submarginal buyers, and this would quickly induce the seller to lower his prices. The fact that they do not do so shows that they *prefer* multiformity to uniformity in the particular case. An example is private school education, which able but poor youths may often attend on scholarships—a principle that the wealthy parents who pay full tuition demonstrably do not consider unjust. If, however, the sellers have received grants of monopolistic privilege by the government, enabling them to restrict competition in the serving of the supramarginal buyers, then they may establish multiformity without enjoying the demonstrable preference of these buyers: for here governmental coercion has entered to inhibit the free expression of preferences.[92]

So far we have discussed price discrimination by sellers in consumers' markets, where consumer surpluses are tapped. Can there be such discrimination in producers' markets? Only when the good is not resalable, total proceeds are greater under multiformity, *and* the supramarginal buyers are willing to pay. The latter will happen when these buyers have a higher DMVP for the good in their firms than other buyers have in theirs. In this case, the seller of the good with multiform prices is absorbing a rent formerly earned by the supramarginal buying firm. The most notable case of such pricing has been railroad freight "discrimination against" the firms shipping a cargo more valuable per unit weight than that of other firms. The gains are not, of course, retained by the railroad in the long run, but absorbed by its own land and labor factors.

Can there be price discrimination by *buyers* when the good is not resalable (and ignorance among sellers is not assumed)? No, there cannot, for the minimum reserve price imposed by, say, a laborer, is determined by the opportunity cost he has forgone elsewhere. In short, if a man earns five gold ounces a week for his labor service in firm A, he will not accept two ounces a week (although he would take two rather than earn nothing at all) since he can earn nearly five ounces somewhere else. And the meaning of price discrimination against sellers is that a buyer would be able to pay less for the same good than the seller can earn elsewhere (cost of moving, etc., omitted). Hence, there can be no price discrimination against sellers. If sellers are ignorant, then, as in the case of the ignorant consumers at a bazaar, we must infer that they prefer the lower income to the cost and trouble of learning more about the market.

7. *Patents and Copyrights*

Turning now to patents and copyrights, we ask: Which of the two, if either, is consonant with the purely free market, and which is a grant of monopoly privilege by the State? In this part, we have been analyzing the economics of the purely free market, where the individual person and property are not subject to molestation. It is therefore important to decide whether patents or copyrights will obtain in the purely free, noninvasive society, or whether they are a function of government interference.

Almost all writers have bracketed patents and copyrights together. Most have considered both as grants of exclusive monopoly privilege by the State; a few have considered both as part and parcel of property right on the free market. But almost everyone has considered patents and copyrights as equivalent: the one as conferring an exclusive property right in the field of mechanical inventions, the other as conferring an exclusive right in the field of literary creations.[93] Yet this bracketing of patents and copyrights is wholly fallacious; the two are completely different in relation to the free market.

It is true that a patent and a copyright are both exclusive property rights and it is also true that they are both property rights in *innovations*. But there is a crucial difference in their *legal enforcement*. If an author or a composer believes his copyright is being infringed, and he takes legal action, he must "prove that the defendant had 'access' to the work allegedly infringed. If the defendant produces something identical with the plaintiff's work by mere chance, there is no infringement." [94] Copyrights, in other words, have their basis in prosecution of implicit theft. The plaintiff must prove that the defendant stole the former's creation by reproducing it and selling it himself in violation of his or someone else's contract with the original seller. But if the defendant independently arrives at the same creation, the plaintiff has no copyright privilege that could prevent the defendant from using and selling his product.

Patents, on the other hand, are completely different. Thus:

> You have patented your invention and you read in the newspaper one day that John Doe, who lives in a city 2,000 miles from your town, has invented an identical or similar device, that he has licensed the EZ company to manufacture it. . . . Neither Doe nor the EZ com-

pany . . . ever heard of your invention. All believe Doe to be the inventor of a new and original device. They may all be guilty of infringing your patent . . . the fact that their infringement was in ignorance of the true facts and unintentional will not constitute a defense.[95]

Patent, then, has nothing to do with implicit theft. It confers an exclusive privilege on the first inventor, and if anyone else should, quite independently, invent the same or similar machine or product, the latter would be debarred by violence from using it in production.

We have seen in chapter 2 that the acid test by which we judge whether or not a certain practice or law is or is not consonant with the free market is this: Is the outlawed practice implicit or explicit theft? If it is, then the free market would outlaw it; if not, then its outlawry is itself government interference in the free market. Let us consider copyright. A man writes a book or composes music. When he publishes the book or sheet of music, he imprints on the first page the word "copyright." This indicates that any man who agrees to purchase this product also agrees as part of the exchange *not* to recopy or reproduce this work for sale. In other words, the author does not sell his property outright to the buyer; he sells it *on condition* that the buyer not reproduce it for sale. Since the buyer does not buy the property outright, but only on this condition, any infringement of the contract by him or a subsequent buyer is *implicit theft* and would be treated accordingly on the free market. The copyright is therefore a logical device of property right on the free market.

Part of the patent protection now obtained by an inventor could be achieved on the free market by a type of "copyright" protection. Thus, inventors must now *mark* their machines as being patented. The mark puts the buyers on notice that the invention is patented and that they cannot sell that article. But the same could be done to extend the copyright system, and without patent. In the purely free market, the inventor could mark his machine *copyright,* and then anyone who buys the machine buys it *on the condition* that he will not reproduce and sell such a machine for profit. Any violation of this contract would constitute implicit theft and be prosecuted accordingly on the free market.

The patent is incompatible with the free market *precisely to the extent that it goes beyond the copyright.* The man who has not bought a machine and who arrives at the same invention independently, will, on the free market, be perfectly able to use and sell his invention. Patents prevent a man from using his invention even though all the property is his and he has not stolen the invention, either explicitly or implicitly, from the first inventor. Patents, therefore, are grants of exclusive monopoly privilege by the State and are *invasive* of property rights on the market.

The crucial distinction between patents and copyrights, then, is not that one is mechanical and the other literary. The fact that they have been applied that way is an historical accident and does not reveal the critical difference between them.[96] The crucial difference is that copyright is a logical attribute of property right on the free market, while patent is a monopoly invasion of that right.

The application of patents to mechanical inventions and copyrights to literary works is peculiarly inappropriate. It would be more in keeping with the free market to be just the reverse. For literary creations are unique products of the individual; it is almost impossible for them to be independently duplicated by someone else. Therefore, a *patent,* instead of a copyright, for literary productions would make little difference in practice. On the other hand, mechanical inventions are discoveries of natural law rather than individual creations, and hence similar independent inventions occur all the time.[97] The simultaneity of inventions is a familiar historical fact. Hence, if it is desired to maintain a free market, it is particularly important to allow *copyrights,* but not patents, for mechanical inventions.

The common law has often been a good guide to the law consonant with the free market. Hence, it is not surprising that common-law copyright prevails for *unpublished* literary manuscripts, while there is no such thing as a common-law *patent.* At common law, the inventor also has the right to keep his invention unpublicized and safe from theft, i.e., he has the equivalent of the copyright protection for unpublicized inventions.

On the free market, there would therefore be no such thing as patents. There would, however, be copyright for any inventor or creator who made use of it, and this copyright would be *perpetual,* not limited to a certain number of years. Obviously, to be fully the property of an individual, a good has to be permanently and perpetually the property of the man and his heirs and assigns. If the State decrees that a man's property ceases at a certain date, this means that the *State* is the real owner and that it simply grants the man use of the property for a certain period of time.[98]

Some defenders of patents assert that they are not monopoly privileges, but simply property rights in inventions or even in "ideas." But, as we have seen, everyone's property right is defended in libertarian law without a patent. If someone has an idea or plan and constructs an invention, and it is stolen from his house, the stealing is an act of theft illegal under general law. On the other hand, patents actually invade the property rights of those *independent* discoverers of an idea or invention who made the discovery after the patentee. Patents, therefore, *invade* rather than defend property rights. The speciousness of this argument that patents protect property rights in ideas is demonstrated by the fact that not all, but only certain types of original ideas, certain types of innovations, are considered patentable.

Another common argument for patents is that "society" is simply making a contract with the inventor to purchase his secret, so that "society" will have use of it. In the first place, "society" could pay a straight subsidy, or price, to the inventor; it would not have to prevent all later inventors from marketing *their* inventions in this field. Secondly, there is nothing in the free economy to prevent any individual or group of individuals from purchasing secret inventions from their creators. No monopolistic patent is necessary.

The most popular argument for patents among economists is the utilitarian one that a patent for a certain number of years is necessary to encourage a sufficient amount of research expenditure for inventions and innovations in processes and products.

This is a curious argument, because the question immediately arises: By what standard do you judge that research expenditures are "too much," "too little," or just about enough? This is a problem faced by *every* governmental intervention in the market's production. Resources—the better lands, laborers, capital goods, time—in society are limited, and they may be used for countless alternative ends. By what standard does someone assert that certain uses are "excessive," that certain uses are "insufficient," etc.? Someone observes that there is little investment in Arizona, but a great deal in Pennsylvania; he indignantly asserts that Arizona deserves more investment. But what standards can he use to make this claim? The *market does* have a rational standard: the highest money incomes and highest profits, for these can be achieved only through maximum service of consumer desires. This principle of maximum service to consumers and producers alike—i.e., to everybody—governs the seemingly mysterious market allocation of resources: how much to devote to one firm or to another, to one area or another, to present or future, to one good or another, to research as compared with other forms of investment. But the observer who criticizes this allocation can have no rational standards for decision; he has only his arbitrary whim. This is especially true of criticism of *production*-relations. Someone who chides *consumers* for buying too much cosmetics may have, rightly or wrongly, some rational basis for his criticism. But someone who thinks that more or less of a certain resource should be used in a certain manner or that business firms are "too large" or "too small" or that too much or too little is spent on research or is invested in a new machine, can have no rational basis for his criticism. Businesses, in short, are producing for a market, guided by the ultimate valuations of consumers on that market. Outside observers may criticize ultimate valuations of consumers if they choose—although if they interfere with consumption based on these valuations they impose a loss of utility upon consumers—but they cannot legitimately criticize the *means:* the production relations, the allocations of factors, etc., by which these ends are served.

Capital funds are limited, and they must be allocated to various uses, one of which is research expenditures. On the market, rational decisions are made in setting research expenditures, in accordance with the best entrepreneurial expectations of an uncertain future. Coercively to encourage research expenditures would distort and hamper the satisfaction of consumers and producers on the market.

Many advocates of patents believe that the ordinary competitive conditions of the market do not sufficiently encourage the adoption of new processes and that therefore innovations must be coercively promoted by the government. But the market decides on the rate of introduction of new processes just as it decides on the rate of industrialization of a new geographic area. In fact, this argument for patents is very similar to the infant-industry argument for tariffs—that market processes are not sufficient to permit the introduction of worthwhile new processes. And the answer to both these arguments is the same: that people must balance the superior productivity of the new processes against the cost of installing them, i.e., against the advantage possessed by the old process in being already built and in existence. Coercively privileging innovation would needlessly scrap valuable plants already in existence and impose an excessive burden upon consumers. For consumers' desires would not be satisfied in the most economic manner.

It is by no means self-evident that patents encourage an increased absolute quantity of research expenditures. But certainly patents distort the *type* of research expenditure being conducted. For while it is true that the *first* discoverer benefits from the privilege, it is also true that his competitors are excluded from production in the area of the patent for many years. And since one patent can build upon a related one in the same field, competitors can often be indefinitely discouraged from *further* research expenditures in the general area covered by the patent. Moreover, the patentee is himself discouraged from engaging in further research in this field, for the privilege permits him to rest on his laurels for the entire period of the patent, with the assurance that no competitor can trespass on his domain. The competitive spur for further research is eliminated. Research expenditures are therefore *overstimulated* in the early stages before anyone has a patent, and they are *unduly restricted* in the period after the patent is received. In addition, some inventions are considered patentable, while others are not. The patent system then has the further effect of artificially stimulating research expenditures in the *patentable* areas, while artificially restricting research in the *nonpatentable* areas.

Manufacturers have by no means unanimously favored patents. R. A. Macfie, leader of England's flourishing patent-abolition movement during the nineteenth century, was president of the Liverpool Chamber of Commerce.[99] Manufacturer I. K. Brunel, before a committee of the House of Lords, deplored the effect of patents in stimulating wasteful expenditure of resources on searching for untried patentable inventions, resources that could have been better used in production. And Austin Robinson has pointed out that many industries get along without patents:

> In practice the enforcement of patent monopolies is often so difficult . . . that competing manufacturers have in some industries preferred to pool patents; and to look for sufficient reward for technical invention in the . . . advantage of priority that earlier experimentation usually gives and in the subsequent good-will that may arise from it.[100]

As Arnold Plant summed up the problem of competitive research expenditures and innovations:

> Neither can it be assumed that inventors would cease to be employed if entrepreneurs lost the monopoly over the use of their inventions. Businesses employ them today for the production of nonpatentable inventions, and they do not do so merely for the profit which priority secures. In active competition . . . no business can afford to lag behind its competitors. The reputation of a firm depends upon its ability to keep ahead, to be first in the market with new improvements in its products and new reductions in their prices.[101]

Finally, of course, the market itself provides an easy and effective course for those who feel that there are not enough expenditures being made in certain directions. *They can make these expenditures themselves.* Those who would like to see more inventions made and exploited, therefore, are at liberty to join together and subsidize such effort in any way they think best. In that way, they would, as consumers, add resources to the research and invention business. And they would not then be forcing other consumers to lose utility by conferring monopoly grants and distorting the market's allocations. Their voluntary expenditures would become *part of the market* and express ultimate consumer valuations. Furthermore, later inventors would not be restricted. The friends of invention could accomplish their aim without calling in the State and imposing losses on a large number of people.

11

Money and Its Purchasing Power

1. *Introduction*

Money has entered into almost all our discussion so far. In chapter 3 we saw how the economy evolved from barter to indirect exchange. We saw the patterns of indirect exchange and the types of allocations of income and expenditure that are made in a monetary economy. In chapter 4 we discussed money prices and their formation, analyzed the marginal utility of money, and demonstrated how monetary theory can be subsumed under utility theory by means of the money regression theorem. In chapter 6 we saw how monetary calculation in markets is essential to a complex, developed economy, and we analyzed the structure of post-income and pre-income demands for and supplies of money on the time market. And from chapter 2 on, all our discussion has dealt with a monetary-exchange economy.

The time has come to draw the threads of our analysis of the market together by completing our study of money and of the effects of changes in monetary relations on the economic system. In this chapter we shall continue to conduct the analysis within the framework of the free-market economy.

2. *The Money Relation: The Demand for and the Supply of Money*

Money is a commodity that serves as a general medium of exchange; its exchanges therefore permeate the economic system. Like all commodities, it has a market demand and a market supply, although its special situation lends it many unique features. We saw in chapter 4 that its "price" has no unique expression on the market. Other commodities are all expressible in terms of units of money and therefore have uniquely identifiable prices. The money commodity, however, can be expressed only by an array of all the other commodities, i.e., all the goods and services that money can buy on the market. This array has no uniquely expressible unit, and, as we shall see, changes in the array cannot be measured. Yet the concept of the "price" or the "value" of money, or the "purchasing power of the monetary unit," is no less real and important for all that. It simply must be borne in mind that, as we saw in chapter 4, there is no single "price level" or measurable unit by which the value-array of money can be expressed. This exchange-value of money also takes on peculiar importance because, unlike other commodities, the prime purpose of the money commodity is to be exchanged, now or in the future, for directly consumable or productive commodities.

The *total demand for money* on the market consists of two parts: the *exchange demand for money* (by sellers of all other goods that wish to purchase money) and the *reservation demand for money* (the demand for money to hold by those who already hold it). Because money is a commodity that permeates the market and is continually being supplied and demanded by everyone, and because the proportion which the existing stock of money bears to new production is high, it will be convenient to analyze the supply of and the demand for money in terms of the *total demand-stock* analysis set forth in chapter 2.[1]

In contrast to other commodities, everyone on the market has both an exchange demand and a reservation demand for money. The exchange demand is his *pre-income demand* (see chapter 6, above). As a seller of labor, land, capital goods, or consumers' goods, he must supply these goods and demand money in exchange to obtain a money income. Aside from speculative considerations, the seller of ready-made goods will tend, as we have seen, to have a perfectly inelastic (vertical) supply curve, since he has no reservation uses for the good. But the supply curve of a good for money is equivalent to a (partial) demand curve for money in terms of the good to be supplied. Therefore, the (exchange) demand curves for money in terms of land, capital goods, and consumers' goods will tend to be perfectly inelastic.

For labor services, the situation is more complicated. Labor, as we have seen, does have a reserved use—satisfying leisure. We have seen that the general supply curve of a labor factor can be either "forward-sloping" or "backward-sloping," depending upon the individuals' marginal utility of money and marginal disutility of leisure forgone. In determining labor's demand curve for money, however, we can be far more certain. To understand why, let us take a hypothetical example of a supply curve of a labor factor (in general use). At a wage rate of 5 gold grains an hour, 40 hours per week of labor service will be sold. Now suppose that the wage rate is raised to 8 gold grains an hour. Some people might work a greater number of hours because they have a greater monetary inducement to sacrifice leisure for labor. They might work 50 hours per week. Others may decide that the increased income permits them to sacrifice some money and take some of the increased earnings in greater leisure. They might work 30 hours. The first would represent a "forward-sloping," the latter a "backward-sloping," supply curve of labor in this price range. But both would have one thing in common. Let us multiply hours by wage rate in each case, to arrive at the total money income of the laborers in the various situations. In the original case, a laborer earned 40 times 5 or 200 gold grains per week. The man with a backward-sloping supply curve will earn 30 times 8 or 240 gold grains a week. The one with a forward-sloping supply curve will earn 50 times 8 or 400 gold grains per week. In both cases, *the man earns more money at the higher wage rate.*

This will always be true. In the first case, it is obvious, for the higher wage rate induces the man to sell more labor. But it is true in the latter case as well. For the higher money income permits a man to gratify his desires for more leisure as well, precisely *because* he is getting an *increased money income*. Therefore, a man's backward-sloping supply curve will never be "backward" enough to make him earn *less money* at higher wage rates.

Thus, a man will always earn more money at a higher wage rate, less money at a lower. But what is *earning* money but another name for *buying* money? And that is precisely what is done. People *buy* money by selling goods and services that they possess or can create. We are now attempting to arrive at the demand schedule for money in relation to various alternative purchasing powers or "exchange-values" of money. A lower exchange-value of money is equivalent to higher goods-prices in terms of money. Conversely, a higher exchange-value of money is equivalent to lower prices of goods. In the labor market, a higher exchange-value of money is translated into lower wage rates, and a lower exchange-value of money into higher wage rates.

Hence, on the labor market, our law may be translated into the following terms: *The higher the exchange-value of money, the lower the quantity of money demanded; the lower the exchange-value of money, the higher the quantity of money demanded* (i.e., the lower the wage rate, the less money earned; the higher the wage rate, the more money earned). Therefore, on the labor market, the demand-for-money schedule is *not* vertical, but falling, when the exchange-value of money increases, as in the case of any demand curve.

Adding the vertical demand curves for money in the other exchange markets to the falling demand curve in the labor market, we arrive at a falling exchange-demand curve for money.

More important, because more volatile, in the total demand for money on the market is the *reservation* demand to hold money. This is everyone's *post-income* demand. After everyone has acquired his income, he must decide, as we have seen, between the allocation of his money assets in three directions: consumption spending, investment spending, and addition to his cash balance ("net hoarding"). Furthermore, he has the additional choice of subtraction from his cash balance ("net dishoarding"). How much he decides to retain in his cash balance is uniquely determined by the marginal utility of money in his cash balance on his value scale. Until now we have discussed at length the sources of the utilities and demands for consumers' goods and for producers' goods. We have now to look at the remaining good: *money in the cash balance,* its utility and demand.

Before discussing the sources of the demand for a cash balance, however, we may determine the shape of the reservation (or "cash balance") demand curve for money. Let us suppose that a man's marginal utilities are such that he wishes to have 10 ounces of money held in his cash balance over a certain period. Suppose now that the exchange-value of money, i.e., the purchasing power of a monetary unit, increases, other things being equal. This means that his 10 gold ounces accomplish more work than they did before the change in the PPM (purchasing power of the monetary unit). As a consequence, he will tend to remove part of the 10 ounces from his cash balance and spend them on goods, the prices of which have now fallen. Therefore, *the higher the PPM (the exchange-value of money), the lower the quantity of money demanded in the cash balance.* Conversely, a lower PPM will mean that the previous cash balance is worth less in real terms than it was before, while the higher prices of goods discourage their purchase. As a result, the lower the PPM, the higher the quantity of money demanded in the cash balance.

As a result, *the reservation demand curve for money in the cash balance falls as the exchange-value of money increases.* This falling demand curve, added to the falling exchange-demand curve for money, yields the market's *total demand curve for money* —also falling in the familiar fashion for every commodity.

There is a third demand curve for the money commodity that deserves mention. This is the demand for *nonmonetary uses* of the monetary metal. This will be relatively unimportant in the advanced monetary economy, but it will exist nevertheless. In the case of gold, this will mean either uses in consumption, as for ornaments, or productive uses, as for industrial purposes. At any rate, this demand curve *also* falls as the PPM increases. As the "price" of money (PPM) increases, more goods can be obtained through expenditure of a unit of money; as a result, the opportunity-cost in using gold for nonmonetary purposes increases, and less is demanded for that purpose. Conversely, as the PPM falls, there is more incentive to use gold for its direct use. This demand curve is added to the total demand curve for money, to obtain the total demand curve for the money commodity.[2]

At any one time there is a *given total stock* of the money commodity. This stock will, at any time, be *owned by someone.* It is therefore dangerously misleading to adopt the custom of American economists since Irving Fisher's day of treating money as somehow "circulating," or worse still, as divided into "circulating money" and "idle money." [3] This concept conjures up the image of the former as moving somewhere at all times, while the latter sits idly in "hoards." This is a grave error. There is, actually, no such thing as "circulation," and there is no mysterious arena where money "moves." At any one time all the money is owned by someone, i.e., rests in someone's cash balance. Whatever the stock of money, therefore, people's actions must bring it into accord with the total demand for money to hold, i.e., the total demand for money that we have just discussed. For even pre-income money acquired in exchange must be held at least momentarily in one's cash balance before being transferred to someone else's balance. All total demand is therefore to hold, and this is in accord with our analysis of total demand in chapter 2.

Total stock must therefore be brought into agreement, on the market, with the total quantity of money demanded. The diagram of this situation is shown in Fig. 74.

On the vertical axis is the PPM, increasing upwards. On the horizontal axis is the quantity of money, increasing rightwards. D_e is the aggregate exchange-demand curve for money, falling and inelastic. D_r is the reservation or cash-balance demand for money. D_t is the total demand for money to hold (the demand for nonmonetary gold being omitted for purposes of convenience).

Somewhere intersecting the D_t curve is the *SS* vertical line—the total stock of money in the community—given at quantity *OS*.

The intersection of the latter two curves determines the equilibrium point, *A*, for the exchange-value of money in the community. The exchange-value, or PPM, will be set at *OB*.

Suppose now that the PPM is slightly higher than *OB*. The demand for money at that point will be less than the stock. People

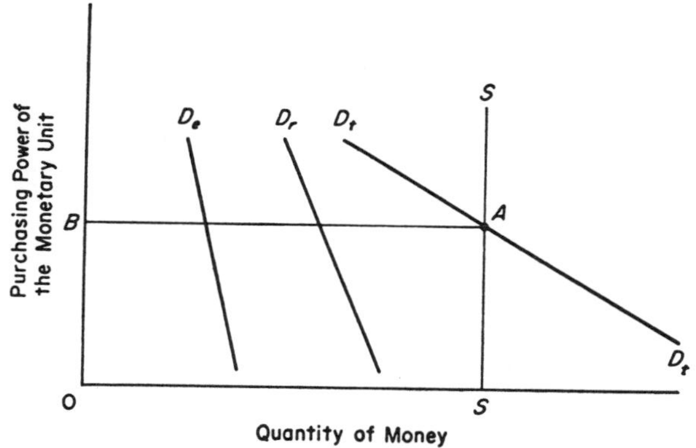

FIG. 74. DETERMINATION OF THE EQUILIBRIUM POINT FOR THE EXCHANGE-VALUE OF MONEY

will become unwilling to hold money at that exchange-value and will be anxious to sell it for other goods. These sales will raise the prices of goods and lower the PPM, until the equilibrium point is reached. On the other hand, suppose that the PPM is lower than *OB*. In that case, more people will demand money, in exchange or in reservation, than there is money stock available. The consequent excess of demand over supply will raise the PPM again to *OB*.

3. *Changes in the Money Relation*

The purchasing power of money is therefore determined by two factors: *the total demand schedule for money to hold* and *the stock of money in existence*. It is easy to see on a diagram what happens when either of these determining elements changes. Thus, suppose that the schedule of total demand increases (shifts to the right). Then (see Fig. 75) the total-demand-for-money curve

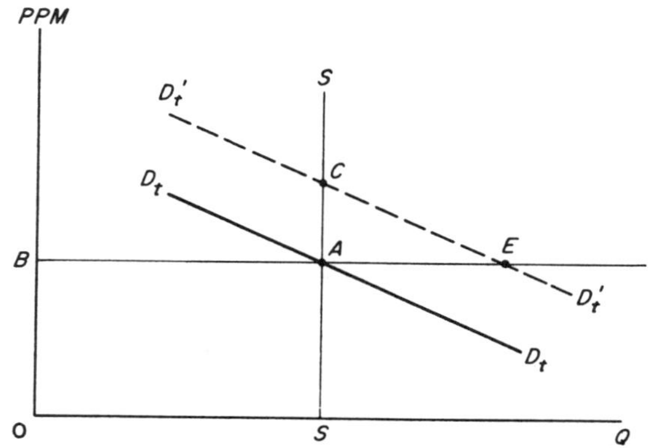

Fig. 75. Effect of a Change in the Total Demand for Money

has shifted from D_tD_t *to* $D_t'D_t'$. At the previous equilibrium PPM point, *A*, the demand for money now exceeds the stock available by *AE*. The bids push the PPM upwards until it reaches the equilibrium point *C*. The converse will be true for a shift of the total demand curve leftward—a decline in the total demand schedule. Then, the PPM will fall accordingly.

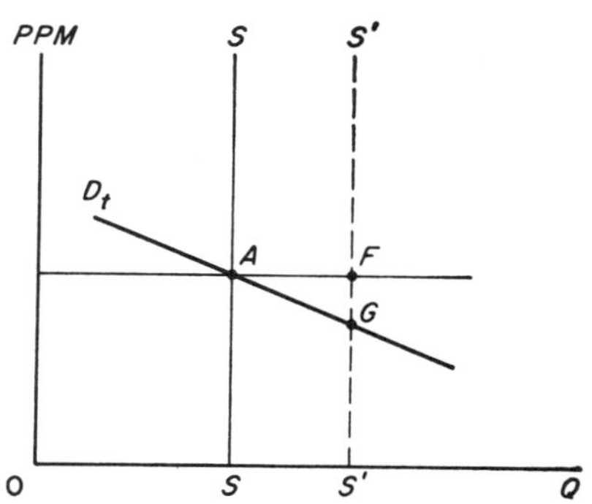

Fig. 76. Effect of a Change in the Total Stock of Money

The effect of a change in the total stock, the demand curve remaining constant, is shown in Fig. 76. Total quantity of stock increases from *OS* to *OS'*. At the new stock level there is an excess of stock, *AF*, over the total demand for money. Money will be sold at a lower PPM to induce people to hold it, and the PPM will fall until it reaches a new equilibrium point *G*. Conversely, if the stock of money is decreased, there will be an excess of demand for money at the existing PPM, and the PPM will rise until the new equilibrium point is reached.

The effect of the quantity of money on its exchange-value is thus simply set forth in our analysis and diagrams.

The absurdity of classifying monetary theories into mutually exclusive divisions (such as "supply and demand theory," "quantity theory," "cash balance theory," "commodity theory," "income and expenditure theory") should now be evident.[4] For all these elements are found in this analysis. Money *is* a commodity; its supply or quantity *is* important in determining its exchange-value; demand for money for the cash balance is also important for this purpose; and the analysis can be applied to income and expenditure situations.

4. *Utility of the Stock of Money*

In the case of consumers' goods, we do not go behind their subjective utilities on people's value scales to investigate why they were preferred; economics must stop once the ranking has been made. In the case of money, however, we are confronted with a different problem. For the utility of money (setting aside the *non*monetary use of the money commodity) depends solely on its prospective use as the general medium of exchange. Hence the subjective utility of money is dependent on the objective exchange-value of money, and we must pursue our analysis of the demand for money further than would otherwise be required.[5] The diagrams above in which we connected the demand for money and its PPM are therefore particularly appropriate. For other goods, demand in the market is a means of routing commodities into the hands of their consumers. For money, on the other hand, the "price" of money is precisely the variable on which the demand schedule depends and to which almost the whole of the demand for money is keyed. To put it in another way: without a price, or an objective exchange-value, any *other* good would be snapped up as a welcome free gift; but money, without a price, would not be used at all, since its entire use consists in its command of other goods on the market. The sole use of money is to be exchanged for goods, and if it had no price and therefore no exchange-value, it could not be exchanged and would no longer be used.

We are now on the threshold of a great economic law, a truth that can hardly be overemphasized, considering the harm its neglect has caused throughout history. An increase in the supply of a producers' good increases, *ceteris paribus,* the supply of a consumers' good. An increase in the supply of a consumers' good (when there has been no decrease in the supply of another good) is demonstrably a clear *social benefit;* for someone's "real income" has increased and no one's has decreased.[6]

Money, on the contrary, is solely useful for exchange purposes. Money, *per se,* cannot be consumed and cannot be used directly as a producers' good in the productive process. Money *per se* is therefore unproductive; it is dead stock and produces nothing. Land or capital is always in the form of some specific good, some specific productive instrument. Money always remains in someone's cash balance.

Goods are useful and scarce, and any increment in goods is a social benefit. But money is useful not directly, but only in exchanges. And we have just seen that as the stock of money in society changes, the objective exchange-value of money changes inversely (though not necessarily proportionally) until the money relation is again in equilibrium. When there is less money, the exchange-value of the monetary unit rises; when there is more money, the exchange-value of the monetary unit falls. We conclude that there is no such thing as "too little" or "too much" money, *that, whatever the social money stock, the benefits of money are always utilized to the maximum extent.* An increase in the supply of money confers no social benefit whatever; it simply benefits some at the expense of others, as will be detailed further below. Similarly, a decrease in the money stock involves no social loss. For money is used only for its purchasing power in exchange, and an increase in the money stock simply dilutes the purchasing power of each monetary unit. Conversely, a fall in the money stock increases the purchasing power of each unit.

David Hume's famous example provides a highly oversimplified view of the effect of changes in the stock of money, but in the present context it is a valid illustration of the absurdity of the belief that an increased money supply can confer a social benefit or relieve any economic scarcity. Consider the magical situation where every man awakens one morning to find that his monetary assets have doubled. Has the wealth, or the real income, of society doubled? Certainly not. In fact, the real income—the actual goods and services supplied—remains unchanged. What has changed is simply the monetary unit, which has been diluted, and the purchasing power of the monetary unit will fall enough (i.e., prices of goods will rise) to bring the new money relation into equilibrium.

One of the most important economic laws, therefore, is: *Every supply of money is always utilized to its maximum extent, and hence no social utility can be conferred by increasing the supply of money.*

Some writers have inferred from this law that any factors devoted to gold mining are being used unproductively, because an increased supply of money does not confer a social benefit. They deduce from this that the government should restrict the amount of gold mining. These critics fail to realize, however, that gold, the money-*commodity,* is used not only as money but also for nonmonetary purposes, either in consumption or in production. Hence, an increase in the supply of gold, although conferring no *monetary* benefit, does confer a social benefit by increasing the supply of gold for direct use.

5. *The Demand for Money*

A. MONEY IN THE ERE AND IN THE MARKET

It is true, as we have said, that the only use for money is in exchange. From this, however, it must not be inferred, as some writers have done, that this exchange must be *immediate.* Indeed, the reason that a reservation demand for money exists and cash balances are kept is that the individual is keeping his money in reserve for *future* exchanges. That is the function of a cash balance—to wait for a propitious time to make an exchange.

Suppose the ERE has been established. In such a world of certainty, there would be no risk of loss in investment and no need to keep cash balances on hand in case an emergency for consumer spending should arise. Everyone would therefore allocate his money stock fully, to the purchase of either present goods or future goods, in accordance with his time preferences. No one would keep his money idle in a cash balance. Knowing that he will want to spend a certain amount of money on consumption in six months' time, a man will lend his money out for that period to be returned at precisely the time it is to be spent. But if no one is willing to keep a cash balance longer than instantaneously, there will be no money held and no use for a money stock. Money, in short, would either be useless or very nearly so in the world of certainty.

In the real world of uncertainty, as contrasted to the ERE, even "idle" money kept in a cash balance performs a use for its owner. Indeed, if it did not perform such a use, it would not be kept in his cash balance. Its uses are based precisely on the fact that the individual is not certain on what he will spend his money or of the precise time that he will spend it in the future.

Economists have attempted mechanically to reduce the demand for money to various sources.[7] There is no such mechanical determination, however. Each individual decides for himself by his own standards his whole demand for cash balances, and we can only trace various influences which different catallactic events may have had on demand.

B. SPECULATIVE DEMAND

One of the most obvious influences on the demand for money is *expectation of future changes in the exchange-value of money*. Thus, suppose that, at a certain point in the future, the PPM of money is expected to drop rapidly. How the demand-for-money schedule now reacts depends on the number of people who hold this expectation and the strength with which they hold it. It also depends on the distance in the future at which the change is expected to take place. The further away in time any economic event, the more its impact will be discounted in the present by the interest rate. Whatever the degree of impact, however, *an expected future fall in the PPM will tend to lower the PPM now.* For an expected fall in the PPM means that present units of money are worth more than they will be in the future, in which case there will be a fall in the demand-for-money schedule as people tend to spend more money now than at the future date. A general expectation of an imminent fall in the PPM will lower the demand schedule for money now and thus tend to bring about the fall at the present moment.

Conversely, an expectation of a rise in the PPM in the near future will tend to raise the demand-for-money schedule as people decide to "hoard" (add money to their cash balance) in expectation of a future rise in the exchange value of a unit of their money. The result will be a *present* rise in the PPM.

An expected fall in the PPM in the future will therefore lower the PPM now, and an expected rise will lead to a rise now. The speculative demand for money functions in the same manner as the speculative demand for any good. An anticipation of a future point speeds the adjustment of the economy toward that future point. Just as the speculative demand for a good speeded adjustment to an equilibrium position, so the anticipation of a change in the PPM speeds the market adjustment toward that position. Just as in the case of any good, furthermore, errors in this speculative anticipation are "self-correcting." Many writers believe that in the case of *money* there is no such self-correction. They assert that while there may be a "real" or underlying demand for goods, money is not consumed and therefore has no such underlying demand. The PPM and the demand for money, they declare, can be explained only as a perpetual and rather meaningless cat-and-mouse race in which everyone is simply trying to anticipate everyone else's anticipations.

There *is,* however, a "real" or underlying demand for money. Money may not be physically consumed, but it is used, and therefore it has utility in a cash balance. Such utility amounts to more than speculation on a rise in the PPM. This is demonstrated by the fact that people *do* hold cash even when they anticipate a fall in the PPM. Such holdings may be reduced, but they still exist, and as we have seen, this must be so in an uncertain world. In fact, without willingness to hold cash, there could be no monetary-exchange economy whatever.

The speculative demand therefore anticipates the underlying nonspeculative demands, whatever their source or inspiration.

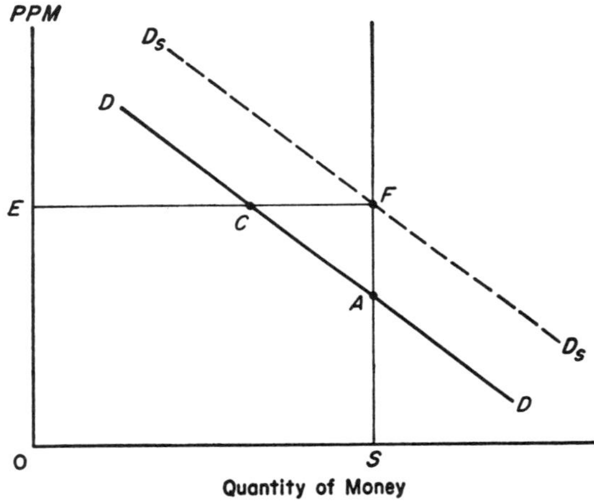

Fig. 77. Self-Correction of Speculative Anticipations of the Demand for Money

Suppose, then, that there is a general anticipation of a rise in the PPM (a fall in prices) not reflected in underlying supply and demand. It is true that, at first, this general anticipation raises, *ceteris paribus,* the demand for money and the PPM. But this situation does not last. For now that a pseudo "equilibrium" has been reached, the speculative anticipators, who did not "really" have an increased demand for money, sell their money (buy goods) to reap their gains. But this means that the underlying demand comes to the fore, and this is less than the money stock at that PPM. The pressure of spending then lowers the PPM again to the true equilibrium point. This may be diagramed as in Fig. 77.

Money stock is *OS*; the true or underlying money demand is *DD,* with true equilibrium point at *A.* Now suppose that the people on the market erroneously anticipate that true demand will be such in the near future that the PPM will be raised to *OE*. The total demand curve for money then shifts to D_sD_s, the new total demand curve including the speculative demand. The PPM does shift to *OE* as predicted. But now the speculators move to cash in their gain, since their true demand for money really reflects *DD* rather than D_sD_s. At the new price *OE*, there is in fact an excess of money stock over quantity demanded, amounting to *CF*. Sellers rush to sell their stock of money and buy goods, and the PPM falls again to equilibrium. Hence, in the field of money as well as in that of specific goods, speculative anticipations are self-correcting, not "self-fulfilling." They speed the market process of adjustment.

C. SECULAR INFLUENCES ON THE DEMAND FOR MONEY

Long-run influences on the demand for money in a progressing economy will tend to be manifold, and in both directions. On the one hand, an advancing economy provides ever more occasions for new exchanges as more and more commodities are offered on the market and as the number of stages of production increases. These greater opportunities tend greatly to increase the demand-for-money schedule. If an economy deteriorates, fewer opportunities for exchange exist, and the demand for money from this source will fall.

The major long-run factor counteracting this tendency and tending toward a *fall* in the demand for money is the growth of the *clearing system*.[8] Clearing is a device by which money is economized and performs the function of a medium of exchange *without being physically present* in the exchange.

A simplified form of clearing may occur between two people. For example, A may buy a watch from B for three gold ounces; at the same time, B buys a pair of shoes from A for one gold ounce. Instead of two transfers of money being made, and a total of four gold ounces changing hands, they decide to perform a clearing operation. A pays B two ounces of money, and they exchange the watch and the shoes. Thus, when a clearing is made, and only the *net* amount of money is actually transferred, all parties can engage in the same transactions at the same prices, but using far less cash. Their demand for cash tends to fall.

There is obviously little scope for clearing, however, as long as all transactions are *cash* transactions. For then people have to exchange one another's goods *at the same time*. But the scope for clearing is vastly increased when *credit* transactions come into play. These credits may be quite short-term. Thus, suppose that A and B deal with each other quite frequently during a year or a month. Suppose they agree not to pay each other immediately in cash, but to give each other credit until the end of each month. Then B may buy shoes from A on one day, and A may buy a watch from B on another. At the end of the period, the debts are canceled and cleared, and the net debtor pays one lump sum to the net creditor.

Once credit enters the picture, the clearing system can be extended to as many individuals as find it convenient. The more people engage in clearing operations (often in places called "clearinghouses") the more cancellations there will be, and the more money will be economized. At the end of the week, for example, there may be five people engaged in clearing, and A may owe B 10 ounces, B owe C 10 ounces, C owe D, etc., and finally E may owe A 10 ounces. In such a case, 50 ounces' worth of debt transactions and potential cash transactions are settled without a single ounce of cash being used.

Clearing, then, is a process of reciprocal cancellations of money debts. It permits a huge quantity of monetary exchanges without actual possession and transfer of money, thereby greatly reducing the demand for money. Clearing, however, cannot be all-encompassing, for there must be some physical money which *could* be used to settle the transaction, and there must be physical money to settle when there is no 100% cancellation (which rarely occurs).

D. Demand for Money Unlimited?

A popular fallacy rejects the concept of "demand for money" because it is allegedly always unlimited. This idea misconceives the very nature of demand and confuses money with wealth or income. It is based on the notion that "people want as much money as they can get." In the first place, this is true for *all* goods.

People would like to have far more goods than they can procure now. But *demand* on the market does not refer to all possible entries on people's value scales; it refers to *effective* demand, to desires made effective by being "demanded," i.e., by the fact that something else is "supplied" for it. Or else it is reservation demand, which takes the form of holding back the good from being sold. Clearly, effective demand for money is not and cannot be unlimited; it is limited by the appraised value of the goods a person can sell in exchange and by the amount of that money which the individual wants to spend on goods rather than keep in his cash balance.

Furthermore, it is, of course, not "money" *per se* that he wants and demands, but money for its purchasing power, or "real" money, money in some way expressed in terms of what it will purchase. (This purchasing power of money, as we shall see below, cannot be *measured*.) More money does him no good if its purchasing power for goods is correspondingly diluted.

E. THE PPM AND THE RATE OF INTEREST

We have been discussing money, and shall continue to do so in the current section, by comparing equilibrium positions, and not yet by tracing step by step how the change from one position to another comes about. We shall soon see that in the case of the price of money, as contrasted with all other prices, the very path toward equilibrium necessarily introduces changes that will change the equilibrium point. This will have important theoretical consequences. We may still talk, however, as if money is "neutral," i.e., does not lead to such changes, because this assumption is perfectly competent to deal with the problems analyzed so far. This is true, in essence, because we are able to use a general concept of the "purchasing power of money" without trying to define it concretely in terms of specific arrays of goods. Since the concept of the PPM is relevant and important even though its specific content changes and cannot be measured, we are justified in assuming that money is neutral as long as we do not need a more precise concept of the PPM.

We have seen how changes in the money relation change the PPM. In the determination of the interest rate, we must now modify our earlier discussion in chapter 6 to take account of allocating one's money stock by adding to or subtracting from one's cash balance. A man may allocate his money to consumption, investment, or addition to his cash balance. His time preferences govern the *proportion* which an individual devotes to present and to future goods, i.e., to *consumption* and to *investment.* Now suppose a man's demand-for-money schedule increases, and he therefore decides to allocate a proportion of his money income to increasing his cash balance. *There is no reason to suppose that this increase affects the consumption/investment proportion at all.* It could, but if so, it would mean a change in his *time preference* schedule as well as in his demand for money.

If the demand for money increases, *there is no reason why a change in the demand for money should affect the interest rate one iota.* There is no necessity at all for an increase in the demand for money to raise the interest rate, or a decline to lower it—no more than the opposite. In fact, there is no causal connection between the two; one is determined by the valuations for money, and the other by valuations for time preference.

Let us return to the section in chapter 6 on Time Preference and the Individual's Money Stock. Did we not see there that an increase in an individual's money stock *lowers* the effective time-preference rate along the time-preference schedule, and conversely that a decrease raises the time-preference rate? Why does this not apply here? Simply because we were dealing with each individual's money stock and assuming that the "real" exchange-value of each unit of money remained the same. His time-preference schedule relates to "real" monetary units, not simply to money itself. If the social stock of money changes or if the demand for money changes, the objective exchange-value of a monetary unit (the PPM) will change also. If the PPM falls, then *more* money in the hands of an individual may not necessarily lower the time-preference rate on his schedule, for the more money may only just compensate him for the fall in the PPM, and his "real money stock" may therefore be the same as before. This again demonstrates that the money relation is *neutral* to time preference and the pure rate of interest.

An increased demand for money, then, tends to lower prices all around without changing time preference or the pure rate of interest. Thus, suppose total social income is 100, with 70 allocated to investment and 30 to consumption. The demand for money increases, so that people decide to hoard a total of 20. Expenditure will now be 80 instead of 100, 20 being added to cash balances. Income in the next period will be only 80, since expenditures in one period result in the identical income to be allocated to the next period.[9] If time preferences remain the same, then the proportion of investment to consumption in the society will remain roughly the same, i.e., 56 invested and 24 consumed. Prices and nominal money values and incomes fall all along the line, and we are left with the same capital structure, the same *real* income, the same interest rate, etc. The only things that have changed are nominal prices, which have fallen, and the proportion of total cash balances to money income, which has increased.

A decreased demand for money will have the reverse effect. Dishoarding will raise expenditure, raise prices, and, *ceteris paribus,* maintain the real income and capital structure intact. The only other change is a *lower* proportion of cash balances to money income.

The only necessary result, then, of a change in the demand-for-money schedule is precisely a change in the same direction of the proportion of total cash balances to total money income and in the real value of cash balances. Given the stock of money, an increased scramble for cash will simply lower money incomes until the desired increase in real cash balances has been attained.

If the demand for money falls, the reverse movement occurs. The desire to reduce cash balances causes an increase in money income. Total cash remains the same, but its proportion to incomes, as well as its real value, declines.[10]

F. HOARDING AND THE KEYNESIAN SYSTEM

1) *Social Income, Expenditures, and Unemployment*

To the great bulk of writers "hoarding"—an increase in the demand for money—has appeared an unmitigated catastrophe.

The very word "hoarding" is a most inappropriate one to use in economics, since it is laden with connotations of vicious antisocial action. But there is nothing at all antisocial about either "hoarding" or "dishoarding." "Hoarding" is simply an increase in the demand for money, and the result of this change in valuations is that people get what they desire, i.e., an increase in the real value of their cash balances and of the monetary unit.[11] Conversely, if the people desire a *lowering* of their real cash balances or in the value of the monetary unit, they may accomplish this through "dishoarding." No other significant economic relation—real income, capital structure, etc.—need be changed at all. The process of hoarding and dishoarding, then, simply means that people want something, either an increase or a decrease in their real cash balances or in the real value of the monetary unit, and that they are able to obtain this result. What is wrong with that? We see here simply another manifestation of consumers' or individuals' "sovereignty" on the free market.

Furthermore, there is no theoretical way of defining "hoarding" beyond a simple addition to one's cash balance in a certain period of time. Yet most writers use the term in a normative fashion, implying that there is some vague standard below which a cash balance is legitimate and above which it is antisocial and vicious. But any quantitative limit set on the demand-for-money schedule would be completely arbitrary and unwarranted.

One of the two major pillars of the Keynesian system (now happily beginning to wane after sweeping the economic world in the 1930's and 1940's) is the proclamation that savings become equal to investment only through the terrible route of a decline in social income. The (implicit) foundation of Keynesianism is the assertion that at a certain level of total social income, total social expenditures out of this income will be lower than income, the remainder going into hoards. This will lower total social income in the next period of time, since, as we have seen, total income in one "day" equals, and is determined by, total expenditures in the previous "day."

The Keynesian "consumption function" plays its part in establishing an alleged law that there exists a certain level of total income, say *A, above which* expenditures will be less than income (net hoarding), and *below which* expenditures will be greater than income (net dishoarding). But the basic Keynesian worry is hoarding, when total income must decline. This situation may be diagramed as in Fig. 78.

In this graph, money income is plotted on both the horizontal and the vertical axes. Hence, a 45° straight line between the axes

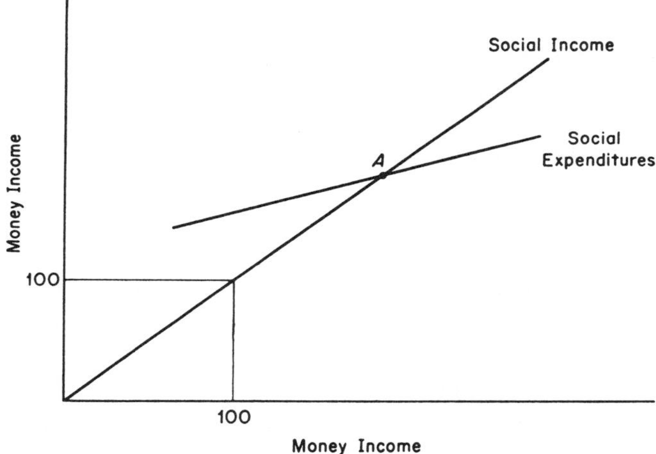

FIG. 78. RELATION BETWEEN SOCIAL INCOME AND SOCIAL EXPENDITURE ACCORDING TO KEYNES

is equal to social income.[12] To illustrate: A social income of 100 on the horizontal axis will correspond to, and equal, a social income of 100 on the vertical axis. The co-ordinates of these figures will meet at a point equidistant between the two axes. The Keynesian law asserts social expenditures to be lower than social income above point *A*, and higher than social income below point *A*, so that *A* will be the equilibrium point for social income to equal expenditure. For if social income is higher than *A*, social expenditures will be lower than income, and income will therefore tend to decline from one day to the next until the equilibrium point *A* is reached. If social income is lower than *A*, dishoarding will occur, expenditures will be higher than income, until finally *A* is reached again.

Below, we shall investigate the validity of this alleged law and the "consumption function" on which it rests. But suppose that we now grant the validity of such a law; the only comment can be an impertinent: So what? What if there is a fall in the national income? Since the fall need only be in *money* terms, and real income, real capital, etc., may remain the same, why any alarm? The only change is that the hoarders have accomplished their objective of increasing their real cash balances and increasing the real value of the monetary unit. It is true that the picture is rather more complex for the transition process until equilibrium is reached, and this will be treated further below (although our final conclusion will be the same). But the Keynesian system attempts to establish the perniciousness of the equilibrium position, and this it cannot do.

Therefore, the elaborate attempts of the Keynesians to demonstrate that free market expenditures will be limited—that consumption is limited by the "function," and investment by stagnation of opportunities and "liquidity preference"—are futile. For even if they were correct (which they are not), the result would be pointless. There is nothing wrong with hoarding or dishoarding, or with "low" or "high" levels (whatever that may mean) of social money income.

The Keynesian attempt to salvage meaning for their doctrine rests on one point and one point alone—the second major pillar of their system. This is the thesis that *money social income and level of employment are correlated,* and that *the latter is a function of the former.* This assumes that a certain "full employment" level of social income exists below which there is correspondingly greater unemployment. This can be diagramed as in Fig. 79.

On the previous diagram is superimposed a vertical *FF* line, which represents the point of alleged "full-employment" social income. If the intersection *A* is below (to the left of) the *FF* line, then there is permanent unemployment corresponding to the distance by which *A* falls short of that line.

Keynesians have also attempted, with little success, to give meaning to an equilibrium position where *A* falls to the right of the *FF* line, identifying this with inflation. Inflation, as we shall see below, is a dynamic process, the essence of which is change. The Keynesian system centers around the equilibrium position and therefore is hardly well equipped to analyze an inflationary situation.

The nub of the Keynesian critique of the free market economy, then, rests on the involuntary unemployment allegedly

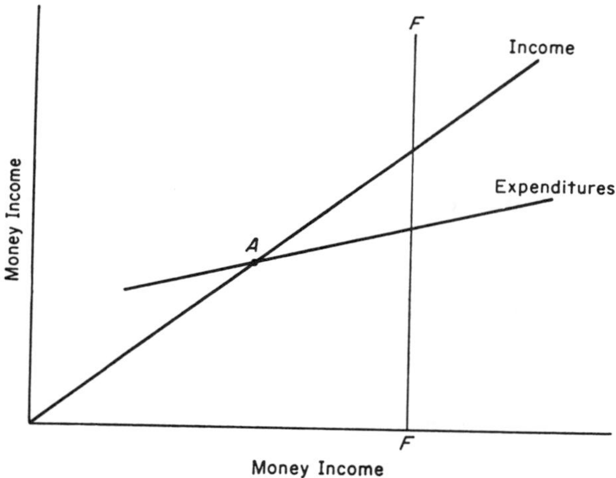

FIG. 79. RELATION BETWEEN FULL EMPLOYMENT AND SOCIAL INCOME AND EXPENDITURES ACCORDING TO KEYNES

caused by too low a level of social expenditures and income. But how can this be, since we have previously explained that there can be no involuntary unemployment in a free market? The answer has become evident (and is admitted in the most intelligent of the Keynesian writings): The Keynesian "under-employment equilibrium" occurs only *if money wage rates are rigid downward,* i.e., if the supply curve of labor below "full employment" is infinitely elastic.[13] Thus, suppose there is a "hoarding" (an increased demand for money), and social income falls. The result is a fall in the monetary demand curves for labor factors, as well as in all other monetary demand curves. We would expect the general supply curve of labor factors to be vertical. Since only *money* wage rates are being changed while *real* wage rates (in terms of purchasing power) remain the same, there will be no shift in labor/leisure preferences, and the total stock of labor offered on the market will remain constant. At any rate, certainly no involuntary unemployment will arise.

How then can the Keynesian case arise? How can the supply of labor remain horizontal at the old money wage rate? In only two ways: (1) if people voluntarily agree with the unions, which insist that no one be employed at lower than the old money wage rate. Since selling prices are falling, maintaining the old money wage rate is equivalent to demanding a higher real wage rate. We have seen above that the unions' raising of real wage rates causes unemployment. But this unemployment is *voluntary,* since the workers acquiesce in the imposition of a higher minimum real wage rate, below which they will not undercut the union and accept employment. Or (2) unions or government coercively impose the minimum wage rate. But this is an example of a *hampered* market, not the free market to which we are confining our analysis here.

Situation (1) or (2) may be diagramed as in Fig. 80.

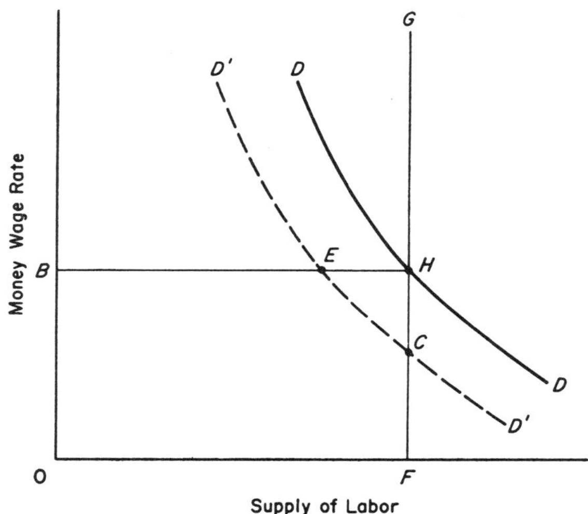

FIG. 80. UNEMPLOYMENT RESULTING FROM FIXING MONEY WAGES AT HIGHER THAN FREE-MARKET RATES

The original demand curve for labor is *DD* (for simplicity of exposition we assume as meaningful the concept of "demand for labor" in general). Total stock of labor in the society is *OF*, or at least that is the stock put forward upon the market. Now an increase in the demand for money shifts all demand curves downwards as all money prices fall. If wage rates are free to fall, the intersection point will move from *H* to *C* and nominal wage rates reduced accordingly, from *FH* to *FC*. There is still "full employment" at level *OF*. Now suppose however, that a union sets a minimum money wage rate of *OB* (or *FH*). Then the supply-of-labor curve becomes *BHG;* horizontal up to *FG* and vertical from there on. The new demand curve *D′D′* will now intersect the supply of labor at point *E* instead of point *C*. Total amount of labor now employed is reduced to *BE*, and *EH* are now unemployed as a result of the union action.

Keynes' own exposition tended to run in terms of real rather than money magnitudes—real social income, real expenditures, etc.[14] Such an analysis obscures dynamic considerations, since transactions take place at least superficially in monetary terms on the market. However, the essential conclusion of our analysis remains unchanged if we pursue it directly in real terms. Instead of falling, demand curves in *real* terms will now remain the same. This is true for the labor market as well. Instead of being depicted on a diagram as a horizontal line at existing wage rates, the effect of union action would have to be shown as a horizontally imposed *increase* in real wage rates (the result of keeping money wage rates constant while selling prices fall). The relevant diagram is shown in Fig. 81. The facts depicted in this diagram are the same as in the previous diagram: unions causing unemployment (*EH*) by insisting on an excessively high money (and therefore real) wage (*OB*).

The sum and substance of the "Keynesian Revolution" was the thesis that there *can* be an unemployment equilibrium on the free market. As we have seen, the only sense in which this is true was known years before Keynes: that widespread union maintenance of excessively high wage rates will cause unemployment.

Keynes believed that while other elements of the economic system, including prices, were set basically in real terms, workers bargained even ultimately only in terms of *money* wages—that unions insisted on minimum money wage rates downward, but would passively accept falling real wages in the form of rising prices, money wage rates remaining the same. The Keynesian prescription for eliminating unemployment therefore rests specifically on the "money illusion"—that unions will impose mini-

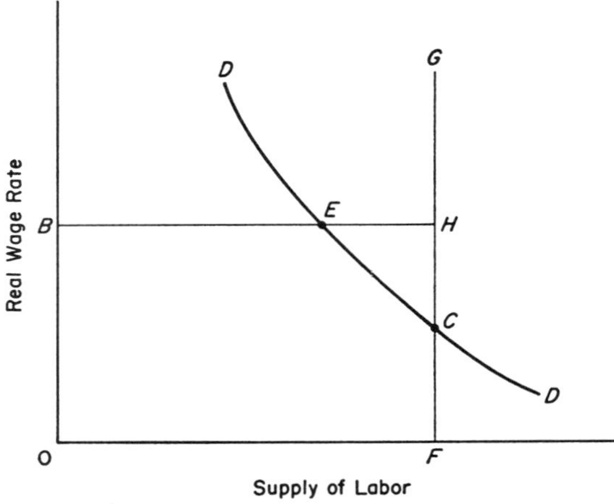

FIG. 81. UNEMPLOYMENT RESULTING FROM FIXING REAL WAGES AT HIGHER THAN FREE-MARKET RATES

mum *money* wage rates, but are too stupid to impose minimum real wage rates *per se*. Unions, however, have learned about purchasing-power problems and the distinction between money and real rates; indeed, it hardly requires much reasoning ability to grasp this distinction.[15] Ironically, Keynes' advocacy of inflation based on the "money illusion" rested on the historical experience (which we shall treat more fully below) that, during an inflation, selling prices rise faster than wage rates. Yet an economy in which unions impose minimum wage rates is precisely an economy in which unions will be alive to any losses in their real, as well as their money, wages. Inflation, therefore, cannot be used as a means of duping unions into relieving unemployment.[16] Keynesianism has been touted as at least a "practical" system. Whatever its theoretical defects, it is alleged to be fit for the modern world of unionism. Yet it is precisely in the modern world that Keynes' doctrine is least appropriate or practical.[17]

The Keynesians object that to allow rigid money wage rates to become flexible downward would further lower monetary demand for goods, and therefore monetary income. But this completely confuses *wage rates* with *aggregate payroll*, or total income going to wages.[18] That the former falls does not mean that the latter falls. On the contrary, total income is, as we have seen, determined by total expenditures in the previous period of time. Lower wage rates will cause the hiring of those made unemployed by the old excessively high wage rates. The fact that labor is now cheaper relatively to land factors will cause investors to expend a greater proportion on labor vis à vis land than before. And the employment of unemployed labor increases production and therefore aggregate real income. Furthermore, even if payrolls also decline, prices and wage rates can adjust—but this will be taken up in the next section on liquidity preference.

2) *"Liquidity Preference"*

Those Keynesians who recognize the grave difficulties of their system fall back on one last string in their bow—"liquidity preference." Intelligent Keynesians will concede that involuntary unemployment is a "special" or rare case, and Lindahl goes even further to say that it could be only a *short*-run and not a long-run equilibrium phenomenon.[19] Neither Modigliani nor Lindahl, however, is thoroughgoing enough in his critique of the Keynesian system, particularly of the "liquidity preference" doctrine.

The Keynesian system, as is quite clear from the mathematical portrayals of it given by its followers, suffers grievously from the mathematical-economic sin of "mutual determination." The use of mathematical functions, which are reversible at will, is appropriate in physics, where we do not know the causes of the observed movements. Since we do not know the causes, any mathematical law explaining or describing movements will be reversible, and, as far as we are concerned, any of the variables in the function is just as much "cause" as another. In praxeology, the science of human action, however, we *know* the original cause—motivated action by individuals. This knowledge provides us with true axioms. From these axioms, true laws are deduced. They are deduced step by step in a logical, cause-and-effect relationship. Since first causes are known, their consequent effects are also known. Economics therefore traces unilinear cause-and-effect relations, not vague "mutually determining" relations.

This methodological reminder is singularly applicable to the Keynesian theory of interest. For the Keynesians consider the rate of interest (*a*) as *determining* investment and (*b*) as being determined by the demand for money to hold "for speculative purposes" (liquidity preference). In practice, however, they treat the latter *not* as determining the rate of interest, but as *being determined* by it. The methodology of "mutual determination" has completely obscured this sleight of hand. Keynesians might object that all demand and supply curves are "mutually determining" in their relation to price. But this facile assertion is not correct. Demand curves are determined by utility scales, and supply curves by speculation and the stock produced by given labor and land factors, which is ultimately governed by time preferences.

The Keynesians therefore treat the rate of interest, *not* as they believe they do—as determined by liquidity preference—but rather as some sort of mysterious and unexplained force imposing itself on the other elements of the economic system. Thus, Keynesian discussion of liquidity preference centers around "inducement to hold cash" as the rate of interest rises or falls. According to the theory of liquidity preference, a fall in the rate of interest increases the quantity of cash demanded for "speculative purposes" (liquidity preferences), and a rise in the rate of interest lowers liquidity preference.

The first error in this concept is the arbitrary separation of the demand for money into two separate parts: a "transactions demand," supposedly determined by the size of social income, and a "speculative demand," determined by the rate of interest. We have seen that all sorts of influences impinge themselves on the demand for money. But they are only influences working *through* the value scales of individuals. And there is only *one* final demand for money, because each individual has only one value scale. There is no way by which we can split the demand up into two parts and speak of them as independent entities. Furthermore, there are far more than two influences on demand. In the final analysis, the demand for money, like all utilities, cannot be reduced to simple determinants; it is the outcome of free, independent decisions on individual value scales. There is, therefore, no "transaction demand" uniquely determined by the size of income.

The "speculative demand" is mysterious indeed. Modigliani explains this "liquidity preference" as follows: ". . . we should expect that any fall in the rate of interest . . . would induce a growing number of potential investors to keep their assets in the form of money, rather than securities; that is to say, we should expect a fall in the rate of interest to increase the demand for money as an asset." [20] This is subject to the criticism, as we have seen, that the rate of interest is here *determining,* and is not *itself* explained by any cause. Furthermore, what does this statement mean? A fall in the rate of interest, according to the Keynesians, means that less interest is being earned from bonds, and therefore there is a greater inducement to hold cash. This is correct (as long as we allow ourselves to think in terms of the interest rate as *determining* instead of *being determined*), but highly inadequate. For if a lower interest rate "induces" greater cash holdings, it also induces greater *consumption,* since consumption also becomes more attractive. In fact, one of the grave defects of the liquidity-preference approach is that the Keynesians never think in terms of *three* "margins" being decided at once. They think only in terms of two at a time. Hence, Modigliani: "Having made his consumption-saving plan, the individual has to make decisions concerning the assets he owns"; i.e., he then allocates them between money and securities.[21] In other words, people first decide between consumption and saving (in the sense of not consuming); and *then* they decide between investing and hoarding these savings. But this is an absurdly artificial construction. People decide on all three of their alternatives, weighing one against each of the others. To say that people first decide between consuming and not consuming and *then* choose between hoarding and investing is just as misleading as to say that people first choose how much to hoard and then decide between consumption and investment.[22]

People, therefore, allocate their money among consumption, investment, and hoarding. *The proportion between consumption and investment reflects individual time preferences.* Consumption reflects desires for present goods, and investment reflects desires for future goods. An increase in the demand-for-money schedule does *not* affect the rate of interest if the proportion between consumption and investment (i.e., time preference) remains the same.

The rate of interest, we must reiterate, is *determined by* time preferences, which also determine the proportions of consumption and investment. To think of the rate of interest as "inducing" more or less saving or hoarding is to misunderstand the problem completely.[23]

Admitting, then, that time preference determines the proportions of consumption and investment and that the demand for money determines the proportion of income hoarded, does the demand for money play a role in determining the interest rate? The Keynesians assert that there is a relation between the rate of interest and a "speculative" demand for cash. Should the schedule of the latter rise, the former rises also. But this is not necessarily true. A greater proportion of funds hoarded can be drawn from three alternative sources: (*a*) from funds that formerly went into consumption, (*b*) from funds that went into investment, and (*c*) from a mixture of both that leaves the old consumption-investment proportion unchanged. Condition (*a*) will bring about a *fall* in the rate of interest; condition (*b*) a *rise* in the rate of interest, and condition (*c*) will leave the rate of interest unchanged. Thus hoarding may reflect either a rise, a fall, or no change in the rate of interest, depending on whether *time preferences* have concomitantly risen, fallen, or remained the same.

The Keynesians contend that the speculative demand for cash

depends upon and determines the rate of interest in this way: if people expect that the rate of interest will rise in the near future, then their liquidity preference increases to await this rise. This, however, can hardly be a part of a long-run *equilibrium* theory, such as Keynes is trying to establish. Speculation, by its very nature, disappears in the ERE, and hence no fundamental causal theory can be based upon it. Furthermore, what *is* an interest rate? One grave and fundamental Keynesian error is to persist in regarding the interest rate as a contract rate on loans, instead of the price spreads between stages of production. The former, as we have seen, is only the reflection of the latter. A strong expectation of a rapid rise in interest rate means a strong expectation of an increase in the price spreads, or rate of net return. A fall in prices means that entrepreneurs generally expect that factor prices will fall *further* in the near future than their selling prices. But it requires no Keynesian labyrinth to explain this phenomenon; all we are confronted with is a situation in which entrepreneurs, expecting that factor prices will soon fall, cease investing and wait for this happy event so that their return will be greater. This is *not* "liquidity preference," but *speculation on price changes.* It involves a modification of our previous discussion of the relation between prices and the demand for money, caused by a fact that we shall explore soon in detail, namely, that prices do not change equally and proportionately.

The expectation of falling factor prices speeds up the movement toward equilibrium and hence toward the pure interest relation as determined by time preference.[24]

If, for example, unions keep wage rates artificially high, "hoarding" will increase as unions keep wage rates ever higher than the equilibrium rate at which "full employment" can be maintained. This induced hoarding lowers the money demand for factors and increases unemployment still further, but only because of wage-rate rigidity.[25]

The final Keynesian bogey is that people may acquire an unlimited demand for money, so that hoards will indefinitely increase. This is termed an "infinite" liquidity preference. And this is the only case in which neo-Keynesians such as Modigliani believe that involuntary unemployment can be compatible with price and wage freedom. The Keynesian worry is that people will hoard instead of buying bonds for fear of a fall in the price of securities. Translating this into more important "natural" terms, this would mean, as we have stated, not investing because of expectation of imminent increases in the natural interest rate. Rather than act as a blockade, however, this expectation *speeds* the ensuing adjustment. Furthermore, the demand for money could not be infinite since people must always continue consuming, whatever their expectations. Of necessity, therefore, the demand for money could never be infinite. The existing level of consumption, in turn, will require a certain level of investment. As long as productive activities are continuing, there is no need or possibility of lasting unemployment, regardless of the degree of hoarding.[26]

A demand for money to hold stems from the general uncertainty of the market. Keynesians, however, attribute liquidity preference, not to *general* uncertainty, but to the specific uncertainty of future bond prices. Surely this is a highly superficial and limiting view.

In the first place, this cause of liquidity preference could occur only on a highly imperfect securities market. As Lachmann pointed out years ago in a neglected article, Keynes' causal pattern—"bearishness" causing "liquidity preference" (demand for cash) and high interest rates—could take place only in the absence of an organized forward or *futures* market for securities. If such a market existed, both bears and bulls on the bond market "could express their expectations by forward transactions which do not require any cash. Where the market for securities is fully organized over time, the owner of 4% bonds who fears a rise in the rate of interest has no incentive to exchange them for cash, for he can always 'hedge' by selling them forward."[27] Bearishness would cause a fall in forward bond prices, followed immediately by a fall in spot prices. Thus, speculative bearishness would, of course, cause at least a temporary rise in the rate of interest, but accompanied by *no* increase in the demand for cash. Hence, any attempted connection between liquidity preference, or demand for cash, and the rate of interest, falls to the ground.

The fact that such a securities market has not been organized indicates that traders are not nearly as worried about rising interest rates as Keynes believes. If they were and this fear loomed as an important phenomenon, then surely a futures market would have developed in securities.

Furthermore, as we have seen, interest rates on loans are merely a reflection of price spreads, so that a prediction of higher interest rates really means the expectation of lower *prices* and, especially, lower costs, resulting in a greater demand for money. And all speculation, on the free market, is self-correcting and speeds adjustment, rather than a cause of economic trouble.

G. THE PURCHASING-POWER AND TERMS-OF-TRADE COMPONENTS IN THE RATE OF INTEREST

Many economists, beginning with Irving Fisher, have asserted that the market rate of interest, in addition to containing specific entrepreneurial components superimposed on the pure rate of interest, also contains a "price" or a "purchasing-power component." When the purchasing power of money is generally expected to rise, the theory asserts that the market rate of interest falls correspondingly; when the PPM is expected to fall, the theory declares that the market rate of interest rises correspondingly.

These economists erred by concentrating on the *loan rate* rather than on the natural rate (the rate of return). The reasoning behind this theory was as follows: If the purchasing power of money is expected to change, then the pure rate of interest (determined by time preference) will no longer be the same in "real terms." Suppose that 100 gold ounces exchange for 105 gold ounces a year from now—i.e., that the rate of interest is 5%. Now, suddenly, let there be a general expectation that the purchasing power of money will increase. In that case, a *lower* amount to be returned, say 102 ounces, may yield 5% real interest in terms of purchasing power. A general expectation of a rise in purchasing power, therefore, will lower the market rate of interest at present, while a general expectation of a fall in purchasing power will raise the rate.[28]

There is a fatal defect in this generally accepted line of reasoning. Suppose, for example, that prices are generally expected to fall by 50% in the next year. Would someone lend 100 gold ounces to exchange for 53 ounces one year from now? Why not? This would certainly preserve the real interest rate at 5%. But then why should the would-be lenders not simply hold on to their money and *double* their real assets as a result of the price fall? And that is precisely what they would do; they certainly would not give money away, even though their real assets would be greater than before. Fisher simply shrugged off this point by saying that the purchasing-power premium could never make the interest rate negative. But this flaw vitiates the entire theory.

The root of the difficulty consists in ignoring the natural rate of interest. Let us consider the interest rate in those terms. Then, suppose 100 ounces are paid for factors that will be transformed in one year into a product that sells for 105 gold ounces, for an interest gain of 5 and an interest return of 5%. Now a general expectation arises of a general *halving* of prices one year from now. The selling price of the product will be 53 ounces in a year's time. What happens now? Will entrepreneurs buy factors for 100 and sell at 53 merely because their real interest rate is preserved? Certainly not. They will do so only if they do not at all anticipate the change in purchasing power. But to the extent that it *is* anticipated, they will hold money rather than buy factors. This will *immediately* lower factor prices to their expected future levels, say from 100 to 50.

What happens to the *loan rate* is analytically quite trivial. It is simply a reflection of the natural rate and depends on how the expectations and judgment of the people on the loan market compare with those on the stock and other markets. For the free economy, there is no point in separately analyzing the loan market. Analysis of the Fisher problem—the relation of the interest rate to price changes—should concentrate on the *natural* rate of interest. Discussion of the relation between price movements and the (natural) rate of interest should be divided into two parts:

first, assuming "neutral money"—that all prices change equally and at the same time—and second, analyzing conditions where factor and product change at different rates. And these changes should first be analyzed without considering that they had been *anticipated* by people on the market.

Suppose, first, that all prices change equally and at the same time. Instead of thinking in terms of 100 ounces borrowed on the loan market, let us consider the natural rate. An investor buys factors in period 1 and then sells the product, say in period 3. Time, as we have seen, is the essence of the production structure. All the processes take time, and capitalists pay money to owners of factors in advance of production and sale. Since factors are bought before products are sold, what is the effect of a period of rising general prices (i.e., falling PPM)? The result is that the entrepreneur reaps an apparent extra profit. Suppose that he normally purchases original factors for 100 and then sells the product for 120 ounces two years later, for an interest return of 10% per annum. Now suppose that a decrease in the demand for money or an increase of money stock propels a general upward movement in prices and that all prices double in two years' time. Then, just because of the passage of time, an entrepreneur who purchases factors for 100 now will sell for 240 ounces in two years' time. Instead of a net return of 20 ounces, or 10% per annum, he reaps 140 ounces, or 70% per annum.

It would seem that a rise in prices creates an inherent tendency for large-scale profits that are not simply individual rewards for more accurate forecasting. However, more careful analysis reveals that this is not an extra profit at all. For the 240 ounces two years from now is roughly equivalent, in terms of purchasing power, to 120 ounces now. The *real* rate of net return, based on money's services, is the same 10% as it has always been. It is clear that any lower net return would amount to a decline in real return. A return of a mere 120 ounces, for example, would amount to a drastic negative real return, for 100 ounces would then be invested for the equivalent gross return of only 60 ounces. It has often been shown that a period of rising prices misleads businessmen into thinking that their increased money profits are also real gains, whereas they only maintain real rates of return. Consider, for example, "replacement costs"—the prices which the businessmen will *now* have to pay for factors. The capitalist who earns 240 ounces on a 100-ounce investment neglects to his sorrow the fact that his factor bundle now costs 200 ounces instead of 100. Businessmen who under such circumstances treat their monetary profits as real profits and consume them soon find that they are really consuming their capital.

The converse occurs in the case of falling prices. The capitalist buys factors in period 1 and sells the product in period 3, when all-around prices are lower. If prices are to fall by a half in two years, an investment of 100, followed by a sale at 60, does not really involve the terrific loss that it appears to be. For the 60 return is equivalent in real terms, both in generalized purchasing power and in replacement of factors, to 120 previous ounces. His real rate of return remains the same. The consequence is that businessmen will be likely to *overstate their losses* in a period of price contraction. Perhaps this is one of the major reasons for the deep-seated belief of most businessmen that they always gain during a general price expansion and lose during a period of general contraction. This belief is purely illusory.

In these examples, the natural interest rate on the market has contained a *purchasing-power component,* which corrects for real rates, positively in money terms during a general expansion, and negatively during a general contraction. The loan rate will be simply a reflection of what has been happening in the natural rate. So far, the discussion is similar to Fisher's, except that these are the effects of *actual,* not anticipated, changes and the Fisher thesis cannot take account of the negative interest rate case. We have seen that rather than take a monetary loss, even though their real return will be the same, entrepreneurs will hold back their purchases of factors until factor prices fall immediately to their future low level. But this process of anticipatory price movement does not occur only in the extreme case of a prospective "negative" return. *It happens whenever a price change is anticipated.* Thus, suppose all entrepreneurs generally anticipate that prices will double in two years. The fact of an anticipated rise will lead to an increase in the price level *now* and an approach immediately toward a doubled price level. An anticipated fall will lead to an immediate fall in factor prices. If all changes were anticipated by everyone, there would be no room for a purchasing-power component to develop. Prices would simply fall immediately to their future level.

The purchasing-power component, then, is *not* the reflection, as has been thought, of *expectations* of changes in purchasing power. It is the reflection of the change itself; indeed, *if the change were completely anticipated, the purchasing power would change immediately, and there would be no room for a purchasing-power component in the rate of interest.* As it is, partial anticipations speed up the adjustment of the PPM to the changed conditions.

So far we have distinguished three components of the natural rate of interest (all reflected in the loan rate of interest). One is the *pure rate* of interest—the result of individual time preferences, tending to be uniform throughout the economy. Second are the specific entrepreneurial rates of interest. These differ from firm to firm and so are not uniform. They are anticipated in advance, and they are the rates that an investor will have to anticipate receiving before he enters the field. A particularly "risky" venture, if successful at all, will therefore tend to earn more in net return than what is generally anticipated to be a "safe" venture. The third component of the natural rate of interest is the purchasing-power component, correcting for general PPM changes because of the inevitable time lags in production. This will be positive in an expansion and negative in a contraction, but will be ephemeral. The more that changes in the PPM are anticipated, the *less* important will be the purchasing-power component and the more rapid will be the adjustment in the PPM *itself*.

There is still a fourth component in the natural rate of interest. This exists to the extent that money changes are *not* neutral (and they never are). Sometimes product prices rise and fall faster than factor prices, sometimes they rise and fall more slowly, and sometimes their behavior is mixed, with some factor prices and some product prices rising more rapidly. Whenever there *is* a general divergence in rates of movement between the prices of the product and of original factors, a *terms-of-trade* component emerges in the natural rate of interest.

Historically, it has often been the case that product prices rise more rapidly and fall more rapidly than the prices of original factors. In the former case, there is, during the period of transition, a favorable change in the terms of trade to the general run of capitalists. For selling prices are increasing *faster* than the buying prices of original factors. This will increase the general rate of return and constitute a general positive terms-of-trade component in the natural rate of interest. This, of course, will also tend to be reflected in the loan rate of interest. In the case of a contraction, a more sluggish fall in the prices of factors creates a general negative terms-of-trade component in the interest rate. The components are precisely the reverse whenever factor prices change more rapidly than product prices. Whenever there is no general change in the "terms of trade" to capitalist-entrepreneurs, no terms-of-trade component will appear in the interest rate.

Changes in terms of trade discussed here are only those resulting purely from differences in the speed of reaction to changing conditions. They do *not* include basic changes in the terms of trade resulting from changes in time preferences, such as we have discussed above.

It is clear that all the interest-rate components aside from the pure rate—entrepreneurial, purchasing power, and terms of trade—are "dynamic" and the result of uncertainty. None of these components would exist in the ERE, and therefore the market interest rate in the ERE would equal the pure rate determined by time preferences alone. In the ERE the only net incomes would be a uniform pure interest return and wages to labor (ground land rents being capitalized into an interest return).

6. *The Supply of Money*

A. THE STOCK OF THE MONEY COMMODITY

The total stock of money in a society is the total number of ounces of the money commodity available. Throughout this volume we have deliberately used "gold ounces" instead of "dollars" or any other name for money, precisely because on the free market the latter would only be a confusing term for *units of weight* of gold or silver.

The total stock, from one period to another, will increase from new production and decrease from being used up—either in industrial production as a nonmonetary factor or from the wear and tear of coins. Since one of the qualities of the money commodity is its durability, the usual tendency is a long-run increase in the money supply and a resulting gradual long-run decline in the PPM. This furthers social utility only in so far as more gold or silver is made available for *nonmonetary* purposes.

We saw in chapter 3 that the physical form of the monetary commodity makes no difference. It can be in nonmonetary use as jewelry, in the form of bars of bullion, or in the form of coins. On the free market, transforming gold from one shape to another would be a business like any other business, charging a market price for its service and earning a pure interest return in the ERE. Since gold begins as bullion and ends as coin, it would seem that the latter would command a small premium over the equivalent weight of the former, the bullion often being a capital good for coin. Sometimes, however, coins are remelted back into bullion for larger transactions, so that a premium for coin over bullion is not a certainty. If, as generally happens, minting coins costs more than melting, coins will command the equivalent premium over bullion. This premium is called *brassage.*

It is impossible for economics to predict the details of the structure of any market. The market for privately issued gold bars or coins might develop as homogeneous, like the market for wheat, or the coins might be stamped and branded by the coinmakers to certify to the quality of their product. Probably the public would buy only branded coins to insure accurate quality.

One argument against permitting free private coinage is that compulsory standardization of the denominations of coins is more convenient than the diversity of coins that would ensue under a free system. But if the market finds it more convenient, private mints will be led by consumer demand to mint certain standard denominations. On the other hand, if greater variety is preferred, consumers will demand and obtain a more varied number of coins.[29]

B. CLAIMS TO MONEY: THE MONEY WAREHOUSE

Chapter 2 described the difference between "claims to present goods" and "claims to future goods." The same analysis applies to money as to barter. A claim to future money is a *bill of exchange*—an evidence of a credit transaction. The holder of the bill—the creditor—redeems it at the date of redemption in exchange for money paid by the debtor. A claim to present money, however, is a completely different good. It is *not* the evidence of an *uncompleted* transaction, an exchange of a present for a future good, as is the bill; it is a simple *evidence of ownership of a present good.* It is not uncompleted, or an exchange on the time market. Therefore, to present this evidence for redemption is not the *completion* of a transaction or equivalent to a creditor's calling his loan; it is a simple *repossessing* of a man's own good. In chapter 2 we gave as examples of a claim to present goods warehouse receipts and shares of stock. Shares of stock, however, cannot be redeemed in parts of a company's fixed assets because of the rules of ownership that the companies themselves set up in their co-operative venture. Furthermore, there is no guarantee that such assets will have a fixed money value. We shall therefore confine ourselves to *warehouse receipts,* which are also more relevant to the supply of money.

When a man deposits goods at a warehouse, he is given a receipt and pays the owner of the warehouse a certain sum for the service of storage. He still retains ownership of the property; the owner of the warehouse is simply guarding it for him. When the warehouse receipt is presented, the owner is obligated to restore the good deposited. A warehouse specializing in money is known as a "bank."

Claims to goods are often treated on the market as equivalent to the goods themselves. If no fraud or theft is suspected, then evidence of ownership of a good in a warehouse is considered as equivalent to the good itself. In many cases, individuals will find it advantageous to exchange the claims or evidences—the *goods-substitutes*—rather than the goods themselves. Paper is more convenient to transfer from person to person, and the expense of moving the goods is eliminated. When Jones sells Smith his wheat, therefore, instead of moving the wheat from one place to another, they may well agree simply to transfer the warehouse receipt itself from Jones to Smith. The goods remain in the same warehouse until Smith needs them or until the receipt is transferred to someone else. Of course, Smith may prefer, for one reason or another, to keep the goods in his own warehouse, in which case they are moved from one to the other.

Let us take the case of a warehouse owned by the Trustee Warehouse Company. It holds various goods in its vaults for safekeeping. Suppose that this company has developed a reputation for being very reliable and theft-free. Consequently, people tend to leave their goods in the Trustee Warehouse for a considerable length of time and, in the case of goods that they do not use frequently, will even tend to transfer the *goods-certificates* (the warehouse receipts, or evidences of ownership of the goods) and not redeem the goods themselves. Thus, the goods-certificates act as goods-substitutes in exchange. Suppose that the Trustee Company sees this happening. It realizes that a good opportunity for fraud presents itself. It can take the depositors' goods, the goods that it holds for safekeeping, and lend them out to people on the market. It can earn interest on these loans, and as long as only a small percentage of depositors ask to redeem their certificates at any one time, no one is the wiser. Or, alternatively, it can issue pseudo warehouse receipts for goods that are not there and lend these on the market. This is the more subtle practice. The pseudo receipts will be exchanged on the market on the same basis as the true receipts, since there is no indication on their face whether they are legitimate or not.

It should be clear that this practice is outright fraud. Someone else's property is taken by the warehouse and used for its own money-making purposes. It is not *borrowed,* since no interest is paid for the use of the money. Or, if spurious warehouse receipts are printed, *evidences of goods* are issued and sold or loaned without any such goods being in existence.

Money is the good most susceptible to these practices. For money, as we have seen, is generally not used directly at all, but only for exchanges. It is, furthermore, a widely homogeneous good, and therefore one ounce of gold is interchangeable with any other. Since it is convenient to transfer paper in exchange rather than carry gold, money warehouses (or banks) that build up public confidence will find that few people redeem their certificates. The banks will be particularly subject to the temptation to commit fraud and issue pseudo money certificates to circulate side by side with genuine money certificates as acceptable money-substitutes. The fact that money is a homogeneous good means that people do not care whether the money they redeem is the original money they deposited. This makes bank frauds easier to accomplish.

"Fraud" is a harsh term, but an accurate one to describe this practice, even if not recognized as such in the law, or by those committing it. It is, in fact, difficult to see the economic or moral difference between the issuance of pseudo receipts and the appropriation of someone else's property or outright embezzlement or, more directly, counterfeiting. Most present legal systems do not outlaw this practice; in fact, it is considered basic banking procedure. Yet the libertarian law of the free market would have to prohibit it. The purely free market is, by definition, one where theft and fraud (implicit theft) are illegal and do not exist.

To part with goods or money held in trust or to issue spurious warehouse receipts is, of course, a dangerous business, even when the law permits it. If the warehouse once failed to meet its contractual obligations, its fraud would be discovered, and a general panic "run" on the warehouse or bank would ensue. It would then be quickly plunged into bankruptcy. Such a bankruptcy, however, would not be similar to the failure of an ordinary speculative business enterprise. It is rather similar to the absconder who gets caught before he has returned the funds he has "borrowed."

Even if the receipt does not say on its face that the warehouse guarantees to keep it in its vaults, such an agreement is *implicit* in the very issuance of the receipt. For it is obvious that if any pseudo receipts are issued, it immediately becomes impossible for the bank to redeem all of them, and therefore fraud is immediately being committed. If a bank has twenty pounds of gold in its vaults, owned by depositors, and gold certificates redeemable on demand for thirty pounds, then notes to the value of ten pounds are fraudulent. *Which* particular receipts are fraudulent can be determined only *after* a run on the bank has occurred and the later claimants are left unsatisfied.

In a purely free market where fraud cannot, by definition, occur, all bank receipts will be genuine, i.e., will represent only actual gold or silver in the vaults. In that case, all the bank's *money-substitutes* (warehouse receipts) will also be *money certificates,* i.e., each receipt genuinely certifies the actual existence of the money in its vaults. The amount of gold kept in bank vaults for redemption purposes is called its "reserves," and the policy of issuing only genuine receipts is therefore a policy of "100% reserves" of cash to demand liabilities (liabilities that must be paid on demand).[30] However, the term "reserve" is a misleading one, because it assumes that the *bank* owns the gold and independently decides how much of it to keep on hand. Actually, it is not the bank that owns the gold, but its depositors.[31]

An enormous literature has developed dealing with the physical form of the money receipts, and yet the physical form is of no economic importance. It may be in the form of a *paper note,* a *token coin* (essentially a note stamped on coin instead of paper), or a book credit (*demand deposit*) in the bank. The demand deposit is not tangibly held by the owner, but can be transferred to anyone he desires by written order to the bank. This order is called a *check.* The depositor has a choice of which form of receipt to take, according to his convenience. Which form he chooses makes no economic difference.

C. Money-Substitutes and the Supply of Money

Since money-substitutes exchange as money on the market, we must consider them as part of the supply of money. It then becomes necessary to distinguish between money (*in the broader sense*)—the common medium of exchange—and *money proper.* Money proper is the ultimate medium of exchange or *standard money*—here the *money commodity*—while the supply of money (in a broader sense) includes all the standard money plus the money-substitutes that are held in individuals' cash balances. In the cases cited above, gold was the money proper or standard money, while the receipts—the demand claims to gold—were the money-substitutes.

The relation between these elements may be illustrated as follows: Assume a community of three persons, A, B, C, and three money warehouses, X, Y, Z. Suppose that each person has 100 ounces of gold in his possession and none on deposit at a warehouse. For the community, then:

Total supply of money proper	= 300 ounces (A's + B's + C's)
Total supply of money-substitutes	= 000 ounces
Total supply of money (in the broader sense)	= 300 ounces

The total supply of money is here identical with the total supply of money proper.

Now assume that A and B each deposits his 100 ounces of gold at warehouses X and Y respectively, while C keeps his gold on hand. The total supply of money is always equal to the total of individual cash balances. Its composition now is:

A—100 ounces of X-Money-Substitute
B—100 ounces of Y-Money-Substitute
C—100 ounces of Gold Money Proper

Total supply of money (in the broader sense) = Total cash balances = 200 ounces of money-substitutes + 100 ounces of money proper.

The effect of the deposit of money proper in the warehouses or banks is to change the *composition* of the total supply of money in cash balances; the total amount, however, remains unchanged at 300 ounces. Money-substitutes of various banks have replaced most of the standard money in individual cash holdings. Similarly, if A and B were to redeem their deposits, the total amount would remain unchanged, while the composition would revert to the original pattern.

What of the 200 ounces of gold deposited in the vaults of the banks? These are no longer part of the money supply; they are held in *reserve* against the outstanding money-substitutes. While in reserve, they form no part of any individual's cash balance; the cash balances consist not of the gold, but of evidences of ownership of the gold. Only the money proper outside of bank reserves forms part of individuals' cash balances and hence part of the community's supply of money.

Thus, as long as all money-substitutes are full money certificates, an increase or decrease in the money-substitutes outstanding can have no effect on the total supply of money. Only the *composition* of that supply is affected, and such changes in composition are of no economic importance.

However, when banks are legally permitted to abandon a 100% reserve and to issue pseudo receipts, the economic effects are quite different. We may call the money-substitutes that are not genuine money certificates, *uncovered* money-substitutes, since they do not genuinely represent money. The issue of uncovered money-substitutes adds to individuals' cash balances and hence to the total supply of money. Uncovered money-substitutes are not offset by new money deposits and so constitute net additions to the total supply. *Any increase or decrease in the supply of uncovered money-substitutes increases or decreases to the same extent the total supply of money (in the broader sense).*

Thus, the total supply of money is composed of the following elements: *supply of money proper outside reserves + supply of money certificates + supply of uncovered money-substitutes.* The supply of money certificates has no effect on the size of the supply of money; an increase in this factor only decreases the size of the first factor. The supply of money proper and the factors determining its size have already been discussed. It depends on annual production compared to annual wear and tear, and thus, on the unhampered market, the supply of money-proper changes only slowly. As for uncovered money-substitutes, since they are essentially a phenomenon of the hampered rather than the free market, factors governing their supply will be further discussed below, in chapter 12.

In the meanwhile, however, let us analyze a little further the difference between a 100%-reserve and a fractional-reserve bank. The Star Bank, let us suppose, is a 100%-reserve bank; it is established with 100 gold ounces of capital invested by its stockholders in building and equipment. In the familiar balance sheet, with assets on the left-hand side and liabilities and capital on the right-hand side, the condition of the bank now appears as follows:

I. Star Bank

Assets		Liabilities	
Equipment	100 oz.		
		Capital	100 oz.

The Star Bank is ready to begin operations. Several people now come and deposit gold in the bank, which in return issues warehouse receipts giving the depositors (the true owners of the gold) the right to redeem their property on demand at any time. Let us assume that after a few months 5,000 gold ounces have been deposited and stored in the bank's vaults. Its balance sheet now appears as follows:

II. Star Bank

Assets		Liabilities	
Gold	5,000 oz.	Warehouse Receipts	5,000 oz.
Equipment	100 oz.		
	5,100 oz.		
		Capital	100 oz.
			5,100 oz.

The warehouse receipts function and exchange as money-substitutes, *replacing,* not adding to, the gold stored in the bank. All the warehouse receipts are money certificates, 100% reserve has been maintained, and no invasion of the free market has occurred. The warehouse receipts may take the form of printed tickets (notes) or book credit (demand deposits) transferable by written order or "check." The two are economically identical.

But now suppose that law enforcement is lax and the bank sees that it can make money easily by engaging in fraud, i.e., by lending some of the depositors' gold (or, rather, issuing pseudo warehouse receipts for nonexistent gold and lending them) to people who wish to borrow it.[32] Let us say that the Star Bank, chafing at the mere interest return earned on its fees for warehouse service, prints 1,000 ounces of pseudo warehouse receipts and lends them on the credit market to businesses and consumers who desire to borrow money. The balance sheet of the Star Bank is now as follows:

III. Star Bank

Assets		Liabilities	
Gold	5,000 oz.	Warehouse Receipts	6,000 oz.
IOU's from debtors	1,000 oz.		
Equipment	100 oz.		
	6,100 oz.		
		Capital	100 oz.
			6,100 oz.

The warehouse receipts still function as money-substitutes on the market. And we see that new money has been created by the bank out of thin air, as if by magic. This process of money creation has also been called the "monetization of debt," an apt term since it describes the only instance where a *liability* can be transformed into money—the supreme *asset.* It is obvious that the more money the bank creates, the more profits it will earn, for any income earned on newly created money is a pure unalloyed gain. The bank has been able to alter the conditions of the free market system, in which money can be obtained only by purchase, mining, or gift. In each of these routes, productive service—either one's own or one's ancestor's or benefactor's—was necessary in order to obtain money. The bank's inflationary intervention has created another route to money: the creation of new money out of thin air, by issuing receipts for nonexistent gold.[33, 34]

D. A Note on Some Criticisms of 100% Reserve

One popular criticism of 100% bank reserves charges that the bank could not then earn any income or cover costs of storage, printing, etc. On the contrary, a bank is perfectly capable of operating like any goods warehouse, i.e., by charging its customers for its services to them and reaping the usual interest return on its operations.

Another popular objection is that a 100%-reserve policy would eliminate all credit. How would businessmen be able to borrow funds for short-term investment? The answer is that businessmen can still borrow *saved funds* from any individual or institution. "Banks" may still lend their own saved funds (capital stock and accumulated surplus) or they may borrow funds from individuals and relend them to business firms, earning the interest differential.[35] Borrowing money (e.g., floating a bond) is a credit transaction; an individual exchanges his present money for a bond—a claim on future money. The borrowing bank pays him interest for this loan and in turn exchanges the money thus gathered for promises by business borrowers to pay money in the future. This is a further credit transaction, in this case the bank acting as the lender and businesses as the borrowers. The bank's income is the interest differential between the two types of credit transactions; the payment is for the services of the bank as an intermediary, channeling the savings of the public into investment. There is, furthermore, no particular reason why the *short-term,* more than any other, credit market should be subsidized by money creation.

Finally, an important criticism of a governmentally enforced policy of 100% reserves is that this measure, though beneficial in itself, would establish a precedent for other governmental intervention in the monetary system, including a change in this very requirement by government edict. These critics advocate "free banking," i.e., no governmental interference with banking apart from enforcing payment of obligations, the banks to be permitted to engage in any fictitious issues they desire. Yet the free market does not mean freedom to commit fraud or any other form of theft. Quite the contrary. The criticism may be obviated by imposing a 100%-reserve requirement, not as an arbitrary administrative fiat of the government, but as part of the general legal defense of property against fraud. As Jevons stated: "It used to be held as a general rule of law, that any present grant or assignment of goods not in existence is without operation," [36] and this general rule need only be revived and enforced to outlaw fictitious money-substitutes. Then banking could be left perfectly free and yet be without departure from 100% reserves.[37]

7. *Gains and Losses during a Change in the Money Relation*

A change in the money relation necessarily involves gains and losses because money is not neutral and price changes do not take place simultaneously. Let us assume—and this will rarely hold in practice—that the final equilibrium position resulting from a change in the money relation is the same in all respects (including relative prices, individual values, etc.) as the previous equilibrium, except for the change in the purchasing power of money. Actually, as we shall see, there will almost undoubtedly be many changes in these factors in the new equilibrium situation. But even if there is not, the *movement* of prices from one equilibrium position to the next will not take place smoothly and simultaneously. It will *not* take place according to the famous example of David Hume and John Stuart Mill, where everyone awakens to find his money supply doubled overnight. Changes in the demand for money or the stock of money occur in step-by-step fashion, first having their effect in one area of the economy and then in the next. Because the market is a complex interacting network, and because some people react more quickly than others, movements of prices will differ in the speed of reaction to the changed situation.

As we have intimated above, the following law can be enunciated: When a change in the money relation causes prices to rise, the man whose selling price rises before his buying prices gains, and the man whose buying prices rise first, loses. The one who gains the most from the transition period is the one whose selling price rises first and buying prices last. Conversely, when prices fall, the man whose buying prices fall before his selling price gains, and the man whose selling price falls before his buying prices, loses.

It should be evident, in the first place, that there is nothing about rising prices that causes gains or about falling prices that causes losses. In either situation, some people gain and some people lose from the change, the gainers being the ones with the greatest and lengthiest positive differential between their selling and their buying prices, and the losers the ones with the greatest and longest negative differential in these movements. Which people gain and which lose from any given change is an empirical question, dependent on the location of changes in elements of the money relation, institutional conditions, anticipations, speeds of reaction, etc.

Let us consider the gains and losses from an increase in money stock. Suppose that we start from a position of monetary equilibrium. Every person's money relation is in equilibrium, with his stock of and demand for money being equal. Now suppose that Mr. Jones finds some new gold never known before. A change in Jones' data has taken place. He now has an excess stock of gold in his cash balance compared with his demand for it. Jones acts to spend his excess cash balance. This new money is spent, let us say, on the products of Smith. Smith now finds that his cash balance exceeds his demand for money, and he spends his excess on the products of someone else.

Jones' increased supply also increases Smith's selling price and income. Smith's selling price has increased before his buying price. He spends the money on the products of Robinson, thus raising the latter's selling prices while most buying prices have not risen. As the money is transferred from hand to hand, buying prices rise more and more. Robinson's selling price increases, for example, but already one of the products he buys—Smith's—has gone up. As the process continues, more and more buying prices rise. The individuals who are far down "on the list" to receive the new money, therefore, find that their buying prices have increased while their selling prices have not yet done so.

Of course, the changes in the money supply and in prices may well be insignificant. But this process occurs, however large or small the change in the money stock. Obviously, the larger the increase in money stock, the greater, *ceteris paribus,* will be its impact on prices.

We have seen above that an increase in the stock of money leads to a fall in the PPM, and a decrease in the stock of money leads to a rise in the PPM. However, there is no simple and uneventful rise and fall in the PPM. For a change in the stock of money is not automatically simultaneous. *New money enters the system at some specific point* and then becomes diffused in this way throughout the economy. The individuals who receive the new money first are the greatest gainers from the increased money; those who receive it last are the greatest losers, since all their buying prices have increased before their selling prices. Monetarily, it is clear that the gains of the approximate first half of the recipients of new money are exactly counterbalanced by the losses of the second half. Conversely, if money should somehow disappear from the system, say through wear and tear or through being misplaced, the initial loser cuts his spending and suffers most, while the last who feel the impact of a decreased money supply gain the most. For a decrease in the money supply results in losses for the first owners, who suffer a cut in selling price before their buying prices are lowered, and gains for the last, who see their buying prices fall before their income is cut.[88]

This analysis bears out our assertion above that there is no social utility in an increased supply, nor any social disutility in a decreased supply, of money. This is true for the transition period as well. An increase in gold is socially useful (i.e., beneficial to some without demonstrably injuring others) only to the extent that it makes possible an increase in the nonmonetary, direct use of gold.

If, as we have been assuming, relative prices and valuations remain the same for all throughout, the new equilibrium will be identical with the old except for an all-round price change. In that case, the gains and losses will be temporary, disappearing upon the advent of the new equilibrium. Actually, however, this will almost never occur. For even if people's values remain frozen, the shift in relative money income during the transition itself changes the structure of demand. The gainers of wealth during the transition period will have a structure of preferences and demand different from that of the losers. As a result, demand itself will shift in structure, and the new equilibrium will have a different set of relative prices. Similarly, the change will probably not be neutral to time preferences. The permanent gainers will undoubtedly have a different structure of time preferences from that of the permanent losers, and, as a result, there may be a permanent shift in general time preferences. What the shift will be or in which direction, it is of course impossible for economics to say.

Money changes have this "driving force," it may be noted, even in the fanciful case of the automatic overnight doubling of the supply of everyone's cash balance. For the fact that everyone's money stock doubles does not at all mean that *all prices* will automatically double! Each individual has a differently shaped demand-for-money schedule, and it is impossible to predict *how* each will be shaped. Some will spend proportionately more of their new money, and others will keep proportionately more in their cash balance. Many people will tend to spend their new cash balances on different goods from those they had bought with their old money. As a result, the structure of demand will change, and a decreased PPM will not double all prices; some will increase by more and some by less than double.[39]

8. *The Determination of Prices: The Goods Side and the Money Side*

We are now in a position to draw together all the strands determining the prices of goods. In chapters 4 through 9 we analyzed all the determinants of the prices of particular goods. In this chapter we have analyzed the determination of the purchasing power of money. Now we can see how both sets of determinants blend together.

A particular price, as we have seen, is determined by the total demand for the good (exchange and reservation) and the stock of the good, increasing as the former increases and decreasing as the latter increases. We may therefore call the demand a "factor of increase" of the price, and the stock a "factor of decrease." The *exchange* demand for each good—the amount of money that will be spent in exchange for the good—equals the stock of money in the society minus the following: the exchange demands for all other goods and the reservation demand for money. In short, the amount spent on *X* good equals the total money supply minus the amount spent on other goods and the amount kept in cash balances.

Suppose we overlook the difficulties involved and now consider the price of "all goods," i.e., the reciprocal of the purchasing power of money. The price of goods-in-general will now be determined by the monetary demand for all goods (factor of increase) and the stock of all goods (factor of decrease). Now, when all goods are considered, the exchange demand for goods equals the stock of money minus the reservation demand for money. (In contrast to any specific good, there is no need to subtract people's expenditures on *other* goods.) The total demand for goods, then, equals the stock of money minus the reservation demand for money, plus the reservation demand for all goods.

The ultimate determinants of the price of all goods are: the stock of money and the reservation demand for goods (factors of increase), and the stock of all goods and the reservation demand for money (factors of decrease). Now let us consider the obverse side: the PPM. The PPM, as we have seen, is determined by the demand for money (factor of increase) and the stock of money (factor of decrease). The exchange demand for money equals the stock of all goods minus the reservation demand for all goods. Therefore, the ultimate determinants of the PPM are: the stock of all goods and the reservation demand for money (factors of increase), and the stock of money and the reservation demand for goods (factors of decrease). We see that this is the exact obverse of the determinants of the price of all goods, which, in turn, is the reciprocal of the PPM.

Thus, the analysis of the money side and the goods side of prices is completely harmonious. No longer is there need for an arbitrary division between a barter-type analysis of relative goods-prices and a holistic analysis of the PPM. Whether we treat one good or all goods, the price or prices will *increase, ceteris paribus,* if the stock of money increases; *decrease* when the stock of the good or goods increases; *decrease* when the reservation demand for money increases; and *increase* when the reservation demand for the good or goods increases. For each individual good, the price will also increase when the specific demand for that good increases; but unless this is a reflection of a drop in the social reservation demand for money, this changed demand will also signify a decreased demand for some other good, and a consequent fall in the price of the latter. Hence, changes in specific demands will not change the value of the PPM.

In a progressing economy, the secular trend for the four determining factors is likely to be: the *money stock* increasing gradually as gold production adds to the previous total; the *stock of goods* increasing as capital investment accumulates; the *reservation demand for goods* disappearing because short-run speculations disappear over the long run, and this is the main reason for such a demand; the *reservation demand for money* unknown, with clearing, for example, working to reduce this demand over a period of time, and the greater number of transactions tending to increase it. The result is that we cannot precisely say how the PPM will move in a progressing economy, though the best summary guess would be that it declines as a result of the influence of the increased stock of goods. Certainly, the influence of the *goods* side is in the direction of falling prices; the money side we cannot predict.

Thus, the ultimate determinants of the PPM as well as of specific prices are the subjective *utilities* of individuals (the determinants of demand) and the given objective stocks of goods—

thereby vindicating the Austrian-Wicksteedian theory of price for all aspects of the economic system.

A final note of warning: It is necessary to remember that *money can never be neutral.* One set of conditions tending to raise the PPM can never precisely offset another set of factors tending to lower it. Thus, suppose that an increase in the stock of goods tends to raise the PPM, while at the same time, an increase in the money supply tends to lower it. One change can never offset the other; for one change will lower one set of prices more than others, while the other will raise a different set within the whole array of prices. The degrees of change in the two cases will depend on the particular goods and individuals affected and on their concrete valuations. Thus, even if we can make an historical (*not* an economic-scientific) judgment that the PPM has remained roughly the same, the price relations have shifted within the array, and therefore the judgment can never be exact.

9. *Interlocal Exchange*

A. UNIFORMITY OF THE GEOGRAPHIC PURCHASING POWER OF MONEY

The price of any commodity tends to be the same throughout the entire area using it. We have seen that this rule is not violated by the fact that cotton in Georgia, for example, is priced lower than cotton in New York. When cotton in New York is a consumers' good, cotton in Georgia is a *capital good* in relation to the former. Cotton in Georgia is not the same commodity as cotton in New York because goods must first be processed in one location and then transported to the places where they are consumed.

Money is no exception to the rule that the price of every commodity will tend to be uniform throughout the entire area in which it is used. In fact, the scope for the money commodity is broader. Other commodities are produced in certain centers and must then be transported to other centers where they are consumed. They are therefore not the same "good" in different geographical locations; in the producing centers they are *capital goods*. Money, it is true, must first be mined and then shipped to places of use. But, once mined, the money commodity is used only for exchange. For these purposes, it is from then on shipped back and forth throughout the world market. Therefore, there is no really important capital-good location for money separate from a consumers'-good location. Whereas all other goods are first produced and then moved to the place where they are used and consumed, money is used interchangeably throughout the entire market area, moving back and forth. Therefore, the tendency toward geographical uniformity in the purchasing power of money holds true for the physical commodity gold or silver, and there is no need for that commodity to be treated as a different good in one place or another.

The purchasing power of money will therefore be identical over the entire area. Should the PPM be lower in New York than in Detroit, the supply of money for the exchange of goods will diminish in New York and increase in Detroit. Prices of goods being higher in New York than in Detroit, people will spend less in New York and more in Detroit than heretofore, this shift being reflected in the movement of money. This action will tend to raise the purchasing power of money in New York and lower it in Detroit, until its purchasing power in the two places is equal. The purchasing power of money will, in this way, tend to remain equal in all places where the money is used, whether or not national boundaries happen to intervene.

Some people contend that, on the contrary, there *do* exist permanent differences in the purchasing power of money from place to place. For example, they point to the fact that prices for food in restaurants are higher in New York City than in Peoria. For most people, however, New York has certain definite advantages over Peoria. It has a vastly wider range of goods and services available to the consumer, including theaters, concerts, colleges, high-quality jewelry and clothing, and stockbrokerage houses. There is a great difference between the commodity "restaurant service in New York" and the commodity "restaurant service in Peoria." The former allows the purchaser to remain in New York and to enjoy its various advantages. Thus, the two are distinct goods, and the fact that the price of restaurant service is greater in New York signifies that the preponderance of individuals on the market value the former more highly and consider it a commodity of higher quality.[40]

Costs of transport, however, do introduce a qualification into this analysis. Suppose that the PPM in Detroit is slightly higher than in Rochester. We would expect gold to flow from Rochester to Detroit, spending relatively more on goods in the latter place, until the PPM's are equalized. If, however, the PPM in Detroit is higher by an amount smaller than the transport cost of shipping the gold from Rochester, then relative PPM's have a leeway to differ within the zone of shipping costs of gold. It would then be too expensive to ship gold to Detroit to take advantage of the higher PPM. The interspatial PPM's may vary in either direction within this cost-of-transport margin.[41]

Many critics allege that the PPM cannot be *uniform* throughout the world because some goods are not transferable from one locale to another. Times Square or Niagara Falls, for example, cannot be transferred from one region to another; they are specific to their locale. Therefore, it is alleged, the equalization process can take place only for those goods which "enter into interregional trade"; it does not apply to the general PPM.

Plausible as it seems, this objection is completely fallacious. In the first place, disparate goods like Times Square and other main streets are *different goods,* so that there is no reason to expect them to have the same price. Secondly, so long as *one* commodity can be traded, the PPM can be equalized. The *composition* of the PPM may well be changed, but this does not refute the fact of equalization. The process of equalization can be deduced from the fact of human action, even though, as we shall see, the PPM cannot be *measured,* since its composition does not remain the same.

Finally, since any good *can* be traded, what is there to prevent, for example, Oshkosh capital from buying a building on Times Square? The Oshkosh capitalists need not literally transport a good back to Oshkosh in order to buy it and make money from their investment. Every good, then, "enters into interregional trade"; no distinction between "domestic" and "interregional" (or "international") goods can be made.

Thus, suppose the PPM is higher in Oshkosh than in New York. New Yorkers tend to buy more in Oshkosh, and Oshkoshians will buy less in New York. This does not only mean that New York will buy more Oshkosh wheat, or that Oshkosh will buy less New York clothing. It also means that New Yorkers will invest in real estate or theaters in Oshkosh, while Oshkoshians will sell some of their New York holdings.

B. CLEARING IN INTERLOCAL EXCHANGE

Clearing is particularly appropriate for interlocal transactions, since costs of transporting money from one locale to another are likely to be heavy. Bills of exchange on each town (i.e., IOU's owed by each town) can be reciprocally canceled. Suppose that there are two traders, A and B in Detroit, and two in Rochester, C and D. A sells C a refrigerator for 200 gold grams, and D sells B a TV set for 200 grams. The two debts can be cleared, and no money need be shipped from one place to the other. On the other hand, D's sale of a TV set may total 120 grams. Suppose for a moment that these are the only traders in the two communities. Then 80 grams will have to be shipped from Rochester to Detroit. In the latter case, the citizens of Detroit have, on net balance, decided to *add* to their cash holdings, while the Rochesterites have decided to diminish their cash holdings.

Economists have often described interlocal trade in terms of "gold export points" and "gold import points." The use of such expressions assumes, however, that even though two localities both use gold money, it makes sense to talk of an "exchange rate" of the money of one locality for that of another. This exchange rate is set between the margins fixed by the cost of transporting money—the "gold import" and "gold export" points. This does *not* hold true on the free market, however. On such a market, all coins and bullion are expressed in terms of weight of gold, and it makes no sense whatever to speak of an "exchange rate" of the money of one place for the same money in another. How can there be an "exchange rate" of an ounce of gold for an ounce of gold? There will be no legal tender or other laws to separate the value of the coins of one area from those of another. Therefore, there may be slight variations in the PPM in each locale, within the limits of the cost of transporting gold, but there could never be deviations from par in interlocal "exchange rates." For there are no exchange rates on the free market, except for two or more coexisting money commodities.

10. *Balances of Payments*

In chapter 3 above, we engaged in an extensive analysis of the individual's balance of payments. We saw there that an individual's *income* can be called his exports, and the physical sources of his income his *goods exported;* while his expenditures can be termed his *imports,* and the goods purchased his *goods imported.*[42] We also saw that it is nonsensical to call a man's balance of trade "favorable" if he chooses to use some of his income to add to his cash balance, or "unfavorable" if he decides to draw down his cash balance, so that expenditures are greater than income. *Every* action and exchange is favorable from the point of view of the person performing the action or exchange; otherwise he would not have engaged in it. A further conclusion is that there is no need for anyone to worry about anyone else's balance of trade.

A person's income and expenditure constitute his "balance of trade," while his credit transactions, added to this balance, comprise his "balance of payment." Credit transactions may complicate the balance, but they do not alter its essentials. When a creditor makes a loan, he adds to his "money paid" column to the extent of the loan—for purchase of a promise to pay in the future. He has purchased the debtor's promise to pay in exchange for transferring part of his present cash balance to the debtor. The debtor adds to his "money receipts" column—from the sale of a promise to pay in the future. These promises to pay may fall due at any future date decided upon by the creditor and the debtor; generally they range from a day to many years. On that date the debtor repays the loan and transfers part of his cash balance to the creditor. This will appear in the debtor's "money paid" column—for repayment of debt—and in the creditor's "money received" column—from repayment of debt. Interest payments made by the debtor to the creditor will be similarly reflected in the respective balances of payments.

More nonsense has been written about balances of payments than about virtually any other aspect of economics. This has been caused by the failure of economists to ground and build their analysis on *individual* balances of payments. Instead they have employed such cloudy, holistic concepts as the "national" balance of payment without basing them on individual actions and balances.

Balances of payments may be consolidated for many individuals, and any number of groupings may be made. In these cases, the balances of payments *only record the monetary transactions between individuals of the group and other individuals, but fail to record the exchanges of individuals within the group.*

For example, suppose that we take the consolidated balance of payments for the Antlers Lodge of Jonesville for a certain period of time. There are three lodge members A, B and C. Suppose their individual balances of payments are as indicated in Table 16.

In the consolidated balance sheet of the Antlers Lodge, the money payments between the members must of necessity cancel out. Thus,

Consolidated Balance of Payments, Antlers Lodge

Money income from "outsiders" (exports)	75 oz.	Money expenditure on goods to "outsiders" (imports)	78 oz.
Reduction of cash balance for transfer to "outsiders"	3 oz.		
	78 oz.		

The consolidated balance tells less about the activities of the members of the group than do the individual balances, since the

TABLE 16

	A	B	C	CONSOLIDATED
Money income from other lodge members.	5 oz.	2 oz.	3 oz.	10 oz.
Money income from "outsiders".	20 oz.	25 oz.	30 oz.	75 oz.
Total Money Income	25 oz.	27 oz.	33 oz.	
Money expenditures on goods of other lodge members.	2 oz.	8 oz.	0 oz.	10 oz.
Money expenditures on goods of "outsiders".	22 oz.	23 oz.	33 oz.	78 oz.
Total Money Expenditures	24 oz.	31 oz.	33 oz.	
Changes in Cash Balance	+1 oz.	−4 oz.	0 oz.	−3 oz.

exchanges *within* the group are not revealed. This discrepancy grows as the number of people grouped in the consolidated balance increases. The consolidated balance of the citizens of a large nation such as the United States conveys less information about their economic activities than is revealed by the consolidated balance of the citizens of Cuba. Finally, if we lump together all the citizens of the world engaged in exchange, their consolidated balance of payments is precisely zero. All the exchanges are internal within the group, and the consolidated balance conveys no information whatever about them. Taken together, the people of the world have zero income from "outside" and zero expenditures on "outside goods."[43]

Fallacies in thinking about foreign trade will disappear if we understand that balances of payment are merely built upon consolidated *individual* transactions and that national balances are merely an arbitrary stopping point between individual balances on the one hand and the simple zeros of a world balance of payments on the other. There is, for example, the perennial worry that a balance of trade will be permanently "unfavorable" so that gold will drain out of the region in question until none is left. Drains of gold, however, are not mysterious acts of God. They are *willed* by people, who, on net balance, wish for one reason or another to reduce their cash balances of gold. The state of the balance is simply the visible manifestation of a voluntary reduction in the cash balance in a certain region or among a certain group.

Worries about *national* balances of payment are the fallacious residue of the accident that statistics of exchange are far more available across national boundaries than elsewhere. It should be clear that the principles applying to the balance of payment of the United States are the same for one region of the country, for one state, for one city, for one block, one house, or one person. Obviously no person or group can suffer because of an "unfavorable" balance; he or the group can suffer only because of a low level of income or assets. Seemingly plausible cries that money "be kept in" the United States, that Americans not be flooded with the "products of cheap foreign labor," etc., take on a new perspective when we apply it, say, to a family of three Jones brothers. Imagine each brother exhorting the others to "buy Jones," to "keep the money circulating *within* the Jones family," to abstain from buying products made by others who earn less than the Jones family! Yet the principle of the argument is precisely the same in both cases.

Another popular argument is that a debtor group or nation cannot possibly repay its debt because its "balance of trade is in fundamental disequilibrium, being inherently unfavorable." This is taken seriously in international affairs; yet how would we regard the individual debtor who used this excuse for defaulting on his loan? The creditor would be justified in bluntly telling the debtor that all he is saying is that he would much rather spend his money income and assets on enjoyable goods and services than on repayment of his debt. Except for the usual holistic analysis, we would see that the same holds true for an international debt.

11. *Monetary Attributes of Goods*

A. QUASI MONEY

We saw in chapter 3 how one or more very easily marketable commodities were chosen by the market as media of exchange, thereby greatly increasing their marketability and becoming more and more generally used until they could be called money. We have implicitly assumed that there are one or two media that are fully marketable—always salable—and other commodities that are simply sold for money. We have omitted mention of the *degrees* of marketability of these goods. Some goods are more readily marketable than others. And some are so easily marketable that they rise practically to the status of *quasi moneys.*

Quasi moneys do not form part of the nation's money supply. The conclusive test is that they are not used to settle debts, nor are they claims to such means of payment at par. However, they are held as assets by individuals and are considered so readily marketable that an extra demand arises for them on the market. Their existence lowers the demand for money, since holders can economize on money by keeping them as assets. The price of these goods is higher than otherwise because of their quasi-monetary status.

In Oriental countries jewels have traditionally been held as quasi moneys. In advanced countries quasi moneys are usually short-term debts or securities that have a broad market and are readily salable at the highest price the market will yield. Quasi moneys include high-grade debentures, some stocks, and some wholesale commodities. Debentures used as quasi moneys have a higher price than otherwise and therefore a *lower interest yield than will accrue on other investments.*[44]

B. BILLS OF EXCHANGE

In previous sections we saw that bills of exchange are not money-substitutes, but *credit* instruments. Money-substitutes are claims to *present* money, equivalent to warehouse receipts. But some critics maintain that in Europe at the turn of the nineteenth century bills *did* circulate as money-substitutes. They circulated as final payment in advance of their due dates, their face value discounted for the period of time left for maturity. Yet these were not money-substitutes. The holder of a bill was a creditor. Each of the acceptors of the bill had to endorse its payment, and the credit standing of each endorser had to be examined to judge the soundness of the bill. In short, as Mises has stated:

> The endorsement of the bill is in fact not a final payment; it liberates the debtor to a limited degree only. If the bill is not paid then his liability is revived in a greater degree than before.[45]

Hence, the bills could not be classed as money-substitutes.

12. *Exchange Rates of Coexisting Moneys*

Up to this point we have analyzed the market in terms of a single money and its purchasing power. This analysis is valid for each and every type of medium of exchange existing on the market. But if there is *more* than one medium coexisting on the market, what determines the exchange ratios between the various media? Although on an unhampered market there is a gradual tendency for one single money to be established, this tendency works very slowly. If two or more commodities offer good facilities and are both especially marketable, they may coexist as moneys. Each will be used by people as media of exchange.

For centuries, gold and silver were two commodities that coexisted as moneys. Both had similar advantages in scarcity, desirability for nonmonetary purposes, portability, durability, etc. Gold, however, being relatively far more valuable per unit of weight, was found to be more useful for larger transactions, and silver better for smaller transactions.

It is impossible to predict whether the market would have continued indefinitely to use gold and silver or whether one would have gradually ousted the other as a general medium of exchange. For, in the late nineteenth century, most Western countries conducted a *coup d'état* against silver, to establish a monometallic standard by coercion.[46] Gold and silver could and did coexist side by side in the same countries or throughout the world market, or one could function as money in one country, and one in another. Our analysis of the exchange rate is the same in both cases.

What determines the exchange rate between two (or more) moneys? Two different kinds of money will exchange in a ratio corresponding *to the ratio of the purchasing power of each in terms of all the other economic goods.* Thus, suppose that there are two coexisting moneys, gold and silver, and the purchasing power of gold is double that of silver, i.e., that the money price of every commodity is double in terms of silver what it is in terms of gold. One ounce of gold exchanges for fifty pounds of butter, and one ounce of silver exchanges for twenty-five pounds of butter. One ounce of gold will then tend to exchange for two ounces of silver; the exchange ratio of gold and silver will tend to be 1:2. If the rate at any time deviates from 1:2, market forces will tend to re-establish the parity between the purchasing powers and the exchange rate between them. This equilibrium exchange rate between two moneys is termed the *purchasing power parity.*

Thus, suppose that the exchange rate between gold and silver is 1:3, three ounces of silver exchanging for one ounce of gold. At the same time, the purchasing power of an ounce of gold is *twice* that of silver. It will now pay people to sell commodities for gold, exchange the gold for silver, and then exchange the silver back into commodities, thereby making a clear arbitrage gain. For example, people will sell fifty pounds of butter for one ounce of gold, exchange the gold for three ounces of silver, and then exchange the silver for seventy-five pounds of butter, gaining twenty-five pounds of butter. Similar gains from this arbitrage action will take place for all other commodities.

Arbitrage will restore the exchange rate between silver and gold to its purchasing power parity. The fact that holders of gold increase their demand for silver in order to profit by the arbitrage action will make silver more expensive in terms of gold and, conversely, gold cheaper in terms of silver. The exchange rate is driven in the direction of 1:2. Furthermore, holders of commodities are increasingly demanding gold to take advantage of the arbitrage, and this raises the purchasing power of gold. In addition, holders of silver are buying more commodities to make the arbitrage profit, and this action lowers the purchasing power of silver. Hence the ratio of the purchasing powers moves from 1:2 in the direction of 1:3. The process stops when the exchange rate is again at purchasing power parity, when arbitrage gains cease. Arbitrage gains tend to eliminate themselves and to bring about equilibrium.

It should be noted that, in the long run, the movement in the purchasing powers will probably not be important in the equilibrating process. With the arbitrage gains over, demands will probably revert back to what they were formerly, and the original ratio of purchasing powers will be restored. In the above case, the equilibrium rate will likely remain at 1:2.

Thus, the exchange rate between any two moneys will tend to be at the purchasing power parity. Any deviation from the parity will tend to eliminate itself and re-establish the parity rate. This holds true for any moneys, including those used mainly in different geographical areas. Whether the exchanges of moneys occur between citizens of the same or different geographical areas makes no economic difference, except for the costs of transport. Of course, if the two moneys are used in two completely isolated geographical areas with no exchanges between the inhabitants, then there is no exchange rate between them. Whenever exchanges *do* take place, however, the rate of exchange will always tend to be set at the purchasing power parity.

It is impossible for economics to state whether, if the money market had remained free, gold and silver would have continued to circulate side by side as moneys. There has been in monetary history a curious reluctance to allow moneys to circulate at freely fluctuating exchange ratios. Whether one of the moneys or both would be used as units of account would be up to the market to decide at its convenience.[47]

13. *The Fallacy of the Equation of Exchange*

The basis on which we have been explaining the purchasing power of money and the changes in and consequences of monetary phenomena has been an analysis of individual action. The behavior of aggregates, such as the aggregate demand for money and aggregate supply, has been constructed out of their individual components. In this way, monetary theory has been integrated into general economics. Monetary theory in American economics, however (apart from the Keynesian system, which we discuss elsewhere), has been presented in entirely different terms—in the quasi-mathematical, holistic equation of exchange, derived especially from Irving Fisher. The prevalence of this fallacious approach makes a detailed critique worth while.

The classic exposition of the equation of exchange was in Irving Fisher's *Purchasing Power of Money*.[48] Fisher describes the chief purpose of his work as that of investigating "the causes determining the purchasing power of money." Money is a generally acceptable medium of exchange, and purchasing power is rightly defined as the "quantities of other goods which a given quantity of goods will buy." [49] He explains that the lower the prices of goods, the larger will be the quantities that can be bought by a given amount of money, and therefore the greater the purchasing power of money. *Vice versa* if the prices of goods rise. This is correct; but then comes this flagrant *non sequitur:* "In short, the purchasing power of money is the reciprocal of the level of prices; so that the study of the purchasing power of money is identical with the study of price levels." [50] From then on, Fisher proceeds to investigate the causes of the "price level"; thus, by a simple "in short," Fisher has leaped from the real world of an array of individual prices for an innumerable list of concrete goods into the misleading fiction of a "price level," without discussing the grave difficulties which any such concept must face. The fallacy of the "price level" concept will be treated further below.

The "price level" is allegedly determined by three aggregative factors: the quantity of money in circulation, its "velocity of circulation"—the average number of times during a period that a unit of money is exchanged for goods—and the total volume of goods bought for money. These are related by the famous equation of exchange: $MV = PT$. This equation of exchange is built up by Fisher in the following way: First, consider an individual exchange transaction—Smith buys ten pounds of sugar for seven cents a pound.[51] An exchange has been made, Smith giving up 70 cents to Jones, and Jones transferring ten pounds of sugar to Smith. From this fact Fisher somehow deduces that "10 pounds of sugar have been regarded as *equal* to 70 cents, and this fact may be expressed thus: 70 cents = 10 pounds multiplied by 7 cents a pound." [52] This off-hand assumption of equality is not self-evident, as Fisher apparently assumes, but a tangle of fallacy and irrelevance. *Who* has "regarded" the ten pounds of sugar as *equal* to the seventy cents? Certainly not Smith, the buyer of the sugar. He bought the sugar precisely because he considered the two quantities as *unequal* in value; to him the value of the sugar was greater than the value of the seventy cents, and that is why he made the exchange. On the other hand, Jones, the seller of the sugar, made the exchange precisely because the values of the two goods were *unequal in the opposite direction,* i.e., he valued the seventy cents more than he did the sugar. There is thus never any equality of values on the part of the two participants. The assumption that an exchange presumes some sort of equality has been a delusion of economic theory since Aristotle, and it is surprising that Fisher, an exponent of the subjective theory of value in many respects, fell into the ancient trap. There is certainly no equality of values between two goods exchanged or, as in this case, between the money and the good. Is there an equality in anything else, and can Fisher's doctrine be salvaged by finding such an equality? Obviously not; there is no equality in weight, length, or any other magnitude. But to Fisher, the equation represents an equality in value between the "money side" and the "goods side"; thus, Fisher states: "The total money paid is equal in value to the total value of the goods bought. The equation thus has a money side and a goods side. The money side is the total money paid . . . The goods side is made up of the products of the quantities of goods exchanged multiplied by respective prices." [53]

We have seen, however, that even for the individual exchange, and setting aside the holistic problem of "total exchanges," there is no such "equality" that tells us anything about the facts of economic life. There is no "value-of-money side" equaling a "value-of-goods side." The equal sign is illegitimate in Fisher's equation.

How, then, account for the general acceptance of the equal sign and the equation? The answer is that, mathematically, the equation is of course an obvious truism: 70 cents = 10 pounds of sugar × 7 cents per pound of sugar. In other words, 70 cents = 70 cents. But this truism conveys no knowledge of economic fact whatsoever.[54] Indeed, it is possible to discover an endless number of such equations, on which esoteric articles and books could be published. Thus:

$$70 \text{ cents} = 100 \text{ grains of sand} \times \frac{\text{number of students in a class}}{100 \text{ grains of sand}} + 70 \text{ cents} - \text{number of students in a class.}$$

Then, we could say that the "causal factors" determining the quantity of money are: the number of grains of sand, the number of students in the class, and the quantity of money. What we have in Fisher's equation, in short, is *two* money sides, each identical with the other. In fact, it is an *identity* and not an equation. To say that such an equation is not very enlightening is self-evident. All that this equation tells us about economic life is that the *total money received in a transaction is equal to the total money given up in a transaction*—surely an uninteresting truism.

Let us reconsider the elements of the equation on the basis of the determinants of price, since that is our center of interest. Fisher's equation of exchange for an individual transaction can be rearranged as follows:

$$\frac{7 \text{ cents}}{1 \text{ pound of sugar}} = \frac{70 \text{ cents}}{10 \text{ pounds of sugar}}$$

Fisher considers that this equation yields the significant information that the price is *determined* by the total money spent divided by the total supply of goods sold. Actually, of course, the equation, as an equation, tells us nothing about the determinants of price; thus, we could set up an equally truistic equation:

$$\frac{7 \text{ cents}}{1 \text{ pound of sugar}} = \frac{70 \text{ cents}}{100 \text{ bushels of wheat}} \times \frac{100 \text{ bushels of wheat}}{10 \text{ pounds of sugar}}$$

This equation is just as mathematically true as the other, and, on Fisher's own mathematical grounds, we could argue cogently that Fisher has "left the important wheat price out of the equation." We could easily add innumerable equations with an infinite number of complex factors that "determine" price.

The *only* knowledge we can have of the determinants of price is the knowledge deduced logically from the axioms of praxeology. Mathematics can at best only translate our previous knowledge into relatively *un*intelligible form; or, usually, it will mislead the reader, as in the present case. The price in the sugar transaction may be made to equal any number of truistic equations; but it is determined by the supply and demand of the participants, and these in turn are governed by the utility of the two goods on the value scales of the participants in exchange. *This* is the fruitful approach in economic theory, not the sterile mathematical one. If we consider the equation of exchange as revealing the determinants of price, we find that Fisher must be implying that the determinants are the "70 cents" and the "10 pounds of sugar." But it should be clear that *things* cannot determine prices. *Things,* whether pieces of money or pieces of sugar or pieces of anything else, can never act; they cannot set prices or supply and demand schedules. All this can be done only by *human action:* only individual actors can decide whether or not to buy; only their value scales determine prices. It is this profound mistake that lies at the root of the fallacies of the Fisher equation of exchange: human action is abstracted out of the picture, and *things* are assumed to be in control of economic life. Thus, either the equation of exchange is a trivial truism—in which case, it is no better than a million other such truistic equations, and has no place in science, which rests on simplicity and economy of methods—or else it is supposed to convey some important truths about economics and the determination of prices. In that case, it makes the profound error of substituting for correct logical analysis of causes based on human action, misleading assumptions based on action by things. At best, the Fisher equation is superfluous and trivial; at worst, it is wrong and misleading, although Fisher himself believed that it conveyed important causal truths.

Thus, Fisher's equation of exchange is pernicious even for the individual transaction. How much more so when he extends it to the "economy as a whole"! For Fisher, this too was a simple step. "The equation of exchange is simply the sum of the equations involved in all individual exchanges" [55] in a period of time. Let us now, for the sake of argument, assume that there is nothing wrong with Fisher's individual equations and consider his "summing up" to arrive at the total equation for the economy as a whole. Let us also abstract from the statistical difficulties involved in discovering the magnitudes for any given historical situation. Let us look at several individual transactions of the sort that Fisher tries to build into a total equation of exchange:

A exchanges 70 cents for 10 pounds of sugar
B exchanges 10 dollars for 1 hat
C exchanges 60 cents for 1 pound of butter
D exchanges 500 dollars for 1 television set.

What is the "equation of exchange" for this community of four? Obviously there is no problem in summing up the total amount of money spent: $511.30. But what about the other side of the equation? Of course, if we wish to be meaninglessly truistic, we could simply write $511.30 on the other side of the equation, without any laborious building up at all. But if we merely do this, there is no point to the whole procedure. Furthermore, as

Fisher wants to get at the determination of prices, or "the price level," he cannot rest content at this trivial stage. Yet he continues on the truistic level:

$$\$511.30 = \frac{7 \text{ cents}}{1 \text{ pound of sugar}} \times 10 \text{ pounds of sugar} + \frac{10 \text{ dollars}}{1 \text{ hat}} \times 1 \text{ hat} + \frac{60 \text{ cents}}{1 \text{ pound of butter}} \times 1 \text{ pound of butter} + \frac{500 \text{ dollars}}{1 \text{ TV set}} \times 1 \text{ TV set}$$

This is what Fisher does, and this is still the same trivial truism that "total money spent equals total money spent." This triviality is not redeemed by referring to $p \times Q$, $p' \times Q'$, etc., with each p referring to a price and each Q referring to the quantity of a good, so that: E = Total money spent $= pQ + p'Q' + p''Q'' + \ldots$ etc. Writing the equation in this symbolic form does not add to its significance or usefulness.

Fisher, attempting to find the causes of the price level, has to proceed further. We have already seen that even for the individual transaction, the equation $p = (E/Q)$ (price equals total money spent divided by the quantity of goods sold) is only a trivial truism and is erroneous when one tries to use it to analyze the *determinants* of price. (This is the equation for the price of sugar in Fisherine symbolic form.) How much worse is Fisher's attempt to arrive at such an equation for the whole community and to use this to discover the *determinants* of a mythical "price level"! For simplicity's sake, let us take only the two transactions of A and B, for the sugar and the hat. Total money spent, E, clearly equals \$10.70, which, of course, equals total money received, $pQ + p'Q'$. But Fisher is looking for an equation to explain the price level; therefore he brings in the concept of an "average price level," P, and a total quantity of goods sold, T, such that E is supposed to equal PT. But the transition from the trivial truism $E = pQ + p'Q' \ldots$ to the equation $E = PT$ cannot be made as blithely as Fisher believes. Indeed, if we are interested in the explanation of economic life, it cannot be made at all.

For example, for the two transactions (or for the four), *what* is *T*? How can 10 pounds of sugar be added to 1 hat or to 1 pound of butter, to arrive at *T*? Obviously, no such addition can be performed, and therefore Fisher's holistic *T*, the total physical quantity of all goods exchanged, is a meaningless concept and cannot be used in scientific analysis. If *T* is a meaningless concept, then *P* must be also, since the two presumably vary inversely if *E* remains constant. And what, indeed, of *P*? Here, we have a whole array of prices, 7 cents a pound, $10 a hat, etc. What is the price *level?* Clearly, there is no price level here; there are only individual prices of specific goods. But here, error is likely to persist. Cannot prices in some way be "averaged" to give us a working definition of a price level? This is Fisher's solution. Prices of the various goods are in some way averaged to arrive at *P*, then $P = (E/T)$, and all that remains is the difficult "satistical" task of arriving at *T*. However, the concept of an average for prices is a common fallacy. It is easy to demonstrate that *prices can never be averaged* for different commodities; we shall use a simple average for our example, but the same conclusion applies to any sort of "weighted average" such as is recommended by Fisher or by anyone else.

What is an average? Reflection will show that for several things to be averaged together, they must first be totaled. In order to be thus added together, the things must have some *unit in common,* and it must be this unit that is added. Only homogeneous units can be added together. Thus, if one object is 10 yards long, a second is 15 yards long, and a third 20 yards long, we may obtain an average length by adding together the number of yards and dividing by three, yielding an average length of 15 yards. Now, money prices are in terms of ratios of units: cents per pound of sugar, cents per hat, cents per pound of butter, etc. Suppose we take the first two prices:

$$\frac{\text{7 cents}}{\text{1 pound sugar}} \quad \text{and} \quad \frac{\text{1000 cents}}{\text{1 hat}}$$

Can these two prices be averaged in any way? Can we add 1,000 and 7 together, get 1,007 cents, and divide by something to get a price level? Obviously not. Simple algebra demonstrates that the only way to add the ratios in terms of cents (certainly there is no other common unit available) is as follows:

$$\frac{\text{(7 hats and 1000 pounds of sugar) cents}}{\text{(hats) (pounds of sugar)}}$$

Obviously, neither the numerator nor the denominator makes sense; the units are incommensurable.

Fisher's more complicated concept of a weighted average, with the prices weighted by the quantities of each good sold, solves the problem of units in the numerator but *not* in the denominator:

$$P = \frac{pQ + p'Q' + p''Q''}{Q + Q' + Q''}$$

The pQ's are all money, but the Q's are still different units. Thus any concept of average price level involves adding or multiplying quantities of completely different units of goods, such as butter hats, sugar, etc., and is therefore meaningless and illegitimate Even pounds of sugar and pounds of butter cannot be added together, because they are two different goods and their valuation is completely different. And if one is tempted to use poundage as the common unit of quantity, what is the pound weight of a concert or a medical or legal service? [56]

It is evident that PT, in the total equation of exchange, is a completely fallacious concept. While the equation $e = pQ$ for an individual transaction is at least a trivial truism, although not very enlightening, the equation $E = PT$ for the whole society is a *false* one. Neither P nor T can be defined meaningfully, and this would be necessary for this equation to have any validity. We are left only with $E = pQ + p'Q'$, etc., which gives us only the useless truism, $E = E$.[57]

Since the P concept is completely fallacious, it is obvious that Fisher's use of the equation to reveal the determinants of prices is also fallacious. He states that if E doubles, and T remains the same, P—the price level—must double. On the holistic level, this is not even a truism; it is false, because neither P nor T can be meaningfully defined. All we can say is that when E doubles, E doubles. For the individual transaction, the equation is at least meaningful; if a man now spends $1.40 on 10 pounds of sugar, it is obvious that the price has doubled from 7 cents to 14 cents a pound. Still, this is only a mathematical truism, telling us nothing of the real causal forces at work. But Fisher never attempted to use this individual equation to explain the determinants of individual prices; he recognized that the logical analysis of supply and demand is far superior here. He used only the *holistic* equation, which he felt explained the determinants of the price level and was uniquely adapted to such an explanation. Yet the holistic equation is false, and the price level remains pure myth, an indefinable concept.

Let us consider the other side of the equation, $E = MV$, the average quantity of money in circulation in the period, multiplied by the average velocity of circulation. V is an absurd concept. Even Fisher, in the case of the other magnitudes, recognized the necessity of building up the total from individual exchanges. He was not successful in building up T out of the individual Q's, P out of the individual p's, etc., but at least he *attempted* to do so. But in the case of V, *what is the velocity of an individual transaction?* Velocity is not an independently defined variable. Fisher, in fact, can derive V only as being equal in every instance and every period to E/M. If I spend in a certain hour $10 for a hat, and I had an average cash balance (or M) for that hour of $200, then, by definition, my V equals $1/20$. I had an average quantity of money in my cash balance of $200, each dollar turned over on the average of one-twentieth of a time, and consequently I spent $10 in this period. But it is absurd to dignify any quantity with a place in an equation *unless it can be defined independently of the other terms in the equation.* Fisher compounds the absurdity by setting up M and V as independent determinants of E, which permits him to go to his desired conclusion that if M doubles, and V and T remain constant, P—the price level—will also double. But since V is defined as equal to E/M, what we actually have is: $M \times (E/M) = PT$ or simply, $E = PT$, our original equation. Thus, Fisher's attempt to arrive at a quantity equation with the price level approximately proportionate to the quantity of money is proved vain by yet another route.

A group of Cambridge economists—Pigou, Robertson, etc.—has attempted to rehabilitate the Fisher equation by eliminating V and substituting the idea that the total supply of money equals the total demand for money. However, their equation is not a particular advance, since they keep the fallacious holistic concepts of P and T, and their k is merely the reciprocal of V, and suffers from the latter's deficiencies.

In fact, since V is not an independently defined variable, M must be eliminated from the equation as well as V, and the Fisherine (and the Cambridge) equation cannot be used to demonstrate the "quantity theory of money." And since M and V must disappear, there are an infinite number of other "equations of exchange" that we could, with equal invalidity, uphold as "determinants of the price level." Thus, the aggregate stock of sugar in the economy may be termed S, and the ratio of E to the total stock of sugar may be called "average sugar turnover," or U. This new "equation of exchange" would be: $SU = PT$, and the stock of sugar would suddenly become a major determinant of the price level. Or we could substitute A = number of salesmen in the country, and X = total expenditures per salesman, or "salesmen turnover," to arrive at a new set of "determinants" in a new equation. And so on.

This example should reveal the fallacy of equations in economic theory. The Fisherine equation has been popular for many years because it has been thought to convey useful economic knowledge. It *appears* to be demonstrating the plausible (on *other* grounds) quantity theory of money. Actually, it has only been misleading.

There are other valid criticisms that could be made of Fisher: his use of index numbers, which even at best could only measure a change in a variable, but never define its actual position; his use of an index of T defined in terms of P and of P defined in terms of T; his denial that money is a commodity; the use of mathematical equations in a field where there can be no constants and therefore no quantitative predictions. In particular, even if the equation of exchange were valid in all other respects, it could at best only describe statically the conditions of an average period. It could never describe the path from one static condition to another. Even Fisher admitted this by conceding that a change in *M* would always affect *V*, so that the influence of *M* on *P* could not be isolated. He contended that after this "transition" period, *V* would revert to a constant and the effect on *P* would be proportional. Yet there is no reasoning to support this assertion. At any rate, enough has been shown to warrant expunging the equation of exchange from the economic literature.

14. *The Fallacy of Measuring and Stabilizing the PPM*

A. MEASUREMENT

In olden times, before the development of economic science, people naively assumed that the value of money remained always unchanged. "Value" was assumed to be an objective quantity inhering in things and their relations, and money was the measure, the fixed yardstick, of the values of goods and their changes. The value of the monetary unit, its purchasing power with respect to other goods, was assumed to be fixed.[58] The analogy of a fixed standard of measurement, which had become familiar to the natural sciences (weight, length, etc.), was unthinkingly applied to human action.

Economists then discovered and made clear that money does not remain stable in value, that the PPM does not remain fixed. The PPM can and does vary, in response to changes in the supply of or the demand for money. These, in turn, can be resolved into the stock of goods and the total demand for money. Individual money prices, as we have seen in section 8 above, are determined by the stock of and demand for money as well as by the stock of and demand for each good. It is clear, then, that the money relation and the demand for and the stock of each individual good are intertwined in each particular price transaction. Thus, when Smith decides whether or not to purchase a hat for two gold ounces, he weighs the utility of the hat against the utility of the two ounces. Entering into every price, then, is the stock of the good, the stock of money, and the demand for money and the good (both ultimately based on individuals' utilities). The money relation is *contained in* particular price demands and supplies and cannot, in practice, be separated from them. If, then, there is a change in the supply of or demand for money, the change will *not* be neutral, but will affect different specific demands for goods and different prices in varying proportions. There is no way of separately measuring changes in the PPM and changes in the specific prices of goods.

The fact that the use of money as a medium of exchange enables us to calculate relative exchange ratios between the different goods exchanged against money has misled some economists into believing that separate measurement of changes in the PPM is possible. Thus, we could say that 1 hat is "worth," or can exchange for, 100 pounds of sugar, or that 1 TV set can exchange for 50 hats. It is a temptation, then, to forget that these exchange ratios are purely hypothetical and can be realized in practice only through monetary exchanges, and to consider them as constituting some barter-world of their own. In this mythical world, the exchange ratios between the various goods are somehow determined separately from the monetary transactions, and it then becomes more plausible to say that some sort of method can be found of isolating the value of money from these relative values and establishing the former as a constant yardstick. Actually, this barter-world is a pure figment; these relative ratios are only historical expressions of past transactions that can be effected only by and with money.

Let us now assume that the following is the array of prices in the PPM on day 1:

10 cents per pound of sugar.
10 dollars per hat.
500 dollars per TV set.
5 dollars per hour legal service of Mr. Jones, lawyer.

Now suppose the following array of prices of the same goods on day 2:

15 cents per pound of sugar.
20 dollars per hat.
300 dollars per TV set.
8 dollars per hour of Mr. Jones' legal service.

Now what can economics say has happened to the PPM over these two periods? All that we can legitimately say is that now 1 dollar can buy 1/20 of a hat instead of 1/10 of a hat, 1/300 of a TV set instead of 1/500 of a set, etc. Thus, we can describe (if we know the figures) what happened to each individual price in the market array. But how much of the price rise of the hat was due to a rise in the demand for hats and how much to a fall in the demand for money? There is no way of answering such a question. *We do not even know for certain whether the PPM has risen or declined.* All we do know is that the purchasing power of money has fallen in terms of sugar, hats, and legal services, and risen in terms of TV sets. Even if all the prices in the array had risen we would not know by *how much* the PPM had fallen, and we would not know how much of the change was due to an increase in the demand for money and how much to changes in stocks. If the supply of money changed during this interval, we would not know how much of the change was due to the increased supply and how much to the other determinants.

Changes are taking place all the time in each of these determinants. In the real world of human action, there is no one determinant that can be used as a fixed benchmark; the whole situation is changing in response to changes in stocks of resources and products and to the changes in the valuations of all the individuals on the market. In fact, one lesson above all should be kept in mind when considering the claims of the various groups of mathematical economists: *in human action there are no quantitative constants.*[59] As a necessary corollary, all praxeological-economic laws are qualitative, not quantitative.

The *index-number* method of measuring changes in the PPM attempts to conjure up some sort of totality of goods whose exchange ratios remain constant among themselves, so that a kind of general averaging will enable a separate measurement of changes in the PPM itself. We have seen, however, that such separation or measurement is impossible.

The only attempt to use index numbers that has any plausibility is the construction of fixed-quantity weights for a base period. Each price is weighted by the quantity of the good sold in the base period, these weighted quantities representing a typical "market basket" proportion of goods bought in that period. The difficulties in such a market-basket concept are insuperable, however. Aside from the considerations mentioned above, there is in the first place *no average buyer or housewife*. There are only individual buyers, and each buyer has bought a different proportion and type of goods. If one person purchases a TV set, and another goes to the movies, each activity is the result of differing value scales, and each has different effects on the various commodities. There is no "average person" who goes partly to the movies and buys part of a TV set. There is therefore no "average housewife" buying some given proportion of a totality of goods. Goods are not bought in their totality against money, but only by individuals in individual transactions, and therefore there can be no scientific method of combining them.

Secondly, even if there were meaning to the market-basket concept, the utilities of the goods in the basket, as well as the basket proportions themselves, are always changing, and this completely eliminates any possibility of a meaningful constant with which to measure price changes. The nonexistent typical housewife would have to have constant valuations as well, an impossibility in the real world of change.

All sorts of index numbers have been spawned in a vain attempt to surmount these difficulties: quantity weights have been chosen that vary for each year covered; arithmetical, geometrical, and harmonic averages have been taken at variable and fixed weights; "ideal" formulas have been explored—all with no realization of the futility of these endeavors. No such index number, no attempt to separate and measure prices and quantities, can be valid.[60]

B. STABILIZATION

The knowledge that the purchasing power of money could vary led some economists to try to improve on the free market by creating, in some way, a monetary unit which would remain stable and constant in its purchasing power. All these stabilization plans, of course, involve in one way or another an attack on the gold or other commodity standard, since the value of gold fluctuates as a result of the continual changes in the supply of and the demand for gold. The stabilizers want the government to keep an arbitrary index of prices constant by pumping money into the economy when the index falls and taking money out when it rises. The outstanding proponent of "stable money," Irving Fisher, revealed the reason for his urge toward stabilization in the following autobiographical passage: "I became increasingly aware of the imperative need of a stable yardstick of value. I had come into economics from mathematical physics, in which fixed units of measure contribute the essential starting point." [61] Apparently, Fisher did not realize that there could be fundamental differences in the nature of the sciences of physics and of purposeful human action.

It is difficult, indeed, to understand what the advantages of a stable value of money are supposed to be. One of the most frequently cited advantages, for example, is that debtors will no longer be harmed by unforeseen rises in the value of money, while creditors will no longer be harmed by unforeseen declines in its value. Yet if creditors and debtors want such a hedge against future changes, they have an easy way out on the free market. When they make their contracts, they can agree that repayment be made in a sum of money corrected by some agreed-upon index number of changes in the value of money. Such a voluntary *tabular standard* for business contracts has long been advocated by stabilizationists, who have been rather puzzled to find that a course which appears to them so beneficial is almost never adopted in business practice. Despite the multitude of index numbers and other schemes that have been proposed to businessmen by these economists, creditors and debtors have somehow failed to take advantage of them. Yet, while stabilization plans have made no headway among the groups that they would supposedly benefit the most, the stabilizationists have remained undaunted in their zeal to force their plans on the whole society by means of State coercion.

There seem to be two basic reasons for this failure of business to adopt a tabular standard: (*a*) As we have seen, there is no scientific, objective means of measuring changes in the value of money. Scientifically, one index number is just as arbitrary and bad as any other. Individual creditors and debtors have not been able to agree on any one index number, therefore, that they can abide by as a measure of change in purchasing power. Each, according to his own interests, would insist on including different commodities at different weights in his index number. Thus, a debtor who is a wheat farmer would want to weigh the price of wheat heavily in his index of the purchasing power of money; a creditor who goes often to night clubs would want to hedge against the price of night-club entertainment, etc. (*b*) A second reason is that businessmen apparently prefer to take their chances in a speculative world rather than agree on some sort of arbitrary hedging device. Stock exchange speculators and commodity speculators are continually attempting to forecast future prices, and, indeed, all entrepreneurs are engaged in anticipating the uncertain conditions of the market. Apparently, businessmen are willing to be entrepreneurs in anticipating future changes in purchasing power as well as any other changes.

The failure of business to adopt voluntarily any sort of tabular standard seems to demonstrate the complete lack of merit in compulsory stabilization schemes. Setting this argument aside, however, let us examine the contention of the stabilizers that somehow they can create certainty in the purchasing power of money, while at the same time leaving freedom and uncertainty in the prices of *particular goods*. This is sometimes expressed in the statement: "Individual prices should be left free to change; the price level should be fixed and constant." This contention rests on the myth that some sort of general purchasing power of money or some sort of price level exists on a plane apart from specific prices in specific transactions. As we have seen, this is purely fallacious. There is no "price level," and there is no way that the exchange-value of money is manifested except in specific purchases of goods, i.e., specific prices. There is no way of separating the two concepts; any array of prices establishes at one and the same time an exchange relation or objective exchange-value between one good and another and between money and a good, and there is no way of separating these elements quantitatively.

It is thus clear that the exchange-value of money cannot be quantitatively separated from the exchange-value of goods. Since the general exchange-value, or PPM, of money cannot be quantitatively defined and isolated in any historical situation, and its changes cannot be defined or measured, it is obvious that it cannot be kept stable. If we do not know what something is, we cannot very well act to keep it constant.[62]

We have seen that the ideal of a stabilized value of money is impossible to attain or even define. Even if it were attainable, however, what would be the result? Suppose, for example, that the purchasing power of money rises and that we disregard the problem of measuring the rise. Why, if this is the result of action on an unhampered market, should we consider it a *bad* result? If the total supply of money in the community has remained constant, falling prices will be caused by a general increase in the demand for money or by an increase in the supply of goods as a result of increased productivity. An increased demand for money stems from the free choice of individuals, say, in the expectation of a more troubled future or of future price declines. Stabilization would deprive people of the chance to increase their *real* cash holdings and the real value of the dollar by free, mutually agreed-upon actions. As in any other aspect of the free market, those entrepreneurs who successfully anticipate the increased demand will benefit, and those who err will lose in their speculations. But even the losses of the latter are purely the consequence of their own voluntarily assumed risks. Furthermore, falling prices resulting from increased productivity are beneficial to all and are precisely the means by which the fruits of industrial progress spread on the free market. Any interference with falling prices blocks the spread of the fruits of an advancing economy; and then real wages could increase only in particular industries, and not, as on the free market, over the economy as a whole.

Similarly, stabilization would deprive people of the chance to *decrease* their real cash holdings and the real value of the dollar, should their demand for money fall. People would be prevented from acting on their expectations of future price increases. Furthermore, if the supply of goods should decline, a stabilization policy would prevent the price rises necessary to clear the various markets.

The intertwining of general purchasing power and specific prices raises another consideration. For money could not be pumped into the system to combat a supposed increase in the value of money without distorting the previous exchange-values between the various goods. We have seen that money cannot be neutral with respect to goods and that, therefore, the whole price structure will change with any change in the supply of money. Hence, the stabilizationist program of fixing the value of money or price level without distorting relative prices is necessarily doomed to failure. It is an impossible program.

Thus, even were it possible to define and measure changes in the purchasing power of money, stabilization of this value would have effects that many advocates consider undesirable. But the magnitudes cannot even be defined, and stabilization would depend on some sort of arbitrary index number. Whichever commodities and weights are included in the index, pricing and production will be distorted.

At the heart of the stabilizationist ideal is a misunderstanding of the nature of money. Money is considered either a mere *numeraire* or a grandiose measure of values. Forgotten is the truth that money is desired and demanded as a useful commodity, even when this use is only as a medium of exchange. When a man holds money in his cash balance, he is deriving utility from it. Those who neglect this fact scoff at the gold standard as a primitive anachronism and fail to realize that "hoarding" performs a useful social function.

15. *Business Fluctuations*

In the real world, there will be continual changes in the pattern of economic activity, changes resulting from shifts in the tastes and demands of consumers, in resources available, technological knowledge, etc. That prices and outputs fluctuate, therefore, is to be expected, and absence of fluctuation would be unusual. *Particular* prices and outputs will change under the impact of shifts in demand and production conditions; the general level of production will change according to individual time preferences. Prices will all tend to move in the same direction, instead of shifting in different directions for different goods, whenever there is a change in the *money relation.* Only a change in the supply of or demand for money will transmit its impulses throughout the entire monetary economy and impel prices in a similar direction, albeit at varying rates of speed. General price fluctuations can be understood only by analyzing the money relation.

Yet simple fluctuations and changes do not suffice to explain that terrible phenomenon so marked in the last century and a half—the "business cycle." The business cycle has had certain definite features which reveal themselves time and again. First, there is a boom period, when prices and productive activity expand. There is a greater boom in the heavy capital-goods and higher-order industries—such as industrial raw materials, machine goods, and construction, and in the markets for titles to these goods, such as the stock market and real estate. Then, suddenly, without warning, there is a "crash." A financial panic with runs on banks ensues, prices fall very sharply, and there is a sudden piling up of unsold inventory, and particularly a revelation of great excess capacity in the higher-order capital-goods industries. A painful period of liquidation and bankruptcy follows, accompanied by heavy unemployment, until recovery to normal conditions gradually takes place.

This is the empirical pattern of the modern business cycle. Historical events can be explained by laws of praxeology, which isolate causal connections. Some of these events can be explained by laws that we have learned: a general price rise could result from an increase in the supply of money or from a fall in demand, unemployment from insistence on maintaining wage rates that have suddenly increased in real value, a reduction in unemployment from a fall in real wage rates, etc. But one thing cannot be explained by any economics of the free market. And this is the crucial phenomenon of the crisis: *Why is there a sudden revelation of business error?* Suddenly, all or nearly all businessmen find that their investments and estimates have been in error, that they cannot sell their products for the prices which they had anticipated. This is the central problem of the business cycle, and this is the problem which any adequate theory of the cycle must explain.

No businessman in the real world is equipped with perfect foresight; all make errors. But the free market process precisely rewards those businessmen who are equipped to make a minimum number of errors. Why should there suddenly be a cluster of errors? Furthermore, why should these errors particularly pervade the capital-goods industries?

Sometimes sharp changes, such as a sudden burst of hoarding or a sudden raising of time preferences and hence a decrease in saving may arrive unanticipated, with a resulting crisis of error. But since the eighteenth century there has been an almost regular pattern of consistent clusters of error which always follow a boom and expansion of money and prices. In the Middle Ages and down to the seventeenth and eighteenth centuries, business crises rarely followed upon booms in this manner. They took place suddenly, in the midst of normal activity, and as the result of some obvious and identifiable external event. Thus, Scott lists crises in sixteenth- and early seventeenth-century England as irregular and caused by some obvious event: famine, plague, seizures of goods in war, bad harvest, crises in the cloth trade as a result of royal manipulations, seizure of bullion by the King, etc.[63] But in the late seventeenth, eighteenth and nineteenth centuries, there developed the aforementioned pattern of the business cycle, and it became obvious that the crisis and ensuing depression could no longer be attributed to some single external event or single act of government.

Since no one event could account for the crisis and depression, observers began to theorize that there must be some deep-seated defect *within* the free market economy that causes these crises and cycles. The blame must rest with the "capitalist system" itself. Many ingenious theories have been put forward to explain the business cycle as an outgrowth of the free-market economy, but none of them has been able to explain the crucial point: the cluster of errors after a boom. In fact, such an explanation can never be found, since no such cluster could appear on the free market.

The nearest attempt at an explanation stressed general swings of "overoptimism" and "overpessimism" in the business community. But put in such fashion, the theory looks very much like a *deus ex machina.* Why should hardheaded businessmen, schooled in trying to maximize their profits, suddenly fall victim to such psychological swings? In fact, the crisis brings bankruptcies regardless of the emotional state of particular entrepreneurs. We shall see in chapter 12 that feelings of optimism *do* play a role, but they are *induced* by certain objective economic conditions. We must search for the objective reasons that cause businessmen to become "overoptimistic." And they cannot be found on the free market.[64] The positive explanation of the business cycle, therefore, will have to be postponed to the next chapter.

16. *Schumpeter's Theory of Business Cycles*

Joseph Schumpeter's business cycle theory is one of the very few that attempt to integrate an explanation of the business cycle with an analysis of the entire economic system. The theory was presented in essence in his *Theory of Economic Development,* published in 1912. This analysis formed the basis for the "first approximation" of his more elaborate doctrine, presented in the two-volume *Business Cycles,* published in 1939.[65] The latter volume, however, was a distinct retrogression from the former, for it attempted to explain the business cycle by postulating three superimposed cycles (each of which was explainable according to his "first approximation"). Each of these cycles is supposed to be roughly periodic in length. They are alleged by Schumpeter to be the three-year "Kitchin" cycle; the nine-year "Juglar"; and the very long (fifty-year) "Kondratieff." These cycles are conceived as independent entities, combining in various ways to yield the aggregate cyclical pattern.[66] Any such "multicyclic" approach must be set down as a mystical adoption of the fallacy of conceptual realism. There is no reality or meaning to the allegedly independent sets of "cycles." The market is one interdependent unit, and the more developed it is, the greater the interrelations among market elements. It is therefore impossible for several or numerous independent cycles to coexist as self-contained units. It is precisely the characteristic of a business cycle that it permeates *all* market activities.

Many theorists have assumed the existence of *periodic* cycles, where the length of each successive cycle is uniform, even down to the precise number of months. The quest for periodicity is a chimerical hankering after the laws of physics; in human action there are no quantitative constants. Praxeological laws can be only qualitative in nature. Therefore, there will be no periodicity in the length of business cycles.

It is best, then, to discard Schumpeter's multicyclical schema entirely and to consider his more interesting one-cycle "approximation" (as presented in his earlier book), which he attempts to derive from his general economic analysis. Schumpeter begins his study with the economy in a state of "circular flow" equilibrium, i.e., what amounts to a picture of an evenly rotating economy. This is proper, since it is only by hypothetically investigating the disturbances of an imaginary state of equilibrium that we can mentally isolate the causal factors of the business cycle. First, Schumpeter describes the ERE, where all anticipations are fulfilled, every individual and economic element is in equilibrium, profits and losses are zero—all based on given values and resources. Then, asks Schumpeter, what can impel changes in this setup? First, there are possible changes in consumer tastes and demands. This is cavalierly dismissed by Schumpeter as unimportant.[67]

There are possible changes in population and therefore in the labor supply; but these are gradual, and entrepreneurs can readily adapt to them. Third, there can be new saving and investment. Wisely, Schumpeter sees that changes in saving-investment rates imply no business cycle; new saving will cause continuous growth. Sudden changes in the rate of saving, when *unanticipated* by the market, can cause dislocations, of course, as may *any* sudden, unanticipated change. But there is nothing *cyclic* or mysterious about these effects. Instead of concluding from this survey, as he should have done, that there *can be no business cycle* on the free market, Schumpeter turned to a fourth element, which for him was the generator of all growth as well as of business cycles—*innovation* in productive techniques.

We have seen above that innovations cannot be considered the prime mover of the economy, since innovations can work their effects only *through* saving and investment and since there are always a great many investments that could improve techniques *within* the corpus of existing knowledge, but which are not made for lack of adequate savings. This consideration alone is enough to invalidate Schumpeter's business-cycle theory.

A further consideration is that Schumpeter's own theory relies specifically for the financing of innovations on newly expanded bank credit, on new money issued by the banks. Without delving into Schumpeter's theory of bank credit and its consequences, it is clear that Schumpeter assumes a hampered market, for we have seen that there could not be any monetary credit expansion on a free market. Schumpeter therefore cannot establish a business-cycle theory for a purely unhampered market.

Finally, Schumpeter's explanation of innovations as the trigger for the business cycle necessarily assumes that there is a recurrent *cluster* of innovations that takes place in each boom period. Why should there be such a cluster of innovations? Why are innovations not more or less continuous, as we would expect? Schumpeter cannot answer this question satisfactorily. The fact that a bold few begin innovating and that they are followed by imitators does not yield a cluster, for this process could be continuous, with new innovators arriving on the scene. Schumpeter offers two explanations for the slackening of innovatory activity toward the end of the boom (a slackening essential to his theory). On the one hand, the release of new products yielded by the new investments creates difficulties for old producers and leads to a period of uncertainty and need for "rest." In contrast, in equilibrium periods, the risk of failure and uncertainty is less than in other periods. But here Schumpeter mistakes the auxiliary construction of the ERE for the real world. There is *never* in existence any actual period of certainty; *all periods are uncertain,* and there is no reason why increased production should cause more uncertainty to develop or any vague needs for rest. Entrepreneurs are always seeking profit-making opportunities, and there is no reason for any periods of "waiting" or of "gathering the harvest" to develop suddenly in the economic system.

Schumpeter's second explanation is that innovations cluster in only one or a few industries and that these innovation opportunities are therefore limited. After a while they become exhausted, and the cluster of innovations ceases. This is obviously related to the Hansen stagnation thesis, in the sense that there are alleged to be a certain limited number of "investment opportunities"—here innovation opportunities—at any time, and that once these are exhausted there is temporarily no further room for investments or innovations. The whole concept of "opportunity" in this connection, however, is meaningless. There is no limit on "opportunity" as long as wants remain unfulfilled. The only other limit on investment or innovation is saved capital available to embark on the projects. But this has nothing to do with vaguely available opportunities which become "exhausted"; the existence of saved capital is a continuing factor. As for innovations, there is no reason why innovations cannot be continuous or take place in many industries, or why the innovatory pace has to slacken.

As Kuznets has shown, a cluster of innovation must assume a cluster of entrepreneurial ability as well, and this is clearly unwarranted. Clemence and Doody, Schumpeterian disciples, countered that entrepreneurial ability *is* exhausted in the act of founding a new firm.[68] But to view entrepreneurship as simply the founding of new firms is completely invalid. Entrepreneurship is not just the founding of new firms, it is not merely innovation; it is *adjustment:* adjustment to the uncertain, changing conditions of the future.[69] This adjustment takes place, perforce, all the time and is not exhausted in any single act of investment.

We must conclude that Schumpeter's praiseworthy attempt to derive a business cycle theory from general economic analysis is a failure. Schumpeter almost hit on the right explanation when he stated that the only other explanation that could be found for the business cycle would be a cluster of *errors* by entrepreneurs, and he saw no reason, no objective cause, why there should be such a cluster of errors. That is perfectly true—for the free, unhampered market!

17. *Further Fallacies of the Keynesian System*

In the text above, we saw that even if the Keynesian functions were correct and social expenditures fell below income above a certain point and *vice versa,* this would have no unfortunate consequences for the economy. The level of national money income, and consequently of hoarding, is an imaginary bogey. In this section, we shall pursue our analysis of the Keynesian system and demonstrate further grave fallacies within the system itself. In other words, we shall see that the consumption function and investment are not ultimate determinants of social income (whereas above we demonstrated that it makes no particular difference if they are or not).

A. INTEREST AND INVESTMENT

Investment, though the dynamic and volatile factor in the Keynesian system, is also the Keynesian stepchild. Keynesians have differed on the causal determinants of investment. Originally, Keynes determined it by the interest rate as compared with the marginal efficiency of capital, or prospect for net return. The interest rate is supposed to be determined by the money relation; we have seen that this idea is fallacious. Actually, the equilibrium net rate of return *is* the interest rate, the natural rate to which the bond rate conforms. Rather than changes in the interest rate *causing* changes in investment, as we have seen before, changes in time preference are reflected in changes in consumption-investment decisions. Changes in the interest rate and in investment are two sides of a coin, both determined by individual valuations and time preferences.

The error of calling the interest rate the cause of investment changes, and itself determined by the money relation, is also adopted by such "critics" of the Keynesian system as Pigou, who asserts that falling prices will release enough cash to lower the interest rate, stimulate investment, and thus finally restore full employment.

Modern Keynesians have tended to abandon the intricacies of the relation between interest and investment and simply declare themselves agnostic on the factors determining investment. They rest their case on an alleged determination of consumption.[70]

B. THE "CONSUMPTION FUNCTION"

If Keynesians are unsure about investment, they have, until very recently, been very emphatic about consumption. Investment is a volatile, uncertain expenditure. Aggregate consumption, on the other hand, is a passive, stable "function" of immediately previous social income. Total net expenditures determining and equaling total net income in a period (gross expenditures *between* stages of production are unfortunately removed from discussion) consist of investment and consumption. Furthermore, consumption always behaves so that below a certain income level consumption will be higher than income, and above that level consumption will be lower. Fig. 82 depicts the relations among consumption, investment, expenditure, and social income.

The relation between income and expenditure is the same as shown in Fig. 78. Now we see why the Keynesians assume the expenditure curve to have a smaller slope than income. *Consumption* is supposed to have the identical slope as expenditures; for investment is unrelated to income, as the determinants are unknown. Hence, investment is depicted as having no functional relation to income and is represented as a constant gap between the expenditure and consumption lines.

The stability of the passive consumption function, as contrasted with the volatility of active investment, is a keystone of the Keynesian system. This assumption is replete with so many grave errors that it is necessary to take them up one at a time.

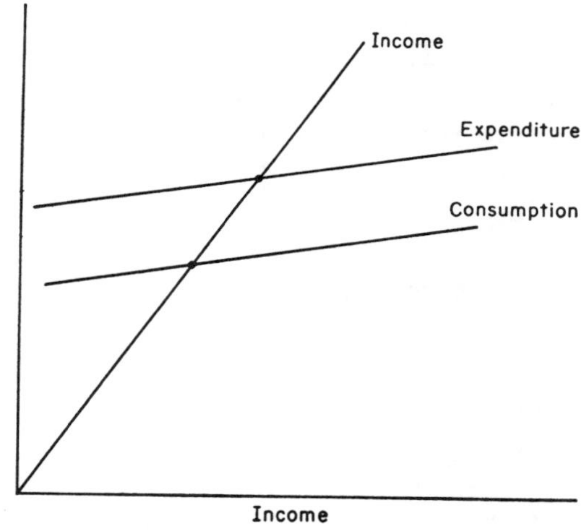

FIG. 82. RELATIONS AMONG CONSUMPTION, INVESTMENT, EXPENDITURE, AND SOCIAL INCOME, ACCORDING TO THE KEYNESIAN SYSTEM

a) How do the Keynesians justify the assumption of a stable consumption function with the shape as shown above? One route was through "budget studies"—cross-sectional studies of the relation between family income and expenditure by income groups in a given year. Budget studies such as that of the National Resources Committee in the mid-1930's yielded similar "consumption functions" with dishoardings increasing below a certain point, and hoardings above it (i.e., income below expenditures below a certain point, and expenditures below income above it).

This is supposed to intimate that those doing the "dissaving," i.e., the dishoarding, are poor people below the subsistence level who incur deficits by borrowing. But how long is this supposed to go on? How can there be a continuous deficit? Who would continue to lend these people the money? It is more reasonable to suppose that the dishoarders are *decumulating* their previously accumulated capital, i.e., that they are wealthy people whose businesses suffered losses during that year.

b) Aside from the fact that budget studies are misinterpreted, there are graver fallacies involved. For the curve given by the budget study has no relation whatever to the Keynesian consumption function! The former, at best, gives a cross section of the relation between *classes* of family expenditure and income for one year; the Keynesian consumption function attempts to establish a relation between *total* social income and total social consumption for *any* given year, holding true over a hypothetical range of social incomes. At best, one entire budget curve can be summed up to yield only *one point* on the Keynesian consumption function. Budget studies, therefore, can in no way confirm the Keynesian assumptions.

c) Another very popular device to confirm the consumption function reached the peak of its popularity during World War II. This was historical-statistical correlation of national income and consumption for a definite period of time, usually the 1930's. This correlation equation was then assumed to be the "stable" consumption function. Errors in this procedure were numerous. In the first place, even assuming such a stable relation, it would only be an *historical* conclusion, *not a theoretical law*. In physics, an experimentally determined law may be assumed to be constant for other identical situations; in human action, historical situations are never the same, and therefore there are no quantitative constants! Conditions and valuations could change at any time, and the "stable" relationship altered. There is here no proof of a stable consumption function. The dismal record of forecasts (such as those of postwar unemployment) made on this assumption should not have been surprising.

Moreover, a stable relation was not even established. Income was correlated with consumption and with investment. Since consumption is a much larger magnitude than (net) investment, no wonder that its *percentage* deviations around the regression equation were smaller! Furthermore, income is here being correlated with 80%–90% *of itself;* naturally, the "stability" is tremendous. If income were correlated with *saving,* of similar magnitude as investment, there would be no greater stability in the income-saving function than in the "income-investment function."

Thirdly, the consumption function is necessarily an *ex ante* relation; it is supposed to tell how much consumers *will* decide to spend given a certain total income. Historical statistics, on the other hand, record only *ex post* data, which give a completely different story. For any *given period of time,* for example, hoarding and dishoarding cannot be recorded *ex post.* In fact, *ex post,* on double-entry accounting records, total social income is always equal to total social expenditures. Yet, in the dynamic, *ex ante,* sense, it is precisely the *divergence* between total social income and total social expenditures (hoarding or dishoarding) that plays the crucial role in the Keynesian theory. But these divergences can never be revealed, as Keynesians believe, by study of *ex post* data. *Ex post,* in fact, saving always equals investment, and social expenditure always equals social income, so that the *ex post* expenditure line coincides with the income line.[71]

d) Actually, the whole idea of stable consumption functions has now been discredited, although many Keynesians do not fully realize this fact.[72] In fact, Keynesians themselves have admitted that, *in the long run,* the consumption function is not stable, since total consumption rises as income rises; and that *in the short run* it is not stable, since it is affected by all sorts of changing factors. But if it is not stable in the short run and not stable in the long run, what kind of stability does it have? Of what use is it? We have seen that the only really important runs are the immediate and the long-run, which shows the direction in which the immediate is tending. There is no use for some sort of separate "intermediate" situation.

e) It is instructive to turn now to the reasons that Keynes himself, in contrast to his followers, gave for assuming his stable consumption function. It is a confused exposition indeed.[73] The "propensity to consume" out of given income, according to Keynes, is determined by two sets of factors, "objective" and "subjective." It seems clear, however, that these are purely *subjective* decisions, so that there can be no separate objective *determinants.* In classifying subjective factors, Keynes makes the mistake of subsuming hoarding and investing motivations under categories of separate "causes": precaution, foresight, improvement, etc. Actually, as we have seen, the demand for money is ultimately determined by each individual for all sorts of reasons, but all tied up with uncertainty; motives for investment are to maintain and increase future standards of living. By a sleight of hand completely unsupported by facts or argument Keynes simply assumes all these subjective factors to be given in the short run, although he admits that they will change in the long run. (If they change in the long run, how can his system yield an equilibrium position?) He simply reduces the subjective motives to current economic organization, customs, standards of living, etc., and assumes them to be given.[74] The "objective factors" (which in reality are subjective, such as time-preference changes, expectations, etc.) can admittedly cause short-run changes in the consumption function (such as windfall changes in capital values). Expectations of future changes in income can affect an individual's consumption, but Keynes simply asserts without discussion that this factor "is likely to average out for the community as a whole." Time preferences are discussed in a very confused way, with interest rate and time preference assumed to be apart from and influencing the propensity to consume. Here again, short-run fluctuations are assumed to have little effect, and Keynes simply leaps to the conclusion that the propensity to consume is, in the short run, a "fairly" stable function.[75]

f) The failure of the consumption-function theory is not only the failure of a specific theory. It is a profound epistemological failure as well. For the concept of a consumption function has no place in economics at all. Economics is *praxeological,* i.e., its propositions are absolutely true given the existence of the axioms —the basic axiom being the existence of human action itself. Economics, therefore, is not and cannot be "empirical" in the positivist sense, i.e., it cannot establish some sort of empirical hypothesis which could or could not be true, and at best is only true approximately. Quantitative, empirico-historical "laws" are worthless in economics, since they may only be coincidences of complex facts, and not isolable, repeatable laws which will hold true in the future. The idea of the consumption function is not only wrong on many counts; it is irrelevant to economics.

Furthermore, the very term "function" is inappropriate in a study of human action. Function implies a quantitative, determined relationship, whereas no such quantitative determinism exists. People act and can change their actions at any time; no causal, constant, external determinants of action can exist. The term "function" is appropriate only to the unmotivated, repeatable motion of inorganic matter.

In conclusion, there is no reason whatever to assume that at some point, expenditures will be below income, while at lower points it will be above income. Economics does not and *cannot* know what *ex ante* expenditure will ever be in relation to income; at any point, it could be equal, or there could be net hoarding or dishoarding. The ultimate decisions are made by the individuals and are not determinable by science. There is, therefore, no stable expenditure function whatever.

C. THE MULTIPLIER

The once highly esteemed "multiplier" has now happily faded in popularity, as economists have begun to realize that it is simply the obverse of the stable consumption function. However, the complete absurdity of the multiplier has not yet been fully appreciated. The theory of the "investment multiplier" runs somewhat as follows:

$$\text{Social Income} = \text{Consumption} + \text{Investment}$$

Consumption is a stable function of income, as revealed by statistical correlation, etc. Let us say, for the sake of simplicity, that Consumption will always be .80 (Income).[76] In that case,

$$\begin{aligned}
&\text{Income} = .80\ (\text{Income}) + \text{Investment}.\\
&.20\ (\text{Income}) = \text{Investment; or}\\
&\text{Income} = 5\ (\text{Investment}).
\end{aligned}$$

The "5" is the "investment multiplier." It is then obvious that all we need to increase social money income by a desired amount is to increase investment by 1/5 of that amount; and the multiplier magic will do the rest. The early "pump primers" believed in approaching this goal through stimulating private investment; later Keynesians realized that if investment is an "active" volatile factor, government spending is no less active and more certain, so that government spending must be relied upon to provide the needed multiplier effect. Creating new money would be most effective, since the government would then be sure not to reduce private funds. Hence the basis for calling all government spending "investment": it is "investment" because it is not tied passively to income.

The following is offered as a far more potent "multiplier," on Keynesian grounds even more potent and effective than the investment multiplier, and *on Keynesian grounds there can be no objection to it.* It is a *reductio ad absurdum,* but it is not simply a parody, for it is in keeping with the Keynesian method.

Social Income = Income of (insert name of any person, say the reader) + Income of everyone else.

Let us use symbols:

Social Income = Y
Income of the Reader = R
Income of everyone else = V

We find that V is a completely stable function of Y. Plot the two on coordinates, and we find historical one-to-one correspondence between them. It is a tremendously stable function, far more stable than the "consumption function." On the other hand, plot R against Y. Here we find, instead of perfect correlation, only the remotest of connections between the fluctuating income of the reader of these lines and the social income. Therefore, this reader's income is the active, volatile, uncertain element in the social income, while everyone else's income is passive, stable, determined by the social income.

Let us say the equation arrived at is:

$$V = .99999\ Y$$

Then, $Y = .99999\ Y + R$

$$.00001\ Y = R$$
$$Y = 100{,}000\ R.$$

This is the reader's own personal multiplier, a far more powerful one than the investment multiplier. To increase social income and thereby cure depression and unemployment, it is only necessary for the government to print a certain number of dollars and give them to the reader of these lines. The reader's spending will prime the pump of a 100,000-fold increase in the national income.[77]

18. *The Fallacy of the Acceleration Principle*

The "acceleration principle" has been adopted by some Keynesians as their explanation of investment, then to be combined with the "multiplier" to yield various mathematical "models" of the business cycle. The acceleration principle antedates Keynesism, however, and may be considered on its own merits. It is almost always used to explain the behavior of investment in the business cycle.

The essence of the acceleration principle may be summed up in the following illustration:

Let us take a certain firm or industry, preferably first-rank producers of consumers' goods. Assume that the firm is producing an output of 100 units of a good during a certain period of time and that 10 machines of a certain type are needed in this production. If the period is a year, consumers demand and purchase 100 units of output per year. The firm has a stock of 10 machines. Suppose that the average life of a machine is 10 years. In equilibrium, the firm buys 1 machine as replacement every year (assuming it had bought a new machine every year to build up to 10).[78] Now suppose that there is a 20% increase in the consumer demand for the firm's output. Consumers now wish to purchase 120 units of output. Assuming a fixed ratio of capital investment to output, it is now necessary for the firm to have 12 machines (maintaining the ratio of 1 machine: 10 units of annual output). In order to have the 12 machines, it must buy 2 additional machines this year. Add this demand to its usual demand of 1 machine, and we see that there has been a 200% increase in demand for the machine. A 20% increase in demand for the product has caused a 200% increase in demand for the capital good. *Hence,* say the proponents of the acceleration principle, an increase in consumption demand *in general* causes an enormously magnified increase in demand for capital goods. Or rather, it causes a magnified increase in demand for "fixed" capital goods, of high *durability*. Obviously, capital goods lasting only one year would receive no magnification effect. The essence of the acceleration principle is the relationship between the increased demand and the low level of replacement demand for a durable good. The more durable the good, the greater the magnification and the greater, therefore, the acceleration effect.

Now suppose that, in the next year, consumer demand for output remains at 120 units. There has been no change in consumer demand from the second year (when it changed from 100 to 120) to the third year. And yet, the accelerationists point out, dire things are happening in the demand for fixed capital. For now there is no longer any need for firms to purchase any new machines beyond what is necessary for replacement. Needed for replacement is still only 1 machine per year. As a result, while there is zero change in demand for consumers' goods, there is a 200% *decline* in demand for fixed capital. And the former is the cause of the latter. In the long run, of course, the situation stabilizes into an equilibrium with 120 units of output and 1 unit of replacement. But in the short run there has been consequent upon a simple increase of 20% in consumer demand, first a 200% increase in the demand for fixed capital, and next a 200% decrease.

To the upholders of the acceleration principle, this illustration provides the key to some of the main features of the business cycle: the greater fluctuations of fixed capital-goods industries as compared with consumers' goods, and the mass of errors revealed by the crisis in the investment goods industries. The acceleration principle leaps boldly from the example of a single firm to a discussion of aggregate consumption and aggregate investment. Everyone knows, the advocates say, that consumption increases in a boom. This increase in consumption accelerates and magnifies increases in investment. Then, the rate of increase of consumption slows down, and a decline is brought about in investment in fixed capital. Furthermore, if consumption demand declines, then there is "excess capacity" in fixed capital—another feature of the depression.

The acceleration principle is rife with error. An important fallacy at the heart of the principle has been uncovered by Professor Hutt.[79] We have seen that consumer demand increases by 20%; but why must 2 extra machines be purchased *in a year?* What does the *year* have to do with it? If we analyze the matter closely, we find that the year is a purely arbitrary and irrelevant unit even within the terms of the example itself. We might just as readily take a *week* as the period of time. Then we would have to say that consumer demand (which, after all, goes on continuously) increases 20% over the first week, thereby necessitating a 200% increase in demand for machines in the first *week* (or even an *infinite* increase if the replacement does not precisely occur in the first week), followed by a 200% (or infinite) decline in the next week, and stability thereafter. A week is never used by the accelerationists because the example would then be glaringly inapplicable to real life, which does not see such enormous fluctuations in the course of a couple of weeks. *But a week is no more arbitrary than a year.* In fact, the only *non*arbitrary period to choose would be the life of the machine (e.g., ten years). Over a *ten*-year period, demand for machines had previously been 10 (in the previous decade), and in the current and succeeding decades it will be 10 plus the extra 2, i.e., 12. In short, over the ten-year period the demand for machines will increase *precisely in* *the same proportion* as the demand for consumers' goods—and there is no magnification effect whatever,

Since businesses buy and produce over planned periods covering the life of their equipment, there is no reason to assume that the market will not plan production suitably and smoothly, without the erratic fluctuations manufactured by the model of the acceleration principle. There is, in fact, no validity in saying that increased consumption *requires* increased production of machines immediately; on the contrary, it is only increased saving and investment in machines, at points of time chosen by entrepreneurs strictly on the basis of expected profit, that *permits* increased production of consumers' goods in the future.

Secondly, the acceleration principle makes a completely unjustified leap from the single firm or industry to the whole economy. A 20% increase in consumption demand at one point must signify a 20% drop in consumption somewhere else. For how can consumption demand in general increase? Consumption demand in general can increase only through a shift from saving. But if saving decreases, then there are less funds available for investment. If there are less *funds* available for investment, how can investment increase even *more* than consumption? In fact, there are *less* funds available for investment when consumption increases. Consumption and investment compete for the use of funds.

Another important consideration is that the proof of the acceleration principle is couched in *physical* rather than *monetary* terms. Actually, consumption demand, particularly *aggregate* consumption demand, as well as demand for capital goods, cannot be expressed in physical terms; it must be expressed in monetary terms, since the demand for goods is the reverse of the *supply* of money on the market for exchange. If consumer demand increases either for one good or for all, it increases in monetary terms, thereby raising prices of consumers' goods. Yet we notice that there has been no discussion whatever of prices or price relationships in the acceleration principle. This neglect of price relationships is sufficient by itself to invalidate the entire principle.[80] The acceleration principle simply glides from a demonstration in *physical* terms to a conclusion in *monetary* terms.

Furthermore, the acceleration principle assumes a constant relationship between "fixed" capital and output, ignoring substitutability, the possibility of a range of output, the more or less intensive working of factors. It also assumes that the new machines are produced practically instantaneously, thus ignoring the requisite period of production.

In fact, the entire acceleration principle is a fallaciously mechanistic one, assuming automatic reactions by entrepreneurs to *present* data, thereby ignoring the most important fact about entrepreneurship: that it is *speculative,* that its essence is estimating the data of the uncertain future. It therefore involves judgment of future conditions by businessmen, and not simply blind reactions to past data. Successful entrepreneurs are those who best forecast the future. Why can't the entrepreneurs foresee the supposed slackening of demand and arrange their investments accordingly? In fact, that is what they will do. If the economist, armed with knowledge of the acceleration principle, thinks that he will be able to operate more profitably than the generally successful entrepreneur, why does he not become an entrepreneur and reap the rewards of success himself? All theories of the business cycle attempting to demonstrate general entrepreneurial error on the free market founder on this problem. They do not answer the crucial question: Why does a whole set of men most able in judging the future suddenly lapse into forecasting error?

A clue to the correct business cycle theory is contained in the fact that buried somewhere in a footnote or minor clause of all business cycle theories is the assumption that the money supply expands during the boom, in particular through credit expansion by the banks. The fact that this is a necessary condition in all the theories should lead us to explore this factor further: perhaps it is a sufficient condition as well. But, as we have seen above, there can be no bank credit expansion on the free market, since this is equivalent to the issue of fraudulent warehouse receipts. The positive discussion of business cycle theory will have to be postponed to the next chapter, since there can be no business cycle in the purely free market.

Business cycle theorists have always claimed to be more "realistic" than general economic theorists. With the exceptions of Mises and Hayek (correctly) and Schumpeter (fallaciously), none has tried to deduce his business cycle theory from general economic analysis.[81] It should be clear that this is required for a satisfactory explanation of the business cycle. Some, in fact, have explicitly discarded economic analysis altogether in their study of business cycles, while most writers use aggregative "models" with no relation to a general economic analysis of individual action. All of these commit the fallacy of "conceptual realism" —i.e., of using aggregative concepts and shuffling them at will, without relating them to actual individual action, while believing that something is being said about the real world. The business-cycle theorist pores over sine curves, mathematical models and curves of all types; he shuffles equations and interactions and thinks that he is saying something about the economic system or about human action. In fact, he is not. The overwhelming bulk of current business cycle theory is not economics at all, but meaningless manipulation of mathematical equations and geometric diagrams.[82]

12

The Economics of Violent Intervention in the Market

1. *Introduction*

Up to this point we have been assuming that no violent invasion of person or property occurs in society; we have been tracing the economic analysis of the free society, the free market, where individuals deal with one another only peacefully and never with violence. This is the construct, or "model," of the purely free market. And this model, imperfectly considered perhaps, has been the main object of study of economic analysis throughout the history of the discipline.

In order to complete the economic picture of our world, however, economic analysis must be extended to the nature and consequences of violent actions and interrelations in society, including intervention in the market and violent abolition of the market ("socialism"). Economic analysis of intervention and socialism has developed much more recently than analysis of the free market.[1] In this book, space limitations prevent us from delving into the economics of intervention to the same extent as we have treated the economics of the free market. But our researches into the former field are summarized more briefly in this final chapter.

One reason why economics has tended to concentrate on the free market is that here is presented the problem of order arising out of a seemingly "anarchic" and "planless" set of actions. We have seen that instead of the "anarchy of production" that a person untrained in economics might see in the free market, there emerges an orderly pattern, structured to meet the desires of all individuals, and yet eminently suited to adapt to changing conditions. In this way we have seen how the free, voluntary actions of individuals combine in an orderly determination of such seemingly mysterious processes as the formation of prices, income, money, economic calculation, profits and losses, and production.

The fact that each man, in pursuing his own self-interest, furthers the interest of everyone else, is a *conclusion* of economic analysis, not an *assumption* on which the analysis is grounded. Many critics have accused economists of being "biased" in favor of the free market economy. But this or any other conclusion of economics is not a bias or prejudice, but a *post-judice* (to use a happy term of Professor E. Merrill Root's)—a judgment made *after* inquiry, and not beforehand.[2] Personal preferences, moreover, are completely separate from the validity of analytic procedures. The personal preferences of the analyst are of no interest for economic science; what is relevant is the validity of the method itself.

2. *A Typology of Intervention*

Intervention is the intrusion of aggressive physical force into society; it means the substitution of coercion for voluntary actions. It must be remembered that, *praxeologically,* it makes no difference what individual or group wields this force; the economic nature and consequences of the action remain the same. Empirically, the vast bulk of interventions are performed by States, since the State is the only organization in society legally equipped to use violence and since it is the only agency that legally derives its revenue from a compulsory levy. It will therefore be convenient to confine our treatment to *government* intervention—bearing in mind, however, that private individuals may illegally use force, or that government may, openly or covertly, permit favored private groups to employ violence against the persons or property of others.

What types of intervention can an individual or group commit? Little or nothing has so far been done to construct a systematic typology of intervention, and economists have simply discussed such seemingly disparate actions as price control, licensing, inflation, etc. We can, however, classify interventions into three broad categories. In the first place, the *intervener,* or "invader," or "aggressor"—the individual or group that initiates violent intervention—may command an individual subject to do or not do certain things, when these actions directly involve the individual's person or property *alone.* In short, the intervener may restrict the subject's use of his property, where exchange with someone else is not involved. This may be called an *autistic intervention,* where the specific order or command involves only the subject himself. Secondly, the intervener may compel an *exchange* between the individual subject and himself or coerce a "gift" from the subject. We may call this a *binary intervention,* since a hegemonic relation is here established between two people: the intervener and the subject. Thirdly, the invader may either compel or prohibit an exchange between a *pair* of subjects (exchanges always take place between *two* people). In this case, we have a *triangular intervention,* where a hegemonic relation is created between the invader and a *pair* of actual or potential exchangers. All these interventions are examples of the *hegemonic* relation (see chapter 2 above)—the relation of command and obedience—in contrast to the contractual, free-market relation of voluntary mutual benefit.

Autistic intervention occurs, therefore, when the intervener coerces a subject without receiving any good or service in return. Simple homicide is an example; another would be the compulsory enforcement or prohibition of a salute, speech, or religious observance. Even if the intervener is the State, issuing an edict to all members of society, the edict in itself is still *autistic,* since the lines of force radiate, so to speak, from the State to each individual alone. Binary intervention, where the intervener forces the subject to make an exchange or gift to the former, is exemplified in taxation, conscription, and compulsory jury service. Slavery is another example of binary, coerced exchange between master and slave.

Examples of triangular intervention, where the intervener compels or prohibits exchanges between sets of two *other* individuals, are price control and licensing. Under price control, the State prohibits any pair of individuals from making an exchange below or above a certain fixed rate; licensing prohibits certain people from making specified exchanges with others. Curiously enough, writers on political economy have recognized only cases in the third category as being "intervention." It is understandable that economists have overlooked autistic intervention, for, in truth, economics can say little about events that lie outside the monetary exchange nexus. There is far less excuse for the neglect of binary intervention.

3. *Direct Effects of Intervention on Utility*

In tracing the effects of intervention, we must explore both the direct and the indirect consequences. In the first place, intervention will have direct, immediate consequences on the utilities of those participating. On the one hand, when the society is free and there is no intervention, everyone will always act in the way that he believes will maximize his utility, i.e., will raise him to the highest possible position on his value scale. In short, everyone's utility *ex ante* will be "maximized" (provided we take care not to interpret "utility" in a cardinal manner). Any exchange on the free market, indeed any action in the free society, occurs because it is expected to benefit each party concerned. If we may use the term "society" to depict the pattern, the array, of all individual exchanges, then we may say that the free market maximizes social utility, since everyone gains in utility from his free actions.[3]

Coercive intervention, on the other hand, signifies *per se* that the individual or individuals coerced *would not have voluntarily done what they are now being forced to do by the intervener.* The person who is coerced into saying or not saying something or into making or not making an exchange with the intervener or with a third party is having his actions changed by a threat of violence. The man being coerced, therefore, *always loses in utility as a result of the intervention,* for his action has been forcibly changed by its impact. In autistic and binary interventions, the individual subjects each lose in utility; in triangular interventions, at least one, and sometimes both, of the pair of would-be exchangers lose in utility.

Who *gains* in utility *ex ante?* Clearly, the intervener; otherwise, he would not have made the intervention. In the case of binary intervention, he himself gains directly in exchangeable goods or services at the expense of his subject.[4] In the case of autistic and triangular interventions, he gains in a sense of psychic well-being from enforcing regulations upon others (or, perhaps, in providing a seeming jusitfication for other, binary interventions).

In contrast to the free market, therefore, all cases of intervention supply one set of men with gains *at the expense* of another set. In binary interventions, the direct gains and losses are "tangible" in the form of exchangeable goods or services; in other cases, the direct gains are nonexchangeable satisfactions to the interveners, and the direct loss is being coerced into less satisfying, if not positively painful, forms of activity.

Before the development of economic science, people tended to think of exchange and the market as always benefiting one party at the expense of the other. This was the root of the mercantilist view of the market, of what Ludwig von Mises calls the "Montaigne fallacy." Economics has shown this to be a fallacy, for on the market *both* parties to an exchange will benefit.[5] On the market, therefore, *there can be no such thing as exploitation.* But the thesis of an inherent conflict of interest *is* true whenever the State or anyone else wielding force intervenes on the market. For then the intervener gains at the expense of the subjects who lose in utility. On the market all is harmony. But as soon as intervention appears on the scene, conflict is created, for each person or group may participate in a scramble to be a net gainer rather than a net loser—to be part of the intervening team, as it were, rather than one of the victims. And the very institution of taxation insures that some will be in the net gaining, and others in the net losing, class.[6] Since all State actions rest on the fundamental binary intervention of taxation, it follows that no State action can increase social utility, i.e., can increase the utility of all affected individuals.[7]

A common objection to the conclusion that the free market, in unique contrast to intervention, increases the utility of every individual in society, points to the fate of the entrepreneur whose product suddenly becomes obsolete. Take, for example, the buggy manufacturer who faces a shift in public demand from buggies to automobiles. Does *he* not lose utility from the operation of the free market? We must realize, however, that we are concerned only with the utilities that are *demonstrated* by the manufacturer's action.[8] In both period 1, when consumers demanded buggies, and in period 2, when they shifted to autos, he acts so as to maximize his utility on the free market. The fact that, in retrospect, he prefers the results of period 1 may be interesting data for the historian, but is irrelevant for the economic theorist. For the manufacturer is *not* living in period 1 any more. He lives always under *present* conditions and in relation to the present value scales of his fellow men. Voluntary exchanges, in any given period, will increase the utility of everyone and will therefore maximize social utility. The buggy manufacturer could not restore the conditions or results of period 1 unless he used force against others to coerce their exchanges, but, in that case, social utility could no longer be maximized, because of his invasive act.

Just as some writers have tried to deny the voluntary nature and the mutual benefits of free exchange, so others have tried to attribute a voluntary quality to actions of the State. Generally, this attempt has been based either on the view that there exists an entity "society," which cheerfully endorses and supports the actions of the State, or that the majority endorses these acts and that this somehow *means* universal support, or finally, that somehow, down deep, even the opposing minority endorses the acts of the State. From these fallacious assumptions, they conclude that the State can increase social utility at least as well as the market can.[9,10]

Having described the unanimity and harmony of the free market, as well as the conflict and losses of utility generated by intervention, let us ask what happens if government is used to check interventions in the market by private criminals—i.e., private imposers of coerced exchanges. It has been asked: Is not this "police" function an act of intervention, and does not the free market itself then necessarily rest on a "framework" of such intervention? And does not the existence of the free market therefore require a loss of utility on the part of the criminals who are being punished by the government? [11] In the first place, we must remember that the purely free market is an array of voluntary exchanges between sets of two persons. If there are no threats of criminal intervention in that market—say because everyone feels duty-bound to respect the private property of others—no "framework" of counterintervention will be needed. The "police" function is therefore solely a secondary derivative problem, not a precondition, of the free market.

Secondly, if governments—or private agencies, for that matter—are employed to check and combat intervention in society by criminals, it is certainly obvious that this combat imposes losses of utility upon the criminals. But these acts of defense are hardly "intervention" in our sense of the term. For the losses of utility are being imposed only upon people who, in turn, have been trying to impose losses of utility on peaceful citizens. In short, the force used by police agencies in defending individual freedom —i.e., in defending the persons and property of the citizens—is purely an *inhibitory* force; it is *counter*intervention against true, initiatory intervention. While such counter action cannot maximize "social utility"—the utility of *everyone* in society involved in interpersonal actions—it *does* maximize the utility of *noncriminals,* i.e., those who have been peacefully maximizing their own utility without inflicting losses upon others. Should these defense agencies do their job perfectly and eliminate all interventions, then their existence will be perfectly compatible with the maximization of social utility.

4. *Utility* Ex Post: *Free Market and Government*

We have thus seen that individuals maximize their utility *ex ante* on the free market, and that they cannot do so when there is intervention, for then the intervener gains in utility only at the expense of a demonstrated loss in utility by his subject. But what of utilities *ex post?* People may *expect* to benefit when they make decisions, but do they *actually* benefit from their results? How do the free market and intervention compare in traveling that vital path from *ante* to *post?*

For the free market, the answer is that the market is constructed so as to reduce error to a minimum. There is, in the first place, a fast-working, highly accurate, easily understandable test that tells the entrepreneur, and also the income-receiver, whether they are succeeding or failing at the task of satisfying the desires of the consumer. For the entrepreneur, who carries the main burden of adjustment to uncertain, fluctuating consumer desires, the test is particularly swift and sure—profits or losses. Large profits are a signal that he has been on the right track, losses that he has been on a wrong one. Profits and losses spur rapid adjustments to consumer demands; at the same time, they perform the function of getting money out of the hands of the inefficient entrepreneurs and into the hands of the good ones. The fact that good entrepreneurs prosper and add to their capital, and poor ones are driven out, insures an ever smoother market adjustment to changes in conditions. Similarly, to a lesser extent, land and labor factors move in accordance with the desire of their owners for higher incomes, and highly value-productive factors are rewarded accordingly.

Consumers also take entrepreneurial risks on the market. Many critics of the market, while willing to concede the *expertise* of the capitalist-entrepreneurs, bewail the prevailing ignorance of consumers, which prevents them from gaining the utility *ex post* that they had expected *ex ante*. Typically, Wesley C. Mitchell entitled one of his famous essays: "The Backward Art of Spending Money." Professor Mises has keenly pointed out the paradox of interventionists who insist that consumers are too ignorant or incompetent to buy products intelligently, while at the same time proclaiming the virtues of democracy, where the same people vote for or against politicians whom they do not know and on policies which they scarcely understand. To put it another way, the partisans of intervention assume that individuals are not competent to run their own affairs or to hire experts to advise them, but also assume that these same individuals *are* competent to vote for these experts at the ballot box. They are further assuming that the mass of supposedly incompetent consumers *are* competent to choose not only those who will rule over themselves, but also over the *competent* individuals in society. Yet such absurd and contradictory assumptions lie at the root of every program for "democratic" intervention in the affairs of the people.[12]

In fact, the truth is precisely the reverse of this popular ideology. Consumers are surely not omnisicient, but they have direct tests by which to acquire and check their knowledge. They buy a certain brand of breakfast food and they do not like it; and so they do not buy it again. They buy a certain type of automobile and like its performance; they buy another one. And in both cases, they tell their friends of this newly won knowledge. Other consumers patronize consumers' research organizations, which can warn or advise them in advance. But, in all cases, the consumers have the direct test of results to guide them. And the firm which satisfied the consumers expands and prospers and thus gains "good will," while the firm failing to satisfy them goes out of business.[13]

On the other hand, voting for politicians and public policies is a completely different matter. Here there are no direct tests of success or failure whatever, neither profits and losses nor enjoyable or unsatisfying consumption. In order to grasp consequences, especially the indirect catallactic consequences of governmental decisions, it is necessary to comprehend complex chains of praxeological reasoning. Very few voters have the ability or the interest to follow such reasoning, particularly, as Schumpeter points out, in political situations. For the minute influence that any one person has on the results, as well as the seeming remoteness of the actions, keeps people from gaining interest in political problems or arguments.[14] Lacking the direct test of success or failure, the voter tends to turn, not to those politicians whose policies have the best chance of success, but to those who can best "sell" their propaganda ability. Without grasping logical chains of deduction, the average voter will never be able to discover the errors that his ruler makes. To borrow an example from a later section of this chapter, suppose that the government inflates the money supply, thereby causing an inevitable rise in prices. The government can blame the price rise on wicked speculators or alien black marketeers, and unless the public knows economics, it will not be able to see the fallacies in the rulers' arguments.

It is curious, once more, that the very writers who complain most of the wiles and lures of advertising never apply their critique to the one area where it is truly correct: the advertising of politicians. As Schumpeter states:

> The picture of the prettiest girl that ever lived will in the long run prove powerless to maintain the sales of a bad cigarette. There is no equally effective safeguard in the case of political decisions. Many decisions of fateful importance are of a nature that makes it impossible for the public to experiment with them at its leisure and at moderate cost. Even if that is possible, judgment is as a rule not so easy to arrive at as in the case of the cigarette, because effects are less easy to interpret.[15]

George J. Schuller, in attempting to refute this argument, protested that: "complex chains of reasoning are required for consumers to select intelligently an automobile or television set." [16] But such knowledge is *not* necessary; for the whole point is that the consumers have always at hand a simple and pragmatic test of success: does the product work and work well? In public economic affairs, there is no such test, for no one can know whether a particular policy has "worked" or not without knowing the a priori reasoning of economics.

It may be objected that, while the average voter may not be competent to decide on *issues* that require chains of praxeological reasoning, he *is* competent to pick the *experts*—the politicians—

who will decide on the issues, just as the individual may select his own private expert adviser in any one of numerous fields. But the critical problem is precisely that in government the individual has no direct, personal test of success or failure of his hired expert such as he has in the market. On the market, individuals tend to patronize those experts whose advice is most successful. Good doctors or lawyers reap rewards on the free market, while poor ones fail; the privately hired expert flourishes in proportion to his ability. In government, on the other hand, there is no market test of the expert's success. Since there is no direct test in government, and, indeed, little or no personal contact or relationship between politician or expert and voter, there is no way by which the voter can gauge the true *expertise* of the man he is voting for. As a matter of fact, the voter is in even greater difficulties in the modern type of issueless election between candidates who agree on all fundamental questions than he is in voting on issues. For issues, after all, *are* susceptible to reasoning; the voter *can,* if he wants to and has the ability, learn about and decide on the issues. But what can any voter, even the most intelligent, know about the true *expertise* or competence of individual candidates, especially when elections are shorn of all important issues? The only thing that the voter can fall back on for a decision are the purely external, advertised "personalities" of the candidates, their glamorous smiles, etc. The result is that voting purely on candidates is bound to be even less rational than voting on the issues themselves.

Not only does government lack a successful test for picking the proper experts, not only is the voter necessarily more ignorant than the consumer, but government itself has other inherent mechanisms which lead to poorer choices of experts and officials. For one thing, the politician and the government expert receive their revenues, not from service voluntarily purchased on the market, but from a compulsory levy on the inhabitants. These officials, then, wholly lack the direct pecuniary incentive to *care* about servicing the public properly and competently. Furthermore, the relative rise of the "fittest" applies in government as in the market, but the criterion of "fitness" is here very different.

In the market, the fittest are those most able to serve the consumers. In government, the fittest are either (1) those most able at wielding coercion or (2) if bureaucratic officials, those best fitted to curry favor with the leading politicians or (3) if politicians, those most adroit at appeals to the voting public.[17]

Another critical divergence between market action and democratic voting is this: the voter has, for example, only a 1/100 billionth power to choose among his potential rulers, who in turn will make decisions affecting him, unchecked until the next election. The individual acting on the market, on the other hand, has absolute sovereign power to make decisions over his property, not just a removed, 1/100 billionth power. Furthermore, the individual is continually demonstrating his choices of whether to buy or not to buy, to sell or not to sell, by making absolute decisions in regard to his property. The voter, by voting for some particular candidate, demonstrates only a relative preference for him over one or two other potential rulers—and he must do this, let us not forget, within the framework of the coercive rule that, whether he votes or not, *one* of these men will rule over him for the next few years. (We should also not forget that, with a secret ballot, the voter does not even demonstrate this much of a constrained and limited preference.)

It may be objected that the shareholder voting in a corporation is in similar straits. But he is not. Aside from the critical point that the corporation does not acquire *its* funds by compulsory levy, the shareholder still has absolute power over his own property by being able to sell his shares on the free market, something that the democratic voter clearly cannot do. Moreover, the shareholder has voting power in the corporation proportionate to his degree of property ownership of the common assets.[18]

Thus, we see that the free market has a smooth, efficient mechanism to bring anticipated, *ex ante* utility into the realization and fruition of *ex post*. The free market always maximizes *ex ante* social utility; it always tends to maximize *ex post* social utility as well. The field of political action, on the other hand, i.e., the field where most intervention takes place, has no such mechanism; indeed, the political process inherently tends to delay and thwart the realization of expected gains. So that the divergence in *ex post* results between free market and intervention is even greater than in *ex ante*, anticipated utility. In fact, the divergence is still greater than we have shown. For, as we analyze the *indirect* consequences of intervention in the remainder of this chapter, we shall find that, in every instance, the consequences of intervention will make the intervention look worse in the eyes of many of its original supporters. Thus, we shall find that the indirect consequence of a price control is to cause unexpected shortages of the product. *Ex post,* many of the interveners themselves will feel that they have lost rather than gained in utility.

In sum, the free market always benefits every participant, and it maximizes social utility *ex ante;* it also tends to do so *ex post,* for it contains an efficient mechanism for speedily converting anticipations into realizations. With intervention, one group gains directly at the expense of another, and therefore social utility is not maximized or even increased; there is no mechanism for speedy translation of anticipation into fruition, but indeed the opposite; and finally, as we shall see, the indirect consequences of intervention will cause many interveners themselves to *lose* utility *ex post.* The remainder of this chapter traces the nature and *indirect* consequences of various forms of intervention.

5. *Triangular Intervention: Price Control*

A triangular intervention occurs when an intervener either compels a pair of people to make an exchange or prohibits them from making an exchange. The coercion may be imposed on the *terms* of the exchange or on the nature of one or both of the products being exchanged or on the people doing the exchanging. The former type of triangular intervention is called a *price control,* because it deals specifically with the terms, i.e., the price, at which the exchange is made; the latter may be called *product control,* as dealing specifically with the nature of the product or of the producer. An example of price control is a decree by the government that no one may buy or sell a certain product at more (or, alternatively, less) than X gold ounces per pound; an example of product control is the prohibition of the sale of this product or prohibition of the sale by any but certain persons selected by the government. Clearly both forms of control have various repercussions on both the price and the nature of the product.

A price control may be effective or ineffective. It will be ineffective if the regulation has no influence on the market price. Thus, if automobiles are selling at 100 gold ounces on the market, and the government decrees that no autos be sold for more than 300 ounces, on pain of punishment inflicted on violators, the decree is at present completely academic and ineffective.[19] However, should a customer wish to order an unusual custom-built automobile for which the seller would charge over 300 ounces, then the regulation *now* becomes effective and changes transactions from what they would have been on the free market.

There are two types of effective price control: a *maximum* price control that prohibits all exchanges of a good above a certain price, with the controlled price being *below* the market equilibrium price; and a *minimum* price control prohibiting exchanges below a certain price, this fixed price being *above* market equilibrium. Let Fig. 83 depict the supply and demand curves

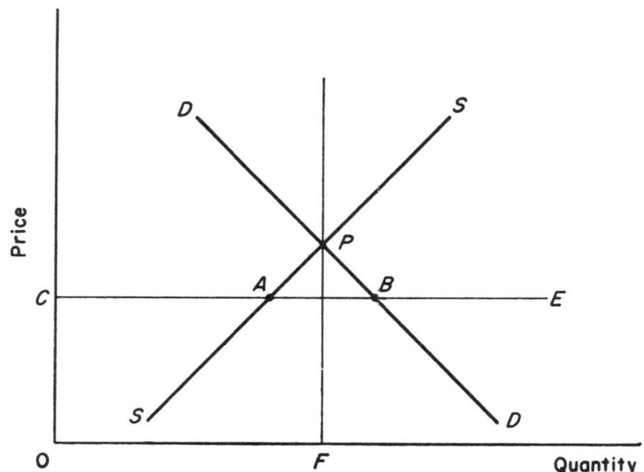

FIG. 83. EFFECT OF A MAXIMUM PRICE CONTROL

for a good subjected to maximum price control: *DD* and *SS* are the demand and supply curves for the good. *FP* is the equilibrium price set by the market. The government, let us assume, imposes a maximum control price *OC*, above which any sale is illegal. At the control price, the market is no longer cleared, and the quantity demanded exceeds the quantity supplied by amount *AB*. In this way, an artificially created shortage of the good has been created. In any shortage, consumers rush to buy goods which are not available at the price. Some must do without, others must patronize the market, revived as illegal or "black," paying a premium for the risk of punishment that sellers now undergo. The chief characteristic of a price maximum is the queue, the endless "lining up" for goods that are not sufficient to supply the people at the rear of the line. All sorts of subterfuges are invented by people desperately seeking to arrive at the clearance of supply and demand once provided by the market. "Under-the-table" deals, bribes, favoritism for older customers, etc., are inevitable features of a market shackled by the price maximum.[20]

It must be noted that, even if the stock of a good is frozen for the foreseeable future and the supply line is vertical, this artificial shortage will still develop and all these consequences ensue. The more "elastic" the supply, i.e., the more resources shift out of production, the more aggravated, *ceteris paribus,* the shortage will be. The firms that leave production are the ones nearest the margin. If the price control is "selective," i.e., is imposed on one or a few products, the economy will not be as universally dislocated as under general maxima, but the artificial shortage created in the particular line will be even more pronounced, since entrepreneurs and factors can shift to the production and sale of other products (preferably substitutes). The prices of the substitutes will go up as the "excess" demand is channeled off in their direction. In the light of this fact, the typical governmental reason for selective price control—"We must impose controls on this necessary product so long as it continues in short supply"—is revealed to be an almost ludicrous error. For the truth is the reverse: price control creates an artificial shortage of the product, which continues *as long as* the control is in existence—

in fact, becomes ever worse as resources have time to shift to other products. If the government were really worried about the short supply of certain products, it would go out of its way *not* to impose maximum price controls upon them.

Before investigating further the effects of general price maxima, let us analyze the consequences of a *minimum* price control, i.e., the imposition of a price *above* the free market price. This may

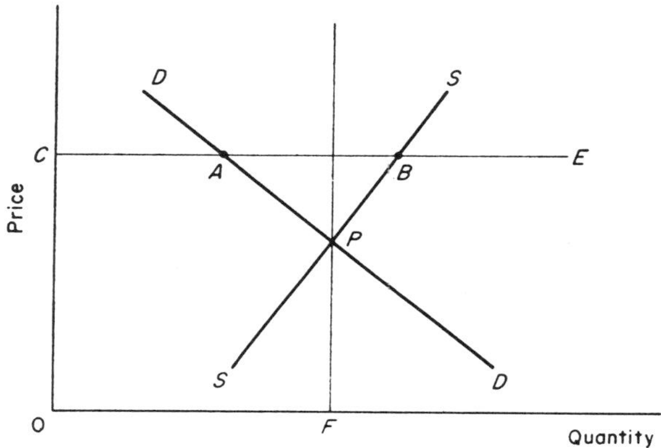

FIG. 84. EFFECT OF A MINIMUM PRICE CONTROL

be depicted in Fig. 84. *DD* and *SS* are the demand and supply curves respectively. *OC* is the control price and *FP* the market equilibrium price. At *OC*, the quantity demanded is less than the quantity supplied, by the amount *AB*. Thus, while the effect of a maximum price is to create an artificial shortage, a minimum price creates an artificial unsold surplus, *AB*. The unsold surplus exists even if the *SS* line is vertical, but a more elastic supply will, *ceteris paribus,* aggravate the surplus. Once again, the market is not cleared. The artificially high price at first attracts resources into the field, while, at the same time, discouraging buyer demand. Under selective price control, resources will leave other fields where they benefit themselves and consumers better, and transfer to this field, where they overproduce and suffer losses as a result.

This offers an interesting example of intervention tampering with the market and causing entrepreneurial losses. Entrepreneurs operate on the basis of certain criteria: prices, interest rate, etc., established by the free market. Interventionary tampering with these signals destroys the continual market tendency to adjustment and brings about losses and misallocation of resources in satisfying consumer wants.

General, over-all price maxima dislocate the entire economy and deny consumers the enjoyment of substitutes. General price

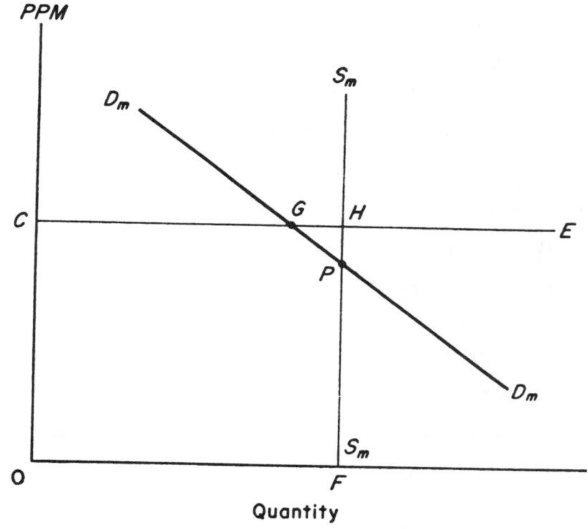

FIG. 85. EFFECT OF IMPOSING GENERAL PRICE MAXIMA

maxima are usually imposed for the announced purpose of "preventing inflation"—invariably while the government is inflating the money supply by a large amount. Over-all price maxima are equivalent to imposing a *minimum* on the PPM (see Fig. 85): *OF* (or S_mS_m) is the money stock in the society; D_mD_m the social demand for money; *FP* is the equilibrium PPM (purchasing power of the monetary unit) set by the market. An imposed minimum PPM above the market (*OC*) injures the clearing "mechanism" of the market. At *OC* the money stock exceeds the money demanded. As a result, people possess a quantity of money *GH* in "unsold surplus." They try to sell their money by buying goods, but they cannot. Their money is anesthetized. To the extent that a government's over-all price maximum is effective, a part of people's money becomes useless, for it cannot be exchanged. But a mad scramble inevitably ensues, with each person hoping that *his* money can be used.[21] Favoritism, lining up, bribes, etc., inevitably abound, as well as great pressure for a "black" market (i.e., *the* market) to provide a channel for the surplus money.

A general price minimum is equivalent to a *maximum* control on the PPM. This sets up an unsatisfied, excess, demand for money over the stock of money available—specifically, in the form of unsold stocks of goods in every field.

The principles of maximum and minimum price control apply to *any* prices, whatever they may be: of consumers' goods, capital goods, land or labor services, or, as we have seen, the "price" of money in terms of other goods. They apply, for example, to minimum wage laws. When a minimum wage law is effective, i.e., where it imposes a wage above the market value of a grade of labor (above the laborer's discounted marginal value product), the supply of labor services exceeds the demand, and the "unsold surplus" of labor services means *involuntary mass unemployment.* Selective, as opposed to general, minimum wage rates, create unemployment in particular industries and tend to perpetuate these pockets by attracting labor to the higher rates. Labor is eventually forced to enter less remunerative, less value-productive lines. This analysis applies whether the minimum wage is imposed by the State or by a labor union.

The reader is referred to chapter 10 above for an analysis of the rare case of a minimum wage imposed by a *voluntary* union. We saw that this creates unemployment and shifts labor to less remunerative and value-productive branches of employment, *but* that these results must be treated as voluntary. To prohibit people from joining unions and agreeing voluntarily on union wage scales and on the *mystique* of unionism would subject workers by force to the dictates of consumers and would impose a welfare loss upon the former. However, as we stated above, a spread among the workers of praxeological knowledge, of a realization that union solidarity causes unemployment and lower wage rates for many workers, would probably weaken this solidarity considerably. Empirically, on the other hand, almost all cases of effective unionism are imposed through coercion exercised by unions, i.e., through union *intervention* in the market.[22] The effects of union intervention are then the same as the same degree of government intervention would have been. As we have pointed out, the analysis of intervention applies to *whatever* agency wields the violence, whether private or governmental. Unemployment and misallocations of many workers to less efficient and lower-paying jobs again occur in this case and again involuntarily.

Our analysis of the effects of price control applies also, as Mises has brilliantly shown, to control over the price ("exchange rate") of one money in terms of another.[23] This was partially seen in Gresham's Law, one of the first economic laws to be discovered. Few have realized that this law is merely a specific instance of the general consequences of price controls. Perhaps this failure is due to the misleading formulation of Gresham's Law, which is usually phrased: "Bad money drives good money out of circulation." Taken at its face value, this is a paradox that violates the general rule of the market that the best methods of satisfying consumers tend to win out over the poorer. The phrasing has been fallaciously used even by those who generally favor the free market, to justify a State monopoly over the coinage of gold and silver. Actually, Gresham's Law should read: "Money overvalued by the State will drive money undervalued by the State out of circulation." Whenever the State sets an arbitrary value or price on one money in terms of another, it thereby establishes an effective *minimum* price control on one money and a *maximum* price control on the other, the "prices" being in terms of each other. This, for example, was the essence of bimetallism. Under bimetallism, a nation recognized gold and silver as moneys, but set an arbitrary price, or exchange ratio, between them. When this arbitrary price differed, as it was bound to do, from the free-market price (and this became ever more likely as time passed and the free-market price changed, while the government's arbitrary price remained the same), one money became overvalued and the other undervalued by the government. Thus, suppose that a country used gold and silver as moneys, and the government set the ratio between them at 16 ounces of silver: 1 ounce of gold. The market price, perhaps 16:1 at the time of the price control, then changes to 15:1. What is the result? Silver is now being arbitrarily undervalued by the government and gold arbitrarily overvalued. In other words, silver is fixed cheaper than it really is in terms of gold on the market, and gold is forced to be more expensive than it really is in terms of silver. The government has imposed a price maximum on silver and a price minimum on gold, in terms of each other.

The same consequences now follow as from any effective price control. With a price maximum on silver, the gold demand for silver in exchange now exceeds the silver demand for gold (conversely, with a price minimum on gold, the silver demand for gold is less than the gold demand for silver). Gold goes begging for silver in unsold surplus, while silver becomes scarce and disappears from circulation. Silver disappears to another country or area where it can be exchanged at the free-market price, and gold, in turn, flows into the country. If the bimetallism is worldwide, then silver disappears into the "black market," and official or open exchanges are made only with gold. No country, therefore, can maintain a bimetallic system in practice, since one money will always be undervalued or overvalued in terms of the other. The overvalued always displaces the other from circulation, the latter being scarce.

Similar consequences follow from such price control as setting arbitrary exchange rates on fiat moneys (see further below) and in setting new and worn coins arbitrarily equal to one another when they discernibly differ in weight.

To sum up our analysis of price control: Directly, the utility of at least one set of exchangers will be injured by the control. Indirectly, as we find by further analysis, hidden, but just as certain, effects injure a substantial number of people who *thought* they would gain in utility from the imposed controls. The announced aim of a maximum price control is to benefit the consumer by giving him his supply at a lower price; yet the objective effect is to prevent many consumers from having the good at all. The announced aim of a minimum price control is to insure higher prices to the sellers; yet the effect will be to prevent many sellers from selling any of their surplus. Furthermore, the price controls inevitably distort the production and allocation of resources and factors in the economy, thereby injuring again the bulk of consumers. And we must not overlook the army of bureaucrats who must be financed by the binary intervention of taxation and who must administer and enforce the myriad of regulations. This army, in itself, withdraws a mass of workers from productive labor and saddles them onto the remaining producers—thereby benefiting the bureaucrats, but injuring the rest of the people.

6. *Triangular Intervention: Product Control*

Triangular interference with an exchange can alter the *terms* of the exchange or else in some way alter the nature of the product or the persons making the exchange. The latter intervention, *product control,* may regulate the product itself (e.g., a law prohibiting all sales of liquor) or the people selling or buying the product (e.g., a law prohibiting Mohammedans from selling —or buying—liquor).

Product control clearly and evidently injures all parties concerned in the exchange: the consumers who lose utility because they cannot purchase the product and satisfy their most urgent wants; and the producers who are prevented from earning a remuneration in this field and must therefore settle for lower earnings elsewhere. Losses by producers are particularly borne by laborers and landowners specific to the industry, who must accept *permanently* lower income. (Entrepreneurial profit is ephemeral anyway, and capitalists tend to earn a uniform interest rate throughout the economy.) Whereas with *price control* one could make out a *prima facie* case that at least *one* set of exchangers gains from the control (the consumers whose buying price is pushed *below* the free-market price, and the producers when the price is pushed *above*), in product control *both* parties to the exchange invariably lose. The direct beneficiaries of product control, then, are the government bureaucrats who administer the regulations: partly from the tax-created jobs that the regulations create, and partly perhaps from satisfactions gained from wielding coercive power over others.

In many cases of product prohibition, of course, inevitable pressure develops, as in price control, for the re-establishment of the market illegally, i.e., a "black market." A black market is always in difficulties because of its illegality. The product will be scarce and costly, to cover the risks to producers involved in violating the law and the costs of bribing government officials; and the more strict the prohibition and penalties, the scarcer the product will be and the higher the price. Furthermore, the illegality greatly hinders the process of distributing information about the existence of the market to consumers (e.g., by way of advertising). As a result, the organization of the market will be far less efficient, the service to the consumer of poorer quality, and prices for this reason alone will be higher than under a legal market. The premium on secrecy in the "black" market also militates against large-scale business, which is likely to be more visible and therefore more vulnerable to law enforcement. Paradoxically, product or price control is apt to serve as a monopolistic grant (see below) of privilege *to* the black marketeers. For they are likely to be very different entrepreneurs from those who would have succeeded in this industry in a legal market (for here the premium is on skill in bypassing the law, bribing government officials, etc.).[24]

Product prohibition may either be *absolute,* as in American liquor prohibition during the 1920's, or *partial.* An example of partial prohibition is compulsory *rationing,* which prohibits consumption beyond a certain amount. The clear effect of rationing is to injure consumers and lower the standard of living of everyone. Since rationing places legal maxima on specific items of consumption, it also distorts the pattern of consumers' spending. Consumer spending is coercively shifted from the goods more heavily to those less heavily rationed. Furthermore, since ration tickets are usually not transferable, the pattern of consumer spending is even more distorted, because people who do not want a certain commodity are not permitted to exchange these coupons for goods not wanted by others. In short, the nonsmoker is not permitted to exchange his cigarette coupons for someone else's gasoline coupons which have been allocated to those who do not own cars. Ration tickets therefore cripple the entire system by introducing a new type of highly inefficient quasi "money," which must be used for purchasing in addition to the regular money.[25]

One form of partial product prohibition is to forbid all but *certain selected* firms from selling a particular product. Such partial exclusion means that these firms are granted a *special privilege* by the government. If such a grant is given to one person or firm, we may call it a *monopoly* grant; if to several persons or firms, it is a *quasi-monopoly* grant.[26] Both types of grant may be called *monopolistic.* An example of this type of grant is *licensing,* where all those to whom the government refuses to give or sell a license are prevented from pursuing the trade or business. Another example is a *protective tariff* or *import quota,* which prevents competition from beyond a country's geographical limits. Of course, outright monopoly grants to a firm or compulsory cartelization of an industry are clear-cut grants of monopolistic privilege.

It is obvious that a monopolistic grant directly and immediately benefits the monopolist or quasi monopolist, whose competitors are debarred by violence from entering the field. It is also evident that would-be competitors are injured and are forced to accept lower remuneration in less efficient and value-productive fields. It is also patently clear that the consumers are injured, for they are prevented from purchasing products from competitors whom they would freely prefer. And this injury takes place, it should be noted, apart from any effect of the grant on prices.

In chapter 10 we buried the theory of monopoly price; we must now resurrect it. The theory of monopoly price, as developed there, is illusory when applied to the free market, but it applies fully in the case of monopoly and quasi-monopoly grants. For *here* we have an identifiable distinction: not the spurious distinction between "competitive" and "monopoly" or "monopolistic" price, but one between the *free-market price* and the *monopoly price.* The "free-market price" is conceptually identifiable and definable, whereas the "competitive price" is not. The theory of monopoly price, therefore, properly contrasts it to the free-market price, and the reader is referred back to chapter 10 for a description of the theory which can now be applied here. The monopolist will be able to achieve a monopoly price for the product if his demand curve is inelastic above the free-market price. We have seen above that on the free market, *every* demand curve to a firm is *elastic* above the free-market price; otherwise the firm would have an incentive to raise its price and increase its revenue. But the grant of monopoly privilege renders the consumer demand curve less elastic, for the consumer is deprived of substitute products from other potential competitors. Whether this lowering of elasticity will be sufficient to make the demand curve to the firm *inelastic* (so that gross revenue will be greater at a price higher than the free-market price) depends on the concrete historical data of the case and is not for economic analysis to determine.

When the demand curve to the firm remains elastic (so that gross revenue will be lower at a higher-than-free-market price), the monopolist will not reap any *monopoly gain* from his grant. Consumers and competitors will still be injured because their trade is prevented, but the monopolist will not gain, because his price and income will be no higher than before. On the other hand, if his demand curve is inelastic, then he institutes a monopoly price so as to maximize his revenue. His production has to be restricted in order to command the higher price. The restriction of production and higher price for the product both injure the consumers. Here the argument of chapter 10 must be reversed. We may no longer say that a restriction of production (such as in a voluntary cartel) benefits the consumers by arriving at the most value-productive point; on the contrary, the consumers are now injured because their free choice would have resulted in the free-market price. Because of coercive force applied by the State, they may not purchase goods freely from all those willing to sell. In other words, any approach *toward* the free-market equilibrium price and output point for any product benefits the consumers and thereby benefits the producers as well. Any departure *away* from the free-market price and output injures the consumers. The monopoly price resulting from a grant of monopoly privilege leads away from the free-market price; it lowers output and raises prices beyond what would be established if consumers and producers could trade freely.

And we cannot *here* use the argument that the restriction is voluntary because the consumers make their own demand curve inelastic. For the consumers are only *fully* responsible for their demand curve on the *free market;* and only *this* demand curve can be fully treated as an expression of their voluntary choice. Once the government steps in to prohibit trade and grant privileges, there is no longer wholly voluntary action. Consumers are forced, willy-nilly, to deal with the monopolist for a certain range of purchases.

All the effects which monopoly-price theorists have mistakenly attributed to voluntary cartels, therefore, *do* apply to governmental monopoly grants. Production is restricted, and factors are released for production elsewhere. But *now* we can say that this production will satisfy the consumers less than under free-market conditions; furthermore, the factors will earn less in the other occupations.

As we saw in chapter 10, there can never be lasting monopoly *profits,* since profits are ephemeral, and all eventually reduce to a uniform interest return. In the long run, monopoly returns are imputed to some *factor.* What is the factor being monopolized in this case? It is obvious that this factor is the *right* to enter the industry. In the free market, this right is unlimited to all and therefore unowned by anyone. The right commands no price on the market because everyone already has it. But here the government has conferred special privileges of entry and sale; and it is these *special* privileges or rights that are responsible for the extra monopoly gain from a monopoly price, and to which we may impute the gain. The monopolist earns a monopoly gain, therefore, *not* for owning any truly productive factor, but from owning a special privilege granted by the government. And this gain does not disappear in the long-run ERE as do profits; it is permanent, so long as the privilege remains and consumer valuations continue as they are.

Of course, the monopoly gain may well be capitalized into the asset value of the firm, so that *subsequent* owners, who invest in the firm after the capitalization took place, will be earning only the equal interest return. A notable example of the capitalization of monopoly (or rather, quasi-monopoly) rights is the New York City taxicab industry. Every taxicab must be licensed, but the city decided, years ago, not to issue any further licenses, or "medallions," so that any new cab owner must purchase his medallion from some previous owner. The (high) price of medallions on the market is then the capitalized value of the monopoly privilege.

As we have seen, all this applies to a quasi monopolist as well as to a monopolist, since the number of the former's competitors is also restricted by the grant of privilege, which makes his demand curve less elastic. Of course, *ceteris paribus,* a monopolist is in a better position than a quasi monopolist, but how much each benefits depends purely on the data of the particular case. In some cases, such as the protective tariff, the quasi monopolist will end, in the long run, by not gaining anything. For since freedom of entry is restricted only to foreign firms, the higher returns accruing to firms newly protected by a tariff will attract more domestic capital to that industry. Eventually, therefore, the new capital will drive the rate of earnings down to the interest rate usual in all of industry, and the monopolistic gain will have been competed away.[27]

Monopolistic grants can be either direct and evident, such as compulsory cartels or licenses; less direct, such as tariffs; or highly indirect, but nevertheless powerful. Ordinances closing businesses at specific hours, for example, or outlawing pushcart peddlers or door-to-door salesmen, are illustrations of laws that forcibly exclude competition and thereby grant monopolistic privileges. Similarly, *antitrust laws* and prosecutions, while seemingly designed to "combat monopoly" and "promote competition," actually do the reverse, for they coercively penalize and repress efficient forms of market structure and activity. Even such a seemingly remote action as conscription has the effect of forcibly withdrawing young men from the labor market and thereby giving their competitors a monopolistic, or rather a *restrictionist,* wage.[28] Unfortunately, we have not the space here to investigate these and other instructive cases.

7. *Binary Intervention: The Government Budget*

Binary intervention occurs, we have seen, when the intervener forces someone to transfer property to him. All government rests on the coerced levy of *taxation,* which is therefore a prime example of binary intervention. Government intervention, consequently, is not only triangular, like price control; it may also be binary, like taxation, and is therefore imbedded into the very nature of government and governmental activity.

For years, writers on public finance have been searching for the "neutral tax," i.e., for that system of taxes which would keep the free market intact. The object of this search is altogether chimerical. For example, economists have often sought uniformity of taxes, so that each person, or at least each person in the same income bracket, pays the same amount of tax. But this is inherently impossible, as we have already seen from Calhoun's demonstration that the community is inevitably divided into tax*payers* and tax-*consumers,* who, of course, cannot be said to pay taxes at all. To repeat the keen analysis of Calhoun (see note 6 above): "nor can it be otherwise; unless what is collected from each individual in the shape of taxes shall be returned to him in disbursements, which would make the process nugatory and absurd." In short, government bureaucrats *do not pay* taxes; they *consume* the tax proceeds. If a private citizen earning $10,000 income pays $2,000 in taxes, the bureaucrat earning $10,000 does not *really* pay $2,000 in taxes also; that he supposedly does is simply a bookkeeping fiction.[29] He is *actually* acquiring an income of $8,000 and paying no taxes at all.

Not only bureaucrats will be tax-consumers, but, to a lesser degree, other, private members of the population as well. For example, suppose that the government taxes $1,000 away from private people who would have spent the money on jewels, and uses it to purchase paper for government offices. This induces a shift in demand away from jewels and toward paper, a decline in the price of jewels, and a flow of resources from the jewelry industry; conversely, paper prices will tend to increase, and resources will flow into the paper industry. Incomes will decline in the jewelry industry and rise in paper.[30] Hence, the paper industry will be, to some extent, beneficiaries of the government budget: of the tax-and-expenditure process of government. But not just the paper industry. For the new money received by the paper firms will be paid out to their suppliers and original factor-owners, and so on as the ripples impinge on other parts of the economy. On the other hand, the jewelry industry, stripped of revenue, reduces *its* demands for factors. Thus the burdens and benefits of the tax-and-expenditure process diffuse themselves throughout the economy, with the strongest impact at the points of first contact—jewelry and paper.[31]

Everyone in the society will be either a net taxpayer or a tax-consumer and this to different degrees, and it will be for the data of each specific case to determine where any particular person or industry stands in this distribution process. The only certainty is that the bureaucrat or politician in office receives 100% of his governmental income from tax proceeds and pays no genuine taxes in return.

The tax-and-expenditure process, therefore, will inevitably distort the allocation of productive factors, the types of goods produced, and the pattern of incomes, from what they would be on the free market. The larger the *level* of taxing and spending, i.e., the bigger the government budget, the greater the distortion will tend to be. And moreover, the larger the budget in relation to market activity, the greater the burden of government on the economy. A larger burden means that more and more resources of society are being coercively siphoned off from the producers into the pockets of government, those who sell to government, and the subsidized favorites of government. In short, the higher the relative level of government, the narrower the base of the producers and the greater the "take" of those expropriating the producers. The higher the level of government, the less resources will be used to satisfy the desires of those consumers who have contributed to production, and the more resources will be used to satisfy the desires of nonproducing consumers.

There has been a great deal of controversy among economists on how to approach the analysis of taxation. Old-fashioned Marshallians insist on the "partial equilibrium" approach of looking only at a particular type of tax, in isolation, and then analyzing its effects; Walrasians, more fashionable today (and exemplified by the late Italian public finance expert, Antonio De Viti De Marco), insist that taxes cannot be considered at all in isolation, that they may be analyzed only in conjunction with what the government does with the proceeds. In all this, what would be the "Austrian" approach, had it been developed, is being neglected. This holds that both procedures are legitimate and necessary to analyze the taxing process fully. In short: the level of taxes-and-expenditures may be analyzed and its inevitable redistributive and distortive effects discussed; and, *within* this aggregate of taxes, individual types of taxes may then be analyzed in isolation. Neither the partial nor the general approaches should be overlooked.

There has also been a great amount of useless controversy about *which* activity of government imposes the burden on the private sector: *taxation* or *government spending*. It is actually futile to separate them, since they are both stages in the same process of burden and redistribution. Thus, suppose the government taxes the betel-nut industry one million dollars in order to buy paper for government bureaus. One million dollars' worth of resources are shifted from betel nuts to paper. This is done in *two* stages, a sort of one-two punch at the free market: first, the betel-nut industry is made poorer by taking away its money; then, the government uses this money to take paper out of the market for its own use, thus extracting resources in the second stage. Both sides of the process are a burden. In a sense, the betel-nut industry is compelled to *pay for* the extraction of paper from society; at least, it bears the immediate brunt of payment. However, even without yet considering the "partial equilibrium" problem of how or whether such taxes are "shifted" by the betel-nut industry onto other shoulders, we should also note that it is not the only one to pay; the consumers of paper certainly pay by finding paper prices raised to them.

The process can be seen more clearly if we consider what happens when taxes and government expenditures are *not* equal, when they are not simply obverse sides of the same coin. When taxes are less than government expenditures (and omitting borrowing from the public for the time being), the government creates new money. It is obvious here that government *expenditures* are the main burden, since this higher amount of resources is being siphoned off. In fact, as we shall see later when considering the binary intervention of *inflation,* creating new money is, anyway, a form of taxation.

But what of that rare case when taxation is higher than government spending? Say that the surplus is either hoarded in the government's gold supply or that the money is liquidated through deflation (see below). Thus, assume that $1,000,000 is taken from the betel-nut industry and only $600,000 is spent on paper. In this case, the larger burden is that of taxation, which pays not only for the extracted paper but also for the hoarded or destroyed money. While the government extracts only $600,000 worth of resources from the economy, the betel-nut industry loses $1,000,000 of potential resources, and this loss should not be forgotten in toting up the burdens imposed by the government's budgetary process. In short, when government expenditures and receipts differ, the "fiscal burden" on society may be very approximately gauged by whichever is the greater total.

Since taxation cannot really be uniform, the government in its budgetary process of tax-and-spend inevitably takes coercively from Peter to give to Paul ("Paul," of course, including itself). In addition to distorting the allocation of resources, therefore, the budgetary process redistributes incomes or, rather, *distributes* incomes. For the free market does *not* distribute incomes; income there arises naturally and smoothly out of the market processes of production and exchange. Thus, the very concept of "distribution" as something separate from production and exchange can arise only from the government's binary intervention. It is often charged, for example, that the free market maximizes the utility of all, and the satisfactions of all consumers, only *"given* a certain existing distribution of income." But this common fallacy is incorrect; *there is no "assumed distribution" on the free market separate from the voluntary activities of every individual's production and exchange.* The only *given* on the free market is the *property right* of every man in his own person and in the resources which he finds, produces, or creates, or which he obtains in voluntary exchange for his products or as a gift from their producers.

The binary intervention of the government's budget, on the other hand, impairs this property right of every one in his own product and *creates* the separate process and the "problem" of distribution. No longer do income and wealth flow purely from service rendered on the market; they now flow to special privilege created by the State and away from those specially burdened by the State.

There are many economists who regard the "free market" as only being free of triangular interference; such binary interference as taxation is not considered intervention in the purity of the "free market." The economists of the Chicago School—headed by Frank H. Knight—have been particularly adept at splitting man's economic activity and confining the "market" to a narrow compass. They can thus favor the "free market" (because they oppose such triangular interventions as price control), while advocating drastic binary interventions in taxes and subsidies to "redistribute" the income determined by that market. In short, the market is to be left "free" in one sphere, while being subject to perpetual harassment and reshuffling by outside coercion. This concept assumes that man is fragmented, that the "market man" is not concerned with what happens to himself as a "subject-to-government" man. This is surely an impermissible myth, which we might call the "tax illusion"—the idea that people do not consider what they earn *after* taxes, but only before taxes. In short, if A earns $9,000 a year on the market, B $5,000, and C $1,000, and the government decides to keep redistributing the incomes so that each earns $5,000, the individuals, apprised of this, are *not* going to keep foolishly assuming that they are still earning what they did before. They are going to take the taxes and subsidies into account.[32]

Thus, we see that the government budgetary process is a coercive shift of resources and incomes from producers on the market to nonproducers; it is also a coercive interference with the free choices of individuals by those constituting the government. Below, we shall analyze the nature and consequences of government spending in more detail. At this time, let us emphasize the important point that government cannot be in any way a fountain of resources; all that it spends, all that it distributes in largesse, it must first acquire in revenue, i.e., it must first extract from the "private sector." The great bulk of the revenues of government, the very nub of its power and its essence, is taxation, to which we turn in the next section. Another method is inflation, the creation of new money, which we shall discuss further below. A third method is borrowing from the public, which will be discussed briefly in Appendix A below.[33]

8. *Binary Intervention: Taxation*

A. INCOME TAXATION

Taxation, as we have seen, takes from producers and gives to others. Any increase in taxation swells the resources, the incomes, and usually the numbers of those living off the producers, while *diminishing* the production base from which these others are drawing their sustenance. Clearly, this is eventually a self-defeating process: there is a limit beyond which the top-heavy burden can no longer be carried by the diminishing stock of producers. Narrower limits are also imposed by the *disincentive* effects of taxation. The greater the amount of taxes imposed on the producers—the tax*payers*—the lower the marginal utility of work will be, for the returns from work are forcibly diminished, and the greater the marginal utility of leisure forgone. Not only that: the greater will be the incentive to shift from the ranks of the burdened taxpayers to the ranks of the tax-*consumers*, either as full-time bureaucrats or as those subsidized by the government. As a result, production will diminish even further, as people retreat to leisure or scramble harder to join the ranks of the privileged tax-consumers.[34] In the market economy, net incomes are derived from wages, interest, ground rents, and profit; and in so far as taxes strike at the earnings from these sources, attempts to earn these incomes will diminish. The laborer, faced with a tax on his wages, has less incentive to work hard; the capitalist, confronting a tax on his interest or profit return, has more incentive to consume rather than to save and invest. The landlord, a tax being imposed on his rents, will have less of a spur to allocate land sites efficiently.

It has been objected that since a man's marginal utility of money assets increases as he holds less of a stock of money, lower money income will mean an increased marginal utility of income. As a result, a tax on money incomes creates both a "substitution effect" against work and in favor of leisure (or against saving in favor of consumption) and an "income effect" working in the opposite direction. This is true, and in rare empirical cases, the latter effect will predominate. In plain language, this means that when extra penalties are placed upon man's efforts he will generally slacken them; but in some cases, he will work harder to try to offset the burdens. In the latter cases, however, we must remember that he will lose the valuable consumption good of "leisure"; he will have less leisure now than he would have if his choices were still free. Working harder under penalty is only a cause for rejoicing if we regard the matter exclusively from the point of view of those living off the producers, who will thereby benefit from the tax. The standard of living of the workers, which must include leisure, has fallen.

The income tax, by taxing income from investments, cripples saving and investment, since it lowers the return from investing below what free-market time preferences would dictate. The lower net interest return leads people to bring their savings-investment into line with the new realities; in short, the marginal savings and investments at the higher return will now be valued below consumption and will no longer be made.

There is another, unheralded reason why an income tax will particularly penalize saving and investment as against consumption. It might be thought that since the income tax confiscates a certain portion of a man's income and leaves him free to allocate the rest between consumption and investment, and since time-preference schedules remain given, the proportion of consumption to saving will remain unchanged. But this ignores the fact that the taxpayer's real income and the real value of his monetary assets have been lowered by paying the tax. We have seen in chapter 6 that, given a man's time-preference schedule, the lower the level of his real monetary assets, the higher his time-preference rate will be, and therefore the higher the proportion of his consumption to investment. The taxpayer's position may be seen in Fig. 86, which is essentially the reverse of the indi-

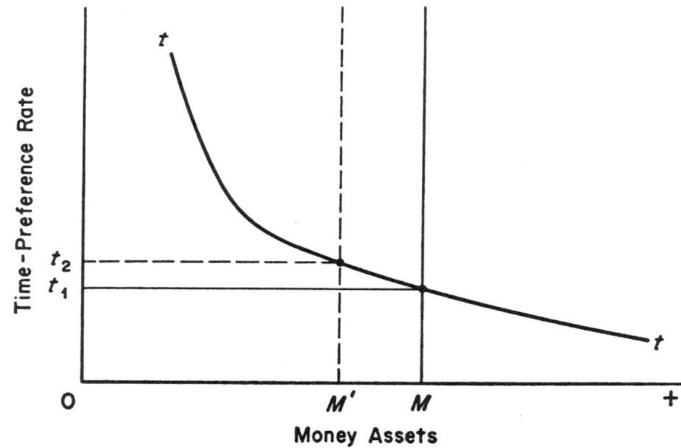

FIG. 86. EFFECT OF INCOME TAX ON TAXPAYER'S RATIO OF CONSUMPTION TO SAVING AND INVESTMENT

vidual time-market diagrams in chapter 6. In the present case, money assets are *increasing* as we go rightward on the horizontal axis, while in chapter 6 money assets were declining. Let us say that the taxpayer's initial position is a money stock of *OM; tt* is his given time-preference curve. His *effective time-preference rate,* determining his consumption/investment proportion, is t_1. Now, suppose that the government levies an income tax, reducing his initial monetary assets at the start of his spending period to *OM′*. His effective time-preference rate, the intersection of *tt* and the *M′* line, is now higher at t_2. He shifts to a higher proportion of consumption and a lower proportion of saving and investment.[35]

We have now seen two reasons why an income tax will shift the social proportion toward more consumption and less saving and investment. It might be objected that the time-preference reason is invalid, since the government officials and the people they subsidize will receive the tax revenues and find that *their* money stock has increased just as that of the taxpayers has declined. We shall see below, however, that no truly productive savings and investments can be made by government, its employees, or the recipients of its subsidies.

Some economists maintain that income taxation reduces savings and investment in society in yet a third way. They assert that income taxation, by its very nature, imposes a "double" tax on savings-investment as against consumption.[36] The reasoning runs as follows: Saving and consumption are really not symmetrical. All saving is directed toward enjoying more consumption in the future; otherwise, there would be no point at all to saving. Saving is abstaining from possible present consumption in return for the expectation of increased consumption at some time in the future. No one wants capital goods for their own sake. They are only the embodiment of increased consumption in the future. Saving-investment is Crusoe's building the stick to obtain more apples at a future date; it fructifies in higher consumption later. Hence, the imposition of an income tax is a "double" tax on consumption, and excessively penalizes saving and investment.[37]

This line of reasoning correctly explains the investment-consumption process. It suffers, however, from a grave defect: it is irrelevant to problems of taxation. It is true that saving is a fructifying agent. But the point is that everyone knows this; that is precisely why people save. Yet, even though they know that saving is a fructifying agent, they do not save all their income. Why? Because of their time-preferences for present consumption. Every individual, given his current income and value scales, allocates that income in the most desirable proportions between consumption, investment, and additions to his cash balance. Any other allocation would satisfy his desires less well and lower his position on his value scale. The fructifying power of saving is *already taken into account* when he makes his allocation. There is therefore no reason to say that an income tax doubly penalizes saving-investment; it penalizes the individual's entire standard of living, encompassing present consumption, future consumption, and his cash balance. It does not *per se* penalize saving any more than the other avenues of income allocation.

This Fisher argument reflects a curious tendency among economists devoted to the free market to be far more concerned about governmental measures penalizing saving and investment than they are about measures hobbling consumption. Surely an economist favoring the free market must grant that the market's voluntary consumption/investment allocations are optimal and that any government interference in this proportion, *from either direction,* is distortive of that market and of production to meet the wants of the consumers. There is nothing, after all, particularly sacred about savings; they are simply the road to future consumption. But they are, then, clearly no more important than *present* consumption, the allocations between the two being determined by the time preferences of all individuals. The economist who balks more at interference with free-market savings than he does at infringement on free-market consumption is therefore implicitly advocating statist interference in the opposite direction. He is implicitly calling for a coerced distortion of resources to lower consumption and increase investment.[38]

B. ATTEMPTS AT NEUTRAL TAXATION

So far, we have discussed the impact of a tax on an individual considered by himself. Equally important is the distortion of the market's *pattern* of factor prices and incomes, created by the way taxes bear down upon different people. The free market determines an intricate, almost infinite array and structure of prices, rates, and incomes. The imposition of different taxes disrupts these patterns and cripples the market's work of allocating resources and output. Thus, if firm A pays $5,000 a year for a certain type of labor, and firm B pays $3,000, laborers will tend to shift from B to A and thereby more efficiently serve the wants of consumers. But if the income earned at firm A is taxed $2,000 per annum, while income at B is taxed negligibly or not at all, the market inducement to move from B to A will totally or virtually disappear, perpetuating a misallocation of productive resources and hampering the growth and even the existence of firm A.

We have seen above that the quest for a *neutral tax*—a tax neutral to the market, leaving the market roughly as it was before the tax was imposed—is a hopeless venture. For there can be no uniformity in paying taxes when some people in society are necessarily taxpayers, while others are privileged tax-consumers. But even if we disregard these objections and fail to consider the redistributionist effects of government *spending* out of tax revenues, we cannot arrive at a system of neutral taxation.[39] Many writers have maintained that uniformly proportional income taxes for all would yield a neutral tax; for then, the relative ratios of incomes in society would remain the same as before. Thus, if A received $6,000 a year, B earned $3,000 and C $2,000, a 10% tax on each man would yield a "distribution" of: A, $5,400; B, $2,700; C, $1,800—the same mutual ratios as before. (This assumes, of course, no disincentive effects of the tax on the various individuals or, rather, equiproportional disincentive effects on each individual in the society—a most unlikely occurrence.) But the trouble is that this "solution" misconceives the nature of what a neutral tax would have to be. For a tax truly neutral to the free market would not be one that left income patterns the same as before; *it would be a tax which would affect the income pattern, and all other aspects of the economy, in the same way as if the tax were really a free-market price.*

This is a very important correction; for we must surely realize that when a service is sold at a certain price on the free market, this sale emphatically does *not* leave income "distribution" the same as before. For, normally, market prices are *not* proportional to each man's income or wealth, but are uniform *in the sense of equal to everyone,* regardless of his income or wealth or even his eagerness for the product. A loaf of bread does *not* cost a multimillionaire a thousand times as much as it costs the average man. If, indeed, the market really behaved in this way, there would soon be no market, for there would be no advantage whatever in earning money. The more money one earned, the more, *pari passu,* the price of every good would be raised to him. Therefore, the entire civilized money economy and the system of production and division of labor based upon it would break down. Far from being "neutral" to the free market, then, a proportional income tax follows a principle which, if consistently applied, would eradicate the market economy and the entire monetary economy itself.

It is clear, then, that equal taxation of everyone—the so-called "head tax" or "poll tax"—would be a far closer approach to the goal of neutrality. But even here, there are serious flaws in its neutrality, entirely apart from the ineluctable taxpayer-tax-consumer dichotomy. For one thing, goods and services on the free market are purchased only by those freely willing to obtain them at the market price. Since a tax is a compulsory levy rather than a free purchase, it can never be assumed that each and every member of society would, in a free market, pay this equal sum to the government. In fact, the very compulsory nature of taxation implies that far less revenue would be paid in to the government were it conducted in a voluntary manner. Rather than being neutral, therefore, the equal tax would distort market results by imposing undue levies on at least three groups of citizens: the poor, the uninterested, and the hostile, i.e., those who, for one reason or another, would *not* have voluntarily paid these equal sums to the government.

Another grave problem in treating the equal tax as akin to a free-market price is that we do not know what "services" of government the people are supposed to be "purchasing." For example, if the government uses the tax to subsidize a certain favored group, it is difficult to know what sort of "service" the payers of the head tax are reaping from this act of government. But let us take a seemingly clear-cut case of pure service, police protection, and let us assume that the head tax is being paid for this expenditure. The free-market rule is that equal prices are paid for equal services; but what, here, is an "equal service"? Surely, the service of police protection is of far greater magnitude in an urban crime center than it is in some sleepy backwater, where crime is rare. Police protection will certainly cost more in the crime-ridden area; hence, if it were supplied on the market, the price paid there would be higher than in the backwater. Furthermore, a person under particular threat of crime, and who might require greater surveillance, would have to pay a higher police fee. A uniform tax would be below market price in the dangerous areas and above it in the peaceful areas. To approach neutrality, then, a tax would have to vary in accordance with the *costs* of services and not be uniform.[40] This is the neglected *cost principle* of taxation.

The cost principle, however, is hardly neutral either. Apart from the inexorable taxpayer-tax-consumer problem, there is, again, the problem of how a "service" is to be defined and isolated. What is the "service" of redistribution from Peter to Paul, and what is the "cost" for which Peter is to be assessed? And even if we confine the discussion to such common services as police protection, there are grave flaws. In the first place, the costs of government, as we shall see further below, are bound to be much higher than those of the free market. Secondly, the State cannot calculate well and therefore cannot gauge its costs accurately. Thirdly, costs are equal to prices only in equilibrium; since the economy is never in equilibrium, costs are never a precise estimate of what the free-market price would have been. And finally, as in the equal tax, and in contrast to the free market, the taxpayer never *demonstrates* his benefit from the governmental act; it is simply and blithely assumed that he would have purchased the service voluntarily at this price.

Still another attempt at neutral taxation is the *benefit principle,* which states that a tax should be levied equal to the benefit which the individuals receive from the government service. It is not always realized what this principle would mean: e.g., that recipients of welfare benefits would have to pay the full costs of these benefits. Each recipient of government welfare would then have to pay *more* than he received, for he would also have to pay the "handling" costs of government bureaucracy. Obviously, there would be no such welfare or any other subsidy payments if the benefit principle were maintained. Even if we again confine the discussion to services like police protection, grave flaws still remain. Let us again disregard the persistent taxpayer-tax-consumer dichotomy. A fatal problem is that we cannot measure benefits or even know whether they exist. As in the head tax and cost principles, there is here no free market where people can *demonstrate* that they are receiving a benefit from the exchange greater than the value of the goods they surrender. In fact, since taxes are levied by coercion, it is clear that people's benefits from government are considerably *less* than the amount that they are required to pay, since, if left free, they would contribute less to government. The "benefit," then, is simply assumed arbitrarily by government officials.

Furthermore, even if the benefit were freely demonstrable, the *benefit principle* would not approach the process of the free market. For, once again, individuals pay a *uniform price* for services on the free market, regardless of the extent of their subjective benefits. The man who would "walk a mile for a Camel" pays no more, ordinarily, than the man who couldn't care less. To tax everyone in accordance with the benefit he receives, then, is diametrically opposed to the market principle. Finally, if everyone's benefit is taxed away, there would be no reason for him to make the exchange or to receive the government service. On the market, not all people, not *even* the marginal buyers, pay the full amount of their benefit. The supramarginal buyers obtain unmeasurable surplus benefit, and *so do* the marginal buyers, for without such a surplus they would not buy the product. Moreover, for such services as police protection, the benefit principle would require the poor and the infirm to pay *more* than the rich and the able, since the former may be said to benefit more from protection. Finally, it should be noted that if each person's benefit from government is to be taxed away, the bureaucrats, who receive all their income from the government, would have to return their whole salary to the government and so serve without pay.[41]

We have thus seen that no principle of taxation can be neutral with respect to the free market. *Progressive* taxation, where each man pays *more* than proportionately to his income, of course makes no attempt at neutrality. If the proportional tax embodies a principle destructive to the entire market economy and the monetary economy itself, then the progressive tax does so still more. For the progressive tax penalizes the able and efficient in even greater proportion than their relative ability and efficiency. Progressive rates are a particular disincentive against especially able work or entrepreneurship. And since such ability is engaged in serving the consumer, a progressive tax levies a particular burden on the consumers as well.

In addition to the two ways discussed above by which income taxation penalizes saving, the progressive tax imposes an added penalty. For empirically, in most cases, the wealthy save and invest proportionately more of their incomes than the lower-income groups. There is, however, no apodictic, praxeological reason why this must always be so. The rule would not hold, for example, in a country where the wealthy bought jewelry while the poor thriftily saved and invested.

While the progressive principle is certainly highly destructive of the market, most conservative, pro-free-market economists tend to overweigh its effects and to underweigh the destructive effects of proportional taxation. Proportional income taxation has many of the same consequences, and therefore the *level* of income taxation is generally more important for the market than the degree of progressivity. Thus, society A may have a proportional income tax requiring every man to pay 50% of his income; society B may have a very steeply progressive tax requiring a poor man to pay ¼% and the richest man 10% of his income. The rich man will certainly prefer society B, *even though* the tax is progressive—demonstrating that it is not so much the progressivity as the height of his tax that burdens the rich man.

Incidentally, the poor producer, with a lower tax upon him, will also prefer society B. This demonstrates the fallacy in the common conservative complaint against progressive taxation that it is a means "for the poor to rob the rich." For both the poor man and the rich man have, in our example, chosen progression! The reason is that the "poor" do not "rob the rich" under progressive taxation. Instead, it is the State that "robs" both through taxation, whether proportional or progressive.

It may be objected that the poor benefit from the State's expenditures and subsidies from the tax proceeds and thus do their "robbing" indirectly. But this overlooks the fact that the State can spend its money in many different ways: it may consume the products of specific industries; it may subsidize some or all of the rich; it may subsidize some or all of the poor. The fact of progressivity does not *in itself* imply that the "poor" are being subsidized en masse. Indeed, if some of the poor are being subsidized, others will probably not be, and so these latter net taxpayers will be "robbed" along with the rich. In fact, since there are usually far more poor than rich, the poor en masse may very well bear the greatest burden of even a progressive tax system.

Of all the possible types of taxes, the one most calculated to cripple and destroy the workings of the market is the *excess profits tax*. For of all productive incomes, profits are a relatively small sum with enormous significance and impact; they are the motor, the driving force, of the entire market economy. Profit-and-loss signals are the prompters of the entrepreneurs and capitalists who direct and ever redirect the productive resources of society in the best possible ways and combinations to satisfy the changing desires of consumers under changing conditions. With the drive for profit crippled, profit and loss no longer serve as an effective incentive, or, therefore, as the means for economic calculation in the market economy.

It is curious that in wartime, precisely when it would seem most urgent to preserve an efficient productive system, the cry invariably goes up for "taking the profits out of war." This zeal never seems to apply so harshly to the clearly war-borne "profits" of steel workers in higher wages—only to the profits of entrepreneurs. There is certainly no better way of crippling a war effort. In addition, the "excess" concept requires some sort of norm above which the profit can be taxed. This norm may either be a certain rate of profit, which involves the numerous difficulties of measuring profit and capital investment in every firm; or it may refer to profits at a base period before the war started. The latter, the general favorite because it specifically taps *war* profits, makes the economy even more chaotic. For it means that while the government strains for more *war* production, the excess profits tax creates every incentive toward lower and inefficient war production. In short, the EPT tends to freeze the process of production as of the peacetime base period. And the longer the war lasts, the more obsolete, the more inefficient and absurd, the base-period structure becomes.

C. SHIFTING AND INCIDENCE: A TAX ON AN INDUSTRY

No discussion of taxation, however brief, can overlook the famous problem of "the shifting and incidence" of taxation. In brief, who pays a tax? The person on whom it is levied, or someone else to whom the former is able to "shift" the tax? There are still economists, incredibly, who hew to the old nineteenth-century "equal diffusion" theory of taxation, which simply closes the problem by proclaiming that "all taxes are shifted to everyone," so that there is no need to analyze each one in particular.[42] This obscurantist tendency is fostered by treating "shifting" in too broad a way. Thus, if an income tax is levied on Jones at 80%, this will hurt *not only* Jones, but also—by decreasing Jones' incentives as well as capacities—other consumers by reducing Jones' work and savings. It is therefore true that the *effects* of taxation diffuse outward from the center of the target. But this is far from saying that Jones can simply shift the tax burden onto the shoulders of others. The concept of "shifting" will here be limited to the case where the payment of a tax can be directly transferred *from* the original payer *to* someone else, and will not be used when others suffer *in addition* to the original taxpayer. The latter may be called the "indirect effects" of the tax.

The first rule of shifting is that *an income tax cannot be shifted.* This formerly accepted truth in economics is now countered with the popular assumption that, for example, a tax on wages will spur unions to demand higher wages to compensate for the tax, and that therefore the tax on wages is shifted "forward" onto the employer, who, in turn, shifts it again forward onto the body of consumers. And yet almost every step in this commonly proclaimed sequence is an egregious fallacy. It is absurd, in the first place, to think that workers or unions wait quietly for a tax to galvanize them into making demands. Workers *always* want higher wages; unions always demand more. The question is: Will they get more? There is no reason to think that they can. A worker can get only the value of the discounted marginal productivity of his labor. No clamor will raise that productivity, and therefore none can raise the wage he earns from his employer. Union demands for higher wages will be treated as usual, i.e., they can be satisfied only at the cost of the unemployment of some of the work force in that industry. But this is true whether or not there has been a tax on wages; the tax will have nothing to do with the final wage set on the market.

The idea that the increased cost will be passed on to the consumer by the employer is an illustration of perhaps the single most widespread fallacy on taxation: that businessmen can simply shift their higher costs forward onto the consumers in the form of higher prices. All the economic theory expounded in this book shows the error of this doctrine. For the price of a given product is set by the demand schedules of the consumers. There is nothing in higher costs or higher taxes which, *per se,* increases these schedules; hence, *any* change in selling prices, whether higher or lower, will *decrease* the revenues of the business involved. For each business, on the market, tends to be, at all times, at its "maximum profit point" in relation to the consumers. Prices are already at their point of maximum return for the business; therefore, higher taxes or other costs imposed on the firm will reduce their net incomes rather than be smoothly and easily passed on to consumers. We thus arrive at this significant conclusion: *no tax* (not just an income tax) *can ever be shifted forward.*

Suppose that a particularly heavy tax—of whatever type—has been laid on a specific industry: say the liquor industry. What will be the effects? As we have noted, the tax will not simply be "passed on" to the consumers.[43] Instead, the price of liquor will remain the same; the net income of the firms will decline. This will mean that returns will be lower to capital and enterprise in liquor than in other industries of the economy; marginal liquor firms will suffer losses and go out of business; and, in general, productive resources of all types will flow out of liquor and into other industries. The *long-run effect,* therefore, is to decrease the supply of liquor produced, and therefore, by the law of supply and demand, to raise the price of liquor on the market. However, as we have said above, this process—this diffusion of suffering over the economy—is hardly "shifting." For the tax is not simply "passed on"; it only permeates to the consumers *through* hurting the industry taxed. The final result will be a distortion of the factors of production; fewer goods are now being produced than the consumers would prefer in the liquor industry; and too many goods, relatively to liquor, are being produced in the other industry.

Taxes, in short, can more readily be "shifted backward" than forward. Strictly, the result is not shifting because it is not a painless process. But it is clear that the backward process (backward to the factors of production) happens more quickly and directly than the effects on consumers. For losses or lowered profits to liquor firms will immediately lower their demand for land, labor and capital factors of production; this falling of demand schedules will lower wages and rents earned in the liquor industry; and these lower earnings will induce a shift of labor, land and capital out of liquor and into other industries. The rapid "backward-shifting" is in harmony with the "Austrian" theory of consumption and production developed in this volume; for prices of factors are determined by the selling prices of the goods which they produce, and *not vice versa* (which would have to be the conclusion of the naive "shifting-forward" doctrine).

It should be noted that, in some cases, the industry itself can welcome a tax upon it, for the sake of conferring an indirect, but effective, monopolistic privilege on the supramarginal firms. Thus, a flat "license" tax will confer a particular privilege on the more heavily capitalized firms, which can more easily afford to pay the fee.

D. SHIFTING AND INCIDENCE: A GENERAL SALES TAX

The most popular example of a tax supposedly shifted forward is the *general sales tax*. Surely, for example, if the government imposes a uniform 20% tax on all retail sales, and if we can make the simplifying assumption that the tax can be equally well enforced everywhere, then business will simply "pass on" the 20% increase in all prices to consumers. In fact, however, there is no way for prices to increase at all! As in the case of one particular industry, prices were previously set, or approximately so, at the points of maximum net revenue for the firms. Stocks of goods or factors have not yet changed, and neither have demand schedules. How then could prices rise? Moreover, if we look at the general array of prices, as is proper when dealing with a general sales tax, these are determined by the supply of and the demand for money, from the goods and money sides. For the general array of prices to rise, there must be either an increase in the supply of money, a decrease in the demand schedule for money, or both. Nothing in a general sales tax causes a change in either of these determinants.[44]

Furthermore, the long-run effects of a general sales tax on prices will be smaller than in the case of an equivalent partial excise tax. A tax on a specific industry, such as liquor, will push resources out of this industry and into others, and therefore the relative price of the taxed commodity will eventually rise. In a general, uniformly enforced sales tax, however, there is no room for such shifts of resources.[45]

The myth that a sales tax can be shifted forward is comparable to the myth that a general union-imposed wage increase can be shifted forward to higher prices for consumers, thereby "causing inflation." There is here no way that the general array of prices can rise, and the only possible result of such a wage increase is mass unemployment.[46]

In considering the general sales tax, many people are misled by the fact that the price paid by the consumer necessarily *includes* the tax. If someone goes to a movie and pays $1.00 admission, and if he sees prominently posted the information that this covers a "price" of $.85 and a tax of $.15, he tends to conclude that the tax has simply been added on to the "price." But $1.00 is the price, not $.85, the latter sum simply being the revenue accruing to the firm after taxes. The revenue to the firm has, in effect, been *reduced* to allow for payment of taxes.

This is precisely the consequence of a general sales tax. Its immediate impact lowers the gross revenue of firms by the amount of the tax. In the long run, of course, firms cannot pay the tax, the loss in gross revenue of firms being imputed backward to interest income by capitalists and to wages and rents earned by owners of original factors—labor and ground land. A decrease in gross revenue to retail firms is reflected back to a decreased demand for the products of all the higher-order firms. The major result of a general sales tax is a general reduction in the net revenues accruing to original factors. The sales tax has been *shifted backwards* to original factor returns—to interest and to all wages and ground rents. No longer does every original factor of production earn its discounted marginal product. Original factors now earn *less* than their DMVP's, the reduction consisting of the sales tax paid to the government.

Let us now integrate this analysis of the incidence of a general sales tax with our previous general analysis of the benefits and burdens of taxation. This is accomplished by remembering that the proceeds of taxation are, in turn, spent by the government. Whether or not the government spends the money for resources for its own activities or simply transfers the money to people it subsidizes, the effect is to *shift* consumption and investment demand from private hands to the government or to government-supported individuals, by the amount of the tax revenue. The tax has been ultimately levied on the *incomes* of original factors, and the money transferred from their hands to the government. The income of the government and of those subsidized by the government has been increased at the expense of the tax producers, and therefore consumption and investment demands on the market have been shifted from the producers to the expropriators by the amount of the tax. As a consequence, the value of the monetary unit will remain unchanged (barring a difference in demands for money between the taxpayers and the tax-consumers), but the *array* of prices will shift in accordance with the shift in demands. Thus, if the market has been spending heavily on clothing, and the government uses the revenue mostly for the purchase of arms, there will be a fall in the price of clothes and a rise in the price of arms, and a tendency for nonspecific factors to shift out of the production of clothing and into the production of armaments.

As a result, there will not finally be, as might be assumed, a proportional 20% fall in all original factor incomes as the result of a 20% general sales tax. Specific factors in industries that have lost business from the shift from private to governmental demand will lose proportionately more in income; specific factors in industries gaining in demand will lose proportionately less—some may gain so much as to gain absolutely from the change. Nonspecific factors will not be affected as much proportionately, but they too will lose and gain according to the difference that the concrete shift in demand makes in their marginal value productivity.

It should be carefully noted that the general sales tax is a conspicuous example of *failure to tax consumption.* The sales tax is commonly *supposed* to penalize consumption, rather than income or capital. Yet we find that the sales tax reduces, not just consumption, but the *incomes* of original factors. *The general sales tax is therefore an income tax,* albeit a rather haphazard one. Many "right-wing" economists have advocated general sales taxation, as opposed to income taxation, on the grounds that the former taxes consumption but not savings-investment; many "left-wing" economists have opposed sales taxation for the same reason. Both are mistaken; the sales tax is an income tax, though of a more haphazard and uncertain incidence. The major effect of the general sales tax will be that of the income tax—to reduce the consumption *and* the saving-investment of the taxpayers.[47] In fact, since, as we have seen, the income tax by its nature falls more heavily on savings-investment than on consumption, we reach the paradoxical and important conclusion that a tax on *consumption* will fall more heavily on *savings-investment* than on consumption in its ultimate incidence.

E. A TAX ON LAND VALUES

Wherever taxes fall, they blight, hamper, and distort the productive activity of the market. Clearly, a tax on wages will distort the allocation of labor effort, a tax on profits will cripple the profit-and-loss motor of the economy, a tax on interest will tend to consume capital, etc. One commonly conceded exception to this rule is the doctrine of Henry George that ground-landowners perform no productive function and that therefore the government may safely tax site value without reducing the supply of productive services on the market. This is the *economic,* as distinguished from the moral, rationale for the famous "single tax." Unhappily, very few economists have challenged this basic assumption, the single-tax proposal being generally rejected on grounds purely pragmatic ("there is no way in practice of distinguishing site from improvement value of land") or conservative ("too much has been invested in land to expropriate the landowners now").[48]

Yet this central Georgist contention is completely fallacious. The owner of ground land performs a very important productive service. He finds, brings into use, and then allocates, land sites to the most value-productive bidders. We must not be misled by the fact that the physical stock of land is fixed at any given time. In the case of land, as of other material goods, it is not just the physical good that is being sold, but a whole bundle of services along with it—among which is the service of transferring ownership from seller to buyer, and doing so efficiently. Ground land does not simply exist; it must be *served to* the user by the owner (one man, of course, can perform both functions when the land is "vertically integrated").[49] The landowner earns the highest ground rents by allocating land sites to their most value-productive uses, i.e., to those uses most desired by consumers. In particular, we must not overlook the importance of *location* and the productive service of the site-owner in assuring the most productive locations for each particular use.

The view that bringing sites into use and deciding upon their location is not really "productive" is a vestige from the old classical view that a service which does not tangibly "create" something physical is not "really" productive.[50] Actually, this function is just as productive as any other, and a particularly vital function it is. To hamper and destroy this function would wreck the market economy.[51]

F. TAXING "EXCESS PURCHASING POWER"

In this necessarily hasty overview of the high spots of taxation theory, we have space for only one more comment: a criticism of the very common view that, in a business boom, the government should increase taxation "in order to sop up excess purchasing power," and thereby halt the inflation and stabilize the economy. We shall discuss the problems of inflation, stabilization, and the business cycle below; here, let us note the oddity of assuming that a *tax* is somehow less of a social cost, less of a burden, than a *price*. Thus, suppose, in a boom, that Messrs. A, B, and C, with the money they have on hand, would spend a certain amount on some commodity—say pipes—at a certain market price, e.g., $10 per pipe. The government decides that this is a most unfortunate situation, that the market price is—by some arbitrary, undivulged standard—"too high," and that therefore it must help its subjects by taxing their money away from them, and thus lowering prices. Suppose, indeed, that A, B, and C are taxed sufficiently to lower the pipe price to, say, $8. By what reasoning are they better off, now that taxes have been increased by precisely the amount that their monetary funds have dwindled? In short, the "tax price" has gone up in order that the prices of other goods may decline. Why is a voluntary price, paid willingly by buyers and accepted by sellers, somehow "bad" or burdensome for the buyers, while at the same time a "price" levied compulsorily on the same buyers for dubious governmental services for which they have not demonstrated a need is somehow "good"? Why are high prices burdensome and high taxes not?

9. *Binary Intervention: Government Expenditures*[52]

A. THE "PRODUCTIVE CONTRIBUTION" OF GOVERNMENT SPENDING

Government expenditures are a coerced transfer of resources from private producers to the uses preferred by government officials. It is customary to classify government spending into two categories: *resource-using,* and *transfer.* Resource-using expenditures frankly shift resources from private persons in society to the use of government: this may take the form of hiring bureaucrats to work for government—which shifts labor resources directly—or of buying products from business firms. Transfer payments are pure subsidy spending—when the government takes from Peter to pay Paul. It is true that, in the latter case, the government gives "Paul" money to decide the allocation as he wishes, and in a sense we may analyze the two types of spending separately. But the similarities here are greater than the differences. For, in both cases, resources are seized from private producers and shifted to the uses which government officials think best. After all, when a bureaucrat receives his government salary, this payment is in the same sense a "transfer payment" from the taxpayers, and the bureaucrat is also free to decide how further to allocate the income at his command. In both cases, money and resources are shifted from producers to nonproducers, who consume or otherwise use them.[53]

This type of analysis of government has been neglected because economists and statisticians tend to assume, rather blithely, that government expenditures are a measure of its productive contribution to society. In the "private sector" of the economy, the value of productive output is sensibly gauged by the amount of money that consumers spend voluntarily on that output. Curiously, on the other hand, the government's "productive output" is gauged, not by what is *spent on* government, but by what government itself spends! No wonder that grandiose claims are often made for the unique productive power of government spending, when a mere increase in that spending serves to raise the government's "productive contribution" to the economy.[54]

What, then, *is* the productive contribution of government? Since the value of government is not gauged on the market, and the payments to the government are not voluntary, it is impossible to estimate. It is impossible to know how much would be paid in to the government were it purely voluntary, or indeed, whether one central government in each geographical area would exist at all. Since, then, the only thing we do know is that the tax-and-spend process diverts income and resources from what they would have been doing in the "private sector," we must conclude that the government's productive contribution to the economy is precisely zero. Furthermore, even if it be objected that governmental services are worth *something,* it would have to be noted that we are again suffering from the error pointed out by Bastiat: a sole emphasis on what is *seen,* to the neglect of what is *not* seen. We may see the government's hydroelectric dam in operation; we do *not* see the things that private individuals would have done with the money—whether buying consumers' goods or investing in producers' goods—but which they were compelled to forgo. In fact, since private consumers would have done something else, something more desired, and therefore from their point of view more *productive,* with the money, we can be sure that the loss in productivity incurred by the government's tax and spending is greater than whatever productivity it has contributed. In short, strictly, the government's productivity is not simply zero, but *negative,* for it has imposed a loss in productivity upon society.[55]

Government expenditure is often referred to as "investment" resulting in "capital." And we have heard much in recent years about Soviet and other multi-Year Plans busily engaged in building up "capital" by government action. Yet it is illegitimate to use the term "capital" for government expenditures. Capital is the status of productive goods along the path to eventual consumption. In any sort of division-of-labor economy, capital goods are built, not for their own sake by the investor, but in order to use them to produce lower-order and eventually consumers' goods. In short, a characteristic of an investment expenditure is that the good in question is not being used to fulfill the needs of the investor, but of someone else—the consumer. Yet, when government confiscates resources from the private market economy, it is precisely defying the wishes of the consumers; when government invests in any good, it does so to serve the whims of government officials, not the desires of consumers. Therefore, no government expenditures can be considered genuine "investment," and no government-owned assets can be considered capital. Government expenditures are divisible into two parts: *consumption* expenditures by government officials, beneficiaries of government subsidies, and other nonproductive recipients; and *waste* expenditures, where government officials really believe that they are "investing" in "capital." These waste expenditures result in *waste assets*.[56] The consumption of the governmentally privileged is, of course, in a different category from private consumption, since it is necessarily *at the expense* of the private consumption of producers. We may therefore call the former "antiproductive consumption." [57]

B. SUBSIDIES AND TRANSFER PAYMENTS

Let us delve a little further into the typology of government spending. Transfer spending or subsidies distort the market by coercively penalizing the efficient for the benefit of the inefficient. (And it does so even if the firm or individual is efficient without a subsidy, for its activities are then being encouraged beyond their most economic point.) Subsidies prolong the life of inefficient firms and prevent the flexibility of the market from fully satisfying consumer wants. The greater the extent of government subsidy, the more the market is prevented from working, the more resources are frozen in inefficient ways, and the lower will be the standard of living of everyone. Furthermore, the more government intervenes and subsidizes, the more caste conflict will be created in society, for individuals and groups will benefit only *at one another's expense*. The more widespread the tax-and-subsidy process, the more people will be induced to abandon production and join the army of those who live coercively off production. Production and living standards will be progressively lowered as energy is diverted from production to politics and as government saddles a dwindling base of production with a growing and more topheavy burden of the State-privileged. This process will be all the more accelerated because those who succeed in any activity will invariably tend to be those who are best at performing it. Those who particularly flourish on the free market, therefore, will be those most adept at production and at serving their fellow men; those who succeed in the political struggle for subsidies, on the other hand, will be those most adept at wielding coercion or at winning favors from wielders of coercion. Generally, different people will be in the different categories of the successful, in accordance with the universal specialization of skills. Furthermore, for those who are skillful at both, the tax-and-subsidy system will encourage and promote their predatory skills and penalize their productive ones.

A common example of direct transfer subsidy is governmental *poor relief.* State poor relief is clearly a *subsidization of poverty,* for men are now automatically entitled to money from the State because of their poverty. Hence, the marginal disutility of income forgone from leisure diminishes, and idleness and poverty tend to increase further, which in turn increases the amount of subsidy that must be extracted from the taxpayers. Thus, a system of legally subsidized poverty tends to call forth more of the very poverty that is supposedly being alleviated. When, as is generally the case, the amount of subsidy depends directly on the number of children possessed by the pauper, there is a further incentive for the pauper to breed more children than otherwise and thereby multiply the number of paupers—and even more dependent paupers—still further.[58] The sincerity of the State's desire to promote charity towards the poor may be gauged by two perennial drives of government: to suppress "charity rackets" and to drive individual beggars off the streets because the "government makes plenty of provision for them." [59] The effect of both measures is to cripple voluntary individual gifts of charity and to force the public to route its giving into the channels approved by, and tied in with, government officialdom.

Similarly, governmental *unemployment relief,* often supposed to help in curing unemployment, has the precisely reverse effect: it subsidizes and intensifies unemployment. We have seen that unemployment arises when laborers or unions set a minimum wage above what they could obtain on the unhampered market. Tax aid helps them to keep this unrealistic minimum and hence prolongs the period of unemployment and aggravates the problem.

C. RESOURCE-USING ACTIVITIES

Let us now return to the resource-using activities of government, where the State professes to be providing a service of some sort to the public. Government "service" may be either furnished free or sold at a price to users. "Free" services are particularly characteristic of government. Police and military protection, fire-fighting, education, parks, some water supply come to mind as examples. The first point to note, of course, is that these services are not and cannot be truly *free*. A free good, as we saw early in this book, would not be a good and hence not an object of human action; it would simply exist in superabundance for all. If a good does not exist aplenty for all, then the resource is scarce, and supplying it costs society other goods forgone. Hence it cannot be free. The resources needed to supply the free governmental service are extracted from the rest of production. Payment is made, however, not by users on the basis of their voluntary purchases, but by a coerced levy on the taxpayers. A basic split is thus effected between *payment* and *receipt of service*. This split is inherent in all government operations.

Many grave consequences follow from the split and from the "free" service as well. As in all cases where price is below the free market price, an enormous and excessive demand is stimulated for the good, far beyond the supply of service available. Consequently, there will always be "shortages" of the free good, constant complaints of insufficiency, overcrowding, etc. An illustration is the perpetual complaints about police insufficiency, particularly in crime-ridden districts, about teacher and school shortages in the public school system, about traffic jams on government-owned streets and highways, etc. In no area of the free market are there such chronic complaints about shortages, insufficiencies, and low quality service. In all areas of private enterprise, firms try to coax and persuade consumers to buy more of their product. Where government owns and operates, on the other hand, there are invariably calls on consumers for patience and sacrifice, and problems of shortages and deficiencies continually abound. It is doubtful if any private enterprise would ever do what the New York City and other governments have done: exhort consumers to use *less* water. It is also characteristic of government operation that when a water shortage develops, it is the *consumers* and not the government "enterprisers" who are blamed for the shortage. The pressure is on consumers to sacrifice, and to use less, while in private industry the (welcome) pressure is on entrepreneurs to supply more.[60]

The well-known inefficiencies of government operation are *not* empirical accidents, resulting perhaps from the lack of a civil-service tradition. They are *inherent* in all government enterprise, and the excessive demand fomented by free and other underpriced services is just one of the many reasons for this condition.

Free supply not only subsidizes the users at the expense of non-using taxpayers; it also misallocates resources by failing to supply the service where it is most needed. The same is true, to a lesser extent, wherever the price is under the free-market price. On the free market, consumers can dictate the pricing and thereby assure the best allocation of productive resources to supply their wants. In a government enterprise, this cannot be done. Let us take again the case of the free service. Since there is no pricing, and therefore no exclusion of submarginal uses, there is no way that the government, even if it wanted to, could allocate its services to their most important uses and to the most eager buyers. All buyers, all uses, are artificially kept on the same plane. As a result, the most important uses will be slighted. The government is faced with insuperable allocation problems, which it cannot solve *even to its own satisfaction*. Thus, the government will be confronted with the problem: Should we build a road in place A or place B? There is no rational way whatever by which it can make this decision. It cannot aid the private consumers of the road in the best way. It can decide only according to the whim of the ruling government official, i.e., only if the *government officials* do the "consuming," and not the public.[61] If the government wishes to do what is best for the public, it is faced with an impossible task.

D. THE FALLACY OF GOVERNMENT ON A "BUSINESS BASIS"

Government may either subsidize deliberately by giving a service away free, or it may genuinely try to find the true market price, i.e., to "operate on a business basis." The latter is often the cry raised by conservatives—that government enterprise be placed on a business footing, that deficits be ended, etc. Almost always this means raising the price. Is this a rational solution, however? It is often stated that a single government enterprise, operating within the sphere of a private market and buying resources from it, can price its services and allocate its resources efficiently. This, however, is incorrect. *There is a fatal flaw* that permeates every conceivable scheme of government enterprise and ineluctably prevents it from rational pricing and efficient allocation of resources. Because of this flaw, government enterprise can *never* be operated on a "business" basis, no matter how ardent a government's intentions.

What is this fatal flaw? It is the fact that government can obtain virtually unlimited resources by means of the coercive tax power (i.e., limited only by the total resources of society). Private businesses must obtain their funds from private investors. This allocation of funds by investors, based on time preference and foresight, "rations" funds and resources to the most profitable and therefore the most serviceable uses. Private firms can get funds *only* from consumers and investors; they can get funds, in other words, only from people who value and buy their services and from savers who are willing to risk investment of their saved funds in anticipation of profit. In short, payment and service are, we repeat, indissolubly linked on the market. But government, on the other hand, can get as much money as it likes. The free market therefore provides a "mechanism," which we have analyzed in detail, for allocating funds for future and present consumption, for directing resources to their most value-productive uses for all the people. It thereby provides a means for businessmen to allocate resources and to price services to insure optimum use. Government, however, has no checkrein on itself, i.e., no requirement of meeting a test of profit-and-loss or valued service to consumers, to permit it to obtain funds. Private enterprise can get funds only from satisfied, valuing customers and from investors guided by present and expected future profits and losses. Government gets more funds at its own whim.

With the checkrein gone, gone also is any opportunity for government to allocate resources rationally. How can it know whether to build road A or road B, whether to "invest" in a road or a school—in fact, how much to spend for all of its activities? There is no rational way that it can allocate funds or even decide how much to have. When there is a shortage of teachers or schoolrooms or police or streets, the government and its supporters have only one answer: more money. The people must relinquish more of their money to the government. Why is this type of answer never offered on the free market? The reason is that money must always be *withdrawn* from some other use in consumption or investment—and this withdrawal must be justified. On the market, justification is provided by the test of profit and loss—the indication that the most urgent wants of the consumers are being satisfied. If an enterprise or product is earning high profits for its owners, and these profits are expected to continue, more money *will be* forthcoming; if not, and losses are being incurred, money will flow *out* of the industry. The profit-and-loss test serves as the critical guide for directing the flow of productive resources. No such guide exists for government, which therefore has no rational way to decide *how much* money to spend in total or in each specific line. The more money it spends, the more service, of course, it can supply—but where to stop?[62]

Proponents of government enterprise may retort that the government should simply tell its bureau to act *as if* it were a profit-making enterprise and to establish itself in the same way as a private business. There are two basic flaws in this theory: (1) It is impossible to *play* enterprise. Enterprise means risking one's own money in investment. Bureaucratic managers and politicians have no real incentive to develop entrepreneurial skills, to really adjust to consumer demands. They do not risk loss of their money in the enterprise. (2) Aside from the question of incentives, even the most eager managers *could not* function as a business. For, regardless of the treatment accorded the operation *after* it is established, the *initial* launching of the firm is made with government money, and therefore by coercive levy. A fatally arbitrary element has been "built into" the very vitals of the enterprise. Furthermore, future decisions on expenditures will be made out of tax funds and will therefore be subject to the same flaw. The ease of obtaining money will inherently distort the operations of government enterprise. Moreover, suppose that the government "invests" in an enterprise E. Either the free market, left alone, would also have invested in this selfsame enterprise, or it would not. If it would have, then the economy suffers, at the very least, from the "take" going to the intermediary bureaucracy. If not, and this is almost certain, then it follows immediately that the expenditure on E is a distortion of private utility on the market—that some other expenditure would have brought greater monetary returns. It follows once again that a government enterprise cannot duplicate the conditions of private business.

In addition, the establishment of government enterprise creates an "unfair" competitive advantage over private firms, for at least part of its capital was gained by coercion rather than service. It is clear that government, with its subsidization, can drive a private business out of the field. Private investment in the same industry will be greatly restricted, since future investors will anticipate losses at the hands of privileged governmental competitors. Moreover, since all services compete for the consumer's dollar, all private firms and all private investment will to some degree be affected and hampered. And when a new government enterprise begins, it generates fears in other industries that they will be next, that they will either be confiscated or forced to compete with government-subsidized enterprises. This fear tends to repress productive investment further and thus lower the general standard of living still more.

Another argument, used quite correctly by "leftist" proponents of government ownership, is this: If business operation is so desirable, why take such a tortuous route? Why not scrap government ownership and turn the whole operation over to private business enterprise? Why go to such elaborate lengths to try to imitate the apparent ideal (private ownership) when the ideal may be pursued directly? The call for business principles in government, therefore, makes little sense, even if that call could be successful.

Many "criteria" have been offered by writers as guides for the pricing of government services. One criterion supports pricing according to "marginal cost." As we have indicated above, however, this is hardly a criterion at all and rests on classical fallacies of price determination by costs. "Marginal" varies according to the period of time surveyed. And costs are not in fact static but flexible; they change according to prices and hence cannot be used as a guide to the setting of prices. Moreover, prices equal average costs only in final equilibrium, and equilibrium cannot be regarded as an ideal for the real world. The market only *tends toward* this goal. Finally, costs of government operation will be higher than for similar operations on the free market.[63]

Government enterprise will not only hamper and repress private investment and entrepreneurship in the same industry and in industries throughout the economy; it will also disrupt the entire labor market. For the government (*a*) will decrease production and living standards in the society by siphoning off potentially productive labor to the bureaucracy; (*b*) using confiscated funds, it will be able to pay more than the market rate for labor and hence set up a clamor by government job-seekers for an expansion of the unproductive bureaucratic machine; and (*c*) the government's high tax-supported wages may well mislead workers into believing that this reflects the market wage in private industry, thus causing unwanted unemployment.

The inefficiencies of government operation are compounded by several other factors. As we have seen, a government enterprise competing in an industry can usually drive out private owners, since the government can subsidize itself in many ways and supply itself with unlimited funds when desired. In cases where it cannot compete even under these conditions, it can arrogate to itself a compulsory monopoly, driving out competitors by force. This was done in the United States in the case of the post office.[64] When the government thus grants itself a monopoly, it may go to the other extreme from free service; it may charge a monopoly price. Charging a monopoly price—now identifiably different from a free-market price—distorts resources again and creates an artificial scarcity of the particular good. It also permits an enormously lowered quality of service. A governmental monopoly need not worry that customers may go elsewhere or that inefficiency may mean its demise.[65] It is particularly absurd to call for "business principles" where a government enterprise functions as a monopoly. Periodically, for example, there are demands that the post office be put on a "business basis" and end its deficit, which must be paid by the taxpayers. But ending the deficit of an inherently and necessarily inefficient government operation does not mean going on a business basis. To cover costs, the price must be raised high enough to achieve a monopoly price and so camouflage and compensate for the government's inefficiencies. A monopoly price will levy an excessive burden on the users of the postal service, especially since the monopoly is compulsory. On the other hand, we have seen that even monopolists must abide by the consumers' demand schedule. If this demand schedule is elastic enough, it may well happen that a monopoly price will reduce revenue so much or cut down so much on its increase that a higher price will *increase* deficits rather than reduce them. An outstanding example has been the New York City subway system in recent years.[66]

E. CENTERS OF CALCULATIONAL CHAOS

We have seen in chapter 10 above that one cartel or one firm could not own all the means of production in the economy, because it could not calculate prices and allocate factors in a rational manner. And we have seen that this is the reason why State socialism could also not plan or allocate rationally. We further noted that two or more stages could not be totally integrated vertically on the market—for total integration would eliminate a whole segment of the market and establish an island of calculational and allocational chaos, an island that would preclude optimal planning for profits and maximum satisfaction for the consumers.

In the case of simple government ownership, still another extension of this thesis becomes evident. For *each* governmental firm introduces its *own* island of chaos into the economy; *there is no need to wait for full socialism for chaos to begin its work.* No government enterprise can ever determine prices or costs or allocate factors or funds in a rational, welfare-maximizing manner. No government enterprise could be established on a "business basis" even if the desire were present. Thus, any governmental operation injects a point of chaos into the economy; and since all markets are interconnected in the economy, every governmental activity disrupts and distorts pricing, the allocation of factors, consumption/investment ratios, etc. Every government enterprise not only lowers the social utilities of the consumers by forcing the allocation of funds to other ends than those desired by the public; it lowers the utility of everyone (including the utilities of some government officials) by distorting the market and spreading calculational chaos. The greater the extent of government ownership, of course, the more powerful will this impact become.

F. CONFLICT AND THE COMMAND POSTS

Aside from its purely economic consequences, government ownership has another kind of impact on society; it necessarily substitutes conflict for the harmony of the free market. Since government service means service by one set of decision-makers, it comes to mean uniform service. The desires of all those forced, directly or indirectly, to pay for the government service cannot be satisfied. Only some forms of the service can or will be produced by the government agency. As a result, government enterprise creates enormous caste conflicts among the citizens, each of whom has different ideas on the best form of service. In the final result, government enterprise can hardly fail to substitute its own values, or the values of one set of customers, for the values of all others. Artificially standardized services of poorer quality—fit to governmental taste or convenience—will hold sway, in contrast to the diversified services of higher quality which the free market supplies to fit the tastes of a multitude of individuals.

In recent years government schools in America have furnished a striking example of such problems and conflicts. Some parents prefer racially segregated schools; others prefer integrated education. Some parents want their children taught socialism; others want antisocialist teaching in the schools. There is no way that the government can resolve these conflicts. It can only impose the will of one group by coercion and leave the others dissatisfied and unhappy. Whichever type of school is chosen, some groups of parents will suffer. On the other hand, there is no such conflict on the free market, which provides any type of service demanded. On the market, those who want segregated or integrated, prosocialist or individualist, schools can have their wants satisfied. It is obvious, therefore, that governmental, as opposed to private, provision of services, lowers the standard of living of much of the population.

The degrees of government ownership in the economy vary from one country to another, but in *all* countries the State has made sure that it owns and monopolizes the vital nerve centers, the command posts of the society. It has acquired compulsory monopoly ownership over these command posts, and it has always asserted, without proof, that private ownership and enterprise in these fields is simply and a priori impossible.

Such vital command posts are defense, money (the mint and, nowadays, note issue), rivers and coastal seas, streets and highways, land generally (the "public domain" and the power of "eminent domain"), and the post office. The defense function is particularly vital to the State's existence, for on its virtual monopoly of force depends its ability to extract taxes from its citizens. Another critical command post held, though not always monopolized by, the State is education. For government schooling permits the influencing of the youthful mind to accept the virtues of the government under which it lives and of the principle of government intervention. Conservatives who often attack "socialistic" teaching in government schools are particularly wide of the mark, for the very fact that a government school exists and is therefore presumed to be good teaches its little charges the virtues of government ownership by example. And if government ownership is good and even preferable in schooling, why not for other educational media, e.g., newspapers—or for other important social services?

Even where the government does not have a compulsory monopoly of schooling, it approaches this ideal by compelling attendance of all children at either a government school or a private school approved by the government. Compulsory attendance brings into the schools those who do not desire or cannot benefit from schooling and forces them out of such competing fields as leisure and business employment.

G. THE FALLACIES OF "PUBLIC" OWNERSHIP

Finally, government ownership is often referred to as "public" ownership (the "public domain," "public" schools, the "public sector"). The implication is that when government owns anything, every member of the public owns equal shares of that property. But we have seen that the important feature of ownership is not legal formality but actual rule, and under government ownership it is the government officialdom that controls and directs, and therefore "owns," the property. Any member of the "public" who thinks he owns the property may test this theory by trying to appropriate for his own *individual* use his aliquot part of government property.[67, 68]

While rulers of government own "public" property, their ownership is not secure in the long run, since they may always be defeated in an election or deposed. Hence government officials will tend to regard themselves as only transitory owners of "public" resources. While a private owner, secure in his property and its capital value, may plan the use of his resource over a long period of time in the future, the government official must exploit "his" property as quickly as he can, since he has no security of tenure. And even the most securely entrenched civil servant must concentrate on present use, because government officials cannot usually sell the capitalized value of their property, as private owners can. In short, except in the case of the "private property" of a hereditary monarch, government officials own the current *use* of resources, but not their capital value. But if a resource itself cannot be owned, but only its current use, there will rapidly ensue an uneconomic exhaustion of the resource, since it will be to no one's benefit to conserve it over a period of time, and yet to each owner's advantage to use it up quickly. It is particularly curious, then, that almost all writers parrot the notion that private owners, possessing time preference, must take the "short view" in using their resources, while only government officials are properly equipped to exercise the "long view." The truth is precisely the reverse. The private individual, secure in his capital ownership, can afford to take the long view because of his interest in maintaining the capital value of his resource. It is the government official who must take and run, who must exploit the property quickly while he is still in command.[69]

H. SOCIAL SECURITY

Before ending our discussion of specific governmental activities, we may note in passing a curiously popular form of government expenditure: "social security." Social security confiscates the income of wage earners, and then, most people presume, it invests the money more wisely than they could themselves, later paying out the money to the former wage earners in their old age. Considered as "social insurance," this is a typical example of government enterprise: there is no relation between premiums and benefits, the latter changing yearly under the impact of political pressures. On the free market, anyone who wishes may invest in an insurance annuity or in stocks or real estate. Compelling everyone to transfer his funds to the government forces him to lose utility. Thus, even on its face, it is difficult to understand the great popularity of the social security program. But the true nature of the program differs greatly from the popular image. For the government does *not* invest the funds it takes in taxes; it simply spends them, giving itself its own bonds which must later be cashed when the benefits fall due. The cash, of course, can be obtained only by *further* taxation. Thus the public must pay *twice* for one payment of social security. The program is essentially one of making more palatable a general taxation of lower-income, wage-earning groups.

I. SOCIALISM AND CENTRAL PLANNING

When government ownership or control extends to the entire productive system, then the economic system is called *socialism*. Socialism, in short, is the violent abolition of the market, the compulsory monopolization of the entire productive sphere by the State. There are two and only two ways that any economy can be organized. One is by freedom and voluntary choice—the way of the market. The other is by force and dictation—the way of the State. To those ignorant of economics, it may seem that the way of the market is only anarchic confusion and chaos, while the way of the State constitutes genuine organization and "central planning." On the contrary, we have seen in this book what an amazing and flexible mechanism the market is for satisfying the wants of all individuals. State operation or intervention is, on the other hand, far less efficient and creates many disruptive and cumulative problems of its own. Moreover, a socialist State, deprived of the real market and its determination of prices for producers' goods, *cannot* calculate and can therefore run a productive system only in chaotic fashion. The economics of socialism—a whole branch of economics of its own—can only be touched upon here; suffice it to say that Mises' demonstration of the impossibility of economic calculation under socialism has never been successfully refuted.[70]

Here we might mention just a few points on the economics of socialism. One, since ownership is, *de facto,* the control of a resource, a Nazi, Fascist or other "centrally planned" system is as much "socialism" as a Communist regime that officially nationalizes property.[71] Secondly, the extent of socialism in the present-day world is at the same time *under*estimated in countries such as the United States and *over*estimated in Soviet Russia. It is underestimated because the expansion of government *lending* to private enterprise in the United States has been generally neglected, and we have seen that the lender, regardless of his legal status, is also an entrepreneur and part owner. The extent of socialism is overestimated because most writers ignore the fact that Russia, socialist as she is, cannot have full socialism as long as she can still refer to the relatively free markets existing in other parts of the world. In short, a single socialist country or bloc of countries, while inevitably experiencing enormous difficulties and wastes in planning, can still buy and sell and refer to the world market and can therefore at least vaguely approximate some sort of rational pricing of producers' goods by extrapolating from that market.[72] The well-known wastes and errors of this partial socialist planning are negligible compared to what would be experienced under the *total* calculational chaos of a world socialist state.

Another neglected factor diminishing the extent of planning in socialist countries is "black market" activities, particularly in commodities (candy, cigarettes, drugs, stockings, etc.) that are easy to conceal. Even in bulkier commodities, falsification of records and extensive graft may bring some sort of limited market—a market violating all the socialist plans—into existence.[73]

Moreover, it should be noted that a centrally "planned" economy is a centrally *prohibited* economy. The concept of "social engineering" is a deceptive metaphor, since in the *social* realm, it is largely *people* who are being planned, rather than the inanimate machinery of engineering blueprints. And since every individual is by nature, if not always by law, a self-owner and self-starter—i.e., a self-energizer, this means that central orders, backed up, as they must be under socialism, by force and violence, effectively *prohibit* all the individuals from doing what they want most or what they believe themselves to be best fitted to do. If the Central Planning Board, in short, orders X and Y to Pinsk to work as truck drivers, this means that X and Y are effectively and coercively *prohibited* from doing what they would have done voluntarily: perhaps X would have gone to Leningrad to be a longshoreman, and perhaps Y would have stayed around to tinker in his workshop and invent a new and highly useful device.

The latter point brings us to another grave defect of central planning: inventions, innovations, technological developments, by their very nature, by definition, cannot be predicted in advance and therefore cannot be centrally and bureaucratically *planned*. Not only does no one know *what* will be invented *when;* no one knows *who* will do the inventing. Clearly, a centrally prohibited economy, irrational and inefficient enough for *given* ends and given means and techniques at any point of time, is all the more incompetent if a flow of inventions and new developments are desired in society. Bureaucracy, incompetent enough to plan a stationary system, is vastly more incompetent at planning a progressive one.[74, 75]

10. *Growth, Affluence, and Government*

A. THE PROBLEM OF GROWTH

In recent years economists and journalists alike have been heavily emphasizing a new concept—"growth," and much economic writing is engaged in a "numbers game" on what percentage, or "rate of growth," "we" should have next year or in the next decade. The discussion is replete with comparisons of the higher rate of country X which "we" must hurriedly counter, etc. Amidst all the interest in growth, there are many grave problems which have hardly been touched upon. First and foremost is the simple query: "What is so good about growth?" The economists, discoursing scientifically about growth, have illegitimately smuggled an ethical judgment into their science—an ethical judgment that remains unanalyzed, as if it were self-evident. But why should growth be the highest value for which we can strive? What is the ethical justification? There is no doubt about the fact that growth, taken over as another dubious metaphor from biology, "sounds" good to most people, but this hardly constitutes an adequate ethical analysis. Many things are considered as good, but on the free market every man must choose between different quantities of them and the price for those forgone. Similarly, growth, as we shall presently see, must be balanced and weighed against competing values. Given due consideration, growth would be considered by few people as the *only* absolute value. If it were, why stop at 5% or 8% growth per year? Why not 50%?

It is completely illegitimate for the economist *qua* economist simply to endorse growth. What he can do is to contrast what growth means in various social conditions. In a free market, for example, every person chooses how much future growth he wants as compared to *present consumption.* "Growth," i.e., a rise in future living standards, can be achieved, as we have implicitly made clear throughout this volume, only in a few definable ways. Either more and better resources can be found, or more and better people can be born, or technology improved, or the capital-goods structure must be lengthened and capital multiplied. In practice, since resources need capital to find and develop them, since technological improvement can be applied to production only via capital investment, since entrepreneurial skills act only through investments, and since an increased labor supply is relatively independent of short-run economic considerations and can backfire in Malthusian fashion by lowering per capita output, the *only* viable way to growth is through increased saving and investment. On the free market, each individual decides how much he wants to save—to increase his future living standards—as against how much he wants to consume in the present. The net resultant of all these voluntary individual decisions is the nation's or world's rate of capital investment. The total is a reflection of the voluntary, free decisions of every consumer, of every person. The economist, therefore, has no business endorsing "growth" as an end; if he does so, he is injecting an unscientific, arbitrary value judgment, especially if he does not present an ethical theory in justification. He should simply say that, in a free market, everyone gets as much "growth" as he chooses to obtain; and that, furthermore, the people as a whole benefit greatly from the voluntary savings of others who do the saving and investing.

What happens if the government decides, either by subsidies or by direct government ownership, to try to spur the social rate of growth? Then, the economist should point out, the entire situation changes. No longer does each person elect to "grow" as he thinks best. Now, with compulsory saving and investing, investment can come only *at the expense* of the *forced* saving of some individuals. In short, if A, B, and C "grow" because their standard of living rises from compulsory investment, they do so at the expense of D, E, and F, the ones who were compelled to save. No longer can we say that the social standard of living, the standard of living of each active person, rises; under compulsory growth, some people—the coerced savers—clearly and demonstrably *lose*. *They* "grow" backward. Here is one reason why government intervention can *never* raise society's rate of "growth." For when individuals act freely on the market, every one of their actions benefits everyone, and so growth is truly "social," i.e., participated in by everyone in the society. But when government acts to force growth, it is only *some* who grow at the expense of the *retrogression* of others. The *wertfrei* economist is therefore not permitted to say that "society" grows at all.

Growth, therefore, is demonstrably not the single absolute value for anyone. People on the market all weigh growth *against* present consumption, just as they weigh work against leisure, and all goods against one another. If we fully realize that there is no such existent entity as "society" apart from individuals, it becomes clear that "society" cannot grow at the expense of imposing losses on some or most of its members. Suppose, for example, that a community exists where the bulk of the population do not *want* to "grow"; they would rather not work very hard or save very much; instead they would loll under the trees, pick berries, and play games. To advocate the government's coming on the scene and forcing these people to work and save, in order to "grow" at some time in the future, means to advocate the compulsory lowering of the standard of living of the bulk of the populace in the present and near future. Any sort of achieved production, under this scheme, however great, would not be "growth" for society; instead it would be retrogression, not only for some but for most people. An economist, therefore, cannot *scientifically* advocate compulsory growth, for what he is really doing is attempting to impose his own ethical views (e.g., more hard work and saving is better than more leisure and berries) on the *other* members of society by force. These members greatly lose utility as a result.

Furthermore, it must be emphasized again that in cases of coerced saving the *saver* reaps none of the benefit of his sacrifice, which is instead reaped by government officials or other beneficiaries. This contrasts to the free market, where people save and invest precisely because *they* will reap some tangible and desired rewards.

In a regime of coerced growth, then, "society" cannot grow, and conditions are totally different from those of the free market. Indeed, what we have is a form of the "free rider" argument against the free market and for government; here the various "free riders" band together to force *other* people to be thrifty so that the former can benefit.[76]

Even if we set these problems aside, it is doubtful how much the coercing free riders can benefit from these measures. Many considerations treated above now come into play. In the first place, the growth and success of the compulsory free riders discourage production and shift more and more people and energy from production to the exploitation of production, i.e., to compulsory free riding. Secondly, we have seen that if government itself does the "investing" out of the confiscated savings of others, the result, for many reasons, is not genuine investment, but *waste assets*. The capital built out of coerced savings, then, instead of benefiting the consumers, is largely wasted and dissipated. Even if government uses the money to subsidize various private investments, the results are still grave; for these investments, being uneconomic in relation to genuine consumers' demand and profit-and-loss signals on the market, will constitute *mal*investment. Once the government removed its subsidies and let all capital compete equally in serving consumers, it is doubtful how much of this investment would survive.

Although we have no intention of dealing here to any extent with an empirical problem like Soviet economic growth, we may illustrate our analysis by noting the hullabaloo that has been raised in recent years over the supposedly enormous rate of Soviet growth. Curiously, one finds that the "growth" seems to be taking place almost exclusively in capital goods, such as iron and steel, hydroelectric dams, etc., whereas little or none of this growth ever seems to filter down to the standard of living of the average Soviet consumer. The consumer's standard of living, however, is the be-all and end-all of the entire production process. *Production* makes no sense whatever except as a means to *consumption.* Investment in capital goods means nothing except as a *necessary way station to increased consumption.* When capital investment takes place in the free market, it deprives no one of consumption goods; for those save who voluntarily choose investment over some present consumption. No one is required to sacrifice present consumption who does not wish to do so. As a result, the standard of living of everyone rises continually and smoothly as investment increases. But a Soviet or other system of compulsory investment *lowers* the standard of living of almost everyone, certainly in the near future. And there is every indication that the "pie-in-the-sky" day when living standards finally rise almost never arrives. In short, government "investment," as we have noted above, turns out to be a peculiar form of wasteful "consumption" by government officials.[77]

There is another consideration that reinforces our conclusion. Professor Lachmann has been diligently reminding us of what economists generally forget: that "capital" is not just a homogeneous blob that can be added to or subtracted from. Capital is an intricate, delicate, interweaving *structure* of capital goods. All of the delicate strands of this structure have to fit, and fit precisely, or else malinvestment occurs. The free market is almost an automatic mechanism for such fitting; and we have seen throughout this volume how the free market, with its price system and profit-and-loss criteria, adjusts the output and variety of the different strands of production, preventing any one from getting long out of alignment.[78] But under socialism or with massive government investment, there is no such mechanism for fitting and harmonizing. Deprived of a free price system and profit-and-loss criteria, the government can only blunder along, blindly "investing" without being able to invest properly in the right fields, the right products, or the right places. A beautiful subway will be built, but no wheels will be available for the trains; a giant dam, but no copper for transmission lines, etc. These sudden surpluses and shortages, so characteristic of government planning, are the result of massive malinvestment by the government.[79]

The current controversy over growth, is, in a sense, the result of a critical error made by "right-wing" economists in their continuing debate with their "left-wing" opponents. Instead of emphasizing freedom and free choice as their highest *political* end, the rightist economists have stressed the importance of freedom *as a utilitarian means* of encouraging saving, investment, and therefore, economic growth. We have seen above that conservative opponents of the progressive income tax have often fallen into the trap of treating saving and investment as somehow a greater and higher good than consumption, and therefore of implicitly criticizing the free market's saving/consumption ratio. Here we have another example of the same lapse into an implicit, arbitrary criticism of the market. What the modern "leftist" proponents of compulsory growth have done is to use the venerable arguments of the conservatives as a boomerang against them, and to say, in effect, to their opponents: "Very well. You have been maintaining that saving and investment are of critical importance because they lead to growth and economic progress. Fine; but, as you yourselves implicitly grant, the free market's proportion of saving and investment is really too slow. Why then rely upon it? Why not speed up growth by using government to coerce even more saving and investment, to speed up capital further?" It is evident that conservatives cannot counter by reiterating their familiar arguments. The proper comment here is the analysis we have been expounding—in short: (*a*) By what right do you maintain that people *should* grow faster than they voluntarily wish to grow? (*b*) Compulsory growth will not benefit the whole of society as will freely chosen growth, and it is therefore not "social growth"; some will gain—and gain at some distant date—at the expense of the retrogression of others. (*c*) Government investment or subsidized investment is either malinvestment or not investment at all, but simply waste assets or "consumption" of waste for the prestige of government officials.

What, in point of fact, *is* economic "growth"? Any proper definition must surely encompass an increase of economic means available for the satisfaction of people's ends—in short, increased satisfactions of people's wants, or as P. T. Bauer has put it, "an increase in the range of effective alternatives open to people." On such a definition, it is clear that compulsory saving, with its imposed losses and restrictions on people's effective choices, cannot spur economic growth; and also that government "investment," with its neglect of voluntary private consumption as its goal, can hardly be said to add to people's alternatives. Quite the contrary.[80]

Finally, the very term "growth" is an illegitimate import of a metaphor from biology into human action.[81] "Growth" and "rate of growth" connote some sort of automatic necessity or inevitability and have for many people a value-loaded connotation of something self-evidently desirable.[82]

Concomitantly with the hubbub about growth there has developed an enormous literature about the "economics of underdeveloped countries." We can here note only a few considerations. First, contrary to a widespread impression, "neoclassical" economics applies just as fully to underdeveloped as to any other countries. In fact, as P. T. Bauer has often stressed, the economic discipline is in some ways sharper in less developed countries because of the extra option that many people have of reverting from a monetary to a barter economy. An underdeveloped country can grow only in the same ways as a more advanced country: largely via capital investment. The economic laws which we have adumbrated throughout this volume are independent of the specific content of any community's or nation's economy, and therefore independent of its level of development. Secondly, underdeveloped countries are especially prone to the wasteful, dramatic, prestigious government "investment" in such projects as steel mills or dams, as contrasted with economic, but undramatic, private investment in improved agricultural tools.[83,84] Thirdly, the term "underdeveloped" is definitely value-loaded to imply that certain countries are "too little" developed below some sort of imposed standard. As Wiggins and Schoeck point out, "undeveloped" would be a more objective term.[85]

Because of its spectacular burst of popularity, something must here be said of the recent "stages of economic growth" doctrine of Professor Rostow. Highly recommended as "the answer to Marx" (as if Marx had never been "answered" before), Rostow divines five stages of economic growth through which each modern nation passes; these center around the "take-off" and include "preconditions" of take-off, drive from take-off to "maturity," and, as the final stage, "high mass-consumption." [86] In addition to committing the common fallacy of assuming some sort of automatic rate of "growth," Rostow adds many others of his own, among which are the following: (*a*) the resumption of the futile modern search for nonexistent "laws of history"; (*b*) the discovery of such "laws" by way of that hoary fallacy of late nineteenth-century German thought, "stages of history," with each arbitrary stage somehow destined to evolve automatically into the next; (*c*) the undue stress—here, as in other ways, closer to Marx than most critics realize—on sheer *technology* as the *fons et origo* of economic development; (*d*) the deliberate mixing of government and private firms as equally capable of "entrepreneurship"; and (*e*) reliance on the fallacious concept of "social overhead capital," which must be mainly supplied by the government before "take-off" is achieved. Actually, as we have seen, there are not different stages of economy, each subject to its own laws, but one single economics which applies to any level of development and explains any degree of "growth." Rostow's final stage of "high mass-consumption" is particularly open to question. What was more characteristic of the early, "take-off" stage of the Industrial Revolution in Britain than precisely the shift of production toward mass consumption of cheap, factory-made textile goods? Mass consumption was a feature of the Industrial Revolution from the beginning; it is not, contrary to a popular myth, some sort of new condition of the 1950's.[87, 88]

B. Professor Galbraith and the Sin of Affluence

In the early part of the twentieth century, the main indictment of the capitalist system by its intellectual critics was the alleged pervasiveness of "monopoly." In the 1930's, mass unemployment and poverty ("one third of a nation") came to the fore.

At the present time growing abundance and prosperity have greatly dimmed the poverty and unemployment theme, and the only serious "monopoly" seems to be that of labor unionism. Let it not be thought, however, that criticism of capitalism has died. Two seemingly contradictory charges are now rife: (*a*) that capitalism is not "growing" fast enough, and (*b*) that the trouble with capitalism is that it makes us too "affluent." Excess wealth has suddenly replaced poverty as the tragic flaw of capitalism.[89] At first sight, these latter charges appear contradictory, for capitalism is at one and the same time accused of producing too many goods, and yet of not increasing its production of goods fast enough. The contradiction seems especially glaring when the same critic presses both lines of attack, as is true of the leading critic of the sin of affluence, Professor Galbraith.[90] But, as the *Wall Street Journal* has aptly pointed out, this is not really a contradiction at all; for the excessive affluence is all in the "private sector," the goods enjoyed by the consumers; the deficiency, or "starvation," is in the "public sector," which needs further growth.[91]

Although *The Affluent Society* is replete with fallacies, backed by dogmatic assertions and time-honored rhetorical devices in place of reasoned argument,[92] the book warrants some consideration here in view of its enormous popularity.

As in the case of most "economists" who attack economic science, Professor Galbraith is an historicist, who believes that economic theory, instead of being grounded on the eternal facts of human nature, is somehow relative to different historical epochs. "Conventional" economic theory, he asserts, was true for the eras before the present, which were times of "poverty"; now, however, we have vaulted from a centuries-long state of poverty into an age of "affluence," and for such an age, a completely new economic theory is needed. Galbraith also makes the philosophical error of believing that ideas are essentially "refuted by events"; on the contrary, in human action, as contrasted with the natural sciences, ideas can be refuted only by *other* ideas; events themselves are complex resultants which need to be interpreted by correct ideas.

One of Galbraith's gravest flaws is the arbitrariness of the categories, which pervade his work, of "poverty" and "affluence." Nowhere does he define what he means by these terms, and therefore nowhere does he lay down standards by which we can know, even in theory, when we have passed the magic borderland between "poverty" and "affluence" that requires an entirely new economic theory to come into being. The present book and most other economic works make it evident that economic science is *not* dependent on some arbitrary level of wealth; the basic praxeological laws are true of all men at all times, and the catallactic laws of the exchange economy are true whenever and wherever exchanges are made.

Galbraith makes much of his supposed discovery, suppressed by other economists, that the marginal utility of goods declines as one's income increases and that therefore a man's final $1,000 is not worth nearly as much to him as his first—the margin of subsistence. But this knowledge is familiar to most economists, and this book, for example, has included it. The marginal utility of goods certainly declines as our income rises; but the very fact that people continue to work for the final $1,000 and work for more money when the opportunity is available, demonstrates conclusively that the marginal utility of goods is still greater than the marginal disutility of leisure forgone. Galbraith's hidden fallacy is a *quantitative* assumption: from the mere fact that the marginal utility of goods *falls* as one's income and wealth rise, Galbraith has somehow concluded that it has *already* fallen to *virtually, or really, zero*. The fact of decline, however, tells us nothing whatever about the *degree* of this decline, which Galbraith arbitrarily assumes has been almost total. All economists, even the most "conventional," know that as incomes have risen in the modern world, workers have chosen to take more and more of that income in the form of leisure. And this should be proof enough that economists have long been familiar with the supposedly suppressed truth that the marginal utility of goods in general tends to decline as their supply increases. But, Galbraith retorts, economists admit that leisure is a consumers' good, but *not* that other goods decline in value as their supply increases.

Yet this is surely an erroneous contention; what economists know is that, as civilization expands the supply of goods, the marginal utility of goods declines *and* the marginal utility of leisure forgone (the opportunity cost of labor) increases, so that more and more real income will be "taken" in the form of leisure. There is nothing at all startling, subversive, or revolutionary about this familiar fact.

According to Galbraith, economists wilfully ignore the spectre of the satiation of wants. Yet they do so quite properly, because when wants—or rather, wants for exchangeable goods—are truly satiated, we shall all know it soon enough; for, at that point, everyone will cease working, will cease trying to transform land resources into final consumers' goods. There will be no need to continue producing, because all needs for consumers' goods will have been supplied—or at least all those which can be produced and exchanged. At this point, everyone will stop work, the market economy—indeed, *all economy*—will come to an end, means will no longer be scarce in relation to ends, and everyone will bask in paradise. I think it self-evident that this time has not yet arrived and shows no signs of arriving; if it some day should arrive, it will be greeted by economists, as by most other people, not with curses, but with rejoicing. Despite their venerable reputation as practitioners of a "dismal science," economists have no vested interests, psychological or otherwise, in scarcity.

But, in the meanwhile, this is still a world of scarcity; scarce means have to be applied to alternate ends; labor is still necessary. People still work for their final $1,000 of income and would be happy to accept another $1,000 should it be offered. We would venture another prediction: An informal poll taken among the people, asking whether they would accept, or know what to do with, an extra few thousand dollars of annual (real) income, would find almost no one who would refuse the offer because of excessive affluence or satiety—or for any other reason. Few would be at a loss about what to do with their increased wealth. Professor Galbraith, of course, has an answer to all this. These wants, he says, are not real or genuine ones; they have been "created" in the populace by advertisers, and their wicked clients, the producing businessmen. The very fact of production, through such advertising, "creates" the supposed wants that it supplies.

Galbraith's entire theory of excess affluence rests on this flimsy assertion that consumer wants are artificially created by business itself. It is an allegation backed only by repetitious assertion and by no evidence whatever—except perhaps for Galbraith's obvious personal dislike for detergents and tailfins. What is more, the attack on wicked advertising as creating wants and degrading the consumer is surely the most conventional of the conventional wisdom in the anticapitalist's arsenal.[93]

There are many fallacies in Galbraith's conventional attack on advertising. In the first place, it is not true that advertising "creates" wants or demands on the part of the consumers. It certainly tries to persuade consumers to buy the product; but it cannot *create* wants or demands, because each person must himself *adopt* the ideas and values on which he acts—whether these ideas or values are sound or unsound. Galbraith here assumes a naive form of determinism—of advertising upon the consumers, and, like all determinists, he leaves an implicit escape clause from the determination for people like himself, who are, unaccountably, *not* determined by advertising. If there is determinism by advertising, how can some people be determined to rush out and buy the product, while Professor Galbraith is free to resist the advertisements with indignation and to write a book denouncing the advertising?[94]

Secondly, Galbraith gives us no standard to decide which wants are so "created" and which are legitimate. By his stress on poverty, one might think that all wants above the subsistence level are false wants created by advertising. Of course, he supplies no evidence for this view. But, as we shall see further below, this is hardly consistent with his views on public or governmentally induced wants.

Thirdly, Galbraith fails to distinguish between fulfilling a given want in a better way and inducing new wants. Unless we are to take the extreme and unsupported view that *all* wants above the subsistence line are "created," we must note the rather odd behavior attributed to businessmen by Galbraith's assumptions.

Why *should* businessmen go to the expense, bother, and uncertainty of trying to create *new* wants, when they could far more easily look for better or cheaper ways of fulfilling wants that consumers *already* have? If consumers, for example, already have a discernible and discoverable want for a "no-rub cleanser," it is surely easier and less costly to produce and then advertise a no-rub cleanser than it would be to create some completely new want—say for *blue* cleansers in particular—and then work very hard and spend a great deal of money on advertising campaigns to try to convince people that they *need* blue cleansers because blue "is the color of the sky" or for some other artificial reason.[95] In short, the Galbraithian view of the business and marketing system makes little or no sense. Rather than go to the expensive, uncertain, and, at bottom, needless, task of trying to find a new want for consumers, business will tend to satisfy those wants that consumers already have, or that they are pretty sure consumers would have if the product were available. Advertising is then used as a means of (*a*) conveying information to the consumers that the product is now available and telling them what the product will do; and (*b*) specifically, trying to convince the consumers that this product *will* satisfy their given want—e.g., *will* be a no-rub cleanser.

Indeed, our view is the only one that makes sense of the increasingly large quantities of money spent by business on marketing research. Why bother investigating in detail *what* consumers really want, if all one need do is to *create* the wants for them by advertising? If, in fact, production *really* created its own demand through advertising, as Galbraith maintains, business would never again have to worry about losses or bankruptcy or a failure to sell automatically any good that it may arbitrarily choose to produce. Certainly there would be no need for marketing research or for any wondering about what consumers will buy. This image of the world is precisely the reverse of what is occurring. Indeed, precisely because people's standards of living are moving ever farther past the subsistence line, businessmen are worrying ever more intensely about what consumers want and what they will buy. It is because the range of goods available to the consumers is expanding so much beyond simple staples needed for subsistence, in quantity, quality, and breadth of product substitutes, that businessmen must compete as never before in paying court to the consumer, in trying to obtain his attention: in short, in advertising. Increasing advertising is a function of the increasingly effective range of competition for the consumer's favor.[96]

Not only will businessmen tend to produce for and satisfy what they believe are the given wants of consumers, but the consumers, in contrast to voters, as we have seen above, have a direct market test for every piece of advertising that they confront. If they buy the cleanser and find that much rubbing is still required, the product will soon fade into oblivion. Thus, any advertising claims for *market* products can be and are quickly and readily tested by the consumers. Confronted with these facts, Galbraith could only maintain that the aversion against rubbing was *itself* generated, in some mysterious and sinister fashion, by business advertising.[97]

Advertising is one of the areas in which Galbraith, curiously and in glaring self-contradiction, treats private business differently from governmental activities. Thus, while business is supposed to be "creating" consumer wants through advertising, thereby generating an artificial affluence, at the same time the neglected "public sector" is increasingly starved and poverty-stricken. Apparently, Galbraith has never heard of, or refuses to acknowledge the existence of, *governmental* propaganda. He makes no mention whatever of the hordes of press agents, publicists and propagandists working for government agencies, bombarding the taxpayers with propaganda which the latter have been *forced* to support. Since a considerable part of the propaganda is for ever-greater increases in the particular government bureau's activities, this means that G, the government officials, expropriate T, the bulk of the taxpayers, in order to hire more propagandists for G, to persuade the taxpayers to permit still more funds to be taken from them. And so forth. It is strange that, while waxing indignant over detergent and automobile commercials over television, Professor Galbraith has never had to endure the tedium of "public service commercials" beamed at him from the government. We may pass over the Washington conferences for influential private organizations that serve as "transmission belts" for government propaganda to the grassroots, the "inside briefings" that perform the same function, the vast quantities of printed matter subsidized by the taxpayer and issued by the government, etc.

Indeed, not only does Galbraith *not* consider government propaganda as artificially want-creating (and this is a realm, let us remember, where consumers *have no market test* of the product), but one of his major proposals is for a vast program of what he calls "investment in men," which turns out to be large-scale governmental "education" to uplift the wants and tastes of the citizenry. In short, Galbraith wants society's objective to be the deliberate expansion of the "New Class" (roughly, intellectuals, who are blithely assumed to be the only ones who really enjoy their work), "with its emphasis on education and its ultimate effect on intellectual, literary, cultural and artistic demands . . ." [98]

It seems evident that, while the free market and business are accused of artificially creating consumer wants, the shoe is precisely on Galbraith's own foot. It is *Galbraith* who is eager to curtail and suppress the consumers' freely chosen wants, and who is advocating a massive and coercive attempt by the government to create artificial wants, to "invest in men" by "educating" them to redirect their wants into those refined and artistic channels of which Professor Galbraith is so fond. Everyone will have to give up his tailfins so that all may be compelled to . . . read books (like *The Affluent Society,* for example?).

There are other grave and fundamental fallacies in Galbraith's approach to government. In particular, after making much ado over the fact that, with poverty conquered, the marginal utility of further goods is lower, he finds that everything somehow works in reverse for "governmental needs." Governmental needs, in some mystical way, are exempt from this law of diminishing marginal wants; instead, *mirabile dictu,* governmental needs *increase* in urgency as society becomes more affluent. From this flagrant and unresolved contradiction, Galbraith leaps to the conclusion that government must compel the massive shifting of resources from superfluous private, to starved public, needs. But on the basis of diminishing marginal utility alone, there is no case for such a shift, since *all* wants at a higher real income are of lower utility than the wants of the poverty-stricken. And when we realize that if we talk about "created" wants at all, governmental propaganda is vastly more likely to "create" wants than is business, a case, even in Galbraith's own terms, can be made for just the reverse: for a shift from the governmental to the private sector. And, finally, Galbraith, in his lament for the starved and underprivileged public sector, somehow neglects to inform his readers that, whatever statistics are used, it is clear that, in the past half-century, government activity has increased far more than private. Government is absorbing and confiscating a far greater share of the national product than in earlier days. How much lower its "utility," and how much greater the case, in Galbraith's terms, for a shift *from* government *to* private activity!

Galbraith also airily assumes, in common with many other writers, that many governmental services are "collective goods" and therefore simply *cannot* be supplied by private enterprise. Without going further into the question of the desirability of private enterprise in these fields, one must note that Galbraith is quite wrong. Not only is his thesis simply a bald assertion, unsupported by facts, but, on the contrary, every single service generally assumed to be suppliable by government *alone* has been historically supplied by private enterprise. This includes such services as education, road building and maintenance, coinage, postal delivery, fire protection, police protection, judicial decisions, and military defense—all of which are often held to be self-evidently and necessarily within the exclusive province of government.[99]

There are many other important fallacies in Galbraith's book, but the central thesis of *The Affluent Society* has now been discussed. Thus, one of the reasons why Galbraith sees great danger in the present high consumption is that much is financed by consumer credit, which Galbraith considers, in the conventional manner, to be "inflationary" and to lead to instability and depression. Yet, as we shall see further, consumer credit that does not add to the money supply is *not* inflationary; it simply permits consumers to *redirect* the pattern of their spending so as to buy more of what they want and ascend higher in their value scales. In short, they may redirect spending from nondurable to durable goods. This is a *transfer* of spending power, not an inflationary rise. The device of consumer credit was a highly productive invention.

Predictably, Galbraith pours much of his scorn on the supply-and-demand explanation of inflation, and especially on the proper monetary explanation, which he terms "mystical." His view of depression is purely Keynesian and assumes that a depression is caused by a deficiency of aggregate demand. "Inflation" is an increase in prices, which he would combat *either* by reducing aggregate demand through high taxes *or* by selective price controls and the fixing, by compulsory arbitration, of important wages and prices. If the former route is chosen, Galbraith, as a Keynesian, believes that unemployment would ensue. But Galbraith is not really worried, for he would take the revolutionary step of separating income from production; production, it seems, is important only because it provides income. (We have seen that government activity has already effected a considerable separation.) He proposes a sliding scale of unemployment insurance provided by the government, to be greater in depression than in boom, the payment in depression rising *almost* to the general prevailing wage (for some reason, Galbraith would not go precisely as high, because of a lingering fear of some disincentive effect on the unemployed's finding jobs). He does not seem to realize that this is merely a way of aggravating and prolonging unemployment during a depression and indirectly subsidizing union wage scales above the market. There is no need to stress the author's other vagaries, such as his adoption of the conventional conservationist concern about using up precious resources—a position, of course, consistent with Galbraith's general attack on the private consumer.[100]

As we have indicated above, there *is* a problem of the "public sector"; scarcities and conflicts keep appearing in government services, and in these fields alone, e.g., juvenile delinquency, traffic jams, overcrowded schools, lack of parking space, etc. We have seen above that the single remedy that proponents of government activity can offer is for more funds to be channeled from private to public activity.[101] We have shown, however, that such scarcity and inefficiency are inherent in government operation of any activity. Instead of taking warning from the inefficiencies of government output, writers like Galbraith turn the blame from government onto the taxpayers and consumers, just as government water officials characteristically blame the *consumers* for water shortages. At no time does Galbraith so much as consider the possibility of mending an ailing public sector by *making that sector private.*

How would Galbraith *know* when his desired "social balance" was achieved? What criteria has he set to guide us in knowing *how much* shift there should be from private to public activity? The answer is, *none;* Galbraith cheerfully concedes that there is no way of finding the point of optimum balance: "No test can be applied, for none exists." But, after all, precise definitions, "precise equilibrium," are not important; for to Galbraith it is crystal "clear" that we must move now from private to public activity, and to a "considerable" extent. We shall know when we arrive, for the public sector will then bask in opulence. And to think that Galbraith accuses the perfectly sound and logical monetary theory of inflation of being "mystical" and "unrevealed magic"! [102]

Before leaving the question of affluence and the recent attack on consumption—the very goal of the entire economic system, let us note two stimulating contributions in recent years on hidden but important functions of luxury consumption, particularly by the "rich." F. A. Hayek has pointed out the important function of the luxury consumption of the rich, at any given time, in pioneering new ways of consumption, and thereby paving the way for later diffusion of such "consumption innovations" to the mass of the consumers.[103] And Bertrand de Jouvenel, stressing the fact that refined esthetic and cultural tastes are concentrated precisely in the more affluent members of society, also points out that these citizens are the ones who could freely and voluntarily give many gratuitous services to others, services which, because they are free, are not counted in the national income statistics.[104]

11. *Binary Intervention: Inflation and Business Cycles*

A. INFLATION AND CREDIT EXPANSION

In chapter 11, we depicted the workings of the monetary system of a purely free market. A free money market adopts specie, either gold or silver or both parallel, as the "standard" or *money proper*. Units of money are simply *units of weight* of the money-stuff. The total stock of the money commodity increases with new production (mining) and decreases from wear and tear and use in industrial employments. Generally, there will be a gradual secular rise in the money stock, with effects as analyzed above. The wealth of some people will increase and of others will decline, and no social usefulness will accrue from an increased supply of money—in its monetary use. However, an increased stock will raise the social standard of living and well-being by further satisfying *nonmonetary* demands for the monetary metal.

Intervention in this money market usually takes the form of issuing pseudo warehouse receipts as money-substitutes. As we saw in chapter 11, demand liabilities such as deposits or paper notes may come into use in a free market, but may equal only the actual value, or weight, of the specie deposited. The demand liabilities are then genuine warehouse receipts, or true money certificates, and they pass on the market as representatives of the actual money, i.e., as money-substitutes. Pseudo warehouse receipts are those issued in excess of the actual weight of specie on deposit. Naturally, their issue can be a very lucrative business. Looking like the genuine certificates, they serve also as money-substitutes, even though not covered by specie. They are fraudulent, because they promise to redeem in specie at face value, a promise that could not possibly be met were all the deposit-holders to ask for their own property at the same time. Only the complacency and ignorance of the public permit the situation to continue.[105]

Broadly, such intervention may be effected either by the government or by private individuals and firms in their role as "banks" or money-warehouses. The process of issuing pseudo warehouse receipts or, more exactly, *the process of issuing money beyond any increase in the stock of specie,* may be called *inflation.*[106] A contraction in the money supply outstanding over any period (aside from a possible net decrease in specie) may be called *deflation.* Clearly, *inflation* is the primary event and the primary purpose of monetary intervention. There can be no deflation without an inflation having occurred in some previous period of time. A priori, almost all intervention will be inflationary. For not only must all monetary intervention *begin* with inflation; the great gain to be derived from inflation comes from the issuer's putting new money into circulation. The profit is practically costless, because, while all other people must either sell goods and services and buy or mine gold, the government or the commercial banks are literally creating money out of thin air. They do not have to buy it. Any profit from the use of this magical money is clear gain to the issuers.

As happens when new specie enters the market, the issue of "uncovered" money-substitutes also has a diffusion effect: the first receivers of the new money gain the most, the next gain slightly less, etc., until the midpoint is reached, and then each receiver loses more and more as he waits for the new money. For the first individuals' selling prices soar while buying prices remain almost the same; but later, buying prices have risen while selling prices remain unchanged. A crucial circumstance, however, differentiates this from the case of increasing specie. The new paper or new demand deposits have no social function whatever; they do not demonstrably benefit some without injuring others in the market society. The increasing money supply is only a social waste and can only advantage some at the expense of others. And the benefits and burdens are distributed as just outlined: the early-comers gaining at the expense of later-comers. Certainly, the business and consumer borrowers from the bank—its clientele—benefit greatly from the new money (at least in the short run), since they are the ones who first receive it.

If inflation is any increase in the supply of money *not* matched by an increase in the gold or silver stock available, the method of inflation just depicted is called *credit expansion*—the creation of new money-substitutes, entering the economy *on the credit market*. As will be seen below, while credit expansion by a bank *seems* far more sober and respectable than outright spending of new money, it actually has far graver consequences for the economic system, consequences which most people would find especially undesirable. This inflationary credit is called *circulating credit,* as distinguished from the lending of *saved funds*—called *commodity credit*. In this book, the term "credit expansion" will apply only to increases in circulating credit.

Credit expansion has, of course, the same effect as any sort of inflation: prices tend to rise as the money supply increases. Like any inflation, it is a process of redistribution, whereby the inflators, and the part of the economy selling to them, gain at the expense of those who come last in line in the spending process. This is the charm of inflation—for the beneficiaries—and the reason why it has been so popular, particularly since modern banking processes have camouflaged its significance for those losers who are far removed from banking operations. The gains to the inflators are visible and dramatic; the losses to others hidden and unseen, but just as effective for all that. Just as half the economy are taxpayers and half tax-consumers, so half the economy are inflation-payers and the rest inflation-consumers.

Most of these gains and losses will be "short-run" or "one-shot"; they will occur during the process of inflation, but will cease after the new monetary equilibrium is reached. The inflators make their gains, but after the new money supply has been diffused throughout the economy, the inflationary gains and losses are ended. However, as we have seen in chapter 11, there are also *permanent* gains and losses resulting from inflation. For the new monetary equilibrium will not simply be the old one multiplied in all relations and quantities by the addition to the money supply. This was an assumption that the old "quantity theory" economists made. The valuations of the individuals making temporary gains and losses will differ. Therefore, each individual will react differently to his gains and losses and alter his relative spending patterns accordingly. Moreover, the new money will form a high ratio to the existing cash balance of some and a low ratio to that of others, and the result will be a variety of changes in spending patterns. Therefore, all prices will *not* have increased uniformly in the new equilibrium; the purchasing power of the monetary unit has fallen, but not equiproportionally over the entire array of exchange-values. Since some prices have risen more than others, therefore, some people will be *permanent* gainers, and some permanent losers, from the inflation.[107]

Particularly hard hit by an inflation, of course, are the relatively "fixed" income groups, who end their losses only after a long period or not at all. Pensioners and annuitants who have contracted for a fixed money income are examples of permanent as well as short-run losers. Life insurance benefits are permanently slashed. Conservative anti-inflationists' complaints about "the widows and orphans" have often been ridiculed, but they are no laughing matter nevertheless. For it is precisely the widows and orphans who bear a main part of the brunt of inflation.[108] Also suffering losses are creditors who have already extended their loans and find it too late to charge a purchasing-power premium on their interest rates.

Inflation also changes the market's consumption/investment ratio. Superficially, it seems that credit expansion greatly increases capital, for the new money enters the market as equivalent to new savings for lending. Since the new "bank money" is apparently added to the supply of savings on the credit market, businesses can now borrow at a lower rate of interest; hence inflationary credit expansion seems to offer the ideal escape from time preference, as well as an inexhaustible fount of added capital. Actually, this effect is illusory. On the contrary, inflation reduces saving and investment, thus lowering society's standard of living. It may even cause large-scale capital consumption. In the first place, as we just have seen, existing creditors are injured. This will tend to discourage lending in the future and thereby discourage saving-investment. Secondly, as we have seen in chapter 11, the inflationary process inherently yields a purchasing-power profit to the businessman, since he purchases factors and sells them at a later time when all prices are higher. The businessman may thus keep abreast of the price increase (we are here exempting from *variations* in price increases the terms-of-trade component), neither losing nor gaining from the inflation. But business accounting is traditionally geared to a world where the value of the monetary unit is stable. Capital goods purchased are entered in the asset column "at cost," i.e., at the price paid for them. When the firm later sells the product, the extra inflationary gain is not really a gain at all; for it must be absorbed in purchasing the replaced capital good at a higher price. Inflation, therefore, tricks the businessman: it destroys one of his main signposts and leads him to believe that he has gained extra profits when he is just able to replace capital. Hence, he will undoubtedly be tempted to consume out of these profits and thereby unwittingly consume capital as well. Thus, inflation tends at once to repress saving-investment and to cause consumption of capital.

The accounting error stemming from inflation has other economic consequences. The firms with the greatest degree of error will be those with capital equipment bought more preponderantly when prices were lowest. If the inflation has been going on for a while, these will be the firms with the oldest equipment. Their seemingly great profits will attract other firms into the field, and there will be a completely unjustified expansion of investment in a seemingly high-profit area. Conversely, there will be a deficiency of investment elsewhere. Thus, the error distorts the market's system of allocating resources and reduces its effectiveness in satisfying the consumer. The error will also be greatest in those firms with a greater proportion of capital equipment to product, and similar distorting effects will take place through excessive investment in heavily "capitalized" industries, offset by underinvestment elsewhere.[109]

B. CREDIT EXPANSION AND THE BUSINESS CYCLE

We have already seen in chapter 8 what happens when there is net saving-investment: an increase in the ratio of gross investment to consumption in the economy. Consumption expenditures fall, and the prices of consumers' goods fall. On the other hand, the production structure is lengthened, and the prices of original factors specialized in the higher stages rise. The prices of capital goods change like a lever being pivoted on a fulcrum at its center; the prices of consumers' goods fall most, those of first-order capital goods fall less; those of highest-order capital goods rise most, and the others less. Thus, the *price differentials* between the stages of production all diminish. Prices of original factors fall in the lower stages and rise in the higher stages, and the nonspecific original factors (mainly labor) shift partly from the lower to the higher stages. Investment tends to be centered in lengthier processes of production. The drop in price differentials is, as we have seen, *equivalent* to a fall in the natural rate of interest, which, of course, leads to a corollary drop in the loan rate. After a while the fruit of the more productive techniques arrives; and the real income of everyone rises.

Thus, an increase in saving resulting from a fall in time preferences leads to a fall in the interest rate and another stable equilibrium situation with a longer and narrower production structure. What happens, however, when the increase in investment is *not* due to a change in time preference and saving, but to credit expansion by the commercial banks? Is this a magic way of expanding the capital structure easily and costlessly, without reducing present consumption? Suppose that 6,000,000 gold ounces are being invested, and 4,000,000 consumed, in a certain period of time. Suppose, now, that the banks in the economy expand credit and increase the money supply by 2,000,000 ounces. What are the consequences? The new money is loaned to businesses.[110] These businesses, now able to acquire the money at a lower rate of interest, enter the capital goods' and original factors' market to bid resources away from the other firms. At any given time, the stock of goods is fixed, and the 2,000,000 new ounces are therefore employed in raising the prices of producers' goods. The rise in prices of capital goods will be imputed to rises in original factors.

The credit expansion reduces the market rate of interest. This means that price differentials are lowered, and, as we have seen in chapter 8, lower price differentials raise prices in the highest stages of production, shifting resources to these stages and also increasing the number of stages. As a result, the production structure is lengthened. The borrowing firms are led to believe that enough funds are available to permit them to embark on projects formerly unprofitable. On the free market, investment will always take place first in those projects that satisfy the most urgent wants of the consumers. Then the next most urgent wants are satisfied, etc. The interest rate regulates the temporal order of choice of projects in accordance with their urgency. A lower rate of interest on the market is a signal that more projects can be undertaken profitably. Increased saving on the free market leads to a stable equilibrium of production at a lower rate of interest. But not so with credit expansion: for the *original factors now receive increased money income.* In the free-market example, total money incomes remained the same. *The increased expenditure on higher stages was offset by decreased expenditure in the lower stages.* The "increased length" of the production structure was compensated by the "reduced width." But credit expansion pumps new money into the production structure: aggregate money incomes increase instead of remaining the same. The production structure has lengthened, but it has also *remained as wide,* without contraction of consumption expenditure.

The owners of the original factors, with their increased money income, naturally hasten to spend their new money. They allocate this spending between consumption and investment in accordance with their time preferences. Let us assume that the time-preference schedules of the people remain unchanged. This is a proper assumption, since there is no reason to assume that they have changed because of the inflation. Production now no longer reflects voluntary time preferences. Business has been led by credit expansion to invest in higher stages, *as if* more savings were available. Since they are not, business has overinvested in the higher stages and underinvested in the lower. Consumers act promptly to re-establish their time preferences—their preferred investment/consumption proportions and price differentials. The *differentials* will be re-established at the old, higher amount, i.e., the rate of interest will return to its free-market magnitude. As a result, the prices at the higher stages of production will fall drastically, the prices at the lower stages will rise again, and the entire new investment at the higher stages will have to be abandoned or sacrificed.

Altering our oversimplified example, which has treated only *two* stages, we see that the highest stages, believed profitable, have proved to be unprofitable. The pure rate of interest, reflecting consumer desires, is shown to have *really* been higher all along. The banks' credit expansion had tampered with that indispensable "signal"—the interest rate—that tells businessmen how much savings are available and what length of projects will be profitable. In the free market the interest rate is an indispensable guide, in the time dimension, to the urgency of consumer wants. But bank intervention in the market disrupts this free price and renders entrepreneurs unable to satisfy consumer desires properly or to estimate the most beneficial time structure of production. As soon as the consumers are able, i.e., as soon as the increased money enters their hands, they take the opportunity to re-establish their time preferences and therefore the old differentials and investment-consumption ratios. *Overinvestment* in the highest stages, and *underinvestment* in the lower stages are now revealed in all their starkness. The situation is analogous to that of a contractor misled into believing that he has more building material than he really has and then awakening to find that he has used up all his material on a capacious foundation (the higher stages), with no material left to complete the house.[111] Clearly, bank credit expansion cannot increase capital investment by one iota. Investment can still come only from savings.

It should not be surprising that the market tends to revert to its preferred ratios. The same process, as we have seen, takes place in all prices after a change in the money stock. Increased money always begins in one area of the economy, raising prices there, and filters and diffuses eventually over the whole economy, which then roughly returns to an equilibrium pattern conforming to the value of the money. If the market then tends to return to its preferred price-ratios after a change in the money supply, it should be evident that this *includes* a return to its preferred saving-investment ratio, reflecting social time preferences.

It is true, of course, that time preferences may alter in the interim, either for each individual or as a result of the redistribution during the change. The gainers may save more or less than the losers would have done. Therefore, the market will not return precisely to the old free-market interest rate and investment/consumption ratio, just as it will not return to its precise pattern of prices. It will revert to whatever the free-market interest rate is *now,* as determined by current time preferences. Some advocates of coercing the market into saving and investing more than it wishes have hailed credit expansion as leading to "forced saving," thereby increasing the capital-goods structure. But this can happen, *not* as a direct consequence of credit expansion, but only because effective time preferences have changed in that direction (i.e., time-preference schedules have shifted, or relatively more money is now in the hands of those with low time preferences). Credit expansion may well lead to the opposite effect: the gainers may have higher time preferences, in which case the free-market interest rate will be higher than before. Because these effects of credit expansion are completely uncertain and depend on the concrete data of each particular case, it is clearly far more cogent for advocates of forced saving to use the *taxation* process to make their redistribution.

The market therefore reacts to a distortion of the free-market interest rate by proceeding to revert to that very rate. The distortion caused by credit expansion deceives businessmen into believing that more savings are available and causes them to *malinvest*—to invest in projects that will turn out to be unprofitable when consumers have a chance to reassert their true preferences. This reassertion takes place fairly quickly—as soon as owners of factors receive their increased incomes and spend them.

This theory permits us to resolve an age-old controversy among economists: whether an increase in the money supply can lower the market rate of interest. To the mercantilists—and to the Keynesians—it was obvious that an increased money stock permanently lowered the rate of interest (given the demand for money). To the classicists it was obvious that changes in the money stock could affect only the value of the monetary unit, and not the rate of interest. The answer is that an increase in the supply of money *does* lower the rate of interest when it enters the market as credit expansion, but only temporarily. In the long run (and this long run is not very "long"), the market reestablishes the free-market time-preference interest rate and eliminates the change. In the long run a change in the money stock affects only the value of the monetary unit.

This process—by which the market reverts to its preferred interest rate and eliminates the distortion caused by credit expansion—*is,* moreover, *the business cycle!* Our analysis therefore permits the solution, not only of the theoretical problem of the relation between money and interest, but also of the problem that has plagued society for the last century and a half and more—the dread business cycle. And, furthermore, the theory of the business cycle can now be explained as a subdivision of our general theory of the economy.

Note the hallmarks of this distortion-reversion process. First, the money supply increases through credit expansion; then businesses are tempted to malinvest—overinvesting in higher-stage and durable production processes. Next, the prices and incomes of original factors increase and consumption increases, and businesses realize that the higher-stage investments have been wasteful and unprofitable. The first stage is the chief landmark of the "boom"; the second stage—the discovery of the wasteful malinvestments—is the "crisis." The *depression* is the next stage, during which malinvested businesses become bankrupt, and original factors must suddenly shift back to the lower stages of production. The liquidation of unsound businesses, the "idle capacity" of the malinvested plant, and the "frictional" unemployment of original factors that must suddenly and *en masse* shift to lower stages of production—these are the chief hallmarks of the depression stage.

We have seen in chapter 11 that the major unexplained features of the business cycle are the mass of error and the concentration of error and disturbance in the capital-goods industries.

Our theory of the business cycle solves both of these problems. The cluster of error suddenly revealed by entrepreneurs is due to the interventionary distortion of a key market signal—the interest rate. The concentration of disturbance in the capital-goods industries is explained by the spur to unprofitable higher-order investments in the boom period. And we have just seen that other characteristics of the business cycle are explained by this theory.

One point should be stressed: the *depression* phase is actually the *recovery* phase. Most people would be happy to keep the boom period, where the inflationary gains are visible and the losses hidden and obscure. This boom euphoria is heightened by the capital consumption that inflation promotes through illusory accounting profits. The stages that people complain about are the crisis and depression. But the latter periods, it should be clear, do not cause the trouble. The trouble occurs during the boom, when malinvestments and distortions take place; the crisis-depression phase is the curative period, after people have been forced to recognize the malinvestments that have occurred. The depression period, therefore, *is* the necessary recovery period; it is the time when bad investments are liquidated and mistaken entrepreneurs leave the market—the time when "consumer sovereignty" and the free market reassert themselves and establish once again an economy that benefits every participant to the maximum degree. The depression period ends when the free-market equilibrium has been restored and expansionary distortion eliminated.

It should be clear that any governmental interference with the depression process can only prolong it, thus making things worse from almost everyone's point of view. Since the depression process *is* the recovery process, any halting or slowing down of the process impedes the advent of recovery. The depression readjustments must work themselves out before recovery can be complete. The more these readjustments are delayed, the longer the depression will have to last, and the longer complete recovery is postponed. For example, if the government keeps wage rates up, it brings about permanent unemployment. If it keeps prices up, it brings about unsold surplus. And if it spurs credit expansion again, then new malinvestment and later depressions are spawned.

Many nineteenth-century economists referred to the business cycle in a biological metaphor, likening the depression to a painful but necessary curative of the alcoholic or narcotic jag which is the boom, and asserting that any tampering with the depression delays recovery. They have been widely ridiculed by present-day economists. The ridicule is misdirected, however, for the biological analogy is in this case correct.

One obvious conclusion from our analysis is the absurdity of the "underconsumptionist" remedies for depression—the idea that the crisis is caused by underconsumption and that the way to cure the depression is to stimulate consumption expenditures. The reverse is clearly the truth. What has brought about the crisis is precisely the fact that entrepreneurial investment erroneously anticipated greater savings, and that this error is revealed by consumers' re-establishing their desired proportion of consumption. "Overconsumption" or "undersaving" has brought about the crisis, although it is hardly fair to pin the guilt on the consumer, who is simply trying to restore his preferences after the market has been distorted by bank credit. The only way to hasten the curative process of the depression is for people to save and invest *more* and consume *less*, thereby finally justifying some of the malinvestments and mitigating the adjustments that have to be made.

One problem has been left unexplained. We have seen that the reversion period is short and that factor incomes increase rather quickly and start restoring the free-market consumption/saving ratios. But why do booms, historically, continue for several years? What delays the reversion process? The answer is that as the boom begins to peter out from an injection of credit expansion, the banks inject a further dose. In short, the only way to *avert* the onset of the depression-adjustment process is to continue inflating money and credit. For only continual doses of new money on the credit market will keep the boom going and the new stages profitable. Furthermore, only *ever increasing* doses can step up the boom, can lower interest rates further, and expand the production structure, for as the prices rise, more and more money will be needed to perform the same amount of work. Once the credit expansion stops, the market ratios are re-established, and the seemingly glorious new investments turn out to be malinvestments, built on a foundation of sand.

How long booms can be kept up, what limits there are to booms in different circumstances, will be discussed below. But it is clear that prolonging the boom by ever larger doses of credit expansion will have only one result: to make the inevitably ensuing depression longer and more grueling. The larger the scope of malinvestment and error in the boom, the greater and longer the task of readjustment in the depression. The way to prevent a depression, then, is simple: avoid starting a boom. And to avoid starting a boom all that is necessary is to pursue a truly free-market policy in money, i.e., a policy of 100% specie reserves for banks and governments.

Credit expansion always generates the business cycle process, even when other tendencies cloak its workings. Thus, many people believe that all is well if prices do not rise or if the actually recorded interest rate does not fall. But prices may well not rise because of some counteracting force—such as an increase in the supply of goods or a rise in the demand for money. But this does not mean that the boom-depression cycle fails to occur. The essential processes of the boom—distorted interest rates, malinvestments, bankruptcies, etc.—continue unchecked. This is one of the reasons why those who approach business cycles from a statistical point of view and try in that way to arrive at a theory are in hopeless error. Any historical-statistical fact is a complex resultant of many causal influences and cannot be used as a simple element with which to construct a causal theory. The point is that credit expansion raises prices *beyond what they would have been in the free market* and thereby creates the business cycle. Similarly, credit expansion does not necessarily lower the interest rate below the rate *previously* recorded; it lowers the rate *below what it would have been in the free market* and thus creates distortion and malinvestment. Recorded interest rates in the boom will generally *rise,* in fact, because of the *purchasing-power component* in the market interest rate. An increase in prices, as we have seen, generates a positive purchasing-power component in the natural interest rate, i.e., the rate of return earned by businessmen on the market. In the free market this would quickly be reflected in the loan rate, which, as we have seen above, is completely dependent on the natural rate. But a continual influx of circulating credit *prevents* the loan rate from catching up with the natural rate, and thereby generates the business-cycle process.[112] A further corollary of this bank-created discrepancy between the loan rate and the natural rate is that creditors on the loan market suffer losses for the benefit of their debtors: the capitalists on the stock market or those who own their own businesses. The latter gain during the boom by the differential between the loan rate and the natural rate, while the creditors (apart from banks, which create their own money) lose to the same extent.

After the boom period is over, what is to be done with the malinvestments? The answer depends on their profitability for further use, i.e., on the degree of error that was committed. Some malinvestments will have to be abandoned, since their earnings from consumer demand will not even cover the current costs of their operation. Others, though monuments of failure, will be able to yield a profit over current costs, although it will not pay to replace them as they wear out. Temporarily working them fulfills the economic principle of always making the best of even a bad bargain.

Because of the malinvestments, however, the boom always leads to general *impoverishment,* i.e., reduces the standard of living below what it would have been in the absence of the boom. For the credit expansion has caused the squandering of scarce resources and scarce capital. Some resources have been completely wasted, and even those malinvestments that continue in use will satisfy consumers less than would have been the case without the credit expansion.

C. Secondary Developments of the Business Cycle

In the previous section we have presented the basic process of the business cycle. This process is often accentuated by other or "secondary" developments induced by the cycle. Thus, the expanding money supply and rising prices are likely to lower the demand for money. Many people begin to anticipate higher prices and will therefore dishoard. The lowered demand for money raises prices further. Since the impetus to expansion comes first in expenditure on capital goods and later in consumption, this "secondary effect" of a lower demand for money may take hold first in producers'-goods industries. This lowers the price-and-profit differentials further and hence widens the distance that the rate of interest will fall below the free-market rate during the boom. The effect is to aggravate the need for readjustment during the depression. The adjustment would cause some fall in the prices of producers' goods anyway, since the essence of the adjustment is to raise price differentials. The extra distortion requires a steeper fall in the prices of producers' goods before recovery is completed.

As a matter of fact, the demand for money generally *rises* at the beginning of an inflation. People are accustomed to thinking of the value of the monetary unit as inviolate and of prices as remaining at some "customary" level. Hence, when prices first begin to rise, most people believe this to be a purely temporary development, with prices soon due to recede. This belief mitigates the extent of the price rise for a time. Eventually, however, people realize that credit expansion has continued and undoubtedly will continue, and their demand for money dwindles, becoming lower than the original level.

After the crisis arrives and the depression begins, various secondary developments often occur. In particular, for reasons that will be discussed further below, the crisis is often marked not only by a *halt* to credit expansion, but by an actual *deflation*—a contraction in the supply of money. The deflation causes a further decline in prices. Any increase in the demand for money will speed up adjustment to the lower prices. Furthermore, when deflation takes place first on the loan market, i.e., as *credit contraction* by the banks—and this is almost always the case—this will have the beneficial effect of speeding up the depression-adjustment process. For credit contraction creates higher price differentials. And the essence of the required adjustment is to return to higher price differentials, i.e., a higher "natural" rate of interest. Furthermore, deflation will hasten adjustment in yet another way: for the accounting error of inflation is here reversed, and businessmen will think their losses are more, and profits less, than they really are. Hence, they will save more than they would have with correct accounting, and the increased saving will speed adjustment by supplying some of the needed deficiency of savings.

It may well be true that the deflationary process will overshoot the free-market equilibrium point and raise price differentials and the interest rate above it. But if so, no harm will be done, since a credit contraction can create no malinvestments and therefore does not generate another boom-bust cycle.[118] And the market will correct the error rapidly. When there is such excessive contraction, and consumption is too high in relation to savings, the money income of businessmen is reduced, and their spending on factors declines—especially in the higher orders. Owners of original factors, receiving lower incomes, will spend less on consumption, price differentials and the interest rate will again be lowered, and the free-market consumption/investment ratios will be speedily restored.

Just as inflation is generally popular for its narcotic effect, deflation is always highly unpopular for the opposite reason. The contraction of money is visible; the benefits to those whose buying prices fall first and who lose money last remain hidden. And the illusory accounting losses of deflation make businesses believe that their losses are greater, or profits smaller, than they actually are, and this will aggravate business pessimism.

It is true that deflation takes from one group and gives to another, as does inflation. Yet not only does credit contraction speed recovery and counteract the distortions of the boom, but it also, in a broad sense, takes away from the original coercive gainers and benefits the original coerced losers. While this will certainly not be true in every case, in the broad sense much the same groups will benefit and lose, but in reverse order from that of the redistributive effects of credit expansion. Fixed-income groups, widows and orphans, will gain, and businesses and owners of original factors previously reaping gains from inflation will lose. The longer the inflation has continued, of course, the less the same individuals will be compensated.[114]

Some may object that deflation "causes" unemployment. However, as we have seen above, deflation can lead to continuing unemployment only if the government or the unions keep wage rates above the discounted marginal value products of labor. If wage rates are allowed to fall freely, no continuing unemployment will occur.

Finally, deflationary credit contraction is, necessarily, severely limited. Whereas credit can expand (barring various economic limits to be discussed below) virtually to infinity, circulating credit can contract only as far down as the total amount of specie in circulation. In short, its maximum possible limit is the eradication of all previous credit expansion.

The business-cycle analysis set forth here has essentially been that of the "Austrian" school, originated and developed by Ludwig von Mises and some of his students.[115] A prominent criticism of this theory is that it "assumes the existence of full employment" or that its analysis holds only *after* "full employment" has been attained. Before that point, say the critics, credit expansion will beneficently put these factors to work and not generate further malinvestments or cycles. But, in the first place, inflation will put no unemployed factors to work unless their owners, though holding out for a money price higher than their marginal value product, are blindly content to accept the necessarily lower real price when it is camouflaged as a rise in the "cost of living." And credit expansion generates further cycles whether or not there are unemployed factors. It creates more distortions and malinvestments, delays indefinitely the process of recovery from the previous boom, and makes necessary an eventually far more grueling recovery to adjust to the new malinvestments as well as to the old. If idle capital goods are now set to work, this "idle capacity" is the hangover effect of previous wasteful malinvestments, and hence is really submarginal and not worth bringing into production. Putting the capital to work again will only redouble the distortions.[116]

D. THE LIMITS OF CREDIT EXPANSION

Having investigated the consequences of credit expansion, we must discuss the important question: If fractional-reserve banking is legal, are there any natural *limits* to credit expansion by the banks? The one basic limit, of course, is the necessity of the banks to redeem their money-substitutes on demand. Under a gold or silver standard, they must redeem in specie; under a government fiat paper standard (see below), the banks have to redeem in government paper. In any case, they must redeem in standard money or its virtual equivalent. Therefore, every fractional reserve bank depends for its very existence on persuading the public—specifically its *clients*—that all is well and that it will be able to redeem its notes or deposits whenever the clients demand. Since this is palpably not the case, the continuance of confidence in the banks is something of a psychological marvel.[117] It is certain, at any rate, that a wider knowledge of praxeology among the public would greatly weaken confidence in the banking system. For the banks are in an inherently weak position. Let just a few of their clients lose confidence and begin to call on the banks for redemption, and this will precipitate a scramble by other clients to make sure that *they* get their money while the banks' doors are still open. The obvious—and justifiable—panic of the banks should any sort of "run" develop encourages other clients to do the same and aggravates the run still further. At any rate, runs on banks can wreak havoc, and, of course, if pursued consistently, could close every bank in the country in a few days.[118]

Runs, therefore, and the constant underlying threat of their occurrence, are one of the prime limits to credit expansion. Runs often develop during a business cycle crisis, when debts are being defaulted and failures become manifest. Runs and the fear of runs help to precipitate deflationary credit contraction.

Runs may be an ever-present threat, but, as effective limitations, they are not generally active. When they do occur, they usually wreck the banks. The fact that a bank is in existence at all signifies that a run has not developed. A more active, everyday limitation is the relatively *narrow range* of a bank's clientele. The clientele of a bank consists of those people willing to hold its deposits or notes (its money-substitutes) in lieu of money proper. It is an empirical fact, in almost all cases, that one bank does not have the patronage of all people in the market society or even of all those who prefer to use bank money rather than specie. It is obvious that the more banks exist, the more restricted will be the clientele of any one bank. People decide which bank to use on many grounds; reputation for integrity, friendliness of service, price of service, and convenience of location may all play a part.

How does the narrow range of a bank's clientele limit its potentiality for credit expansion? The newly issued money-substitutes are, of course, loaned to a bank's clients. The client then spends the new money on goods and services. The new money begins to be diffused throughout the society. Eventually—usually very quickly—it is spent on the goods or services of people who use a *different* bank. Suppose that the Star Bank has expanded credit; the newly issued Star Bank's notes or deposits find their way into the hands of Mr. Jones, who uses the City Bank. Two alternatives may occur, either of which has the same economic effect: (*a*) Jones accepts the Star Bank's notes or deposits, and deposits them in the City Bank, which calls on the Star Bank for redemption; or (*b*) Jones refuses to accept the Star Bank's notes and insists that the Star client—say Mr. Smith—who bought something from Jones, redeem the note himself and pay Jones in acceptable standard money.

Thus, while gold or silver is acceptable throughout the market, a bank's money-substitutes are acceptable only to its own clientele. Clearly, a single bank's credit expansion is limited, and this limitation is stronger (*a*) the narrower the range of its clientele, and (*b*) the greater its issue of money-substitutes in relation to that of competing banks. In illustration of the first point, let us assume that each bank has only one client. Then it is obvious that there will be very little room for credit expansion. At the opposite extreme, if one bank is used by everybody in the economy, there will be no demands for redemption resulting from its clients' purchasing from nonclients. It is obvious that, *ceteris paribus,* a numerically smaller clientele is more restrictive of credit expansion.

As regards the second point, the greater the degree of relative credit expansion by any one bank, the sooner will the day of redemption—and potential bankruptcy—be at hand. Suppose that the Star Bank expands credit, while none of the competing banks do. This means that the Star Bank's clientele have added considerably to their cash balances; as a result the marginal utility to them of each unit of money to hold declines, and they are impelled to spend a great proportion of the new money. Some of this increased spending will be on one another's goods and services, but it is clear that the greater the credit expansion, the greater will be the tendency for their spending to "spill over" onto the goods and services of nonclients. This tendency to spill over, or "drain," is greatly enhanced when increased spending by clients on the goods and services of other clients raises their prices. In the meanwhile, the prices of the goods sold by nonclients remain the same. As a consequence, clients are impelled to buy more from nonclients and less from one another; while nonclients buy less from clients and more from one another. The result is an "unfavorable" balance of trade from clients to nonclients.[119] It is clear that this tendency of money to seek a uniform level of exchange value throughout the entire market is an example of the process by which new money (in this case, new money-substitutes) is diffused through the market. The greater the relative credit expansion by the bank, then, the greater and more rapid will be the drain and consequent pressure on an expanding bank for redemption.

The purpose of banks' keeping any specie reserves in their vaults (assuming no legal reserve requirements) now becomes manifest. It is not to meet bank runs—since no fractional-reserve bank can be equipped to withstand a run. It is to meet the demands for redemption which will inevitably come from nonclients.

Mises has brilliantly shown that a subdivision of this process was discovered by the British Currency School and by the classical "international trade" theorists of the nineteenth century. These older economists assumed that all the banks in a certain region or country expanded credit together. The result was a rise in the prices of goods produced in that country. A further result was an "unfavorable" balance of trade, i.e., an outflow of standard specie to other countries. Since other countries did not patronize the expanding country's banks, the consequence was a "specie drain" from the expanding country and increased pressure for redemption on its banks.

Like all parts of the overstressed and overelaborated theory of "international trade," this analysis is simply a special subdivision of "general" economic theory. And cataloging it as "international trade" theory, as Mises has shown, underestimates its true significance.[120, 121]

Thus, the more freely competitive and numerous are the banks, the less they will be able to expand fiduciary media, even if they are left free to do so. As we have noted in chapter 11, such a system is known as "free banking." [122] A major objection to this analysis of free banking has been the problem of bank "cartels." If banks get together and agree to expand their credits simultaneously, the clientele limitation vis-à-vis competing banks will be removed, and the clientele of each bank will, in effect, increase to include all bank users. Mises points out, however, that the sounder banks with higher fractional reserves will not wish to lose the good will of their own clients and risk bank runs by entering into collusive agreements with weaker banks.[123] This consideration, while placing limits on such agreements, does not rule them out altogether. For, after all, no fractional-reserve banks are *really* sound, and if the public can be led to believe that, say, an 80%-specie reserve is sound, it can believe the same about 60%- or even 10%-reserve banks. Indeed, the fact that the weaker banks are allowed by the public to exist at all demonstrates that the more conservative banks may not lose much good will by agreeing to expand with them.

As Mises has demonstrated, there is no question that, from the point of view of opponents of inflation and credit expansion, free banking is superior to a central banking system (see below). But, as Amasa Walker stated:

> Much has been said, at different times, of the desirableness of *free banking*. Of the propriety and rightfulness of allowing any person who chooses to carry on banking, as freely as farming or any other branch of business, there can be no doubt. But, while banking, as at present, means the issuing of inconvertible paper, the more it is guarded and restricted the better. But when such issues are entirely forbidden, and only notes equivalent to certificates of so much coin are issued, banking may be as free as brokerage. The only thing to be secured would be that no issues should be made except upon specie in hand.[124]

E. THE GOVERNMENT AS PROMOTER OF CREDIT EXPANSION

Historically, governments have fostered and encouraged credit expansion to a great degree. They have done so by *weakening* the limitations that the market places on bank credit expansion. One way of weakening is to anesthetize the bank against the threat of bank runs. In nineteenth-century America, the government permitted banks, when they got into trouble in a business crisis, to suspend specie payment while continuing in operation. They were temporarily freed from their contractual obligation of paying their debts, while they could continue lending and even force their debtors to repay in their own bank notes. This is a powerful way to eradicate limitations on credit expansion, since the banks know that if they overreach themselves, the government will permit them blithely to avoid payment of their contractual obligations.

Under a fiat money standard, governments (or their central banks) may obligate themselves to bail out, with increased issues of standard money, any bank or any major bank in distress. In the late nineteenth century, the principle became accepted that the central bank must act as the "lender of last resort," which will lend money freely to banks threatened with failure. Another recent American device to abolish the confidence limitation on bank credit is "deposit insurance," whereby the government guarantees to furnish paper money to redeem the banks' demand liabilities. These and similar devices remove the market brakes on rampant credit expansion.

A second device, now so legitimized that any country lacking it is considered hopelessly "backward," is the central bank. The central bank, while often nominally owned by private individuals or banks, is run directly by the national government. Its purpose, not always stated explicitly, is to remove the competitive check on bank credit provided by a multiplicity of independent banks. Its aim is to make sure that all the banks in the country are co-ordinated and will therefore expand or contract together—at the will of the government. And we have seen that co-ordination of expansion greatly weakens the market's limits.

The crucial way by which governments have established central bank control over the commercial banking system is by granting the bank *a monopoly of the note issue* in the country. As we have seen, money-substitutes may be issued in the form of notes or book deposits. Economically, the two forms are identical. The State has found it convenient, however, to distinguish between the two and to outlaw all note issue by private banks. Such nationalizing of the note-issue business forces the commercial banks to go to the central bank whenever their customers desire to exchange demand deposits for paper notes. To obtain notes to furnish their clients, commercial banks must buy them from the central bank. Such purchases can be made only by selling their gold coin or other standard money or by drawing on the banks' deposit accounts with the central bank.

Since the public always wishes to hold some of its money in the form of notes and some in demand deposits, the banks must establish a continuing relationship with the central bank to be assured a supply of notes. Their most convenient procedure is to establish demand deposit accounts with the central bank, which thereby becomes the "bankers' bank." These demand deposits (added to the gold in their vaults) become the reserves of the banks. The central bank can also more freely create demand liabilities not backed 100% by gold, and these increased liabilities add to the reserves and demand deposits held by banks or else increase central bank notes outstanding. The rise in reserves of banks throughout the country will spur them to expand credit, while any decrease in these reserves will induce a general contraction in credit.

The central bank can increase the reserves of a country's banks in three ways: (*a*) by simply lending them reserves; (*b*) by purchasing their assets, thereby adding directly to the banks' deposit accounts with the central bank, or (*c*) by purchasing the IOU's of the public, which will then deposit the drafts on the central bank in the various banks that serve the public directly, thereby enabling them to use the credits on the central bank to add to their own reserves. The second process is known as *discounting;* the latter as *open market purchase*. A lapse in discounts as the loans mature will lower reserves, as will *open market sales*. In open market sales, the people will pay the central bank for its assets, purchased with checks drawn on their accounts at the banks; and the central bank exacts payment by reducing bank reserves on its books. In most cases, the assets purchased or sold on the open market are government IOU's.[125]

Thus, the banking system becomes co-ordinated under the aegis of the government. The central bank is always accorded a great deal of prestige by its creator government. Often the government makes its notes legal tender. Under the gold standard, the wide resources which it commands, added to the fact that the whole country is its clientele, usually make negligible any trouble the bank may have in redeeming its liabilities in gold. Furthermore, it is certain that no government will let its own central bank (i.e., itself) go bankrupt; the central bank will always be permitted to suspend specie payment in times of serious difficulty. It can therefore inflate and expand credit itself (through rediscounts and open market purchases) and, by adding to bank reserves, spur a *multiple* bank credit expansion throughout the country. The effect is multiple because banks will generally keep a certain proportion of reserves to liabilities—based on estimates of nonclient redemption—and a general increase in their reserves will induce a multiple expansion of fiduciary media. In fact, the multiple will even increase, for the knowledge that all the banks are co-ordinated and expanding together decreases the possibility of nonclient redemption and therefore the proportion of reserves that each bank will wish to keep.

When the government "goes off" the gold standard, central bank notes then become legal tender and virtually the standard money. It then cannot possibly fail, and this, of course, practically eliminates limitations on its credit expansion. In the present-day United States, for example, the current basically fiat standard (also known as a "restricted international gold bullion standard") virtually eliminates pressure for redemption, while the central bank's ready provision of reserves as well as deposit insurance eliminates the threat of bank failure.[126] In order to insure centralized control by the government over bank credit, the United States enforces on banks a certain minimum ratio of reserves (almost wholly deposits with the central bank) to deposits.

So long as a country is in any sense "on the gold standard," the central bank and the banking system must worry about an external drain of specie should the inflation become too great. Under an unrestricted gold standard, it must also worry about an internal drain resulting from the demands of those who do not use the banks. A shift in public taste from deposits to notes will embarrass the commercial banks, though not the central bank. Assiduous propaganda on the conveniences of banking, however, has reduced the ranks of those not using banks to a few malcontents. As a result, the only limitation on credit expansion is now external. Governments, of course, are always anxious to remove all checks on their powers of inducing monetary expansion. One way of removing the external threat is to foster international cooperation, so that all governments and central banks expand their money supply at a uniform rate. The "ideal" condition for unlimited inflation is, of course, a world fiat paper money, issued by a world central bank or other governmental authority. Pure fiat money on a national scale would serve almost as well, but there would then be the embarrassment of national moneys depreciating in terms of other moneys, and imports becoming much more expensive.[127]

F. THE ULTIMATE LIMIT: THE RUNAWAY BOOM

With the establishment of fiat money by a State or by a World State, it would seem that all limitations on credit expansion, or on any inflation, are eliminated. The central bank can issue limitless amounts of nominal units of paper, unchecked by any necessity of digging a commodity out of the ground. They may be supplied to banks to bolster their credit at the pleasure of the government. No problems of internal or external drain exist. And if there existed a World State, or a co-operating cartel of States, with a world bank and world paper money, and gold and silver money were outlawed, could not the World State then expand the money supply at will with no foreign exchange or foreign trade difficulties, permanently redistributing wealth from the market's choice to its own favorites, from voluntary producers to the ruling castes?

Many economists and most other people assume that the State could accomplish this goal. Actually, it could not, for there is an ultimate limit on inflation, a very wide one, to be sure, but a terrible limit that will in the end conquer any inflation. Paradoxically, this is the phenomenon of *runaway inflation,* or *hyperinflation.*

When the government and the banking system begin inflating, the public will usually aid them unwittingly in this task. The public, not cognizant of the true nature of the process, believes that the rise in prices is transient and that prices will soon return to "normal." As we have noted above, people will therefore hoard more money, i.e., keep a greater proportion of their income in the form of cash balances. The social demand for money, in short, increases. As a result, prices tend to increase less than proportionately to the increase in the quantity of money. The government obtains *more real* resources from the public than it had expected, since the public's demand for these resources has declined.

Eventually, the public begins to realize what is taking place. It seems that the government is attempting to use inflation as a permanent form of taxation. But the public has a weapon to combat this depredation. Once people realize that the government will continue to inflate, and therefore that prices will continue to rise, they will step up their purchases of goods. For they will realize that they are gaining by buying now, instead of waiting until a future date when the value of the monetary unit will be lower and prices higher. In other words, the social demand for money falls, and prices now begin to rise more rapidly than the increase in the supply of money. When this happens, the confiscation by the government, or the "taxation" effect of inflation, will be lower than the government had expected, for the increased money will be reduced in purchasing power by the greater rise in prices. This stage of the inflation is the beginning of hyperinflation, of the runaway boom.[128]

The lower demand for money allows fewer resources to be extracted by the government, but the government can still obtain resources so long as the market continues to use the money. The accelerated price rise will, in fact, lead to complaints of a "scarcity of money" and stimulate the government to greater efforts of inflation, thereby causing even more accelerated price increases. This process will not continue long, however. As the rise in prices continues, the public begins a "flight from money," getting rid of money as soon as possible in order to invest in real goods—almost *any* real goods—as a store of value for the future. This mad scramble away from money, lowering the demand for money to hold practically to zero, causes prices to rise upward in astronomical proportions. The value of the monetary unit falls practically to zero. The devastation and havoc that the runaway boom causes among the populace is enormous. The relatively fixed-income groups are wiped out. Production declines drastically (sending up prices further), as people lose the incentive to work—since they must spend much of their time getting rid of money. The main desideratum becomes getting hold of real goods, whatever they may be, and spending money as soon as received. When this runaway stage is reached, the economy in effect breaks down, the market is virtually ended, and society reverts to a state of virtual barter and complete impoverishment.[129] Commodities are then slowly built up as media of exchange. The public has rid itself of the inflation burden by its ultimate weapon: lowering the demand for money to such an extent that the government's money has become worthless. When all other limits and forms of persuasion fail, this is the only way—through chaos and economic breakdown—for the people to force a return to the "hard" commodity money of the free market.

The most famous runaway inflation was the German experience of 1923. It is particularly instructive because it took place in one of the world's most advanced industrial countries.[130] The chaotic events of the German hyperinflation and other accelerated booms, however, are only a pale shadow of what would happen under a World State inflation. For Germany was able to recover and return to a full monetary market economy quickly, since it could institute a new currency based on exchanges with other pre-existing moneys (gold or foreign paper). As we have seen, however, Mises' regression theorem shows that no money can be established on the market except as it can be exchanged for a previously-existing money (which in turn must have ultimately related back to a commodity in barter). If a World State outlaws gold and silver and establishes a unitary fiat money, which it proceeds to inflate until a runaway boom destroys it, *there will be no pre-existing money on the market.* The task of reconstruction will then be enormously more difficult.

G. INFLATION AND COMPENSATORY FISCAL POLICY

Inflation, in recent years, has been generally defined as an increase in prices. This is a highly unsatisfactory definition. Prices are highly complex phenomena, activated by many different causal factors. They may increase or decrease from the goods side—i.e., as a result of a change in the supply of goods on the market. They may increase or decrease because of a change in the social demand for money to hold; or they may rise or fall from a change in the supply of money. To lump all of these causes together is misleading, for it glosses over the separate influences, the isolation of which is the goal of science. Thus, the money supply may be increasing, while at the same time the social demand for money is increasing from the goods side, in the form of increased supplies of goods. Each may offset the other, with no general price changes occurring. Yet both processes perform their work nevertheless. Resources will still shift as a result of inflation, and the business cycle caused by credit expansion will still appear. It is, therefore, highly inexpedient to define inflation as a rise in prices.

Movements in the supply-of-goods and in the demand-for-money schedules are all the results of voluntary changes of preferences on the market. The same is true for increases in the supply of gold or silver. But increases in fiduciary or fiat media are acts of fraudulent intervention in the market, distorting voluntary preferences and the voluntarily determined pattern of income and wealth. Therefore, the most expedient definition of "inflation" is one we have set forth above: an increase in the supply of money beyond any increase in specie.[131]

The absurdity of the various governmental programs for "fighting inflation" now becomes evident. Most people believe that government officials must constantly pace the ramparts, armed with a huge variety of "control" programs designed to combat the inflation enemy. Yet all that is really necessary is that the government and the banks (nowadays controlled almost completely by the government) cease *inflating.*[132] The absurdity of the term "inflationary pressure" also becomes clear. Either the government and banks *are inflating* or they are not; there is no such thing as "inflationary pressure." [133]

The idea that the government has the duty to tax the public in order to "sop up excess purchasing power" is particularly ludicrous.[134] If inflation has been under way, this "excess purchasing power" is precisely the result of previous governmental inflation. In short, the government is supposed to burden the public twice: once in appropriating the resources of society by inflating the money supply, and again, by taxing back the new money from the public. Rather than "checking inflationary pressure," then, a tax surplus in a boom will simply place an additional burden upon the public. If the taxes are used for further government spending, or for repaying debts to the public, then there is not even a deflationary effect. If the taxes are used to redeem government debt held by the banks, the deflationary effect will not be a credit contraction and therefore will not correct maladjustments brought about by the previous inflation. It will, indeed, create further dislocations and distortions of its own.

Keynesian and neo-Keynesian "compensatory fiscal policy" advocates that government deflate during an "inflationary" period and inflate (incur deficits, financed by borrowing from the banks) to combat a depression. It is clear that government inflation can relieve unemployment and unsold stocks only if the process dupes the owners into accepting lower *real* prices or wages. This "money illusion" relies on the owners' being too ignorant to realize when their real incomes have declined—a slender basis on which to ground a cure. Furthermore, the inflation will benefit part of the public at the expense of the rest, and any credit expansion will only set a further "boom-bust" cycle into motion. The Keynesians depict the free market's monetary-fiscal system as minus a steering wheel, so that the economy, though readily adjustable in other ways, is constantly walking a precarious tightrope between depression and unemployment on the one side and inflation on the other. It is then necessary for the government, in its wisdom, to step in and steer the economy on an even course. After our completed analysis of money and business cycles, however, it should be evident that the true picture is just about the reverse. The free market, unhampered, would not be in danger of suffering inflation, deflation, depression, or unemployment. But the intervention of government *creates* the tightrope for the economy and is constantly, if sometimes unwittingly, pushing the economy into these pitfalls.

12. *Conclusion: The Free Market and Coercion*

We have thus concluded our analysis of voluntary and free action and its consequences in the free market, and of violent and coercive action and *its* consequences in economic intervention. Superficially, it looks to many people as if the free market is a chaotic and anarchic place, while government intervention imposes order and community values upon this anarchy. Actually, praxeology—economics—shows us that the truth is quite the reverse. We may divide our analysis into the direct, or palpable, effects, and the indirect, hidden effects of the two principles. Directly, voluntary action—free exchange—leads to the mutual benefit of both parties to the exchange. Indirectly, as our investigations have shown, the network of these free exchanges in society—known as the "free market"—creates a delicate and even awe-inspiring mechanism of harmony, adjustment, and precision in allocating productive resources, deciding upon prices, and gently but swiftly guiding the economic system toward the greatest possible satisfaction of the desires of all the consumers. In short, not only does the free market *directly* benefit all parties and leave them free and uncoerced; it also creates a mighty and efficient instrument of social *order*. Proudhon, indeed, wrote better than he knew when he called "Liberty, the Mother, not the Daughter, of Order."

On the other hand, coercion has diametrically opposite features. Directly, coercion benefits one party only at the expense of others. Coerced exchange is a system of exploitation of man by man, in contrast to the free market, which is a system of cooperative exchanges in the exploitation of *nature* alone. And not only does coerced exchange mean that some live at the expense of others, but, indirectly, as we have just observed, coercion leads only to further problems: it is inefficient and chaotic, it cripples production, and it leads to cumulative and unforeseen difficulties. Seemingly orderly, coercion is not only exploitative; it is also profoundly *disorderly*.

The major function of praxeology—of economics—is to bring to the world the knowledge of these indirect, these hidden, consequences of the different forms of human action. The hidden order, harmony, and efficiency of the voluntary free market, the hidden disorder, conflict, and gross inefficiency of coercion and intervention—these are the great truths that economic science, through deductive analysis from self-evident axioms, reveals to us. Praxeology cannot, by itself, pass ethical judgment or make policy decisions. Praxeology, through its *wertfrei* laws, informs us that the workings of the voluntary principle and of the free market lead inexorably to freedom, prosperity, harmony, efficiency, and order; while coercion and government intervention lead inexorably to hegemony, conflict, exploitation of man by man, inefficiency, poverty, and chaos. At this point, praxeology retires from the scene; and it is up to the citizen—the ethicist—to choose his political course according to the values that he holds dear.

APPENDIX A: GOVERNMENT BORROWING

The major source of government revenue is taxation. Another source is government borrowing. Government borrowing from the banking system is really a form of inflation: it creates new money-substitutes that go first to the government and then diffuse, with each step of spending, into the community. Inflation is discussed in the text above. This is a process entirely different from borrowing from the public, which is not inflationary, for the latter transfers saved funds from private to governmental hands rather than creates new funds. Its economic effect is to divert savings from the channels most desired by the consumers and to shift them to the uses desired by government officials. Hence, from the point of view of the consumers, borrowing from the public wastes savings. The consequences of this waste are a lowering of the capital structure of the society and a lowering of the general standard of living in the present and the future. Diversion and waste of savings from investment causes interest rates to be higher than they otherwise would, since now private uses must compete with government demands. Public borrowing strikes at individual *savings* more effectively even than taxation, for it specifically lures away *savings* rather than taxing income in general.

It might be objected that lending to the government is voluntary and is therefore equivalent to any other voluntary contribution to the government; the "diversion" of funds is something desired by the consumers and hence by society.[135] Yet the process is "voluntary" only in a one-sided way. For we must not forget that the government enters the time market as a bearer of coercion and as a guarantor that it will use this coercion to obtain funds for repayment. The government is armed by coercion with a crucial power denied to all other people on the market; it is always assured of funds, whether by taxation or by inflation. The government will therefore be able to divert considerable funds from savers, and at an interest rate lower than any paid elsewhere. For the risk component in the interest rate paid by the government will be lower than that paid by any other borrowers.[136]

Lending to government, therefore, may be voluntary, but the process is hardly voluntary when considered as a whole. It is rather a voluntary participation in future confiscation to be committed by the government. In fact, lending to government *twice* involves diversion of private funds to the government: once when the loan is made, and private savings are diverted to government spending; and again when the government taxes or inflates (or borrows again) to obtain the money to repay the loan. Then, once more, a coerced diversion takes place from private producers to the government, the proceeds of which, after payment of the bureaucracy for handling services, accrues to the government bondholders. The latter have thus become a part of the State apparatus and are engaging in a "relation of State" with the tax-paying producers.[137]

The ingenious slogan that the public debt does not matter because "we owe it to ourselves" is clearly absurd. The crucial question is: Who is the "we" and who are the "ourselves"? Analysis of the world must be individualistic and not holistic. Certain people owe money to certain other people, and it is precisely this fact that makes the borrowing as well as the taxing process important. For we might just as well say that taxes are unimportant for the same reason.[138]

Many "right-wing" opponents of public borrowing, on the other hand, have greatly exaggerated the dangers of the public debt and have raised persistent alarms about imminent "bankruptcy." It is obvious that the government cannot become "insolvent" like private individuals—for it can always obtain money by coercion, while private citizens cannot. Further, the periodic agitation that the government "reduce the public debt" generally forgets that—short of outright repudiation—the debt can be reduced only by *increasing,* at least for a time, the tax and/or inflation in society. Social utility can therefore not be enhanced by debt-reduction, *except* by the method of *repudiation*—the one way that the public debt can be lowered without a concomitant increase in fiscal coercion. Repudiation would also have the further merit (from the standpoint of the free market) of casting a pall on all future government credit, so that the government could no longer so easily divert savings to government use. It is therefore one of the most curious and inconsistent features of the history of politico-economic thought that it is precisely the "right-wingers," the presumed champions of the free market, who attack repudiation most strongly and who insist on as swift a payment of the public debt as possible.[139]

APPENDIX B: "COLLECTIVE GOODS" AND "EXTERNAL BENEFITS": TWO ARGUMENTS FOR GOVERNMENT ACTIVITY

One of the most important philosophical problems of recent centuries is whether ethics is a rational discipline, or instead a purely arbitrary, unscientific set of personal values. Whichever side one may take in this debate, it would certainly be generally agreed that economics—or praxeology—cannot *by itself* suffice to establish an ethical, or politico-ethical, doctrine. Economics *per se* is therefore a *wertfrei* science, which does not engage in ethical judgments. Yet, while economists will generally agree to this flat statement, it is certainly curious how much energy they have spent trying to justify—in some tortuous, presumably scientific, and *wertfrei* manner—various activities and expenditures of government. The consequence is the widespread smuggling of *unanalyzed,* undefended ethical judgments into a supposedly *wertfrei* system of economics.[140, 141]

Two favorite, seemingly scientific, justifications for government activity and enterprise are (*a*) what we might call the argument of "external benefits" and (*b*) the argument of "collective goods" or "collective wants." Stripped of seemingly scientific or quasi-mathematical trappings, the first argument reduces to the contention that A, B, and C do not seem to be able to do certain things without benefiting D, who may try to evade his "just share" of the payment. This and other "external benefit" arguments will be discussed shortly. The "collective goods" argument is, on its face, even more scientific; the economist simply asserts that some goods or services, by their very nature, must be supplied "collectively," and "therefore" government must supply them out of tax revenue.

This seemingly simple, existential statement, however, cloaks a good many unanalyzed politico-ethical assumptions. In the first place, even if there *were* "collective goods," it by no means follows *either* (1) that one agency must supply them or (2) that everyone in the collectivity *must* be forced to pay for them. In short, if X is a collective good, needed by most people in a certain community, and which can be supplied only to all, it by no means follows that every beneficiary must be forced to pay for the good, which, incidentally, he may not even want. In short, we are back squarely in the moral problem of external benefits, which we shall discuss below. The "collective goods" argument turns out, upon analysis, to reduce to the "external benefit" argument. Furthermore, even if only one agency must supply the good, it has not been proved that the *government,* rather than some voluntary agency, or even some private corporation, cannot supply that good.[142]

Secondly, the very concept of "collective goods" is a highly dubious one. How, first of all, can a "collective" want, think, or act? Only an individual exists, and can do these things. There is no existential referent of the "collective" that supposedly wants and then receives goods. Many attempts have been made, nevertheless, to salvage the concept of the "collective" good, to provide a seemingly ironclad, scientific justification for government operations. Molinari, for example, trying to establish defense as a collective good, asserted: "A police force serves every inhabitant of the district in which it acts, but the mere establishment of a bakery does not appease their hunger." But, on the contrary, there is no absolute necessity for a police force to defend *every* inhabitant of an area or, still more, to give each one the same *degree* of protection. Furthermore, an absolute pacifist, a believer in total nonviolence, living in the area, would *not* consider himself protected by, or receiving defense service from, the police. On the contrary, he would consider any police in his area a detriment to him. Hence, defense cannot be considered a "collective good" or "collective want." Similarly for such projects as dams, which cannot be simply assumed to benefit everyone in the area.[143]

Antonio De Viti De Marco defined "collective wants" as consisting of two categories: wants arising when an individual is not in isolation and wants connected with a conflict of interest. The first category, however, is so broad as to encompass most market products. There would be no point, for example, in putting on plays unless a certain number went to see them or in publishing newspapers without a certain wide market. Must all these industries therefore be nationalized and monopolized by the government? The second category is presumably meant to apply to defense. This, however, is incorrect. Defense, itself, does not reflect a conflict of interest, but a threat of *invasion,* against which defense is needed. Furthermore, it is hardly sensible to call "collective" that want which is precisely the *least* likely to be unanimous, since robbers will hardly desire it! [144] Other economists write as if defense is necessarily collective because it is an immaterial service, whereas bread, autos, etc., are materially divisible and salable to individuals. But "immaterial" services to individuals abound in the market. Must concert-giving be monopolized by the State because its services are immaterial?

In recent years, Professor Samuelson has offered his own definition of "collective consumption goods," in a so-called "pure" theory of government expenditures. Collective consumption goods, according to Samuelson, are those "which all enjoy in common in the sense that each individual's consumption of such a good leads to no subtraction from any other individual's consumption of that good." For some reason, these are supposed to be the proper goods (or *at least* these) for government, rather than the free market, to provide.[145] Samuelson's category has been attacked with due severity. Professor Enke, for example, pointed out that most governmental services simply do not fit Samuelson's classification—including highways, libraries, judicial services, police, fire, hospitals, and military protection. In fact, we may go further and state that *no* goods would ever fit into Samuelson's category of "collective consumption goods." Margolis, for example, while critical of Samuelson, concedes the inclusion of national defense and lighthouses in this category. But "national defense" is surely not an absolute good with only one unit of supply. It consists of specific resources committed in certain definite and concrete ways—and these resources are necessarily scarce. A ring of defense bases around New York, for example, cuts down the amount possibly available around San Francisco. Furthermore, a lighthouse shines over a certain fixed area only. Not only does a ship within the area prevent others from entering the area at the same time, but also the construction of a lighthouse in one place limits its construction elsewhere. In fact, if a good is really technologically "collective" in Samuelson's sense, it is *not a good at all,* but a natural condition of human welfare, like air—superabundant to all, and therefore *unowned* by anyone. Indeed, it is not the *lighthouse,* but the *ocean itself*—when the lanes are not crowded—which is the "collective consumption good," and which *therefore* remains unowned. Obviously, neither government nor anyone else is normally needed to produce or allocate the ocean.[146]

Tiebout, conceding that there is no "pure" way to establish an optimum level for government expenditures, tries to salavage such a theory specifically for *local* government. Realizing that the taxing, and even voting, process precludes voluntary demonstration of consumer choice in the governmental field, he argues that decentralization and freedom of internal migration renders *local* government expenditures more or less optimal—as we can say that free market expenditures by firms are "optimal"—since the residents can move in and out as they please. Certainly, it is true that the consumer will be better off if he can move readily out of a high-tax, and into a low-tax, community. But this helps the consumer only to a degree; it does not solve the problem of government expenditures, which remains otherwise the same. There are, indeed, other factors than government entering into a man's choice of residence, and enough people may be attached to a certain geographical area, for one reason or another, to permit a great deal of government depredation before they move. Furthermore, a major problem is that the world's total land area is fixed, and that governments have universally pre-empted all the land and thus universally burden consumers.[147]

We come now to the problem of external benefits—the major justification for government activities expounded by economists.[148] Where individuals simply benefit themselves by their actions, many writers concede that the free market may be safely left unhampered. But men's actions may often, even inadvertently, benefit others. While one might think this a cause for rejoicing, critics charge that from this fact flow evils in abundance. A free exchange, where A and B mutually benefit, may be all very well, say these economists; but what if A does something voluntarily which benefits B as well as himself, but for which B pays nothing in exchange?

There are two general lines of attack on the free market, using external benefits as the point of criticism. Taken together, these arguments against the market and for governmental intervention or enterprise cancel each other out, but each must, in all fairness, be examined separately. The first type of criticism is to *attack A for not doing enough for B*. The benefactor is, in effect, denounced for taking his own selfish interests exclusively into account, and thereby neglecting the potential indirect recipient waiting silently in the wings.[149] The second line of attack is to *denounce B for accepting a benefit without paying A in return*. The recipient is denounced as an ingrate and a virtual thief for accepting the free gift. The free market, then, is accused of injustice and distortion by both groups of attackers: the first believes that the selfishness of man is such that A will not act enough in ways to benefit B; the second that B will receive too much "unearned increment" without paying for it. Either way, the call is for remedial State action; on the one hand, to use violence in order to force or induce A to act more in ways which will aid B; on the other, to force B to pay A for his gift.

Generally, these ethical views are clothed in the "scientific" opinion that, in these cases, free-market action is no longer optimal, but should be brought back into optimality by corrective State action. Such a view completely misconceives the way in which economic science asserts that free-market action is *ever* optimal. It is optimal, not from the standpoint of the personal ethical views of an economist, but from the standpoint of the free, voluntary actions of all participants and in satisfying the freely expressed needs of the consumers. Government interference, therefore, will necessarily and always move *away* from such an optimum.

It is amusing that while each line of attack is quite widespread, each can be rather successfully rebutted by using the essence of the *other* attack! Take, for example, the first—*the attack on the benefactor.* To denounce the benefactor and implicitly call for State punishment for insufficient good deeds is to advance a moral claim by the recipient upon the benefactor. We do not intend to argue ultimate values in this book. But it should be clearly understood that to adopt this position is to say that B is entitled peremptorily to call on A to do something to benefit him, and for which B does not pay anything in return. We do not have to go all the way with the second line of attack (on the "free rider"), but we can say perhaps that it is presumptuous of the free rider to assert his right to a post of majesty and command. For what the first line of attack asserts is the moral right of B to exact gifts from A, by force if necessary.

Compulsory thrift, or attacks on potential savers for not saving and investing enough, are examples of this line of attack. Another is an attack on the user of a natural resource that is being depleted. Anyone who uses such a resource at all, whatever the extent, "deprives" some future descendant of the use. "Conservationists," therefore, call for lower present use of such resources in favor of greater future use. Not only is this compulsory benefaction an example of the first line of attack, but, if this argument is adopted, logically no resource subject to depletion could *ever* be used at all. For when the future generation comes of age, *it too* faces a future generation. This entire line of argument is therefore a peculiarly absurd one.

The second line of attack is of the opposite form—a denunciation of the recipient of the "gift." The recipient is denounced as a "free rider," as a man who wickedly enjoys the "unearned increment" of the productive actions of others. This, too, is a curious line of attack. It is an argument which has cogency only when directed against the first line of attack, i.e., against the free rider *who wants compulsory free rides*. But here we have a situation where A's actions, taken purely because they benefit himself, *also* have the happy effect of benefiting someone else. Are we to be indignant because happiness is being diffused throughout society? Are we to be critical because more than one person benefits from someone's actions? After all, the free rider did not ask for his ride. He received it, unasked, as a boon because A benefits from his own action. To adopt the second line of attack is to call in the gendarmes to apply punishment because too many people in the society are happy. In short, am I to be taxed for enjoying the view of my neighbor's well-kept garden? [150]

One striking instance of this second line of attack is the nub of the Henry Georgist position: an attack on the "unearned increment" derived from a rise in the capital values of ground land. We have seen above that as the economy progresses, real land rents will rise with real wage rates, and the result will be increases in the real capital values of land. Growing capital structure, division of labor, and population tend to make site land relatively more scarce and hence cause the increase. The argument of the Georgists is that the landowner is not morally responsible for this rise, which comes about from events external to his landholding; yet he reaps the benefit. The landowner is therefore a free rider, and his "unearned increment" rightfully belongs to "society." Setting aside the problem of the reality of society and whether "it" can own anything, we have here a moral attack on a free-rider situation.

The difficulty with this argument is that it proves far too much. For which one of us would earn anything like our present real income were it not for external benefits that we derive from the actions of others? Specifically, the great modern accumulation of capital goods is an inheritance from all the net savings of our ancestors. Without them, we would, regardless of the quality of our own moral character, be living in a primitive jungle. The inheritance of money capital from our ancestors is, of course, simply inheritance of shares in this capital structure. We are all, therefore, free riders on the past. We are also free riders on the present, because we benefit from the continuing investment of our fellow men and from their specialized skills on the market. Certainly the vast bulk of our wages, if they could be so imputed, would be due to this heritage on which we are free riders.

The landowner has no more of an unearned increment than any one of us. Are all of us to suffer confiscation, therefore, and to be taxed for our happiness? And *who* then is to receive the loot? Our dead ancestors, who were our benefactors in investing the capital? [151]

An important case of external benefits is "external economies," which could be reaped by investment in certain industries, but which would not accrue as profit to the entrepreneurs. There is no need to dwell on the lengthy discussion in the literature on the actual range of such external economies, although they are apparently negligible. The suggestion has been persistently advanced that the government subsidize these investments so that "society" can reap the external economies. Such is the Pigou argument for subsidizing external economies, as well as the old and still dominant "infant industries" argument for a protective tariff.

The call for state subsidization of external economy investments amounts to a *third line* of attack on the free market, i.e., *that B, the potential beneficiaries, be forced to subsidize the benefactors A, so that the latter will produce the former's benefits.* This third line is the favorite argument of economists for such proposals as government-aided dams or reclamations (recipients taxed to pay for their benefits) or compulsory schooling (the taxpayers will eventually benefit from others' education), etc. The recipients are again bearing the onus of the policy; but here they are not criticized for free riding. They are now being "saved" from a situation in which they would not have obtained certain benefits. Since they would not have paid for them, it is difficult to understand exactly *what* they are being saved from. The third line of attack therefore agrees with the first that the free market does not, because of human selfishness, produce enough external-economy actions; but it joins the second line of attack in placing the cost of remedying the situation on the strangely unwilling recipients. If this subsidy takes place, it is obvious that the recipients are no longer free riders: indeed, they are simply being coerced into buying benefits for which, acting by free choice, they would not have paid.

The absurdity of the third approach may be revealed by pondering the question: Who benefits from the suggested policy? The benefactor A receives a subsidy, it is true. But it is often doubtful if he benefits, since he would otherwise have acted and invested profitably in some other direction. The State has simply compensated him for losses which he would have received and has adjusted the proceeds so that he receives the equivalent of an opportunity forgone. Therefore A, if a business firm, does not benefit. As for the recipients, they are being forced by the State to pay for benefits that they otherwise would not have purchased. How can we say that they "benefit"?

A standard reply is that the recipients "could not" have obtained the benefit even if they had wanted to buy it voluntarily. The first problem here is by what mysterious process the critics know that the recipients would have liked to purchase the "benefit." Our only way of knowing the content of preference scales is to see them revealed in concrete choices. Since the choice concretely was *not* to buy the benefit, there is no justification for outsiders to assert that B's preference scale was "really" different from what was revealed in his actions.

Secondly, there is no reason why the prospective recipients *could* not have bought the benefit. In all cases a benefit produced can be sold on the market and earn its value product to consumers. The fact that producing the benefit would not be profitable to the investor signifies that the consumers do not value it as much as they value the uses of nonspecific factors in alternative lines of production. For costs to be higher than prospective selling price means that the nonspecific factors earn more in *other* channels of production. Furthermore, in possible cases where some consumers are not satisfied with the extent of the market production of some benefit, they are at perfect liberty to subsidize the investors *themselves.* Such a voluntary subsidy would be equivalent to paying a higher market price for the benefit and would reveal their willingness to pay that price. The fact that, in any case, such a subsidy has not emerged eliminates any justification for a coerced subsidy by the government. Rather than providing a benefit to the taxed "beneficiaries," in fact, the coerced subsidy inflicts a loss upon them, for they could have spent their funds themselves on goods and services of greater utility.[152]

Notes

NOTES TO CHAPTER 8

1. "One thing I miss . . . in discussion generally in the field, is any use of words recognizing that profit means profit *or loss* and is in fact as likely to be a loss as a gain." Frank H. Knight, "An Appraisal of Economic Change: Discussion," *American Economic Review, Papers and Proceedings,* May, 1954, p. 63. Professor Knight's great contributions to profit theory are in sharp contrast to his errors in capital and interest theory. See his famous work, *Risk, Uncertainty, and Profit* (3rd ed.; London: London School of Economics, 1940). Perhaps the best presentation of profit theory is in Ludwig von Mises, "Profit and Loss," in *Planning for Freedom* (South Holland, Ill.: Libertarian Press, 1952), pp. 108–51.
2. We may make such value judgments, of course, only to the extent that we believe it is "good" to correct maladjustments and to serve the consumers, and "bad" to create such maladjustments. These value judgments, therefore, are not at all praxeological truths, though most people would probably subscribe to them. Those who *prefer* maladjustments in serving consumers will adopt the opposite value judgments.
3. On all this, *see* Mises, "Profit and Loss," in *Planning for Freedom.* On the role of the fallacy of capital's automatically yielding profit in public utility regulation, *see* Arthur S. Dewing, *The Financial Policy of Corporations* (5th ed.; New York: Ronald Press, 1953), I, 308–53.
4. Mises, *Planning for Freedom,* p. 114.
5. Hayek, *Prices and Production,* pp. 48–49.
6. *See* Hayek, "The 'Paradox' of Saving" in *Profits, Interest, and Investment,* pp. 199–263.
7. This production structure diagram differs from our usual ones; it presents both the capital structure and the payment to owners of original factors as amalgamated in the same bar, to represent total investment at each stage. The steps in the diagram, then, represent the interest spreads to the capitalists (in rough, not exact, fashion).
8. Hayek, *Prices and Production,* pp. 75–76.
9. Of course, the productivity of a labor factor will differ from one task to another. No one disputes this; indeed, if this were not so, the factor would be *purely nonspecific,* and we have seen that this is an impossibility. "Specific" is here used to mean pure specificity for one production process.
10. See below for discussion of this point.
11. Historically, the advancing capitalist economy has coincided with an expanding money supply, so that we have rarely had an empirical illustration of the above "pure" process described in the text. We must remember that we have throughout been making the implicit assumption that

the "money relation"—the demand for, and particularly the supply of, money—remains unchanged. Effects of changes in this relation will be considered in chapter 11. The only relaxation of this assumption here is that the number of stages increases, and this tends to increase the demand for money to that extent.

12. The demand for money increases to the extent that each gold unit must "turn over" more times in the increased number of stages, thus tending to lower the "general level" of prices.
13. For a view of capitalized gains similar to the one presented here, *see* Roy F. Harrod, *Economic Essays* (New York: Harcourt, Brace & Co., 1952), pp. 198–205.
14. This is not the same as assuming an ERE, for in the ERE there are *no changes* to be foreseen.
15. The rise in general money prices. in monetary terms, is accounted for by the decreased demand for money as a result of the lower number of stages for the monetary unit to "turn over" in.
16. The definitions of the progressing and the retrogressing economy differ from those of Mises in *Human Action*. They are defined here as an increase or a decrease in capital in society, while Mises defines them as an increase or a decrease in total capital *per person* in the society. The present definitions focus on the analysis of saving and investment, population growth or decline being a very different phase of the subject. When we are making an historical "welfare" assessment of the conditions of the economy, however, the question of production *per capita* becomes important.
17. It is possible that the changes in investment were anticipated in the market. To the extent that an increase or a decrease was anticipated, the aggregate profits or losses will accrue in the form of a gain in capital value before the actual change in investment takes place. Losses arise during retrogression because previously employed processes have to be abandoned. The fact that the highest stages, already begun, have to be abandoned is an indication that the shift was not fully anticipated by the producers.
18. It is this assumption, coupled with a completely unjustifiable dichotomizing of "consumers' goods industries" and "capital goods industries" (whereas, in fact. there are *stages* of capital goods leading to consumers' goods, and not an arbitrary dichotomy) that is at the bottom of Nurkse's criticism of the structure of production analysis. *See* Ragnar Nurkse, "The Schematic Representation of the Structure of Production," *Review of Economic Studies*, II (1935).
19. The popular assumption now, in fact, is that a hidden hand somehow guarantees that capital will automatically increase continually, so that factor productivity will increase by "2–3% per year."
20. An illustration from modern times: "Austria was successful in pushing through policies which are popular all over the world. Austria has most impressive records in five lines: she increased public expenditures. she increased wages, she increased social benefits, she increased bank credits, she increased consumption. After all those achievements she was on the

verge of ruin." Fritz Machlup, "The Consumption of Capital in Austria," *Review of Economic Statistics* (1935), p. 19.

21. It is often assumed that only depreciation funds for durable capital goods are available for capital consumption. But this overlooks a very large part of capital—so-called "circulation capital," the less durable capital goods which pass quickly from one stage to another. As each stage receives funds from its sale of these or other goods, it is not necessary for the producer to continue to repurchase circulation capital. These funds too may be immediately spent on consumption. *See* Hayek, *Pure Theory of Capital,* pp. 47 ff., for a contrast between the correct and the fashionable approaches toward capital.
22. Frank H. Knight, "Professor Hayek and the Theory of Investment," *Economic Journal,* March, 1935, p. 85 n. *Also see* Knight, *Risk, Uncertainty, and Profit,* pp. xxxvii–xxxix.
23. Very few writers have realized this. *See* Hayek, "The 'Paradox' of Saving," in *Profits, Interest, and Investment,* pp. 214 ff., 253 ff.
24. Böhm-Bawerk, *Positive Theory of Capital,* p. 82.
25. Mises, *Human Action,* pp. 478–79.
26. *See* Hayek, *Pure Theory of Capital,* pp. 60 ff. Similarly, there are numerous long processes which are not productive at all or which are less productive than shorter processes. *These* longer processes will obviously not be chosen at all. In sum, while all new investment will be in longer processes, it certainly does not follow that all longer processes are more productive and therefore worthy of investment. For Böhm-Bawerk's strictures on this point, *see* Eugen von Böhm-Bawerk, *Further Essays on Capital and Interest,* in *Capital and Interest* (South Holland, Ill.: Libertarian Press, 1959), III, 2.
27. It should be clear that, as Mises lucidly put it, "originary [pure] interest is not a price determined on the market by the interplay of the demand for and the supply of capital or capital goods. Its height does not depend on the extent of this demand and supply. It is rather the rate of originary interest that determines both the demand for and the supply of capital and capital goods. It determines how much of the available supply of goods is to be devoted to consumption in the immediate future and how much to provision for remoter periods of the future." Mises, *Human Action,* pp. 523–24.
28. Eugen von Böhm-Bawerk, "The Positive Theory of Capital and Its Critics, Part III," *Quarterly Journal of Economics,* January, 1896, pp. 121–35. Also see *id., Further Essays, etc.,* pp. 31 ff.
29. Böhm-Bawerk, "The Positive Theory of Capital and Its Critics, Part III," *op. cit.,* pp. 128 ff.
30. Mises, *Human Action, op. cit.,* pp. 492 ff.
31. The futility of "Point 4" and "technical assistance" in furthering production in the backward countries should be evident from this discussion. As Böhm-Bawerk commented, in discussing advanced techniques: "There are always thousands of persons who know of the existence of the machines, who would be glad to secure the advantage of their use, but who

do not dispose of the capital necessary for their purchase." Böhm-Bawerk, "The Positive Theory of Capital and Its Critics, Part III," *op. cit.*, p. 127. Also see *id., Further Essays, etc.*, pp. 4–10.

32. "It is frequently supposed that all the increases in the quantity of capital per head . . . must mean that some commodities will now be produced by longer processes than before. But so long as the processes used in different industries are of different lengths, this is by no means a necessary consequence. . . . If input is transferred from industries using shorter processes to industries using longer processes, there will be no change in the length of the period of production in any industry, nor any change in the methods of production of any particular commodity, but merely an increase in the periods for which particular units of input are invested. The significance of these changes in the investment periods of particular units of input will, however, be exactly the same as it would be if they were the consequence of a change in the length of particular processes of production." Hayek, *Pure Theory of Capital*, pp. 77–78. Also see *id., Prices and Production*, p. 77, and Böhm-Bawerk, *Further Essays, etc.*, pp. 57–71.
33. *And* if there had been fewer land grants and other governmental subsidies to railroads! Thus, *see* E. Renshaw, "Utility Regulation: A Reexamination," *Journal of Business*, October, 1958, pp. 339–40.
34. "The fact that not every technological improvement is instantly applied in the whole field is not more conspicuous than the fact that not everyone throws away his old car or his old clothes as soon as a better car is on the market or new patterns become fashionable." Mises, *Human Action*, pp. 504 and 502–10. Specifically, the old equipment will continue in use as long as its operating costs are lower than the total costs of installing the new equipment. If, in addition, total costs (including replacement costs for wear and tear on capital goods) are greater for the old equipment, then the firm will gradually abandon old equipment as it wears out and will invest in the new technique. For an extensive discussion, *see* Hayek, *Pure Theory of Capital*, pp. 310–20.
35. "Technocrats" condemn the market for rewarding investments according to their (marginal) *value-productivity* instead of their (marginal) *physical productivity*. But we see here an excellent example of a technique more physically productive but less value-productive, and for a very good reason: that the given specific capital goods already produced lend an advantage to the old technique, so that "out-of-pocket" operating costs of the old technique are lower, until the equipment wears out, than total costs for the new project. Consumers are benefited by continuing the old techniques while they remain profitable, for then factors are spared for more valuable production elsewhere.
36. As will be seen below, actuarial risks can be "insured" against, but not the entrepreneurial uncertainty of the market.
37. It is evident that Mises' strictures in *Human Action*, p. 530, apply to the doctrine that the quantity of capital determines the pure rate of interest, and not to the present argument.

38. The loan market will diverge from the "natural" market to the extent that conditions for repayment of loans, etc., establish such differences. The two would be the same if the loans were clearly recognized as entrepreneurial, so that in cases where there was no deliberate fraud, the borrower would not be considered criminal if he did not repay the loan. However, if, as discussed in chapter 2 above, there are no bankruptcy laws and defaulting borrowers are considered criminal, then obviously the "safety" of all loans would increase in relation to "natural" investments, and the interest rates on loans would decline accordingly. In the free society, however, there would be nothing to prevent borrowers and lenders from agreeing, at the time the contract is made, that borrowers would *not* be held criminally responsible and that the loan would really be an entrepreneurial one. Or they could make any sort of arrangement in dividing gains or losses that they might choose.
39. Knight, *Risk, Uncertainty, and Profit,* pp. 212–55, especially p. 233.
40. Mises, *Human Action,* pp. 106–16, which also contains a discussion of the fallacies of the "calculus of probability" as applied to human action.
41. *See* Richard von Mises, *Probability, Statistics, and Truth* (2nd ed.; New York: Macmillan, 1957).
42. Ludwig von Mises, *Human Action,* p. 107.
43. *Ibid.,* p. 110.
44. There is a distinction between gambling and betting. Gambling refers to wagering on events of class probability, such as throws of dice, where there is no knowledge of the unique event. Betting refers to wagering on unique events about which both parties to the bet know something—such as a horse race or a Presidential election. In either case, however, the wagerer is creating a new risk or uncertainty.

NOTES TO CHAPTER 9

1. *Net* rents equal *gross* rents earned minus gross rents paid to owners of factors.
2. Its capital value will be positive, however, if people *expect* the land to earn rents in the near future.
3. "The last unit of product of any finite amount would . . . have to pay its corresponding rent. The only product obtained, in the strict theory of the case, without paying rent, would be one unit infinitesimally small—in plain Anglo-Saxon, would be nothing at all. No finite unit of product can be shown to be a no-rent unit." Frank A. Fetter, "The Passing of the Old Rent Concept," *Quarterly Journal of Economics,* May, 1901, p. 439.
4. The terms "marginal," "supramarginal," etc., are rather differently used here from the way they are used above. Instead of dealing with the supply and demand for a homogeneous good or factor, we are here referring to one *class* of factors, such as lands, and comparing different *qualities* of the various factors in that class. The near-zero-earning land is "marginal" because it is the one just barely put to use.

5. Here we shift the definition of progressing economy to mean increasing capital *per person,* so that we can contrast the effects of changes in the supply of one type of factor to changes in the supply of another.
6. There is, of course, no reason to assume that maximum real income per head is necessarily the best ethical ideal; for some, the ideal might be maximum real income plus maximum population. In a free society, parents are free to choose their own ethical principles in the matter.
7. Economics can say little else about population and its size. The inclusion of a corpus of "population theory" under economics instead of biology or psychology is the unfortunate result of the historical accident that the early economists were the first to delve into demographic problems.
8. The Lausanne way (of Walras and Pareto) of phrasing this distinction would be to say that, in the former case (when we are moving along the curve), we implicitly assumed that "(the supply of) tastes, techniques, and resources remains given in the economy." In the present case, we are considering a change in a resource (e.g., an increase in the supply of labor). We would amend this to say that only *tastes* and resources were considered given. As we saw in the previous section, techniques are not immediate determinants of production changes. The techniques must be put to use via saving and investment. In fact, we may deal with tastes and resources *alone,* provided that we include time preferences among the "tastes."
9. When an owner performs, and earns a return for, an essentially labor activity which he could *also* perform as an employee (e.g., the owner-manager), that return is an implicit wage. On definitions of "labor," *see* Spencer Heath, *Citadel, Market, and Altar* (Baltimore: Science of Society Foundation, 1957), pp. 235–36.
10. When we use the term "quality" here and in other parts of catallactic analysis, we are not employing it in some metaphysical sense or from some "higher" ethical point of view. We mean quality *as expressed by choice of the market,* in the form of a higher MVP and therefore a higher wage.
11. For an example of an interesting work on bargaining with unions based squarely on the false labor-management dichotomy, *see* Lee H. Hill and Charles R. Hook, Jr., *Management at the Bargaining Table* (New York: McGraw-Hill, 1945). On foremen's unions, *see* Theodore R. Iserman, *Industrial Peace and the Wagner Act* (New York: McGraw-Hill, 1947), pp. 49–58.
12. This "rule" by consumers' valuations holds in so far as entrepreneurs and owners of factors aim at maximum money income. To the extent that they abstain from higher money income to pursue *nonmonetary ends* (e.g., looking at one's untilled land or enjoying leisure), the producers' own valuations will be determining. From the general praxeological point of view, these producers are to that extent acting as *consumers.* Therefore, the full rule of consumers' value scales would hold even here. However, for purposes of catallactic market analysis, it may be

convenient to separate man as a producer from man as a consumer, even though, considered in his entirety, the same man performs both functions. In that event, we may say that to the extent that nonmonetary goals enter, not consumers' values are determining, but the values of *all individuals* in society. For further discussion of this question and of "consumer sovereignty," see chapter 10 below.

13. In the free society, as we have indicated above, the site could not originally become the property of anyone until it had been "used" in some way, such as being cleared, cultivated, etc. There need be no subsequent use, however, until rents can be obtained.
14. There will be such a backward supply curve if the marginal utility of money falls rapidly enough and the marginal disutility of leisure forgone rises rapidly enough as units of labor are sold for higher prices in money.
15. It will be noted that we have avoided using the very fashionable term "model" to apply to the analyses in this book. The term "model" is an example of an unfortunate bias in favor of the methodology of physics and engineering, as applied to the sciences of human action. The constructs are imaginary because their various elements never coexist in reality; yet they are necessary in order to draw out, by deductive reasoning and *ceteris paribus* assumptions, the tendencies and causal relations of the real world. The "model" of engineering, on the other hand, is a mechanical construction in miniature, *all parts of which* can and must coexist in reality. The engineering model portrays in itself all the elements and the relations among them that will coexist in reality. For this distinction between an imaginary construct and a model, the writer is indebted to Professor Ludwig von Mises.
16. For some philosophical discussions of human variation, *see* Harper, *Liberty,* pp. 61–83, 135–41; Roger J. Williams, *Free and Unequal* (Austin, Tex.: University of Texas Press, 1953): George Harris, *Inequality and Progress* (Boston: Houghton Mifflin, 1898); Herbert Spencer, *Social Statics* (New York: D. Appleton & Co., 1890), pp. 474-82; A. H. Hobbs, *The Claims of Sociology* (Harrisburg, Pa.: The Stackpole Co., 1951), pp. 23–64; Hobbs, *Social Problems and Scientism* (Harrisburg, Pa.: The Stackpole Co., 1953), pp. 254–304.
17. Cf. Van Sickle and Rogge, *op. cit.,* pp. 178–81.
18. For a treatment of wage rates and geography, see the section below on "The Economics of Location and Spatial Relations."
19. It should be understood throughout that when we refer to increases in wage rates or ground rents in the expanding economy, we are referring to real, and not necessarily to money, wage rates or ground rents.
20. This assumes, of course, that there is no offsetting *decline* in capital elsewhere. If there is, then there will be no *general* rise in wages.
21. For a discussion of these problems, *see* Mises, *Human Action,* pp. 598–600.
22. Capital goods will remain unemployed because of previous entrepreneurial error, i.e., investing in the wrong type of capital goods.

23. *See* Mises, *Human Action,* pp. 595–98. As Mises concludes, "Unemployment in the unhampered market is always voluntary." Particularly recommended is Mises' critique of the theory of "frictional unemployment."
24. Economics does not "assume mobility of labor." It simply analyzes the consequences of a laborer's decision to be "mobile" or "immobile," the latter amounting to a voluntary choice of at least temporary unemployment.
25. The "idleness" referred to here is catallactic, and not necessarily total. In other words, it means that a man does not seek to sell his labor services for money and therefore does not enter the societal labor market. He might well be very "busy" working at hobbies, etc.
26. Hayek, *Prices and Production,* pp. 91–93.
27. Cf. Fred R. Fairchild and Thomas J. Shelly, *Understanding Our Free Economy* (New York: D. Van Nostrand, 1952), pp. 478–81.
28. Hence, when the economist considers only the single firm (as in recent years), he goes completely astray by ignoring the generality of economic interrelations. To analyze means-ends relations logically, as economics does, requires taking all relations into account. Failure to do so, either by treating the single firm only or by treating unreal holistic aggregates or by taking refuge in the irrelevant mathematics of the Lausanne "general equilibrium" school, is equivalent to abandoning economics.
29. Many beginning students come away with the impression that economics consists of an indigestible brew of "cost curves" to be memorized by rote and drawn neatly on the blackboard.
30. E. T. Weiler, *The Economic System* (New York: Macmillan, 1952). pp. 141–61; Stigler, *op. cit.,* pp. 126 ff.
31. Stigler, *op. cit.,* p. 126.
32. Robbins points out that the length of a period of productive activity depends upon the expectations of entrepreneurs concerning the permanence of a change and the technical obstacles to a change. Robbins, "Remarks, etc.," *op cit.,* pp. 17–18.
33. For a critique of cost-curve theory, see the articles by Robbins, Thirlby, and Gabor and Pearce cited above, especially Gabor and Pearce, "A New Approach, etc.," *loc. cit. Also see* Milton Friedman, "Survey of the Empirical Evidence on Economies of Scale: Comment" in *Business Concentration and Price Policy* (Princeton: National Bureau of Economic Research, 1955), pp. 230–38; Armen Alchian, "Costs and Outputs" in *The Allocation of Economic Resources* (Stanford: Stanford University Press, 1959), pp. 23–40; F. A. Hayek, "Unions, Inflation, and Prices" in Philip D. Bradley, ed., *The Public Stake in Union Power* (Charlottesville, Va.: University of Virginia Press, 1959), pp. 55 f.; Hayek, *Pure Theory of Capital,* pp. 14, 20–21; Harrod, "Theory of Imperfect Competition Revised" in *Economic Essays,* pp. 139–87; G. Warren Nutter, "Competition: Direct and Devious," *American Economic Review, Papers and Proceedings,* May, 1954, pp. 69 ff.; Scott, *op. cit.,* p. 5.
34. This law follows from the natural law that every quantitatively observable cause-effect relation can be duplicated. For example, if $x + 2y + 3z$

are necessary and sufficient to form $1p$, *another* set will form another p, so that $2x + 4y + 6z$ will yield $2p$.

35. See chapter 10 for more on the theory of pure competition.
36. For example, suppose that 1,000 gold ounces invested in factors yield 100 units of product and that 1,100 ounces yield 101 units. All the points in the gap between 1,000 and 1,100 will yield no more than 100 units. The excess of investment over 1,000 and under 1,100 ounces is clearly sheer waste, and no businessman will invest within the gap. Instead, investments will be made at such trough points for average cost as 1,000 and 1,100.
37. Stigler, *Theory of Price,* pp. 132 ff.
38. We are not discussing the fact that the railroad could, of course, cut down or increase the mileage of its track by including less or more geographic area in its service. The example assumes a given geographic area in which the railroad operates.
39. *See* Mises, *Human Action,* pp. 338–40. This is the unrealistic condition implicitly assumed by textbook "cost curves."
40. *Ibid.,* p. 340.
41. Stigler, *Theory of Price,* p. 136.
42. It is particularly important not to limit possible efficiencies from large-scale production to narrow technological factors such as the "size of the plant." There are also efficiencies derived from the *organization of a firm* owning several plants—e.g., management utilization, specialization, efficiency of large-scale purchasing and selling. research expenditures, etc. Cf. George G. Hagedorn, *Studies on Concentration* (New York: National Association of Manufacturers, 1951), pp. 14 ff.
43. *See* Friedman, *loc. cit.*
44. For a good, largely empirical, study of size of firm, *see* George G. Hagedorn, *Business Size and the Public Interest* (New York: National Association of Manufacturers, 1949). Also see *id., Studies on Concentration,* and John G. McLean and Robert W. Haigh, "How Business Corporations Grow," *Harvard Business Review,* Nov.–Dec., 1954, pp. 81–93.
45. Plans are relevant, not only in the ERE, but also to all decisions on maintenance or replacement, as well as additions to capital goods when they wear out or fall into disrepair.
46. It is costless only if no rise in the price of the good is foreseen for the near future. If it is, then there will arise the opportunity cost of forgoing a higher price. Hence, if there is no hope of a higher price, the businessman will sell, however low the price (adjusting for the costs of selling minus the costs of continued storage).
47. Conventional "cost-curve" analysis depicts average cost and demand curves as tangential in the ERE—i.e., that price = average cost. *But* (aside from the unreality of assuming smooth curves rather than discontinuous angles), interest return—as well as return to the owner's decision-making ability—will accrue to the entrepreneurs even in the ERE. Hence, no such tangency can arise. See chapter 10 below for the implications of this revision for "monopolistic competition" theory.

48. For further readings on cost, *see* G. F. Thirlby, "The Marginal Cost Controversy: A Note on Mr. Coase's Model," *Economica,* February, 1947, pp. 48–53; F. A. Fetter's classic "The Passing of the Old Rent Concept," *loc. cit.;* R. H. Coase, "Business Organization and the Accountant," *The Accountant,* October 1–November 26, 1938; and *id.,* "Full Costs, Cost Changes, and Prices" in *Business Concentration and Price Policy,* pp. 392–94; John E. Hodges, "Some Economic Implications of Cost-Plus Pricing," *Southwestern Social Science Quarterly,* December, 1954, pp. 225–34; I. F. Pearce, "A Study in Price Policy," *Economica,* May, 1956, pp. 114–27; I. F. Pearce and Lloyd R. Amey, "Price Policy with a Branded Product," *Review of Economic Studies,* Vol. XXIV (1956–57), No. 1, pp. 49–60; James S. Earley, "Recent Developments in Cost Accounting and the 'Marginal Analysis,'" *Journal of Political Economy,* June, 1955, pp. 227–42; and David Green, Jr., "A Moral to the Direct-Costing Controversy?" *Journal of Business,* July, 1960, pp. 218–26.
49. This implicit wage will equal the DMVP of the owner's managerial services, which will tend to equal the "opportunity wage forgone" that he could be earning as a manager elsewhere.
50. In one of those extremely fertile but neglected hints of his, Böhm-Bawerk wrote: "But even where he [the businessman] does not personally take part in the carrying out of the production, he yet contributes a certain amount of personal trouble in the shape of intellectual superintendence—say, in planning the business, or, at the least, in the act of will by which he devotes his means of production to a definite undertaking." Böhm-Bawerk, *Capital and Interest,* p. 8.
51. For an interesting contribution to the theory of business income, though not coinciding with the one presented here, *see* Harrod, "Theory of Profit" in *Economic Essays,* pp. 190–95. *Also see* Friedman, *loc. cit.*
52. Since the scope of their business property and decisions is relatively negligible compared to their labor services, we may neglect their decision rents here.
53. It is a managerial wage, even though the only employee may be the owner himself. It may seem strange to classify a domestic servant as "self-employed," but actually he is no different from a doctor or a lawyer to the extent that the latter sell their services to *consumers* rather than to capitalists.
54. Another reason why an economy of producers' co-operatives could not calculate is that every original factor would be tied indissolubly to a specific line of production. There can be no calculation where all factors are purely specific.
55. Vertical integration, we might note, tends to reduce the demand for money (to "turn over" at various stages) and thereby to lower the purchasing power of the monetary unit. For the effect of vertical integration on the analysis of investment and the production structure, *see* Hayek, *Prices and Production,* pp. 62–68.
56. The implicit price, or opportunity cost of selling to oneself, might be less than the existing market price, since the entry of the Jones Com-

pany on the market might have lowered the price of the good, say to 102 ounces. There would be no way at all, however, to estimate the implicit price if there were no external market and external price.

57. On the size of a firm, see the challenging article by R. H. Coase, "The Nature of the Firm" in George J. Stigler and Kenneth E. Boulding, eds., *Readings in Price Theory* (Chicago: R. D. Irwin, 1952), pp. 331–51. In an illuminating passage Coase pointed out that State "planning is imposed on industry, while firms arise voluntarily because they represent a more efficient method of organizing production. In a competitive system there is an 'optimum' amount of planning." *Ibid.*, p. 335 n.
58. Capital goods are stressed here because they are the product for which the calculability problem becomes important. Consumers' goods *per se* are no problem, since there are always many consumers buying goods, and therefore consumers' goods will always have a market.
59. See the classic presentation of the position in Ludwig von Mises, "Economic Calculation in the Socialist Commonwealth," reprinted in F. A. Hayek, ed., *Collectivist Economic Planning* (London: George Routledge & Sons, 1935), pp. 87–130. *Also see* in the Hayek volume the other essays by Hayek, Pierson, and Halm. Mises continued his argument in *Socialism* (2nd ed.; New Haven: Yale University Press, 1951), pp. 135–63, and refutes more recent criticisms in his *Human Action,* pp. 694–711. Aside from these works, the best book on the subject of economic calculation under socialism is Trygve J. B. Hoff, *Economic Calculation in the Socialist Society* (London: William Hodge, 1949). *Also see* F. A. Hayek, "Socialist Calculation III, the Competitive 'Solution'" in *Individualism and the Economic Order,* pp. 181–208, and Henry Hazlitt's remarkable essay in fictional form, *The Great Idea* (New York: Appleton-Century-Crofts, 1951).
60. It is remarkable that so many antisocialist writers have never become aware of this critical point.
61. Far from being refuted, Mises had already disposed of this argument in his original article. See *Collectivist Economic Planning,* p. 109. Further, Barone's article was written in 1908, twelve years before Mises'. A careful perusal of Mises' original article, in fact, reveals that he there disposed of almost all the alleged "solutions" which decades later were brought forth as "new" attempts to refute his argument.
62. Part of the confusion stems from an unfortunate position taken by two followers of Mises in this debate—Hayek and Robbins. They argued that a socialist government could not calculate because it simply could not compute the millions of equations that would be necessary. This left them open to the obvious retort that now, with high-speed computers available to the government, this practical objection is no longer relevant. In reality, the job of rational calculation has nothing to do with computing equations. Nobody has to worry about "equations" in real life except mathematical economists. Cf. Lionel Robbins, *The Great Depression* (New York: Macmillan, 1934), p. 151, and Hayek in *Collectivist Economic Planning,* pp. 212 f.

63. *See* Gottfried von Haberler, *The Theory of International Trade* (London: William Hodge, 1936), pp. 3–8.
64. "The fact that the production of raw materials and foodstuffs cannot be centralized and forces people to disperse over the various parts of the earth's surface enjoins also upon the processing industries a certain degree of decentralization. It makes it necessary to consider the problems of transportation as a particular factor of production costs. The costs of transportation must be weighed against the economies to be expected from more thoroughgoing specialization." Mises, *Human Action,* pp. 341–42.
65. *See* Mises, *Human Action,* pp. 622–24.
66. For the weighty implications of this "Misesian" analysis for the theory of "international trade," cf. not only Mises' *Theory of Money and Credit,* but also the excellent, though neglected, Chi-Yuen Wu, *An Outline of International Price Theories* (London: George Routledge & Sons, 1939), pp. 115, 233–35, and *passim.*
67. This error lies at the root of attacks on the "basing-point system" of pricing in some industries. The critics assume that *uniform pricing* of a good means uniform pricing *at the various mills,* whereas it really implies uniform "delivered prices" of the various firms at any given *consumer center.* On the basing-point question, see also the analysis in *United States Steel Corporation T. N. E. C. Papers* (New York: United States Steel Corporation, 1940), II, 102–35.
68. For purposes of simplification, we have omitted the consumers in Rochester, Detroit, and elsewhere, but the same law applies to them. For consumers in Rochester and Detroit, in equilibrium:

$$P(C_r) \text{ in Rochester} = P(C_d) \text{ in Rochester, and}$$
$$P(C_r) \text{ in Detroit} = P(C_d) \text{ in Detroit, etc.}$$

69. For a critique of some aspects of this separation in the "new welfare economics," *see* B. R. Rairikar, "Welfare Economics and Welfare Criteria," *Indian Journal of Economics,* July, 1953, pp. 1–15.
70. The last few years have seen signs of a revival of "Austrian" production theory—the tradition in which these chapters have been written. In addition to works cited above, *see* Ludwig M. Lachmann, *Capital and Its Structure* (London: London School of Economics, 1956) and *id.,* "Mrs. Robinson on the Accumulation of Capital," *South African Journal of Economics,* June, 1958, pp. 87–100. Robert Dorfman's "Waiting and the Period of Production," *Quarterly Journal of Economics,* August, 1959, pp. 351–72, and his "A Graphical Exposition of Böhm-Bawerk's Interest Theory," *Review of Economic Studies,* February, 1959, pp. 153–58, are interesting chiefly as a groping attempt by a leading mathematical economist to return to the Austrian road. For an incisive critique of Dorfman, *see* Egon Neuberger, "Waiting and the Period of Production: Comment," *Quarterly Journal of Economics,* February, 1960, pp. 150–53.

NOTES TO CHAPTER 10

1. This applies not only to specific types of goods, but also to the allocation between present and future goods, in accordance with the time preferences of the consumers.
2. Of course, we may formally salvage the concept of "consumers' sovereignty" by asserting that all these psychic elements and evaluations constitute "consumption" and that the concept therefore still has validity. However, it would seem to be more appropriate in the *catallactic context of the market* (which is the area here under discussion) to reserve "consumption" to mean the enjoyment of *exchangeable goods.* Naturally, in the final sense, everyone is an ultimate consumer—both of exchangeable and of nonexchangeable goods. However, the market deals only in exchangeable goods (by definition), and when we separate the consumer and the producer in terms of the market, we distinguish the demanding, as compared to the supplying, of exchangeable goods. It is more appropriate, then, not to consider a nonexchangeable good as an object of consumption in this particular context. This is important in order to discuss the contention that individual producers are somehow subject to the sovereign rule of *other* individuals—the "consumers."
3. W. H. Hutt, "The Concept of Consumers' Sovereignty," *Economic Journal,* March, 1940, pp. 66–77. Hutt originated the term in an article in 1934. For an interesting use of a similar concept, cf. Charles Coquelin, "Political Economy" in *Lalor's Cyclopedia,* III, 222–23.
4. To be consistent, currently fashionable theory would have to accuse Crusoe and Friday of being vicious "bilateral monopolists," busily charging each other "monopoly prices" and therefore ripe for State intervention!
5. See chapter 8, p. 469 above.
6. In the words of Professor Mises: "That the production of a commodity *p* is not larger than it really is, is due to the fact that the complementary factors of production required for an expansion were employed for the production of other commodities. . . . Neither did the producers of *p* intentionally restrict the production of *p*. Every entrepreneur's capital is limited; he employs it for those projects which, he expects, will, by filling the most urgent demand of the public, yield the highest profit.

   "An entrepreneur at whose disposal are 100 units of capital employs, for instance, 50 units for the production of *p* and 50 units for the production of *q*. If both lines are profitable, it is odd to blame him for not having employed more, e.g., 75 units, for the production of *p*. He could increase the production of *p* only by curtailing correspondingly the production of *q*. But with regard to *q* the same fault could be found by the grumblers. If one blames the entrepreneur for not having produced more *p,* one must blame him also for not having produced more *q*. This means: one blames the entrepreneur for the fact that there is a scarcity of the factors of production and that the earth is not a land of Cockaigne." Mises, *Planning for Freedom,* pp. 115–16.

7. *Ibid.,* p. 115.
8. Much error would have been avoided if economists had heeded the words of Arthur Latham Perry: "Every man who puts forth an effort to satisfy the desire of another, with the expectation of a return, is . . . a Producer. The Latin word *producere* means *to expose anything to sale.* . . . We must rid ourselves at the outset of the notion . . . that it is only to be applied to forms of *matter,* that it means . . . to *transform* something only. . . . The fundamental meaning of the root-word, both in Latin and in English, is *effort with reference to a sale.* A product is a service ready to be rendered. A producer is any person who gets something ready to sell and sells it. . . ." Perry, *op. cit.,* pp. 165–66.
9. R. H. Coase, in an illuminating article, has pointed out that the extent to which transactions take place *within* a firm or *between* firms is dependent on the balancing of the necessary costs of using the price mechanism as against the costs of organizing a structure of production within a firm. Coase, "The Nature of the Firm," *loc. cit.*
10. This spurious distinction was brought into wide currency by Thorstein Veblen and continued in the happily short-lived "technocracy" movement of the early 1930's. According to his biographer, this distinction was the keynote of all Veblen's writings. Cf. Joseph Dorfman, *The Economic Mind in American Civilization* (New York: Viking Press, 1949), III, 438 ff.
11. On the "orthodox" neglect of cost limitations, *see* Robbins, "Remarks, etc.," *loc. cit.*
12. Cf. Mises, *Human Action,* p. 367.
13. As Professor Benham states: "Firms which have produced a relatively large share of output in the past will demand the same share in the future. Firms which are expanding—owing, for example, to an unusually efficient management—will demand a larger share than they obtained in the past. Firms with a greater 'capacity' for producing, as measured by the size of their . . . plant will demand a correspondingly greater share." Benham, *op. cit.,* p. 232. On the difficulties faced by cartels, *see also* Bjarke Fog, "How Are Cartel Prices Determined?" *Journal of Industrial Economics,* November, 1956, pp. 16–23; Donald Dewey, *Monopoly in Economics and Law* (Chicago: Rand McNally, 1959), pp. 14–24; and Wieser, *Social Economics,* p. 225.
14. For illustrations of this instability in the history of cartels, *see* Fairchild, Furniss, and Buck, *Elementary Economics,* II, 54–55; Charles Norman Fay, *Too Much Government, Too Much Taxation* (New York: Doubleday, Page, 1923) p. 41, and *Big Business and Government* (New York: Doubleday, Page, 1912); A. D. H. Kaplan, *Big Enterprise in a Competitive System* (Washington: Brookings Institute, 1954), pp. 11–12.
15. These terms will be explained below.

16. Clearly, the very term "equal" is unusable here. What does it mean to say that lawyer Jones' ability is "equal" to teacher Smith's?
17. From his Address to the Civic Federation Conference on Trusts, held in Chicago, September 13–16, 1899, *Chicago Conference on Trusts* (Chicago, 1900), pp. 253–54, reprinted in Benjamin R. Tucker, *Individual Liberty* (New York: Vanguard Press, 1926), pp. 248–57. Said a lawyer at the conference: "The control of prices can be brought about permanently only by such a superiority in the methods of manufacture as will successfully defy competition. Any price established by a combination which enables competitors to make a reasonable profit will soon encourage such competition as will reduce the price." Azel F. Hatch, *Chicago Conference,* p. 70. See also the excellent article by A. Leo Weil, *ibid.,* pp. 77–96; and W. P. Potter, *ibid.,* pp. 299–305; F. B. Thurber, *ibid.,* pp. 124–36; Horatio W. Seymour, *ibid.,* pp. 188–93; J. Sterling Morton, *ibid.,* pp. 225–230.
18. Does our discussion imply, as Dorfman has charged (J. Dorfman, *op. cit.,* III, 247), that "whatever is, is right"? We cannot enter into a discussion of the relation of economics to ethics at this point, but we can state briefly that our answer, pertaining to the free market, is a qualified Yes. Specifically, our statement would be: *Given the ends* on the value scales of individuals, as revealed by their real actions, the maximum satisfaction of those ends for every person is achieved only on the free market. Whether individuals have the "proper" ends or not is another question entirely and cannot be decided by economics.
19. If all the factors and resources are absolutely *controlled* by the State, it makes little difference if, legally, the State *owns* these resources. For ownership connotes control, and if the nominal owner is coercively deprived of control, it is the controller who is the real owner of the resource.
20. The only author, to our knowledge, that looks forward to One (voluntary) Big Cartel as a potential ideal is Heath, *op. cit.,* pp. 184–87.
21. Cf. Mises, *Human Action,* p. 592.
22. The same confusion exists in the laws concerning monopoly. Despite constitutional warnings against vagueness, the Sherman Anti-Trust Act outlaws "monopolizing" actions without once defining the concept. To this day there has been no clear legislative decision concerning what constitutes illegal monopolistic action.
23. We are, of course, not considering here particular uncertainties of agriculture resulting from climate, etc.
24. For further discussion, *see* Murray N. Rothbard, "The Bogey of Administered Prices," *The Freeman,* September, 1959, pp. 39–41.
25. On the contrary, the consumers control Macy's to the extent that the store desires monetary income. Cf. John W. Scoville and Noel Sargent, eds., *Fact and Fancy in the T. N. E. C. Monographs* (New York: National Association of Manufacturers, 1942), p. 312.
26. One reason often given for ascribing "control over price" to Ford and not the small wheat grower is that Ford is so large that his actions affect the market price of his product, while the farmer is so small that

his actions do not affect the price. On this, see the critique below of "monopolistic competition" theories.

27. Economists have often charged, for example, that consumers who will pay a higher price for the same good at a store with a more pleasant atmosphere are acting "irrationally." Actually, they are by no means doing so, since consumers are buying not just a physical can of beans, but a can of beans sold in a certain store by certain clerks, and these factors may (or may not) make a difference to them. Businessmen are far less motivated by such "nonphysical" considerations (although good will affects their purchases too), *not* because they are "more rational" than consumers, but because they are not concerned, as consumers are, with their *own* value scales in deciding their purchases. As we have seen above, businessmen are generally motivated purely by the expected revenue that goods will bring on the market. For an excellent treatment of the definition of "homogeneous product," *see* G. Warren Nutter, "The Plateau Demand Curve and Utility Theory," *Journal of Political Economy,* December, 1955, pp. 526–28. *Also see* Alex Hunter, "Product Differentiation and Welfare Economics," *Quarterly Journal of Economics,* November, 1955, pp. 533–52.

28. Professor Lawrence Abbott, in one of the outstanding theoretical works of recent years, demonstrates also that as civilization and the economy advance, products will become more and more differentiated and less and less homogeneous. For one thing, greater differentiation occurs at the consumer than at the producer level, and the expanding economy takes over an increasing proportion of goods once made by the consumer himself and therefore supplies more finished goods than raw materials to the consumer than formerly (bread rather than flour, sweaters rather than wool yarn, etc.). Thus, there is greater opportunity for differentiation.

Furthermore, to the familiar charge that business advertising tends to create differentiation in the consumer's mind that is not "really" there, Abbott replies incisively that the *reverse* is more likely to be true and that advancing civilization increases the consumer's perception and discrimination of differences of which he was previously ignorant. Writes Abbott: ". . . as man becomes more civilized, he develops greater powers of perception with regard to quality differences. Subjective homogeneity may exist even when objective homogeneity does not, due to the inability or unwillingness of buyers to perceive differences between almost identical products and discriminate between them. . . . As a society matures and education improves, people learn to develop more acute powers of discrimination. Their wants become more detailed. They begin . . . to develop a preference, say, not simply for white wine, but for 1948 Chablis. . . . People generally tend to underestimate the significance of apparently trivial differences in fields in which they are not expert. An unmusical person may be unwilling to concede that there is any difference in tone between a Steinway and a Chickering piano, being unable himself to detect it. A nongolfer is more likely than a habitual player to believe that all brands of golf balls are virtually alike." Lawrence Abbott, *Quality and Competition* (New York: Columbia University Press, 1955), pp. 18–19, and chap. I. Also see *ibid.*, pp. 45–46 and Edward H. Chamberlin, "Product Heterogeneity and Public Policy" in *Towards a More General Theory of Value* (New York: Oxford University Press, 1957), p. 96.

29. Oddly, despite the reams of literature on monopolies, very few economists have bothered to *define* monopoly, and these problems have therefore been overlooked. Mrs. Robinson, in the beginning of her famous *Economics of Imperfect Competition,* saw the difficulty and then evaded the issue throughout the rest of the book. She concedes that under careful analysis either a monopoly would be defined as every producer's control over his own product or monopoly could simply not exist on the free market at all. For competition exists among all products for the consumer's dollar, while very few articles are rigorously homogeneous. Mrs. Robinson then tries to evade the issue by falling back on "common sense" and defining monopoly as existing where there is a "marked gap" between the product and other substitutes the consumer may buy. But this will not do. Economics, in the first place, can establish no quantitative laws, so that there is nothing we can say about sizes of gaps. When does the gap become "marked"? Secondly, even if such "laws" were meaningful, there would be no way to measure the cross-elasticities of demands, the elasticity of substitution between the products, etc. These elasticities of substitution are changing all the time and could not be measured successfully even if they all remained constant, since supply conditions are always changing. No laboratory exists where all economic factors may be held fixed. After this point in her discussion, Mrs. Robinson practically forgets all about heterogeneity of product. Joan Robinson, *Economics of Imperfect Competition* (London: Macmillan, 1933), pp. 4–6. Also cf. Hunter, *op. cit.*, pp. 547 ff.
30. Quoted in Richard T. Ely and others, *Outlines of Economics* (3rd ed.; New York: Macmillan, 1917), pp. 190–91. Blackstone gave almost the same definition and called monopoly a "license or privilege allowed by the king." *Also see* A. Leo Weil, *Chicago Conference,* p. 86.
31. The onrush of monopoly grants by Queen Elizabeth I and Charles I provoked resistance from even the Crown's subservient judges, and, in 1624, Parliament declared that "all monopolies are altogether contrary to the laws of this realm and are and shall be void." This antimonopoly spirit was deeply ingrained in America, and the original Maryland constitution declared that monopolies were "odious" and "contrary to . . . principles of commerce." Ely, *op. cit.,* pp. 191–92. *Also see* Francis A. Walker, *Political Economy* (New York: Henry Holt & Co., 1911), pp. 483–84.
32. Francis Wayland, *The Elements of Political Economy* (Boston: Gould & Lincoln, 1854), p. 116. Cf. this later definition by Arthur Latham Perry: "A monopoly, as the derivation of the word implies, is a restriction imposed by a government upon the sale of certain services." Perry, *op. cit.*, p. 190. In recent years this definition has all but died out. A rare current example is: "Monopoly exists when government by

its coercive power limits to a particular person or organization, or combination of them, the right to sell particular goods or services . . . It is an infringement of the right to make a living." Heath, *op. cit.*, p. 237.

33. As Weil stated: "Monopolies cannot be created by association or agreement. We now have no letters patent giving exclusive right. . . . It is therefore wholly unjustifiable to use the term monopoly as applied to the effects of industrial consolidation." Weil, *Chicago Conference*, pp. 86 f.
34. For example, Edward H. Chamberlin, *Theory of Monopolistic Competition* (7th ed.; Cambridge: Harvard University Press, 1956), pp. 57 ff., 270 ff.
35. It might be objected that these concepts are vague and give rise to problems. Problems do arise, but they are not insuperable. Thus, if one man is named Joseph Williams, does this preclude anyone else from having the same name, and is any future Joseph Williams to be considered a criminal? The answer is clearly: No, so long as there is no attempt by one to impersonate the other. In short, it is not so much the name *per se* which an individual owns, but the name as an affiliate of his person.
36. For clear expositions of the theory of monopoly price, *see* Mises, *Socialism,* pp. 385–92, and *Human Action,* pp. 278, 354–84; Menger, *op. cit.,* pp. 207–25; Fetter, *Economic Principles,* pp. 73–85, 381–85; Harry Gunnison Brown, "Competitive and Monopolistic Price-Making," *Quarterly Journal of Economics,* XXII (1908), 626–39; and Wieser, *Social Economics,* pp. 204, 211–12. In this particular case, "neoclassical" includes "Austrian."
37. Mises, *Human Action,* p. 278.
38. Thus: "The mere existence of monopoly does not mean anything. The publisher of a copyright book is a monopolist. But he may not be able to sell a single copy, no matter how low the price he asks. Not every price at which a monopolist sells a monopolized commodity is a monopoly price. Monopoly prices are only prices at which it is more advantageous for the monopolist to restrict the total amount to be sold than to expand sales to the limit which a competitive market would allow." *Ibid.,* p. 356.
39. Here we abstract from monetary expense or "money cost" considerations. When the producer is considering sale of *already produced* stock, such past monetary expenses are completely irrelevant. When he is considering present and future production for future sale, present money-cost considerations become important, and the producer strives for maximum *net* returns. At any rate, some A′ point will be set, whatever the actual configuration of money costs, unless, indeed, average money costs are falling rapidly enough in this region to make the "competitive point" the most remunerative after all. It is curious that it is precisely the condition of falling average cost that has given the most worry to antimonopoly writers, who have been concerned that one given firm in any industry might grow to "monopoly" size because of

this condition. And yet, if it is "monopoly price," not monopoly, that is particularly important, such worry is clearly unfounded. On the general unimportance of cost considerations in monopoly theory, *see* Chamberlin, *Theory of Monopolistic Competition,* pp. 193–94.

40. We are devoting space to analysis of monopoly-price theory and its consequences because the theory, though invalid on the *free* market, will prove very useful in analyzing the consequences of monopoly grants by government.

41. As Mises warns: "It would be a serious blunder to deduce from the antithesis between monopoly price and competitive price that the monopoly price is the outgrowth of the absence of competition. There is always catallactic competition on the market. Catallactic competition is no less a factor in the determination of monopoly prices than it is in the determination of competitive prices. The shape of the demand curve that makes the appearance of monopoly prices possible and directs the monopolists' conduct is determined by the competition of all other commodities competing for the buyers' dollars. The higher the monopolist fixes the price at which he is ready to sell, the more potential buyers turn their dollars toward other vendible goods. On the market, every commodity competes with all other commodities." Mises, *Human Action,* p. 278.

42. We are not discussing here the generally conceded point that monopoly profits are capitalized in capital gains to the shares of the firm's stock.

43. To attain a monopoly price, the factor-owner must meet two conditions: (*a*) He must be a monopolist (in the sense of definition 1) over the factor; if he were not, the monopoly gain could be bid away by competitors entering the field; and (*b*) the demand curve for the factor must be inelastic above the competitive-price point.

44. This is the underlying assumption in Mrs. Joan Robinson's *Economics of Imperfect Competition.*

45. Bidding takes place among numerous firms in various industries, not only among firms in the same industry.

46. An amusing instance of this concern is this argument for compulsory legal cartelization by West German industrialists: "that the so-called unrestricted competition would produce a catastrophe in which the stronger industries would destroy the weaker and establish themselves as monopolies." Create an *inefficient* monopoly now to avoid an *efficient* monopoly later! M. S. Handler, "German Unionism Supports Cartels," *New York Times,* March 17, 1954, p. 12. For other such instances, *see* Charles F. Phillips, *Competition? Yes, but . . .* (Irvington-on-Hudson: Foundation for Economic Education, 1955).

47. What of the allegedly vast "financial power" of a big firm, rendering it impervious to cost? In a brilliant article, Professor Wayne Leeman has pointed out that a larger firm will also have larger volume and will therefore suffer greater losses when selling below cost. Having a larger volume, it has more to lose. What is relevant, therefore, is not the *absolute* size of the financial resources of the competing firms, but the size of their resources in relation to their volume of sales and expendi-

tures. And this changes the conventional picture drastically. Wayne A. Leeman, "The Limitations of Local Price-Cutting as a Barrier to Entry," *Journal of Political Economy,* August, 1956, pp. 331–32.

48. After investigating conditions in the retail gasoline industry (one particularly subject to allegedly "cutthroat" competition), an economist declared: "Some people think that leading marketers occasionally reduce prices to drive out competition so that they may later enjoy a monopoly. But, as one oil man has put it, 'That is like trying to sweep back the ocean to get a dry place to sit down. . . .' [Competitors] . . . never scare, and never hesitate for long, and would move in immediately when prices were restored, offering little opportunity to a single marketer to recoup his losses." Harold Fleming, *Oil Prices and Competition* (American Petroleum Institute, 1953), p. 54.
49. Leeman, *op. cit.,* pp. 330–31.
50. A leading oil executive told Leeman: "We have invested too much in plant and equipment in this area to want to invite in a host of competitors under an umbrella of high prices." *Ibid.,* p. 331.
51. Leeman points out, in a striking refutation of one of the myths of our age, that this is *precisely* what happened to John D. Rockefeller. "According to a widely accepted view, he softened up small competitors in the oil business by a period of intensive price competition, bought them out for a song, and then raised prices to consumers to make up his losses. Actually, the softening-up process did not work . . . for Rockefeller usually ended up paying . . . so handsomely that the sellers, often in violation of promises made, proceeded to build another plant for its nuisance value, hoping again to collect a reward from their benefactor. . . . Rockefeller after a time got tired of paying . . . 'blackmail' and . . . decided that the best way to hold the dominant position he wanted was to keep profit margins small all the time." *Ibid.,* p. 332. *Also see* Marian V. Sears, "The American Businessman at the Turn of the Century," *The Business History Review,* December, 1956, p. 391. Moreover, Professor McGee has shown, after an intensive investigation, that in not one instance did Standard Oil attempt "predatory price-cutting," thus destroying the Standard Oil myth once and for all. John S. McGee, "Predatory Price-Cutting: The Standard Oil (New Jersey) Case," *The Journal of Law and Economics,* October, 1958, pp. 137–69.
52. Leeman concludes, quite correctly, that large rather than small firms dominate many markets, *not* as a result of victorious cutthroat competition and monopolistic pricing, but by taking advantage of the low costs of much large-scale production and keeping prices low in fear of *potential* as well as actual rivals. Leeman, *op. cit.,* pp. 333–34.
53. We have found in the literature only one hint of the discovery of this illusion: Scoville and Sargent, *op. cit.,* p. 302. *See also* Bradford B. Smith, "Monopoly and Competition," *Ideas on Liberty,* No. 3 (November, 1955), pp. 66 ff.
54. In the case of depletable natural resources, *any* allocation of use necessarily involves the use of some of the resource in the present (even considering the resource as homogeneous) and the "withholding" of the

remainder for allocation to future use. But there is no way of conceptually distinguishing such withholding from "monopolistic" withholding and therefore of discussing a "monopoly price."

55. See the reference to Abbott, *op. cit.*, in note 28 above.
56. On "natural monopoly" doctrine as applied to the electrical industry, *see* Dean Russell, *The TVA Idea* (Irvington-on-Hudson: Foundation for Economic Education, 1949), pp. 79–85. For an excellent discussion of the regulation of public utilities, *see* Dewing, *op. cit.*, I, 308–68.
57. "Prices are a market phenomenon. . . . They are the resultant of a certain constellation of market data, of actions and reactions of the members of a market society. It is vain to meditate what prices would have been if some of their determinants had been different. . . . It is no less vain to ponder on what prices ought to be. Everybody is pleased if the prices of things he wants to buy drop and the prices of the things he wants to sell rise. . . . Any price determined on a market is the necessary outgrowth of the interplay of the forces operating, that is, demand and supply. Whatever the market situation which generated this price may be, with regard to it the price is always adequate, genuine, and real. It cannot be higher if no bidder ready to offer a higher price turns up, and it cannot be lower if no seller ready to deliver at a lower price turns up. Only the appearance of such people ready to buy or sell can alter prices. Economics . . . does not develop formulas which would enable anybody to compute a 'correct' price different from that established on the market by the interaction of buyers and sellers. . . . This refers also to monopoly prices. . . . *No alleged 'fact finding' and no armchair speculation can discover another price at which demand and supply would become equal.* The failure of all experiments to find a satisfactory solution for the limited-space monopoly of public utilities clearly proves this truth." (Italics added.) Mises, *Human Action,* pp. 392–94.
58. The first to point out the error in the common talk of "monopoly wage rates" of unions was Professor Mises. *See* his brilliant discussion in *Human Action,* pp. 373–74. *Also see* P. Ford, *The Economics of Collective Bargaining* (Oxford: Basil Blackwell, 1958), pp. 35–40. Ford also refutes the thesis advanced by the recent "Chicago School" that unions perform a service as sellers of labor: "But a union does not itself produce or sell the commodity, labour, nor receive payment for it. . . . It could be more fitly described as . . . fixing the wages and other conditions on which its individual members are permitted to sell their services to the individual employers." *Ibid.*, p. 36.
59. A restrictionist, rather than a monopoly, price can be achieved because the number of laborers is so important in relation to the possible variation in *hours* of work by an individual laborer that the latter can be ignored here. If, however, the total labor supply is limited originally to a few people, then an imposed higher wage rate will cut down the number of hours purchased from the workers who remain working, perhaps so much as to render a restrictionist price unprofitable to them.

In such a case it would be more appropriate to speak of a *monopoly* price.

60. Cf. Mises, *Human Action,* p. 764.
61. *See* Charles E. Lindblom, *Unions and Capitalism* (New Haven: Yale University Press, 1949), pp. 78 ff., 92–97, 108, 121, 131–32, 150–52, 155. *Also see* Henry C. Simons, "Some Reflections on Syndicalism" in *Economic Policy for a Free Society* (Chicago: University of Chicago Press, 1948), pp. 131 f., 139 ff.; Martin Bronfenbrenner, "The Incidence of Collective Bargaining," *American Economic Review, Papers and Proceedings,* May, 1954, pp. 301–02; Fritz Machlup, "Monopolistic Wage Determination as a Part of the General Problem of Monopoly" in *Wage Determination and the Economics of Liberalism* (Washington, D. C.: Chamber of Commerce of the United States, 1947), pp. 64–65.
62. *See* Murray N. Rothbard, "Mises' 'Human Action': Comment," *American Economic Review,* March, 1951, pp. 183–84.
63. The same is true, to an even greater extent, of measures of governmental intervention in the market. See chapter 12 below.
64. *See* James Birks, *Trade Unionism in Relation to Wages* (London, 1897), p. 30.
65. *See* James Birks, *Trades' Unionism: A Criticism and a Warning* (London, 1894), p. 22.
66. We can deal here only with the directly catallactic consequences of labor unionism. Unionism also has other consequences which many might consider even more deplorable. Prominent is the fusing of the able and the incompetent into one group. Seniority rules, for example, are invariable favorites of unions. They set restrictively high wages for less able workers and also lower the productivity of all. But they also *reduce* the wages of the more able workers—those who must be chained to the stultifying march of seniority for their jobs and promotions. Seniority also decreases the mobility of workers and creates a kind of industrial serfdom by establishing vested rights in jobs according to the length of time the employees have worked. Cf. David McCord Wright, "Regulating Unions" in Bradley, *op. cit.,* pp. 113–21.
67. Students of labor unions have almost universally ignored the systematic use of violence by unions. For a welcome exception, *see* Sylvester Petro, *Power Unlimited* (New York: Ronald Press, 1959). Also cf. F. A. Hayek, "Unions, Inflation, and Profits," *op. cit.,* p. 47.
68. On the nature and consequences of these various criteria of wage determination, *see* Ford, *op. cit.,* pp. 85–110.
69. See the excellent critique by Hutt, *The Theory of Collective Bargaining, passim.*
70. On the Ricardo effect, *see* Mises, *Human Action,* pp. 767–70. Also see the detailed critique by Ford, *op. cit.,* pp. 56–66, who also points to the union record of hindering mechanization by imposing restrictive work rules and by moving quickly to absorb any possible gain from the new equipment.
71. In particular, *see* Edward H. Chamberlin, *Theory of Monopolistic Competition,* and Mrs. Joan Robinson, *Economics of Imperfect Com-*

petition. For a lucid discussion and comparison of the two works, *see* Robert Triffin, *Monopolistic Competition and General Equilibrium Theory* (Cambridge: Harvard University Press, 1940). The differences between the "monopolistic" and the "imperfect" formulations are not important here.

72. Recently, Professor Chamberlin has conceded this point and has, in a series of remarkable articles, astounded his followers by repudiating the concept of pure competition as a welfare ideal. Chamberlin now declares: "The welfare ideal itself . . . is correctly described as one of monopolistic competition . . . [This] seems to follow very directly from the recognition that human beings are individual, diverse in their tastes and desires, and moreover, widely dispersed spatially." Chamberlin, *Towards a More General Theory of Value*, pp. 93–94; also *ibid.*, pp. 70–83; E. H. Chamberlin and J. M. Clark, "Discussion," *American Economic Review, Papers and Proceedings*, May, 1950, pp. 102–04; Hunter, *op. cit.*, pp. 533–52; Hayek, "The Meaning of Competition" in *Individualism and the Economic Order*, p. 99; and Marshall I. Goldman, "Product Differentiation and Advertising: Some Lessons from Soviet Experience," *Journal of Political Economy*, August, 1960, pp. 346–57. Also see note 28 above.

73. This definition of the demand curve to the firm was Mrs. Robinson's outstanding contribution, unfortunately repudiated by her recently. Triffin castigated Mrs. Robinson for evading the problem of "oligopolistic indeterminacy," whereas actually she had neatly solved this pseudo problem. *See* Robinson, *op. cit.*, p. 21. For other aspects of oligopoly, *see* Willard D. Arant, "Competition of the Few among the Many," *Quarterly Journal of Economics*, August, 1956, pp. 327–45.

74. For an acute criticism of monopolistic-competition theory, *see* L. M. Lachmann, "Some Notes on Economic Thought, 1933–53," *South African Journal of Economics*, March, 1954, pp. 26 ff., especially pp. 30–31. Lachmann points out that economists generally treat types of "perfect" or "monopolistic" competition as static market forms, whereas competition is actually a dynamic process.

75. And the product differentiation associated with the falling demand curve may well lower costs of distribution and of inspection (as well as improve consumer knowledge) to more than offset the supposed rise in production costs. In short, the *AC* curve above is *really* a production-cost, rather than a total-cost, curve, neglecting distribution costs. Cf. Goldman, *loc. cit.* Furthermore, a genuine total-cost curve would then not be independent of the firm's demand curve, thus vitiating the usual "cost-curve" analysis. *See* Dewey, *op. cit.*, p. 87. Also see section C below.

76. *See* Chamberlin, "Measuring the Degree of Monopoly and Competition" and "Monopolistic Competition Revisited" in *Towards a More General Theory of Value*, pp. 45–83.

77. *See* J. M. Clark, "Competition and the Objectives of Government Policy" in E. H. Chamberlin, ed., *Monopoly and Competition and Their Regulation* (London: Macmillan, 1954), pp. 317–27; Clark, "Toward a

Concept of Workable Competition" in *Readings in the Social Control of Industry* (Philadelphia: Blakiston, 1942), pp. 452–76; Clark, "Discussion," *loc. cit.;* Abbott, *op. cit., passim;* Joseph A. Schumpeter, *Capitalism, Socialism and Democracy* (New York: Harper & Bros., 1942); Hayek, "The Meaning of Competition," *loc. cit.*, and Lachmann, *loc. cit.*

78. See the above citations by Clark; and Richard B. Heflebower, "Toward a Theory of Industrial Markets and Prices" in R. B. Heflebower and G. W. Stocking, eds., *Readings on Industrial Organization and Public Policy* (Homewood, Ill.: R. D. Irwin, 1958), pp. 297–315. A more dubious argument—the flatness of the firm's demand curve in the relevant range—has been stressed by other economists, notably A. J. Nichol, "The Influence of Marginal Buyers on Monopolistic Competition," *Quarterly Journal of Economics,* November, 1934, pp. 121–34; Alfred Nicols, "The Rehabilitation of Pure Competition," *Quarterly Journal of Economics,* November, 1947, pp. 31–63; and Nutter, *loc. cit.*
79. But cf. Abbott, *op. cit.*, pp. 180–81.
80. The author first learned this particular piece of analysis from the classroom lectures of Professor Arthur F. Burns, and, to our knowledge, it has never seen print.
81. Roy Harrod, *Economic Essays* (New York: Harcourt, Brace, 1952), p. 149.
82. After arriving at this conclusion, the author came across a brilliant but neglected article pointing out that interest is a return and not a cost, and showing the devastating implications of this fact for cost-curve theory. The article does not, however, apply the theory satisfactorily to the problem of monopolistic competition. *See* Gabor and Pearce, "A New Approach to the Theory of the Firm," *loc. cit.*, and *id.*, "The Place of Money Capital, etc.," *loc. cit.* While there are a few similarities, Professor Dewey's critique of the "excess capacity" doctrine is essentially very different from ours and based on far more "orthodox" considerations. Dewey, *op. cit.*, pp. 96 ff.
83. Since the erroneous but popular theory of "countervailing power," propounded by J. K. Galbraith, falls with the monopolistic-competition theory, it is unnecessary to discuss it here. For a more detailed critique of its numerous fallacies, *see* Simon N. Whitney, "Errors in the Concept of Countervailing Power," *Journal of Business,* October, 1953, pp. 238–53; George J. Stigler, "The Economist Plays with Blocs," *American Economic Review, Papers and Proceedings,* May, 1954, pp. 8–14; and David McC. Wright, "Discussion," *ibid.*, pp. 26–30.
84. Chamberlin, *Theory of Monopolistic Competition,* pp. 123 ff. Chamberlin includes in selling costs advertising, sales expenses, and store displays.
85. *See* Mises, *Human Action,* p. 319. *Also see* Kermit Gordon, "Concepts of Competition and Monopoly—Discussion," *American Economic Review, Papers and Proceedings,* May, 1955, pp. 486–87.
86. It is surely highly artificial to call bright ribbons on a packaged good a "production cost," while labeling bright ribbons decorating the store selling the good as a "selling cost."

87. Cf. Alfred Nicols, "The Development of Monopolistic Competition and the Monopoly Problem," *Review of Economics and Statistics,* May, 1949, pp. 118–23.
88. "The consumer is, according to . . . legend, simply defenseless against 'high-pressure' advertising. If this were true, success or failure in business would depend on the mode of advertising only. However, nobody believes that any kind of advertising would have succeeded in making the candlemakers hold the field against the electric bulb, the horse-drivers against the motor cars. . . . But this implies that the quality of the commodity advertised is instrumental in bringing about the success of an advertising campaign. . . . The tricks and artifices of advertising are available to the seller of the better product no less than to the seller of the poorer product. But only the former enjoys the advantages derived from the better quality of his product." Mises, *Human Action,* pp. 317–18.
89. *See* Wicksteed, *op. cit.,* I, 253 ff.
90. It is difficult to conceive of a case, in reality, to which such a restriction imposed on buyers (called "perfect price-discrimination") would apply. Mrs. Robinson cites as an example a ransom charged by a kidnapper, but this, of course, does not obtain on the free, unhampered market, which precludes kidnapping. Robinson *op. cit.,* p. 187 n.
91. *See* Mises, *Human Action,* pp. 385 ff.
92. An example is medicine, where the government helps to restrict the supply and thus to prevent price-cutting. See the illuminating article by Reuben A. Kessel, "Price Discrimination in Medicine," *The Journal of Law and Economics,* October, 1958, pp. 20–53. Also see chapter 12 below on grants of monopoly privilege.
93. Henry George was a notable exception. See his excellent discussion in *Progress and Poverty* (New York: Modern Library, 1929), p. 411 n.
94. Richard Wincor, *How to Secure Copyright* (New York: Oceana Publishers, 1950), p. 37.
95. Irving Mandell, *How to Protect and Patent Your Invention* (New York: Oceana Publishers, 1951), p. 34.
96. This can be seen in the field of *designs,* which can be either copyrighted or patented.
97. For a legal hint on the proper distinction between copyright and monopoly, *see* F. E. Skone James, "Copyright" in *Encyclopædia Britannica* (14th ed.; London, 1929), VI, 415–16. For the views of nineteenth-century economists on patents, *see* Fritz Machlup and Edith T. Penrose, "The Patent Controversy in the Nineteenth Century," *Journal of Economic History,* May, 1950, pp. 1–29. *Also see* Fritz Machlup, *An Economic Review of the Patent System* (Washington, D. C.: United States Government Printing Office, 1958).
98. Of course, there would be nothing to prevent the creator or his heirs from voluntarily abandoning this property right and throwing it into the "public domain" if they so desired.
99. See the illuminating article by Machlup and Penrose, *op. cit.,* pp. 1–29,
100. Cited in Edith Penrose, *Economics of the International Patent System* (Baltimore: Johns Hopkins Press, 1951), p. 36; also see *ibid.,* pp. 19–41.

101. Arnold Plant, "The Economic Theory concerning Patents for Inventions," *Economica*, February, 1934, p. 44.

NOTES TO CHAPTER 11

1. Cf. Edwin Cannan, "The Application of the Theoretical Analysis of Supply and Demand to Units of Currency" in F. A. Lutz and L. W. Mints, eds., *Readings in Monetary Theory* (Philadelphia: Blakiston, 1951), pp. 3–12, and Cannan, *Money* (6th ed.; London: Staples Press, 1929), pp. 10–19, 65–78.
2. From this point on, this nonmonetary demand is included, for convenience, in the "total demand for money."
3. Cf. Irving Fisher, *The Purchasing Power of Money* (2nd ed.; New York: Macmillan, 1913).
4. A typical such classification can be found in Lester V. Chandler, *An Introduction to Monetary Theory* (New York: Harper & Bros., 1940).
5. *See* Mises, *Theory of Money and Credit,* p. 98. The entire volume is indispensable for the analysis of money. *Also see* Mises, *Human Action,* ch. xvii and ch. xx.
6. See chapter 12 below for a discussion of the concept of social benefit or social utility.
7. J. M. Keynes' *Treatise on Money* (New York: Harcourt, Brace, 1930) is a classic example of this type of analysis.
8. On the clearing system, *see* Mises, *Theory of Money and Credit,* pp. 281–86.
9. Since no one can receive a money *income* unless someone else makes a money *expenditure* on his services. (See chapter 3 above.)
10. Strictly, the *ceteris paribus* condition will tend to be violated. An increased demand for money tends to lower money prices and will therefore lower money costs of gold mining. This will stimulate gold mining production until the interest return on mining is again the same as in other industries. Thus, the increased demand for money will also call forth new money to meet the demand. A decreased demand for money will raise money costs of gold mining and at least lower the rate of new production. It will not actually decrease the total money stock unless the new production rate falls below the wear-and-tear rate. Cf. Jacques Rueff, "The Fallacies of Lord Keynes' General Theory" in Henry Hazlitt, ed., *The Critics of Keynesian Economics* (Princeton: D. Van Nostrand, 1960), pp. 238–63.
11. See the excellent article by W. H. Hutt, "The Significance of Price Flexibility" in Hazlitt, *The Critics, etc.,* pp. 383–406.
12. The term generally used is "national" income. However, in a free-market economy the nation will no more be an important economic boundary than the village or region. It is more convenient, then, to set aside regional problems for other analysis and to concentrate on aggregate social income; this is especially true since regions do not present a problem to economic theory until their governments begin intervening in the free market.

13. Thus, see the revealing article by Franco Modigliani, "Liquidity Preference and the Theory of Interest and Money" in Hazlitt, *The Critics, etc.*, pp. 156–69. Also see the articles by Erik Lindahl, "On Keynes' Economic System," *The Economic Record,* May, 1954, pp. 19–32; November, 1954, pp. 159–71; and Wassily W. Leontief, "Postulates: Keynes' *General Theory* and the Classicists" in S. Harris, ed., *The New Economics* (New York: Knopf, 1952), pp. 232–42. For an empirical critique of the assumed Keynesian correspondence between aggregate output and employment, *see* George W. Wilson, "The Relationship between Output and Employment," *Review of Economics and Statistics,* February, 1960, pp. 37–43.
14. This is what Keynes' discussion of "wage units" amounted to. Cf. Lindahl, "On Keynes' Economic System—Part I," *op. cit.,* p. 20.
15. Cf. Lindahl, *op. cit.,* pp. 25, 159 ff. Lindahl's articles provide a good summary as well as a critique of the Keynesian system.
16. Furthermore, inflation is, at best, an inefficient and distortive substitute for flexible wage rates. For inflation affects the entire economy and its prices, while particular wage rates will fall only to the extent necessary to "clear" the market for the particular labor factor. Thus, freely flexible wage rates will fall only in those fields necessary to eliminate unemployment in those particular areas. Cf. Henry Hazlitt, *The Failure of the "New Economics"* (Princeton: D. Van Nostrand, 1959), pp. 278 ff.
17. Cf. L. Albert Hahn, *The Economics of Illusion* (New York: Squier Publishing Co., 1949), pp. 50 ff., 166 ff., and *passim.*
18. Cf. Hutt, "The Significance of Price Flexibility," *loc. cit.*
19. Cf. Lindahl's critique of Lawrence Klein's *The Keynesian Revolution* in *op. cit.,* p. 162. *Also see* Leontief, *loc. cit.*
20. Modigliani, *op. cit.,* pp. 139–40.
21. *Ibid.,* p. 137.
22. See the critique of the Keynesian doctrine by Tjardus Greidanus, *The Value of Money* (2nd ed.; London: Staples Press, 1950), pp. 194–215, and of the liquidity-preference theory by D. H. Robertson, "Mr. Keynes and the Rate of Interest" in *Readings in the Theory of Income Distribution,* pp. 439–41. In contrast to Keynes' famous phrase that the rate of interest is "the reward for parting with liquidity," Greidanus points out that buying consumers' goods (or even producers' goods in Keynes' sense of "interest") sacrifices liquidity and yet earns no interest "reward." Greidanus, *op. cit.,* p. 211. *Also see* Hazlitt, *The Failure, etc.,* pp. 186 ff.
23. Mises, *Human Action,* pp. 529–30.
24. Hutt concludes that equilibrium "is secured when all services and products are so priced that they are (i) brought within the reach of people's pockets (i.e., so that they are purchasable by existing money incomes) or (ii) brought into such a relation to predicted prices that no postponement of expenditure on them is induced. For instance, the products and services used in the manufacture of investment goods must be so priced that anticipated future money incomes will be able to buy the services and depreciation of new equipment or replacements." Hutt, "The Significance of Price Flexibility," *op. cit.,* p. 394.

25. "Postponements (in purchases) arise because it is judged that a cut in costs (or other prices) is less than will eventually have to take place, or because the rate of fall of costs is insufficiently rapid." *Ibid.,* p. 395.
26. As Hutt points out, if we can conceive of a situation of infinitely elastic liquidity preference (and no such situation has ever existed), then "we can conceive of prices falling rapidly, keeping pace with expectations of price changes, but never reaching zero, with full utilization of resources persisting all the way." *Ibid.,* p. 398.
27. L. M. Lachmann, "Uncertainty and Liquidity Preference," *Economica,* August, 1937, p. 301.
28. Irving Fisher, *The Rate of Interest* (New York, 1907), ch. v, xiv; *id., The Purchasing Power of Money,* pp. 56–59.
29. For an exposition of the feasibility of private coinage, *see* Spencer, *op. cit.,* pp. 438–39; Charles A. Conant, *The Principles of Money and Banking* (New York: Harper & Bros., 1905), I, 127–32; Lysander Spooner, *A Letter to Grover Cleveland* (Boston: B. R. Tucker, 1886), p. 79; B. W. Barnard, "The Use of Private Tokens for Money in the United States," *The Quarterly Journal of Economics,* 1916–17, pp. 617–26.

    Recent writers favorable to private coinage include: Everett Ridley Taylor, *Progress Report on a New Bill of Rights* (Diablo, California: the author, 1954); Oscar B. Johannsen, "Advocates Unrestricted Private Control over Money and Banking," *The Commercial and Financial Chronicle,* June 12, 1958, pp. 2622 f.; Leonard E. Read, *Government—An Ideal Concept* (Irvington-on-Hudson: Foundation for Economic Education, 1954), pp. 82 ff. An economist hostile to market-controlled commodity money has recently conceded the feasibility of private coinage under a commodity standard. Milton Friedman, *A Program for Monetary Stability* (New York: Fordham University Press, 1960), p. 5.
30. Time deposits are, legally, future claims, since banks have a legal right to delay payment thirty days. Moreover, they do not pass as final media of exchange. The latter fact is not determining, however, since a secure claim to a money-substitute is itself part of the money supply. "Idle" cash balances are kept as "time deposits," just as gold bullion is a more "idle" form of money than coins. The deciding factor, perhaps, is that the thirty-day limit is virtually a dead letter, for if a "savings" bank should impose it, a bankrupting "run" on the bank would ensue. Furthermore, actual payments are sometimes made by "cashiers' checks" on time deposits. Thus, "time" deposits now function as *demand* deposits and should be treated as part of the money supply. If banks wished to act as genuine *savings* banks, borrowing and lending *credit,* they could issue IOU's for specified lengths of time, due at definite future dates. Then no confusion or possible "counterfeiting" could arise.
31. Such items as bills of lading, pawn tickets, and dock warrants have been warehouse receipts rooted in the specific objects deposited, in contrast to the loose "general deposits" where a homogeneous good can be returned. *See* W. Stanley Jevons, *Money and the Mechanism of Exchange* (16th ed.; London: Kegan Paul, Trench, Trübner & Co., 1907), pp. 201–11.

32. We might ask why the owners of the bank do not really reap the spoils and lend the money to themselves. The answer is that they once did so profusely, as the history of early American banking shows. Legal regulations forced the banks to abandon this practice.
33. This discussion is not meant to imply that bankers, particularly at the present time, are always knowingly engaged in fraudulent practices. So embedded, indeed, have these practices become, and always with the sanction of law as well as of sophisticated but fallacious economic doctrines, that it is undoubtedly a rare banker who regards his standard occupational procedure as fraudulent.
34. For a brilliant discussion of fractional-reserve banking, *see* Amasa Walker, *The Science of Wealth* (3rd ed.; Boston: Little, Brown & Co., 1867), pp. 138–68, 184–232.
35. Swiss banks have successfully and for a long time been issuing debentures to the public at varying maturities, and banks in Belgium and Holland have recently followed suit. On the purely free market, such practices would undoubtedly be greatly extended. Cf. Benjamin H. Beckhart, "To Finance Term Loans," *The New York Times,* May 31, 1960.
36. Jevons, *Money and the Mechanism of Exchange,* pp. 211–12.
37. "If pecuniary promises were always of a special character, there could be no possible harm in allowing perfect freedom in the issue of promissory notes. The issuer would merely constitute himself a warehouse keeper and would be bound to hold each special lot of coin ready to pay each corresponding note." *Ibid.,* p. 208.
38. *See* Mises, *Theory of Money and Credit,* pp. 131–45.
39. *See* Mises, *Human Action,* pp. 413–16.
40. For an appreciation of Mises' achievement in clarifying this problem, *see* Wu, *op. cit.,* pp. 127, 232–34.
41. As we shall see below, however, interlocal *clearing* can greatly narrow these limits.
42. To say that "exports pay for imports" is simply to say that income pays for expenditures.
43. For an excellent and original analysis of balances of payments along these lines, *see* Mises, *Human Action,* pp. 447–49.
44. Cf. Mises, *Human Action,* pp. 459–61.
45. Mises, *Theory of Money and Credit,* pp. 285–86.
46. For recent evidence that this action in the United States was a deliberate "crime against silver," and not sheer accident, *see* Paul M. O'Leary, "The Scene of the Crime of 1873 Revisited," *Journal of Political Economy,* August, 1960, pp. 388–92. One argument in favor of such action holds that the government thereby simplified accounts in the economy. However, the market could easily have done so itself by keeping all accounts in gold.
47. *See* Mises, *Theory of Money and Credit,* pp. 179 ff., and Jevons, *Money and the Mechanism of Exchange,* pp. 88–96. For advocacy of such parallel standards, *see* Isaiah W. Sylvester, *Bullion Certificates as Currency* (New York, 1882) and William Brough, *Open Mints and Free Banking* (New York: G. P. Putnam's Sons, 1894). Sylvester, who also advocated

100% specie-reserve currency, was an official of the United States Assay Office.

For historical accounts of the successful working of parallel standards, *see* Luigi Einaudi, "The Theory of Imaginary Money from Charlemagne to the French Revolution" in F. C. Lane and J. C. Riemersma, eds., *Enterprise and Secular Change* (Homewood, Ill.: R. D. Irwin, 1953), pp. 229–61; Robert Sabatino Lopez, "Back to Gold, 1252," *Economic History Review,* April, 1956, p. 224; and Arthur N. Young, "Saudi Arabian Currency and Finance," *The Middle East Journal,* Summer, 1953, pp. 361–80.

48. Fisher, *The Purchasing Power of Money,* especially pp. 13 ff.
49. *Ibid.,* p. 13.
50. *Ibid.,* p. 14.
51. We are using "dollars" and "cents" here instead of weights of gold for the sake of simplicity and because Fisher himself uses these expressions.
52. *Ibid.,* p. 16.
53. *Ibid.,* p. 17.
54. Greidanus justly calls this sort of equation "in all its absurdity the prototype of the equations set up by the equivalubrists," in the modern mode of the "economics of the bookkeeper, not of the economist. . . ." Greidanus, *op. cit.,* p. 196.
55. Fisher, *The Purchasing Power of Money,* p. 16.
56. For a brilliant critique of the disturbing effects of averaging even when a commensurable unit *does* exist, *see* Louis M. Spadaro, "Averages and Aggregates in Economics" in *On Freedom and Free Enterprise,* pp. 140–60.
57. *See* Clark Warburton, "Elementary Algebra and the Equation of Exchange," *American Economic Review,* June, 1953, pp. 358–61. *Also see* Mises, *Human Action,* p. 396; B. M. Anderson, Jr., *The Value of Money* (New York: Macmillan, 1926), pp. 154–64; and Greidanus, *op. cit.,* pp. 59–62.
58. Conventional accounting practice is based on a fixed value of the monetary unit.
59. Professor Mises has pointed out that the assertion of the mathematical economists that their task is made difficult by the existence of "many variables" in human action grossly understates the problem; for the point is that *all* the determinants are variables and that in contrast to the natural sciences *there are no constants.*
60. See the brilliant critique of index numbers by Mises, *Theory of Money and Credit,* pp. 187–94. *Also see* R. S. Padan, "Review of C. M. Walsh's *Measurement of General Exchange Value,*" *Journal of Political Economy,* September, 1901, p. 609.
61. Irving Fisher, *Stabilised Money* (London: George Allen & Unwin, 1935), p. 375.
62. The fact that the purchasing power of the monetary unit is not quantitatively definable does not negate the fact of its *existence,* which is established by prior praxeological knowledge. It thereby differs, for example, from the "competitive price–monopoly price" dichotomy, which cannot

be independently established by praxeological deduction for free-market conditions.

63. Cited in Wesley C. Mitchell, *Business Cycles, the Problem and Its Setting* (New York: National Bureau of Economic Research, 1927), pp. 76–77.
64. "The whole psychological theory of the business cycle appears to be hardly more than an inversion of the real causal sequence. Expectations more nearly derive from objective conditions than produce them. . . . It is not the wave of optimism that makes times good. Good times are almost bound to bring a wave of optimism with them. On the other hand, when the decline comes, it comes not because anyone loses confidence, but because the basic economic forces are changing." V. Lewis Bassie, "Recent Development in Short-Term Forecasting," *Studies in Income and Wealth,* XVII (Princeton: National Bureau of Economic Research, 1955), 10–12.
65. Joseph A. Schumpeter, *The Theory of Economic Development* (Cambridge: Harvard University Press, 1936) and *id., Business Cycles* (New York: McGraw-Hill, 1939).
66. Warren and Pearson, as well as Dewey and Dakin, conceive of the business cycle as made up of superimposed, independent, periodic cycles from *each field* of production activity. *See* George F. Warren and Frank A. Pearson, *Prices* (New York: John Wiley and Sons, 1933); E. R. Dewey and E. F. Dakin, *Cycles: The Science of Prediction* (New York: Holt, 1949).
67. On the tendency to neglect the consumer's role in innovation, cf. Ernst W. Swanson, "The Economic Stagnation Thesis, Once More," *The Southern Economic Journal,* January, 1956, pp. 287–304.
68. S. S. Kuznets, "Schumpeter's *Business Cycles,*" *American Economic Review,* June, 1940, pp. 262–63; Richard V. Clemence and Francis S. Doody, *The Schumpeterian System* (Cambridge: Addison-Wesley Press, 1950), pp. 52 ff.
69. In so far as innovation is a regularized business procedure of research and development, rents from innovations will accrue to the research and development workers in firms, rather than to entrepreneurial profits. Cf. Carolyn Shaw Solo, "Innovation in the Capitalist Process: A Critique of the Schumpeterian Theory," *Quarterly Journal of Economics,* August, 1951, pp. 417–28.
70. Some Keynesians account for investment by the "acceleration principle" (see below). The Hansen "stagnation" thesis—that investment is determined by population growth, the rate of technological improvement, etc.—seems happily to be a thing of the past.
71. *See* Lindahl, *op. cit.,* p. 169 n. Lindahl shows the difficulties of mixing an *ex post* income line with *ex ante* consumption and spending, as the Keynesians do. Lindahl also shows that the expenditure and income lines coincide if the divergence between expected and realized income affects income and not stocks. Yet it cannot affect stocks, for, contrary to Keynesian assertion, there is no such thing as hoarding or any other unexpected event leading to "unintended increase in inventories." An increase in inventories is never unintended, since the seller has the alter-

native of selling the good at the market price. The fact that his inventory increases means that he has voluntarily *invested* in larger inventory, hoping for a future price rise.

72. Summing up disillusionment with the consumption function are two significant articles: Murray E. Polakoff, "Some Critical Observations on the Major Keynesian Building Blocks," *Southern Economic Journal,* October, 1954, pp. 141–51, and Leo Fishman, "Consumer Expectations and the Consumption Function," *ibid.,* January, 1954, pp. 243–51.
73. Keynes, *General Theory, etc.,* pp. 89–112.
74. *Ibid.,* pp. 109–10.
75. What is "fairly" supposed to mean? How can a theoretical law be based on "fair" stability? More stable than other functions? What are the grounds for this assumption, particularly as a law of human action? *Ibid.,* pp. 89–96.
76. Actually, the form of the Keynesian function is generally "linear," e.g., Consumption = .80 (Income) + 20. The form given in the text simplifies the exposition without, however, changing its essence.
77. *Also see* Hazlitt, *The Failure, etc.,* pp. 135–55.
78. It is usually overlooked that this replacement pattern, necessary to the acceleration principle, could apply only to those firms or industries that had been growing in size rapidly and continuously.
79. See his brilliant critique of the acceleration principle in W. H. Hutt, *Co-ordination and the Price System* (unpublished, but available from the Foundation for Economic Education, Irvington-on-Hudson, 1955), pp. 73–117.
80. Neglect of prices and price relations is at the core of a great many economic fallacies.
81. *See* Mises, *Human Action,* pp. 581 f.; S. S. Kuznets, "Relations between Capital Goods and Finished Products in the Business Cycle" in *Economic Essays in Honor of Wesley Clair Mitchell* (New York: Columbia University Press, 1935), p. 228; and Hahn, *Commonsense Economics,* pp. 139–43.
82. See the excellent critique by Leland B. Yeager of the neostagnationist Keynesian versions of "growth economics" of Harrod and Domar, which make use of the acceleration principle. Yeager, *op. cit.,* pp. 53–63.

NOTES TO CHAPTER 12

1. Some economists, notably Edwin Cannan, have denied that economic analysis could be applied to acts of violent intervention. But, on the contrary, economics is the praxeological analysis of human actions, and violent interrelations are forms of action which can be analyzed.
2. Is it, then, surprising that the early economists, all religious men, marveled at their epochal discovery of the harmony pervading the free market and tended to ascribe this beneficence to a "hidden hand" or divine harmony? It is easier for us to scoff at their enthusiasm than to realize that it does not detract from the validity of their analysis.

   Conventional writers charge, for example, that the French "optimistic" school of the nineteenth century were engaging in a naive *Harmonielehre*—a mystical idea of a divinely ordained harmony. But this charge ignores the fact that the French optimists were building on the very sound "welfare-economic" insight that voluntary exchanges on the free market conduce harmoniously to the benefit of all. For example, *see* About, *op. cit.,* pp. 104–12.

3. The study of the direct consequences for utility of intervention or nonintervention is peculiarly the realm of "welfare economics." For a critique and outline of a reconstruction of welfare economics, *see* Rothbard, "Toward a Reconstruction of Utility and Welfare Economics," *loc. cit.*
4. Perhaps we may note here the German sociologist Franz Oppenheimer's distinction between the free market and binary intervention as the "economic" as against the "political" means to the satisfaction of one's wants: "There are two fundamentally opposed means whereby man, requiring sustenance, is impelled to obtain the necessary means for satisfying his desires. These are work and robbery, one's own labor and the forcible appropriation of the labor of others . . . I propose . . . to call one's own labor and the equivalent exchange of one's own labor for the labor of others, the 'economic means' for the satisfaction of needs, while the unrequited appropriation of the labor of others will be called the 'political means' . . . The state is an organization of the political means." Oppenheimer, *op. cit.,* pp. 24–27.
5. One of the roots of this fallacy is the idea that in an exchange the two things exchanged are or should be "equal" in value and that "inequality" of value demonstrates "exploitation." We have seen, on the contrary, that any exchange involves inequality of the values of each commodity between buyer and seller, and that it is this very double inequality of values that brings about the exchange. An example of stress on this fallacy is the well-known work by Yves Simon, *Philosophy of Democratic Government* (Chicago: University of Chicago Press, 1951), ch. iv.
6. It has become fashionable to assert that John C. Calhoun anticipated the Marxian doctrine of class exploitation, but actually, Calhoun's "classes" were *castes:* creatures of State intervention itself. In particular, Calhoun saw that the binary intervention of taxation must always be spent so that some people in the community become net payers of tax funds, and the others net recipients. Calhoun defined the latter as the "ruling class" and the former as the "ruled." Thus:

   "Few, comparatively, as they are, the agents and employees of the government constitute that portion of the community who are the exclusive recipients of the proceeds of the taxes. . . . But as the recipients constitute only a portion of the community, it follows . . . that the action [of the fiscal process] must be unequal between the payers of the taxes and the recipients of their proceeds. Nor can it be otherwise; unless what is collected from each individual in the shape of taxes shall be returned to him in that of disbursements, which would make the process nugatory and absurd. . . . It must necessarily follow that some one portion of the community must pay in taxes more than it receives in disbursements, while another receives in disbursements more than it pays in taxes. It is, then, manifest . . . that taxes must be, in effect, bounties to that portion of the community which receives more in disbursements than it pays in taxes, while to the other which pays in taxes more than it receives in disbursements they are taxes in reality—burdens instead of bounties. This consequence is unavoidable. It results from the nature of the process, be the taxes ever so equally laid . . .

"The necessary result, then, of the unequal fiscal action of the government is to divide the community into two great classes: one consisting of those who, in reality, pay the taxes and, of course, bear exclusively the burden of supporting the government; and the other, of those who are the recipients of their proceeds through disbursements, and who are, in fact, supported by the government; or, the effect of this is to place them in antagonistic relations in reference to the fiscal action of the government. . . . For the greater the taxes and disbursements, the greater the gain of the one and the loss of the other, and vice versa. . . ." John C. Calhoun, *A Disquisition on Government* (New York: Liberal Arts Press, 1953), pp. 16–18.

7. See Rothbard, "Toward a Reconstruction of Utility and Welfare Economics," *loc. cit.* For an analysis of State action, *see* Gustave de Molinari, *The Society of Tomorrow* (New York: G. P. Putnam's Sons, 1904), pp. 19 ff., 65–96.
8. We have seen above that praxeology may deal with utilities only as deduced from the concrete actions of human beings. Elsewhere we have named this concept "demonstrated preference," have traced its history, and criticized competing concepts. Rothbard, "Toward a Reconstruction of Utility and Welfare Economics," *op. cit.*, pp. 224 ff.
9. For a critique of the first assumption, *see* Murray N. Rothbard, "The Mantle of Science" in Helmut Schoeck and James W. Wiggins, eds., *Scientism and Values* (Princeton: D. Van Nostrand, 1960); on the latter arguments, *see* Rothbard, "Toward a Reconstruction of Utility and Welfare Economics," *op. cit.*, pp. 256 ff.
10. Schumpeter's insights on the fallacy of attributing a voluntary nature to the State deserve to be heeded: ". . . ever since the princes' feudal incomes ceased to be of major importance, the State has been living on a revenue which was being produced in the private sphere for private purposes and had to be deflected from these purposes by political force. The theory which construes taxes on the analogy of club dues or of the purchase of the services of, say, a doctor only proves how far removed this part of the social sciences is from scientific habits of mind." Schumpeter, *Capitalism, Socialism, and Democracy*, p. 198 and 198 n.
11. I am deeply indebted to Professor Ludwig M. Lachmann, Mr. L. D. Goldblatt, and other members of Professor Lachmann's Honours Seminar in Economics at the University of Witwatersrand, South Africa, for raising these questions in their discussion of my "Reconstruction" paper cited above.

12. Neither are these contradictions removed by abandoning democracy in favor of dictatorship. For even if the mass of the public do not vote under a dictatorship, they must still consent to the rule of the dictator and his chosen experts, and therefore their unique competence in the *political* field as against other spheres of their daily life must still be assumed.
13. *See* Rothbard, "Mises' *Human Action:* Comment," *op. cit.,* pp. 383–84. Also cf. George H. Hildebrand, "Consumer Sovereignty in Modern Times," *American Economic Review, Papers and Proceedings,* May, 1951, p. 26.
14. Cf. the excellent discussion of the contrast between daily life and politics in Schumpeter, *Capitalism, Socialism, and Democracy,* pp. 258–60.
15. *Ibid.,* p. 263.
16. Schuller, "Rejoinder," *op. cit.,* p. 189.
17. We might say that this insight underlies F. A. Hayek's famous chapter, "Why the Worst Get on Top" in *The Road to Serfdom* (Chicago: University of Chicago Press, 1944), ch. x. Also see the recent brief discussion by Jack Hirshleifer, "Capitalist Ethics—Tough or Soft?" *Journal of Law and Economics,* October, 1959, p. 118.
18. Cf. the interesting definition of "democracy" in Heath, *op. cit.,* p. 234.
19. Of course, even a completely ineffective triangular control is likely to increase the government bureaucracy dealing with the matter and therefore increase the total amount of *binary* intervention over the taxpayer. But more on this below.
20. A "bribe" is only payment of the market price by a buyer.
21. Ironically, the government's destruction of part of the people's money almost always takes place *after* the government has pumped in new money and used it for its own purposes. The injury that the government imposes on the public is twofold: (1) it takes resources away from the public by inflating the currency (see below); and (2) after the money has percolated down to the public, it destroys part of the money's usefulness.
22. In the present-day United States, much of the task of coercion has been assumed on the unions' behalf by the government. This was the essence of the Wagner Act, the law of the land since 1935. (The Taft-Hartley Act was only a relatively unimportant amendment to the Wagner Act, which continues on the books.) The crucial provisions of this act are: (1) to coerce all workers in a certain production unit (arbitrarily defined *ad hoc* by the government) into being represented by a union in bargaining with an employer, if a majority of workers agree; (2) to prohibit the employer from refusing to hire union members or union organizers; and (3) to compel the employer to bargain with this union. Thus, unions have been invested with governmental authority, and the strong arm of the government uses coercion to force workers and employers alike to deal with the unions. On special coercive privilege granted to unions, *see also* Roscoe Pound, "Legal Immunities of Labor Unions" in *Labor Unions and Public Policy* (Washington: American

Enterprise Association, 1958), pp. 145–73; and Frank H. Knight, "Wages and Labor Union Action in the Light of Economic Analysis" in Bradley, *op. cit.*, p. 43. *Also see* Petro, *op. cit.*, and chapter 10, p. 628 above.

23. Mises, *Human Action,* pp. 432 n., 447, 469, 776.
24. It was notorious, for example, that the bootleggers, a caste created by Prohibition, were one of the main groups *opposing* repeal of Prohibition in America.
25. The workings of rationing (as well as the socialist system in general) have never been more vividly portrayed than in Henry Hazlitt's *The Great Idea, op. cit.*
26. We might well call the latter an *oligopoly* grant, but this would engender hopeless confusion with existing oligopoly theory. On the latter, see chapter 10 above.
27. Monopoly privilege is granted by a government, which has power only over its own geographic area. Therefore, monopoly prices achieved within an area are always, on the market, subject to devastating competition from other countries. This is increasingly true as civilization advances and transportation costs decline, thus subjecting local monopolies to ever greater threats of competition from other areas. Hence, any domestic monopoly will tend to reach out to restrict foreign competition and block efficient interregional trade: It is no wonder that the tariff used to be called "The Mother of Trusts."

    We might note here that on a truly free market there would be no need for any separate "theory of international trade." Nations become significant economically only with government intervention, either by way of monetary intervention or barriers to trade.
28. Monopolistic privileges to *businesses may* confer a monopoly price, depending on the elasticity of the firm's demand curve. Privileges to workers, on the other hand, *always* confer a higher, restrictionist price at lower than free-market output. The reason is that a business can expand or contract its production at will; if, then, a few firms are granted the privilege of producing in a certain field, they may expand production, if conditions are ripe, and *not* reduce total supply. On the other hand, aside from hours worked, which is not very flexible, restriction of entry into a labor market must *always* reduce the total supply of labor in that industry and therefore confer a restrictionist price. Of course, a *direct* restriction on production such as conservation laws always reduces supply and thereby confers a restrictionist price.
29. It will be more convenient to use dollars rather than gold ounces in this section; but we still assume complete equivalence of dollars and gold weights. We do not consider *monetary* intervention until the end of this chapter.
30. This does not mean that resources will flow directly out of jewelry and into paper. It is more likely that resources will flow into and out of industries similar to each other, occupationally and geographically, and that resources will readjust, step by step, from one industry to the next.

31. In the long run of the ERE, of course, all firms in all industries earn a uniform interest return, and the bulk of the gains or losses are imputed back to the original specific factors.
32. For a further discussion of the economic effects of taxation, see the next section below.
33. A fourth method, revenue from sale of governmental goods or services, is a peculiar form of taxation; at the very least, to *acquire* the original assets for this "business," taxation is needed.
34. In the less developed countries, where a money economy is still emerging from barter, any given amount of taxation will have a still more drastic effect: for it will make *monetary* incomes much less worthwhile and will shift people's efforts from trying to make money back to untaxed barter arrangements. Taxation can therefore decisively retard development from a barter to a monetary economy, or even reverse the process. *See* C. Lowell Harriss, "Public Finance" in Bernard F. Haley, ed., *A Survey of Contemporary Economics* (Homewood, Ill.: Richard D. Irwin, 1952), p. 264. For a practical application, *see* P. T. Bauer, "The Economic Development of Nigeria," *Journal of Political Economy,* October, 1955, pp. 400 ff.

    If any government taxes in *kind,* there is then no span of time between taxation and the extraction of physical resources from the private sector. Both take place in the same act.
35. For this shift to occur, the individual's *real* monetary assets must decline, not just the nominal amount in terms of money. If, then, instead of this tax, there is deflation in the society, and the value of the monetary unit increases roughly proportionately everywhere, then the *nominal* fall in each individual's money stock will not be a *real* fall, and hence effective time-preference ratios will remain unchanged. In the case of income taxation, deflation will not occur, since the government will spend the revenue rather than contract the money supply. (Even in the rare case where all the tax money is liquidated by the government, the individuals taxed will lose more than others and hence will lose some real monetary assets.)
36. Thus, cf. Irving and Herbert W. Fisher, *Constructive Income Taxation* (New York: Harper & Bros., 1942). "Double" is used in the sense of *two* instances, not arithmetically twice.
37. These economists generally conclude that not income, but only consumption, should be taxed as the only "real" income.
38. The bias in favor of investment, or "growth," as against present consumption, is similar to the conservationist attack on present consumption. What is so worthy about *future* consumption and so unworthy about consuming in the *present?* Perhaps what we have here is an illicit smuggling of the less rational aspects of the "Protestant ethic" into economic science. Of the many problems involved, we may mention one here: What nonarbitrary quantitative standards for thrift can the economist establish once the free market's decision is overridden?
39. This is true if we also disregard the grave conceptual difficulties of arriving at a definition of "income," in accounting for the imputed

monetary value of work done within a household, of averaging fluctuating incomes over various years, etc.

40. We are not here conceding that "costs" determine "prices." The general array of final prices determines the general array of cost prices, but *then* the viability of firms is determined by whether the price that people will pay for their particular products will be enough to cover the costs, which are determined throughout the market.
41. Ever since Adam Smith, economists have tried, fallaciously, to use the benefit principle to justify proportional, and even progressive, taxation, on the ground that people benefit "from society" in proportion, or even more than in proportion, to their incomes. But it is clear that the rich benefit *less* from such services as police protection, since they could more afford to pay for their own than the poor. And the rich derive no benefit from welfare expenditures. Therefore, the rich derive *fewer* benefits, absolutely, from government than the poor, and the benefit principle cannot be used to justify proportional or progressive taxation.

    But, it might be objected, can't we say that everyone derives proportional benefits to his income from "society," though not from government? In the first place, this cannot be established. In fact, the opposite argument would be more accurate: for since both A and B participate in society and its benefits, any differential income between A and B must be due to their own *particular* worths rather than to society. Certainly equal benefits from society cannot be used to imply a proportional tax. And, furthermore, even if the argument were true, by what legerdemain can we say that "society" is equivalent to the State? If A, B, C, producers on the market, benefit from each other's existence as "society," how can G, the government, use this fact to establish *its* claim to *their* wealth?
42. For a critique of this doctrine, *see* E. R. A. Seligman, *The Shifting and Incidence of Taxation* (New York: Macmillan, 1899), pp. 122–36.
43. Businessmen are particularly prone to this "passing on" argument—obviously in an attempt to convince consumers that *they* are really paying any tax on that industry. Yet the argument is clearly belied by the very zeal of each industry to have its taxes lowered and to fight against a tax increase. If taxes could really be shifted so easily and businessmen were simply unpaid collection agents for the government, they would never protest a tax on their industry. (Perhaps this is the reason why almost no businessmen have protested being collection agents for withholding taxes on their *workers!*)
44. It might be objected that the firms can pass along the sales tax because it is a *general* increase for all firms. Aside from the fact that no relevant general factor (supply, demand for money) has increased, the individual firm is still concerned only with its individual demand curve, and these curves have not shifted. A tax increase has done nothing to make a higher price *more profitable* than it was before.
45. Resources can now shift only from work into idleness (or into barter). This, of course, may and probably will happen; since, as we shall see

further, a sales tax is a tax on incomes, the rise in opportunity cost of leisure may push some workers into idleness and thereby lower the quantity of goods produced. To this extent, prices *will* eventually rise, although hardly in the smooth, immediate, proportionate way of "shifting." See the pioneering article by Harry Gunnison Brown, "The Incidence of a General Output or a General Sales Tax," reprinted in R. A. Musgrave and C. S. Shoup, eds., *Readings in the Economics of Taxation* (Homewood, Ill.: Richard D. Irwin, 1959), pp. 330–39. While this was the first modern attack on the fallacy that sales taxes are shifted forward, Brown unfortunately weakened the implications of this thesis toward the end of his article.

46. Of course, if the money supply is increased after a wage rise, and credit expanded, prices can be raised so that money wages are again not above their discounted marginal value products.

47. Mr. Frank Chodorov, in his *The Income Tax—Root of All Evil* (New York: Devin-Adair, 1954), fails to indicate what other type of tax would be "better" from a free-market point of view, than the income tax. It is clear from our discussion that there are few taxes indeed that will not be as bad as the income tax from the viewpoint of the free market. Certainly sales or excise taxation will not fill the bill.

    Mr. Chodorov, furthermore, is surely wrong when he terms income and inheritance taxes *unique* denials of the right of individual property. Any tax whatever infringes on property right, and there is nothing in an "indirect tax" which makes the infringement any less clear. It is true that an income tax forces the subject to keep records and disclose his personal dealings, thus imposing a further loss in his utility. The sales tax, however, also forces record-keeping; the difference again is one of degree rather than of kind, since here the directness covers only retail storekeepers instead of the bulk of the population.

48. Thus, even so eminent an economist as F. A. Hayek has recently written: "This scheme [the single tax] for the socialization of land is, in its logic, probably the most seductive and plausible of all socialist schemes. If the factual assumptions on which it is based were correct, i.e., if it were possible to distinguish clearly between the value of the 'permanent and indestructible powers' of the soil . . . and . . . the value due to . . . improvement . . . the argument for its adoption would be very strong." F. A. Hayek, *The Constitution of Liberty* (Chicago: University of Chicago Press, 1960), pp. 352–53. Also see a somewhat similar concession by the Austrian economist von Wieser. Friedrich Freiherr von Wieser, "The Theory of Urban Ground Rent" in Louise Sommer, ed., *Essays in European Economic Thought* (Princeton: D. van Nostrand, 1960), pp. 78 ff.

49. I do not know anyone who has brought out the productivity of landowners as clearly as Mr. Spencer Heath, an ex-Georgist. *See* Spencer Heath, *How Come That We Finance World Communism?* (mimeographed MS., New York; Science of Society Foundation, 1953); *id., Rejoinder to 'Vituperation Well Answered' by Mr. Mason Gaffney*

(New York; Science of Society Foundation, 1953); *id., Progress and Poverty Reviewed* (New York: The Freeman, 1952).

50. Spencer Heath comments on Henry George as follows: "Wherever the services of land owners are concerned he is firm in his dictum that *all* values are physical . . . In the exchange services performed by [landowners], their social distribution of sites and resources, no physical production is involved; hence he is unable to see that they are entitled to any share in the distribution of physical things and that the rent they receive . . . is but recompense for their non-coercive distributive or exchange services . . . He rules out all creation of values by the services performed in [land] distribution by free contract and exchange, which is the sole alternative to either a violent and disorderly or an arbitrary and tyrannical distribution of land." Heath, *Progress and Poverty Reviewed,* pp. 9–10.

51. For the effects of the "single tax" and for other criticisms, *see* Murray N. Rothbard, *The Single Tax: Economic and Moral Implications* (Irvington-on-Hudson: Foundation for Economic Education, 1957); Rothbard, "A Reply to Georgist Criticisms" (mimeographed MS., Foundation for Economic Education, 1957); and Frank H. Knight, "The Fallacies in the 'Single Tax,'" *The Freeman* (August 10, 1953), pp. 810–11. One of the more amusing objections is that of the dean of Georgist economists, Dr. Harry Gunnison Brown. Although the Georgists base much of their economic case on a sharp distinction between ownership of land and ownership of improvements on that land, Brown tries to refute the disruptive economic effects of the single tax by implicitly assuming that land and improvements are owned by the same people anyway! Actually, of course, the disruptive effects remain; vertical integration by individuals or firms does not remove the economic principle from either of the integrated stages of production. *See* Harry Gunnison Brown, "Foundations, Professors and 'Economic Education,'" *The American Journal of Economics and Sociology,* January, 1958, pp. 150–52.

52. Government expenditures are made from government revenue. In the preceding section we have dealt with the major source of governmental revenue, taxation. Below we shall deal with inflation, or money creation, and in the present section a discussion of government "enterprise" is included. For a brief treatment of the final major source of government revenue—borrowing from the public—see Appendix A below.

53. It may be objected that while bureaucrats may not be producers, other "Pauls" who receive subsidies on occasion are basically producers on the market. To the extent that they receive subsidies from the government, however, they are being nonproductive and living off the producers by compulsion. What is relevant, in short, is the extent to which they are in a *relation of State* to their fellow men. We might add that, in this work, the term "State" is never meant in an anthropomorphic manner. "State" really means people acting toward one another in a systematically "stateish" relationship.

I am indebted to Mr. Ralph Raico, of the University of Chicago, for the "relation of State" concept.

54. Originally, Professor Simon Kuznets contended that only *taxes* should gauge the government's productive output, thus measuring product by revenue as in the case of private firms. But taxes, being compulsory, cannot be used as a productive gauge. In contrast to the present method of national income accounting, Kuznets would have eliminated all government *deficits* from its "productive contribution."
55. Even for those who do not accept this analysis, any who believe, empirically, that waste in government exceeds 50% of its expenditures would have to agree that our assumption is more accurate than the current estimate of 100% productivity by the government.
56. If a waste asset owned by the government is sold to private enterprise, *then* all or part of it might become a capital good. But this potential does not make the good capital while used by the government. It might be objected that government purchases are genuine investments when used by a government "enterprise" that charges prices on the market. We shall see, however, that this is not really enterprise but *playing at* enterprise.

    See below for a more detailed discussion of the waste involved in waste assets.
57. This is to be distinguished from the classical concept of "nonproductive consumption" as all consumption above that needed to maintain the productive capacity of the laborer.
58. As Thomas Mackay aptly stated: "We can have exactly as many paupers as the country chooses to pay for." Thomas Mackay, *Methods of Social Reform* (London: John Murray, 1896), p. 210. Private charity to the poor, on the other hand, would not have the same vicious-circle effect, since the poor would not have a continuing compulsory claim on the rich. This is particularly true where private charity is given only to the "deserving" poor. On the nineteenth-century concept of the "deserving poor," cf. Barbara Wootton, *Social Science and Social Pathology* (London: George Allen and Unwin, 1959), pp. 51, 55, and 268 ff.
59. The reader may gauge from the following anecdote by an admirer of such a drive just *who* was the true friend of the poor organ-grinder—his customer or the government:

    "During a similar campaign to clean up the streets of organ-grinders (most of whom were simply licensed beggars) a woman came up to LaGuardia at a social function and begged him not to deprive her of her favorite organ-grinder.

    " 'Where do you live?' he asked her.

    " 'On Park Avenue!'

    "LaGuardia successfully pushed through his plan to eliminate the organ-grinders and the peddlers, despite the pleas of the penthouse slummers." Newbold Morris and Dana Lee Thomas, *Let the Chips Fall* (New York, 1955), pp. 119–20.
60. See Murray N. Rothbard, "Government in Business" in *Essays on Liberty* (Irvington-on-Hudson: Foundation for Economic Education,

1958), IV, 186 ff. It is therefore characteristic of government ownership and "enterprise" that the consumer becomes, not a "king" to be courted, but a troublesome fellow bent on using up the "social" product.

61. Thus, the government official may select a road that will yield him or his allies more votes.
62. Cf. Ludwig von Mises, *Bureaucracy* (New Haven: Yale University Press, 1946), pp. 50, 53.
63. Various fallacious criteria have been advanced for deciding between private and state action. One common rule is to weigh "marginal social costs" and benefits against "marginal private costs" and benefits. Apart from other flaws, there is no such entity as "society" separate from constituent individuals, so that this proferred criterion is simply meaningless.
64. See the interesting pamphlet by Frank Chodorov, *The Myth of the Post Office* (Hinsdale, Ill.: Henry Regnery Co., 1948). On a similar situation in England, *see* Frederick Millar, "The Evils of State Trading as Illustrated by the Post Office" in Thomas Mackay, ed., *A Plea for Liberty* (New York: D. Appleton Co., 1891), pp. 305–25. For a portrayal of the political factors that have systematically distorted economic considerations in setting postal rates in the United States, *see* Jane Kennedy, "Development of Postal Rates; 1845–1955," *Land Economics,* May, 1957, pp. 93–112; and Kennedy, "Structure and Policy in Postal Rates," *Journal of Political Economy,* June, 1957, pp. 185–208.
65. Only governments can make self-satisfied announcements of cuts in service in order to effect economies. In private business, economies must be made as corollaries to improvements in service. A recent example of a cut in government service—in the midst of improving private services in most other fields—was the decline in American postal deliveries from two to one a day, coupled, of course, with perennial requests for higher rates. When France nationalized the important Western Railway system in 1908, freight was increasingly damaged, trains slowed down, and accidents grew at such a pace that an economist caustically observed that the French government had added railway accidents to its growing list of monopolies. *See* Murray N. Rothbard, "The Railroads of France," *Ideas on Liberty,* September, 1955, p. 42.
66. Ironically enough, the higher fares have driven many customers to buying and driving their own cars, thus aggravating the perennial traffic problem (shortage of government street space) even further. Another example of government intervention creating and multiplying its own difficulties! On the subways, *see* Ludwig von Mises, "The Agony of the Welfare State," *The Freeman,* May 4, 1953, pp. 556–57.
67. It might be objected that individual stockholders of corporations cannot do this either, e.g., a General Motors stockholder is not allowed to seize a car in lieu of cash dividends or in exchange for his stock. Yet stockholders *do* own their company, and this example precisely proves our point. For the individual stockholder can contract out of his company; he can *sell* his aliquot shares of General Motors stock to someone else. The subject of government *cannot* contract out of that government; he

cannot sell his "shares" in the post office, for example, because he has no such shares. As F. A. Harper has succintly stated: "The corollary of the right of ownership is the right of disownership. So if I cannot sell a thing, it is evident that I do not really own it." Harper, *op. cit.*, pp. 106, 32. Also *see* Isabel Paterson, *The God of the Machine* (New York: Putnam's, 1943), pp. 179 ff., and T. Robert Ingram, *Schools: Government or Public?* (Houston: St. Thomas Press, n.d.).

68. It might be noted that even if all the fallacious planks of the Henry George structure were conceded, the Single Tax program would still not follow from the premises. As Benjamin Tucker brilliantly demonstrated years ago, the most that could possibly be established would be *each man's* "right" to his tiny aliquot part of the site value of every plot of land—*not* the *State's* right to the whole value. Tucker, *Individual Liberty*, pp. 241–43.

69. Those who object that private individuals are mortal, while "governments are immortal," indulge in the fallacy of conceptual realism at its starkest. "Government" is not a real acting entity, but rather a type of interpersonal action adopted by actual individuals.

70. See the literature referred to in chap. 10, above, on the economics of socialism. Also John Jewkes, *Ordeal by Planning* (New York: Macmillan, 1948). For application to Soviet practice, *see* Boris Brutzkus, *Economic Planning in Soviet Russia* (London: Routledge, 1935) and such recent material as G. F. Ray, "Industrial Planning in Hungary," *Scottish Journal of Political Economy*, June, 1960; E. Stuart Kirby, "Economic Planning and Policy in Communist China," *International Affairs*, April, 1958; P. J. D. Wiles, "Changing Economic Thought in Poland," *Oxford Economic Papers*, June, 1957; Alec Nove, "The Politics of Economic Rationality," *Social Research*, Summer, 1958; and especially, Nove, "The Problem of 'Success Indicators' in Soviet Industry," *Economica*, February, 1958. See below on socialist planning in connection with growth and underdevelopment.

71. A chief difference is that a formal Communist-style expropriation makes it far more difficult to *desocialize* later.

72. The first one to point this out was Ludwig von Mises, in his *Human Action*, pp. 698–99. It is particularly interesting to find an empirical confirmation in Wiles, dealing with Communist planning: "What actually happens is that 'world prices,' i.e., *capitalist world prices*, are used in all intra-[Soviet] bloc trade. They are translated into rubles . . . and entered into bilateral clearing accounts. To the question, 'What would you do if there were no capitalist world?' came only the answer 'We'll cross that bridge when we come to it.' In the case of electricity the bridge is already under their feet; there has been great difficulty in pricing it since there is no world market." Wiles, *loc. cit.*, pp. 202–03. On the difficulties encountered by the Soviet bloc in using world market prices, *see especially* Horst Mendershausen, "The Terms of Soviet-Satellite Trade: A Broadened Analysis," *Review of Economics and Statistics*, May, 1960, pp. 152–63.

73. For an interesting account of the recent growth of organized private enterprises in Soviet Russia, illegal but protected by local graft, *see* Edward Crankshaw, "Breaking the Law in a Police State; Regimentation Can't Curb Russians' Anarchic Spirit," *New York Herald-Tribune,* August 17, 1960.
74. Recent researches have shown the fallacy of the common view that modern inventions and applied technological developments can take place only in very large-scale, even centrally planned, laboratories. See particularly the brilliant work of John Jewkes, David Sawers, and Richard Stillerman, *The Sources of Invention* (London: Macmillan Co., 1958). *Also see* John R. Baker, *Science and the Planned State* (New York: Macmillan Co., 1945). For a useful summary of recent literature in this field, *see* Richard R. Nelson, "The Economics of Invention: A Survey of the Literature," *The Journal of Business,* April, 1959, pp. 101–27. Soviet science has, of course, been able to copy the technical achievements of the West; yet, on the inefficiencies of Soviet science, *see* Baker, *op. cit.,* and Baker, *Science and the Sputniks* (London: Society for Freedom in Science, December, 1958). Of interest on the inherent inefficiencies of governmental military research is the Hoover Commission Task Force Report: Subcommittee of the Commission on Organization of the Executive Branch of Government, *Research Activities in the Department of Defense and Defense-Related Agencies* (Washington, D. C.: April, 1955). On atomic energy and government, *see,* in addition to Jewkes, Sawers, and Stillerman, Alfred Bornemann, "Atomic Energy and Enterprise Economics," *Land Economics,* August, 1954.

    Virtually the central theme of Hayek's *Constitution of Liberty* is the importance of freedom for innovations and progress, in the widest sense.
75. Two of the arguments for government activity most favored by economists are the "collective goods" and "external benefit" arguments. For a critique, see Appendix B below.
76. This is the first line of argument for government intervention analyzed in Appendix B below.
77. In many cases, these "investments" are not simply bureaucratic errors; they pay welcome gains to government officials in "prestige." Every "underdeveloped" government seems to insist on its steel mill or its dam, for example, regardless whether it is economic or not (therefore usually *not*). As Professor Friedman astutely points out: "The Pharaohs raised enormous sums of capital to build the Pyramids; this was capital formation on a grand scale; it certainly did not promote economic development in the fundamental sense of contributing to a self-sustaining growth in the standard of life of the Egyptian masses. Modern Egypt has under government auspices built a steel mill; this involves capital formation; but it is a drain on the economic resources of Egypt . . . since the cost of making steel in Egypt is very much greater than the cost of buying it elsewhere; it is simply a modern equivalent of the Pyramids, except that maintenance expenses are higher." Milton Friedman, "Foreign Economic Aid: Means and Objectives," *Yale Review,* Summer, 1958, p. 505.

78. Cf. L. M. Lachmann, *Capital and Its Structure, op. cit. Also see* P. T. Bauer and B. S. Yamey, *The Economics of Under-Developed Countries* (London: James Nisbet and Co., 1957), pp. 129 ff.
79. On the subject of compulsory saving and government investment, see the noteworthy article of P. T. Bauer, "The Political Economy of Non-Development" in James W. Wiggins and Helmut Schoeck, eds., *Foreign Aid Re-examined* (Washington, D. C.: Public Affairs Press, 1958), pp. 129–38. Bauer writes: " . . . if development has meaning as a desirable process, it must refer to an increase in *desired* output. Governmental collection and investment of saving effect production which is not subject to the test of voluntary purchase at market price . . . Increased output through this method is at best an ambiguous indicator of economic improvement . . . If the capital is not provided voluntarily, this suggests that the population prefers an alternative use of resources, whether current consumption or other forms of investment." *Ibid.,* pp. 133–34.
80. P. T. Bauer, *Economic Analysis and Policy in Underdeveloped Countries* (Duke University Press, 1957), pp. 113 ff. On Soviet economic growth Bauer and Yamey make this salutary comment: "The meaning of national income, industrial output and capital formation is also debatable in an economy when so large a part of output is not governed by consumers' choices in the market; the difficulties of interpretation are particularly obvious in connection with the huge capital expenditure undertaken by government without reference to the valuation of output by consumers." Bauer and Yamey, *op. cit.,* p. 162. *Also see* Friedman, "Foreign Economic Aid," *op. cit.,* p. 510.
81. For a critique of various metaphors illegitimately and misleadingly imported from the natural sciences into economics, *see* Rothbard, "The Mantle of Science," *loc. cit.*
82. The presumably excessive growth of cancerous cells, for example, is generally overlooked.
83. The prolific writings of Professor Bauer are a particularly fruitful source of analysis of the problems of the underdeveloped countries. In addition to the references above, *see* especially Bauer's excellent *United States Aid and Indian Economic Development* (Washington: American Enterprise Association, November, 1959); his *West African Trade* (Cambridge University Press, 1954); "Lewis' *Theory of Economic Growth,*" *American Economic Review,* September, 1956, pp. 632–41; "A Reply," *Journal of Political Economy,* October, 1956, pp. 435–41; and P. T. Bauer and B. S. Yamey, "The Economics of Marketing Reform," *Journal of Political Economy,* June, 1954, pp. 210–34.

    The following quotation from Bauer's study on India is instructive for its analysis of central planning as well as development: "As a corollary of reserving a large (and increasing) sector of the economy for the government, private enterprise and investment, both Indian and foreign, are banned from a wide range of industrial and commercial activity. These restrictions and barriers affect not only private Indian investment, but also the entry of foreign capital, enterprise and skill, which inevitably retards economic development. Such measures are thus paradoxical in view of the alleged emphasis on economic advance." Bauer, *United States Aid, etc.,* p. 43.

Bauer's chief defect is a tendency to underweigh the role of capital in economic development.

84. It is fascinating to discover, in 1925–26, before Soviet Russia became committed to full socialism and coerced industrialization, Soviet leaders and economists attacking central planning and forced industry and calling for economic reliance on private peasantry. After 1926, however, the Soviet planned economy deliberately planned *uneconomically* for forced heavy industry in order to establish an autarkic socialism. *See* Edward H. Carr, *Socialism In One Country, 1924–1926* (New York: Macmillan Co., 1958), I, 259 f., 316, 351, 503–13. On the Hungarian experience, *see* Ray, *op. cit.,* pp. 134 ff.

85. Wiggins and Schoeck, *op. cit.,* p. v. This symposium has many illuminating articles on the whole problem of underdevelopment. In addition to the Bauer article cited above, see especially the contributions of Rippy, Groseclose, Stokes, Schoeck, Haberler and Wiggins. Also see the critique of the concept of underdevelopment in Jacob Viner, *International Trade and Economic Development* (Glencoe, Ill.: Free Press, 1952), pp. 120 ff.

86. W. W. Rostow, *The Stages of Economic Growth* (Cambridge University Press, 1960). Perhaps some of the popularity may be due to the term "take-off," which is certainly in tune with our aeronautical and space-minded age.

87. On the complex of fallacies involved in the search for "laws of history," *see* Ludwig von Mises, *Theory and History* (New Haven: Yale University Press, 1957); for a critique of earlier "stage theories" of economic history, see T. S. Ashton, "The Treatment of Capitalism by Historians" in F. A. Hayek, ed., *Capitalism and the Historians* (Chicago: University of Chicago Press, 1954), pp. 57–62. Some of the fallacies of the "social overhead" concept are refuted in Wilson Schmidt, "Social Overhead Mythology" in Wiggins and Schoeck, *op. cit.,* pp. 111–28, although Schmidt himself clings to several. On the superiority of private over government entrepreneurship and innovation, and its significance for development, *see* Yale Brozen, "Business Leadership and Technological Change," *American Journal of Economics and Sociology,* 1954, pp. 13–30; and Brozen, "Technological Change, Ideology and Productivity," *Political Science Quarterly,* December, 1955, pp. 522–42.

Another Rostow fallacy is the adoption of the late nineteenth-century German theory that a strong centralized state was a necessary precondition for the emergence of Western capitalism. For a partial critique, see Jelle C. Riemersma, "Economic Enterprise and Political Powers After the Reformation," *Economic Development and Cultural Change,* July, 1955, pp. 297–308.

Finally, for a keen and pioneering discussion of many aspects of coerced development, *see* S. Herbert Frankel, *The Economic Impact of Under-Developed Societies* (Oxford: Basil Blackwell, 1953). For a contrasting case study of the free-market road to development, *see* F. C. Benham, "The Growth of Manufacturing in Hong Kong," *International Affairs*, October, 1956, pp. 456–63.

88. For a critique of Rostow, stressing his mechanistic view of history and a technological determinism that neglects the vital *ideas* creating technology and political institutions, *see* David McCord Wright, "True Growth Must Come Through Freedom," *Fortune*, December, 1959, pp. 137–38, 209–12.

89. This performance leads one to believe that Schumpeter was right when he declared: ". . . capitalism stands its trial before judges who have the sentence of death in their pockets. They are going to pass it, whatever the defense they may hear; the only success victorious defense may produce is a change in the indictment." Schumpeter, *Capitalism, Socialism, and Democracy*, p. 144.

90. John Kenneth Galbraith, *The Affluent Society* (Boston: Houghton Mifflin Co., 1958).

91. "Fable for Our Times," *Wall Street Journal*, April 21, 1960, p. 12. Thus Galbraith, *op. cit.*, deplores the government's failure to "invest more" in scientists and scientific research to promote our growth, while also attacking American affluence. It turns out, however, that Galbraith wants more of precisely that kind of research which can have no possible commercial application.

92. Galbraith's major rhetorical device may be called "the sustained sneer," which includes (*a*) presenting an opposing argument so sardonically as to make it seem patently absurd, with no need for reasoned refutation; (*b*) coining and reiterating Veblenesque names of disparagement, e.g., "the conventional wisdom"; and (*c*) ridiculing the opposition further by psychological *ad hominem* attacks, i.e., accusing opponents of having a psychological vested interest in their absurd doctrines—this mode of attack being now more fashionable than older accusations of economic venality. The "conventional wisdom" encompasses just about everything with which Galbraith disagrees.

93. In addition to wicked advertising, wants are also artificially created, according to Galbraith, by emulation of one's neighbor: "Keeping up with the Joneses." But, in the first place, what is *wrong* with such emulation, except an unsupported ethical judgment of Galbraith's? Galbraith pretends to ground his theory, not on his private ethical judgment, but on the alleged creation of wants by production itself. Yet simple emulation would not be a function of producers, but of consumers themselves—unless emulation, too, were inspired by advertising. But this reduces to the criticism of advertising discussed in the text. And secondly, where did the original *Jones* obtain his wants? Regardless of how many people have wants purely in emulation of others, *some* person or persons must have originally had these wants as genuine needs of their very own. Otherwise the argument is hopelessly circular. Once this is conceded, it is impossible for economics to decide to what extent each want is pervaded by emulation.

94. For more on determinism and the sciences of human action, *see* Rothbard, "The Mantle of Science," *op. cit.*, and Mises, *Theory and History*.
95. Professor Abbott, in his important book on competition, quality of products, and the business system, put it this way: "The producers will generally find it easier and less costly to gain sales by adapting the product as closely as possible to existing tastes and by directing advertising to those whose wants it is already well equipped to satisfy than by attempting to alter human beings to fit the product." Abbott, *op. cit.*, p. 74.
96. Recent writings by marketing experts on "the marketing revolution" now under way stress precisely this increasing competition for, and courting of, the favor and custom of the consumer. Thus, *see* Robert J. Keith, "The Marketing Revolution," *Journal of Marketing*, January, 1960, pp. 35–38; Goldman, *loc. cit.*, and Goldman, "Marketing—a Lesson for Marx," *Harvard Business Review*, January–February, 1960, pp. 79–86.
97. On the alleged powers of business advertising, it is well to note these pungent comments of Ludwig von Mises: "It is a widespread fallacy that skillful advertising can talk the consumers into buying everything that the advertiser wants them to buy . . . However, nobody believes that any kind of advertising would have succeeded in making the candlemakers hold the field against the electric bulb, the horse-drivers against the motorcars, the goose quill against the steel pen and later against the fountain pen." *Human Action*, p. 317. For a critique of the notion of the "hidden persuaders," *see* Raymond A. Bauer, "Limits of Persuasion," *Harvard Business Review*, September–October, 1958, pp. 105–10.
98. Galbraith, *op. cit.*, p. 345. In proposing this large-scale creation of an intellectual class, Galbraith virtually ignores the artificiality of educating people beyond their interests, capacities, or job opportunities available.
99. Since this would take us far afield indeed, we can mention here only one reference: to the successful development of the road and canal networks of eighteenth-century England by private road, canal, and navigation improvement companies. *See* T. S. Ashton, *An Economic History of England: The 18th Century* (New York: Barnes and Noble, n.d.), pp. 72–81. On the fallacy of "collective goods," only suppliable by the government, see Appendix B below.
100. Amidst the tangle of Galbraith's remaining fallacies and errors, we might mention one: his curious implication that Professor von Mises is a businessman. For first Galbraith talks of the age-old hostility between businessmen and intellectuals, backs this statement by quoting Mises as critical of many intellectuals, and then concedes that "most businessmen" would regard Mises as "rather extreme." But since Mises is certainly not a businessman, it is odd to see his statements used as evidence for businessman-intellectual enmity. Galbraith, *op. cit.*, pp. 184–85. This peculiar error is shared by Galbraith's Harvard colleagues, whose work he cites favorably, and who persist in quoting such non-

businessmen as Henry Hazlitt and Dr. F. A. Harper as spokesmen for the "classical business creed." *See* Francis X. Sutton, Seymour E. Harris, Carl Kaysen, and James Tobin, *The American Business Creed* (Cambridge: Harvard University Press, 1956).

The Affluent Society is a work that particularly lends itself to satire, and this has been cleverly supplied in "The Sumptuary Manifesto," *The Journal of Law and Economics,* October, 1959, pp. 120–23.

101. See pp. 819 ff. of this chapter.

102. A brief, and therefore bald, version of Galbraith's thesis may be found in John Kenneth Galbraith, "Use of Income That Economic Growth Makes Possible . . ." in *Problems of United States Economic Development* (New York: Committee for Economic Development, January, 1958), pp. 201–06. In the same collection of essays there is in some ways a more extreme statement of the same position by Professor Moses Abramovitz, who presses even further to denounce *leisure* as threatening to deprive us of that "modicum of purposive, disciplined activity which . . . gives savor to our lives." Moses Abramovitz, "Economic Goals and Social Welfare in the Next Generation," *ibid.,* p. 195. It is perhaps apropos to note a strong resemblance between coerced deprivation of leisure and slavery, as well as to remark that the only society that can genuinely "invest in men" is a society where slavery abounds. In fact, Galbraith writes almost wistfully of a slave system for this reason. *The Affluent Society,* pp. 274–75.

In addition to Galbraith and Abramovitz, other "Galbraithian" papers in the CED Symposium are those of Professor David Riesman and especially Sir Roy Harrod, who is angry at "touts," the British brand of advertiser. Like Galbraith, Harrod would also launch a massive government education program to "teach" people how to use their leisure in the properly refined and esthetic manner. This contrasts to Abramovitz, who would substitute a bracing discipline of work for expanding leisure. But then again, one suspects that the bulk of the people would find a coerced Harrodian esthetic just as disciplinary. *Problems of United States Economic Development,* I, 207–13, 223–34.

103. Hayek, *The Constitution of Liberty,* pp. 42 ff. As Hayek puts it: "A large part of the expenditure of the rich, though not intended for that end, thus serves to defray the cost of the experimentation with the new things that, as a result, can later be made available to the poor.

"The important point is not merely that we gradually learn to make cheaply on a large scale what we already know how to make expensively in small quantities but that only from an advanced position does the next range of desires and possibilities become visible, so that the selection of new goals and the effort toward their achievement will begin long before the majority can strive for them." *Ibid.,* pp. 43–44. Also see the similar point made by Mises thirty years before. Ludwig von Mises, "The Nationalization of Credit" in Sommer, *op. cit.,* pp. 111 f. And *see* Bertrand De Jouvenel, *The Ethics of Redistribution* (Cambridge: Cambridge University Press, 1952), pp. 38 f.

104. *Ibid.,* especially pp. 67 ff. If all housewives suddenly stopped doing their own housework and, instead, hired themselves out to their next-door neighbors, the supposed increase in national product, as measured by statistics, would be very great, even though the actual increase would be nil. For more on this point, *see* De Jouvenel, "The Political Economy of Gratuity," *The Virginia Quarterly Review,* Autumn, 1959, pp. 515 ff.
105. Although it has obvious third-person effects, this type of intervention is essentially binary because the issuer, or intervener, gains at the expense of individual holders of legitimate money. The "lines of force" radiate from the interveners to each of those who suffer losses.
106. Inflation, in this work, is explicitly defined to exclude increases in the stock of specie. While these increases have such similar effects as raising the prices of goods, they also differ sharply in other effects: (*a*) simple increases in specie do not constitute an intervention in the free market, penalizing one group and subsidizing another; and (*b*) they do not lead to the processes of the business cycle.
107. Cf. Mises, *The Theory of Money and Credit,* pp. 140–42.
108. The avowed goal of Keynes' inflationist program was the "euthanasia of the rentier." Did Keynes realize that he was advocating the not-so-merciful annihilation of some of the most unfit-for-labor groups in the entire population—groups whose marginal value productivity consisted almost exclusively in their savings? Keynes, *General Theory, etc.,* p. 376.
109. For an interesting discussion of some aspects of the accounting error, *see* W. T. Baxter, "The Accountant's Contribution to the Trade Cycle," *Economica,* May, 1955, pp. 99–112. *Also see* Mises, *Theory of Money and Credit,* pp. 202–04; *Human Action,* pp. 546 f.
110. To the extent that the new money is loaned to *consumers* rather than businesses, the cycle effects discussed in this section do not occur.
111. *See* Mises, *Human Action,* p. 557.
112. Since Knut Wicksell is one of the fathers of this business-cycle approach, it is important to stress that our usage of "natural rate" differs from his. Wicksell's "natural rate" was akin to our "free-market rate"; our "natural rate" is the rate of return earned by businesses on the existing market without considering loan interest. It corresponds to what has been misleadingly called the "normal profit rate," but is actually the basic rate of interest. See chapter 6 above.
113. If some readers are tempted to ask why credit contraction will not lead to the opposite type of malinvestment to that of the boom—overinvestment in lower-order capital goods and underinvestment in higher-order goods—the answer is that there is no arbitrary choice open of investing in higher-order or lower-order goods. Increased investment *must* be made in the higher-order goods—in lengthening the structure of production. A decreased amount of investment simply cuts down on higher-order investment. There will thus be no excess of investment in the lower orders, but simply a shorter structure than would otherwise be the case. Contraction, unlike expansion, does not create positive malinvestments.

114. If the economy is on a gold or silver standard, then many advocates of a free market will argue for credit contraction for the following additional reasons: (*a*) to preserve the principle of paying one's contractual obligations and (*b*) to punish the banks for their expansion and force them back toward a 100%-specie reserve policy.
115. Mises first presented the "Austrian theory" in a notable section of his *Theory of Money and Credit,* pp. 346–66. For a more developed statement, see his *Human Action,* pp. 547–83. For F. A. Hayek's important contributions, see especially his *Prices and Production,* and also his *Monetary Theory and the Trade Cycle* (London, 1933), and *Profits, Interest, and Investment.* Other works in the Misesian tradition include Robbins, *The Great Depression,* and Fritz Machlup, *The Stock Market, Credit, and Capital Formation* (New York: Macmillan, 1940).
116. *See* Mises, *Human Action,* pp. 577–78; and Hayek, *Prices and Production,* pp. 96–99.
117. Perhaps one reason for continuing confidence in the banking system is that people generally believe that fraud is prosecuted by the government and that, therefore, any practice *not* so prosecuted must be sound. Governments, indeed (as we shall see below), always go out of their way to bolster the banking system.
118. All this, of course, assumes no further government intervention in banking than permitting fractional reserve banking. Since the advent of deposit "insurance" during the New Deal, for example, the bank-run limitation has been virtually eliminated by this act of special privilege.
119. In the consolidated balance of payments of the clients, money income from sales to nonclients (exports) will decline, and money expenditures on the goods and services of nonclients (imports) will increase. The excess cash balances of the clients are transferred to nonclients.
120. Older economists also distinguished an "internal drain" as well as the "external drain," but included in the former only the drain from bank users to those who insist on standard money.
121. See *Human Action,* pp. 434–35.
122. For various views on free and central banking, *see* Vera C. Smith, *The Rationale of Central Banking* (London: P. S. King and Son, 1936).
123. *Human Action,* p. 444.
124. Amasa Walker, *op. cit.,* pp. 230–31.
125. There is a fourth way by which a central bank may increase bank reserves: in countries, such as the United States, where banks must keep a legally required minimum ratio of reserves to deposits, the bank may simply lower the required ratio.
126. Foreign central banks and governments are still permitted to redeem in gold bullion, but this is hardly a consolation for either foreign *citizens* or Americans. The result is that gold is still an ultimate "balancing" item between national governments, and therefore a kind of medium of exchange *for governments* and central banks in international transactions.
127. The transition from gold to fiat money will be greatly smoothed if the State has previously abandoned ounces, grams, grains, and other units

of weight in naming its monetary units and substituted unique names, such as dollar, mark, franc, etc. It will then be far easier to eliminate the public's association of monetary units with *weight* and to teach the public to value the *names themselves.* Furthermore, if each national government sponsors its own unique name, it will be far easier for each State to control its own fiat issue absolutely.

128. Cf. the analysis by John Maynard Keynes in his *A Tract on Monetary Reform* (London: Macmillan, 1923), ch. ii, section 1.
129. On runaway inflation, *see* Mises, *Theory of Money and Credit,* pp. 227–31.
130. Costantino Bresciani-Turroni, *The Economics of Inflation* (London: George Allen and Unwin, 1937), is a brilliant and definitive work on the German inflation.
131. Inflation is here defined as *any* increase in the money supply greater than an increase in specie, not as a *big* change in that supply. As here defined, therefore, the terms "inflation" and "deflation" *are* praxeological categories. *See* Mises, *Human Action,* pp. 419–20. But also see Mises' remarks in Aaron Director, ed., *Defense, Controls, and Inflation* (Chicago: University of Chicago Press, 1952), p. 3 n.
132. *See* George Ferdinand, "Review of Albert G. Hart, *Defense without Inflation,*" *Christian Economics,* Vol. III, No. 19 (October 23, 1951).
133. *See* Mises in Director, *op. cit.,* p. 334.
134. See section 8F above.
135. A recent objection of this sort appears in James M. Buchanan, *Public Principles of Public Debt* (Homewood, Ill.: Richard D. Irwin, 1958), especially pp. 104–05.
136. It is incorrect, however, to say that government loans are "riskless" and therefore that the interest yield on government bonds may be taken to be the pure interest rate. Governments may always repudiate their obligations if they wish, or they may be overturned and their successors may refuse to honor the IOU's.
137. Hence, despite Buchanan's criticism, the classical economists such as Mill were right: the public debt is a *double* burden on the free market; in the present, because resources are withdrawn from private to unproductive governmental employment; and in the future, when private citizens are taxed to pay the debt. Indeed, for Buchanan to be right, and the public debt to be no burden, two extreme conditions would have to be met: (1) the bondholder would have to tear up his bond, so that the loan would be a genuinely voluntary contribution to the government; *and* (2) the government would have to be a totally voluntary institution, subsisting on voluntary payments alone, not just for this particular debt, but for all its transactions with the rest of society. Cf. Buchanan, *op. cit.*
138. In the same way, we would have to assert that the Jews killed by the Nazis during World War II really committed suicide: "They did it to themselves."

139. For the rare exception of a libertarian who recognizes the merit of repudiation from a free-market point of view, *see* Frank Chodorov, "Don't Buy Bonds," *analysis,* Vol. IV, No. 9 (July, 1948), pp. 1–2.
140. One venerable example, used constantly in texts on public finance (an area particularly prone to camouflaged ethical judgments) is the "canons of justice" for taxation propounded by Adam Smith. For a critique of these supposedly "self-evident" canons, *see* Rothbard, "The Mantle of Science," *loc. cit.*
141. The analysis of the economic nature and consequences of government ownership in this book is *wertfrei* and does not involve ethical judgments. It is a mistake, for example, to believe that anyone, knowing the economic laws demonstrating the great inefficiencies of government ownership, would *necessarily* have to choose private over government ownership, although, of course, he may well do so. Those who place a high moral value, for example, on social conflict or on poverty or on inefficiency, or those who greatly desire to wield bureaucratic power over others (or to see people subjected to bureaucratic power) may well opt even more enthusiastically for government ownership. Ultimate ethical principles and choices are outside the scope of this book. This, of course, does not mean that the present author deprecates their importance. On the contrary, he believes that ethics *is* a rational discipline.
142. Thus, cf. Molinari, *op. cit.,* pp. 47–95.
143. *Ibid.,* p. 63. On the fallacy of collective goods, *see* S. R., "Spencer As His Own Critic," *Liberty,* June, 1904, and Merlin H. Hunter and Harry K. Allen, *Principles of Public Finance* (New York: Harpers, 1940), p. 22. Molinari had not always believed in the existence of "collective goods," as can be seen from his remarkable "De la production de la sécurité," *Journal des Economistes,* February 15, 1849, and Molinari, "Onzième soirée" in *Les soirées de la Rue Saint Lazare* (Paris, 1849).
144. Antonio De Viti De Marco, *First Principles of Public Finance* (London: Jonathan Cape, 1936), pp. 37–41. Similar to De Viti's first category is Baumol's attempted criterion of "jointly" financed goods, for a critique of which *see* Rothbard, "Toward A Reconstruction of Utility and Welfare Economics," *op. cit.,* pp. 255–60.
145. Paul A. Samuelson, "The Pure Theory of Public Expenditures," *Review of Economics and Statistics* (November, 1954), pp. 387–89.
146. Stephen Enke, "More on the Misuse of Mathematics in Economics: A Rejoinder," *Review of Economics and Statistics,* May, 1955, pp. 131–33; Julius Margolis, "A Comment On the Pure Theory of Public Expenditures," *Review of Economics and Statistics,* November, 1955, pp. 347–49. In his reply to critics, Samuelson, after hastening to deny any possible implication that he wished to *confine* the sphere of government to collective goods alone, asserts that his category is really a "polar" concept. Goods in the real world are supposed to be only blends of the "polar extremes" of public and private goods. But these concepts, even in Samuelson's own terms, are decidedly not polar, but exhaustive. Either A's consumption of a good diminishes B's possible consumption, or it does

not: these two alternatives are mutually exclusive and exhaust the possibilities. In effect, Samuelson has abandoned his category either as a theoretical or as a practical device. Paul A. Samuelson, "Diagrammatic Exposition of a Theory of Public Expenditure," *Review of Economics and Statistics,* November, 1955, pp. 350–56.

147. Charles M. Tiebout, "A Pure Theory of Local Expenditures," *Journal of Political Economy,* October, 1956, pp. 416–24. At one point, Tiebout seems to admit that his theory would be valid only if each person could somehow be "his own municipal government." *Ibid.,* p. 421.

In the course of an acute critique of the idea of competition in government, the Colorado Springs *Gazette-Telegraph* wrote as follows: "Were the taxpayer free to act as a customer, buying only those services he deemed useful to himself and which were priced within his reach, then this competition between governments would be a wonderful thing. But because the taxpayer is not a customer, but only the governed, he is not free to choose. He is only compelled to pay . . . With government there is no producer-customer relationship. There is only the relation that always exists between those who rule and those who are ruled. The ruled are never free to refuse the services of the products of the ruler . . . Instead of trying to see which government could best serve the governed, each government began to vie with every other government on the basis of its tax collections . . . The victim of this competition is always the taxpayer . . . The taxpayer is now set upon by the federal, state, school board, county and city governments. Each of these is competing for the last dollar he has." Colorado-Springs *Gazette-Telegraph,* July 16, 1958.

148. The problem of "external costs," usually treated as symmetrical with external benefits, is not really related: it is a consequence of failure to enforce fully the rights of property. If A's actions injure B's property, and the government refuses to stop the act and enforce damages, property rights and hence the free market are not being fully defended and maintained. Hence, external costs (e.g., smoke damage) are failures to maintain a fully free market, rather than *defects of* that market. *See* Mises, *Human Action,* pp. 650–53; and De Jouvenel, "The Political Economy of Gratuity," *op. cit.,* pp. 522–26.

149. For some unexplained reason, the benefits worried over are only the *indirect* ones, where B benefits inadvertently from A's action. Direct *gifts,* or charity, where A simply donates money to B, are not attacked under the category of external benefits.

150. "If my neighbors hire private watchmen they benefit me indirectly and incidentally. If my neighbors build fine houses or cultivate gardens, they indirectly minister to my leisure. Are they entitled to tax me for these benefits because I cannot 'surrender' them?" S.R., "Spencer As His Own Critic," *loc. cit.*

151. There is justice as well as bluntness in Benjamin Tucker's criticism: " 'What gives value to land?' asks Rev. Hugh O. Pentecost [a Georgist]. And he answers: 'The presence of population—the community. Then rent, or the value of land, morally belongs to the community.' What

gives value to Mr. Pentecost's preaching? The presence of population —the community. Then Mr. Pentecost's salary, or the value of his preaching, morally belongs to the community." Tucker, *Instead of a Book*, p. 357.

152. As Mises states: ". . . the means which a government needs in order to run a plant at a loss or to subsidize an unprofitable project must be withdrawn either from the taxpayers' spending and investing power or from the loan market . . . What the government spends more, the public spends less. Public works . . . are paid for by funds taken away from the citizens. If the government had not interfered, the citizens would have employed them for the realization of profit-promising projects the realization of which is neglected merely on account of the government's intervention. Yet this nonrealized project would have been profitable, i.e., it would have employed the scarce means of production in accordance with the most urgent needs of the consumers. From the point of view of the consumers the employment of these means of production for the realization of an unprofitable project is wasteful. It deprives them of satisfactions which they prefer to those which the government-sponsored project can furnish them." Mises, *Human Action*, p. 655.

Ellis and Fellner, in their discussion of external economies, ignore the primordial fact that the subsidization of these economies must be at the expense of funds usable for greater satisfactions elsewhere. Ellis and Fellner do not realize that their refutation of the Pigou thesis that increasing-cost industries are over-expanded destroys any possible basis for a subsidy to the decreasing-cost industries. Howard S. Ellis and William Fellner, "External Economies and Diseconomies" in *Readings in Price Theory* (Chicago: Blakiston Co., 1952), pp. 242–63.

Index of Authors

Prepared by Vernelia A. Crawford

Note: This index includes the titles of parts, chapters, and sections, each listed under appropriate subject classifications. With the exception of these specific page references, which are hyphenated, the numbers in each instance refer to the *first* page of a discussion. A page number followed by a figure in parentheses indicates the number of a footnote reference.

Index of Subjects